Ethical and Professional Standards, Quantitative Methods, and Economics

CFA® PROGRAM CURRICULUM • VOLUME 1

LEVEL II
2011

Learning Solutions

New York   Boston   San Francisco
London   Toronto   Sydney   Tokyo   Singapore   Madrid
Mexico City   Munich   Paris   Cape Town   Hong Kong   Montreal

Cover photograph courtesy of Hector Emanuel.

1 2 3 4 5 6 7 8 9 10 V313 15 14 13 12 11 10

0999900000270552065

AG/JW

Please visit our website at *www.pearsoned.com*

ISBN 10: 0-558-52187-8
ISBN 13: 978-0-558-52187-5

Mixed Sources
Product group from well-managed forests, controlled sources and recycled wood or fiber
www.fsc.org Cert no. SW-COC-002985
©1996 Forest Stewardship Council

CONTENTS

iii

ECONOMICS

⊘ indicates an optional segment   www.cfainstitute.org/toolkit—Your online preparation resource

HOW TO USE THE CFA PROGRAM CURRICULUM

Congratulations on passing Level I of the Chartered Financial Analyst (CFA®) Program. This exciting and rewarding program of study reflects your desire to become a serious investment professional. You are participating in a program noted for its high ethical standards and the breadth of knowledge, skills, and abilities it develops. Your commitment to the CFA Program should be educationally and professionally rewarding.

The credential you seek is respected around the world as a mark of accomplishment and dedication. Each level of the program represents a distinct achievement in professional development. Successful completion of the program is rewarded with membership in a prestigious global community of investment professionals. CFA charterholders are dedicated to life-long learning and maintaining currency with the ever-changing dynamics of a challenging profession.

The CFA examination measures your degree of mastery of the assigned CFA Program curriculum. Therefore, the key to your success on the examination is reading and studying the CFA Program curriculum. The remaining sections provide background on the Candidate Body of Knowledge (CBOK™), the organization of the curriculum and tips for developing an effective study program.

Curriculum Development

The CFA Program curriculum is grounded in the practice of the investment profession. Utilizing the Global Body of Investment Knowledge (GBIK) collaborative website, CFA Institute performs a continuous practice analysis with investment professionals around the world to determine the knowledge, skills, and abilities that are relevant to the profession. Regional panels and targeted surveys are conducted annually to verify and reinforce the continuous feedback. The practice analysis process ultimately defines the Candidate Body of Knowledge (CBOK). The CBOK consists of four components:

► A broad topic outline that lists the major knowledge areas

► Topic area weights that indicate the relative exam weightings of the top-level topic areas

► Learning Outcome Statements (LOS) that advise candidates as to what they should be able to do with this knowledge (LOS are provided in candidate study sessions and at the beginning of each reading)

► The curriculum of material that candidates receive upon exam registration and are expected to master

A committee made up of practicing charterholders, in conjunction with CFA Institute staff, designs the CFA Program curriculum to deliver the CBOK to candidates. The examinations, also written by practicing charterholders, are designed to allow you to demonstrate your mastery of the CBOK as set forth in the CFA Program curriculum. As you structure your personal study program, you should emphasize mastery of the CBOK and the practical application of that knowledge. For more information on the practice analysis, CBOK, and development of the CFA Program curriculum, please visit www.cfainstitute.org/toolkit.

Organization of the Curriculum

The Level II CFA Program curriculum is organized into 10 topic areas. Each topic area begins with a brief statement of the material and the depth of knowledge expected.

Each topic area is then divided into one or more study sessions. These study sessions—18 sessions in the Level II curriculum—should form the basic structure of your reading and preparation.

Each study session includes a statement of its structure and objective, and is further divided into specific reading assignments. The outline on the inside front cover of each volume illustrates the organization of these 18 study sessions.

The reading assignments are the basis for all examination questions, and are selected or developed specifically to teach the CBOK. These readings are drawn from CFA Program-commissioned content, textbook chapters, professional journal articles, research analyst reports, and cases. Readings include problems and solutions as well as appendices to help you learn.

Reading-specific Learning Outcome Statements (LOS) are listed at the beginning of each reading. These LOS indicate what you should be able to accomplish after studying the reading. We encourage you to review how to properly use LOS, and the descriptions of commonly used LOS "command words," at www.cfainstitute.org/toolkit. The command words signal the depth of learning you are expected to achieve from the reading. You should use the LOS to guide and focus your study, as each examination question is based on an assigned reading and one or more LOS. However, the readings provide context for the LOS and enable you to apply a principle or concept in a variety of scenarios. The candidate is responsible for the entirety of all of the required material in a study session, the assigned readings as well as the end-of-reading questions and problems.

Features of the Curriculum

► **Required vs. Optional Segments** - You should read all of the pages for an assigned reading. In some cases, however, we have reprinted an entire chapter or article and marked those parts of the reading that are not required as "optional." The CFA examination is based only on the required segments, and the optional segments are included only when they might help you to better understand the required segments (by seeing the required material in its full context). When an optional segment begins, you will see an icon and a solid vertical bar in the outside margin that will continue until the optional segment ends, accompanied by another icon. *Unless the material is specifically marked as optional, you should assume it is required.* Keep in mind that the optional material is provided strictly for your convenience and will not be tested. You should rely on the required segments and the reading-specific LOS in preparing for the examination.

► **Problems/Solutions** - *All questions and problems in the readings as well as their solutions (which are provided directly following the problems) are part of the curriculum and required material for the exam.* When appropriate, we have included problems within and after the readings to demonstrate practical application and reinforce your understanding of the concepts presented. The questions and problems are designed to help you learn these concepts and may serve as a basis for exam questions. Many of the questions are adapted from past CFA examinations.

- ▶ **Margins** - The wide margins in each volume provide space for your note-taking.

- ▶ **Two-Color Format** - To enrich the visual appeal and clarity of the exhibits, tables, and text, the curriculum is printed in a two-color format.

- ▶ **Six-Volume Structure** - For portability of the curriculum, the material is spread over six volumes.

- ▶ **Glossary and Index** - For your convenience, we have printed a glossary and index in each volume. Throughout the curriculum, a **bolded blue** word in a reading denotes a term defined in the glossary.

- ▶ **Source Material** - The authorship, publisher, and copyright owners are given for each reading for your reference. We recommend that you use this CFA Institute curriculum rather than the original source materials because the curriculum may include only selected pages from outside readings, updated sections within the readings, and has problems and solutions tailored to the CFA Program.

- ▶ **LOS Self-Check** - We have inserted checkboxes next to each LOS that you can use to track your progress in mastering the concepts in each reading.

Designing Your Personal Study Program

Create a Schedule - An orderly, systematic approach to examination preparation is critical. You should dedicate a consistent block of time every week to reading and studying. Complete all reading assignments and the associated problems and solutions in each study session. Review the LOS both before and after you study each reading to ensure that you have mastered the applicable content and can demonstrate the knowledge, skill, or ability described by the LOS and the assigned reading. Use the new LOS self-check to track your progress and highlight areas of weakness for later review.

You will receive periodic e-mail communications that contain important study tips and preparation strategies. Be sure to read these carefully.

CFA Institute estimates that you will need to devote a minimum of 10–15 hours per week for 18 weeks to study the assigned readings. Allow a minimum of one week for each study session, and plan to complete them all at least 30–45 days prior to the examination. This schedule will allow you to spend the final four to six weeks before the examination reviewing the assigned material and taking online sample and mock examinations.

At CFA Institute, we believe that candidates need to commit to a *minimum* of 270–300 hours reading and reviewing the curriculum and end-of-reading questions and problems. Many candidates have also incorporated the online sample examinations into their preparations during the final weeks before the exam. This recommendation, however, may substantially underestimate the hours needed for appropriate examination preparation depending on your individual circumstances, relevant experience, and academic background. You will undoubtedly adjust your study time to conform to your own strengths and weaknesses, and your educational and professional background.

You will probably spend more time on some study sessions than on others, but on average you should plan on devoting 15 hours per study session. You should allow ample time for both in-depth study of all topic areas and additional concentration on those topic areas for which you feel least prepared.

Candidate Preparation Toolkit - We have created the online toolkit to provide a single comprehensive location with resources and guidance for candidate preparation. In addition to in-depth information on study program planning, the CFA Program curriculum, and the online sample and mock examinations, the toolkit also contains curriculum errata, printable study session outlines, sample examination questions, and more. Errata that we have identified in the curriculum are corrected and listed periodically in the errata listing in the toolkit. We encourage you to use the toolkit as your central preparation resource during your tenure as a candidate. Visit the toolkit at www.cfainstitute.org/toolkit.

Online Sample Examinations - CFA Institute online sample examinations are intended to assess your exam preparation as you progress toward the end of your study. After each question, you will receive immediate feedback noting the correct response and indicating the relevant assigned reading, so you'll be able to identify areas of weakness for further study. The 120-minute sample examinations reflect the question formats, topics, and level of difficulty of the actual CFA examinations. Aggregate data indicate that the CFA examination pass rate was higher among candidates who took one or more online sample examinations than among candidates who did not take the online sample examinations. For more information on the online sample examinations, please visit www.cfainstitute.org/toolkit.

Online Mock Examinations - In response to candidate requests, CFA Institute has developed mock examinations that mimic the actual CFA examinations not only in question format and level of difficulty, but also in length. The three-hour online mock exams are intended to be taken after you complete your study of the full curriculum, so you can test your understanding of the CBOK and your readiness for the exam. To further differentiate, feedback is provided at the end of the exam, rather than after each question as with the sample exams. CFA Institute recommends that you take these mock exams at the final stage of your preparation toward the actual CFA examination. For more information on the online mock examinations, please visit www.cfainstitute.org/toolkit.

Tools to Measure Your Comprehension of the Curriculum

With the addition of the online mock exams, CFA Institute now provides three distinct ways you can practice for the actual CFA exam. The full descriptions are above, but below is a brief summary of each:

End-of-Reading Questions and Problems - These are found at the end of each reading in the printed curriculum, and should be used to test your understanding of the concepts.

Online Sample Exams - Available in Fall 2010, online sample exams are designed to assess your exam preparation, and can help you target areas of weakness for further study.

Online Mock Exams - In contrast to the sample exams, mock exams will be available in Spring 2011. Mock exams are designed to replicate the exam day experience, and should be taken near the end of your study period to prepare for exam day.

Preparatory Providers - After you enroll in the CFA Program, you may receive numerous solicitations for preparatory courses and review materials. When considering a prep course, make sure the provider is in compliance with the CFA Institute Prep Provider Guidelines Program. Just remember, there are no shortcuts to success on the CFA examinations; reading and studying the CFA curriculum is the key to success on the examination. The CFA examinations reference only the CFA Institute assigned curriculum—no preparatory course or review course materials are consulted or referenced. For more information on the Prep Provider Guidelines Program, visit www.cfainstitute.org/cfaprog/resources/prepcourse.html.

SUMMARY

Every question on the CFA examination is based on specific pages in the required readings and on one or more LOS. Frequently, an examination question is also tied to a specific example highlighted within a reading or to a specific end-of-reading question and/or problem and its solution. To make effective use of the curriculum, please remember these key points:

1. All pages printed in the Custom Curriculum are required reading for the examination except for occasional sections marked as optional. You may read optional pages as background, but you will not be tested on them.

2. All questions, problems, and their solutions - printed at the end of readings - are part of the curriculum and required study material for the examination.

3. You should make appropriate use of the CFA Candidate Toolkit and the online sample/mock examinations.

4. You should schedule and commit sufficient study time to cover the 18 study sessions, review the materials, and take sample/mock examinations.

5. **Note:** Some of the concepts in the study sessions may be superseded by updated rulings and/or pronouncements issued after a reading was published. Candidates are expected to be familiar with the overall analytical framework contained in the assigned readings. Candidates are not responsible for changes that occur after the material was written.

Feedback

At CFA Institute, we are committed to delivering a comprehensive and rigorous curriculum for the development of competent, ethically grounded investment professionals. We rely on candidate and member feedback as we work to incorporate content, design, and packaging improvements. You can be assured that we will continue to listen to your suggestions. Please send any comments or feedback to curriculum@cfainstitute.org. Ongoing improvements in the curriculum will help you prepare for success on the upcoming examinations, and for a lifetime of learning as a serious investment professional.

ETHICAL AND PROFESSIONAL STANDARDS

STUDY SESSIONS

Study Session 1   Ethical and Professional Standards
Study Session 2   Application

TOPIC LEVEL LEARNING OUTCOME

The candidate should be able to apply a thorough knowledge of the CFA Institute Code of Ethics and Standards of Professional Conduct to recognize unprofessional practices and recommend appropriate corrective measures.

STUDY SESSION 1
ETHICAL AND PROFESSIONAL STANDARDS

The readings in this study session present a framework for ethical conduct in the investment profession by focusing on the CFA Institute Code of Ethics and Standards of Professional Conduct (the Code and Standards) as well as the CFA Institute Soft Dollar Standards and the CFA Institute Research Objectivity Standards.

The principles and guidance presented in the CFA Institute *Standards of Practice Handbook* (*Handbook*) form the basis for the CFA Institute self-regulatory program to maintain the highest professional standards among investment practitioners. A clear understanding of the CFA Institute Code of Ethics and Standards of Professional Conduct (both found in the *Handbook*) should allow the practitioner to identify and appropriately resolve ethical conflicts. The resulting recognition for integrity should benefit both the individual and the profession. "Guidance" in the *Handbook* addresses the practical application of the Code of Ethics and Standards of Professional Conduct. The guidance reviews the purpose and scope of each Standard, presents recommended procedures for compliance, and provides examples of the Standard in practice.

The CFA Institute Soft Dollar Standards and CFA Institute Research Objectivity Standards address contemporary issues for which CFA Institute has believed further, more specific guidance is warranted. Both documents are consistent with and complement the CFA Institute Code of Ethics and Standards of Professional Conduct.

Soft-dollar payment arrangements, involving the investment manager's use of client brokerage to obtain services related to the manager's investment decision-making process, have become extremely complex. As a consequence, ethically ambiguous situations can arise in which it is not immediately clear that the manager remains in compliance with the obligation, under the CFA Institute Code of Ethics, to place client interests ahead of personal or firm interests. The Soft Dollar Standards provide guidance on what services and products are

3

appropriate for purchase with client brokerage, the appropriate disclosure of soft-dollar practices, and the necessary record keeping.

Investment research objectivity should be the logical consequence of ethical conduct, consistent with the CFA Institute Code of Ethics and Standards of Professional Conduct, in which client interests are placed first and conflicts of interest are fully disclosed. When temptation or pressure leads to biased or misleading research reports, the integrity of all financial professionals is tainted. The CFA Institute Research Objectivity Standards present specific policies and procedures designed to create a research environment where conflicts of interests and opportunities for ethical lapses are minimized and disclosed.

READING ASSIGNMENTS

Reading 1   Code of Ethics and Standards of Professional Conduct
Standards of Practice Handbook, Tenth Edition

Reading 2   Guidance for Standards I–VII
Standards of Practice Handbook, Tenth Edition

Reading 3   CFA Institute Soft Dollar Standards
CFA Institute Soft Dollar Standards

Reading 4   CFA Institute Research Objectivity Standards

CODE OF ETHICS AND STANDARDS OF PROFESSIONAL CONDUCT

LEARNING OUTCOMES

The candidate should be able to:	Mastery
a. state the six components of the Code of Ethics and the seven Standards of Professional Conduct;	☐
b. explain the ethical responsibilities required by the Code and Standards.	☐

PREFACE

The *Standards of Practice Handbook* (*Handbook*) provides guidance to the people who grapple with real ethical dilemmas in the investment profession on a daily basis; the *Handbook* addresses the professional intersection where theory meets practice and where the concept of ethical behavior crosses from the abstract to the concrete. The *Handbook* is intended for a diverse and global audience: CFA Institute members navigating ambiguous ethical situations; supervisors and direct/indirect reports determining the nature of their responsibilities to each other, to existing and potential clients, and to the broader financial markets; and candidates preparing for the Chartered Financial Analyst (CFA) examinations.

Recent events in the global financial markets have tested the ethical mettle of financial market participants, including CFA Institute members. The standards taught in the CFA Program and by which CFA Institute members and candidates must abide represent timeless ethical principles and professional conduct for all market conditions. Through adherence to these standards, which continue to serve as the model for ethical behavior in the investment profession globally, each market participant does his or her part to improve the integrity and efficient operations of the financial markets.

The *Handbook* provides guidance in understanding the interconnectedness of the principles and provisions of the Code of Ethics and Standards of Professional Conduct (Code and Standards). Individually, the principles outline the high level of ethical conduct required from CFA Institute members and candidates. However, applying the principles individually may not capture the complexity of ethical requirements related to the investment industry. The Code and Standards should be viewed and interpreted as an interwoven tapestry of ethical requirements. Through members' and candidates' adherence to these principles as a whole, the integrity of and trust in the capital markets are improved.

Evolution of the CFA Institute Code of Ethics and Standards of Professional Conduct

Generally, changes to the Code and Standards over the years have been minor. CFA Institute has revised the language of the Code and Standards and occasionally added a new standard to address a prominent issue of the day. For instance, in 1992, CFA Institute added the standard addressing performance presentation to the existing list of standards.

Major changes came in 2005 with the ninth edition of the *Handbook*. CFA Institute adopted new standards, revised some existing standards, and reorganized the standards. The revisions were intended to clarify the requirements of the Code and Standards and effectively convey to its global membership what constitutes "best practice" in a number of areas relating to the investment profession.

The Code and Standards must be regularly reviewed and updated if they are to remain effective and continue to represent the highest ethical standards in the global investment industry. CFA Institute strongly believes that revisions of the Code and Standards are not undertaken for cosmetic change but to add value by addressing legitimate concerns and improving comprehension.

Changes to the Code and Standards have far-reaching implications for the CFA Institute membership, the CFA Program, and the investment industry as a whole. CFA Institute members and candidates are *required* to adhere to the Code and Standards. In addition, the Code and Standards are increasingly being adopted, in whole or in part, by firms and regulatory authorities. Their relevance goes well beyond CFA Institute members and candidates.

Standards of Practice Handbook

The periodic revisions to the Code and Standards have come in conjunction with updates of the *Standards of Practice Handbook*. The *Handbook* is the fundamental element of the ethics education effort of CFA Institute and the primary resource for guidance in interpreting and implementing the Code and Standards. The *Handbook* seeks to educate members and candidates on how to apply the Code and Standards to their professional lives and thereby benefit their clients, employers, and the investing public in general. The *Handbook* explains the purpose of the Code and Standards and how they apply in a variety of situations. The sections discuss and amplify each standard and suggest procedures to prevent violations.

Examples in the "Application of the Standard" sections are meant to illustrate how the standard applies to hypothetical but factual situations. The names contained in the examples are fictional and are not meant to refer to any actual person or entity. Unless otherwise stated, individuals in each example are CFA

Institute members and holders of the CFA designation. Because factual circumstances vary so widely and often involve gray areas, the explanatory material and examples are not intended to be all inclusive. Many examples set forth in the application sections involve standards that have legal counterparts; *members are strongly urged to discuss with their supervisors and legal and compliance departments the content of the Code and Standards and the members' general obligations under the Code and Standards.*

CFA Institute recognizes that the presence of any set of ethical standards may create a false sense of security unless the documents are fully understood, enforced, and made a meaningful part of everyday professional activities. The *Handbook* is intended to provide a useful frame of reference that suggests ethical professional behavior in the investment decision-making process. This selection cannot cover every contingency or circumstance, however, and it does not attempt to do so. The development and interpretation of the Code and Standards are evolving processes; the Code and Standards will be subject to continuing refinement.

Summary of Changes in the Tenth Edition

The comprehensive review of the Code and Standards in 2005 resulted in principle requirements that remain applicable today. The review carried out for the tenth edition focused on updates to the guidance and examples within the *Handbook*. In the tenth edition, the changes relate primarily to the growing diversity of the CFA Institute membership and CFA Program candidate base and aim to make specific guidance easier to understand.

Clarification of Standard III(A)

Standard III(A) Duties to Clients—Loyalty, Prudence, and Care was shortened to improve clarity. The third sentence was deleted to avoid possible misinterpretations of the members' or candidates' required duties to their clients. The principle contained in the deleted sentence already has been established in Standard I(A) regarding the responsibility to adhere to the most strict legal, regulatory, or CFA Institute requirements.

> Deletion:
> In relationships with clients, Members and Candidates must determine applicable fiduciary duty and must comply with such duty to persons and interests to whom it is owed.

Why Ethics Matters

A new section was added to the *Handbook* to broaden the discussion of the importance of ethics to the investment profession. The chapter addresses market integrity and sustainability, the role of CFA Institute, and the importance of ongoing awareness of and education about changes in the investment industry.

Text Revisions

As the investment industry and, as a result, CFA Institute membership have become more global, the use of English that can be easily understood and translated into different languages has become critical. Therefore, in some places, CFA Institute has eliminated, modified, or added language for clarity, even though it is not the intent to change the meaning of a particular provision.

Guidance Table

To keep the *Handbook* as a primary resource for members and candidates as they tackle ethical dilemmas, bulleted tables were added to help the reader locate the guidance within a standard that is most applicable to the situations that may occur in daily professional life. The Code and Standards must not be viewed as something solely to be learned to pass the CFA examinations; its principles are intended to play an active role in everyday decision making.

Example Highlight

In a continued effort to assist readers in locating examples of situations similar to issues they are facing, this update includes a brief descriptive heading for each example in the "Application of the Standard" sections. The heading notes the principle being addressed or the nature of the example.

Cross-Standard Examples

To further highlight the applicability of multiple standards to a single set of facts, some examples are used several times. The single or slightly modified facts are accompanied by comments directed to the standard in question. The other standards using the same example are noted at the end of the comments.

CFA Institute Professional Conduct Program

All CFA Institute members and candidates enrolled in the CFA Program are required to comply with the Code and Standards. The CFA Institute Board of Governors maintains oversight and responsibility for the Professional Conduct Program (PCP), which, in conjunction with the Disciplinary Review Committee (DRC), is responsible for enforcement of the Code and Standards. The CFA Institute Bylaws and Rules of Procedure for Proceedings Related to Professional Conduct (Rules of Procedure) form the basic structure for enforcing the Code and Standards. The Rules of Procedure are based on two primary principles: 1) fair process to the member and candidate and 2) confidentiality of proceedings.

Professional Conduct staff, under the direction of the CFA Institute Designated Officer, conducts professional conduct inquiries. Several circumstances can prompt an inquiry. First, members and candidates must self-disclose on the annual Professional Conduct Statement all matters that question their professional conduct, such as involvement in civil litigation or a criminal investigation or being the subject of a written complaint. Second, written complaints received by Professional Conduct staff can bring about an investigation. Third, CFA Institute staff may become aware of questionable conduct by a member or candidate through the media or another public source. Fourth, CFA examination proctors may submit a violation report for any candidate suspected to have compromised his or her professional conduct during the examination.

When an inquiry is initiated, the Professional Conduct staff conducts an investigation that may include requesting a written explanation from the member or candidate; interviewing the member or candidate, complaining parties, and third parties; and collecting documents and records in support of its investigation. The Designated Officer, upon reviewing the material obtained during the investigation, may conclude the inquiry with no disciplinary sanction, issue a cautionary letter, or continue proceedings to discipline the member or candidate. If the Designated Officer finds that a violation of the Code and Standards occurred, the Designated Officer proposes a disciplinary sanction, which may be rejected or accepted by the member or candidate.

If the member or candidate does not accept the proposed sanction, the matter is referred to a hearing panel composed of DRC members and CFA Institute member volunteers affiliated with the DRC. The hearing panel reviews materials and presentations from the Designated Officer and from the member or candidate. The hearing panel's task is to determine whether a violation of the Code and Standards occurred and, if so, what sanction should be imposed.

Sanctions imposed by CFA Institute may have significant consequences; they include public censure, suspension of membership and use of the CFA designation, and revocation of the CFA charter. Candidates enrolled in the CFA Program who have violated the Code and Standards may be suspended from further participation in the CFA Program.

Adoption of the Code and Standards

The Code and Standards apply to individual members of CFA Institute and candidates in the CFA Program. CFA Institute does encourage firms to adopt the Code and Standards, however, as part of a firm's code of ethics. Those who claim compliance should fully understand the requirements of each of the principles of the Code and Standards.

Once a party—nonmember or firm—ensures its code of ethics meets the principles of the Code and Standards, that party should make the following statement whenever claiming compliance:

> *"[Insert name of party] claims compliance with the CFA Institute Code of Ethics and Standards of Professional Conduct. This claim has not been verified by CFA Institute."*

CFA Institute welcomes public acknowledgement, when appropriate, that firms are complying with the CFA Institute Code of Ethics and Standards of Professional Conduct and encourages firms to notify us of the adoption plans. For firms that would like to distribute the Code and Standards to clients and potential clients, attractive one-page copies of the Code and Standards, including translations, are available on the CFA Institute website (www. cfainstitute.org).

CFA Institute has also published the Asset Manager Code of Professional Conduct (AMC), which is designed, in part, to help asset managers comply with the regulations mandating codes of ethics for investment advisers. Whereas the Code and Standards are aimed at individual investment professionals who are members of CFA Institute or candidates in the CFA Program, the AMC was drafted specifically for firms. The AMC provides specific, practical guidelines for asset managers in six areas: loyalty to clients, the investment process, trading, compliance, performance evaluation, and disclosure. The AMC and the appropriate steps to acknowledge adoption or compliance can be found on the CFA Institute website (www.cfainstitute.org).

Acknowledgments

CFA Institute is a not-for-profit organization that is heavily dependent on the expertise and intellectual contributions of member volunteers. Members devote their time as they share a mutual interest in the organization's mission to promote and achieve ethical practice in the investment profession. CFA Institute owes much to the volunteers' abundant generosity and energy in extending ethical integrity.

The CFA Institute Standards of Practice Council (SPC), a group consisting of CFA charterholder volunteers from many different countries, is charged with maintaining and interpreting the Code and Standards and ensuring that they are effective. The SPC draws its membership from a broad spectrum of organizations in the securities field, including brokers, investment advisers, banks, and insurance companies. In most instances, the SPC members have important supervisory responsibilities within their firms.

The SPC continually evaluates the Code and Standards, as well as the guidance in the *Handbook*, to ensure that they are:

▶ representative of high standards of professional conduct;

▶ relevant to the changing nature of the investment profession;

▶ globally applicable;

▶ sufficiently comprehensive, practical, and specific;

▶ enforceable; and

▶ testable for the CFA Program.

The SPC has spent countless hours reviewing and discussing revisions to the Code and Standards and updates to the guidance that makes up the tenth edition of the *Handbook*. Following is a list of the current and former members of the SPC who generously donated their time and energy to this effort.

Christopher C. Loop, CFA, Chair	Toshihiko Saito, CFA, Prior Chair
Karin B. Bonding, CFA	Jinliang Li, CFA
Jean-Francois Bouilly, CFA	Lynn S. Mander, CFA
Terence E. Burns, CFA	James M. Meeth, CFA
Sharon Craggs, CFA	Brian O'Keefe, CFA
Mario Eichenberger, CFA	Guy G. Rutherfurd, Jr., CFA
James E. Hollis, CFA	Sunil B. Singhania, CFA
Samuel B. Jones, CFA	Peng Lian Wee, CFA
Ulrike Kaiser-Boeing, CFA	

The chair and members of the SPC would like to thank the CFA Institute staff who supported this revision for their efforts to keep the process smooth and well organized.

This tenth edition of the *Standards of Practice Handbook* is dedicated to the late Mildred Hermann, who served in a variety of capacities with the CFA Institute predecessor organizations, the Financial Analysts Federation (FAF) and the Association for Investment Management and Research (AIMR). With a work ethic that knew no limits, she possessed an unfailing sense of fairness and uncompromising integrity—attributes she expected in all investment professionals.

As FAF/AIMR staff representative to the predecessor committees to the Standards of Practice Council, Mildred was instrumental in the development of the first edition of the *Standards of Practice Handbook* and continued her direct involvement with the four subsequent editions published up to her retirement in 1991. She proved to be a passionate and skilled technician whose prodigious intellect, range of knowledge, and seasoned judgment fused seamlessly to create a deeply informed understanding of regulatory trends and their implications for FAF/AIMR members and the investment profession at large.

Mildred's tenure was marked by her special brand of leadership, vision, and commitment in promoting the highest standards of ethical conduct and professional practice. As Rossa O'Reilly, CFA, former chair of the Board of Governors, aptly observed at her retirement, "Very few professionals have contributed as much or worked as diligently toward furthering the goals of the profession of investment analysis and portfolio management as Mildred Hermann." For those of us fortunate enough to have worked with Mildred, she is fondly remembered as a unique talent, quick wit, valued colleague, model of human decency, and a humble, beloved friend.

WHY ETHICS MATTERS

The adherence of investment professionals to ethical practices benefits all market participants and increases investor confidence in global financial markets. Clients are reassured that the investment professionals they hire operate with the clients' best interests in mind, and investment professionals benefit from the more efficient and transparent operation of the market that integrity promotes. Ethical practices instill public trust in markets and support the development of markets. Sound ethics is fundamental to capital markets and the investment profession.

The first decade of the 21st century has been but one of many times of crisis for the investment industry. This period, unfortunately, has encompassed many instances of unethical behavior—by business executives and investment professionals. The newspapers and airwaves have brimmed with a succession of accounting frauds and manipulations, Ponzi schemes, insider trading, and other misdeeds. Each case has resulted in heavy financial losses and stained reputations. Equally important has been the terrible toll these actions have taken on investors' trust. Trust is hard earned and easily lost; corporations and individuals can safeguard themselves by committing to the highest standards of ethics and professional conduct.

Ethics is not merely a virtue to be demonstrated by CFA Institute members and candidates. Ethics must permeate all levels of our profession. Serving the best interests of the investing clients and employers lies at the heart of what collectively must be done to ensure a sense of trust and integrity in the financial markets. Although the drive to achieve such a lofty collective objective is critically important, the drive must ultimately start in the workplace. It is imperative that top management foster a strong culture of ethics not just among CFA charterholders and candidates but among all staff members who are involved directly or indirectly with client relations, the investment process, record keeping, and beyond. In such a culture, all participants can see clear evidence of how extremely important ethics is when woven into the fabric of an organization, or in other words, all participants in the process will know that ethics genuinely matters.

Ethics and CFA Institute

An important goal of CFA Institute is to ensure that the organization and its members develop, promote, and follow the highest ethical standards in the investment industry. The CFA Institute Code of Ethics (Code) and Standards of Professional Conduct (Standards) are the foundation supporting the organization's quest to advance the interests of the global investment community by establishing and maintaining the highest standards of professional excellence and integrity. The Code is a set of principles that define the professional conduct CFA Institute expects from its members and candidates in the CFA Program. The Code works in tandem with the Standards, which outline conduct that constitutes fair and ethical business practices.

For more than 40 years, CFA Institute members and candidates in the CFA Program have been required to abide by the organization's Code and Standards. Periodically, CFA Institute has revised and updated its Code and Standards to ensure that they remain relevant to the changing nature of the investment profession and representative of the "highest standard" of professional conduct. Recent events have highlighted unethical actions in the areas of governance, investment ratings, financial product packaging and distribution, and outright investment fraud. Finance is a sophisticated and interconnected global industry; new investment opportunities and new financial instruments to make the most of those opportunities are constantly developing. Although the investment world has become a far more complex place since the first publication of the *Handbook*, distinguishing right from wrong remains the paramount principle of the Code and Standards.

Ethics and Market Sustainability

The increasingly interconnected nature of global finance brings to the fore an added consideration that was, perhaps, less relevant in years past. This consideration is that of *market sustainability*. In addition to committing to the highest levels of ethical behavior, today's investment professional, when making decisions, should consider the long-term health of the market as a whole. As recent events have demonstrated, the sum of apparently isolated and unrelated decisions, however innocuous when considered on an individual basis, when aggregated, can precipitate a market crisis. In an interconnected global economy and marketplace, each participant should strive to be aware of how his or her actions or products may be distributed to, used in, or have an impact on other regions or countries.

The much-discussed credit crisis that buffeted global financial markets highlights these concerns. Relying on esoteric structures, certain banks developed financial instruments that extended credit to consumers and companies that otherwise would not have had access to those monies. Clients purchased these instruments in a quest for yield in a low-interest-rate environment. But some of the higher-risk borrowers could not afford their loans and were not able to refinance them. Defaults soared, and some of the instruments collapsed. Many of the institutions that had purchased the instruments or retained stakes in them had not completed sufficient diligence on the instruments' structures and suffered horrendous losses. Established institutions toppled into ruin, wrecking lives and reputations. Had members of the investment profession considered with greater foresight the question of market sustainability in tandem with the needs and expectations of their clients, the magnitude of the crisis might have been lessened.

CFA Institute encourages all members and candidates to consider in their investment decision-making process the promotion and protection of the global financial markets as an aspect of the broader context of the application of the Code and Standards. Those in positions of authority have a special responsibility to consider the broader context of market sustainability in their development and approval of corporate policies, particularly those involving risk management and product development. In addition, corporate compensation strategies should not encourage otherwise ethically sound individuals to engage in unethical or questionable conduct for financial gain. Ethics, sustainability, and properly functioning capital markets are components of the same concept of protecting the interests of all.

Ethics and Regulation

Regulation alone will never fully anticipate and eliminate the causes of financial crises. Some individuals will try to and may well be able to circumvent the regulatory rules. Only strong ethical principles, at the level of the individual and the level of the firm, will limit abuses. Knowing the rules or regulations to apply in a particular situation, although important, is not sufficient to ensure ethical decision making. Individuals must be able both to recognize areas that are prone to ethical pitfalls and to identify those circumstances and influences that can impair ethical judgment.

The Code and Standards, as well as other voluntary ethical standards of the CFA Institute (e.g., the Global Investment Performance Standards, Soft Dollar Standards, Trade Management Guidelines, Research Objectivity Standards, and the Asset Manager Code of Professional Conduct), offer a foundation to adopt and build on in promoting an ethical corporate culture. The adoption of these standards is not limited to investment professionals and their firms affiliated with CFA Institute. National regulators might consider the *Handbook*'s guidance in fostering ethical identities within organizations and national systems.

In the future, the nature and level of regulation will depend on how companies comply with the rules already in place. Greater adherence to the spirit of current rules may well require fewer regulatory changes. Conversely, continued short-sightedness and disregard for the outcomes of particularly adverse practices may necessitate more stringent regulation. In this respect, the investment industry can have a positive effect on evolving regulation and, in that way, on its own operational environment. Through continuing education, investment professionals can reinforce and evaluate their personal ethical conduct.

Ethics Education and Awareness

New challenges will continually arise for members and candidates in applying the Code and Standards because ethical dilemmas are not unambiguously right or wrong. The dilemma exists because the choice between right and wrong is not always clear. Even well-intentioned investment professionals can find themselves in circumstances that may tempt them to cut corners. Situational influences can overpower the best of intentions.

To assist members and candidates in adhering to the principles of the Code and Standards, CFA Institute has made a significant commitment to provide members and candidates with the resources to extend and deepen their understanding of the principles' applications. The publications from CFA Institute offer a wealth of material. *CFA Magazine* contains a section on ethics in most issues. The magazine contains not only vignettes describing potentially questionable situations and guidance related to the Code and Standards but also frequent articles on broad topics relevant to current and developing ethical issues. The *Financial Analysts Journal* also publishes articles related to ethics and professional conduct. Archived issues of these publications are available on the CFA Institute website (www.cfainstitute.org).

CFA Institute includes presentations on ethics in many of its sponsored conferences. These presentations vary as widely as the articles do, from staff-led training courses to discussion of market events by outside professionals with a view toward ethical education. These presentations highlight current trends and how improved ethical decision making may lead to different or even preferred outcomes in the future.

These various resources are available to members and candidates and the investment community at large. Those unable to attend an actual conference will find podcasts, webcasts, or transcripts available on the CFA Institute website (www.cfainstitute.org). Conferences and the presentations offered in the *CFA Institute Conference Proceedings Quarterly* also provide continuing education credits for those members participating in the program.

The Research Foundation of CFA Institute, a not-for-profit organization established to promote the development and dissemination of relevant research for investment practitioners worldwide, has contributed to continued ethical education through the commission and publication in 2007 of *The Psychology of Ethics in the Finance and Investment Industry*. In this monograph, Thomas Oberlechner, professor of psychology at Webster University in Vienna, discusses the role psychology plays in individuals' ethical or unethical decision making. He concludes that understanding the dynamic nature of ethical decision making allows us to understand why unethical decisions can be made by anyone and, hence, how to manage our ethical conduct.

Markets function to an important extent on trust. Recent events have shown the fragility of this foundation and the devastating consequences that can ensue when this foundation is fundamentally questioned. Investment professionals should remain mindful of the long-term health of financial markets and incorporate this concern for the market's sustainability in their investment decision making. CFA Institute and the Standards of Practice Council hope this edition of the *Handbook* will assist and guide investment professionals in meeting the ethical demands of the highly interconnected global capital markets.

CFA INSTITUTE CODE OF ETHICS AND STANDARDS OF PROFESSIONAL CONDUCT

Preamble

The CFA Institute Code of Ethics and Standards of Professional Conduct are fundamental to the values of CFA Institute and essential to achieving its mission to lead the investment profession globally by setting high standards of education, integrity, and professional excellence. High ethical standards are critical to maintaining the public's trust in financial markets and in the investment profession. Since their creation in the 1960s, the Code and Standards have promoted the integrity of CFA Institute members and served as a model for measuring the ethics of investment professionals globally, regardless of job function, cultural differences, or local laws and regulations. All CFA Institute members (including holders of the Chartered Financial Analyst [CFA] designation) and CFA candidates must abide by the Code and Standards and are encouraged to notify their employer of this responsibility. Violations may result in disciplinary sanctions by CFA Institute. Sanctions can include revocation of membership, revocation of candidacy in the CFA Program, and revocation of the right to use the CFA designation.

The Code of Ethics

Members of CFA Institute (including CFA charterholders) and candidates for the CFA designation ("Members and Candidates") must:

▶ Act with integrity, competence, diligence, respect, and in an ethical manner with the public, clients, prospective clients, employers, employees, colleagues in the investment profession, and other participants in the global capital markets.

▶ Place the integrity of the investment profession and the interests of clients above their own personal interests.

▶ Use reasonable care and exercise independent professional judgment when conducting investment analysis, making investment recommendations, taking investment actions, and engaging in other professional activities.

▶ Practice and encourage others to practice in a professional and ethical manner that will reflect credit on themselves and the profession.

▶ Promote the integrity of and uphold the rules governing capital markets.

▶ Maintain and improve their professional competence and strive to maintain and improve the competence of other investment professionals.

Standards of Professional Conduct

I. PROFESSIONALISM

A. **Knowledge of the Law.** Members and Candidates must understand and comply with all applicable laws, rules, and regulations (including the CFA Institute Code of Ethics and Standards of Professional Conduct) of any government, regulatory organization, licensing agency, or professional association governing their professional activities. In the event of conflict, Members and Candidates must comply with the more strict law, rule, or regulation. Members and Candidates must not knowingly participate or assist in and must dissociate from any violation of such laws, rules, or regulations.

B. **Independence and Objectivity.** Members and Candidates must use reasonable care and judgment to achieve and maintain independence and objectivity in their professional activities. Members and Candidates must not offer, solicit, or accept any gift, benefit, compensation, or consideration that reasonably could be expected to compromise their own or another's independence and objectivity.

C. **Misrepresentation.** Members and Candidates must not knowingly make any misrepresentations relating to investment analysis, recommendations, actions, or other professional activities.

D. **Misconduct.** Members and Candidates must not engage in any professional conduct involving dishonesty, fraud, or deceit or commit any act that reflects adversely on their professional reputation, integrity, or competence.

II. INTEGRITY OF CAPITAL MARKETS

A. **Material Nonpublic Information.** Members and Candidates who possess material nonpublic information that could affect the value of an investment must not act or cause others to act on the information.

B. Market Manipulation. Members and Candidates must not engage in practices that distort prices or artificially inflate trading volume with the intent to mislead market participants.

III. DUTIES TO CLIENTS

A. Loyalty, Prudence, and Care. Members and Candidates have a duty of loyalty to their clients and must act with reasonable care and exercise prudent judgment. Members and Candidates must act for the benefit of their clients and place their clients' interests before their employer's or their own interests.

B. Fair Dealing. Members and Candidates must deal fairly and objectively with all clients when providing investment analysis, making investment recommendations, taking investment action, or engaging in other professional activities.

C. Suitability.

1. When Members and Candidates are in an advisory relationship with a client, they must:

   a. Make a reasonable inquiry into a client's or prospective client's investment experience, risk and return objectives, and financial constraints prior to making any investment recommendation or taking investment action and must reassess and update this information regularly.

   b. Determine that an investment is suitable to the client's financial situation and consistent with the client's written objectives, mandates, and constraints before making an investment recommendation or taking investment action.

   c. Judge the suitability of investments in the context of the client's total portfolio.

2. When Members and Candidates are responsible for managing a portfolio to a specific mandate, strategy, or style, they must make only investment recommendations or take only investment actions that are consistent with the stated objectives and constraints of the portfolio.

D. Performance Presentation. When communicating investment performance information, Members and Candidates must make reasonable efforts to ensure that it is fair, accurate, and complete.

E. Preservation of Confidentiality. Members and Candidates must keep information about current, former, and prospective clients confidential unless:

1. The information concerns illegal activities on the part of the client or prospective client,

2. Disclosure is required by law, or

3. The client or prospective client permits disclosure of the information.

IV. DUTIES TO EMPLOYERS

A. Loyalty. In matters related to their employment, Members and Candidates must act for the benefit of their employer and not deprive their employer of the advantage of their skills and abilities, divulge confidential information, or otherwise cause harm to their employer.

B. Additional Compensation Arrangements. Members and Candidates must not accept gifts, benefits, compensation, or consideration that competes with or might reasonably be expected to create a conflict of interest with their employer's interest unless they obtain written consent from all parties involved.

C. **Responsibilities of Supervisors.** Members and Candidates must make reasonable efforts to detect and prevent violations of applicable laws, rules, regulations, and the Code and Standards by anyone subject to their supervision or authority.

V. INVESTMENT ANALYSIS, RECOMMENDATIONS, AND ACTIONS

A. **Diligence and Reasonable Basis.** Members and Candidates must:

1. Exercise diligence, independence, and thoroughness in analyzing investments, making investment recommendations, and taking investment actions.

2. Have a reasonable and adequate basis, supported by appropriate research and investigation, for any investment analysis, recommendation, or action.

B. **Communication with Clients and Prospective Clients.** Members and Candidates must:

1. Disclose to clients and prospective clients the basic format and general principles of the investment processes they use to analyze investments, select securities, and construct portfolios and must promptly disclose any changes that might materially affect those processes.

2. Use reasonable judgment in identifying which factors are important to their investment analyses, recommendations, or actions and include those factors in communications with clients and prospective clients.

3. Distinguish between fact and opinion in the presentation of investment analysis and recommendations.

C. **Record Retention.** Members and Candidates must develop and maintain appropriate records to support their investment analyses, recommendations, actions, and other investment-related communications with clients and prospective clients.

VI. CONFLICTS OF INTEREST

A. **Disclosure of Conflicts.** Members and Candidates must make full and fair disclosure of all matters that could reasonably be expected to impair their independence and objectivity or interfere with respective duties to their clients, prospective clients, and employer. Members and Candidates must ensure that such disclosures are prominent, are delivered in plain language, and communicate the relevant information effectively.

B. **Priority of Transactions.** Investment transactions for clients and employers must have priority over investment transactions in which a Member or Candidate is the beneficial owner.

C. **Referral Fees.** Members and Candidates must disclose to their employer, clients, and prospective clients, as appropriate, any compensation, consideration, or benefit received from or paid to others for the recommendation of products or services.

VII. RESPONSIBILITIES AS A CFA INSTITUTE MEMBER OR CFA CANDIDATE

A. **Conduct as Members and Candidates in the CFA Program.** Members and Candidates must not engage in any conduct that compromises the reputation or integrity of CFA Institute or the CFA designation or the integrity, validity, or security of the CFA examinations.

B. Reference to CFA Institute, the CFA Designation, and the CFA Program.
When referring to CFA Institute, CFA Institute membership, the CFA designation, or candidacy in the CFA Program, Members and Candidates must not misrepresent or exaggerate the meaning or implications of membership in CFA Institute, holding the CFA designation, or candidacy in the CFA program.

GUIDANCE FOR STANDARDS I–VII

LEARNING OUTCOMES

The candidate should be able to:	Mastery
a. demonstrate a thorough knowledge of the Code of Ethics and Standards of Professional Conduct by applying the Code and Standards to specific situations;	☐
b. recommend practices and procedures designed to prevent violations of the Code of Ethics and Standards of Professional Conduct.	☐

STANDARD I—PROFESSIONALISM

A. Knowledge of the Law

Members and Candidates must understand and comply with all applicable laws, rules, and regulations (including the CFA Institute Code of Ethics and Standards of Professional Conduct) of any government, regulatory organization, licensing agency, or professional association governing their professional activities. In the event of conflict, Members and Candidates must comply with the more strict law, rule, or regulation. Members and Candidates must not knowingly participate or assist in and must dissociate from any violation of such laws, rules, or regulations.

Guidance

Highlights:

► *Relationship between the Code and Standards and Applicable Law*
► *Participation in or Association with Violations by Others*
► *Investment Products and Applicable Laws*

Members and candidates must understand the applicable laws and regulations of all the countries in which they trade securities or provide investment advice or other investment services. On the basis of their understanding, members and candidates must comply with the laws and regulations that directly govern their work. When questions arise, members and candidates should know their firm's policies and procedures for accessing compliance guidance. This standard does not require members and candidates to become experts, however, in compliance. Additionally, investment professionals are not required to have detailed knowledge of or be experts on all the laws that could potentially govern the member's or candidate's activities.

During times of changing regulations, members and candidates must remain vigilant in maintaining their knowledge of the requirements for their professional activities. The financial and ethical missteps in the first decade of the 21st century created an environment for swift and wide-ranging regulatory changes. As new local, regional, and global requirements are updated, members, candidates, and their firms must adjust their procedures and practices to remain in compliance.

Relationship between the Code and Standards and Applicable Law

Some members or candidates may live, work, or provide investment services to clients living in a country that has no law or regulation governing a particular action or that has laws or regulations that differ from the requirements of the Code and Standards. When applicable law and the Code and Standards require different conduct, members and candidates must follow the more strict of the applicable law or the Code and Standards.

"Applicable law" is the law that governs the member's or candidate's conduct. Which law applies will depend on the particular facts and circumstances of each case. The "more strict" law or regulation is the law or regulation that imposes greater restrictions on the action of the member or candidate or calls for the member or candidate to exert a greater degree of action that protects the interests of investors. For example, applicable law or regulation may not require members and candidates to disclose referral fees received from or paid to others for the recommendation of investment products or services. Because the Code and Standards impose this obligation, however, members and candidates must disclose the existence of such fees.

Members and candidates must adhere to the following principles:

▶ Members and candidates must comply with applicable law or regulation related to their professional activities.

▶ Members and candidates must not engage in conduct that constitutes a violation of the Code and Standards, even though it may otherwise be legal.

▶ In the absence of any applicable law or regulation or when the Code and Standards impose a higher degree of responsibility than applicable laws and regulations, members and candidates must adhere to the Code and Standards. Applications of these principles are outlined in Exhibit 1.

CFA Institute members are obligated to abide by the CFA Institute Articles of Incorporation, Bylaws, Code of Ethics, Standards of Professional Conduct,

Rules of Procedure, Membership Agreement, and other applicable rules promulgated by CFA Institute, all as amended from time to time. CFA candidates who are not members must also abide by these documents (except for the Membership Agreement) as well as rules and regulations related to the administration of the CFA examination, the Candidate Responsibility Statement, and the Candidate Pledge.

Participation in or Association with Violations by Others

Members and candidates are responsible for violations in which they *knowingly* participate or assist. Although members and candidates are presumed to have knowledge of all applicable laws, rules, and regulations, CFA Institute acknowledges that members may not recognize violations if they are not aware of all the facts giving rise to the violations. Standard I(A) applies when members and candidates know or should know that their conduct may contribute to a violation of applicable laws, rules, regulations, or the Code and Standards.

If a member or candidate has reasonable grounds to believe that imminent or ongoing client or employer activities are illegal or unethical, the member or candidate must dissociate, or separate, from the activity. In extreme cases, dissociation may require a member or candidate to leave his or her employment. Members and candidates may take the following intermediate steps to dissociate from ethical violations of others when direct discussions with the person or persons committing the violation are unsuccessful. The first step should be to attempt to stop the behavior by bringing it to the attention of the employer through a supervisor or the firm's compliance department. If this attempt is unsuccessful, then members and candidates have a responsibility to step away and dissociate from the activity. Dissociation practices will differ on the basis of the member's or candidate's role in the investment industry. It may include removing one's name from written reports or recommendations, asking for a different assignment, or refusing to accept a new client or continue to advise a current client. Inaction combined with continuing association with those involved in illegal or unethical conduct may be construed as participation or assistance in the illegal or unethical conduct.

CFA Institute strongly encourages members and candidates to report potential violations of the Code and Standards committed by fellow members and candidates. Although a failure to report is less likely to be construed as a violation than a failure to dissociate from unethical conduct, the impact of inactivity on the integrity of capital markets can be significant. Although the Code and Standards do not compel members and candidates to report violations to their governmental or regulatory organizations unless such disclosure is mandatory under applicable law, such disclosure may be prudent under certain circumstances. Members and candidates should consult their legal and compliance advisers for guidance.

Additionally, CFA Institute encourages members, nonmembers, clients, and the investing public to report violations of the Code and Standards by CFA Institute members or CFA candidates by submitting a complaint in writing to the CFA Institute Professional Conduct Program via e-mail (pcprogram@cfainstitute.org) or the CFA Institute website (www.cfainstitute.org).

Investment Products and Applicable Laws

Members and candidates involved in creating or maintaining investment services or investment products or packages of securities and/or derivatives should be mindful of where these products or packages will be sold as well as their places of origination. The applicable laws and regulations of the countries or regions of origination and expected sale should be understood by those responsible for the supervision of the services or creation and maintenance of the products or packages. Members and candidates should make reasonable efforts to review whether associated firms that are distributing products or services developed by their employing firm also abide by the laws and regulations of the countries and regions of distribution. Members and candidates should undertake the necessary due diligence when transacting cross-border business to understand the multiple applicable laws and regulations in order to protect the reputation of their firm and themselves.

EXHIBIT 1	Global Application of the Code and Standards

Members and candidates who practice in multiple jurisdictions may be subject to varied securities laws and regulations. If applicable law is stricter than the requirements of the Code and Standards, members and candidates must adhere to applicable law; otherwise, they must adhere to the Code and Standards. The following chart provides illustrations involving a member who may be subject to the securities laws and regulations of three different types of countries:

NS: country with no securities laws or regulations

LS: country with *less* strict securities laws and regulations than the Code and Standards

MS: country with *more* strict securities laws and regulations than the Code and Standards

Applicable Law	Duties	Explanation
Member resides in NS country, does business in LS country; LS law applies.	Member must adhere to the Code and Standards.	Because applicable law is less strict than the Code and Standards, the member must adhere to the Code and Standards.
Member resides in NS country, does business in MS country; MS law applies.	Member must adhere to the law of MS country.	Because applicable law is stricter than the Code and Standards, member must adhere to the more strict applicable law.
Member resides in LS country, does business in NS country; LS law applies.	Member must adhere to the Code and Standards.	Because applicable law is less strict than the Code and Standards, member must adhere to the Code and Standards.
Member resides in LS country, does business in MS country; MS law applies.	Member must adhere to the law of MS country.	Because applicable law is stricter than the Code and Standards, member must adhere to the more strict applicable law.

(Exhibit continued on next page . . .)

EXHIBIT 1   (continued)

Applicable Law	Duties	Explanation
Member resides in LS country, does business in NS country; LS law applies, but it states that law of locality where business is conducted governs.	Member must adhere to the Code and Standards.	Because applicable law states that the law of the locality where the business is conducted governs and there is no local law, the member must adhere to the Code and Standards.
Member resides in LS country, does business in MS country; LS law applies, but it states that law of locality where business is conducted governs.	Member must adhere to the law of MS country.	Because applicable law of the locality where the business is conducted governs and local law is stricter than the Code and Standards, member must adhere to the more strict applicable law.
Member resides in MS country, does business in LS country; MS law applies.	Member must adhere to the law of MS country.	Because applicable law is stricter than the Code and Standards, member must adhere to the more strict applicable law.
Member resides in MS country, does business in LS country; MS law applies, but it states that law of locality where business is conducted governs.	Member must adhere to the Code and Standards.	Because applicable law states that the law of the locality where the business is conducted governs and local law is less strict than the Code and Standards, member must adhere to the Code and Standards.
Member resides in MS country, does business in LS country with a client who is a citizen of LS country; MS law applies, but it states that the law of the client's home country governs.	Member must adhere to the Code and Standards.	Because applicable law states that the law of the client's home country governs (which is less strict than the Code and Standards), member must adhere to the Code and Standards.
Member resides in MS country, does business in LS country with a client who is a citizen of MS country; MS law applies, but it states that the law of the client's home country governs.	Member must adhere to the law of MS country.	Because applicable law states that the law of the client's home country governs and the law of the client's home country is stricter than the Code and Standards, the member must adhere to the more strict applicable law.

Recommended Procedures for Compliance

Members and Candidates

Suggested methods by which members and candidates can acquire and maintain understanding of applicable laws, rules, and regulations include the following:

► *Stay informed:* Members and candidates should establish or encourage their employers to establish a procedure by which employees are regularly informed about changes in applicable laws, rules, regulations, and case law. In many instances, the employer's compliance department or legal counsel can provide such information in the form of memorandums distributed to employees in the organization. Also, participation in an internal or external continuing education program is a practical method of staying current.

► *Review procedures:* Members and candidates should review, or encourage their employers to review, the firm's written compliance procedures on a regular basis to ensure that the procedures reflect current law and provide adequate guidance to employees about what is permissible conduct under the law and/or the Code and Standards. Recommended compliance procedures for specific items of the Code and Standards are discussed in this *Handbook* in the "Guidance" sections associated with each standard.

► *Maintain current files:* Members and candidates should maintain or encourage their employers to maintain readily accessible current reference copies of applicable statutes, rules, regulations, and important cases.

Distribution Area Laws

Members and candidates should make reasonable efforts to understand the applicable laws—both country and regional—for the countries and regions where their investment products are developed and are most likely to be distributed to clients.

Legal Counsel

When in doubt about the appropriate action to undertake, it is recommended that a member or candidate seek the advice of compliance personnel or legal counsel concerning legal requirements. If a potential violation is being committed by a fellow employee, it may also be prudent for the member or candidate to seek the advice of the firm's compliance department or legal counsel.

Dissociation

When dissociating from an activity that violates the Code and Standards, members and candidates should document the violation and urge their firms to attempt to persuade the perpetrator(s) to cease such conduct. To dissociate from the conduct, a member or candidate may have to resign his or her employment.

Firms

The formality and complexity of compliance procedures for firms depend on the nature and size of the organization and the nature of its investment operations. Members and candidates should encourage their firms to consider the following policies and procedures to support the principles of Standard I(A):

▶ *Develop and/or adopt a code of ethics*: The ethical culture of an organization starts at the top. Members and candidates should encourage their supervisors or managers to adopt a code of ethics. Adhering to a code of ethics facilitates solutions when people face ethical dilemmas and can prevent the need for employees to resort to a "whistleblowing" solution publicly alleging concealed misconduct. CFA Institute has published the *Asset Manager Code of Professional Conduct*, which firms may adopt or use as the basis for their codes (visit www.cfapubs.org/loi/ccb).

▶ *Provide information on applicable laws*: Pertinent information that highlights applicable laws and regulations might be distributed to employees or made available in a central location. Information sources might include primary information developed by the relevant government, governmental agencies, regulatory organizations, licensing agencies, and professional associations (e.g., from their websites); law firm memorandums or newsletters; and association memorandums or publications (e.g., *CFA Magazine*).

▶ *Establish procedures for reporting violations*: Firms might provide written protocols for reporting suspected violations of laws, regulations, or company policies.

Application of the Standard

Example 1 (Notification of Known Violations): Michael Allen works for a brokerage firm and is responsible for an underwriting of securities. A company official gives Allen information indicating that the financial statements Allen filed with the regulator overstate the issuer's earnings. Allen seeks the advice of the brokerage firm's general counsel, who states that it would be difficult for the regulator to prove that Allen has been involved in any wrongdoing.

> *Comment*: Although it is recommended that members and candidates seek the advice of legal counsel, the reliance on such advice does not absolve a member or candidate from the requirement to comply with the law or regulation. Allen should report this situation to his supervisor, seek an independent legal opinion, and determine whether the regulator should be notified of the error.

Example 2 (Dissociating from a Violation): Lawrence Brown's employer, an investment banking firm, is the principal underwriter for an issue of convertible debentures by the Courtney Company. Brown discovers that the Courtney Company has concealed severe third-quarter losses in its foreign operations. The preliminary prospectus has already been distributed.

> *Comment*: Knowing that the preliminary prospectus is misleading, Brown should report his findings to the appropriate supervisory persons in his firm. If the matter is not remedied and Brown's employer does not dissociate from the underwriting, Brown should sever all his connections with the underwriting. Brown should also seek legal advice to determine whether additional reporting or other action should be taken.

Example 3 (Dissociating from a Violation): Kamisha Washington's firm advertises its past performance record by showing the 10-year return of a composite of its client accounts. Washington discovers, however, that the composite omits the performance of accounts that have left the firm during the 10-year period, whereas the description of the composite indicates the inclusion of all firm accounts. This omission has led to an inflated performance figure. Washington is asked to use promotional material that includes the erroneous performance number when soliciting business for the firm.

> *Comment*: Misrepresenting performance is a violation of the Code and Standards. Although she did not calculate the performance herself, Washington would be assisting in violating Standard I(A) if she were to use the inflated performance number when soliciting clients. She must dissociate herself from the activity. If discussing the misleading number with the person responsible is not an option for correcting the problem, she can bring the situation to the attention of her supervisor or the compliance department at her firm. If her firm is unwilling to recalculate performance, she must refrain from using the misleading promotional material and should notify the firm of her reasons. If the firm insists that she use the material, she should consider whether her obligation to dissociate from the activity requires her to seek other employment.

Example 4 (Following the Highest Requirements): James Collins is an investment analyst for a major Wall Street brokerage firm. He works in a developing country with a rapidly modernizing economy and a growing capital market. Local securities laws are minimal—in form and content—and include no punitive prohibitions against insider trading.

> *Comment*: Collins must abide by the requirements of the Code and Standards that might be more strict than the rules of the developing country. He should be aware of the risks that a small market and the absence of a fairly regulated flow of information to the market represent to his ability to obtain information and make timely judgments. He should include this factor in formulating his advice to clients. In handling material nonpublic information that accidentally comes into his possession, he must follow Standard II(A)—Material Nonpublic Information.

Example 5 (Following the Highest Requirements): Laura Jameson works for a multinational investment adviser based in the United States. Jameson lives and works as a registered investment adviser in the tiny, but wealthy, island nation of Karramba. Karramba's securities laws state that no investment adviser registered and working in that country can participate in initial public offerings (IPOs) for the adviser's personal account. Jameson, believing that as a U.S. citizen working for a U.S.-based company she should comply only with U.S. law, has ignored this Karrambian law. In addition, Jameson believes that, as a charterholder, as long as she adheres to the Code and Standards requirement that she disclose her participation in any IPO to her employer and clients when such ownership creates a conflict of interest, she is meeting the highest ethical requirements.

> *Comment*: Jameson is in violation of Standard I(A). As a registered investment adviser in Karramba, Jameson is prevented by Karrambian securities law from participating in IPOs regardless of the law of her home country. In addition, because the law of the country where she is working is stricter than the Code and Standards, she must follow the stricter requirements of the local law rather than the requirements of the Code and Standards.

Example 6 (Laws and Regulations Based on Religious Tenets): Amanda Janney is employed as a fixed-income portfolio manager for a large international firm. She is on a team within her firm that is responsible for creating and managing a fixed-income hedge fund to be sold throughout the firm's distribution centers to high-net-worth clients. Her firm receives expressions of interest from potential clients from the Middle East who are seeking investments that comply with Islamic law. The marketing and promotional materials for the fixed-income hedge fund do not specify whether or not the fund is a suitable investment for an investor seeking compliance with Islamic law. Because the fund is being distributed globally, Janney is concerned about the reputation of the fund and the firm and believes disclosure of whether or not the fund complies with Islamic law could help minimize potential mistakes with placing this investment.

> *Comment*: As the financial market continues to become globalized, members and candidates will need to be aware of the differences between cultural and religious laws and requirements as well as the different governmental laws and regulations. Janney and the firm could be proactive in their efforts to acknowledge areas where the new fund may not be suitable for clients.

Example 7 (Reporting Potential Unethical Actions): Krista Blume is a junior portfolio manager for high-net-worth portfolios at a large global investment manager. She observes a number of new portfolios and relationships coming from a country in Europe where the firm did not have previous business and is told that a broker in that country is responsible for this new business. At a meeting on allocation of research resources to third-party research firms, Blume notes that this broker has been added to the list and is allocated payments for research. However, she knows the portfolios do not invest in securities in the broker's country. And she has not seen any research come from this broker. Blume asks her supervisor about the name being on the list and is told that someone in marketing is receiving the research and that the name being on the list is OK. She believes that what is going on may be that the broker is being paid for new business through the inappropriate research payments and wishes to dissociate from the misconduct.

> *Comment*: Blume should follow the firm's policies and procedures for reporting potential unethical activity, which may include discussions with her supervisor or someone in a designated compliance department. She should communicate her concerns appropriately while advocating for disclosure between the new broker relationship and the research payments.

B. Independence and Objectivity

Members and Candidates must use reasonable care and judgment to achieve and maintain independence and objectivity in their professional activities. Members and Candidates must not offer, solicit, or accept any gift, benefit, compensation, or consideration that reasonably could be expected to compromise their own or another's independence and objectivity.

Guidance

Highlights:

▶ *Buy-Side Clients*
▶ *Fund Manager Relationships*
▶ *Investment Banking Relationships*

► *Public Companies*

► *Credit Rating Agency Opinions*

► *Issuer-Paid Research*

► *Travel Funding*

Standard I(B) states the responsibility of CFA Institute members and candidates in the CFA Program to maintain independence and objectivity so that their clients will have the benefit of their work and opinions unaffected by any potential conflict of interest or other circumstance adversely affecting their judgment. Every member and candidate should endeavor to avoid situations that could cause or be perceived to cause a loss of independence or objectivity in recommending investments or taking investment action.

External sources may try to influence the investment process by offering analysts and portfolio managers a variety of benefits. Corporations may seek expanded research coverage; issuers and underwriters may wish to promote new securities offerings; brokers may want to increase commission business; and independent rating agencies may be influenced by the company requesting the rating. Benefits may include gifts, invitations to lavish functions, tickets, favors, or job referrals. One type of benefit is the allocation of shares in oversubscribed IPOs to investment managers for their personal accounts. This practice affords managers the opportunity to make quick profits that may not be available to their clients. Such a practice is prohibited under Standard I(B). Modest gifts and entertainment are acceptable, but special care must be taken by members and candidates to resist subtle and not-so-subtle pressures to act in conflict with the interests of their clients. Best practice dictates that members and candidates reject any offer of gift or entertainment that could be expected to threaten their independence and objectivity.

Receiving a gift, benefit, or consideration from a *client* can be distinguished from gifts given by entities seeking to influence a member or candidate to the detriment of other clients. In a client relationship, the client has already entered some type of compensation arrangement with the member, candidate, or his or her firm. A gift from a client could be considered supplementary compensation. The potential for obtaining influence to the detriment of other clients, although present, is not as great as in situations where no compensation arrangement exists. When possible, prior to accepting "bonuses" or gifts from clients, members and candidates should disclose to their employers such benefits offered by clients. If notification is not possible prior to acceptance, members and candidates must disclose to their employers benefits previously accepted from clients. Disclosure allows the employer of a member or candidate to make an independent determination about the extent to which the gift may affect the member's or candidate's independence and objectivity.

Members and candidates may also come under pressure from their own firms to, for example, issue favorable research reports or recommendations for certain companies with potential or continuing business relationships with the firm. The situation may be aggravated if an executive of the company sits on the bank or investment firm's board and attempts to interfere in investment decision making. Members and candidates acting in a sales or marketing capacity must be especially mindful of their objectivity in promoting appropriate investments for their clients.

Left unmanaged, pressures that threaten independence place research analysts in a difficult position and may jeopardize their ability to act independently and objectively. One of the ways that research analysts have coped with these pressures in the past is to use subtle and ambiguous language in their recommendations or to temper the tone of their research reports. Such subtleties are lost on some investors, however, who reasonably expect research reports and recommendations to be straightforward and transparent, and to communicate clearly an analyst's views based on unbiased analysis and independent judgment.

Members and candidates are personally responsible for maintaining independence and objectivity when preparing research reports, making investment recommendations, and taking investment action on behalf of clients. Recommendations must convey the member's or candidate's true opinions, free of bias from internal or external pressures, and be stated in clear and unambiguous language.

Members and candidates also should be aware that some of their professional or social activities within CFA Institute or its member societies may subtly threaten their independence or objectivity. When seeking corporate financial support for conventions, seminars, or even weekly society luncheons, the members or candidates responsible for the activities should evaluate both the actual effect of such solicitations on their independence and whether their objectivity might be perceived to be compromised in the eyes of their clients.

Buy-Side Clients

One source of pressure on sell-side analysts is buy-side clients. Institutional clients are traditionally the primary users of sell-side research, either directly or with soft dollar brokerage. Portfolio managers may have significant positions in the security of a company under review. A rating downgrade may adversely affect the portfolio's performance, particularly in the short term, because the sensitivity of stock prices to ratings changes has increased in recent years. A downgrade may also affect the manager's compensation, which is usually tied to portfolio performance. Moreover, portfolio performance is subject to media and public scrutiny, which may affect the manager's professional reputation. Consequently, some portfolio managers implicitly or explicitly support sell-side ratings inflation.

Portfolio managers have a responsibility to respect and foster the intellectual honesty of sell-side research. Therefore, it is improper for portfolio managers to threaten or engage in retaliatory practices, such as reporting sell-side analysts to the covered company in order to instigate negative corporate reactions. Although most portfolio managers do not engage in such practices, the perception by the research analyst that a reprisal is possible may cause concern and make it difficult for the analyst to maintain independence and objectivity.

Fund Manager Relationships

Research analysts are not the only people who must be concerned with maintaining their independence. Members and candidates who are responsible for hiring and retaining outside managers should not accepts gifts, entertainment, or travel funding that may be perceived as impairing their decisions. The use of secondary fund managers has evolved into a common practice to manage specific asset allocations. Both the primary and secondary fund managers often arrange educational and marketing events to inform others about their business strategies or investment process. Members and candidates must review the merits of each offer individually in determining whether they may attend yet maintain their independence.

Investment Banking Relationships

Some sell-side firms may exert pressure on their analysts to issue favorable research reports on current or prospective investment banking clients. For many of these firms, income from investment banking has become increasingly important to overall firm profitability because brokerage income has declined as a result of price competition. Consequently, firms offering investment banking services work hard to develop and maintain relationships with investment banking clients and prospects. These companies are often covered by the firm's research analysts because companies often select their investment banks on the basis of the reputation of their research analysts, the quality of their work, and their standing in the industry.

In some countries, research analysts frequently work closely with their investment banking colleagues to help evaluate prospective investment banking clients. In other countries, because of past abuses in managing the obvious conflicts of interest, regulators have established clear rules prohibiting the interaction of these groups. Although collaboration between research analysts and investment banking colleagues may benefit the firm and enhance market efficiency (e.g., by allowing firms to assess risks more accurately and make better pricing assumptions), it requires firms to carefully balance the conflicts of interest inherent in the collaboration. Having analysts work with investment bankers is appropriate only when the conflicts are adequately and effectively managed and disclosed. Firm managers have a responsibility to provide an environment in which analysts are neither coerced nor enticed into issuing research that does not reflect their true opinions. Firms should require public disclosure of actual conflicts of interest to investors.

Members, candidates, and their firms must adopt and follow perceived best practices in maintaining independence and objectivity in the corporate culture and protecting analysts from undue pressure by their investment banking colleagues. The "firewalls" traditionally built between these two functions must be managed to minimize conflicts of interest; indeed, enhanced firewall policies may go as far as prohibiting all communications between these groups. A key element of an enhanced firewall is separate reporting structures for personnel on the research side and personnel on the investment banking side. For example, investment banking personnel should not have any authority to approve, disapprove, or make changes to research reports or recommendations. Another element should be a compensation arrangement that minimizes the pressures on research analysts and rewards objectivity and accuracy. Compensation arrangements should not link analyst remuneration directly to investment banking assignments in which the analyst may participate as a team member. Firms should also regularly review their policies and procedures to determine whether analysts are adequately safeguarded and to improve the transparency of disclosures relating to conflicts of interest. The highest level of transparency is achieved when disclosures are prominent and specific rather than marginalized and generic.

Public Companies

Analysts may be pressured to issue favorable reports and recommendations by the companies they follow. Not every stock is a "buy," and not every research report is favorable—for many reasons, including the cyclical nature of many business activities and market fluctuations. For instance, a "good company" does not always translate into a "good stock" rating if the current stock price is fully valued. In making an investment recommendation, the analyst is responsible for anticipating, interpreting, and assessing a company's prospects and stock price performance in a factual manner. Many company managers, however, believe that their company's stock is undervalued, and these managers may find it difficult to accept critical research reports or ratings downgrades. Company managers' compensation may also be dependent on stock performance.

Due diligence in financial research and analysis involves gathering information from a wide variety of sources, including public disclosure documents (such as proxy statements, annual reports, and other regulatory filings) and also company management and investor-relations personnel, suppliers, customers, competitors, and other relevant sources. Research analysts may justifiably fear that companies will limit their ability to conduct thorough research by denying analysts who have "negative" views direct access to company managers and/or barring them from conference calls and other communication venues. Retaliatory practices include companies bringing legal action against analysts personally and/or their firms to seek monetary damages for the economic effects of negative reports and recommendations. Although few companies engage in such behavior, the perception that a reprisal is possible is a reasonable concern for analysts. This concern may make it difficult for them to conduct the comprehensive research needed to make objective recommendations. For further information and guidance, members and candidates should refer to the CFA Institute publication *Best Practice Guidelines Governing Analyst/Corporate Issuer Relations* (www.cfainstitute.org).

Credit Rating Agency Opinions

Credit rating agencies provide a service by grading the fixed-income products offered by companies. Analysts face challenges related to incentives and compensation schemes that may be tied to the final rating and successful placement of the product. Members and candidates employed at rating agencies should ensure that procedures and processes at the agencies prevent undue influences from a sponsoring company during the analysis. Members and candidates should abide by their agencies' and the industry's standards of conduct regarding the analytical process and the distribution of their reports.

The work of credit rating agencies also raises concerns similar to those inherent in investment banking relationships. Analysts may face pressure to issue ratings at a specific level because of other services the agency offers companies, namely, advising on the development of structured products. The rating agencies need to develop the necessary firewalls and protections to allow the independent operations of their different business lines.

When using information provided by credit rating agencies, members and candidates should be mindful of the potential conflicts of interest. And because of the potential conflicts, members and candidates may need to independently validate the rating granted.

Issuer-Paid Research

In light of the recent reduction of sell-side research coverage, many companies, seeking to increase visibility both in the financial markets and with potential investors, have hired analysts to produce research reports analyzing their companies. These reports bridge the gap created by the lack of coverage and can be an effective method of communicating with investors.

Issuer-paid research conducted by independent analysts, however, is fraught with potential conflicts. Depending on how the research is written and distributed, investors may be misled into believing that the research is from an independent source when, in reality, it has been paid for by the subject company.

Members and candidates must adhere to strict standards of conduct that govern how the research is to be conducted and what disclosures must be made in the report. Analysts must engage in thorough, independent, and unbiased analysis and must fully disclose potential conflicts of interest, including the nature of their compensation. Otherwise, analysts risk misleading investors.

Investors need clear, credible, and thorough information about companies, and they need research based on independent thought. At a minimum, issuer-paid research should include a thorough analysis of the company's financial statements based on publicly disclosed information, benchmarking within a peer group, and industry analysis. Analysts must exercise diligence, independence, and thoroughness in conducting their research in an objective manner. Analysts must distinguish between fact and opinion in their reports. Conclusions must have a reasonable and adequate basis and must be supported by appropriate research.

Independent analysts must also strictly limit the type of compensation that they accept for conducting issuer-paid research. Otherwise, the content and conclusions of the reports could reasonably be expected to be determined or affected by compensation from the sponsoring companies. Compensation that might influence the research report could be direct, such as payment based on the conclusions of the report, or indirect, such as stock warrants or other equity instruments that could increase in value on the basis of positive coverage in the report. In such instances, the independent analyst has an incentive to avoid including negative information or making negative conclusions. Best practice is for independent analysts, prior to writing their report, to negotiate only a flat fee for their work that is not linked to their conclusions or recommendations.

Travel Funding

The benefits related to accepting paid travel extend beyond the cost savings to the member or candidate, such as the chance to talk exclusively with the executives of a company. The problem is that members and candidates may be influenced by these discussions when flying on a corporate or chartered jet. Best practice dictates that members and candidates always use commercial transportation rather than accept paid travel arrangements from an outside company. Should commercial transportation be unavailable, members and candidates may accept modestly arranged travel to participate in appropriate information-gathering events, such as a property tour.

Recommended Procedures for Compliance

Members and candidates should adhere to the following practices and should encourage their firms to establish procedures to avoid violations of Standard I(B):

▶ *Protect the integrity of opinions*: Members, candidates, and their firms should establish policies stating that every research report concerning the securities of a corporate client should reflect the unbiased opinion of the analyst. Firms should also design compensation systems that protect the integrity of the investment decision process by maintaining the independence and objectivity of analysts.

▶ *Create a restricted list*: If the firm is unwilling to permit dissemination of adverse opinions about a corporate client, members and candidates should encourage the firm to remove the controversial company from the research universe and put it on a restricted list so that the firm disseminates only factual information about the company.

▶ *Restrict special cost arrangements*: When attending meetings at an issuer's headquarters, members and candidates should pay for commercial transportation and hotel charges. No corporate issuer should reimburse members or candidates for air transportation. Members and candidates should encourage issuers to limit the use of corporate aircraft to situations in which commercial transportation is not available or in which efficient movement could not otherwise be arranged. Members and candidates should take particular care that when frequent meetings are held between an individual issuer and an individual member or candidate, the issuer should not always host the member or candidate.

▶ *Limit gifts*: Members and candidates must limit the acceptance of gratuities and/or gifts to token items. Standard I(B) does not preclude customary, ordinary business-related entertainment as long as its purpose is not to influence or reward members or candidates. Firms should consider a strict value limit for acceptable gifts that is based on the local or regional customs and should address whether the limit is per gift or an aggregate annual value.

▶ *Restrict investments*: Members and candidates should encourage their investment firms to develop formal polices related to employee purchases of equity or equity-related IPOs. Firms should require prior approval for employee participation in IPOs, with prompt disclosure of investment actions taken following the offering. Strict limits should be imposed on investment personnel acquiring securities in private placements.

▶ *Review procedures*: Members and candidates should encourage their firms to implement effective supervisory and review procedures to ensure that analysts and portfolio managers comply with policies relating to their personal investment activities.

▶ *Independence policy*: Members, candidates, and their firms should establish a formal written policy on the independence and objectivity of research and implement reporting structures and review procedures to ensure that research analysts do not report to and are not supervised or controlled by any department of the firm that could compromise the independence of the analyst. More detailed recommendations related to a firm's policies regarding research objectivity are set forth in the CFA Institute statement *Research Objectivity Standards* (www.cfainstitute.org).

▶ *Appointed officer*: Firms should appoint a senior officer with oversight responsibilities for compliance with the firm's code of ethics and all regulations concerning its business. Firms should provide every employee with the procedures and policies for reporting potentially unethical behavior, violations of regulations, or other activities that may harm the firm's reputation.

Application of the Standard

Example 1 (Travel Expenses): Steven Taylor, a mining analyst with Bronson Brokers, is invited by Precision Metals to join a group of his peers in a tour of mining facilities in several western U.S. states. The company arranges for chartered group flights from site to site and for accommodations in Spartan Motels, the only chain with accommodations near the mines, for three nights. Taylor allows Precision Metals to pick up his tab, as do the other analysts, with one exception—John Adams, an employee of a large trust company who insists on following his company's policy and paying for his hotel room himself.

Comment: The policy of the company where Adams works complies closely with Standard I(B) by avoiding even the appearance of a conflict of interest, but Taylor and the other analysts were not necessarily violating Standard I(B).

In general, when allowing companies to pay for travel and/or accommodations in these circumstances, members and candidates must use their judgment. They must be on guard that such arrangements not impinge on a member's or candidate's independence and objectivity. In this example, the trip was strictly for business and Taylor was not accepting irrelevant or lavish hospitality. The itinerary required chartered flights, for which analysts were not expected to pay. The accommodations were modest. These arrangements are not unusual and did not violate Standard I(B) as long as Taylor's independence and objectivity were not compromised. In the final analysis, members and candidates should consider both whether they can remain objective and whether their integrity might be perceived by their clients to have been compromised.

Example 2 (Research Independence): Susan Dillon, an analyst in the corporate finance department of an investment services firm, is making a presentation to a potential new business client that includes the promise that her firm will provide full research coverage of the potential client.

Comment: Dillon may agree to provide research coverage, but she must not commit her firm's research department to providing a favorable recommendation. The firm's recommendation (favorable, neutral, or unfavorable) must be based on an independent and objective investigation and analysis of the company and its securities.

Example 3 (Research Independence and Intrafirm Pressure): Walter Fritz is an equity analyst with Hilton Brokerage who covers the mining industry. He has concluded that the stock of Metals & Mining is overpriced at its current level, but he is concerned that a negative research report will hurt the good relationship between Metals & Mining and the investment banking division of his firm. In fact, a senior manager of Hilton Brokerage has just sent him a copy of a proposal his firm has made to Metals & Mining to underwrite a debt offering. Fritz needs to produce a report right away and is concerned about issuing a less-than-favorable rating.

Comment: Fritz's analysis of Metals & Mining must be objective and based solely on consideration of company fundamentals. Any pressure from other divisions of his firm is inappropriate. This conflict could have been eliminated if, in anticipation of the offering, Hilton Brokerage had placed Metals & Mining on a restricted list for its sales force.

Example 4 (Research Independence and Issuer Relationship Pressure): As in Example 3, Walter Fritz has concluded that Metals & Mining stock is overvalued at its current level, but he is concerned that a negative research report might jeopardize a close rapport that he has nurtured over the years with Metals & Mining's CEO, chief finance officer, and investment relations officer. Fritz is concerned that a negative report might result also in management retaliation—for instance, cutting him off from participating in conference calls when a quarterly earnings release is made, denying him the ability to ask questions on such calls, and/or denying him access to top management for arranging group meetings between Hilton Brokerage clients with top Metals & Mining managers.

Comment: As in Example 3, Fritz's analysis must be objective and based solely on consideration of company fundamentals. Any pressure from Metals & Mining is inappropriate. Fritz should reinforce the integrity of his conclusions by stressing that his investment recommendation is based on relative valuation, which may include qualitative issues with respect to Metals & Mining's management.

Example 5 (Research Independence and Sales Pressure): As support for the sales effort of her corporate bond department, Lindsey Warner offers credit guidance to purchasers of fixed-income securities. Her compensation is closely linked to the performance of the corporate bond department. Near the quarter's end, Warner's firm has a large inventory position in the bonds of Milton, Ltd., and has been unable to sell the bonds because of Milton's recent announcement of an operating problem. Salespeople have asked her to contact large clients to push the bonds.

> *Comment*: Unethical sales practices create significant potential violations of the Code and Standards. Warner's opinion of the Milton bonds must not be affected by internal pressure or compensation. In this case, Warner must refuse to push the Milton bonds unless she is able to justify that the market price has already adjusted for the operating problem.

Example 6 (Research Independence and Prior Coverage): Jill Jorund is a securities analyst following airline stocks and a rising star at her firm. Her boss has been carrying a "buy" recommendation on International Airlines and asks Jorund to take over coverage of that airline. He tells Jorund that under no circumstances should the prevailing buy recommendation be changed.

> *Comment*: Jorund must be independent and objective in her analysis of International Airlines. If she believes that her boss's instructions have compromised her, she has two options: Tell her boss that she cannot cover the company under these constraints or take over coverage of the company, reach her own independent conclusions, and if they conflict with her boss's opinion, share the conclusions with her boss or other supervisors in the firm so that they can make appropriate recommendations. Jorund must issue only recommendations that reflect her independent and objective opinion.

Example 7 (Gifts and Entertainment from Related Party): Edward Grant directs a large amount of his commission business to a New York-based brokerage house. In appreciation for all the business, the brokerage house gives Grant two tickets to the World Cup in South Africa, two nights at a nearby resort, several meals, and transportation via limousine to the game. Grant fails to disclose receiving this package to his supervisor.

> *Comment*: Grant has violated Standard I(B) because accepting these substantial gifts may impede his independence and objectivity. Every member and candidate should endeavor to avoid situations that might cause or be perceived to cause a loss of independence or objectivity in recommending investments or taking investment action. By accepting the trip, Grant has opened himself up to the accusation that he may give the broker favored treatment in return.

Example 8 (Gifts and Entertainment from Client): Theresa Green manages the portfolio of Ian Knowlden, a client of Tisbury Investments. Green achieves an annual return for Knowlden that is consistently better than that of the benchmark she and the client previously agreed to. As a reward, Knowlden offers Green two tickets to Wimbledon and the use of Knowlden's flat in London for a week. Green discloses this gift to her supervisor at Tisbury.

> *Comment*: Green is in compliance with Standard I(B) because she disclosed the gift from one of her clients in accordance with the firm's policies. Members and candidates may accept bonuses or gifts from clients as long as they disclose them to their employers, because gifts in a client relationship are deemed less likely to affect a member's or candidate's objectivity and

independence than gifts in other situations. Disclosure is required, however, so that supervisors can monitor such situations to guard against employees favoring a gift-giving client to the detriment of other fee-paying clients (such as by allocating a greater proportion of IPO stock to the gift-giving client's portfolio).

Best practices for monitoring include comparing the transaction costs of the Knowlden account with the costs of other accounts managed by Green and other similar accounts within Tisbury. The supervisor could also compare the performance returns with the returns of other clients with the same mandate. This comparison will assist in determining whether a pattern of favoritism by Green is disadvantaging other Tisbury clients or the possibility that this favoritism could affect her future behavior.

Example 9 (Travel Expenses from External Manager): Tom Wayne is the investment manager of the Franklin City Employees Pension Plan. He recently completed a successful search for a firm to manage the foreign equity allocation of the plan's diversified portfolio. He followed the plan's standard procedure of seeking presentations from a number of qualified firms and recommended that his board select Penguin Advisors because of its experience, well-defined investment strategy, and performance record. The firm claims compliance with the Global Investment Performance Standards (GIPS) and has been verified. Following the selection of Penguin, a reporter from the *Franklin City Record* calls to ask if there was any connection between this action and the fact that Penguin was one of the sponsors of an "investment fact-finding trip to Asia" that Wayne made earlier in the year. The trip was one of several conducted by the Pension Investment Academy, which had arranged the itinerary of meetings with economic, government, and corporate officials in major cities in several Asian countries. The Pension Investment Academy obtains support for the cost of these trips from a number of investment managers, including Penguin Advisors; the Academy then pays the travel expenses of the various pension plan managers on the trip and provides all meals and accommodations. The president of Penguin Advisors was also one of the travelers on the trip.

> *Comment*: Although Wayne can probably put to good use the knowledge he gained from the trip in selecting portfolio managers and in other areas of managing the pension plan, his recommendation of Penguin Advisors may be tainted by the possible conflict incurred when he participated in a trip partly paid for by Penguin Advisors and when he was in the daily company of the president of Penguin Advisors. To avoid violating Standard I(B), Wayne's basic expenses for travel and accommodations should have been paid by his employer or the pension plan; contact with the president of Penguin Advisors should have been limited to informational or educational events only; and the trip, the organizer, and the sponsor should have been made a matter of public record. Even if his actions were not in violation of Standard I(B), Wayne should have been sensitive to the public perception of the trip when reported in the newspaper and the extent to which the subjective elements of his decision might have been affected by the familiarity that the daily contact of such a trip would encourage. This advantage would probably not be shared by firms competing with Penguin Advisors.

Example 10 (Research Independence and Compensation Arrangements): Javier Herrero recently left his job as a research analyst for a large investment adviser. While looking for a new position, he was hired by an investor-relations firm to write a research report on one of its clients, a small educational software company. The investor-relations firm hopes to generate investor interest in the technology company. The firm will pay Herrero a flat fee plus a bonus if any new investors buy stock in the company as a result of Herrero's report.

> *Comment*: If Herrero accepts this payment arrangement, he will be in violation of Standard I(B) because the compensation arrangement can reasonably be expected to compromise his independence and objectivity. Herrero will receive a bonus for attracting investors, which provides an incentive to draft a positive report regardless of the facts and to ignore or play down any negative information about the company. Herrero should accept only a flat fee that is not tied to the conclusions or recommendations of the report. Issuer-paid research that is objective and unbiased can be done under the right circumstances as long as the analyst takes steps to maintain his or her objectivity and includes in the report proper disclosures regarding potential conflicts of interest.

Example 11 (Recommendation Objectivity and Service Fees): Two years ago, Bob Wade, trust manager for Central Midas Bank, was approached by Western Funds about promoting its family of funds, with special interest in the service-fee class of funds. To entice Central to promote this class, Western Funds offered to pay the bank a service fee of 0.25 percent. Without disclosing the fee being offered to the bank, Wade asked one of the investment managers to review Western's funds to determine whether they were suitable for clients of Central Midas Bank. The manager completed the normal due diligence review and determined that the new funds were fairly valued in the market with fee structures on a par with competitors. Wade decided to accept Western's offer and instructed the team of portfolio managers to exclusively promote these funds and the service-fee class to clients seeking to invest new funds or transfer from their current investments.

Now, two years later, the funds managed by Western begin to underperform their peers. Wade is counting on the fees to reach his profitability targets and continues to push these funds as acceptable investments for Central's clients.

> *Comment*: Wade is violating Standard I(B) because the fee arrangement has affected the objectivity of his recommendations. Wade is relying on the fee as a component of the department's profitability and is unwilling to offer other products that may affect the fees received.
>
> See also Standard VI(A)—Disclosure of Conflicts.

Example 12 (Recommendation Objectivity): Bob Thompson has been doing research for the portfolio manager of the fixed-income department. His assignment is to do sensitivity analysis on securitized subprime mortgages. He has discussed with the manager possible scenarios to use to calculate expected returns. A key assumption in such calculations is housing price appreciation (HPA) because it drives "prepays" (prepayments of mortgages) and losses. Thompson is concerned with the significant appreciation experienced over the previous five years as a result of the increased availability of funds from subprime mortgages. Thompson insists that the analysis should include a scenario run with negative 10 percent for the first year, negative 5 percent for the second year, and then (to project a worst-case scenario) 0 percent for Years 3 through 5. The manager replies that these assumptions are too dire because there has never been a time in their available database when HPA was negative.

Thompson conducts his research to better understand the risks inherent in these securities and evaluates these securities in the worst-case scenario, an unlikely but possible environment. Based on the results of the enhanced scenarios, Thompson does not recommend the purchase of the securitization. Against the general market trends, the manager follows Thompson's recommendation and does not invest. The following year, the housing market collapses. In avoiding the subprime investments, the manager's portfolio outperforms its peer group that year.

> *Comment*: Thompson's actions in running the worst-case scenario against the protests of the portfolio manager are in alignment with the principles of Standard I(B). Thompson did not allow his research to be pressured by the general trends of the market or the manager's desire to limit the research to historical norms.
>
> See also Standard V(A)—Diligence and Reasonable Basis.

C. Misrepresentation

Members and Candidates must not knowingly make any misrepresentations relating to investment analysis, recommendations, actions, or other professional activities.

Guidance

Highlights:

▶ *Impact on Investment Practice*
▶ *Plagiarism*
▶ *Work Completed for Employer*

Trust is the foundation of the investment profession. Investors must be able to rely on the statements and information provided to them by those with whom the investors have trusted their financial well-being. Investment professionals who make false or misleading statements not only harm investors but also reduce the level of investor confidence in the investment profession and threaten the integrity of capital markets as a whole.

A misrepresentation is any untrue statement or omission of a fact or any statement that is otherwise false or misleading. A member or candidate must not knowingly omit or misrepresent information or give a false impression of a firm, organization, or security in the member's or candidate's oral representations, advertising (whether in the press or through brochures), electronic communications, or written materials (whether publicly disseminated or not). In this context, "knowingly" means that the member or candidate either knows or should have known that the misrepresentation was being made or that omitted information could alter the investment decision-making process.

Written materials include, but are not limited to, research reports, underwriting documents, company financial reports, market letters, newspaper columns, and books. Electronic communications include, but are not limited to, internet communications, webpages, chat rooms, and e-mails. Members and candidates who use webpages should regularly monitor materials posted on the site to ensure that the site contains current information. Members and candidates should also ensure that all reasonable precautions have been taken to protect the site's integrity and security and that the site does not misrepresent any information and does provide full disclosure.

The omission of a fact or outcome has increased in importance because of the growing use of technical analysis. Many members and candidates rely on models to scan for new investment opportunities, to develop investment vehicles, and to produce investment recommendations and ratings. Although not every model can test for every factor or outcome, members and candidates should ensure that their analyses incorporate a broad range of assumptions—from very positive scenarios to extremely negative scenarios. The omission from the analysis of potentially negative outcomes or of levels of risk outside the norm may misrepresent the true economic value of the investment.

Impact on Investment Practice

Members and candidates must not misrepresent any aspect of their practice, including (but not limited to) their qualifications or credentials, the qualifications or services provided by their firm, their performance record and the record of their firm, and the characteristics of an investment. Any misrepresentation made by a member or candidate relating to the member's or candidate's professional activities is a breach of this standard.

Members and candidates should exercise care and diligence when incorporating third-party information. Misrepresentations resulting from the use of the credit ratings, research, testimonials, or marketing materials of these outside parties become the responsibility of the investment professional when it affects that professional's business practices.

Investing through outside managers continues to expand as an acceptable method of investing in areas outside a firm's core competencies. Members and candidates must disclose their intended use of external managers and must not represent those managers' investment practices as their own. Although the level of involvement of outside managers may change over time, appropriate disclosures by members and candidates are important to avoiding misrepresentations, especially if the primary activity is to invest directly with a single external manager. Standard V(B)—Communication with Clients and Prospective Clients discusses in further detail communicating the firm's investment practices.

Standard I(C) prohibits members and candidates from guaranteeing clients any specific return on volatile investments. Most investments contain some element of risk that makes their return inherently unpredictable. For these investments, guaranteeing either a particular rate of return or a guaranteed preservation of investment capital (e.g., "I can guarantee that you will earn 8 percent on equities this year" or "I can guarantee that you will not lose money on this investment") is misleading to investors. Standard I(C) does not prohibit members and candidates from providing clients with information on investment products that have guarantees built into the structure of the product itself or for which an institution has agreed to cover any losses.

Plagiarism

Standard I(C) also prohibits plagiarism in the preparation of material for distribution to employers, associates, clients, prospects, or the general public. Plagiarism is defined as copying or using in substantially the same form materials prepared by others without acknowledging the source of the material or identifying the author and publisher of such material. Members and candidates must not copy (or represent as their own) original ideas or material without permission and must acknowledge and identify the source of ideas or material that is not their own.

The investment profession uses a myriad of financial, economic, and statistical data in the investment decision-making process. Through various publications and presentations, the investment professional is constantly exposed to the work of others and to the temptation to use that work without proper acknowledgment.

Misrepresentation through plagiarism in investment management can take various forms. The simplest and most flagrant example is to take a research report or study done by another firm or person, change the names, and release the material as one's own original analysis. This action is a clear violation of Standard I(C). Other practices include 1) using excerpts from articles or reports prepared by others either verbatim or with only slight changes in wording without acknowledgment, 2) citing specific quotations as attributable to "leading analysts" and "investment experts" without naming the specific references, 3) presenting statistical estimates of forecasts prepared by others and identifying the sources but without including the qualifying statements or caveats that may have been used, 4) using charts and graphs without stating their sources, and 5) copying proprietary computerized spreadsheets or algorithms without seeking the cooperation or authorization of their creators.

In the case of distributing third-party, outsourced research, members and candidates may use and distribute these reports as long as they do not represent themselves as the authors of such a report. Indeed, the member or candidate may add value for the client by sifting through research and repackaging it for clients. In such cases, clients should be fully informed that they are paying for the ability of the member or candidate to find the best research from a wide variety of sources. Members and candidates must not misrepresent their abilities, the extent of their expertise, or the extent of their work in a way that would mislead their clients or prospective clients. Members and candidates should disclose whether the research being presented to clients comes from another source, from either within or outside the member's or candidate's firm. This allows clients to understand who has the expertise behind the report or if the work is being done by the analyst, other members of the firm, or an outside party.

Standard I(C) also applies to plagiarism in oral communications, such as through group meetings; visits with associates, clients, and customers; use of audio/video media (which is rapidly increasing); and telecommunications, including electronic data transfer and the outright copying of electronic media.

One of the most egregious practices in violation of this standard is the preparation of research reports based on multiple sources of information without acknowledging the sources. Examples of information from such sources include ideas, statistical compilations, and forecasts combined to give the appearance of original work. Although there is no monopoly on ideas, members and candidates must give credit where it is clearly due. Analysts should not use undocumented forecasts, earnings projections, asset values, and so on. Sources must be revealed to bring the responsibility directly back to the author of the report or the firm involved.

Work Completed for Employer

The preceding paragraphs address actions that would constitute a violation of Standard I(C). In some situations, however, members or candidates may use research conducted or models developed by others within the same firm without committing a violation. The most common example relates to the situation in which one (or more) of the original analysts is no longer with the firm. Research and models developed while employed by a firm are the property of the firm. The firm retains the right to continue using the work completed after a member or candidate has left the organization. The firm may issue future reports without providing attribution to the prior analysts. A member or candidate cannot, however, reissue a previously released report solely under his or her name.

Recommended Procedures for Compliance

Factual Presentations

Members and candidates can prevent unintentional misrepresentations of the qualifications or services they or their firms provide if each member and candidate understands the limit of the firm's or individual's capabilities and the need to be accurate and complete in presentations. Firms can provide guidance for employees who make written or oral presentations to clients or potential clients by providing a written list of the firm's available services and a description of the firm's qualifications. This list should suggest ways of describing the firm's services, qualifications, and compensation that are both accurate and suitable for client or customer presentations. Firms can also help prevent misrepresentation by specifically designating which employees are authorized to speak on behalf of the firm. Whether or not the firm provides guidance, members and candidates should make certain that they understand the services the firm can perform and its qualifications.

Qualification Summary

In addition, to ensure accurate presentations to clients, each member and candidate should prepare a summary of his or her own qualifications and experience and a list of the services the member or candidate is capable of performing. Firms can assist member and candidate compliance by periodically reviewing employee correspondence and documents that contain representations of individual or firm qualifications.

Verify Outside Information

When providing information to clients from third parties, members and candidates share a responsibility for the accuracy of the marketing and distribution materials that pertain to the third party's capabilities, services, and products. Misrepresentation by third parties can damage the member's or candidate's reputation, the reputation of the firm, and the integrity of the capital markets. Members and candidates should encourage their employers to develop procedures for verifying information of third-party firms.

Maintain Webpages

Members and candidates who publish webpages should regularly monitor materials posted on the site to ensure that the site contains current information. Members and candidates should also ensure that all reasonable precautions have been taken to protect the site's integrity, confidentiality, and security and that the site does not misrepresent any information and provides full disclosure.

Plagiarism Policy

To avoid plagiarism in preparing research reports or conclusions of analysis, members and candidates should take the following steps:

► *Maintain copies*: Keep copies of all research reports, articles containing research ideas, material with new statistical methodologies, and other materials that were relied on in preparing the research report.

▶ *Attribute quotations*: Attribute to their sources any direct quotations, including projections, tables, statistics, model/product ideas, and new methodologies prepared by persons other than recognized financial and statistical reporting services or similar sources.

▶ *Attribute summaries*: Attribute to their sources any paraphrases or summaries of material prepared by others. For example, to support his analysis of Brown Company's competitive position, the author of a research report on Brown might summarize another analyst's report on Brown's chief competitor, but the author of the Brown report must acknowledge in his own report the reliance on the other analyst's report.

Application of the Standard

Example 1 (Representing the Firm's Abilities): Allison Rogers is a partner in the firm of Rogers and Black, a small firm offering investment advisory services. She assures a prospective client who has just inherited US$1 million that "we can perform all the financial and investment services you need." Rogers and Black is well equipped to provide investment advice but, in fact, cannot provide asset allocation assistance or a full array of financial and investment services.

> *Comment*: Rogers has violated Standard I(C) by orally misrepresenting the services her firm can perform for the prospective client. She must limit herself to describing the range of investment advisory services Rogers and Black can provide and offer to help the client obtain elsewhere the financial and investment services that her firm cannot provide.

Example 2 (Disclosure of Issuer-Paid Research): Anthony McGuire is an issuer-paid analyst hired by publicly traded companies to electronically promote their stocks. McGuire creates a website that promotes his research efforts as a seemingly independent analyst. McGuire posts a profile and a strong buy recommendation for each company on the website indicating that the stock is expected to increase in value. He does not disclose the contractual relationships with the companies he covers on his website, in the research reports he issues, or in the statements he makes about the companies in internet chat rooms.

> *Comment*: McGuire has violated Standard I(C) because the internet site is misleading to potential investors. Even if the recommendations are valid and supported with thorough research, his omissions regarding the true relationship between himself and the companies he covers constitute a misrepresentation. McGuire has also violated Standard VI(A)—Disclosure of Conflicts by not disclosing the existence of an arrangement with the companies through which he receives compensation in exchange for his services.

Example 3 (Correction of Unintentional Errors): Hijan Yao is responsible for the creation and distribution of the marketing materials for his firm, which claims compliance with the GIPS standards. Yao creates and distributes a presentation of performance by the firm's Asian equity composite that states the composite has ¥350 billion in assets. In fact, the composite has only ¥35 billion in assets, and the higher figure on the presentation is a result of a typographical error. Nevertheless, the erroneous material is distributed to a number of clients before Yao catches the mistake.

> *Comment*: Once the error is discovered, Yao must take steps to cease distribution of the incorrect material and correct the error by informing those who have received the erroneous information. Because Yao did not know-

ingly make the misrepresentation, however, he did not violate Standard I(C). Since his firm claims compliance with the GIPS standards, it must also comply with the GIPS Guidance Statement on Error Correction in relation to the error.

Example 4 (Noncorrection of Known Errors): Syed Muhammad is the president of an investment management firm. The promotional material for the firm, created by the firm's marketing department, incorrectly claims that Muhammad has an advanced degree in finance from a prestigious business school in addition to the CFA designation. Although Muhammad attended the school for a short period of time, he did not receive a degree. Over the years, Muhammad and others in the firm have distributed this material to numerous prospective clients and consultants.

> *Comment*: Even though Muhammad may not have been directly responsible for the misrepresentation of his credentials in the firm's promotional material, he used this material numerous times over an extended period and should have known of the misrepresentation. Thus, Muhammad has violated Standard I(C).

Example 5 (Plagiarism): Cindy Grant, a research analyst for a Canadian brokerage firm, has specialized in the Canadian mining industry for the past 10 years. She recently read an extensive research report on Jefferson Mining, Ltd., by Jeremy Barton, another analyst. Barton provided extensive statistics on the mineral reserves, production capacity, selling rates, and marketing factors affecting Jefferson's operations. He also noted that initial drilling results on a new ore body, which had not been made public, might show the existence of mineral zones that could increase the life of Jefferson's main mines, but Barton cited no specific data as to the initial drilling results. Grant called an officer of Jefferson, who gave her the initial drilling results over the telephone. The data indicated that the expected life of the main mines would be tripled. Grant added these statistics to Barton's report and circulated it as her own report within her firm.

> *Comment*: Grant plagiarized Barton's report by reproducing large parts of it in her own report without acknowledgment.

Example 6 (Misrepresentation of Information): When Ricki Marks sells mortgage-backed derivatives called "interest-only strips" (IOs) to public pension plan clients, she describes them as "guaranteed by the U.S. government." Purchasers of the IOs are entitled only to the interest stream generated by the mortgages, however, not the notional principal itself. One particular municipality's investment policies and local law require that securities purchased by its public pension plans be guaranteed by the U.S. government. Although the underlying mortgages are guaranteed, neither the investor's investment nor the interest stream on the IOs is guaranteed. When interest rates decline, causing an increase in prepayment of mortgages, interest payments to the IOs' investors decline, and these investors lose a portion of their investment.

> *Comment*: Marks violated Standard I(C) by misrepresenting the terms and character of the investment.

Example 7 (Potential Information Misrepresentation): Khalouck Abdrabbo manages the investments of several high-net-worth individuals in the United States who are approaching retirement. Abdrabbo advises these individuals that a portion of their investments be moved from equity to bank-sponsored certificates of deposit and money market accounts so that the principal will be "guaranteed" up to a certain amount. The interest is not guaranteed.

Comment: Although there is risk that the institution offering the certificates of deposits and money market accounts could go bankrupt, in the United States, these accounts are insured by the U.S. government through the Federal Deposit Insurance Corporation. Therefore, using the term "guaranteed" in this context is not inappropriate as long as the amount is within the government-insured limit. Abdrabbo should explain these facts to the clients.

Example 8 (Plagiarism): Steve Swanson is a senior analyst in the investment research department of Ballard and Company. Apex Corporation has asked Ballard to assist in acquiring the majority ownership of stock in the Campbell Company, a financial consulting firm, and to prepare a report recommending that stockholders of Campbell agree to the acquisition. Another investment firm, Davis and Company, had already prepared a report for Apex analyzing both Apex and Campbell and recommending an exchange ratio. Apex has given the Davis report to Ballard officers, who have passed it on to Swanson. Swanson reviews the Davis report and other available material on Apex and Campbell companies. From his analysis, he concludes that the common stocks of Campbell and Apex represent good value at their current prices; he believes, however, that the Davis report does not consider all the factors a Campbell stockholder would need to know to make a decision. Swanson reports his conclusions to the partner in charge, who tells him to "use the Davis report, change a few words, sign your name, and get it out."

Comment: If Swanson does as requested, he will violate Standard I(C). He could refer to those portions of the Davis report that he agrees with if he identifies Davis as the source; he could then add his own analysis and conclusions to the report before signing and distributing it.

Example 9 (Plagiarism): Claude Browning, a quantitative analyst for Double Alpha, Inc., returns in great excitement from a seminar. In that seminar, Jack Jorrely, a well-publicized quantitative analyst at a national brokerage firm, discussed one of his new models in great detail, and Browning is intrigued by the new concepts. He proceeds to test the model, making some minor mechanical changes but retaining the concepts, until he produces some very positive results. Browning quickly announces to his supervisors at Double Alpha that he has discovered a new model and that clients and prospective clients should be informed of this positive finding as ongoing proof of Double Alpha's continuing innovation and ability to add value.

Comment: Although Browning tested Jorrely's model on his own and even slightly modified it, he must still acknowledge the original source of the idea. Browning can certainly take credit for the final, practical results; he can also support his conclusions with his own test. The credit for the innovative thinking, however, must be awarded to Jorrely.

Example 10 (Plagiarism): Fernando Zubia would like to include in his firm's marketing materials some "plain-language" descriptions of various concepts, such as the price-to-earnings (P/E) multiple and why standard deviation is used as a measure of risk. The descriptions come from other sources, but Zubia wishes to use them without reference to the original authors. Would this use of material be a violation of Standard I(C)?

Comment: Copying verbatim any material without acknowledgement, including plain-language descriptions of the P/E multiple and standard deviation, violates Standard I(C). Even though these concepts are general, best practice would be for Zubia to describe them in his own words or cite the sources from which the descriptions are quoted. Members and candidates would be violating Standard I(C) if they were either responsible for creating market-ing materials without attribution or knowingly use plagiarized materials.

Example 11 (Plagiarism): Through a mainstream media outlet, Erika Schneider learns about a study that she would like to cite in her research. Should she cite both the mainstream intermediary source as well as the author of the study itself when using that information?

> *Comment*: In all instances, a member or candidate must cite the actual source of the information. Best practice for Schneider would be to obtain the information directly from the author and review it before citing it in a report. In that case, Schneider would not need to report how she found out about the information. For example, suppose Schneider read in the *Financial Times* about a study issued by CFA Institute; best practice for Schneider would be to obtain a copy of the study from CFA Institute, review it, and then cite it in her report. If she does not use any interpretation of the report from the *Financial Times* and the newspaper does not add value to the report itself, the news-paper is merely a conduit to the original information and does not need to be cited. If she does not obtain the report and review the information, Schnei-der runs the risk of relying on second-hand information that may misstate facts. If, for example, the *Financial Times* erroneously reported some informa-tion from the original CFA Institute study and Schneider copied that erroneous information without acknowledging CFA Institute, she could be the object of complaints. Best practice would be either to obtain the complete study from its original author and cite only that author or to use the information provided by the intermediary and cite both sources.

Example 12 (Misrepresentation of Information): Paul Ostrowski runs a two-person investment management firm. Ostrowski's firm subscribes to a service from a large investment research firm that provides research reports that can be repackaged by smaller firms for those firms' clients. Ostrowski's firm distributes these reports to clients as its own work.

> *Comment*: Ostrowski can rely on third-party research that has a reasonable and adequate basis, but he cannot imply that he is the author of such research. If he does, Ostrowski is misrepresenting the extent of his work in a way that misleads the firm's clients or prospective clients.

Example 13 (Misrepresentation of Information): Tom Stafford is part of a team within Appleton Investment Management responsible for managing a pool of assets for Open Air Bank, which distributes structured securities to offshore clients. He becomes aware that Open Air is promoting the structured securities as a much less risky investment than the investment management policy followed by him and the team to manage the original pool of assets. Also, Open Air has procured an independent rating for the pool that significantly overstates the quality of the investments. Stafford communicates his concerns to his team leader and supervisor, who responds that Open Air owns the product and is responsible for all marketing and distribution. Stafford's supervisor goes on to say that the product is outside of the U.S. regulatory regime that Appleton fol-lows and that all risks of the product are disclosed at the bottom of page 184 of the prospectus.

> *Comment*: As a member of the investment team, Stafford is qualified to rec-ognize the degree of accuracy of the materials that characterize the portfo-lio, and he is correct to be worried about Appleton's responsibility for a misrepresentation of the risks. Thus, he should continue to pursue the issue of Open Air's inaccurate promotion of the portfolio according to the firm's policies and procedures.

The Code and Standards stress protecting the reputation of the firm and the sustainability and integrity of the capital markets. Misrepresenting the quality and risks associated with the investment pool may lead to negative consequences for others well beyond the direct investors.

Example 14 (Avoiding a Misrepresentation): Trina Smith is a fixed-income portfolio manager at a pension fund. She has observed that the market for highly structured mortgages is the focus of salespeople she meets and that these products represent a significant number of trading opportunities. In discussions about this topic with her team, Smith learns that calculating yields on changing cash flows within the deal structure requires very specialized vendor software. After more research, they find out that each deal is unique and that deals can have more than a dozen layers and changing cash flow priorities. Smith comes to the conclusion that, because of the complexity of these securities, the team cannot effectively distinguish between potentially good and bad investment options. To avoid misrepresenting their understanding, the team decides that the highly structured mortgage segment of the securitized market should not become part of the core of the fund's portfolio; they will allow some of the less complex securities to be part of the core.

Comment: Smith is in compliance with Standard I(C) by not investing in securities that she and her team cannot effectively understand. Because she is not able to describe the risk and return profile of the securities to the pension fund beneficiaries and trustees, she appropriately limits the fund's exposure to this sector.

D. Misconduct

Members and Candidates must not engage in any professional conduct involving dishonesty, fraud, or deceit or commit any act that reflects adversely on their professional reputation, integrity, or competence.

Guidance

Whereas Standard I(A) addresses the obligation of members and candidates to comply with applicable law that governs their professional activities, Standard I(D) addresses *all* conduct that reflects poorly on the professional integrity, good reputation, or competence of members and candidates. Any act that involves lying, cheating, stealing, or other dishonest conduct is a violation of this standard if the offense reflects adversely on a member's or candidate's professional activities. Although CFA Institute discourages any sort of unethical behavior by members and candidates, the Code and Standards are primarily aimed at conduct and actions related to a member's or candidate's professional life.

Conduct that damages trustworthiness or competence may include behavior that, although it is not illegal, nevertheless negatively affects a member's or candidate's ability to perform his or her responsibilities. For example, abusing alcohol during business hours might constitute a violation of this standard because it could have a detrimental effect on the member's or candidate's ability to fulfill his or her professional responsibilities. Personal bankruptcy may not reflect on the integrity or trustworthiness of the person declaring bankruptcy, but if the circumstances of the bankruptcy involve fraudulent or deceitful business conduct, the bankruptcy may be a violation of this standard.

In some cases, the absence of appropriate conduct or the lack of sufficient effort may be a violation of Standard I(D). The integrity of the investment profession is built on trust. A member or candidate—whether an investment banker, rating or research analyst, or portfolio manager—is expected to conduct the necessary due diligence to properly understand the nature and risks of an investment before making an investment recommendation. By not taking these steps and, instead, relying on someone else in the process to have performed them, members or candidates may violate the trust their clients have placed in them. This loss of trust may have a significant impact on the reputation of the member or candidate and the operations of the financial market as a whole.

Individuals may attempt to abuse the CFA Institute Professional Conduct Program by actively seeking CFA Institute enforcement of the Code and Standards, and Standard I(D) in particular, as a method of settling personal, political, or other disputes unrelated to professional ethics. CFA Institute is aware of this issue, and appropriate disciplinary policies, procedures, and enforcement mechanisms are in place to address misuse of the Code and Standards and the Professional Conduct Program in this way.

Recommended Procedures for Compliance

In addition to ensuring that their own behavior is consistent with Standard I(D), to prevent general misconduct, members and candidates should encourage their firms to adopt the following policies and procedures to support the principles of Standard I(D):

▶ *Code of ethics*: Develop and/or adopt a code of ethics to which every employee must subscribe and make clear that any personal behavior that reflects poorly on the individual involved, the institution as a whole, or the investment industry will not be tolerated.

▶ *List of violations*: Disseminate to all employees a list of potential violations and associated disciplinary sanctions, up to and including dismissal from the firm.

▶ *Employee references*: Check references of potential employees to ensure that they are of good character and not ineligible to work in the investment industry because of past infractions of the law.

Application of the Standard

Example 1 (Professionalism and Competence): Simon Sasserman is a trust investment officer at a bank in a small affluent town. He enjoys lunching every day with friends at the country club, where his clients have observed him having numerous drinks. Back at work after lunch, he clearly is intoxicated while making investment decisions. His colleagues make a point of handling any business with Sasserman in the morning because they distrust his judgment after lunch.

> *Comment*: Sasserman's excessive drinking at lunch and subsequent intoxication at work constitute a violation of Standard I(D) because this conduct has raised questions about his professionalism and competence. His behavior reflects poorly on him, his employer, and the investment industry.

Example 2 (Fraud and Deceit): Howard Hoffman, a security analyst at ATZ Brothers, Inc., a large brokerage house, submits reimbursement forms over a two-year period to ATZ's self-funded health insurance program for more than two dozen bills, most of which have been altered to increase the amount due. An investigation by the firm's director of employee benefits uncovers the inappropriate conduct. ATZ subsequently terminates Hoffman's employment and notifies CFA Institute.

> *Comment*: Hoffman violated Standard I(D) because he engaged in intentional conduct involving fraud and deceit in the workplace that adversely reflected on his integrity.

Example 3 (Fraud and Deceit): Jody Brink, an analyst covering the automotive industry, volunteers much of her spare time to local charities. The board of one of the charitable institutions decides to buy five new vans to deliver hot lunches to low-income elderly people. Brink offers to donate her time to handle purchasing agreements. To pay a long-standing debt to a friend who operates an automobile dealership—and to compensate herself for her trouble—she agrees to a price 20 percent higher than normal and splits the surcharge with her friend. The director of the charity ultimately discovers the scheme and tells Brink that her services, donated or otherwise, are no longer required.

> *Comment*: Brink engaged in conduct involving dishonesty, fraud, and misrepresentation and has violated Standard I(D).

Example 4 (Personal Actions and Integrity): Carmen Garcia manages a mutual fund dedicated to socially responsible investing. She is also an environmental activist. As the result of her participation in nonviolent protests, Garcia has been arrested on numerous occasions for trespassing on the property of a large petrochemical plant that is accused of damaging the environment.

> *Comment*: Generally, Standard I(D) is not meant to cover legal transgressions resulting from acts of civil disobedience in support of personal beliefs because such conduct does not reflect poorly on the member's or candidate's professional reputation, integrity, or competence.

Example 5 (Professional Misconduct): Meredith Rasmussen works on a buy-side trading desk of an investment management firm and concentrates on in-house trades for a hedge fund subsidiary managed by a team at the investment management firm. The hedge fund has been very successful and is marketed globally by the firm. From her experience as the trader for much of the activity of the fund, Rasmussen has become quite knowledgeable about the hedge fund's strategy, tactics, and performance. When a distinct break in the market occurs, however, and many of the securities involved in the hedge fund's strategy decline markedly in value, Rasmussen observes that the reported performance of the hedge fund does not reflect this decline. In her experience, the lack of effect is a very unlikely occurrence. She approaches the head of trading about her concern and is told that she should not ask any questions, that the fund is big and successful and is not her concern. She is fairly sure something is not right, so she contacts the compliance officer, who also tells her to stay away from the issue of the hedge fund's reporting.

> *Comment*: Rasmussen has clearly come upon an error in policies, procedures, and compliance practices within the firm's operations. According to the firm's procedures for reporting potentially unethical activity, she should pursue the issue by gathering some proof of her reason for doubt. Should all internal communications within the firm not satisfy her concerns, Rasmussen should consider reporting the potential unethical activity to the appropriate regulator.
>
> See also Standard IV(A) for guidance on whistleblowing and Standard IV(C) for the duties of a supervisor.

STANDARD II—INTEGRITY OF CAPITAL MARKETS

A. Material Nonpublic Information

Members and Candidates who possess material nonpublic information that could affect the value of an investment must not act or cause others to act on the information.

Guidance

Highlights:

▶ *What Is "Material" Information?*

▶ *What Constitutes "Nonpublic" Information?*

▶ *Mosaic Theory*

▶ *Investment Research Reports*

Trading or inducing others to trade on material nonpublic information erodes confidence in capital markets, institutions, and investment professionals by supporting the idea that those with inside information and special access can take unfair advantage of the general investing public. Although trading on inside information may lead to short-term profits, in the long run, individuals and the profession as a whole will suffer from such trading. It will cause investors to avoid capital markets because the markets are perceived to be "rigged" in favor of the knowledgeable insider. Standard II(A) promotes and maintains a high level of confidence in market integrity, which is one of the foundations of the investment profession.

The prohibition on using this information goes beyond the direct buying and selling of individual securities or bonds. Members and candidates must not use material nonpublic information to influence their investment actions related to derivatives (e.g., swaps or option contracts), mutual funds, or other alternative investments. *Any* trading based on material nonpublic information constitutes a violation of Standard II(A). The expansion of financial products and the increasing interconnectivity of financial markets globally have resulted in new potential opportunities for trading on material nonpublic information.

What Is "Material" Information?

Information is "material" if its disclosure would probably have an impact on the price of a security or if reasonable investors would want to know the information before making an investment decision. In other words, information is material if it would significantly alter the total mix of information currently available about a security in such a way that the price of the security would be affected.

The specificity of the information, the extent of its difference from public information, its nature, and its reliability are key factors in determining whether a particular piece of information fits the definition of material. For example, material information may include, but is not limited to, information on the following:

▶ earnings;

▶ mergers, acquisitions, tender offers, or joint ventures;

▶ changes in assets or asset quality;

► innovative products, processes, or discoveries;

► new licenses, patents, registered trademarks, or regulatory approval/rejection of a product;

► developments regarding customers or suppliers (e.g., the acquisition or loss of a contract);

► changes in management;

► change in auditor notification or the fact that the issuer may no longer rely on an auditor's report or qualified opinion;

► events regarding the issuer's securities (e.g., defaults on senior securities, calls of securities for redemption, repurchase plans, stock splits, changes in dividends, changes to the rights of security holders, public or private sales of additional securities, and changes in credit ratings);

► bankruptcies;

► significant legal disputes;

► government reports of economic trends (employment, housing starts, currency information, etc.);

► orders for large trades before they are executed.

In addition to the substance and specificity of the information, the source or relative reliability of the information also determines materiality. The less reliable a source, the less likely the information provided would be considered material. For example, factual information from a corporate insider regarding a significant new contract for a company is likely to be material, whereas an assumption based on speculation by a competitor about the same contract is likely to be less reliable and, therefore, not material.

Also, the more ambiguous the effect of the information on price, the less material that information is considered. If it is unclear whether the information will affect the price of a security and to what extent, the information may not be considered material. The passage of time may also render information that was once important immaterial.

What Constitutes "Nonpublic" Information?

Information is "nonpublic" until it has been disseminated or is available to the marketplace in general (as opposed to a select group of investors). Dissemination can be defined as "made known to." For example, a company report of profits that is posted on the internet and distributed widely through a press release or accompanied by a filing has been effectively disseminated to the marketplace. Members and candidates must have a reasonable expectation that people have received the information before it can be considered public. It is not necessary, however, to wait for the slowest method of delivery. Once the information is disseminated to the market, it is public information that is no longer covered by this standard.

Members and candidates must be particularly aware of information that is selectively disclosed by corporations to a small group of investors, analysts, or other market participants. Information that is made available to analysts remains nonpublic until it is made available to investors in general. Corporations that disclose information on a limited basis create the potential for insider-trading violations.

Issues of selective disclosure often arise when a corporate insider provides material information to analysts in a briefing or conference call before that information is released to the public. Analysts must be aware that a disclosure made to a room full of analysts does not necessarily make the disclosed information "public." Analysts should also be alert to the possibility that they are selectively receiving material nonpublic information when a company provides them with guidance or interpretation of such publicly available information as financial statements or regulatory filings.

Mosaic Theory

A financial analyst gathers and interprets large quantities of information from many sources. The analyst may use significant conclusions derived from the analysis of public and nonmaterial nonpublic information as the basis for investment recommendations and decisions even if those conclusions would have been material inside information had they been communicated directly to the analyst by a company. Under the "mosaic theory," financial analysts are free to act on this collection, or mosaic, of information without risking violation.

The practice of financial analysis depends on the free flow of information. For the fair and efficient operation of the capital markets, analysts and investors must have the greatest amount of information possible to facilitate making well-informed investment decisions about how and where to invest capital. Accurate, timely, and intelligible communication is essential if analysts and investors are to obtain the data needed to make informed decisions about how and where to invest capital. These disclosures must go beyond the information mandated by the reporting requirements of the securities laws and should include specific business information about items used to guide a company's future growth, such as new products, capital projects, and the competitive environment. Analysts seek and use such information to compare and contrast investment alternatives.

Much of the information used by analysts comes directly from companies. Analysts often receive such information through contacts with corporate insiders, especially investor-relations staff and financial officers. Information may be disseminated in the form of press releases, through oral presentations by company executives in analysts' meetings or conference calls, or during analysts' visits to company premises. In seeking to develop the most accurate and complete picture of a company, analysts should also reach beyond contacts with companies themselves and collect information from other sources, such as customers, contractors, suppliers, and the companies' competitors.

Analysts are in the business of formulating opinions and insights that are not obvious to the general investing public about the attractiveness of particular securities. In the course of their work, analysts actively seek out corporate information not generally known to the market for the express purpose of analyzing that information, forming an opinion on its significance, and informing their clients, who can be expected to trade on the basis of the recommendation. Analysts' initiatives to discover and analyze information and communicate their findings to their clients significantly enhance market efficiency, thus benefiting all investors (see *Dirks v. Securities and Exchange Commission*). Accordingly, violations of Standard II(A) will *not* result when a perceptive analyst reaches a conclusion about a corporate action or event through an analysis of public information and items of nonmaterial nonpublic information.

Investment professionals should note, however, that although analysts are free to use mosaic information in their research reports, they should save and document all their research [see Standard V(C)—Record Retention]. Evidence of the analyst's knowledge of public and nonmaterial nonpublic information about a corporation strengthens the assertion that the analyst reached his or her conclusions solely through appropriate methods rather than through the use of material nonpublic information.

Investment Research Reports

When a particularly well-known or respected analyst issues a report or makes changes to his or her recommendation, that information alone may have an effect on the market and thus may be considered material. Theoretically, under Standard II(A), such a report would have to be made public before it was distributed to clients. The analyst is not a company insider, however, and does not have access to inside information. Presumably, the analyst created the report from information available to the public (mosaic theory) and by using his or her expertise to interpret the information. The analyst's hard work, paid for by the client, generated the conclusions. Simply because the public in general would find the conclusions material does not require that the analyst make his or her work public. Investors who are not clients of the analyst can either do the work themselves or become clients of the analyst for access to the analyst's expertise.

Recommended Procedures for Compliance

Achieve Public Dissemination

If a member or candidate determines that information is material, the member or candidate should make reasonable efforts to achieve public dissemination of the information. This effort usually entails encouraging the issuer company to make the information public. If public dissemination is not possible, the member or candidate must communicate the information only to the designated supervisory and compliance personnel within the member's or candidate's firm and must not take investment action or alter current investment recommendations on the basis of the information. Moreover, members and candidates must not knowingly engage in any conduct that may induce company insiders to privately disclose material nonpublic information.

Adopt Compliance Procedures

Members and candidates should encourage their firms to adopt compliance procedures to prevent the misuse of material nonpublic information. Particularly important is improving compliance in such areas as the review of employee and proprietary trading, documentation of firm procedures, and the supervision of interdepartmental communications in multiservice firms. Compliance procedures should suit the particular characteristics of a firm, including its size and the nature of its business.

Adopt Disclosure Procedures

Members and candidates should encourage their firms to develop and follow disclosure policies designed to ensure that information is disseminated to the marketplace in an equitable manner. For example, analysts from small firms should receive the same information and attention from a company as analysts from large firms receive. Similarly, companies should not provide certain information to buy-side analysts but not to sell-side analysts, or vice versa. Furthermore, a company should not discriminate among analysts in the provision of information or "blackball" particular analysts who have given negative reports on the company in the past.

Issue Press Releases

Companies should consider issuing press releases prior to analyst meetings and conference calls and scripting those meetings and calls to decrease the chance that further information will be disclosed. If material nonpublic information is disclosed for the first time in an analyst meeting or call, the company should promptly issue a press release or otherwise make the information publicly available.

Firewall Elements

An information barrier commonly referred to as a "firewall" is the most widely used approach to preventing the communication of material nonpublic information within firms. It restricts the flow of confidential information to those who need to know the information to perform their jobs effectively. The minimum elements of such a system include, but are not limited to, the following:

- ▶ substantial control of relevant interdepartmental communications, preferably through a clearance area within the firm in either the compliance or legal department;
- ▶ review of employee trading through the maintenance of "watch," "restricted," and "rumor" lists;
- ▶ documentation of the procedures designed to limit the flow of information between departments and of the actions taken to enforce those procedures;
- ▶ heightened review or restriction of proprietary trading while a firm is in possession of material nonpublic information.

Appropriate Interdepartmental Communications

Although documentation requirements must, for practical reasons, take into account the differences between the activities of small firms and those of large, multiservice firms, firms of all sizes and types benefit by improving the documentation of their internal enforcement of firewall procedures. Therefore, even at small firms, procedures concerning interdepartmental communication, the review of trading activity, and the investigation of possible violations should be compiled and formalized.

Physical Separation of Departments

As a practical matter, to the extent possible, firms should consider the physical separation of departments and files to prevent the communication of sensitive information that should not be shared. For example, the investment banking and corporate finance areas of a brokerage firm should be separated from the sales and research departments, and a bank's commercial lending department should be segregated from its trust and research departments.

Prevention of Personnel Overlap

There should be no overlap of personnel between the investment banking and corporate finance areas of a brokerage firm and the sales and research departments or between a bank's commercial lending department and its trust and research departments. For a firewall to be effective in a multiservice firm, an employee can be allowed to be on only one side of the firewall at any time. Inside knowledge may not be limited to information about a specific offering or the current financial condition of a company. Analysts may be exposed to much information about the company, including new product developments or future budget projections that clearly constitute inside knowledge and thus preclude the analyst from returning to his or her research function. For example, an analyst who follows a particular company may provide limited assistance to the investment bankers under carefully controlled circumstances when the firm's investment banking department is involved in a deal with the company. That analyst must then be treated as though he or she were an investment banker; the analyst must remain on the investment banking side of the wall until any information he or she learns is publicly disclosed. In short, the analyst cannot use any information learned in the course of the project for research purposes and cannot share that information with colleagues in the research department.

A Reporting System

A primary objective of an effective firewall procedure is to establish a reporting system in which authorized people review and approve communications between departments. If an employee behind a firewall believes that he or she needs to share confidential information with someone on the other side of the wall, the employee should consult a designated compliance officer to determine whether sharing the information is necessary and how much information should be shared. If the sharing is necessary, the compliance officer should coordinate the process of "looking over the wall" so that the necessary information will be shared and the integrity of the procedure will be maintained.

A single supervisor or compliance officer should have the specific authority and responsibility of deciding whether or not information is material and whether it is sufficiently public to be used as the basis for investment decisions. Ideally, the supervisor or compliance officer responsible for communicating information to a firm's research or brokerage area would not be a member of that area.

Personal Trading Limitations

Firms should consider restrictions or prohibitions on personal trading by employees and should carefully monitor both proprietary trading and personal trading by employees. Firms should require employees to make periodic reports (to the extent that such reporting is not already required by securities laws) of their own transactions and transactions made for the benefit of family members. Securities should be placed on a restricted list when a firm has or may have material nonpublic information. The broad distribution of a restricted list often triggers the sort of trading the list was developed to avoid. Therefore, a watch list shown to only the few people responsible for compliance should be used to monitor transactions in specified securities. The use of a watch list in combination with a restricted list is an increasingly common means of ensuring effective control of personal trading.

Record Maintenance

Multiservice firms should maintain written records of the communications between various departments. Firms should place a high priority on training and should consider instituting comprehensive training programs, particularly for employees in sensitive areas.

Proprietary Trading Procedures

Procedures concerning the restriction or review of a firm's proprietary trading while it possesses material nonpublic information will necessarily depend on the types of proprietary trading in which a firm may engage. A prohibition on all types of proprietary activity when a firm comes into possession of material nonpublic information is *not* appropriate. For example, when a firm acts as a market maker, a prohibition on proprietary trading may be counterproductive to the goals of maintaining the confidentiality of information and market liquidity. This concern is particularly important in the relationships between small, regional broker/dealers and small issuers. In many situations, a firm will take a small issuer public with the understanding that the firm will continue to be a market maker in the stock. In such instances, a withdrawal by the firm from market-making acts would be a clear tip to outsiders. Firms that continue market-making activity while in the possession of material nonpublic information should, however, instruct their market makers to remain passive to the market—that is, to take only the contra side of unsolicited customer trades.

In risk-arbitrage trading, the case for a trading prohibition is more compelling than it is in the case of market making. The impetus for arbitrage trading is neither passive nor reactive, and the potential for illegal profits is greater than in market making. The most prudent course for firms is to suspend arbitrage activity when a security is placed on the watch list. Those firms that continue arbitrage activity face a high hurdle in proving the adequacy of their internal procedures for preventing trading on material nonpublic information and must demonstrate a stringent review and documentation of firm trades.

Communication to All Employees

Written compliance policies and guidelines should be circulated to all employees of a firm. Policies and guidelines should be used in conjunction with training programs aimed at enabling employees to recognize material nonpublic information. Such information is not always clearly identifiable. Employees must be given sufficient training to either make an informed decision or to realize they need to consult a supervisor or compliance officer before engaging in questionable transactions.

Application of the Standard

Example 1 (Acting on Nonpublic Information): Frank Barnes, the president and controlling shareholder of the SmartTown clothing chain, decides to accept a tender offer and sell the family business at a price almost double the market price of its shares. He describes this decision to his sister (SmartTown's treasurer), who conveys it to her daughter (who owns no stock in the family company at present), who tells her husband, Staple. Staple, however, tells his stockbroker, Alex Halsey, who immediately buys SmartTown stock for himself.

> *Comment*: The information regarding the pending sale is both material and nonpublic. Staple has violated Standard II(A) by communicating the inside information to his broker. Halsey also has violated the standard by buying the shares on the basis of material nonpublic information.

Example 2 (Acting on Nonpublic Information): Josephine Walsh is riding an elevator up to her office when she overhears the chief financial officer (CFO) for the Swan Furniture Company tell the president of Swan that he has just calculated the company's earnings for the past quarter and they have unexpectedly and significantly dropped. The CFO adds that this drop will not be released to the public until next week. Walsh immediately calls her broker and tells him to sell her Swan stock.

> *Comment*: Walsh has sufficient information to determine that the information is both material and nonpublic. By trading on the inside information, she has violated Standard II(A).

Example 3 (Controlling Nonpublic Information): Samuel Peter, an analyst with Scotland and Pierce Incorporated, is assisting his firm with a secondary offering for Bright Ideas Lamp Company. Peter participates, via telephone conference call, in a meeting with Scotland and Pierce investment banking employees and Bright Ideas' CEO. Peter is advised that the company's earnings projections for the next year have significantly dropped. Throughout the telephone conference call, several Scotland and Pierce salespeople and portfolio managers walk in and out of Peter's office, where the telephone call is taking place. As a result, they are aware of the drop in projected earnings for Bright Ideas. Before the conference call is concluded, the salespeople trade the stock of the company on behalf of the firm's clients and other firm personnel trade the stock in a firm proprietary account and in employee personal accounts.

> *Comment*: Peter has violated Standard II(A) because he failed to prevent the transfer and misuse of material nonpublic information to others in his firm. Peter's firm should have adopted information barriers to prevent the communication of nonpublic information between departments of the firm. The salespeople and portfolio managers who traded on the information have also violated Standard II(A) by trading on inside information.

Example 4 (Acting on Nonpublic Information): Madison & Lambeau, a well-respected broker/dealer, submits a weekly column to *Securities Weekly* magazine. Once published, the column usually affects the value of the stocks discussed. Ron George, an employee of Madison & Lambeau, knows that *Securities Weekly* is published by Ziegler Publishing, for which his nephew is the night foreman. George's nephew faxes him an advance copy of the weekly column before it is printed. George regularly trades in the securities mentioned in the Madison & Lambeau column prior to its distribution, and to date, he has realized a personal profit of US$42,000 as well as significant profits for his clients.

> *Comment*: George has violated Standard II(A) by trading on material nonpublic information. The Madison & Lambeau article is considered nonpublic until the magazine is distributed through the normal channels.

Example 5 (Acting on Nonpublic Information): Greg Newman and his wife, Nancy Newman, volunteer at a local charitable organization that delivers meals to the elderly. One morning, Nancy Newman receives a telephone call from Betsy Sterling, another volunteer, who asks if the Newmans can fill in for her and her husband that afternoon. Betsy Sterling indicates that her husband is busy at work because his company has just fired its chief financial officer for misappropriation of funds. Nancy Newman agrees to perform the volunteer work for the Sterlings and advises her husband of the situation. Greg Newman knows that Betsy Sterling's husband is the CEO at O'Hara Brothers Incorporated, and he determines that this information is not public. Then, he sells his entire holding of 3,000 shares of O'Hara Brothers. Three days later, the firing is announced and O'Hara Brothers stock drops in value.

> *Comment*: Because the information is material and nonpublic, Greg Newman has violated Standard II(A) by trading on this information.

Example 6 (Selective Disclosure of Material Information): Elizabeth Levenson is based in Taipei and covers the Taiwanese market for her firm, which is based in Singapore. She is invited, together with the other 10 largest shareholders of a manufacturing company, to meet the finance director of that company. During the meeting, the finance director states that the company expects its workforce to strike next Friday, which will cripple productivity and distribution. Can Levenson use this information as a basis to change her rating on the company from "buy" to "sell"?

> *Comment*: Levenson must first determine whether the material information is public. According to Standard II(A), if the company has not made this information public (a small-group forum does not qualify as a method of public dissemination), she cannot use the information.

Example 7 (Determining Materiality): Leah Fechtman is trying to decide whether to hold or sell shares of an oil-and-gas exploration company that she owns in several of the funds she manages. Although the company has underperformed the index for some time already, the trends in the industry sector signal that companies of this type might become takeover targets. While she is considering her decision, her doctor, who casually follows the markets, mentions that she thinks that the company in question will soon be bought out by a large multinational conglomerate and that it would be a good idea to buy the stock right now. After talking to various investment professionals and checking their opinions on the company as well as checking industry trends, Fechtman decides the next day to accumulate more stock in the oil-and-gas exploration company.

> *Comment*: Although information on an expected takeover bid may be of the type that is generally material and nonpublic, in this case, the source of information is unreliable, so the information cannot be considered material. Therefore, Fechtman is not prohibited from trading the stock on the basis of this information.

Example 8 (Applying the Mosaic Theory): Jagdish Teja is a buy-side analyst covering the furniture industry. Looking for an attractive company to recommend as a buy, he analyzes several furniture makers by studying their financial reports and visiting their operations. He also talks to some designers and retailers to find out which furniture styles are trendy and popular. Although none of the companies that he analyzes are a clear buy, he discovers that one of them, Swan Furniture Company (SFC), may be in trouble financially. Swan's extravagant new designs have been introduced at substantial cost. Even though these designs initially attracted attention, in the long run, the public is buying more conservative furniture from other makers. Based on this information and on a profit-and-loss analysis, Teja believes that Swan's next quarter's earnings will drop substantially. He issues a sell recommendation for SFC. Immediately after receiving that recommendation, investment managers start reducing the SFC stock in their portfolios.

> *Comment*: Information on quarterly earnings data is material and nonpublic. Teja arrived at his conclusion about the earnings drop on the basis of public information and on pieces of nonmaterial nonpublic information (such as opinions of designers and retailers). Therefore, trading based on Teja's correct conclusion is not prohibited by Standard II(A).

Example 9 (Applying the Mosaic Theory): Roger Clement is a senior financial analyst who specializes in the European automobile sector at Rivoli Capital. Because he has been repeatedly nominated by many leading industry magazines and newsletters as "best analyst" for the automobile industry, he is widely regarded as an authority on the sector. After speaking with representatives of Turgot Chariots, a European auto manufacturer with sales primarily in South Korea, as well as interviews with salespeople, labor leaders, his firm's Korean currency analysts, and banking officials, Clement has analyzed Turgot Chariots and concluded that 1) its newly introduced model will probably not meet sales anticipation, 2) its corporate restructuring strategy may well face serious opposition from the unions, 3) the depreciation of the Korean won should lead to pressure on margins for the industry in general and Turgot's market segment in particular, and 4) banks could take a tougher-than-expected stance in the upcoming round of credit renegotiations with the company. For these reasons, he changes his conclusion about the company from "market outperform" to "market underperform."

> *Comment*: To reach a conclusion about the value of the company, Clement has pieced together a number of nonmaterial or public bits of information that affect Turgot Chariots. Therefore, under the mosaic theory, Clement has not violated Standard II(A) in drafting the report.

Example 10 (Analyst Recommendations as Material Nonpublic Information): The next day, Clement is preparing to be interviewed on a global financial news television program where he will discuss his changed recommendation on Turgot Chariots for the first time in public. While preparing for the program, he mentions to the show's producers and Mary Zito, the journalist who will be interviewing him, the information he will be discussing. Just prior to going on the air, Zito sells her holdings in Turgot Chariots.

> *Comment*: When Zito receives advance notice of Clement's change of opinion, she knows it will have a material impact on the stock price, even if she is not totally aware of Clement's underlying reasoning. She is not a client of Clement but obtains early access to the material nonpublic information prior to publication. Her trades are thus based on material nonpublic information and violate Standard II(A).

Example 11 (Acting on Nonpublic Information): Timothy Holt is a portfolio manager for the Toro Aggressive Growth Fund, a large mutual fund with an aggressive-growth mandate. Because of its mandate, the fund is heavily invested in small-cap companies with strong growth potential. Based on an unfavorable analysis of McCardell Industries by his research department, Holt decides to liquidate the fund's holdings in this company. Holt knows that this action will be widely viewed as negative by the market and that the company's stock is likely to plunge. He contacts several family members to tell them to liquidate any of their holdings before Toro's holdings are sold.

> *Comment*: When Holt tells his family to sell stock in advance of Toro's trade, he is violating Standard II(A) by causing others to trade on material nonpublic information.

Example 12 (Acting on Nonpublic Information): Holt executes his sell order of McCardell Industries with Toro's broker, Karim Ahmed. Ahmed immediately recognizes the likely effect this order will have on the stock price of McCardell and sells his own holdings in the company prior to placing the order.

> *Comment*: Ahmed has violated Standard II(A) by trading on material nonpublic information.

Example 13 (Acting on Nonpublic Information): Ashton Kellogg is a retired investment professional who manages his own portfolio. He owns shares in National Savings, a large local bank. A close friend and golfing buddy, John Mayfield, is a senior executive at National. National has seen its stock drop considerably, and the news and outlook are not good. In a conversation about the economy and the banking industry on the golf course, Mayfield drops the information that National will surprise the investment community in a few days when it announces excellent earnings for the quarter. Kellogg is pleasantly surprised by this information, and thinking that Mayfield, as a senior executive, knows the law and would not disclose inside information, he doubles his position in the bank. Subsequently, National announces that it had good operating earnings but had to set aside reserves for anticipated significant losses on its loan portfolio. The combined news causes the stock to go down 60 percent.

> *Comment*: Even though Kellogg believes that Mayfield would not break the law by disclosing insider information and money was lost on the purchase, Kellogg should not have purchased additional shares of National. It is the member's or candidate's responsibility to make sure, before executing investment actions, that comments about earnings are not material nonpublic information. Kellogg has violated Standard II(A).

B. Market Manipulation

Members and Candidates must not engage in practices that distort prices or artificially inflate trading volume with the intent to mislead market participants.

Guidance

Highlights:

▶ *Information-Based Manipulation*
▶ *Transaction-Based Manipulation*

Standard II(B) requires that members and candidates uphold market integrity by prohibiting market manipulation. Market manipulation includes practices that distort security prices or trading volume with the intent to deceive people or entities that rely on information in the market. Market manipulation damages the interests of all investors by disrupting the smooth functioning of financial markets and lowering investor confidence. Although market manipulation may be less likely to occur in mature financial markets than in emerging markets, cross-border investing increasingly exposes all global investors to the potential for such practices.

Market manipulation includes 1) the dissemination of false or misleading information and 2) transactions that deceive or would be likely to mislead market participants by distorting the price-setting mechanism of financial instruments. The development of new products and technologies increases the incentives, means, and opportunities for market manipulation.

Information-Based Manipulation

Information-based manipulation includes, but is not limited to, spreading false rumors to induce trading by others. For example, members and candidates must refrain from "pumping up" the price of an investment by issuing misleading positive information or overly optimistic projections of a security's worth only to later "dump" the investment (sell ownership in it) once the price of the stock, fueled by the misleading information's effect on other market participants, reaches an artificially high level.

Transaction-Based Manipulation

Transaction-based manipulation involves instances where the member or candidate knew or should have known that his or her actions could very well affect the pricing of a security. This includes, but is not limited to, the following:

▶ transactions that artificially affect prices or volume to give the impression of activity or price movement in a financial instrument, which represent a diversion from the expectations of a fair and efficient market; and

▶ securing a controlling, dominant position in a financial instrument to exploit and manipulate the price of a related derivative and/or the underlying asset.

Standard II(B) is not intended to preclude transactions undertaken on legitimate trading strategies based on perceived market inefficiencies. The intent of the action is critical to determining whether it is a violation of this standard.

Application of the Standard

Example 1 (Independent Analysis and Company Promotion): The principal owner of Financial Information Services (FIS) entered into an agreement with two microcap companies to promote the companies' stock in exchange for stock and cash compensation. The principal owner caused FIS to disseminate e-mails, design and maintain several internet sites, and distribute an online investment newsletter—all of which recommended investment in the two companies. The systematic publication of purportedly independent analyses and recommendations containing inaccurate and highly promotional and speculative statements increased public investment in the companies and led to dramatically higher stock prices.

> *Comment*: The principal owner of FIS violated Standard II(B) by using inaccurate reporting and misleading information under the guise of independent analysis to artificially increase the stock price of the companies. Furthermore, the principal owner violated Standard V(A)—Diligence and Reasonable Basis by not having a reasonable and adequate basis for recommending the two companies and violated Standard VI(A)—Disclosure of Conflicts by not disclosing to investors the compensation agreements (which constituted a conflict of interest).

Example 2 (Personal Trading Practices and Price): An employee of a broker/dealer acquired a significant ownership interest in several publicly traded microcap stocks and held the stock in various brokerage accounts in which the broker/dealer had a controlling interest. The employee orchestrated the manipulation of the stock price by artificially increasing the bid price for the stock through transactions among the various accounts.

> *Comment*: The employee of the broker/dealer violated Standard II(B) by distorting the price of the stock through false trading and manipulative sales practices.

Example 3 (Creating Artificial Price Volatility): Matthew Murphy is an analyst at Divisadero Securities & Co., which has a significant number of hedge funds among its most important brokerage clients. Some of the hedge funds hold short positions on Wirewolf Semiconductor. Two trading days before the publication of the quarter-end report, Murphy alerts his sales force that he is about to issue a research report on Wirewolf that will include the following opinion:

▶ quarterly revenues are likely to fall short of management's guidance;

▶ earnings will be as much as 5 cents per share (or more than 10 percent) below consensus; and

▶ Wirewolf's highly respected chief financial officer may be about to join another company.

Knowing that Wirewolf has already entered its declared quarter-end "quiet period" before reporting earnings (and thus would be reluctant to respond to rumors), Murphy times the release of his research report specifically to sensationalize the negative aspects of the message in order to create significant downward pressure on Wirewolf's stock—to the distinct advantage of Divisadero's hedge fund clients. The report's conclusions are based on speculation, not on fact. The next day, the research report is broadcast to all of Divisadero's clients and to the usual newswire services.

Before Wirewolf's investor-relations department can assess the damage on the final trading day of the quarter and refute Murphy's report, its stock opens trading sharply lower, allowing Divisadero's clients to cover their short positions at substantial gains.

> *Comment*: Murphy violated Standard II(B) by aiming to create artificial price volatility designed to have a material impact on the price of an issuer's stock. Moreover, by lacking an adequate basis for the recommendation, Murphy also violated Standard V(A)—Diligence and Reasonable Basis.

Example 4 (Personal Trading and Volume): Rajesh Sekar manages two funds—an equity fund and a balanced fund—whose equity components are supposed to be managed in accordance with the same model. According to that model, the funds' holdings in stock of Digital Design Inc. (DD) are excessive. Reduction of the DD holdings would not be easy, however, because the stock has low liquidity in the stock market. Sekar decides to start trading larger portions of DD stock back and forth between his two funds to slowly increase the price; he believes market participants will see growing volume and increasing price and become interested in the stock. If other investors are willing to buy the DD stock because of such interest, then Sekar will be able to get rid of at least some of his overweight position without inducing price decreases. In this way, the whole transaction will be for the benefit of fund participants, even if additional brokers' commissions are incurred.

> *Comment*: Sekar's plan would be beneficial for his funds' participants but is based on artificial distortion of both trading volume and the price of the DD stock and thus constitutes a violation of Standard II(B).

Example 5 ("Pump-Priming" Strategy): Sergei Gonchar is chairman of the ACME Futures Exchange, which is launching a new bond futures contract. To convince investors, traders, arbitrageurs, hedgers, and so on, to use its contract, the exchange attempts to demonstrate that it has the best liquidity. To do so, it enters into agreements with members in which they commit to a substantial minimum trading volume on the new contract over a specific period in exchange for substantial reductions of their regular commissions.

> *Comment*: The formal liquidity of a market is determined by the obligations set on market makers, but the actual liquidity of a market is better estimated

by the actual trading volume and bid–ask spreads. Attempts to mislead participants about the actual liquidity of the market constitute a violation of Standard II(B). In this example, investors have been intentionally misled to believe they chose the most liquid instrument for some specific purpose, but they could eventually see the actual liquidity of the contract significantly reduced after the term of the agreement expires. If the ACME Futures Exchange fully discloses its agreement with members to boost transactions over some initial launch period, it will not violate Standard II(B). ACME's intent is not to harm investors but, on the contrary, to give them a better service. For that purpose, it may engage in a liquidity-pumping strategy, but the strategy must be disclosed.

Example 6 (Creating Artificial Price Volatility): Emily Gordon, an analyst of household products companies, is employed by a research boutique, Picador & Co. Based on information that she has gathered during a trip through Latin America, she believes that Hygene, Inc., a major marketer of personal care products, has generated better-than-expected sales from its new product initiatives in South America. After modestly boosting her projections for revenue and for gross profit margin in her worksheet models for Hygene, Gordon estimates that her earnings projection of US$2.00 per diluted share for the current year may be as much as 5 percent too low. She contacts the chief financial officer (CFO) of Hygene to try to gain confirmation of her findings from her trip and to get some feedback regarding her revised models. The CFO declines to comment and reiterates management's most recent guidance of US$1.95 to US$2.05 for the year.

Gordon decides to try to force a comment from the company by telling Picador & Co. clients who follow a momentum investment style that consensus earnings projections for Hygene are much too low; she explains that she is considering raising her published estimate by an ambitious US$0.15 to US$2.15 per share. She believes that when word of an unrealistically high earnings projection filters back to Hygene's investor-relations department, the company will feel compelled to update its earnings guidance. Meanwhile, Gordon hopes that she is at least correct with respect to the earnings direction and that she will help clients who act on her insights to profit from a quick gain by trading on her advice.

Comment: By exaggerating her earnings projections in order to try to fuel a quick gain in Hygene's stock price, Gordon is in violation of Standard II(B). Furthermore, by virtue of previewing her intentions of revising upward her earnings projections to only a select group of clients, she is in violation of Standard III(B)—Fair Dealing. Instead of what she did, it would have been acceptable for Gordon to write a report that:

▶ framed her earnings projection in a range of possible outcomes;

▶ outlined clearly the assumptions used in her Hygene models that took into consideration the findings from her trip through Latin America; and

▶ distributed the report to all Picador & Co. clients in an equitable manner.

Example 7 (Pump and Dump Strategy): In an effort to pump up the price of his holdings in Moosehead & Belfast Railroad Company, Steve Weinberg logs on to several investor chat rooms on the internet to start rumors that the company is about to expand its rail network in anticipation of receiving a large contract for shipping lumber.

Comment: Weinberg has violated Standard II(B) by disseminating false information about Moosehead & Belfast with the intent to mislead market participants.

Example 8 (Manipulating Model Inputs): Bill Mandeville supervises a structured financing team for Superior Investment Bank. His responsibilities include packaging new structured investment products and managing Superior's relationship with relevant rating agencies. To achieve the best rating possible, Mandeville uses mostly positive scenarios as model inputs—scenarios that reflect minimal downside risk in the assets underlying the structured products. The resulting output statistics in the rating request and underwriting prospectus support the idea that the new structured products have minimal potential downside risk. Additionally, Mandeville's compensation from Superior is partially based on both the level of the rating assigned and the successful sale of new structured investment products but does not have a link to the long-term performance of the instruments.

Mandeville is extremely successful and leads Superior as the top originator of structured investment products for the next two years. In the third year, the economy experiences difficulties and the values of the assets underlying structured products significantly decline. The subsequent defaults lead to major turmoil in the capital markets, the demise of Superior Investment Bank, and Mandeville's loss of employment.

Comment: Mandeville manipulates the inputs of a model to minimize associated risk to achieve higher ratings. His understanding of structured products allows him to skillfully decide which inputs to include in support of the desired rating and price. This information manipulation for short-term gain, which is in violation of Standard II(B), ultimately causes significant damage to many parties and the capital markets as a whole. Mandeville should have realized that promoting a rating and price with inaccurate information could cause not only a loss of price confidence in the particular structured product but also a loss of investor trust in the system. Such loss of confidence affects the ability of the capital markets to operate efficiently.

STANDARD III—DUTIES TO CLIENTS

A. Loyalty, Prudence, and Care

Members and Candidates have a duty of loyalty to their clients and must act with reasonable care and exercise prudent judgment. Members and Candidates must act for the benefit of their clients and place their clients' interests before their employer's or their own interests.

Guidance

Highlights:

► *Identifying the Actual Investment Client*
► *Developing the Client's Portfolio*
► *Soft Commission Policies*
► *Proxy Voting Policies*

Standard III(A) clarifies that client interests are paramount. A member's or candidate's responsibility to a client includes a duty of loyalty and a duty to exercise reasonable care. Investment actions must be carried out for the sole benefit of the client and in a manner the member or candidate believes, given the known facts and circumstances, to be in the best interest of the client. Members and candidates must exercise the same level of prudence, judgment, and care that they would apply in the management and disposition of their own interests in similar circumstances.

Prudence requires caution and discretion. The exercise of prudence by investment professionals requires that they act with the care, skill, and diligence in the circumstances that a reasonable person acting in a like capacity and familiar with such matters would use. In the context of managing a client's portfolio, prudence requires following the investment parameters set forth by the client and balancing risk and return. Acting with care requires members and candidates to act in a prudent and judicious manner in avoiding harm to clients.

Standard III(A) sets minimum expectations for members and candidates when fulfilling their responsibilities to their clients. Regulatory and legal requirements for such duties can vary across the investment industry depending on a variety of factors, including job function of the investment professional, the existence of an adviser/client relationship, and the nature of the recommendations being offered. From the perspective of the end user of financial services, these different standards can be arcane and confusing, leaving investors unsure of what level of service to expect from investment professionals they employ. The single standard of conduct described in Standard III(A) benefits investors by establishing a benchmark for the duties of loyalty, prudence, and care and clarifies that all CFA Institute members and candidates, regardless of job title, local laws, or cultural differences, are required to comply with these fundamental responsibilities. Investors hiring members or candidates who must adhere to the duty of loyalty, prudence, and care set forth in this standard can be confident that these responsibilities are a requirement regardless of any legally imposed fiduciary duties.

Standard III(A), however, is not a substitute for a member's or candidate's legal or regulatory obligations. Members and candidates must also understand and adhere to any legally imposed fiduciary responsibility they assume with each client. Fiduciary duties are often imposed by law or regulation when an individual or institution is charged with the duty of acting for the benefit of another party, such as managing investment assets. The duty required in fiduciary relationships exceeds what is acceptable in many other business relationships because a fiduciary is in an enhanced position of trust.

As stated in Standard I(A), members and candidates must abide by the most strict requirements imposed on them by regulators or the Code and Standards, including any legally imposed fiduciary duty. Standard III(A) establishes a minimum benchmark for the duties of loyalty, prudence, and care that are required of all members and candidates regardless of whether a legal fiduciary duty applies.

Members and candidates must also be aware of whether they have "custody" or effective control of client assets. If so, a heightened level of responsibility arises. Members and candidates are considered to have custody if they have any direct or indirect access to client funds. Members and candidates must manage any pool of assets in their control in accordance with the terms of the governing documents (such as trust documents and investment management agreements), which are the primary determinant of the manager's powers and duties. Whenever their actions are contrary to provisions of those instruments or applicable law, members and candidates are at risk of violating Standard III(A).

Identifying the Actual Investment Client

The first step for members and candidates in fulfilling their duty of loyalty to clients is to determine the identity of the "client" to whom the duty of loyalty is owed. In the context of an investment manager managing the personal assets of an individual, the client is easily identified. When the manager is responsible for the portfolios of pension plans or trusts, however, the client is not the person or entity who hires the manager but, rather, the beneficiaries of the plan or trust. The duty of loyalty is owed to the ultimate beneficiaries.

In some situations, an actual client or group of beneficiaries may not exist. Members and candidates managing a fund to an index or an expected mandate owe the duty of loyalty, prudence, and care to invest in a manner consistent with the stated mandate. The decisions of a fund's manager, although benefitting all fund investors, do not have to be based on an individual investor's requirements and risk profile. Client loyalty and care for those investing in the fund are the responsibility of members and candidates who have an advisory relationship with those individuals.

Situations involving potential conflicts of interest with respect to responsibilities to clients may be extremely complex because they may involve a number of competing interests. The duty of loyalty, prudence, and care applies to a large number of persons in varying capacities, but the exact duties may differ in many respects in accord with the relationship with each client or each type of account in which the assets are managed. Members and candidates must not only put their obligations to clients first in all dealings but must also endeavor to avoid all real or potential conflicts of interest.

Members and candidates with positions whose responsibilities do not include direct investment management also have "clients" that must be considered. Just as there are various types of advisory relationships, members and candidates must look at their roles and responsibilities when making a determination of who their clients are. Sometimes the client is easily identifiable; such is the case in the relationship between a company executive and the firm's public shareholders. At other times, the client may be the investing public as a whole, in which case, the goals of independence and objectivity of research surpass the goal of loyalty to a single organization.

Developing the Client's Portfolio

The duty of loyalty, prudence, and care owed to the individual client is especially important because the professional investment manager typically possesses greater knowledge in the investment arena than the client does. This disparity places the individual client in a vulnerable position; the client must trust the manager. The manager in these situations should ensure that the client's objectives and expectations for the performance of the account are realistic and suitable to the client's circumstances and that the risks involved are appropriate. In most circumstances, recommended investment strategies should relate to the long-term objectives and circumstances of the client.

Particular care must be taken to detect whether the goals of the investment manager or the firm in placing business, selling products, and executing security transactions potentially conflict with the best interests and objectives of the client. When members and candidates cannot avoid potential conflicts between their firm and clients' interests, they must provide clear and factual disclosures of the circumstances to the clients.

Members and candidates must follow any guidelines set by their clients for the management of their assets. Some clients, such as charitable organizations and pension plans, have strict investment policies that limit investment options to certain types or classes of investment or prohibit investment in certain securities. Other organizations have aggressive policies that do not prohibit investments by type but, instead, set criteria on the basis of the portfolio's total risk and return.

Investment decisions must be judged in the context of the total portfolio rather than by individual investment within the portfolio. The member's or candidate's duty is satisfied with respect to a particular investment if the individual has thoroughly considered the investment's place in the overall portfolio, the risk of loss and opportunity for gains, tax implications, and the diversification, liquidity, cash flow, and overall return requirements of the assets or the portion of the assets for which the manager is responsible.

Soft Commission Policies

An investment manager often has discretion over the selection of brokers executing transactions. Conflicts arise when an investment manager uses client brokerage to purchase research services that benefit the investment manager, a practice commonly called "soft dollars" or "soft commissions." Whenever members or candidates use client brokerage to purchase goods or services that do not benefit the client, they should disclose to clients the methods or policies followed in addressing the potential conflict. A member or candidate who pays a higher commission than he or she would normally pay to purchase goods or services, without corresponding benefit to the client, violates the duty of loyalty to the client.

From time to time, a client will direct a manager to use the client's brokerage to purchase goods or services for the client, a practice that is commonly called "directed brokerage." Because brokerage commission is an asset of the client and is used to benefit that client, not the manager, such a practice does not violate any duty of loyalty. A member or candidate is obligated to seek "best price" and "best execution," however, and be assured by the client that the goods or services purchased from the brokerage will benefit the account beneficiaries. "Best execution" refers to a trading process that seeks to maximize the value of the client's portfolio within the client's stated investment objectives and constraints. In addition, the member or candidate should disclose to the client that the client may not be getting best execution from the directed brokerage.

Proxy Voting Policies

The duty of loyalty, prudence, and care may apply in a number of situations facing the investment professional other than issues related directly to investing assets.

Part of a member's or candidate's duty of loyalty includes voting proxies in an informed and responsible manner. Proxies have economic value to a client, and members and candidates must ensure that they properly safeguard and maximize this value. An investment manager who fails to vote, casts a vote without considering the impact of the question, or votes blindly with management on nonroutine governance issues (e.g., a change in company capitalization) may violate this standard. Voting of proxies is an integral part of the management of investments.

A cost–benefit analysis may show that voting all proxies may not benefit the client, so voting proxies may not be necessary in all instances. Members and candidates should disclose to clients their proxy voting policies.

Recommended Procedures for Compliance

Regular Account Information

Members and candidates with control of client assets should submit to each client, at least quarterly, an itemized statement showing the funds and securities in the custody or possession of the member or candidate plus all debits, credits, and transactions that occurred during the period; should disclose to the client where the assets are to be maintained, as well as where or when they are moved; and should separate the client's assets from any other party's assets, including the member's or candidate's own assets.

Client Approval

If a member or candidate is uncertain about the appropriate course of action with respect to a client, the member or candidate should ask what he or she would expect or demand if the member or candidate were the client. If in doubt, a member or candidate should disclose the questionable matter in writing to the client and obtain client approval.

Firm Policies

Members and candidates should address and encourage their firms to address the following topics when drafting the statements or manuals containing their policies and procedures regarding responsibilities to clients:

- ▶ *Follow all applicable rules and laws*: Members and candidates must follow all legal requirements and applicable provisions of the Code and Standards.
- ▶ *Establish the investment objectives of the client*: Make a reasonable inquiry into a client's investment experience, risk and return objectives, and financial constraints prior to making investment recommendations or taking investment actions.
- ▶ *Consider all the information when taking actions*: When taking investment actions, members and candidates must consider the appropriateness and suitability of the investment relative to 1) the client's needs and circumstances, 2) the investment's basic characteristics, and 3) the basic characteristics of the total portfolio.
- ▶ *Diversify*: Members and candidates should diversify investments to reduce the risk of loss, unless diversification is not consistent with plan guidelines or is contrary to the account objectives.
- ▶ *Carry out regular reviews*: Members and candidates should establish regular review schedules to ensure that the investments held in the account adhere to the terms of the governing documents.
- ▶ *Deal fairly with all clients with respect to investment actions*: Members and candidates must not favor some clients over others and should establish policies for allocating trades and disseminating investment recommendations.
- ▶ *Disclose conflicts of interest*: Members and candidates must disclose all actual and potential conflicts of interest so that clients can evaluate those conflicts.
- ▶ *Disclose compensation arrangements*: Members and candidates should make their clients aware of all forms of manager compensation.

► *Vote proxies*: In most cases, members and candidates should determine who is authorized to vote shares and vote proxies in the best interests of the clients and ultimate beneficiaries.

► *Maintain confidentiality*: Members and candidates must preserve the confidentiality of client information.

► *Seek best execution*: Unless directed by the client as ultimate beneficiary, members and candidates must seek best execution for their clients. (Best execution is defined in the preceding text.)

► *Place client interests first*: Members and candidates must serve the best interests of clients.

Application of the Standard

Example 1 (Identifying the Client—Plan Participants): First Country Bank serves as trustee for the Miller Company's pension plan. Miller is the target of a hostile takeover attempt by Newton, Inc. In attempting to ward off Newton, Miller's managers persuade Julian Wiley, an investment manager at First Country Bank, to purchase Miller common stock in the open market for the employee pension plan. Miller's officials indicate that such action would be favorably received and would probably result in other accounts being placed with the bank. Although Wiley believes the stock to be overvalued and would not ordinarily buy it, he purchases the stock to support Miller's managers, to maintain Miller's good favor toward the bank, and to realize additional new business. The heavy stock purchases cause Miller's market price to rise to such a level that Newton retracts its takeover bid.

> *Comment*: Standard III(A) requires that a member or candidate, in evaluating a takeover bid, act prudently and solely in the interests of plan participants and beneficiaries. To meet this requirement, a member or candidate must carefully evaluate the long-term prospects of the company against the short-term prospects presented by the takeover offer and by the ability to invest elsewhere. In this instance, Wiley, acting on behalf of his employer, which was the trustee for a pension plan, clearly violated Standard III(A). He used the pension plan to perpetuate existing management, perhaps to the detriment of plan participants and the company's shareholders, and to benefit himself. Wiley's responsibilities to the plan participants and beneficiaries should have taken precedence over any ties of his bank to corporate managers and over his self-interest. Wiley had a duty to examine the takeover offer on its own merits and to make an independent decision. The guiding principle is the appropriateness of the investment decision to the pension plan, not whether the decision benefitted Wiley or the company that hired him.

Example 2 (Client Commission Practices): JNI, a successful investment counseling firm, serves as investment manager for the pension plans of several large regionally based companies. Its trading activities generate a significant amount of commission-related business. JNI uses the brokerage and research services of many firms, but most of its trading activity is handled through a large brokerage company, Thompson, Inc. The reason is that the executives of the two firms have a close friendship. Thompson's commission structure is high in comparison with charges for similar brokerage services from other firms. JNI considers Thompson's research services and execution capabilities average. In exchange for JNI directing its brokerage to Thompson, Thompson absorbs a number of JNI overhead expenses, including those for rent.

Comment: JNI executives are breaching their responsibilities by using client brokerage for services that do not benefit JNI clients and by not obtaining best price and best execution for their clients. Because JNI executives are not upholding their duty of loyalty, they are violating Standard III(A).

Example 3 (Brokerage Arrangements): Charlotte Everett, a struggling independent investment adviser, serves as investment manager for the pension plans of several companies. One of her brokers, Scott Company, is close to consummating management agreements with prospective new clients whereby Everett would manage the new client accounts and trade the accounts exclusively through Scott. One of Everett's existing clients, Crayton Corporation, has directed Everett to place securities transactions for Crayton's account exclusively through Scott. But to induce Scott to exert efforts to send more new accounts to her, Everett also directs transactions to Scott from other clients without their knowledge.

Comment: Everett has an obligation at all times to seek best price and best execution on all trades. Everett may direct new client trades exclusively through Scott Company as long as Everett receives best price and execution on the trades or receives a written statement from new clients that she is *not* to seek best price and execution and that they are aware of the consequence for their accounts. Everett may trade other accounts through Scott as a reward for directing clients to Everett only if the accounts receive best price and execution and the practice is disclosed to the accounts. Because Everett does not disclose the directed trading, Everett has violated Standard III(A).

Example 4 (Brokerage Arrangements): Emilie Rome is a trust officer for Paget Trust Company. Rome's supervisor is responsible for reviewing Rome's trust account transactions and her monthly reports of personal stock transactions. Rome has been using Nathan Gray, a broker, almost exclusively for trust account brokerage transactions. When Gray makes a market in stocks, he has been giving Rome a lower price for personal purchases and a higher price for sales than he gives to Rome's trust accounts and other investors.

Comment: Rome is violating her duty of loyalty to the bank's trust accounts by using Gray for brokerage transactions simply because Gray trades Rome's personal account on favorable terms. Rome is placing her own interests before those of her clients.

Example 5 (Client Commission Practices): Lauren Parker, an analyst with Provo Advisors, covers South American equities for her firm. She likes to travel to the markets for which she is responsible and decides to go on a trip to Chile, Argentina, and Brazil. The trip is sponsored by SouthAM, Inc., a research firm with a small broker/dealer affiliate that uses the clearing facilities of a larger New York brokerage house. SouthAM specializes in arranging South American trips for analysts during which they can meet with central bank officials, government ministers, local economists, and senior executives of corporations. SouthAM accepts commission dollars at a ratio of 2 to 1 against the hard dollar costs of the research fee for the trip. Parker is not sure that SouthAM's execution is competitive, but without informing her supervisor, she directs the trading desk at Provo to start giving commission business to SouthAM so she can take the trip. SouthAM has conveniently timed the briefing trip to coincide with the beginning of Carnival season, so Parker also decides to spend five days of vacation in Rio de Janeiro at the end of the trip. Parker uses commission dollars to pay for the five days of hotel expenses.

Comment: Parker is violating Standard III(A) by not exercising her duty of loyalty to her clients. She should have determined whether the commissions charged by SouthAM are reasonable in relation to the benefit of the research provided by the trip. She also should have determined whether best execution and prices could be received from SouthAM. In addition, the five extra days are not part of the research effort because they do not assist in the investment decision making. Thus, the hotel expenses for the five days should not be paid for with client assets.

Example 6 (Excessive Trading): Vida Knauss manages the portfolios of a number of high-net-worth individuals. A major part of her investment management fee is based on trading commissions. Knauss engages in extensive trading for each of her clients to ensure that she attains the minimum commission level set by her firm. Although the securities purchased and sold for the clients are appropriate and fall within the acceptable asset classes for the clients, the amount of trading for each account exceeds what is necessary to accomplish the client's investment objectives.

> *Comment*: Knauss has violated Standard III(A) because she is using the assets of her clients to benefit her firm and herself.

Example 7 (Managing Family Accounts): Adam Dill recently joined New Investments Asset Managers. To assist Dill in building a book of clients, both his father and brother opened new fee-paying accounts. Dill followed all the firm's procedures in noting his relationships with these clients and in developing their investment policy statements.

After several years, the number of Dill's clients has grown, but he still manages the original accounts of his family members. An IPO is coming to market that is a suitable investment for many of his clients, including his brother. Dill does not receive the amount of stock he requested, so to avoid any appearance of a conflict of interest, he does not allocate any shares to his brother's account.

> *Comment*: Dill has violated Standard III(A) because he is not acting for the benefit of his brother's account as well as his other accounts. The brother's account is a regular fee-paying account comparable to the accounts of his other clients. By not allocating the shares proportionately across *all* accounts for which he thought the IPO was suitable, Dill is disadvantaging specific clients.
>
> Dill would have been correct in not allocating shares to his brother's account if that account was being managed outside the normal fee structure of the firm.

Example 8 (Identifying the Client): Donna Hensley has been hired by a law firm to testify as an expert witness. Although the testimony is intended to represent impartial advice, she is concerned that her work may have negative consequences for the law firm. If the law firm is Hensley's client, how does she ensure that her testimony will not violate the required duty of loyalty, prudence, and care to one's client?

> *Comment*: In this situation, the law firm represents Hensley's employer and the aspect of "who is the client" is not well defined. When acting as an expert witness, Hensley is bound by the standard of independence and objectivity in the same manner as an independent research analyst would be bound. Hensley must not let the law firm influence the testimony she is to provide in the legal proceedings.

Example 9 (Identifying the Client): Jon Miller is a mutual fund portfolio manager. The fund is focused on the global financial services sector. Wanda Spears is a private wealth manager in the same city as Miller and is a friend of Miller. At a local CFA Institute society meeting, Spears mentions to Miller that her new client is an investor in Miller's fund. She states that the two of them now share a responsibility to this client.

> *Comment*: Spears' statement is not totally correct. Because she provides the advisory services to her new client, she alone is bound by the duty of loyalty to this client. Miller's responsibility is to manage the fund according to the investment policy statement of the fund. His actions should not be influenced by the needs of any particular fund investor.

B. Fair Dealing

Members and Candidates must deal fairly and objectively with all clients when providing investment analysis, making investment recommendations, taking investment action, or engaging in other professional activities.

Guidance

Highlights:

▶ *Investment Recommendations*
▶ *Investment Action*

Standard III(B) requires members and candidates to treat all clients fairly when disseminating investment recommendations or making material changes to prior investment recommendations or when taking investment action with regard to general purchases, new issues, or secondary offerings. Only through the fair treatment of all parties can the investment management profession maintain the confidence of the investing public.

When an investment adviser has multiple clients, the potential exists for the adviser to favor one client over another. This favoritism may take various forms—from the quality and timing of services provided to the allocation of investment opportunities.

The term "fairly" implies that the member or candidate must take care not to discriminate against any clients when disseminating investment recommendations or taking investment action. Standard III(B) does not state "equally" because members and candidates could not possibly reach all clients at exactly the same time—whether by printed mail, telephone (including text messaging), computer (including internet updates and e-mail distribution), facsimile (fax), or wire. Each client has unique needs, investment criteria, and investment objectives, so not all investment opportunities are suitable for all clients. In addition, members and candidates may provide more personal, specialized, or in-depth service to clients who are willing to pay for premium services through higher management fees or higher levels of brokerage. Members and candidates may differentiate their services to clients, but different levels of service must not disadvantage or negatively affect clients. In addition, the different service levels should be disclosed to clients and prospective clients and should be available to everyone (i.e., different service levels should not be offered selectively).

Standard III(B) covers conduct in two broadly defined categories—investment recommendations and investment action.

Investment Recommendations

The first category of conduct involves members and candidates whose primary function is the preparation of investment recommendations to be disseminated either to the public or within a firm for the use of others in making investment decisions. This group includes members and candidates employed by investment counseling, advisory, or consulting firms as well as banks, brokerage firms, and insurance companies. The criterion is that the member's or candidate's primary responsibility is the preparation of recommendations to be acted on by others, including those in the member's or candidate's organization.

An investment recommendation is any opinion expressed by a member or candidate in regard to purchasing, selling, or holding a given security or other investment. The opinion may be disseminated to customers or clients through an initial detailed research report, through a brief update report, by addition to or deletion from a list of recommended securities, or simply by oral communication. A recommendation that is distributed to anyone outside the organization is considered a communication for general distribution under Standard III(B).

Standard III(B) addresses the manner in which investment recommendations or changes in prior recommendations are disseminated to clients. Each member or candidate is obligated to ensure that information is disseminated in such a manner that all clients have a fair opportunity to act on every recommendation. Communicating with all clients on a uniform basis presents practical problems for members and candidates because of differences in timing and methods of communication with various types of customers and clients. Members and candidates should encourage their firms to design an equitable system to prevent selective or discriminatory disclosure and should inform clients about what kind of communications they will receive.

The duty to clients imposed by Standard III(B) may be more critical when members or candidates change their recommendations than when they make initial recommendations. Material changes in a member's or candidate's prior investment recommendations because of subsequent research should be communicated to all current clients; particular care should be taken that the information reaches those clients who the member or candidate knows have acted on or been affected by the earlier advice. Clients who do not know that the member or candidate has changed a recommendation and who, therefore, place orders contrary to a current recommendation should be advised of the changed recommendation before the order is accepted.

Investment Action

The second category of conduct includes those members and candidates whose primary function is taking investment action (portfolio management) on the basis of recommendations prepared internally or received from external sources. Investment action, like investment recommendations, can affect market value. Consequently, Standard III(B) requires that members or candidates treat all clients fairly in light of their investment objectives and circumstances. For example, when making investments in new offerings or in secondary financings, members and candidates should distribute the issues to all customers for whom the investments are appropriate in a manner consistent with the policies of the firm for allocating blocks of stock. If the issue is oversubscribed, then the issue should be prorated to all subscribers. This action should be taken on a round-lot basis to avoid odd-lot distributions. In addition, if the issue is oversubscribed, members and candidates should forgo any sales to themselves or their immediate families in order to free up additional shares for clients. If the investment professional's family-member accounts are managed similarly to the accounts of other clients of the firm, however, the family-member accounts should not be excluded from buying such shares.

Members and candidates must make every effort to treat all individual and institutional clients in a fair and impartial manner. A member or candidate may have multiple relationships with an institution; for example, the member or candidate may be a corporate trustee, pension fund manager, manager of funds for individuals employed by the customer, loan originator, or creditor. A member or candidate must exercise care to treat all clients fairly.

Members and candidates should disclose to clients and prospective clients the documented allocation procedures they or their firms have in place and how the procedures would affect the client or prospect. The disclosure should be clear and complete so that the client can make an informed investment decision. Even when complete disclosure is made, however, members and candidates must put client interests ahead of their own. A member's or candidate's duty of fairness and loyalty to clients can never be overridden by client consent to patently unfair allocation procedures.

Treating clients fairly also means that members and candidates should not take advantage of their position in the industry to the detriment of clients. For instance, in the context of IPOs, members and candidates must make bona fide public distributions of "hot issue" securities (defined as securities of a public offering that are trading at a premium in the secondary market whenever such trading commences because of the great demand for the securities). Members and candidates are prohibited from withholding such securities for their own benefit and must not use such securities as a reward or incentive to gain benefit.

Recommended Procedures for Compliance

Develop Firm Policies

Although Standard III(B) refers to a member's or candidate's responsibility to deal fairly and objectively with clients, members and candidates should also encourage their firms to establish compliance procedures requiring all employees who disseminate investment recommendations or take investment actions to treat customers and clients fairly. At the very least, a member or candidate should recommend appropriate procedures to management if none are in place. And the member or candidate should make management aware of possible violations of fair-dealing practices within the firm when they come to the attention of the member or candidate.

The extent of the formality and complexity of such compliance procedures depends on the nature and size of the organization and the type of securities involved. An investment adviser who is a sole proprietor and handles only discretionary accounts might not disseminate recommendations to the public, but that adviser should have formal written procedures to ensure that all clients receive fair investment action.

Good business practice dictates that initial recommendations be made available to all customers who indicate an interest. Although a member or candidate need not communicate a recommendation to all customers, the selection process by which customers receive information should be based on suitability and known interest, not on any preferred or favored status. A common practice to assure fair dealing is to communicate recommendations simultaneously within the firm and to customers.

Members and candidates should consider the following points when establishing fair-dealing compliance procedures:

▶ *Limit the number of people involved*: Members and candidates should make reasonable efforts to limit the number of people who are privy to the fact that a recommendation is going to be disseminated.

▶ *Shorten the time frame between decision and dissemination*: Members and candidates should make reasonable efforts to limit the amount of time that elapses between the decision to make an investment recommendation and the time the actual recommendation is disseminated. If a detailed institutional recommendation is in preparation that might take two or three weeks to publish, a short summary report including the conclusion might be published in advance. In an organization where both a research committee and an investment policy committee must approve a recommendation, the meetings should be held on the same day if possible. The process of reviewing, printing, and mailing reports or faxing or distributing them by e-mail necessarily involves the passage of time, sometimes long periods of time. In large firms with extensive review processes, the time factor is usually not within the control of the analyst who prepares the report. Thus, many firms and their analysts communicate to customers and firm personnel the new or changed recommendations by an update or "flash" report. The communication technique might be fax, e-mail, wire, or short written report.

▶ *Publish guidelines for pre-dissemination behavior*: Guidelines are needed that prohibit personnel who have prior knowledge of an investment recommendation from discussing or taking any action on the pending recommendation.

▶ *Simultaneous dissemination*: Members and candidates should establish procedures for the timing of dissemination of investment recommendations so that all clients are treated fairly—that is, are informed at approximately the same time. For example, if a firm is going to announce a new recommendation, supervisory personnel should time the announcement to avoid placing any client or group of clients at unfair advantage relative to other clients. A communication to all branch offices should be sent at the time of the general announcement. (When appropriate, the firm should accompany the announcement of a new recommendation with a statement that trading restrictions for the firm's employees are now in effect.) The trading restrictions should stay in effect until the recommendation is widely distributed to all relevant clients. Once this distribution has occurred, the member or candidate may follow up separately with individual clients, but members and candidates should not give favored clients advance information when such advance notification may disadvantage other clients.

▶ *Maintain a list of clients and their holdings*: Members and candidates should maintain a list of all clients and the securities or other investments each client holds in order to facilitate notification of customers or clients of a change in an investment recommendation. If a particular security or other investment is to be sold, such a list can be used to ensure that all holders are treated fairly in the liquidation of that particular investment.

▶ *Develop and document trade allocation procedures*: When formulating procedures for allocating trades, members and candidates should develop a set of guiding principles that ensure:

  ▶ fairness to advisory clients, both in priority of execution of orders and in the allocation of the price obtained in execution of block orders or trades;

▶ timeliness and efficiency in the execution of orders; and

▶ accuracy of the member's or candidate's records as to trade orders and client account positions.

With these principles in mind, members and candidates should develop or encourage their firm to develop written allocation procedures, with particular attention to procedures for block trades and new issues. Procedures to consider are as follows:

▶ requiring orders and modifications or cancellations of orders to be documented and time stamped;

▶ processing and executing orders on a first-in, first-out basis with consideration of bundling orders for efficiency as appropriate for the asset class or the security;

▶ developing a policy to address such issues as calculating execution prices and "partial fills" when trades are grouped, or in a block, for efficiency;

▶ giving all client accounts participating in a block trade the same execution price and charging the same commission;

▶ when the full amount of the block order is not executed, allocating partially executed orders among the participating client accounts pro rata on the basis of order size while not going below an established minimum lot size for some securities (e.g., bonds);

▶ when allocating trades for new issues, obtaining advance indications of interest, allocating securities by client (rather than portfolio manager), and providing a method for calculating allocations.

Disclose Trade Allocation Procedures

Members and candidates should disclose to clients and prospective clients how they select accounts to participate in an order and how they determine the amount of securities each account will buy or sell. Trade allocation procedures must be fair and equitable, and disclosure of inequitable allocation methods does not relieve the member or candidate of this obligation.

Establish Systematic Account Review

Member and candidate supervisors should review each account on a regular basis to ensure that no client or customer is being given preferential treatment and that the investment actions taken for each account are suitable for each account's objectives. Because investments should be based on individual needs and circumstances, an investment manager may have good reasons for placing a given security or other investment in one account while selling it from another account and should fully document the reasons behind both sides of the transaction. Members and candidates should encourage firms to establish review procedures, however, to detect whether trading in one account is being used to benefit a favored client.

Disclose Levels of Service

Members and candidates should disclose to all clients whether the organization offers different levels of service to clients for the same fee or different fees. Different levels of service should not be offered to clients selectively.

Application of the Standard

Example 1 (Selective Disclosure): Bradley Ames, a well-known and respected analyst, follows the computer industry. In the course of his research, he finds that a small, relatively unknown company whose shares are traded over the counter has just signed significant contracts with some of the companies he follows. After a considerable amount of investigation, Ames decides to write a research report on the small company and recommend purchase of its shares. While the report is being reviewed by the company for factual accuracy, Ames schedules a luncheon with several of his best clients to discuss the company. At the luncheon, he mentions the purchase recommendation scheduled to be sent early the following week to all the firm's clients.

> *Comment*: Ames has violated Standard III(B) by disseminating the purchase recommendation to the clients with whom he has lunch a week before the recommendation is sent to all clients.

Example 2 (Fair Dealing between Funds): Spencer Rivers, president of XYZ Corporation, moves his company's growth-oriented pension fund to a particular bank primarily because of the excellent investment performance achieved by the bank's commingled fund for the prior five-year period. Later, Rivers compares the results of his pension fund with those of the bank's commingled fund. He is startled to learn that, even though the two accounts have the same investment objectives and similar portfolios, his company's pension fund has significantly underperformed the bank's commingled fund. Questioning this result at his next meeting with the pension fund's manager, Rivers is told that, as a matter of policy, when a new security is placed on the recommended list, Morgan Jackson, the pension fund manager, first purchases the security for the commingled account and then purchases it on a pro rata basis for all other pension fund accounts. Similarly, when a sale is recommended, the security is sold first from the commingled account and then sold on a pro rata basis from all other accounts. Rivers also learns that if the bank cannot get enough shares (especially of hot issues) to be meaningful to all the accounts, its policy is to place the new issues only in the commingled account.

Seeing that Rivers is neither satisfied nor pleased by the explanation, Jackson quickly adds that nondiscretionary pension accounts and personal trust accounts have a lower priority on purchase and sale recommendations than discretionary pension fund accounts. Furthermore, Jackson states, the company's pension fund had the opportunity to invest up to 5 percent in the commingled fund.

> *Comment*: The bank's policy does not treat all customers fairly, and Jackson has violated her duty to her clients by giving priority to the growth-oriented commingled fund over all other funds and to discretionary accounts over nondiscretionary accounts. Jackson must execute orders on a systematic basis that is fair to all clients. In addition, trade allocation procedures should be disclosed to all clients when they become clients. Of course, in this case, disclosure of the bank's policy would not change the fact that the policy is unfair.

Example 3 (Fair Dealing and IPO Distribution): Dominic Morris works for a small regional securities firm. His work consists of corporate finance activities and investing for institutional clients. Arena, Ltd., is planning to go public. The partners have secured rights to buy an arena football league franchise and are planning to use the funds from the issue to complete the purchase. Because arena football is the current rage, Morris believes he has a hot issue on his hands.

He has quietly negotiated some options for himself for helping convince Arena to do the financing through his securities firm. When he seeks expressions of interest, the institutional buyers oversubscribe the issue. Morris, assuming that the institutions have the financial clout to drive the stock up, then fills all orders (including his own) and decreases the institutional blocks.

> *Comment*: Morris has violated Standard III(B) by not treating all customers fairly. He should not have taken any shares himself and should have pro-rated the shares offered among all clients. In addition, he should have disclosed to his firm and to his clients that he received options as part of the deal [see Standard VI(A)—Disclosure of Conflicts].

Example 4 (Fair Dealing and Transaction Allocation): Eleanor Preston, the chief investment officer of Porter Williams Investments (PWI), a medium-sized money management firm, has been trying to retain a client, Colby Company. Management at Colby, which accounts for almost half of PWI's revenues, recently told Preston that if the performance of its account did not improve, it would find a new money manager. Shortly after this threat, Preston purchases mortgage-backed securities (MBS) for several accounts, including Colby's. Preston is busy with a number of transactions that day, so she fails to allocate the trades immediately or write up the trade tickets. A few days later, when Preston is allocating trades, she notes that some of the MBS have significantly increased in price and some have dropped. Preston decides to allocate the profitable trades to Colby and spread the losing trades among several other PWI accounts.

> *Comment*: Preston has violated Standard III(B) by failing to deal fairly with her clients in taking these investment actions. Preston should have allocated the trades prior to executing the orders, or she should have had a systematic approach to allocating the trades, such as pro rata, as soon as practical after they were executed. Among other things, Preston must disclose to the client that the adviser may act as broker for, receive commissions from, and have a potential conflict of interest regarding both parties in agency cross-transactions. After the disclosure, she should obtain from the client consent authorizing such transactions in advance.

Example 5 (Selective Disclosure): Saunders Industrial Waste Management (SIWM) publicly indicates to analysts that it is comfortable with the somewhat disappointing earnings per share projection of US$1.16 for the quarter. Bernard Roberts, an analyst at Coffey Investments, is confident that SIWM management has understated the forecasted earnings so that the real announcement will cause an "upside surprise" and boost the price of SIWM stock. The "whisper number" (rumored) estimate based on extensive research and discussed among knowledgeable analysts is higher than US$1.16. Roberts repeats the US$1.16 figure in his research report to all Coffey clients but informally tells his large clients that he expects the earnings per share to be higher, making SIWM a good buy.

> *Comment*: By not sharing his opinion regarding the potential for a significant upside earnings surprise with all clients, Roberts is not treating all clients fairly and has violated Standard III(B).

Example 6 (Additional Services for Select Clients): Jenpin Weng uses e-mail to issue a new recommendation to all his clients. He then calls his three largest institutional clients to discuss the recommendation in detail.

> *Comment*: Weng has not violated Standard III(B) because he widely disseminated the recommendation and provided the information to all his clients prior to discussing it with a select few. Weng's largest clients received

additional personal service because they presumably pay higher fees or because they have a large amount of assets under Weng's management. If Weng had discussed the report with a select group of clients prior to distributing it to all his clients, he would have violated Standard III(B).

Example 7 (Minimum Lot Allocations): Lynn Hampton is a well-respected private wealth manager in her community with a diversified client base. She determines that a new 10-year bond being offered by Healthy Pharmaceuticals is appropriate for five of her clients. Three clients request to purchase US$10,000 each, and the other two request US$50,000 each. The minimum lot size is established at US$5,000, and the issue is oversubscribed at the time of placement. Her firm's policy is that odd-lot allocations, especially those below the minimum, should be avoided because they may affect the liquidity of the security at the time of sale.

Hampton is informed she will receive only US$55,000 of the offering for all accounts. Hampton distributes the bond investments as follows: The three accounts that requested US$10,000 are allocated US$5,000 each, and the two accounts that requested US$50,000 are allocated US$20,000 each.

Comment: Hampton has not violated Standard III(B), even though the distribution is not on a complete pro rata basis because of the required minimum lot size. With the total allocation being significantly below the amount requested, Hampton ensured that each client received at least the minimum lot size of the issue. This approach allowed the clients to efficiently sell the bond later if necessary.

C. Suitability

1. **When Members and Candidates are in an advisory relationship with a client, they must:**

   a. **Make a reasonable inquiry into a client's or prospective client's investment experience, risk and return objectives, and financial constraints prior to making any investment recommendation or taking investment action and must reassess and update this information regularly.**

   b. **Determine that an investment is suitable to the client's financial situation and consistent with the client's written objectives, mandates, and constraints before making an investment recommendation or taking investment action.**

   c. **Judge the suitability of investments in the context of the client's total portfolio.**

2. **When Members and Candidates are responsible for managing a portfolio to a specific mandate, strategy, or style, they must make only investment recommendations or take only investment actions that are consistent with the stated objectives and constraints of the portfolio.**

Guidance

Highlights:

▶ *Developing an Investment Policy*
▶ *Understanding the Client's Risk Profile*

▶ *Updating an Investment Policy*
▶ *The Need for Diversification*
▶ *Managing to an Index or Mandate*

Standard III(C) requires that members and candidates who are in an investment advisory relationship with clients consider carefully the needs, circumstances, and objectives of the clients when determining the appropriateness and suitability of a given investment or course of investment action. An appropriate suitability determination will not, however, prevent some investments or investment actions from losing value.

In judging the suitability of a potential investment, the member or candidate should review many aspects of the client's knowledge, experience related to investing, and financial situation. These aspects include, but are not limited to, the risk profile of the investment as compared with the constraints of the client, the impact of the investment on the diversity of the portfolio, and whether the client has the means or net worth to assume the associated risk. The investment professional's determination of suitability should reflect only the investment recommendations or actions that a prudent person would be willing to undertake. Not every investment opportunity will be suitable for every portfolio, regardless of the potential return being offered.

The responsibilities of members and candidates to gather information and make a suitability analysis prior to making a recommendation or taking investment action fall on those members and candidates who provide investment advice in the course of an advisory relationship with a client. Other members and candidates may be simply executing specific instructions for retail clients when buying or selling securities, such as shares in mutual funds. These members and candidates and some others, such as sell-side analysts, may not have the opportunity to judge the suitability of a particular investment for the ultimate client. In cases of unsolicited trade requests that a member or candidate knows are unsuitable for the client, the member or candidate should refrain from making the trade or should seek an affirmative statement from the client that suitability is not a consideration.

Developing an Investment Policy

When an advisory relationship exists, members and candidates must gather client information at the inception of the relationship. Such information includes the client's financial circumstances, personal data (such as age and occupation) that are relevant to investment decisions, attitudes toward risk, and objectives in investing. This information should be incorporated into a written investment policy statement (IPS) that addresses the client's risk tolerance, return requirements, and all investment constraints (including time horizon, liquidity needs, tax concerns, legal and regulatory factors, and unique circumstances). Without identifying such client factors, members and candidates cannot judge whether a particular investment or strategy is suitable for a particular client. The IPS also should identify and describe the roles and responsibilities of the parties to the advisory relationship and investment process, as well as schedules for review and evaluation of the IPS. After formulating long-term capital market expectations, members and clients can assist in developing an appropriate strategic asset allocation and investment program for the client, whether these are presented in separate documents or incorporated in the IPS or in appendices to the IPS.

Understanding the Client's Risk Profile

One of the most important factors to be considered in matching appropriateness and suitability of an investment with a client's needs and circumstances is measuring that client's tolerance for risk. The investment professional must consider the possibilities of rapidly changing investment environments and their likely impact on a client's holdings, both individual securities and the collective portfolio. The risk of many investment strategies can and should be analyzed and quantified in advance.

The use of synthetic investment vehicles and derivative investment products has introduced particular issues of risk. Members and candidates should pay careful attention to the leverage inherent in many of these vehicles or products when considering them for use in a client's investment program. Such leverage and limited liquidity, depending on the degree to which they are hedged, bear directly on the issue of suitability for the client.

Updating an Investment Policy

Updating the IPS should be repeated at least annually and also prior to material changes to any specific investment recommendations or decisions on behalf of the client. The effort to determine the needs and circumstances of each client is not a one-time occurrence. Investment recommendations or decisions are usually part of an ongoing process that takes into account the diversity and changing nature of portfolio and client characteristics. The passage of time is bound to produce changes that are important with respect to investment objectives.

For an individual client, important changes might include the number of dependents, personal tax status, health, liquidity needs, risk tolerance, amount of wealth beyond that represented in the portfolio, and extent to which compensation and other income provide for current-income needs. With respect to an institutional client, such changes might relate to the magnitude of unfunded liabilities in a pension fund, the withdrawal privileges in an employee savings plan, or the distribution requirements of a charitable foundation. Without efforts to update information concerning client factors, one or more factors could change without the investment manager's knowledge.

Suitability review can be done effectively only if the client fully discloses his or her complete financial portfolio, including those portions not managed by the member or candidate. If clients withhold information about their financial portfolio, the suitability analysis conducted by members and candidates cannot be expected to be complete; it must be based on the information provided.

The Need for Diversification

The investment profession has long recognized that the combination of several different investments is likely to provide a more acceptable level of risk exposure than having all assets in a single investment. The unique characteristics (or risks) of an individual investment may become partially or entirely neutralized when it is combined with other individual investments within a portfolio. Some reasonable amount of diversification is thus the norm for many portfolios, especially those managed by individuals or institutions that have some degree of legal fiduciary responsibility.

An investment with high relative risk on its own may be a suitable investment in the context of the entire portfolio or when the client's stated objectives contemplate speculative or risky investments. The manager may be responsible for only a portion of the client's total portfolio, or the client may not have provided a full financial picture. Members and candidates can be responsible for assessing the suitability of an investment only on the basis of the information and criteria actually provided by the client.

Managing to an Index or Mandate

Some members and candidates do not manage money for individuals but are responsible for managing a fund to an index or an expected mandate. The responsibility of these members and candidates is to invest in a manner consistent with the stated mandate. For example, a member or candidate who serves as the fund manager for a large-cap income fund would not be following the fund mandate by investing heavily in small-cap or start-up companies whose stock is speculative in nature. Members and candidates who manage pooled assets to a specific mandate are not responsible for determining the suitability of the fund as an investment for investors who may be purchasing shares in the fund. The responsibility for determining the suitability of an investment for clients can only be conferred on members and candidates who have an advisory relationship with clients.

Recommended Procedures for Compliance

Investment Policy Statement

To fulfill the basic provisions of Standard III(C), a member or candidate should put the needs and circumstances of each client and the client's investment objectives into a written investment policy statement. In formulating an investment policy for the client, the member or candidate should take the following into consideration:

- ▶ client identification—1) type and nature of client, 2) the existence of separate beneficiaries, and 3) approximate portion of total client assets that the member or candidate is managing;
- ▶ investor objectives—1) return objectives (income, growth in principal, maintenance of purchasing power) and 2) risk tolerance (suitability, stability of values);
- ▶ investor constraints—1) liquidity needs, 2) expected cash flows (patterns of additions and/or withdrawals), 3) investable funds (assets and liabilities or other commitments), 4) time horizon, 5) tax considerations, 6) regulatory and legal circumstances, 7) investor preferences, prohibitions, circumstances, and unique needs, and 8) proxy voting responsibilities and guidance;
- ▶ performance measurement benchmarks.

Regular Updates

The investor's objectives and constraints should be maintained and reviewed periodically to reflect any changes in the client's circumstances. Members and candidates should regularly compare client constraints with capital market expectations to arrive at an appropriate asset allocation. Changes in either factor may result in a fundamental change in asset allocation. Annual review is reasonable unless business or other reasons, such as a major change in market conditions, dictate more frequent review. Members and candidates should document attempts to carry out such a review if circumstances prevent it.

Suitability Test Policies

With the increase in regulatory required suitability tests, members and candidates should encourage their firms to develop related policies and procedures. The procedures will differ according to the size of the firm and scope of the services offered to its clients.

The test procedures should require the investment professional to look beyond the potential return of the investment and include the following:

► an analysis on the impact on the portfolio's diversification;

► a comparison of the investment risks with the client's assessed risk tolerance; and

► the fit of the investment with the required investment strategy.

Application of the Standard

Example 1 (Investment Suitability—Risk Profile): Caleb Smith, an investment adviser, has two clients: Larry Robertson, 60 years old, and Gabriel Lanai, 40 years old. Both clients earn roughly the same salary, but Robertson has a much higher risk tolerance because he has a large asset base. Robertson is willing to invest part of his assets very aggressively; Lanai wants only to achieve a steady rate of return with low volatility to pay for his children's education. Smith recommends investing 20 percent of both portfolios in zero-yield, small-cap, high-technology equity issues.

> *Comment*: In Robertson's case, the investment may be appropriate because of his financial circumstances and aggressive investment position, but this investment is not suitable for Lanai. Smith is violating Standard III(C) by applying Robertson's investment strategy to Lanai because the two clients' financial circumstances and objectives differ.

Example 2 (Investment Suitability—Entire Portfolio): Jessica Walters, an investment adviser, suggests to Brian Crosby, a risk-averse client, that covered call options be used in his equity portfolio. The purpose would be to enhance Crosby's income and partially offset any untimely depreciation in the portfolio's value should the stock market or other circumstances affect his holdings unfavorably. Walters educates Crosby about all possible outcomes, including the risk of incurring an added tax liability if a stock rises in price and is called away and, conversely, the risk of his holdings losing protection on the downside if prices drop sharply.

> *Comment*: When determining suitability of an investment, the primary focus should be on the characteristics of the client's entire portfolio, not the characteristics of single securities on an issue-by-issue basis. The basic characteristics of the entire portfolio will largely determine whether investment recommendations are taking client factors into account. Therefore, the most important aspects of a particular investment are those that will affect the characteristics of the total portfolio. In this case, Walters properly considers the investment in the context of the entire portfolio and thoroughly explains the investment to the client.

Example 3 (IPS Updating): In a regular meeting with client Seth Jones, the portfolio managers at Blue Chip Investment Advisors are careful to allow some time to review his current needs and circumstances. In doing so, they learn that some significant changes have recently taken place in his life. A wealthy uncle left Jones an inheritance that increased his net worth fourfold, to US$1,000,000.

Comment: The inheritance has significantly increased Jones's ability (and possibly his willingness) to assume risk and has diminished the average yield required to meet his current-income needs. Jones's financial circumstances have definitely changed, so Blue Chip managers must update Jones's investment policy statement to reflect how his investment objectives have changed. Accordingly, the Blue Chip portfolio managers should consider a somewhat higher equity ratio for his portfolio than was called for by the previous circumstances, and the managers' specific common stock recommendations might be heavily tilted toward low-yield, growth-oriented issues.

Example 4 (Following an Investment Mandate): Louis Perkowski manages a high-income mutual fund. He purchases zero-dividend stock in a financial services company because he believes the stock is undervalued and is in a potential growth industry, which makes it an attractive investment.

Comment: A zero-dividend stock does not seem to fit the mandate of the fund that Perkowski is managing. Unless Perkowski's investment fits within the mandate or is within the realm of allowable investments the fund has made clear in its disclosures, Perkowski has violated Standard III(C).

Example 5 (IPS Requirements and Limitations): Max Gubler, chief investment officer of a property/casualty insurance subsidiary of a large financial conglomerate, wants to improve the diversification of the subsidiary's investment portfolio and increase its returns. The subsidiary's investment policy statement provides for highly liquid investments, such as large-cap equities and government, supranational, and corporate bonds with a minimum credit rating of AA and maturity of no more than five years. In a recent presentation, a venture capital group offered very attractive prospective returns on some of its private equity funds that provide seed capital to ventures. An exit strategy was already contemplated, but investors would have to observe a minimum three-year lock-up period and a subsequent laddered exit option for a maximum of one-third of their shares per year. Gubler does not want to miss this opportunity. After extensive analysis, with the intent to optimize the return on the equity assets within the subsidiary's current portfolio, he invests 4 percent in this seed fund, leaving the portfolio's total equity exposure still well below its upper limit.

Comment: Gubler is violating Standard III(A)—Loyalty, Prudence, and Care as well as Standard III(C). His new investment locks up part of the subsidiary's assets for at least three years and up to as many as five years and possibly beyond. The IPS requires investments in highly liquid investments and describes accepted asset classes; private equity investments with a lock-up period certainly do not qualify. Even without a lock-up period, an asset class with only an occasional, and thus implicitly illiquid, market may not be suitable for the portfolio. Although an IPS typically describes objectives and constraints in great detail, the manager must also make every effort to understand the client's business and circumstances. Doing so should enable the manager to recognize, understand, and discuss with the client other factors that may be or may become material in the investment management process.

Example 6 (Submanager and IPS Reviews): Paul Ostrowski's investment management business has grown significantly over the past couple of years, and some clients want to diversify internationally. Ostrowski decides to find a submanager to handle the expected international investments. Because this will be his first subadviser, Ostrowski uses the CFA Institute model "request for proposal" to design a questionnaire for his search. By his deadline, he receives seven completed questionnaires from a variety of domestic and international firms trying to gain his business. Ostrowski reviews all the applications in detail and decides to select the firm that charges the lowest fees because doing so will have the least impact on his firm's bottom line.

> *Comment*: When selecting an external or subadviser, Ostrowski needs to ensure that the new manager's services are appropriate for his clients. This due diligence includes comparing the risk profile of the clients with the investment strategy of the manager. In basing the decision on the fee structure alone, Ostrowski may be violating Standard III(C).
>
> When clients ask to diversify into international products, it is an appropriate time to review and update the clients' IPS. Ostrowski's review may determine that the risk of international investments modifies the risk profiles of the clients or does not represent an appropriate investment.
>
> See also Standard V(A)—Diligence and Reasonable Basis for further discussion of the review process needed in selecting appropriate submanagers.

Example 7 (Investment Suitability—Risk Profile): Samantha Snead, a portfolio manager for Thomas Investment Counsel, Inc., specializes in managing public retirement funds and defined-benefit pension plan accounts, all of which have long-term investment objectives. A year ago, Snead's employer, in an attempt to motivate and retain key investment professionals, introduced a bonus compensation system that rewards portfolio managers on the basis of quarterly performance relative to their peers and to certain benchmark indices. In an attempt to improve the short-term performance of her accounts, Snead changes her investment strategy and purchases several high-beta stocks for client portfolios. These purchases are seemingly contrary to the clients' investment policy statements. Following their purchase, an officer of Griffin Corporation, one of Snead's pension fund clients, asks why Griffin Corporation's portfolio seems to be dominated by high-beta stocks of companies that often appear among the most actively traded issues. No change in objective or strategy has been recommended by Snead during the year.

> *Comment*: Snead violated Standard III(C) by investing the clients' assets in high-beta stocks. These high-risk investments are contrary to the long-term risk profile established in the clients' IPS. Snead has changed the investment strategy of the clients in an attempt to reap short-term rewards offered by her firm's new compensation arrangement, not in response to changes in clients' investment policy statements.
>
> See also Standard VI(A)—Disclosure of Conflicts.

Example 8 (Investment Suitability): Andre Shrub owns and operates Conduit, an investment advisory firm. Prior to opening Conduit, Shrub was an account manager with Elite Investment, a hedge fund managed by his good friend Adam Reed. To attract clients to a new Conduit fund, Shrub offers lower-than-normal management fees. He can do so because the fund consists of two top-performing funds managed by Reed. Given his personal friendship with Reed and the prior performance record of these two funds, Shrub believes this new fund is a winning combination for all parties. Clients quickly invest with Conduit to gain access to the Elite funds. No one is turned away because Conduit is seeking to expand its assets under management.

> *Comment*: Shrub has violated Standard III(C) because the risk profile of the new fund may not be suitable for every client. As an investment adviser, Shrub needs to establish an investment policy statement for each client and recommend only investments that match that client's risk and return profile in that client's IPS. Shrub is required to act as more than a simple sales agent for Elite.

Although Shrub cannot disobey the direct request of a client to purchase a specific security, he should fully discuss the risks of a planned purchase and provide reasons why it might not be suitable for a client. This requirement may lead members and candidates to decline new customers if those customers' requested investment decisions are significantly out of line with their stated requirements.

See also Standard V(A)—Diligence and Reasonable Basis.

D. Performance Presentation

When communicating investment performance information, Members and Candidates must make reasonable efforts to ensure that it is fair, accurate, and complete.

Guidance

Standard III(D) requires members and candidates to provide credible performance information to clients and prospective clients and to avoid misstating performance or misleading clients and prospective clients about the investment performance of members or candidates or their firms. This standard encourages full disclosure of investment performance data to clients and prospective clients.

Standard III(D) covers any practice that would lead to misrepresentation of a member's or candidate's performance record, whether the practice involves performance presentation or performance measurement. This standard prohibits misrepresentations of past performance or reasonably expected performance. A member or candidate must give a fair and complete presentation of performance information whenever communicating data with respect to the performance history of individual accounts, composites or groups of accounts, or composites of an analyst's or firm's performance results. Furthermore, members and candidates should not state or imply that clients will obtain or benefit from a rate of return that was generated in the past.

The requirements of this standard are not limited to members and candidates managing separate accounts. Whenever a member or candidate provides performance information for which the manager is claiming responsibility, such as for pooled funds, the history must be accurate. Research analysts promoting the success or accuracy of their recommendations must ensure that their claims are fair, accurate, and complete.

If the presentation is brief, the member or candidate must make available to clients and prospects, on request, the detailed information supporting that communication. Best practice dictates that brief presentations include a reference to the limited nature of the information provided.

Recommended Procedures for Compliance

Apply GIPS Standards. For members and candidates who are showing the performance history of the assets they manage, compliance with the GIPS standards is the best method to meet their obligations under Standard III(D). Members and candidates should encourage their firms to comply with the GIPS standards.

Compliance without Applying GIPS Standards

Members and candidates can also meet their obligations under Standard III(D) by:

▶ considering the knowledge and sophistication of the audience to whom a performance presentation is addressed;

▶ presenting the performance of the weighted composite of similar portfolios rather than using a single representative account;

▶ including terminated accounts as part of performance history with a clear indication of when the accounts were terminated;

▶ including disclosures that fully explain the performance results being reported (for example, stating, when appropriate, that results are simulated when model results are used, clearly indicating when the performance record is that of a prior entity, or disclosing whether the performance is gross of fees, net of fees, or after tax); and

▶ maintaining the data and records used to calculate the performance being presented.

Application of the Standard

Example 1 (Performance Calculation and Length of Time): Kyle Taylor of Taylor Trust Company, noting the performance of Taylor's common trust fund for the past two years, states in a brochure sent to his potential clients, "You can expect steady 25 percent annual compound growth of the value of your investments over the year." Taylor Trust's common trust fund did increase at the rate of 25 percent per year for the past year, which mirrored the increase of the entire market. The fund has never averaged that growth for more than one year, however, and the average rate of growth of all of its trust accounts for five years is 5 percent per year.

> *Comment*: Taylor's brochure is in violation of Standard III(D). Taylor should have disclosed that the 25 percent growth occurred only in one year. Additionally, Taylor did not include client accounts other than those in the firm's common trust fund. A general claim of firm performance should take into account the performance of all categories of accounts. Finally, by stating that clients can expect a steady 25 percent annual compound growth rate, Taylor is also violating Standard I(C)—Misrepresentation, which prohibits assurances or guarantees regarding an investment.

Example 2 (Performance Calculation and Asset Weighting): Anna Judd, a senior partner of Alexander Capital Management, circulates a performance report for the capital appreciation accounts for the years 1988 through 2004. The firm claims compliance with the GIPS standards. Returns are not calculated in accordance with the requirements of the GIPS standards, however, because the composites are not asset weighted.

> *Comment*: Judd is in violation of Standard III(D). When claiming compliance with GIPS standards, firms must meet all of the requirements, make mandatory disclosures, and meet any other requirements that apply to that firm's specific situation. Judd's violation is not from any misuse of the data but from a false claim of GIPS compliance.

Example 3 (Performance Presentation and Prior Fund/Employer): Aaron McCoy is vice president and managing partner of the equity investment group of

Mastermind Financial Advisors, a new business. Mastermind recruited McCoy because he had a proven six-year track record with G&P Financial. In developing Mastermind's advertising and marketing campaign, McCoy prepares an advertisement that includes the equity investment performance he achieved at G&P Financial. The advertisement for Mastermind does not identify the equity performance as being earned while at G&P. The advertisement is distributed to existing clients and prospective clients of Mastermind.

> *Comment*: McCoy has violated Standard III(D) by distributing an advertisement that contains material misrepresentations about the historical performance of Mastermind. Standard III(D) requires that members and candidates make every reasonable effort to ensure that performance information is a fair, accurate, and complete representation of an individual's or firm's performance. As a general matter, this standard does not prohibit showing past performance of funds managed at a prior firm as part of a performance track record as long as showing that record is accompanied by appropriate disclosures about where the performance took place and the person's specific role in achieving that performance. If McCoy chooses to use his past performance from G&P in Mastermind's advertising, he should make full disclosure of the source of the historical performance.

Example 4 (Performance Presentation and Simulated Results): Jed Davis has developed a mutual fund selection product based on historical information from the 1990–95 period. Davis tested his methodology by applying it retroactively to data from the 1996–2003 period, thus producing simulated performance results for those years. In January 2004, Davis's employer decided to offer the product and Davis began promoting it through trade journal advertisements and direct dissemination to clients. The advertisements included the performance results for the 1996–2003 period but did not indicate that the results were simulated.

> *Comment*: Davis violated Standard III(D) by failing to clearly identify simulated performance results. Standard III(D) prohibits members and candidates from making any statements that misrepresent the performance achieved by them or their firms and requires members and candidates to make every reasonable effort to ensure that performance information presented to clients is fair, accurate, and complete. Use of simulated results should be accompanied by full disclosure as to the source of the performance data, including the fact that the results from 1995 through 2003 were the result of applying the model retroactively to that time period.

Example 5 (Performance Calculation and Selected Accounts Only): In a presentation prepared for prospective clients, William Kilmer shows the rates of return realized over a five-year period by a "composite" of his firm's discretionary accounts that have a "balanced" objective. This composite consisted of only a few of the accounts, however, that met the balanced criterion set by the firm, excluded accounts under a certain asset level without disclosing the fact of their exclusion, and included accounts that did not have the balanced mandate because those accounts would boost the investment results. In addition, to achieve better results, Kilmer manipulated the narrow range of accounts included in the composite by changing the accounts that made up the composite over time.

> *Comment*: Kilmer violated Standard III(D) by misrepresenting the facts in the promotional material sent to prospective clients, distorting his firm's performance record, and failing to include disclosures that would have clarified the presentation.

E. Preservation of Confidentiality

Members and Candidates must keep information about current, former, and prospective clients confidential unless:

1. **The information concerns illegal activities on the part of the client;**
2. **Disclosure is required by law; or**
3. **The client or prospective client permits disclosure of the information.**

Guidance

Highlights:

▶ *Status of Client*

▶ *Compliance with Laws*

▶ *Electronic Information and Security*

▶ *Professional Conduct Investigations by CFA Institute*

Standard III(E) requires that members and candidates preserve the confidentiality of information communicated to them by their clients, prospective clients, and former clients. This standard is applicable when 1) the member or candidate receives information because of his or her special ability to conduct a portion of the client's business or personal affairs and 2) the member or candidate receives information that arises from or is relevant to that portion of the client's business that is the subject of the special or confidential relationship. If disclosure of the information is required by law or the information concerns illegal activities by the client, however, the member or candidate may have an obligation to report the activities to the appropriate authorities.

Status of Client

This standard protects the confidentiality of client information even if the person or entity is no longer a client of the member or candidate. Therefore, members and candidates must continue to maintain the confidentiality of client records even after the client relationship has ended. If a client or former client expressly authorizes the member or candidate to disclose information, however, the member or candidate may follow the terms of the authorization and provide the information.

Compliance with Laws

As a general matter, members and candidates must comply with applicable law. If applicable law requires disclosure of client information in certain circumstances, members and candidates must comply with the law. Similarly, if applicable law requires members and candidates to maintain confidentiality, even if the information concerns illegal activities on the part of the client, members and candidates should not disclose such information. When in doubt, members and candidates should consult with their employer's compliance personnel or legal counsel before disclosing confidential information about clients.

Electronic Information and Security

Because of the ever increasing volume of electronically stored information, members and candidates need to be particularly aware of possible accidental disclosures. Many employers have strict policies about storing client information on personal laptops or portable drives. Standard III(E) does not require members or candidates to become experts in information security technology, but they should have a thorough understanding of the policies of their employers. The size and operations of the firm will lead to differing policies for ensuring the security of confidential information maintained within the firm.

Professional Conduct Investigations by CFA Institute

The requirements of Standard III(E) are not intended to prevent members and candidates from cooperating with an investigation by the CFA Institute Professional Conduct Program (PCP). When permissible under applicable law, members and candidates shall consider the PCP an extension of themselves when requested to provide information about a client in support of a PCP investigation into their own conduct. Members and candidates are encouraged to cooperate with investigations into the conduct of others. Any information turned over to the PCP is kept in the strictest confidence. Members and candidates will not be considered in violation of this standard by forwarding confidential information to the PCP.

Recommended Procedures for Compliance

The simplest, most conservative, and most effective way to comply with Standard III(E) is to avoid disclosing any information received from a client except to authorized fellow employees who are also working for the client. In some instances, however, a member or candidate may want to disclose information received from clients that is outside the scope of the confidential relationship and does not involve illegal activities. Before making such a disclosure, a member or candidate should ask the following:

► In what context was the information disclosed? If disclosed in a discussion of work being performed for the client, is the information relevant to the work?

► Is the information background material that, if disclosed, will enable the member or candidate to improve service to the client?

Members and candidates need to understand and follow their firm's electronic information storage procedures. If the firm does not have procedures in place, members and candidates should encourage the development of procedures that appropriately reflect the firm's size and business operations.

Application of the Standard

Example 1 (Possessing Confidential Information): Sarah Connor, a financial analyst employed by Johnson Investment Counselors, Inc., provides investment advice to the trustees of City Medical Center. The trustees have given her a number of internal reports concerning City Medical's needs for physical plant renovation and expansion. They have asked Connor to recommend investments that would generate capital appreciation in endowment funds to meet projected capital expenditures. Connor is approached by a local businessman, Thomas Kasey, who is considering a substantial contribution either to City Medical Center or to another local hospital. Kasey wants to find out the building plans of both institutions before making a decision, but he does not want to speak to the trustees.

Comment: The trustees gave Connor the internal reports so she could advise them on how to manage their endowment funds. Because the information in the reports is clearly both confidential and within the scope of the confidential relationship, Standard III(E) requires that Connor refuse to divulge information to Kasey.

Example 2 (Disclosing Confidential Information): Lynn Moody is an investment officer at the Lester Trust Company. She has an advisory customer who has talked to her about giving approximately US$50,000 to charity to reduce her income taxes. Moody is also treasurer of the Home for Indigent Widows (HIW), which is planning its annual giving campaign. HIW hopes to expand its list of prospects, particularly those capable of substantial gifts. Moody recommends that HIW's vice president for corporate gifts call on her customer and ask for a donation in the US$50,000 range.

Comment: Even though the attempt to help the Home for Indigent Widows was well intended, Moody violated Standard III(E) by revealing confidential information about her client.

Example 3 (Disclosing Possible Illegal Activity): Government officials approach Casey Samuel, the portfolio manager for Garcia Company's pension plan, to examine pension fund records. They tell her that Garcia's corporate tax returns are being audited and the pension fund is being reviewed. Two days earlier, Samuel had learned in a regular investment review with Garcia officers that potentially excessive and improper charges were being made to the pension plan by Garcia. Samuel consults her employer's general counsel and is advised that Garcia has probably violated tax and fiduciary regulations and laws.

Comment: Samuel should inform her supervisor of these activities, and her employer should take steps, with Garcia, to remedy the violations. If that approach is not successful, Samuel and her employer should seek advice of legal counsel to determine the appropriate steps to be taken. Samuel may well have a duty to disclose the evidence she has of the continuing legal violations and to resign as asset manager for Garcia.

Example 4 (Disclosing Possible Illegal Activity): David Bradford manages money for a family-owned real estate development corporation. He also manages the individual portfolios of several of the family members and officers of the corporation, including the chief financial officer (CFO). Based on the financial records of the corporation and some questionable practices of the CFO that Bradford has observed, Bradford believes that the CFO is embezzling money from the corporation and putting it into his personal investment account.

Comment: Bradford should check with his firm's compliance department or appropriate legal counsel to determine whether applicable securities regulations require reporting the CFO's financial records.

STANDARD IV—DUTIES TO EMPLOYERS

A. Loyalty

In matters related to their employment, Members and Candidates must act for the benefit of their employer and not deprive their employer of the advantage of their skills and abilities, divulge confidential information, or otherwise cause harm to their employer.

Guidance

Highlights:

▶ *Employer Responsibilities*
▶ *Independent Practice*
▶ *Leaving an Employer*
▶ *Whistleblowing*
▶ *Nature of Employment*

Standard IV(A) requires members and candidates to protect the interests of their firm by refraining from any conduct that would injure the firm, deprive it of profit, or deprive it of the member's or candidate's skills and ability. Members and candidates must always place the interests of clients above the interests of their employer but should also consider the effects of their conduct on the sustainability and integrity of the employer firm. In matters related to their employment, members and candidates must not engage in conduct that harms the interests of their employer. Implicit in this standard is the obligation of members and candidates to comply with the policies and procedures established by their employers that govern the employer–employee relationship—to the extent that such policies and procedures do not conflict with applicable laws, rules, regulations, or the Code and Standards.

This standard is not meant to be a blanket requirement to place employer interests ahead of personal interests in all matters. The standard does not require members and candidates to subordinate important personal and family obligations to their work. Members and candidates should enter into a dialogue with their employer about balancing personal and employment obligations when personal matters may interfere with their work on a regular or significant basis.

Employer Responsibilities

The employer–employee relationship imposes duties and responsibilities on both parties. Employers must recognize the duties and responsibilities that they owe to their employees if they expect to have contented and productive employees.

Members and candidates are encouraged to provide their employers with a copy of the Code and Standards. These materials will inform the employer of the responsibilities of a CFA Institute member or candidate in the CFA Program. The Code and Standards also serve as a basis for questioning employer policies and practices that conflict with these responsibilities.

Employers are not obligated to adhere to the Code and Standards. In expecting to retain competent employees who are members and candidates, however, they should not develop conflicting policies and procedures. The employer is responsible for a positive working environment, which includes an ethical workplace. Senior management has the additional responsibility to devise compensation structures and incentive arrangements that do not encourage unethical behavior.

Independent Practice

Included in Standard IV(A) is the requirement that members and candidates abstain from independent competitive activity that could conflict with the interests of their employer. Although Standard IV(A) does not preclude members or candidates from entering into an independent business while still employed, members and candidates who plan to engage in independent practice for compensation must notify their employer and describe the types of services the members or candidates will render to prospective independent clients, the expected duration of the services, and the compensation for the services. Members and candidates should not render services until they receive consent from their employer to all of the terms of the arrangement. "Practice" means any service that the employer currently makes available for remuneration. "Undertaking independent practice" means engaging in competitive business, as opposed to making preparations to begin such practice.

Leaving an Employer

When members and candidates are planning to leave their current employer, they must continue to act in the employer's best interest. They must not engage in any activities that would conflict with this duty until their resignation becomes effective. It is difficult to define specific guidelines for those members and candidates who are planning to compete with their employer as part of a new venture. The circumstances of each situation must be reviewed to distinguish permissible preparations from violations of duty. Activities that might constitute a violation, especially in combination, include the following:

▶ misappropriation of trade secrets;

▶ misuse of confidential information;

▶ solicitation of employer's clients prior to cessation of employment;

▶ self-dealing (appropriating for one's own property a business opportunity or information belonging to one's employer); and

▶ misappropriation of clients or client lists.

A departing employee is generally free to make arrangements or preparations to go into a competitive business before terminating the relationship with his or her employer as long as such preparations do not breach the employee's duty of loyalty. Members and candidates who are contemplating seeking other employment must not contact existing clients or potential clients prior to leaving their employer for purposes of soliciting their business for the new employer. Once notice is provided to the employer of the intent to resign, the member or candidate must follow the employer's policies and procedures related to notifying clients of his or her planned departure. In addition, the member or candidate must not take records or files to a new employer without the written permission of the previous employer.

Once an employee has left the firm, the skills and experience that an employee obtained while employed are not "confidential" or "privileged" information. Similarly, simple knowledge of the names and existence of former clients is generally not confidential information unless deemed such by an agreement or by law. Standard IV(A) does not prohibit experience or knowledge gained at one employer from being used at another employer. Firm records, however, or work performed on behalf of the firm that is stored in paper copy or electronically for the member's or candidate's convenience while employed should be erased or returned to the employer unless the firm gives permission to keep those records after employment ends.

The standard does not prohibit former employees from contacting clients of their previous firm as long as the contact information does not come from the records of the former employer or violate an applicable "noncompete agreement." Members and candidates are free to use public information after departing to contact former clients without violating Standard IV(A) as long as there is no specific agreement not to do so.

Employers often require employees to sign noncompete agreements that preclude a departing employee from engaging in certain conduct. Members and candidates should take care to review the terms of any such agreement when leaving their employer to determine what, if any, conduct those agreements may prohibit.

Whistleblowing

A member's or candidate's personal interests, as well as the interests of his or her employer, are secondary to protecting the integrity of capital markets and the interests of clients. Therefore, circumstances may arise (e.g., when an employer is engaged in illegal or unethical activity) in which members and candidates must act contrary to their employer's interests in order to comply with their duties to the market and clients. In such instances, activities that would normally violate a member's or candidate's duty to his or her employer (such as contradicting employer instructions, violating certain policies and procedures, or preserving a record by copying employer records) may be justified. Such action would be permitted only if the intent is clearly aimed at protecting clients or the integrity of the market, not for personal gain.

Nature of Employment

A wide variety of business relationships exists within the investment industry. For instance, a member or candidate may be an employee or an independent contractor. Members and candidates must determine whether they are employees or independent contractors in order to determine the applicability of Standard IV(A). This issue will be decided largely by the degree of control exercised by the employing entity over the member or candidate. Factors determining control include whether the member's or candidate's hours, work location, and other parameters of the job are set; whether facilities are provided to the member or candidate; whether the member's or candidate's expenses are reimbursed; whether the member or candidate seeks work from other employers; and the number of clients or employers the member or candidate works for.

A member's or candidate's duties within an independent contractor relationship are governed by the oral or written agreement between the member and the client. Members and candidates should take care to define clearly the scope of their responsibilities and the expectations of each client within the context of each relationship. Once the member or candidate establishes a relationship with a client, the member or candidate has a duty to abide by the terms of the agreement.

Recommended Procedures for Compliance

Employers may establish codes of conduct and operating procedures for their employees to follow. Members and candidates should fully understand the policies to ensure that they are not in conflict with the Code and Standards. The following topics identify policies that members and candidates should encourage their firms to adopt if the policies are not currently in their procedures.

Competition Policy

Members and candidates must understand any restrictions placed by the employer on offering similar services outside the firm while employed by the firm. The policy may outline the procedures for requesting approval to under-take the outside service or may be a strict prohibition of such service. If a member's or candidate's employer elects to have its employees sign a noncompete agreement as part of the employment agreement, members and candidates should ensure that the details are clear and fully explained prior to signing the agreement.

Termination Policy

Members and candidates should clearly understand the termination policies of their employer. The policy should establish clear procedures regarding the resig-nation process, including addressing how the termination will be disclosed to clients and staff. The firm's policy may also outline the procedures for transferring responsibilities of ongoing research responsibilities and account management.

Incident-Reporting Procedures

Members and candidates should be aware of their firm's policies related to whistleblowing and encourage their firms to adopt industry best practices in this area. Many firms are required by regulatory mandates to establish confidential and anonymous reporting procedures that allow employees to report potentially unethical and illegal activities in the firm.

Employee Classification

Members and candidates should understand their status within their employer firm. Firms are encouraged to adopt a standardized classification structure—e.g., part time, full time, outside contractor—for their employees and indicate how each of the firm's policies applies to each employee class.

Application of the Standard

Example 1 (Soliciting Former Clients): Samuel Magee manages pension accounts for Trust Assets, Inc., but has become frustrated with the working envi-ronment and has been offered a position with Fiduciary Management. Before resigning from Trust Assets, Magee asks four big accounts to leave that firm and open accounts with Fiduciary. Magee also persuades several prospective clients to sign agreements with Fiduciary Management. Magee had previously made presentations to these prospects on behalf of Trust Assets.

> *Comment*: Magee violated the employee–employer principle requiring him to act solely for his employer's benefit. Magee's duty is to Trust Assets as long as he is employed there. The solicitation of Trust Assets' current clients and prospective clients is unethical and violates Standard IV(A).

Example 2 (Former Employer's Documents and Files): James Hightower has been employed by Jason Investment Management Corporation for 15 years. He began as an analyst but assumed increasing responsibilities and is now a senior portfolio manager and a member of the firm's investment policy committee. Hightower has decided to leave Jason Investment and start his own investment management business. He has been careful not to tell any of Jason's clients that he is leaving; he does not want to be accused of breaching his duty to Jason by soliciting Jason's clients before his departure. Hightower is planning to copy and take with him the following documents and information he developed or worked on while at Jason: 1) the client list, with addresses, telephone numbers, and other pertinent client information; 2) client account statements; 3) sample marketing presentations to prospective clients containing Jason's performance record; 4) Jason's recommended list of securities; 5) computer models to determine asset allocations for accounts with various objectives; 6) computer models for stock selection; and 7) personal computer spreadsheets for Hightower's major corporate recommendations, which he developed when he was an analyst.

> *Comment*: Except with the consent of their employer, departing members and candidates may not take employer property, which includes books, records, reports, and other materials, because taking such materials may interfere with their employer's business opportunities. Taking any employer records, even those the member or candidate prepared, violates Standard IV(A). Employer records include items stored in hard copy or any other medium (e.g., home computers, portable storage devices, cell phones).

Example 3 (Addressing Rumors): Reuben Winston manages all-equity portfolios at Target Asset Management (TAM), a large, established investment counselor. Ten years previously, Philpott & Company, which manages a family of global bond mutual funds, acquired TAM in a diversification move. After the merger, the combined operations prospered in the fixed-income business but the equity management business at TAM languished. Lately, a few of the equity pension accounts that had been with TAM before the merger have terminated their relationships with TAM. One day, Winston finds on his voice mail a message from a concerned client, "Hey! I just heard that Philpott is close to announcing the sale of your firm's equity management business to Rugged Life. What is going on?" Not being aware of any such deal, Winston and his associates are stunned. Their internal inquiries are met with denials from Philpott management, but the rumors persist. Feeling left in the dark, Winston contemplates leading an employee buyout of TAM's equity management business.

> *Comment*: An employee-led buyout of TAM's equity asset management business would be consistent with Standard IV(A) because it would rest on the permission of the employer and, ultimately, the clients. In this case, however, in which employees suspect the senior managers or principals are not truthful or forthcoming, Winston should consult legal counsel to determine appropriate action.

Example 4 (Ownership of Completed Prior Work): Laura Clay, who is unemployed, wants part-time consulting work while seeking a full-time analyst position. During an interview at Bradley Associates, a large institutional asset manager, Clay is told that the firm has no immediate research openings but would be willing to pay her a flat fee to complete a study of the wireless communications industry within a given period of time. Clay would be allowed unlimited access to Bradley's research files and would be welcome to come to the offices and use whatever support facilities are available during normal working hours. Bradley's research director does not seek any exclusivity for Clay's output, and the two agree to the arrangement on a handshake. As Clay nears completion of the study, she is offered an analyst job in the research department of Winston & Company, a brokerage firm, and she is pondering submitting the draft of her wireless study for publication by Winston.

Comment: Although she is under no written contractual obligation to Bradley, Clay has an obligation to let Bradley act on the output of her study before Winston & Company or Clay use the information to their advantage. That is, unless Bradley gives permission to Clay and waives its rights to her wireless report, Clay would be in violation of Standard IV(A) if she were to immediately recommend to Winston the same transactions recommended in the report to Bradley. Furthermore, Clay must not take from Bradley any research file material or other property that she may have used.

Example 5 (Ownership of Completed Prior Work): Emma Madeline, a recent college graduate and a candidate in the CFA Program, spends her summer as an unpaid intern at Murdoch and Lowell. The senior managers at Murdoch are attempting to bring the firm into compliance with the GIPS standards, and Madeline is assigned to assist in its efforts. Two months into her internship, Madeline applies for a job at McMillan & Company, which has plans to become GIPS compliant. Madeline accepts the job with McMillan. Before leaving Murdoch, she copies the firm's software that she helped develop because she believes this software will assist her in her new position.

Comment: Even though Madeline does not receive monetary compensation for her services at Murdoch, she has used firm resources in creating the software and is considered an employee because she receives compensation and benefits in the form of work experience and knowledge. By copying the software, Madeline violated Standard IV(A) because she misappropriated Murdoch's property without permission.

Example 6 (Soliciting Former Clients): Dennis Elliot has hired Sam Chisolm, who previously worked for a competing firm. Chisolm left his former firm after 18 years of employment. When Chisolm begins working for Elliot, he wants to contact his former clients because he knows them well and is certain that many will follow him to his new employer. Is Chisolm in violation of Standard IV(A) if he contacts his former clients?

Comment: Because client records are the property of the firm, contacting former clients for any reason through the use of client lists or other information taken from a former employer without permission would be a violation of Standard IV(A). In addition, the nature and extent of the contact with former clients may be governed by the terms of any noncompete agreement signed by the employee and the former employer that covers contact with former clients after employment.

Simple knowledge of the names and existence of former clients is not confidential information, just as skills or experience that an employee obtains while employed are not "confidential" or "privileged" information. The Code and Standards do not impose a prohibition on the use of experience or knowledge gained at one employer from being used at another employer. The Code and Standards also do not prohibit former employees from contacting clients of their previous firm, in the absence of a noncompete agreement. Members and candidates are free to use public information about their former firm after departing to contact former clients without violating Standard IV(A).

In the absence of a noncompete agreement, as long as Chisolm maintains his duty of loyalty to his employer before joining Elliot's firm, does not take steps to solicit clients until he has left his former firm, and does not make use of material from his former employer without its permission after he has left, he is not in violation of the Code and Standards.

Example 7 (Starting a New Firm): Geraldine Allen currently works at a registered investment company as an equity analyst. Without notice to her employer, she registers with government authorities to start an investment company that will compete with her employer, but she does not actively seek clients. Does registration of this competing company with the appropriate regulatory authorities constitute a violation of Standard IV(A)?

> *Comment*: Allen's preparation for the new business by registering with the regulatory authorities does not conflict with the work for her employer if the preparations have been done on Allen's own time outside the office and if Allen will not be soliciting clients for the business or otherwise operating the new company until she has left her current employer.

Example 8 (Competing with Current Employer): Several employees are planning to depart their current employer within a few weeks and have been careful to not engage in any activities that would conflict with their duty to their current employer. They have just learned that one of their employer's clients has undertaken a request for proposal (RFP) to review and possibly hire a new investment consultant. The RFP has been sent to the employer and all of its competitors. The group believes that the new entity to be formed would be qualified to respond to the RFP and be eligible for the business. The RFP submission period is likely to conclude before the employees' resignations are effective. Is it permissible for the group of departing employees to respond to the RFP for their anticipated new firm?

> *Comment*: A group of employees responding to an RFP that their employer is also responding to would lead to direct competition between the employees and the employer. Such conduct violates Standard IV(A) unless the group of employees receives permission from their employer as well as the entity sending out the RFP.

Example 9 (Externally Compensated Assignments): Alfonso Mota is a research analyst with Tyson Investments. He works part time as a mayor for his hometown, a position for which he receives compensation. Must Mota seek permission from Tyson to serve as mayor?

> *Comment*: If Mota's mayoral duties are so extensive and time-consuming that they might detract from his ability to fulfill his responsibilities at Tyson, he should discuss his outside activities with his employer and come to a mutual agreement regarding how to manage his personal commitments with his responsibilities to his employer.

Example 10 (Soliciting Former Clients): After leaving her employer, Shawna McQuillen establishes her own money management business. While with her former employer, she did not sign a noncompete agreement that would have prevented her from soliciting former clients. Upon her departure, she does not take any of her client lists or contact information and she clears her personal computer of any employer records, including client contact information. She obtains the phone numbers of her former clients through public records and contacts them to solicit their business.

> *Comment*: McQuillen is not in violation of Standard IV(A) because she has not used information or records from her former employer and is not prevented by an agreement with her former employer from soliciting her former clients.

Example 11 (Whistleblowing Actions): Meredith Rasmussen works on a buy-side trading desk and concentrates on in-house trades for a hedge fund subsidiary managed by a team at the investment management firm. The hedge fund has been very successful and is marketed globally by the firm. From her experience as the trader for much of the activity of the fund, Rasmussen has become quite knowledgeable about the hedge fund's strategy, tactics, and performance. When a distinct break in the market occurs, however, and many of the securities involved in the hedge fund's strategy decline markedly in value, Rasmussen observes that the reported performance of the hedge fund does not reflect this decline. In her experience, the lack of any effect is a very unlikely occurrence. She approaches the head of trading about her concern and is told that she should not ask any questions, that the fund is big and successful and is not her concern. She is fairly sure something is not right, so she contacts the compliance officer, who also tells her to stay away from the issue of this hedge fund's reporting.

> *Comment*: Rasmussen has clearly come upon an error in policies, procedures, and compliance practices in the firm's operations. Having been unsuccessful in finding a resolution with her supervisor and the compliance officer, Rasmussen should consult the firm's whistleblowing policy to determine the appropriate next step toward informing management of her concerns. The potentially unethical actions of the investment management division are appropriate grounds for further disclosure, so Rasmussen's whistleblowing would not represent a violation of Standard IV(A).
>
> See also Standard I(D)—Misconduct and Standard IV(C)—Responsibilities of Supervisors.

Example 12 (Soliciting Former Clients): Angel Crome has been a private banker for YBSafe Bank for the past eight years. She has been very successful and built a considerable client portfolio during that time but is extremely frustrated by the recent loss of reputation by her current employer and subsequent client insecurity. A locally renowned headhunter contacted Crome a few days ago and offered her an interesting job with a competing private bank. This bank offers a substantial signing bonus for advisers with their own client portfolios. Crome figures that she can solicit at least 70 percent of her clients to follow her and gladly enters into the new employment contract.

> *Comment*: Crome may contact former clients upon termination of her employment with YBSafe Bank, but she is prohibited from using client records built and kept with her in her capacity as an employee of YBSafe Bank. Client lists are proprietary information of her former employer and must not be used for her or her new employer's benefit. The use of written, electronic, or any other form of records, other than publicly available information, to contact her former clients at YBSafe Bank will be a violation of Standard IV(A).

Example 13 (Notification of Code and Standards): Krista Smith is a relatively new assistant trader for the fixed-income desk of a major investment bank. She is on a team responsible for structuring collateralized debt obligations (CDOs) made up of securities in the inventory of the trading desk. At a meeting of the team, senior executives explain the opportunity to eventually separate the CDO into various risk-rated tranches to be sold to the clients of the firm. After the senior executives leave the meeting, the head trader announces various responsibilities of each member of the team and then says, "This is a good time to unload some of the junk we have been stuck with for a while and disguise it with ratings and a thick, unreadable prospectus, so don't be shy in putting this CDO together. Just kidding." Smith is worried by this remark and asks some of her colleagues what the head trader meant. They all respond that he was just kidding but that there is some truth in the remark because the CDO is seen by management as an opportunity to improve the quality of the securities in the firm's inventory.

Concerned about the ethical environment of the workplace, Smith decides to talk to her supervisor about her concerns and provides the head trader with a copy of the Code and Standards. Smith discusses the principle of placing the client above the interest of the firm and the possibility that the development of the new CDO will not adhere to this responsibility. The head trader assures Smith that the appropriate analysis will be conducted when determining the appropriate securities for collateral. Furthermore, the ratings are assigned by an independent firm and the prospectus will include full and factual disclosures. Smith is reassured by the meeting, but she also reviews the company's procedures and requirements for reporting potential violations of company policy and securities laws.

Comment: Smith's review of the company policies and procedures for reporting violations allows her to be prepared to report through the appropriate whistleblower process if she decides that the CDO development process involves unethical actions by others. Smith's actions comply with the Code and Standards principles of placing the clients' interests first and being loyal to her employer. In providing her supervisor with a copy of the Code and Standards, Smith is highlighting the high level of ethical conduct she is required to adhere to in her professional activities.

B. Additional Compensation Arrangements

Members and Candidates must not accept gifts, benefits, compensation, or consideration that competes with or might reasonably be expected to create a conflict of interest with their employer's interest unless they obtain written consent from all parties involved.

Guidance

Standard IV(B) requires members and candidates to obtain permission from their employer before accepting compensation or other benefits from third parties for the services rendered to the employer or for any services that might create a conflict with their employer's interest. Compensation and benefits include direct compensation by the client and any indirect compensation or other benefits received from third parties. "Written consent" includes any form of communication that can be documented (for example, communication via computer e-mail that can be retrieved and documented).

Members and candidates must obtain permission for additional compensation/benefits because such arrangements may affect loyalties and objectivity and create potential conflicts of interest. Disclosure allows an employer to consider the outside arrangements when evaluating the actions and motivations of members and candidates. Moreover, the employer is entitled to have full knowledge of all compensation/benefit arrangements so as to be able to assess the true cost of the services members or candidates are providing.

Recommended Procedures for Compliance

Members and candidates should make an immediate written report to their employer specifying any compensation they propose to receive for services in addition to the compensation or benefits received from their employer. The details of the report should be confirmed by the party offering the additional compensation, including performance incentives offered by clients. This written report should state the terms of any agreement under which a member or candidate will receive additional compensation; "terms" include the nature of the compensation, the approximate amount of compensation, and the duration of the agreement.

Application of the Standard

Example 1 (Notification of Client Bonus Compensation): Geoff Whitman, a portfolio analyst for Adams Trust Company, manages the account of Carol Cochran, a client. Whitman is paid a salary by his employer, and Cochran pays the trust company a standard fee based on the market value of assets in her portfolio. Cochran proposes to Whitman that "any year that my portfolio achieves at least a 15 percent return before taxes, you and your wife can fly to Monaco at my expense and use my condominium during the third week of January." Whitman does not inform his employer of the arrangement and vacations in Monaco the following January as Cochran's guest.

> *Comment*: Whitman violated Standard IV(B) by failing to inform his employer in writing of this supplemental, contingent compensation arrangement. The nature of the arrangement could have resulted in partiality to Cochran's account, which could have detracted from Whitman's performance with respect to other accounts he handles for Adams Trust. Whitman must obtain the consent of his employer to accept such a supplemental benefit.

Example 2 (Notification of Outside Compensation): Terry Jones sits on the board of directors of Exercise Unlimited, Inc. In return for his services on the board, Jones receives unlimited membership privileges for his family at all Exercise Unlimited facilities. Jones purchases Exercise Unlimited stock for the client accounts for which it is appropriate. Jones does not disclose this arrangement to his employer because he does not receive monetary compensation for his services to the board.

> *Comment*: Jones has violated Standard IV(B) by failing to disclose to his employer benefits received in exchange for his services on the board of directors. The nonmonetary compensation may create a conflict of interest in the same manner as being paid to serve as a director.

Example 3 (Prior Approval for Outside Compensation): Jonathan Hollis is an analyst of oil-and-gas companies for Specialty Investment Management. He is currently recommending the purchase of ABC Oil Company shares and has published a long, well-thought-out research report to substantiate his recommendation. Several weeks after publishing the report, Hollis received a call from the investor-relations office of ABC Oil saying that Thomas Andrews, CEO of the company, saw the report and really liked the analyst's grasp of the business and his company. The investor-relations officer invited Hollis to visit ABC Oil to discuss the industry further. ABC Oil offers to send a company plane to pick Hollis up and arrange for his accommodations while visiting. Hollis, after gaining the appropriate approvals, accepts the meeting with the CEO but declines the offered travel arrangements.

Several weeks later, Andrews and Hollis meet to discuss the oil business and Hollis's report. Following the meeting, Hollis joins Andrews and the investment relations officer for dinner at an upscale restaurant near ABC Oil's headquarters.

Upon returning to Specialty Investment Management, Hollis provides a full review of the meeting to the director of research, including a disclosure of the dinner attended.

Comment: Hollis's actions did not violate Standard IV(B). Through gaining approval before accepting the meeting and declining the offered travel arrangements, Hollis sought to avoid any potential conflicts of interest between his company and ABC Oil. Because the location of the dinner was not available prior to arrival and Hollis notified his company of the dinner upon his return, accepting the dinner should not impair his objectivity. By disclosing the dinner, Hollis has enabled Specialty Investment Management to assess whether it has any impact on future reports and recommendations by Hollis related to ABC Oil.

C. Responsibilities of Supervisors

Members and Candidates must make reasonable efforts to detect and prevent violations of applicable laws, rules, regulations, and the Code and Standards by anyone subject to their supervision or authority.

Guidance

Highlights:

▶ *Detection Procedures*

▶ *Compliance Procedures*

▶ *Inadequate Procedures*

▶ *Enforcement of Non-Investment-Related Policies*

Standard IV(C) states that members and candidates must take steps to prevent persons acting under their supervision from violating laws, rules, regulations, firm policies, or the Code and Standards.

Any investment professional who has employees subject to her or his control or influence—whether or not the employees are CFA Institute members, CFA charterholders, or candidates in the CFA Program—exercises supervisory responsibility. Members and candidates acting as supervisors must also have in-depth knowledge of the Code and Standards so that they can apply this knowledge in discharging their supervisory responsibilities.

The conduct that constitutes reasonable supervision in a particular case depends on the number of employees supervised and the work performed by those employees. Members and candidates who supervise large numbers of employees cannot personally evaluate the conduct of their employees on a continuing basis. Although these members and candidates may delegate supervisory duties, such delegation does not relieve them of their supervisory responsibility. Their responsibilities under Standard IV(C) include instructing those subordinates to whom supervision is delegated about methods to prevent and detect violations of laws, rules, regulations, firm policies, and the Code and Standards.

Detection Procedures

Members and candidates with supervisory responsibility must make reasonable efforts to detect violations of laws, rules, regulations, firm policies, and the Code and Standards. They exercise reasonable supervision by establishing and implementing written compliance procedures and ensuring that those procedures are followed through periodic review. If a member or candidate has adopted reasonable procedures and taken steps to institute an effective compliance pro-gram, then the member or candidate may not be in violation of Standard IV(C) if he or she does not detect violations that occur despite these efforts. The fact that violations do occur may indicate, however, that the compliance procedures are inadequate. In addition, in some cases, merely enacting such procedures may not be sufficient to fulfill the duty required by Standard IV(C). A member or candidate may be in violation of Standard IV(C) if he or she knows or should know that the procedures designed to detect and prevent violations are not being followed.

Compliance Procedures

Members and candidates with supervisory responsibility must understand what constitutes an adequate compliance system for their firms and make reasonable efforts to see that appropriate compliance procedures are established, docu-mented, communicated to covered personnel, and followed. "Adequate" proce-dures are those designed to meet industry standards, regulatory requirements, the requirements of the Code and Standards, and the circumstances of the firm. Once compliance procedures are established, the supervisor must also make rea-sonable efforts to ensure that the procedures are monitored and enforced.

To be effective, compliance procedures must be in place prior to the occur-rence of a violation of the law or the Code and Standards. Although compliance procedures cannot be designed to anticipate every potential violation, they should be designed to anticipate the activities most likely to result in misconduct. Each compliance program must be appropriate for the size and nature of the organization. The member or candidate should review model compliance pro-cedures or other industry programs to ensure that the firm's procedures meet the minimum industry standards.

Once a supervisor learns that an employee has violated or may have violated the law or the Code and Standards, the supervisor must promptly initiate an inves-tigation to ascertain the extent of the wrongdoing. Relying on an employee's statements about the extent of the violation or assurances that the wrongdoing will not recur is not enough. Reporting the misconduct up the chain of command and warning the employee to cease the activity are also not enough. Pending the outcome of the investigation, a supervisor should take steps to ensure that the vio-lation will not be repeated, such as placing limits on the employee's activities or increasing the monitoring of the employee's activities.

Inadequate Procedures

A member or candidate with supervisory responsibility should bring an inade-quate compliance system to the attention of the firm's senior managers and rec-ommend corrective action. If the member or candidate clearly cannot discharge supervisory responsibilities because of the absence of a compliance system or because of an inadequate compliance system, the member or candidate should decline in writing to accept supervisory responsibility until the firm adopts rea-sonable procedures to allow adequate exercise of supervisory responsibility.

Enforcement of Non-Investment-Related Policies

A member or candidate with supervisory responsibility should enforce policies related to investment and non-investment-related activities equally. Firms regu-larly establish policies related to attendance and acceptable workplace actions, such as mandatory vacations for specific positions. The equal enforcement of all firm policies assists in creating a strong ethical work environment where all rules are demonstrated to be important.

Recommended Procedures for Compliance

Codes of Ethics or Compliance Procedures

Members and candidates are encouraged to recommend that their employers adopt a code of ethics. Adoption of a code of ethics is critical to establishing a strong ethical foundation for investment advisory firms and their employees. Codes of ethics formally emphasize and reinforce the client loyalty responsibilities of investment firm personnel, protect investing clients by deterring misconduct, and protect the firm's reputation for integrity.

There is a distinction, however, between codes of ethics and the specific policies and procedures needed to ensure compliance with the codes and with securities laws and regulations. Although both are important, codes of ethics should consist of fundamental, principle-based ethical and fiduciary concepts that are applicable to all of the firm's employees. In this way, firms can best convey to employees and clients the ethical ideals that investment advisers strive to achieve. These concepts need to be implemented, however, by detailed, firmwide compliance policies and procedures. Compliance procedures assist the firm's personnel in fulfilling the responsibilities enumerated in the code of ethics and make probable that the ideals expressed in the code of ethics will be adhered to in the day-to-day operation of the firm.

Stand-alone codes of ethics should be written in plain language and should address general fiduciary concepts. They should be unencumbered by numerous detailed procedures. Codes presented in this way are the most effective in stressing to employees that they are in positions of trust and must act with integrity at all times. Mingling compliance procedures in the firm's code of ethics goes against the goal of reinforcing the ethical obligations of employees.

Separating the code of ethics from compliance procedures will also reduce, if not eliminate, the legal terminology and "boilerplate" language that can make the underlying ethical principles incomprehensible to the average person. Above all, to ensure that a culture of ethics and integrity is created rather than merely a focus on following the rules, the principles in the code of ethics must be stated in a way that is accessible and understandable to everyone in the firm.

Members and candidates should encourage their employers to provide their codes of ethics to clients. In this case also, a simple, straightforward code of ethics will be best understood by clients. Unencumbered by the compliance procedures, the code of ethics will be effective in conveying that the firm is committed to conducting business in an ethical manner and in the best interests of the clients.

Adequate Compliance Procedures

A supervisor complies with Standard IV(C) by identifying situations in which legal violations or violations of the Code and Standards are likely to occur and by establishing and enforcing compliance procedures to prevent such violations. Adequate compliance procedures should:

► be contained in a clearly written and accessible manual that is tailored to the firm's operations;

- be drafted so that the procedures are easy to understand;
- designate a compliance officer whose authority and responsibility are clearly defined and who has the necessary resources and authority to implement the firm's compliance procedures;
- describe the hierarchy of supervision and assign duties among supervisors;
- implement a system of checks and balances;
- outline the scope of the procedures;
- outline procedures to document the monitoring and testing of compliance procedures;
- outline permissible conduct; and
- delineate procedures for reporting violations and sanctions.

Once a compliance program is in place, a supervisor should:

- disseminate the contents of the program to appropriate personnel;
- periodically update procedures to ensure that the measures are adequate under the law;
- continually educate personnel regarding the compliance procedures;
- issue periodic reminders of the procedures to appropriate personnel;
- incorporate a professional conduct evaluation as part of an employee's performance review;
- review the actions of employees to ensure compliance and identify violators; and
- take the necessary steps to enforce the procedures once a violation has occurred.

Once a violation is discovered, a supervisor should:

- respond promptly;
- conduct a thorough investigation of the activities to determine the scope of the wrongdoing; and
- increase supervision or place appropriate limitations on the wrongdoer pending the outcome of the investigation.

Application of the Standard

Example 1 (Supervising Research Activities): Jane Mattock, senior vice president and head of the research department of H&V, Inc., a regional brokerage firm, has decided to change her recommendation for Timber Products from buy to sell. In line with H&V's procedures, she orally advises certain other H&V executives of her proposed actions before the report is prepared for publication. As a result of Mattock's conversation with Dieter Frampton, one of the executives of H&V accountable to Mattock, Frampton immediately sells Timber's stock from his own account and from certain discretionary client accounts. In addition, other personnel inform certain institutional customers of the changed recommendation before it is printed and disseminated to all H&V customers who have received previous Timber reports.

> *Comment*: Mattock has violated Standard IV(C) by failing to reasonably and adequately supervise the actions of those accountable to her. She did not

prevent or establish reasonable procedures designed to prevent dissemination of or trading on the information by those who knew of her changed recommendation. She must ensure that her firm has procedures for reviewing or recording any trading in the stock of a corporation that has been the subject of an unpublished change in recommendation. Adequate procedures would have informed the subordinates of their duties and detected sales by Frampton and selected customers.

Example 2 (Supervising Research Activities): Deion Miller is the research director for Jamestown Investment Programs. The portfolio managers have become critical of Miller and his staff because the Jamestown portfolios do not include any stock that has been the subject of a merger or tender offer. Georgia Ginn, a member of Miller's staff, tells Miller that she has been studying a local company, Excelsior, Inc., and recommends its purchase. Ginn adds that the company has been widely rumored to be the subject of a merger study by a well-known conglomerate and discussions between them are under way. At Miller's request, Ginn prepares a memo recommending the stock. Miller passes along Ginn's memo to the portfolio managers prior to leaving for vacation, and he notes that he has not reviewed the memo. As a result of the memo, the portfolio managers buy Excelsior stock immediately. The day Miller returns to the office, he learns that Ginn's only sources for the report were her brother, who is an acquisitions analyst with Acme Industries, the "well-known conglomerate," and that the merger discussions were planned but not held.

> *Comment*: Miller violated Standard IV(C) by not exercising reasonable supervision when he disseminated the memo without checking to ensure that Ginn had a reasonable and adequate basis for her recommendations and that Ginn was not relying on material nonpublic information.

Example 3 (Supervising Trading Activities): David Edwards, a trainee trader at Wheeler & Company, a major national brokerage firm, assists a customer in paying for the securities of Highland, Inc., by using anticipated profits from the immediate sale of the same securities. Despite the fact that Highland is not on Wheeler's recommended list, a large volume of its stock is traded through Wheeler in this manner. Roberta Ann Mason is a Wheeler vice president responsible for supervising compliance with the securities laws in the trading department. Part of her compensation from Wheeler is based on commission revenues from the trading department. Although she notices the increased trading activity, she does nothing to investigate or halt it.

> *Comment*: Mason's failure to adequately review and investigate purchase orders in Highland stock executed by Edwards and her failure to supervise the trainee's activities violate Standard IV(C). Supervisors should be especially sensitive to actual or potential conflicts between their own self-interests and their supervisory responsibilities.

Example 4 (Supervising Trading Activities and Record Keeping): Samantha Tabbing is senior vice president and portfolio manager for Crozet, Inc., a registered investment advisory and registered broker/dealer firm. She reports to Charles Henry, the president of Crozet. Crozet serves as the investment adviser and principal underwriter for ABC and XYZ public mutual funds. The two funds' prospectuses allow Crozet to trade financial futures for the funds for the limited purpose of hedging against market risks. Henry, extremely impressed by Tabbing's performance in the past two years, directs Tabbing to act as portfolio manager for the funds. For the benefit of its employees, Crozet has also organized the Crozet Employee Profit-Sharing Plan (CEPSP), a defined-contribution retirement plan. Henry assigns Tabbing to manage 20 percent of the assets of CEPSP.

Tabbing's investment objective for her portion of CEPSP's assets is aggressive growth. Unbeknownst to Henry, Tabbing frequently places S&P 500 Index purchase and sale orders for the funds and the CEPSP without providing the futures commission merchants (FCMs) who take the orders with any prior or simultaneous designation of the account for which the trade has been placed. Frequently, neither Tabbing nor anyone else at Crozet completes an internal trade ticket to record the time an order was placed or the specific account for which the order was intended. FCMs often designate a specific account only after the trade, when Tabbing provides such designation. Crozet has no written operating procedures or compliance manual concerning its futures trading, and its compliance department does not review such trading. After observing the market's movement, Tabbing assigns to CEPSP the S&P 500 positions with more-favorable execution prices and assigns positions with less-favorable execution prices to the funds.

> *Comment*: Henry violated Standard IV(C) by failing to adequately supervise Tabbing with respect to her S&P 500 trading. Henry further violated Standard IV(C) by failing to establish record-keeping and reporting procedures to prevent or detect Tabbing's violations.

Example 5 (Accepting Responsibility): Meredith Rasmussen works on a buy-side trading desk and concentrates on in-house trades for a hedge fund subsidiary managed by a team at the investment management firm. The hedge fund has been very successful and is marketed globally by the firm. From her experience as the trader for much of the activity of the fund, Rasmussen has become quite knowledgeable about the hedge fund's strategy, tactics, and performance. When a distinct break in the market occurs and many of the securities involved in the hedge fund's strategy decline markedly in value, however, Rasmussen observes that the reported performance of the hedge fund does not at all reflect this decline. From her experience, this lack of an effect is a very unlikely occurrence. She approaches the head of trading about her concern and is told that she should not ask any questions, that the fund is too big and successful and is not her concern. She is fairly sure something is not right, so she contacts the compliance officer and is again told to stay away from the hedge fund reporting issue.

> *Comment*: Rasmussen has clearly come upon an error in policies, procedures, and compliance practices within the firm's operations. According to Standard IV(C), the supervisor and the compliance officer have the responsibility to review the concerns brought forth by Rasmussen. Supervisors have the responsibility of establishing and encouraging an ethical culture in the firm. The dismissal of Rasmussen's question violates Standard IV(C) and undermines the firm's ethical operations.
>
> See also Standard I(D)—Misconduct and, for guidance on whistleblowing, Standard IV(A)—Loyalty.

Example 6 (Inadequate Procedures): Brendan Witt, a former junior sell-side technology analyst, decided to return to school to earn an MBA. To keep his research skills and industry knowledge sharp, Witt accepted a position with On-line and Informed, an independent internet-based research company. The position requires the publication of a recommendation and report on a different company every month. Initially, Witt is a regular contributor of new research and a participant in the associated discussion boards that generally have positive comments on the technology sector. Over time, his ability to manage his educational requirements and his work requirements begin to conflict with one another. Knowing a recommendation is due the next day for On-line, Witt creates a report based on a few news articles and what the conventional wisdom of the markets has deemed the "hot" security of the day.

Comment: Allowing the report submitted by Witt to be posted highlights a lack of compliance procedures by the research firm. Witt's supervisor needs to work with the management of On-line to develop an appropriate review process to ensure that all contracted analysts comply with the requirements.

See also Standard V(A)—Diligence and Reasonable Basis, as it relates to Witt's responsibility for substantiating a recommendation.

Example 7 (Inadequate Supervision): Michael Papis is the chief investment officer of his state's retirement fund. The fund has always used outside advisers for the real estate allocation, and this information is clearly presented in all fund communications. Thomas Nagle, a recognized sell-side research analyst and Papis's business school classmate, recently left the investment bank he worked for to start his own asset management firm, Accessible Real Estate. Nagle is trying to build his assets under management and contacts Papis about gaining some of the retirement fund's allocation. In the previous few years, the performance of the retirement fund's real estate investments was in line with the fund's benchmark but was not extraordinary. Papis decides to help out his old friend and also to seek better returns by moving the real estate allocation to Accessible. The only notice of the change in adviser appears in the next annual report in the listing of associated advisers.

Comment: Papis's actions highlight the need for supervision and review at all levels in an organization. His responsibilities may include the selection of external advisers, but the decision to change advisers appears arbitrary. Members and candidates should ensure that their firm has appropriate policies and procedures in place to detect inappropriate actions such as the action taken by Papis.

See also Standard V(A)—Diligence and Reasonable Basis, Standard V(B)—Communication with Clients and Prospective Clients, and Standard VI(A)—Disclosure of Conflicts.

STANDARD V—INVESTMENT ANALYSIS, RECOMMENDATIONS, AND ACTIONS

A. Diligence and Reasonable Basis

Members and Candidates must:

1. **Exercise diligence, independence, and thoroughness in analyzing investments, making investment recommendations, and taking investment actions.**
2. **Have a reasonable and adequate basis, supported by appropriate research and investigation, for any investment analysis, recommendation, or action.**

Guidance

Highlights:

▶ *Defining Diligence and Reasonable Basis*
▶ *Using Secondary or Third-Party Research*

► *Quantitatively Oriented Research*

► *Selecting External Advisers and Subadvisers*

► *Group Research and Decision Making*

The application of Standard V(A) depends on the investment philosophy the member, candidate, or firm is following, the role of the member or candidate in the investment decision-making process, and the support and resources provided by the member's or candidate's employer. These factors will dictate the nature of the diligence and thoroughness of the research and the level of investigation required by Standard V(A).

The requirements for issuing conclusions based on research will vary in relation to the member's or candidate's role in the investment decision-making process, but the member or candidate must make reasonable efforts to cover all pertinent issues when arriving at a recommendation. Members and candidates enhance transparency by providing or offering to provide supporting information to clients when recommending a purchase or sale or when changing a recommendation.

Defining Diligence and Reasonable Basis

Every investment decision is based on a set of facts known and understood at the time. Clients turn to members and candidates for advice and expect these advisers to have more information and knowledge than they do. This information and knowledge is the basis from which members and candidates apply their professional judgment in taking investment actions and making recommendations.

At a basic level, clients want assurance that members and candidates are putting forth the necessary effort to support the recommendations they are making. Communicating the level and thoroughness of the information reviewed before the member or candidate makes a judgment allows clients to understand the reasonableness of the recommended investment actions.

As with determining the suitability of an investment for the client, the necessary level of research and analysis will differ with the product, security, or service being offered. In providing an investment service, members and candidates typically use a variety of resources, including company reports, third-party research, and results from quantitative models. A reasonable basis is formed through a balance of these resources appropriate for the security or decision being analyzed.

The following list provides some, but definitely not all, examples of attributes to consider while forming the basis for a recommendation:

► company's operating and financial history;

► current stage of the industry's business cycle;

► mutual fund's fee structure and management history;

► output and potential limitations of quantitative models;

► quality of the assets included in a securitization; and

► appropriateness of selected peer-group comparisons.

Even though an investment recommendation may be well-informed, downside risk remains for any investment. Members and candidates can base their decision only on the information available at the time the decision is made. The steps taken in developing a diligent and reasonable recommendation should minimize unexpected downside events.

Using Secondary or Third-Party Research

If members and candidates rely on secondary or third-party research, they must make reasonable and diligent efforts to determine whether such research is sound. Secondary research is defined as research conducted by someone else in the member's or candidate's firm. Third-party research is research conducted by entities outside the member's or candidate's firm, such as a brokerage firm, bank, or research firm. If a member or candidate has reason to suspect that either secondary or third-party research or information comes from a source that lacks a sound basis, the member or candidate must not rely on that information. Criteria that a member or candidate can use in forming an opinion on whether research is sound include the following:

▶ assumptions used;

▶ rigor of the analysis performed;

▶ date/timeliness of the research; and

▶ evaluation of the objectivity and independence of the recommendations.

A member or candidate may rely on others in his or her firm to determine whether secondary or third-party research is sound and use the information in good faith unless the member or candidate has reason to question its validity or the processes and procedures used by those responsible for the research. For example, a portfolio manager may not have a choice of a data source because the firm's senior managers conducted due diligence to determine which vendor would provide services; the member or candidate can use the information in good faith assuming the due diligence process was deemed adequate.

A member or candidate should verify that the firm has a policy about the timely and consistent review of approved research providers to ensure that the quality of the research continues to meet the necessary standards. If such a policy is not in place at the firm, the member or candidate should encourage the development and adoption of a formal review practice.

Quantitatively Oriented Research

Standard V(A) applies to the rapidly expanding use of quantitatively oriented research models, such as computer-generated screening and ranking of equity securities and the creation or valuation of derivative instruments. Models are being used for more than the back testing of investment strategies, and the continued development of models is an important part of capital market developments.

The importance and limitations of financial models became clear as the credit crisis unfolded in 2007 and 2008. In many cases the financial models used to value collateralized debt securities and related derivative products were poorly understood. Members and candidates need to have an understanding of the parameters used in the model or quantitative research. Although they are not required to become experts in the technical aspects of the models, they must be able to explain to their clients the importance of the quantitative research and how the results were used in the decision-making process.

Members and candidates need to consider the time horizon of the data used as inputs in financial models. The information from many commercially available databases may not effectively incorporate both positive and negative market cycles. In the development of a recommendation, the member or candidate may need to test the models by using volatility and performance expectations that represent scenarios outside the observable databases. In reviewing the computer models or the resulting output, members and candidates need to pay particular attention to the assumptions used in the analysis and the rigor of the analysis to ensure that the model incorporates negative market events.

Selecting External Advisers and Subadvisers

Financial instruments and asset allocation techniques continue to develop and evolve. This progression has led to the use of specialized managers to invest in specific asset classes or diversification strategies that complement a firm's in-house expertise. Standard V(A) applies to the level of review necessary in selecting an external adviser or subadviser.

Members and candidates need to ensure that their firms have standardized criteria for reviewing external advisers. Such criteria would include, but would not be limited to, the following:

► reviewing the adviser's established code of ethics;
► understanding the adviser's compliance and internal control procedures;
► assessing the quality of the published return information; and
► reviewing the adviser's adherence to its stated strategy.

CFA Institute published codes, standards, and guides to best practice provide members and candidates with examples of acceptable practices for external advisers and advice in selecting a new adviser. The following guides are available at the CFA Institute website (www.cfainstitute.org): Asset Manager Code of Professional Conduct, Global Investment Performance Standards, and Model Request for Proposal (for equity, credit, or real estate managers).

Group Research and Decision Making

Commonly, members and candidates are part of a group or team that is collectively responsible for producing investment analysis or research. The conclusions or recommendations of the group report represent the consensus of the group and are not necessarily the views of the member or candidate, even though the name of the member or candidate is included on the report. In some instances, the member or candidate will not agree with the view of the group. If, however, the member or candidate believes that the consensus opinion has a reasonable and adequate basis and is independent and objective, the member or candidate need not decline to be identified with the report. If the member or candidate is confident in the process, the member or candidate does not need to dissociate from the report even if it does not reflect his or her opinion.

Recommended Procedures for Compliance

Members and candidates should encourage their firms to consider the following policies and procedures to support the principles of Standard V(A):

► Establish a policy requiring that research reports, credit ratings, and investment recommendations have a basis that can be substantiated as reasonable and adequate. An individual employee (a supervisory analyst) or a group of employees (a review committee) should be appointed to review and approve such items prior to external circulation to determine whether the criteria established in the policy have been met.

▶ Develop detailed, written guidance for analysts (research, investment, or credit), supervisory analysts, and review committees that establishes the due diligence procedures for judging whether a particular recommendation has a reasonable and adequate basis.

▶ Develop measurable criteria for assessing the quality of research, the reasonableness and adequacy of the basis for any recommendation or rating, and the accuracy of recommendations over time. In some cases, firms may consider implementing compensation arrangements that depend on these measurable criteria and that are applied consistently to all related analysts.

▶ Develop detailed, written guidance that establishes minimum levels of scenario testing of all computer-based models used in developing, rating, and evaluating financial instruments. The policy should contain criteria related to the breadth of the scenarios tested, the accuracy of the output over time, and the analysis of cash flow sensitivity to inputs.

▶ Develop measurable criteria for assessing outside providers, including the quality of information being provided, the reasonableness and adequacy of the provider's collection practices, and the accuracy of the information over time. The established policy should outline how often the provider's products are reviewed.

▶ Adopt a standardized set of criteria for evaluating the adequacy of external advisers. The policy should include how often and on what basis the allocation of funds to the adviser will be reviewed.

Application of the Standard

Example 1 (Sufficient Due Diligence): Helen Hawke manages the corporate finance department of Sarkozi Securities, Ltd. The firm is anticipating that the government will soon close a tax loophole that currently allows oil-and-gas exploration companies to pass on drilling expenses to holders of a certain class of shares. Because market demand for this tax-advantaged class of stock is currently high, Sarkozi convinces several companies to undertake new equity financings at once before the loophole closes. Time is of the essence, but Sarkozi lacks sufficient resources to conduct adequate research on all the prospective issuing companies. Hawke decides to estimate the IPO prices on the basis of the relative size of each company and to justify the pricing later when her staff has time.

> *Comment*: Sarkozi should have taken on only the work that it could adequately handle. By categorizing the issuers by general size, Hawke has bypassed researching all the other relevant aspects that should be considered when pricing new issues and thus has not performed sufficient due diligence. Such an omission can result in investors purchasing shares at prices that have no actual basis. Hawke has violated Standard V(A).

Example 2 (Sufficient Scenario Testing): Babu Dhaliwal works for Heinrich Brokerage in the corporate finance group. He has just persuaded Feggans Resources, Ltd., to allow his firm to do a secondary equity financing at Feggans Resources' current stock price. Because the stock has been trading at higher multiples than similar companies with equivalent production, Dhaliwal presses the Feggans Resources managers to project what would be the maximum production they could achieve in an optimal scenario. Based on these numbers, he is able to justify the price his firm will be asking for the secondary issue. During a sales pitch to the brokers, Dhaliwal then uses these numbers as the base-case production levels that Feggans Resources will achieve.

Comment: When presenting information to the brokers, Dhaliwal should have given a range of production scenarios and the probability of Feggans Resources achieving each level. By giving the maximum production level as the likely level of production, he has misrepresented the chances of achieving that production level and seriously misled the brokers. Dhaliwal has violated Standard V(A).

Example 3 (Developing a Reasonable Basis): Brendan Witt, a former junior sell-side technology analyst, decided to return to school to earn an MBA. To keep his research skills and industry knowledge sharp, Witt accepted a position with On-line and Informed, an independent internet-based research company. The position requires the publication of a recommendation and report on a different company every month. Initially, Witt is a regular contributor of new research and a participant in the associated discussion boards that generally have positive comments on the technology sector. Over time, his ability to manage his educational requirements and his work requirements begin to conflict with one another. Knowing a recommendation is due the next day for On-line, Witt creates a report based on a few news articles and what the conventional wisdom of the markets has deemed the "hot" security of the day.

Comment: Witt's knowledge of and exuberance for technology stocks, a few news articles, and the conventional wisdom of the markets do not constitute, without more information, a reasonable and adequate basis for a stock recommendation that is supported by appropriate research and investigation. Therefore, Witt has violated Standard V(A).

See also Standard IV(C)—Responsibilities of Supervisors as it relates to the firm's inadequate procedures.

Example 4 (Timely Client Updates): Kristen Chandler is an investment consultant in the London office of Dalton Securities, a major global investment consultant firm. One of her U.K. pension funds has decided to appoint a specialist U.S. equity manager. Dalton's global manager of research relies on local consultants to cover managers within their regions and, after conducting thorough due diligence, puts their views and ratings in Dalton's manager database. Chandler accesses Dalton's global manager research database and conducts a screen of all U.S. equity managers on the basis of a match with the client's desired philosophy/style, performance, and tracking-error targets. She selects the five managers that meet these criteria and puts them in a briefing report that is delivered to the client 10 days later. Between the time of Chandler's database search and the delivery of the report to the client, Chandler is told that Dalton has updated the database with the information that one of the firms that Chandler has recommended for consideration lost its chief investment officer, the head of its U.S. equity research, and the majority of its portfolio managers on the U.S. equity product—all of whom have left to establish their own firm. Chandler does not revise her report with this updated information.

Comment: Chandler has failed to satisfy the requirement of Standard V(A). Although Dalton updated the manager ratings to reflect the personnel turnover at one of the firms, Chandler did not update her report to reflect the new information.

Example 5 (Group Research Opinions): Evelyn Mastakis is a junior analyst who has been asked by her firm to write a research report predicting the expected interest rate for residential mortgages over the next six months. Mastakis submits her report to the fixed-income investment committee of her firm for review, as required by firm procedures. Although some committee members support Mastakis's conclusion, the majority of the committee disagrees with her conclusion, and the report is significantly changed to indicate that interest rates are likely to increase more than originally predicted by Mastakis. Should Mastakis ask that her name be taken off the report when it is disseminated?

Comment: The results of research are not always clear, and different people may have different opinions based on the same factual evidence. In this case, the committee may have valid reasons for issuing a report that differs from the analyst's original research. The firm can issue a report that is different from the original report of an analyst as long as there is a reasonable or adequate basis for its conclusions.

Generally, analysts must write research reports that reflect their own opinion and can ask the firm not to put their name on reports that ultimately differ from that opinion. When the work is a group effort, however, not all members of the team may agree with all aspects of the report. Ultimately, members and candidates can ask to have their names removed from the report, but if they are satisfied that the process has produced results or conclusions that have a reasonable or adequate basis, members or candidates do not have to dissociate from the report even when they do not agree with its contents. If Mastakis is confident in the process, she does not need to dissociate from the report even if it does not reflect her opinion.

Example 6 (Reliance on Third-Party Research): Gary McDermott runs a two-person investment management firm. McDermott's firm subscribes to a service from a large investment research firm that provides research reports. McDermott's firm makes investment recommendations on the basis of these reports.

Comment: Members and candidates can rely on third-party research but must make reasonable and diligent efforts to determine that such research is sound. If McDermott undertakes due diligence efforts on a regular basis to ensure that the research produced by the large firm is objective and reasonably based, McDermott can rely on that research when making investment recommendations to clients.

Example 7 (Due Diligence in Submanager Selection): Paul Ostrowski's business has grown significantly over the past couple of years, and some clients want to diversify internationally. Ostrowski decides to find a submanager to handle the expected international investments. Because this will be his first subadviser, Ostrowski uses the CFA Institute model "request for proposal" to design a questionnaire for his search. By his deadline, he receives seven completed questionnaires from a variety of domestic and international firms trying to gain his business. Ostrowski reviews all the applications in detail and decides to select the firm that charges the lowest fees because doing so will have the least impact on his firm's bottom line.

Comment: The selection of an external adviser or subadviser should be based on a full and complete review of the advisers' services, performance history, and cost structure. In basing the decision on the fee structure alone, Ostrowski may be violating Standard V(A).

See also Standard III(C)—Suitability as it relates to the ability of the selected adviser to meet the needs of the clients.

Example 8 (Sufficient Due Diligence): Michael Papis is the chief investment officer of his state's retirement fund. The fund has always used outside advisers for the real estate allocation, and this information is clearly presented in all fund communications. Thomas Nagle, a recognized sell-side research analyst and Papis's business school classmate, recently left the investment bank he worked for to start his own asset management firm, Accessible Real Estate. Nagle is trying to build his assets under management and contacts Papis about gaining some of the retirement fund's allocation. In the previous few years, the performance of the retirement fund's real estate investments was in line with the fund's benchmark but was not extraordinary. Papis decides to help out his old friend and also to seek better returns by moving the real estate allocation to Accessible. The only notice of the change in adviser appears in the next annual report in the listing of associated advisers.

> *Comment*: Papis violated Standard V(A) in this example. His responsibilities may include the selection of the external advisers, but the decision to change advisers appears to have been arbitrary. If Papis was dissatisfied with the current real estate adviser, he should have conducted a proper solicitation to select the most appropriate adviser.
>
> See also Standard IV(C)—Responsibilities of Supervisors, Standard V(B)—Communication with Clients and Prospective Clients, and Standard VI(A)—Disclosure of Conflicts.

Example 9 (Sufficient Due Diligence): Andre Shrub owns and operates Conduit, an investment advisory firm. Prior to opening Conduit, Shrub was an account manager with Elite Investment, a hedge fund managed by his good friend Adam Reed. To attract clients to a new Conduit fund, Shrub offers lower-than-normal management fees. He can do so because the fund consists of two top-performing funds managed by Reed. Given his personal friendship with Reed and the prior performance record of these two funds, Shrub believes this new fund is a winning combination for all parties. Clients quickly invest with Conduit to gain access to the Elite funds. No one is turned away because Conduit is seeking to expand its assets under management.

> *Comment*: Shrub violated Standard V(A) by not conducting a thorough analysis of the funds managed by Reed before developing the new Conduit fund. Due diligence must be applied more deeply than review of a single security. It includes a review of outside managers and investment funds. Shrub's reliance on his personal relationship with Reed and his prior knowledge of Elite are insufficient justification for the investments. The funds may be appropriately considered, but a full review of their operating procedures, reporting practices, and transparency are some elements of the necessary due diligence.
>
> See also Standard III(C)—Suitability.

Example 10 (Sufficient Due Diligence): Bob Thompson has been doing research for the portfolio manager of the fixed-income department. His assignment is to do sensitivity analysis on securitized subprime mortgages. He has discussed with the manager possible scenarios to use to calculate expected returns. A key assumption in such calculations is housing price appreciation (HPA) because it drives "prepays" (prepayments of mortgages) and losses. Thompson is concerned with the significant appreciation experienced over the previous five years as a result of the increased availability of funds from subprime mortgages. Thompson insists that the analysis should include a scenario run with negative 10 percent for the first year, negative 5 percent for the second year, and then (to project a worst-case scenario) 0 percent for Years 3 through 5. The manager replies that these assumptions are too dire because there has never been a time in their available database when HPA was negative.

Thompson conducts his research to better understand the risks inherent in these securities and evaluates these securities in the worst-case scenario, an unlikely but possible environment. Based on the results of the enhanced scenarios, Thompson does not recommend the purchase of the securitization. Against the general market trends, the manager follows Thompson's recommendation and does not invest. The following year, the housing market collapses. In avoiding the subprime investments, the manager's portfolio outperforms its peer group that year.

> *Comment*: Thompson's actions in running the scenario test with inputs beyond the historical trends available in the firm's databases adheres to the principles of Standard V(A). His concerns over recent trends provide a sound basis for further analysis. Thompson understands the limitations of his model, when combined with the limited available historical information, to accurately predict the performance of the funds if market conditions change negatively.
>
> See also Standard I(B)—Independence and Objectivity.

Example 11 (Use of Quantitatively Oriented Models): Espacia Liakos works in sales for Hellenica Securities, a firm specializing in developing intricate derivative strategies to profit from particular views on market expectations. One of her clients is Eugenie Carapalis, who has become convinced that commodity prices will become more volatile over the coming months. Carapalis asks Liakos to quickly engineer a strategy that will benefit from this expectation. Liakos turns to Hellenica's modelling group to fulfil this request. Because of the tight deadline, the modelling group outsources parts of the work to several trusted third parties. Liakos implements the disparate components of the strategy as the firms complete them.

Within a month, Carapalis is proven correct: Volatility across a range of commodities increases sharply. But her derivatives position with Hellenica returns huge losses, and the losses increase daily. Liakos investigates and realizes that, although each of the various components of the strategy had been validated, they had never been evaluated as an integrated whole. In extreme conditions, portions of the model worked at cross-purposes with other portions, causing the overall strategy to fail dramatically.

> *Comment*: Liakos violated Standard V(A). Members and candidates must understand the statistical significance of the results of the models they recommend and must be able to explain them to clients. Liakos did not take adequate care to ensure a thorough review of the whole model; its components were evaluated only individually. Because Carapalis clearly intended to implement the strategy as a whole rather than as separate parts, Liakos should have tested how the components of the strategy interacted as well as how they performed individually.

Example 12 (Successful Due Diligence/Failed Investment): Alton Newbury is an investment adviser to high-net-worth clients. A client with an aggressive risk profile in his investment policy statement asks about investing in the Top Shelf hedge fund. This fund, based in Calgary, Alberta, Canada, has reported 20 percent returns for the first three years. The fund prospectus states that its strategy involves long and short positions in the energy sector and extensive leverage. Based on his analysis of the fund's track record, the principals involved in managing the fund, the fees charged, and the fund's risk profile, Newbury recommends the fund to the client and secures a position in it. The next week, the fund announces that it has suffered a loss of 60 percent of its value and is suspending operations and redemptions until after a regulatory review. Newbury's client calls him in a panic and asks for an explanation.

> *Comment*: Newbury's actions were consistent with Standard V(A). Analysis of an investment that results in a reasonable basis for recommendation does not guarantee that the investment will have no downside risk. Newbury should discuss the analysis process with the client while reminding him or her that past performance does not lead to guaranteed future gains and that losses in an aggressive investment portfolio should be expected.

B. Communication with Clients and Prospective Clients

Members and Candidates must:

1. **Disclose to clients and prospective clients the basic format and general principles of the investment processes they use to analyze investments, select securities, and construct portfolios and must promptly disclose any changes that might materially affect those processes.**
2. **Use reasonable judgment in identifying which factors are important to their investment analyses, recommendations, or actions and include those factors in communications with clients and prospective clients.**
3. **Distinguish between fact and opinion in the presentation of investment analyses and recommendations.**

Guidance

Highlights:

▶ *Informing Clients of the Investment Process*
▶ *Different Forms of Communication*
▶ *Identifying Limitations of Analysis*
▶ *Distinction between Facts and Opinions in Reports*

Standard V(B) addresses member and candidate conduct with respect to communicating with clients. Developing and maintaining clear, frequent, and thorough communication practices is critical to providing high-quality financial services to clients. When clients understand the information communicated to them, they also can understand exactly how members and candidates are acting on their behalf, which gives clients the opportunity to make well-informed decisions about their investments. Such understanding can be accomplished only through clear communication.

Standard V(B) states that members and candidates should communicate in a recommendation the factors that were instrumental in making the investment recommendation. A critical part of this requirement is to distinguish clearly between opinions and facts. In preparing a research report, the member or candidate must present the basic characteristics of the security(ies) being analyzed, which will allow the reader to evaluate the report and incorporate information the reader deems relevant to his or her investment decision-making process.

Similarly, in preparing a recommendation about, for example, an asset allocation strategy, alternative investment vehicle, or structured investment product, the member or candidate should include factors that are relevant to whatever asset classes are being discussed. In all cases, the upside potential and downside risk expressed in terms of expected total returns should be among the factors communicated. Follow-on communication of any changes in the risk characteristics of a security or asset strategy would also be advisable.

Informing Clients of the Investment Process

Members and candidates must adequately describe to clients and prospective clients the manner in which the member or candidate conducts the investment decision-making process. The member or candidate must keep clients and other interested parties informed on an ongoing basis about changes to the investment process. Only by thoroughly understanding the nature of the investment product or service can a client determine whether changes to that product or service could materially affect his or her investment objectives.

Understanding the basic characteristics of an investment is of great importance in judging the suitability of that investment on a stand-alone basis, but it is especially important in determining the impact each investment will have on the characteristics of a portfolio. Although the risk and return characteristics of a common stock might seem to be essentially the same for any investor when the stock is viewed in isolation, the effects of those characteristics greatly depend on the other investments held. For instance, if the particular stock will represent 90 percent of an individual's investments, the stock's importance in the portfolio is vastly different from what it would be to an investor with a highly diversified portfolio for whom the stock will represent only 2 percent of the holdings.

A firm's investment policy may include the use of outside advisers to manage various portions of the clients' assets under management. Members and candidates should inform the clients about the specialization or diversification expertise provided by the external adviser(s). This information allows clients to understand the full mix of products and strategies being applied that may affect their investment objectives.

Different Forms of Communication

For purposes of Standard V(B), communication is not confined to a written report of the type traditionally generated by an analyst researching a security, company, or industry. A presentation of information can be made via any means of communication, including in-person recommendation or description, telephone conversation, media broadcast, or transmission by computer (e.g., on the internet). Furthermore, the nature of these communications is highly diverse— from one word ("buy" or "sell") to in-depth reports of more than 100 pages.

A communication may contain a general recommendation about the market, asset allocations, or classes of investments (e.g., stocks, bonds, real estate) or may relate to a specific security. If recommendations are contained in capsule form (such as a recommended stock list), members and candidates should notify clients that additional information and analyses are available from the producer of the report.

Identifying Limitations of Analysis

Investment advice based on quantitative research and analysis must be supported by readily available reference material and should be applied in a manner consistent with previously applied methodology; if changes in methodology are made, they should be highlighted. Members and candidates should outline known limitations of the analysis and conclusions contained in their investment advice. In evaluating the basic characteristics of the investment being recommended, members and candidates should consider in the report the potential total returns and the principal risks inherent in the expected returns, which may include credit risk, financial risk (specifically, the use of leverage or financial derivatives), and overall market risk.

Once the process has been completed, the member or candidate who prepares the report must include those elements that are important to the analysis and conclusions of the report so that the reader can follow and challenge the report's reasoning. A report writer who has done adequate investigation may emphasize certain areas, touch briefly on others, and omit certain aspects deemed unimportant. For instance, a report may dwell on a quarterly earnings release or new-product introduction and omit other matters as long as the analyst clearly stipulates the limits to the scope of the report.

Distinction between Facts and Opinions in Reports

Standard V(B) requires that opinion be separated from fact. Violations often occur when reports fail to separate the past from the future by not indicating that earnings estimates, changes in the outlook for dividends, and/or future market price information are *opinions* subject to future circumstances. In the case of complex quantitative analyses, analysts must clearly separate fact from statistical conjecture and should identify the known limitations of an analysis. Analysts may violate Standard V(B) by failing to identify the limits of statistically developed projections, because this omission leaves readers unaware of the limits of the published projections.

Recommended Procedures for Compliance

Because the selection of relevant factors is an analytical skill, determination of whether a member or candidate has used reasonable judgment in excluding and including information in research reports depends heavily on case-by-case review rather than a specific checklist. To assist in the after-the-fact review of a report, the member or candidate must maintain records indicating the nature of the research and should, if asked, be able to supply additional information to the client (or any user of the report) covering factors not included in the report.

Application of the Standard

Example 1 (Sufficient Disclosure of Investment System): Sarah Williamson, director of marketing for Country Technicians, Inc., is convinced that she has found the perfect formula for increasing Country Technician's income and diversifying its product base. Williamson plans to build on Country Technician's reputation as a leading money manager by marketing an exclusive and expensive investment advice letter to high-net-worth individuals. One hitch in the plan is the complexity of Country Technician's investment system—a combination of technical trading rules (based on historical price and volume fluctuations) and portfolio construction rules designed to minimize risk. To simplify the newsletter, she decides to include only each week's top-five "buy" and "sell" recommendations and to leave out details of the valuation models and the portfolio structuring scheme.

> *Comment*: Williamson's plans for the newsletter violate Standard V(B). Williamson need not describe the investment system in detail in order to implement the advice effectively, but she must inform clients of Country Technician's basic process and logic. Without understanding the basis for a recommendation, clients cannot possibly understand its limitations or its inherent risks.

Example 2 (Providing Opinions as Facts): Richard Dox is a mining analyst for East Bank Securities. He has just finished his report on Boisy Bay Minerals. Included in his report is his own assessment of the geological extent of mineral reserves likely to be found on the company's land. Dox completed this calculation on the basis of the core samples from the company's latest drilling. According to Dox's calculations, the company has more than 500,000 ounces of gold on the property. Dox concludes his research report as follows: "Based on the fact that the company has 500,000 ounces of gold to be mined, I recommend a strong BUY."

> *Comment*: If Dox issues the report as written, he will violate Standard V(B). His calculation of the total gold reserves for the property is an opinion, not a fact. Opinion must be distinguished from fact in research reports.

Example 3 (Proper Description of a Security): Olivia Thomas, an analyst at Government Brokers, Inc., which is a brokerage firm specializing in government bond trading, has produced a report that describes an investment strategy designed to benefit from an expected decline in U.S. interest rates. The firm's derivative products group has designed a structured product that will allow the firm's clients to benefit from this strategy. Thomas's report describing the strategy indicates that high returns are possible if various scenarios for declining interest rates are assumed. Citing the proprietary nature of the structured product underlying the strategy, the report does not describe in detail how the firm is able to offer such returns or the related risks in the scenarios, nor does the report address the likely returns of the strategy if, contrary to expectations, interest rates rise.

> *Comment*: Thomas has violated Standard V(B) because her report fails to describe properly the basic characteristics of the actual and implied risks of the investment strategy, including how the structure was created and the degree to which leverage was embedded in the structure. The report should include a balanced discussion of how the strategy would perform in the case of rising as well as falling interest rates, preferably illustrating how the strategies might be expected to perform in the event of a reasonable variety of interest rate and credit-risk-spread scenarios. If liquidity issues are relevant with regard to the valuation of either the derivatives or the underlying securities, provisions the firm has made to address those risks should also be disclosed.

Example 4 (Notification of Fund Mandate Change): May & Associates is an aggressive-growth manager that has represented itself since its inception as a specialist at investing in small-cap U.S. stocks. One of May's selection criteria is a maximum capitalization of US$250 million for any given company. After a string of successful years of superior performance relative to its peers, May has expanded its client base significantly, to the point at which assets under management now exceed $3 billion. For liquidity purposes, May's chief investment officer (CIO) decides to lift the maximum permissible market-cap ceiling to US$500 million and change the firm's sales and marketing literature accordingly to inform prospective clients and third-party consultants.

> *Comment*: Although May's CIO is correct about informing potentially interested parties as to the change in investment process, he must also notify May's existing clients. Among the latter group might be a number of clients who not only retained May as a small-cap manager but also retained midcap and large-cap specialists in a multiple-manager approach. Such clients could regard May's change of criteria as a style change that distorts their overall asset allocations.

Example 5 (Notification of Fund Mandate Change): Rather than lifting the ceiling for its universe from US$250 million to US$500 million, May & Associates extends its small-cap universe to include a number of non-U.S. companies.

Comment: Standard V(B) requires that May's CIO advise May's clients of this change because the firm may have been retained by some clients specifically for its prowess at investing in U.S. small-cap stocks. Other changes that require client notification are introducing derivatives to emulate a certain market sector or relaxing various other constraints, such as portfolio beta. In all such cases, members and candidates must disclose changes to all interested parties.

Example 6 (Notification of Changes to the Investment Process): RJZ Capital Management is an active value-style equity manager that selects stocks by using a combination of four multifactor models. The firm has found favorable results when back testing the most recent 10 years of available market data in a new dividend discount model (DDM) designed by the firm. This model is based on projected inflation rates, earnings growth rates, and interest rates. The president of RJZ decides to replace its simple model that uses price to trailing 12-months earnings with the new DDM.

Comment: Because the introduction of a new and different valuation model represents a material change in the investment process, RJZ's president must communicate the change to the firm's clients. RJZ is moving away from a model based on hard data toward a new model that is at least partly dependent on the firm's forecasting skills. Clients would likely view such a model as a significant change rather than a mere refinement of RJZ's process.

Example 7 (Notification of Changes to the Investment Process): RJZ Capital Management loses the chief architect of its multifactor valuation system. Without informing its clients, the president of RJZ decides to redirect the firm's talents and resources toward developing a product for passive equity management—a product that will emulate the performance of a major market index.

Comment: By failing to disclose to clients a substantial change to its investment process, the president of RJZ has violated Standard V(B).

Example 8 (Notification of Changes to the Investment Process): At Fundamental Asset Management, Inc., the responsibility for selecting stocks for addition to the firm's "approved" list has just shifted from individual security analysts to a committee consisting of the research director and three senior portfolio managers. Eleanor Morales, a portfolio manager with Fundamental Asset Management, thinks this change is not important enough to communicate to her clients.

Comment: Morales must disclose the process change to all her clients. Some of Fundamental's clients might be concerned about the morale and motivation among the firm's best research analysts after such a change. Moreover, clients might challenge the stock-picking track record of the portfolio managers and might even want to monitor the situation closely.

Example 9 (Sufficient Disclosure of Investment System): Amanda Chinn is the investment director for Diversified Asset Management, which manages the endowment of a charitable organization. Because of recent staff departures, Diversified has decided to limit its direct investment focus to large-cap securities and supplement the needs for small-cap and midcap management by hiring outside fund managers. In describing the planned strategy change to the charity, Chinn's update letter states, "As investment director, I will directly oversee the investment team managing the endowment's large-capitalization allocation. I will coordinate the selection and ongoing review of external managers responsible for allocations to other classes." The letter also describes the reasons for the change and the characteristics external managers must have to be considered.

> *Comment*: Standard V(B) requires the disclosure of the investment process used to construct the portfolio of the fund. Changing the investment process from managing all classes of investments within the firm to the use of external managers is one example of information that needs to be communicated to clients. Chinn and her firm have embraced the principles of Standard V(B) by providing their client with relevant information. The charity can now make a reasonable decision about whether Diversified Asset Management remains the appropriate manager for its fund.

Example 10 (Notification of Changes to the Investment Process): Michael Papis is the chief investment officer of his state's retirement fund. The fund has always used outside advisers for the real estate allocation, and this information is clearly presented in all fund communications. Thomas Nagle, a recognized sell-side research analyst and Papis's business school classmate, recently left the investment bank he worked for to start his own asset management firm, Accessible Real Estate. Nagle is trying to build his assets under management and contacts Papis about gaining some of the retirement fund's allocation. In the previous few years, the performance of the retirement fund's real estate investments was in line with the fund's benchmark but was not extraordinary. Papis decides to help out his old friend and also to seek better returns by moving the real estate allocation to Accessible. The only notice of the change in adviser appears in the next annual report in the listing of associated advisers.

> *Comment*: Papis has violated Standard V(B). He attempted to hide the nature of his decision to change external managers by making only a limited disclosure. The plan recipients and the fund's trustees need to be aware when changes are made to ensure that operational procedures are being followed.
>
> See also Standard IV(C)—Responsibilities of Supervisors, Standard V(A)—Diligence and Reasonable Basis, and Standard VI(A)—Disclosure of Conflicts.

C. Record Retention

> **Members and Candidates must develop and maintain appropriate records to support their investment analyses, recommendations, actions, and other investment-related communications with clients and prospective clients.**

Guidance

Highlights:

▶ *Records Are Property of the Firm*
▶ *Local Requirements*

Members and candidates must retain records that substantiate the scope of their research and reasons for their actions or conclusions. Which records are required to support recommendations and/or investment actions depends on the role of the member or candidate in the investment decision-making process. Records may be maintained either in hard copy or electronic form.

Some examples of supporting documentation that assists the member or candidate in meeting the requirements for retention are as follows:

► personal notes from meetings with the covered company;
► press releases or presentations issued by the covered company;
► computer-based model outputs and analyses;
► computer-based model input parameters;
► risk analyses of securities' impacts on a portfolio;
► selection criteria for external advisers;
► notes from clients from meetings to review investment policy statements;
► outside research reports.

Records Are Property of the Firm

As a general matter, records created as part of a member's or candidate's professional activity on behalf of his or her employer are the property of the firm. When a member or candidate leaves a firm to seek other employment, the member or candidate cannot take the property of the firm, including originals or copies of supporting records of the member's or candidate's work, to the new employer without the express consent of the previous employer. The member or candidate cannot use historical recommendations or research reports created at the previous firm because the supporting documentation is unavailable. For future use, the member or candidate must re-create the supporting records at the new firm with information gathered through public sources or directly from the covered company and not from memory or sources obtained at the previous employer.

Local Requirements

Local regulators often impose requirements on members, candidates, and their firms related to record retention that must be followed. Fulfilling such regulatory requirements also may satisfy the requirements of Standard V(C), but members and candidates should explicitly determine whether it does. In the absence of regulatory guidance, CFA Institute recommends maintaining records for at least seven years.

Recommended Procedures for Compliance

The responsibility to maintain records that support investment action generally falls with the firm rather than individuals. Members and candidates must, however, archive research notes and other documents, either electronically or in hard copy, that support their current investment-related communications. Doing so will assist their firms in complying with requirements for preservation of internal or external records.

Application of the Standard

Example 1 (Record Retention and IPS Objectives and Recommendations): One of Nikolas Lindstrom's clients is upset by the negative investment returns in his equity portfolio. The investment policy statement for the client requires that the portfolio manager follow a benchmark-oriented approach. The benchmark for the client includes a 35 percent investment allocation in the technology sector. The client acknowledges that this allocation was appropriate, but over the past three years, technology stocks have suffered severe losses. The client complains to the investment manager that so much money was allocated to this sector.

> *Comment*: For Lindstrom, having appropriate records is important to show that over the past three years the percentage of technology stocks in the benchmark index was 35 percent as called for in the IPS. Lindstrom should also have the IPS for the client stating that the benchmark was appropriate for the client's investment objectives. He should also have records indicating that the investment has been explained appropriately to the client and that the IPS was updated on a regular basis. Taking these actions, Lindstrom would be in compliance with Standard V(C).

Example 2 (Record Retention and Research Process): Malcolm Young is a research analyst who writes numerous reports rating companies in the luxury retail industry. His reports are based on a variety of sources, including interviews with company managers, manufacturers, and economists; onsite company visits; customer surveys; and secondary research from analysts covering related industries.

> *Comment*: Young must carefully document and keep copies of all the information that goes into his reports, including the secondary or third-party research of other analysts. Failure to maintain such files would violate Standard V(C).

Example 3 (Records as Firm, Not Employee, Property): Martin Blank develops an analytical model while he is employed by Grosse Point Investment Management, LLP (GPIM). While at the firm, he systematically documents the assumptions that make up the model as well as his reasoning behind the assumptions. As a result of the success of his model, Blank is hired to be the head of the research department of one of GPIM's competitors. Blank takes copies of the records supporting his model to his new firm.

> *Comment*: The records created by Blank supporting the research model he developed at GPIM are the records of GPIM. Taking the documents with him to his new employer without GPIM's permission violates Standard V(C). To use the model in the future, Blank must re-create the records supporting his model at the new firm.

STANDARD VI—CONFLICTS OF INTEREST

A. Disclosure of Conflicts

Members and Candidates must make full and fair disclosure of all matters that could reasonably be expected to impair their independence and objectivity or interfere with respective duties to their clients, prospective clients, and employer. Members and Candidates must ensure that such disclosures are prominent, are delivered in plain language, and communicate the relevant information effectively.

Guidance

Highlights:

► *Disclosure of Conflicts to Employers*
► *Disclosure to Clients*
► *Cross-Departmental Conflicts*
► *Conflicts with Stock Ownership*
► *Conflicts as a Director*

Best practice is to avoid actual conflicts or the appearance of conflicts of interest when possible. Conflicts of interest often arise in the investment profession. Conflicts can occur between the interests of clients, the interests of employers, and the member's or candidate's own personal interests. Common sources for conflict are compensation structures, especially incentive and bonus structures that provide immediate returns for members and candidates with little or no consideration of long-term value creation.

Identifying and managing these conflicts is a critical part of working in the investment industry and can take many forms. When conflicts cannot be reasonably avoided, clear and complete disclosure of their existence is necessary.

Standard VI(A) protects investors and employers by requiring members and candidates to fully disclose to clients, potential clients, and employers all actual and potential conflicts of interest. Once a member or candidate has made full disclosure, the member's or candidate's employer, clients, and prospective clients will have the information needed to evaluate the objectivity of the investment advice or action taken on their behalf.

To be effective, disclosures must be prominent and must be made in plain language and in a manner designed to effectively communicate the information. Members and candidates have the responsibility of determining how often, in what manner, and in what particular circumstances the disclosure of conflicts must be made. Best practices dictate updating disclosures when the nature of a conflict of interest changes materially—for example, if the nature of a conflict of interest deepens through the introduction of bonuses based on each quarter's profits as opposed to the previous review based on annual profits. In making and updating disclosures of conflicts of interest, members and candidates should err on the side of caution to ensure that conflicts are effectively communicated.

Disclosure of Conflicts to Employers

Disclosure of conflicts to employers may be appropriate in many instances. When reporting conflicts of interest to employers, members and candidates should give their employers enough information to assess the impact of the conflict. By complying with employer guidelines, members and candidates allow their employers to avoid potentially embarrassing and costly ethical or regulatory violations.

Reportable situations include conflicts that would interfere with rendering unbiased investment advice and conflicts that would cause a member or candidate to act not in the employer's best interest. The same circumstances that generate conflicts to be reported to clients and prospective clients also would dictate reporting to employers. Ownership of stocks analyzed or recommended, participation on outside boards, and financial or other pressures that could influence a decision are to be promptly reported to the employer so that their impact can be assessed and a decision made on how to resolve the conflict.

The mere appearance of a conflict of interest may create problems for members, candidates, and their employers. Therefore, many of the conflicts previously mentioned could be explicitly prohibited by an employer. For example, many employers restrict personal trading, outside board membership, and related activities to prevent situations that might not normally be considered problematic from a conflict-of-interest point of view but that could give the appearance of a conflict of interest. Members and candidates must comply with these restrictions. Members and candidates must take reasonable steps to avoid conflicts and, if they occur inadvertently, must report them promptly so that the employer and the member or candidate can resolve them as quickly and effectively as possible.

Standard VI(A) also deals with a member's or candidate's conflicts of interest that might be detrimental to the employer's business. Any potential conflict situation that could prevent clear judgment about or full commitment to the execution of the member's or candidate's duties to the employer should be reported to the member's or candidate's employer and promptly resolved.

Disclosure to Clients

Members and candidates must maintain their objectivity when rendering investment advice or taking investment action. Investment advice or actions may be perceived to be tainted in numerous situations. Can a member or candidate remain objective if, on behalf of the firm, the member or candidate obtains or assists in obtaining fees for services? Can a member or candidate give objective advice if he or she owns stock in the company that is the subject of an investment recommendation or if the member or candidate has a close personal relationship with the company managers? Requiring members and candidates to disclose all matters that reasonably could be expected to impair the member's or candidate's objectivity allows clients and prospective clients to judge motives and possible biases for themselves.

Often in the investment industry, a conflict, or the perception of a conflict, cannot be avoided. The most obvious conflicts of interest, which should always be disclosed, are relationships between an issuer and the member, candidate, or their firm (such as a directorship or consultancy by a member; investment banking, underwriting, and financial relationships; broker/dealer market-making activities; and material beneficial ownership of stock). For the purposes of Standard VI(A), members and candidates beneficially own securities or other investments if they have a direct or indirect pecuniary interest in the securities; have the power to vote or direct the voting of the shares of the securities or investments; or have the power to dispose or direct the disposition of the security or investment.

A member or candidate must take reasonable steps to determine whether a conflict of interest exists and disclose to clients any known conflicts of the member's or candidate's firm. Disclosure of broker/dealer market-making activities alerts clients that a purchase or sale might be made from or to the firm's principal account and that the firm has a special interest in the price of the stock.

Additionally, disclosures should be made to clients of fee arrangements, subadvisory agreements, or other situations involving nonstandard fee structures. Equally important is the disclosure of arrangements in which the firm benefits directly from investment recommendations. An obvious conflict of interest is the rebate of a portion of the service fee some classes of mutual funds charge to investors. Members and candidates should ensure that their firms disclose such relationships so clients can fully understand the costs of their investments and the benefits received by their investment manager's employer.

Cross-Departmental Conflicts

Other circumstances can give rise to actual or potential conflicts of interest. For instance, a sell-side analyst working for a broker/dealer may be encouraged, not only by members of her or his own firm but by corporate issuers themselves, to write research reports about particular companies. The buy-side analyst is likely to be faced with similar conflicts as banks exercise their underwriting and security-dealing powers. The marketing division may ask an analyst to recommend the stock of a certain company in order to obtain business from that company.

The potential for conflicts of interest also exists with broker-sponsored limited partnerships formed to invest venture capital. Increasingly, members and candidates are expected not only to follow issues from these partnerships once they are offered to the public but also to promote the issues in the secondary market after public offerings. Members, candidates, and their firms should attempt to resolve situations presenting potential conflicts of interest or disclose them in accordance with the principles set forth in Standard VI(A).

Conflicts with Stock Ownership

The most prevalent conflict requiring disclosure under Standard VI(A) is a member's or candidate's ownership of stock in companies that he or she recommends to clients and/or that clients hold. Clearly, the easiest method for preventing a conflict is to prohibit members and candidates from owning any such securities, but this approach is overly burdensome and discriminates against members and candidates.

Therefore, sell-side members and candidates should disclose any materially beneficial ownership interest in a security or other investment that the member or candidate is recommending. Buy-side members and candidates should disclose their procedures for reporting requirements for personal transactions. Conflicts arising from personal investing are discussed more fully in the guidance for Standard VI(B).

Conflicts as a Director

Service as a director poses three basic conflicts of interest. First, a conflict may exist between the duties owed to clients and the duties owed to shareholders of the company. Second, investment personnel who serve as directors may receive the securities or options to purchase securities of the company as compensation for serving on the board, which could raise questions about trading actions that might increase the value of those securities. Third, board service creates the opportunity to receive material nonpublic information involving the company. Even though the information is confidential, the perception could be that information not available to the public is being communicated to a director's firm—whether a broker, investment adviser, or other type of organization. When members or candidates providing investment services also serve as directors, they should be isolated from those making investment decisions by the use of firewalls or similar restrictions.

Recommended Procedures for Compliance

Members or candidates should disclose special compensation arrangements with the employer that might conflict with client interests, such as bonuses based on short-term performance criteria, commissions, incentive fees, performance fees, and referral fees. If the member's or candidate's firm does not permit such disclosure, the member or candidate should document the request and may consider dissociating from the activity.

Members' and candidates' firms are encouraged to include information on compensation packages in firms' promotional literature. If a member or candidate manages a portfolio for which the fee is based on capital gains or capital appreciation (a performance fee), this information should be disclosed to clients. If a member, candidate, or a member's or candidate's firm has outstanding agent options to buy stock as part of the compensation package for corporate financing activities, the amount and expiration date of these options should be disclosed as a footnote to any research report published by the member's or candidate's firm.

Application of the Standard

Example 1 (Conflict of Interest and Business Relationships): Hunter Weiss is a research analyst with Farmington Company, a broker and investment banking firm. Farmington's merger and acquisition department has represented Vimco, a conglomerate, in all of Vimco's acquisitions for 20 years. From time to time, Farmington officers sit on the boards of directors of various Vimco subsidiaries. Weiss is writing a research report on Vimco.

> *Comment*: Weiss must disclose in his research report Farmington's special relationship with Vimco. Broker/dealer management of and participation in public offerings must be disclosed in research reports. Because the position of underwriter to a company entails a special past and potential future relationship with a company that is the subject of investment advice, it threatens the independence and objectivity of the report writer and must be disclosed.

Example 2 (Conflict of Interest and Business Stock Ownership): The investment management firm of Dover & Roe sells a 25 percent interest in its partnership to a multinational bank holding company, First of New York. Immediately after the sale, Margaret Hobbs, president of Dover & Roe, changes her recommendation for First of New York's common stock from "sell" to "buy" and adds First of New York's commercial paper to Dover & Roe's approved list for purchase.

> *Comment*: Hobbs must disclose the new relationship with First of New York to all Dover & Roe clients. This relationship must also be disclosed to clients by the firm's portfolio managers when they make specific investment recommendations or take investment actions with respect to First of New York's securities.

Example 3 (Conflict of Interest and Personal Stock Ownership): Carl Fargmon, a research analyst who follows firms producing office equipment, has been recommending purchase of Kincaid Printing because of its innovative new line of copiers. After his initial report on the company, Fargmon's wife inherits from a distant relative US$3 million of Kincaid stock. He has been asked to write a follow-up report on Kincaid.

> *Comment*: Fargmon must disclose his wife's ownership of the Kincaid stock to his employer and in his follow-up report. Best practice would be to avoid the conflict by asking his employer to assign another analyst to draft the follow-up report.

Example 4 (Conflict of Interest and Personal Stock Ownership): Betty Roberts is speculating in penny stocks for her own account and purchases 100,000 shares of Drew Mining, Inc., for 30 cents a share. She intends to sell these shares at the sign of any substantial upward price movement of the stock. A week later, her employer asks her to write a report on penny stocks in the mining industry to be published in two weeks. Even without owning the Drew stock, Roberts would recommend it in her report as a "buy." A surge in the price of the stock to the US$2 range is likely to result once the report is issued.

> *Comment*: Although this holding may not be material, Roberts must disclose it in the report and to her employer before writing the report because the gain for her will be substantial if the market responds strongly to her recommendation. The fact that she has only recently purchased the stock adds to the appearance that she is not entirely objective.

Example 5 (Conflict of Interest and Compensation Arrangement): Samantha Snead, a portfolio manager for Thomas Investment Counsel, Inc., specializes in managing public retirement funds and defined-benefit pension plan accounts, all of which have long-term investment objectives. A year ago, Snead's employer, in an attempt to motivate and retain key investment professionals, introduced a bonus compensation system that rewards portfolio managers on the basis of quarterly performance relative to their peers and to certain benchmark indices. In an attempt to improve the short-term performance of her accounts, Snead changes her investment strategy and purchases several high-beta stocks for client portfolios. These purchases are seemingly contrary to the clients' investment policy statements. Following their purchase, an officer of Griffin Corporation, one of Snead's pension fund clients, asks why Griffin Corporation's portfolio seems to be dominated by high-beta stocks of companies that often appear among the most actively traded issues. No change in objective or strategy has been recommended by Snead during the year.

> *Comment*: Snead has violated Standard VI(A) by failing to inform her clients of the changes in her compensation arrangement with her employer, which created a conflict of interest between her compensation and her clients' IPS. Firms may pay employees on the basis of performance, but pressure by Thomas Investment Counsel to achieve short-term performance goals is in basic conflict with the objectives of Snead's accounts.
>
> See also Standard III(C)—Suitability.

Example 6 (Conflict of Interest and Options and Compensation Arrangements): Wayland Securities works with small companies doing IPOs and/or secondary offerings. Typically, these deals are in the US$10 million to US$50 million range, and as a result, the corporate finance fees are quite small. To compensate for the small fees, Wayland Securities usually takes "agents options"—that is, rights (exercisable within a two-year time frame) to acquire up to an additional 10 percent of the current offering. Following an IPO performed by Wayland for Falk Resources, Ltd., Darcy Hunter, the head of corporate finance at Wayland, is concerned about receiving value for her Falk Resources options. The options are one month from expiring, and the stock is not doing well. She contacts John Fitzpatrick in the research department of Wayland Securities, reminds him that he is eligible for 30 percent of these options, and indicates that now would be a good time to give some additional coverage to Falk Resources. Fitzpatrick agrees and immediately issues a favorable report.

> *Comment*: For Fitzpatrick to avoid being in violation of Standard VI(A), he must indicate in the report the volume and expiration date of agent options outstanding. Furthermore, because he is personally eligible for some of the options, Fitzpatrick must disclose the extent of this compensation. He also must be careful that he does not violate his duty of independence and objectivity under Standard I(B).

Example 7 (Conflict of Interest and Compensation Arrangements): Gary Carter is a representative with Bengal International, a registered broker/dealer. Carter is approached by a stock promoter for Badger Company, who offers to pay Carter additional compensation for sales of Badger Company's stock to Carter's clients. Carter accepts the stock promoter's offer but does not disclose the arrangements to his clients or to his employer. Carter sells shares of the stock to his clients.

> *Comment*: Carter has violated Standard VI(A) by failing to disclose to clients that he is receiving additional compensation for recommending and selling Badger stock. Because he did not disclose the arrangement with Badger to his clients, the clients were unable to evaluate whether Carter's recommendations to buy Badger were affected by this arrangement. Carter's conduct also violated Standard VI(A) by failing to disclose to his employer monetary compensation received in addition to the compensation and benefits conferred by his employer. Carter was required by Standard VI(A) to disclose the arrangement with Badger to his employer so that his employer could evaluate whether the arrangement affected Carter's objectivity and loyalty.

Example 8 (Conflict of Interest and Directorship): Carol Corky, a senior portfolio manager for Universal Management, recently became involved as a trustee with the Chelsea Foundation, a large not-for-profit foundation in her hometown. Universal is a small money manager (with assets under management of approximately US$100 million) that caters to individual investors. Chelsea has assets in excess of US$2 billion. Corky does not believe informing Universal of her involvement with Chelsea is necessary.

> *Comment*: By failing to inform Universal of her involvement with Chelsea, Corky violated Standard VI(A). Given the large size of the endowment at Chelsea, Corky's new role as a trustee can reasonably be expected to be time-consuming, to the possible detriment of Corky's portfolio responsibilities with Universal. Also, as a trustee, Corky may become involved in the investment decisions at Chelsea. Therefore, Standard VI(A) obligates Corky to discuss becoming a trustee at Chelsea with her compliance officer or supervisor at Universal before accepting the position, and she should have disclosed the degree to which she would be involved in investment decisions at Chelsea.

Example 9 (Conflict of Interest and Personal Trading): Bruce Smith covers East European equities for Marlborough Investments, an investment management firm with a strong presence in emerging markets. While on a business trip to Russia, Smith learns that investing in Russian equity directly is difficult but that equity-linked notes that replicate the performance of the underlying Russian equity can be purchased from a New York–based investment bank. Believing that his firm would not be interested in such a security, Smith purchases a note linked to a Russian telecommunications company for his own account without informing Marlborough. A month later, Smith decides that the firm should consider investing in Russian equities by way of the equity-linked notes. He prepares a write-up on the market that concludes with a recommendation to purchase several of the notes. One note he recommends is linked to the same Russian telecom company that Smith holds in his personal account.

> *Comment*: Smith has violated Standard VI(A) by failing to disclose his purchase and ownership of the note linked to the Russian telecom company. Smith is required by the standard to disclose the investment opportunity to

his employer and look to his company's policies on personal trading to determine whether it was proper for him to purchase the note for his own account. By purchasing the note, Smith may or may not have impaired his ability to make an unbiased and objective assessment of the appropriateness of the derivative instrument for his firm, but Smith's failure to disclose the purchase to his employer impaired his employer's ability to decide whether his ownership of the security is a conflict of interest that might affect Smith's future recommendations. Then, when he recommended the particular telecom notes to his firm, Smith compounded his problems by not disclosing that he owned the notes in his personal account—a clear conflict of interest.

Example 10 (Conflict of Interest and Requested Favors): Michael Papis is the chief investment officer of his state's retirement fund. The fund has always used outside advisers for the real estate allocation, and this information is clearly presented in all fund communications. Thomas Nagle, a recognized sell-side research analyst and Papis's business school classmate, recently left the investment bank he worked for to start his own asset management firm, Accessible Real Estate. Nagle is trying to build his assets under management and contacts Papis about gaining some of the retirement fund's allocation. In the previous few years, the performance of the retirement fund's real estate investments was in line with the fund's benchmark but was not extraordinary. Papis decides to help out his old friend and also to seek better returns by moving the real estate allocation to Accessible. The only notice of the change in adviser appears in the next annual report in the listing of associated advisers.

> *Comment*: Papis has violated Standard VI(A) by not disclosing to his employer his personal relationship with Nagle. Disclosure of his past history with Nagle would allow his firm to determine whether the conflict may have impaired Papis's independence in deciding to change managers.
>
> See also Standard IV(C)—Responsibilities of Supervisors, Standard V(A)—Diligence and Reasonable Basis, and Standard V(B)—Communication with Clients and Prospective Clients.

Example 11 (Conflict of Interest and Business Relationships): Bob Wade, trust manager for Central Midas Bank, was approached by Western Funds about promoting its family of funds, with special interest in the service-fee class. To entice Central to promote this class, Western Funds offered to pay the bank a service fee of 0.25 percent. Without disclosing the fee being offered to the bank, Wade asked one of the investment managers to review the Western Funds family of funds to determine whether they were suitable for clients of Central. The manager completed the normal due diligence review and determined that the funds were fairly valued in the market with fee structures on a par with their competitors. Wade decided to accept Western's offer and instructed the team of portfolio managers to exclusively promote these funds and the service-fee class to clients seeking to invest new funds or transfer from their current investments. So as to not influence the investment managers, Wade did not disclose the fee offer and allowed that income to flow directly to the bank.

> *Comment*: Wade is violating Standard VI(A) by not disclosing the portion of the service fee being paid to Central. Although the investment managers may not be influenced by the fee, neither they nor the client have the proper information about Wade's decision to exclusively market this fund family and class of investments. Central may come to rely on the new fee as a component of the firm's profitability and may be unwilling to offer other products in the future that could affect the fees received.
>
> See also Standard I(B)—Independence and Objectivity.

B. Priority of Transactions

Investment transactions for clients and employers must have priority over investment transactions in which a Member or Candidate is the beneficial owner.

Guidance

Highlights:

▶ *Avoiding Potential Conflicts*
▶ *Personal Trading Secondary to Trading for Clients*
▶ *Standards for Nonpublic Information*
▶ *Impact on All Accounts with Beneficial Ownership*

Standard VI(B) reinforces the responsibility of members and candidates to give the interests of their clients and employers priority over their personal financial interests. This standard is designed to prevent any potential conflict of interest or the appearance of a conflict of interest with respect to personal transactions. Client interests have priority. Client transactions must take precedence over transactions made on behalf of the member's or candidate's firm or personal transactions.

Avoiding Potential Conflicts

Conflicts between the client's interest and an investment professional's personal interest may occur. Although conflicts of interest exist, nothing is inherently unethical about individual managers, advisers, or mutual fund employees making money from personal investments as long as 1) the client is not disadvantaged by the trade, 2) the investment professional does not benefit personally from trades undertaken for clients, and 3) the investment professional complies with applicable regulatory requirements.

Some situations occur where a member or candidate may need to enter a personal transaction that runs counter to current recommendations or what the portfolio manager is doing for client portfolios. For example, a member or candidate may be required at some point to sell an asset to make a college tuition payment or a down payment on a home, to meet a margin call, or so on. The sale may be contrary to the long-term advice the member or candidate is currently providing to clients. In these situations, the same three criteria given in the preceding paragraph should be applied in the transaction so as to not violate Standard VI(B).

Personal Trading Secondary to Trading for Clients

Standard VI(B) states that transactions for clients and employers must have priority over transactions in securities or other investments of which a member or candidate is the beneficial owner. The objective of the standard is to prevent personal transactions from adversely affecting the interests of clients or employers. A member or candidate having the same investment positions or being co-invested with clients does not always create a conflict. Some clients in certain investment situations require members or candidates to have aligned interests. Personal investment positions or transactions of members or candidates or their firm should never, however, adversely affect client investments.

Standards for Nonpublic Information

Standard VI(B) covers the activities of members and candidates who have knowledge of pending transactions that may be made on behalf of their clients or employers, who have access to nonpublic information during the normal preparation of research recommendations, or who take investment actions. Members and candidates are prohibited from conveying nonpublic information to any person whose relationship to the member or candidate makes the member or candidate a beneficial owner of the person's securities. Members and candidates must not convey this information to any other person if the nonpublic information can be deemed material.

Impact on All Accounts with Beneficial Ownership

Members or candidates may undertake transactions in accounts for which they are a beneficial owner only after their clients and employers have had adequate opportunity to act on a recommendation. Personal transactions include those made for the member's or candidate's own account, for family (including spouse, children, and other immediate family members) accounts, and for accounts in which the member or candidate has a direct or indirect pecuniary interest, such as a trust or retirement account. Family accounts that are client accounts should be treated like any other firm account and should neither be given special treatment nor be disadvantaged because of the family relationship. If a member or candidate has a beneficial ownership in the account, however, the member or candidate may be subject to preclearance or reporting requirements of the employer or applicable law.

Recommended Procedures for Compliance

Policies and procedures designed to prevent potential conflicts of interest, and even the appearance of a conflict of interest, with respect to personal transactions are critical to establishing investor confidence in the securities industry. Therefore, members and candidates should urge their firms to establish such policies and procedures. Because investment firms vary greatly in assets under management, types of clients, number of employees, and so on, each firm should have policies regarding personal investing that are best suited to the firm. Members and candidates should then prominently disclose these policies to clients and prospective clients.

The specific provisions of each firm's standards will vary, but all firms should adopt certain basic procedures to address the conflict areas created by personal investing. These procedures include the following:

▶ *Limited participation in equity IPOs*: Some eagerly awaited IPOs rise significantly in value shortly after the issue is brought to market. Because the new issue may be highly attractive and sought after, the opportunity to participate in the IPO may be limited. Therefore, purchases of IPOs by investment personnel create conflicts of interest in two principal ways. First, participation in an IPO may have the appearance of taking away an attractive investment opportunity from clients for personal gain—a clear breach of the duty of loyalty to clients. Second, personal purchases in IPOs may have the appearance that the investment opportunity is being bestowed as an incentive to make future investment decisions for the benefit of the party providing the opportunity. Members and candidates can avoid these conflicts or appearances of conflicts of interest by not participating in IPOs.

Reliable and systematic review procedures should be established to ensure that conflicts relating to IPOs are identified and appropriately dealt with by supervisors. Members and candidates should preclear their participation in IPOs, even in situations without any conflict of interest between a member's or candidate's participation in an IPO and the client's interests. Members and candidates should not benefit from the position that their clients occupy in the marketplace—through preferred trading, the allocation of limited offerings, and/or oversubscription.

▶ *Restrictions on private placements*: Strict limits should be placed on investment personnel acquiring securities in private placements, and appropriate supervisory and review procedures should be established to prevent noncompliance.

Firms do not routinely use private placements for clients (e.g., venture capital deals) because of the high risk associated with them. Conflicts related to private placements are more significant to members and candidates who manage large pools of assets or act as plan sponsors because these managers may be offered special opportunities, such as private placements, as a reward or an enticement for continuing to do business with a particular broker.

Participation in private placements raises conflict-of-interest issues that are similar to issues surrounding IPOs. Investment personnel should not be involved in transactions, including (but not limited to) private placements that could be perceived as favors or gifts that seem designed to influence future judgment or to reward past business deals.

Whether the venture eventually proves to be good or bad, managers have an immediate conflict concerning private placement opportunities. If and when the investments go public, participants in private placements have an incentive to recommend the investments to clients regardless of the suitability of the investments for their clients. Doing so increases the value of the participants' personal portfolios.

▶ *Establish blackout/restricted periods*: Investment personnel involved in the investment decision-making process should establish blackout periods prior to trades for clients so that managers cannot take advantage of their knowledge of client activity by "front-running" client trades (trading for one's personal account before trading for client accounts).

Individual firms must decide who within the firm should be required to comply with the trading restrictions. At a minimum, all individuals who are involved in the investment decision-making process should be subject to the same restricted period. Each firm must determine specific requirements related to blackout and restricted periods that are most relevant to the firm while ensuring that the procedures are governed by the guiding principles set forth in the Code and Standards. Size of firm and type of securities purchased are relevant factors. For example, in a large firm, a blackout requirement is, in effect, a total trading ban because the firm is continually trading in most securities. In a small firm, the blackout period is more likely to prevent the investment manager from front-running.

▶ *Reporting requirements*: Supervisors should establish reporting procedures for investment personnel, including disclosure of personal holdings/beneficial ownerships, confirmations of trades to the firm and the employee, and preclearance procedures. Once trading restrictions are in place, they must be enforced. The best method for monitoring and enforcing procedures to eliminate conflicts of interest in personal trading is through reporting requirements, including the following:

▶ **Disclosure of holdings in which the employee has a beneficial interest.** Disclosure by investment personnel to the firm should be made upon commencement of the employment relationship and at least annually thereafter. To address privacy considerations, disclosure of personal holdings should be handled in a confidential manner by the firm.

▶ **Providing duplicate confirmations of transactions.** Investment personnel should be required to direct their brokers to supply to firms duplicate copies or confirmations of all their personal securities transactions and copies of periodic statements for all securities accounts. The duplicate confirmation requirement has two purposes: 1) The requirement sends a message that there is independent verification, which reduces the likelihood of unethical behavior, and 2) it enables verification of the accounting of the flow of personal investments that cannot be determined from merely looking at holdings.

▶ **Preclearance procedures.** Investment personnel should examine all planned personal trades to identify possible conflicts prior to the execution of the trades. Preclearance procedures are designed to identify possible conflicts before a problem arises.

▶ *Disclosure of policies*: Upon request, members and candidates should fully disclose to investors their firm's policies regarding personal investing. The information about employees' personal investment activities and policies will foster an atmosphere of full and complete disclosure and calm the public's legitimate concerns about the conflicts of interest posed by investment personnel's personal trading. The disclosure must provide helpful information to investors; it should not be simply boilerplate language such as "investment personnel are subject to policies and procedures regarding their personal trading."

Application of the Standard

Example 1 (Personal Trading): Research analyst Marlon Long does not recommend purchase of a common stock for his employer's account because he wants to purchase the stock personally and does not want to wait until the recommendation is approved and the stock purchased by his employer.

> *Comment*: Long has violated Standard VI(B) by taking advantage of his knowledge of the stock's value before allowing his employer to benefit from that information.

Example 2 (Trading for Family Member Account): Carol Baker, the portfolio manager of an aggressive-growth mutual fund, maintains an account in her husband's name at several brokerage firms with which the fund and a number of Baker's other individual clients do a substantial amount of business. Whenever a hot issue becomes available, she instructs the brokers to buy it for her husband's account. Because such issues normally are scarce, Baker often acquires shares in hot issues but her clients are not able to participate in them.

> *Comment*: To avoid violating Standard VI(B), Baker must acquire shares for her mutual fund first and acquire them for her husband's account only after doing so, even though she might miss out on participating in new issues via her husband's account. She also must disclose the trading for her husband's

account to her employer because this activity creates a conflict between her personal interests and her employer's interests.

Example 3 (Family Accounts as Equals): Erin Toffler, a portfolio manager at Esposito Investments, manages the retirement account established with the firm by her parents. Whenever IPOs become available, she first allocates shares to all her other clients for whom the investment is appropriate; only then does she place any remaining portion in her parents' account, if the issue is appropriate for them. She has adopted this procedure so that no one can accuse her of favoring her parents.

Comment: Toffler has violated Standard VI(B) by breaching her duty to her parents by treating them differently from her other accounts simply because of the family relationship. As fee-paying clients of Esposito Investments, Toffler's parents are entitled to the same treatment as any other client of the firm. If Toffler has beneficial ownership in the account, however, and Esposito Investments has preclearance and reporting requirements for personal transactions, she may have to preclear the trades and report the transactions to Esposito.

Example 4 (Personal Trading and Disclosure): Gary Michaels is an entry-level employee who holds a low-paying job serving both the research department and the investment management department of an active investment management firm. He purchases a sports car and begins to wear expensive clothes after only a year of employment with the firm. The director of the investment management department, who has responsibility for monitoring the personal stock transactions of all employees, investigates and discovers that Michaels has made substantial investment gains by purchasing stocks just before they were put on the firm's recommended "buy" list. Michaels was regularly given the firm's quarterly personal transaction form but declined to complete it.

Comment: Michaels violated Standard VI(B) by placing personal transactions ahead of client transactions. In addition, his supervisor violated the Standard IV(C)—Responsibilities of Supervisors by permitting Michaels to continue to perform his assigned tasks without having signed the quarterly personal transaction form. Note also that if Michaels had communicated information about the firm's recommendations to a person who traded the security, that action would be a misappropriation of the information and a violation of Standard II(A)—Material Nonpublic Information.

Example 5 (Trading Prior to Report Dissemination): A brokerage's insurance analyst, Denise Wilson, makes a closed-circuit TV report to her firm's branches around the country. During the broadcast, she includes negative comments about a major company in the insurance industry. The following day, Wilson's report is printed and distributed to the sales force and public customers. The report recommends that both short-term traders and intermediate investors take profits by selling that insurance company's stock. Seven minutes after the broadcast, however, Ellen Riley, head of the firm's trading department, had closed out a long "call" position in the stock. Then, shortly thereafter, Riley established a sizable "put" position in the stock. When asked about her activities, Riley claimed she took the actions to facilitate anticipated sales by institutional clients.

Comment: Riley did not give customers an opportunity to buy or sell in the options market before the firm itself did. By taking action before the report was disseminated, Riley's firm may have depressed the price of the calls and increased the price of the puts. The firm could have avoided a conflict of interest if it had waited to trade for its own account until its clients had an opportunity to receive and assimilate Wilson's recommendations. As it is, Riley's actions violated Standard VI(B).

C. Referral Fees

Members and Candidates must disclose to their employer, clients, and prospective clients, as appropriate, any compensation, consideration, or benefit received from or paid to others for the recommendation of products or services.

Guidance

Standard VI(C) states the responsibility of members and candidates to inform their employer, clients, and prospective clients of any benefit received for referrals of customers and clients. Such disclosures allow clients or employers to evaluate 1) any partiality shown in any recommendation of services and 2) the full cost of the services. Members and candidates must disclose when they pay a fee or provide compensation to others who have referred prospective clients to the member or candidate.

Appropriate disclosure means that members and candidates must advise the client or prospective client, before entry into any formal agreement for services, of any benefit given or received for the recommendation of any services provided by the member or candidate. In addition, the member or candidate must disclose the nature of the consideration or benefit—for example, flat fee or percentage basis; one-time or continuing benefit; based on performance; benefit in the form of provision of research or other noncash benefit—together with the estimated dollar value. Consideration includes all fees, whether paid in cash, in soft dollars, or in kind.

Recommended Procedures for Compliance

Members and candidates should encourage their employers to develop procedures related to referral fees. The firm may completely restrict such fees. If the firm does not adopt a strict prohibition of such fees, the procedures should indicate the appropriate steps for requesting approval.

Employers should have investment professionals provide to the clients notification of approved referral fee programs and provide the employer regular (at least quarterly) updates on the amount and nature of compensation received.

Application of the Standard

Example 1 (Disclosure of Referral Arrangements and Outside Parties): Brady Securities, Inc., a broker/dealer, has established a referral arrangement with Lewis Brothers, Ltd., an investment counseling firm. In this arrangement, Brady Securities refers all prospective tax-exempt accounts, including pension, profit-sharing, and endowment accounts, to Lewis Brothers. In return, Lewis Brothers makes available to Brady Securities on a regular basis the security recommendations and reports of its research staff, which registered representatives of Brady Securities use in serving customers. In addition, Lewis Brothers conducts monthly economic and market reviews for Brady Securities personnel and directs all stock commission business generated by referral accounts to Brady Securities.

Willard White, a partner in Lewis Brothers, calculates that the incremental costs involved in functioning as the research department of Brady Securities are US$20,000 annually.

Referrals from Brady Securities last year resulted in fee income of US$200,000 for Brady Securities, and directing all stock trades through Brady Securities resulted in additional costs to Lewis Brothers' clients of US$10,000.

Diane Branch, the chief financial officer of Maxwell Inc., contacts White and says that she is seeking an investment manager for Maxwell's profit-sharing plan. She adds, "My friend Harold Hill at Brady Securities recommended your firm without qualification, and that's good enough for me. Do we have a deal?" White accepts the new account but does not disclose his firm's referral arrangement with Brady Securities.

> *Comment*: White has violated Standard VI(C) by failing to inform the prospective customer of the referral fee payable in services and commissions for an indefinite period to Brady Securities. Such disclosure could have caused Branch to reassess Hill's recommendation and make a more critical evaluation of Lewis Brothers' services.

Example 2 (Disclosure of Interdepartmental Referral Arrangements): James Handley works for the trust department of Central Trust Bank. He receives compensation for each referral he makes to Central Trust's brokerage department and personal financial management department that results in a sale. He refers several of his clients to the personal financial management department but does not disclose the arrangement within Central Trust to his clients.

> *Comment*: Handley has violated Standard VI(C) by not disclosing the referral arrangement at Central Trust Bank to his clients. Standard VI(C) does not distinguish between referral payments paid by a third party for referring clients to the third party and internal payments paid within the firm to attract new business to a subsidiary. Members and candidates must disclose all such referral fees. Therefore, Handley is required to disclose, at the time of referral, any referral fee agreement in place among Central Trust Bank's departments. The disclosure should include the nature and the value of the benefit and should be made in writing.

Example 3 (Disclosure of Referral Arrangements and Informing Firm): Katherine Roberts is a portfolio manager at Katama Investments, an advisory firm specializing in managing assets for high-net-worth individuals. Katama's trading desk uses a variety of brokerage houses to execute trades on behalf of its clients. Roberts asks the trading desk to direct a large portion of its commissions to Naushon, Inc., a small broker/dealer run by one of Roberts' business school classmates. Katama's traders have found that Naushon is not very competitive on pricing, and although Naushon generates some research for its trading clients, Katama's other analysts have found most of Naushon's research to be not especially useful. Nevertheless, the traders do as Roberts asks, and in return for receiving a large portion of Katama's business, Naushon recommends the investment services of Roberts and Katama to its wealthiest clients. This arrangement is not disclosed to either Katama or the clients referred by Naushon.

> *Comment*: Roberts is violating Standard VI(C) by failing to inform her employer of the referral arrangement.

Example 4 (Disclosure of Referral Arrangements and Employer Compensation): Yeshao Wen is a portfolio manager for a bank. He receives additional monetary compensation from his employer when he is successful in assisting in the sales process and generation of assets under management. The assets in question will be invested in proprietary products, such as affiliate company mutual funds.

> *Comment*: Standard VI(C) is meant to address instances where the investment advice provided by a member or candidate appears to be objective and independent but in fact is influenced by an unseen referral arrangement. It is not meant to cover compensation by employers to employees for generating new business when it would be obvious to potential clients that the employees are "referring" potential clients to the services of their employers.
>
> If Wen is selling the bank's investment management services in general, he does not need to disclose to potential clients that he will receive a bonus for finding new clients and acquiring new assets under management for the bank. Potential clients are probably aware that it would be financially beneficial both to the portfolio manager and the manager's firm for the portfolio manager to sell the services of the firm and attract new clients.
>
> In this example, however, the assets will be managed in "proprietary product offerings" of the manager's company (for example, an in-house mutual fund) and Wen will receive additional compensation for selling firm products. Some sophisticated investors may realize that it would be financially beneficial to the portfolio manager and the manager's firm if the investor were to buy the product offerings of the firm. Best practice dictates, however, that members or candidates acting as portfolio managers disclose to clients that they are compensated for selling firm products to clients. Such disclosure will meet the purpose of Standard VI(C), which is to allow investors to determine whether there is any partiality on the part of the portfolio manager making investment advice.

Example 5 (Disclosure of Referral Arrangements and Outside Organizations): Alex Burl is a portfolio manager at Helpful Investments, a local investment advisory firm. Burl is on the advisory board of his child's school, which is looking for ways to raise money to purchase new playground equipment for the school. Burl discusses a plan with his supervisor in which he will donate to the school a portion of his service fee from new clients referred by the parents of students at the school. Upon getting the approval from Helpful, Burl presents the idea to the school's advisory board and directors. The school agrees to announce the program at the next parent event and asks Burl to provide the appropriate written materials to be distributed. A week following the distribution of the flyers, Burl receives the first school-related referral. In establishing the client's investment policy statement, Burl clearly discusses the school's referral and outlines the plans for distributing the donation back to the school.

> *Comment*: Burl has not violated Standard VI(C) because he secured the permission of his employer, Helpful Investments, and the school prior to beginning the program and because he discussed the arrangement with the client at the time the investment policy statement was designed.

Example 6 (Disclosure of Referral Arrangements and Outside Parties): The sponsor of a state employee pension is seeking to hire a firm to manage the pension plan's emerging market allocation. To assist in the review process, the sponsor has hired Thomas Arrow as a consultant to solicit proposals from various advisers. Arrow is contracted by the sponsor to represent its best interest in selecting the most appropriate new manager. The process runs smoothly, and Overseas Investments is selected as the new manager.

The following year, news breaks that Arrow is under investigation by the local regulator for accepting kickbacks from investment managers after they are awarded new pension allocations. Overseas Investments is included in the list of firms allegedly making these payments. Although the sponsor is happy with the performance of Overseas since it has been managing the pension plan's emerging market funds, the sponsor still decides to have an independent review of the proposals and the selection process to ensure that Overseas was the appropriate firm for its needs. This review confirms that, even though Arrow was being paid by both parties, the recommendation of Overseas appeared to be objective and appropriate.

Comment: Arrow has violated Standard VI(C) because he did not disclose the fee being paid by Overseas. Withholding this information raises the question of a potential lack of objectivity in the recommendations Overseas is making; this aspect is in addition to questions about the legality of having firms pay to be considered for an allocation.

Regulators and governmental agencies may adopt requirements concerning allowable consultant activities. Local regulations sometimes include having a consultant register with the regulatory agency's ethics board. Regulator policies may include a prohibition on acceptance of payments from investment managers receiving allocations and require regular reporting of contributions made to political organizations and candidates. Arrow would have to adhere to these requirements as well as the Code and Standards.

STANDARD VII—RESPONSIBILITIES AS A CFA INSTITUTE MEMBER OR CFA CANDIDATE

A. Conduct as Members and Candidates in the CFA Program

Members and Candidates must not engage in any conduct that compromises the reputation or integrity of CFA Institute or the CFA designation or the integrity, validity, or security of the CFA examinations.

Guidance

Highlights:

▶ *Confidential Program Information*

▶ *Additional CFA Program Restrictions*

▶ *Expressing an Opinion*

Standard VII(A) covers the conduct of CFA Institute members and candidates involved with the CFA Program and prohibits any conduct that undermines the public's confidence that the CFA charter represents a level of achievement based on merit and ethical conduct. The standard's function is to hold members and candidates to a high ethical criterion while they are participating in or involved with the CFA Program. Conduct covered includes but is not limited to:

▶ cheating or assisting others on the CFA examination or any other CFA Institute examination;

▶ disregarding the rules and policies of the CFA Program related to exam administration;

▶ providing confidential program or exam information to candidates or the public;

▶ disregarding or attempting to circumvent security measures established by CFA Institute for the CFA exam;

▶ improperly using the CFA designation in any form of communication;

▶ improperly using an association with CFA Institute to further personal or professional goals;

▶ misrepresenting information on the Professional Conduct Statement or in the CFA Institute Continuing Education Program.

Confidential Program Information

CFA Institute is vigilant about protecting the integrity of the CFA Program content and examination process. The CFA Program prohibits candidates from disclosing confidential material gained during the exam process.

Examples of information that cannot be disclosed by candidates sitting for an exam include but are not limited to:

▶ specific details of questions appearing on the exam, and

▶ broad topical areas and formulas tested or not tested on the exam.

All aspects of the exam, including questions, broad topical areas, and formulas, tested or not tested, are considered confidential until such time as CFA Institute elects to release them publicly. This confidentiality requirement allows CFA Institute to maintain the integrity and rigor of the exam for future candidates. Standard VII(A) does not prohibit candidates from discussing nonconfidential information or curriculum material with others or in study groups in preparation for the exam.

Candidates increasingly use online forums and new technology as part of their exam preparations. CFA Institute actively polices blogs, forums, and related social networking groups for information considered confidential. The organization works with both individual candidates and the sponsors of online or offline services to promptly remove any and all violations. As noted in the discussion of Standard I(A)—Knowledge of the Law, candidates, members, and the public are encouraged to report suspected violations to CFA Institute.

Additional CFA Program Restrictions

The CFA Program examination administration policies define additional allowed and disallowed actions concerning the exams. Violating any of the testing policies, such as the calculator policy, personal belongings policy, or the Candidate Pledge, constitutes a violation of Standard VII(A). Candidates will find all of these policies on the CFA Program portion of the CFA Institute website (www.cfainstitute.org). Exhibit 2 provides the Candidate Pledge, which highlights the respect candidates must have for the integrity, validity, and security of the CFA exam.

Members may participate as volunteers in various aspects of the CFA Program. Standard VII(A) prohibits members from disclosing and/or soliciting confidential material gained prior to or during the exam and grading processes with those outside the CFA exam development process.

Examples of information that cannot be shared by members involved in developing, administering, or grading the exams include but are not limited to:

► questions appearing on the exam or under consideration;

► deliberation related to the exam process; and

► information related to the scoring of questions.

Expressing an Opinion

Standard VII(A) does *not* cover expressing opinions regarding the CFA Program or CFA Institute. Members and candidates are free to disagree and express their disagreement with CFA Institute on its policies, procedures, or any advocacy positions taken by the organization. When expressing a personal opinion, a candidate is prohibited from disclosing content-specific information, including any actual exam question and the information as to subject matter covered or not covered in the exam.

EXHIBIT 2	**Sample of CFA Program Testing Policies**
Candidate Pledge	As a candidate in the CFA Program, I am obligated to follow Standard VII(A) of the CFA Institute Standards of Professional Conduct, which states that members and candidates must not engage in any conduct that compromises the reputation or integrity of CFA Institute or the CFA designation or the integrity, validity, or security of the CFA exam.
	► Prior to this exam, I have not given or received information regarding the content of this exam. During this exam, I will not give or receive any information regarding the content of this exam.
	► After this exam, I will not **disclose any portion of this exam** and I will not remove **any exam materials** from the testing room in original or copied form. I understand that all exam materials, including my answers, are the property of CFA Institute and will not be returned to me in any form.
	► I will follow **all** rules of the CFA Program as stated on the CFA Institute website and the back cover of the exam book. My violation of any rules of the CFA Program will result in CFA Institute voiding my exam results and may lead to suspension or termination of my candidacy in the CFA Program.

Application of the Standard

Example 1 (Sharing Exam Questions): Travis Nero serves as a proctor for the administration of the CFA examination in his city. In the course of his service, he reviews a copy of the Level II exam on the evening prior to the exam's administration and provides information concerning the exam questions to two candidates who use it to prepare for the exam.

Comment: Nero and the two candidates have violated Standard VII(A). By giving information about the exam questions to two candidates, Nero provided an unfair advantage to the two candidates and undermined the integrity and validity of the Level II exam as an accurate measure of the knowledge, skills, and abilities necessary to earn the right to use the CFA designation. By accepting the information, the candidates also compromised the integrity and validity of the Level II exam and undermined the ethical framework that is a key part of the designation.

Example 2 (Bringing Written Material into Exam Room): Loren Sullivan is enrolled to take the Level II CFA examination. He has been having difficulty remembering a particular formula, so prior to entering the exam room, he writes the formula on the palm of his hand. During the afternoon section of the exam, a proctor notices Sullivan looking at the palm of his hand. She asks to see his hand and finds the formula to be readable.

Comment: Because Sullivan wrote down information from the Candidate Body of Knowledge (CBOK) and took that written information into the exam room, his conduct compromised the validity of his exam performance and violated Standard VII(A). Sullivan's conduct was also in direct contradiction of the rules and regulations of the CFA Program, the Candidate Pledge, and the CFA Institute Code and Standards.

Example 3 (Writing after Exam Period End): At the conclusion of the morning section of the Level I CFA examination, the proctors announce that all candidates are to stop writing immediately. John Davis has not completed the exam, so he continues to randomly fill in ovals on his answer sheet. A proctor approaches Davis's desk and reminds him that he should stop writing immediately. Davis, however, continues to complete the answer sheet. After the proctor asks him to stop writing two additional times, Davis finally puts down his pencil.

Comment: By continuing to complete his exam after time was called, Davis has violated Standard VII(A). By continuing to write, Davis took unfair advantage of other candidates, and his conduct compromised the validity of his exam performance. Additionally, by not heeding the proctor's repeated instructions, Davis violated the rules and regulations of the CFA Program.

Example 4 (Sharing Exam Content): After completing Level II of the CFA Exam, Annabelle Rossi writes in her blog about her experience. She posts the following: "Level II is complete! I think I did fairly well on the exam. It was really difficult, but fair. I think I did especially well on the derivatives questions. And there were tons of them! I think I counted 18! The ethics questions were really hard. I'm glad I spent so much time on the Code and Standards. I was surprised to see there were no questions at all about IPO allocations. I expected there to be a couple. Well, off to celebrate getting through it. See you tonight?"

Comment: Rossi did not violate Standard VII(A) when she wrote about how difficult she found the exam or how well she thinks she may have done. By revealing portions of the CBOK covered on the exam and areas not covered, however, she did violate Standard VII(A) and the Candidate Pledge. Depending on the time frame in which the comments were posted, Rossi not only may have assisted future candidates but also may have provided an unfair advantage to candidates sitting for the same exam, thereby undermining the integrity and validity of the Level II exam.

Example 5 (Sharing Exam Content): Level I candidate Etienne Gagne has been a frequent visitor to an internet forum designed specifically for CFA Program candidates. The week after completing the Level I examination, Gagne and several others begin a discussion thread on the forum about the most challenging questions and attempt to determine the correct answers.

> *Comment*: Gagne has violated Standard VII(A) by providing and soliciting confidential exam information, which compromises the integrity of the exam process and violates the Candidate Pledge. In trying to determine correct answers to specific questions, the group's discussion included question-specific details considered to be confidential to the CFA Program. CFA Institute works with candidates and the sponsors of such online discussion boards and forums to remove information of this specific nature from these websites.

Example 6 (Sharing Exam Content): CFA4Sure is a company that produces test-preparation materials for CFA Program candidates. Many candidates register for and use the company's products. The day after the CFA examination, CFA4Sure sends an e-mail to all its customers asking them to share with the company the hardest questions from the exam so that CFA4Sure can better prepare its customers for the next exam administration. Marisol Pena e-mails a summary of the questions she found most difficult on the exam.

> *Comment*: Pena has violated Standard VII(A) by disclosing a portion of the exam questions. The information provided is considered confidential until publicly released by CFA Institute. CFA4Sure is likely to use such feedback to refine its review materials for future candidates. Pena's sharing of the specific questions undermines the integrity of the exam while potentially making the exam easier for future candidates.
>
> If the CFA4Sure employees who participated in the solicitation of confidential CFA Program information are CFA Institute members or candidates, they also have violated Standard VII(A).

Example 7 (Sharing Exam Questions): Ashlie Hocking is in London writing Level II of the CFA examination. After completing the exam, she immediately attempts to contact her friend in Sydney, Australia, to tip him off about specific questions on the exam.

> *Comment*: Hocking has violated Standard VII(A) by attempting to give her friend an unfair advantage, thereby compromising the integrity of the CFA exam process.

Example 8 (Discussion of Exam Grading Guidelines and Results): Prior to participating in grading CFA examinations, Wesley Whitcomb is required to sign a CFA Institute Grader Agreement. As part of the Grader Agreement, Whitcomb agrees not to reveal or discuss the exam materials with anyone except CFA Institute staff or other graders. Several weeks after the conclusion of the CFA exam grading, Whitcomb tells several colleagues who are candidates in the CFA Program which question he graded. He also discusses the guideline answer and adds that few candidates scored well on the question.

> *Comment*: Whitcomb violated Standard VII(A) by breaking the Grader Agreement and disclosing information related to a specific question on the exam, which compromised the integrity of the exam process.

Example 9 (Compromising CFA Institute Integrity as a Volunteer): Jose Ramirez is an investor-relations consultant for several small companies that are seeking greater exposure to investors. He is also the program chair for the CFA Institute society in the city where he works. Ramirez schedules only companies that are his clients to make presentations to the society and excludes other companies.

Comment: Ramirez, by using his volunteer position at CFA Institute to benefit himself and his clients, compromises the reputation and integrity of CFA Institute and thus violates Standard VII(A).

Example 10 (Compromising CFA Institute Integrity as a Volunteer): Marguerite Warrenski is a member of the CFA Institute GIPS Executive Committee, which oversees the creation, implementation, and revision of the GIPS standards. As a member of the Executive Committee, she has advance knowledge of confidential information regarding the GIPS standards, including any new or revised standards the committee is considering. She tells her clients that her Executive Committee membership will allow her to better assist her clients in keeping up with changes to the Standards and facilitating their compliance with the changes.

Comment: Warrenski is using her association with the GIPS Executive Committee to promote her firm's services to clients and potential clients. In defining her volunteer position at CFA Institute as a strategic business advantage over competing firms and implying to clients that she would use confidential information to further their interests, Warrenski is compromising the reputation and integrity of CFA Institute and thus violating Standard VII(A). She may factually state her involvement with the Executive Committee but cannot infer any special advantage to her clients from such participation.

B. Reference to CFA Institute, the CFA Designation, and the CFA Program

When referring to CFA Institute, CFA Institute membership, the CFA designation, or candidacy in the CFA Program, Members and Candidates must not misrepresent or exaggerate the meaning or implications of membership in CFA Institute, holding the CFA designation, or candidacy in the CFA Program.

Guidance

Highlights:

▶ *CFA Institute Membership*
▶ *Using the CFA Designation*
▶ *Referring to Candidacy in the CFA Program*
▶ *Proper Usage of the CFA Marks*

Standard VII(B) is intended to prevent promotional efforts that make promises or guarantees that are tied to the CFA designation. Individuals may refer to their CFA designation, CFA Institute membership, or candidacy in the CFA Program but must not exaggerate the meaning or implications of membership in CFA Institute, holding the CFA designation, or candidacy in the CFA Program.

Standard VII(B) is not intended to prohibit factual statements related to the positive benefit of earning the CFA designation. However, statements referring to CFA Institute, the CFA designation, or the CFA Program that overstate the competency of an individual or imply, either directly or indirectly, that superior performance can be expected from someone with the CFA designation are not allowed under the standard.

Statements that highlight or emphasize the commitment of CFA Institute members, CFA charterholders, and CFA candidates to ethical and professional conduct or mention the thoroughness and rigor of the CFA Program are appropriate. Members and candidates may make claims about the relative merits of CFA Institute, the CFA Program, or the Code and Standards as long as those statements are implicitly or explicitly stated as the opinion of the speaker. Statements that do not express opinions have to be supported by facts.

Standard VII(B) applies to any form of communication, including but not limited to communications made in electronic or written form (such as on firm letterhead, business cards, professional biographies, directory listings, printed advertising, firm brochures, or personal resumes) and oral statements made to the public, clients, or prospects.

CFA Institute Membership

The term "CFA Institute member" refers to "regular" and "affiliate" members of CFA Institute who have met the membership requirements as defined in the CFA Institute Bylaws. Once accepted as a CFA Institute member, the member must satisfy the following requirements to maintain his or her status:

▶ remit annually to CFA Institute a completed Professional Conduct Statement, which renews the commitment to abide by the requirements of the Code and Standards and the CFA Institute Professional Conduct Program, and

▶ pay applicable CFA Institute membership dues on an annual basis.

If a CFA Institute member fails to meet any of these requirements, the individual is no longer considered an active member. Until membership is reactivated, individuals must not present themselves to others as active members. They may state, however, that they were CFA Institute members in the past or refer to the years when their membership was active.

Using the CFA Designation

Those who have earned the right to use the Chartered Financial Analyst designation may use the trademarks or registered marks "Chartered Financial Analyst" or "CFA" and are encouraged to do so but only in a manner that does not misrepresent or exaggerate the meaning or implications of the designation. The use of the designation may be accompanied by an accurate explanation of the requirements that have been met to earn the right to use the designation.

"CFA charterholders" are those individuals who have earned the right to use the CFA designation granted by CFA Institute. These people have satisfied certain requirements, including completion of the CFA Program and required years of acceptable work experience. Once granted the right to use the designation, individuals must also satisfy the CFA Institute membership requirements (see above) to maintain their right to use the designation.

If a CFA charterholder fails to meet any of the membership requirements, he or she forfeits the right to use the CFA designation. Until membership is reactivated, individuals must not present themselves to others as CFA charterholders. They may state, however, that they were charterholders in the past.

Referring to Candidacy in the CFA Program

Candidates in the CFA Program may refer to their participation in the CFA Program, but the reference must clearly state that an individual is a candidate in the CFA Program and must not imply that the candidate has achieved any type of partial designation. A person is a candidate in the CFA Program if:

► the person's application for registration in the CFA Program has been accepted by CFA Institute, as evidenced by issuance of a notice of acceptance, and the person is enrolled to sit for a specified examination; or

► the registered person has sat for a specified examination but exam results have not yet been received.

If an individual is registered for the CFA Program but declines to sit for an exam or otherwise does not meet the definition of a candidate as described in the CFA Institute Bylaws, then that individual is no longer considered an active candidate. Once the person is enrolled to sit for a future examination, his or her CFA candidacy resumes.

CFA candidates must never state or imply that they have a partial designation as a result of passing one or more levels or cite an expected completion date of any level of the CFA Program. Final award of the charter is subject to meeting the CFA Program requirements and approval by the CFA Institute Board of Governors.

If a candidate passes each level of the exam in consecutive years and wants to state that he or she did so, that is not a violation of Standard VII(B) because it is a statement of fact. If the candidate then goes on to claim or imply superior ability by obtaining the designation in only three years, however, he or she is in violation of Standard VII(B).

Exhibit 3 provides examples of proper and improper references to the CFA designation.

EXHIBIT 3	Proper and Improper References to the CFA Designation
Proper References	**Improper References**
"Completion of the CFA Program has enhanced my portfolio management skills."	"CFA charterholders achieve better performance results."
"John Smith passed all three CFA examinations in three consecutive years."	"John Smith is among the elite, having passed all three CFA examinations in three consecutive attempts."
"The CFA designation is globally recognized and attests to a charterholder's success in a rigorous and comprehensive study program in the field of investment management and research analysis."	"As a CFA charterholder, I am the most qualified to manage client investments."
"The credibility that the CFA designation affords and the skills the CFA Program cultivates are key assets for my future career development."	As a CFA charterholder, Jane White provides the "best value in trade execution."
"I enrolled in the CFA Program to obtain the highest set of credentials in the global investment management industry."	"Enrolling as a candidate in the CFA Program ensures one of becoming better at valuing debt securities."
"I passed Level I of the CFA exam."	"CFA, Level II"

(Exhibit continued on next page . . .)

EXHIBIT 3	(continued)

Proper References	Improper References
"I am a 2010 Level III CFA candidate." "I passed all three levels of the CFA Program and will be eligible for the CFA charter upon completion of the required work experience." "As a CFA charterholder, I am committed to the highest ethical standards."	"CFA, Expected 2011"

Proper Usage of the CFA Marks

Upon obtaining the CFA charter from CFA Institute, charterholders are given the right to use the CFA marks, including Chartered Financial Analyst®, CFA®, and the CFA Logo (a certification mark):

These marks are registered by CFA Institute in countries around the world.

The Chartered Financial Analyst and CFA marks must always be used either after a charterholder's name or as adjectives (never as nouns) in written documents or oral conversations. For example, to refer to oneself as "a CFA" or "a Chartered Financial Analyst" is improper.

The CFA Logo certification mark is used by charterholders as a distinctive visual symbol of the CFA designation that can be easily recognized by employers, colleagues, and clients. As a certification mark, it must be used only to directly refer to an individual charterholder or group of charterholders.

Exhibit 4 provides examples of correct and incorrect use of the marks. CFA charterholders should refer to the complete guidelines published by CFA Institute for additional and up-to-date information and examples illustrating proper and improper use of the CFA Logo, Chartered Financial Analyst mark, and CFA mark. These guidelines and the CFA logo are available on the CFA Institute website at www.cfainstitute.org/aboutus/policies/cfaguide.html.

EXHIBIT 4	Correct and Incorrect Use of the Chartered Financial Analyst and CFA Marks

Correct	Incorrect	Principle
He is one of two CFA charterholders in the company.	He is one of two CFAs in the company.	The CFA and Chartered Financial Analyst designations must always be used as adjectives, never as nouns or common names.
He earned the right to use the Chartered Financial Analyst designation.	He is a Chartered Financial Analyst.	

(Exhibit continued on next page . . .)

EXHIBIT 4	**(continued)**	

Correct	Incorrect	Principle
Jane Smith, CFA	Jane Smith, C.F.A. John Doe, cfa	No periods. Always capitalize the letters "CFA".
John Jones, CFA	John, a CFA-type portfolio manager. The focus is on Chartered Financial Analysis. CFA-equivalent program. Swiss-CFA	Do not alter the designation to create new words or phrases.
John Jones, Chartered Financial Analyst	Jones Chartered Financial Analysts, Inc.	The designation must not be used as part of the name of a firm.
Jane Smith, CFA John Doe, Chartered Financial Analyst	Jane Smith, **CFA** John Doe, **Chartered Financial Analyst**	The CFA designation should not be given more prominence (e.g., larger, bold) than the charterholder's name.
Level I candidate in the CFA Program.	Chartered Financial Analyst (CFA), September 2011.	Candidates in the CFA Program must not cite the expected date of exam completion and award of charter.
Passed Level I of the CFA examination in 2010.	CFA Level I. CFA degree expected in 2011.	No designation exists for someone who has passed Level I, Level II, or Level III of the exam. The CFA designation should not be referred to as a degree.
I have passed all three levels of the CFA Program and may be eligible for the CFA charter upon completion of the required work experience.	CFA (Passed Finalist)	A candidate who has passed Level III but has not yet received his or her charter cannot use the CFA or Chartered Financial Analyst designation.
CFA, 2009, CFA Institute, (optional: Charlottesville, Virginia, USA)	CFA, 2009, CFA Society of the UK	In citing the designation in a resume, a charterholder should use the date that he or she received the designation and should cite CFA Institute as the conferring body.

Recommended Procedures for Compliance

Misuse of a member's CFA designation or CFA candidacy or improper reference to it is common by those in a member's or candidate's firm who do not possess knowledge of the requirements of Standard VII(B). As an appropriate step to reduce this risk, members and candidates should disseminate written information about Standard VII(B) and the accompanying guidance to their firm's legal, compliance, public relations, and marketing departments (see www.cfainstitute.org/aboutus/policies/cfaguide.html).

For materials that refer to employees' affiliation with CFA Institute, members and candidates should encourage their firms to create templates that are approved by a central authority (such as the compliance department) as being consistent with Standard VII(B). This practice promotes consistency and accuracy in the firm of references to CFA Institute membership, the CFA designation, and CFA candidacy.

Application of the Standard

Example 1 (Passing Exams in Consecutive Years): An advertisement for AZ Investment Advisors states that all the firm's principals are CFA charterholders and all passed the three examinations on their first attempt. The advertisement prominently links this fact to the notion that AZ's mutual funds have achieved superior performance.

> *Comment*: AZ may state that all principals passed the three examinations on the first try as long as this statement is true, but it must not be linked to performance or imply superior ability. Implying that 1) CFA charterholders achieve better investment results and 2) those who pass the exams on the first try may be more successful than those who do not violates Standard VII(B).

Example 2 (Right to Use CFA Designation): Five years after receiving his CFA charter, Louis Vasseur resigns his position as an investment analyst and spends the next two years traveling abroad. Because he is not actively engaged in the investment profession, he does not file a completed Professional Conduct Statement with CFA Institute and does not pay his CFA Institute membership dues. At the conclusion of his travels, Vasseur becomes a self-employed analyst accepting assignments as an independent contractor. Without reinstating his CFA Institute membership by filing his Professional Conduct Statement and paying his dues, he prints business cards that display "CFA" after his name.

> *Comment*: Vasseur has violated Standard VII(B) because his right to use the CFA designation was suspended when he failed to file his Professional Conduct Statement and stopped paying dues. Therefore, he no longer is able to state or imply that he is an active CFA charterholder. When Vasseur files his Professional Conduct Statement, resumes paying CFA Institute dues to activate his membership, and completes the CFA Institute reinstatement procedures he will be eligible to use the CFA designation.

Example 3 ("Retired" CFA Institute Membership Status): After a 25-year career, James Simpson retires from his firm. Because he is not actively engaged in the investment profession, he does not file a completed Professional Conduct Statement with CFA Institute and does not pay his CFA Institute membership dues. Simpson designs a plain business card (without a corporate logo) to hand out to friends with his new contact details, and he continues to put "CFA" after his name.

Comment: Simpson has violated Standard VII(B). Because he failed to file his Professional Conduct Statement and ceased paying dues, his membership has been suspended and he must give up the right to use the CFA designation. CFA Institute has procedures, however, for reclassifying a member and charterholder as "retired" and reducing the annual dues. If he wants to obtain retired status, he needs to file the appropriate paperwork with CFA Institute. When Simpson receives his notification from CFA Institute that his membership has been reclassified as retired and he resumes paying reduced dues, his membership will be reactivated and his right to use the CFA designation will be reinstated.

Example 4 (CFA Logo—Individual Use Only): Asia Futures Ltd is a small quantitative investment advisory firm. The firm takes great pride in the fact that all its employees are CFA charterholders. To underscore this fact, the firm's senior partner is proposing to change the firm's letterhead to include the following:

Asia Futures Ltd.

Comment: The CFA Logo is a certification mark intended to identify *individual* charterholders and must not be incorporated in a company name, confused with a company logo, or placed in such close proximity to a company name or logo as to give the reader the idea that the certification mark certifies the company. The only appropriate use of the CFA logo is on the business card or letterhead of each individual CFA charterholder.

Example 5 (Stating Facts about CFA Designation and Program): Rhonda Reese has been a CFA charterholder since 2000. In a conversation with a friend who is considering enrolling in the CFA Program, she states that she has learned a great deal from the CFA Program and that many firms require their employees to be CFA charterholders. She would recommend the CFA Program to anyone pursuing a career in investment management.

Comment: Reese's comments comply with Standard VII(B). Her statements refer to facts: The CFA Program enhanced her knowledge, and many firms require the CFA designation for their investment professionals.

Example 6 (Order of Professional and Academic Designations): Tatiana Prittima has earned both her CFA designation and a PhD in finance. She would like to cite both her accomplishments on her business card but is unsure of the proper method for doing so.

Comment: The order of designations cited on such items as resumes and business cards is a matter of personal preference. Prittima is free to cite the CFA designation either before or after citing her PhD.

PRACTICE PROBLEMS FOR READING 2

Unless otherwise stated in the question, all individuals in the following questions are CFA Institute members or candidates in the CFA Program and, therefore, are subject to the CFA Institute Code of Ethics and Standards of Professional Conduct.

1. Smith, a research analyst with a brokerage firm, decides to change his recommendation for the common stock of Green Company, Inc., from a "buy" to a "sell." He mails this change in investment advice to all the firm's clients on Wednesday. The day after the mailing, a client calls with a buy order for 500 shares of Green Company. In this circumstance, Smith should:

   A. accept the order.

   B. advise the customer of the change in recommendation before accepting the order.

   C. not accept the order because it is contrary to the firm's recommendation.

2. Which statement about a manager's use of client brokerage commissions violates the Code and Standards?

   A. A client may direct a manager to use that client's brokerage commissions to purchase goods and services for that client.

   B. Client brokerage commissions should be used to benefit the client and should be commensurate with the value of the brokerage and research services received.

   C. Client brokerage commissions may be directed to pay for the investment manager's operating expenses.

3. Jamison is a junior research analyst with Howard & Howard, a brokerage and investment banking firm. Howard & Howard's mergers and acquisitions department has represented the Britland Company in all of its acquisitions for the past 20 years. Two of Howard & Howard's senior officers are directors of various Britland subsidiaries. Jamison has been asked to write a research report on Britland. What is the best course of action for her to follow?

   A. Jamison may write the report but must refrain from expressing any opinions because of the special relationships between the two companies.

   B. Jamison should not write the report because the two Howard & Howard officers serve as directors for subsidiaries of Britland.

   C. Jamison may write the report if she discloses the special relationships with the company in the report.

4. Which of the following statements clearly *conflicts* with the recommended procedures for compliance presented in the CFA Institute *Standards of Practice Handbook*?

   A. Firms should disclose to clients the personal investing policies and procedures established for their employees.

   B. Prior approval must be obtained for the personal investment transactions of all employees.

   C. For confidentiality reasons, personal transactions and holdings should not be reported to employers unless mandated by regulatory organizations.

5. Bronson provides investment advice to the board of trustees of a private university endowment fund. The trustees have provided Bronson with the fund's financial information, including planned expenditures. Bronson receives a phone call on Friday afternoon from Murdock, a prominent alumnus, requesting that Bronson fax him comprehensive financial information about the fund. According to Murdock, he has a potential contributor but needs the information that day to close the deal and cannot contact any of the trustees. Based on the CFA Institute Standards, Bronson should:

   A. send Murdock the information because disclosure would benefit the client.

   B. not send Murdock the information to preserve confidentiality.

   C. send Murdock the information, provided Bronson promptly notifies the trustees.

6. Miller heads the research department of a large brokerage firm. The firm has many analysts, some of whom are subject to the Code and Standards. If Miller delegates some supervisory duties, which statement best describes her responsibilities under the Code and Standards?

   A. Miller's supervisory responsibilities do not apply to those subordinates who are not subject to the Code and Standards.

   B. Miller no longer has supervisory responsibility for those duties delegated to her subordinates.

   C. Miller retains supervisory responsibility for all subordinates despite her delegation of some duties.

7. Willier is the research analyst responsible for following Company X. All the information he has accumulated and documented suggests that the outlook for the company's new products is poor, so the stock should be rated a weak "hold." During lunch, however, Willier overhears a financial analyst from another firm whom he respects offer opinions that conflict with Willier's forecasts and expectations. Upon returning to his office, Willier releases a strong "buy" recommendation to the public. Willier:

   A. violated the Standards by failing to distinguish between facts and opinions in his recommendation.

   B. violated the Standards because he did not have a reasonable and adequate basis for his recommendation.

   C. was in full compliance with the Standards.

8. An investment management firm has been hired by ETV Corporation to work on an initial public offering for the company. The firm's brokerage unit now has a "sell" recommendation on ETV, but the head of the investment banking department has asked the head of the brokerage unit to change the recommendation from "sell" to "buy." According to the Standards, the head of the brokerage unit would be permitted to:

   A. increase the recommendation by no more than one increment (in this case, to a "hold" recommendation).

   B. place the company on a restricted list and give only factual information about the company.

   C. assign a new analyst to decide if the stock deserves a higher rating.

9. Albert and Tye, who recently started their own investment advisory business, have registered to take the Level III CFA examination. Albert's business card reads, "Judy Albert, CFA Level II." Tye has not put anything about the CFA designation on his business card, but promotional material that he designed for the business describes the CFA requirements and indicates that Tye participates in the CFA Program and has completed Levels I and II. According to the Standards:

   A. Albert has violated the Standards but Tye has not.

   B. Tye has violated the Standards but Albert has not.

   C. both Albert and Tye have violated the Standards.

10. Scott works for a regional brokerage firm. He estimates that Walkton Industries will increase its dividend by US$1.50 a share during the next year. He realizes that this increase is contingent on pending legislation that would, if enacted, give Walkton a substantial tax break. The U.S. representative for Walkton's home district has told Scott that, although she is lobbying hard for the bill and prospects for its passage are favorable, concern of the U.S. Congress over the federal deficit could cause the tax bill to be voted down. Walkton Industries has not made any statements about a change in dividend policy. Scott writes in his research report, "We expect Walkton's stock price to rise by at least US$8.00 a share by the end of the year because the dividend will increase by US$1.50 a share. Investors buying the stock at the current time should expect to realize a total return of at least 15 percent on the stock." According to the Standards:

    A. Scott violated the Standards because he used material inside information.

    B. Scott violated the Standards because he failed to separate opinion from fact.

    C. Scott violated the Standards by basing his research on uncertain predictions of future government action.

11. Which *one* of the following actions will help to ensure the fair treatment of brokerage firm clients when a new investment recommendation is made?

    A. Informing all people in the firm in advance that a recommendation is to be disseminated.

    B. Distributing recommendations to institutional clients prior to individual accounts.

    C. Minimizing the time between the decision and the dissemination of a recommendation.

12. The mosaic theory holds that an analyst:

    A. violates the Code and Standards if the analyst fails to have knowledge of and comply with applicable laws.

    B. can use material public information and nonmaterial nonpublic information in the analyst's analysis.

    C. should use all available and relevant information in support of an investment recommendation.

13. Jurgen is a portfolio manager. One of her firm's clients has told Jurgen that he will compensate her beyond the compensation provided by her firm on the basis of the capital appreciation of his portfolio each year. Jurgen should:

    A. turn down the additional compensation because it will result in conflicts with the interests of other clients' accounts.

    B. turn down the additional compensation because it will create undue pressure on her to achieve strong short-term performance.

    C. obtain permission from her employer prior to accepting the compensation arrangement.

14. One of the discretionary accounts managed by Farnsworth is the Jones Corporation employee profit-sharing plan. Jones, the company president, recently asked Farnsworth to vote the shares in the profit-sharing plan in favor of the slate of directors nominated by Jones Corporation and against the directors sponsored by a dissident stockholder group. Farnsworth does not want to lose this account because he directs all the account's trades to a brokerage firm that provides Farnsworth with useful information about tax-free investments. Although this information is not of value in managing the Jones Corporation account, it does help in managing several other accounts. The brokerage firm providing this information also offers the lowest commissions for trades and provides best execution. Farnsworth investigates the director issue, concludes that the management-nominated slate is better for the long-run performance of the company than the dissident group's slate, and votes accordingly. Farnsworth:

    A. violated the Standards in voting the shares in the manner requested by Jones but not in directing trades to the brokerage firm.

    B. did not violate the Standards in voting the shares in the manner requested by Jones or in directing trades to the brokerage firm.

    C. violated the Standards in directing trades to the brokerage firm but not in voting the shares as requested by Jones.

15. Brown works for an investment counseling firm. Green, a new client of the firm, is meeting with Brown for the first time. Green used another counseling firm for financial advice for years, but she has switched her account to Brown's firm. After spending a few minutes getting acquainted, Brown explains to Green that she has discovered a highly undervalued stock that offers large potential gains. She recommends that Green purchase the stock. Brown has committed a violation of the Standards. What should she have done differently?

  A. Brown should have determined Green's needs, objectives, and tolerance for risk before making a recommendation of any type of security.

  B. Brown should have thoroughly explained the characteristics of the company to Green, including the characteristics of the industry in which the company operates.

  C. Brown should have explained her qualifications, including her education, training, experience, and the meaning of the CFA designation.

16. Grey recommends the purchase of a mutual fund that invests solely in long-term U.S. Treasury bonds. He makes the following statements to his clients:

  Statement 1:   "The payment of the bonds is guaranteed by the U.S. government; therefore, the default risk of the bonds is virtually zero."

  Statement 2:   "If you invest in the mutual fund, you will earn a 10 percent rate of return each year for the next several years based on historical performance of the market."

  Did Grey's statements violate the CFA Institute Code and Standards?

  A. Neither statement violated the Code and Standards.

  B. Only Statement 1 violated the Code and Standards.

  C. Only Statement 2 violated the Code and Standards.

17. Anderb, a portfolio manager for XYZ Investment Management Company—a registered investment organization that advises investment firms and private accounts—was promoted to that position three years ago. Bates, her supervisor, is responsible for reviewing Anderb's portfolio account transactions and her required monthly reports of personal stock transactions. Anderb has been using Jonelli, a broker, almost exclusively for brokerage transactions for the portfolio account. For securities in which Jonelli's firm makes a market, Jonelli has been giving Anderb lower prices for personal purchases and higher prices for personal sales than Jonelli gives to Anderb's portfolio accounts and other investors. Anderb has been filing monthly reports with Bates only for those months in which she has no personal transactions, which is about every fourth month. Which of the following is *most likely* to be a violation of the Code and Standards?

  A. Anderb failed to disclose to her employer her personal transactions.

  B. Anderb owned the same securities as those of her clients.

  C. Bates allowed Anderb to use Jonelli as her broker for personal trades.

18. Which of the following is a correct statement of a member's or candidate's duty under the Code and Standards?

    A. In the absence of specific applicable law or other regulatory requirements, the Code and Standards govern the member's or candidate's actions.

    B. A member or candidate is required to comply only with applicable local laws, rules, regulations, or customs, even though the Code and Standards may impose a higher degree of responsibility or a higher duty on the member or candidate.

    C. A member or candidate who trades securities in a securities market where no applicable local laws or stock exchange rules regulate the use of material nonpublic information may take investment action based on material nonpublic information.

19. Ward is scheduled to visit the corporate headquarters of Evans Industries. Ward expects to use the information he obtains there to complete his research report on Evans stock. Ward learns that Evans plans to pay all of Ward's expenses for the trip, including costs of meals, hotel room, and air transportation. Which of the following actions would be the *best* course for Ward to take under the Code and Standards?

    A. Accept the expense-paid trip and write an objective report.

    B. Pay for all travel expenses, including costs of meals and incidental items.

    C. Accept the expense-paid trip but disclose the value of the services accepted in the report.

20. Which of the following statements is *correct* under the Code and Standards?

    A. CFA Institute members and candidates are prohibited from undertaking independent practice in competition with their employer.

    B. Written consent from the employer is necessary to permit independent practice that could result in compensation or other benefits in competition with a member's or candidate's employer.

    C. Members and candidates are prohibited from making arrangements or preparations to go into a competitive business before terminating their relationship with their employer.

21. Smith is a financial analyst with XYZ Brokerage Firm. She is preparing a purchase recommendation on JNI Corporation. Which of the following situations is *most likely* to represent a conflict of interest for Smith that would have to be disclosed?

    A. Smith frequently purchases items produced by JNI.

    B. XYZ holds for its own account a substantial common stock position in JNI.

    C. Smith's brother-in-law is a supplier to JNI.

22. Michelieu tells a prospective client, "I may not have a long-term track record yet, but I'm sure that you'll be very pleased with my recommendations and service. In the three years that I've been in the business, my equity-oriented clients have averaged a total return of more than 26 percent a year." The statement is true, but Michelieu only has a few clients, and one of his clients took a large position in a penny stock (against Michelieu's advice) and realized a huge gain. This large return caused the average of all of Michelieu's clients to exceed 26 percent a year. Without this one investment, the average gain would have been 8 percent a year. Has Michelieu violated the Standards?

    A. No, because Michelieu is not promising that he can earn a 26 percent return in the future.

    B. No, because the statement is a true and accurate description of Michelieu's track record.

    C. Yes, because the statement misrepresents Michelieu's track record.

23. An investment banking department of a brokerage firm often receives material nonpublic information that could have considerable value if used in advising the firm's brokerage clients. In order to conform to the Code and Standards, which one of the following is the best policy for the brokerage firm?

    A. Permanently prohibit both "buy" and "sell" recommendations of the stocks of clients of the investment banking department.

    B. Establish physical and informational barriers within the firm to prevent the exchange of information between the investment banking and brokerage operations.

    C. Monitor the exchange of information between the investment banking department and the brokerage operation.

24. Stewart has been hired by Goodner Industries, Inc., to manage its pension fund. Stewart's duty of loyalty, prudence, and care is owed to:

    A. the management of Goodner.

    B. the participants and beneficiaries of Goodner's pension plan.

    C. the shareholders of Goodner.

25. Which of the following statements is a stated purpose of disclosure in Standard VI(C)—Referral Fees?

    A. Disclosure will allow the client to request discounted service fees.

    B. Disclosure will help the client evaluate any possible partiality shown in the recommendation of services.

    C. Disclosure means advising a prospective client about the referral arrangement once a formal client relationship has been established.

26. Rose, a portfolio manager for a local investment advisory firm, is planning to sell a portion of his personal investment portfolio to cover the costs of his child's academic tuition. Rose wants to sell a portion of his holdings in Household Products, but his firm recently upgraded the stock to "strong buy." Which of the following describes Rose's options under the Code and Standards?

   A. Based on his firm's "buy" recommendation, Rose cannot sell the shares because he would be improperly prospering from the inflated recommendation.

   B. Rose is free to sell his personal holdings once his firm is properly informed of his intentions.

   C. Rose can sell his personal holdings but only when a client of the firm places an order to buy shares of Household.

27. A former hedge fund manager, Jackman, has decided to launch a new private wealth management firm. From his prior experiences, he believes the new firm needs to achieve US$1 million in assets under management in the first year. Jackman offers a $10,000 incentive to any adviser who joins his firm with the minimum of $200,000 in committed investments. Jackman places notice of the opening on several industry web portals and career search sites. Which of the following is *correct* according to the Code and Standards?

   A. A member or candidate is eligible for the new position and incentive if he or she can arrange for enough current clients to switch to the new firm and if the member or candidate discloses the incentive fee.

   B. A member or candidate may not accept employment with the new firm because Jackman's incentive offer violates the Code and Standards.

   C. A member or candidate is not eligible for the new position unless he or she is currently unemployed because soliciting the clients of the member's or candidate's current employer is prohibited.

28. Carter works for Invest Today, a local asset management firm. A broker that provides Carter with proprietary research through client brokerage arrangements is offering a new trading service. The broker is offering low-fee, execution-only trades to complement its traditional full-service, execution-and-research trades. To entice Carter and other asset managers to send additional business its way, the broker will apply the commissions paid on the new service toward stratifying the brokerage commitment of the prior full-service arrangements. Carter has always been satisfied with the execution provided on the full-service trades, and the new low-fee trades are comparable to the fees of other brokers currently used for the accounts that prohibit soft dollar arrangements.

   A. Carter can trade for his accounts that prohibit soft dollar arrangements under the new low-fee trading scheme.

   B. Carter cannot use the new trading scheme because the commissions are prohibited by the soft dollar restrictions of the accounts.

   C. Carter should trade only through the new low-fee scheme and should increase his trading volume to meet his required commission commitment.

29. Rule has worked as a portfolio manager for a large investment management firm for the past 10 years. Rule earned his CFA charter last year and has decided to open his own investment management firm. After leaving his current employer, Rule creates some marketing material for his new firm. He states in the material, "In earning the CFA charter, a highly regarded credential in the investment management industry, I further enhanced the portfolio management skills learned during my professional career. While completing the examination process in three consecutive years, I consistently received the highest possible scores on the topics of Ethics, Alternative Investments, and Portfolio Management." Has Rule violated Standard VII(B)—Reference to CFA Institute, the CFA Designation, and the CFA Program in his marketing material?

    A. Rule violated Standard VII(B) in stating that he completed the exams in three consecutive years.

    B. Rule violated Standard VII(B) in stating that he received the highest scores in the topics of Ethics, Alternative Investments, and Portfolio Management.

    C. Rule did not violate Standard VII(B).

30. Stafford is a portfolio manager for a specialized real estate mutual fund. Her firm clearly describes in the fund's prospectus its soft dollar policies. Stafford decides that entering the CFA Program will enhance her investment decision-making skill and decides to use the fund's soft dollar account to pay the registration and exam fees for the CFA Program. Which of the following statements is *most likely* correct?

    A. Stafford did not violate the Code and Standards because the prospectus informed investors of the fund's soft dollar policies.

    B. Stafford violated the Code and Standards because improving her investment skills is not a reasonable use of the soft dollar account.

    C. Stafford violated the Code and Standards because the CFA Program does not meet the definition of research allowed to be purchased with brokerage commissions.

31. Long has been asked to be the keynote speaker at an upcoming investment conference. The event is being hosted by one of the third-party investment managers currently used by his pension fund. The manager offers to cover all conference and travel costs for Long and make the conference registrations free for three additional members of his investment management team. To ensure that the conference obtains the best speakers, the host firm has arranged for an exclusive golf outing for the day following the conference on a local championship-caliber course. Which of the following is *least likely* to violate Standard I(B)?

    A. Long may accept only the offer to have his conference-related expenses paid by the host firm.

    B. Long may accept the offer to have his conference-related expenses paid and may attend the exclusive golf outing at the expense of the hosting firm.

    C. Long may accept the entire package of incentives offered to speak at this conference.

32. Andrews, a private wealth manager, is conducting interviews for a new research analyst for his firm. One of the candidates is Wright, an analyst with a local investment bank. During the interview, while Wright is describing his analytical skills, he mentions a current merger in which his firm is acting as the adviser. Andrews has heard rumors of a possible merger between the two companies, but no releases have been made by the companies concerned. Which of the following actions by Andrews is *least likely* a violation of the Code and Standards?

   A. Waiting until the next day before trading on the information to allow time for it to become public.

   B. Notifying all investment managers in his firm of the new information so none of their clients are disadvantaged.

   C. Placing the securities mentioned as part of the merger on the firm's restricted trading list.

33. Pietro, president of Local Bank, has hired the bank's market maker, Vogt, to seek a merger partner. Local is currently not listed on a stock exchange and has not reported that it is seeking strategic alternatives. Vogt has discussed the possibility of a merger with several firms, but they have all decided to wait until after the next period's financial data are available. The potential buyers believe the results will be worse than the results of prior periods and will allow them to pay less for Local Bank.

Pietro wants to increase the likelihood of structuring a merger deal quickly. Which of the following actions would *most likely* be a violation of the Code and Standards?

   A. Pietro could instruct Local Bank to issue a press release announcing that it has retained Vogt to find a merger partner.

   B. Pietro could place a buy order for 2,000 shares (or four times the average weekly volume) through Vogt for his personal account.

   C. After confirming with Local's chief financial officer, Pietro could instruct Local to issue a press release reaffirming the firm's prior announced earnings guidance for the full fiscal year.

34. ABC Investment Management acquires a new, very large account with two concentrated positions. The firm's current policy is to add new accounts for the purpose of performance calculation after the first full month of management. Cupp is responsible for calculating the firm's performance returns. Before the end of the initial month, Cupp notices that one of the significant holdings of the new accounts is acquired by another company, causing the value of the investment to double. Because of this holding, Cupp decides to account for the new portfolio as of the date of transfer, thereby allowing ABC Investment to reap the positive impact of that month's portfolio return.

   A. Cupp did not violate the Code and Standards because the GIPS standards allow composites to be updated on the date of large external cash flows.

   B. Cupp did not violate the Code and Standards because companies are allowed to determine when to incorporate new accounts into their composite calculation.

   C. Cupp violated the Code and Standards because the inclusion of the new account produces an inaccurate calculation of the monthly results according to the firm's stated policies.

35. Cannan has been working from home on weekends and occasionally saves correspondence with clients and completed work on her home computer. Because of worsening market conditions, Cannan is one of several employees released by her firm. While Cannan is looking for a new job, she uses the files she saved at home to request letters of recommendation from former clients. She also provides to prospective clients some of the reports as examples of her abilities.

   A. Cannan is violating the Code and Standards because she did not receive permission from her former employer to keep or use the files after her employment ended.

   B. Cannan did not violate the Code and Standards because the files were created and saved on her own time and computer.

   C. Cannan violated the Code and Standards because she is prohibited from saving files on her home computer.

36. Quinn sat for the Level III CFA exam this past weekend. He updates his resume with the following statement:
"In finishing the CFA Program, I improved my skills related to researching investments and managing portfolios. I will be eligible for the CFA charter upon completion of the required work experience."

   A. Quinn violated the Code and Standards by claiming he improved his skills through the CFA Program.

   B. Quinn violated the Code and Standards by incorrectly stating that he is eligible for the CFA charter.

   C. Quinn did not violate the Code and Standards with his resume update.

37. During a round of golf, Rodriguez, chief financial officer of Mega Retail, mentions to Hart, a local investment adviser and long-time personal friend, that Mega is having an exceptional sales quarter. Rodriguez expects the results to be almost 10 percent above the current estimates. The next day, Hart initiates the purchase of a large stake in the local exchange-traded retail fund for her personal account.

   A. Hart violated the Code and Standards by investing in the exchange-traded fund that included Mega Retail.

   B. Hart did not violate the Code and Standards because she did not invest directly in securities of Mega Retail.

   C. Rodriguez did not violate the Code and Standards because the comments made to Hart were not intended to solicit an investment in Mega Retail.

38. Park is very frustrated after taking her Level II exam. While she was studying for the exam, to supplement the curriculum provided, she ordered and used study material from a third-party provider. Park believes the additional material focused her attention on specific topic areas that were not tested while ignoring other areas. She posts the following statement on the provider's discussion board: "I am very dissatisfied with your firm's CFA Program Level II material. I found the exam extremely difficult and myself unprepared for specific questions after using your product. How could your service provide such limited instructional resources on the analysis of inventories and taxes when the exam had multiple questions about them? I will not recommend your products to other candidates."

   A. Park violated the Code and Standards by purchasing third-party review material.

   B. Park violated the Code and Standards by providing her opinion on the difficulty of the exam.

   C. Park violated the Code and Standards by providing specific information on topics tested on the exam.

39. Paper was recently terminated as one of a team of five managers of an equity fund. The fund had two value-focused managers and terminated one of them to reduce costs. In a letter sent to prospective employers, Paper presents, with written permission of the firm, the performance history of the fund to demonstrate his past success.

   A. Paper did not violate the Code and Standards.

   B. Paper violated the Code and Standards by claiming the performance of the entire fund as his own.

   C. Paper violated the Code and Standards by including the historical results of his prior employer.

40. Townsend was recently appointed to the board of directors of a youth golf program that is the local chapter of a national not-for-profit organization. The program is beginning a new fund-raising campaign to expand the number of annual scholarships it provides. Townsend believes many of her clients make annual donations to charity. The next week in her regular newsletter to all clients, she includes a small section discussing the fund-raising campaign and her position on the organization's board.

   A. Townsend did not violate the Code and Standards.

   B. Townsend violated the Code and Standards by soliciting donations from her clients through the newsletter.

   C. Townsend violated the Code and Standards by not getting approval of the organization before soliciting her clients.

The following information relates to Questions 41–46[1]

Anne Boswin, CFA, is a senior fixed-income analyst at Greenfield Financial Corporation. Boswin develops financial models for predicting changes in bond prices. On the premise that bonds of firms targeted for leveraged buyouts (LBOs) often decline in value, Boswin develops a model to predict which firms are likely to be subject to LBOs.

---

[1] This case was written by Sarah W. Peck, PhD.

Boswin works closely with another analyst, Robert Acertado, CFA. Acertado uses Boswin's model frequently to identify potential LBO targets for further research. Using the model and his extensive research skills, Acertado makes timely investment recommendations and develops a strong track record.

Based on this record, Acertado receives an employment offer from the asset management division of Smith & Garner Investments, Inc., a diversified financial services firm. With Boswin's consent, Acertado downloads the model before leaving Greenfield.

At Smith & Garner, Acertado presents the idea of predicting LBO targets as a way to identify bonds that might decline in value and thus be good sell recommendations. After Acertado walks his boss through the model, the supervisor comments, "I like your idea and your model, Robert. I can see that we made the right decision in hiring you."

Because Smith & Garner has both an Investment Banking (IB) and Asset Management (AM) division, Acertado's supervisor reminds him that he should not attempt to contact or engage in conversation with anyone from the Investment Banking division. The supervisor also directs him to eat in the East end of the company cafeteria. "The West end is reserved for the IB folks, and you may laugh at this, but we actually put up a wall, between the two ends. If anyone were to accuse us of not having a firewall, we could actually point to it!" Robert's supervisor also tells him, "There should be absolutely no conversation about divisional business while in the hall and elevator that serves as a common access to the cafeteria for both divisions. We are very strict about this."

The following week, Acertado is riding alone in the elevator when it stops on an IB floor. As the doors begin to slide open, Acertado hears a voice whispering, "I am so pleased that we were able to put the financing together for Country Industries. I was concerned because the leverage will go to 80%—higher than our typical deal." As soon as the doors open enough to reveal that the elevator is occupied, all conversation stops.

Late that afternoon, Acertado uses the LBO model to measure the probability of Country Industries receiving an LBO offer. According to the model, the probability is 62%—slightly more than the 60% Acertado generally requires before conducting additional research. It is late in the afternoon and Acertado has little time to research the matter fully before the end of the trading day. He checks his inputs to the model. In the interest of time, Acertado immediately recommends selling Country Industries' senior bonds held in any long-only accounts. He also recommends establishing positions in derivatives contracts that will benefit from a decline in the value of Country Industries' bonds.

The next morning, after the firm has established the derivatives positions he recommended, Acertado calls Boswin. Knowing that his former associate will be preparing Greenfield's monthly newsletter, he tells her, "I ran Country Industries through your model and I think it is likely that they will receive an LBO offer." Acertado explains some of the inputs he used in the model. At the conclusion of the conversation Boswin responds, "You may be right. Country Industries sounds like a possible LBO candidate, and thus, a sell rating on their senior bonds would be in order. If I'm lucky, I can finish researching the issue in time to include the recommendation in the upcoming newsletter. Thanks. It was good talking with you, Robert."

After the conversation with Acertado, Boswin quickly runs Country Industries through the model. Based on her inputs, the model calculates that the probability of an LBO is 40 percent—not enough, in Boswin's opinion, to justify further research. She wonders if there is a discrepancy between her inputs and Acertado's. Pressed for time, Boswin resumes her work on the upcoming newsletter rather than investigating the matter.

Acertado soon begins searching the internet for information on companies that the model predicts have more than a 60% probability of an LBO offer. He scours blogs and company websites looking for signs of a potential offer. He uses evidence of rumored offers in developing sell recommendations on various corporations' bonds.

41. When downloading the model from Greenfield Financial Corporation, does Acertado violate any CFA Institute Standards of Practice and Professional Conduct?
    A. No.
    B. Yes, because he does not have written permission from Boswin.
    C. Yes, because he does not have permission from Greenfield Financial Corporation.

42. When using the model at Smith & Garner, Acertado is *least likely* to violate the Standard relating to:
    A. misrepresentation.
    B. loyalty to employer.
    C. material nonpublic information.

43. When making the recommendation regarding Country Industries, does Acertado violate any CFA Institute Standards?
    A. No.
    B. Yes, relating to diligence and reasonable basis.
    C. Yes, relating to material nonpublic information.

44. In his phone conversation with Boswin, Acertado *least likely* violates the CFA Institute Standard relating to:
    A. suitability.
    B. integrity of capital markets.
    C. preservation of confidentiality.

45. When analyzing the probability of an LBO of Country Industries, does Boswin violate any CFA Institute Standards?
    A. No.
    B. Yes, relating to independence and objectivity.
    C. Yes, relating to diligence and reasonable basis.

46. When searching blogs does Acertado violate any CFA Institute Standards?
    A. No.
    B. Yes, because he misuses company resources.
    C. Yes, because he seeks inside information on the blogs.

The following information relates to Questions 47–52[2]

Erik Brecksen, CFA, a portfolio manager at Apfelbaum Kapital, is a strong advocate of the CFA program. He displays the CFA logo on both his letterhead and business cards and prefers to hire only CFA candidates or charterholders. Brecksen recently recruited Hans Grohl, a CFA candidate and recent MBA

---

[2] This case was written by David S. Krause, PhD, and Dorothy C. Kelly, CFA.

graduate from a top university with excellent quantitative analysis skills. After receiving Grohl's letter of acceptance, Brecksen instructs the personnel department to order business cards and letterhead for Grohl, telling them, "Use mine as a template. Just change the name, title, and other information as necessary." When Grohl arrives for his first day of work, he receives business cards and letterhead displaying his name, the firm name, and the CFA logo.

Apfelbaum Kapital stresses "top-down" fundamental analysis and uses a team approach to investment management. The firm's investment professionals, all of whom are CFA charterholders or candidates, attend weekly investment committee meetings. At the meetings, analysts responsible for different industrial sectors present their research and recommendations. Following each presentation, the investment committee, consisting of senior portfolio managers, questions the analyst about the recommendation. If the majority of the committee agrees with the recommendation, the recommendation is approved and the stock is placed on a restricted list while the firm executes the necessary trades.

Apfelbaum considers its research proprietary. It is intended for the sole use of its investment professionals and is not distributed outside the firm. The names of all the investment personnel associated with the sector or investment class are listed on each research report regardless of their actual level of contribution to the report.

On Grohl's first day of work, Brecksen assigns him responsibility for a company that Brecksen covered previously. He provides Grohl with his past research including all of his files and reports. Brecksen instructs Grohl to report back when he has finished his research and is ready to submit his own research report on the company.

Grohl reads Brecksen's old reports before studying the financial statements of the company and its competitors. Taking advantage of his quantitative analysis skills, Grohl then conducts a detailed multi-factor analysis. Afterward, he produces a written buy recommendation using Brecksen's old research reports as a guide for format and submits a draft to Brecksen for review.

Brecksen reviews the work and indicates that he is not familiar with multi-factor analysis. He tells Grohl that he agrees with the buy recommendation, but instructs Grohl to omit the multi-factor analysis from the report. Grohl attempts to defend his research methodology, but is interrupted when Brecksen accepts a phone call. Grohl follows Brecksen's instructions and removes all mention of the multi-factor analysis from the final report. Brecksen presents the completed report at the weekly meeting with both his and Grohl's names listed on the document. After Brecksen's initial presentation, the committee turns to Grohl and asks about his research. Grohl takes the opportunity to mention the multi-factor analysis. Satisfied, the committee votes in favor of the recommendation and congratulates Grohl on his work.

Ottie Zardt, CFA, has worked as a real estate analyst for Apfelbaum for the past 18 months. A new independent rating service has determined that Zardt's recommendations have resulted in an excess return of 12% versus the industry's return of 2.7% for the past twelve months. After learning about the rating service, Zardt immediately updates the promotional material he is preparing for distribution at an upcoming industry conference. He includes a reference to the rating service and quotes its returns results and other information. Before distributing the material at the conference, he adds a footnote stating "Past performance is no guarantee of future success."

47. According to the CFA Institute Standards of Professional Conduct, may Brecksen and Grohl both use the letterhead and business cards provided by Apfelbaum Kapital?

    A. Yes.

    B. No, because candidates may not use the logo.

    C. No, because the logo may not be used on company letterhead.

48. When preparing the initial draft for Brecksen's review, does Grohl violate any CFA Standards?

    A. No.

    B. Yes, because he used Brecksen's research reports without permission.

    C. Yes, because he did not use reasonable judgment in identifying which factors were important to the analyses.

49. When instructing Grohl to eliminate the multi-factor analysis from the research report, does Brecksen violate any CFA Standards?

    A. No.

    B. Yes, relating to record retention.

    C. Yes, relating to diligence and reasonable basis.

50. When removing the multi-factor analysis from his research report, does Grohl violate any CFA Standards?

    A. No.

    B. Yes, because he no longer has a reasonable basis for his recommendation.

    C. Yes, because he is required to make full and fair disclosure of all relevant information.

51. When listing their names on the research report, do Brecksen and Grohl violate any CFA Standards?

    A. No.

    B. Yes, because Brecksen misrepresents his authorship.

    C. Yes, because Grohl should dissociate from the report.

52. When distributing the material at the industry conference, does Zardt violate any CFA Standards?

    A. No.

    B. Yes, because Zardt does not verify the accuracy of the information.

    C. Yes, because analysts can not claim performance or promote the accuracy of their recommendations.

The following information relates to Questions 53–58[3]

Samuel Telline, CFA, is a portfolio manager at Aiklin Investments with discretionary authority over all of his accounts. One of his clients, Alan Caper, Chief Executive Officer (CEO) of Ellipse Manufacturing, invites Telline to lunch.

At the restaurant, the CEO reveals the reason for the lunch. "As you know Reinhold Partners has made an unsolicited cash offer for all outstanding shares

---

[3] This case was written by Sarah W. Peck, PhD.

of Ellipse Manufacturing. Reinhold has made it clear that I will not be CEO if they are successful. I can assure you that our shareholders will be better off in the long term if I'm in charge." Caper then shows Telline his projections for a new plan designed to boost both sales and operating margins.

"I know that your firm is the trustee for our firm's Employee Stock Ownership Plan (ESOP). I hope that the trustee will vote in the best interest of our shareholders—and that would be a vote against the takeover offer."

After looking through Caper's business plans, Telline says, "This plan looks good. I will recommend that the trustee vote against the offer."

Caper responds, "I remember my friend Karen Leighton telling me that the Leighton Family's Trust is managed by your firm. Perhaps the trustee could vote those shares against the acquisition as well. Karen Leighton is a close friend. I am sure that she would agree."

Telline responds, "The Family Trust is no longer managed by Aiklin." He adds, "I understand that the Trust is very conservatively managed. I doubt it that it would have holdings in Ellipse Manufacturing." Telline does not mention that although the Family Trust has changed investment managers, Karen Leighton remains an important client at Aiklin with significant personal holdings in Ellipse.

After lunch, Telline meets with Sydney Brown, CFA, trustee of the Eclipse ESOP. He shows her Caper's plan for improvements. "I think the plan is a good one and Caper is one of the firm's most profitable accounts. We don't want to lose him." Brown agrees to analyze the plan. After thoroughly analyzing both the plan and the takeover offer, Brown concludes that the takeover offer is best for the shareholders in the ESOP and votes the plan's shares in favor of the takeover offer.

A few months later the acquisition of Ellipse by Reinhold Partners is completed. Caper again meets Telline for lunch. "I received a generous severance package and I'm counting on you to manage my money well for me. While we are on the subject, I would like to be more aggressive with my portfolio. With my severance package, I can take additional risk." Telline and Caper discuss his current financial situation, risk tolerance, and financial objectives throughout lunch. Telline agrees to adjust Caper's investment policy statement (IPS) to reflect his greater appetite for risk and his increased wealth.

Back at the office, Telline realizes that with the severance package, Caper is now his wealthiest client. He also realizes that Caper's increased appetite for risk gives him a risk profile similar to that of another client. He pulls a copy of the other client's investment policy statement (IPS) and reviews it quickly before realizing that the two clients have very different tax situations. Telline quickly revises Caper's IPS to reflect the changes in his financial situation. He uses the other client's IPS as a reference when revising the section relating to Caper's risk tolerance. He then files the revised IPS in Caper's file.

The following week, an Aiklin analyst issues a buy recommendation on a small technology company with a promising software product. Telline reads the report carefully and concludes it would be suitable under Caper's new IPS. Telline places an order for 10,000 shares in Caper's account and then calls Caper to discuss the stock in more detail. Telline does not purchase the stock for any other clients. Although the one client has the same risk profile as Caper, that client does not have cash available in his account and Telline determines that selling existing holdings does not make sense.

In a subsequent telephone conversation, Caper expresses his lingering anger over the takeover. "You didn't do enough to persuade Aiklin's clients to vote against the takeover. Maybe I should look for an investment manager who is more loyal." Telline tries to calm Caper but is unsuccessful. In an attempt to change the topic of conversation, Telline states, "The firm was just notified of our allocation of a long-awaited IPO. Your account should receive a significant allocation. I would hate to see you lose out by moving your account." Caper seems mollified and concludes the phone call, "I look forward to a long-term relationship with you and your firm."

Aiklin distributes a copy of its firm policies regarding IPO allocations to all clients annually. According to the policy, Aiklin allocates IPO shares to each investment manager and each manager has responsibility for allocating shares to accounts for which the IPO is suitable. The statement also discloses that Aiklin offers different levels of service for different fees.

After carefully reviewing the proposed IPO and his client accounts, Telline determines that the IPO is suitable for 11 clients including Caper. Because the deal is oversubscribed, he receives only half of the shares he expected. Telline directs 50% of his allocation to Caper's account and divides the remaining 50% between the other ten accounts, each with a value equal to half of Caper's account.

53. When discussing the Leighton Family Trust, does Telline violate any CFA Institute Standards of Professional Conduct?
   A. No.
   B. Yes, relating to duties to clients.
   C. Yes, relating to misrepresentation.

54. When deciding how to vote the ESOP shares, does Brown violate any CFA Institute Standards?
   A. No.
   B. Yes, relating to loyalty, prudence, and care.
   C. Yes, relating to diligence and reasonable basis.

55. The Standard *least likely* to provide guidance for Telline when working with the clients' investment policy statements would be the Standard relating to:
   A. suitability.
   B. fair dealing.
   C. loyalty, prudence, and care.

56. Does Telline violate any CFA Institute Standards when he places the buy order for shares in the technology company for Caper's account?
   A. No.
   B. Yes, relating to fair dealing.
   C. Yes, relating to diligence and reasonable basis.

57. Is Aiklin's policy with respect to IPO allocations consistent with required and recommended CFA Institute Standards?
   A. Yes.
   B. No, because the IPO policy disadvantages certain clients.
   C. No, because the different levels of service disadvantage certain clients.

58. Does Telline violate any CFA Institute Standards in his allocation of IPO shares to Caper's account?
   A. No.
   B. Yes, because the IPO is not suitable for Caper.
   C. Yes, because he does not treat all his clients fairly.

The following information relates to Questions 59–64[4]

Adam Craw, CFA, is chief executive officer (CEO) of Crawfood, a European private equity firm specializing in food retailers. The retail food industry has been consolidating during the past two years as private equity funds have closed numerous deals and taken many companies private.

Crawfood recently hired Lillian Voser, a CFA Level II candidate, as a controller. On Voser's first day of work, the head of personnel informs her that by signing the employment contract, Voser agrees to comply with the company's code of ethics and compliance manual. She hands Voser copies of the code and compliance manual without further comment. Voser spends the next hour reading both documents. An excerpt from the compliance manual appears in Exhibit 1.

EXHIBIT 1	Crawfood Company Compliance Manual Excerpts

1. Employees must not accept gifts, benefits, compensation, or consideration that competes with, or might reasonably be expected to create a conflict of interest with their employer's interest unless they obtain written consent from all parties involved.

2. Officers have responsibility for ensuring that their direct reports—that is, employees whom they directly supervise—adhere to applicable laws, rules, and regulations.

3. Employees in possession of material nonpublic information should make reasonable efforts to achieve public dissemination of the information if such actions would not breach a duty.

4. Employees shall not trade or cause others to trade in securities of food retailers that may be potential takeover targets of their employer.

When she enters her new office that afternoon, Voser finds a large gift basket sent by her sister. The card reads "Congratulations on your new position." The basket is filled with expensive high-quality food items from Greenhornfood—a local small, publicly-traded food retailer, which produces many delicatessen products under its own brand name.

During the next two weeks, Voser meets with all of Crawfood's upper management, including the CEO. In his office, Craw praises Voser's efforts to complete the CFA program. "The program is demanding, but it is worthwhile." Craw then explains his investment strategy for choosing Crawfood's acquisition targets. He points to a large map on the wall with multi-colored pins marking Crawfood's previous takeovers. The map shows acquisitions in all the major cities of Germany with one exception—the home of Crawfood headquarters. Craw remarks, "We are currently in talks for another purchase. Confidentiality prohibits me from discussing it any further, but you will hear more about it soon."

Introduced to Greenhornfood by her sister, Voser quickly becomes a loyal customer. She considers it the best food retailer in the vicinity and she frequently purchases its products.

---

[4] This case was written by Anne-Katrin Scherer, CFA.

The following week, the local newspaper features an article about Greenhornfood and its young founders. The article describes the company's loyal and growing customer base as well as its poor quarterly financial results. Voser notes that the stock has steadily declined during the past twelve months. She concludes that the company has an inexperienced management team, but its popular product line and loyal customer base make the company a potential acquisition target. Voser calls her sister and recommends that she purchase Greenhornfood shares because "it would be an attractive acquisition for a larger company." Based on Voser's recommendation, her sister buys €3,000 worth of shares.

During the following two weeks the stock price of Greenhornfood continues to decline. Voser's sister is uncertain of what she should do with her position. She seeks Voser's advice. Voser recommends that her sister wait another few days before making her decision and promises to analyze the situation in the meantime.

While walking by Craw's office the following day, Voser sees a document with Greenhornfood's distinctive logo and overhears the company's name through an open office door. That evening, Voser tells her sister, "with the price decline, the stock is even more attractive." She recommends that her sister increase her position. Based on her recommendation her sister buys an additional €3,000 worth of Greenhornfood shares.

One month later, Crawfood publicly announces the acquisition of Greenhornfood Company at a 20% premium to the previous day's closing price. Following the announcement, Voser's sister boasts about Voser's excellent recommendation and timing to her broker.

Regulatory authorities initiate an investigation into suspicious trading in Greenhornfood shares and options preceding the formal announcement of the acquisition. Craw receives a letter from regulatory authorities stating that he is the subject of a formal investigation into his professional conduct surrounding the acquisition. He learns from the compliance officer that Voser is also under investigation. The compliance officer provides no details and out of respect for Voser's privacy, Craw makes no inquiries.

The situation remains unchanged and the matter is still pending with regulatory authorities several months later when Craw receives his annual Professional Conduct Statement (PCS) from CFA Institute. He reviews the text asking "In the last two years, have you been . . . the subject of . . . any investigation . . . in which your professional conduct, in either a direct or supervisory capacity, was at issue?"

59. Are Excerpts 2 and 3 of Crawfood's compliance procedures consistent with the CFA Institute Standards of Professional Conduct?

    A. Yes.

    B. No, because Excerpt 2 applies only to officers and their direct reports.

    C. No, because Excerpt 3 does not require employees to achieve public dissemination.

60. According to the CFA Institute Standards, must Voser obtain permission from her supervisor before accepting the Greenhornfood gift basket?

    A. No.

    B. Yes, because the value of the basket is higher than €50.

    C. Yes, because consent is required by the company's compliance procedures.

61. When making her initial recommendation to purchase Greenhornfood company shares, Voser *most likely* violates the Standard relating to:

   A. loyalty to employer.

   B. integrity of capital markets.

   C. diligence and reasonable basis.

62. When recommending the purchase of additional Greenhornfood company shares, Voser *least likely* violates the Standard relating to:

   A. loyalty to employer.

   B. integrity of capital markets.

   C. diligence and reasonable basis.

63. Does Craw violate any CFA Institute Standards?

   A. No.

   B. Yes, because he passes material nonpublic information to Voser.

   C. Yes, because he does not make reasonable efforts to prevent violations of applicable law.

64. According to the CFA Standards, Craw must disclose to CFA Institute the investigation into:

   A. his conduct.

   B. Voser's conduct.

   C. neither his conduct nor Voser's conduct.

SOLUTIONS FOR READING 2

1. **B is correct.** This question involves Standard III(B)—Fair Dealing. Smith disseminated a change in the stock recommendation to his clients but then received a request contrary to that recommendation from a client who probably had not yet received the recommendation. Prior to executing the order, Smith should take additional steps to ensure that the customer has received the change of recommendation. Answer A is incorrect because the client placed the order prior to receiving the recommendation and, therefore, does not have the benefit of Smith's most recent recommendation. Answer C is also incorrect; simply because the client request is contrary to the firm's recommendation does not mean a member can override a direct request by a client. After Smith contacts the client to ensure that the client has received the changed recommendation, if the client still wants to place a buy order for the shares, Smith is obligated to comply with the client's directive.

2. **C is correct.** This question involves Standard III(A)—Loyalty, Prudence, and Care and the specific topic of soft dollars or soft commissions. Answer C is the correct choice because client brokerage commissions may not be directed to pay for the investment manager's operating expenses. Answer B describes how members and candidates should determine how to use brokerage commissions—that is, if the use is in the best interests of clients and is commensurate with the value of the services provided. Answer A describes a practice that is commonly referred to as "directed brokerage." Because brokerage is an asset of the client and is used to benefit the client, not the manager, such practice does not violate a duty of loyalty to the client. Members and candidates are obligated in all situations to disclose to clients their practices in the use of client brokerage commissions.

3. **C is correct.** This question involves Standard VI(A)—Disclosure of Conflicts. The question establishes a conflict of interest in which an analyst, Jamison, is asked to write a research report on a company that is a client of the analyst's employer. In addition, two directors of the company are senior officers of Jamison's employer. Both facts establish that there are conflicts of interest that must be disclosed by Jamison in her research report. Answer B is incorrect because an analyst is not prevented from writing a report simply because of the special relationship the analyst's employer has with the company as long as that relationship is disclosed. Answer A is incorrect because whether or not Jamison expresses any opinions in the report is irrelevant to her duty to disclose a conflict of interest. Not expressing opinions does not relieve the analyst of the responsibility to disclose the special relationships between the two companies.

4. **C is correct.** This question asks about compliance procedures relating to personal investments of members and candidates. The statement in answer C clearly conflicts with the recommended procedures in the *Standards of Practice Handbook*. Employers should compare personal transactions of employees with those of clients on a regular basis regardless of the existence of a requirement by any regulatory organization. Such comparisons ensure that employees' personal trades do not conflict with their duty to their clients, and the comparisons can be conducted in a confidential manner. The statement in answer A does not conflict with the procedures in the *Handbook*. Disclosure of such policies will give full information to clients regarding potential conflicts of interest on the part

of those entrusted to manage their money. Answer B is incorrect because firms are encouraged to establish policies whereby employees clear their personal holdings and transactions with their employers.

5. B is correct. This question relates to Standard III(A)—Loyalty, Prudence, and Care and Standard III(E)—Preservation of Confidentiality. In this case, the member manages funds of a private endowment. Clients, who are, in this case, the trustees of the fund, must place some trust in members and candidates. Bronson cannot disclose confidential financial information to anyone without the permission of the fund, regardless of whether the disclosure may benefit the fund. Therefore, answer A is incorrect. Answer C is incorrect because Bronson must notify the fund and obtain the fund's permission before publicizing the information.

6. C is correct. Under Standard IV(C)—Responsibilities of Supervisors, members and candidates may delegate supervisory duties to subordinates but such delegation does not relieve members or candidates of their supervisory responsibilities. As a result, answer B is incorrect. Moreover, whether or not Miller's subordinates are subject to the Code and Standards is irrelevant to her supervisory responsibilities. Therefore, answer A is incorrect.

7. B is correct. This question relates to Standard V(A)—Diligence and Reasonable Basis. The opinion of another financial analyst is not an adequate basis for Willier's action in changing the recommendation. Answer C is thus incorrect. So is answer A because, although it is true that members and candidates must distinguish between facts and opinions in recommendations, the question does not illustrate a violation of that nature. If the opinion overheard by Willier had sparked him to conduct additional research and investigation that justified a change of opinion, then a changed recommendation would be appropriate.

8. B is correct. This question relates to Standard I(B)—Independence and Objectivity. When asked to change a recommendation on a company stock to gain business for the firm, the head of the brokerage unit must refuse in order to maintain his independence and objectivity in making recommendations. He must not yield to pressure by the firm's investment banking department. To avoid the appearance of a conflict of interest, the firm should discontinue issuing recommendations about the company. Answer A is incorrect; changing the recommendation in any manner that is contrary to the analyst's opinion violates the duty to maintain independence and objectivity. Answer C is incorrect because merely assigning a new analyst to decide whether the stock deserves a higher rating will not address the conflict of interest.

9. A is correct. Standard VII(B)—Reference to CFA Institute, the CFA Designation, and the CFA Program is the subject of this question. The reference on Albert's business card implies that there is a "CFA Level II" designation; Tye merely indicates in promotional material that he is participating in the CFA Program and has completed Levels I and II. Candidates may not imply that there is some sort of partial designation earned after passing a level of the CFA exam. Therefore, Albert has violated Standard VII(B). Candidates may communicate that they are participating in the CFA Program, however, and may state the levels that they have completed. Therefore, Tye has not violated Standard VII(B).

10. B is correct. This question relates to Standard V(B)—Communication with Clients and Prospective Clients. Scott has issued a research report stating that he expects the price of Walkton Industries stock to rise by US$8 a share "because the dividend will increase" by US$1.50 per share. He has made this statement knowing that the dividend will increase only if Congress enacts certain legislation, an uncertain prospect. By stating that the dividend will increase, Scott failed to separate fact from opinion.

    The information regarding passage of legislation is not material nonpublic information because it is conjecture, and the question does not state whether the U.S. Representative gave Scott her opinion on the passage of the legislation in confidence. She could have been offering this opinion to anyone who asked. Therefore, statement A is incorrect. It may be acceptable to base a recommendation, in part, on an expectation of future events, even though they may be uncertain. Therefore, answer C is incorrect.

11. C is correct. This question, which relates to Standard III(B)—Fair Dealing, tests the knowledge of the procedures that will assist members and candidates in treating clients fairly when making investment recommendations. The steps listed in C will all help ensure the fair treatment of clients. Answer A may have negative effects on the fair treatment of clients. The more people who know about a pending change, the greater the chance that someone will inform some clients before the information's release. The firm should establish policies that limit the number of people who are aware in advance that a recommendation is to be disseminated. Answer B, distributing recommendations to institutional clients before distributing them to individual accounts, discriminates among clients on the basis of size and class of assets and is a violation of Standard III(B).

12. B is correct. This question deals with Standard II(A)—Material Nonpublic Information. The mosaic theory states that an analyst may use material public information and nonmaterial nonpublic information in creating a larger picture than shown by any individual piece of information and the conclusions the analyst reaches become material only after the pieces are assembled. Answers A and C are accurate statements relating to the Code and Standards but do not describe the mosaic theory.

13. C is correct. This question involves Standard IV(B)—Additional Compensation Arrangements. The arrangement described in the question—whereby Jurgen would be compensated beyond the compensation provided by her firm, on the basis of an account's performance—is not a violation of the Standards as long as Jurgen discloses the arrangement in writing to her employer and obtains permission from her employer prior to entering into the arrangement. Answers A and B are incorrect; although the private compensation arrangement could conflict with the interests of other clients and lead to short-term performance pressures, members and candidates may enter into such agreements as long as they have disclosed the arrangements to their employer and obtained permission for the arrangement from their employer.

14. B is correct. This question relates to Standard III(A)—Loyalty, Prudence, and Care—specifically, a member's or candidate's responsibility for voting proxies and the use of client brokerage. According to the facts stated in the question, Farnsworth did not violate Standard III(A). Although the company president asked Farnsworth to vote the shares of the Jones Corporation profit-sharing plan a certain way, Farnsworth investigated the

issue and concluded, independently, the best way to vote. Therefore, even though his decision coincided with the wishes of the company president, Farnsworth is not in violation of his responsibility to be loyal and to provide care to his clients. In this case, the participants and the beneficiaries of the profit-sharing plan are the clients, not the company's management. Had Farnsworth not investigated the issue or had he yielded to the president's wishes and voted for a slate of directors that he had determined was not in the best interest of the company, Farnsworth would have violated his responsibilities to the beneficiaries of the plan. In addition, because the brokerage firm provides the lowest commissions and best execution for securities transactions, Farnsworth has met his obligations to the client in using this brokerage firm. It does not matter that the brokerage firm also provides research information that is not useful for the account generating the commission, because Farnsworth is not paying extra money of the client's for that information.

15. A is correct. In this question, Brown is providing investment recommendations before making inquiries about the client's financial situation, investment experience, or investment objectives. Brown is thus violating Standard III(C)—Suitability. Answers B and C provide examples of information members and candidates should discuss with their clients at the outset of the relationship, but these answers do not constitute a complete list of those factors. Answer A is the best answer.

16. C is correct. This question involves Standard I(C)—Misrepresentation. Statement 1 is a factual statement that discloses to clients and prospects accurate information about the terms of the investment instrument. Statement 2, which guarantees a specific rate of return for a mutual fund, is an opinion stated as a fact and, therefore, violates Standard I(C). If Statement 2 were rephrased to include a qualifying statement, such as "in my opinion, investors may earn. . .," it would not be in violation of the Standards.

17. A is correct. This question involves three of the Standards. Anderb, the portfolio manager, has been obtaining more favorable prices for her personal securities transactions than she gets for her clients, which is a breach of Standard III(A)—Loyalty, Prudence, and Care. In addition, she violated Standard I(D)—Misconduct by failing to adhere to company policy and by hiding her personal transactions from her firm. Anderb's supervisor, Bates, violated Standard IV(C)—Responsibilities of Supervisors; although the company had requirements for reporting personal trading, Bates failed to adequately enforce those requirements. Answer B does not represent a violation because Standard VI(B)—Priority of Transactions requires that personal trading in a security be conducted after the trading in that security of clients and the employer. The Code and Standards do not prohibit owning such investments, although firms may establish policies that limit the investment opportunities of members and candidates. Answer B does not represent a violation because the Code and Standards do not contain a prohibition against employee's using the same broker they use for their personal accounts that they also use for their client accounts. This arrangement should be disclosed to the employer so that the employer may determine whether a conflict of interest exists.

18. A is correct. This question relates to Standard I(A)—Knowledge of the Law—specifically, global application of the Code and Standards. Members and candidates who practice in multiple jurisdictions may be subject to various securities laws and regulations. If applicable law is more strict than

the requirements of the Code and Standards, members and candidates must adhere to applicable law; otherwise, members and candidates must adhere to the Code and Standards. Therefore, answer A is correct. Answer B is incorrect because members and candidates must adhere to the higher standard set by the Code and Standards if local applicable law is less strict. Answer C is incorrect because when no applicable law exists, members and candidates are required to adhere to the Code and Standards, and the Code and Standards prohibit the use of material nonpublic information.

19. B is correct. The best course of action under Standard I(B)—Independence and Objectivity is to avoid a conflict of interest whenever possible. Therefore, for Ward to pay for all his expenses is the correct answer. Answer C details a course of action in which the conflict would be disclosed, but the solution is not as appropriate as avoiding the conflict of interest. Answer A would not be the best course because it would not remove the appearance of a conflict of interest; even though the report would not be affected by the reimbursement of expenses, it could appear to be.

20. B is correct. Under Standard IV(A)—Loyalty, members and candidates may undertake independent practice that may result in compensation or other benefit in competition with their employer as long as they obtain consent from their employer. Answer C is also consistent with the Standards because the Standards allow members and candidates to make arrangements or preparations to go into competitive business as long as those arrangements do not interfere with their duty to their current employer. Answer A is not consistent with the Standards because the Standards do not include a complete prohibition against undertaking independent practice.

21. B is correct. This question involves Standard VI(A)—Disclosure of Conflicts—specifically, the holdings of an analyst's employer in company stock. Answers A and C do not describe conflicts of interest that Smith would have to disclose. Answer A describes the use of a firm's products, which would not be a required disclosure. In answer C, the relationship between the analyst and the company through a relative is so tangential that it does not create a conflict of interest necessitating disclosure.

22. C is correct. This question relates to Standard I(C)—Misrepresentation. Although Michelieu's statement about the total return of his clients' accounts on average may be technically true, it is misleading because the majority of the gain resulted from one client's large position taken against Michelieu's advice. Therefore, this statement misrepresents the investment performance the member is responsible for. He has not taken steps to present a fair, accurate, and complete presentation of performance. Answer B is thus incorrect. Answer A is incorrect because although Michelieu is not guaranteeing future results, his words are still a misrepresentation of his performance history.

23. B is correct. The best policy to prevent violation of Standard II(A)—Material Nonpublic Information is the establishment of firewalls in a firm to prevent exchange of insider information. The physical and informational barrier of a firewall between the investment banking department and the brokerage operation prevents the investment banking department from providing information to analysts on the brokerage side who may be writing recommendations on a company stock. Prohibiting recommendations of the stock of companies that are clients of the investment banking department is an alternative, but answer A states that this prohibition would be permanent, which is not the best answer. Once an

offering is complete and the material nonpublic information obtained by the investment banking department becomes public, resuming publishing recommendations on the stock is not a violation of the Code and Standards because the information of the investment banking department no longer gives the brokerage operation an advantage in writing the report. Answer C is incorrect because no exchange of information should be occurring between the investment banking department and the brokerage operation, so monitoring of such exchanges is not an effective compliance procedure for preventing the use of material nonpublic information.

24. B is correct. Under Standard III(A)—Loyalty, Prudence, and Care, members and candidates who manage a company's pension fund owe these duties to the participants and beneficiaries of the pension plan, not the management of the company or the company's shareholders.

25. B is correct. Answer B gives one of the two primary reasons listed in the *Handbook* for disclosing referral fees to clients under Standard VI(C)—Referral Fees. (The other is to allow clients and employers to evaluate the full cost of the services.) Answer A is inconsistent because Standard VI(C) does not require members or candidates to discount their fees when they receive referral fees. Answer C is inconsistent with Standard VI(C) because disclosure of referral fees, to be effective, should be made to prospective clients before entering into a formal client relationship with them.

26. B is correct. Standard VI(B)—Priority of Transactions does not limit transactions of company employees that differ from current recommendations as long as the sale does not disadvantage current clients. Thus, answer A is incorrect. Answer C is incorrect because the Standard does not require the matching of personal and client trades.

27. C is correct. Standard IV(A)—Loyalty discusses activities permissible to members and candidates when they are leaving their current employer; soliciting clients is strictly prohibited. Thus, answer A is inconsistent with the Code and Standards even with the required disclosure. Answer B is incorrect because the offer does not directly violate the Code and Standards. There may be out-of-work members and candidates who can arrange the necessary commitments without violating the Code and Standards.

28. A is correct. The question relates to Standard III(A)—Loyalty, Prudence, and Care. Carter believes the broker offers effective execution at a fee that is comparable with those of other brokers, so he is free to use the broker for all accounts. Answer B is incorrect because the accounts that prohibit soft dollar arrangements do not want to fund the purchase of research by Carter. The new trading scheme does not incur additional commissions from clients, so it would not go against the prohibitions. Answer C is incorrect because Carter should not incur unnecessary or excessive "churning" of the portfolios (excessive trading) for the purpose of meeting the brokerage commitments of soft dollar arrangements.

29. B is correct. According to Standard VII(B)—Reference to CFA Institute, the CFA Designation, and the CFA Program, CFA Program candidates do not receive their actual scores on the exam. Topic and subtopic results are grouped into three broad categories, and the exam is graded only as "pass" or "fail." Although a candidate may have achieved a topical score of "above 70 percent," she or he cannot factually state that she or he received the highest possible score because that information is not reported. Thus, answer C is incorrect. Answer A is incorrect as long as the member or candidate actually completed the exams consecutively. Standard VII(B)

does not prohibit the communication of factual information about completing the CFA Program in three consecutive years.

30. C is correct. According to Standard III(A)—Loyalty, Prudence, and Care, the CFA Program would be considered a personal or firm expense and should not be paid for with the fund's brokerage commissions. Soft dollar accounts should be used only to purchase research services that directly assist the investment manager in the investment decision-making process, not to assist the management of the firm or to further education. Thus, answer A is incorrect. Answer B is incorrect because the reasonableness of how the money is used is not an issue; the issue is that educational expense is not research.

31. A is correct. Standard I(B)—Independence and Objectivity emphasizes the need for members and candidates to maintain their independence and objectivity. Best practices dictate that firms adopt a strict policy not to accept compensation for travel arrangements. At times, however, accepting paid travel would not compromise one's independence and objectivity. Answers B and C are incorrect because the added benefits—free conference admission for additional staff members and an exclusive golf retreat for the speaker—could be viewed as inducements related to the firm's working arrangements and not solely related to the speaking engagement. Should Long wish to bring other team members or participate in the golf outing, he or his firm should be responsible for the associated fees.

32. C is correct. The guidance to Standard II(A)—Material Nonpublic Information recommends adding securities to the firm's restricted list when the firm has or may have material nonpublic information. By adding these securities to this list, Andrews would uphold this standard. Because waiting until the next day will not ensure that news of the merger is made public, answer A is incorrect. Negotiations may take much longer between the two companies, and the merger may never happen. Andrews must wait until the information is disseminated to the market before he trades on that information. Answer B is incorrect because Andrews should not disclose the information to other managers; no trading is allowed on material nonpublic information.

33. B is correct. Through placing a personal purchase order that is significantly greater than the average volume, Pietro is violating Standard IIB—Market Manipulation. He is attempting to manipulate an increase in the share price and thus bring a buyer to the negotiating table. The news of a possible merger and confirmation of the firm's earnings guidance may also have positive effects on the price of Local Bank, but Pietro's action in instructing the release of the information does not represent a violation through market manipulation. Announcements of this nature are common and practical to keep investors informed. Thus, answers A and C are incorrect.

34. C is correct. Cupp violated Standard III(D)—Performance Presentations when he deviated from the firm's stated policies solely to capture the gain from the holding being acquired. Answer A is incorrect because the firm does not claim GIPS compliance and the GIPS standards require external cash flows to be treated in a consistent manner with the firm's documented policies. Answer B is incorrect because the firm does not state that it is updating its composite policies. If such a change were to occur, all cash flows for the month would have to be reviewed to ensure their consistent treatment under the new policy.

35. A is correct. According to Standard V(C)—Record Retention, Cannan needed the permission of her employer to maintain the files at home after her employment ended. Without that permission, she should have deleted the files. All files created as part of a member's or candidate's professional activity are the property of the firm, even those created outside normal work hours. Thus, answer B is incorrect. Answer C is incorrect because the Code and Standards do not prohibit using one's personal computer to complete work for one's employer.

36. B is correct. According to Standard VII(B)—Reference to CFA Institute, the CFA Designation, and the CFA Program, Quinn cannot claim to have finished the CFA Program or be eligible for the CFA charter until he officially learns that he has passed the Level III exam. Until the results for the most recent exam are released, those who sat for the exam should continue to refer to themselves as "candidates." Thus, answer C is incorrect. Answer A is incorrect because members and candidates may discuss areas of practice in which they believe the CFA Program improved their personal skills.

37. A is correct. Hart's decision to invest in the retail fund appears directly correlated with Rodriguez's statement about the successful quarter of Mega Retail and thus violates Standard II(A)—Material Nonpublic Information. Rodriguez's information would be considered material because it would influence the share price of Mega Retail and probably influence the price of the entire exchange-traded retail fund. Thus, answer B is incorrect. Answer C is also incorrect because Rodriguez shared information that was both material and nonpublic. Company officers regularly have such knowledge about their firms, which is not a violation. The sharing of such information, however, even in a conversation between friends, does violate Standard II(A).

38. C is correct. Standard VII(A)—Conduct as Members and Candidates in the CFA Program prohibits providing information to candidates or the public that is considered confidential to the CFA Program. In revealing that questions related to the analysis of inventories and analysis of taxes were on the exam, Park has violated this standard. Answer B is incorrect because the guidance for the standard explicitly acknowledges that members and candidates are allowed to offer their opinions about the CFA Program. Answer A is incorrect because candidates are not prohibited from using outside resources.

39. B is correct. Paper has violated Standard III(D)—Performance Presentation by not disclosing that he was part of a team of managers that achieved the results shown. If he had also included the return of the portion he directly managed, he would not have violated the standard. Thus, answer A is incorrect. Answer C is incorrect because Paper received written permission from his prior employer to include the results.

40. A is correct. Townsend has not provided any information about her clients to the leaders or managers of the golf program; thus, she has not violated Standard III(E)—Preservation of Confidentiality. Providing contact information about her clients for a direct-mail solicitation would have been a violation. Answer B is incorrect because the notice in the newsletter does not violate Standard III(E). Answer C is incorrect because the golf program's fund-raising campaign had already begun, so discussing the opportunity to donate was appropriate.

41. C is correct. Boswin, as an employee, developed the model on behalf of Greenfield. Therefore, Greenfield, not Boswin, is the owner of the model. Acertado violates Standard IV(A) Duties to Employers: Loyalty when he downloads the model without proper written permission from Greenfield Financial. Acertado is misappropriating employer assets.

42. C is correct. Acertado is least likely to violate Standard II(A) regarding Material Nonpublic Information when using the model at Smith and Garner. Acertado likely violated Standard IV(A), Loyalty, when he used the model. The Standard prohibits members who leave an employer from taking records or files—such as the model—without the written permission of the employer. Acertado also likely violated Standard I(C)—Misrepresentation when he failed to correct his supervisor's impression that the investment idea and the model were Acertado's creation.

43. C is correct. Acertado violates Standard II(A)—Material Nonpublic Information. He has a reasonable belief that the conversation that he overhears is from a reliable source and would have a material impact on security prices. According to the CFA Standards, he must not act, nor cause others to act on the information. Acertado does not violate the Standard relating to Diligence and Reasonable Basis because he bases the recommendation on a reliable model and checks his inputs prior to making the recommendation.

44. A is correct. Acertado least likely violates Standard III(C), which relates to suitability during his phone conversation with Boswin. According to the Standard, members in an advisory relationship with a client must determine an investment's suitability within the context of the client's portfolio. The Standard also requires that members make reasonable inquiries into a client or prospective client's investment experience; risk and return objectives; and financial constraints prior to making investment recommendations. Boswin is neither a client nor a prospective client, thus Acertado is not bound by the Standard of Suitability during their conversation. Acertado is, however, in jeopardy of violating other Standards—specifically those relating to Integrity of Capital Markets and Preservation of Confidentiality by revealing material nonpublic information about a Smith & Garner client. According to Standard II(A), Acertado, who is in possession of material nonpublic information, must not act, nor cause others to act on the information. According to Standard III(E), members must keep information about current, former, and prospective clients confidential.

45. A is correct. Boswin uses her usual process in researching Country Industries. She is not in possession of material nonpublic information and she maintains her objectivity. Her use of the model provides a reasonable basis for the decision not to pursue additional research or make an investment recommendation regarding Country Industries.

46. A is correct. Blogs and company websites are in the public domain and thus do not constitute inside information. Acertado's use of blog sites to supplement his current research process is acceptable.

47. B is correct. The CFA logo is a certification mark intended to identify individual charterholders and may not be incorporated into a company's name or logo. Standard VII(B) indicates that the use of the CFA logo is appropriate on the business card or letterhead of an individual CFA charterholder.

48. A is correct. Grohl exercised diligence, independence, and thoroughness in analyzing the company and its competitors. Brecksen provided his research reports for Grohl's use and using the reports as a guide was appropriate. Standard V(A) requires that members distinguish between fact and opinion in communicating investment recommendations to clients. The Standard does not apply to investment recommendations communicated to supervisors or internal investment committees.

49. A is correct. Brecksen does not consider the multi-factor analysis a critical component of the analysis or the resulting investment recommendation and thus, under Standards V(A) and (C), is not required to maintain a record of the analysis within the completed report.

Apfelbaum uses traditional "top-down" fundamental analysis in the investment process. The report followed the traditional format of previous reports on the same company. It contained a complete fundamental analysis and recommendation—indicating diligence and reasonable basis. The report also contained a multi-factor analysis—which is a quantitative analysis tool. If quantitative analysis were the basis of the investment recommendation, it would constitute a change in the general investment principles used by the firm. According to Standard V(B)—Communications with Clients and Prospective Clients, Brecksen and Grohl would be required to promptly disclose those changes to clients and prospective clients.

50. A is correct. Removing the multi-factor analysis from the research report does not constitute a violation. Grohl diligently prepared the internal document according to the firm's traditional format with a complete fundamental analysis and recommendation—indicating diligence and a reasonable basis for his recommendation. It would be wise for Grohl to retain records of the multi-factor analysis but he need not retain the analysis in the research report to comply with Standards V(A)—Diligence and Reasonable Basis or V(C)—Record Retention.

51. A is correct. According to Standard V(A)—Diligence and Reasonable Basis, research report conclusions or recommendations may represent the consensus of a group and not necessarily the views of the individual members listed. If the member believes that the consensus opinion has a reasonable basis, then he need not dissociate from the report.

52. B is correct. Zardt violated the Standard relating to Performance Presentation because he did not verify the accuracy of the return information before its distribution. According to Standard III(D), analysts may promote the success or accuracy of their recommendations, but they must make reasonable efforts to ensure that the information is fair, accurate, and complete. In addition to providing attribution, Zardt should take steps to ensure the accuracy of the data prior to distributing the material.

53. B is correct. Telline has a duty to preserve the confidentiality of current, former, and prospective clients. Telline violates Standard III(E)—Preservation of Confidentiality when he reveals that the firm managed the assets of Leighton Family Trust.

54. A is correct. Brown conducts an independent and careful analysis of the plans' benefits for shareholders as well as the takeover offer. In doing so she puts the client's interests ahead of the firm's. Brown's actions are consistent with Standard III(A)—Loyalty, Prudence, and Care; Standard V(A)—Diligence and Reasonable Basis; and Standard III(B)—Fair Dealing.

55. B is correct. Telline is not likely to receive appropriate guidance on developing or revising investment policy statements from the Standard relating to Fair Dealing. Standard III(B) provides members with guidance on treating clients fairly when making investment recommendations, providing investment analysis, or taking investment action. Telline could obtain guidance from the Standards relating to Loyalty, Prudence, and Care and Suitability. Both Standard III(A) and (C) provide guidance for members in determining client objectives and the suitability of investments.

56. A is correct. Telline determines that the other client does not have the cash available in his account and selling existing holdings does not make sense. Moreover, Telline is careful to consider the investment's suitability for Caper's account. Telline's actions are consistent with CFA Institute Standards III(A)—Loyalty, Prudence, and Care and III(B)—Fair Dealing.

57. B is correct. The firm violates Standard III(B)—Fair Dealing. Under Aiklin's policy, some clients for whom an IPO is suitable may not receive their pro-rata share of the issue. CFA Standards recommend that firms allocate IPOs on a pro-rata basis to clients, not to portfolio managers.

58. C is correct. Telline violates Standard III(B)—Fair Dealing by over-allocating shares to Caper. Telline carefully reviews both the proposed IPO and his client accounts to determine suitability. He fails to allocate the IPO shares on a pro-rata basis to all clients for whom the investment is suitable.

59. B is correct. Excerpt 2 is inconsistent with CFA Standards because it addresses only officers and only their direct reports, that is, employees whom they directly supervise. Standard IV (C) states that "any investment professionals who have employees subject to their control or influence" exercise supervisory responsibility. According to *The Standards of Practice Handbook*, "members and candidates who supervise large numbers of employees cannot personally evaluate the conduct of their employees on a continuing basis. Although these members . . . may delegate supervisory duties, such delegation does not relieve them of their supervisory responsibility." Excerpt 3 is consistent with CFA Standards. It is based on a quote from the *Standards of Practice Handbook* stating that "if a member or candidate determines that information is material, the member . . . should make reasonable efforts to achieve public dissemination." Members are not required to achieve public dissemination and those bound by a duty of loyalty or a duty to preserve confidentiality would refrain from doing so because it would breach their duty.

60. A is correct. According to Standard I(B)—Independence and Objectivity, members must use reasonable care and judgment to achieve and maintain independence and objectivity in their professional activities. Although it was sent to Voser's office, the gift basket is a private gift from Voser's sister and not likely to affect Voser's professional activities. According to Excerpt 4 of the Crawfood compliance manual and Standard IV(B)— Additional Compensation Arrangements, employees must obtain permission from their employer before accepting gifts, compensation, or other benefits that compete with, or might create a conflict of interest with, the employer's interests. The gift basket does not create a conflict or compete with the employer's interests.

61. A is correct. Voser most likely violated the Standard relating to loyalty to employer, Standard IV(A). While Voser used public information to develop the recommendation to purchase Greenhornfood shares, the company compliance guide states that she should not trade or cause others to trade

in securities of companies that may be potential takeover targets. Voser's recommendation caused her sister to trade in Greenhornfood, violating the company's compliance policies, and possibly harming her employer in its attempt to acquire Greenhornfood.

By advising others to invest in a food retailer that she considered an attractive acquisition target, Voser deprived her employer of the advantage of her skills and abilities and may have caused harm to her employer. Voser could have recommended Greenhornfood to Craw rather than her sister as an acquisition target. Although the sister's trade in Greenhornfood was small, a large trade might have moved the stock price and caused harm to Crawfood in terms of additional cost.

62. C is correct. Voser least likely violated the Standard relating to diligence and reasonable basis. Voser initially applied the mosaic theory and had a reasonable basis for the trade as required by Standard V(A). Eventually, she came into possession of material nonpublic information (corporate logo on a document, overheard conversation). According to Standard II(A), once in possession of material nonpublic information, she is prohibited from acting or causing others to act. Voser also violated her duty of loyalty to her employer, Standard IV(A), by encouraging others to trade in Greenhornfood and possibly harming Crawfood's attempts to acquire the smaller company at an attractive price.

63. C is correct. Craw did not adequately fulfill his responsibilities as a supervisor. While he may have delegated supervisory duties to Voser's immediate supervisor, such delegation does not relieve him of his supervisory responsibility. As stated in the *Standards of Practice Handbook*, members and candidates with supervisory responsibility also must understand what constitutes an adequate compliance system for their firms and make reasonable efforts to see that appropriate compliance procedures are established, documented, communicated to covered personnel, and followed. "Adequate" procedures are those designed to meet industry standards, regulatory requirements, the requirements of the Code and Standards, and the circumstances of the firm. Once compliance procedures are established, the supervisor must also make reasonable efforts to ensure that the procedures are monitored and enforced. According to Standard IV(C)—Responsibilities of Supervisors, adequate compliance procedures require that once a violation is discovered, Craw conduct a thorough investigation to determine the scope of wrongdoing.

64. A is correct. As stated on page ix of the *Standards of Practice Handbook*, "Members and candidates must self disclose on the annual Professional Conduct Statement all matters that question their professional conduct, such as involvement in civil litigation, a criminal investigation, or being the subject of a written complaint." Standard VII(A)—Conduct as Members and Candidates in the CFA Program prohibits conduct that compromises the reputation of the CFA designation including misrepresenting information on the Professional Conduct Statement. Members are encouraged but not required to report violations of others. At a minimum, Craw should remind Voser of her duty to report the investigation.

CFA INSTITUTE SOFT DOLLAR STANDARDS

LEARNING OUTCOMES

The candidate should be able to:	Mastery
a. define soft-dollar arrangements and state the general principles of the Soft Dollar Standards;	☐
b. critique company soft-dollar practices and policies;	☐
c. determine whether a product or service qualifies as "permissible research" that can be purchased with client brokerage.	☐

INTRODUCTION 1

CFA Institute Soft Dollar Standards provide guidance to investment professionals worldwide through the articulation of high ethical standards for CFA Institute members dealing with "soft dollar" issues. CFA Institute Soft Dollar Standards are consistent with and complement the existing CFA Institute Standards of Professional Conduct that all CFA Institute members and candidates in the CFA Program are required to follow.

The purposes of the Standards are to define "soft dollars," identify what is "allowable" research, establish standards for soft dollar use, create model disclosure guidelines, and provide guidance for client-directed brokerage arrangements.

The Soft Dollar Standards are *voluntary* standards for members. If a CFA Institute member claims compliance with the Standards, then certain of these Standards are mandatory (i.e., they *must* be followed to claim compliance) and

185

others are recommended (i.e., they *should* be followed). CFA Institute strongly encourages members to adopt the required and recommended Standards. If the Soft Dollar Standards are adopted, compliance will not supplant the responsibility to comply with applicable law.[1] CFA Institute members should comply at all times with the relevant laws of the countries in which they do business. In situations in which these Standards impose a higher degree of responsibility or disclosure than, but do not conflict with, local law, the member is held to the mandatory provisions of these Standards.

2 BACKGROUND

In 1975, the U.S. Congress created a "safe harbor" under Section 28(e) of the Securities and Exchange Act of 1934 to protect investment managers from claims that they had breached their fiduciary duties by using their client commissions to pay a higher commission to acquire investment research than they might have paid for "execution" services. According to Securities and Exchange Commission (SEC) Staff, the protection of Section 28(e) is available only for securities transactions conducted on an agency basis.[2] Since that time, the soft dollar area has undergone considerable expansion, both in terms of actual usage and the types of products and services for which safe harbor protection is claimed. The complexity of these practices, including technologically sophisticated research tools and the existence of "mixed-use" products, has resulted in a fair amount of legitimate confusion surrounding the appropriate use of soft dollars.

CFA Institute seeks to provide ethical standards for CFA Institute members and those in the industry that engage in soft dollar practices and also emphasizes the paramount duty of the investment manager, as a fiduciary, to place the interests of clients before those of the investment manager. In particular, the Soft Dollar Standards focus on six key areas:

▶ Definitions—to enable all parties dealing with soft dollar practices to have a common understanding of all of the different aspects of soft dollars.

▶ Research—to give clear guidance to investment managers on what products and services are appropriate for a manager to purchase with client brokerage.

▶ Mixed-Use Products—to clarify the manager's duty to clearly justify the use of client brokerage to pay a portion of a mixed-use product.

▶ Disclosure—to obligate investment managers to clearly disclose their soft dollar practices and give detailed information to each client when requested.

---

[1] For example, in the United States, the Securities Exchange Act of 1934, Investment Company Act of 1940, and Investment Advisers Act of 1940 all address the use of client commissions in soft dollar arrangements. The U.S. Department of Labor also provides regulations regarding directed brokerage practices concerning ERISA-covered pension plans.

[2] According to the SEC staff, securities transactions conducted on a principal basis cannot claim Section 28(e) "safe harbor" protection. Both principal transactions and those agency transactions unable to qualify for "safe harbor" protection are not necessarily illegal but are evaluated based on the existence of full disclosure, informed client consent, and other fundamental fiduciary principles, including placing the client's interests first.

- ▶ Record Keeping—to ensure that the client can 1) receive assurances that what the investment manager is doing with the client's brokerage can be supported in an "audit," and 2) receive important information on request.
- ▶ Client-Directed Brokerage—to clarify the manager's role and fiduciary responsibilities with respect to clients.

OVERVIEW　　　　　　　　3

CFA Institute Soft Dollar Standards focus on the member's obligations to its clients. Although the Standards primarily focus on the obligations of the member as investment manager, they may be applicable to other parties involved in soft dollar practices, including brokers, plan sponsors, and trustees. Each of these parties, however, has its own set of obligations that should be considered prior to participating in any soft dollar arrangement.

CFA Institute Soft Dollar Standards are ethical principles intended to ensure:

- ▶ full and fair disclosure of an investment manager's use of a client's brokerage[3];
- ▶ consistent presentation of information so that the client, broker, and other applicable parties can clearly understand an investment manager's brokerage practices;
- ▶ uniform disclosure and record keeping to enable an investment manager's client to have a clear understanding of how the investment manager is using the client's brokerage; and
- ▶ high standards of ethical practices within the investment industry.

No finite set of standards can cover all potential situations or anticipated future developments concerning the types of investment research available to investment managers. However, meeting the objective of full and fair disclosure and ensuring that the "client comes first" obligates an investment manager to disclose fully and clearly to its client the investment manager's practice when addressing any potential conflict concerning the payment methods for investment research.

CFA Institute Soft Dollar Standards are based on the following set of fundamental principles that an investment manager should consider when attempting to comply:

- ▶ an investment manager is a fiduciary and, as such, must disclose all relevant aspects concerning any benefit the manager receives through a client's brokerage;
- ▶ proprietary research and third-party research are to be treated the same in evaluating soft dollar arrangements, because the research that an investment manager receives from each is paid for with client brokerage;
- ▶ research should be purchased with client brokerage only if the primary use of the research, whether a product or a service, directly assists the investment manager in its investment decision-making process and not in the management of the investment firm; and
- ▶ when in doubt, the research should be paid for with investment manager assets, not client brokerage.

---

[3] The term "Brokerage" is described in the definitions section of the Standards.

4   COMPARISON WITH CURRENT PRACTICES

CFA Institute Soft Dollar Standards seek to clarify certain areas of brokerage practices that have been a source of confusion for CFA Institute members. By emphasizing the basic fiduciary responsibilities of CFA Institute members with respect to their client's assets, the Soft Dollar Standards are intended to illuminate the line between permissible and impermissible uses of client brokerage. In this respect, the Standards do not create "new law" but address well-established principles applicable to the investment manager–client relationship.

In other respects, a reiteration of the current "soft dollar" practices would fail to adequately address the issues raised by the complexity of current brokerage practices faced by CFA Institute members. The Soft Dollar Standards, therefore, depart from certain well-established practices in the soft dollar area and address practices beyond those that currently claim Section 28(e) safe harbor protection.

The Soft Dollar Standards are not to be read as in any way changing the scope of activities that the SEC determines to fall within the safe harbor. Instead they are separate, ethical standards applicable to a variety of practices implicated in Soft Dollar Arrangements. Thus, these Standards will impose higher standards of conduct in certain areas on CFA Institute members that voluntarily elect to comply with the Standards, as follows:

1. **Definition of Soft Dollar Arrangements**

    a. *Proprietary, in addition to third-party, research.*

    Traditionally, soft dollar arrangements are understood to address those products or services provided to the investment manager by someone other than the executing broker, products or services that are commonly known as "third-party" research. Such an approach is deficient in light of the range of products and services provided by both third-party research providers and "in-house" research departments of brokerage firms. Thus, any meaningful Standards must also recognize the importance of research provided by the executing broker, commonly known as "proprietary" or "in-house" research.

    For purposes of the Soft Dollar Standards, "soft dollar arrangements" include proprietary, as well as third-party, research arrangements and seek to treat both categories the same. Although these Standards do *not* suggest an "unbundling" of proprietary research, they do require the investment manager to provide certain basic information regarding the types of research obtained with client brokerage through proprietary research arrangements. Moreover, these Standards should not be read to require research obtained either through third-party or proprietary arrangements to be attributed on an account-by-account basis or otherwise to require a "tracing" of products or services.

    b. *Principal, in addition to agency, trades.*

    Traditionally, the term "soft dollars" refers to commissions generated by trades conducted on an agency basis.[4] However, such an approach fails to recognize that research may be obtained through the use of "spreads" or "discounts" generated by trades conducted on a principal basis. For the purposes of the Soft Dollar Standards, soft dollar arrangements include transactions conducted on an agency *or* principal basis.

---

[4] As noted above, the "safe harbor" provided by Section 28(e) of the Securities Exchange Act of 1934, as interpreted by the SEC staff, applies only to those transactions conducted on an agency, not principal, basis.

2. Definition of Research

Traditionally, "allowable" research in the soft dollar context is evaluated by whether it provides lawful and appropriate assistance to an investment manager in the investment decision-making process. This approach, however, leaves CFA Institute members with inadequate guidance. Consequently, the Soft Dollar Standards embrace a definition of research that requires the primary use of the soft dollar product or service to directly assist the investment manager in its investment decision-making process and not in the management of the investment firm.

In many cases, this determination may not lend itself to absolute precision, but an investment manager must use its best judgment as a fiduciary to justify the use of client brokerage to pay for a product or service. The Standards suggest the use of a three-tiered analysis to aid CFA Institute members in determining whether a product or service is research. Such an approach is intended to provide needed guidance for CFA Institute members in determining when it is appropriate to use client brokerage to purchase a product or service.

3. Enhanced Disclosure

Disclosure of a CFA Institute member's brokerage practices will provide the member's client with a means of evaluating the member's soft dollar practices and how client brokerage is used. Under the Soft Dollar Standards, the CFA Institute member must disclose to its clients certain information, the majority of which the member is already required under current law to disclose, or to maintain, in order to meet federal disclosure requirements. Moreover, although the Soft Dollar Standards require the CFA Institute member to disclose the *availability* of additional information, this information does not actually have to be provided, unless it is specifically requested by the client.

4. Compliance Statement

Finally, the Soft Dollar Standards contemplate the use of a voluntary statement of compliance. Only a claim of compliance with these Standards requires an investment manager to comply with all of the mandatory provisions of these Standards and only as to the client brokerage that its compliance statement relates. Thus, an investment manager that claims compliance with the Soft Dollar Standards must provide the client with a statement that any brokerage arrangement with respect to *that* client's account comports with the mandatory provisions of these Standards. Such a compliance statement will help to ensure the continued integrity of the Standards and provide clients with additional assurance with respect to how their brokerage is used by their investment manager.

DEFINITIONS   5

For purposes of the CFA Institute Soft Dollar Standards, the following terms apply:

Agency Trade refers to a transaction involving the payment of a commission.

Best Execution refers to executing Client transactions so that the Client's total cost is the most favorable under the particular circumstances at that time.

Broker refers to any person or entity that provides securities execution services.

Brokerage refers to the amount on any trade retained by a Broker to be used directly or indirectly as payment for execution services and, when applicable, Research supplied to the Investment Manager or its Client in connection with Soft Dollar Arrangements or for benefits provided to the Client in Client-Directed Brokerage Arrangements. For these purposes, trades may be conducted on an agency *or* principal basis.

Brokerage Arrangement refers to an arrangement whereby a Broker provides services or products that are in addition to execution. Brokerage Arrangements include Investment Manager-Directed and Client-Directed Brokerage Arrangements.

Brokerage and Research Services refers to services and/or products provided by a Broker to an Investment Manager through a Brokerage Arrangement.

Client refers to the entity, including a natural person, investment fund, or separate account, designated to receive the benefits, including income, from the Brokerage generated through Securities Transactions. A Client may be represented by a trustee or other Fiduciary, who may or may not have Investment Discretion.

Client-Directed Brokerage Arrangement refers to an arrangement whereby a Client directs that trades for its account be executed through a specific Broker in exchange for which the Client receives a benefit in addition to execution services. Client-Directed Brokerage Arrangements include rebates, commission banking, and commission recapture programs through which the Broker provides the Client with cash or services or pays certain obligations of the Client. A Client may also direct the use of limited lists of brokers—not for the purpose of reducing Brokerage costs but to effect various other goals (e.g., increased diversity by using minority-owned brokers) or geographical concentration.

Commission refers to the amount paid to the Broker in addition to the price of the security and applicable regulatory fees on an Agency Trade.

Fiduciary refers to any entity, or a natural person, including a CFA Institute member, that has discretionary authority or responsibility for the management of a Client's assets or other relationships of special trust.

Investment Decision-Making Process refers to the quantitative and qualitative processes and related tools used by the Investment Manager in rendering investment advice to its Clients, including financial analysis, trading and risk analysis, securities selection, broker selection, asset allocation, and suitability analysis.

Investment Discretion refers to the sole or shared authority (whether or not exercised) to determine what securities or other assets to purchase or sell on behalf of a Client.

Investment Manager refers to any entity, or a natural person, including a CFA Institute member, that serves in the capacity of asset manager to a Client. The Investment Manager may have sole, shared, or no Investment Discretion over an account.

Investment Manager-Directed Brokerage Arrangement refers to Proprietary and Third-Party Research Arrangements.

Member refers to any individual who is required to comply with the CFA Institute Code of Ethics and Standards of Professional Conduct in accordance with the CFA Institute Bylaws.

Mixed-Use refers to services and/or products, provided to an Investment Manager by a Broker through a Brokerage Arrangement, that have the capacity to be used for both the Investment Decision-Making Process *and* management of the investment firm.

Principal Trade refers to a transaction involving a "discount" or a "spread."

Proprietary Research Arrangement refers to an arrangement whereby the Investment Manager directs a Broker to effect Securities Transactions for Client accounts in exchange for which the Investment Manager receives Research from, and/or access to, the "in-house" staffs of the brokerage firms.

Provided by a Broker refers to 1) in Proprietary Research Arrangements, Research developed by the Broker and 2) in Third-Party Research Arrangements, Research for which the obligation to pay is between the Broker and Third-Party Research Provider, not between the Investment Manager and Third-Party Research Provider.

Research refers to services and/or products provided by a Broker, the primary use of which must directly assist the Investment Manager in its Investment Decision-Making Process and not in the management of the investment firm.

Section 28(e) Safe Harbor refers to the "safe harbor" set forth in Section 28(e) of the U.S. Securities Exchange Act of 1934, which provides that an Investment Manager that has Investment Discretion over a Client account is not in breach of its fiduciary duty when paying more than the lowest Commission rate available if it determines in good faith that the rate paid is commensurate with the value of Brokerage and Research Services provided by the Broker.

Securities Transactions refers to any transactions involving a Broker, whether conducted on an agency basis or principal basis.

Soft Dollar Arrangement refers to an arrangement whereby the Investment Manager directs transactions to a Broker, in exchange for which the Broker provides Brokerage and Research Services to the Investment Manager. Soft Dollar Arrangements include Proprietary and Third-Party Research Arrangements but do *not* include Client-Directed Brokerage Arrangements. Soft Dollar Arrangements are sometimes referred to herein as Investment Manager-Directed Brokerage Arrangements, where applicable.

Third-Party Research Arrangement refers to an arrangement whereby the Investment Manager directs a Broker to effect Securities Transactions for Client accounts in exchange for which the Investment Manager receives Research provided by the Broker, which has been generated by an entity *other than* the executing Broker.

CFA INSTITUTE SOFT DOLLAR STANDARDS 6

I. General

Principles

A. These Soft Dollar Standards apply to all CFA Institute Members' Proprietary and Third-Party Research Arrangements, with or without Commissions, and recognize two fundamental principles:

1. Brokerage is the property of the Client.

2. The Investment Manager has an ongoing duty to ensure the quality of transactions effected on behalf of its Client, including:

   a. seeking to obtain Best Execution;

   b. minimizing transaction costs; and

   c. using Client Brokerage to benefit Clients.

Required

B. An Investment Manager in Soft Dollar Arrangements must always act for the benefit of its Clients and place Clients' interests before its own.

C. An Investment Manager may not allocate a Client's Brokerage based on the amount of Client referrals the Investment Manager receives from a Broker.

   Clarification: With respect to mutual funds, the Investment Manager's Client is the fund. However, in this context, the fund's board, not the fund, establishes the policies with respect to the use of certain brokers.

II. Relationships with Clients

Required

A. The Investment Manager must disclose to the Client that it may engage in Soft Dollar Arrangements prior to engaging in such Arrangements involving that Client's account.

Recommended

B. The Investment Manager should assure that, over time, all Clients receive the benefits of Research purchased with Client Brokerage.

   1. *Agency Trades.* While it is permissible for the Investment Manager to use a Client's Brokerage derived from Agency Trades to obtain Research that may not directly benefit that particular Client at that particular time, the Investment Manager should endeavor to ensure that, over a reasonable period of time, the Client receives the benefit of Research purchased with other Clients' Brokerage.

   2. *Principal Trades.* The Investment Manager should determine if the particular Principal Trade is subject to certain fiduciary requirements (e.g., ERISA, Investment Company Act of 1940) which require that Client Brokerage derived from Principal Trades must benefit the Client account generating the Brokerage. If such requirements do not apply, it is permissible to use Client Brokerage derived from Principal Trades to benefit Client accounts other than the account generating the Brokerage if the Investment Manager discloses this practice and obtains prior consent from the Client.

   Clarification: Certain fiduciary statutes require that brokerage derived from a Principal Trade must directly benefit the Client account generating the Trade. In such situations, even consent by the Client will not waive this legal requirement. Compliance with the Soft Dollar Standards should not be read to, in any way, absolve one's responsibilities to comply fully with the applicable law regarding Principal Trades.

III. Selection of Brokers

Principle

A. Selecting Brokers to execute Clients' Securities Transactions is a key component of the Investment Manager's ability to add value to its Client portfolios. The failure to obtain Best Execution may result in impaired performance for the Client.

Required

B. In selecting Brokers, the Investment Manager must consider the capabilities of the Broker to provide Best Execution.

Recommended

C. In evaluating the Broker's capability to provide Best Execution, the Investment Manager should consider the Broker's financial responsibility, the Broker's responsiveness to the Investment Manager, the Commission rate or spread involved, and the range of services offered by the Broker.
Clarification: These criteria are relevant components to the Broker's ability to obtain the most favorable total cost under the particular circumstances at that time.

IV. Evaluation of Research

Required

A. In determining whether to use Client Brokerage to pay for Research, the Investment Manager must use the following criteria:

1. Whether the Research under consideration meets the definition of Research contained in these Standards.

2. Whether the Research benefits the Investment Manager's Client(s).

3. Whether the Investment Manager is able to document the basis for the determinations.

4. Whether under certain fiduciary regulations (e.g., ERISA, the Investment Company Act of 1940) for Principal Trades, the Research directly benefits the Client account generating the trade. If the Principal Trades are not subject to such regulations, the Research may benefit Client accounts other than those generating the trade if the Investment Manager has made disclosure and obtained prior Client consent.

B. The inability to decide and document that the Research meets the above criteria requires that the Investment Manager *not* pay for such Research with Client Brokerage.

C. In determining the portion of Mixed-Use Research to be paid with Client Brokerage, the Investment Manager must:

1. Be able to make a reasonable, justifiable, and documentable allocation of the cost of the Research according to its expected usage.

2. Pay with Client Brokerage only the portion of the Research that is actually used by the Investment Manager in the Investment Decision-Making Process.

3. Reevaluate the Mixed-Use Research allocation at least annually.

V. Client-Directed Brokerage

Principle

A. Because Brokerage is an asset of the Client, not the Investment Manager, the practice of Client-Directed Brokerage does not violate any investment manager duty per se.

B. In a Client-Directed Brokerage Arrangement:

Required

    1. The Investment Manager must not use Brokerage from another Client account to pay for a product or service purchased under the Client-Directed Brokerage Arrangement.

Recommended

    2. The Investment Manager should disclose to the Client:

        a. the Investment Manager's duty to continue to seek to obtain Best Execution, and

        b. that arrangements that require the Investment Manager to commit a certain percentage of Brokerage may affect the Investment Manager's ability to i) seek to obtain Best Execution and ii) obtain adequate Research.

    3. The Investment Manager should attempt to structure the Client-Directed Brokerage Arrangement in a manner that comports with Appendix 3A to the Soft Dollar Standards.

VI. Disclosure

In addition to disclosure required elsewhere in the Soft Dollar Standards:

Required

A. An Investment Manager must clearly disclose, with specificity and in "plain language," its policies with respect to all Soft Dollar Arrangements, including:

    1. *To Clients and potential Clients.* An Investment Manager must disclose whether it may use the Research to benefit Clients other than those whose trades generated the Brokerage. This disclosure must address whether the trades generating the Brokerage involved transactions conducted on a principal basis.

    2. *To Clients.* An Investment Manager must disclose i) the types of Research received through Proprietary or Third-Party Research Arrangements; ii) the extent of use; and iii) whether any affiliated Broker is involved.

    Clarification: Description of the types and use of Research should be appropriate to the type of Research Arrangement involved. The disclosures required or recommended in the Soft Dollar Standards do not contemplate an "unbundling" of Proprietary Research Arrangements. Instead, the description of Research should, in the judgment of the Investment Manager, provide Clients with the ability to understand the type of Research involved *in the degree of detail* appropriate to the source of the Research.

B. To claim compliance with these Standards for any Client account, an Investment Manager must provide the Client with a statement that any Soft Dollar Arrangements with respect to the particular Client account comport with the CFA Institute Soft Dollar Standards. This statement must be provided at least annually.

Clarification: This statement is required only if the Investment Manager is claiming compliance with the Soft Dollar Standards. If applicable, the statement is to be provided to the individual Client to which the claim is being made.

C. An Investment Manager must prominently disclose in writing to its Client that additional information in accordance with the CFA Institute Soft Dollar Standards concerning the Investment Manager's Soft Dollar Arrangements is available on request. Such additional information should include the following on at least an annual basis.

Clarification: Although certain additional information is suggested, the Soft Dollar Standards are intended to preserve the ability of the Client and Investment Manager to determine what other information may be relevant in light of particular Client needs or types of accounts.

   1. *On a firmwide basis.* A description of the products and services that were received from Brokers pursuant to a Soft Dollar Arrangement, regardless of whether the product or service derives from Proprietary or Third-Party Research Arrangements, detailed by Broker.

   2. *For a specific Client account:*

      a. the total amount of Commissions generated for that Client through a Soft Dollar Arrangement, detailed by Broker; and

      b. the total amount of Brokerage directed by that Client through Directed Brokerage Arrangements.

Clarification: The disclosure required in this section is intended to provide the requesting Client with certain basic items of information: a description of what the entire firm obtained through Soft Dollar Arrangements, the identity of brokers providing those products and services, the total amount of Directed Brokerage attributable to the Client, and the total amount of Commissions generated for the requesting Client's account.

   3. The aggregate percentage of the Investment Manager's Brokerage derived from Client-Directed Brokerage Arrangements and the amount of that Client's Directed Brokerage, as a percentage of that aggregate.

      a. The Investment Manager is not obligated to report amounts of Client-Directed Brokerage that constitute less than 10 percent of the Manager's aggregate amount of Client-Directed Brokerage.

Recommended

When requested by a Client:

D. The Investment Manager should provide a description of the product or service obtained through Brokerage generated from the Client's account.

E. The Investment Manager should provide the aggregate dollar amount of Brokerage paid from all accounts over which the Manager has Investment Discretion.

VII. Record Keeping

Required

The Investment Manager must maintain, when applicable, all records that:

A. are required by applicable law;

B. are necessary to supply Clients on a timely basis with the information required by Soft Dollar Standard VI;

C. document arrangements, oral or written, obligating the Investment Manager to generate a specific amount of Brokerage;

D. document arrangements with Clients pertaining to Soft Dollar or Client-Directed Brokerage Arrangements;

E. document any agreements with Brokers pertaining to Soft Dollar Arrangements;

F. document transactions with Brokers involving Soft Dollar Arrangements, including 1) a list of Proprietary or Third-Party Research providers and 2) a description of the service or product obtained from the provider;

G. document the bases of allocation in determining to use Client Brokerage to pay for any portion of a Mixed-Use service or product;

H. indicate how the services and products obtained through Soft Dollar Arrangements directly assist the Investment Manager in the Investment Decision-Making Process;

I. show compliance with the CFA Institute Soft Dollar Standards, including the identity of the Investment Manager personnel responsible for determining such compliance;

J. copies of all Client disclosures and authorizations.

APPENDIX 3A—RECOMMENDED PRACTICES FOR CLIENT-DIRECTED BROKERAGE ARRANGEMENTS

In Client-Directed Brokerage Arrangements:

A. When directed by a Fiduciary, the Investment Manager should receive written assurance from the Fiduciary that the Client-Directed Brokerage Arrangement will solely benefit the Client's account.

B. The Investment Manager should attempt to structure Client-Directed Brokerage Arrangements so that:

   1. they do not require the commitment of a certain portion of Brokerage to a single Broker, and

   2. Commissions are negotiated and seeking to obtain Best Execution is still relevant.

C. The Investment Manager should request from its Client in any Client-Directed Brokerage Arrangement written instructions that:

   1. restate the Investment Manager's continuing responsibility for seeking to obtain Best Execution,

   2. list the eligible Brokers,

3. specify the approximate target percentage or dollar amount of transactions to be directed, and

4. state procedures for monitoring the Arrangements.

D. The Investment Manager should regularly communicate with the Client for the purpose of jointly evaluating the Client-Directed Brokerage Arrangement, including:

1. the potential for achieving Best Execution,

2. the list of Brokers and their trading skills,

3. the target percentage of transactions to be directed to the selected Brokers, and

4. the Investment Manager's trading style and liquidity needs.

APPENDIX 3B—PERMISSIBLE RESEARCH GUIDANCE

Central to whether a product or service constitutes "Research" that can be paid for with Client Brokerage is whether the product or service provides lawful and appropriate assistance to the Investment Manager in carrying out its investment decision-making responsibilities. This determination pivots on whether the product or service aids the Investment Decision-Making Process instead of the general operation of the firm.

CFA Institute Soft Dollar Standards add guidance by requiring that the primary use of the Research must directly assist the Investment Manager in its Investment Decision-Making Process and not in the management of the investment firm.

Formulating what is allowable Research is not subject to hard and fast rules. Rather, the context in which something is used and the particulars of an Investment Manager's business form the framework for this determination. In evaluating a practice, the substance of *actual* usage will prevail over the *form* of some possible usage.

Three-Level Analysis

CFA Institute Soft Dollar Standards assist the Investment Manager in making this determination by setting forth a three-level analysis to assist the Investment Manager in determining whether a product or service is Research. In the vast majority of cases, if the criteria of all three levels are satisfied, the Investment Manager can then feel comfortable in using Client Brokerage to pay for the Research. When conducting the analysis, the Investment Manager must consider the ethical framework of the Soft Dollar Standards. In conjunction with the Soft Dollar Standards' Client disclosure requirements, an Investment Manager must be able to explain to its Client how the Research—and when applicable, its component parts—assists in the Investment Decision-Making Process. Stated another way, the Investment Manager should only obtain Research with Client Brokerage if the Manager would feel comfortable disclosing and explaining the decision in a face-to-face meeting with the Client.

Level I—Define the Product or Service The first step is for the Investment Manager to define the product or service to be purchased with Client Brokerage. In most instances, the product or service is clearly defined (e.g., an industry report). However, many products and services consist of different components that are related only to the ability of the product or service to assist the Investment Manager in its Investment Decision-Making Process (e.g., a computer work station that runs Research software). For such multicomponent products or services, the Investment Manager, consistent with the Soft Dollar Standards' ethical framework, must narrowly construe the component parts that are necessary for the products or services to directly assist the Investment Manager in the Investment Decision-Making Process.

For example, the computer work station could be considered a closely related component of the product or service that constitutes the "Research." The electricity needed to run the computer, however, is not closely related and, if paid with Client Brokerage, would violate the ethical principles of the Soft Dollar Standards.

Level II—Determine Usage   The second step is for the Investment Manager to determine that the primary use of the product or service, as defined by the Investment Manager in the Level I analysis, will directly assist the Investment Manager in its Investment Decision-Making Process.

For example, an Investment Manager subscribes to the Bloomberg Service and uses this service only to enable all persons visiting the Investment Manager's offices to look up the price of securities and analyze market trends. Under the Level I analysis, the Investment Manager defines the service as the market data received from Bloomberg, plus the Bloomberg supplied terminal and the dedicated line necessary to receive the Bloomberg service in the Investment Manager's offices. However, under the Level II analysis, the Investment Manager does not use the Bloomberg service to directly assist it in its Investment Decision-Making Process. To the contrary, the Investment Manager subscribes to the Bloomberg Service as a benefit to the firm. The Bloomberg Service, therefore, cannot be paid for with Client Brokerage.

Level III—Mixed-Use Analysis   The third step occurs only after the Investment Manager determines that the product or service is Research by completing the Level I and Level II analysis above. The Investment Manager must then determine what portion of the Research is used by the Investment Manager to directly assist it in the Investment Decision-Making Process. If less than 100 percent of the Research is used for assistance in its Investment Decision-Making Process, the Investment Manager must consider the Research as Mixed-Use Research. With Mixed-Use Research, the Investment Manager can use Client Brokerage to pay for only that portion of the Research used by the Investment Manager in the Investment Decision-Making Process and not in the management of the investment firm.

For example, if the Bloomberg service discussed in the Level III analysis was actually used 50 percent of the time to determine market and industry trends as part of the Investment Manager's Investment Decision-Making Process, the Investment Manager could pay for 50 percent of the Bloomberg service with Client Brokerage.

Conclusion

The Investment Manager can establish that the product or service is Research that can be purchased with Client Brokerage only after the Investment Manager has taken two steps. First, the Investment Manager must have defined the product or service (Level I analysis). Second, the Investment Manager must have determined that the primary use of the product or service will directly assist the

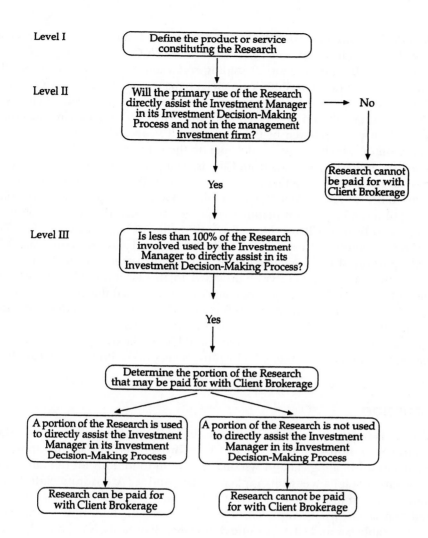

Level I — Define the product or service constituting the Research

Level II — Will the primary use of the Research directly assist the Investment Manager in its Investment Decision-Making Process and not in the management investment firm? — No — Research cannot be paid for with Client Brokerage

Yes

Level III — Is less than 100% of the Research involved used by the Investment Manager to directly assist in its Investment Decision-Making Process?

Yes

Determine the portion of the Research that may be paid for with Client Brokerage

A portion of the Research is used to directly assist the Investment Manager in its Investment Decision-Making Process — Research can be paid for with Client Brokerage

A portion of the Research is not used to directly assist the Investment Manager in its Investment Decision-Making Process — Research cannot be paid for with Client Brokerage

Investment Manager in the Investment Decision-Making Process rather than in the management of the investment firm (Level II analysis). The final step is for the Investment Manager to determine what portion of the Research will be used by the Investment Manager in the Investment Decision-Making Process and pay only for that portion with Client Brokerage (Level III analysis).

APPENDIX 3C—CASE STUDY UNDER THE CFA INSTITUTE SOFT DOLLAR STANDARDS

XYZ Firm is an Investment Manager that seeks to comply with the CFA Institute Soft Dollar Standards and claim such compliance. XYZ, a member of CFA Institute, manages a variety of accounts: separate accounts, including accounts of employee benefit plans subject to ERISA, accounts of non-ERISA institutional investors, and accounts of wealthy individuals; several collective investment vehicles, including a group trust for employee benefit plans subject to ERISA and/or governmental plans; a "hedge fund" for institutional and other "sophisticated" individual investors; and three SEC-registered investment companies, including an equity fund, a fixed-income fund, and a money market fund.

XYZ executes trades for its Client accounts with several broker-dealers who conduct trades for XYZ on both a principal and agency basis. Some of the broker–dealers have offered to provide XYZ with the following products and/or services for XYZ's own use, to be paid for with XYZ's Client Brokerage business: 1) desks and office equipment; 2) trading room television sets that receive the Financial News Network and other financial news services supplied by cable and satellite television services; 3) the Bloomberg Service, which includes a Bloomberg terminal; and 4) software that will assist XYZ in analyzing economic trends in industries followed by the Firm, as well as a widely available computer work station on which to install and operate the software. In addition, XYZ has received the following requests from Clients: 5) a pension fund Client subject to ERISA has requested that XYZ direct a portion of its Brokerage from its separate account to Broker ABC to obtain research information to be provided to the plan trustees; 6) a public pension plan has requested that XYZ direct a portion of its Brokerage to Broker ABC in return for cash credits to be paid to the Plan; 7) a non-ERISA institutional investor in XYZ's hedge fund has requested that XYZ direct a portion of the hedge fund's brokerage to Broker ABC to compensate Broker ABC for research services provided to the institutional investor; and, 8) the SEC-registered investment companies have requested that XYZ direct a portion of the equity fund's Brokerage to Broker ABC in return for credits to be used to reduce or eliminate all of the registered investment companies' custodian fees.

What steps or other actions must or should XYZ take to comply with the Soft Dollar Standards and/or other CFA Institute Standards of Professional Conduct?

Discussion

XYZ Firm is facing a set of decisions that typically confronts Investment Managers in connection with their use of Client Brokerage. XYZ should approach these decisions in a logical and systematic fashion to identify all relevant issues and ensure compliance with applicable law and CFA Institute Soft Dollar Standards. As an initial matter, XYZ should clearly isolate and identify the proposed transactions contemplated. Then, in order to determine compliance with applicable law and CFA Institute Soft Dollar Standards, XYZ should 1) consider fundamental principles that apply to the conduct of CFA Institute members, 2) identify applicable laws and regulations and analyze the proposed transactions in light of those laws and regulations, and 3) identify the CFA Institute Soft Dollar Standards and analyze the proposed transactions in light of those Standards. XYZ may pursue the proposed transactions only after satisfying itself that the transactions pass this systematic, multilevel analysis.

Isolate and Define the Proposed Transactions. One of the benefits of the CFA Institute Soft Dollar Standards is that they help Investment Managers to clearly define their practices as they relate to their Clients' Brokerage. By referring to the definitions contained in the Soft Dollar Standards, XYZ should determine that the broker–dealers' offer to provide the products and services in Transactions 1–4 described in the "Facts" section possibly constitutes a Soft Dollar Arrangement. Because XYZ is contemplating directing transactions to the broker–dealers to receive execution on trades and to receive products and services that will benefit XYZ directly, this offer may meet the CFA Institute Soft Dollar Standards definition of a Soft Dollar Arrangement. An additional measure of whether Transactions 1–4 qualify as Soft Dollar Arrangements under the CFA Institute Soft Dollar Standards is whether the products and services received by XYZ qualify as Research as defined in the Soft Dollar Standards. Transactions 5–8 may constitute Client-Directed Brokerage Arrangements, as defined in the CFA Institute Soft Dollar Standards, if XYZ determines that the *clients* are directing that their trades be routed through specific broker–dealers in order that the *clients* may receive benefits *in addition to* execution services.

Fundamental Principles. In considering the transactions that have been proposed, XYZ should adhere to a set of fundamental principles contained in three of the CFA Institute Standards that generally govern a member's conduct in this area. Standard I (Fundamental Responsibilities) of the CFA Institute Standards of Professional Conduct requires that a member be familiar and comply with all applicable laws governing their professional activities. XYZ is thus charged with a duty to know and apply the provisions of law that are implicated by the proposed transactions. Even if XYZ has adopted the CFA Institute Soft Dollar Standards, compliance with these Standards does not absolve XYZ of the responsibility to comply with applicable law. For situations in which the CFA Institute Standards impose a higher degree of responsibility or disclosure than, but do not conflict with, applicable law, XYZ must adhere to the provisions of the CFA Institute Standards *in addition to* any provisions of applicable law.

Moreover, Standard I of the CFA Institute Soft Dollar Standards contains fundamental principles that govern any of XYZ's activities involving Soft Dollar Arrangements. Standard I states that 1) Brokerage is the property of the Client and 2) XYZ has an ongoing duty to ensure the quality of transactions effected on behalf of its Clients, which includes:

▶ seeking to obtain Best Execution;

▶ minimizing transactions costs; and

▶ using Client Brokerage to benefit Clients.

These principles are reflected in the CFA Institute Soft Dollar Standards' requirement that XYZ, in considering a Soft Dollar Arrangement, must act for the benefit of its Clients and place its Clients' interests before its own.

Finally, Standard V of the CFA Institute Soft Dollar Standards, governing Client-Directed Brokerage Arrangements, requires that XYZ must not use Brokerage from another Client account to pay for a product or service purchased under the Client-Directed Brokerage Arrangement.

Applicable Laws and Regulations. Members are expected at all times to comply with the applicable laws of the countries in which they do business. For example, in the United States, the Securities Exchange Act of 1934, Investment Company Act of 1940, Investment Advisers Act of 1940, and Employment Retirement Income Security Act of 1974 would govern certain or possibly all of the transactions that XYZ is considering. Regardless of the country in which XYZ is doing business, as a threshold matter, it must analyze each transaction for compliance with applicable law. Only those transactions that comply with local laws are eligible for subsequent analysis under the CFA Institute Soft Dollar Standards.

Applicable Relevant Standards. Assuming each of the proposed transactions has "survived" the first two stages of analysis, they must still comply with provisions of the CFA Institute Soft Dollar Standards in order for XYZ to pursue them. Because XYZ has previously determined that each of the transactions qualifies as a possible Soft Dollar Arrangement (depending on whether the products or services qualify as Research under the CFA Institute Soft Dollar Standards) or a Client-Directed Brokerage Arrangement (depending on whether XYZ's Client is directing its trades to receive a benefit), XYZ must satisfy the following three broad requirements to claim compliance with the Soft Dollar Standards:

▶ Determine that each arrangement is permitted by the CFA Institute Soft Dollar Standards.

▶ Disclose the Investment Manager's Soft Dollar policies to its Clients.

▶ Maintain the specified records.

A. *Determinations of Eligibility.* Standard III of the CFA Institute Soft Dollar Standards requires that, as an initial matter in selecting any broker, XYZ must consider the capabilities of the broker to provide Best Execution. Once XYZ has satisfied itself that a particular broker will provide Best Execution, XYZ must next evaluate any additional research provided by the broker under the following four criteria specified in Soft Dollar Standard IV:

▶ The research under consideration must meet the definition of Research contained in the Soft Dollar Standards.

▶ The Research must benefit XYZ's clients.

▶ XYZ must be able to document the basis for its determination.

▶ Under certain fiduciary regulations (i.e., ERISA, the Investment Company Act of 1940), for trades conducted on a principal basis, the Research must directly benefit the Client account generating the trade. If not so limited by such regulations, the Research must directly benefit the Client account generating the trade, unless XYZ has made disclosure and obtained prior Client consent.

The meaning of the term "Research" is crucial to XYZ's evaluation under Soft Dollar Standard IV. "Research" is defined in the CFA Institute Soft Dollar Standards to mean services and/or products the primary use of which must directly assist the Investment Manager in its Investment Decision-Making Process and not in the management of the investment firm.

Transaction 1—Use of Client Brokerage to Pay for Desks and Office Equipment
Transaction 1 would not qualify for Research as defined in the Soft Dollar Standards because desks and office equipment would not satisfy the Soft Dollar Standards' definition of Research. Although XYZ should be able to determine that desks and office equipment do not qualify as Research based on the plain terms of the definition, the result becomes clear when XYZ applies the three-level analysis. Under that analysis, XYZ would first define the products or services that it desires to purchase with Client Brokerage. The desks are a discrete and simple product that can be clearly identified. Although office equipment is a somewhat general term, XYZ should also be able to clearly identify the office equipment being offered (e.g., photocopier, fax machine, etc.). XYZ next would analyze the primary use of these products to determine whether they will directly assist XYZ's Investment Decision-Making Process. At this point, XYZ clearly should understand that desks and most office equipment cannot be considered to aid directly in the Investment Decision-Making Process and hence do not qualify as Research under the CFA Institute Soft Dollar Standards. Because the Soft Dollar Standards only permit XYZ to receive Research as defined in the CFA Institute Soft Dollar Standards, XYZ could not engage in Transaction 1 and claim compliance with the CFA Institute Soft Dollar Standards.

Transaction 2—Use of Client Brokerage to Pay for Trading Room Television Sets   Transaction 2 involves a service that is more difficult than office equipment to analyze under the definition of Research contained in the Soft Dollar Standards. The service that XYZ desires to purchase is really a composite of products and services that may or may not qualify as Research under the definition provided in the Soft Dollar Standards. XYZ's first task is to define the service under the first level of analysis. Accordingly, XYZ should narrowly construe the component parts that are *necessary* for the service at issue in this example (i.e., financial news networks) to assist XYZ in its Investment Decision-Making Process.

In this situation, XYZ could reasonably conclude that the component parts (i.e., television sets, individual financial news services, and cable or satellite providers) are necessary for the total service to assist XYZ in its Investment Decision-Making Process. Thus, the service is potentially eligible to be paid for with client brokerage, *provided* that the total service satisfies the next level of analysis.

Applying the next level of analysis would allow XYZ to conclude that the service may qualify as Research if the primary use of the service is to directly aid the Investment Manager in its Investment Decision-Making Process. Even if financial news services have a broader use than to provide data to Investment Managers for purposes of making investment decisions, it would be consistent with the Soft Dollar Standards for XYZ to conclude that such services meet the primary use analysis—if based on actual use.

Transaction 3—Use of Client Brokerage to Pay for the Bloomberg Service Transaction 3 involves a similar analysis under the definition of Research contained in the CFA Institute Soft Dollar Standards. As with Transaction 2, XYZ's first step is to define the products or services that XYZ proposes to purchase with Client Brokerage. Again, XYZ should narrowly construe the component parts and could reasonably conclude that the Bloomberg terminal is a necessary component to receive the Bloomberg Service.

In applying the next level of analysis, XYZ may also reasonably conclude that the primary use of the Bloomberg Service, with its specific focus on real-time market news and analysis, does directly aid in the Investment Decision-Making Process. The service, therefore, may satisfy the first two levels of analyzing the definition of Research contained in the Soft Dollar Standards. However, if XYZ uses the Bloomberg Service and terminal to allow Clients to access financial information, the primary use of the service would not be to assist XYZ in its Investment Decision-Making Process, and the service would not qualify as Research under the CFA Institute Soft Dollar Standards. If XYZ uses the Bloomberg Service and terminal both in its own Investment Decision-Making Process and for Client purposes, at the third level of analysis, XYZ must make a good faith determination as to what portion of the service is actually used in the Investment Decision-Making Process. Only this portion may be paid for with Client Brokerage. XYZ must reevaluate this allocation on an annual basis.

Transaction 4—Use of Client Brokerage to Pay for Software and Computer Workstations At this point, XYZ should be comfortable applying the three-level analysis required to define Research under the Soft Dollar Standards. Transaction 4 involves the same analysis that confronted XYZ in the first three transactions. In defining the product in Transaction 4 (i.e., the research software), XYZ might reasonably determine that each of the component parts (the software and workstation) is necessary for the product to assist in the Investment Decision-Making Process.

Furthermore, XYZ might reasonably conclude under the second level of analysis that the software (and its component parts) will directly aid XYZ's Investment Decision-Making Process. If the primary use of the software is to directly assist XYZ in its Investment Decision-Making Process (as indicated by Level II analysis), XYZ may purchase the software using Client Brokerage. However, as with Transaction 3, only that portion actually used by XYZ in its Investment Decision-Making Process (as determined by Level III analysis) may be paid for with Client Brokerage, and any mixed-use allocation must be reevaluated annually.

Client-Directed Transactions. The eligibility of Transactions 5–8 must be determined under the portions of the CFA Institute Soft Dollar Standards related to Client-Directed Brokerage Arrangements. Standard V of the CFA

Institute Soft Dollar Standards requires that, in considering Transactions 5–8, XYZ must not use Brokerage from another Client account to pay for a product or service purchased under the Client-Directed Brokerage Arrangement. Standard V also recommends that XYZ attempt to structure the Client-Directed Brokerage Arrangement in accordance with certain recommended practices under the CFA Institute Soft Dollar Standards.

Transaction 5—Directing of Brokerage by ERISA Client to Benefit Plan Trustees
In considering Transaction 5, XYZ must be particularly cognizant of the definition of Client contained in the Soft Dollar Standards. The Standards define Client to refer to "the entity, including a natural person, investment fund, or separate account, designated to receive the benefits, including income, from the Brokerage generated through Securities Transactions."

Although this definition of Client also recognizes that a Client may be represented by a trustee or other Fiduciary, XYZ must be sensitive to the fundamental principle contained in Standard I of the CFA Institute Soft Dollar Standards that stresses that Brokerage is the property of the *Client*, not the trustee or Fiduciary representing the Client. XYZ should immediately question whether Transaction 5 qualifies as a Client-Directed Brokerage Arrangement because the additional benefit flows not to the Client but to the Client's trustees. Because Transaction 5 likely does not qualify as a proper Client-Directed Brokerage Arrangement, if XYZ were to pursue it, XYZ would be violating the fundamental principle that requires the use of Client Brokerage to benefit Clients. XYZ should, therefore, decline to pursue Transaction 5.

Transaction 6—Directing of Brokerage by Public Pension Plan to Obtain Cash Credits for the Plan Transaction 6, however, would be a permissible Client-Directed Brokerage Arrangement under the Soft Dollar Standards because Client Brokerage would be used to generate cash credits that solely benefit the Client. XYZ should attempt to structure the arrangement in conformity with the recommended practices for Client-Directed Brokerage Arrangements that are contained in the Soft Dollar Standards, which would require XYZ to:

▶ Disclose to the Client XYZ's duty to continue to seek to obtain Best Execution.

▶ Disclose to the Client that committing a certain percentage of the Client's Brokerage to a particular broker–dealer may affect XYZ's ability to seek to obtain Best Execution and purchase adequate Research.

▶ XYZ should receive written assurance from the plan trustees that the Client-Directed Brokerage Arrangement will solely benefit plan beneficiaries.

▶ XYZ should attempt to structure the Client-Directed Brokerage Arrangement so that it does not require the commitment of a certain portion of Brokerage to a single broker and so that commissions are negotiated and seeking to obtain Best Execution is still relevant.

▶ XYZ should request from the Client written instructions that 1) restate XYZ's continuing responsibility for seeking to obtain Best Execution, 2) list eligible brokers; 3) specify the target percentage of transactions to be directed, and 4) state procedures for monitoring the arrangement.

▶ XYZ should regularly communicate with the Client for the purpose of jointly evaluating the Client-Directed Brokerage Arrangement, including 1) the potential for achieving Best Execution, 2) the list of brokers and their trading skills, 3) the target percentage of transactions to be directed to selected brokers, 4) XYZ's trading style and liquidity needs, and 5) other factors identified by the Client as relevant to the selection of brokers.

Transaction 7—Directing of Brokerage by Institutional Investor in Hedge Fund to Compensate Broker for Research Provided to Investor Transaction 7 raises issues under Standard V of the CFA Institute Soft Dollar Standards because Standard V requires that XYZ not use Brokerage from another Client account to pay for a product or service purchased under the Client-Directed Brokerage Arrangement. In Transaction 7, XYZ's hedge fund is a commingled pool containing numerous investors. The CFA Institute Soft Dollar Standards define Client to refer to the beneficiaries of an *entity*, including, as in this case, *all* of the beneficiaries of an investment fund. However, the product or service purchased under this particular Client-Directed Brokerage Arrangement has benefited *only* the institutional investor in the hedge fund, not all of the Client's underlying investors and thus may be construed to violate the principles in Standard V of the CFA Institute Soft Dollar Standards. XYZ, therefore, should not pursue Transaction 7.

Transaction 8—Directing of a Portion of One Fund's Brokerage by Three Investment Companies to Benefit All Three Companies Transaction 8 raises similar concerns as Transactions 5 and 7. XYZ is apparently directed by three distinct Clients (each of the three registered funds) to direct brokerage of one Client (i.e., the equity fund) to benefit all three Clients. XYZ should not pursue this arrangement because it would violate the principle in Standard V of the CFA Institute Soft Dollar Standards, which states that brokerage from another Client account should not be used to pay for a product or service purchased under a Client-Directed Brokerage Arrangement.

B. *Disclosure.* In order to claim compliance with the CFA Institute Soft Dollar Standards, XYZ must also meet specific disclosure obligations relating to its Brokerage practices. In addition to XYZ's disclosure obligations described above in the discussion of the transactions, XYZ must clearly disclose the following information relating to its Soft Dollar and Client-Directed Brokerage Arrangements:

 ► XYZ must disclose to Clients and potential Clients whether XYZ may use the Research to benefit Clients other than those whose trades generated the Brokerage and whether the trades generating the Brokerage involved transactions conducted on a principal basis.

 ► XYZ must disclose to Clients 1) a description of the types of Research received through the arrangements, 2) the extent of its use, and 3) whether any broker affiliate of XYZ was involved.

 ► XYZ must provide each Client with a statement that any Soft Dollar or Client-Directed Brokerage Arrangements with respect to its account comport with the CFA Institute Soft Dollar Standards (this statement must be provided at least annually).

 ► XYZ must disclose in writing to its Clients that additional information in accordance with the CFA Institute Soft Dollar Standards concerning XYZ's Soft Dollar and Client-Directed Brokerage Arrangements is available on request. Such additional information should include 1) a firmwide description of the products and services that were received from each broker pursuant to a Soft Dollar Arrangement, including the identity of those Brokers; 2) for a specific Client account, the total amount of Commissions generated for the Client through Soft Dollar Arrangements, detailed by Broker and reporting the amount of

Brokerage directed by the Client to specific brokers; and 3) the aggregate percentage of XYZ Brokerage derived from Client-Directed Brokerage Arrangements and the amount of the particular Client's Directed Brokerage as a percentage of the aggregate, subject to a 10 percent *de minimis* amount.

C. *Record Keeping.* In addition to the eligibility determinations and disclosure obligations, in order to claim compliance with the CFA Institute Soft Dollar Standards, XYZ must also maintain, when applicable, all records that:

► are required by applicable law;

► are necessary to supply Clients on a timely basis with the information required by Soft Dollar Standard VI;

► document arrangements, oral or written, obligating the Investment Manager to generate a specific amount of Brokerage;

► document arrangements with Clients pertaining to Soft Dollar or Client-Directed Brokerage Arrangements;

► document any agreements with Brokers pertaining to Soft Dollar Arrangements;

► document transactions with Brokers involving Soft Dollar Arrangements, including 1) a list of Proprietary or Third-Party Research providers and 2) a description of the service or product obtained from the provider;

► document the bases of allocation in determining to use Client Brokerage to pay for any portion of a Mixed-Use service or product;

► indicate how the services and products obtained through Soft Dollar Arrangements directly assist XYZ in the Investment Decision-Making Process;

► show compliance with the CFA Institute Soft Dollar Standards, including the identity of XYZ personnel responsible for determining such compliance;

► are copies of all Client disclosures and authorizations.

PRACTICE PROBLEMS FOR READING 3

The following information relates to Questions 1–6[1]

Portfolio manager Elsa Wirk, CFA, is a partner at LEV Capital Management, a long-only domestic equity manager. In addition to her portfolio management duties, Wirk is responsible for determining compliance with CFA Institute Soft Dollar Standards. In her morning mail, Wirk receives a notice that the local regulatory agency has issued a new rule about the use of client brokerage. According to the new rule, research to be paid with client brokerage "must include value-added analysis."

As part of her compliance duties, on a periodic basis Wirk evaluates the various brokers and research services used by LEV. Her assistant develops a worksheet of the brokerage firms' quoted commission rates for domestic stock trades. In addition, Wirk studies trading reports on each firm showing the average spread for all trades for each of the past 12 months and ranks the firms on an aggregate basis. Finally, Wirk evaluates research and other services available through soft dollars. Several firms offer proprietary and third-party research arrangements which LEV believes are valuable to the firm and its clients. Wirk polls staff members on the value of the services provided. After completing the research, Wirk develops a list of "preferred brokers" based on their commission structure, execution history, and research services. She instructs the firm's trading desk to direct trades to the preferred brokers whenever possible.

Babbit Financial is one of Wirk's preferred brokers. Babbit charges commissions of $0.05 per share and offers a variety of products and services including proprietary research. For firms that generate a minimum dollar amount of brokerage commissions, Babbit offers a subscription service that provides raw data feeds of historic price and economic information. Wirk is confident that the amount of brokerage directed to its preferred brokers will exceed the required minimum. LEV will be able to use the raw data feeds for research activities as well as valuing client portfolios.

Norton Investments, which recently launched a new hedge fund, is also a preferred broker. Norton charges commissions of $0.06 per share and provides third-party research including reports from Anderson Financial. Anderson produces excellent research in the area of derivatives and Wirk believes its reports will be useful to LEV in developing proprietary structured products.

Wirk is planning a meeting with a prospective client. The prospective client, a pension fund, requires that its advisers comply with CFA Institute Soft Dollar Standards. In preparation, Wirk sends the pension fund a packet containing the following information:

Soft Dollar Arrangements

LEV engages in soft dollar arrangements with brokers in which commission dollars generated by client trades pay for investment research and brokerage products and services. The commission paid to such brokers may be higher than the commission another broker would charge for the same transaction. The research purchased with brokerage benefits all clients and not only those whose trades generated the brokerage.

---

[1]This case was written by Sarah W. Peck, PhD, and Dorothy C. Kelly, CFA.

End-of-reading problems and solutions copyright © CFA Institute. Reprinted with permission.

LEV uses commissions on securities purchased or sold in client accounts to pay for the following services:

Research Provider	Broker	Description of Service
Alpha Financial	ABC	Stock market quotations and monitoring
Statbase	LMN	Statistical database
Mod-Allocator	ABC	Asset allocation modeling
Performance Analyst	PQR	Asset allocation backtesting

At the meeting, the pension fund trustees inform LEV that, by law, 20% of the fund's brokerage must be directed to three local minority-owned brokers. Wirk tells the pension fund board that, "We have a fiduciary duty to seek best execution for all client trades. The requirement to commit 20% of brokerage to specific firms may affect our ability to seek and obtain best execution. It may also adversely affect our ability to obtain adequate research for the fund."

The trustees respond that they "will continue to increase diversity by using minority-owned brokers and to support the regional economy by using local brokers." They also inform Wirk that they have entered into commission recapture programs with all three minority-owned firms. The commission recapture programs provide the pension fund with cash rebates that the pension fund uses to pay certain administrative expenses.

Wirk replies that to comply with the trustees' request, she will need written instructions identifying the eligible brokers, the approximate target percentage to be directed to each, and procedures for monitoring the arrangements. The pension fund soon signs a contract with LEV naming Wirk as portfolio manager.

The following month, Wirk directs the trading desk to purchase 10,000 shares of a mid-capitalization stock for the pension fund. The trading desk has three choices. Babbit would execute the trade on a principal basis rather than charge its normal commission. Norton would charge its normal commission of $0.06 to execute the trade. Framer, an agency broker that is not on Wirk's list of preferred brokers, specializes in the stock and would charge a commission of $0.05 per share. The head trader believes that Framer will execute the shares with minimal market impact.

1. Is directing brokerage to Wirk's preferred brokers consistent with both the required and recommended CFA Institute Soft Dollar Standards?
    A. Yes.
    B. Only if the preferred broker offers best execution.
    C. Only if the preferred broker offers research services of appropriate value.

2. According to the CFA Institute Soft Dollar Standards, is it permissible for Wirk to pay for some portion of Babbit's subscription service with client brokerage?
    A. Yes.
    B. No, because the service does not include value-added analysis.
    C. No, because the service requires a minimum dollar amount of transactions.

3. Is the purchase of Anderson reports with client brokerage consistent with both the required and recommended CFA Institute Soft Dollar Standards?

   A. Yes.

   B. No, because the reports are from a third-party.

   C. No, because the reports do not support the investment decision-making process.

4. Is the written information that Wirk provides to the potential client consistent with both the required and recommended CFA Institute Soft Dollar Standards?

   A. Yes.

   B. No, because it does not address whether trades generating brokerage involve transactions conducted on a principal basis.

   C. No, because it does not indicate that all soft dollar arrangements comply with the CFA Institute Soft Dollar Standards.

5. Are Wirk's oral statements about the pension fund's proposed directed brokerage arrangement consistent with both the required and recommended CFA Institute Soft Dollar Standards?

   A. Yes.

   B. No, because Wirk should disclose the information in writing.

   C. No, because Wirk was misrepresenting the facts—the arrangement will not affect Wirk's ability to obtain adequate research.

6. Are the written instructions that Wirk requests from the pension plan consistent with recommended practices of the CFA Institute Soft Dollar Standards?

   A. Yes.

   B. No, because Wirk should also request written instructions that relieve LEV of responsibility to seek best execution.

   C. No, because Wirk should also request written instructions that restate LEV's responsibility to seek best execution.

SOLUTIONS FOR READING 3

1. B is correct. According to the general principles of the CFA Institute Soft Dollar Standards, LEV has an ongoing duty to ensure the quality of transactions made on its behalf including seeking to obtain best execution.

2. B is correct. Compliance with the Soft Dollar Standards does not absolve Wirk of her responsibility to comply fully with applicable law. According to the local regulatory authority, permissible research must include value-added analysis. Raw data feeds of historical prices would not qualify as permissible research according to the regulatory agency's rules.

3. C is correct. According to the Standards, research paid by client brokerage must directly assist the investment manager in investment decision-making. Anderson's research on structured products will not assist LEV, a long-only domestic equity manager, in its current investment decision-making, but more likely will benefit new product development.

4. B is correct. The Standards require that an investment manager disclose its policies with respect to soft dollar arrangements to both clients and potential clients. The disclosure must address whether trades generating brokerage involve transactions conducted on a principal basis.

5. A is correct. In cases of client-directed brokerage, the Standards recommend that the manager disclose his duty to continue to seek to obtain best execution; the client-directed brokerage arrangement may affect the manager's ability to seek to obtain best execution.

6. C is correct. In a client-directed brokerage arrangement, the Standards recommend that investment managers request written instructions that restate the manager's continuing responsibility to seek to obtain best execution.

CFA INSTITUTE RESEARCH OBJECTIVITY STANDARDS

LEARNING OUTCOMES

The candidate should be able to:	Mastery
a. explain the objectives of the Research Objectivity Standards;	☐
b. critique company policies and practices related to research objectivity, and distinguish between changes required and changes recommended for compliance with the Research Objectivity Standards.	☐

GUIDING PRINCIPLES   1

CFA Institute has been concerned for some time that allegations of ethical misconduct and lack of objectivity and independence of research analysts weaken investor confidence in the financial markets and taint the reputations of all investment professionals. CFA Institute believes that the vast majority of investment professionals, particularly CFA Institute members who must attest annually to their adherence to the CFA Institute Code of Ethics and Standards of Professional Conduct, have professional integrity and should be able to conduct their professional activities free from pressure to bias their research and recommendations.

Therefore, the guiding principles that support the CFA Institute-ROS (Research Objectivity Standards) directly reflect the CFA Institute Code of Ethics:

▶ To act with integrity, competence, dignity, and in an ethical manner when dealing with the public, clients, prospects, employers, employees, and fellow CFA Institute members.

▶ To practice and encourage others to practice in a professional and ethical manner that will reflect credit on CFA Institute members and their profession.

▶ To strive to maintain and improve their competence and the competence of others in the profession.

▶ To use reasonable care and exercise independent judgment.

These principles, in concert with the CFA Institute mission "to advance the interests of the global investment community by establishing and maintaining the highest standards of professional excellence and integrity," provide the motivation and philosophical basis for undertaking this project to develop the CFA Institute-ROS.

2 COMPARISON WITH THE NEW YORK STOCK EXCHANGE AND NATIONAL ASSOCIATION OF SECURITIES DEALERS RULES

In the United States, the New York Stock Exchange (NYSE) and the National Association of Securities Dealers (NASD) recently issued new rules for their members relating to the issues of analyst independence and objectivity. CFA Institute commented on the adequacy of these rules when proposed by the NYSE, NASD, and the U.S. Securities and Exchange Commission. CFA Institute was generally supportive of these rules, which closely reflect the recommendations of the CFA Institute Task Force on Analyst Independence and the CFA Institute-ROS in their draft form. (The CFA Institute comment letter is posted on the CFA Institute website: www.aimr.org/advocacy/.)

Despite the implementation of the NYSE/NASD rules, CFA Institute still sees a definite need to go forward with the CFA Institute-ROS. As a global organization, CFA Institute believes that the ethical conflicts facing research analysts are worldwide and not just relevant to those working in the United States. The CFA Institute-ROS are designed so that there will be no conflict for firms between the NYSE/NASD rules and the CFA Institute-ROS.

3 OVERVIEW OF THE CFA INSTITUTE RESEARCH OBJECTIVITY STANDARDS

The CFA Institute-ROS are intended to be specific, measurable standards for managing and disclosing conflicts of interest that may impede a research analyst's ability to conduct independent research and make objective recommendations. Based on the ethical principles of placing the interests of investing clients before one's own, or the firm's, and of full and fair disclosure of conflicts of interest, the CFA Institute-ROS provide ethical standards and accompanying specific recommended practices to guide investment firms worldwide, and their respective employees, in achieving objectivity and independence of research reports.

Firms that adopt the CFA Institute-ROS demonstrate their commitment to manage conflicts of interest effectively and to provide full and fair disclosure of these conflicts to all investors who have access to their research. CFA Institute believes that firms that claim adoption will benefit from the competitive advantage that a commitment to, and reputation for, integrity yields.

A fundamental principle of ethical investment practice is that the best interests of the investing client must always take precedence over the interests of investment professionals and their employers. Every investment professional is personally responsible for ensuring that his or her independence and objectivity is maintained when preparing research reports, making investment recommendations, and taking investment action on behalf of clients. The CFA Institute Code of Ethics and Standards of Professional Conduct (CFA Institute Code and Standards), to which all CFA Institute members, Chartered Financial Analyst™ (CFA®) charterholders, and CFA candidates must adhere, already embody these principles. Therefore, the CFA Institute-ROS are designed to complement, not replace, the CFA Institute Code and Standards. CFA Institute believes that firms that comply with the CFA Institute-ROS will provide an appropriate working environment for their investment professionals—one that promotes ethical behavior and facilitates compliance with the CFA Institute Code and Standards.

Adoption of the CFA Institute-ROS cannot ensure the accuracy of research reports and recommendations. Future events are inherently uncertain. Regardless of the comprehensiveness and sophistication of the methodology used in the financial analysis, the actual event will often differ from the forecast on which investment recommendations are made. However, CFA Institute believes that firms that adopt the CFA Institute-ROS will instill confidence in investors and demonstrate that their research and recommendations have a reasonable and adequate basis, clearly differentiate between fact and opinion, and fully convey the opinion of the author(s).

Finally, CFA Institute recognizes that no finite set of guidelines or recommended practices will be exhaustive, nor will it address all future developments in the investment industry's structure and practices. Good ethics is always a work-in-progress. Therefore, CFA Institute encourages firms that adopt the CFA Institute-ROS to strive continuously to comply not only with the principles set forth in the Standards themselves, but also with the recommended procedures for compliance. In doing so, CFA Institute recommends that firms work to achieve the following objectives when designing policies and procedures to implement the CFA Institute-ROS:

A. To prepare research reports, make investment recommendations, and take investment actions; and develop policies, procedures, and disclosures that always place the interests of investing clients before their employees' or the firm's interests.

B. To facilitate full, fair, meaningful, and specific disclosures of potential and actual conflicts of interest of the firm or its employees to its current and prospective clients.

C. To promote the creation and maintenance of effective policies and procedures that would minimize and manage conflicts of interest that may jeopardize the independence and objectivity of research.

D. To support self-regulation through voluntary industry development of, and adherence to, specific, measurable, and demonstrable standards that promote and reward independent and objective research.

E. To provide a work environment for all investment professionals that supports, encourages, and rewards ethical behavior and supports CFA Institute members, CFA charterholders, and CFA candidates in their adherence to the CFA Institute Code and Standards.

DEFINITIONS

The following terms are used in the CFA Institute-ROS with the meanings specified:

Compliance and legal department: Department within a firm responsible for 1) implementing and enforcing a firm's policies and procedures and 2) ensuring that a firm and its employees are in compliance with applicable laws, rules, and regulations.

Corporate issuer: Company or corporation obtaining funding from public capital markets.

Covered employee: Firm employee who 1) conducts research, writes research reports, and/or makes investment recommendations; or assists in the research process; 2) takes investment action on behalf of clients or the firm, or who comes in contact with investment recommendations or decisions during the decision-making process; or 3) may benefit, personally or professionally, from influencing research reports or recommendations.

Immediate family: Individual(s) whose principal residence is the same as the principal residence of the subject person.

Investment advisory relationship: Asset management relationship that entails entire, shared, or partial investment discretion over client funds.

Investment banking: Corporate finance activities, such as acting as an underwriter in an offering for a subject company, acting as a financial adviser in a merger or acquisition, providing venture capital, lines of credit or other similar products, making a market in a security, or serving as a placement agent for corporate issuers.

Investment manager: Individual employed by an investment management firm (e.g., mutual fund, investment adviser, pension funds) to research securities and/or take investment action to purchase or sell securities for client accounts or for the firm's own account, whether or not such person has the title of "investment manager."

Personal investments and trading: Purchases and sales of a particular security including maintaining long-, short-, and other derivative positions in which an individual has a financial interest.

Public appearance: Participation in a seminar; open forum (including an interactive electronic forum); radio, television, or other media interview; or other public speaking activity in which a research analyst or investment manager makes a recommendation or offers an opinion.

Quiet period: Period during which covered employees are prohibited from issuing research reports or recommendations on, and publicly speaking about, a specific subject company.

Research analyst: Person who is primarily responsible for, contributes to, or is connected with, the preparation of the substance of a research report or the basis for a recommendation, whether or not any such person has the title of "research analyst."

Research report: Written or electronic communication that firms sell or distribute to clients or the general public, which presents information about a corporate issuer and may express an opinion or make a recommendation about the investment potential of the corporate issuer's equity securities, fixed income securities, or derivatives of such securities.

Restricted period: A period of time during which a firm prohibits its covered employees from trading specified securities.

Subject company: Corporate issuer whose securities are the subject of a research report or recommendation.

Supervisory analyst: Designated person responsible for reviewing research reports to assess and maintain the quality and integrity of research reports.

INVESTMENT BANKS, BROKER-DEALERS AND OTHER FIRMS THAT SELL RESEARCH

4

The following standards are applicable to firms, such as investment banks, broker-dealers, and independent research firms, that employ investment professionals to research issuers and make recommendations about these issuers' securities, and that sell these research reports and recommendations for either hard currency or soft commissions ("sell-side" firms).

Requirements

1.0 Research Objectivity Policy

Firms must have:

a. a formal written policy on the independence and objectivity of research (Policy) that must be:
  i. made available to clients and prospective clients (both investing and corporate); and
  ii. disseminated to all firm employees;
b. supervisory procedures that reasonably ensure that the firm and its covered employees comply with the provisions of the policy and all applicable laws and regulations; and
c. a senior officer of the firm who attests annually to clients and prospective clients to the firm's implementation of, and adherence to, the Policy.

2.0 Public Appearances

Firms that permit research analysts and other covered employees to present and discuss their research and recommendations in public appearances must require these employees to fully disclose personal and firm conflicts of interest to the host or interviewer and, whenever possible, to the audience.

3.0 Reasonable and Adequate Basis

Firms must require research reports and recommendations to have a basis that can be substantiated as reasonable and adequate. An individual employee (supervisory analyst who is someone other than the author) or a group of employees (review committee) must be appointed to review and approve all research reports and recommendations.

4.0 Investment Banking

Firms that engage in, or collaborate on, investment banking activities must:

a. establish and implement effective policies and procedures that:

    i. segregate research analysts from the investment banking department; and

    ii. ensure that investment banking objectives or employees do not have the ability to influence or affect research or recommendations;

b. implement reporting structures and review procedures that ensure that research analysts do not report to, and are not supervised or controlled by, investment banking or another department of the firm that could compromise the independence of the analyst; and

c. implement procedures that prevent investment banking or corporate finance departments from reviewing, modifying, approving, or rejecting research reports and recommendations on their own authority.

5.0 Research Analyst Compensation

Firms must establish and implement salary, bonus, and other compensation for research analysts that:

a. align compensation with the quality of the research and the accuracy of the recommendations over time; and

b. do not directly link compensation to investment banking or other corporate finance activities on which the analyst collaborated (either individually or in the aggregate).

6.0 Relationships with Subject Companies

Firms must implement policies and procedures that manage the working relationships that research analysts develop with the management of subject companies. Research analysts must be prohibited from:

a. sharing with, or communicating to, a subject company, prior to publication, any section of a research report that might communicate the research analyst's proposed recommendation, rating, or price target; and

b. directly or indirectly promising a subject company or other corporate issuer a favorable report or a specific price target, or from threatening to change reports, recommendations, or price targets.

7.0 Personal Investments and Trading

Firms must have policies and procedures that:

a. manage covered employees' "personal investments and trading activities" effectively;

b. ensure that covered employees do not share information about the subject company or security with any person who could have the ability to trade in advance of ("front run") or otherwise disadvantage investing clients;

c. ensure that covered employees and members of their immediate families do not have the ability to trade in advance of or otherwise disadvantage investing clients relative to themselves or the firm;

d. prohibit covered employees and members of their immediate families from trading in a manner that is contrary to, or inconsistent with, the employees' or the firm's most recent, published recommendations or ratings, except in circumstances of extreme financial hardship; and

e. prohibit covered employees and members of their immediate families from purchasing or receiving securities prior to an IPO for subject companies and other companies in the industry or industries assigned.

8.0 Timeliness of Research Reports and Recommendations

Firms must issue research reports on subject companies on a timely and regular basis.

9.0 Compliance and Enforcement

Firms must:

a. have effective enforcement of their policies and compliance procedures to ensure research objectivity;

b. implement appropriate disciplinary sanctions for covered employees, up to and including dismissal from the firm, for violations;

c. monitor and audit the effectiveness of compliance procedures; and

d. maintain records of the results of internal audits.

10.0 Disclosure

Firms must provide full and fair disclosure of all conflicts of interest to which the firm or its covered employees are subject.

11.0 Rating System

Firms must establish a rating system that:

a. is useful for investors and for investment decision-making; and

b. provides investors with information for assessing the suitability of the security to their own unique circumstances and constraints.

Recommended Procedures for Compliance

1.0 Research Objectivity Policy

An effective Research Objectivity Policy would clearly identify and describe the job title, function and department of covered employees. It should also identify whether covered employees are personally subject to a code of ethics and standards of professional conduct and provide the code and standards, if applicable. Covered employees should include those who conduct research, write research reports, and make recommendations, those who come in contact with research and recommendations, and those who may benefit from influencing research and recommendations.

Covered employees should be regularly trained on their responsibilities under the Policy and be required to attest annually in writing to their understanding of and adherence to it.

Full disclosure of the conflicts of interest that covered employees may face is a critical element of any Policy. These conflicts may include collaboration with investment banking or corporate finance; participation in marketing activities; necessary ongoing working relationships with corporate issuers; personal investments and trading; and firm investments and trading. The Policy should discuss each conflict that a firm's covered employees may face and how the firm's policies and procedures manage those conflicts effectively.

Since compensation is a major motivator of employee decision-making and actions, the Policy should clearly describe the factors on which compensation of research analysts is based.

Firms should also disclose in the Policy the conditions under which a research report can be purchased or acquired by clients, prospective clients, and investors in general.

It is recommended that firms post the Policy on their website for easy access by clients and prospective clients.

2.0 Public Appearances

A public appearance includes participation in a seminar; forum (including an interactive electronic forum); radio, television, or other media interview; or other public speaking activity in which a research analyst makes a recommendation or offers an opinion.

At a minimum, firms that permit covered employees to present and discuss research and recommendations in public or open forums (whether the audience consists of investment professionals, investing clients, or the general investing public) have a responsibility to ensure that the audience of such presentations has sufficient information to make informed judgments about the objectivity of the research and recommendations. Firms should also recognize that their employees have a responsibility to provide sufficient information to the audience to assess the suitability of the investment in light of their specific circumstances and constraints. Speakers should remind audience members to judge the suitability of the investment in light of their own unique situation.

Covered employees who make public appearances should be prepared to make full disclosure of all conflicts of interest, either their own or their firms', about which they could reasonably be expected to know. Firms should require research analysts who participate in public appearances to make the following disclosures to the interviewer or the audience as appropriate: 1) whether the research analyst knows (or has reason to know) whether the subject company is an investment banking or other corporate finance client of the firm; and 2) whether the research analyst has participated, or is participating, in marketing activities for the subject company.

Firms should provide the full research reports on the subject companies discussed to members of the audience at a reasonable price. At a minimum, the covered employee should disclose to the interviewer or audience whether a written research report is available to members of the audience who are not clients of the firm, the approximate cost, and how a viewer, listener, or reader might acquire the report.

Firms should make copies of the full research report available for purchase or review; for example via the firm's website.

3.0 Reasonable and Adequate Basis

Firms should develop detailed, written guidance for research analysts, supervisory analysts, and review committees that establish due diligence procedures for judging whether or not there is a reasonable and adequate basis for a particular recommendation.

When recommending a purchase, sale, or change in recommendation, firms should provide, or offer to provide, supporting information to investing clients. When making a recommendation, firms should disclose the current market price of the security in question.

4.0 Investment Banking

Collaboration between the research and investment banking activities of the firm creates severe conflicts of interest for research analysts. Firms need effective policies and procedures in place to safeguard the independence and objectivity of research analysts. Specifically, firms should prohibit research analysts from sharing with, or communicating to, members of the investment banking or corporate finance department, prior to publication, any section of the research report that might communicate the research analyst's proposed recommendation. The compliance or legal department should act as an intermediary for all communications between the research analyst and investment banking or corporate finance. Firms may permit investment banking or corporate finance personnel to review a research report only to verify factual information or to identify potential conflicts of interest. It is recommended that all written and oral communications between a research analyst and investment banking or corporate finance be documented and conducted with the compliance or legal department acting as an intermediary.

Firms should implement quiet periods for initial public offerings (IPOs) and secondary offerings of securities. Quiet periods should be of sufficient length to ensure that research reports and recommendations will not be based on inside information gained by the research analyst through investment banking sources. However, firms may issue an information-only research report concerning the effects of a significant event on a subject company if authorized by the compliance or legal departments. Quiet periods of 30 calendar days from issuance for IPOs and at least 10 calendar days from issuance for secondary offerings are recommended.

It is recommended that firms prohibit research analysts from participating in marketing activities, including "roadshows," for IPOs and secondary offerings in order to further the integrity of the ensuing quiet period. If firms permit research analysts to participate in such activities, the research analysts should disclose this participation in all interviews and public appearances.

5.0 Research Analyst Compensation

Firms should develop measurable criteria for assessing the quality of research including the reasonableness and adequacy of the basis for any recommendation and the accuracy of recommendations over time. Firms should implement compensation arrangements that depend on these measurable criteria and that are applied consistently to all research analysts. It is recommended that such criteria form a part of the Policy and be made available to clients and prospective clients.

Although direct linking of analyst's compensation with investment banking and corporate finance activities is prohibited, firms should disclose the extent to which research analyst compensation in general is dependent upon the firm's investment banking revenues.

6.0 Relationships with Subject Companies

In order to conduct quality research and develop a reasonable and adequate basis for a recommendation, research analysts, who rely on company financial reports and other documents for their research and as part of the basis for their recommendation, need the ability to communicate with subject-company management and participate fully in conference calls and other subject-company investor and analyst-relations activities. Maintaining appropriate working relationships with subject-company personnel is an important aspect of the research analyst's responsibilities.

Firms should establish and implement policies and procedures that govern these relationships, including policies regarding material gifts, company-sponsored and -paid trips, and communications with company management. Firms should have a clear, written definition of what constitutes "material."

Firms should implement procedures that ensure that only those sections of the report containing facts that could be reasonably checked or verified by the subject company are shared prior to publication.

It is recommended that the compliance or legal department receive a draft research report before sections are shared with the subject company, approve in advance all changes to a research report or recommendation that occur as a consequence of subject-company verification, and that the research analyst provide written justification for any changes that occur after verification by the subject company. It is also recommended that firms retain supporting documentation including the original report, the sections shared with the subject company, and any subsequent changes to the report or recommendation.

7.0 Personal Investments and Trading

Permitting research analysts and other covered employees to invest and trade in the securities of subject companies and industries may better align their personal interests with the interests of investing clients provided that precautions are taken to ensure that the interests of investing clients are always placed before the interests of the employee, members of their immediate families, and the firm.

Firms that permit covered employees and members of their immediate families to invest and trade in the securities, including derivative securities, of subject companies should require notification to, and approval by, the compliance or legal department in advance of all trades of securities in subject companies in the industry or industries assigned to that covered employee.

Firms should have specific policies and procedures that adequately prevent "front running" of investing client trades. These procedures should include restricted periods before and after issuing a research report. Restricted periods of at least 30 calendar days before and five calendar days after report issuance are recommended, with exceptions permitted on the announcement of significant news or events by the subject company if investing clients are given adequate notice and the ability to trade. However, restrictions on purchases or sales of securities need not apply to the securities of a diversified investment company or other investment fund over which the covered employees or members of their immediate families have no investment discretion or control.

When research analysts are permitted to invest and trade in the securities of the companies they cover, it is critical that firms prohibit them from trading contrary to the published recommendations of the firm on these companies. When research analysts trade contrary to their own investment recommendations, investing clients and prospective investing clients are rightly concerned about the quality and independence of the recommendation. Although there may be legitimate investment-management objectives for selling a security that the analyst recommends that investing clients purchase (e.g., the need to re-balance a diversified portfolio), investors are sent a mixed message that may cause concern and confusion.

There is one instance in which research analysts may be permitted to sell contrary to their recommendation. This is the case where the analyst would suffer "extreme financial hardship" if he or she could not liquidate these securities. To be clear and consistent about how this exception is applied, firms should have clear definitions of what constitutes extreme financial hardship and should also require a significant change in the employee's personal financial circumstances. Advance approval by the compliance or legal departments should be required. Appropriate documentation of the hardship conditions and the decision process should be retained.

Firms should require covered employees to provide to the firm or its compliance or legal department a complete list of all personal investments in which they or members of their immediate families have a financial interest. This list should be provided on a regular basis, but at least annually.

Firms should establish policies and procedures that prevent short-term trading of securities by covered employees. It is recommended that covered employees be required to hold securities for a minimum of 60 calendar days, except in the case of extreme financial hardship.

8.0 Timeliness of Research Reports and Recommendations

Firms have a fiduciary responsibility to investing clients to provide them with adequate and timely information on subject companies. To this end, firms should require research reports to be issued and recommendations or ratings to be confirmed or updated on a regular basis. It is recommended that reports and recommendations be issued at least quarterly, with additional updates recommended when there is an announcement of significant news or events by, or that might impact, the subject company.

Firms should not quietly and unobtrusively discontinue coverage of a subject company. When coverage of a subject company is being discontinued, firms should require the research analyst to issue a "final" research report that includes a recommendation. The final report should clearly explain the reason for discontinuing coverage.

9.0 Compliance and Enforcement

Firms should disseminate a list of activities that would be considered violations and resulting disciplinary sanctions to all covered employees. Firms should also disseminate a list of activities that would be considered violations and resulting disciplinary sanctions to all clients (both investing and corporate) and prospective clients. It is recommended that firms provide this information on their websites in conjunction with the publication of the research objectivity policy.

10.0 Disclosure

To be full and fair, disclosures should be comprehensive and complete, be presented prominently in the supporting documents or on the firm's website, be written in plain language that is easily understood by the average reader, and be designed to inform rather than obscure the nature of the conflicts of interest faced by the covered employee or the firm. It is recommended that such disclosure, or a page reference to the disclosure, be made on the front of the research report.

Firms that engage in investment banking or other corporate finance activities should disclose whether the subject company is currently an investment banking or other corporate finance client (corporate client) of the firm. It is recommended that firms disclose in the research report whether they have received compensation during the previous 12 months or expect to receive compensation in the next 3 months from a subject company that is a corporate client.

Firms should review all of their communications with investing clients to determine the most appropriate method of communicating conflicts of interest. Such communications would include advertisements, market letters, research reports, sales literature, electronic communications, and communications with the press and other media. In addition to disclosures in research reports, firms should determine the appropriate communications method(s) to inform investing clients of the following:

1. whether the firm makes a market in securities of a subject company;
2. whether the firm managed or co-managed a recent initial public or secondary offering of a subject company;
3. whether the research analyst or firm owns securities or any financial instrument that might reasonably be expected to benefit from the recommendation; or
4. whether the firm, an allied or affiliated firm, or the covered employee or a member of that employee's immediate family is a director, officer, or advisory board member of the subject company.

Firms should ensure that all conflicts of interest are disclosed in research reports. It is recommended that firms disclose the following in the research reports of all subject companies:

1. whether the subject company is a corporate client;
2. whether the firm or any of its affiliates holds one percent (1%) or more of any class of the outstanding common equity of the subject company as of five (5) business days prior to the issuance of the research report;
3. whether the firm makes a market in the securities of the subject company;
4. whether the firm permits the author(s) or members of their immediate families to invest or trade in the securities of the subject company;
5. whether the author(s) or members of their immediate families have a financial interest in any financial instrument that might reasonably be expected to benefit from the recommendation;
6. whether firm management, or the author(s) or members of their immediate families, are directors, officers, or advisory board members of the subject company; and
7. whether the author(s) of the report received a material gift from the subject company in the previous 12 months.

When the subject company is also a corporate client, it is recommended that firms also disclose the following in research reports and on their websites:

1. the nature of the corporate client relationship (e.g., initial public offering, merger and acquisition, etc.);
2. whether the firm received fees or revenues from the subject company in the previous 12 months or is expected to receive fees or revenues in the next 3 months;

3. whether the author(s) of the report assisted the firm in non-research activities and the specific nature of those activities (e.g., evaluated a subject company for acceptability as a corporate client, marketing activities); and

4. whether the compensation of the author(s) was dependent upon participation in investment banking or corporate finance activities.

Firms should provide appropriate statistical or other quantitative and qualitative presentations of information about their recommendations or ratings. In some jurisdictions, firms are required to provide distributions of their ratings by category and how these ratings have changed over time. Firms should provide information about prices of the securities of the subject company. It is recommended that price information be presented for a period of at least three years prior to the issuance of the research report. Firms should also provide information in connection with these price charts that identifies ratings and the dates of rating changes and provide information that identifies when and if the author(s) or research analysts changed the rating during that period.

Firms should disclose the valuation methods used to determine price targets and provide a description of the risk that may impede achieving those targets.

11.0 Rating System

One-dimensional rating systems do not provide sufficient information with which investors can make informed investment decisions. Therefore, firms should implement a rating system that incorporates the following: 1) recommendation or rating categories, 2) time horizon categories, and 3) risk categories.

Recommendation or rating categories may be absolute (e.g., buy, hold, sell) or relative (e.g., market outperform, neutral, or underperform). If the recommendation categories are relative, the firm should clearly identify the relevant benchmark, index, or objective.

Time horizon categories should clearly identify whether the time horizon measures the period over which the expected price target would be achieved or sustained.

Firms should require that communications of a firm's rating or recommendation, including discussions in public appearances, always include all three elements of the rating.

Firms should prohibit covered employees from communicating a rating or recommendation that is different from the current published rating or recommendation.

Firms should provide clients and prospective clients with a complete description of the firm's rating system on request. Firms should regularly inform clients and prospective clients of the availability of this description and how a client or prospective client can acquire this description.

PRACTICE PROBLEMS FOR READING 4

The following information relates to Questions 1–6

CVG is a regional investment firm that provides investment banking and brokerage services. The firm has a small investment research staff and has recently adopted the CFA Institute Research Objectivity Standards, including both the required and recommended policies and procedures.

Andrei Kepsh is a junior research analyst at CVG. The director of research has assigned Kepsh to initiate coverage on a local biotechnology company, GeoTech. CVG owns and makes a market in GeoTech shares. CVG recently participated in the selling group, but was not an underwriter, for GeoTech's initial public offering. Kepsh was not personally involved in the sale of the IPO. As part of his research, Kepsh meets with GeoTech's director of investor relations, Nils Olsen.

Two weeks later, on 2 May, Kepsh gives Olsen a copy of his completed GeoTech report containing a "buy" recommendation, and asks Olsen to correct any misstatements of fact before the report is released to CVG's clients. The next morning, Kepsh sends a copy of the GeoTech report to CVG's director of research. Kepsh also delivers the GeoTech report to CVG's investment banking department, and requests a review of his report for any conflicts of interest before it is released to CVG's clients on 5 May.

On 5 May, Kepsh has lunch with Gentura Hirai, one of the firm's senior analysts. Hirai explains the CFA Institute Research Objectivity Standards and CVG's policies and procedures regarding research reports and recommendations. Hirai states that CVG requires that reports be updated annually, or more frequently if there is substantive new information on the subject company. Also, because the research staff is small, CVG initiates coverage based on availability of the analytical staff and prioritizes companies to be covered on the basis of expected market attraction. Coverage is discontinued on the same basis, with a final report sent to clients if staff time permits.

After the appropriate waiting period, Kepsh purchases GeoTech shares for his personal account. On 11 May, Kepsh is one of the speakers at a biotechnology investment conference that is open to the public. By the time Kepsh presents his report on GeoTech, the conference is behind schedule. To save time, Kepsh summarizes his report and recommendation and does not make any disclosure statements. After the presentation, a conference participant requests a copy of his report. Kepsh responds that the report is available to the audience for a nominal fee.

On 25 May, Kepsh sells shares of GeoTech to pay for a wedding anniversary gift for his wife. In the future, Kepsh expects that, based on CVG's policy, he will receive large bonuses from increased investment banking fees and brokerage commissions attributable to his recommendations.

1. In giving his report to Olsen, does Kepsh comply with the CFA Institute Research Objectivity Standards?

   A. No.

   B. Yes, because he submitted a copy to the director of research.

   C. Yes, because he asked Olsen to correct any misstatements of facts.

2. Does Kepsh's interaction with the investment banking department comply with the CFA Institute Research Objectivity Standards?

   A. Yes.

   B. No, only because the investment banking department has been provided with the report containing the recommendation.

   C. No, both because the investment banking department has been provided with the report containing the recommendation, and because he does not direct the report through the compliance department.

3. Do CVG's policies regarding updating reports and discontinuing coverage, respectively, conform with the CFA Institute Research Objectivity Standards?

	Updating of Reports	Discontinuing Coverage
A.	No	No
B.	No	Yes
C.	Yes	No

4. To be in compliance with the CFA Institute Research Objectivity Standards, Kepsh must inform the conference audience about all of the following, *except*:

   A. CVG's ownership of GeoTech shares.

   B. CVG's making a market in GeoTech shares.

   C. CVG's participation in the selling group for the public offering of GeoTech.

5. Does Kepsh's response to the conference participant's question about the availability of the GeoTech report conform to the CFA Institute Research Objectivity Standards?

   A. Yes.

   B. No, because CVG should provide its research reports only to its clients.

   C. No, because CVG should provide research reports at no charge to all members of the audience.

6. Are Kepsh's sale of shares and CVG's bonus policy, respectively, in conformity with the CFA Institute Research Objectivity Standards?

	Sale of Shares	Bonus Policy
A.	No	No
B.	No	Yes
C.	Yes	No

SOLUTIONS FOR READING 4

1. A is correct. The Standards prohibit sharing the entire report and the recommendation with the subject company.

2. C is correct. The Standards recommend that any contact with the investment banking department regarding a research report be documented in writing, directed through the compliance department, and limited only to verification of facts, such as conflicts of interest.

3. A is correct. The Standards recommend that reports and recommendations be updated at least quarterly and that when coverage of a subject company is being discontinued, firms should issue a final research report and recommendation.

4. C is correct. The Standards require disclosure only if the firm managed or co-managed an offering of GeoTech securities.

5. A is correct. The Standards recommend that an analyst making a public appearance to discuss a report should disclose to the audience that the report is available at a reasonable price.

6. A is correct. The Standards prohibit Kepsh from trading in a manner that is contrary to the employee's or firm's most recent published recommendations. The Standards also prohibit direct linking of analyst compensation with investment banking activities.

STUDY SESSION 2
ETHICAL AND PROFESSIONAL STANDARDS:
Application

This study session uses case studies as an aid to understanding and internalizing the values and standards presented in the CFA Institute Code of Ethics and Standards of Professional Conduct.

The cases present realistic but fictional situations that closely approximate how individuals practicing in the investment industry encounter ethical issues in their day-to-day activities. The discussions following each case identify key violations of the Standards of Professional Conduct, recommend corrective actions, and when appropriate, formulate policy statements a firm could use in seeking to prevent the violations. The *Standards Reporter* readings present regulatory actions taken in response to actual occurrences and explain how the violations would be viewed from the perspective of the Code of Ethics and Standards of Professional Conduct.

Widespread recognition exists that certain situations create a "fiduciary" relationship in which an elevated level of fidelity, due diligence, and prudence is required of the investment manager. Historically, the term "fiduciary" has been defined in country-specific laws and regulations, making generic definitions difficult. Nonetheless, the underlying principles of the prudent investor rule, presented in "Prudence in Perspective," capture much of what is expected of investment professionals entrusted with the prudent management of client assets.

READING ASSIGNMENTS

THE GLENARM COMPANY

by Glen A. Holden Jr., CFA

LEARNING OUTCOMES

The candidate should be able to:	Mastery
a. critique the practices and policies presented;	☐
b. explain the appropriate action to take in response to conduct that violates the CFA Institute Code of Ethics and Standards of Professional Conduct.	☐

CASE FACTS   1

Peter Sherman, CFA, recently joined the Glenarm Company after five years at Pearl Investment Management. He is very excited about the new job and believes he will make a big contribution to Glenarm. His first task is to identify attractive Latin American companies for Glenarm's emerging markets portfolio. Sherman, knowing many of these companies through his consulting contacts, approaches the task enthusiastically. He believes the Glenarm Company will clearly benefit from his knowledge about these companies and has no need to know about his consulting on the side.

Sherman's Background

Sherman had joined Pearl Investment Management, a small equity-oriented firm, as a junior research analyst. Pearl entered the international investing arena shortly after Sherman arrived, and Sherman performed well as he gained experience, particularly in researching emerging market securities. Sherman also spent some time handling client relations in the account administration department. More than a year ago, Sherman had earned his CFA designation.

Sherman's role at Pearl grew when several of his boss's foreign investment banking contacts hired Pearl to research companies and industries in Latin America in order to better position themselves vis-à-vis their local competitors.

When Pearl expanded its research department to accommodate these new projects, the company made Sherman its primary analyst for emerging markets. The firm encouraged Sherman to develop expertise in this area, and he capitalized on his position by serving as a consultant to several third-world companies to assist them in attracting U.S. and European investors, an arrangement that Sherman fully disclosed to Pearl. Pearl did not own stock in any of the companies that Sherman consulted with.

Shortly after Sherman's research responsibilities at Pearl expanded, he received a call from John Lawrence, an acquaintance in the local CFA Institute financial analysts society and a partner of the Glenarm Company, one of Pearl's competitors. Lawrence indicated that his company was looking for an individual with Sherman's background and asked him if he would be interested in becoming a portfolio manager at Glenarm.

Glenarm

The Glenarm Company is a small equity-oriented management firm. Glenarm was recently investigated, censured, and fined by the U.S. Securities and Exchange Commission for a number of violations related to its portfolio management practices. The latest censure was Glenarm's third in the past 13 years. The firm's partners are desperate to rehabilitate their reputation and stem the steady outflow of clients.

No one in the firm other than Lawrence is a member of CFA Institute or the local society, but the Glenarm partners have accepted Lawrence's reasoning that hiring a CFA charterholder as a portfolio manager will enhance the credentials of the firm, will demonstrate a commitment to professionalism in their practice, and is their best chance to expand their client base. Lawrence believes Sherman is an excellent prospect.

The Glenarm partners believe Sherman may be able to bring some business with him if he joins the firm. While at Pearl, Sherman developed client contacts through his duties with the research department and through handling client relations. He also has some knowledge of investment management clients by virtue of his interaction with the portfolio managers. To entice him, Glenarm offers Sherman a large portion of the first-year investment management fee for all the Pearl clients he is able to solicit and bring to Glenarm. Although he has reservations because of Glenarm's past problems with the SEC, Sherman decides that the opportunity is too good to pass up. Also, he can continue his consulting work. So, he agrees to join Glenarm as a portfolio manager.

The Transition

In preparation for his move to Glenarm but while he is still at Pearl, Sherman pays social calls on several local Pearl clients after business hours to inform them that he will be leaving Pearl and encourage them to switch their accounts to Glenarm. He also contacts a number of accounts that Pearl has been actively soliciting but that have not yet committed to hire Pearl as their investment manager. He also contacts prospects that Pearl has rejected in the past as too small or incompatible with the firm's business to determine if they are interested in hiring Glenarm. As a result of this activity, Sherman convinces several of Pearl's clients and prospects to hire Glenarm as their investment management company but to delay any action until he has joined Glenarm.

In his last week at Pearl, Sherman identifies material that he has worked on to take with him to his new job, including:

▶ sample marketing presentations he prepared;

▶ computer program models for stock selection and asset allocation that he developed;

▶ research material on several companies Sherman has been following;

▶ news articles he collected that contain potential research ideas; and

▶ a list of companies that Sherman suggested in the past deserved further research and possible investment and that were rejected by Pearl.

Several activities in the case are or could be in violation of the CFA Institute Code of Ethics and Standards of Professional Conduct (Code and Standards). Identify possible violations and state what actions are required by Sherman and/or Glenarm to correct the potential violations, and make a short policy statement a firm could use to prevent the violations.

CASE DISCUSSION   2

This case depicts violations or possible violations of the CFA Institute Code and Standards related to a member's duties toward the member's employer: the duty to disclose to one's employer additional compensation arrangements and the duty to disclose conflicts of interest to the employer.

Loyalty to One's Employer

Standard IV(A)—Duties to Employer: Loyalty, states that in matters related to their employment, members and candidates must act for the benefit of their employer and not deprive their employer of the advantage of their skills and abilities, divulge confidential information, or otherwise cause harm to their employer. Sherman's solicitation of clients and prospects and his plans to take Pearl property for the benefit of Glenarm are a breach of Standard IV(A).

Standard IV(A) does not preclude members from seeking alternative employment, but it does obligate a member to protect the interests of the employer by refraining from any conduct that could deprive an employer of profit or the benefits of the member's skills and abilities. An employee is free to make arrangements to leave any employer and go into competitive business—so long as the employee's preparations to leave do not breach the employee's duty of loyalty to the current employer.

In this instance, Sherman had an obligation to act in the best interests of Pearl while he was still an employee of Pearl. He had a duty not to engage in any activities that would be detrimental to Pearl's business until his resignation date became effective. The following activities by Sherman violated this duty of loyalty and, as a result, violated Standard IV(A).

Solicitation of clients and prospects. Sherman's solicitation of clients on behalf of Glenarm while he was still employed at Pearl is a clear violation of Standard IV(A). Attempting to lure clients from Pearl to another investment company undermined Pearl's business, and the fact that such activity was carried out "after hours" or in a social context is irrelevant; the damage to Pearl's business was the same. Even after leaving Pearl, Sherman must abide by any additional legal and contractual obligations between him and Pearl that would prevent solicitation of clients.

Soliciting potential clients of Pearl was also a violation of Standard IV(A). When engaging in such activity, Sherman was attempting to interfere with Pearl's business opportunities for his own benefit and the benefit of his future employer. Solicitation of clients and prospects cannot begin until Sherman has left Pearl and begun to work for Glenarm.

Sherman's contact of prospects that Pearl had not pursued because of their size or investment objectives does not constitute a violation of Standard IV(A) so long as the contacts were not in competition with Pearl in any way. Sherman could solicit business for his new employer on his own time when that activity did not interfere with his responsibilities at Pearl or take away a business opportunity from Pearl.

Misappropriation of employer property. Except with the consent of the employer, departing employees may not take property of the employer. Even material prepared by the departing employee is the property of the employer, and taking that property is a violation of the employee's duty to the employer. Employees must obtain permission to take with them any work or work product prepared in the course of the employee's employment or on behalf of the employer.

In this case, all the material mentioned as taken by Sherman was the property of Pearl. Sample marketing material prepared by Sherman, computer program models for stock selection and asset allocation that he developed, and research material and news articles that he collected are all Pearl's property because Sherman's efforts in creating or gathering these materials were undertaken in the context of his employment with and for the benefit of Pearl. Even the list of rejected research ideas was Pearl's property; those ideas were generated by Sherman for Pearl's consideration and use. The analyst that Pearl hires to replace Sherman might benefit by reviewing the list of ideas considered and rejected by the firm.

Actions Required

Sherman should have refrained from solicitation of any of Pearl's clients or prospects until he had left Pearl. Sherman should have obtained Pearl's permission to take copies of any work he prepared on behalf of Pearl in the course of his employment there. Without such permission, Sherman should not have taken any material that could have even remotely been considered Pearl's property.

Policy Statement for a Firm

"Employees shall not undertake any independent practice that could result in compensation or other benefit in competition with the firm unless they obtain written consent from the firm and the person or entity for whom they undertake independent practice. Departing employees shall not engage in any activities that would be in conflict with this policy, including soliciting firm clients or prospects, removing firm property, or misuse of confidential information."

Disclosure of Additional Compensation and Conflicts

Under Standard IV(B)—Duties to Employers: Disclosure of Additional Compensation Arrangements, CFA Institute members and candidates must not accept gifts, benefits, compensation, or consideration that competes with, or might reasonably be expected to create a conflict of interest with, their employer's interest unless they obtain written consent from all parties involved. Because such arrangements may affect an employee's loyalties and objectivity and may create conflicts of interest, employers must receive notice of these arrangements so that they can evaluate employees' actions and motivations.

In the case, Sherman disclosed his consulting arrangements to Pearl but not to Glenarm. Thus, he was violating Standard IV(B). Although Sherman's consulting activities might have uncovered investment opportunities for Glenarm clients, the arrangements had the potential to affect Sherman's ability to render objective advice and to divert Sherman's energies away from managing Glenarm clients' portfolios. Sherman should have given Glenarm written information on his independent practice so that the firm could make an informed determination about whether the outside activities impaired his ability to perform his responsibilities with the firm.

Sherman's consulting arrangements are also a violation of Standard VI(A)—Disclosure of Conflicts, and Standard I(B)—Independence and Objectivity. Under Standard VI(A), Sherman must make full and fair disclosure of all matters that could reasonably be expected to impair their independence and objectivity or interfere with respective duties to their employer, clients, and prospective clients. Members and candidates must ensure that such disclosures are prominent, are delivered in plain language, and communicate the relevant information effectively. Sherman could wind up receiving consulting fees from the same companies about which he is writing research reports for Glenarm's internal use. Thus, the consulting could compromise Sherman's independence and objectivity and would violate Standard I(B).

Actions Required

Sherman must disclose to Glenarm all outside compensation arrangements and describe in detail the activities that gave rise to this compensation. He must obtain written permission in advance of entering into these relationships.

Policy Statement for a Firm

"Employees shall disclose to the firm in writing all monetary compensation or other benefits that they receive for their services that are in addition to compensation or benefits conferred by the firm. Employees shall also disclose all matters that reasonably could be expected to interfere with their duty to this firm or ability to make unbiased and objective recommendations."

PRESTON PARTNERS

by Jules A. Huot, CFA

LEARNING OUTCOMES

The candidate should be able to:	Mastery
a. critique the practices and policies presented;	☐
b. explain the appropriate action to take in response to conduct that violates the CFA Institute Code of Ethics and Standards of Professional Conduct.	☐

CASE FACTS — 1

Sheldon Preston, CFA, the senior partner in Preston Partners, is sitting in his office and pondering the actions he should take in light of the activities of one of his portfolio managers, Gerald Smithson, CFA.

Preston Partners is a medium-sized investment management firm that specializes in managing large-capitalization portfolios of U.S. equities for pension funds and personal accounts. As president, Preston has made it a habit to review each day all the Preston Partner trades and the major price changes in the portfolios. Yesterday, he discovered some deeply disturbing information. Several weeks previously, when Preston was on a two-week vacation, Smithson had added to all his clients' portfolios the stock of Utah BioChemical Company, a client of Preston Partners, and of Norgood PLC, a large northern European manufacturer and distributor of drugs and laboratory equipment headquartered in the United Kingdom. Preston had known of a strong, long-standing relationship between Smithson and the president of Utah BioChemical. Indeed, among Smithson's clients were the personal portfolio of Arne Okapuu, president and CEO of Utah BioChemical, and the Utah BioChemical pension fund. Yesterday came the announcement that Utah BioChemical intended to merge with Norgood PLC, and with that news, the share prices of both companies increased more than 40 percent.

Preston Partners had adopted the CFA Institute Code of Ethics and Standards of Professional Conduct as part of the firm's own policy and procedures

235

manual. Preston had written the manual himself but, because he had been pressed for time, had stuck to the key elements rather than addressing all policies in detail. He made sure that every employee received a copy of the manual when he or she joined the firm. Preston thought surely Smithson knew the local securities laws and the Code and Standards even if he hadn't read the manual. Extremely upset, Preston called Smithson into his office for an explanation.

While on vacation in Britain, Smithson narrated, he had seen Okapuu in a restaurant dining with someone he recognized as the chairman of Norgood. Their conversation appeared to be intense but very upbeat. Smithson did not attempt to greet Okapuu. Later, Smithson called on an old analyst friend in London, Andrew Jones, and asked him for some information on Norgood, the stock of which was trading as American Depositary Receipts (ADRs) on the New York Stock Exchange. Jones sent Smithson his firm's latest research report, which was recommending a "hold" on the Norgood stock.

Smithson was already somewhat familiar with the biochemical industry because his large accounts owned other stocks in the industry. Nevertheless, when he returned to the United States, he gathered together several trade journals for background, obtained copies of the two companies' annual reports, and carried out his own due diligence on Utah BioChemical and Norgood.

After thoroughly analyzing both companies' financial history, product lines, and market positions, Smithson concluded that each company's stock was selling at an attractive price based on his valuation. The earnings outlook for Norgood was quite positive, primarily because of the company's presence in the European Union and its strong supplier relationships. Norgood's stock price had shown little volatility but had risen consistently in the past, and the company currently had a strong balance sheet. Utah BioChemical, a leader in the biochemical industry, at one time had been a high-growth stock but had been in a slump in recent years. Based on his analysis of the new products in Utah's pipeline, however, and their market potential, Smithson projected strong sales and cash flow for Utah BioChemical in the future.

Through his research, Smithson also recognized that Utah BioChemical and Norgood were in complementary businesses. Reflecting on what he had seen on his trip to London, Smithson began to wonder if Okapuu was negotiating a merger with or takeover of Norgood. Convinced of the positive prospects for Utah BioChemical and Norgood, Smithson put in a block trade for 50,000 shares of each company. The purchase orders were executed during the next two weeks.

Smithson had not personally executed a block trade for some time; he usually left execution up to an assistant. Because this trade was so large, however, he decided to handle it himself. He glanced at the section on block trades in Preston Partners' policy and procedures manual, but the discussion was not clear on methods for allocating shares. So, he decided to allocate the shares by beginning with his largest client accounts and working down to the small accounts. Smithson's clients ranged from very conservative personal trust accounts to pension funds with aggressive objectives and guidelines.

At the time of Smithson's decision to make the share purchases, Utah BioChemical was trading at $10 a share and the Norgood ADRs were trading at $12 a share. During the next two weeks, the price for each company's shares rose several dollars, but no merger or takeover announcement was made—until yesterday.

Several activities in this case are or could be violations of the CFA Institute Code and Standards. Identify possible violations, state what actions Preston and/or Smithson should take to correct the potential violations, and make a short policy statement a firm could use to prevent the violations.

CASE DISCUSSION   2

Gerald Smithson's story describes some perfectly legitimate actions but also some actions in clear violation of the CFA Institute Code and Standards. In researching and making the decision to purchase shares of Utah BioChemical and Norgood for his client accounts, Smithson complied with Standard V(A)—Diligence and Reasonable Basis. He observed a meeting between the heads of two public companies in related businesses, which sparked his interest in researching the companies further. He already had some knowledge of the biochemical industry through some clients' investments and through his relationship with Arne Okapuu, and he carried out his own due diligence on the companies. Smithson had a reasonable basis, supported by appropriate research and investigation, for his investment decision, and he exercised diligence and thoroughness in taking investment action.

Smithson neither possessed nor acted on insider information. He did not actually overhear a conversation; rather, after his research was complete, he "put two and two together" and speculated that the executives might have been discussing a merger or takeover. Viewing the two company leaders together was only one piece of his "mosaic" and was only a small factor in his investment decision-making process. If Smithson had based his decisions solely on his chance viewing of the dinner meeting, the investment decisions would have been inappropriate. Smithson failed to comply, however, with aspects of the Standards related to the suitability of the investments for his clients and the allocation of trades. In addition, Sheldon Preston failed to exercise his supervisory responsibilities.

Responsibilities to Clients and Interactions with Clients

Smithson purchased shares in Utah BioChemical Company and Norgood PLC for all of his client portfolios without first determining the suitability or appropriateness of the shares for each account. The case states that the investment objectives and guidelines for Smithson's accounts ranged from conservative, for his personal trust accounts, to aggressive, for his pension fund clients. Norgood, with its stable stock price, financial strength, and positive earnings outlook, appears to be a conservative stock that would fit within the guidelines of Smithson's more conservative accounts. It may or may not fit the more aggressive guidelines established for some of Smithson's pension fund clients.

Utah BioChemical, however, is probably too volatile to be included in a conservative account and thus may not have been appropriate or suitable for some of the firm's personal trust clients. Therefore, Smithson may have violated Standard III(C)—Suitability, in regard to the appropriateness and suitability of the investment actions he took. Under Standard III(C), an investment manager must consider the client's tolerance for risk, needs, circumstances, goals, and preferences, in matching a client with an investment.

Actions Required

The case does not make clear whether Smithson's clients have written investment objectives and guideline policy statements. If they do not, Preston should direct Smithson to prepare such written guidelines for all accounts. Smithson should review the guidelines for every account for which he bought shares of Utah BioChemical and Norgood and assess the characteristics of those investments in light of the objectives of the clients and their portfolios. In those accounts for which either investment is unsuitable and inappropriate, he should sell those shares, and Preston Partners should reimburse the accounts for any losses sustained by them.

Policy Statement for a Firm

"For each client of the firm, portfolio managers, in consultation with the client, shall prepare a written investment policy statement setting out the objectives, the constraints, and the asset-mix policy that meets the needs and circumstances of the client. Managers shall insert this analysis in each client's file. Portfolio managers shall review and confirm the investment policy statements at least annually and whenever the client's business or personal circumstances create a need to review them. In their client relationships, portfolio managers should be alert to any changes in the clients' circumstances that would require a policy review. When taking investment action, portfolio managers shall consider the appropriateness and suitability of an investment to the needs and circumstances of the client. Managers must satisfy themselves that the basic characteristics of the investment meet the written guidelines for the client's account."

Allocation of Trades

Standard III(B)—Fair Dealing, states that members shall deal fairly with clients when taking investment actions. In this case, the firm did not have detailed written guidelines for allocating block trades to client accounts. So, Smithson simply allocated trades to his largest accounts first, at more favorable prices, which discriminated against the smaller accounts. Certain small clients were disadvantaged financially because of Smithson's block-trade allocation method.

Standard III(B) arises out of the investment manager's duty of loyalty to clients embodied in the CFA Institute Code and Standards. Without loyalty, the client cannot trust or rely on the investment manager.

Whenever an investment manager has two or more clients, he or she faces the possibility of showing one client preference over the other. The Code and Standards require that the investment advisor treat each client fairly but do not specify the allocation method to be used. Moreover, treating all clients fairly does not mean that all clients must be treated equally. Equal treatment, given clients' different needs, objectives, and constraints, would be impossible.

Action Required

Because Preston Partners has only vague policies for portfolio managers on allocating block trades, Preston needs to formulate some detailed guidelines. The trade allocation procedures should be based on guiding principles that ensure 1) fairness to clients, both in priority of execution of orders and in the allocation of the price obtained in the execution of block trades, 2) timeliness and efficiency in the execution of trades, and 3) accuracy in the investment manager's records for trade orders and maintenance of client account positions. In advance of each trade, portfolio managers should be required to write down the account for which the trade is being made and the number of shares being traded.

Block trades are often executed throughout a day or week, which results in many small trades at different prices. To assure that all accounts receive the same average price for each segment of the trade, trades should be allocated to the appropriate accounts just prior to or immediately following each segment of the block trade on a pro rata basis. For example, if 5,000 shares of Norgood and 5,000 shares of Utah BioChemical traded on Day 1, Smithson would have immediately allocated each set of shares to each appropriate account according to the relative size of the account. Each account would thus pay the same average price. If 10,000 more shares traded later that day, or the next day, or so on, Smithson would follow the same procedure. Procedures for trade allocation should be disclosed to clients in writing at the outset of the client's relationship with the firm. Obtaining full disclosure and the client's consent does not, however, relieve the manager of the responsibility to deal fairly with clients under the Code and Standards.

Policy Statement for a Firm

"All client accounts participating in a block trade shall receive the same execution price and be charged the same commission, if any. All trade allocations to client accounts shall be made on a pro rata basis prior to or immediately following part or all of a block trade."

Responsibilities of Supervisors

Preston Partners did not have in place supervisory procedures that would have prevented Smithson's allocation approach. Preston's failure to adopt adequate procedures violated Standard IV(C)—Responsibilities of Supervisors. Preston Partners had adopted the Code and Standards; thus, anyone in the firm with supervisory responsibility should have been thoroughly familiar with the obligation of supervisors under the Code and Standards to make reasonable efforts to detect and prevent violations of applicable laws, rules, and regulations. Supervisors and managers should understand what constitutes an adequate compliance program and must establish proper compliance procedures, preferably designed to prevent rather than simply uncover violations.

The case notes that certain sections of the policy and procedures manual were unclear. Supervisors have a responsibility to ensure that compliance policies are clear and well developed. Supervisors and managers must document the procedures and disseminate them to staff. In addition to distributing the policy and procedures manual, they have a responsibility to ensure adequate training of each new employee concerning the key policies and procedures of the firm. Periodic refresher training sessions for all staff are also recommended.

Ultimately, supervisors must take the necessary steps to monitor the actions of all investment professionals and enforce the established policies and procedures.

Actions Required

Preston should assure that proper procedures are established that would have prevented the violation committed by Smithson. Preston should assume the responsibility or appoint someone within the firm to become the designated compliance officer whose responsibility is to assure that all policies, procedures, laws, and regulations are being followed by employees.

Policy Statement for a Firm

"Employees in a supervisory role are responsible for the actions of those under their supervision with regard to compliance with the firm's policies and procedures and any securities laws and regulations that govern employee activities."

SUPER SELECTION
by Paul F. Van Schyndel, CFA

LEARNING OUTCOMES

The candidate should be able to:	Mastery
a. critique the practices and policies presented;	☐
b. explain the appropriate action to take in response to conduct that violates the CFA Institute Code of Ethics and Standards of Professional Conduct.	☐

CASE FACTS 1

Patricia Cuff, chief financial officer and compliance officer for Super Selection Investment Advisors, has just finished reviewing the brokerage account statement for one of Super Selection's portfolio managers, Karen Trader. When a disgruntled board member of Atlantis Medical Devices (AMD) informed her of Trader's possible misconduct, Cuff decided to investigate Trader's relationship with AMD, a company whose stocks Trader recently bought for all her portfolios. As a result, Cuff obtained and is now reviewing Trader's brokerage statements, which were not previously submitted by Trader. Cuff is concerned about possible violations of the company's standards of professional conduct and her responsibilities as a compliance officer and member of CFA Institute to act on those violations.

Super Selection is a medium-size, rapidly growing money manager registered with the U.S. Securities and Exchange Commission to manage both separate accounts and mutual funds. Super Selection has subscribed to the CFA Institute Code of Ethics and Standards of Professional Conduct by incorporating the CFA Institute Code and Standards into the firm's compliance manual.

Trader has been a portfolio manager for Super Selection for almost five years. She loves the job because of the people she meets and the money she is able to earn. She has been particularly pleased to keep up her friendship with Josey James, a former college classmate and now the president of AMD, a rapidly growing local biotech company.

241

Over the past five years, James has provided Trader with information on attractive stocks in Trader's field—biotechnology—on which Trader capitalized for her Super Selection portfolios and her personal portfolio. Because she was able to act more quickly on her personal trades than her Super Selection trades, Trader has often purchased stocks of the companies recommended by James for her own account prior to purchasing them for her clients. As a result, the performance of her personal portfolio has been better than the performance of her other portfolios.

Three years ago, James asked Trader to serve as an outside director for AMD and, despite AMD's uncertain prospects at the time, Trader eagerly accepted the offer. Because AMD was in shaky financial condition until recently, the company compensated its directors with stock options rather than cash payments. For the past several years, directors received options exercisable into 200,000 shares in AMD stock. AMD's shares were not traded anywhere, however, so this compensation was essentially worthless, and Trader has not reported her relationship with AMD to Super Selection. This year, with AMD's sales setting records and earnings up, directors started receiving quarterly director fees of $5,000.

Several months ago, the AMD board voted to issue shares of stock to the public to raise needed cash. The market for initial public offerings (IPOs) was very hot, with valuations of biotech companies at record levels; so, AMD top managers believed the moment was opportune to go public. A public market for AMD shares was very appealing to many board members. Trader, for example, was eager to exercise her stock options so that she could cash in on their value. She had just begun construction of a new home, which was putting significant pressure on her cash flow. Trader voted, with the majority of the board, to go public as soon as possible—before the new-issue market soured.

Shortly before the public offering date, Trader received a frantic phone call from James asking for a favor. James indicated that the IPO market had reversed course in the preceding few days; valuations of biotech companies were falling rapidly. James was afraid that investor interest in AMD had slowed so much that the IPO would be threatened. James asked Trader to commit to purchasing a large amount of the AMD offering for her Super Selection accounts to provide enough support for the offering to proceed as planned.

Trader had previously decided that AMD was a questionable investment for her accounts. As an AMD director, however, she also wanted to see a successful IPO, so she offered to reevaluate that decision. In this reevaluation, AMD's stock price seemed high to Trader. Moreover, if she wanted to achieve the desired volume, AMD stock would then represent a higher percentage of Trader's Super Selection portfolios than most holdings. Nevertheless, Trader decided to purchase the shares as James suggested, and when the IPO was effective, she placed the order for the separate accounts and the mutual funds that she managed.

> Explain what violations of the CFA Institute Code and Standards have occurred and the steps that Trader should have taken to avoid the violations. What responsibility does Cuff, as compliance officer, have? What actions should Cuff take now?

2 CASE DISCUSSION

Several violations of the Code and Standards have occurred as a result of Karen Trader's involvement with an outside company.

Trader is neither a CFA charterholder nor a member of CFA Institute, but she is bound by the CFA Institute Code and Standards to the extent that they are incorporated in her firm's compliance policies. Patricia Cuff's responsibility to take action regarding violations of the Code and Standards arises from her duties as a CFA Institute member, as a compliance officer, and as a senior manager of Super Selection.

Responsibilities of Supervisors

Those with legal or compliance responsibilities, such as the designated compliance officer, do not become supervisors solely because they occupy such named positions. Generally, determining whether an individual has supervisory responsibilities depends on whether employees are subject to that individual's control or influence. In other words, does the individual have the authority, for example, to hire, fire, reward, and punish an employee. In this case, even though Trader does not report directly to Cuff, we assume Cuff supervises the actions of all employees of the firm (and has the power to hire, fire, reward, and punish them) in her dual responsibilities as CFO and compliance officer. Therefore, she must comply with the Standard IV(C)—Responsibilities of Supervisors.

As a supervisor, Cuff has a responsibility to take appropriate steps to prevent any violation by those she oversees of applicable statutes, regulations, or CFA Institute Standards. As compliance officer, she must also ensure that the firm's compliance policies are being followed and that violations of these policies are addressed.

Actions Required

As a supervisor, Cuff should take corrective action after discovering the violations by reporting them to senior management. Cuff and Super Selection's senior managers should then take affirmative steps to ensure that the appropriate action is taken to address the misconduct.

As compliance officer, Cuff should direct or monitor a thorough investigation of Trader's actions, recommend limitations on Trader's activities (such as monitoring all trading done in her client accounts, prohibiting her from personal trading, and imposing sanctions on her, including fines), implement procedures designed to prevent and detect future misconduct, and ensure that her recommendations are carried out.

The senior managers should also consult an attorney to determine whether Trader's actions should be reported to local legal or regulatory bodies. If senior management fails to act, Cuff may need to take additional steps, such as disclosing the incident to Super Selection's board of directors and to the appropriate regulatory authorities, and may need to resign from the firm.

Policy Statement for the Firm

"Employees in a supervisory role are responsible for the actions of the employees they supervise regarding compliance with the firm's policies and procedures and any securities laws and regulations that govern the employees' activities. When supervisors become aware of a violation of securities laws or firm policies, they must notify the compliance officer and senior management and/or ensure that appropriate steps are taken to address the violation."

Employees and the Employer/Supervisor

Trader has responsibilities under Standard VI(A)—Disclosure of Conflicts. Trader violated this standard by 1) failing to disclose the conflict of interest that she had as a result of her ownership of AMD stock options and 2) failing to disclose to her employer the compensation she received as a director of AMD. The stock options and the cash compensation both should have been disclosed.

Actions Required

To avoid the violation, Trader should have disclosed to her employer the compensation she was receiving as an AMD director, whether cash or any other benefit, and should have disclosed her ownership of the AMD stock options and her directorship. This disclosure would have provided her employer and clients the information necessary to evaluate the objectivity of her investment advice and actions.

Cuff, since discovering the violation, needs to ensure that proper disclosure is made to clients and a thorough review is made of Trader's client accounts and her personal accounts to determine whether any conflicts have occurred in addition to the IPO violation. If conflicts are discovered, Cuff has a responsibility to take appropriate action—e.g., limit behavior, impose sanctions, and so on.

Policy Statement for the Firm

"All personnel are required to inform their supervisors of any outside activities, such as board directorships, in which they are engaged or into which they propose to enter and receive approval for these activities prior to engaging in them. Employees shall disclose all conflicts of interest to clients and Super Selection prior to engaging in any activity that could be influenced by such conflicts."

Reasonable Basis

Trader had previously determined that AMD was not a suitable investment for her clients. Under pressure from James, Trader has reversed her stance on AMD and has thus violated Standard V(A)—Diligence and Reasonable Basis.

Actions Required

Trader should have diligently and thoroughly researched AMD again prior to making a decision on investing in this security for her clients' accounts. Once having concluded that AMD was not appropriate, she should not change her opinion, without adequate foundation. Trader must also inform clients of any conflicts she has as an AMD director and as an owner of AMD stock options.

Cuff should periodically—at least annually—review investment actions taken for clients by Super Selection employees to determine whether those actions were taken on a reasonable and adequate basis.

Policy Statement for the Firm

"Portfolio managers must consider all applicable relevant factors for each investment recommendation. Recommendations should be made in view of client objectives and the basic characteristics of the investment to be bought or sold."

Fiduciary Duty

By investing in and influencing the public offering of AMD in order to boost the price of this stock, Trader misused her professional position for personal benefits and breached her fiduciary duty to her clients, thus violating Standard III(A)—Loyalty, Prudence and Care.

Although Trader, as a director of AMD, has a duty to that companies' shareholders, she cannot void her obligation to her clients at Super Selection and in the case situation, should have acted in client interests first.

Actions Required

Trader should have taken investment actions that were for the sole benefit of her clients. She should not have been swayed by her ownership of any company into taking an investment action for her clients that she might not have taken in the absence of that ownership. Cuff must thoroughly investigate Trader's activities to see whether other breaches of fiduciary duty have occurred. Following this type of breach and any others, Cuff must limit the activities of the wrongdoers, ensure the implementation of procedures to prevent and detect future occurrences, and follow up to make sure that her recommendations are carried out.

Policy Statement for the Firm

"Employees have a responsibility to identify those persons and interests to which they owe a fiduciary duty. Employees must comply with these identified fiduciary duties."

Investment Recommendations and Actions

Trader violated Standard III(C.1)—Suitability, when she purchased AMD stock for her clients and did not take into consideration their needs and circumstances.

Actions Required

Trader should have considered clients' needs and circumstances prior to taking investment actions and should not have taken these actions to benefit herself or her friends. Cuff should establish a periodic review—to occur at least annually— to compare the suitability of investment actions taken for client accounts with their written investment policy statements.

Policy Statement for the Firm

"The objectives and constraints of each client's portfolio should be put into a written investment policy statement. In taking action or making investment recommendations for clients, employees should consider the needs and circumstances of the client and the basic characteristics of the investment and portfolio involved. No recommendation should be made unless it has been reasonably determined to be suitable for the client's financial situation, investment experience, and objectives."

Priority of Transactions

Trader violated Standard VI(B)—Priority of Transactions, by trading prior to her clients' trades and may have benefited from the impact of her clients' trades on the stock price.

Actions Required

In this instance, Trader circumvented Super Selection's procedures by not reporting trades and brokerage accounts. Nevertheless, Cuff should have made efforts to ensure that Super Selection's policies were being followed. Cuff should review her firm's policies and procedures to make sure they are adequate and determine whether any adjustments should be made to implement or improve them. If adjustments are necessary, she should carry them out. Cuff should also make sure that employees of Super Selection are periodically informed of the Code and Standards and its requirements so as to eliminate any uncertainty about which employees are covered and what responsibilities they have to comply with these standards. Cuff needs to investigate Trader's personal transactions thoroughly and recommend appropriate sanctions for Trader's behavior. Cuff must also ensure that her recommended sanctions are followed to completion.

Policy Statement for the Firm

"The interests of customers will always be given priority over the personal financial interests of the firm's personnel—particularly when securities are being traded or investment actions are being taken. All personal trades by employees of the firm will be pre-cleared in accordance with the firm's compliance policies. In addition, personal trades will be monitored for suspicious activity, such as conflicts of interest and trading on material nonpublic information. Any violator of these priority and pre-clearance policies will be subject to sanctions, including loss of employment."

TRADE ALLOCATION: FAIR DEALING AND DISCLOSURE

LEARNING OUTCOMES

The candidate should be able to:	Mastery
a. critique trade allocation practices, and determine whether compliance exists with the CFA Institute Standards of Professional Conduct addressing fair dealing and client loyalty;	☐
b. discuss appropriate actions to take in response to trade allocation practices that do not adequately respect client interests.	☐

The U.S. Securities and Exchange Commission (SEC) continues to focus its enforcement efforts on trade allocation issues. In the most recent enforcement action involving trade allocation practices, *In the Matter of McKenzie Walker Investment Management, Inc. and Richard McKenzie, Jr.*, the SEC censured and fined a registered investment advisor for failing to disclose its trade allocation practices. However, the SEC order in the *McKenzie Walker* matter makes clear that the firm's trade allocation practices themselves came under scrutiny.

The SEC found that McKenzie Walker did not prescribe any objective procedures or formulas for allocating trades among clients or maintain any internal control mechanism to ensure that portfolio managers allocated trades fairly. Instead, the firm allocated trades on an *ad hoc* basis according to clients' needs and objectives, the profitability of the trade, the type of client account, and in some instances, the client's relationship with the firm or its principal. Neither McKenzie Walker's compliance officer nor anyone else at the firm was required to review trade allocation practices to assess whether all accounts received an equitable allocation of trades consistent with their internal objectives.

According to the SEC, in allocating trades, McKenzie Walker significantly favored the firm's performance-based fee accounts over its asset-based fee accounts. The firm used profitable equity trades as well as hot initial public offerings (IPOs) to boost the performance of performance-based accounts in general and certain accounts in particular. The performance-based fee accounts received profitable equity trades (trades that resulted in a gain during the time interval between the execution of a trade and its allocation to an account at the end of the day) at approximately twice the rate of the asset-based fee accounts. The asset-based fee accounts received only 2 percent of the approximately $910,000 gross trading profits that McKenzie Walker earned for its clients by trading hot IPOs in the calendar year 1992. The asset-based accounts were also allocated all of the trading losses for poorly performing IPOs, which resulted in net losses for those accounts. In contrast, the performance-based fee accounts received 98 percent of the gross IPO trading profits and no trading losses. Among the performance-based fee accounts, the firm favored certain clients, including a former colleague and a former business partner of Richard McKenzie, Jr., and one of the firm's lawyers.

The SEC found that McKenzie Walker failed to disclose its practice of favoring its performance-based fee clients in the allocation of equity trades and hot IPOs. The SEC concluded that McKenzie Walker willfully violated Section 206(2) of the Investment Advisers Act of 1940 by "failing to disclose to its clients, current or prospective, that it engaged in a practice of generally favoring its performance-based fee clients in the allocation of equity trades and hot IPOs, and specifically favoring certain of its performance-based fee clients over such clients." The SEC censured the firm, ordered that the firm disgorge $224,683 plus $35,974 in prejudgment interest, and pay a $100,000 civil fine.

It is interesting to note that McKenzie Walker was not censured for the firm's trade allocation practices per se but, rather, for failing to disclose its trade allocation practices.

Under the CFA Institute Standards of Professional Conduct, however, in addition to fully disclosing their procedures, members must also adopt trade allocation procedures that treat clients in an equitable manner.

CFA Institute Standard III(B)—Fair Dealing states that members must deal fairly and objectively with all clients. To fulfill these duties, members must draft and adhere to allocation procedures that ensure that investment opportunities are allocated to all clients in an appropriate and fair manner. All clients for whom a new issue or secondary offering is suitable should have an opportunity to participate in the offering if they so choose. Members or their firms should adopt an objective formula or procedure for allocating investments to all customers for whom the investments are appropriate.

The CFA Institute *Standards of Practice Handbook* suggests steps to ensure that adequate trade allocation practices are followed. CFA Institute members and their firms are encouraged to:

► obtain advance indications of client interest for new issues;

► allocate new issues by client rather than by portfolio manager;

► adopt a pro rata or similar objective method or formula for allocating trades;

► treat clients fairly in terms of both trade execution order and price;

► execute orders timely and efficiently;

► keep accurate records of trades and client accounts; and

► periodically review all accounts to ensure that all clients are being treated fairly.

Without adequate trade allocation procedures, members and their firms risk breaching the fiduciary duties owed to their investment management clients. CFA Institute Standard III(A)—Loyalty, Prudence, and Care, states that members have a duty of loyalty to their clients and must place clients' interests above their own. Members should strive to avoid all real or potential conflicts of interest. Allocating hot IPOs to selected clients in the hopes of receiving additional future business or increased fees creates an obvious conflict of interest and breaches members' duty to clients. Such practices are detrimental to the interests of those clients not given the opportunity to participate in the offering. The establishment of objective allocation procedures assists members in complying with their fiduciary duties.

Once trade allocation procedures are established, they must be disclosed. As the SEC stated in its order in the *McKenzie Walker* case, a reasonable investor would consider it important to know these allocation procedures. Disclosure must be sufficient to give the client or potential client full knowledge of the procedures and enable the client to make an informed decision regarding the handling of his or her account.

In summary, full and fair disclosure of a firm's allocation procedures is a minimum step toward meeting the goal of fair dealing. Disclosure of unfair allocation procedures does not, however, relieve CFA Institute members of their duties of fair dealing and fiduciary trust to all clients.

CHANGING INVESTMENT OBJECTIVES

The U.S. Securities and Exchange Commission (SEC) sanctioned Mitchell Hutchins Asset Management (Mitchell Hutchins), a registered broker-dealer and investment adviser, for the failure to trade securities for an investment fund within the limits of the stated fund objectives.

Mitchell Hutchins commenced management of the PaineWebber Short-Term U.S. Government Income Fund (the Fund) in 1993, marketing it as a higher-yield and somewhat higher-risk alternative to money market funds and bank certificates of deposit. The prospectus disclosed that the Fund's investment objective was to achieve the highest level of income consistent with preservation of capital and low volatility of net asset value. The appendix to the prospectus also disclosed that the Fund had "no present intention" of investing in certain classes of interest only (IO) and principal only (PO) stripped mortgage-backed securities.

Contrary to the Fund's low-volatility investment objective and "no present intention" statement, the Fund's portfolio manager began investing in certain IO and PO securities in the fall of 1993. When interest rates increased sharply in February 1994, the Fund incurred significant losses, performing well below comparable funds.

The SEC found that the fund manager improperly deviated from the investment policy recited in its registration statement without shareholder approval. The SEC also found that Mitchell Hutchins violated the antifraud provisions of the federal securities laws by marketing the Fund as a low-volatility investment, when ultimately it was not.

By investing in securities outside the Fund's stated objectives, the portfolio manager's conduct violated Standard III(C.2)—Duties to Clients and Standard V(B.1)—Communication with Clients and Prospective Clients, of CFA Institute's Standards of Professional Conduct. Standard III(C.2) states that when members and candidates are responsible for managing a portfolio to a specific mandate, strategy, or style, they must only make investment recommendations or take investment actions that are consistent with the stated objectives and constraints of the portfolio. Standard V(B.1) states that members must disclose to clients the basic format and general principles of the investment processes by which securities are selected and portfolios are constructed and shall promptly disclose to clients and prospects any change that might materially affect those processes.

Standard III(C.2) protects investors by ensuring that when members manage a portfolio to a specific mandate or strategy, such as in the case of a mutual fund, that they adhere to the stated investment strategy. This allows investors to judge the suitability of the fund for themselves and protects them from style drift and exposure to investment strategies, asset classes, and risks other than those explicitly stated.

In much the same way, Standard V(B.1) protects investors by supplying them with enough information to have an adequate understanding of and to make informed decisions about an investment product or service that is being offered. Undisclosed changes by a manager in the investment strategy of a portfolio may be contrary to the investor's goals. Knowing the key elements of and principles behind the investment allows investors to choose investment products and services that are suitable and appropriate to their investment objectives.

CFA Institute members can take several steps to help ensure that they abide by the principles of Standard III(C.2) and V(B.1). First, when managing a separate portfolio, members should make a reasonable inquiry into a client's financial situation, investment experience, and investment objectives. This information should be updated at least annually. Second, members should disclose the basic format and general principles of the investment processes by which securities are selected and portfolios are constructed at the outset of the relationship, and on a regular basis thereafter. Third, members should implement regular internal checks for each account to ensure that portfolio characteristics meet the account's investment mandate, or the stated investment strategy in the case of pooled funds. Finally, if members wish to change the investment objectives or strategies of portfolios they manage, then members must notify clients and investors of the potential change. Members should fully disclose the impact that the change will have on the portfolio and secure documented authorization of the change in strategy from the client.

The SEC censured the firm, issued a cease-and-desist order, imposed a civil penalty of $500,000, and ordered the appointment of an independent consultant to review and make any appropriate recommendations concerning Mitchell Hutchins' policies and procedures.

PRUDENCE IN PERSPECTIVE
by John Train and Thomas A. Melfe

LEARNING OUTCOMES

The candidate should be able to:	Mastery
a. explain the basic principles of the new Prudent Investor Rule;	☐
b. explain the general fiduciary standards to which a trustee must adhere;	☐
c. differentiate between the old Prudent Man Rule and the new Prudent Investor Rule;	☐
d. explain the key factors that a trustee should consider when investing and managing trust assets.	☐

THE MEANING OF PRUDENCE

Prudence is a process, not a result. A trustee must act prudently in all he does for a trust and its beneficiaries.

Prudence is a flexible and unspecific standard of care, permitting wide discretion within general rules. It lacks the "safe harbor" features found in some other regulatory areas, such as federal securities and tax law, which tell you exactly what you should do.

CARE, SKILL, AND CAUTION

The principle of prudence consists of the three elements, care, skill, and caution.

Administrative prudence means exercising care, skill, and caution in safekeeping trust assets, disposing of trust income and principal, maintaining trust records and keeping beneficiaries informed, and treating beneficiaries impartially.

There is also *investment prudence*, which means exercising care, skill, and caution when dealing with any aspect of a trust's investments. For instance, before investing any funds, a trustee should establish investment objectives that suit the purposes of the trust and needs of the beneficiaries; act diligently in selecting investments; determine the risk tolerance of a trust and choose only investments that suit that risk level; diversify the trust's holdings; focus on the portfolio's liquidity; determine whether to ask the advice of experts; and make certain that the investments themselves are advantageous to both the income and the remainder beneficiaries.

It helps greatly in understanding the new Prudent Investor Rule to see how it evolved from the old Prudent Man Rule, so we include a section to elucidate that background.

3   THE OLD PRUDENT MAN RULE: *HARVARD V. AMORY*

The new Prudent Investor Rule, the subject of this reading, derives from the old Prudent Man Rule. The Old Rule arose from a celebrated 1830 Massachusetts court decision, *Harvard College v. Amory*. Amory was a trustee of a $50,000 testamentary trust. The income went to the decedent's widow for life. At her death the remainder passed to Harvard and Massachusetts General Hospital in equal shares. The will gave Amory broad power to invest the trust fund, including in stocks according to "his best judgment and discretion." Amory invested the entire $50,000 fund in stocks that yielded 8 percent in dividends. Five years after the trust was established, the widow died. Amory filed his account with the court, showing a trust value of only $38,000. When he asked the court for his discharge, Harvard and Massachusetts General Hospital objected, demanding that he restore the $12,000 of lost capital. Judge Putnam, who heard the case, ruled in favor of Amory. The keystone of his decision was a phrase that has become graven in trust lore: "Do what you will, the capital is at hazard." He went on to pronounce a legal principle that became a universal standard for fiduciary conduct, known as the "Prudent Man Rule":

> All that can be required of a trustee to invest, is, that he shall conduct himself faithfully and exercise a sound discretion. He is to observe how men of prudence, discretion, and intelligence manage their own affairs, not in regard to speculation, but in regard to the permanent disposition of their funds, considering the probable income, as well as the probable safety of the capital to be invested.

Over the next century the philosophies of state legislatures and courts changed from favoring flexibility in trust investing to a desire for more certainty and conservatism. In the first half of the twentieth century, most states enacted lists of specific types of investments that trustees were permitted to make, and courts established a series of subrules on what was prudent and what was not. Thus the flexibility and discretion of *Harvard v. Amory* rule gave way to rules and restrictions.

The following are some examples of restrictions tacked on to the Old Rule by state courts and legislatures:

► Certain types of investments were imprudent per se and thus not allowed for trusts.

► Each investment in a trust portfolio, rather than the portfolio as a whole, had to satisfy the tests of prudence.

▶ A trustee was required to perform duties personally, not delegate them to others.

▶ Investment in mutual funds or index funds was an improper delegation of duty by the trustee.

The various restrictions grafted onto *Harvard v. Amory* by state legislatures and courts ultimately impaired its value by reducing its flexibility. They tended to backtrack toward earlier conservative and protective theories of trust investing, although not without struggles. Some institutions attempted to buck the restrictive trend by adopting model language echoing Judge Putnam's opinion.

In 1942 the American Bankers Association promulgated its Model Prudent Man Investment Statute, which both parroted and slightly modified Judge Putnam's words:

> In acquiring, investing, reinvesting, exchanging, retaining, selling, and managing property for the benefit of another, a fiduciary shall exercise the judgment and care under the circumstances then prevailing, which men of prudence, discretion, and intelligence exercise in the management of their own affairs, not in regard to speculation but in regard to the permanent disposition of their funds, considering the probable income as well as probable safety of their capital.

In 1959 the *Restatement of the Law, Trusts* (Second)—the Bible of American trust law principles—used different language with the same impact:

> In making investments of trust funds the trustee is under a duty to the beneficiary in the absence of provisions in the terms of the trust or of a statute otherwise providing, to make such investments and only such investments as a prudent man would make of his own property having in view the preservation of the estate and the amount and regularity of the income to be derived.

In 1972 the National Conference of Commissioners on Uniform State Laws issued a model Uniform Management of Institutional Funds (*not* private trusts) Act, which at this writing has been adopted by many states. This model legislation imposed a variation of the Prudent Man Rule on trustees and directors of not-for-profit institutions such as universities, hospitals, museums, and charitable foundations.

As recently as 1974, the National Conference of Commissioners on Uniform State Laws adopted the following wording for its Uniform Probate Code Prudent Man Rule:

> Except as otherwise provided by the terms of the trust, the trustee shall observe the standards in dealing with the trust assets that would be observed by a prudent man dealing with the property of another, and if the trustee has special skills or expertise, he is under duty to use those skills.

Also in 1974, Congress rejected many of these restrictive subrules when it enacted the Employee Retirement Income Security Act (ERISA), governing employee benefit trusts. ERISA incorporated its own prudent man rule, adopting many recommendations of the legal and investment communities. In its formulation, Congress sought to "avoid repeating the mistake of freezing its rules against future learning and developments." Its prudent man section states:

> The fiduciary shall discharge his duties with the care, skill, prudence, and diligence under the circumstances then prevailing that a prudent man acting in a like capacity and familiar with such matters would use in the conduct of an enterprise of a like

character and with like aims; and by diversifying the investments of the plans so as to minimize the risk of large losses, unless under the circumstances it is clearly prudent not to do so.

Over time the states' additions and restrictions had resulted in so many prohibitions that trust investing departed from how the real-life prudent man was handling his own investments—the heart of the Old Rule! By the late 1950s, the *accretions* to the Rule *became* the Rule. In reaction to the restrictive court rulings and legislation, a counterreformation arose. The trust industry and the legal profession disagreed with the ultraconservatism of the modified Rule. Feminism influenced a name change to the "Prudent Person Rule." Lawyers countered its strictures by writing investment powers into wills and trust agreements that authorized the trustee to invest in his sole discretion, without regard to state law restrictions, even if the securities were non-income-producing, unseasoned, or speculative, essentially drafting out the constricting parts of a state's Prudent Man Rule. Some banks included in their specimen clauses for wills and trusts a provision that the trustee could invest in any securities that were eligible for the bank's own investment management accounts. Some drafters of wills and trusts allowed the trustee to invest in "alternative investments, such as venture capital, covered options, precious metals and natural resources."

Eventually, the entire trust community accepted the view that the old Prudent Man Rule placed trusts at a disadvantage by depriving them of newer investment variations. State legislatures began to join the movement, eliminating the legal lists that dictated what trusts could invest in, and replacing them with Prudent Man standards similar to *Harvard v. Amory*. In 1970 New York State adopted the following Prudent Man Rule:

> A fiduciary holding funds for investment may invest the same in such securities as would be acquired by prudent men of discretion and intelligence in such matters who are seeking a reasonable income and preservation of their capital, provided, however, that nothing in this subparagraph shall limit the effect of any will, agreement court order or other instrument creating or defining the investment powers of a fiduciary, or shall restrict the authority of a court of proper jurisdiction to instruct the fiduciary in the interpretation or administration of the express terms of any will, agreement or other instrument or in the administration of the property under the fiduciary's care.

Finally, in 1994 the National Conference of Commissioners of Uniform State Laws published its Uniform Prudent Investor Act, with the stated purpose of updating private trust investment law "in recognition of the alterations that have occurred in investment practice . . ." This Act draws upon the revised standards for prudent trust investment promulgated by the American Law Institute in its Third Restatement (1992), Section 227. It reads as follows:

> The trustee is under a duty to the beneficiaries to invest and manage the funds of the trust as a prudent investor would, in light of the purposes, terms, distribution requirements, and other circumstances of the trust.
>
> **a.** This standard requires the exercise of reasonable care, skill, and caution, and is to be applied to investments not in isolation but in the context of the trust portfolio and as a part of an overall investment strategy, which should incorporate risk and return objectives reasonably suitable to the trust.
>
> **b.** In making and implementing investment decisions, the trustee has a duty to diversify the investments of the trust unless, under the circumstances, it is prudent not to do so.
>
> **c.** In addition, the trustee must:
>
> > **1.** conform to fundamental fiduciary duties of loyalty and impartiality;

2. act with prudence in deciding whether and how to delegate authority and in the selection and supervision of agents; and

3. incur only costs that are reasonable in amount and appropriate to the investment responsibilities of the trusteeship.

 d. The trustee's duties under this Section are subject to the rule of § 228, dealing primarily with contrary investment provisions of a trust or statute.

The Old Rule, lumbered with so many restrictions over the years, was thus finally freed up.

THE NEW PRUDENT INVESTOR RULE   **4**

The American Law Institute's 1992 Restatement of the Law Third, Trusts is not itself the law, but it is the definitive commentary on the law. Lawyers, professional trustees, and the courts often turn to it for guidance. It has greatly influenced the development of American trust law.

The sponsors of the Third Restatement concluded that the inflexibility imposed by the courts had placed unjustified liability upon trustees and inhibited the exercise of investment judgment. The American Law Institute's reporter says that the New Rule liberates expert trustees "to pursue challenging, rewarding, nontraditional strategies" and provides unsophisticated trustees with reasonably clear guidance to practical courses of investment.

So the essence of the New Rule is that no investments or techniques are imprudent per se—a radical departure, considering that the Old Rule held that investments that were speculative or non-income-producing were intrinsically imprudent.

The New Rule contains five basic principles:

1. Diversification is fundamental to risk minimization and is therefore ordinarily required of trustees.

2. Risk and return are so directly related that trustees have a duty to analyze and make conscious decisions concerning the levels of risk appropriate to the purposes of the trust.

3. Trustees have a duty to avoid fees, transaction costs, and other expenses that are not justified by the objectives of the investment program.

4. The fiduciary's duty of impartiality requires a conscious balancing of current income and growth.

5. Trustees may have a duty, as well as the authority, to delegate as prudent investors would.

The Third Restatement's new Prudent Investor Rule is intended for a trust only if it is consistent with the terms of a trust and with state law. Generally, the terms of the trust will control. Assuming that a state has adopted the New Rule, or permits a trust to adopt it, then the terms of the trust will dictate whether the New Rule applies to its investment activity.

The terms of a trust may expand or limit the provisions of the Third Restatement's New Rule. In general, a trustee can properly make investments as expressly or implicitly authorized by the terms of the trust. Thus a trust's terms will control a trustee's investment duties and authorities, even if different from the Rule, so long as they do not conflict with the law. But absent contrary provisions (or silence) in the terms of the trust, the Restatement's New Rule will govern, if a state has adopted it.

While the Restatement mainly addresses the administration of private trusts, it is also generally appropriate to charitable or public funds. The New Rule is also intended to guide executors and administrators of estates, guardians, conservators, and the like.

Even though the Restatement's New Rule does not directly apply to nonprivate trustees, it is the safest route for them to follow, since courts and regulators who supervise these other fiduciaries will probably turn to the Restatement for guidance, just as they looked to the previous Restatement in the days of the Old Rule.

Duty to Conform to General Fiduciary Standards

Of the standards to which a trustee must adhere, the most important are that he must exercise care, skill, and caution, and must manifest loyalty and impartiality. His compliance with these duties is judged as of the time an investment decision is made, and *not* with the benefit of hindsight or subsequent developments, nor on the outcome of his investment decisions. This is just as it was under Judge Putnam's rule.

Loyalty means that a trustee must be free of conflicts of interest in managing a trust's investments, and must act solely in the interests of the beneficiaries. Impartiality means that a trustee must recognize the divergent interests of different beneficiaries. He must resolve these differences "in a fair and reasonable manner," whatever that may mean.

Care includes obtaining relevant information on the circumstances and requirements of the trust and its beneficiaries, on the contents and resources of the trust estate, and about the available investment choices. The duty of care may also require a trustee to seek the advice of others.

Skill means that although a person of ordinary intelligence, without financial experience, may serve as a trustee, he should obtain the guidance of specialists in order to meet the skill criterion. Furthermore, unlike the Old Rule, which in general forbade investment delegation, the Restatement holds that a trustee may in some instances have a duty to delegate investment authority to others. In so delegating, "the trustee must exercise appropriate care and skill in selecting and supervising agents and in determining the degree and terms of the delegation." If, on the other hand, a trustee possesses more than ordinary skill, he must use it.

The New Rule requires caution when investing trust funds, with a view to both safety of capital and securing a reasonable return. Safety of capital includes preserving its real, as against nominal, value; that is, seeking to limit the erosion of the trust's purchasing power due to inflation.

In a major departure from the Old Rule, the New Rule defines reasonable return as total return: capital growth as well as income. Furthermore, under the New Rule, capital growth does not necessarily mean only preservation of the trust's purchasing power but may extend to growth in the real value of principal in appropriate cases.[1] The Restatement continues:

> In balancing the return objectives between flow of income and growth of principal, emphasis depends not only on the purposes and distribution requirements of the trust, but also on its other circumstances and specific terms, such as the beneficiaries' tax positions and whether the trustee has power to invade principal.

---

[1] We note that this is a remarkable line of reasoning. It is in reality quite enough to preserve buying power in real terms while providing a reasonable income that rises to offset inflation. Seeking much more than this—swinging for the fences—may achieve much less. Nevertheless, says the New Rule, it is permissible to try, if this endeavor is consistent with the situation of the trust. And these days many of the finest growth companies pay very low dividends, while rewarding their shareholders by reducing the number of shares outstanding through open-market purchases.

Caution and Risk Management

The Old Rule requires caution in making investments. This has been interpreted as a duty to avoid speculation and undue risk and follows from the "risk-averse" duty of caution.

That duty survives under the New Rule, but it is altered. After declaring that all investments, even U.S. Treasury obligations, and all investment strategies involve some risk, the Restatement asserts that the duty of caution does not call for the total avoidance of risk by trustees but rather for its "prudent management," taking account of inflation, volatility, illiquidity, and the like, in addition to potential loss.

This emphasis on active risk management in trusts is new. Its importance is shown by its specific inclusion in the Restatement's phrase "an overall investment strategy, which should incorporate risk and return objectives reasonably suitable to the trust." Risk management by a trustee is viewed by the Restatement as requiring that careful attention be given to each trust's particular "risk tolerance," defined as its tolerance for volatility, given the needs of the beneficiaries. Under the New Rule, the trustee has an affirmative duty to assess its risk tolerance and actively manage the risk element of its investments.

Diversification

The Restatement declares:

> In making and implementing investment decisions, the trustee has a duty to diversify the investments of the trust unless, under the circumstances, it is prudent not to do so.

This duty was included as a separate one in the preceding Second Restatement, but not as part of that edition's prudent investment standard. In the Third Restatement, the duty is elevated to the standard itself, to show "its centrality in fiduciary investing," and perhaps to encourage the states to adopt diversification as a requirement in their Prudent Investor statutes. Strange as it seems, trust portfolio diversification has not always been mandated by state law, even though it has for many years been almost universally followed in trust portfolios.

The Third Restatement also declares that "no objective, general legal standard can be set for a degree of risk that is or is not prudent," and it acknowledges that "the degree of risk permitted for a particular trust is ultimately a matter for interpretation and judgment. This requires that a trustee make reasonable efforts to ascertain the purposes of the trust and to understand the types of investments suitable to those purposes in light of all the relevant circumstances."

THE UNIFORM PRUDENT INVESTOR ACT   5

The Third Restatement is dedicated exclusively to the *investment* and related duties of trustees. Based on its new Prudent Investor Rule, another institution, the National Conference of Commissioners on Uniform State Laws, whose charter is to promote uniformity among the fifty states in certain areas of the law, in 1994 promulgated the Uniform Prudent Investor Act, which we will call the Model Act.

Many states responded to the Model Act by revising their Prudent Man statutes to conform to the Act. Others adopted the entire Model Act with only slight modifications.

The Model Act is the wave of the future. All trustees of private trusts must understand its provisions, even trustees in states that have not yet adopted it. To that end we will describe its more important sections.

Like the Third Restatement from which it flows, the Model Act makes five fundamental changes in the old rules governing private trust investing:

1. The standard of prudence applies to the trust portfolio as a whole, rather than to each individual investment on its own.

2. The trade-off between investment risk and return is the fiduciary's central consideration.

3. All specific restrictions on the types of investments that a trustee may use are abrogated; a trustee may invest in anything that plays an appropriate role in achieving the risk/return objectives of the trust and that meets the requirements of prudent investing.

4. The traditional duty to diversify investments is integrated into the Prudent Investment Standard.

5. Delegation by a trustee is permissible, subject to certain safeguards.

For the text of the Model Act, see Appendix 10B.

6　SUMMARY OF THE MODEL ACT

The heart of the Model Act is its Section 2, setting forth a new standard of prudence to which the trustees it governs must adhere, unless the trust instrument provides otherwise. The Act's prudence standard provides that:

a. A trustee shall invest and manage trust assets as a prudent investor would, by considering the purpose, terms, distribution requirements, and other circumstances of the trust. In satisfying this standard, the trustee shall exercise reasonable care, skill, and caution.

b. A trustee's investment and management decisions respecting individual assets must be evaluated not in isolation but in the context of the trust portfolio as a whole and as a part of an overall investment strategy having risk and return objectives reasonably suited to the trust.

Risk/Reward

The Act incorporates a risk-reward ratio concept into the Model Act's new Prudence Standard. A Comment invokes "the main theme of modern investment practice, sensitivity to the risk/return curve." The Comment explains that risk varies with financial and other circumstances, and thus with a trust's purpose and the circumstances of the beneficiaries.

Strategy

A trustee must 1) develop an overall portfolio strategy designed to achieve expected present and future distributions to its beneficiaries and 2) do so with proper regard for risk and return. Unlike the Old Rule's focus on the prudence of individual investment holdings and avoiding risk, the new standard recognizes the relationship of the potential for reward to a trust from accepting risk and focuses on the trustee's duty to manage that risk over the portfolio as a whole, not taking each holding in isolation. This departure is a most noteworthy feature of the Model Act and New Rule.

The Act identifies *key factors* that a trustee should consider when investing and managing trust assets, notably:

► general economic conditions

► the possible effect of inflation or deflation

► the expected tax consequences for the beneficiaries of investment decisions or strategies

► the role that each investment or course of action plays within the overall trust portfolio

► the expected total return from income and capital appreciation

► the beneficiaries' other resources

► needs for liquidity, regularity of income, and preservation or appreciation of capital

► an asset's special relationship or special value, if any, to the purposes of the trust or to the beneficiaries

The Model Act further states a trustee need not satisfy all of these factors for each investment but only those "as are relevant to the trust or its beneficiaries."

The Model Act also includes three *investment policy* provisions:

1. A trustee shall make a reasonable effort to verify the facts relevant to the investment and management of trust assets.

2. A trustee may invest in any kind of property or type of investment consistent with the standards of the Act.

3. A trustee possessing special skills or expertise, or who is selected as trustee based upon the representation of having such skills, has a duty to use those special skills or expertise.

The first provision invokes a trustee's traditional duty to investigate before investing; that is, to analyze information likely to bear on an investment's value or safety. Examples offered are financial reports, auditor's reports, records of title, and the like—routine steps taken by investment analysts.

The second, in a major change for trustees of private trusts, declares the policy that no kind of property or investment is inherently imprudent. Under the Old Rule a variety of investments had been categorized by the courts as imprudent, such as venture capital, futures, options, lower-rated bonds, and stocks of new and untried enterprises. Conversely, the Model Act's Commentary also points out that long-term bonds, which were historically considered ideal for trusts, are now thought to incur a level of risk and volatility perhaps inappropriate for some trusts.

In underscoring its belief that no specific investments or techniques should be deemed imprudent per se, the Model Act's Commentary opines that trust beneficiaries are better protected by the Act's emphasis on close attention to risk/return objectives than by an attempt to predict categories of investment that are intrinsically imprudent. The Act espouses the view that the trustee's task is to invest at a risk level suitable to the purposes of the trust, whether that level is speculative or conservative.

The third provision reaffirms a policy of the old Prudent Man Rule. That policy distinguished between amateur and professional trustees, holding that the standard of prudence is "relational," meaning that the standard for professional trustees is higher than that for laymen.

Diversification

The Model Act and the Third Restatement both emphasize the importance of diversification to reduce risk in a trust portfolio. A trustee should diversify a trust's investments unless, owing to special circumstances, he reasonably determines that the purposes of the trust are better served by putting most of his eggs in a single basket. They even acknowledge that there is no automatic rule or method for identifying how much diversification is enough.

The duty to diversify might not apply if a trust held a block of low-basis stock, where the capital gains tax cost of selling it would outweigh the benefit of diversifying, or if by selling a stock the trust would lose control of a business.

Initial Review

The Act provides that the trustee of a new trust, or of an old trust to which new assets are being added, or a successor trustee, should conduct a review immediately and decide whether to retain or dispose of those assets. This provision applies to investments that were suitable when acquired but subsequently became unsuitable. The provision derives from the Restatement's admonition that a trustee must constantly monitor a trust's investments.

Loyalty

The Model Act includes a separate section on the duty of loyalty, which it calls "the most characteristic rule of trust law," namely to "invest and manage the trust assets solely in the interest of the beneficiaries."

Impartiality

Another traditional duty, also subject to a separate section in the Model Act, is the duty of a trustee to act impartially, taking into account any differing interests of the beneficiaries, whether successive, such as income beneficiaries and remaindermen, or simultaneous, as within a class of income beneficiaries.

This duty is the hardest for a trustee to fulfill to all the beneficiaries' satisfaction. It often forces him to adopt compromise investment strategies: to play it safe as between an income beneficiary wanting high income and prospective remaindermen wanting high growth. The supposed failure to meet this duty of impartiality often gives rise to remaindermens' claims when the trust terminates that the trustee violated the impartiality duty by giving the income beneficiaries too much income.

Some trusts avoid the problem by eliminating the duty of impartiality. For example, if the settlor's widow is the income beneficiary, and clearly the preferred beneficiary, and if the testator wants the trustee to pursue a high-income investment strategy, he can simply relieve the trustee of the duty to be impartial vis-à-vis the remaindermen. A fine solution is to distribute 4 percent a year, say, of the running three-year average total capital.

Costs

The Act provides that a trustee may only incur costs that are appropriate and reasonable. Trustees are thus obliged to make comparisons on transaction and agent costs such as brokerage commissions, and to calculate the cost-benefit ratio, considering the trust's size and ability to bear such costs. These costs include the trustee's own compensation. Although he has a duty to *control* costs, a trustee is not obliged to pay only the *lowest* costs.

The Model Act preserves the time-honored principle that compliance with the Prudent Investor Rule is to be determined in light of the circumstances at the time of the trustee's action, not by hindsight. A trustee is not an insurer or guarantor.

Delegation

A key feature of the Model Act breaks with the past and permits a trustee to delegate investment and management functions that he previously had to perform personally if a prudent investor with similar skills would reasonably delegate them under the circumstances. Still, a trustee must act prudently in the following:

► selecting the agent

► establishing the scope and terms of the delegation

► periodically reviewing the agent's actions

An agent who accepts delegation by a trustee is subject to the jurisdiction of the courts of the state in which the trust is resident.

The Model Act provides that a trustee who complies with its requirements for delegating investment and management functions to an agent will *not* be liable to the beneficiaries or to the trust for the agent's decisions or actions. Not every state is likely to accept this provision. New York's version of the Model Act, for instance, omits it.

The Model Act provides that it shall apply to trusts in existence upon, and created after, the date it is enacted by an adopting state. As to existing trusts, it applies only to investment decisions and actions made after its effective date.

APPENDIX 10A

THE NEW PRUDENT INVESTOR RULE

From the *Restatement of the Law Third, Trusts* (Prudent Investor Rule):

§ 227. General Standard of Prudent Investment

The trustee is under a duty to the beneficiaries to invest and manage the funds of the trust as a prudent investor would, in light of the purposes, terms, distributions requirements, and other circumstances of the trust.

a. This standard requires the exercise of reasonable care, skill, and caution, and is to be applied to investments not in isolation but in the context of the trust portfolio and as a part of an overall investment strategy, which should incorporate risk and return objectives reasonably suitable to the trust.

b. In making and implementing investment decisions, the trustee has a duty to diversify the investments of the trust unless, under the circumstances, it is prudent not to do so.

c. In addition, the trustee must:

1. conform to fundamental fiduciary duties of loyalty (§ 170) and impartiality (§ 183);

2. act with prudence in deciding whether and how to delegate authority and in the selection and supervision of agents (§ 171); and

3. incur only costs that are reasonable in amount and appropriate to the investment responsibilities of the trusteeship (§ 188).

d. The trustee's duties under this Section are subject to the rule of § 228, dealing primarily with contrary investment provisions of a trust or statute.

UNIFORM PRUDENT INVESTOR ACT OF 1994

Section

1. Prudent Investor Rule.

2. Standard of Care; Portfolio Strategy; Risk and Return Objectives.

3. Diversification.

4. Duties at Inception of Trusteeship.

5. Loyalty.

6. Impartiality.

7. Investment Costs.

8. Reviewing Compliance.

9. Delegation of Investment and Management Functions.

Section

10. Language Invoking Standard of [Act].

11. Application to Existing Trusts.

12. Uniformity of Application and Construction.

13. Short Title.

14. Severability.

15. Effective Date.

16. Repeals.

§ 1. Prudent Investor Rule.

a. Except as otherwise provided in subsection (b), a trustee who invests and manages trust assets owes a duty to the beneficiaries of the trust to comply with the prudent investor rule set forth in this [Act].

b. The prudent investor rule, a default rule, may be expanded, restricted, eliminated, or otherwise altered by the provisions of a trust. A trustee is not liable to a beneficiary to the extent that the trustee acted in reasonable reliance on the provisions of the trust.

Reprinted by permission of HBS Press. From *Investing and Managing Trusts under the New Prudent Investor Rule: A Guide for Trustees, Investment Advisors, and Lawyers,* by John Train and Thomas A. Melfe, pages 165–169. Copyright © 1999.

§ 2. Standard of Care; Portfolio Strategy; Risk and Return Objectives.

a. A trustee shall invest and manage trust assets as a prudent investor would, but considering the purposes, terms, distribution requirements, and other circumstances of the trust. In satisfying this standard, the trustee shall exercise reasonable care, skill, and caution.

b. A trustee's investment and management decisions respecting individual assets must be evaluated not in isolation but in the context of the trust portfolio as a whole and as a part of an overall investment strategy having risk and return objectives reasonably suited to the trust.

c. Among circumstances that a trustee shall consider in investing and managing trust assets are such of the following as are relevant to the trust or its beneficiaries:

1. general economic conditions;

2. the possible effect of inflation or deflation;

3. the expected tax consequences of investment decisions or strategies;

4. the role that each investment or course of action plays within the overall trust portfolio, which may include financial assets, interests in closely held enterprises, tangible and intangible personal property, and real property;

5. the expected total return from income and the appreciation of capital;

6. other resources of the beneficiaries;

7. needs for liquidity, regularity of income, and preservation or appreciation of capital; and

8. an asset's special relationship or special value, if any, to the purposes of the trust or to one or more of the beneficiaries.

d. A trustee shall make a reasonable effort to verify facts relevant to the investment and management of trust assets.

e. A trustee may invest in any kind of property or type of investment consistent with the standards of this [Act].

f. A trustee who has special skills or expertise, or is named trustee in reliance upon the trustee's representation that the trustee has special skills or expertise, has a duty to use those special skills or expertise.

§ 3. Diversification.

A trustee shall diversify the investments of the trust unless the trustee reasonably determines that, because of special circumstances, the purposes of the trust are better served without diversifying.

§ 4. Duties at Inception of Trusteeship.

Within a reasonable time after accepting a trusteeship or receiving trust assets, a trustee shall review the trust assets and make and implement decisions concerning the retention and disposition of assets, in order to bring the trust portfolio into compliance with the purposes, terms, distribution requirements, and other circumstances of the trust, and with the requirements of this [Act].

§ 5. Loyalty.

A trustee shall invest and manage the trust assets solely in the interest of the beneficiaries.

§ 6. Impartiality.

If a trust has two or more beneficiaries, the trustee shall act impartially in investing and managing the trust assets, taking into account any differing interests of the beneficiaries.

§ 7. Investment Costs.

In investing and managing trust assets, a trustee may only incur costs that are appropriate and reasonable in relation to the assets, the purposes of the trust, and the skills of the trustee.

§ 8. Reviewing Compliance.

Compliance with the prudent investor rule is determined in light of the facts and circumstances existing at the time of a trustee's decision or action and not by hindsight.

§ 9. Delegation of Investment and Management Functions.

a. A trustee may delegate investment and management functions that a prudent trustee of comparable skills could properly delegate under the circumstances. The trustee shall exercise reasonable care, skill, and caution in:

   1. selecting an agent;
   2. establishing the scope and terms of the delegation, consistent with the purposes and terms of the trust; and
   3. periodically reviewing the agent's actions in order to monitor the agent's performance and compliance with the terms of the delegation.

b. In performing a delegated function, an agent owes a duty to the trust to exercise reasonable care to comply with the terms of the delegation.

c. A trustee who complies with the requirements of subsection (a) is not liable to the beneficiaries or to the trust for the decisions or actions of the agent to whom the function was delegated.

d. By accepting the delegation of a trust function from the trustee of a trust that is subject to the law of this State, an agent submits to the jurisdiction of the courts of this State.

§ 10. Language Invoking Standard of [Act].

The following terms or comparable language in the provisions of a trust, unless otherwise limited or modified, authorizes any investment or strategy permitted under this [Act]: "investments permissible by law for investment of trust funds," "legal investments," "authorized investments," "using the judgment and care under the circumstances then prevailing that persons of prudence, discretion, and intelligence exercise in the management of their own affairs, not in regard to speculation but in regard to the permanent disposition of their funds, considering the probable income as well as the probable safety of their capital," "prudent man rule," "prudent trustee rule," "prudent person rule," and "prudent investor rule."

§ 11. Application to Existing Trusts.

This [Act] applies to trusts existing on and created after its effective date. As applied to trusts existing on its effective date, this [Act] governs only decisions or actions occurring after that date.

§ 12. Uniformity of Application and Construction.

This [Act] shall be applied and construed to effectuate its general purpose to make uniform the law with respect to the subject of this [Act] among the States enacting it.

§ 13. Short Title.

This [Act] may be cited as the "[Name of Enacting State] Uniform Prudent Investor Act."

§ 14. Severability.

If any provision of this [Act] or its application to any person or circumstance is held invalid, the invalidity does not affect other provisions or applications of this [Act] which can be given effect without the invalid provision or application, and to this end the provisions of this [Act] are severable.

§ 15. Effective Date.

This [Act] takes effect _____.

§ 16. Repeals.

The following acts and parts of acts are repealed:

1.
2.
3.

PRACTICE PROBLEMS FOR READING 10

The following information relates to Questions 1–6

Praveen Shankar is employed as an analyst for Front Hall Investments (FHI), an asset management firm. Shankar is also a CFA candidate studying for the Level III exam.

Based on the past four monthly observations, Shankar observes that auto industry stock returns show a strong positive correlation with changes in hourly wages. As a result, his latest investment strategy report recommends that, in his opinion, adjustments to portfolio holdings of auto industry common stocks should be based on the national labor department's monthly release of hourly wage data.

The national labor department was scheduled to release hourly wage data on Thursday, 17 August. However, a clerical error causes the news of a dramatic increase in hourly wages to be released on the labor department's website on Tuesday, 15 August. Shankar assumes that he is the only analyst who notices the information on the website, and recommends that FHI's clients increase their holdings in auto industry common stocks. When the investment community subsequently learns of the wage data, the prices of auto industry common stocks rise significantly. During the following week, Shankar and FHI receive favorable publicity as a result of his timely recommendation.

Norah Pankow, CFA, Shankar's supervisor, is program director for the local CFA Society. Pankow selects only her own clients and brokers as seminar speakers for the society, and she tells Shankar, "Just as I had hoped, the seminars have been very positive for FHI's business." One of Pankow's other initiatives for the society is to create a publicly available web log (blog) on the internet. The blog's purpose is to give local society members a forum to discuss matters related to the CFA Program. To help generate discussion among the members, Shankar participates in the blog by listing several of the most recent, unpublished, Level II exam questions nearly word for word. He notes in his blog posting that the questions are from the exam that took place earlier.

At the end of August, Shankar sits in on a meeting between Pankow and Gerry Byrd, president of FHI. Pankow, who serves as a trustee for a pension plan, expresses concern that one of the pension plan's largest equity investments has underperformed. Pankow fears that, based on the results of this investment, her actions as a fiduciary will be criticized. Shankar states, "A trustee's compliance with the trustee's fiduciary duty is evaluated as of the date the investment decisions are made." Pankow responds, "I believe that a trustee's fiduciary compliance is based on whether the investment turned out to produce total returns that increased the wealth of the trust beneficiaries." Byrd responds, "I think that both of your views are valid and defensible, and at FHI we have supported either approach depending on the circumstances."

Impressed with Shankar's knowledge, Byrd requests that Shankar review FHI's compliance policy and compare it with the CFA Institute Code of Ethics and Standards of Professional Conduct. Key components of FHI's compliance policy are presented in Exhibit 1.

EXHIBIT 1	Front Hall Investments Key Components of Compliance Policy

1. Employees must not knowingly make any misrepresentation related to their investment analyses, recommendations, actions, and other professional activities.

2. Employees must not engage in any dishonest, fraudulent, or deceitful professional conduct, or commit any act that reflects adversely on their professional reputation, integrity, or competence.

Shankar offers to prepare a list of possible improvements to FHI's code if he sees that any are needed. As the conversation concludes, Byrd shows Shankar FHI's proposed new corporate letterhead, which Byrd says "will demonstrate our strong commitment to comply with CFA Institute Standards." Exhibit 2 shows the proposed letterhead.

EXHIBIT 2	Proposed Corporate Letterhead for Front Hall Investments

Front Hall Investments, committed to the highest standards of practice

One month later, Shankar advises Pankow that he will be leaving FHI for a new job. Prior to leaving FHI, at social events during nonworking hours, Shankar approaches two individuals to become clients of his new firm:

▶ Bill Homan oversees the investment of assets for a large nonprofit organization. Homan is not a client of FHI, but FHI employees had met with Homan several times over the last three months and were hoping he would hire FHI to manage the large-capitalization value portion of the nonprofit organization's equity portfolio.

▶ Lin Cheung had recently approached FHI concerning the overall management of an endowment fund. FHI had decided not to accept this fund as a client because of its small size and an investment objective that differed from the expertise and focus of FHI.

1. Does Shankar violate any CFA Institute Standards of Professional Conduct in recommending that clients increase their holdings of auto industry common stocks?

   A. No.

   B. Yes, because his recommendation did not have a reasonable basis.

   C. Yes, because his recommendation did not distinguish between fact and opinion.

2. Are Pankow and Shankar, respectively, in compliance with CFA Institute Standards with respect to:

	Pankow's selection of seminar leaders?	Shankar's blog posting?
A.	No	No
B.	No	Yes
C.	Yes	No

3. Are Shankar's statement and Pankow's response about fiduciary responsibility consistent with the New Prudent Investor Rule?

	Shankar's Statement	Pankow's Response
A.	No	No
B.	No	Yes
C.	Yes	No

4. Is the FHI compliance policy in Exhibit 1 consistent with CFA Institute Standards?

   A. Only component #1 is compliant with CFA Institute Standards.

   B. Only component #2 is compliant with CFA Institute Standards.

   C. Both components #1 and #2 are consistent with CFA Institute Standards.

5. Would FHI be in compliance with CFA Institute Standards if it used its proposed new letterhead?

   A. Yes.

   B. No, because not all of FHI's employees are CFA charterholders.

   C. No, because the CFA logo is not to be used by any firm on its corporate letterhead.

6. Did Shankar violate CFA Institute Standards in his discussions with Homan and/or Cheung?

   A. Yes, with Cheung only.

   B. Yes, with Homan only.

   C. Yes, with both Cheung and Homan.

The following information relates to Questions 7–12 and is based on "Guidance for Standards I–VII" and this reading

Jorge Aznar, the newly-hired compliance officer at Scott Bancorp (SB), is updating the firm's compliance manual. Aznar sets up a meeting with Anita Portillo, CFA, a portfolio manager at SB who specializes in individually-managed equity portfolios, to learn more about some of the daily processes of the firm's employees.

During the meeting, Aznar discusses the firm's policies related to proxy voting. With respect to portfolios managed for individuals, SB does not require that all proxies be voted in every instance and does not disclose its proxy-voting policies to clients. Portillo explains that SB recently conducted a cost-benefit analysis and found that the costs of evaluating all proxy-related issues outweigh the potential benefit to the clients.

Aznar turns the discussion to the firm's policies related to personal investing. SB requires investment personnel to disclose holdings in which the employee has a beneficial interest when he or she begins employment and on an annual basis thereafter. While employees are required to obtain preclearance for all personal trades and provide copies of periodic statements for all securities accounts, they are not required to direct their brokers to supply duplicate confirmations.

Portillo mentions to Aznar that she has substantially increased the bank's assets under management this year. This was the result of a relationship she established with a small advisory firm that specializes in structuring portfolios for individuals with conservative investment profiles. She states that in addition to these new individual accounts, JNR Manufacturing has hired her to manage a portion of its pension plan.

In reviewing Portillo's accounts, Aznar expresses concern over some high-risk alternative investments in some of the portfolios. He believes these high-risk assets are unsuitable for investors with conservative profiles and is concerned that Portillo may be violating her fiduciary duty by purchasing these assets. Portillo explains that she frequently includes small amounts of these types of investments in portfolios that do not have explicit prohibitions against them in an effort to boost the expected return and enhance diversification, and only does so after a thorough analysis of the investments and their place in each client's overall portfolio, including any tax implications, liquidity needs, and the overall return requirements for each account.

Aznar is unconvinced and worries about any legal implications that might arise with respect to these types of high-risk investments, particularly with regard to JNR Manufacturing's pension plan, for which SB is trustee. Portillo remarks, "According to the new Prudent Investor Rule, diversification is normally required of trustees unless it is clearly imprudent to do so. Moreover, unlike the old Prudent Man Rule, the new Prudent Investor Rule holds that no investments and/or techniques are necessarily considered imprudent." Portillo also explains that the new Prudent Investor Rule requires trustees to use care, skill, and caution. Portillo states, "While a trustee may not delegate investment authority, he may seek the guidance of specialists in order to meet the skill criterion."

The following day, Portillo receives a call from Wayne Seboro, president of JNR Manufacturing. Seboro informs Portillo that JNR is being targeted for a hostile takeover and attempts to persuade Portillo to support the company's resistance by voting the shares held in JNR's pension portfolio in opposition to the bid. Seboro indicates that Portillo's support would likely prompt JNR to commit a large amount of additional funds to the portfolio. While Portillo's initial analysis suggests the takeover would be beneficial to shareholders, she believes that the additional business could decrease overall costs to all clients of SB, including JNR Manufacturing's pension plan participants. After further consideration, Portillo decides to vote the shares in favor of the bid.

7. Is SB's proxy-voting policy consistent with the requirements and recommendations of the CFA Institute Standards with respect to voting and disclosure?

   A. Yes.

   B. No, it is not consistent with respect to voting only.

   C. No, it is not consistent with respect to disclosure only.

8. Are SB's policies related to personal investing consistent with the required and recommended procedures provided for by the CFA Institute Standards?

    A. Yes.

    B. No, they are not consistent with respect to the requirement to supply duplicate confirmations.

    C. No, they are not consistent with respect to the disclosure of holdings in which the employee has a beneficial interest.

9. Does Portillo's inclusion of high-risk alternative investments in the accounts she manages for individuals violate any CFA Institute Standards?

    A. No.

    B. Yes, with respect to suitability.

    C. Yes, with respect to diligence and reasonable basis.

10. Are Portillo's remarks consistent with the new Prudent Investor Rule with respect to diversification and investments?

    A. Yes.

    B. No, they are not consistent with respect to investments only.

    C. No, they are not consistent with respect to diversification only.

11. Are Portillo's statements regarding the skill criterion consistent with the new Prudent Investor Rule with respect to the delegation of investment authority and seeking the guidance of specialists?

    A. Yes.

    B. No, they are not consistent with respect to seeking the guidance of specialists only.

    C. No, they are not consistent with respect to the delegation of investment authority only.

12. Regarding her vote on the takeover bid for JNR Manufacturing, has Portillo violated any CFA Institute Standards?

    A. No.

    B. Yes, by failing to act in the best interest of her employer.

    C. Yes, by failing to act in the best interest of JNR Manufacturing management.

SOLUTIONS FOR READING 10

1. B is correct. Shankar's analysis based on four observations does not constitute a reasonable basis for making an investment recommendation.

2. A is correct. Both have compliance issues. Improperly using one's position as a society leader to benefit oneself or one's clients is a violation. Posting exam questions, even after the exam is completed, compromises the integrity of the examination.

3. C is correct. The view expressed in Shankar's statement is consistent with the New Prudent Investor Rule which states that compliance is judged as of the time an investment decision is made, and *not* with the benefit of hindsight or subsequent developments, nor on the outcome of investment decisions. The view expressed in Pankow's response is inconsistent with the New Prudent Investor Rule.

4. C is correct. Both elements of the compliance policy are consistent with the CFA Institute Standard relating to Professionalism.

5. C is correct. Firms are not permitted to incorporate the CFA logo in their corporate names or letterheads.

6. B is correct. The Standard relating to Duties to Employers prohibits members who are contemplating other employment from soliciting either existing or potential clients prior to leaving the employer. Shankar is permitted to solicit Cheung on behalf of the new firm because Cheung is not a prospective FHI client. Homan, however, is clearly a prospective client.

7. C is correct. Members and candidates should disclose their proxy-voting policies to clients.

8. B is correct. Standard VI(B) provides recommended procedures for compliance that state that investment personnel should be required to direct their brokers to supply duplicate copies or confirmations to their firms of all their personal securities transactions.

9. A is correct. No violations took place. Standard III(A) states, "Investment decisions may be judged in the context of the total portfolio rather than by individual investments within the portfolio." The member or candidate's duty is satisfied with respect to a particular investment if he or she has thoroughly considered the investment's place in the overall portfolio, the risk of loss and opportunity for gains, tax implications, and the diversification, liquidity, cash flow, and overall return requirements of the assets or the portion of the assets for which the manager is responsible.

10. A is correct. Under the New Prudent Investor Rule, both of these remarks are correct; diversification is one of the basic investment principles that determine prudent practice, and is normally required of trustees unless it is clearly imprudent to do so. Additionally, unlike the old Prudent Man Rule which held that investments that were speculative or non-income-producing were intrinsically imprudent, the New Prudent Investor Rule holds that no investments are imprudent per se.

11. C is correct. Unlike the old Prudent Man Rule, which in general forbade investment delegation, the Restatement holds that a trustee may in some instance have a duty to delegate investment authority to others.

12. A is correct. Standard III(A) requires that a member or candidate, in evaluating a takeover bid, act prudently and solely in the interests of plan participants and beneficiaries. In the case, Portillo acted in the best interests of the shareholders of JNR who were her clients.

QUANTITATIVE METHODS

STUDY SESSION

Study Session 3   Quantitative Methods for Valuation

TOPIC LEVEL LEARNING OUTCOME

The candidate should be able to demonstrate a thorough knowledge of, and the ability to apply, linear and multiple regression analysis and time series analysis to the valuation of securities.

STUDY SESSION 3
QUANTITATIVE METHODS FOR VALUATION

This study session begins with a discussion of linear correlation and then focuses on linear regression, one of the most widely used statistical techniques in financial modeling. In addition to a discussion of building and interpreting multiple regression models, the readings present information about testing the significance of the estimated parameters and verifying the whole regression model. Equally important is understanding the assumptions behind the structure of regression models, making corrections if the observed variables do not exhibit the assumed properties, and avoiding misspecification of the models.

Time-series analysis is used to describe the dynamic behavior of an economic or financial variable, to forecast its future values, and to detect relations between the time series of different variables. Indeed, regression models must be treated within a time-series context if the variables are measured over time. Regression reports for such models should include standard time-series tests to ensure that the results of the regression are interpreted correctly. Using time-series analysis to explain the past and predict the future of a data series is useful in analyzing company and industry data. Model assumptions and the consequences of model misspecification must be considered in any application. In addition, time-series properties, such as stationarity and mean reversion, have important consequences for security valuation.

READING ASSIGNMENTS

Reading 11	Correlation and Regression *Quantitative Methods for Investment Analysis,* Second Edition, by Richard A. DeFusco, CFA, Dennis W. McLeavey, CFA, Jerald E. Pinto, CFA, and David E. Runkle, CFA
Reading 12	Multiple Regression and Issues in Regression Analysis *Quantitative Methods for Investment Analysis,* Second Edition, by Richard A. DeFusco, CFA, Dennis W. McLeavey, CFA, Jerald E. Pinto, CFA, and David E. Runkle, CFA

277

Reading 13   Time-Series Analysis
Quantitative Methods for Investment Analysis, Second Edition,
by Richard A. DeFusco, CFA, Dennis W. McLeavey, CFA, Jerald E.
Pinto, CFA, and David E. Runkle, CFA

CORRELATION AND REGRESSION

by Richard A. DeFusco, CFA, Dennis W. McLeavey, CFA,
Jerald E. Pinto, CFA, and David E. Runkle, CFA

LEARNING OUTCOMES

The candidate should be able to:	Mastery
a. calculate and interpret a sample covariance and a sample correlation coefficient, and interpret a scatter plot;	☐
b. explain the limitations to correlation analysis, including outliers and spurious correlation;	☐
c. formulate a test of the hypothesis that the population correlation coefficient equals zero, and determine whether the hypothesis is rejected at a given level of significance;	☐
d. distinguish between the dependent and independent variables in a linear regression;	☐
e. explain the assumptions underlying linear regression, and interpret the regression coefficients;	☐
f. calculate and interpret the standard error of estimate, the coefficient of determination, and a confidence interval for a regression coefficient;	☐
g. formulate a null and alternative hypothesis about a population value of a regression coefficient, select the appropriate test statistic, and determine whether the null hypothesis is rejected at a given level of significance;	☐
h. calculate a predicted value for the dependent variable, given an estimated regression model and a value for the independent variable, and calculate and interpret a confidence interval for the predicted value of a dependent variable;	☐
i. describe the use of analysis of variance (ANOVA) in regression analysis, interpret ANOVA results, and calculate and interpret an *F*-statistic;	☐
j. discuss the limitations of regression analysis.	☐

1

INTRODUCTION

As a financial analyst, you will often need to examine the relationship between two or more financial variables. For example, you might want to know whether returns to different stock market indexes are related and, if so, in what way. Or you might hypothesize that the spread between a company's return on invested capital and its cost of capital helps to explain the company's value in the marketplace. Correlation and regression analysis are tools for examining these issues.

This reading is organized as follows. In Section 2, we present correlation analysis, a basic tool in measuring how two variables vary in relation to each other. Topics covered include the calculation, interpretation, uses, limitations, and statistical testing of correlations. Section 3 introduces basic concepts in regression analysis, a powerful technique for examining the ability of one or more variables (independent variables) to explain or predict another variable (the dependent variable).

2

CORRELATION ANALYSIS

We have many ways to examine how two sets of data are related. Two of the most useful methods are scatter plots and correlation analysis. We examine scatter plots first.

2.1 Scatter Plots

A **scatter plot** is a graph that shows the relationship between the observations for two data series in two dimensions. Suppose, for example, that we want to graph the relationship between long-term money growth and long-term inflation in six industrialized countries to see how strongly the two variables are related. Table 1 shows the average annual growth rate in the money supply and the average annual inflation rate from 1970 to 2001 for the six countries.

To translate the data in Table 1 into a scatter plot, we use the data for each country to mark a point on a graph. For each point, the *x*-axis coordinate is the country's annual average money supply growth from 1970–2001, and the *y*-axis coordinate is the country's annual average inflation rate from 1970–2001. Figure 1 shows a scatter plot of the data in Table 1.

Note that each observation in the scatter plot is represented as a point, and the points are not connected. The scatter plot does not show which observation comes from which country; it shows only the actual observations of both data series plotted as pairs. For example, the rightmost point shows the data for the United Kingdom. The data plotted in Figure 1 show a fairly strong linear relationship with a positive slope. Next we examine how to quantify this linear relationship.

2.2 Correlation Analysis

In contrast to a scatter plot, which graphically depicts the relationship between two data series, **correlation analysis** expresses this same relationship using a single

TABLE 1 Annual Money Supply Growth Rate and Inflation Rate by Country, 1970–2001		
Country	Money Supply Growth Rate (%)	Inflation Rate (%)
Australia	11.66	6.76
Canada	9.15	5.19
New Zealand	10.60	8.15
Switzerland	5.75	3.39
United Kingdom	12.58	7.58
United States	6.34	5.09
Average	9.35	6.03

Source: International Monetary Fund.

number. The correlation coefficient is a measure of how closely related two data series are. In particular, the correlation coefficient measures the direction and extent of **linear association** between two variables. A correlation coefficient can have a maximum value of 1 and a minimum value of -1. A correlation coefficient greater than 0 indicates a positive linear association between the two variables: When one variable increases (or decreases), the other also tends to increase (or decrease). A correlation coefficient less than 0 indicates a negative linear association between the two variables: When one increases (or decreases), the other tends to decrease (or increase).

FIGURE 1   Scatter Plot of Annual Money Supply Growth Rate and Inflation Rate by Country, 1970–2001

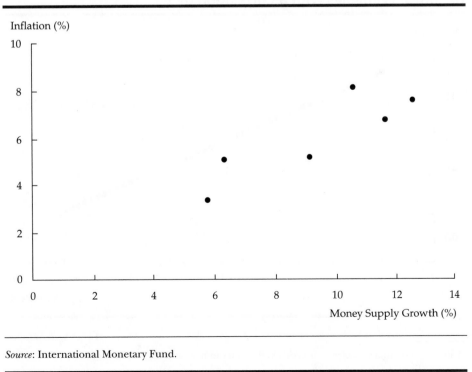

Source: International Monetary Fund.

FIGURE 2   Variables with a Correlation of 1

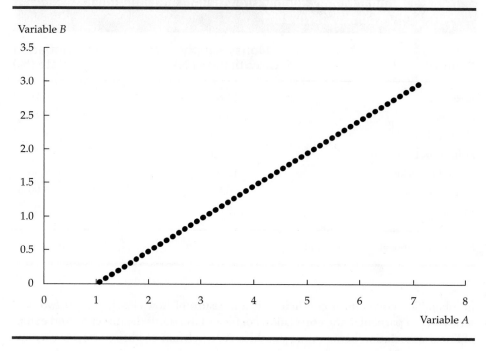

A correlation coefficient of 0 indicates no linear relation between the two variables.[1] Figure 2 shows the scatter plot of two variables with a correlation of 1.

Note that all the points on the scatter plot in Figure 2 lie on a straight line with a positive slope. Whenever variable *A* increases by one unit, variable *B* increases by half a unit. Because all of the points in the graph lie on a straight line, an increase of one unit in *A* is associated with exactly the same half-unit

FIGURE 3   Variables with a Correlation of −1

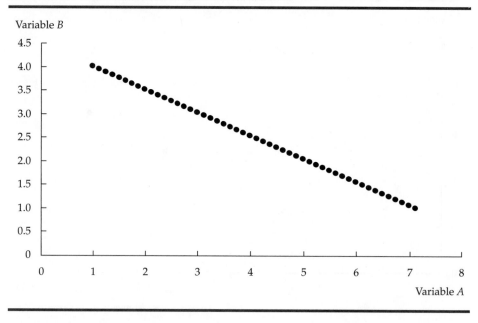

---

[1] Later, we show that variables with a correlation of 0 can have a strong nonlinear relation.

FIGURE 4   Variables with a Correlation of 0

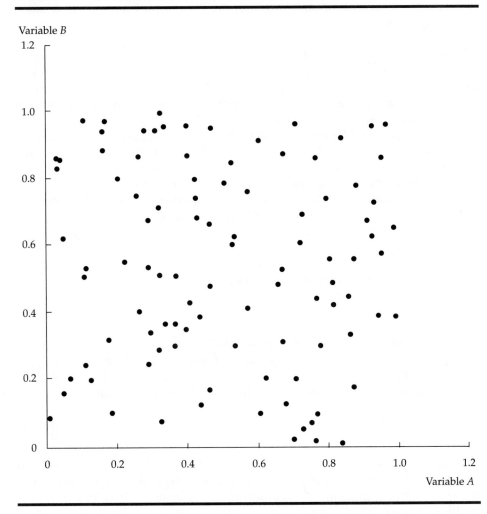

increase in *B*, regardless of the level of *A*. Even if the slope of the line in the figure were different (but positive), the correlation between the two variables would be 1 as long as all the points lie on that straight line.

Figure 3 shows a scatter plot for two variables with a correlation coefficient of −1. Once again, the plotted observations fall on a straight line. In this graph, however, the line has a negative slope. As *A* increases by one unit, *B* decreases by half a unit, regardless of the initial value of *A*.

Figure 4 shows a scatter plot of two variables with a correlation of 0; they have no linear relation. This graph shows that the value of *A* tells us absolutely nothing about the value of *B*.

2.3 Calculating and Interpreting the Correlation Coefficient

To define and calculate the correlation coefficient, we need another measure of linear association: covariance. We have previously defined covariance as the expected value of the product of the deviations of two random variables from their respective population means. That was the definition of population covariance, which we would also use in a forward-looking sense. To study historical or sample correlations, we need to use sample covariance. The sample covariance of X and Y, for a sample of size n, is

$$\text{Cov}(X, Y) = \sum_{i=1}^{n} (X_i - \overline{X})(Y_i - \overline{Y})/(n-1) \tag{1}$$

The sample covariance is the average value of the product of the deviations of observations on two random variables from their sample means.[2] If the random variables are returns, the unit of covariance would be returns squared.

The sample correlation coefficient is much easier to explain than the sample covariance. To understand the sample correlation coefficient, we need the expression for the sample standard deviation of a random variable X. We need to calculate the sample variance of X to obtain its sample standard deviation. The variance of a random variable is simply the covariance of the random variable with itself. The expression for the sample variance of X, s_X^2, is

$$s_X^2 = \sum_{i=1}^{n} (X_i - \overline{X})^2/(n-1)$$

The sample standard deviation is the positive square root of the sample variance:

$$s_X = \sqrt{s_X^2}$$

Both the sample variance and the sample standard deviation are measures of the dispersion of observations about the sample mean. Standard deviation uses the same units as the random variable; variance is measured in the units squared.

The formula for computing the sample correlation coefficient is

$$r = \frac{\text{Cov}(X, Y)}{s_X s_Y} \tag{2}$$

The correlation coefficient is the covariance of two variables (X and Y) divided by the product of their sample standard deviations (s_X and s_Y). Like covariance, the correlation coefficient is a measure of linear association. The correlation coefficient, however, has the advantage of being a simple number, with no unit of measurement attached. It has no units because it results from dividing the covariance by the product of the standard deviations. Because we will be using sample variance, standard deviation, and covariance in this reading, we will repeat the calculations for these statistics.

Table 2 shows how to compute the various components of the correlation equation (Equation 2) from the data in Table 1.[3] The individual observations on countries' annual average money supply growth from 1970–2001 are denoted X_i, and individual observations on countries' annual average inflation rate from 1970–2001 are denoted Y_i. The remaining columns show the calculations for the inputs to correlation: the sample covariance and the sample standard deviations.

---

[2] The use of $n-1$ in the denominator is a technical point; it ensures that the sample covariance is an unbiased estimate of population covariance.

[3] We have not used full precision in the table's calculations. We used the average value of the money supply growth rate of $0.5608/6 = 0.0935$, rounded to four decimal places, in the cross-product and squared deviation calculations, and similarly, we used the mean inflation rate as rounded to 0.0603 in those calculations. We computed standard deviation as the square root of variance rounded to six decimal places, as shown in the table. Had we used full precision in all calculations, some of the table's entries would be different and the computed value of correlation would be 0.8709 rather than 0.8702, not materially affecting our conclusions.

	Money Supply Growth Rate	Inflation Rate	Cross-Product	Squared Deviations	Squared Deviations
Country	X_i	Y_i	$(X_i - \bar{X})(Y_i - \bar{Y})$	$(X_i - \bar{X})^2$	$(Y_i - \bar{Y})^2$

TABLE 2 Sample Covariance and Sample Standard Deviations: Annual Money Supply Growth Rate and Inflation Rate by Country, 1970–2001

Country	Money Supply Growth Rate X_i	Inflation Rate Y_i	Cross-Product $(X_i - \bar{X})(Y_i - \bar{Y})$	Squared Deviations $(X_i - \bar{X})^2$	Squared Deviations $(Y_i - \bar{Y})^2$
Australia	0.1166	0.0676	0.000169	0.000534	0.000053
Canada	0.0915	0.0519	0.000017	0.000004	0.000071
New Zealand	0.1060	0.0815	0.000265	0.000156	0.000449
Switzerland	0.0575	0.0339	0.000950	0.001296	0.000697
United Kingdom	0.1258	0.0758	0.000501	0.001043	0.000240
United States	0.0634	0.0509	0.000283	0.000906	0.000088
Sum	0.5608	0.3616	0.002185	0.003939	0.001598
Average	0.0935	0.0603			
Covariance			0.000437		
Variance				0.000788	0.000320
Standard deviation				0.028071	0.017889

Notes:
1. Divide the cross-product sum by $n - 1$ (with $n = 6$) to obtain the covariance of X and Y.
2. Divide the squared deviations sums by $n - 1$ (with $n = 6$) to obtain the variances of X and Y.

Source: International Monetary Fund.

Using the data shown in Table 2, we can compute the sample correlation coefficient for these two variables as follows:

$$r = \frac{\text{Cov}(X, Y)}{s_x s_y} = \frac{0.000437}{(0.028071)(0.017889)} = 0.8702$$

The correlation coefficient of approximately 0.87 indicates a strong linear association between long-term money supply growth and long-term inflation for the countries in the sample. The correlation coefficient captures this strong association numerically, whereas the scatter plot in Figure 1 shows the information graphically.

What assumptions are necessary to compute the correlation coefficient? Correlation coefficients can be computed validly if the means and variances of X and Y, as well as the covariance of X and Y, are finite and constant. Later, we will show that when these assumptions are not true, correlations between two different variables can depend greatly on the sample that is used.

2.4 Limitations of Correlation Analysis

Correlation measures the linear association between two variables, but it may not always be reliable. Two variables can have a strong **nonlinear relation** and still have a very low correlation. For example, the relation $B = (A - 4)^2$ is a nonlinear relation contrasted to the linear relation $B = 2A - 4$. The nonlinear relation between variables A and B is shown in Figure 5. Below a level of 4 for A, variable B decreases with increasing values of A. When A is 4 or greater, however,

FIGURE 5   Variables with a Strong Nonlinear Association

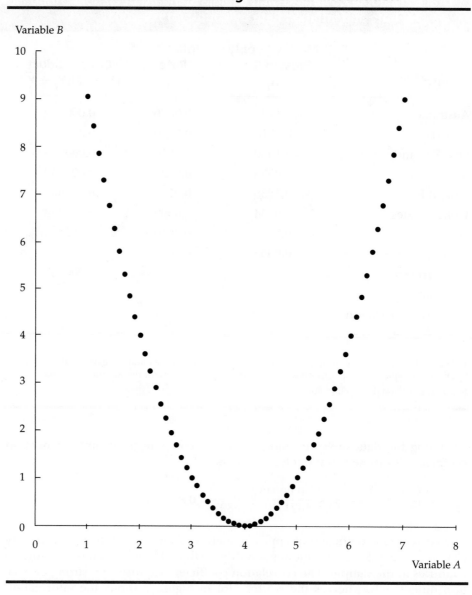

Variable B

Variable A

B increases whenever A increases. Even though these two variables are perfectly associated, the correlation between them is 0.[4]

Correlation also may be an unreliable measure when outliers are present in one or both of the series. Outliers are small numbers of observations at either extreme (small or large) of a sample. Figure 6 shows a scatter plot of the monthly returns to the Standard & Poor's 500 Index and the monthly inflation rate in the United States during the 1990s (January 1990 through December 1999).

---

[4] The perfect association is the quadratic relationship $B = (A - 4)^2$.

In the scatter plot in Figure 6, most of the data lie clustered together with little discernible relation between the two variables. In three cases, however (the three circled observations), inflation was greater than 0.8 percent in a particular month and stock returns were strongly negative. These observations are outliers. If we compute the correlation coefficient for the entire data sample, that correlation is −0.2997. If we eliminate the three outliers, however, the correlation is −0.1347.

The correlation in Figure 6 is quite sensitive to excluding only three observations. Does it make sense to exclude those observations? Are they noise or news? One possible partial explanation of Figure 6 is that during the 1990s, whenever inflation was very high during a month, market participants became concerned that the Federal Reserve would raise interest rates, which would cause the value of stocks to decline. This story offers one plausible explanation for how investors reacted to large inflation announcements. Consequently, the outliers may provide important information about market reactions during this period. Therefore, the correlation that includes the outliers may make more sense than the correlation that excludes them.

As a general rule, we must determine whether a computed sample correlation changes greatly by removing a few outliers. But we must also use judgment to determine whether those outliers contain information about the two variables' relationship (and should thus be included in the correlation analysis) or contain no information (and should thus be excluded).

Keep in mind that correlation does not imply causation. Even if two variables are highly correlated, one does not necessarily cause the other in the sense that certain values of one variable bring about the occurrence of certain values of the other. Furthermore, correlations can be spurious in the sense of misleadingly pointing towards associations between variables.

FIGURE 6 U.S. Inflation and Stock Returns in the 1990s

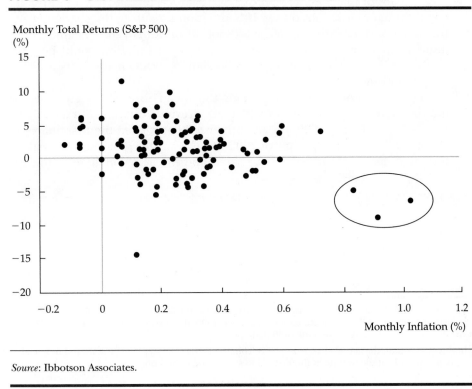

Source: Ibbotson Associates.

The term **spurious correlation** has been used to refer to 1) correlation between two variables that reflects chance relationships in a particular data set, 2) correlation induced by a calculation that mixes each of two variables with a third, and 3) correlation between two variables arising not from a direct relation between them but from their relation to a third variable. As an example of the second kind of spurious correlation, two variables that are uncorrelated may be correlated if divided by a third variable. As an example of the third kind of spurious correlation, height may be positively correlated with the extent of a person's vocabulary, but the underlying relationships are between age and height and between age and vocabulary. Investment professionals must be cautious in basing investment strategies on high correlations. Spurious correlation may suggest investment strategies that appear profitable but actually would not be so, if implemented.

2.5 Uses of Correlation Analysis

In this section, we give examples of correlation analysis for investment. Because investors' expectations about inflation are important in determining asset prices, inflation forecast accuracy will serve as our first example.

EXAMPLE 1

Evaluating Economic Forecasts (1)

Investors closely watch economists' forecasts of inflation, but do these forecasts contain useful information? In the United States, the Survey of Professional Forecasters (SPF) gathers professional forecasters' predictions about many economic variables.[5] Since the early 1980s, SPF has gathered predictions on the U.S. inflation rate using the change in the U.S. consumer price index (CPI) for all urban consumers and all items to measure inflation. If these forecasts of inflation could perfectly predict actual inflation, the correlation between forecasts and inflation would be 1.

Figure 7 shows a scatter plot of the mean forecast of current-quarter percentage change in CPI from previous quarter and actual percentage change in CPI, on an annualized basis, from the first quarter of 1983 to the last quarter of 2002.[6] In this scatter plot, the forecast for each quarter is plotted on the x-axis and the actual change in the CPI is plotted on the y-axis.

---

[5] The survey was originally developed by Victor Zarnowitz for the American Statistical Association and the National Bureau of Economic Research. Starting in 1990, the survey has been directed by Dean Croushire of the Federal Reserve Bank of Philadelphia.

[6] In this scatter plot, the actual change in CPI is from the Federal Reserve's economic and financial database, available at the website of the Federal Reserve Bank of St. Louis.

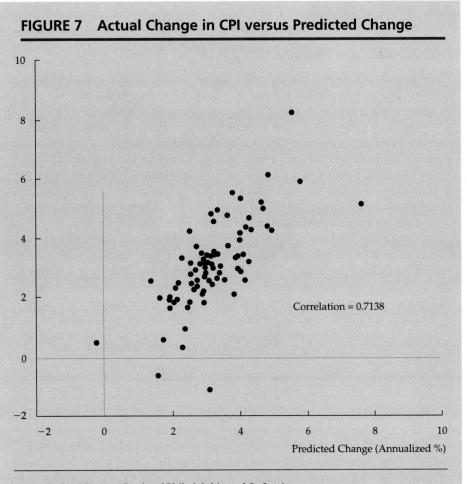

FIGURE 7   Actual Change in CPI versus Predicted Change

Correlation = 0.7138

Predicted Change (Annualized %)

Source: Federal Reserve Banks of Philadelphia and St. Louis.

As Figure 7 shows, a fairly strong linear association exists between the forecast and the actual inflation rate, suggesting that professional forecasts of inflation might be useful in investment decision-making. In fact, the correlation between the two series is 0.7138. Although there is no causal relation here, there is a direct relation because forecasters assimilate information to forecast inflation.

One important issue in evaluating a portfolio manager's performance is determining an appropriate benchmark for the manager. In recent years, style analysis has been an important component of benchmark selection.[7]

---

[7] See, for example, Sharpe (1992) and Buetow, Johnson, and Runkle (2000).

EXAMPLE 2

Style Analysis Correlations

Suppose a portfolio manager uses small-cap stocks in an investment portfolio. By applying style analysis, we can try to determine whether the portfolio manager uses a small-cap growth style or a small-cap value style.

In the United States, the Russell 2000 Growth Index and the Russell 2000 Value Index are often used as benchmarks for small-cap growth and small-cap value managers, respectively. Correlation analysis shows, however, that the returns to these two indexes are very closely associated with each other. For the 20 years ending in 2002 (January 1983 to December 2002), the correlation between the monthly returns to the Russell 2000 Growth Index and the Russell 2000 Value Index was 0.8526.

If the correlation between the returns to the two indexes were 1, there would be absolutely no difference in equity management style between small-cap value and small-cap growth. If we knew the return to one style, we could be certain about the return to the other style. Because the returns to the two indexes are highly correlated, we can say that very little difference exists between the two return series, and therefore, we may not be able to justify distinguishing between small-cap growth and small-cap value as different investment styles.

The previous examples in this reading have examined the correlation between two variables. Often, however, investment managers need to understand the correlations among many asset returns. For example, investors who have any exposure to movements in exchange rates must understand the correlations of the returns to different foreign currencies and other assets in order to determine their optimal portfolios and hedging strategies.[8] In the following example, we see how a correlation matrix shows correlation between pairs of variables when we have more than two variables. We also see one of the main challenges to investment managers: Investment return correlations can change substantially over time.

EXAMPLE 3

Exchange Rate Return Correlations

The exchange rate return measures the periodic domestic currency return to holding foreign currency. Suppose a change in inflation rates in the United Kingdom and the United States results in the U.S. dollar price of a pound changing from $1.50 to $1.25. If this change occurred in one month, the return in that month to holding pounds would be $(1.25 - 1.50)/1.50 = -16.67$ percent, in terms of dollars.

Table 3 shows a correlation matrix of monthly returns in U.S. dollars to holding Canadian, Japanese, Swedish, or British currencies.[9] To interpret a correlation matrix, we first examine the top panel of this table.

---

[8] See, for example, Clarke and Kritzman (1996).

[9] Data for the 1980s run from January 1980 through December 1989. Data for the 1990s run from January 1990 through December 1999.

The first column of numbers of that panel shows the correlations between USD returns to holding the Canadian dollar and USD returns to holding Canadian, Japanese, Swedish, and British currencies. Of course, any variable is perfectly correlated with itself, and so the correlation between USD returns to holding the Canadian dollar and USD returns to holding the Canadian dollar is 1. The second row of this column shows that the correlation between USD returns to holding the Canadian dollar and USD returns to holding the Japanese yen was 0.2593 from 1980 to 1989. The remaining correlations in the panel show how the USD returns to other combinations of currency holdings were correlated during this period.

TABLE 3 Correlations of Monthly U.S. Dollar Returns to Selected Foreign Currency Returns

1980–1989	Canada	Japan	Sweden	United Kingdom
Canada	1.0000			
Japan	0.2593	1.0000		
Sweden	0.2834	0.6576	1.0000	
United Kingdom	0.3925	0.6068	0.6840	1.0000

1990–1999	Canada	Japan	Sweden	United Kingdom
Canada	1.0000			
Japan	−0.0734	1.0000		
Sweden	0.1640	0.2860	1.0000	
United Kingdom	0.0475	0.2906	0.6444	1.0000

Source: Ibbotson Associates.

Note that Table 3 omits many of the correlations. For example, Column 2 of the panel omits the correlation between USD returns to holding yen and USD returns to holding Canadian dollars. This correlation is omitted because it is identical to the correlation between USD returns to holding Canadian dollars and USD returns to holding yen shown in Row 2 of Column 1. Other omitted correlations would also have been duplicative. In fact, correlations are always symmetrical: The correlation between X and Y is always the same as the correlation between Y and X.

If you compare the two panels of this table, you will find that many of the currency return correlations changed dramatically between the 1980s and the 1990s. In the 1980s, for example, the correlation between the return to holding Japanese yen and the return to holding either Swedish kronor (0.6576) or British pounds (0.6068) was almost as high as the correlation between the return to holding kronor and the return to holding pounds (0.6840). In the 1990s, however, the correlation between yen returns and either krona or pound returns dropped by more than half (to 0.2860 and 0.2906, respectively), but the correlation between krona and pound returns hardly changed at all (0.6444). Some of the correlations between returns to the Canadian dollar and returns to other currencies dropped even more dramatically. In the 1980s, the correlation between Canadian dollar returns and Japanese yen returns was 0.2593. By the 1990s, that correlation actually became negative (-0.0734). The correlation between the Canadian dollar returns and British pound returns dropped from 0.3925 in the 1980s to 0.0475 in the 1990s.

Optimal asset allocation depends on expectations of future correlations. With less than perfect positive correlation between two assets' returns, there are potential risk-reduction benefits to holding both assets. Expectations of future correlation may be based on historical sample correlations, but the variability in historical sample correlations poses challenges. We discuss these issues in detail in the reading on portfolio concepts.

In the next example, we extend the discussion of the correlations of stock market indexes begun in Example 2 to indexes representing large-cap, small-cap, and broad-market returns. This type of analysis has serious diversification and asset allocation consequences because the strength of the correlations among the assets tells us how successfully the assets can be combined to diversify risk.

EXAMPLE 4

Correlations among Stock Return Series

Table 4 shows the correlation matrix of monthly returns to three U.S. stock indexes during the period January 1971 to December 1999 and in three subperiods (the 1970s, 1980s, and 1990s).[10] The large-cap style is represented by the return to the S&P 500 Index, the small-cap style is represented by the return to the Dimensional Fund Advisors U.S. Small-Stock Index, and the broad-market returns are represented by the return to the Wilshire 5000 Index.

TABLE 4 Correlations of Monthly Returns to Various U.S. Stock Indexes

1971–1999	S&P 500	U.S. Small-Stock	Wilshire 5000
S&P 500	1.0000		
U.S. Small-Stock	0.7615	1.0000	
Wilshire 5000	0.9894	0.8298	1.0000

(Table continued on next page . . .)

[10] The 1970s data have an initiation date of January 1971 because that is the starting date of the Wilshire 5000 total return series.

TABLE 4 (continued)			
1971–1979	**S&P 500**	**U.S. Small-Stock**	**Wilshire 5000**
S&P 500	1.0000		
U.S. Small-Stock	0.7753	1.0000	
Wilshire 5000	0.9906	0.8375	1.0000
1980–1989	**S&P 500**	**U.S. Small-Stock**	**Wilshire 5000**
S&P 500	1.0000		
U.S. Small-Stock	0.8440	1.0000	
Wilshire 5000	0.9914	0.8951	1.0000
1990–1999	**S&P 500**	**U.S. Small-Stock**	**Wilshire 5000**
S&P 500	1.0000		
U.S. Small-Stock	0.6843	1.0000	
Wilshire 5000	0.9858	0.7768	1.0000

Source: Ibbotson Associates.

The first column of numbers in the top panel of Table 4 shows nearly perfect positive correlation between returns to the S&P 500 and returns to the Wilshire 5000: The correlation between the two return series is 0.9894. This result should not be surprising, because both the S&P 500 and the Wilshire 5000 are value-weighted indexes, and large-cap stock returns receive most of the weight in both indexes. In fact, the companies that make up the S&P 500 have about 80 percent of the total market value of all companies included in the Wilshire 5000.

Small stocks also have a reasonably high correlation with large stocks. In the total sample, the correlation between the S&P 500 returns and the U.S. Small-Stock returns is 0.7615. The correlation between U.S. Small-Stock returns and returns to the Wilshire 5000 is slightly higher (0.8298). This result is also not too surprising because the Wilshire 5000 contains small-cap stocks and the S&P 500 does not. The second, third, and fourth panels of Table 4 show that correlations among the various stock market return series show some variation from decade to decade. For example, the correlation between returns to the S&P 500 and U.S. small-cap stocks dropped from 0.8440 in the 1980s to 0.6843 in the 1990s.[11]

For asset allocation purposes, correlations among asset classes are studied carefully with a view toward maintaining appropriate diversification based on forecasted correlations.

---

[11] The correlation coefficient for the 1990s was less than that for the 1980s at the 0.01 significance level. A test for this type of hypothesis on the correlation coefficient can be conducted using Fisher's *z*-transformation. See Daniel and Terrell (1995) for information on this method.

EXAMPLE 5

Correlations of Debt and Equity Returns

Table 5 shows the correlation matrix for various U.S. debt returns and S&P 500 returns using monthly data from January 1926 to December 2002.

TABLE 5 Correlations among U.S. Stock and Debt Returns, 1926–2002

All	S&P 500	U.S. Long-Term Corp.	U.S. Long-Term Govt.	U.S. 30-Day T-Bill	High-Yield Corp.
S&P 500	1.0000				
U.S. Long-Term Corp.	0.2143	1.0000			
U.S. Long-Term Govt.	0.1466	0.8480	1.0000		
U.S. 30-Day T-bill	−0.0174	0.0970	0.1119	1.0000	
High-Yield Corp.	0.6471	0.4274	0.3131	0.0174	1.0000

Source: Ibbotson Associates.

The first column of numbers, in particular, shows the correlations of S&P 500 returns with various debt returns. Note that S&P 500 returns are almost completely uncorrelated (−0.0174) with 30-day Treasury bill returns for this period. Long-term corporate debt returns are somewhat more correlated (0.2143) with S&P 500 returns. Returns on high-yield corporate bonds have the highest correlation (0.6471) with S&P 500 total returns. This high correlation is understandable; high-yield debt securities behave partially as equities because of their high default risk. If a company defaults, holders of high-yield debt typically lose most of their investment.

Long-term government bonds, however, have a low correlation (0.1466) with S&P 500 returns. We expect some correlation between these variables because interest rate increases reduce the present value of future cash flows for both bonds and stocks. The relatively low correlation between these two return series, however, shows that other factors affect the returns on stocks besides interest rates. Without these other factors, the correlation between bond and stock returns would be higher.

The second column of numbers in Table 5 shows that the correlation between long-term government bond and corporate bond returns is quite high (0.8480) for this time period. Although this correlation is the highest in the entire matrix, it is not 1. The correlation is less than 1 because the default premium for long-term corporate bonds changes, whereas U.S. government bonds do not incorporate a default premium. As a result, changes in required yields for government bonds have a correlation less than 1 with changes in required yields for corporate bonds, and return correlations between government bonds and corporate bonds are also below 1. Note also that the correlation of high-yield corporate bond returns with long-term government bond returns

(0.3131), indicated in the third column of numbers, is less than half the correlation of high-yield corporate bond returns with S&P 500 returns. This relatively low correlation is another indicator that high-yield bond returns behave more similarly to equity returns than to debt returns.

Note finally that 30-day T-bill returns have a very low correlation with all other return series. In fact, the correlations between T-bill returns and other return series are lower than any of the other correlations in this table.

In the final example of this section, correlation is used in a financial statement setting to show that net income is an inadequate proxy for cash flow.

EXAMPLE 6

Correlations among Net Income, Cash Flow from Operations, and Free Cash Flow to the Firm

Net income (NI), cash flow from operations (CFO), and free cash flow to the firm (FCFF) are three measures of company performance that analysts often use to value companies. Differences in these measures for given companies would not cause differences in the relative valuation if the measures were highly correlated.

CFO equals net income plus the net noncash charges that were subtracted to obtain net income, minus the company's investment in working capital during the same time period. FCFF equals CFO plus net-of-tax interest expense, minus the company's investment in fixed capital over the time period. FCFF may be interpreted as the cash flow available to the company's suppliers of capital (debtholders and shareholders) after all operating expenses have been paid and necessary investments in working and fixed capital have been made.[12]

Some analysts base their valuations only on NI, ignoring CFO and FCFF. If the correlations among NI, CFO, and FCFF were very high, then an analyst's decision to ignore CFO and FCFF would be easy to understand because NI would then appear to capture everything one needs to know about cash flow.

Table 6 shows the correlations among NI, CFO, and FCFF for a group of six publicly traded U.S. companies involved in retailing women's clothing for 2001. Before computing the correlations, we normalized all of the data by dividing each company's three performance measures by the company's revenue for the year.[13]

---

[12] For more on these three measures and their use in equity valuation, see Stowe, Robinson, Pinto, and McLeavey (2002). The statements in the footnoted paragraph explain the relationships among these measures according to U.S. GAAP. Stowe et al. also discuss the relationships among these measures according to international accounting standards.

[13] The results in this table are based on data for all women's clothing stores (U.S. Occupational Health and Safety Administration Standard Industrial Classification 5621) with a market capitalization of more than $250 million at the end of 2001. The market-cap criterion was used to eliminate microcap firms, whose performance-measure correlations may be different from those of higher-valued firms.

**TABLE 6 Correlations among Performance Measures:
U.S. Women's Clothing Stores, 2001**

	NI	CFO	FCFF
NI	1.0000		
CFO	0.6959	1.0000	
FCFF	0.4045	0.8217	1.0000

Source: Compustat.

Because CFO and FCFF include NI as a component (in the sense that CFO and FCFF can be obtained by adding and subtracting various quantities from NI), we might expect that the correlations between NI and CFO and between NI and FCFF would be positive. Table 6 supports that conclusion. These correlations with NI, however, are much smaller than the correlation between CFO and FCFF (0.8217). The lowest correlation in the table is between NI and FCFF (0.4045). This relatively low correlation shows that NI contained some but far from all the information in FCFF for these companies in 2001. Later in this reading, we will test whether the correlation between NI and FCFF is significantly different from zero.

2.6 Testing the Significance of the Correlation Coefficient

Significance tests allow us to assess whether apparent relationships between random variables are the result of chance. If we decide that the relationships do not result from chance, we will be inclined to use this information in predictions because a good prediction of one variable will help us predict the other variable. Using the data in Table 2, we calculated 0.8702 as the sample correlation between long-term money growth and long-term inflation in six industrialized countries between 1970 and 2001. That estimated correlation seems high, but is it significantly different from 0? Before we can answer this question, we must know some details about the distribution of the underlying variables themselves. For purposes of simplicity, let us assume that both of the variables are normally distributed.[14]

We propose two hypotheses: the null hypothesis, H_0, that the correlation in the population is 0 ($\rho = 0$); and the alternative hypothesis, H_a, that the correlation in the population is different from 0 ($\rho \neq 0$).

The alternative hypothesis is a test that the correlation is not equal to 0; therefore, a two-tailed test is appropriate. As long as the two variables are

---

[14] Actually, we must assume that the variables come from a bivariate normal distribution. If two variables, X and Y, come from a bivariate normal distribution, then for each value of X the distribution of Y is normal. See, for example, Ross (1997) or Greene (2003).

distributed normally, we can test to determine whether the null hypothesis should be rejected using the sample correlation, r. The formula for the t-test is

$$t = \frac{r\sqrt{n-2}}{\sqrt{1-r^2}} \qquad \textbf{(3)}$$

This test statistic has a t-distribution with $n-2$ degrees of freedom if the null hypothesis is true. One practical observation concerning Equation 3 is that the magnitude of r needed to reject the null hypothesis H_0: $\rho = 0$ decreases as sample size n increases, for two reasons. First, as n increases, the number of degrees of freedom increases and the absolute value of the critical value t_c decreases. Second, the absolute value of the numerator increases with larger n, resulting in larger-magnitude t-values. For example, with sample size $n = 12$, $r = 0.58$ results in a t-statistic of 2.252 that is just significant at the 0.05 level ($t_c = 2.228$). With a sample size $n = 32$, a smaller sample correlation $r = 0.35$ yields a t-statistic of 2.046 that is just significant at the 0.05 level ($t_c = 2.042$); the $r = 0.35$ would not be significant with a sample size of 12 even at the 0.10 significance level. Another way to make this point is that sampling from the same population, a false null hypothesis H_0: $\rho = 0$ is more likely to be rejected as we increase sample size, all else equal.

EXAMPLE 7

Testing the Correlation between Money Supply Growth and Inflation

Earlier in this reading, we showed that the sample correlation between long-term money supply growth and long-term inflation in six industrialized countries was 0.8702 during the 1970–2001 period. Suppose we want to test the null hypothesis, H_0, that the true correlation in the population is 0 ($\rho = 0$) against the alternative hypothesis, H_a, that the correlation in the population is different from 0 ($\rho \neq 0$). Recalling that this sample has six observations, we can compute the statistic for testing the null hypothesis as follows:

$$t = \frac{0.8702\sqrt{6-2}}{\sqrt{1-0.8702^2}} = 3.532$$

The value of the test statistic is 3.532. As the table of critical values of the t-distribution for a two-tailed test shows, for a t-distribution with $n - 2 = 6 - 2 = 4$ degrees of freedom at the 0.05 level of significance, we can reject the null hypothesis (that the population correlation is equal to 0) if the value of the test statistic is greater than 2.776 or less than -2.776. The fact that we can reject the null hypothesis of no correlation based on only six observations is quite unusual; it further demonstrates the strong relation between long-term money supply growth and long-term inflation in these six countries.

EXAMPLE 8

Testing the Krona–Yen Return Correlation

The data in Table 3 showed that the sample correlation between the USD monthly returns to Swedish kronor and Japanese yen was 0.2860 for the period from January 1990 through December 1999. If we observe this sample correlation, can we reject a null hypothesis that the underlying or population correlation equals 0?

With 120 months from January 1990 through December 1999, we use the following statistic to test the null hypothesis, H_0, that the true correlation in the population is 0, against the alternative hypothesis, H_a, that the correlation in the population is different from 0:

$$t = \frac{0.2860 \sqrt{120 - 2}}{\sqrt{1 - 0.2860^2}} = 3.242$$

At the 0.05 significance level, the critical level for this test statistic is 1.98 ($n = 120$, degrees of freedom = 118). When the test statistic is either larger than 1.98 or smaller than -1.98, we can reject the hypothesis that the correlation in the population is 0. The test statistic is 3.242, so we can reject the null hypothesis.

Note that the sample correlation coefficient in this case is significantly different from 0 at the 0.05 level, even though the coefficient is much smaller than that in the previous example. The correlation coefficient, though smaller, is still significant because the sample is much larger (120 observations instead of 6 observations).

The above example shows the importance of sample size in tests of the significance of the correlation coefficient. The following example also shows the importance of sample size and examines the relationship at the 0.01 level of significance as well as at the 0.05 level.

EXAMPLE 9

The Correlation between Bond Returns and T-Bill Returns

Table 5 showed that the sample correlation between monthly returns to U.S. government bonds and monthly returns to 30-day T-bills was 0.1119 from January 1926 through December 2002. Suppose we want to test whether the correlation coefficient is statistically significantly different from zero. There are 924 months during the period January 1926 to December 2002. Therefore, to test the null hypothesis, H_0 (that the true correlation in the population is 0), against the alternative hypothesis, H_a (that the correlation in the population is different from 0), we use the following test statistic:

$$t = \frac{0.1119 \sqrt{924 - 2}}{\sqrt{1 - 0.1119^2}} = 3.4193$$

At the 0.05 significance level, the critical value for the test statistic is approximately 1.96. At the 0.01 significance level, the critical value for the test statistic is approximately 2.58. The test statistic is 3.4193, so we can reject the null hypothesis of no correlation in the population at both the 0.05 and 0.01 levels. This example shows that, in large samples, even relatively small correlation coefficients can be significantly different from zero.

In the final example of this section, we explore another situation of small sample size.

EXAMPLE 10

Testing the Correlation between Net Income and Free Cash Flow to the Firm

Earlier in this reading, we showed that the sample correlation between NI and FCFF for six women's clothing stores was 0.4045 in 2001. Suppose we want to test the null hypothesis, H_0, that the true correlation in the population is 0 ($\rho = 0$) against the alternative hypothesis, H_a, that the correlation in the population is different from 0 ($\rho \neq 0$). Recalling that this sample has six observations, we can compute the statistic for testing the null hypothesis as follows:

$$t = \frac{0.4045 \sqrt{6 - 2}}{\sqrt{1 - 0.4045^2}} = 0.8846$$

With $n - 2 = 6 - 2 = 4$ degrees of freedom and a 0.05 significance level, we reject the null hypothesis that the population correlation equals 0 for values of the test statistic greater than 2.776 or less than -2.776. In this case, however, the t-statistic is 0.8846, so we cannot reject the null hypothesis. Therefore, for this sample of women's clothing stores, there is no **statistically significant** correlation between NI and FCFF, when each is normalized by dividing by sales for the company.[15]

---

[15] It is worth repeating that the smaller the sample, the greater the evidence in terms of the magnitude of the sample correlation needed to reject the null hypothesis of zero correlation. With a sample size of 6, the absolute value of the sample correlation would need to be greater than 0.81 (carrying two decimal places) for us to reject the null hypothesis. Viewed another way, the value of 0.4045 in the text would be significant if the sample size were 24, because $0.4045(24 - 2)^{1/2}/(1 - 0.4045^2)^{1/2} = 2.075$, which is greater than the critical t-value of 2.074 at the 0.05 significance level with 22 degrees of freedom.

The scatter plot creates a visual picture of the relationship between two variables, while the correlation coefficient quantifies the existence of any linear relationship. Large absolute values of the correlation coefficient indicate strong linear relationships. Positive coefficients indicate a positive relationship and negative coefficients indicate a negative relationship between two data sets. In Examples 8 and 9, we saw that relatively small sample correlation coefficients (0.2860 and 0.1119) can be statistically significant and thus might provide valuable information about the behavior of economic variables.

Next we will introduce linear regression, another tool useful in examining the relationship between two variables.

3   LINEAR REGRESSION

3.1 Linear Regression with One Independent Variable

As a financial analyst, you will often want to understand the relationship between financial or economic variables, or to predict the value of one variable using information about the value of another variable. For example, you may want to know the impact of changes in the 10-year Treasury bond yield on the earnings yield of the S&P 500 (the earnings yield is the reciprocal of the price-to-earnings ratio). If the relationship between those two variables is linear, you can use linear regression to summarize it.

Linear regression allows us to use one variable to make predictions about another, test hypotheses about the relation between two variables, and quantify the strength of the relationship between the two variables. The remainder of this reading focuses on linear regression with a single independent variable. In the next reading, we will examine regression with more than one independent variable.

Regression analysis begins with the dependent variable (denoted Y), the variable that you are seeking to explain. The independent variable (denoted X) is the variable you are using to explain changes in the dependent variable. For example, you might try to explain small-stock returns (the dependent variable) based on returns to the S&P 500 (the independent variable). Or you might try to explain inflation (the dependent variable) as a function of growth in a country's money supply (the independent variable).

Linear regression assumes a linear relationship between the dependent and the independent variables. The following regression equation describes that relation:

$$Y_i = b_0 + b_1 X_i + \varepsilon_i, \ i = 1, \dots, n \tag{4}$$

This equation states that the **dependent variable**, Y, is equal to the intercept, b_0, plus a slope coefficient, b_1, times the **independent variable**, X, plus an **error term**, ε. The error term represents the portion of the dependent variable that cannot be explained by the independent variable. We refer to the intercept b_0 and the slope coefficient b_1 as the **regression coefficients**.

Regression analysis uses two principal types of data: cross-sectional and time series. Cross-sectional data involve many observations on X and Y for the same time period. Those observations could come from different companies, asset classes, investment funds, people, countries, or other entities, depending on the regression model. For example, a cross-sectional model might use data from many companies to test whether predicted earnings-per-share growth explains differences in price-to-earnings ratios (P/Es) during a specific time period. The word "explain" is frequently used in describing regression relationships. One estimate of a company's P/E that does not depend on any other variable is the average P/E. If a regression of a P/E on an independent variable tends to give more accurate estimates of P/E than just assuming that the company's P/E equals the average P/E, we say that the independent variable helps *explain* P/Es because using that independent variable improves our estimates. Finally, note that if we use cross-sectional observations in a regression, we usually denote the observations as $i = 1, 2, \ldots, n$.

Time-series data use many observations from different time periods for the same company, asset class, investment fund, person, country, or other entity, depending on the regression model. For example, a time-series model might use monthly data from many years to test whether U.S. inflation rates determine U.S. short-term interest rates.[16] If we use time-series data in a regression, we usually denote the observations as $t = 1, 2, \ldots, T$.[17]

Exactly how does linear regression estimate b_0 and b_1? Linear regression, also known as linear least squares, computes a line that best fits the observations; it chooses values for the intercept, b_0, and slope, b_1, that minimize the sum of the squared vertical distances between the observations and the regression line. Linear regression chooses the **estimated** or fitted **parameters** $\hat{b}_0$ and $\hat{b}_1$ in Equation 4 to minimize[18]

$$\sum_{i=1}^{n} (Y_i - \hat{b}_0 - \hat{b}_1 X_i)^2 \qquad\qquad \textbf{(5)}$$

In this equation, the term $(Y_i - \hat{b}_0 - \hat{b}_1 X_i)^2$ means (dependent variable − predicted value of dependent variable)^2. Using this method to estimate the values of $\hat{b}_0$ and $\hat{b}_1$, we can fit a line through the observations on X and Y that best explains the value that Y takes for any particular value of X.[19]

Note that we never observe the population parameter values b_0 and b_1 in a regression model. Instead, we observe only $\hat{b}_0$ and $\hat{b}_1$, which are estimates of the population parameter values. Thus predictions must be based on the parameters' estimated values, and testing is based on estimated values in relation to the hypothesized population values.

Figure 8 gives a visual example of how linear regression works. The figure shows the linear regression that results from estimating the regression relation between the annual rate of inflation (the dependent variable) and annual rate of money supply growth (the independent variable) for six industrialized countries from 1970 to 2001 ($n = 6$).[20] The equation to be estimated is Long-term rate of inflation = $b_0 + b_1$ (Long-term rate of money supply growth) + ε.

The distance from each of the six data points to the fitted regression line is the regression residual, which is the difference between the actual value of the dependent variable and the predicted value of the dependent variable made by the regression equation. Linear regression chooses the estimated coefficients $\hat{b}_0$

---

[16] A mix of time-series and cross-sectional data, also known as panel data, is now frequently used in financial analysis. The analysis of panel data is an advanced topic that Greene (2003) discusses in detail.

[17] In this reading, we primarily use the notation $i = 1, 2, \ldots, n$ even for time series to prevent confusion that would be caused by switching back and forth between different notations.

[18] Hats over the symbols for coefficients indicate estimated values.

[19] For a discussion of the precise statistical sense in which the estimates of b_0 and b_1 are optimal, see Greene (2003).

[20] These data appear in Table 2.

FIGURE 8   Fitted Regression Line Explaining the Inflation Rate Using Growth in the Money Supply by Country, 1970–2001

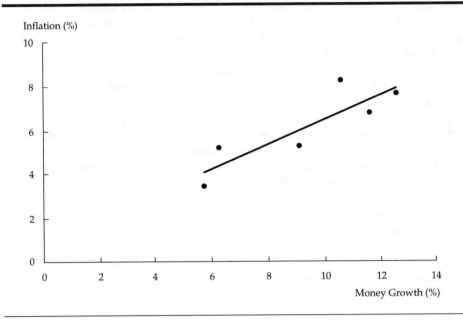

Source: International Monetary Fund.

and $\hat{b}_1$ in Equation 4 such that the sum of the squared vertical distances is minimized. The estimated regression equation is Long-term inflation = 0.0084 + 0.5545 (Long-term money supply growth).[21]

According to this regression equation, if the long-term money supply growth is 0 for any particular country, the long-term rate of inflation in that country will be 0.84 percent. For every 1-percentage-point increase in the long-term rate of money supply growth for a country, the long-term inflation rate is predicted to increase by 0.5545 percentage points. In a regression such as this one, which contains one independent variable, the slope coefficient equals $\text{Cov}(Y, X)/\text{Var}(X)$. We can solve for the slope coefficient using data from Table 2, excerpted here:

TABLE 2 (excerpted)				
	Money Supply Growth Rate X_i	**Inflation Rate** Y_i	**Cross-Product** $(X_i - \bar{X})(Y_i - \bar{Y})$	**Squared Deviations** $(X_i - \bar{X})^2$	**Squared Deviations** $(Y_i - \bar{Y})^2$
Sum	0.5608	0.3616	0.002185	0.003939	0.001598
Average	0.0935	0.0603			
Covariance			**0.000437**		
Variance				**0.000788**	0.000320
Standard deviation				0.028071	0.017889

---

[21] We entered the monthly returns as decimals.

$$\text{Cov}(Y, X) = 0.000437$$
$$\text{Var}(X) = 0.000788$$
$$\text{Cov}(Y, X)/\text{Var}(X) = 0.000437/0.000788$$
$$\hat{b}_1 = 0.5545$$

In a linear regression, the regression line fits through the point corresponding to the means of the dependent and the independent variables. As shown in Table 1 (excerpted below), from 1970 to 2001, the mean long-term growth rate of the money supply for these six countries was 9.35 percent, whereas the mean long-term inflation rate was 6.03 percent.

TABLE 1 (excerpted)		
	Money Supply Growth Rate	**Inflation Rate**
Average	9.35%	6.03%

Because the point (9.35, 6.03) lies on the regression line $\hat{b}_0 = \overline{Y} - \hat{b}_1\overline{X}$, we can solve for the intercept using this point as follows:

$$\hat{b}_0 = 0.0603 - 0.5545(0.0935) = 0.0084$$

We are showing how to solve the linear regression equation step by step to make the source of the numbers clear. Typically, an analyst will use the data analysis function on a spreadsheet or a statistical package to perform linear regression analysis. Later, we will discuss how to use regression residuals to quantify the uncertainty in a regression model.

3.2 Assumptions of the Linear Regression Model

We have discussed how to interpret the coefficients in a linear regression model. Now we turn to the statistical assumptions underlying this model. Suppose that we have n observations on both the dependent variable, Y, and the independent variable, X, and we want to estimate Equation 4:

$$Y_i = b_0 + b_1 X_i + \varepsilon_i, \ i = 1, \ldots, n$$

To be able to draw valid conclusions from a linear regression model with a single independent variable, we need to make the following six assumptions, known as the classic normal linear regression model assumptions:

1. The relationship between the dependent variable, Y, and the independent variable, X is linear in the parameters b_0 and b_1. This requirement means that b_0 and b_1 are raised to the first power only and that neither b_0 nor b_1 is multiplied or divided by another regression parameter (as in b_0/b_1, for example). The requirement does not exclude X from being raised to a power other than 1.

2. The independent variable, X, is not random.[22]

3. The expected value of the error term is 0: $E(\varepsilon) = 0$.

4. The variance of the error term is the same for all observations: $E(\varepsilon_i^2) = \sigma_\varepsilon^2$, $i = 1, \ldots, n$.

5. The error term, ε, is uncorrelated across observations. Consequently, $E(\varepsilon_i\varepsilon_j) = 0$ for all i not equal to j.[23]

6. The error term, ε, is normally distributed.[24]

Now we can take a closer look at each of these assumptions.

Assumption 1 is critical for a valid linear regression. If the relationship between the independent and dependent variables is nonlinear in the parameters, then estimating that relation with a linear regression model will produce invalid results. For example, $Y_i = b_0 e^{b_1 X_i} + \varepsilon_i$ is nonlinear in b_1, so we could not apply the linear regression model to it.[25]

Even if the dependent variable is nonlinear, linear regression can be used as long as the regression is linear in the parameters. So, for example, linear regression can be used to estimate the equation $Y_i = b_0 + b_1 X_i^2 + \varepsilon_i$.

Assumptions 2 and 3 ensure that linear regression produces the correct estimates of b_0 and b_1.

Assumptions 4, 5, and 6 let us use the linear regression model to determine the distribution of the estimated parameters $\hat{b}_0$ and $\hat{b}_1$ and thus test whether those coefficients have a particular value.

► Assumption 4, that the variance of the error term is the same for all observations, is also known as the homoskedasticity assumption. The reading on regression analysis discusses how to test for and correct violations of this assumption.

► Assumption 5, that the errors are uncorrelated across observations, is also necessary for correctly estimating the variances of the estimated parameters $\hat{b}_0$ and $\hat{b}_1$. The reading on multiple regression discusses violations of this assumption.

► Assumption 6, that the error term is normally distributed, allows us to easily test a particular hypothesis about a linear regression model.[26]

---

[22] Although we assume that the independent variable in the regression model is not random, that assumption is clearly often not true. For example, it is unrealistic to assume that the monthly returns to the S&P 500 are not random. If the independent variable is random, then is the regression model incorrect? Fortunately, no. Econometricians have shown that even if the independent variable is random, we can still rely on the results of regression models given the crucial assumption that the error term is uncorrelated with the independent variable. The mathematics underlying this reliability demonstration, however, are quite difficult. See, for example, Greene (2003) or Goldberger (1998).

[23] $\mathrm{Var}(\varepsilon_i) = E[\varepsilon_i - E(\varepsilon_i)]^2 = E(\varepsilon_i - 0)^2 = E(\varepsilon_i)^2$. $\mathrm{Cov}(\varepsilon_i, \varepsilon_j) = E\{[\varepsilon_i - E(\varepsilon_i)][\varepsilon_j - E(\varepsilon_j)]\} = E[(\varepsilon_i - 0)(\varepsilon_j - 0)] = E(\varepsilon_i\varepsilon_j) = 0$.

[24] If the regression errors are not normally distributed, we can still use regression analysis. Econometricians who dispense with the normality assumption use chi-square tests of hypotheses rather than F-tests. This difference usually does not affect whether the test will result in a particular null hypothesis being rejected.

[25] For more information on nonlinearity in the parameters, see Gujarati (2003).

[26] For large sample sizes, we may be able to drop the assumption of normality by appeal to the central limit theorem; see Greene (2003). Asymptotic theory shows that, in many cases, the test statistics produced by standard regression programs are valid even if the error term is not normally distributed. Non-normality of some financial time series can be quite severe. With severe non-normality, even with a relatively large number of observations, invoking asymptotic theory to justify using test statistics from linear regression models may be inappropriate.

EXAMPLE 11

Evaluating Economic Forecasts (2)

If economic forecasts were completely accurate, every prediction of change in an economic variable in a quarter would exactly match the actual change that occurs in that quarter. Even though forecasts can be inaccurate, we hope at least that they are unbiased—that is, that the expected value of the forecast error is zero. An unbiased forecast can be expressed as E(Actual change − Predicted change) = 0. In fact, most evaluations of forecast accuracy test whether forecasts are unbiased.[27]

Figure 9 repeats Figure 7 in showing a scatter plot of the mean forecast of current-quarter percentage change in CPI from the previous quarter and actual percentage change in CPI, on an annualized basis, from the first quarter of 1983 to the last quarter of 2002, but it adds the fitted regression line for the equation Actual percentage change = b_0 + b_1 (Predicted percentage change) + ε. If the forecasts are unbiased, the intercept, b_0, should be 0 and the slope, b_1, should be 1. We should also find E(Actual change − Predicted change) = 0. If forecasts are actually unbiased, as long as b_0 = 0 and b_1 = 1, the error term [Actual change − b_0 − b_1(Predicted change)] will have an expected value of 0, as required by Assumption 3 of the linear regression model. With unbiased forecasts, any other values of b_0 and b_1 would yield an error term with an expected value different from 0.

FIGURE 9   Actual Change in CPI versus Predicted Change

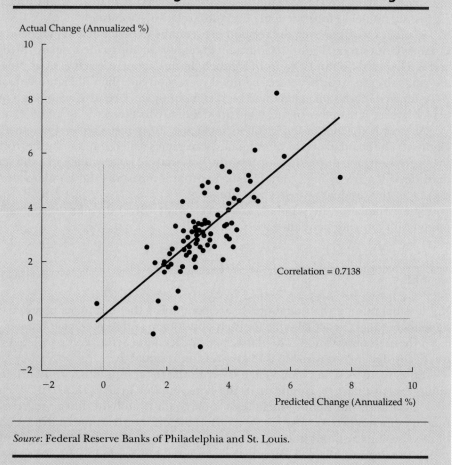

Source: Federal Reserve Banks of Philadelphia and St. Louis.

---

[27] See, for example, Keane and Rumble (1990).

> If $b_0 = 0$ and $b_1 = 1$, our best guess of actual change in CPI would be 0 if professional forecasters' predictions of change in CPI were 0. For every 1-percentage-point increase in the prediction of change by the professional forecasters, the regression model would predict a 1-percentage-point increase in actual change.
>
> The fitted regression line in Figure 9 comes from the equation Actual change = −0.0140 + 0.9637(Predicted change). Note that the estimated values of both b_0 and b_1 are close to the values $b_0 = 0$ and $b_1 = 1$ that are consistent with unbiased forecasts. Later in this reading, we discuss how to test the hypotheses that $b_0 = 0$ and $b_1 = 1$.

3.3 The Standard Error of Estimate

The linear regression model sometimes describes the relationship between two variables quite well, but sometimes it does not. We must be able to distinguish between these two cases in order to use regression analysis effectively. Therefore, in this section and the next, we discuss statistics that measure how well a given linear regression model captures the relationship between the dependent and independent variables.

Figure 9, for example, shows a strong relation between predicted inflation and actual inflation. If we knew professional forecasters' predictions for inflation in a particular quarter, we would be reasonably certain that we could use this regression model to forecast actual inflation relatively accurately.

In other cases, however, the relation between the dependent and independent variables is not strong. Figure 10 adds a fitted regression line to the data on inflation and stock returns in the 1990s from Figure 6. In this figure, the actual observations are generally much farther from the fitted regression line than in Figure 9. Using the estimated regression equation to predict monthly stock returns assuming a particular level of inflation might result in an inaccurate forecast.

As noted, the regression relation in Figure 10 is less precise than that in Figure 9. The standard error of estimate (sometimes called the standard error of the regression) measures this uncertainty. This statistic is very much like the standard deviation for a single variable, except that it measures the standard deviation of $\hat{\varepsilon}_i$, the residual term in the regression.

The formula for the standard error of estimate (SEE) for a linear regression model with one independent variable is

$$\text{SEE} = \left(\frac{\sum_{i=1}^{n}(Y_i - \hat{b}_0 - \hat{b}_1 X_i)^2}{n-2} \right)^{1/2} = \left(\frac{\sum_{i=1}^{n}(\hat{\varepsilon}_i)^2}{n-2} \right)^{1/2} \tag{6}$$

In the numerator of this equation, we are computing the difference between the dependent variable's actual value for each observation and its predicted value ($\hat{b}_0 + \hat{b}_1 X_i$) for each observation. The difference between the actual and predicted values of the dependent variable is the regression residual, $\hat{\varepsilon}_i$.

Equation 6 looks very much like the formula for computing a standard deviation, except that $n - 2$ appears in the denominator instead of $n - 1$. We use $n - 2$ because the sample includes n observations and the linear regression model estimates two parameters ($\hat{b}_0$ and $\hat{b}_1$); the difference between the number of observations and the number of parameters is $n - 2$. This difference is also called the degrees of freedom; it is the denominator needed to ensure that the estimated standard error of estimate is unbiased.

FIGURE 10   Fitted Regression Line Explaining Stock Returns by Inflation during the 1990s

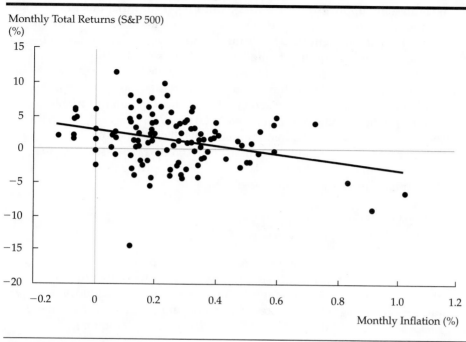

Source: Ibbotson Associates.

EXAMPLE 12

Computing the Standard Error of Estimate

Recall that the estimated regression equation for the inflation and money supply growth data shown in Figure 8 was $Y_i = 0.0084 + 0.5545X_i$. Table 7 uses this estimated equation to compute the data needed for the standard error of estimate.

TABLE 7 Computing the Standard Error of Estimate

Country	Money Supply Growth Rate X_i	Inflation Rate Y_i	Predicted Inflation Rate $\hat{Y}_i$	Regression Residual $Y_i - \hat{Y}_i$	Squared Residual $(Y_i - \hat{Y}_i)^2$
Australia	0.1166	0.0676	0.0731	−0.0055	0.000030
Canada	0.0915	0.0519	0.0591	−0.0072	0.000052
New Zealand	0.1060	0.0815	0.0672	0.0143	0.000204
Switzerland	0.0575	0.0339	0.0403	−0.0064	0.000041
United Kingdom	0.1258	0.0758	0.0782	−0.0024	0.000006
United States	0.0634	0.0509	0.0436	0.0073	0.000053
Sum					0.000386

Source: International Monetary Fund.

The first and second columns of numbers in Table 7 show the long-term money supply growth rates, X_i, and long-term inflations rates, Y_i, for the six countries. The third column of numbers shows the predicted value of the dependent variable from the fitted regression equation for each observation. For the United States, for example, the predicted value of long-term inflation is $0.0084 + 0.5545(0.0634) = 0.0436$ or 4.36 percent. The next-to-last column contains the regression residual, which is the difference between the actual value of the dependent variable, Y_i, and the predicted value of the dependent variable, $(\hat{Y}_i = \hat{b}_0 + \hat{b}_1 X_i)$. So for the United States, the residual is equal to $0.0509 - 0.0436 = 0.0073$ or 0.73 percent. The last column contains the squared regression residual. The sum of the squared residuals is 0.000386. Applying the formula for the standard error of estimate, we obtain

$$\left(\frac{0.000386}{6-2}\right)^{1/2} = 0.009823$$

Thus the standard error of estimate is about 0.98 percent.

Later, we will combine this estimate with estimates of the uncertainty about the parameters in this regression to determine confidence intervals for predicting inflation rates from money supply growth. We will see that smaller standard errors result in more accurate predictions.

3.4 The Coefficient of Determination

Although the standard error of estimate gives some indication of how certain we can be about a particular prediction of Y using the regression equation, it still does not tell us how well the independent variable explains variation in the dependent variable. The coefficient of determination does exactly this: It measures the fraction of the total variation in the dependent variable that is explained by the independent variable.

We can compute the coefficient of determination in two ways. The simpler method, which can be used in a linear regression with one independent variable, is to square the correlation coefficient between the dependent and independent variables. For example, recall that the correlation coefficient between the long-term rate of money growth and the long-term rate of inflation between 1970 and 2001 for six industrialized countries was 0.8702. Thus the coefficient of determination in the regression shown in Figure 8 is $(0.8702)^2 = 0.7572$. So in this regression, the long-term rate of money supply growth explains approximately 76 percent of the variation in the long-term rate of inflation across the countries between 1970 and 2001. (Relatedly, note that the square root of the coefficient of determination in a one-independent-variable linear regression, after attaching the sign of the estimated slope coefficient, gives the correlation coefficient between the dependent and independent variables.)

The problem with this method is that it cannot be used when we have more than one independent variable.[28] Therefore, we need an alternative method of computing the coefficient of determination for multiple independent variables. We now present the logic behind that alternative.

---

[28] We will discuss such models in the reading on multiple regression.

If we did not know the regression relationship, our best guess for the value of any particular observation of the dependent variable would simply be $\bar{Y}$, the mean of the dependent variable. One measure of accuracy in predicting Y_i based on $\bar{Y}$ is the sample variance of Y_i, $\sum_{i=1}^{n} \frac{(Y_i - \bar{Y})^2}{n-1}$. An alternative to using $\bar{Y}$ to predict a particular observation Y_i is using the regression relationship to make that prediction. In that case, our predicted value would be $\hat{Y}_i = \hat{b}_0 + \hat{b}_1 X_i$. If the regression relationship works well, the error in predicting Y_i using $\hat{Y}_i$ should be much smaller than the error in predicting Y_i using $\bar{Y}$. If we call $\sum_{i=1}^{n} (Y_i - \bar{Y})^2$ the total variation of Y and $\sum_{i=1}^{n} (Y_i - \hat{Y}_i)^2$ the unexplained variation from the regression, then we can measure the explained variation from the regression using the following equation:

$$\text{Total variation} = \text{Unexplained variation} + \text{Explained variation} \quad \textbf{(7)}$$

The coefficient of determination is the fraction of the total variation that is explained by the regression. This gives us the relationship

$$R^2 = \frac{\text{Explained variation}}{\text{Total variation}} = \frac{\text{Total variation} - \text{Unexplained variation}}{\text{Total variation}} \quad \textbf{(8)}$$
$$= 1 - \frac{\text{Unexplained variation}}{\text{Total variation}}$$

Note that total variation equals explained variation plus unexplained variation, as shown in Equation 7. Most regression programs report the coefficient of determination as R^2.[29]

EXAMPLE 13

Inflation Rate and Growth in the Money Supply

Using the data in Table 7, we can see that the unexplained variation from the regression, which is the sum of the squared residuals, equals 0.000386. Table 8 shows the computation of total variation in the dependent variable, the long-term rate of inflation.

---

[29] As we illustrate in the tables of regression output later in this reading, regression programs also report multiple R, which is the correlation between the actual values and the forecast values of Y. The coefficient of determination is the square of multiple R.

TABLE 8 Computing Total Variation

Country	Money Supply Growth Rate X_i	Inflation Rate Y_i	Deviation from Mean $Y_i - \bar{Y}$	Squared Deviation $(Y_i - \bar{Y})^2$
Australia	0.1166	0.0676	0.0073	0.000053
Canada	0.0915	0.0519	−0.0084	0.000071
New Zealand	0.1060	0.0815	0.0212	0.000449
Switzerland	0.0575	0.0339	−0.0264	0.000697
United Kingdom	0.1258	0.0758	0.0155	0.000240
United States	0.0634	0.0509	−0.0094	0.000088
	Average:	0.0603	Sum:	0.001598

Source: International Monetary Fund.

The average inflation rate for this period is 6.03 percent. The next-to-last column shows the amount each country's long-term inflation rate deviates from that average; the last column shows the square of that deviation. The sum of those squared deviations is the total variation in Y for the sample (0.001598), shown in Table 8.

The coefficient of determination for the regression is

$$\frac{\text{Total variation} - \text{Unexplained variation}}{\text{Total variation}} = \frac{0.001598 - 0.000386}{0.001598} = 0.7584$$

Note that this method gives the same result rounded to two decimal places, 0.76, that we obtained earlier (the difference at greater decimal places results from rounding). We will use this method again in the reading on multiple regression; when we have more than one independent variable, this method is the only way to compute the coefficient of determination.

3.5 Hypothesis Testing

In this section, we address testing hypotheses concerning the population values of the intercept or slope coefficient of a regression model. This topic is critical in practice. For example, we may want to check a stock's valuation using the capital asset pricing model; we hypothesize that the stock has a market-average beta or level of systematic risk. Or we may want to test the hypothesis that economists' forecasts of the inflation rate are unbiased (not overestimates or underestimates, on average). In each case, does the evidence support the hypothesis? Questions such as these can be addressed with hypothesis tests within a regression model. Such tests are often t-tests of the value of the intercept or slope coefficient(s). To understand the concepts involved in this test, it is useful to first review a simple, equivalent approach based on confidence intervals.

We can perform a hypothesis test using the confidence interval approach if we know three things: 1) the estimated parameter value, $\hat{b}_0$ or $\hat{b}_1$, 2) the hypothesized value of the parameter, b_0 or b_1, and 3) a confidence interval around the estimated parameter. A confidence interval is an interval of values that we believe includes the true parameter value, b_1, with a given degree of confidence. To compute a confidence interval, we must select the significance level for the test and know the standard error of the estimated coefficient.

Suppose we regress a stock's returns on a stock market index's returns and find that the slope coefficient ($\hat{b}_1$) is 1.5 with a standard error ($s_{\hat{b}_1}$) of 0.200. Assume we used 62 monthly observations in our regression analysis. The hypothesized value of the parameter (b_1) is 1.0, the market average slope coefficient. The estimated and the population slope coefficients are often called beta, because the population coefficient is often represented by the Greek symbol beta (β) rather than the b_1 we use in this reading. Our null hypothesis is that $b_1 = 1.0$ and $\hat{b}_1$ is the estimate for b_1. We will use a 95 percent confidence interval for our test, or we could say that the test has a significance level of 0.05.

Our confidence interval will span the range $\hat{b}_1 - t_c s_{\hat{b}_1}$ to $\hat{b}_1 + t_c s_{\hat{b}_1}$, or

$$\hat{b}_1 \pm t_c s_{\hat{b}_1} \tag{9}$$

where t_c is the critical t value.[30] The critical value for the test depends on the number of degrees of freedom for the t-distribution under the null hypothesis. The number of degrees of freedom equals the number of observations minus the number of parameters estimated. In a regression with one independent variable, there are two estimated parameters, the intercept term and the coefficient on the independent variable. For 62 observations and two parameters estimated in this example, we have 60 degrees of freedom ($62 - 2$). For 60 degrees of freedom, the table of critical values in the back of the book shows that the critical t-value at the 0.05 significance level is 2.00. Substituting the values from our example into Equation 9 gives us the interval

$$\begin{aligned}
\hat{b}_1 \pm t_c s_{\hat{b}_1} &= 1.5 \pm 2.00(0.200) \\
&= 1.5 \pm 0.400 \\
&= 1.10 \text{ to } 1.90
\end{aligned}$$

Under the null hypothesis, the probability that the confidence interval includes b_1 is 95 percent. Because we are testing $b_1 = 1.0$ and because our confidence interval does not include 1.0, we can reject the null hypothesis. Therefore, we can be 95 percent confident that the stock's beta is different from 1.0.

In practice, the most common way to test a hypothesis using a regression model is with a t-test of significance. To test the hypothesis, we can compute the statistic

$$t = \frac{\hat{b}_1 - b_1}{s_{\hat{b}_1}} \tag{10}$$

---

[30] We use the t-distribution for this test because we are using a sample estimate of the standard error, s_b, rather than its true (population) value.

This test statistic has a *t*-distribution with $n - 2$ degrees of freedom because two parameters were estimated in the regression. We compare the absolute value of the *t*-statistic to t_c. If the absolute value of *t* is greater than t_c, then we can reject the null hypothesis. Substituting the values from the above example into this relationship gives the *t*-statistic associated with the probability that the stock's beta equals 1.0 ($b_1 = 1.0$).

$$t = \frac{\hat{b}_1 - b_1}{s_{\hat{b}_1}}$$

$$= (1.5 - 1.0)/0.200$$

$$= 2.50$$

Because $t > t_c$, we reject the null hypothesis that $b_1 = 1.0$.

The *t*-statistic in the example above is 2.50, and at the 0.05 significance level, $t_c = 2.00$; thus we reject the null hypothesis because $t > t_c$. This statement is equivalent to saying that we are 95 percent confident that the interval for the slope coefficient does not contain the value 1.0. If we were performing this test at the 0.01 level, however, t_c would be 2.66 and we would not reject the hypothesis because *t* would not be greater than t_c at this significance level. A 99 percent confidence interval for the slope coefficient does contain the value 1.0.

The choice of significance level is always a matter of judgment. When we use higher levels of confidence, the t_c increases. This choice leads to wider confidence intervals and to a decreased likelihood of rejecting the null hypothesis. Analysts often choose the 0.05 level of significance, which indicates a 5 percent chance of rejecting the null hypothesis when, in fact, it is true (a Type I error). Of course, decreasing the level of significance from 0.05 to 0.01 decreases the probability of Type I error, but it increases the probability of Type II error— failing to reject the null hypothesis when, in fact, it is false.

Often, financial analysts do not simply report whether or not their tests reject a particular hypothesis about a regression parameter. Instead, they report the *p*-value or probability value for a particular hypothesis. The *p*-value is the smallest level of significance at which the null hypothesis can be rejected. It allows the reader to interpret the results rather than be told that a certain hypothesis has been rejected or accepted. In most regression software packages, the *p*-values printed for regression coefficients apply to a test of null hypothesis that the true parameter is equal to 0 against the alternative that the parameter is not equal to 0, given the estimated coefficient and the standard error for that coefficient. For example, if the *p*-value is 0.005, we can reject the hypothesis that the true parameter is equal to 0 at the 0.5 percent significance level (99.5 percent confidence).

The standard error of the estimated coefficient is an important input for a hypothesis test concerning the regression coefficient (and for a confidence interval for the estimated coefficient). Stronger regression results lead to smaller standard errors of an estimated parameter and result in tighter confidence intervals. If the standard error ($s_{\hat{b}_1}$) in the above example were 0.100 instead of 0.200, the confidence interval range would be half as large and the *t*-statistic twice as large. With a standard error this small, we would reject the null hypothesis even at the 0.01 significance level because we would have $t = (1.5 - 1)/0.1 = 5.00$ and $t_c = 2.66$.

With this background, we can turn to hypothesis tests using actual regression results. The next three examples illustrate hypothesis tests in a variety of typical investment contexts.

EXAMPLE 14

Estimating Beta for General Motors Stock

You are an investor in General Motors stock and want an estimate of its beta. As in the text example, you hypothesize that GM has an average level of market risk and that its required return in excess of the risk-free rate is the same as the market's required excess return. One regression that summarizes these statements is

$$(R - R_F) = \alpha + \beta(R_M - R_F) + \varepsilon \qquad \textbf{(11)}$$

where R_F is the periodic risk-free rate of return (known at the beginning of the period), R_M is the periodic return on the market, R is the periodic return to the stock of the company, and β is the covariance of stock and market return divided by the variance of the market return, $\text{Cov}(R, R_M)/\sigma_M^2$. Estimating this equation with linear regression provides an estimate of β, $\hat{\beta}$, which tells us the size of the required return premium for the security, given expectations about market returns.[31]

Suppose we want to test the null hypothesis, H_0, that $\beta = 1$ for GM stock to see whether GM stock has the same required return premium as the market as a whole. We need data on returns to GM stock, a risk-free interest rate, and the returns to the market index. For this example, we use data from January 1998 through December 2002 ($n = 60$). The return to GM stock is R. The monthly return to 30-day Treasury bills is R_F. The return to the S&P 500 is R_M.[32] We are estimating two parameters, so the number of degrees of freedom is $n - 2 = 60 - 2 = 58$. Table 9 shows the results from the regression $(R - R_F) = \alpha + \beta(R_M - R_F) + \varepsilon$.

TABLE 9   Estimating Beta for GM Stock

Regression Statistics

Multiple R	0.5549
R-squared	0.3079
Standard error of estimate	0.0985
Observations	60

(Table continued on next page…)

---

[31] Beta (β) is typically estimated using 60 months of historical data, but the data-sample length sometimes varies. Although monthly data is typically used, some financial analysts estimate β using daily data. For more information on methods of estimating β, see Reilly and Brown (2003). The expected excess return for GM stock above the risk-free rate $(R - R_F)$ is $\beta(R_M - R_F)$, given a particular excess return to the market above the risk-free rate $(R_M - R_F)$. This result holds because we regress $(R - R_F)$ against $(R_M - R_F)$. For example, if a stock's beta is 1.5, its expected excess return is 1.5 times that of the market portfolio.

[32] Data on GM stock returns came from Bloomberg. Data on T-bill returns and S&P 500 returns came from Ibbotson Associates.

TABLE 9 (continued)			
	Coefficients	**Standard Error**	***t*-Statistic**
Alpha	0.0036	0.0127	0.2840
Beta	1.1958	0.2354	5.0795

Source: Ibbotson Associates and Bloomberg L.P.

We are testing the null hypothesis, H_0, that β for GM equals 1 ($\beta = 1$) against the alternative hypothesis that β does not equal 1 ($\beta \neq 1$). The estimated $\hat{\beta}$ from the regression is 1.1958. The estimated standard error for that coefficient in the regression, $s_{\hat{\beta}}$ is 0.2354. The regression equation has 58 degrees of freedom ($60 - 2$), so the critical value for the test statistic is approximately $t_c = 2.00$ at the 0.05 significance level. Therefore, the 95 percent confidence interval for the data for any particular hypothesized value of β is shown by the range

$$\hat{\beta} \pm t_c s_{\hat{\beta}}$$

$$1.1958 \pm 2.00(0.2354)$$

$$0.7250 \text{ to } 1.6666$$

In this case, the hypothesized parameter value is $\beta = 1$, and the value 1 falls inside this confidence interval, so we cannot reject the hypothesis at the 0.05 significance level. This means that we cannot reject the hypothesis that GM stock has the same systematic risk as the market as a whole.

Another way of looking at this issue is to compute the *t*-statistic for the GM beta hypothesized parameter using Equation 10:

$$t = \frac{\hat{\beta} - \beta}{s_{\hat{\beta}}} = \frac{1.1958 - 1.0}{0.2354} = 0.8318$$

This *t*-statistic is less than the critical *t*-value of 2.00. Therefore, neither approach allows us to reject the null hypothesis. Note that the *t*-statistic associated with $\hat{\beta}$ in the regression results in Table 9 is 5.0795. Given the significance level we are using, we cannot reject the null hypothesis that $\beta = 1$, but we can reject the hypothesis that $\beta = 0$.[33]

Note also that the R^2 in this regression is only 0.3079. This result suggests that only about 31 percent of the total variation in the excess return to GM stock (the return to GM above the risk-free rate) can be explained by excess return to the market portfolio. The remaining 69 percent of GM stock's excess return variation is the nonsystematic component, which can be attributed to company-specific risk.

---

[33] The *t*-statistics for a coefficient automatically reported by statistical software programs assume that the null hypothesis states that the coefficient is equal to 0. If you have a different null hypothesis, as we do in this example ($\beta = 1$), then you must either construct the correct test statistic yourself or instruct the program to compute it.

In the next example, we show a regression hypothesis test with a one-sided alternative.

EXAMPLE 15

Explaining Company Value Based on Returns to Invested Capital

Some financial analysts have argued that one good way to measure a company's ability to create wealth is to compare the company's return on invested capital (ROIC) to its weighted-average cost of capital (WACC). If a company has an ROIC greater than its cost of capital, the company is creating wealth; if its ROIC is less than its cost of capital, it is destroying wealth.[34]

Enterprise value (EV) is a market-price-based measure of company value defined as the market value of equity and debt minus the value of cash and investments. Invested capital (IC) is an accounting measure of company value defined as the sum of the book values of equity and debt. Higher ratios of EV to IC should reflect greater success at wealth creation in general. Mauboussin (1996) argued that the spread between ROIC and WACC helps explains the ratio of EV to IC. Using data on companies in the food-processing industry, we can test the relationship between EV/IC and (ROIC–WACC) using the regression model given in Equation 12.

$$EV_i/IC_i = b_0 + b_1(ROIC_i - WACC_i) + \varepsilon_i \qquad \textbf{(12)}$$

where the subscript i is an index to identify the company. Our null hypothesis is $H_0: b_1 \leq 0$, and we specify a significance level of 0.05. If we reject the null hypothesis, we have evidence of a statistically significant relationship between EV/IC and (ROIC–WACC). We estimate Equation 12 using data from nine food-processing companies for 2001.[35] The results of this regression are displayed in Table 10 and Figure 11.

TABLE 10 Explaining Enterprise Value/Invested Capital by the ROIC–WACC Spread

Regression Statistics

Multiple R	0.9469
R-squared	0.8966
Standard error of estimate	0.7422
Observations	9

(Table continued on next page…)

---

[34] See, for example, Stewart (1991) and Mauboussin (1996).

[35] Our data comes from Nelson (2003). Many sell-side analysts use this type of regression. It is one of the most frequently used cross-sectional regressions in published analyst reports.

TABLE 10 (continued)			
	Coefficients	**Standard Error**	**t-Statistic**
Intercept	1.3478	0.3511	3.8391
Spread	30.0169	3.8519	7.7928

Source: Nelson (2003).

FIGURE 11   Fitted Regression Line Explaining Enterprise Value/Invested Capital Using ROIC–WACC Spread for the Food Industry

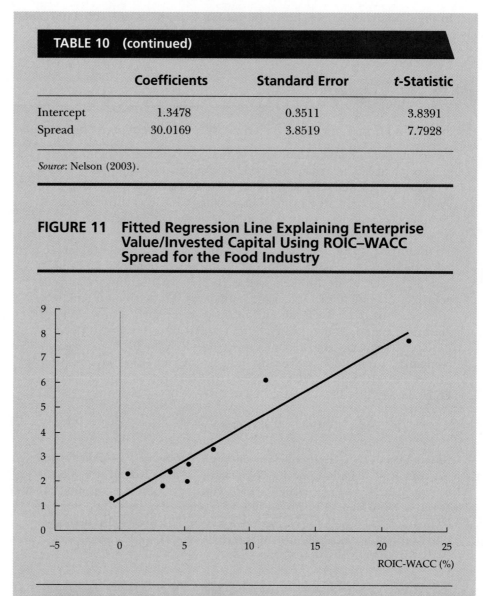

Source: CSFB Food Investors Handbook 2003.

We reject the null hypothesis based on the *t*-statistic of approximately 7.79 on estimated slope coefficient. There is a strong positive relationship between the return spread (ROIC–WACC) and the ratio of EV to IC in our sample of companies. Figure 11 illustrates the strong positive relationship. The R^2 of 0.8966 indicates that the return spread explains about 90 percent of the variation in the ratio of EV to IC among the food-processing companies in the sample in 2001. The coefficient on the return spread of 30.0169 implies that the predicted increase in EV/IC is 0.01 (30.0169) = 0.3002 or about 30 percent for a 1-percentage-point increase in the return spread, for our sample of companies.

In the final example of this section, we show that the null hypothesis can involve a slope coefficient of 1 just as well as a slope of 0.

EXAMPLE 16

Testing whether Inflation Forecasts Are Unbiased

Example 11 introduced the concept of testing for bias in forecasts. That example showed that if a forecast is unbiased, its expected error is 0. We can examine whether a time-series of forecasts for a particular economic variable is unbiased by comparing the forecast at each date with the actual value of the economic variable announced after the forecast. If the forecasts are unbiased, then, by definition, the average realized forecast error should be close to 0. In that case, the value of b_0 (the intercept) should be 0 and the value of b_1 (the slope) should be 1, as discussed in Example 11.

Refer once again to Figure 9, which shows the current-quarter predictions of percentage change in CPI made by professional economic forecasters and the actual percentage change from the first quarter of 1983 through the fourth quarter of 2002 ($n = 80$). To test whether the forecasts are unbiased, we must estimate the regression shown in Example 11. We report the results of this regression in Table 11. The equation to be estimated is

$$\text{Actual percentage change in CPI}_t = b_0 + b_1(\text{Predicted change}_t) + \varepsilon_t$$

This regression estimates two parameters (the intercept and the slope); therefore, the regression has $n - 2 = 80 - 2 = 78$ degrees of freedom.

TABLE 11 Testing whether Forecasts of CPI Are Unbiased (Dependent Variable: CPI Change Expressed in Percent)

Regression Statistics

Multiple R	0.7138
R-squared	0.5095
Standard error of estimate	1.0322
Observations	80

	Coefficients	Standard Error	t-Statistic
Intercept	−0.0140	0.3657	−0.0384
Forecast (slope)	0.9637	0.1071	9.0008

Sources: Federal Reserve Banks of Philadelphia and St. Louis.

We can now test two null hypotheses about the parameters in this regression. Our first null hypothesis is that the intercept in this regression is 0 (H_0: $b_0 = 0$). The alternative hypothesis is that the intercept does not equal 0 (H_a: $b_0 \neq 0$). Our second null hypothesis is that the slope coefficient in this regression is 1 (H_0: $b_1 = 1$). The alternative hypothesis is that the slope coefficient does not equal 1 (H_a: $b_1 \neq 1$).

To test the hypotheses about b_0 and b_1, we must first decide on a critical value based on a particular significance level and then construct the confidence intervals for each parameter. If we choose the 0.05 significance level, with 78 degrees of freedom, the critical value, t_c, is approximately 1.99. The estimated value of the parameter $\hat{b}_0$ is -0.0140, and the estimated value of the standard error for $\hat{b}_0(s_{\hat{b}_0})$ is 0.3657. Let B_0 stand for any particular hypothesized value. Therefore, under the null hypothesis that $b_0 = B_0$, a 95 percent confidence interval for b_0 is

$$\hat{b}_0 \pm t_c s_{\hat{b}_0}$$

$$-0.0140 \pm 1.99(0.3657)$$

$$-0.7417 \text{ to } 0.7137$$

In this case, B_0 is 0. The value of 0 falls within this confidence interval, so we cannot reject the first null hypothesis that $b_0 = 0$. We will explain how to interpret this result shortly.

Our second null hypothesis is based on the same sample as our first null hypothesis. Therefore, the critical value for testing that hypothesis is the same as the critical value for testing the first hypothesis ($t_c = 1.99$). The estimated value of the parameter $\hat{b}_1$ is 0.9637, and the estimated value of the standard error for $\hat{b}_1$, $s_{\hat{b}_1}$, is 0.1071. Therefore, the 95 percent confidence interval for any particular hypothesized value of b_1 can be constructed as follows:

$$\hat{b}_1 \pm t_c s_{\hat{b}_1}$$

$$0.9637 \pm 1.99(0.1071)$$

$$0.7506 \text{ to } 1.1768$$

In this case, our hypothesized value of b_1 is 1. The value 1 falls within this confidence interval, so we cannot reject the null hypothesis that $b_1 = 1$ at the 0.05 significance level. Because we did not reject either of the null hypotheses ($b_0 = 0$, $b_1 = 1$) about the parameters in this model, we cannot reject the hypothesis that the forecasts of CPI change were unbiased.[36]

As an analyst, you often will need forecasts of **economic growth** to help you make recommendations about asset allocation, expected returns, and other investment decisions. The hypothesis tests just conducted suggest that you cannot reject the hypothesis that the CPI predictions in the Survey of Professional Forecasters are unbiased. If you need an unbiased forecast of future percentage change in CPI for your asset-allocation decision, you might want to use these forecasts.

---

[36] Jointly testing the hypothesis $b_0 = 0$ and $b_1 = 1$ would require us to take into account the covariance of $\hat{b}_0$ and $\hat{b}_1$. For information on testing joint hypotheses of this type, see Greene (2003).

3.6 Analysis of Variance in a Regression with One Independent Variable

Analysis of variance (ANOVA) is a statistical procedure for dividing the total variability of a variable into components that can be attributed to different sources.[37] In regression analysis, we use ANOVA to determine the usefulness of the independent variable or variables in explaining variation in the dependent variable. An important statistical test conducted in analysis of variance is the F-test. The F-statistic tests whether all the slope coefficients in a linear regression are equal to 0. In a regression with one independent variable, this is a test of the null hypothesis H_0: $b_1 = 0$ against the alternative hypothesis H_a: $b_1 \neq 0$.

To correctly determine the test statistic for the null hypothesis that the slope coefficient equals 0, we need to know the following:

▶ the total number of observations (n);

▶ the total number of parameters to be estimated (in a one-independent-variable regression, this number is two: the intercept and the slope coefficient);

▶ the sum of squared errors or residuals, $\sum_{i=1}^{n} (Y_i - \hat{Y}_i)^2$, abbreviated SSE.

This value is also known as the residual sum of squares; and

▶ the regression sum of squares, $\sum_{i=1}^{n} (\hat{Y}_i - \overline{Y})^2$, abbreviated RSS. This value

is the amount of total variation in Y that is explained in the regression equation. Total variation (TSS) is the sum of SSE and RSS.

The F-test for determining whether the slope coefficient equals 0 is based on an F-statistic, constructed using these four values. The F-statistic measures how well the regression equation explains the variation in the dependent variable. The F-statistic is the ratio of the average regression sum of squares to the average sum of the squared errors. The average regression sum of squares is computed by dividing the regression sum of squares by the number of slope parameters estimated (in this case, one). The average sum of squared errors is computed by dividing the sum of squared errors by the number of observations, n, minus the total number of parameters estimated (in this case, two: the intercept and the slope). These two divisors are the degrees of freedom for an F-test. If there are n observations, the F-test for the null hypothesis that the slope coefficient is equal to 0 is here denoted $F_{\text{# slope parameters}, \, n - \text{# parameters}} = F_{1, n-2}$, and the test has 1 and $n - 2$ degrees of freedom.

Suppose, for example, that the independent variable in a regression model explains none of the variation in the dependent variable. Then the predicted value for the regression model, $\hat{Y}_i$, is the average value of the dependent variable $\overline{Y}$. In this case, the regression sum of squares $\sum_{i=1}^{n} (\hat{Y}_i - \overline{Y})^2$ is 0. Therefore, the F-statistic is 0. If the independent variable explains little of the variation in the dependent variable, the value of the F-statistic will be very small.

---

[37] In this reading, we focus on regression applications of ANOVA, the most common context in which financial analysts will encounter this tool. In this context, ANOVA is used to test whether all the regression slope coefficients are equal to 0. Analysts also use ANOVA to test a hypothesis that the means of two or more populations are equal. See Daniel and Terrell (1995) for details.

The formula for the F-statistic in a regression with one independent variable is

$$F = \frac{\text{RSS}/1}{\text{SSE}/(n-2)} = \frac{\text{Mean regression sum of squares}}{\text{Mean squared error}} \qquad (13)$$

If the regression model does a good job of explaining variation in the dependent variable, then this ratio should be high. The explained regression sum of squares per estimated parameter will be high relative to the unexplained variation for each degree of freedom. Critical values for this F-statistic are given in Appendix D at the end of this volume.

Even though the F-statistic is commonly computed by regression software packages, analysts typically do not use ANOVA and F-tests in regressions with just one independent variable. Why not? In such regressions, the F-statistic is the square of the t-statistic for the slope coefficient. Therefore, the F-test duplicates the t-test for the significance of the slope coefficient. This relation is not true for regressions with two or more slope coefficients. Nevertheless, the one-slope coefficient case gives a foundation for understanding the multiple-slope coefficient cases.

Often, mutual fund performance is evaluated based on whether the fund has positive alpha—significantly positive excess risk-adjusted returns.[38] One commonly used method of risk adjustment is based on the capital asset pricing model. Consider the regression

$$(R_i - R_F) = \alpha_i + \beta_i(R_M - R_F) + \varepsilon_i \qquad (14)$$

where R_F is the periodic risk-free rate of return (known at the beginning of the period), R_M is the periodic return on the market, R_i is the periodic return to Mutual Fund i, and β_i is the fund's beta. A fund has zero risk-adjusted excess return if $\alpha_i = 0$. If $\alpha_i = 0$, then $(R_i - R_F) = \beta_i(R_M - R_F) + \varepsilon_i$ and taking expectations, $E(R_i) = R_F + \beta_i(R_M - R_F)$, implying that β_i completely explains the fund's mean excess returns. If, for example, $\alpha_i > 0$, the fund is earning higher returns than expected given its beta.

In summary, to test whether a fund has a positive alpha, we must test the null hypothesis that the fund has no risk-adjusted excess returns (H_0: $\alpha = 0$) against the alternative hypothesis of nonzero risk-adjusted returns (H_a: $\alpha \neq 0$).

EXAMPLE 17

Performance Evaluation: The Dreyfus Appreciation Fund

Table 12 presents results evaluating the excess return to the Dreyfus Appreciation Fund from January 1998 through December 2002. Note that the estimated beta in this regression, $\hat{\beta}_i$, is 0.7902. The Dreyfus Appreciation Fund was estimated to be about 0.8 times as risky as the market as a whole.

---

[38] Note that the Greek letter alpha, α, is traditionally used to represent the intercept in Equation 14 and should not be confused with another traditional usage of α to represent a significance level.

TABLE 12 Performance Evaluation of Dreyfus Appreciation Fund, January 1998 to December 2002

Regression Statistics

Multiple R	0.9280
R-squared	0.8611
Standard error of estimate	0.0174
Observations	60

ANOVA	Degrees of Freedom (df)	Sum of Squares (SS)	Mean Sum of Squares (MSS)	F
Regression	1	0.1093	0.1093	359.64
Residual	58	0.0176	0.0003	
Total	59	0.1269		

	Coefficients	Standard Error	t-Statistic
Alpha	0.0009	0.0023	0.4036
Beta	0.7902	0.0417	18.9655

Source: Center for Research in Security Prices, University of Chicago.

Note also that the estimated alpha ($\hat{\alpha}$) in this regression is positive (0.0009). The value of the coefficient is only a little more than one-third the size of the standard error for that coefficient (0.0023), so the t-statistic for the coefficient is only 0.4036. Therefore, we cannot reject the null hypothesis ($\alpha = 0$) that the fund did not have a significant excess return beyond the return associated with the market risk of the fund. This result means that the returns to the fund were explained by the market risk of the fund and there was no additional statistical significance to the excess returns to the fund during this period.[39]

Because the t-statistic for the slope coefficient in this regression is 18.9655, the p-value for that coefficient is less than 0.0001 and is approximately zero. Therefore, the probability that the true value of this coefficient is actually 0 is microscopic.

How can we use an F-test to determine whether the slope coefficient in this regression is equal to 0? The ANOVA portion of Table 12 provides the data we need. In this case:

▶ the total number of observations (n) is 60;
▶ the total number of parameters to be estimated is 2 (intercept and slope);

---

[39] This example introduces a well-known investment use of regression involving the capital asset pricing model. Researchers, however, recognize qualifications to the interpretation of alpha from a linear regression. The systematic risk of a managed portfolio is controlled by the portfolio manager. If, as a consequence, portfolio beta is correlated with the return on the market (as could result from market timing), inferences on alpha based on least-squares beta, as here, can be mistaken. This advanced subject is discussed in Dybvig and Ross (1985a) and (1985b).

> ► the sum of squared errors or residuals, SSE, is 0.0176; and
>
> ► the regression sum of squares, RSS, is 0.1093.
>
> Therefore, the F-statistic to test whether the slope coefficient is equal to 0 is
>
> $$\frac{0.1093/1}{0.0176/(60-2)} = 360.19$$
>
> (The slight difference from the F-statistic in Table 12 is due to rounding.) The ANOVA output would show that the p-value for this F-statistic is less than 0.0001 and is exactly the same as the p-value for the t-statistic for the slope coefficient. Therefore, the F-test tells us nothing more than we already knew from the t-test. Note also that the F-statistic (359.64) is the square of the t-statistic (18.9655).

3.7 Prediction Intervals

Financial analysts often want to use regression results to make predictions about a dependent variable. For example, we might ask, "How fast will the sales of XYZ Corporation grow this year if real GDP grows by 4 percent?" But we are not merely interested in making these forecasts; we also want to know how certain we should be about the forecasts' results. For example, if we predicted that sales for XYZ Corporation would grow by 6 percent this year, our prediction would mean more if we were 95 percent confident that sales growth would fall in the interval from 5 percent to 7 percent, rather than only 25 percent confident that this outcome would occur. Therefore, we need to understand how to compute confidence intervals around regression forecasts.

We must take into account two sources of uncertainty when using the regression model $Y_i = b_0 + b_1 X_i + \varepsilon_i$, $i = 1, \ldots , n$ and the estimated parameters, $\hat{b}_0$ and $\hat{b}_1$, to make a prediction. First, the error term itself contains uncertainty. The standard deviation of the error term, σ_ε, can be estimated from the standard error of estimate for the regression equation. A second source of uncertainty in making predictions about Y, however, comes from uncertainty in the estimated parameters $\hat{b}_0$ and $\hat{b}_1$.

If we knew the true values of the regression parameters, b_0 and b_1, then the variance of our prediction of Y, given any particular predicted (or assumed) value of X, would simply be s^2, the squared standard error of estimate. The variance would be s^2 because the prediction, $\hat{Y}$, would come from the equation $\hat{Y} = b_0 + \hat{b}_1 X$ and $(Y - \hat{Y}) = \varepsilon$.

Because we must estimate the regression parameters $\hat{b}_0$ and $\hat{b}_1$ however, our prediction of $Y, \hat{Y}$, given any particular predicted value of X, is actually $\hat{Y} = \hat{b}_0 + \hat{b}_1 X$. The estimated variance of the prediction error, s_f^2 of Y, given X, is

$$s_f^2 = s^2 \left[1 + \frac{1}{n} + \frac{(X - \overline{X})^2}{(n-1)s_x^2} \right] \qquad \textbf{(15)}$$

This estimated variance depends on:

► the squared standard error of estimate, s^2;

► the number of observations, n;

▶ the value of the independent variable, X, used to predict the dependent variable;

▶ the estimated mean, $\overline{X}$; and

▶ variance, s_x^2 of the independent variable.[40]

Once we have this estimate of the variance of the prediction error, determining a prediction interval around the prediction is very similar to estimating a confidence interval around an estimated parameter, as shown earlier in this reading. We need to take the following four steps to determine the prediction interval for the prediction:

1. Make the prediction.

2. Compute the variance of the prediction error using Equation 15.

3. Choose a significance level, α, for the forecast. For example, the 0.05 level, given the degrees of freedom in the regression, determines the critical value for the forecast interval, t_c.

4. Compute the $(1 - \alpha)$ percent prediction interval for the prediction, namely $\hat{Y} \pm t_c s_f$.

EXAMPLE 18

Predicting the Ratio of Enterprise Value to Invested Capital

We continue with the example of explaining the ratio of enterprise value to invested capital among food-processing companies by the spread between the return to invested capital and the weighted-average cost of capital (ROIC–WAAC). In Example 15, we estimated the regression given in Table 10.

TABLE 10 Explaining Enterprise Value/Invested Capital by the ROIC–WACC Spread (repeated)

Regression Statistics

Multiple R	0.9469
R-squared	0.8966
Standard error of estimate	0.7422
Observations	9

	Coefficients	Standard Error	t-Statistic
Intercept	1.3478	0.3511	3.8391
Spread	30.0169	3.8519	7.7928

Source: Nelson (2003).

---

[40] For a derivation of this equation, see Pindyck and Rubinfeld (1998).

You are interested in predicting the ratio of enterprise value to invested capital for a company if the return spread between ROIC and WACC is 10 percentage points. What is the 95 percent confidence interval for the ratio of enterprise value to invested capital for that company? Using the data provided in Table 10, take the following steps:

1. Make the prediction: Expected EV/IC = 1.3478 + 30.0169(0.10) = 4.3495. This regression suggests that if the return spread between ROIC and WACC (X_i) is 10 percent, the EV/IC ratio will be 4.3495.

2. Compute the variance of the prediction error. To compute the variance of the forecast error, we must know:

   ▶ the standard error of the estimate of the equation, $s = 0.7422$ (as shown in Table 10);

   ▶ the mean return spread, $\overline{X} = 0.0647$ (this computation is not shown in the table); and

   ▶ the variance of the mean return spread in the sample, $s_{\overline{x}}^2 = 0.004641$ (this computation is not shown in the table).

   Using these data, you can compute the variance of the forecast error (s_f^2) for predicting EV/IC for a company with a 10 percent spread between ROIC and WACC.

$$s_f^2 = 0.7422^2 \left[1 + \frac{1}{9} + \frac{(0.10 - 0.0647)^2}{(9-1)0.004641} \right]$$
$$= 0.630556$$

   In this example, the variance of the forecast error is 0.630556, and the standard deviation of the forecast error is $s_f = (0.630556)^{1/2} = 0.7941$.

3. Determine the critical value of the t-statistic. Given a 95 percent confidence interval and $9 - 2 = 7$ degrees of freedom, the critical value of the t-statistic, t_c, is 2.365 using the tables in the back of this volume.

4. Compute the prediction interval. The 95 percent confidence interval for EV/IC extends from $4.3495 - 2.365(0.7941)$ to $4.3495 + 2.365(0.7941)$, or 2.4715 to 6.2275.

In summary, if the spread between the ROIC and the WACC is 10 percent, the 95 percent prediction interval for EV/IC will extend from 2.4715 to 6.2275. The small sample size is reflected in the relatively large prediction interval.

3.8 Limitations of Regression Analysis

Although this reading has shown many of the uses of regression models for financial analysis, regression models do have limitations. First, regression relations can change over time, just as correlations can. This fact is known as the issue of **parameter instability**, and its existence should not be surprising as the economic, tax, regulatory, political, and institutional contexts in which financial markets operate change. Whether considering cross-sectional or time-series regression, the analyst will probably face this issue. As one example, cross-sectional regression relationships between stock characteristics may differ between growth-led and value-led markets. As a second example, the time-series regression estimating the beta often yields significantly different estimated betas depending on the time period selected. In both cross-sectional and time-series contexts, the most common problem is sampling from more than one population, with the challenge of identifying when doing so is an issue.

A second limitation to the use of regression results specific to investment contexts is that public knowledge of regression relationships may negate their future usefulness. Suppose, for example, an analyst discovers that stocks with a certain characteristic have had historically very high returns. If other analysts discover and act upon this relationship, then the prices of stocks with that characteristic will be bid up. The knowledge of the relationship may result in the relation no longer holding in the future.

Finally, if the regression assumptions listed in Section 3.2 are violated, hypothesis tests and predictions based on linear regression will not be valid. Although there are tests for violations of regression assumptions, often uncertainty exists as to whether an assumption has been violated. This limitation will be discussed in detail in the reading on multiple regression.

SUMMARY

▶ A scatter plot shows graphically the relationship between two variables. If the points on the scatter plot cluster together in a straight line, the two variables have a strong linear relation.

▶ The sample correlation coefficient for two variables X and Y is $r = \dfrac{\text{Cov}(X, Y)}{s_x s_y}$.

▶ If two variables have a very strong linear relation, then the absolute value of their correlation will be close to 1. If two variables have a weak linear relation, then the absolute value of their correlation will be close to 0.

▶ The squared value of the correlation coefficient for two variables quantifies the percentage of the variance of one variable that is explained by the other. If the correlation coefficient is positive, the two variables are directly related; if the correlation coefficient is negative, the two variables are inversely related.

▶ If we have n observations for two variables, we can test whether the population correlation between the two variables is equal to 0 by using a t-test. This test statistic has a t-distribution with $n - 2$ degrees of freedom if the null hypothesis of 0 correlation is true.

▶ Even one outlier can greatly affect the correlation between two variables. Analysts should examine a scatter plot for the variables to determine whether outliers might affect a particular correlation.

▶ Correlations can be spurious in the sense of misleadingly pointing toward associations between variables.

▶ The dependent variable in a linear regression is the variable that the regression model tries to explain. The independent variables are the variables that a regression model uses to explain the dependent variable.

▶ If there is one independent variable in a linear regression and there are n observations on the dependent and independent variables, the regression model is $Y_i = b_0 + b_1 X_i + \varepsilon_i$, $i = 1, \ldots, n$, where Y_i is the dependent variable, X_i is the independent variable, and ε_i is the error term. In this model, the coefficient b_0 is the intercept. The intercept is the predicted value of the dependent variable when the independent variable has a value of zero. In this model, the coefficient b_1 is the slope of the regression line. If the value of the independent variable increases by one unit, then the model predicts that the value of the dependent variable will increase by b_1 units.

▶ The assumptions of the classic normal linear regression model are the following:

    ▶ A linear relation exists between the dependent variable and the independent variable.

    ▶ The independent variable is not random.

    ▶ The expected value of the error term is 0.

    ▶ The variance of the error term is the same for all observations (homoskedasticity).

    ▶ The error term is uncorrelated across observations.

    ▶ The error term is normally distributed.

▶ The estimated parameters in a linear regression model minimize the sum of the squared regression residuals.

▶ The standard error of estimate measures how well the regression model fits the data. If the SEE is small, the model fits well.

▶ The coefficient of determination measures the fraction of the total variation in the dependent variable that is explained by the independent variable. In a linear regression with one independent variable, the simplest way to compute the coefficient of determination is to square the correlation of the dependent and independent variables.

▶ To calculate a confidence interval for an estimated regression coefficient, we must know the standard error of the estimated coefficient and the critical value for the t-distribution at the chosen level of significance, t_c.

▶ To test whether the population value of a regression coefficient, b_1, is equal to a particular hypothesized value, B_1, we must know the estimated coefficient, $\hat{b}_1$, the standard error of the estimated coefficient, $s_{\hat{b}_1}$, and the critical value for the t-distribution at the chosen level of significance, t_c. The test statistic for this hypothesis is $(\hat{b}_1 - B_1)/s_{\hat{b}_1}$. If the absolute value of this statistic is greater than t_c, then we reject the null hypothesis that $b_1 = B_1$.

▶ In the regression model $Y_i = b_0 + b_1 X_i + \varepsilon_i$, if we know the estimated parameters, $\hat{b}_0$ and $\hat{b}_1$, for any value of the independent variable, X, then the predicted value of the dependent variable Y is $\hat{Y} = \hat{b}_0 + \hat{b}_1 X$.

▶ The prediction interval for a regression equation for a particular predicted value of the dependent variable is $\hat{Y} \pm t_c s_f$ where s_f is the square root of the estimated variance of the prediction error and t_c is the critical level for the t-statistic at the chosen significance level. This computation specifies a $(1 - \alpha)$ percent confidence interval. For example, if $\alpha = 0.05$, then this computation yields a 95 percent confidence interval.

PRACTICE PROBLEMS FOR READING 11

1. Variable X takes on the values shown in the following table for five observations. The table also shows the values for five other variables, Y_1 through Y_5. Which of the variables Y_1 through Y_5 have a zero correlation with variable X?

X	Y_1	Y_2	Y_3	Y_4	Y_5
1	7	2	4	4	1
2	7	4	2	1	2
3	7	2	0	0	3
4	7	4	2	1	4
5	7	2	4	4	5

2. Use the data sample below to answer the following questions.

$$\sum_{i=1}^{n} X_i = 220 \qquad \sum_{i=1}^{n} (X_i - \overline{X})^2 = 440 \qquad \sum_{i=1}^{n} (X_i - \overline{X})(Y_i - \overline{Y}) = -568$$

$$\sum_{i=1}^{n} Y_i = 385 \qquad \sum_{i=1}^{n} (Y_i - \overline{Y})^2 = 1120 \qquad n = 11$$

   A. Calculate the sample mean, variance, and standard deviation for X.

   B. Calculate the sample mean, variance, and standard deviation for Y.

   C. Calculate the sample covariance between X and Y.

   D. Calculate the sample correlation between X and Y.

3. Statistics for three variables are given below. X is the monthly return for a large-stock index, Y is the monthly return for a small-stock index, and Z is the monthly return for a corporate bond index. There are 60 observations.

$$\overline{X} = 0.760 \qquad \sum_{i=1}^{n} (X_i - \overline{X})^2 = 769.081 \qquad \sum_{i=1}^{n} (X_i - \overline{X})(Y_i - \overline{Y}) = 720.535$$

$$\overline{Y} = 1.037 \qquad \sum_{i=1}^{n} (Y_i - \overline{Y})^2 = 1243.309 \qquad \sum_{i=1}^{n} (X_i - \overline{X})(Z_i - \overline{Z}) = 231.007$$

$$\overline{Z} = 0.686 \qquad \sum_{i=1}^{n} (Z_i - \overline{Z})^2 = 183.073 \qquad \sum_{i=1}^{n} (Y_i - \overline{Y})(Z_i - \overline{Z}) = 171.816$$

   A. Calculate the sample variance and standard deviation for X, Y, and Z.

   B. Calculate the sample covariance between X and Y, X and Z, and Y and Z.

   C. Calculate the sample correlation between X and Y, X and Z, and Y and Z.

4. Home sales and interest rates should be negatively related. The following table gives the number of annual unit sales for Packard Homes and mortgage rates for four recent years. Calculate the sample correlation between sales and mortgage rates.

Year	Unit Sales	Interest Rate (%)
2000	50	8.0
2001	70	7.0
2002	80	6.0
2003	60	7.0

5. The following table shows the sample correlations between the monthly returns for four different mutual funds and the S&P 500. The correlations are based on 36 monthly observations. The funds are as follows:

Fund 1	Large-cap fund
Fund 2	Mid-cap fund
Fund 3	Large-cap value fund
Fund 4	Emerging markets fund
S&P 500	U.S. domestic stock index

	Fund 1	Fund 2	Fund 3	Fund 4	S&P 500
Fund 1	1				
Fund 2	0.9231	1			
Fund 3	0.4771	0.4156	1		
Fund 4	0.7111	0.7238	0.3102	1	
S&P 500	0.8277	0.8223	0.5791	0.7515	1

Test the null hypothesis that each of these correlations, individually, is equal to zero against the alternative hypothesis that it is not equal to zero. Use a 5 percent significance level.

6. Juan Martinez, Dieter Osterburg, and Sara Durbin are discussing the correlations between monthly stock returns. Martinez believes that returns are random and that the correlation between stock returns from one month to the next should be zero. Osterburg believes that high or low returns are followed by strong reversals, causing monthly returns to have a negative month-to-month correlation. Durbin believes that positive or negative returns tend to be followed by returns in the same direction, resulting in positive month-to-month correlation.

They give you a series of 60 monthly returns for the S&P 500 during the 1994–98 time period. You create two variables: X represents the first 59 monthly returns, and Y the last 59 monthly returns. For the first observation, X is the January 1994 return and Y is the February 1994 return; for the second observation, X is the February 1994 return and Y is the March 1994 return, etc. The result is 59 paired, contiguous monthly returns. The calculated sample correlation coefficient between X and Y is -0.0641.

A. Interpret the meaning of the negative correlation.

B. Is this correlation significantly different from 0? Use a two-tailed test and a 5 percent significance level.

7. You have monthly returns for four indexes and want to test for serial correlation. You have 29 years of data, or 348 monthly observations. When you compare monthly returns, your sample is reduced to 347 because Month 1 is compared with Month 2, Month 2 with Month 3, until Month 347 is compared with Month 348. Below are the sample correlations calculated for the indexes:

Index	S&P 500	MSCI Europe	MSCI Pacific	MSCI Far East
Serial correlation	0.0034	0.0335	0.1121	0.1052

For each index, test the hypothesis that its serial correlation is equal to 0. Use a 10 percent significance level.

8. Bouvier Co. is a Canadian company that sells forestry products to several Pacific Rim customers. Bouvier's sales are very sensitive to exchange rates. The following table shows recent annual sales (in millions of Canadian dollars) and the average exchange rate for the year (expressed as the units of foreign currency needed to buy one Canadian dollar).

Year i	Exchange Rate X_i	Sales Y_i
1	0.40	20
2	0.36	25
3	0.42	16
4	0.31	30
5	0.33	35
6	0.34	30

A. Calculate the sample mean and standard deviation for X (the exchange rate) and Y (sales).

B. Calculate the sample covariance between the exchange rate and sales.

C. Calculate the sample correlation between the exchange rate and sales.

D. Calculate the intercept and coefficient for an estimated linear regression with the exchange rate as the independent variable and sales as the dependent variable.

9. Julie Moon is an energy analyst examining electricity, oil, and natural gas consumption in different regions over different seasons. She ran a regression explaining the variation in energy consumption as a function of temperature. The total variation of the dependent variable was 140.58, the explained variation was 60.16, and the unexplained variation was 80.42. She had 60 monthly observations.

A. Compute the coefficient of determination.

B. What was the sample correlation between energy consumption and temperature?

C. Compute the standard error of the estimate of Moon's regression model.

D. Compute the sample standard deviation of monthly energy consumption.

10. You are examining the results of a regression estimation that attempts to explain the unit sales growth of a business you are researching. The analysis of variance output for the regression is given in the table below. The regression was based on five observations ($n = 5$).

ANOVA

	df	SS	MSS	F	Significance F
Regression	1	88.0	88.0	36.667	0.00904
Residual	3	7.2	2.4		
Total	4	95.2			

   A. How many independent variables are in the regression to which the ANOVA refers?

   B. Define Total SS.

   C. Calculate the sample variance of the dependent variable using information in the above table.

   D. Define Regression SS and explain how its value of 88 is obtained in terms of other quantities reported in the above table.

   E. What hypothesis does the F-statistic test?

   F. Explain how the value of the F-statistic of 36.667 is obtained in terms of other quantities reported in the above table.

   G. Is the F-test significant at the 5 percent significance level?

11. The first table below contains the regression results for a regression with monthly returns on a large-cap mutual fund as the dependent variable and monthly returns on a market index as the independent variable. The analysis is performed using only 12 monthly returns (in percent). The second table provides summary statistics for the dependent and independent variables.

   A. What is the predicted return on the large-cap mutual fund for a market index return of 8.00 percent?

   B. Find a 95 percent prediction interval for the expected mutual fund return.

Regression Statistics

Multiple R	0.776
R-squared	0.602
Standard error	4.243
Observations	12

	Coefficients	Standard Error	t-Statistic	p-Value
Intercept	−0.287	1.314	−0.219	0.831
Slope coefficient	0.802	0.206	3.890	0.003

Statistic	Market Index Return	Large-Cap Fund Return
Mean	2.30%	1.56%
Standard deviation	6.21%	6.41%
Variance	38.51	41.13
Count	12	12

12. Industry automobile sales should be related to consumer sentiment. The following table provides a regression analysis in which sales of automobiles and light trucks (in millions of vehicles) are estimated as a function of a consumer sentiment index.

Regression Statistics

Multiple R	0.80113
R-squared	0.64181
Standard error	0.81325
Observations	120

	Coefficients	Standard Error	t-Statistic	p-Value
Intercept	6.071	0.58432	10.389	0
Slope coefficient	0.09251	0.00636	14.541	0

For the independent variable and dependent variable, the means, standard deviations, and variances are as follows:

	Sentiment Index X	Automobile Sales (Millions of Units) Y
Mean	91.0983	14.4981
Standard deviation	11.7178	1.35312
Variance	137.3068	1.83094

A. Find the expected sales and a 95 percent prediction interval for sales if the sentiment index has a value of 90.

B. Find the expected sales and a 95 percent prediction interval for sales if the sentiment index has a value of 100.

13. Use the following information to create a regression model:

$$\sum_{i=1}^{n} X_i = 81 \qquad \sum_{i=1}^{n} (X_i - \overline{X})^2 = 60 \qquad \sum_{i=1}^{n} (X_i - \overline{X})(Y_i - \overline{Y}) = 84$$

$$\sum_{i=1}^{n} X_i^2 = 789$$

$$\sum_{i=1}^{n} Y_i = 144 \qquad \sum_{i=1}^{n} (Y_i - \overline{Y})^2 = 144 \qquad \sum_{i=1}^{n} (Y_i - \hat{b}_0 - \hat{b}_1 X_i)^2 = 26.4$$

$$n = 9$$

A. Calculate the sample mean, variance, and standard deviation for X and for Y.

B. Calculate the sample covariance and the correlation between X and Y.

C. Calculate $\hat{b}_0$ and $\hat{b}_1$ for a regression of the form $Y_i = \hat{b}_0 + \hat{b}_1 X_i$.

For the remaining three parts of this question, assume that the calculations shown above already incorporate the correct values for $\hat{b}_0$ and $\hat{b}_1$.

D. Find the total variation, explained variation, and unexplained variation.

E. Find the coefficient of determination.

F. Find the standard error of the estimate.

14. The bid–ask spread for stocks depends on the market liquidity for stocks. One measure of liquidity is a stock's trading volume. Below are the results of a regression analysis using the bid–ask spread at the end of 2002 for a sample of 1,819 NASDAQ-listed stocks as the independent variable and the natural log of trading volume during December 2002 as the dependent variable. Several items in the regression output have been intentionally omitted. Use the reported information to fill in the missing values.

Regression Statistics

Multiple R	X2
R-squared	X1
Standard error	X3
Observations	1819

ANOVA	df	SS	MSS	F	Significance F
Regression	X5	14.246	X7	X9	0
Residual	X6	45.893	X8		
Total	X4	60.139			

	Coefficients	Standard Error	t-Statistic	p-Value	Lower 95%	Upper 95%
Intercept	0.55851	0.018707	29.85540	0	0.52182	0.59520
Slope coefficient	−0.04375	0.001842	X10	0	X11	X12

15. An economist collected the monthly returns for KDL's portfolio and a diversified stock index. The data collected are shown below:

Month	Portfolio Return (%)	Index Return (%)
1	1.11	−0.59
2	72.10	64.90
3	5.12	4.81
4	1.01	1.68
5	−1.72	−4.97
6	4.06	−2.06

The economist calculated the correlation between the two returns and found it to be 0.996. The regression results with the KDL return as the dependent variable and the index return as the independent variable are given as follows:

Regression Statistics

Multiple R	0.996
R-squared	0.992
Standard error	2.861
Observations	6

ANOVA	df	SS	MSS	F	Significance F
Regression	1	4101.62	4101.62	500.79	0
Residual	4	32.76	8.19		
Total	5	4134.38			

	Coefficients	Standard Error	t-Statistic	p-Value
Intercept	2.252	1.274	1.768	0.1518
Slope	1.069	0.0477	22.379	0

When reviewing the results, Andrea Fusilier suspected that they were unreliable. She found that the returns for Month 2 should have been 7.21 percent and 6.49 percent, instead of the large values shown in the first table. Correcting these values resulted in a revised correlation of 0.824 and the revised regression results shown as follows:

Regression Statistics

Multiple R	0.824
R-squared	0.678
Standard error	2.062
Observations	6

ANOVA	df	SS	MSS	F	Significance F
Regression	1	35.89	35.89	8.44	0.044
Residual	4	17.01	4.25		
Total	5	52.91			

	Coefficients	Standard Error	t-Statistic	p-Value
Intercept	2.242	0.863	2.597	0.060
Slope	0.623	0.214	2.905	0.044

Explain how the bad data affected the results.

16. Diet Partners charges its clients a small management fee plus a percentage of gains whenever portfolio returns are positive. Cleo Smith believes that strong incentives for portfolio managers produce superior returns for clients. In order to demonstrate this, Smith runs a regression with the Diet Partners' portfolio return (in percent) as the dependent variable and its management fee (in percent) as the independent variable. The estimated regression for a 60-month period is

$$\text{RETURN} = -3.021 + 7.062 \text{ (FEE)}$$
$$(-7.28) \quad (14.95)$$

The calculated t-values are given in parentheses below the intercept and slope coefficients. The coefficient of determination for the regression model is 0.794.

A. What is the predicted RETURN if FEE is 0 percent? If FEE is 1 percent?

B. Using a two-tailed test, is the relationship between RETURN and FEE significant at the 5 percent level?

C. Would Smith be justified in concluding that high fees are good for clients?

The following information relates to Questions 17–22

Kenneth McCoin, CFA, is a fairly tough interviewer. Last year, he handed each job applicant a sheet of paper with the information in the following table, and he then asked several questions about regression analysis. Some of McCoin's questions, along with a sample of the answers he received to each, are given below. McCoin told the applicants that the independent variable is the ratio of net income to sales for restaurants with a market cap of more than $100 million and the dependent variable is the ratio of cash flow from operations to sales for those restaurants. Which of the choices provided is the best answer to each of McCoin's questions?

Regression Statistics

Multiple R	0.8623	
R-squared	0.7436	
Standard error	0.0213	
Observations	24	

ANOVA	df	SS	MSS	F	Significance F
Regression	1	0.029	0.029000	63.81	0
Residual	22	0.010	0.000455		
Total	23	0.040			

	Coefficients	Standard Error	t-Statistic	p-Value
Intercept	0.077	0.007	11.328	0
Slope	0.826	0.103	7.988	0

17. What is the value of the coefficient of determination?

    A. 0.8261.

    B. 0.7436.

    C. 0.8623.

18. Suppose that you deleted several of the observations that had small residual values. If you re-estimated the regression equation using this reduced sample, what would likely happen to the standard error of the estimate and the R-squared?

	Standard Error of the Estimate	R-Squared
A.	Decrease	Decrease
B.	Decrease	Increase
C.	Increase	Decrease

19. What is the correlation between X and Y?

    A. −0.7436.

    B. 0.7436.

    C. 0.8623.

20. Where did the *F*-value in the ANOVA table come from?

    A. You look up the *F*-value in a table. The *F* depends on the numerator and denominator degrees of freedom.

    B. Divide the "Mean Square" for the regression by the "Mean Square" of the residuals.

    C. The *F*-value is equal to the reciprocal of the *t*-value for the slope coefficient.

21. If the ratio of net income to sales for a restaurant is 5 percent, what is the predicted ratio of cash flow from operations to sales?

    A. $0.007 + 0.103(5.0) = 0.524$.

    B. $0.077 - 0.826(5.0) = -4.054$.

    C. $0.077 + 0.826(5.0) = 4.207$.

22. Is the relationship between the ratio of cash flow to operations and the ratio of net income to sales significant at the 5 percent level?

    A. No, because the *R*-squared is greater than 0.05.

    B. No, because the *p*-values of the intercept and slope are less than 0.05.

    C. Yes, because the *p*-values for *F* and *t* for the slope coefficient are less than 0.05.

The following information relates to Questions 23–28

Howard Golub, CFA, is preparing to write a research report on Stellar Energy Corp. common stock. One of the world's largest companies, Stellar is in the business of refining and marketing oil. As part of his analysis, Golub wants to evaluate the sensitivity of the stock's returns to various economic factors. For example, a client recently asked Golub whether the price of Stellar Energy Corporation stock has tended to rise following increases in retail energy prices. Golub believes the association between the two variables to be negative, but he does not know the strength of the association.

Golub directs his assistant, Jill Batten, to study the relationships between Stellar monthly common stock returns versus the previous month's percent change in the U.S. Consumer Price Index for Energy (CPIENG), and Stellar monthly common stock returns versus the previous month's percent change in the U.S. Producer Price Index for Crude Energy Materials (PPICEM). Golub wants Batten to run both a correlation and a linear regression analysis. In response, Batten compiles the summary statistics shown in Exhibit 1 for the 248 months between January 1980 and August 2000. All of the data are in decimal form, where 0.01 indicates a 1 percent return. Batten also runs a regression analysis using Stellar monthly returns as the dependent variable and the monthly change in CPIENG as the independent variable. Exhibit 2 displays the results of this regression model.

EXHIBIT 1	Descriptive Statistics		
	Monthly Return Stellar Common Stock	Lagged Monthly Change	
		CPIENG	PPICEM
Mean	0.0123	0.0023	0.0042
Standard Deviation	0.0717	0.0160	0.0534
Covariance, Stellar vs. CPIENG	−0.00017		
Covariance, Stellar vs. PPICEM	−0.00048		
Covariance, CPIENG vs. PPICEM	0.00044		
Correlation, Stellar vs. CPIENG	−0.1452		

EXHIBIT 2	Regression Analysis with CPIENG

Regression Statistics

Multiple R	0.1452
R-squared	0.0211
Standard error of the estimate	0.0710
Observations	248

	Coefficients	Standard Error	t-Statistic
Intercept	0.0138	0.0046	3.0275
Slope coefficient	−0.6486	0.2818	−2.3014

23. Batten wants to determine whether the sample correlation between the Stellar and CPIENG variables (−0.1452) is statistically significant. The critical value for the test statistic at the 0.05 level of significance is approximately 1.96. Batten should conclude that the statistical relationship between Stellar and CPIENG is:

　A. significant, because the calculated test statistic has a lower absolute value than the critical value for the test statistic.

　B. significant, because the calculated test statistic has a higher absolute value than the critical value for the test statistic.

　C. not significant, because the calculated test statistic has a higher absolute value than the critical value for the test statistic.

24. Did Batten's regression analyze cross-sectional or time-series data, and what was the expected value of the error term from that regression?

	Data Type	Expected Value of Error Term
A.	Time-series	0
B.	Time-series	ε_i
C.	Cross-sectional	0

25. Based on the regression, which used data in decimal form, if the CPIENG *decreases* by 1.0 percent, what is the expected return on Stellar common stock during the next period?

A. 0.0073 (0.73 percent).

B. 0.0138 (1.38 percent).

C. 0.0203 (2.03 percent).

26. Based on Batten's regression model, the coefficient of determination indicates that:

A. Stellar's returns explain 2.11 percent of the variability in CPIENG.

B. Stellar's returns explain 14.52 percent of the variability in CPIENG.

C. Changes in CPIENG explain 2.11 percent of the variability in Stellar's returns.

27. For Batten's regression model, the standard error of the estimate shows that the standard deviation of:

A. the residuals from the regression is 0.0710.

B. values estimated from the regression is 0.0710.

C. Stellar's observed common stock returns is 0.0710.

28. For the analysis run by Batten, which of the following is an *incorrect* conclusion from the regression output?

A. The estimated intercept coefficient from Batten's regression is statistically significant at the 0.05 level.

B. In the month after the CPIENG declines, Stellar's common stock is expected to exhibit a positive return.

C. Viewed in combination, the slope and intercept coefficients from Batten's regression are not statistically significant at the 0.05 level.

SOLUTIONS FOR READING 11

1. The four variables Y_1 through Y_4 have a zero correlation with X. Notice that although Y_3 and Y_4 are clearly nonlinearly related to X (decreasing and then increasing as the value of X increases), their overall linear relationship with X is zero. Variable Y_5 has a correlation of 1.0 with X.

2. A. The sample mean, variance, and standard deviation of X are

$$\overline{X} = \sum_{i=1}^{n} X_i/n = 220/11 = 20$$

$$s_X^2 = \sum_{i=1}^{n} (X_i - \overline{X})^2/(n-1) = 440/10 = 44$$

$$s_X = \sqrt{s_X^2} = \sqrt{44} = 6.633$$

B. The sample mean, variance, and standard deviation of Y are

$$\overline{Y} = \sum_{i=1}^{n} Y_i/n = 385/11 = 35$$

$$s_Y^2 = \sum_{i=1}^{n} (Y_i - \overline{Y})^2/(n-1) = 1120/10 = 112$$

$$s_Y = \sqrt{s_Y^2} = \sqrt{112} = 10.583$$

C. The sample covariance between X and Y is

$$\text{Cov}(X,Y) = \sum_{i=1}^{n} [(X_i - \overline{X})(Y_i - \overline{Y})]/(n-1) = -568/10 = -56.8$$

D. The sample correlation between X and Y is

$$r = \frac{\text{Cov}(X, Y)}{s_x s_y} = \frac{-56.8}{6.633 \times 10.583} = -0.809$$

3. A. The sample variances and standard deviations are

$$s_X^2 = \sum_{i=1}^{n} (X_i - \overline{X})^2/(n-1) = 769.081/59 = 13.035$$

$$s_X = \sqrt{13.035} = 3.610$$

$$s_Y^2 = \sum_{i=1}^{n} (Y_i - \overline{Y})^2/(n-1) = 1243.309/59 = 21.073$$

$$s_Y = \sqrt{21.073} = 4.591$$

$$s_Z^2 = \sum_{i=1}^{n} (Z_i - \overline{Z})^2/(n-1) = 183.073/59 = 3.103$$

$$s_Z = \sqrt{3.103} = 1.762$$

B. The sample covariances are

$$\text{Cov}(X,Y) = \sum_{i=1}^{n} (X_i - \overline{X})(Y_i - \overline{Y})/(n-1) = 720.535/59 = 12.212$$

$$\text{Cov}(X,Z) = \sum_{i=1}^{n} (X_i - \overline{X})(Z_i - \overline{Z})/(n-1) = 231.007/59 = 3.915$$

$$\text{Cov}(Y,Z) = \sum_{i=1}^{n} (Y_i - \overline{Y})(Z_i - \overline{Z})/(n-1) = 171.816/59 = 2.912$$

C. The sample correlations are

$$r_{XY} = \frac{\text{Cov}(X,Y)}{s_X s_Y} = \frac{12.212}{(3.610)(4.591)} = 0.737$$

$$r_{XZ} = \frac{\text{Cov}(X,Z)}{s_X s_Z} = \frac{3.915}{(3.610)(1.762)} = 0.615$$

$$r_{YZ} = \frac{\text{Cov}(Y,Z)}{s_Y s_Z} = \frac{2.912}{(4.591)(1.762)} = 0.360$$

4. Sample mean sales are $(50 + 70 + 80 + 60)/4 = 260/4 = 65$.

Sample mean interest rate is $(8.0 + 7.0 + 6.0 + 7.0)/4 = 28.0/4 = 7.0$.

Sample variance of sales is $[(50 - 65)^2 + (70 - 65)^2 + (80 - 65)^2 + (60 - 65)^2]/3 = 500/3 = 166.7$.

Sample standard deviation of sales is the square root of the variance, or 12.91.

Sample variance of interest rates is $[(8 - 7)^2 + (7 - 7)^2 + (6 - 7)^2 + (7 - 7)^2]/3 = 2/3 = 0.666667$.

Sample standard deviation of interest rates is the square root of this result, or 0.8165.

Sample covariance between sales and interest rates is $[(50 - 65)(8 - 7) + (70 - 65)(7 - 7) + (80 - 65)(6 - 7) + (60 - 65)(7 - 7)]/3 = -30/3 = -10$.

Sample correlation is the covariance divided by the product of the standard deviations:

$$r = \frac{\text{Cov}(X, Y)}{s_x s_y} = \frac{-10}{(12.91)(0.8165)} = -0.9487$$

5. The critical t-value for $n - 2 = 34$ df, using a 5 percent significance level and a two-tailed test, is 2.032. First, take the smallest correlation in the table, the correlation between Fund 3 and Fund 4, and see if it is significantly different from zero. Its calculated t-value is

$$t = \frac{r\sqrt{n - 2}}{\sqrt{1 - r^2}} = \frac{0.3102\sqrt{36 - 2}}{\sqrt{1 - 0.3102^2}} = 1.903$$

This correlation is not significantly different from zero. If we take the next lowest correlation, between Fund 2 and Fund 3, this correlation of 0.4156 has a calculated t-value of 2.664. So this correlation is significantly different from zero at the 5 percent level of significance. All of the other correlations in the table (besides the 0.3102) are greater than 0.4156, so they too are significantly different from zero.

6. A. The negative correlation, as Osterburg hypothesizes, is consistent with reversals. An above-average return tends to be followed by a below-average return. Similarly, a below-average return tends to be followed by an above-average return.

B. The null hypothesis, H_0, is that the correlation is 0 ($\rho = 0$); the alternative hypothesis, H_a, is that the correlation is different from 0 ($\rho \neq 0$). We can test this hypothesis with a t-test. The calculated value of the t-test is as follows:

$$t = \frac{r\sqrt{n - 2}}{\sqrt{1 - r^2}} = \frac{-0.0641\sqrt{59 - 2}}{\sqrt{1 - (-0.0641)^2}} = -0.485$$

This test statistic has a t-distribution with $n - 2 = 59 - 2 = 57$ df, so the critical t-value (for a two-tailed test and 5 percent significance) is approximately 2.00. So we cannot reject the hypothesis that $\rho = 0$ with 95 percent confidence. We thus cannot reject Martinez's opinion that the returns are random.

7. The null hypothesis, H_0, is that the correlation is 0 ($\rho = 0$); the alternative hypothesis, H_a, is that the correlation is different from 0 ($\rho \neq 0$). The calculated value of the t-test for the S&P 500 is

$$t = \frac{r\sqrt{n-2}}{\sqrt{1-r^2}} = \frac{0.0034\sqrt{347-2}}{\sqrt{1-0.0034^2}} = 0.063$$

The t-values for the other indices are calculated similarly, as follows:

MSCI Europe	0.623
MSCI Pacific	2.095
MSCI Far East	1.965

The critical t-value for $n - 2 = 347 - 2 = 345$ df is approximately 1.65. At a 10 percent significance level (two-tailed test with 345 df), the correlations for the S&P 500 and MSCI Europe are not significantly different from zero. The MSCI Pacific and MSCI Far East correlations apparently are significantly different from zero.

8. The following table provides several useful calculations:

Year i	Exchange Rate X_i	Sales Y_i	$(X_i - \bar{X})^2$	$(Y_i - \bar{Y})^2$	$(X_i - \bar{X})(Y_i - \bar{Y})$
1	0.4	20	0.0016	36	−0.24
2	0.36	25	0.0000	1	0.00
3	0.42	16	0.0036	100	−0.60
4	0.31	30	0.0025	16	−0.20
5	0.33	35	0.0009	81	−0.27
6	0.34	30	0.0004	16	−0.08
Sum	2.16	156	0.0090	250	−1.39

A. The sample mean and standard deviation of the exchange rate are

$$\bar{X} = \sum_{i=1}^{n} X_i / n = 2.16/6 = 0.36$$

and

$$s_X = \sqrt{\sum_{i=1}^{n} (X_i - \bar{X})^2 / (n-1)} = \sqrt{0.009/5} = 0.042426$$

The sample mean and standard deviation of sales are

$$\bar{Y} = \sum_{i=1}^{n} Y_i / n = 156/6 = 26$$

and

$$s_Y = \sqrt{\sum_{i=1}^{n} (Y_i - \bar{Y})^2 / (n-1)} = \sqrt{250/5} = 7.0711$$

B. The sample covariance between the exchange rate and sales is

$$\text{Cov}(X, Y) = \sum_{i=1}^{n} (X_i - \bar{X})(Y_i - \bar{Y}) / (n-1) = -1.39/5 = -0.278$$

C. The sample correlation between the exchange rate and sales is

$$r = \frac{\text{Cov}(X, Y)}{s_x s_y} = \frac{-0.278}{(0.042426)(7.0711)} = -0.927$$

D. We want to estimate a regression equation of the form $Y_i = b_0 + b_1 X_i + \varepsilon_i$. Noting that division by $(n-1)$ in the numerator cancels with division by $(n-1)$ in the denominator in the expression for the slope coefficient, the estimates of the slope coefficient and the intercept are

$$\hat{b}_1 = \frac{\sum_{i=1}^{n}(Y_i - \bar{Y})(X_i - \bar{X})}{\sum_{i=1}^{n}(X_i - \bar{X})^2} = \frac{-1.39}{0.009} = -154.44$$

and

$$\hat{b}_0 = \bar{Y} - \hat{b}_1 \bar{X} = 26 - (-154.44)(0.36) = 26 + 55.6 = 81.6$$

So the regression equation is $Y_i = 81.6 - 154.44 X_i$.

9. A. The coefficient of determination is

$$\frac{\text{Explained variation}}{\text{Total variation}} = \frac{60.16}{140.58} = 0.4279$$

B. For a linear regression with one independent variable, the absolute value of correlation between the independent variable and the dependent variable equals the square root of the coefficient of determination, so the correlation is $\sqrt{0.4279} = 0.6542$. (The correlation will have the same sign as the slope coefficient.)

C. The standard error of the estimate is

$$\left(\sum_{i=1}^{n} \frac{(Y_i - \hat{b}_0 - \hat{b}_1 X_i)^2}{n-2} \right)^{1/2} = \left(\frac{\text{Unexplained variation}}{n-2} \right)^{1/2}$$

$$= \sqrt{\frac{80.42}{60-2}} = 1.178$$

D. The sample variance of the dependent variable is

$$\sum_{i=1}^{n} \frac{(Y_i - \overline{Y})^2}{n-1} = \frac{\text{Total variation}}{n-1} = \frac{140.58}{60-1} = 2.3827$$

The sample standard deviation is $\sqrt{2.3827} = 1.544$.

10. A. The degrees of freedom for the regression is the number of slope parameters in the regression, which is the same as the number of independent variables in the regression. Because regression df = 1, we conclude that there is one independent variable in the regression.

B. Total SS is the sum of the squared deviations of the dependent variable Y about its mean.

C. The sample variance of the dependent variable is the total SS divided by its degrees of freedom ($n - 1 = 5 - 1 = 4$ as given). Thus the sample variance of the dependent variable is $95.2/4 = 23.8$.

D. The Regression SS is the part of total sum of squares explained by the regression. Regression SS equals the sum of the squared differences between predicted values of the Y and the sample mean of Y: $\sum_{i=1}^{n} (\hat{Y}_i - \overline{Y})^2$. In terms of other values in the table, Regression SS is equal to Total SS minus Residual SS: $95.2 - 7.2 = 88$.

E. The F-statistic tests whether all the slope coefficients in a linear regression are equal to 0.

F. The calculated value of F in the table is equal to the Regression MSS divided by the Residual MSS: $88/2.4 = 36.667$.

G. Yes. The significance of 0.00904 given in the table is the p-value of the test (the smallest level at which we can reject the null hypothesis). This value of 0.00904 is less than the specified significance level of 0.05, so we reject the null hypothesis. The regression equation has significant explanatory power.

11. A. For the large-cap fund, the predicted rate of return, $\hat{Y}$, is

$$\hat{Y} = \hat{b}_0 + \hat{b}_1 X = -0.287 + 0.802(8.00) = 6.129$$

B. The estimated variance of the prediction error, s_f^2, of Y, given X, is

$$s_f^2 = s^2 \left[1 + \frac{1}{n} + \frac{(X - \overline{X})^2}{(n-1)s_x^2} \right]$$

$$= 4.243^2 \left[1 + \frac{1}{12} + \frac{(8.00 - 2.30)^2}{(12-1)(38.51)} \right] = 20.884$$

The standard deviation of the prediction error is the square root of this number: 4.57. For 10 degrees of freedom, the critical t-value is 2.228. A 95 percent prediction interval is $\hat{Y} \pm t_c s_f$, or $6.129 \pm 2.228(4.57)$, or 6.129 ± 10.182.

$$\text{Prob}(-4.053 < Y < 16.311) = 0.95$$

12. A. For a sentiment index of 90, predicted auto sales, $\hat{Y}$, are $\hat{Y} = \hat{b}_0 + \hat{b}_1 X = 6.071 + 0.09251(90) = 14.397$ (about 14.4 million vehicles). The estimated variance of the prediction error, s_f^2, of Y, given X, is

$$s_f^2 = s^2 \left[1 + \frac{1}{n} + \frac{(X - \overline{X})^2}{(n-1)s_x^2} \right]$$

$$= 0.81325^2 \left[1 + \frac{1}{120} + \frac{(90 - 91.0983)^2}{(120 - 1)(137.3068)} \right] = 0.66694$$

The standard deviation of the prediction error is the square root of this number: 0.8167. For 118 degrees of freedom and a 0.05 level of significance, the critical t-value is approximately 1.98. The 95 percent prediction interval for $X = 90$ is $\hat{Y} \pm t_c s_f$, or $14.397 \pm 1.98(0.8167)$, or 14.397 ± 1.617.

$$\text{Prob}(12.780 < Y < 16.014) = 0.95$$

B. For a sentiment index of 100, predicted auto sales, $\hat{Y}$, are

$$Y = \hat{b}_0 + \hat{b}_1 X = 6.071 + 0.09251(100) = 15.322$$

The estimated variance of the prediction error, s_f^2, of Y, given X, is

$$s_f^2 = s^2 \left[1 + \frac{1}{n} + \frac{(X - \overline{X})^2}{(n-1)s_x^2} \right]$$

$$= 0.81325^2 \left[1 + \frac{1}{120} + \frac{(100 - 91.0983)^2}{(120 - 1)(137.3068)} \right] = 0.67009$$

The standard deviation of the prediction error is the square root of this number: 0.81859. For 118 degrees of freedom, the critical t-value is approximately 1.98. A 95 percent prediction interval would be $\hat{Y} \pm t_c s_f$, or $15.322 \pm 1.98(0.81859)$, or 15.322 ± 1.621.

$$\text{Prob}(13.701 < Y < 16.943) = 0.95$$

13. A. The sample size is $n = 9$.

For X, the sample mean is $\overline{X} = \sum_{i=1}^{n} X_i / n = 81/9 = 9$, the sample variance is $s_X^2 = \sum_{i=1}^{n} (X_i - \overline{X})^2 / (n - 1) = 60/8 = 7.5$, and the sample standard deviation is $s_X = \sqrt{7.5} = 2.7386$.

For Y, the sample mean is $\overline{Y} = \sum_{i=1}^{n} Y_i / n = 144/9 = 16$, the sample variance is $s_Y^2 = \sum_{i=1}^{n} (Y_i - \overline{Y})^2 / (n - 1) = 144/8 = 18$, and the sample standard deviation is $s_Y = \sqrt{18} = 4.2426$.

B. The sample covariance is

$$\text{Cov}(X, Y) = \sum_{i=1}^{n} (X_i - \overline{X})(Y_i - \overline{Y}) / (n - 1) = 84/8 = 10.5$$

The sample correlation between X and Y is

$$r = \frac{\text{Cov}(X, Y)}{s_x s_y}$$

$$= \frac{10.5}{(2.7386)(4.2426)} = 0.9037$$

C. The coefficients for the regression equation are

$$\hat{b}_1 = \frac{\sum_{i=1}^{n}(Y_i - \overline{Y})(X_i - \overline{X})}{\sum_{i=1}^{n}(X_i - \overline{X})^2} = \frac{84}{60} = 1.4, \text{ and}$$

$$\hat{b}_0 = \overline{Y} - \hat{b}_1\overline{X} = 16 - 1.4(9) = 3.4$$

So the regression equation is $\hat{Y}_i = 3.4 + 1.4X_i$.

D. The total variation is $\sum_{i=1}^{n}(Y_i - \overline{Y})^2 = 144$, and the unexplained variation is

$$\sum_{i=1}^{n}(Y_i - \hat{b}_0 - \hat{b}_1X_i)^2 = 26.4. \text{ So the explained variation is } 144 - 26.4 = 117.6.$$

E. The coefficient of variation, the R-squared, is

$$\frac{\text{Explained variation}}{\text{Total variation}} = \frac{117.6}{144} = 0.81667$$

F. The standard error of the estimate is

$$\text{SEE} = \left[\sum_{i=1}^{n}\frac{(Y_i - \hat{b}_0 - \hat{b}_1X_i)^2}{n-2}\right]^{1/2}$$

$$= \left(\frac{26.4}{9-2}\right)^{1/2} = 1.942$$

14. The R-squared (**X1**) is Explained variation/Total variation = 14.246/60.139 = 0.2369. The Multiple R (**X2**) is the correlation between the two variables, which is the square root of the R-squared, or $\sqrt{0.2369} = 0.4867$. The standard error (**X3**) is the square root of unexplained variation divided by $(n-2)$, which is $\sqrt{45.893/(1819-2)} = 0.1589$.

The Total df, **X4**, is the sample size minus 1, or $n-1 = 1{,}819 - 1 = 1{,}818$. The Regression df (**X5**) is equal to the number of independent variables, which is 1. The Residual df (**X6**) is the difference between the Total df and Regression df, which is also $n - (k+1)$ where n is the sample size (1,819) and k is the number of independent variables (1). X6 is $1{,}819 - (1+1) = 1{,}817$. MSS is the "mean square," which is the sum of squares divided by the degrees of freedom. For **X7**, the MSS regression is $14.246/1 = 14.246$. For **X8**, the MSS residual is $45.893/1{,}817 = 0.025258$. The F (**X9**) is testing the hypothesis that the regression coefficient equals zero, and it is equal to MSS regression/MSS residual, or $14.246/0.025258 = 564.02$. This F has 1 df in the numerator and 1817 df in the denominator. This value for F is extremely large, and the probability of an F this large is practically zero.

X10, the calculated t-value for the slope coefficient, is the coefficient divided by its standard error: $t = -0.04375/0.00184 = -23.75$. This is an extremely large negative t, with a probability of practically zero. (Notice that the square root of the F is equal to the t for a regression with one independent variable.) Finally, **X11** and **X12** are the upper and lower bounds for a 95 percent confidence interval for the slope coefficient. The critical t for a two-tailed test at the 5 percent significance level with 1,817 degrees of freedom is approximately 1.96. The lower bound, **X11**, is $\hat{b}_1 - t_c s_{\hat{b}_1} = -0.04375 - 1.96(0.001842) = -0.04736$. The upper bound, **X12**, is $\hat{b}_1 + t_c s_{\hat{b}_1} = -0.04375 + 1.96(0.001842) = -0.04014$.

15. The Month 2 data point is an outlier, lying far away from the other data values. Because this outlier was caused by a data entry error, correcting the outlier improves the validity and reliability of the regression. In this case, the true correlation is reduced from 0.996 to 0.824. The revised R-squared is substantially lower (0.678 versus 0.992). The significance of the regression is also lower, as can be seen in the decline of the F-value from 500.79 to 8.44 and the decline in the t-statistic of the slope coefficient from 22.379 to 2.905.

    The total sum of squares and regression sum of squares were greatly exaggerated in the incorrect analysis. With the correction, the slope coefficient changes from 1.069 to 0.623. This change is important. When the index moves up or down, the original model indicates that the portfolio return goes up or down by 1.069 times as much, while the revised model indicates that the portfolio return goes up or down by only 0.623 times as much. In this example, incorrect data entry caused the outlier. Had it been a valid observation, not caused by a data error, then the analyst would have had to decide whether the results were more reliable including or excluding the outlier.

16. **A.** If FEE = 0%, RETURN = $-3.021 + 7.062(0) = -3.021\%$.

    If FEE = 1%, RETURN = $-3.021 + 7.062(1) = 4.041\%$.

    B. The calculated t-value for the coefficient of FEE is 14.95. The critical t-value for 58 degrees of freedom, a two-tailed test, and a 5 percent significance level is 2.00. Because the calculated t exceeds the critical t, we may conclude that the coefficient of FEE is not equal to zero and that the relationship between RETURN and FEE is significant.

    C. Smith's analysis is inadequate to conclude that high fees are good. Clearly, high returns cause high fees (because of the compensation contract that Diet Partners has with its clients). The regression may be recognizing this relationship. Unfortunately, the reverse may not be true—that fees cause returns. As an analogy, assume that income taxes are a function of income. A regression of income as a function of income taxes would find a strong positive relationship. Does this mean that taxes cause income, or the reverse? Smith's experiment is too simplistic to address the issue of whether a particular compensation contract is good or bad for client returns.

17. B is correct. The coefficient of determination is the same as R-squared.

18. C is correct. Deleting observations with small residuals will degrade the strength of the regression, resulting in an *increase* in the standard error and a *decrease* in R-squared.

19. C is correct. For a regression with one independent variable, the correlation is the same as the Multiple R with the sign of the slope coefficient. Because the slope coefficient is positive, the correlation is 0.8623.

20. B is correct. This answer describes the calculation of the F-statistic.

21. C is correct. To make a prediction using the regression model, multiply the slope coefficient by the forecast of the independent variable and add the result to the intercept.

22. C is correct. The p-value reflects the strength of the relationship between the two variables. In this case the p-value is less than 0.05, and thus the regression of the ratio of cash flow from operations to sales on the ratio of net income to sales is significant at the 5 percent level.

23. B is correct because the calculated test statistic is

$$t = \frac{r\sqrt{n-2}}{\sqrt{1-r^2}}$$

$$= \frac{-0.1452\sqrt{248-2}}{\sqrt{1-(-0.1452)^2}} = -2.3017$$

Because the absolute value of $t = -2.3017$ is greater than 1.96, the correlation coefficient is statistically significant. For a regression with one independent variable, the t-value (and significance) for the slope coefficient (which is -2.3014) should equal the t-value (and significance) of the correlation coefficient. The slight difference between these two t-values is caused by rounding error.

24. A is correct because the data are time series, and the expected value of the error term, $E(\varepsilon)$, is 0.

25. C is correct. From the regression equation, Expected return = 0.0138 + $-0.6486(-0.01)$ = 0.0138 + 0.006486 = 0.0203, or 2.03 percent.

26. C is correct. R-squared is the coefficient of determination. In this case, it shows that 2.11 percent of the variability in Stellar's returns is explained by changes in CPIENG.

27. A is correct, because the standard error of the estimate is the standard deviation of the regression residuals.

28. C is the correct response, because it is a false statement. The slope and intercept are both statistically significant.

MULTIPLE REGRESSION AND ISSUES IN REGRESSION ANALYSIS

by Richard A. DeFusco, CFA, Dennis W. McLeavey, CFA, Jerald E. Pinto, CFA, and David E. Runkle, CFA

LEARNING OUTCOMES

The candidate should be able to:	Mastery
a. formulate a multiple regression equation to describe the relation between a dependent variable and several independent variables, determine the statistical significance of each independent variable, and interpret the estimated coefficients and their p-values;	☐
b. formulate a null and an alternative hypothesis about the population value of a regression coefficient, calculate the value of the test statistic, determine whether to reject the null hypothesis at a given level of significance by using a one-tailed or two-tailed test, and interpret the results of the test;	☐
c. calculate and interpret 1) a confidence interval for the population value of a regression coefficient and 2) a predicted value for the dependent variable, given an estimated regression model and assumed values for the independent variables;	☐
d. explain the assumptions of a multiple regression model;	☐
e. calculate and interpret the F-statistic, and discuss how it is used in regression analysis;	☐
f. distinguish between and interpret the R^2 and adjusted R^2 in multiple regression;	☐
g. infer how well a regression model explains the dependent variable by analyzing the output of the regression equation and an ANOVA table;	☐
h. formulate a multiple regression equation by using dummy variables to represent qualitative factors, and interpret the coefficients and regression results;	☐
i. discuss the types of heteroskedasticity and the effects of heteroskedasticity and serial correlation on statistical inference;	☐
j. describe multicollinearity, and discuss its causes and effects in regression analysis;	☐
k. discuss the effects of model misspecification on the results of a regression analysis, and explain how to avoid the common forms of misspecification;	☐

351

l.	discuss models with qualitative dependent variables;	☐
m.	interpret the economic meaning of the results of multiple regression analysis and critique a regression model and its results.	☐

1　INTRODUCTION

As financial analysts, we often need to use more-sophisticated statistical methods than correlation analysis or regression involving a single independent variable. For example, a trading desk interested in the costs of trading NASDAQ stocks might want information on the determinants of the bid–ask spread on the NASDAQ. A mutual fund analyst might want to know whether returns to a technology mutual fund behaved more like the returns to a growth stock index or like the returns to a value stock index. An investor might be interested in the factors that determine whether analysts cover a stock. We can answer these questions using linear regression with more than one independent variable—multiple linear regression.

In Sections 2 and 3, we introduce and illustrate the basic concepts and models of multiple regression analysis. These models rest on assumptions that are sometimes violated in practice. In Section 4, we discuss three major violations of a regression assumption. We address practical concerns such as how to diagnose an assumption violation and what remedial steps to take when a model assumption has been violated. Section 5 outlines some guidelines for building good regression models and discusses ways that analysts sometimes go wrong in this endeavor. In a number of investment applications, we are interested in the probability that one of two outcomes occurs: For example, we may be interested in whether a stock has analyst coverage or not. Section 6 discusses a class of models, qualitative dependent variable models, that addresses such questions.

2　MULTIPLE LINEAR REGRESSION

As investment analysts, we often hypothesize that more than one variable explains the behavior of a variable in which we are interested. The variable we seek to explain is called the dependent variable. The variables that we believe explain the dependent variable are called the independent variables.[1] A tool that permits us to examine the relationship (if any) between the two types of variables is multiple linear regression. **Multiple linear regression** allows us to determine the effect of more than one independent variable on a particular dependent variable.

To give an example of how we might use this tool, suppose we want to know whether the bid–ask spread for stocks trading in a dealer market is affected by the number of market makers (dealers) for that stock and the market capitalization of the stock. We can address this question using the following **multiple linear regression model:**

$$Y_i = b_0 + b_1 X_{1i} + b_2 X_{2i} + \epsilon_i$$

[1] Independent variables are also called explanatory variables or regressors.

where

Y_i = the natural logarithm of the bid–ask spread for stock i (the dependent variable)

X_{1i} = the natural logarithm of the number of market makers for stock i

X_{2i} = the natural logarithm of the market capitalization of company i

ϵ_i = the error term

Of course, linear regression models can use more than two independent variables to explain the dependent variable. A **multiple linear regression model** has the general form

$$Y_i = b_0 + b_1 X_{1i} + b_2 X_{2i} + \ldots + b_k X_{ki} + \epsilon_i, \, i = 1, 2, \ldots, n \qquad \textbf{(1)}$$

where

Y_i = the ith observation of the dependent variable Y

X_{ji} = the ith observation of the independent variable X_j, $j = 1, 2, \ldots, k$

b_0 = the intercept of the equation

$b_1, \ldots, b_k$ = the slope coefficients for each of the independent variables

ϵ_i = the error term

n = the number of observations

A slope coefficient, b_j, measures how much the dependent variable, Y, changes when the independent variable, X_j, changes by one unit, holding all other independent variables constant. For example, if $b_1 = 1$ and all of the other independent variables remain constant, then we predict that if X_1 increases by one unit, Y will also increase by one unit. If $b_1 = -1$ and all of the other independent variables are held constant, then we predict that if X_1 increases by one unit, Y will decrease by one unit. Multiple linear regression estimates $b_0, \ldots, b_k$. In this reading, we will refer to both the intercept, b_0, and the slope coefficients, $b_1, \ldots, b_k$, as **regression coefficients**. As we proceed with our discussion, keep in mind that a regression equation has k slope coefficients and $k + 1$ regression coefficients.

In practice, we use software to estimate a multiple regression model. Example 1 presents an application of multiple regression analysis in investment practice. In the course of discussing a hypothesis test, Example 1 presents typical regression output and its interpretation.

EXAMPLE 1

Explaining the Bid–Ask Spread

As the manager of the trading desk at an investment management firm, you have noticed that the average bid–ask spreads of different NASDAQ-listed stocks can vary widely. When the ratio of a stock's bid–ask spread to its price is higher than for another stock, your firm's costs of trading in that stock tend to be higher. You have formulated the hypothesis that NASDAQ stocks' percentage bid–ask spreads are related to the number of market makers and the company's stock market capitalization. You have decided to investigate your hypothesis using multiple regression analysis.

You specify a regression model in which the dependent variable measures the percentage bid–ask spread and the independent variables measure the number of market makers and the company's stock market capitalization. The regression is estimated using data from December 2002 for 1,819 NASDAQ-listed stocks. Based on earlier published research exploring bid–ask spreads, you express the dependent and independent variables as natural logarithms, a so-called **log-log regression model**. A log-log regression model may be appropriate when one believes that proportional changes in the dependent variable bear a constant relationship to proportional changes in the independent variable(s), as we illustrate below. You formulate the multiple regression:

$$Y_i = b_0 + b_1 X_{1i} + b_2 X_{2i} + \epsilon_i \tag{2}$$

where

Y_i = the natural logarithm of (bid–ask spread/stock price) for stock i
X_{1i} = the natural logarithm of the number of NASDAQ market makers for stock i
X_{2i} = the natural logarithm of the market capitalization (measured in millions of dollars) of company i

In a log-log regression such as Equation 2, the slope coefficients are interpreted as elasticities, assumed to be constant. For example, $b_2 = -0.75$ means that for a 1 percent increase in the market capitalization, we expect bid–ask spread/stock price to decrease by 0.75 percent, holding all other independent variables constant.[2]

Reasoning that greater competition tends to lower costs, you suspect that the greater the number of market makers, the smaller the percentage bid–ask spread. Therefore, you formulate a first null hypothesis and alternative hypothesis:

$H_0: b_1 \geq 0$
$H_a: b_1 < 0$

The null hypothesis is the hypothesis that the "suspected" condition is not true. If the evidence supports rejecting the null hypothesis and accepting the alternative hypothesis, you have statistically confirmed your suspicion.[3]

You also believe that the stocks of companies with higher market capitalization may have more-liquid markets, tending to lower percentage bid–ask spreads. Therefore, you formulate a second null hypothesis and alternative hypothesis:

$H_0: b_2 \geq 0$
$H_a: b_2 < 0$

[2] Note that $\Delta(\ln X) \approx \Delta X/X$, where Δ represents "change in" and $\Delta X/X$ is a proportional change in X. We discuss the model further in Example 11.

[3] An alternative valid formulation is a two-sided test ($H_0: b_1 = 0$ versus $H_a: b_1 \neq 0$) which reflects the beliefs of the researcher less strongly. A two-sided test could also be conducted for the hypothesis on market capitalization that we discuss next.

TABLE 1 Results from Regressing ln(Bid–Ask Spread/Price) on ln(Number of Market Makers) and ln(Market Cap)

	Coefficient	Standard Error	t-Statistic
Intercept	−0.7586	0.1369	−5.5416
ln(Number of NASDAQ market makers)	−0.2790	0.0673	−4.1427
ln(Company's market cap)	−0.6635	0.0246	−27.0087

ANOVA	df	SS	MSS	F	Significance F
Regression	2	2,681.6482	1,340.8241	1,088.8325	0.00
Residual	1,816	2,236.2820	1.2314		
Total	1,818	4,917.9302			

Residual standard error	1.1097
Multiple R-squared	0.5453
Observations	1,819

Source: FactSet, NASDAQ.

For both tests, we use a t-test, rather than a z-test, because we do not know the population variance of b_1 and b_2. Suppose that you choose a 0.01 significance level for both tests. Table 1 shows the results of estimating this linear regression using data from December 2002.

If the regression result is not significant, we follow the useful principle of not proceeding to interpret the individual regression coefficients. Thus the analyst might look first at the ANOVA section, which addresses the regression's overall significance.

► The ANOVA (analysis of variance) section reports quantities related to the overall explanatory power and significance of the regression. SS stands for sum of squares, and MSS stands for mean sum of squares (SS divided by df). The F-test reports the overall significance of the regression. For example, an entry of 0.01 for the significance of F means that the regression is significant at the 0.01 level. In Table 1, the regression is even more significant because the significance of F is 0 at two decimal places. Later in the reading, we will present more information on the F-test.

Having ascertained that the overall regression is highly significant, an analyst might turn to the first listed column in the first section of the regression output.

▶ The Coefficients column gives the estimates of the intercept, b_0, and the slope coefficients, b_1 and b_2. These estimates are all negative, but are they significantly negative? The Standard Error column gives the standard error (the standard deviation) of the estimated regression coefficients. The test statistic for hypotheses concerning the population value of a regression coefficient has the form (Estimated regression coefficient − Hypothesized population value of the regression coefficient)/(Standard error of the regression coefficient). This is a *t*-test. Under the null hypothesis, the hypothesized population value of the regression coefficient is 0. Thus (Estimated regression coefficient)/(Standard error of the regression coefficient) is the *t*-statistic given in the third column. For example, the *t*-statistic for the intercept is $-0.7586/0.1369 = -5.5416$, ignoring the effects of rounding errors. To evaluate the significance of the *t*-statistic we need to determine a quantity called degrees of freedom (df).[4] The calculation is Degrees of freedom = Number of observations − (Number of independent variables + 1) = $n - (k + 1)$.

▶ The final section of Table 1 presents two measures of how well the estimated regression fits or explains the data. The first is the standard deviation of the regression residual, the residual standard error. This standard deviation is called the standard error of estimate (SEE). The second measure quantifies the degree of linear association between the dependent variable and all of the independent variables jointly. This measure is known as multiple R^2 or simply R^2 (the square of the correlation between predicted and actual values of the dependent variable).[5] A value of 0 for R^2 indicates no linear association; a value of 1 indicates perfect linear association. The final item in Table 1 is the number of observations in the sample (1,819).

Having reviewed the meaning of typical regression output, we can return to complete the hypothesis tests.

The estimated regression supports the hypothesis that the greater the number of market makers, the smaller the percentage bid–ask spread: We reject H_0: $b_1 \geq 0$ in favor of H_a: $b_1 < 0$. The results also support the belief that the stocks of companies with higher market capitalization have lower percentage bid–ask spreads: We reject H_0: $b_2 \geq 0$ in favor of H_a: $b_2 < 0$. To see that the null hypothesis is rejected for both tests, we can use *t*-test tables. For both tests, df = $1,819 - 3 = 1,816$. The tables do not give critical values for degrees of freedom that large. The critical value for a one-tailed test with df = 200 at the 0.01 significance level is 2.345; for a larger number of degrees of freedom, the critical value would be even smaller in magnitude. Therefore, in our one-sided tests, we reject the null hypothesis in favor of the alternative hypothesis if

$$t = \frac{\hat{b}_j - b_j}{s_{\hat{b}_j}} = \frac{\hat{b}_j - 0}{s_{\hat{b}_j}} < -2.345$$

---

[4] To calculate the degrees of freedom lost in the regression, we add 1 to the number of independent variables to account for the intercept term.

[5] Multiple R^2 is also known as the multiple coefficient of determination, or simply the coefficient of determination.

where

$\hat{b}_j$ = the regression estimate of b_j, $j = 1, 2$
b_j = the hypothesized value[6] of the coefficient (0)
$s_{\hat{b}_j}$ = the estimated standard error of $\hat{b}_j$

The t-values of -4.1427 and -27.0087 for the estimates of b_1 and b_2, respectively, are both less than -2.345.

Before proceeding further, we should address the interpretation of a prediction stated in natural logarithm terms. We can convert a natural logarithm to the original units by taking the antilogarithm. To illustrate this conversion, suppose that a particular stock has five NASDAQ market makers and a market capitalization of $100 million. The natural logarithm of the number of NASDAQ market makers is equal to ln 5 = 1.6094, and the natural logarithm of the company's market cap (in millions) is equal to ln 100 = 4.6052. With these values, the regression model predicts that the natural log of the ratio of the bid–ask spread to the stock price will be $-0.7586 + (-0.2790 \times 1.6094) + (-0.6635 \times 4.6052) = -4.2632$. We take the antilogarithm of -4.2632 by raising e to that power: $e^{-4.2632} = 0.0141$. The predicted bid–ask spread will be 1.41 percent of the stock price.[7] Later we state the assumptions of the multiple regression model; before using an estimated regression to make predictions in actual practice, we should assure ourselves that those assumptions are satisfied.

In Table 1, we presented output common to most regression software programs. Many software programs also report p-values for the regression coefficients.[8] For each regression coefficient, the p-value would be the smallest level of significance at which we can reject a null hypothesis that the population value of the coefficient is 0, in a two-sided test. The lower the p-value, the stronger the evidence against that null hypothesis. A p-value quickly allows us to determine if an independent variable is significant at a conventional significance level such as 0.05, or at any other standard we believe is appropriate.

Having estimated Equation 1, we can write

$$\hat{Y}_i = \hat{b}_0 + \hat{b}_1 X_{1i} + \hat{b}_2 X_{2i}$$
$$= -0.7586 - 0.2790 X_{1i} - 0.6635 X_{2i}$$

where $\hat{Y}_i$ stands for the predicted value of Y_i, and $\hat{b}_0$, $\hat{b}_1$, and $\hat{b}_2$, stand for the estimated values of b_0, b_1, and b_2, respectively. How should we interpret the estimated slope coefficients -0.2790 and -0.6635?

Interpreting the slope coefficients in a multiple linear regression model is different than doing so in the one-independent-variable regressions explored in the reading on correlation and regression. Suppose we have a one-independent-variable regression that we estimate as $\hat{Y}_i = 0.50 + 0.75 X_{1i}$. The interpretation of the slope estimate 0.75 is that for every 1 unit increase in X_1, we expect Y to increase

[6] To economize on notation in stating test statistics, in this context we use b_j to represent the hypothesized value of the parameter (elsewhere we use it to represent the unknown population parameter).

[7] The operation illustrated (taking the antilogarithm) recovers the value of a variable in the original units as $e^{\ln X} = X$.

[8] The entry 0.00 for the significance of F was a p-value for the F-test.

by 0.75 units. If we were to add a second independent variable to the equation, we would generally find that the estimated coefficient on X_1 is *not* 0.75 unless the second independent variable were uncorrelated with X_1. The slope coefficients in a multiple regression are known as **partial regression coefficients** or **partial slope coefficients** and need to be interpreted with care.[9] Suppose the coefficient on X_1 in a regression with the second independent variable was 0.60. Can we say that for every 1-unit increase in X_1, we expect Y to increase by 0.60 units? Not without qualification. For every 1-unit increase in X_1, we still expect Y to increase by 0.75 units when X_2 is not held constant. We would interpret 0.60 as the expected increase in Y for a 1-unit increase X_1 *holding the second independent variable constant.*

To explain what the shorthand reference "holding the second independent constant" refers to, if we were to regress X_1 on X_2, the residuals from that regression would represent the part of X_1 that is uncorrelated with X_2. We could then regress Y on those residuals in a 1-independent-variable regression. We would find that the slope coefficient on the residuals would be 0.60; by construction, 0.60 would represent the expected effect on Y of a 1-unit increase in X_1 after removing the part of X_1 that is correlated with X_2. Consistent with this explanation, we can view 0.60 as the expected net effect on Y of a 1-unit increase in X_1, after accounting for any effects of the other independent variables on the expected value of Y. To reiterate, a partial regression coefficient measures the expected change in the dependent variable for a one-unit increase in an independent variable, holding all the other independent variables constant.

To apply this process to the regression in Table 1, we see that the estimated coefficient on the natural logarithm of market capitalization is −0.6635. Therefore, the model predicts that an increase of 1 in the natural logarithm of the company's market capitalization is associated with a −0.6635 change in the natural logarithm of the ratio of the bid–ask spread to the stock price, holding the natural logarithm of the number of market makers constant. We need to be careful not to expect that the natural logarithm of the ratio of the bid–ask spread to the stock price would differ by −0.6635 if we compared two stocks for which the natural logarithm of the company's market capitalization differed by 1, because in all likelihood the number of market makers for the two stocks would differ as well, which would affect the dependent variable. The value −0.6635 is the expected net effect of difference in log market capitalizations, net of the effect of the log number of market makers on the expected value of the dependent variable.

2.1 Assumptions of the Multiple Linear Regression Model

Before we can conduct correct statistical inference on a multiple linear regression model (a model with more than one independent variable estimated using ordinary least squares), we need to know the assumptions underlying that model.[10] Suppose we have n observations on the dependent variable, Y, and the independent variables, $X_1, X_2, \ldots, X_k$, and we want to estimate the equation $Y_i = b_0 + b_1 X_{1i} + b_2 X_{2i} + \ldots + b_k X_{ki} + \epsilon_i$.

In order to make a valid inference from a multiple linear regression model, we need to make the following six assumptions, which as a group define the classical normal multiple linear regression model:

---

[9] The terminology comes from the fact that they correspond to the partial derivatives of Y with respect to the independent variables. Note that in this usage, the term "regression coefficients" refers just to the slope coefficients.

[10] Ordinary least squares (OLS) is an estimation method based on the criterion of minimizing the sum of the squared residuals of a regression.

1. The relationship between the dependent variable, Y, and the independent variables, $X_1, X_2, \ldots, X_k$, is linear as described in Equation 1.

2. The independent variables $(X_1, X_2, \ldots, X_k)$ are not random.[11] Also, no exact linear relation exists between two or more of the independent variables.[12]

3. The expected value of the error term, conditioned on the independent variables, is 0: $E(\epsilon | X_1, X_2, \ldots, X_k) = 0$.

4. The variance of the error term is the same for all observations:[13] $E(\epsilon_i^2) = \sigma_\epsilon^2$.

5. The error term is uncorrelated across observations: $E(\epsilon_i \epsilon_j) = 0, j \neq i$.

6. The error term is normally distributed.

Note that these assumptions are almost exactly the same as those for the single-variable linear regression model. Assumption 2 is modified such that no exact linear relation exists between two or more independent variables or combinations of independent variables. If this part of Assumption 2 is violated, then we cannot compute linear regression estimates.[14] Also, even if no exact linear relationship exists between two or more independent variables, or combinations of independent variables, linear regression may encounter problems if two or more of the independent variables or combinations thereof are highly correlated. Such a high correlation is known as multicollinearity, which we will discuss later in this reading. We will also discuss the consequences of supposing that Assumptions 4 and 5 are met if, in fact, they are violated.

Although Equation 1 may seem to apply only to cross-sectional data because the notation for the observations is the same ($i = 1, \ldots, n$), all of these results apply to time-series data as well. For example, if we analyze data from many time periods for one company, we would typically use the notation $Y_t, X_{1t}, X_{2t}, \ldots, X_{kt}$, in which the first subscript denotes the variable and the second denotes the tth time period.

EXAMPLE 2

Factors Explaining Pension Fund Performance

Ambachtsheer, Capelle, and Scheibelhut (1998) tested to see which factors affect the performance of pension funds. Specifically, they wanted to know whether the risk-adjusted net value added (RANVA) of 80 U.S. and Canadian pension funds depended on the size of the individual fund and the proportion of the fund's assets that were passively managed (indexed). Using data from 80 funds for four years (1993 to 1996),

---

[11] As discussed in the reading on correlation and regression, even though we assume that independent variables in the regression model are not random, often that assumption is clearly not true. For example, the monthly returns to the S&P 500 are not random. If the independent variable is random, then is the regression model incorrect? Fortunately, no. Even if the independent variable is random but uncorrelated with the error term, we can still rely on the results of regression models. See, for example, Greene (2003) or Goldberger (1998).

[12] No independent variable can be expressed as a linear combination of any set of the other independent variables. Technically, a constant equal to 1 is included as an independent variable associated with the intercept in this condition.

[13] $\text{Var}(\epsilon) = E(\epsilon^2)$ and $\text{Cov}(\epsilon_i \epsilon_j) = E(\epsilon_i \epsilon_j)$ because $E(\epsilon) = 0$.

[14] When we encounter this kind of linear relationship (called perfect collinearity), we cannot compute the matrix inverse needed to compute the linear regression estimates. See Greene (2003) for a further description of this issue.

the authors regressed RANVA on the size of the pension fund and the fraction of pension fund assets that were passively managed.[15] They used the equation

$$\text{RANVA}_i = b_0 + b_1\text{Size}_i + b_2\text{Passive}_i + \epsilon_i$$

where

RANVA_i = the average RANVA (in percent) for fund i from 1993 to 1996

Size_i = the $\log_{10}$ of average assets under management for fund i

Passive_i = the fraction (decimal) of passively managed assets in fund i

Table 2 shows the results of their analysis.[16]

TABLE 2   Results from Regressing RANVA on Size and Passive Management

	Coefficients	Standard Error	t-Statistic
Intercept	−2.1	0.45	−4.7
Size	0.4	0.14	2.8
Passive management	0.8	0.42	1.9

Source: Ambachtsheer, Capelle, and Scheibelhut (1998).

Suppose we use the results in Table 2 to test the null hypothesis that a pension fund's size had no effect on its RANVA. Our null hypothesis is that the coefficient on the size variable equals 0 (H_0: $b_1 = 0$), and our alternative hypothesis is that the coefficient does not equal 0 (H_a: $b_1 \neq 0$). The t-statistic for testing that hypothesis is

$$\frac{\hat{b}_1 - b_1}{s_{\hat{b}_1}} = \frac{0.4 - 0}{0.14} = 2.8$$

With 80 observations and three coefficients, the t-statistic has $80 - 3 = 77$ degrees of freedom. At the 0.05 significance level, the critical value for t is about 1.99. The computed t-statistic on the size coefficient is 2.8,

[15] As mentioned in an earlier footnote, technically a constant equal to 1 is included as an independent variable associated with the intercept term in a regression. Because all the regressions reported in this reading include an intercept term, we will not separately mention a constant as an independent variable in the remainder of this reading.

[16] Size is the log base 10 of average assets. A log transformation is commonly used for independent variables that can take a wide range of values; company size and fund size are two such variables. One reason to use the log transformation is to improve the statistical properties of the residuals. If the authors had not taken the log of assets and instead used assets as the independent variable, the regression model probably would not have explained RANVA as well.

which suggests strongly that we can reject the null hypothesis that size is unrelated to RANVA. The estimated coefficient of 0.4 implies that every 10-fold increase in fund size (an increase of 1 in $Size_i$) is associated with an expected 0.4 percentage point increase (40 basis points) in $RANVA_i$, *holding constant the fraction of passively managed assets*. Because $Size_i$ is the base 10 log of average assets, an increase of 1 in Size is the same as a 10-fold increase in fund assets.

Of course, no causal relation between size and RANVA is clear: Funds that are more successful may attract more assets. This regression equation is consistent with that result, as well as the result that larger funds perform better. On one hand, we could argue that larger funds are more successful. On the other hand, we could argue that more successful funds attract more assets and become larger.

Now suppose we want to test the null hypothesis that passive management is not related to RANVA; we want to test whether the coefficient on the fraction of assets under passive management equals 0 (H_0: $b_2 = 0$) against the alternative hypothesis that the coefficient on the fraction of assets under passive management does not equal 0 (H_a: $b_2 \neq 0$). The t-statistic to test this hypothesis is

$$\frac{\hat{b}_2 - b_2}{s_{\hat{b}_2}} = \frac{0.8 - 0}{0.42} = 1.9$$

The critical value of the t-test is 1.99 at the 0.05 significance level and about 1.66 at the 0.10 level. Therefore, at the 0.10 significance level, we can reject the null hypothesis that passive management has no effect on fund returns; however, we cannot do so at the 0.05 significance level. Although researchers typically use a significance level of 0.05 or smaller, these results and others like them are strong enough that many pension plan sponsors have increased the use of passive management for pension fund assets. We can interpret the coefficient on passive management of 0.8 as implying that an increase of 0.10 in the proportion of a fund's passively managed assets is associated with an expected 0.08 percentage point increase (8 basis points) in RANVA for the fund, holding Size constant.

EXAMPLE 3

Explaining Returns to the Fidelity Select Technology Fund

Suppose you are considering an investment in the Fidelity Select Technology Fund (FSPTX), a U.S. mutual fund specializing in technology stocks. You want to know whether the fund behaves more like a large-cap growth fund or a large-cap value fund.[17] You decide to estimate the regression

$$Y_t = b_0 + b_1 X_{1t} + b_2 X_{2t} + \epsilon_t$$

---

[17] This regression is related to return-based style analysis, one of the most frequent applications of regression analysis in the investment profession. For more information, see Sharpe (1988), who pioneered this field, and Buetow, Johnson, and Runkle (2000).

where

Y_t = the monthly return to the FSPTX
X_{1t} = the monthly return to the S&P 500/BARRA Growth Index
X_{2t} = the monthly return to the S&P 500/BARRA Value Index

The S&P 500/BARRA Growth and Value indexes represent predominantly large-cap growth and value stocks, respectively.

Table 3 shows the results of this linear regression using monthly data from January 1998 through December 2002. The estimated intercept in the regression is 0.0079. Thus, if both the return to the S&P 500/BARRA Growth Index and the return to the S&P 500/BARRA Value Index equal 0 in a specific month, the regression model predicts that the return to the FSPTX will be 0.79 percent. The coefficient on the large-cap growth index is 2.2308, and the coefficient on the large-cap value index return is −0.4143. Therefore, if in a given month the return to the S&P 500/BARRA Growth Index was 1 percent and the return to the S&P 500/BARRA Value Index was −2 percent, the model predicts that the return to the FSPTX would be 0.0079 + 2.2308(0.01) −0.4143(−0.02) = 3.85 percent.

TABLE 3   Results from Regressing the FSPTX Returns on the S&P 500/BARRA Growth and Value Indexes

	Coefficient	Standard Error	t-Statistic
Intercept	0.0079	0.0091	0.8635
S&P 500/BARRA Growth Index	2.2308	0.2299	9.7034
S&P 500/BARRA Value Index	−0.4143	0.2597	−1.5953

ANOVA	df	SS	MSS	F	Significance F
Regression	2	0.8649	0.4324	86.4483	5.48E-18
Residual	57	0.2851	0.0050		
Total	59	1.1500			

Residual standard error	0.0707
Multiple R-squared	0.7521
Observations	60

Source: Ibbotson Associates.

We may want to know whether the coefficient on the returns to the S&P 500/BARRA Value Index is statistically significant. Our null hypothesis states that the coefficient equals 0 ($H_0: b_2 = 0$); our alternative hypothesis states that the coefficient does not equal 0 ($H_a: b_2 \neq 0$).

Our test of the null hypothesis uses a *t*-test constructed as follows:

$$t = \frac{\hat{b}_2 - b_2}{s_{\hat{b}_2}} = \frac{-0.4143 - 0}{0.2597} = -1.5953$$

where

$\hat{b}_2$ = the regression estimate of b_2

b_2 = the hypothesized value[18] of the coefficient (0)

$s_{\hat{b}_2}$ = the estimated standard error of $\hat{b}_2$

This regression has 60 observations and three coefficients (two independent variables and the intercept); therefore, the *t*-test has $60 - 3 = 57$ degrees of freedom. At the 0.05 significance level, the critical value for the test statistic is about 2.00. The absolute value of the test statistic is 1.5953. Because the test statistic's absolute value is less than the critical value ($1.5953 < 2.00$), we fail to reject the null hypothesis that $b_2 = 0$. (Note that the *t*-tests reported in Table 3, as well as the other regression tables, are tests of the null hypothesis that the population value of a regression coefficient equals 0.)

Similar analysis shows that at the 0.05 significance level, we cannot reject the null hypothesis that the intercept equals 0 (H_0: $b_0 = 0$) in favor of the alternative hypothesis that the intercept does not equal 0 (H_a: $b_0 \neq 0$). Table 3 shows that the *t*-statistic for testing that hypothesis is 0.8635, a result smaller in absolute value than the critical value of 2.00. However, at the 0.05 significance level we *can* reject the null hypothesis that the coefficient on the S&P 500/BARRA Growth Index equals 0 (H_0: $b_1 = 0$) in favor of the alternative hypothesis that the coefficient does not equal 0 (H_a: $b_1 \neq 0$). As Table 3 shows, the *t*-statistic for testing that hypothesis is 9.70, a result far above the critical value of 2.00. Thus multiple regression analysis suggests that returns to the FSPTX are very closely associated with the returns to the S&P 500/BARRA Growth Index, but they are not related to S&P 500/BARRA Value Index (the *t*-statistic of -1.60 is not statistically significant).

2.2 Predicting the Dependent Variable in a Multiple Regression Model

Financial analysts often want to predict the value of the dependent variable in a multiple regression based on assumed values of the independent variables. We have previously discussed how to make such a prediction in the case of only one independent variable. The process for making that prediction with multiple linear regression is very similar.

To predict the value of a dependent variable using a multiple linear regression model, we follow these three steps:

---

[18] To economize on notation in stating test statistics, in this context we use b_2 to represent the hypothesized value of the parameter (elsewhere we use it to represent the unknown population parameter).

1. Obtain estimates $\hat{b}_0$, $\hat{b}_1$, $\hat{b}_2$, . . . , $\hat{b}_k$ of the regression parameters b_0, b_1, b_2, . . . , b_k.

2. Determine the assumed values of the independent variables, $\hat{X}_{1i}$, $\hat{X}_{2i}$, . . . , $\hat{X}_{ki}$.

3. Compute the predicted value of the dependent variable, $\hat{Y}_i$, using the equation

$$\hat{Y}_i = \hat{b}_0 + \hat{b}_1\hat{X}_{1i} + \hat{b}_2\hat{X}_{2i} + \ldots + \hat{b}_k\hat{X}_{ki}$$

(3)

Two practical points concerning using an estimated regression to predict the dependent variable are in order. First, we should be confident that the assumptions of the regression model are met. Second, we should be cautious about predictions based on values of the independent variables that are outside the range of the data on which the model was estimated; such predictions are often unreliable.

EXAMPLE 4

Predicting a Pension Fund's RANVA

In Example 2, we explained the RANVA for U.S. and Canadian pension funds based on the log base 10 of the assets under management for a fund (Size$_i$) and the fraction of assets in the fund that were passively managed (Passive$_i$).

$$\text{RANVA}_i = b_0 + b_1\text{Size}_i + b_2\text{Passive}_i + \epsilon_i$$

Now we can use the results of the regression reported in Table 2 (excerpted here) to predict the performance (RANVA) for a pension fund.

TABLE 2   (excerpt)

	Coefficients
Intercept	−2.1
Size	0.4
Passive management	0.8

Suppose that a particular fund has assets under management of $10 million, and 25 percent of the assets are passively managed. The log base 10 of the assets under management equals log(10,000,000) = 7. The fraction of assets in the fund that are passively managed is 0.25. Accordingly, the predicted RANVA for that fund, based on the regression, is −2.1 + (0.4 × 7) + (0.8 × 0.25) = 0.9 percent (90 basis points). The regression predicts that the RANVA will be 90 basis points for a pension fund with assets under management of $10 million, 25 percent of which are passively managed.

When predicting the dependent variable using a linear regression model, we encounter two types of uncertainty: uncertainty in the regression model itself, as reflected in the standard error of estimate, and uncertainty about the estimates of the regression model's parameters. In the reading on correlation and regression, we presented procedures for constructing a prediction interval for linear regression with one independent variable. For multiple regression, however, computing a prediction interval to properly incorporate both types of uncertainty requires matrix algebra, which is outside the scope of this reading.[19]

2.3 Testing whether All Population Regression Coefficients Equal Zero

Earlier, we illustrated how to conduct hypothesis tests on regression coefficients individually. But what about the significance of the regression as a whole? As a group, do the independent variables help explain the dependent variable? To address this question, we test the null hypothesis that all the slope coefficients in a regression are simultaneously equal to 0. In this section, we discuss **analysis of variance (ANOVA)**, which provides information about a regression's explanatory power and the inputs for an *F*-test of the above null hypothesis.

If none of the independent variables in a regression model helps explain the dependent variable, the slope coefficients should all equal 0. In a multiple regression, however, we cannot test the null hypothesis that *all* slope coefficients equal 0 based on *t*-tests that *each individual* slope coefficient equals 0, because the individual tests do not account for the effects of interactions among the independent variables. For example, a classic symptom of multicollinearity is that we can reject the hypothesis that all the slope coefficients equal 0 even though none of the *t*-statistics for the individual estimated slope coefficients is significant. Conversely, we can construct unusual examples in which the estimated slope coefficients are significantly different from 0 although jointly they are not.

To test the null hypothesis that all of the slope coefficients in the multiple regression model are jointly equal to 0 (H_0: $b_1 = b_2 = \ldots = b_k = 0$) against the alternative hypothesis that at least one slope coefficient is not equal to 0 we must use an *F*-test. The *F*-test is viewed as a test of the regression's overall significance.

To correctly calculate the test statistic for the null hypothesis, we need four inputs:

- total number of observations, n;

- total number of regression coefficients to be estimated, $k + 1$, where k is the number of slope coefficients;

- sum of squared errors or residuals, $\sum_{i=1}^{n} (Y_i - \hat{Y}_i)^2 = \sum_{i=1}^{n} \hat{\epsilon}_i^2$, abbreviated SSE, also known as the residual sum of squares (unexplained variation);[20] and

- regression sum of squares, $\sum_{i=1}^{n} (\hat{Y}_i - \overline{Y})^2$, abbreviated RSS.[21] This amount is the variation in Y from its mean that the regression equation explains (explained variation).

---

[19] For more information, see Greene (2003).

[20] In a table of regression output, this is the number under "SS" column in the row "Residual."

[21] In a table of regression output, this is the number under the "SS" column in the row "Regression."

The *F*-test for determining whether the slope coefficients equal 0 is based on an *F*-statistic calculated using the four values listed above. The *F*-statistic measures how well the regression equation explains the variation in the dependent variable; it is the ratio of the mean regression sum of squares to the mean squared error.

We compute the mean regression sum of squares by dividing the regression sum of squares by the number of slope coefficients estimated, *k*. We compute the mean squared error by dividing the sum of squared errors by the number of observations, *n*, minus $(k + 1)$. The two divisors in these computations are the degrees of freedom for calculating an *F*-statistic. For *n* observations and *k* slope coefficients, the *F*-test for the null hypothesis that the slope coefficients are all equal to 0 is denoted $F_{k, n - (k + 1)}$. The subscript indicates that the test should have *k* degrees of freedom in the numerator (numerator degrees of freedom) and $n - (k + 1)$ degrees of freedom in the denominator (denominator degrees of freedom).

The formula for the *F*-statistic is

$$F = \frac{\dfrac{\text{RSS}}{k}}{\dfrac{\text{SSE}}{[n - (k + 1)]}} = \frac{\text{Mean regression sum of squares}}{\text{Mean squared error}} = \frac{\text{MSR}}{\text{MSE}} \qquad (4)$$

where MSR is the mean regression sum of squares and MSE is the mean squared error. In our regression output tables, MSR and MSE are the first and second quantities under the MSS (mean sum of squares) column in the ANOVA section of the output. If the regression model does a good job of explaining variation in the dependent variable, then the ratio MSR/MSE will be large.

What does this *F*-test tell us when the independent variables in a regression model explain none of the variation in the dependent variable? In this case, each predicted value in the regression model, $\hat{Y}_i$, has the average value of the dependent variable, $\overline{Y}$, and the regression sum of squares, $\sum_{i=1}^{n} (\hat{Y}_i - \overline{Y})^2$ is 0. Therefore, the *F*-statistic for testing the null hypothesis (that all the slope coefficients are equal to 0) has a value of 0 when the independent variables do not explain the dependent variable at all.

To specify the details of making the statistical decision when we have calculated *F*, we reject the null hypothesis at the α significance level if the calculated value of *F* is greater than the upper α critical value of the *F* distribution with the specified numerator and denominator degrees of freedom. Note that we use a one-tailed *F*-test.[22]

We can illustrate the test using Example 1, in which we investigated whether the natural log of the number of NASDAQ market makers and the natural log of the stock's market capitalization explained the natural log of the bid–ask spread divided by price. Assume that we set the significance level for this test to α = 0.05 (i.e., a 5 percent probability that we will mistakenly reject the null hypothesis if it is true). Table 1 (excerpted here) presents the results of variance computations for this regression.

---

[22] We use a one-tailed test because MSR necessarily increases relative to MSE as the explanatory power of the regression increases.

ANOVA	df	SS	MSS	F	Significance F
Regression	2	2,681.6482	1,340.8241	1,088.8325	0.00
Residual	1,816	2,236.2820	1.2314		
Total	1,818	4,917.9302			

TABLE 1   (excerpt)

This model has two slope coefficients ($k = 2$), so there are two degrees of freedom in the numerator of this F-test. With 1,819 observations in the sample, the number of degrees of freedom in the denominator of the F-test is $n - (k + 1) = 1,819 - 3 = 1,816$. The sum of the squared errors is 2,236.2820. The regression sum of squares is 2,681.6482. Therefore, the F-test for the null hypothesis that the two slope coefficients in this model equal 0 is

$$\frac{2681.6482/2}{2236.2820/1,816} = 1,088.8325$$

This test statistic is distributed as an $F_{2, \, 1,816}$ random variable under the null hypothesis that the slope coefficients are equal to 0. In the table for the 0.05 significance level, we look at the second column, which shows F-distributions with two degrees of freedom in the numerator. Near the bottom of the column, we find that the critical value of the F-test needed to reject the null hypothesis is between 3.00 and 3.07.[23] The actual value of the F-test statistic at 1,088.83 is much greater, so we reject the null hypothesis that coefficients of both independent variables equal 0. In fact, Table 1 under "Significance F," reports a p-value of 0. This p-value means that the smallest level of significance at which the null hypothesis can be rejected is practically 0. The large value for this F-statistic implies a minuscule probability of incorrectly rejecting the null hypothesis (a mistake known as a Type I error).

2.4 Adjusted R^2

In the reading on correlation and regression, we presented the coefficient of determination, R^2, as a measure of the goodness of fit of an estimated regression to the data. In a multiple linear regression, however, R^2 is less appropriate as a measure of whether a regression model fits the data well (goodness of fit). Recall that R^2 is defined as

$$\frac{\text{Total variation} - \text{Unexplained variation}}{\text{Total variation}}$$

The numerator equals the regression sum of squares, RSS. Thus R^2 states RSS as a fraction of the total sum of squares, $\sum_{i=1}^{n} (Y_i - \overline{Y})^2$. If we add regression variables to the model, the amount of unexplained variation will decrease, and RSS will

---

[23] We see a range of values because the denominator has more than 120 degrees of freedom but less than an infinite number of degrees of freedom.

increase, if the new independent variable explains any of the unexplained variation in the model. Such a reduction occurs when the new independent variable is even slightly correlated with the dependent variable and is not a linear combination of other independent variables in the regression.[24] Consequently, we can increase R^2 simply by including many additional independent variables that explain even a slight amount of the previously unexplained variation, even if the amount they explain is not statistically significant.

Some financial analysts use an alternative measure of goodness of fit called **adjusted R^2**, or $\overline{R}^2$. This measure of fit does not automatically increase when another variable is added to a regression; it is adjusted for degrees of freedom. Adjusted R^2 is typically part of the multiple regression output produced by statistical software packages.

The relation between R^2 and $\overline{R}^2$ is

$$\overline{R}^2 = 1 - \left(\frac{n-1}{n-k-1}\right)(1-R^2)$$

where n is the number of observations and k is the number of independent variables (the number of slope coefficients). Note that if $k \geq 1$, then R^2 is strictly greater than adjusted R^2. When a new independent variable is added, $\overline{R}^2$ can decrease if adding that variable results in only a small increase in R^2. In fact, $\overline{R}^2$ can be negative, although R^2 is always nonnegative.[25] If we use $\overline{R}^2$ to compare regression models, it is important that the dependent variable be defined the same way in both models and that the sample sizes used to estimate the models are the same.[26] For example, it makes a difference for the value of $\overline{R}^2$ if the dependent variable is GDP (gross domestic product) or ln(GDP), even if the independent variables are identical. Furthermore, we should be aware that a high $\overline{R}^2$ does not necessarily indicate that the regression is well specified in the sense of including the correct set of variables.[27] One reason for caution is that a high $\overline{R}^2$ may reflect peculiarities of the dataset used to estimate the regression. To evaluate a regression model, we need to take many other factors into account, as we discuss in Section 5.1.

3

USING DUMMY VARIABLES IN REGRESSIONS

Often, financial analysts need to use qualitative variables as independent variables in a regression. One type of qualitative variable, called a **dummy variable**, takes on a value of 1 if a particular condition is true and 0 if that condition is false.[28] For example, suppose we want to test whether stock returns were different in January than during the remaining months of a particular year. We include one independent variable in the regression, X_{1t}, that has a value of 1 for

---

[24] We say that variable y is a linear combination of variables x and z if $y = ax + bz$ for some constants a and b. A variable can also be a linear combination of more than two variables.

[25] When $\overline{R}^2$ is negative, we can effectively consider its value to be 0.

[26] See Gujarati (2003). The value of adjusted R^2 depends on sample size. These points hold if we are using R^2 to compare two regression models.

[27] See Mayer (1975, 1980).

[28] Not all qualitative variables are simple dummy variables. For example, in a trinomial choice model (a model with three choices), a qualitative variable might have the value 0, 1, or 2.

each January and a value of 0 for every other month of the year. We estimate the regression model

$$Y_t = b_0 + b_1 X_{1t} + \epsilon_t$$

In this equation, the coefficient b_0 is the average value of Y_t in months other than January, and b_1 is the difference between the average value of Y_t in January and the average value of Y_t in months other than January.

We need to exercise care in choosing the number of dummy variables in a regression. The rule is that if we want to distinguish among n categories, we need $n - 1$ dummy variables. For example, to distinguish between *during January* and *not during January* above ($n = 2$ categories), we used one dummy variable ($n - 1 = 2 - 1 = 1$). If we want to distinguish between each of the four quarters in a year, we would include dummy variables for three of the four quarters in a year. If we make the mistake of including dummy variables for four rather than three quarters, we have violated Assumption 2 of the multiple regression model and cannot estimate the regression. The next example illustrates the use of dummy variables in a regression with monthly data.

EXAMPLE 5

Month-of-the-Year Effects on Small-Stock Returns

For many years, financial analysts have been concerned about seasonality in stock returns.[29] In particular, analysts have researched whether returns to small stocks differ during various months of the year. Suppose we want to test whether total returns to one small-stock index, the Russell 2000 Index, differ by month. Using data from January 1979 (the first available date for the Russell 2000 data) through the end of 2002, we can estimate a regression including an intercept and 11 dummy variables, one for each of the first 11 months of the year. The equation that we estimate is

$$\text{Returns}_t = b_0 + b_1 \text{Jan}_t + b_2 \text{Feb}_t + \ldots + b_{11} \text{Nov}_t + \epsilon_t$$

where each monthly dummy variable has a value of 1 when the month occurs (e.g., $\text{Jan}_1 = \text{Jan}_{13} = 1$, as the first observation is a January) and a value of 0 for the other months. Table 4 shows the results of this regression.

The intercept, b_0, measures the average return for stocks in December because there is no dummy variable for December.[30] This equation estimates that the average return in December is 3.01 percent ($\hat{b}_0 = 0.0301$). Each of the estimated coefficients for the dummy variables shows the estimated difference between returns in that month and returns for December. So, for example, the estimated additional return in January is 0.03 percent higher than December ($\hat{b}_1 = 0.0003$). This gives a January return prediction of 3.04 percent (3.01 December + 0.03 additional).

---

[29] For a discussion of this issue, see Siegel (1998).

[30] When $\text{Jan}_t = \text{Feb}_t = \ldots = \text{Nov}_t = 0$, the return is not associated with January through November so the month is December and the regression equation simplifies to $\text{Returns}_t = b_0 + \epsilon_t$. Because $E(\text{Returns}_t) = b_0 + E(\epsilon_t) = b_0$, the intercept b_0 represents the mean return for December.

TABLE 4 Results from Regressing Russell 2000 Returns on Monthly Dummy Variables

	Coefficient	Standard Error	*t*-Statistic
Intercept	0.0301	0.0116	2.5902
January	0.0003	0.0164	0.0176
February	−0.0111	0.0164	−0.6753
March	−0.0211	0.0164	−1.2846
April	−0.0141	0.0164	−0.8568
May	−0.0137	0.0164	−0.8320
June	−0.0200	0.0164	−1.2164
July	−0.0405	0.0164	−2.4686
August	−0.0230	0.0164	−1.4025
September	−0.0375	0.0164	−2.2864
October	−0.0393	0.0164	−2.3966
November	−0.0059	0.0164	−0.3565

ANOVA	df	SS	MSS	F	Significance F
Regression	11	0.0543	0.0049	1.5270	0.1213
Residual	276	0.8924	0.0032		
Total	287	0.9467			

Residual standard error	0.0569
Multiple R-squared	0.0574
Observations	288

Source: Ibbotson Associates.

The low R^2 in this regression (0.0574), however, suggests that a month-of-the-year effect in small-stock returns may not be very important for explaining small-stock returns. We can use the F-test to analyze the null hypothesis that jointly, the monthly dummy variables all equal 0 (H_0: $b_1 = b_2 = \ldots = b_{11} = 0$). We are testing for significant monthly variation in small-stock returns. Table 4 shows the data needed to perform an analysis of variance. The number of degrees of freedom in the numerator of the F-test is 11; the number of degrees of freedom in the denominator is $[288 - (11 + 1)] = 276$. The regression sum of squares equals 0.0543, and the sum of squared errors equals 0.8924. Therefore, the F-statistic to determine whether all of the regression slope coefficients are jointly equal to 0 is

$$\frac{0.0543/11}{0.8924/276} = 1.53$$

Appendix D (the *F*-distribution table) at the end of this volume shows the critical values for this *F*-test. If we choose a significance level of 0.05 and look in Column 11 (because the numerator has 11 degrees of freedom), we see that the critical value is 1.87 when the denominator has 120 degrees of freedom. The denominator actually has 276 degrees of freedom, so the critical value of the *F*-statistic is smaller than 1.87 (for df = 120) but larger than 1.79 (for an infinite number of degrees of freedom). The value of the test statistic is 1.53, so we clearly cannot reject the null hypothesis that all of the coefficients jointly are equal to 0.

The *p*-value of 0.1213 shown for the *F*-test in Table 4 means that the smallest level of significance at which we can reject the null hypothesis is roughly 0.12, or 12 percent—above the conventional level of 5 percent. Among the 11 monthly dummy variables, July, September, and October have a *t*-statistic with an absolute value greater than 2. Although the coefficients for these dummy variables are statistically significant, we have so many insignificant estimated coefficients that we cannot reject the null hypothesis that returns are equal across the months. This test suggests that the significance of a few coefficients in this regression model may be the result of random variation. We may thus want to avoid portfolio strategies calling for differing investment weights for small stocks in different months.

EXAMPLE 6

Determinants of Spreads on New High-Yield Bonds

Fridson and Garman (1998) used data from 1995 and 1996 to examine variables that may explain the initial yield spread between a newly issued high-yield bond and a Treasury bond with similar maturity. They built a model of yield spreads using variables that affect the creditworthiness and interest-rate risk of the bond. Their model included the following factors:

▶ rating: Moody's senior-equivalent rating;
▶ zero-coupon status: Dummy variable (0 = no, 1 = yes);
▶ BB-B spread: Yield differential (Merrill Lynch Single-B Index minus Double-B Index, in basis points);
▶ seniority: Dummy variable (0 = senior, 1 = subordinated);
▶ callability: Dummy variable (0 = noncallable, 1 = callable);
▶ term: Maturity (years);
▶ first-time issuer: Dummy variable (0 = no, 1 = yes);
▶ underwriter type: Dummy variable (0 = investment bank, 1 = commercial bank);
▶ interest rate change.

Table 5 shows the authors' results.

TABLE 5	Multiple Regression Model of New High-Yield Issue Spread, 1995–96		
	Coefficient	**Standard Error**	***t*-Statistic**
Intercept	−213.67	63.03	−3.39
Rating	66.19	4.13	16.02
Zero-coupon status	136.54	32.82	4.16
BB-B spread	95.31	24.82	3.84
Seniority	41.46	11.95	3.47
Callability	51.65	15.42	3.35
Term	−8.51	2.71	−3.14
First-time issuer	25.23	10.97	2.30
Underwriter type	28.13	12.67	2.22
Interest rate change	40.44	19.08	2.12
R-squared	0.56		
Observations	428		

Source: Fridson and Garman (1998).

We can summarize Fridson and Garman's findings as follows:

► Bond rating has the highest significance level of any coefficient in the regression. This result should not be surprising, because the rating captures rating agencies' estimates of the risk involved with the bond.

► Zero-coupon status increases the yield spread because zero-coupon bonds have more interest rate risk than coupon bonds of a similar maturity.

► The BB-B spread affects yields because it captures the market's evaluation of how much influence rating differentials have on credit risk.

► Seniority affects yields because subordinated debt has a much lower recovery rate in the case of default.

► Callability increases yields because it limits upside potential on the bond if yields decline.

► Term actually reduces the yield spread. Perhaps term enters with a negative coefficient because the market is willing to buy long-term debt only from high-quality companies; lower-quality companies must issue shorter-term debt.

► First-time issuers must pay a premium because the market does not know much about them.

► Bonds underwritten by commercial banks have a premium over bonds underwritten by investment banks, most likely because the market believes that investment banks have a competitive edge in attracting high-quality corporate clients.

> ▶ Interest-rate increases in Treasuries during the previous month cause yield spreads to widen, presumably because the market believes that increasing interest rates will worsen the economic prospects of companies issuing high-yield debt.
>
> Note that all of the coefficients in this regression model are statistically significant at the 0.05 level. The smallest absolute value of a *t*-statistic in this table is 2.12.

VIOLATIONS OF REGRESSION ASSUMPTIONS   4

In Section 2.1, we presented the assumptions of the multiple linear regression model. Inference based on an estimated regression model rests on those assumptions being satisfied. In applying regression analysis to financial data, analysts need to be able to diagnose violations of regression assumptions, understand the consequences of violations, and know the remedial steps to take. In the following sections we discuss three regression violations: heteroskedasticity, serial correlation, and multicollinearity.

4.1 Heteroskedasticity

So far, we have made an important assumption that the variance of error in a regression is constant across observations. In statistical terms, we assumed that the errors were homoskedastic. Errors in financial data, however, are often **heteroskedastic**: the variance of the errors differs across observations. In this section, we discuss how heteroskedasticity affects statistical analysis, how to test for heteroskedasticity, and how to correct for it.

We can see the difference between homoskedastic and heteroskedastic errors by comparing two graphs. Figure 1 shows the values of the dependent and independent variables and a fitted regression line for a model with homoskedastic errors. There is no systematic relationship between the value of the independent variable and the regression residuals (the vertical distance between a plotted point and the fitted regression line). Figure 2 shows the values of the dependent and independent variables and a fitted regression line for a model with heteroskedastic errors. Here, a systematic relationship is visually apparent: On average, the regression residuals grow much larger as the size of the independent variable increases.

4.1.1 The Consequences of Heteroskedasticity

What are the consequences when the assumption of constant error variance is violated? Although heteroskedasticity does not affect the consistency[31] of the regression parameter estimators, it can lead to mistakes in inference. When errors are heteroskedastic, the *F*-test for the overall significance of the regression

---

[31] Informally, an estimator of a regression parameter is consistent if the probability that estimates of a regression parameter differ from the true value of the parameter decreases as the number of observations used in the regression increases. The regression parameter estimates from ordinary least squares are consistent regardless of whether the errors are heteroskedastic or homoskedastic. For a more advanced discussion, see Greene (2003).

FIGURE 1 **Regression with Homoskedasticity**

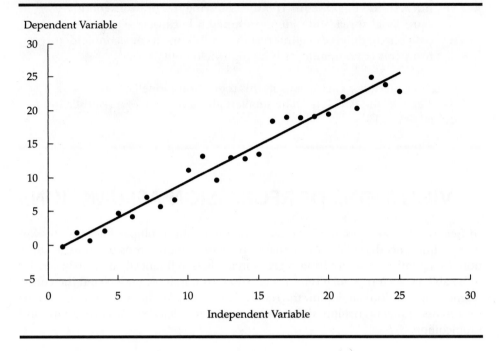

FIGURE 2 **Regression with Heteroskedasticity**

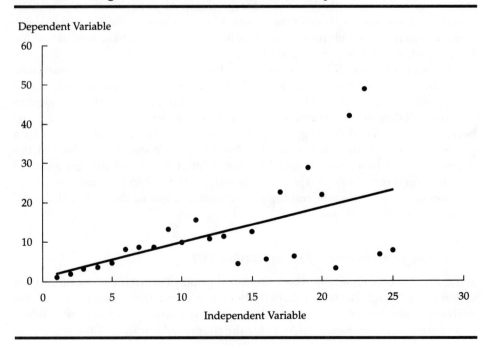

is unreliable.[32] Furthermore, t-tests for the significance of individual regression coefficients are unreliable because heteroskedasticity introduces bias into estimators of the standard error of regression coefficients. If a regression shows significant heteroskedasticity, the standard errors and test statistics computed by regression programs will be incorrect unless they are adjusted for heteroskedasticity.

In regressions with financial data, the most likely result of heteroskedasticity is that the estimated standard errors will be underestimated and the t-statistics will be inflated. When we ignore heteroskedasticity, we tend to find significant relationships where none actually exist.[33] The consequences in practice may be serious if we are using regression analysis in the development of investment strategies. As Example 7 shows, the issue impinges even on our understanding of financial models.

EXAMPLE 7

Heteroskedasticity and Tests of an Asset Pricing Model

MacKinlay and Richardson (1991) examined how heteroskedasticity affects tests of the capital asset pricing model (CAPM).[34] These authors argued that if the CAPM is correct, they should find no significant differences between the risk-adjusted returns for holding small stocks versus large stocks. To implement their test, MacKinlay and Richardson grouped all stocks on the New York and American exchanges by market-value decile with annual reassignment. They then tested for systematic differences in risk-adjusted returns across market-capitalization-based stock portfolios. They estimated the following regression:

$$r_{i,t} = \alpha_i + \beta_i r_{m,t} + \epsilon_{i,t}$$

where

$r_{i,t}$ = excess return (return above the risk-free rate) to portfolio i in period t

$r_{m,t}$ = excess return to the market as a whole in period t

The CAPM formulation hypothesizes that excess returns on a portfolio are explained by excess returns on the market as a whole. That hypothesis implies that $\alpha_i = 0$ for every i; on average, no excess return accrues to any portfolio after taking into account its systematic (market) risk.

Using data from January 1926 to December 1988 and a market index based on equal-weighted returns, MacKinlay and Richardson failed to reject the CAPM at the 0.05 level when they assumed that the errors in the regression model are normally distributed and homoskedastic. They found, however, that they could reject the CAPM when they corrected their test statistics to account for heteroskedasticity. They rejected the hypothesis that there are no size-based, risk-adjusted excess returns in historical data.[35]

---

[32] This unreliability occurs because the mean squared error is a biased estimator of the true population variance given heteroskedasticity.

[33] Sometimes, however, failure to adjust for heteroskedasticity results in standard errors that are too large (and t-statistics that are too small).

[34] For more on the CAPM, see Bodie, Kane, and Marcus (2001), for example.

[35] MacKinlay and Richardson also show that when using value-weighted returns, one can reject the CAPM whether or not one assumes normally distributed returns and homoskedasticity.

We have stated that effects of heteroskedasticity on statistical inference can be severe. To be more precise about this concept, we should distinguish between two broad kinds of heteroskedasticity: unconditional and conditional.

Unconditional heteroskedasticity occurs when heteroskedasticity of the error variance is not correlated with the independent variables in the multiple regression. Although this form of heteroskedasticity violates Assumption 4 of the linear regression model, it creates no major problems for statistical inference.

The type of heteroskedasticity that causes the most problems for statistical inference is **conditional heteroskedasticity**—heteroskedasticity in the error variance that is correlated with (conditional on) the values of the independent variables in the regression. Fortunately, many statistical software packages easily test and correct for conditional heteroskedasticity.

4.1.2 Testing for Heteroskedasticity

Because of conditional heteroskedasticity's consequences on inference, the analyst must be able to diagnose its presence. The Breusch–Pagan test is widely used in finance research because of its generality.[36]

Breusch and Pagan (1979) suggested the following test for conditional heteroskedasticity: Regress the squared residuals from the estimated regression equation on the independent variables in the regression. If no conditional heteroskedasticity exists, the independent variables will not explain much of the variation in the squared residuals. If conditional heteroskedasticity is present in the original regression, however, the independent variables will explain a significant portion of the variation in the squared residuals. The independent variables can explain the variation because each observation's squared residual will be correlated with the independent variables if the independent variables affect the variance of the errors.

Breusch and Pagan showed that under the null hypothesis of no conditional heteroskedasticity, nR^2 (from the regression of the squared residuals on the independent variables from the original regression) will be a χ^2 random variable with the number of degrees of freedom equal to the number of independent variables in the regression.[37] Therefore, the null hypothesis states that the regression's squared error term is uncorrelated with the independent variables. The alternative hypothesis states that the squared error term is correlated with the independent variables. Example 8 illustrates the Breusch–Pagan test for conditional heteroskedasticity.

EXAMPLE 8

Testing for Conditional Heteroskedasticity in the Relation between Interest Rates and Expected Inflation

Suppose an analyst wants to know how closely nominal interest rates are related to expected inflation to determine how to allocate assets in a fixed income portfolio. The analyst wants to test the Fisher effect, the hypothesis suggested by Irving Fisher that nominal interest rates increase

---

[36] Some other tests require more-specific assumptions about the functional form of the heteroskedasticity. For more information, see Greene (2003).

[37] The Breusch–Pagan test is distributed as a χ^2 random variable in large samples. The constant 1 technically associated with the intercept term in a regression is not counted here in computing the number of independent variables. For more on the Breusch–Pagan test, see Greene (2003).

by 1 percentage point for every 1 percentage point increase in expected inflation.[38] The Fisher effect assumes the following relation between nominal interest rates, real interest rates, and expected inflation:

$$i = r + \pi^e$$

where

i = the nominal interest rate
r = the real interest rate (assumed constant)
π^e = the expected rate of inflation

To test the Fisher effect using time-series data, we could specify the following regression model for the nominal interest rate:

$$i_t = b_0 + b_1 \pi_t^e + \epsilon_t \qquad \textbf{(5)}$$

Noting that the Fisher effect predicts that the coefficient on the inflation variable is 1, we can state the null and alternative hypotheses as

$$H_0: b_1 = 1$$
$$H_a: b_1 \neq 1$$

We might also specify a 0.05 significance level for the test. Before we estimate Equation 5, we must decide how to measure expected inflation (π_t^e) and the nominal interest rate (i_t).

The Survey of Professional Forecasters (SPF) has compiled data on the quarterly inflation expectations of professional forecasters.[39] We use those data as our measure of expected inflation. We use three-month Treasury bill returns as our measure of the (risk-free) nominal interest rate.[40] We use quarterly data from the fourth quarter of 1968 to the fourth quarter of 2002 to estimate Equation 5. Table 6 shows the regression results.

To make the statistical decision on whether the data support the Fisher effect, we calculate the following t-statistic, which we then compare to its critical value.

$$t = \frac{\hat{b}_1 - b_1}{s_{\hat{b}_1}} = \frac{0.8774 - 1}{0.0812} = -1.5099$$

With a t-statistic of -1.5099 and $137 - 2 = 135$ degrees of freedom, the critical t-value is about 1.98. If we have conducted a valid test, we cannot reject at the 0.05 significance level the hypothesis that the true coefficient in this regression is 1 and that the Fisher effect holds. The t-test assumes that the errors are homoskedastic. Before we accept the validity

---

[38] For more on the Fisher effect, see, for example, Mankiw (2000).

[39] For this example, we use the annualized median SPF prediction of current-quarter growth in the GDP deflator (GNP deflator before 1992).

[40] Our data on Treasury bill returns are based on three-month T-bill yields in the secondary market. Because those yields are stated on a discount basis, we convert them to a compounded annual rate so they will be measured on the same basis as our data on inflation expectations. These returns are risk-free because they are known at the beginning of the quarter and there is no default risk.

TABLE 6   Results from Regressing T-Bill Returns on Predicted Inflation

	Coefficient	Standard Error	t-Statistic
Intercept	0.0304	0.0040	7.6887
Inflation prediction	0.8774	0.0812	10.8096
Residual standard error		0.0220	
Multiple R-squared		0.4640	
Observations		137	
Durbin–Watson statistic		0.4673	

Source: Federal Reserve Bank of Philadelphia, U.S. Department of Commerce.

of the t-test, therefore, we should test whether the errors are conditionally heteroskedastic. If those errors prove to be conditionally heteroskedastic, then the test is invalid.

We can perform the **Breusch–Pagan test** for conditional heteroskedasticity on the squared residuals from the Fisher effect regression. The test regresses the squared residuals on the predicted inflation rate. The R^2 in the squared residuals regression (not shown here) is 0.1651. The test statistic from this regression, nR^2, is $137 \times 0.1651 = 22.619$. Under the null hypothesis of no conditional heteroskedasticity, this test statistic is a χ^2 random variable with one degree of freedom (because there is only one independent variable).

We should be concerned about heteroskedasticity only for large values of the test statistic. Therefore, we should use a one-tailed test to determine whether we can reject the null hypothesis. The critical value of the test statistic for a variable from a χ^2 distribution with one degree of freedom at the 0.05 significance level is 3.84. The test statistic from the Breusch–Pagan test is 22.619, so we can reject the hypothesis of no conditional heteroskedasticity at the 0.05 level. In fact, we can even reject the hypothesis of no conditional heteroskedasticity at the 0.01 significance level, because the critical value of the test statistic in the case is 6.63. As a result, we conclude that the error term in the Fisher effect regression is conditionally heteroskedastic. The standard errors computed in the original regression are not correct, because they do not account for heteroskedasticity. Therefore, we cannot accept the t-test as valid.

In Example 8, we concluded that a t-test that we might use to test the Fisher effect was not valid. Does that mean that we cannot use a regression model to investigate the Fisher effect? Fortunately, no. A methodology is available to adjust regression coefficients' standard error to correct for heteroskedasticity. Using an adjusted standard error for $\hat{b}_1$, we can reconduct the t-test. As we shall see in the next section, using this valid t-test we still do not reject the null hypothesis in Example 8.

4.1.3 Correcting for Heteroskedasticity

Financial analysts need to know how to correct for heteroskedasticity, because such a correction may reverse the conclusions about a particular hypothesis test—and thus affect a particular investment decision. In Example 7, for instance, MacKinlay and Richardson reversed their investment conclusions after correcting their model's significance tests for heteroskedasticity.

We can use two different methods to correct the effects of conditional heteroskedasticity in linear regression models. The first method, computing **robust standard errors**, corrects the standard errors of the linear regression model's estimated coefficients to account for the conditional heteroskedasticity. The second method, **generalized least squares**, modifies the original equation in an attempt to eliminate the heteroskedasticity. The new, modified regression equation is then estimated under the assumption that heteroskedasticity is no longer a problem.[41] The technical details behind these two methods of correcting for conditional heteroskedasticity are outside the scope of this volume.[42] Many statistical software packages can easily compute robust standard errors, however, and we recommend using them.[43]

Returning to the subject of Example 8 concerning the Fisher effect, recall that we concluded that the error variance was heteroskedastic. If we correct the regression coefficients' standard errors for conditional heteroskedasticity, we get the results shown in Table 7. In comparing the standard errors in Table 7 with those in Table 6, we see that the standard error for the intercept changes very little, but the standard error for the coefficient on predicted inflation (the slope coefficient) increases by about 25.5 percent (from 0.0812 to 0.1019). Note also that the regression coefficients are the same in both tables, because the results in Table 7 correct only the standard errors in Table 6.

TABLE 7 Results from Regressing T-Bill Returns on Predicted Inflation (Standard Errors Corrected for Conditional Heteroskedasticity)			
	Coefficients	**Standard Error**	**t-Statistic**
Intercept	0.0304	0.0038	8.0740
Inflation prediction	0.8774	0.1019	8.6083
Residual standard error		0.0220	
Multiple R-squared		0.4640	
Observations		137	

Source: Federal Reserve Bank of Philadelphia, U.S. Department of Commerce.

[41] Generalized least squares requires econometric expertise to implement correctly on financial data. See Greene (2003), Hansen (1982), and Keane and Runkle (1998).

[42] For more details on both methods, see Greene (2003).

[43] Robust standard errors are also known as **heteroskedasticity-consistent standard errors** or **White-corrected standard errors**.

We can now conduct a valid t-test of the null hypothesis that the slope coefficient has a true value of 1, using the robust standard error for $\hat{b}_1$. We find that $t = (0.8774 - 1)/0.1019 = -1.2031$. In absolute value, this number is still much smaller than the critical value of 1.98 needed to reject the null hypothesis that the slope equals 1.[44] Thus, in this particular example, even though conditional heteroskedasticity was statistically significant, correcting for it had no effect on the result of the hypothesis test about the slope of the predicted inflation coefficient. In other cases, however, our statistical decision might change based on using robust standard errors in the t-test. Example 7 concerning tests of the CAPM is a case in point.

4.2 Serial Correlation

A more common—and potentially more serious—problem than violation of the homoskedasticity assumption is the violation of the assumption that regression errors are uncorrelated across observations. Trying to explain a particular financial relation over a number of periods is risky, because errors in financial regression models are often correlated through time.

When regression errors are correlated across observations, we say that they are **serially correlated** (or autocorrelated). Serial correlation most typically arises in time-series regressions. In this section, we discuss three aspects of serial correlation: its effect on statistical inference, tests for it, and methods to correct for it.

4.2.1 The Consequences of Serial Correlation

As with heteroskedasticity, the principal problem caused by serial correlation in a linear regression is an incorrect estimate of the regression coefficient standard errors computed by statistical software packages. As long as none of the independent variables is a lagged value of the dependent variable (a value of the dependent variable from a previous period), then the estimated parameters themselves will be consistent and need not be adjusted for the effects of serial correlation. If, however, one of the independent variables is a lagged value of the dependent variable—for example, if the T-bill return from the previous month was an independent variable in the Fisher effect regression—then serial correlation in the error term will cause all the parameter estimates from linear regression to be inconsistent and they will not be valid estimates of the true parameters.[45]

In this reading, we assume that none of the independent variables is a lagged value of the dependent variable. When that is the case, the effect of serial correlation appears in the regression coefficient standard errors. We will examine it here for the positive serial correlation case, because that case is so common. **Positive serial correlation** is serial correlation in which a positive error for one observation increases the chance of a positive error for another observation. Positive serial correlation also means that a negative error for one observation increases the chance of a negative error for another observation.[46] In examining positive serial correlation, we make the common assumption that serial correla-

---

[44] Remember, this is a two-tailed test.

[45] We address this issue in the reading on time-series analysis.

[46] In contrast, with **negative serial correlation**, a positive error for one observation increases the chance of a negative error for another observation, and a negative error for one observation increases the chance of a positive error for another.

tion takes the form of **first-order serial correlation**, or serial correlation between adjacent observations. In a time-series context, that assumption means the sign of the error term tends to persist from one period to the next.

Although positive serial correlation does not affect the consistency of the estimated regression coefficients, it does affect our ability to conduct valid statistical tests. First, the F-statistic to test for overall significance of the regression may be inflated because the mean squared error (MSE) will tend to underestimate the population error variance. Second, positive serial correlation typically causes the ordinary least squares (OLS) standard errors for the regression coefficients to underestimate the true standard errors. As a consequence, if positive serial correlation is present in the regression, standard linear regression analysis will typically lead us to compute artificially small standard errors for the regression coefficient. These small standard errors will cause the estimated t-statistics to be inflated, suggesting significance where perhaps there is none. The inflated t-statistics may, in turn, lead us to incorrectly reject null hypotheses about population values of the parameters of the regression model more often than we would if the standard errors were correctly estimated. This Type I error could lead to improper investment recommendations.[47]

4.2.2 Testing for Serial Correlation

We can choose from a variety of tests for serial correlation in a regression model,[48] but the most common is based on a statistic developed by Durbin and Watson (1951); in fact, many statistical software packages compute the Durbin–Watson statistic automatically. The equation for the Durbin–Watson test statistic is

$$DW = \frac{\sum_{t=2}^{T} (\hat{\epsilon}_t - \hat{\epsilon}_{t-1})^2}{\sum_{t=1}^{T} \hat{\epsilon}_t^2} \qquad (6)$$

where $\hat{\epsilon}_t$ is the regression residual for period t. We can rewrite this equation as

$$\frac{\frac{1}{T-1}\sum_{t=2}^{T} (\hat{\epsilon}_t^2 - 2\hat{\epsilon}_t\hat{\epsilon}_{t-1} + \hat{\epsilon}_{t-1}^2)}{\frac{1}{T-1}\sum_{t=1}^{T} \hat{\epsilon}_t^2}$$

$$\approx \frac{Var(\hat{\epsilon}_t) - 2\,Cov(\hat{\epsilon}_t, \hat{\epsilon}_{t-1}) + Var(\hat{\epsilon}_{t-1})}{Var(\hat{\epsilon}_t)}$$

If the variance of the error is constant through time, then we expect $Var(\hat{\epsilon}_t) = \hat{\sigma}_\epsilon^2$ for all t, where we use $\hat{\sigma}_\epsilon^2$ to represent the estimate of the constant error variance. If, in addition, the errors are also not serially correlated, then we expect $Cov(\hat{\epsilon}_t, \hat{\epsilon}_{t-1}) = 0$. In that case, the Durbin–Watson statistic is approximately equal to

$$\frac{\hat{\sigma}_\epsilon^2 - 0 + \hat{\sigma}_\epsilon^2}{\hat{\sigma}_\epsilon^2} = 2$$

---

[47] OLS standard errors need not be underestimates of actual standard errors if negative serial correlation is present in the regression.

[48] See Greene (2003) for a detailed discussion of tests of serial correlation.

This equation tells us that if the errors are homoskedastic and not serially correlated, then the Durbin–Watson statistic will be close to 2. Therefore, we can test the null hypothesis that the errors are not serially correlated by testing whether the Durbin–Watson statistic differs significantly from 2.

If the sample is very large, the Durbin–Watson statistic will be approximately equal to $2(1 - r)$, where r is the sample correlation between the regression residuals from one period and those from the previous period. This approximation is useful because it shows the value of the Durbin–Watson statistic for differing levels of serial correlation. The Durbin–Watson statistic can take on values ranging from 0 (in the case of serial correlation of $+1$) to 4 (in the case of serial correlation of -1):

▶ If the regression has no serial correlation, then the regression residuals will be uncorrelated through time and the value of the Durbin–Watson statistic will be equal to $2(1 - 0) = 2$.

▶ If the regression residuals are positively serially correlated, then the Durbin–Watson statistic will be less than 2. For example, if the serial correlation of the errors is 1, then the value of the Durbin–Watson statistic will be 0.

▶ If the regression residuals are negatively serially correlated, then the Durbin–Watson statistic will be greater than 2. For example, if the serial correlation of the errors is -1, then the value of the Durbin–Watson statistic will be 4.

Returning to Example 8, which explored the Fisher effect, as shown in Table 6 the Durbin–Watson statistic for the OLS regression is 0.4673. This result means that the regression residuals are positively serially correlated:

$$
\begin{aligned}
DW &= 0.4673 \\
&\approx 2(1 - r) \\
r &\approx 1 - DW/2 \\
&= 1 - 0.4673/2 \\
&= 0.766
\end{aligned}
$$

This outcome raises the concern that OLS standard errors may be incorrect because of positive serial correlation. Does the observed Durbin–Watson statistic (0.4673) provide enough evidence to warrant rejecting the null hypothesis of no positive serial correlation?

We should reject the null hypothesis of no serial correlation if the Durbin–Watson statistic is below a critical value, d^*. Unfortunately, Durbin and Watson also showed that, for a given sample, we cannot know the true critical value, d^*. Instead, we can determine only that d^* lies either between two values, d_u (an upper value) and d_l (a lower value), or outside those values. Figure 3 depicts the upper and lower values of d^* as they relate to the results of the Durbin–Watson statistic.

FIGURE 3   Value of the Durbin–Watson Statistic

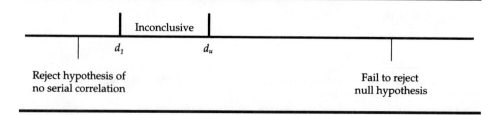

From Figure 3, we learn the following:

▶ When the Durbin–Watson (DW) statistic is less than d_l, we reject the null hypothesis of no positive serial correlation.

▶ When the DW statistic falls between d_l and d_u, the test results are inconclusive.

▶ When the DW statistic is greater than d_u, we fail to reject the null hypothesis of no positive serial correlation.[49]

Returning to Example 8, the Fisher effect regression has one independent variable and 137 observations. The Durbin–Watson statistic is 0.4673. We can reject the null hypothesis of no correlation in favor of the alternative hypothesis of positive serial correlation at the 0.05 level because the Durbin–Watson statistic is far below d_l for $k = 1$ and $n = 100$ (1.65). The level of d_l would be even higher for a sample of 137 observations. This finding of significant positive serial correlation suggests that the OLS standard errors in this regression probably significantly underestimate the true standard errors.

4.2.3 Correcting for Serial Correlation

We have two alternative remedial steps when a regression has significant serial correlation. First, we can adjust the coefficient standard errors for the linear regression parameter estimates to account for the serial correlation. Second, we can modify the regression equation itself to eliminate the serial correlation. We recommend using the first method for dealing with serial correlation; the second method may result in inconsistent parameter estimates unless implemented with extreme care.

The most prevalent method for adjusting standard errors was developed by Hansen (1982) and is a standard feature in many statistical software packages.[50] An additional advantage of Hansen's method is that it simultaneously corrects for conditional heteroskedasticity.[51]

Table 8 shows the results of correcting the standard errors from Table 6 for serial correlation and heteroskedasticity using Hansen's method. Note that the coefficients for both the intercept and the slope are exactly the same as in the original regression. The robust standard errors are now much larger, however— about twice the OLS standard errors. Because of the severe serial correlation in the regression error, OLS greatly underestimates the uncertainty about the estimated parameters in the regression.

Note also that the Durbin–Watson statistic has not changed from Table 6. The serial correlation has not been eliminated, but the standard error has been corrected to account for the serial correlation.

---

[49] Of course, sometimes serial correlation in a regression model is negative rather than positive. For a null hypothesis of no serial correlation, the null hypothesis is rejected if DW < d_l (indicating significant positive serial correlation) or if DW > $4 - d_l$ (indicating significant negative serial correlation).

[50] This correction is known by various names, including serial-correlation consistent standard errors, serial correlation and heteroskedasticity adjusted standard errors, robust standard errors, and Hansen–White standard errors. Analysts may also say that they use the Newey–West method for computing robust standard errors.

[51] We do not always use Hansen's method to correct for serial correlation and heteroskedasticity because sometimes the errors of a regression are not serially correlated.

TABLE 8	Results from Regressing T-Bill Returns on Predicted Inflation (Standard Errors Corrected for Conditional Heteroskedasticity and Serial Correlation)		
	Coefficient	**Standard Error**	**t-Statistic**
Intercept	0.0304	0.0069	4.4106
Inflation prediction	0.8774	0.1729	5.0730
Residual standard error		0.0220	
Multiple R-squared		0.4640	
Observations		137	
Durbin–Watson statistic		0.4673	

Source: Federal Reserve Bank of Philadelphia, U.S. Department of Commerce.

Now suppose we want to test our original null hypothesis (the Fisher effect) that the coefficient on the predicted inflation term equals 1 (H_0: $b_1 = 1$) against the alternative that the coefficient on the inflation term is not equal to 1 (H_a: $b_1 \neq 1$). With the corrected standard errors, the value of the test statistic for this null hypothesis is

$$\frac{\hat{b}_1 - b_1}{s_{\hat{b}_1}} = \frac{0.8774 - 1}{0.1729} = -0.7091$$

The critical values for both the 0.05 and 0.01 significance level are much larger than 0.7091 (absolute value of the t-test statistic), so we cannot reject the null hypothesis.

In this particular case, our conclusion about the Fisher effect was not affected by serial correlation, but the standard error on the slope coefficient after taking into account serial correlation and conditional heteroskedasticity (0.1729) is more than double the OLS standard error (0.0812). Therefore, for some hypotheses, serial correlation and conditional heteroskedasticity could have had a big effect on whether we accepted or rejected those hypotheses.[52]

4.3 Multicollinearity

The second assumption of the multiple linear regression model is that no exact linear relationship exists between two or more of the independent variables. When one of the independent variables is an exact linear combination of other independent variables, it becomes mechanically impossible to estimate the regression. That case, known as perfect collinearity, is much less of a practical concern than multicollinearity.[53] **Multicollinearity** occurs when two or more

---

[52] Serial correlation can also affect forecast accuracy.

[53] To give an example of perfect collinearity, suppose we tried to explain a company's credit ratings with a regression that included net sales, cost of goods sold, and gross profit as independent variables. Because Gross profit = Net sales − Cost of goods sold by definition, there is an exact linear relationship between these variables. This type of blunder is relatively obvious (and easy to avoid).

independent variables (or combinations of independent variables) are highly (but not perfectly) correlated with each other. With multicollinearity we can estimate the regression, but the interpretation of the regression output becomes problematic. Multicollinearity is a serious practical concern because approximate linear relationships among financial variables are common.

4.3.1 The Consequences of Multicollinearity

Although the presence of multicollinearity does not affect the consistency of the OLS estimates of the regression coefficients, the estimates become extremely imprecise and unreliable. Furthermore, it becomes practically impossible to distinguish the individual impacts of the independent variables on the dependent variable. These consequences are reflected in inflated OLS standard errors for the regression coefficients. With inflated standard errors, t-tests on the coefficients have little power (ability to reject the null hypothesis).

4.3.2 Detecting Multicollinearity

In contrast to the cases of heteroskedasticity and serial correlation, we shall not provide a formal statistical test for multicollinearity. In practice, multicollinearity is often a matter of degree rather than of absence or presence.[54]

The analyst should be aware that using the magnitude of pairwise correlations among the independent variables to assess multicollinearity, as has occasionally been suggested, is generally not adequate. Although very high pairwise correlations among independent variables can indicate multicollinearity, it is not necessary for such pairwise correlations to be high for there to be a problem of multicollinearity.[55] Stated another way, high pairwise correlations among the independent variables are not a necessary condition for multicollinearity, and low pairwise correlations do not mean that multicollinearity is not a problem. The only case in which correlation between independent variables may be a reasonable indicator of multicollinearity occurs in a regression with exactly two independent variables.

The classic symptom of multicollinearity is a high R^2 (and significant F-statistic) even though the t-statistics on the estimated slope coefficients are not significant. The insignificant t-statistics reflect inflated standard errors. Although the coefficients might be estimated with great imprecision, as reflected in low t-statistics, the independent variables *as a group* may do a good job of explaining the dependent variable, and a high R^2 would reflect this effectiveness. Example 9 illustrates this diagnostic.

EXAMPLE 9

Multicollinearity in Explaining Returns to the Fidelity Select Technology Fund

In Example 3 we regressed returns to the Fidelity Select Technology Fund (FSPTX) on returns to the S&P 500/BARRA Growth Index and the S&P 500/BARRA Value Index. Table 9 shows the results of our

---

[54] See Kmenta (1986).

[55] Even if pairs of independent variables have low correlation, there may be linear combinations of the independent variables that are very highly correlated, creating a multicollinearity problem.

TABLE 9   Results from Regressing the FSPTX Returns on the S&P 500/BARRA Growth and Value Indexes

	Coefficient	Standard Error	t-Statistic
Intercept	0.0079	0.0091	0.8635
S&P 500/BARRA Growth Index	2.2308	0.2299	9.7034
S&P 500/BARRA Value Index	−0.4143	0.2597	−1.5953

ANOVA	df	SS	MSS	F	Significance F
Regression	2	0.8649	0.4324	86.4483	5.48E-18
Residual	57	0.2851	0.0050		
Total	59	1.1500			

Residual standard error	0.0707
Multiple R-squared	0.7521
Observations	60

Source: Ibbotson Associates.

regression, which uses data from January 1998 through December 2002. The t-statistic of 9.7034 on the growth index return is greater than 2.0, indicating that the coefficient on the growth index differs significantly from 0 at standard significance levels. On the other hand, the t-statistic on the value index return is −1.5953 and thus is not statistically significant. This result suggests that the returns to the FSPTX are linked to the returns to the growth index and not closely associated with the returns to the value index. The coefficient on the growth index, however, is 2.23. This result implies that returns on the FSPTX are more volatile than are returns on the growth index.

Note also that this regression explains a significant amount of the variation in the returns to the FSPTX. Specifically, the R^2 from this regression is 0.7521. Thus approximately 75 percent of the variation in the returns to the FSPTX is explained by returns to the S&P 500/BARRA growth and value indexes.

Now suppose we run another linear regression that adds returns to the S&P 500 itself to the returns to the S&P 500/BARRA Growth and Value indexes. The S&P 500 includes the component stocks of these two style indexes, so we are introducing a severe multicollinearity problem.

Table 10 shows the results of that regression. Note that the R^2 in this regression has changed almost imperceptibly from the R^2 in the previous regression (increasing from 0.7521 to 0.7539), but now the standard errors of the coefficients are much larger. Adding the return to the S&P 500 to the previous regression does not explain any more of the variance in the returns to the FSPTX than the previous regression did, but now none of the coefficients is statistically significant. This is the classic case of multicollinearity mentioned in the reading.

TABLE 10   Results from Regressing the FSPTX Returns on Returns to the S&P 500/BARRA Growth and Value Indexes and the S&P 500 Index

	Coefficient	Standard Error	t-Statistic
Intercept	0.0072	0.0092	0.7761
S&P 500/BARRA Growth Index	−1.1324	5.2443	−0.2159
S&P 500/BARRA Value Index	−3.4912	4.8004	−0.7273
S&P 500 Index	6.4436	10.0380	0.6419

ANOVA	df	SS	MSS	F	Significance F
Regression	3	0.8670	0.2890	57.1751	4.73E-17
Residual	56	0.2830	0.0051		
Total	59	1.1500			

Residual standard error	0.0711
Multiple R-squared	0.7539
Observations	60

Source: Ibbotson Associates.

Multicollinearity may be a problem even when we do not observe the classic symptom of insignificant *t*-statistics but a highly significant *F*-test. Advanced textbooks provide further tools to help diagnose multicollinearity.[56]

4.3.3 Correcting for Multicollinearity

The most direct solution to multicollinearity is excluding one or more of the regression variables. In the example above, we can see that the S&P 500 total returns should not be included if both the S&P 500/BARRA Growth and Value Indexes are included, because the returns to the entire S&P 500 Index are a weighted average of the return to growth stocks and value stocks. In many cases, however, no easy solution is available to the problem of multicollinearity, and you will need to experiment with including or excluding different independent variables to determine the source of multicollinearity.

4.4 Heteroskedasticity, Serial Correlation, Multicollinearity: Summarizing the Issues

We have discussed some of the problems that heteroskedasticity, serial correlation, and multicollinearity may cause in interpreting regression results. These violations of regression assumptions, we have noted, all lead to problems in

---

[56] See Greene (2003).

TABLE 11   Problems in Linear Regression and Their Solutions

Problem	Effect	Solution
Heteroskedasticity	Incorrect standard errors	Use robust standard errors (corrected for conditional heteroskedasticity)
Serial correlation	Incorrect standard errors (additional problems if a lagged value of the dependent variable is used as an independent variable)	Use robust standard errors (corrected for serial correlation)
Multicollinearity	High R^2 and low t-statistics	Remove one or more independent variables; often no solution based in theory

making valid inferences. The analyst should check that model assumptions are fulfilled before interpreting statistical tests.

Table 11 gives a summary of these problems, the effect they have on the linear regression results (an analyst can see these effects using regression software), and the solutions to these problems.

5 MODEL SPECIFICATION AND ERRORS IN SPECIFICATION

Until now, we have assumed that whatever regression model we estimate is correctly specified. **Model specification** refers to the set of variables included in the regression and the regression equation's functional form. In the following, we first give some broad guidelines for correctly specifying a regression. Then we turn to three types of model misspecification: misspecified functional form, regressors that are correlated with the error term, and additional time-series misspecification. Each of these types of misspecification invalidates statistical inference using OLS; most of these misspecifications will cause the estimated regression coefficients to be inconsistent.

5.1 Principles of Model Specification

In discussing the principles of model specification, we need to acknowledge that there are competing philosophies about how to approach model specification. Furthermore, our purpose for using regression analysis may affect the specification we choose. The following principles have fairly broad application, however.

► *The model should be grounded in cogent economic reasoning.* We should be able to supply the economic reasoning behind the choice of variables, and the reasoning should make sense. When this condition is fulfilled, we increase the chance that the model will have predictive value with new data. This approach contrasts to the variable-selection process known as **data mining**. With data mining, the investigator essentially develops a model that maximally exploits the characteristics of a specific dataset.

▶ *The functional form chosen for the variables in the regression should be appropriate given the nature of the variables.* As one illustration, consider studying mutual fund **market timing** based on fund and market returns alone. One might reason that for a successful timer, a plot of mutual fund returns against market returns would show curvature, because a successful timer would tend to increase (decrease) beta when market returns were high (low). The model specification should reflect the expected nonlinear relationship.[57] In other cases, we may transform the data such that a regression assumption is better satisfied.

▶ *The model should be parsimonious.* In this context, "parsimonious" means accomplishing a lot with a little. We should expect each variable included in a regression to play an essential role.

▶ *The model should be examined for violations of regression assumptions before being accepted.* We have already discussed detecting the presence of heteroskedasticity, serial correlation, and multicollinearity. As a result of such diagnostics, we may conclude that we need to revise the set of included variables and/or their functional form.

▶ *The model should be tested and be found useful out of sample before being accepted.* The term "out of sample" refers to observations outside the dataset on which the model was estimated. A plausible model may not perform well out of sample because economic relationships have changed since the sample period. That possibility is itself useful to know. A second explanation, however, may be that relationships have not changed but that the model explains only a specific dataset.

Having given some broad guidance on model specification, we turn to a discussion of specific model specification errors. Understanding these errors will help an analyst develop better models and be a more informed consumer of investment research.

5.2 Misspecified Functional Form

Whenever we estimate a regression, we must assume that the regression has the correct functional form. This assumption can fail in several ways:

▶ One or more important variables could be omitted from regression.

▶ One or more of the regression variables may need to be transformed (for example, by taking the natural logarithm of the variable) before estimating the regression.

▶ The regression model pools data from different samples that should not be pooled.

---

[57] This example is based on Treynor and Mazuy (1966), an early regression study of mutual fund timing. To capture curvature, they included a term in the squared market excess return, which does not violate the assumption of the multiple linear regression model that relationship between the dependent and independent variables is linear *in the coefficients*.

First, consider the effects of omitting an important independent variable from a regression (omitted variable bias). If the true regression model was

$$Y_i = b_0 + b_1 X_{1i} + b_2 X_{2i} + \epsilon_i \tag{7}$$

but we estimate the model[58]

$$Y_i = a_0 + a_1 X_{1i} + \epsilon_i$$

then our regression model would be misspecified. What is wrong with the model?

If the omitted variable (X_2) is correlated with the remaining variable (X_1), then the error term in the model will be correlated with (X_1), and the estimated values of the regression coefficients a_0 and a_1 would be biased and inconsistent. In addition, the estimates of the standard errors of those coefficients will also be inconsistent, so we can use neither the coefficients estimates nor the estimated standard errors to make statistical tests.

EXAMPLE 10

Omitted Variable Bias and the Bid–Ask Spread

In this example, we extend our examination of the bid–ask spread to show the effect of omitting an important variable from a regression. In Example 1, we showed that the natural logarithm of the ratio [(Bid–ask spread)/Price] was significantly related to both the natural logarithm of the number of market makers and the natural logarithm of the market capitalization of the company. We repeat Table 1 from Example 1 below.

TABLE 1   Results from Regressing ln(Bid–Ask Spread/Price) on ln(Number of Market Makers) and ln(Market Cap) (repeated)

	Coefficients	Standard Error	t-Statistic
Intercept	−0.7586	0.1369	−5.5416
ln(Number of NASDAQ market makers)	−0.2790	0.0673	−4.1427
ln(Company's market cap)	−0.6635	0.0246	−27.0087

(Table continued on next page . . .)

---

[58] We use a different regression coefficient notation when X_{2i} is omitted, because the intercept term and slope coefficient on X_{1i} will generally not be the same as when X_{2i} is included.

TABLE 1 (continued)					
ANOVA	df	SS	MSS	F	Significance F
Regression	2	2,681.6482	1,340.8241	1,088.8325	0.00
Residual	1,816	2,236.2820	1.2314		
Total	1,818	4,917.9302			

Residual standard error	1.1097
Multiple R-squared	0.5453
Observations	1,819

Source: FactSet, NASDAQ.

If we did not include the natural log of market capitalization as an independent variable in the regression, and we regressed the natural logarithm of the ratio [(Bid–ask spread)/Price] only on the natural logarithm of the number of market makers for the stock, the results would be as shown in Table 12.

TABLE 12 Results from Regressing ln(Bid–Ask Spread/Price) on ln(Number of Market Makers)			
	Coefficients	Standard Error	*t*-Statistic
Intercept	−0.1229	0.1596	−0.7698
ln(Number of NASDAQ market makers)	−1.6629	0.0517	−32.1519

ANOVA	df	SS	MSS	F	Significance F
Regression	1	1,783.3549	1,783.3549	1,033.7464	0.00
Residual	1,817	3,134.5753	1.7251		
Total	1,818	4,917.9302			

Residual standard error	1.3134
Multiple R-squared	0.3626
Observations	1,819

Source: FactSet, NASDAQ.

Note that the coefficient on ln(Number of NASDAQ market makers) fell from -0.2790 in the original (correctly specified) regression to -1.6629 in the misspecified regression. Also, the intercept rose from -0.7586 in the correctly specified regression to -0.1229 in the misspecified regression. These results illustrate that omitting an independent variable that should be in the regression can cause the remaining regression coefficients to be inconsistent.

A second common cause of misspecification in regression models is the use of the wrong form of the data in a regression, when a transformed version of the data is appropriate. For example, sometimes analysts fail to account for curvature or nonlinearity in the relationship between the dependent variable and one or more of the independent variables, instead specifying a linear relation among variables. When we are specifying a regression model, we should consider whether economic theory suggests a nonlinear relation. We can often confirm the nonlinearity by plotting the data, as we will illustrate in Example 11 below. If the relationship between the variables becomes linear when one or more of the variables is represented as a proportional change in the variable, we may be able to correct the misspecification by taking the natural logarithm of the variable(s) we want to represent as a proportional change. Other times, analysts use unscaled data in regressions, when scaled data (such as dividing net income or cash flow by sales) are more appropriate. In Example 1, we scaled the bid–ask spread by stock price because what a given bid–ask spread means in terms of transactions costs for a given size investment depends on the price of the stock; if we had not scaled the bid–ask spread, the regression would have been misspecified.

EXAMPLE 11

Nonlinearity and the Bid–Ask Spread

In Example 1, we showed that the natural logarithm of the ratio [(Bid–ask spread)/Price] was significantly related to both the natural logarithm of the number of market makers and the natural logarithm of the company's market capitalization. But why did we take the natural logarithm of each of the variables in the regression? We began a discussion of this question in Example 1, which we continue now.

What does theory suggest about the nature of the relationship between the ratio (Bid–ask spread)/Price, or the percentage bid–ask spread, and its determinants (the independent variables)? Stoll (1978) builds a theoretical model of the determinants of percentage bid–ask spread in a dealer market. In his model, the determinants enter multiplicatively in a particular fashion. In terms of the independent variables introduced in Example 1, the functional form assumed is

$$[(\text{Bid–ask spread})/\text{Price}]_i = c(\text{Number of market makers})_i^{b_1} \times (\text{Market capitalization})_i^{b_2}$$

where c is a constant. The relationship of the percentage bid–ask spread with the number of market makers and market capitalization is not linear in the original variables.[59] If we take natural log of both sides of the above model, however, we have a log-log regression that is linear in the transformed variables:[60]

$$Y_i = b_0 + b_1 X_{1i} + b_2 X_{2i} + \epsilon_i$$

where

Y_i = the natural logarithm of the ratio (Bid–ask spread)/Price for stock i

b_0 = a constant that equals $\ln(c)$

X_{1i} = the natural logarithm of the number of market makers for stock i

X_{2i} = the natural logarithm of the market capitalization of company i

ϵ_i = the error term

As mentioned in Example 1, a slope coefficient in the log-log model is interpreted as an elasticity, precisely, the partial elasticity of the dependent variable with respect to the independent variable ("partial" means holding the other independent variables constant).

We can plot the data to assess whether the variables are linearly related after the logarithmic transformation. For example Figure 4 shows a scatterplot of the natural logarithm of the number of market makers for a stock (on the X axis) and the natural logarithm of (Bid–ask spread)/Price (on the Y axis), as well as a regression line showing the linear relation between the two transformed variables. The relation between the two transformed variables is clearly linear.

FIGURE 4   Linear Regression When Two Variables Have a Linear Relation

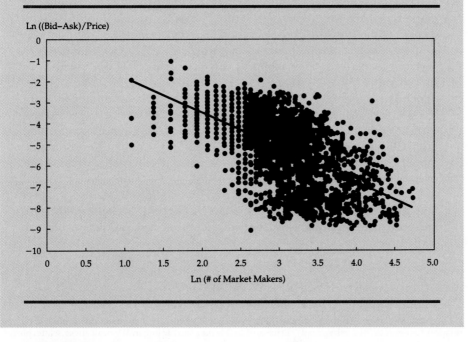

---

[59] The form of the model is analogous to the Cobb–Douglas production function in economics.

[60] We have added an error term to the model.

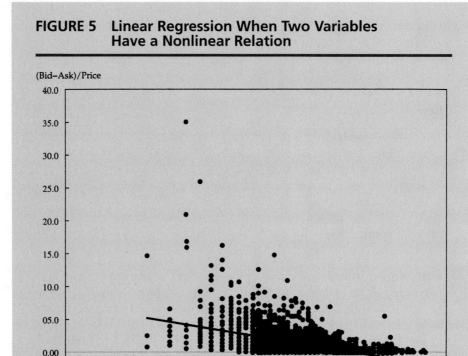

FIGURE 5 Linear Regression When Two Variables Have a Nonlinear Relation

If we do not take log of the ratio (Bid–ask spread)/Price, the plot is not linear. Figure 5 shows a plot of the natural logarithm of the number of market makers for a stock (on the X axis) and the ratio (Bid–ask spread)/Price (on the Y axis), as well as a regression line that attempts to show a linear relation between the two variables. We see that the relation between the two variables is very nonlinear.[61] Consequently, we should not estimate a regression with (Bid–ask spread)/Price as the dependent variable. Consideration of the need to ensure that predicted bid–ask spreads are positive would also lead us to not use (Bid–ask spread)/Price as the dependent variable. If we use the nontransformed ratio (Bid–ask spread)/Price as the dependent variable, the estimated model could predict negative values of the bid–ask spread. This result would be nonsensical; in reality, no bid–ask spread is negative (it is hard to motivate traders to simultaneously buy high and sell low), so a model that predicts negative bid–ask spreads is certainly misspecified.[62] We illustrate the problem of negative values of the predicted bid–ask spreads now.

---

[61] The relation between (Bid–ask spread)/Price and ln(Market cap) is also nonlinear, while the relation between ln(Bid–ask spread)/Price and ln(Market cap) is linear. We omit these scatterplots to save space.

[62] In our data sample, the bid–ask spread for each of the 1,819 companies is positive.

Table 13 shows the results of a regression with (Bid–ask spread)/ Price as the dependent variable and the natural logarithm of the number of market makers and the natural logarithm of the company's market capitalization as the independent variables.

TABLE 13 Results from Regressing Bid–Ask Spread/Price on ln(Number of Market Makers) and ln(Market Cap)

	Coefficients	Standard Error	t-Statistic
Intercept	0.0658	0.0024	27.6430
ln(Number of NASDAQ market makers)	−0.0045	0.0012	−3.8714
ln(Company's market cap)	−0.0068	0.0004	−15.8679

ANOVA	df	SS	MSS	F	Significance F
Regression	2	0.3185	0.1592	427.8174	0.00
Residual	1816	0.6760	0.0004		
Total	1818	0.9944			

Residual standard error	0.0193
Multiple R-squared	0.3203
Observations	1,819

Source: FactSet, NASDAQ.

Suppose that for a particular NASDAQ-listed stock, the number of market makers is 20 and the market capitalization is $5 billion. Therefore, the natural log of the number of market makers equals ln 20 = 2.9957 and the natural log of the stock's market capitalization (in millions) is ln 5,000 = 8.5172. In this case, the predicted ratio of bid–ask spread to price is 0.0658 + (2.9957 × − 0.0045) + (−0.0068 × 8.5172) = −0.0056. Therefore, the model predicts that the ratio of bid–ask spread to stock price is −0.0056 or −0.56 percent of the stock price. Thus the predicted bid–ask spread is negative, which does not make economic sense. This problem could be avoided by using log of (Bid–ask spread)/Price as the dependent variable.[63]

[63] Whether the natural log of the percentage bid–ask spread, Y, is positive or negative, the percentage bid–ask spread found as e^Y is positive, because a positive number raised to any power is positive. The constant e is positive ($e \approx 2.7183$).

Often, analysts must decide whether to scale variables before they compare data across companies. For example, in financial statement analysis, analysts often compare companies using **common size statements**. In a common size income statement, all the line items in a company's income statement are divided by the company's revenues.[64] Common size statements make comparability across companies much easier. An analyst can use common size statements to quickly compare trends in gross margins (or other income statement variables) for a group of companies.

Issues of comparability also appear for analysts who want to use regression analysis to compare the performance of a group of companies. Example 12 illustrates this issue.

EXAMPLE 12

Scaling and the Relation between Cash Flow from Operations and Free Cash Flow

Suppose an analyst wants to explain free cash flow to the firm as a function of cash flow from operations in 2001 for 11 family clothing stores in the United States with market capitalizations of more than $100 million as of the end of 2001.

To investigate this issue, the analyst might use free cash flow as the dependent variable and cash flow from operations as the independent variable in single-independent-variable linear regression. Table 14 shows the results of that regression. Note that the t-statistic for the slope coefficient for cash flow from operations is quite high (6.5288), the significance level for the F-statistic for the regression is very low (0.0001), and the R-squared is quite high. We might be tempted to believe that this regression is a success and that for a family clothing store, if cash flow from operations increased by $1.00, we could confidently predict that free cash flow to the firm would increase by $0.3579.

TABLE 14	Results from Regressing the Free Cash Flow on Cash Flow from Operations for Family Clothing Stores

	Coefficients	Standard Error	t-Statistic
Intercept	0.7295	27.7302	0.0263
Cash flow from operations	0.3579	0.0548	6.5288

ANOVA	df	SS	MSS	F	Significance F
Regression	1	245,093.7836	245,093.7836	42.6247	0.0001
Residual	9	51,750.3139	5,750.0349		
Total	10	296,844.0975			

(Table continued on next page . . .)

---

[64] For more on common size statements, see White, Sondhi, and Fried (2003). Free cash flow and cash flow from operations are discussed in Stowe, Robinson, Pinto, and McLeavey (2002).

TABLE 14 (continued)	
Residual standard error	75.8290
Multiple *R*-squared	0.8257
Observations	11

Source: Compustat.

But is this specification correct? The regression does not account for size differences among the companies in the sample.

We can account for size differences by using common size cash flow results across companies. We scale the variables by dividing cash flow from operations and free cash flow to the firm by the company's sales before using regression analysis. We will use (Free cash flow to the firm/Sales) as the dependent variable and (Cash flow from operations/Sales) as the independent variable. Table 15 shows the results of this regression. Note that the *t*-statistic for the slope coefficient on (Cash flow from operations/Sales) is 1.6262, so it is not significant at the 0.05 level. Note also that the significance level of the *F*-statistic is 0.1383, so we cannot reject at the 0.05 level the hypothesis that the regression does not explain variation in (Free cash flow/Sales) among family clothing stores. Finally, note that the *R*-squared in this regression is much lower than that of the previous regression.

TABLE 15 Results from Regressing the Free Cash Flow/Sales on Cash Flow from Operations/Sales for Family Clothing Stores

	Coefficient	Standard Error	*t*-Statistic
Intercept	−0.0121	0.0221	−0.5497
Cash flow from operations/Sales	0.4749	0.2920	1.6262

ANOVA	df	SS	MSS	F	Significance F
Regression	1	0.0030	0.0030	2.6447	0.1383
Residual	9	0.0102	0.0011		
Total	10	0.0131			

Residual standard error	0.0336
Multiple *R*-squared	0.2271
Observations	11

Source: Compustat.

> Which regression makes more sense? Usually, the scaled regression makes more sense. We want to know what happens to free cash flow (as a fraction of sales) if a change occurs in cash flow from operations (as a fraction of sales). Without scaling, the results of the regression can be based solely on scale differences across companies, rather than based on the companies' underlying economics.

A third common form of misspecification in regression models is pooling data from different samples that should not be pooled. This type of misspecification can best be illustrated graphically. Figure 6 shows two clusters of data on variables X and Y, with a fitted regression line. The data could represent the relationship between two financial variables at two stages of a company's growth, for example.

FIGURE 6   Plot of Two Series with Changing Means

In each cluster of data on X and Y, the correlation between the two variables is virtually 0. Because the means of both X and Y are different for the two clusters of data in the combined sample, X and Y are highly correlated. The correlation is spurious (misleading), however, because it reflects scale differences across companies.

5.3 Time-Series Misspecification (Independent Variables Correlated with Errors)

In the previous section, we discussed the misspecification that arises when a relevant independent variable is omitted from a regression. In this section, we discuss problems that arise from the kinds of variables included in the regression, particularly in a time-series context. In models that use time-series data to explain the relations among different variables, it is particularly easy to violate Regression Assumption 3, that the error term has mean 0, conditioned on the independent variables. If this assumption is violated, the estimated regression coefficients will be biased and inconsistent.

Three common problems that create this type of time-series misspecification are:

▶ including lagged dependent variables as independent variables in regressions with serially correlated errors;

▶ including a function of a dependent variable as an independent variable, sometimes as a result of the incorrect dating of variables; and

▶ independent variables that are measured with error.

The next examples demonstrate these problems.

Suppose that an analyst has estimated a linear regression with significant serial correlation in the errors. That serial correlation could be corrected by the methods discussed previously in this reading. Nevertheless, suppose that the analyst includes as an additional independent variable the first lagged value of the dependent variable. For example, the analyst might use the regression equation

$$Y_t = b_0 + b_1 X_{1t} + b_2 Y_{t-1} + \epsilon_t \qquad \textbf{(8)}$$

Because we assume that the error term is serially correlated, by definition the error term is correlated with the dependent variable. Consequently, the lagged dependent variable, Y_{t-1}, will be correlated with the error term, violating the assumption that the independent variables are uncorrelated with the error term. As a result, the estimates of the regression coefficients will be biased and inconsistent.

EXAMPLE 13

Fisher Effect with a Lagged Dependent Variable

In our discussion of serial correlation, we concluded from a test using the Durbin–Watson test that the error term in the Fisher effect equation (Equation 5) showed positive (first-order) serial correlation, using three-month T-bill returns as the dependent variable and inflation expectations of professional forecasters as the independent variable. Observations on the dependent and independent variables were quarterly. Table 16 modifies that regression by including the previous quarter's three-month T-bill returns as an additional independent variable.

TABLE 16   **Results from Regressing T-Bill Returns on Predicted Inflation and Lagged T-Bill Returns**

	Coefficient	Standard Error	*t*-Statistic
Intercept	0.0046	0.0040	1.5718
Inflation prediction	0.2753	0.0631	4.3610
Lagged T-bill return	0.7553	0.0495	15.2510
Residual standard error		0.0134	
Multiple *R*-squared		0.8041	
Observations		137	

Source: Federal Reserve Bank of Philadelphia, U.S. Department of Commerce.

At first glance, these regression results look very interesting—the coefficient on the lagged T-bill return appears to be highly significant. But on closer consideration, we must ignore these regression results, because the regression is fundamentally misspecified. As long as the error term is serially correlated, including lagged T-bill returns as an independent variable in the regression will cause all the coefficient estimates to be biased and inconsistent. Therefore, this regression is not usable for either testing a hypothesis or for forecasting.

A second common time-series misspecification in investment analysis is to forecast the past. What does that mean? If we forecast the future (say we predict at time t the value of variable Y in period $t + 1$), we must base our predictions on information we knew at time t. We could use a regression to make that forecast using the equation

$$Y_{t+1} = b_0 + b_1 X_{1t} + \epsilon_{t+1} \tag{9}$$

In this equation, we predict the value of Y in time $t + 1$ using the value of X in time t. The error term, ϵ_{t+1}, is unknown at time t and thus should be uncorrelated with X_{1t}.

Unfortunately, analysts sometimes use regressions that try to forecast the value of a dependent variable at time $t + 1$ based on independent variable(s) that are functions of the value of the dependent variable at time $t + 1$. In such a model, the independent variable(s) would be correlated with the error term, so the equation would be misspecified. As an example, an analyst may try to explain the cross-sectional returns for a group of companies during a particular year using the market-to-book ratio and the market capitalization for those companies at the end of the year.[65] If the analyst believes that such a regression predicts whether companies with high market-to-book ratios or high market capitalizations will have high returns, the analyst is mistaken. For any given period, the

---

[65] "Market-to-book ratio" is the ratio of price per share divided by book value per share.

higher the return during the period, the higher the market capitalization at the end of the period. It is also true that the higher the return during the period, the higher the market-to-book ratio at the end of the period. So in this case, if all the cross-sectional data come from period $t + 1$, a high value of the dependent variable (returns) actually causes a high value of the independent variables (market cap and market-to-book), rather than the other way around. In this type of misspecification, the regression model effectively includes the dependent variable on both the right- and left-hand sides of the regression equation.

The third common time-series misspecification arises when an independent variable is measured with error. Suppose a financial theory tells us that a particular variable X_t, such as expected inflation, should be included in the regression model. We do not observe X_t; instead, we observe actual inflation, $Z_t = X_t + u_t$, where u_t is an error term that is uncorrelated with X_t. Even in this best of circumstances, using Z_t in the regression instead of X_t will cause the regression coefficient estimates to be biased and inconsistent. Let's see why. If we want to estimate the regression

$$Y_t = b_0 + b_1 X_t + \epsilon_t$$

but we observe Z_t not X_t, then we would estimate

$$Y_t = b_0 + b_1 Z_t + (-b_1 u_t + \epsilon_t)$$

But because $Z_t = X_t + u_t$, Z_t is correlated with the error term $(-b_1 u_t + \epsilon_t)$. Therefore, our estimated model violates the assumption that the error term is uncorrelated with the independent variable. Consequently, the estimated regression coefficients will be biased and inconsistent.

EXAMPLE 14

The Fisher Effect with Measurement Error

Recall from Example 8 on the Fisher effect that we could not reject the hypothesis that three-month T-bill returns moved one-for-one with expected inflation.

TABLE 6 Results from Regressing T-Bill Returns on Predicted Inflation (repeated)

	Coefficient	Standard Error	t-Statistic
Intercept	0.0304	0.0040	7.6887
Inflation prediction	0.8774	0.0812	10.8096
Residual standard error	0.0220		
Multiple R-squared	0.4640		
Observations	137		
Durbin–Watson statistic	0.4673		

Source: Federal Reserve Bank of Philadelphia, U.S. Department of Commerce.

What if we used actual inflation instead of expected inflation as the independent variable? Note first that

$$\pi = \pi^e + \nu$$

where

π = actual rate of inflation
π^e = expected rate of inflation
ν = the difference between actual and expected inflation

Because actual inflation measures expected inflation with error, the estimators of the regression coefficients using T-bill yields as the dependent variable and actual inflation as the dependent variable will not be consistent.[66]

Table 17 shows the results of using actual inflation as the independent variable. The estimates in this table are quite different from those presented in the previous table. Note that the slope coefficient on actual inflation is much lower than the slope coefficient on predicted inflation in the previous regression. This result is an illustration of a general proposition: In a single-independent-variable regression, if we select a version of that independent variable that is measured with error, the estimated slope coefficient on that variable will be biased toward 0.[67]

TABLE 17 Results from Regressing T-Bill Returns on Actual Inflation

	Coefficient	Standard Error	t-Statistic
Intercept	0.0432	0.0034	12.7340
Actual inflation	0.5066	0.0556	9.1151
Residual standard error		0.0237	
Multiple R-squared		0.3810	
Observations		137	

Source: Federal Reserve Bank of Philadelphia, U.S. Department of Commerce.

[66] A consistent estimator is one for which the probability of estimates close to the value of the population parameter increases as sample size increases.

[67] This proposition does not generalize to regressions with more than one independent variable. Of course, we ignore serially-correlated errors in this example, but because the regression coefficients are inconsistent (due to measurement error), testing or correcting for serial correlation is not worthwhile.

5.4 Other Types of Time-Series Misspecification

By far the most frequent source of misspecification in linear regressions that use time series from two or more different variables is nonstationarity. Very roughly **nonstationarity** means that a variable's properties, such as mean and variance, are not constant through time. We will postpone our discussion about stationarity, but we can list some examples in which we need to use stationarity tests before we use regression statistical inference.[68]

▶ Relations among time series with trends (for example, the relation between consumption and GDP).

▶ Relations among time series that may be **random walks** (time series for which the best predictor of next period's value is this period's value). Exchange rates are often random walks.

The time-series examples in this reading were carefully chosen such that nonstationarity was unlikely to be an issue for any of them. But nonstationarity can be a very severe problem for analyzing the relations among two or more time series in practice. Analysts must understand these issues before they apply linear regression to analyzing the relations among time series. Otherwise, they may rely on invalid statistical inference.

MODELS WITH QUALITATIVE DEPENDENT VARIABLES

6

Financial analysts often need to be able to explain the outcomes of a qualitative dependent variable. **Qualitative dependent variables** are dummy variables used as dependent variables instead of as independent variables.

For example, to predict whether or not a company will go bankrupt, we need to use a qualitative dependent variable (bankrupt or not) as the dependent variable and use data on the company's financial performance (e.g., return on equity, debt-to-equity ratio, or debt rating) as independent variables. Unfortunately, linear regression is not the best statistical method to use for estimating such a model. If we use the qualitative dependent variable bankrupt (1) or not bankrupt (0) as the dependent variable in a regression with financial variables as the independent variables, the predicted value of the dependent variable could be much greater than 1 or much lower than 0. Of course, these results would be invalid. The probability of bankruptcy (or of anything, for that matter) cannot be greater than 100 percent or less than 0 percent. Instead of a linear regression model, we should use probit, logit, or discriminant analysis for this kind of estimation.

Probit and **logit models** estimate the probability of a discrete outcome given the values of the independent variables used to explain that outcome. The probit model, which is based on the normal distribution, estimates the probability that $Y = 1$ (a condition is fulfilled) given the value of the independent variable X. The logit model is identical, except that it is based on the logistic distribution rather than the normal distribution.[69] Both models must be estimated using maximum likelihood methods.[70]

---

[68] We include both unit root tests and tests for cointegration in the term "stationarity tests."

[69] The logistic distribution $e^{(b_0 + b_1 X)}/[1 + e^{(b_0 + b_1 X)}]$ is easier to compute than the cumulative normal distribution. Consequently, logit models gained popularity when computing power was expensive.

[70] For more on probit and logit models, see Greene (2003).

Another technique to handle qualitative dependent variables is **discriminant analysis**. In his Z-score and Zeta analysis, Altman (1968, 1977) reported on the results of discriminant analysis. Altman uses financial ratios to predict the qualitative dependent variable bankruptcy. Discriminant analysis yields a linear function, similar to a regression equation, which can then be used to create an overall score. Based on the score, an observation can be classified into the bankrupt or not bankrupt category.

Qualitative dependent variable models can be useful not only for portfolio management but also for business management. For example, we might want to predict whether a client is likely to continue investing in a company or to withdraw assets from the company. We might also want to explain how particular demographic characteristics might affect the probability that a potential investor will sign on as a new client, or evaluate the effectiveness of a particular direct-mail advertising campaign based on the demographic characteristics of the target audience. These issues can be analyzed with either probit or logit models.

EXAMPLE 15

Explaining Analyst Coverage

Suppose we want to investigate what factors determine whether at least one analyst covers a company. We can employ a probit model to address the question. The sample consists of 2,047 observations on public companies in 1999. All data come from Disclosure, Inc. The analyst coverage data on Disclosure come from I/B/E/S.

The variables in the probit model are as follows:

ANALYSTS = the discrete dependent variable, which takes on a value of 1 if at least one analyst covers the company and a value of 0 if no analysts cover the company

LNVOLUME = the natural log of trading volume in the most recent week

LNMV = the natural log of market value

ESTABLISHED = a dummy independent variable that takes on a value of 1 if the company's financial data has been audited for at least five years

LNTA = the natural log of total assets (book value)

LNSALES = the natural log of net sales

In this attempt to explain analyst coverage, the market (volume and value) and the book (value and sales) variables might be expected to explain coverage through various dimensions of size and, hence, importance.[71] The audit history variable reflects a possible comfort level that analysts could be expected to have with audited statements. The model includes three variables (LNMV, LNTA, and LNSALES) that we may expect to be correlated. Based on analysis not shown here, our probit regression did not exhibit the classic symptom of multicollinearity. Table 18 shows the results of the probit estimation.

---

[71] For more information on tests of multicollinearity, see Greene (2003).

TABLE 18   Explaining Analyst Coverage Using a Probit Model

	Coefficient	Standard Error	*t*-Statistic
Intercept	−7.9738	0.4362	−18.2815
LNVOLUME	0.1574	0.0158	9.9482
LNMV	0.4442	0.0369	12.0268
ESTABLISHED	0.3168	0.1045	3.0320
LNTA	0.0548	0.0296	1.8494
LNSALES	0.0507	0.0266	1.9059
Percent correctly predicted		73.67	

Source: Disclosure, Inc.

As Table 18 shows, three coefficients (besides the intercept) have *t*-statistics with an absolute value greater than 2.0. The coefficient on LNVOLUME has a *t*-statistic of 9.95. That value is far above the critical value at the 0.05 level for the *t*-statistic (1.96), so we can reject at the 0.05 level of significance the null hypothesis that the coefficient on LNVOLUME equals 0, in favor of the alternative hypothesis that the coefficient is not equal to 0. The second coefficient with an absolute value greater than 2 is LNMV, which has a *t*-statistic of 12.03. We can also reject at the 0.05 level of significance the null hypothesis that the coefficient on LNMV is equal to 0, in favor of the alternative hypothesis that the coefficient is not equal to 0. Finally, the coefficient on ESTABLISHED has a *t*-statistic of 3.03. We can reject at the 0.05 level of significance the null hypothesis that the coefficient on ESTABLISHED is equal to 0.

Neither of the two remaining independent variables is statistically significant at the 0.05 level in this probit analysis. Neither of the *t*-statistics on these two variables is larger in absolute value than 1.91, so neither one reaches the critical value of 1.96 needed to reject the null hypothesis (that the associated coefficient is significantly different from 0). This result shows that once we take into account a company's market value, trading volume, and the existence of a five-year audit history, the other factors—book value of assets and value of sales—have no power to explain whether at least one analyst will cover the company.

SUMMARY

In this reading, we have presented the multiple linear regression model and discussed violations of regression assumptions, model specification and misspecification, and models with qualitative variables.

▶ The general form of a multiple linear regression model is $Y_i = b_0 + b_1 X_{1i} + b_2 X_{2i} + \ldots + b_k X_{ki} + \epsilon_i$

▶ We conduct hypothesis tests concerning the population values of regression coefficients using t-tests of the form

$$t = \frac{\hat{b}_j - b_j}{s_{\hat{b}_j}}$$

▶ The lower the p-value reported for a test, the more significant the result.

▶ The assumptions of classical normal multiple linear regression model are as follows:

  1. A linear relation exists between the dependent variable and the independent variables.

  2. The independent variables are not random. Also, no exact linear relation exists between two or more of the independent variables.

  3. The expected value of the error term, conditioned on the independent variables, is 0.

  4. The variance of the error term is the same for all observations.

  5. The error term is uncorrelated across observations.

  6. The error term is normally distributed.

▶ To make a prediction using a multiple linear regression model, we take the following three steps:

  1. Obtain estimates of the regression coefficients.

  2. Determine the assumed values of the independent variables.

  3. Compute the predicted value of the dependent variable.

▶ When predicting the dependent variable using a linear regression model, we encounter two types of uncertainty: uncertainty in the regression model itself, as reflected in the standard error of estimate, and uncertainty about the estimates of the regression coefficients.

▶ The F-test is reported in an ANOVA table. The F-statistic is used to test whether at least one of the slope coefficients on the independent variables is significantly different from 0.

$$F = \frac{\text{RSS}/k}{\text{SSE}/[n - (k + 1)]} = \frac{\text{Mean regression sum of squares}}{\text{Mean squared error}}$$

Under the null hypothesis that all the slope coefficients are jointly equal to 0, this test statistic has a distribution of $F_{k, n - (k + 1)}$, where the regression has n observations and k independent variables. The F-test measures the overall significance of the regression.

▶ R^2 is nondecreasing in the number of independent variables, so it is less reliable as a measure of goodness of fit in a regression with more than one independent variable than in a one-independent-variable regression.

Analysts often choose to use adjusted R^2 because it does not necessarily increase when one adds an independent variable.

▶ Dummy variables in a regression model can help analysts determine whether a particular qualitative independent variable explains the model's dependent variable. A dummy variable takes on the value of 0 or 1. If we need to distinguish among n categories, the regression should include $n-1$ dummy variables. The intercept of the regression measures the average value of the dependent variable of the omitted category, and the coefficient on each dummy variable measures the average incremental effect of that dummy variable on the dependent variable.

▶ If a regression shows significant conditional heteroskedasticity, the standard errors and test statistics computed by regression programs will be incorrect unless they are adjusted for heteroskedasticity.

▶ One simple test for conditional heteroskedasticity is the Breusch–Pagan test. Breusch and Pagan showed that, under the null hypothesis of no conditional heteroskedasticity, nR^2 (from the regression of the squared residuals on the independent variables from the original regression) will be a χ^2 random variable with the number of degrees of freedom equal to the number of independent variables in the regression.

▶ The principal effect of serial correlation in a linear regression is that the standard errors and test statistics computed by regression programs will be incorrect unless adjusted for serial correlation. Positive serial correlation typically inflates the t-statistics of estimated regression coefficients as well as the F-statistic for the overall significance of the regression.

▶ The most commonly used test for serial correlation is based on the Durbin–Watson statistic. If the Durbin–Watson statistic differs sufficiently from 2, then the regression errors have significant serial correlation.

▶ Multicollinearity occurs when two or more independent variables (or combinations of independent variables) are highly (but not perfectly) correlated with each other. With multicollinearity, the regression coefficients may not be individually statistically significant even when the overall regression is significant as judged by the F-statistic.

▶ Model specification refers to the set of variables included in the regression and the regression equation's functional form. The following principles can guide model specification:

  ▶ The model should be grounded in cogent economic reasoning.

  ▶ The functional form chosen for the variables in the regression should be appropriate given the nature of the variables.

  ▶ The model should be parsimonious.

  ▶ The model should be examined for violations of regression assumptions before being accepted.

  ▶ The model should be tested and be found useful out of sample before being accepted.

▶ If a regression is misspecified, then statistical inference using OLS is invalid and the estimated regression coefficients may be inconsistent.

▶ Assuming that a model has the correct functional form, when in fact it does not, is one example of misspecification. There are several ways this assumption may be violated:

  ▶ One or more important variables could be omitted from the regression.

  ▶ One or more of the regression variables may need to be transformed before estimating the regression.

> ▶ The regression model pools data from different samples that should not be pooled.

▶ Another type of misspecification occurs when independent variables are correlated with the error term. This is a violation of Regression Assumption 3, that the error term has a mean of 0, and causes the estimated regression coefficients to be biased and inconsistent. Three common problems that create this type of time-series misspecification are:

▶ including lagged dependent variables as independent variables in regressions with serially correlated errors;

▶ including a function of dependent variable as an independent variable, sometimes as a result of the incorrect dating of variables; and

▶ independent variables that are measured with error.

▶ Probit and logit models estimate the probability of a discrete outcome (the value of a qualitative dependent variable, such as whether a company enters bankruptcy) given the values of the independent variables used to explain that outcome. The probit model, which is based on the normal distribution, estimates the probability that $Y = 1$ (a condition is fulfilled) given the values of the independent variables. The logit model is identical, except that it is based on the logistic distribution rather than the normal distribution.

PRACTICE PROBLEMS FOR READING 12

1. With many U.S. companies operating globally, the effect of the U.S. dollar's strength on a U.S. company's returns has become an important investment issue. You would like to determine whether changes in the U.S. dollar's value and overall U.S. equity market returns affect an asset's returns. You decide to use the S&P 500 Index to represent the U.S. equity market.

A. Write a multiple regression equation to test whether changes in the value of the dollar and equity market returns affect an asset's returns. Use the notations below.

R_{it} = return on the asset in period t

R_{Mt} = return on the S&P 500 in period t

ΔX_t = change in period t in the log of a trade-weighted index of the foreign exchange value of the U.S. dollar against the currencies of a broad group of major U.S. trading partners.

B. You estimate the regression for Archer Daniels Midland Company (NYSE: ADM). You regress its monthly returns for the period January 1990 to December 2002 on S&P 500 Index returns and changes in the log of the trade-weighted exchange value of the U.S. dollar. The table below shows the coefficient estimates and their standard errors.

Coefficient Estimates from Regressing ADM's Returns: Monthly Data, January 1990–December 2002

	Coefficient	Standard Error
Intercept	0.0045	0.0062
R_{Mt}	0.5373	0.1332
ΔX_t	−0.5768	0.5121
$n = 156$		

Source: FactSet, Federal Reserve Bank of Philadelphia.

Determine whether S&P 500 returns affect ADM's returns. Then determine whether changes in the value of the U.S. dollar affect ADM's returns. Use a 0.05 significance level to make your decisions.

C. Based on the estimated coefficient on R_{Mt}, is it correct to say that "for a 1 percentage point increase in the return on the S&P 500 in period t, we expect a 0.5373 percentage point increase in the return on ADM"?

2. One of the most important questions in financial economics is what factors determine the cross-sectional variation in an asset's returns. Some have argued that book-to-market ratio and size (market value of equity) play an important role.

A. Write a multiple regression equation to test whether book-to-market ratio and size explain the cross-section of asset returns. Use the notations below.

$$(B/M)_i = \text{book-to-market ratio for asset } i$$
$$R_i = \text{return on asset } i \text{ in a particular month}$$
$$\text{Size}_i = \text{natural log of the market value of equity for asset } i$$

B. The table below shows the results of the linear regression for a cross-section of 66 companies. The size and book-to-market data for each company are for December 2001. The return data for each company are for January 2002.

Results from Regressing Returns on the Book-to-Market Ratio and Size

	Coefficient	Standard Error
Intercept	0.0825	0.1644
$(B/M)_i$	−0.0541	0.0588
Size_i	−0.0164	0.0350
$n = 66$		

Source: FactSet.

Determine whether the book-to-market ratio and size are each useful for explaining the cross-section of asset returns. Use a 0.05 significance level to make your decision.

3. There is substantial cross-sectional variation in the number of financial analysts who follow a company. Suppose you hypothesize that a company's size (market cap) and financial risk (debt-to-equity ratios) influence the number of financial analysts who follow a company. You formulate the following regression model:

$$(\text{Analyst following})_i = b_0 + b_1 \text{Size}_i + b_2 (\text{D/E})_i + \epsilon_i$$

where

$(\text{Analyst following})_i$ = the natural log of $(1 + n)$, where n_i is the number of analysts following company i

Size_i = the natural log of the market capitalization of company i in millions of dollars

$(\text{D/E})_i$ = the debt-to-equity ratio for company$_i$

In the definition of Analyst following, 1 is added to the number of analysts following a company because some companies are not followed by any analysts, and the natural log of 0 is indeterminate. The following table gives the coefficient estimates of the above regression model for a randomly selected sample of 500 companies. The data are for the year 2002.

Coefficient Estimates from Regressing Analyst Following on Size and Debt-to-Equity Ratio			
	Coefficient	**Standard Error**	**t-Statistic**
Intercept	−0.2845	0.1080	−2.6343
Size_i	0.3199	0.0152	21.0461
$(\text{D/E})_i$	−0.1895	0.0620	−3.0565
$n = 500$			

Source: First Call/Thomson Financial, Compustat.

A. Consider two companies, both of which have a debt-to-equity ratio of 0.75. The first company has a market capitalization of $100 million, and the second company has a market capitalization of $1 billion. Based on the above estimates, how many more analysts will follow the second company than the first company?

B. Suppose the p-value reported for the estimated coefficient on $(\text{D/E})_i$ is 0.00236. State the interpretation of 0.00236.

4. In early 2001, U.S. equity marketplaces started trading all listed shares in minimal increments (ticks) of $0.01 (decimalization). After decimalization, bid–ask spreads of stocks traded on the NASDAQ tended to decline. In response, spreads of NASDAQ stocks cross-listed on the Toronto Stock Exchange (TSE) tended to decline as well. Researchers Oppenheimer and Sabherwal (2003) hypothesized that the percentage decline in TSE spreads of cross-listed stocks was related to company size, the predecimalization ratio of spreads on NASDAQ to those on the TSE, and the percentage decline in NASDAQ spreads. The following table gives the regression coefficient estimates from estimating that relationship for a sample of 74 companies. Company size is measured by the natural logarithm of the book value of company's assets in thousands of Canadian dollars.

Coefficient Estimates from Regressing Percentage Decline in TSE Spreads on Company Size, Predecimalization Ratio of NASDAQ to TSE Spreads, and Percentage Decline in NASDAQ Spreads

	Coefficient	t-Statistic
Intercept	−0.45	−1.86
$Size_i$	0.05	2.56
(Ratio of spreads)$_i$	−0.06	−3.77
(Decline in NASDAQ spreads)$_i$	0.29	2.42
$n = 74$		

Source: Oppenheimer and Sabherwal (2003).

The average company in the sample has a book value of assets of C$900 million and a predecimalization ratio of spreads equal to 1.3. Based on the above model, what is the predicted decline in spread on the TSE for a company with these average characteristics, given a 1 percent decline in NASDAQ spreads?

5. The "neglected-company effect" claims that companies that are followed
by fewer analysts will earn higher returns on average than companies that
are followed by many analysts. To test the neglected-company effect, you
have collected data on 66 companies and the number of analysts providing
earnings estimates for each company. You decide to also include size as an
independent variable, measuring size as the log of the market value of the
company's equity, to try to distinguish any small-company effect from a
neglected-company effect. The small-company effect asserts that
small-company stocks may earn average higher risk-adjusted returns than
large-company stocks.

The table below shows the results from estimating the model $R_i = b_0 +
b_1 \text{Size}_i + b_2 (\text{Number of analysts})_i + \epsilon_i$ for a cross-section of 66 companies.
The size and number of analysts for each company are for December 2001.
The return data are for January 2002.

Results from Regressing Returns on Size and Number of Analysts

	Coefficient	Standard Error	t-Statistic
Intercept	0.0388	0.1556	0.2495
Size$_i$	−0.0153	0.0348	−0.4388
(Number of analysts)$_i$	0.0014	0.0015	0.8995

ANOVA	df	SS	MSS
Regression	2	0.0094	0.0047
Residual	63	0.6739	0.0107
Total	65	0.6833	

Residual standard error	0.1034
R-squared	0.0138
Observations	66

Source: First Call/Thomson Financial, FactSet.

A. What test would you conduct to see whether the two independent
variables are *jointly* statistically related to returns ($H_0: b_1 = b_2 = 0$)?

B. What information do you need to conduct the appropriate test?

C. Determine whether the two variables jointly are statistically related to
returns at the 0.05 significance level.

D. Explain the meaning of adjusted R^2 and state whether adjusted R^2 for
the regression would be smaller than, equal to, or larger than 0.0138.

6. Some developing nations are hesitant to open their equity markets to foreign investment because they fear that rapid inflows and outflows of foreign funds will increase volatility. In July 1993, India implemented substantial equity market reforms, one of which allowed foreign institutional investors into the Indian equity markets. You want to test whether the volatility of returns of stocks traded on the Bombay Stock Exchange (BSE) increased after July 1993, when foreign institutional investors were first allowed to invest in India. You have collected monthly return data for the BSE from February 1990 to December 1997. Your dependent variable is a measure of return volatility of stocks traded on the BSE; your independent variable is a dummy variable that is coded 1 if foreign investment was allowed during the month and 0 otherwise.

You believe that market return volatility actually *decreases* with the opening up of equity markets. The table below shows the results from your regression.

Results from Dummy Regression for Foreign Investment in India with a Volatility Measure as the Dependent Variable

	Coefficient	Standard Error	t-Statistic
Intercept	0.0133	0.0020	6.5351
Dummy	−0.0075	0.0027	−2.7604
$n = 95$			

Source: FactSet.

A. State null and alternative hypotheses for the slope coefficient of the dummy variable that are consistent with testing your stated belief about the effect of opening the equity markets on stock return volatility.

B. Determine whether you can reject the null hypothesis at the 0.05 significance level (in a one-sided test of significance).

C. According to the estimated regression equation, what is the level of return volatility before and after the market-opening event?

7. Both researchers and the popular press have discussed the question as to which of the two leading U.S. political parties, Republicans or Democrats, is better for the stock market.

A. Write a regression equation to test whether overall market returns, as measured by the annual returns on the S&P 500 Index, tend to be higher when the Republicans or the Democrats control the White House. Use the notations below.

R_{Mt} = return on the S&P 500 Index in period t

$Party_t$ = the political party controlling the White House (1 for a Republican president; 0 for a Democratic president) in period t

B. The table below shows the results of the linear regression from Part A using annual data for the S&P 500 and a dummy variable for the party that controlled the White House. The data are from 1926 to 2002.

Results from Regressing S&P 500 Returns on a Dummy Variable for the Party That Controlled the White House, 1926–2002

	Coefficient	Standard Error	t-Statistic
Intercept	0.1494	0.0323	4.6270
$Party_t$	−0.0570	0.0466	−1.2242

ANOVA	df	SS	MSS	F	Significance F
Regression	1	0.0625	0.0625	1.4987	0.2247
Residual	75	3.1287	0.0417		
Total	76	3.1912			

Residual standard error	0.2042
R-squared	0.0196
Observations	77

Source: FactSet.

Based on the coefficient and standard error estimates, verify to two decimal places the t-statistic for the coefficient on the dummy variable reported in the table.

C. Determine at the 0.05 significance level whether overall U.S. equity market returns tend to differ depending on the political party controlling the White House.

8. Problem 3 addressed the cross-sectional variation in the number of financial analysts who follow a company. In that problem, company size and debt-to-equity ratios were the independent variables. You receive a suggestion that membership in the S&P 500 Index should be added to the model as a third independent variable; the hypothesis is that there is greater demand for analyst coverage for stocks included in the S&P 500 because of the widespread use of the S&P 500 as a benchmark.

A. Write a multiple regression equation to test whether analyst following is systematically higher for companies included in the S&P 500 Index. Also include company size and debt-to-equity ratio in this equation. Use the notations below.

$$(\text{Analyst following})_i = \text{natural log of } (1 + \text{Number of analysts following company } i)$$
$$\text{Size}_i = \text{natural log of the market capitalization of company } i \text{ in millions of dollars}$$
$$(\text{D/E})_i = \text{debt-to-equity ratio for company } i$$
$$\text{S\&P}_i = \text{inclusion of company } i \text{ in the S\&P 500 Index} \\ (1 \text{ if included, } 0 \text{ if not included})$$

In the above specification for analyst following, 1 is added to the number of analysts following a company because some companies are not followed by any analyst, and the natural log of 0 is indeterminate.

B. State the appropriate null hypothesis and alternative hypothesis in a two-sided test of significance of the dummy variable.

C. The following table gives estimates of the coefficients of the above regression model for a randomly selected sample of 500 companies. The data are for the year 2002. Determine whether you can reject the null hypothesis at the 0.05 significance level (in a two-sided test of significance).

Coefficient Estimates from Regressing Analyst Following on Size, Debt-to-Equity Ratio, and S&P 500 Membership, 2002

	Coefficient	Standard Error	t-Statistic
Intercept	−0.0075	0.1218	−0.0616
Size_i	0.2648	0.0191	13.8639
$(\text{D/E})_i$	−0.1829	0.0608	−3.0082
$\text{S\&P}_i$	0.4218	0.0919	4.5898
$n = 500$			

Source: First Call/Thomson Financial, Compustat.

D. Consider a company with a debt-to-equity ratio of 2/3 and a market capitalization of $10 billion. According to the estimated regression equation, how many analysts would follow this company if it were not included in the S&P 500 Index, and how many would follow if it were included in the index?

E. In Problem 3, using the sample, we estimated the coefficient on the size variable as 0.3199, versus 0.2648 in the above regression. Discuss whether there is an inconsistency in these results.

9. You believe there is a relationship between book-to-market ratios and subsequent returns. The output from a cross-sectional regression and a graph of the actual and predicted relationship between the book-to-market ratio and return are shown below.

Results from Regressing Returns on the Book-to-Market Ratio

	Coefficient	Standard Error	*t*-Statistic
Intercept	12.0130	3.5464	3.3874
$\left(\dfrac{\text{Book value}}{\text{Market value}}\right)_i$	−9.2209	8.4454	−1.0918

ANOVA	df	SS	MSS	F	Significance F
Regression	1	154.9866	154.9866	1.1921	0.2831
Residual	32	4162.1895	130.0684		
Total	33	4317.1761			

Residual standard error	11.4048
R-squared	0.0359
Observations	34

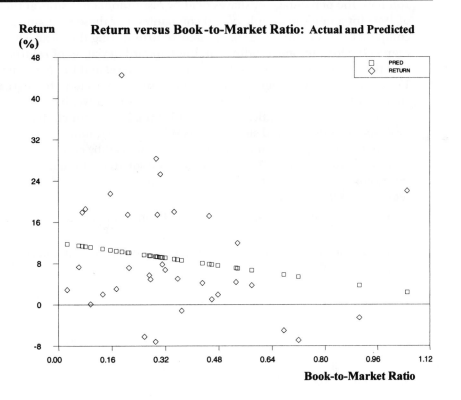

Return versus Book-to-Market Ratio: Actual and Predicted

A. You are concerned with model specification problems and regression assumption violations. Focusing on assumption violations, discuss symptoms of conditional heteroskedasticity based on the graph of the actual and predicted relationship.

B. Describe in detail how you could formally test for conditional heteroskedasticity in this regression.

C. Describe a recommended method for correcting for conditional heteroskedasticity.

10. You are examining the effects of the January 2001 NYSE implementation of the trading of shares in minimal increments (ticks) of $0.01 (decimalization). In particular, you are analyzing a sample of 52 Canadian companies cross-listed on both the NYSE and the Toronto Stock Exchange (TSE). You find that the bid–ask spreads of these shares decline on both exchanges after the NYSE decimalization. You run a linear regression analyzing the decline in spreads on the TSE, and find that the decline on the TSE is related to company size, predecimalization ratio of NYSE to TSE spreads, and decline in the NYSE spreads. The relationships are statistically significant. You want to be sure, however, that the results are not influenced by conditional heteroskedasticity. Therefore, you regress the squared residuals of the regression model on the three independent variables. The R^2 for this regression is 14.1 percent. Perform a statistical test to determine if conditional heteroskedasticity is present.

11. You are analyzing if institutional investors such as mutual funds and pension funds prefer to hold shares of companies with less volatile returns. You have the percentage of shares held by institutional investors at the end of 1998 for a random sample of 750 companies. For these companies, you compute the standard deviation of daily returns during that year. Then you regress the institutional holdings on the standard deviation of returns. You find that the regression is significant at the 0.01 level and the F-statistic is 12.98. The R^2 for this regression is 1.7 percent. As expected, the regression coefficient of the standard deviation of returns is negative. Its t-statistic is -3.60, which is also significant at the 0.01 level. Before concluding that institutions prefer to hold shares of less volatile stocks, however, you want to be sure that the regression results are not influenced by conditional heteroskedasticity. Therefore, you regress the squared residuals of the regression model on the standard deviation of returns. The R^2 for this regression is 0.6 percent.

A. Perform a statistical test to determine if conditional heteroskedasticity is present.

B. In view of your answer to Part A, what remedial action, if any, is appropriate?

12. In estimating a regression based on monthly observations from January 1987 to December 2002 inclusive, you find that the coefficient on the independent variable is positive and significant at the 0.05 level. You are concerned, however, that the t-statistic on the independent variable may be inflated because of serial correlation between the error terms. Therefore, you examine the Durbin–Watson statistic, which is 1.8953 for this regression.

A. Based on the value of the Durbin–Watson statistic, what can you say about the serial correlation between the regression residuals? Are they positively correlated, negatively correlated, or not correlated at all?

B. Compute the sample correlation between the regression residuals from one period and those from the previous period.

C. Perform a statistical test to determine if serial correlation is present. Assume that the critical values for 192 observations when there is a single independent variable are about 0.09 above the critical values for 100 observations.

13. The book-to-market ratio and the size of a company's equity are two factors that have been asserted to be useful in explaining the cross-sectional variation in subsequent returns. Based on this assertion, you want to estimate the following regression model:

$$R_i = b_0 + b_1 \left(\frac{\text{Book}}{\text{Market}} \right)_i + b_2 \text{Size}_i + \epsilon_i$$

where

R_i = Return of Company i's shares (in the following period)

$\left(\dfrac{\text{Book}}{\text{Market}} \right)_i$ = Company i's book-to-market ratio

Size_i = Market value of Company i's equity

A colleague suggests that this regression specification may be erroneous, because he believes that the book-to-market ratio may be strongly related to (correlated with) company size.

A. To what problem is your colleague referring, and what are its consequences for regression analysis?

B. With respect to multicollinearity, critique the choice of variables in the regression model above.

Regression of Return on Book-to-Market and Size

	Coefficient	Standard Error	*t*-Statistic
Intercept	14.1062	4.220	3.3427
$\left(\dfrac{\text{Book}}{\text{Market}}\right)_i$	−12.1413	9.0406	−1.3430
Size_i	−0.00005502	0.00005977	−0.92047
R-squared	0.06156		
Observations	34		

Correlation Matrix

	Book-to-Market Ratio	Size
Book-to-Market Ratio	1.0000	
Size	−0.3509	1.0000

C. State the classic symptom of multicollinearity and comment on that basis whether multicollinearity appears to be present, given the additional fact that the *F*-test for the above regression is not significant.

14. You are analyzing the variables that explain the returns on the stock of the Boeing Company. Because overall market returns are likely to explain a part of the returns on Boeing, you decide to include the returns on a value-weighted index of all the companies listed on the NYSE, AMEX, and NASDAQ as an independent variable. Further, because Boeing is a large company, you also decide to include the returns on the S&P 500 Index, which is a value-weighted index of the larger market-capitalization companies. Finally, you decide to include the changes in the U.S. dollar's value. To conduct your test, you have collected the following data for the period 1990–2002.

R_t = monthly return on the stock of Boeing in month t

R_{ALLt} = monthly return on a value-weighted index of all the companies listed on the NYSE, AMEX, and NASDAQ in month t

R_{SPt} = monthly return on the S&P 500 Index in month t

ΔX_t = change in month t in the log of a trade-weighted index of the foreign exchange value of the U.S. dollar against the currencies of a broad group of major U.S. trading partners

The following table shows the output from regressing the monthly return on Boeing stock on the three independent variables.

Regression of Boeing Returns on Three Explanatory Variables: Monthly Data, January 1990–December 2002			
	Coefficient	**Standard Error**	**t-Statistic**
Intercept	0.0026	0.0066	0.3939
R_{ALLt}	−0.1337	0.6219	−0.2150
R_{SPt}	0.8875	0.6357	1.3961
ΔX_t	0.2005	0.5399	0.3714

ANOVA	**df**	**SS**	**MSS**
Regression	3	0.1720	0.0573
Residual	152	0.8947	0.0059
Total	155	1.0667	

Residual standard error	0.0767
R-squared	0.1610
Observations	156

Source: FactSet, Federal Reserve Bank of Philadelphia.

From the *t*-statistics, we see that none of the explanatory variables is statistically significant at the 5 percent level or better. You wish to test, however, if the three variables *jointly* are statistically related to the returns on Boeing.

A. Your null hypothesis is that all three population slope coefficients equal 0—that the three variables *jointly* are statistically not related to the returns on Boeing. Conduct the appropriate test of that hypothesis.

B. Examining the regression results, state the regression assumption that may be violated in this example. Explain your answer.

C. State a possible way to remedy the violation of the regression assumption identified in Part B.

15. You are analyzing the cross-sectional variation in the number of financial analysts that follow a company (also the subject of Problems 3 and 8). You believe that there is less analyst following for companies with a greater debt-to-equity ratio and greater analyst following for companies included in the S&P 500 Index. Consistent with these beliefs, you estimate the following regression model.

$$(\text{Analyst following})_i = b_0 + b_1 (\text{D/E})_i + b_2 (\text{S\&P})_i + \epsilon_i$$

where

$$
\begin{aligned}
(\text{Analyst following})_i &= \text{natural log of } (1 + \text{Number of analysts following} \\
&\quad\ \text{company } i) \\
(\text{D/E})_i &= \text{debt-to-equity ratio for company } i \\
\text{S\&P}_i &= \text{inclusion of company } i \text{ in the S\&P 500 Index} \\
&\quad\ (1 \text{ if included; } 0 \text{ if not included})
\end{aligned}
$$

In the preceding specification, 1 is added to the number of analysts following a company because some companies are not followed by any analysts, and the natural log of 0 is indeterminate. The following table gives the coefficient estimates of the above regression model for a randomly selected sample of 500 companies. The data are for the year 2002.

Coefficient Estimates from Regressing Analyst Following on Debt-to-Equity Ratio and S&P 500 Membership, 2002			
	Coefficient	**Standard Error**	**t-Statistic**
Intercept	1.5367	0.0582	26.4038
$(\text{D/E})_i$	-0.1043	0.0712	-1.4649
$\text{S\&P}_i$	1.2222	0.0841	14.5327
$n = 500$			

Source: First Call/Thomson Financial, Compustat.

You discuss your results with a colleague. She suggests that this regression specification may be erroneous, because analyst following is likely to be also related to the size of the company.

A. What is this problem called, and what are its consequences for regression analysis?

B. To investigate the issue raised by your colleague, you decide to collect data on company size also. You then estimate the model after including an additional variable, $Size_i$, which is the natural log of the market capitalization of company i in millions of dollars. The following table gives the new coefficient estimates.

Coefficient Estimates from Regressing Analyst Following on Size, Debt-to-Equity Ratio, and S&P 500 Membership, 2002

	Coefficient	Standard Error	t-Statistic
Intercept	−0.0075	0.1218	−0.0616
$Size_i$	0.2648	0.0191	13.8639
$(D/E)_i$	−0.1829	0.0608	−3.0082
$S\&P_i$	0.4218	0.0919	4.5898
$n = 500$			

Source: First Call/Thomson Financial, Compustat.

What do you conclude about the existence of the problem mentioned by your colleague in the original regression model you had estimated?

16. You have noticed that hundreds of non-U.S. companies are listed not only on a stock exchange in their home market but also on one of the exchanges in the United States. You have also noticed that hundreds of non-U.S. companies are listed only in their home market and not in the United States. You are trying to predict whether or not a non-U.S. company will choose to list on a U.S. exchange. One of the factors that you think will affect whether or not a company lists in the United States is its size relative to the size of other companies in its home market.

A. What kind of a dependent variable do you need to use in the model?

B. What kind of a model should be used?

The following information relates to Questions 17–22

Gary Hansen is a securities analyst for a mutual fund specializing in small-capitalization growth stocks. The fund regularly invests in initial public offerings (IPOs). If the fund subscribes to an offer, it is allocated shares at the offer price. Hansen notes that IPOs frequently are underpriced, and the price rises when open market trading begins. The initial return for an IPO is calculated as the change in price on the first day of trading divided by the offer price. Hansen is developing a regression model to predict the initial return for IPOs. Based on past research, he selects the following independent variables to predict IPO initial returns:

Underwriter rank	=	1–10, where 10 is highest rank
Pre-offer price adjustment[a]	=	(Offer price−Initial filing price)/ Initial filing price
Offer size ($ millions)	=	Shares sold × Offer price
Fraction retained[a]	=	Fraction of total company shares retained by insiders

[a] Expressed as a decimal

Hansen collects a sample of 1,725 recent IPOs for his regression model. Regression results appear in Exhibit 1, and ANOVA results appear in Exhibit 2.

EXHIBIT 1	Hansen's Regression Results Dependent Variable: IPO Initial Return (Expressed in Decimal Form, i.e., 1% = 0.01)		
Variable	**Coefficient (b_j)**	**Standard Error**	**t-Statistic**
Intercept	0.0477	0.0019	25.11
Underwriter rank	0.0150	0.0049	3.06
Pre-offer price adjustment	0.4350	0.0202	21.53
Offer size	−0.0009	0.0011	−0.82
Fraction retained	0.0500	0.0260	1.92

EXHIBIT 2	Selected ANOVA Results for Hansen's Regression	
	Degrees of Freedom (df)	**Sum of Squares (SS)**
Regression	4	51.433
Residual	1,720	91.436
Total	1,724	142.869
	Multiple R-squared = 0.36	

Hansen wants to use the regression results to predict the initial return for an upcoming IPO. The upcoming IPO has the following characteristics:

► underwriter rank = 6;
► pre-offer price adjustment = 0.04;
► offer size = $40 million;
► fraction retained = 0.70.

Because he notes that the pre-offer price adjustment appears to have an important effect on initial return, Hansen wants to construct a 95 percent confidence interval for the coefficient on this variable. He also believes that for each 1 percent increase in pre-offer price adjustment, the initial return will increase by less than 0.5 percent, holding other variables constant. Hansen wishes to test this hypothesis at the 0.05 level of significance.

Before applying his model, Hansen asks a colleague, Phil Chang, to review its specification and results. After examining the model, Chang concludes that the model suffers from two problems: 1) conditional heteroskedasticity, and 2) omitted variable bias. Chang makes the following statements:

Statement 1:   "Conditional heteroskedasticity will result in consistent coefficient estimates, but both the t-statistics and F-statistic will be biased, resulting in false inferences."

Statement 2:   "If an omitted variable is correlated with variables already included in the model, coefficient estimates will be biased and inconsistent and standard errors will also be inconsistent."

Selected values for the t-distribution and F-distribution appear in Exhibits 3 and 4, respectively.

EXHIBIT 3	Selected Values for the t-Distribution (df = ∞)
Area in Right Tail	**t-Value**
0.050	1.645
0.025	1.960
0.010	2.326
0.005	2.576

EXHIBIT 4	Selected Values for the F-Distribution (α = 0.01) (df1/df2: Numerator/ Denominator Degrees of Freedom)	
	df1	
	4	∞
df2 4	16.00	13.50
∞	3.32	1.00

17. Based on Hansen's regression, the predicted initial return for the upcoming IPO is *closest* to:

  A. 0.0943.

  B. 0.1064.

  C. 0.1541.

18. The 95 percent confidence interval for the regression coefficient for the pre-offer price adjustment is *closest* to:

  A. 0.156 to 0.714.

  B. 0.395 to 0.475.

  C. 0.402 to 0.468.

19. The *most* appropriate null hypothesis and the *most* appropriate conclusion regarding Hansen's belief about the magnitude of the initial return relative to that of the pre-offer price adjustment (reflected by the coefficient b_j) are:

	Null Hypothesis	Conclusion about b_j (0.05 Level of Significance)
A.	$H_0: b_j = 0.5$	Reject H_0
B.	$H_0: b_j \geq 0.5$	Fail to reject H_0
C.	$H_0: b_j \geq 0.5$	Reject H_0

20. The *most* appropriate interpretation of the multiple R-squared for Hansen's model is that:

   A. unexplained variation in the dependent variable is 36 percent of total variation.

   B. correlation between predicted and actual values of the dependent variable is 0.36.

   C. correlation between predicted and actual values of the dependent variable is 0.60.

21. Is Chang's Statement 1 correct?

   A. Yes.

   B. No, because the model's F-statistic will not be biased.

   C. No, because the model's t-statistics will not be biased.

22. Is Chang's Statement 2 correct?

   A. Yes.

   B. No, because the model's coefficient estimates will be unbiased.

   C. No, because the model's coefficient estimates will be consistent.

The following information relates to Questions 23–28

Adele Chiesa is a money manager for the Bianco Fund. She is interested in recent findings showing that certain business condition variables predict excess U.S. stock market returns (one-month market return minus one-month T-bill return). She is also familiar with evidence showing how U.S. stock market returns differ by the political party affiliation of the U.S. President. Chiesa estimates a multiple regression model to predict monthly excess stock market returns accounting for business conditions and the political party affiliation of the U.S. President:

$$\text{Excess stock market return}_t$$
$$= a_0 + a_1 \text{Default spread}_{t-1} + a_2 \text{Term spread}_{t-1} + a_3 \text{Pres party dummy}_{t-1} + e_t$$

Default spread is equal to the yield on Baa bonds minus the yield on Aaa bonds. Term spread is equal to the yield on a 10-year constant-maturity U.S. Treasury index minus the yield on a 1-year constant-maturity U.S. Treasury index. Pres party dummy is equal to 1 if the U.S. President is a member of the Democratic Party and 0 if a member of the Republican Party.

Chiesa collects 432 months of data (all data are in percent form, i.e., 0.01 = 1 percent). The regression is estimated with 431 observations because the independent variables are lagged one month. The regression output is in Exhibit 1. Exhibits 2 through 5 contain critical values for selected test statistics.

EXHIBIT 1	Multiple Regression Output (the Dependent Variable Is the One-Month Market Return in Excess of the One-Month T-Bill Return)		
	Coefficient	*t*-Statistic	*p*-Value
Intercept	−4.60	−4.36	<0.01
Default spread$_{t-1}$	3.04	4.52	<0.01
Term spread$_{t-1}$	0.84	3.41	<0.01
Pres party dummy$_{t-1}$	3.17	4.97	<0.01

Number of observations = 431

Test statistic from Breusch–Pagan (BP) test = 7.35

$R^2 = 0.053$

Adjusted $R^2 = 0.046$

Durbin–Watson (DW) = 1.65

Sum of squared errors (SSE) = 19,048

Regression sum of squares (SSR) = 1,071

An intern working for Chiesa has a number of questions about the results in Exhibit 1:

Question 1: How do you test to determine whether the overall regression model is significant?

Question 2: Does the estimated model conform to standard regression assumptions? For instance, is the error term serially correlated, or is there conditional heteroskedasticity?

Question 3: How do you interpret the coefficient for the Pres party dummy variable?

Question 4: Default spread appears to be quite important. Is there some way to assess the precision of its estimated coefficient? What is the economic interpretation of this variable?

After responding to her intern's questions, Chiesa concludes with the following statement: "Predictions from Exhibit 1 are subject to parameter estimate uncertainty, but not regression model uncertainty."

EXHIBIT 2	Critical Values for the Durbin–Watson Statistic ($\alpha = 0.05$)

	K = 3	
N	d_l	d_u
420	1.825	1.854
430	1.827	1.855
440	1.829	1.857

EXHIBIT 3	Table of the Student's t-Distribution (One-Tailed Probabilities for df = ∞)

p	t
0.10	1.282
0.05	1.645
0.025	1.960
0.01	2.326
0.005	2.576

EXHIBIT 4	Values of χ^2

Probability in Right Tail

df	0.975	0.95	0.05	0.025
1	0.0001	0.0039	3.841	5.024
2	0.0506	0.1026	5.991	7.378
3	0.2158	0.3518	7.815	9.348
4	0.4840	0.7110	9.488	11.14

EXHIBIT 5	Table of the F-Distribution (Critical Values for Right-Hand Tail Area Equal to 0.05) Numerator: df1 and Denominator: df2

df2	df1				
	1	2	3	4	427
1	161	200	216	225	254
2	18.51	19.00	19.16	19.25	19.49
3	10.13	9.55	9.28	9.12	8.53
4	7.71	6.94	6.59	6.39	5.64
427	3.86	3.02	2.63	2.39	1.17

23. Regarding the intern's Question 1, is the regression model as a whole significant at the 0.05 level?

   A. No, because the calculated F-statistic is less than the critical value for F.

   B. Yes, because the calculated F-statistic is greater than the critical value for F.

   C. Yes, because the calculated χ^2 statistic is greater than the critical value for χ^2.

24. Which of the following is Chiesa's *best* response to Question 2 regarding serial correlation in the error term? At a 0.05 level of significance, the test for serial correlation indicates that there is:

   A. no serial correlation in the error term.

   B. positive serial correlation in the error term.

   C. negative serial correlation in the error term.

25. Regarding Question 3, the Pres party dummy variable in the model indicates that the mean monthly value for the excess stock market return is:

   A. 1.43 percent larger during Democratic presidencies than Republican presidencies.

   B. 3.17 percent larger during Democratic presidencies than Republican presidencies.

   C. 3.17 percent larger during Republican presidencies than Democratic presidencies.

26. In response to Question 4, the 95 percent confidence interval for the regression coefficient for the default spread is *closest* to:

   A. 0.13 to 5.95.

   B. 1.72 to 4.36.

   C. 1.93 to 4.15.

27. With respect to the default spread, the estimated model indicates that when business conditions are:

   A. strong, expected excess returns will be higher.

   B. weak, expected excess returns will be lower.

   C. weak, expected excess returns will be higher.

28. Is Chiesa's concluding statement correct regarding parameter model uncertainty and regression model uncertainty?

   A. Yes.

   B. No, predictions are not subject to parameter estimate uncertainty.

   C. No, predictions are subject to regression model uncertainty and parameter model uncertainty.

SOLUTIONS FOR READING 12

1. A. $R_{it} = b_0 + b_1 R_{Mt} + b_2 \Delta X_t + \epsilon_{it}$

B. We can test whether the coefficient on the S&P 500 Index returns is statistically significant. Our null hypothesis is that the coefficient is equal to 0 (H_0: $b_1 = 0$); our alternative hypothesis is that the coefficient is not equal to 0 (H_a: $b_1 \neq 0$). We construct the t-test of the null hypothesis as follows:

$$\frac{\hat{b}_1 - b_1}{s_{\hat{b}_1}} = \frac{0.5373 - 0}{0.1332} = 4.0338$$

where

$\hat{b}_1$ = regression estimate of b_1
b_1 = the hypothesized value of the coefficient (here, 0)
$s_{\hat{b}_1}$ = the estimated standard error of $\hat{b}_1$

Because this regression has 156 observations and three regression coefficients, the t-test has $156 - 3 = 153$ degrees of freedom. At the 0.05 significance level, the critical value for the test statistic is between 1.98 and 1.97. The absolute value of the test statistic is 4.0338; therefore, we can reject the null hypothesis that $b_1 = 0$.

Similarly, we can test whether the coefficient on the change in the value of the U.S. dollar is statistically significant in this regression. Our null hypothesis is that the coefficient is equal to 0 (H_0: $b_2 = 0$); our alternative hypothesis is that the coefficient is not equal to 0 (H_a: $b_2 \neq 0$). We construct the t-test as follows:

$$\frac{\hat{b}_2 - b_2}{s_{\hat{b}_2}} = \frac{-0.5768 - 0}{0.5121} = -1.1263$$

As before, the t-test has 153 degrees of freedom, and the critical value for the test statistic is between 1.98 and 1.97 at the 0.05 significance level. The absolute value of the test statistic is 1.1263; therefore, we cannot reject the null hypothesis that $b_2 = 0$.

Based on the above t-tests, we conclude that S&P 500 Index returns do affect ADM's returns but that changes in the value of the U.S. dollar do not affect ADM's returns.

C. The statement is not correct. To make it correct, we need to add the qualification "holding ΔX constant" to the end of the quoted statement.

2. A. $R_i = b_0 + b_1 (B/M)_i + b_2 Size_i + \epsilon_i$

B. We can test whether the coefficients on the book-to-market ratio and size are individually statistically significant using t-tests. For the book-to-market ratio, our null hypothesis is that the coefficient is equal to 0 (H_0: $b_1 = 0$); our alternative hypothesis is that the coefficient is not equal to 0 (H_a: $b_1 \neq 0$). We can test the null hypothesis using a t-test constructed as follows:

$$\frac{\hat{b}_1 - b_1}{s_{\hat{b}_1}} = \frac{-0.0541 - 0}{0.0588} = -0.9201$$

where

$\hat{b}_1$ = regression estimate of b_1

b_1 = the hypothesized value of the coefficient (here, 0)

$s_{\hat{b}_1}$ = the estimated standard error of $\hat{b}_1$

This regression has 66 observations and three coefficients, so the t-test has $66 - 3 = 63$ degrees of freedom. At the 0.05 significance level, the critical value for the test statistic is about 2.0. The absolute value of the test statistic is 0.9201; therefore, we cannot reject the null hypothesis that $b_1 = 0$. We can conclude that the book-to-market ratio is not useful in explaining the cross-sectional variation in returns for this sample.

We perform the same analysis to determine whether size (as measured by the log of the market value of equity) can help explain the cross-sectional variation in asset returns. Our null hypothesis is that the coefficient is equal to 0 (H_0: $b_2 = 0$); our alternative hypothesis is that the coefficient is not equal to 0 (H_a: $b_2 \neq 0$). We can test the null hypothesis using a t-test constructed as follows:

$$\frac{\hat{b}_2 - b_2}{s_{\hat{b}_2}} = \frac{-0.0164 - 0}{0.0350} = -0.4686$$

where

$\hat{b}_2$ = regression estimate of b_1

b_2 = the hypothesized value of the coefficient (here, 0)

$s_{\hat{b}_2}$ = the estimated standard error of $\hat{b}_2$

Again, because this regression has 66 observations and three coefficients, the t-test has $66 - 3 = 63$ degrees of freedom. At the 0.05 significance level, the critical value for the test statistic is about 2.0. The absolute value of the test statistic is 0.4686; therefore, we cannot reject the null hypothesis that $b_2 = 0$. We can conclude that asset size is not useful in explaining the cross-sectional variation of asset returns in this sample.

3. A. The estimated regression is (Analyst following)$_i$ = $-0.2845 +$ $0.3199 \text{Size}_i - 0.1895 (\text{D}/\text{E})_i + \epsilon_i$. Therefore, the prediction for the first company is

$$\begin{aligned} (\text{Analyst following})_i &= -0.2845 + 0.3199(\ln 100) - 0.1895(0.75) \\ &= -0.2845 + 1.4732 - 0.1421 = 1.0466 \end{aligned}$$

Recalling that (Analyst following)$_i$ is the natural log of $(1 + n_i)$, where n_i is the number of analysts following company i; it follows that $1 + n_1 = e^{1.0466} = 2.848$, approximately. Therefore, $n_1 = 2.848 - 1 = 1.848$, or about two analysts. Similarly, the prediction for the second company is as follows:

$$\begin{aligned} (\text{Analyst following})_i &= -0.2845 + 0.3199(\ln 1,000) - 0.1895(0.75) \\ &= -0.2845 + 2.2098 - 0.1421 = 1.7832 \\ &= 1.7832 \end{aligned}$$

Thus, $1 + n_2 = e^{1.7832} = 5.949$, approximately. Therefore, $n_2 = 5.949 - 1 = 4.949$, or about five analysts.

The model predicts that $5 - 2 = 3$ more analysts will follow the second company than the first company.

B. We would interpret the p-value of 0.00236 as the smallest level of significance at which we can reject a null hypothesis that the population value of the coefficient is 0, in a two-sided test. Clearly, in this regression the debt-to-equity ratio is a highly significant variable.

4. The estimated model is

Percentage decline in TSE spread of company i
$$= -0.45 + 0.05\text{Size}_i - 0.06(\text{Ratio of spreads})_i$$
$$+ 0.29(\text{Decline in NASDAQ spreads})_i$$

Therefore, the prediction is

Percentage decline in TSE spread
$$= -0.45 + 0.05(\ln 900,000) - 0.06(1.3) + 0.29(1)$$
$$= -0.45 + 0.69 - 0.08 + 0.29 = 0.45$$

The model predicts that for a company with average sample characteristics, the spread on the TSE declines by 0.45 percent for a 1 percent decline in NASDAQ spreads.

5. A. To test the null hypothesis that all the slope coefficients in the regression model are equal to 0 ($H_0: b_1 = b_2 = 0$) against the alternative hypothesis that at least one slope coefficient is not equal to 0, we must use an F-test.

B. To conduct the F-test, we need four inputs, all of which are found in the ANOVA section of the table in the statement of the problem:

   i. total number of observations, n

   ii. total number of regression coefficients to be estimated, $k + 1$

   iii. sum of squared errors or residuals, $\sum_{i=1}^{n}(Y_i - \hat{Y}_i)^2$ abbreviated SSE, and

   iv. regression sum of squares, $\sum_{i=1}^{n}(\hat{Y}_i - \overline{Y})^2$, abbreviated RSS

C. The F-test formula is

$$F = \frac{\text{RSS}/k}{\text{SSE}/[n - (k + 1)]} = \frac{0.0094/2}{0.6739/[66 - (2 + 1)]} = 0.4394$$

The F-statistic has degrees of freedom $F\{k, [n - (k + 1)]\} = F(2, 63)$. From the F-test table, for the 0.05 significance level, the critical value for $F(2, 63)$ is about 3.15, so we cannot reject the hypothesis that the slope coefficients are both 0. The two independent variables are jointly statistically unrelated to returns.

D. Adjusted R^2 is a measure of goodness of fit that takes into account the number of independent variables in the regression, in contrast to R^2. We can assert that adjusted R^2 is smaller than $R^2 = 0.0138$ without the need to perform any calculations. (However, adjusted R^2 can be shown to equal -0.0175 using an expression in the text on the relationship between adjusted R^2 and R^2.)

6. A. You believe that opening markets actually reduces return volatility; if that belief is correct, then the slope coefficient would be negative, $b_1 < 0$. The null hypothesis is that the belief is not true: $H_0: b_1 \geq 0$. The alternative hypothesis is that the belief is true: $H_a: b_1 < 0$.

B. The critical value for the t-statistic with $95 - 2 = 93$ degrees of freedom at the 0.05 significance level in a one-sided test is about 1.66. For the one-sided test stated in Part A, we reject the null hypothesis if the t-statistic on the slope coefficient is less than -1.66. As the t-statistic of $-2.7604 < -1.66$, we reject the null. Because the dummy variable takes on a value of 1 when foreign investment is allowed, we can conclude that the volatility was lower with foreign investment.

C. According to the estimated regression, average return volatility was 0.0133 (the estimated value of the intercept) before July 1993 and $0.0058 (= 0.0133 - 0.0075)$ after July 1993.

7. A. The appropriate regression model is $R_{Mt} = b_0 + b_1 \text{Party}_t + \epsilon_t$.

B. The t-statistic reported in the table for the dummy variable tests whether the coefficient on Party_t is significantly different from 0. It is computed as follows:

$$\frac{\hat{b}_1 - b_1}{s_{\hat{b}_1}} = \frac{-0.0570 - 0}{0.0466} = -1.22$$

where

$\hat{b}_1$ = regression estimate of b_1
b_1 = the hypothesized value of the coefficient (here, 0)
$s_{\hat{b}_1}$ = the estimated standard error of $\hat{b}_1$

To two decimal places, this value is the same as the t-statistic reported in the table for the dummy variable, as expected. The problem specified two decimal places because the reported regression output reflects rounding; for this reason, we often cannot exactly reproduce reported t-statistics.

C. Because the regression has 77 observations and two coefficients, the t-test has $77 - 2 = 75$ degrees of freedom. At the 0.05 significance level, the critical value for the two-tailed test statistic is about 1.99. The absolute value of the test statistic is 1.2242; therefore, we do not reject the null hypothesis that $b_1 = 0$. We can conclude that the political party in the White House does not, on average, affect the annual returns of the overall market as measured by the S&P 500.

8. A. The regression model is as follows:

$$(\text{Analyst following})_i = b_0 + b_1 \text{Size}_i + b_2 (\text{D/E})_i + b_3 \text{S\&P}_i + \epsilon_i$$

where $(\text{Analyst following})_i$ is the natural log of $(1 + \text{number of analysts following company } i)$; Size_i is the natural log of the market capitalization of company i in millions of dollars; $(\text{D/E})_i$ is the debt-to-equity ratio for company i, and $\text{S\&P}_i$ is a dummy variable with a value of 1 if the company i belongs to the S&P 500 Index and 0 otherwise.

B. The appropriate null and alternative hypotheses are H_0: $b_3 = 0$ and H_a: $b_3 \neq 0$, respectively.

C. The t-statistic to test the null hypothesis can be computed as follows:

$$\frac{\hat{b}_3 - b_3}{s_{\hat{b}_3}} = \frac{0.4218 - 0}{0.0919} = 4.5898$$

This value is, of course, the same as the value reported in the table. The regression has 500 observations and 4 regression coefficients, so the t-test has $500 - 4 = 496$ degrees of freedom. At the 0.05 significance level, the critical value for the test statistic is between 1.96 and 1.97. Because the value of the test statistic is 4.5898 we can reject the null hypothesis that $b_3 = 0$. Thus a company's membership in the S&P 500 appears to significantly influence the number of analysts who cover that company.

D. The estimated model is

$$(\text{Analyst following})_i = -0.0075 + 0.2648\text{Size}_i - 0.1829(\text{D/E})_i \\ + 0.4218\text{S\&P}_i + \epsilon_i$$

Therefore the prediction for number of analysts following the indicated company that is not part of the S&P 500 Index is

$$\begin{aligned}(\text{Analyst following})_i &= -0.0075 + 0.2648(\text{In } 10{,}000) \\ &\quad - 0.1829(2/3) + 0.4218(0) \\ &= -0.0075 + 2.4389 - 0.1219 + 0 = 2.3095\end{aligned}$$

Recalling that $(\text{Analyst following})_i$ is the natural log of $(1 + n_i)$, where n_i is the number of analysts following company i; it ensues (coding the company under consideration as 1) that $1 + n_1 = e^{2.3095} = 10.069$, approximately. Therefore, the prediction is that $n_1 = 10.069 - 1 = 9.069$, or about nine analysts.

Similarly, the prediction for the company that is included in the S&P 500 Index is

$$\begin{aligned}(\text{Analyst following})_i &= -0.0075 + 0.2648(\text{In } 10{,}000) \\ &\quad - 0.1829(2/3) + 0.4218(1) \\ &= -0.0075 + 2.4389 - 0.1219 + 0.4218 \\ &= 2.7313\end{aligned}$$

Coding the company that does belong to the S&P 500 as 2, $1 + n_2 = e^{2.7313} = 15.353$. Therefore, the prediction is that $n_2 = 15.353 - 1 = 14.353$, or about 14 analysts.

E. There is no inconsistency in the coefficient on the size variable differing between the two regressions. The regression coefficient on an independent variable in a multiple regression model measures the expected net effect on the expected value of the dependent variable for a one-unit increase in that independent variable, after accounting for any effects of the other independent variables on the expected value of the dependent variable. The earlier regression had one fewer independent variable; after the effect of S&P 500 membership on the expected value of the dependent variable is taken into account, it is to be expected that the effect of the size variable on the dependent variable will change. What the regressions appear to indicate is that the net effect of the size variable on the expected analyst following diminishes when S&P 500 membership is taken into account.

9. A. In a well-specified regression, the differences between the actual and predicted relationship should be random; the errors should not depend on the value of the independent variable. In this regression, the errors seem larger for smaller values of the book-to-market ratio.

This finding indicates that we may have conditional heteroskedasticity in the errors, and consequently, the standard errors may be incorrect. We cannot proceed with hypothesis testing until we test for and, if necessary, correct for heteroskedasticity.

B. A test for heteroskedasticity is to regress the squared residuals from the estimated regression equation on the independent variables in the regression. As seen in Section 4.1.2, Breusch and Pagan showed that, under the null hypothesis of no conditional heteroskedasticity, $n \times R^2$ (from the regression of the squared residuals on the independent variables from the original regression) will be a χ^2 random variable, with the number of degrees of freedom equal to the number of independent variables in the regression.

C. One method to correct for heteroskedasticity is to use robust standard errors. This method uses the parameter estimates from the linear regression model but corrects the standard errors of the estimated parameters to account for the heteroskedasticity. Many statistical software packages can easily compute robust standard errors.

10. The test statistic is nR^2, where n is the number of observations and R^2 is the R^2 of the regression of squared residuals. So, the test statistic is $52 \times 0.141 = 7.332$. Under the null hypothesis of no conditional heteroskedasticity, this test statistic is a χ^2 random variable. There are three degrees of freedom, the number of independent variables in the regression. Appendix C, at the end of this volume, shows that for a one-tailed test, the test statistic critical value for a variable from a χ^2 distribution with 3 degrees of freedom at the 0.05 significance level is 7.815. The test statistic from the Breusch–Pagan test is 7.332. So, we cannot reject the hypothesis of no conditional heteroskedasticity at the 0.05 level. Therefore, we do not need to correct for conditional heteroskedasticity.

11. A. The test statistic is nR^2, where n is the number of observations and R^2 is the R^2 of the regression of squared residuals. So, the test statistic is $750 \times 0.006 = 4.5$. Under the null hypothesis of no conditional heteroskedasticity, this test statistic is a χ^2 random variable. Because the regression has only one independent variable, the number of degrees of freedom is equal to 1. Appendix C, at the end of this volume, shows that for a one-tailed test, the test statistic critical value for a variable from a χ^2 distribution with one degree of freedom at the 0.05 significance level is 3.841. The test statistic is 4.5. So, we can reject the hypothesis of no conditional heteroskedasticity at the 0.05 level. Therefore, we need to correct for conditional heteroskedasticity.

B. Two different methods can be used to correct for the effects of conditional heteroskedasticity in linear regression models. The first method involves computing robust standard errors. This method corrects the standard errors of the linear regression model's estimated parameters to account for the conditional heteroskedasticity. The second method is generalized least squares. This method modifies the original equation in an attempt to eliminate the heteroskedasticity. The new, modified regression equation is then estimated under the assumption that heteroskedasticity is no longer a problem.

Many statistical software packages can easily compute robust standard errors (the first method), and we recommend using them.

12. A. Because the value of the Durbin–Watson statistic is less than 2, we can say that the regression residuals are positively correlated. Because this statistic is fairly close to 2, however, we cannot say without a statistical test if the serial correlation is statistically significant.

B. From January 1987 through December 2002, there are 16 years, or $16 \times 12 = 192$ monthly returns. Thus the sample analyzed is quite large. Therefore, the Durbin–Watson statistic is approximately equal to $2(1 - r)$, where r is the sample correlation between the regression residuals from one period and those from the previous period.

$$DW = 1.8953 \approx 2(1 - r)$$

So, $r \approx 1 - DW/2 = 1 - 1.8953/2 = 0.0524$. Consistent with our answer to Part A, the correlation coefficient is positive.

C. Appendix E indicates that the critical values d_l and d_u for 100 observations when there is one independent variable are 1.65 and 1.69, respectively. Based on the information given in the problem, the critical values d_l and d_u for about 200 observations when there is one independent variable are about 1.74 and 1.78, respectively. Because the DW statistic of 1.8953 for our regression is above d_u, we fail to reject the null hypothesis of no positive serial correlation. Therefore, we conclude that there is no evidence of positive serial correlation for the error term.

13. A. This problem is known as multicollinearity. When some linear combinations of the independent variables in a regression model are highly correlated, the standard errors of the independent coefficient estimates become quite large, even though the regression equation may fit rather well.

B. The choice of independent variables presents multicollinearity concerns because market value of equity appears in both variables.

C. The classic symptom of multicollinearity is a high R^2 (and significant F-statistic) even though the t-statistics on the estimated slope coefficients are insignificant. Here a significant F-statistic does not accompany the insignificant t-statistics, so the classic symptom is not present.

14. A. To test the null hypothesis that all of the regression coefficients except for the intercept in the multiple regression model are equal to 0 (H_0: $b_1 = b_2 = b_3 = 0$) against the alternative hypothesis that at least one slope coefficient is not equal to 0, we must use an F-test.

$$F = \frac{RSS/k}{SSE/[n - (k + 1)]} = \frac{0.1720/3}{0.8947/[156 - (3 + 1)]} = 9.7403$$

The F-statistic has degrees of freedom $F\{k, [n - (k + 1)]\} = F(3, 152)$. From the F-test table, the critical value for $F(3, 120) = 2.68$ and $F(3, 152)$ will be less than $F(3, 120)$, so we can reject at the 0.05 significance level the null hypothesis that the slope coefficients are all 0. Changes in the three independent variables are jointly statistically related to returns.

B. None of the t-statistics are significant, but the F-statistic is significant. This suggests the possibility of multicollinearity in the independent variables.

C. The apparent multicollinearity is very likely related to the inclusion of *both* the returns on the S&P 500 Index *and* the returns on a value-weighted index of all the companies listed on the NYSE, AMEX, and NASDAQ as independent variables. The value-weighting of the latter index, giving relatively high weights to larger companies such as those included in the S&P 500, may make one return series an approximate linear function of the other. By dropping one or the other of these two variables, we might expect to eliminate the multicollinearity.

15. A. Your colleague is indicating that you have omitted an important variable from the regression. This problem is called the omitted variable bias. If the omitted variable is correlated with an included variable, the estimated values of the regression coefficients would be biased and inconsistent. Moreover, the estimates of standard errors of those coefficients would also be inconsistent. So, we cannot use either the coefficient estimates or the estimates of their standard errors to perform statistical tests.

B. A comparison of the new estimates with the original estimates clearly indicates that the original model suffered from the omitted variable bias due to the exclusion of company size from that model. As the t-statistics of the new model indicate, company size is statistically significant. Further, for the debt-to-equity ratio, the absolute value of the estimated coefficient substantially increases from 0.1043 to 0.1829, while its standard error declines. Consequently, it becomes significant in the new model, in contrast to the original model, in which it is not significant at the 5 percent level. The value of the estimated coefficient of the S&P 500 dummy substantially declines from 1.2222 to 0.4218. These changes imply that size should be included in the model.

16. A. You need to use a qualitative dependent variable. You could give a value of 1 to this dummy variable for a listing in the United States and a value of 0 for not listing in the United States.

B. Because you are using a qualitative dependent variable, linear regression is not the right technique to estimate the model. One possibility is to use either a probit or a logit model. Both models are identical, except that the logit model is based on logistic distribution while the probit model is based on normal distribution. Another possibility is to use discriminant analysis.

17. C is correct. The predicted initial return (IR) is:

$$IR = 0.0477 + (0.0150 \times 6) + (0.435 \times 0.04) - (0.0009 \times 40) + (0.05 \times 0.70) = 0.1541$$

18. B is correct. The 95% confidence interval is $0.435 \pm (0.0202 \times 1.96) = (0.395, 0.475)$.

19. C is correct. To test Hansen's belief about the direction and magnitude of the initial return, the test should be a one-tailed test. The alternative hypothesis is $H_1: b_j < 0.5$, and the null hypothesis is $H_0: b_j \geq 0.5$. The correct test statistic is: $t = (0.435 - 0.50)/0.0202 = -3.22$, and the critical value of the t-statistic for a one-tailed test at the 0.05 level is -1.645. The test statistic is significant, and the null hypothesis can be rejected at the 0.05 level of significance.

20. C is correct. The multiple R-squared for the regression is 0.36; thus, the model explains 36 percent of the variation in the dependent variable. The correlation between the predicted and actual values of the dependent variable is the square root of the R-squared or $\sqrt{0.36} = 0.60$.

21. A is correct. Chang is correct because the presence of conditional heteroskedasticity results in consistent parameter estimates, but biased (up or down) standard errors, t-statistics, and F-statistics.

22. A is correct. Chang is correct because a correlated omitted variable will result in biased and inconsistent parameter estimates and inconsistent standard errors.

23. B is correct.
The F-test is used to determine if the regression model as a whole is significant.

$$F = \text{Mean square regression (MSR)} \div \text{Mean squared error (MSE)}$$
$$\text{MSE} = \text{SSE}/[n-(k+1)] = 19{,}048 \div 427 = 44.60$$
$$\text{MSR} = \text{SSR}/k = 1071 \div 3 = 357$$
$$F = 357 \div 44.60 = 8.004$$

The critical value for degrees of freedom of 3 and 427 with $\alpha = 0.05$ (one-tail) is $F = 2.63$ from Exhibit 5. The calculated F is greater than the critical value, and Chiesa should reject the null hypothesis that all regression coefficients are equal to zero.

24. B is correct. The Durbin–Watson test used to test for serial correlation in the error term, and its value reported in Exhibit 1 is 1.65. For no serial correlation, DW is approximately equal to 2. If DW $< d_l$, *the error terms are positively serially correlated.* Because the DW = 1.65 is less than $d_l = 1.827$ for $n = 431$ (see Exhibit 2), Chiesa should reject the null hypothesis of no serial correlation and conclude that there is evidence of positive serial correlation among the error terms.

25. B is correct. The coefficient for the Pres party dummy variable (3.17) represents the increment in the mean value of the dependent variable related to the Democratic Party holding the presidency. In this case, the excess stock market return is 3.17 percent greater in Democratic presidencies than in Republican presidencies.

26. B is correct. The confidence interval is computed as $a_1 \pm s(a_1) \times t(95\%, \infty)$. From Exhibit 1, $a_1 = 3.04$ and $t(a_1) = 4.52$, resulting in a standard error of $a_1 = s(a_1) = 3.04/4.52 = 0.673$. The critical value for t from Exhibit 3 is 1.96 for $p = 0.025$. The confidence interval for a_1 is $3.04 \pm 0.673 \times 1.96 = 3.04 \pm 1.31908$ or from 1.72092 to 4.35908.

27. C is correct. The default spread is typically larger when business conditions are poor, i.e., a greater probability of default by the borrower. The positive sign for default spread (see Exhibit 1) indicates that expected returns are positively related to default spreads, meaning that excess returns are greater when business conditions are poor.

28. C is correct. Predictions in a multiple regression model are subject to both parameter estimate uncertainty and regression model uncertainty.

TIME-SERIES ANALYSIS
by Richard A. DeFusco, CFA, Dennis W. McLeavey, CFA,
Jerald E. Pinto, CFA, and David E. Runkle, CFA

LEARNING OUTCOMES

The candidate should be able to:	Mastery
a. calculate and evaluate the predicted trend value for a time series, modeled as either a linear trend or a log-linear trend, given the estimated trend coefficients;	☐
b. discuss the factors that determine whether a linear or a log-linear trend should be used with a particular time series, and evaluate the limitations of trend models;	☐
c. explain the requirement for a time series to be covariance stationary, and discuss the significance of a series that is not stationary;	☐
d. discuss the structure of an autoregressive (AR) model of order p, and calculate one- and two-period-ahead forecasts given the estimated coefficients;	☐
e. explain how autocorrelations of the residuals can be used to test whether the autoregressive model fits the time series;	☐
f. explain mean reversion, and calculate a mean-reverting level;	☐
g. contrast in-sample and out-of-sample forecasts, and compare the forecasting accuracy of different time-series models based on the root mean squared error criterion;	☐
h. discuss the instability of coefficients of time-series models;	☐
i. describe the characteristics of random walk processes, and contrast them to covariance stationary processes;	☐
j. discuss the implications of unit roots for time-series analysis, explain when unit roots are likely to occur and how to test for them, and demonstrate how a time series with a unit root can be transformed so it can be analyzed with an AR model;	☐
k. discuss the steps of the unit root test for nonstationarity, and explain the relation of the test to autoregressive time-series models;	☐
l. discuss how to test and correct for seasonality in a time-series model, and calculate and interpret a forecasted value using an AR model with a seasonal lag;	☐

Quantitative Methods for Investment Analysis, Second Edition, by Richard A. DeFusco, CFA, Dennis W. McLeavey, CFA, Jerald E. Pinto, CFA, and David E. Runkle, CFA. Copyright © 2004 by CFA Institute. Reprinted with permission.

439

m. explain autoregressive conditional heteroskedasticity (ARCH), and discuss how ARCH models can be applied to predict the variance of a time series; ☐

n. explain how time-series variables should be analyzed for nonstationarity and/or cointegration before use in a linear regression; ☐

o. select and justify the choice of a particular time-series model from a group of models. ☐

1 INTRODUCTION TO TIME-SERIES ANALYSIS

As financial analysts, we often use time-series data to make investment decisions. A **time series** is a set of observations on a variable's outcomes in different time periods: the quarterly sales for a particular company during the past five years, for example, or the daily returns on a traded security. In this reading, we explore the two chief uses of time-series models: to explain the past and to predict the future of a time series. We also discuss how to estimate time-series models, and we examine how a model describing a particular time series can change over time. The following two examples illustrate the kinds of questions we might want to ask about time series.

Suppose it is the beginning of 2003 and we are managing a U.S.-based investment portfolio that includes Swiss stocks. Because the value of this portfolio would decrease if the Swiss franc depreciates with respect to the dollar, and vice-versa, holding all else constant, we are considering whether to hedge the portfolio's exposure to changes in the value of the franc. To help us in making this decision, we decide to model the time series of the franc/dollar exchange rate. Figure 1 shows monthly data on the franc/dollar exchange rate. (The data are monthly averages of daily exchange rates.) Has the exchange rate been more stable since 1987 than it was in previous years? Has the exchange rate shown a long-term trend? How can we best use past exchange rates to predict future exchange rates?

As another example, suppose it is the beginning of 2001. We cover retail stores for a sell-side firm and want to predict retail sales for the coming year. Figure 2 shows monthly data on U.S. real retail sales. The data are inflation adjusted but not seasonally adjusted, hence the spikes around the holiday season at the turn of each year. Because the reported sales in the stores' financial statements are not seasonally adjusted, we model seasonally unadjusted retail sales. How can we model the trend in retail sales? How can we adjust for the extreme seasonality reflected in the peaks and troughs occurring at regular intervals? How can we best use past retail sales to predict future retail sales?

Some fundamental questions arise in time-series analysis: How do we model trends? How do we predict the future value of a time series based on its past

**FIGURE 1   Swiss Franc/U.S. Dollar Exchange Rate, Monthly
                Average of Daily Data**

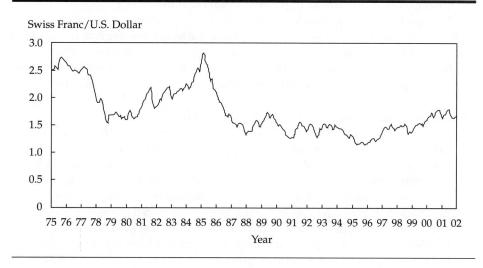

Source: Board of Governors of the Federal Reserve System.

FIGURE 2   Monthly U.S. Real Retail Sales

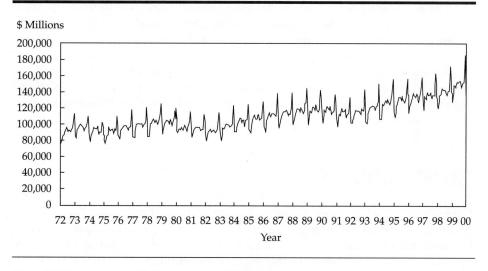

Source: U.S. Department of Commerce, Census Bureau.

values? How do we model seasonality? How do we choose among time-series models? And how do we model changes in the variance of time series over time? We address each of these issues in this reading.

CHALLENGES OF WORKING WITH TIME SERIES

2

Throughout the reading, our objective will be to apply linear regression to a given time series. Unfortunately, in working with time series we often find that the assumptions of the linear regression model are not satisfied. To apply time-series analysis, we need to assure ourselves that the linear regression model assumptions are met. When those assumptions are not satisfied, in many cases we can transform the time series, or specify the regression model differently, so that the assumptions of the linear regression model are met.

We can illustrate assumption difficulties in the context of a common time-series model, an autoregressive model. Informally, an autoregressive model is one in which the independent variable is a lagged (that is, past) value of the dependent variable, such as the model $x_t = b_0 + b_1 x_{t-1} + \epsilon_t$.[1] Specific problems that we often encounter in dealing with time series include the following:

► The residual errors are correlated instead of being uncorrelated. In the calculated regression, the difference between x_t and $b_0 + b_1 x_{t-1}$ is called the residual error. The linear regression assumes that this error term is not correlated across observations. The violation of that assumption is frequently more critical in terms of its consequences in the case of time-series models involving past values of the time series as independent variables than for other models (such as cross-sectional) in which the dependent and independent variables are distinct. As we discussed in the reading on multiple regression, in a regression in which the dependent and independent variables are distinct, serial correlation of the errors in this model does not affect the consistency of our estimates of intercept or slope coefficients. By contrast, in an autoregressive time-series regression such as $x_t = b_0 + b_1 x_{t-1} + \epsilon_t$, serial correlation in the error term causes estimates of the intercept (b_0) and slope coefficient (b_1) to be inconsistent.

► The mean and/or variance of the time series changes over time. Regression results are invalid if we estimate an autoregressive model for a time series with mean and/or variance that changes over time.

Before we try to use time series for forecasting, we may need to transform the time-series model so that it is well specified for linear regression. With this objective in mind, you will observe that time-series analysis is relatively straightforward and logical.

3   TREND MODELS

Estimating a trend in a time series and using that trend to predict future values of the time series is the simplest method of forecasting. For example, we saw in Figure 2 that monthly U.S. real retail sales show a long-term pattern of upward movement—that is, a **trend**. In this section, we examine two types of trends—linear trends and log-linear trends—and discuss how to choose between them.

3.1 Linear Trend Models

The simplest type of trend is a **linear trend**, one in which the dependent variable changes at a constant rate with time. If a time series, y_t, has a linear trend, then we can model the series using the following regression equation:

$$y_t = b_0 + b_1 t + \epsilon_t, \qquad t = 1, 2, \ldots, T \tag{1}$$

---

[1] We could also write the equation as $y_t = b_0 + b_1 y_{t-1} + \epsilon_t$.

where

y_t = the value of the time series at time t (value of the dependent variable)
b_0 = the y-intercept term
b_1 = the slope coefficient
t = time, the independent or explanatory variable
ϵ_t = a random-error term

In Equation 1, the trend line, $b_0 + b_1 t$, predicts the value of the time series at time t (where t takes on a value of 1 in the first period of the sample and increases by 1 in each subsequent period). Because the coefficient b_1 is the slope of the trend line, we refer to b_1 as the trend coefficient. We can estimate the two coefficients, b_0 and b_1, using ordinary least squares, denoting the estimated coefficients as $\hat{b}_0$ and $\hat{b}_1$.[2]

Now we demonstrate how to use these estimates to predict the value of the time series in a particular period. Recall that t takes on a value of 1 in Period 1. Therefore, the predicted or fitted value of y_t in Period 1 is $\hat{y}_1 = \hat{b}_0 + \hat{b}_1(1)$. Similarly, in a subsequent period, say the sixth period, the fitted value is $\hat{y}_6 = \hat{b}_0 + \hat{b}_1(6)$. Now suppose that we want to predict the value of the time series for a period outside the sample, say period $T + 1$. The predicted value of y_t for period $T + 1$ is $\hat{y}_{T+1} = \hat{b}_0 + \hat{b}_1(T + 1)$. For example, if $\hat{b}_0$ is 5.1 and $\hat{b}_1$ is 2, then at $t = 5$ the predicted value of y_5 is 15.1 and at $t = 6$ the predicted value of y_6 is 17.1. Note that each consecutive observation in this time series increases by $\hat{b}_1 = 2$ irrespective of the level of the series in the previous period.

EXAMPLE 1

The Trend in the U.S. Consumer Price Index

It is January 2001. As a fixed income analyst in the trust department of a bank, Lisette Miller is concerned about the future level of inflation and how it might affect portfolio value. Therefore, she wants to predict future inflation rates. For this purpose, she first needs to estimate the linear trend in inflation. To do so, she uses the monthly U.S. Consumer Price Index (CPI) inflation data, expressed as an annual percentage rate,[3] shown in Figure 3. The data include 192 months from January 1985 to December 2000, and the model to be estimated is $y_t = b_0 + b_1 t + \epsilon_t$, $t = 1, 2, \ldots, 192$. Table 1 shows the results of estimating this equation. With 192 observations and two parameters, this model has 190 degrees of freedom. At the 0.05 significance level, the critical value for a t-statistic is 1.97. Both the intercept ($\hat{b}_0 = 4.1342$) and the trend coefficient ($\hat{b}_1 = -0.0095$) are statistically significant because the absolute values of t-statistics for both coefficients are well above the critical value. The estimated regression equation can be written as

$$y_t = 4.1342 - 0.0095t$$

---

[2] Recall that ordinary least squares is an estimation method based on the criterion of minimizing the sum of a regression's squared residuals.

[3] In these data, 1 percent is represented as 1.0.

FIGURE 3   Monthly CPI Inflation, Not Seasonally Adjusted

Source: Bureau of Labor Statistics.

TABLE 1	Estimating a Linear Trend in Inflation Monthly Observations, January 1985–December 2000

Regression Statistics

R-squared	0.0408
Standard error	2.5544
Observations	192
Durbin–Watson	1.38

	Coefficient	Standard Error	t-Statistic
Intercept	4.1342	0.3701	11.1693
Trend	−0.0095	0.0033	−2.8445

Source: U.S. Bureau of Labor Statistics.

Because the trend line slope is estimated to be −0.0095, Miller concludes that the linear trend model's best estimate is that the annualized rate of inflation declined at a rate of about one one-hundredth of a percentage point per month during the sample time period.

In January 1985, the first month of the sample, the predicted value of inflation is $\hat{y}_1 = 4.1342 - 0.0095(1) = 4.1247$ percent. In December 2000, the 192nd or last month of the sample, the predicted value of inflation is $\hat{y}_{192} = 4.1342 - 0.0095(192) = 2.3177$ percent.[4] Note, though, that these predicted values are for in-sample periods. A comparison of these values with the actual values indicates how well Miller's model fits the data; however, a main purpose of the estimated model is to predict the level of inflation for out-of-sample periods. For example, for December 2001 (12 months after the end of the sample), $t = 192 + 12 = 204$, and the predicted level of inflation is $\hat{y}_{204} = 4.1342 - 0.0095(204) = 2.2041$ percent.

Figure 4 shows the inflation data along with the fitted trend. Note that inflation does not appear to be above or below the trend line for a long period of time. No persistent differences exist between the trend and actual inflation. The residuals (actual minus trend values) appear to be unpredictable and uncorrelated in time. Therefore, it is reasonable to use a linear trend line to model inflation rates from 1985 through 2000. Furthermore, we can conclude that inflation has been steadily decreasing during that time period. Note also that the R^2 in this model is quite low, indicating great uncertainty in the inflation forecasts from this model. In fact, the trend explains only 4.08 percent of the variation in monthly inflation. Later in this reading, we will examine whether we can build a better model of inflation than a model that uses only a trend line.

FIGURE 4 Monthly CPI Inflation with Trend

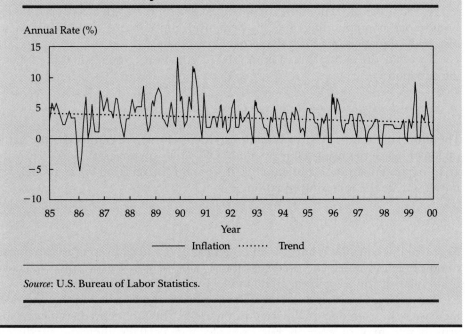

Source: U.S. Bureau of Labor Statistics.

---

[4] In reporting the final result (here, 2.3177), we use estimated regression coefficients without rounding; in stating the calculation, we use the regression coefficients with rounding, so carrying out the calculation with the rounded coefficients often results in slightly different answers.

3.2 Log-Linear Trend Models

Sometimes a linear trend does not correctly model the growth of a time series. In those cases, we often find that fitting a linear trend to a time series leads to persistent rather than uncorrelated errors. If the residuals from a linear trend model are persistent, we then need to employ an alternative model satisfying the conditions of linear regression. For financial time series, an important alternative to a linear trend is a log-linear trend. Log-linear trends work well in fitting time series that have exponential growth.

Exponential growth means constant growth at a particular rate. So, annual growth at a constant rate of 5 percent is exponential because the series continues to increase without an upper bound. How does exponential growth work? Suppose we describe a time series by the following equation:

$$y_t = e^{b_0 + b_1 t}, \quad t = 1, 2, \ldots, T \tag{2}$$

Exponential growth is growth at a constant rate $(e^{b_1} - 1)$ with continuous compounding. For instance, consider values of the time series in two consecutive periods. In Period 1, the time series has the value $y_1 = e^{b_0 + b_1(1)}$, and in Period 2, it has the value $y_2 = e^{b_0 + b_1(2)}$. The resulting ratio of the values of the time series in the first two periods is $y_2/y_1 = (e^{b_0 + b_1(2)})/(e^{b_0 + b_1(1)}) = e^{b_1(1)}$. Generally, in any period t, the time series has the value $y_t = e^{b_0 + b_1(t)}$. In period $t + 1$, the time series has the value $y_{t+1} = e^{b_0 + b_1(t+1)}$. The ratio of the values in the periods $(t + 1)$ and t is $y_{t+1}/y_t = e^{b_0 + b_1(t+1)}/e^{b_0 + b_1(t)} = e^{b_1(1)}$. Thus, the proportional rate of growth in the time series over two consecutive periods is always the same: $(y_{t+1} - y_t)/y_t = y_{t+1}/y_t - 1 = e^{b_1} - 1$.[5] Therefore, exponential growth is growth at a constant rate. Continuous compounding is a mathematical convenience that allows us to restate the equation in a form that is easy to estimate.

If we take the natural log of both sides of Equation 2, the result is the following equation:

$$\ln y_t = b_0 + b_1 t, \quad t = 1, 2, \ldots, T$$

Therefore, if a time series grows at an exponential rate, we can model the natural log of that series using a linear trend.[6] Of course, no time series grows exactly at an exponential rate. Consequently, if we want to use a **log-linear model**, we must estimate the following equation:

$$\ln y_t = b_0 + b_1 t + \epsilon_t, \quad t = 1, 2, \ldots, T \tag{3}$$

Note that this equation is linear in the coefficients b_0 and b_1. In contrast to a linear trend model, in which the predicted trend value of y_t is $\hat{b}_0 + \hat{b}_1 t$, the predicted trend value of y_t in a log-linear trend model is $e^{\hat{b}_0 + \hat{b}_1 t}$ because $e^{\ln y_t} = y_t$.

Examining Equation 3, we see that a log-linear model predicts that $\ln y_t$ will increase by b_1 from one time period to the next. The model predicts a constant growth rate in y_t of $e^{b_1} - 1$. For example, if $b_1 = 0.05$, then the predicted growth rate of y_t in each period is $e^{0.05} - 1 = 0.051271$ or 5.13 percent. In contrast, the linear trend model (Equation 1) predicts that y_t grows by a constant amount from one period to the next.

---

[5] For example, if we use annual periods and $e^{b_1} = 1.04$ for a particular series, then that series grows by $1.04 - 1 = 0.04$, or 4 percent a year.

[6] An exponential growth rate is a compound growth rate with continuous compounding.

Example 2 illustrates the problem of nonrandom residuals in a linear trend model, and Example 3 shows a log-linear regression specification fit to the same data.

EXAMPLE 2

A Linear Trend Regression for Quarterly Sales at Intel

In January 2000, technology analyst Ray Benedict wants to use Equation 1 to fit the data on quarterly sales for Intel Corporation shown in Figure 5. He uses 60 observations on Intel's sales from the first quarter of 1985 to the fourth quarter of 1999 to estimate the linear trend regression model $y_t = b_0 + b_1 t + \epsilon_t$, $t = 1, 2, \ldots, 60$. Table 2 shows the results of estimating this equation.

FIGURE 5 Intel Quarterly Sales

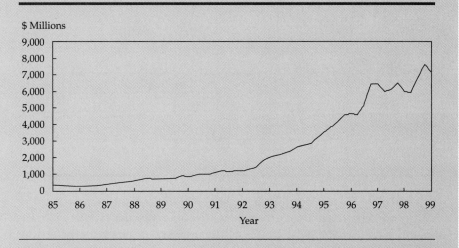

Source: Compustat.

TABLE 2 Estimating a Linear Trend in Intel Sales

Regression Statistics

R-squared	0.8774
Standard error	871.6858
Observations	60
Durbin–Watson	0.13

	Coefficient	Standard Error	*t*-Statistic
Intercept	–1,318.7729	227.9585	–5.7852
Trend	132.4005	6.4994	20.3712

Source: Compustat.

At first glance, the results shown in Table 2 seem quite reasonable: Both the intercept and the trend coefficient are highly statistically significant. When Benedict plots the data on Intel's sales and the trend line, however, he sees a different picture. As Figure 6 shows, before 1989 the trend line is persistently below sales. Between 1989 and 1996, the trend line is persistently above sales, but after 1996, the trend line is once again persistently below sales.

FIGURE 6   Intel Quarterly Sales with Trend

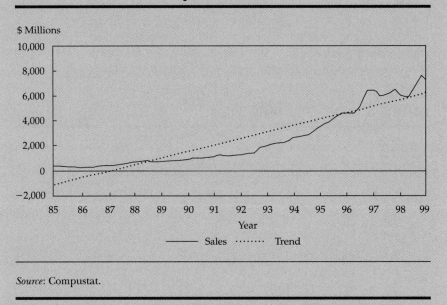

Source: Compustat.

Recall a key assumption underlying the regression model: that the regression errors are not correlated across observations. If a trend is persistently above or below the value of the time series, however, the residuals (the difference between the time series and the trend) are serially correlated. Figure 7 shows the residuals (the difference between sales

FIGURE 7   Residual from Predicting Intel Sales with a Trend

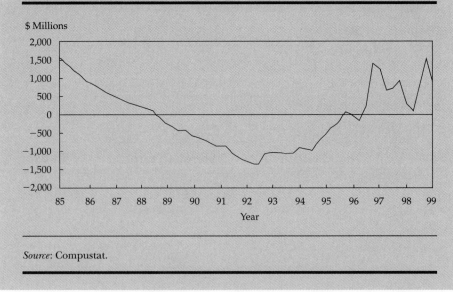

Source: Compustat.

and the trend) from estimating a linear trend model with the raw sales data. The figure shows that the residuals are persistent. Because of this persistent serial correlation in the errors of the trend model, using a linear trend to fit sales at Intel would be inappropriate, even though the R^2 of the equation is high (0.88). The assumption of uncorrelated residual errors has been violated. Because the dependent and independent variables are not distinct, as in cross-sectional regressions, this assumption violation is serious and causes us to search for a better model.

EXAMPLE 3

A Log-Linear Regression for Quarterly Sales at Intel

Having rejected a linear trend model in Example 2, technology analyst Benedict now tries a different model for the quarterly sales for Intel Corporation from the first quarter of 1985 to the fourth quarter of 1999. The curvature in the data plot shown in Figure 5 is a hint that an exponential curve may fit the data. Consequently, he estimates the following linear equation:

$$\ln y_t = b_0 + b_1 t + \epsilon_t, \qquad t = 1, 2, \ldots, 60$$

This equation seems to fit the sales data much better than did Equation 1. As Table 3 shows, the R^2 for this equation is 0.98 (the R^2 with Equation 1 was 0.88). An R^2 of 0.98 means that 98 percent of the variation in the natural log of Intel's sales is explained solely by a linear trend.

TABLE 3   Estimating a Linear Trend in Lognormal Intel Sales

Regression Statistics

R-squared	0.9831
Standard error	0.1407
Observations	60
Durbin–Watson	0.30

	Coefficient	Standard Error	*t*-Statistic
Intercept	5.5529	0.0368	150.9809
Trend	0.0609	0.0010	58.0680

Source: Compustat.

Figure 8 shows how well a linear trend fits the natural log of Intel's sales. The natural logs of the sales data lie very close to the linear trend during the sample period, and log sales are not above or below the trend for long periods of time. Thus, a log-linear trend model seems much better suited for modeling Intel's sales than does a linear trend model.

How can Benedict use the results of estimating Equation 3 to predict Intel's sales in the future? Suppose Benedict wants to predict Intel's sales for the first quarter of 2000 ($t = 61$). The estimated value $\hat{b}_0$ is 5.5529, and the estimated value $\hat{b}_1$ is 0.0609. Therefore, the estimated model predicts that $\ln \hat{y}_{61} = 5.5529 + 0.0609(61) = 9.2673$ and that predicted sales are $\hat{y}_{61} = e^{\ln \hat{y}_{61}} = e^{9.2673} = \$10,585.63$ million.[7]

FIGURE 8   Natural Log of Intel Quarterly Sales

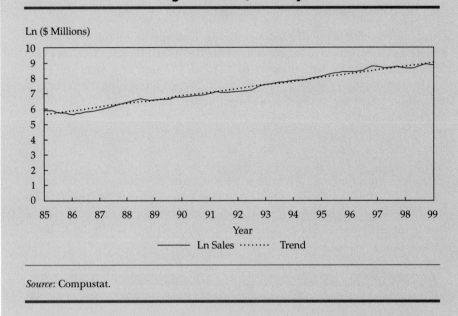

Ln ($ Millions)

Source: Compustat.

How much different is this forecast from the prediction of the linear trend model? Table 2 showed that for the linear trend model, the estimated value of $\hat{b}_0$ is -1318.7729 and the estimated value of $\hat{b}_1$ is 132.4005. Thus, if we predict Intel's sales for the first quarter of 2000 ($t = 61$) using the linear trend model, the forecast is $\hat{y}_{61} = -1318.7729 + 132.4005(61) = \$6,757.66$ million. This forecast is far below the prediction made by the log-linear regression model. Later in this reading, we will examine whether we can build a better model of Intel's quarterly sales than a model that uses only a log-linear trend.

---

[7] Note that $\hat{b}_1 = 0.0609$ implies that the exponential growth rate per quarter in Intel's sales will be 6.28 percent ($e^{0.0609} - 1 = 0.062793$).

3.3 Trend Models and Testing for Correlated Errors

Both the linear trend model and the log-linear trend model are single-variable regression models. If they are to be correctly specified, the regression-model assumptions must be satisfied. In particular, the regression error for one period must be uncorrelated with the regression error for all other periods.[8] In Example 2 in the previous section, we could infer an obvious violation of that assumption from a visual inspection of a plot of residuals (Figure 7). The log-linear trend model of Example 3 appeared to fit the data much better, but we still need to confirm that the uncorrelated errors assumption is satisfied. To address that question formally, we must carry out a Durbin–Watson test on the residuals.

In the reading on regression analysis, we showed how to test whether regression errors are serially correlated using the Durbin–Watson statistic. For example, if the trend models shown in Examples 1 and 3 really capture the time-series behavior of inflation and the log of Intel's sales, then the Durbin–Watson statistic for both of those models should not differ significantly from 2.0. Otherwise, the errors in the model are either positively or negatively serially correlated, and that correlation can be used to build a better forecasting model for those time series.

In Example 1, estimating a linear trend in the monthly CPI inflation yielded a Durbin–Watson statistic of 1.38. Is this result significantly different from 2.0? To find out, we need to test the null hypothesis of no positive serial correlation. For a sample with 192 observations and one independent variable, the critical value, d_l, for the Durbin–Watson test statistic at the 0.05 significance level is above 1.65. Because the value of the Durbin–Watson statistic (1.38) is below this critical value, we can reject the hypothesis of no positive serial correlation in the errors. We can conclude that a regression equation that uses a linear trend to model inflation has positive serial correlation in the errors.[9] We will need a different kind of regression model because this one violates the least-squares assumption of no serial correlation in the errors.

In Example 3, estimating a linear trend with the natural logarithm of sales for the Intel example yielded a Durbin–Watson statistic of 0.30. Suppose we wish to test the null hypothesis of no positive serial correlation. The critical value, d_l, is 1.55 at the 0.05 significance level. The value of the Durbin–Watson statistic (0.30) is below this critical value, so we can reject the null hypothesis of no positive serial correlation in the errors. We can conclude that a regression equation that uses a trend to model the log of Intel's quarterly sales has positive serial correlation in the errors. So, for this series as well, we need to build a different kind of model.

Overall, we conclude that the trend models sometimes have the limitation that errors are serially correlated. Existence of serial correlation suggests that we can build better forecasting models for such time series than trend models.

---

[8] Note that time-series observations, in contrast to cross-sectional observations, have a logical ordering: They must be processed in chronological order of the time periods involved. For example, we should not make a prediction of the inflation rate using a CPI series in which the order of the observations had been scrambled, because time patterns such as growth in the independent variables can negatively affect the statistical properties of the estimated regression coefficients.

[9] Significantly small values of the Durbin–Watson statistic indicate positive serial correlation; significantly large values point to negative serial correlation. Here the DW statistic of 1.38 indicates positive serial correlation. For more information, see the readings on regression analysis.

AUTOREGRESSIVE (AR) TIME-SERIES MODELS

4

A key feature of the log-linear model's depiction of time series and a key feature of time series in general is that current-period values are related to previous-period values. For example, Intel's sales for the current period are related to its sales in the previous period. An **autoregressive model (AR)**, a time series regressed on its own past values, represents this relationship effectively. When we use this model, we can drop the normal notation of y as the dependent variable and x as the independent variable because we no longer have that distinction to make. Here we simply use x_t. For example, Equation 4 shows a first-order autoregression, AR(1), for the variable x_t:

$$x_t = b_0 + b_1 x_{t-1} + \epsilon_t \tag{4}$$

Thus, in an AR(1) model, we use only the most recent past value of x_t to predict the current value of x_t. In general, a pth-order autoregression, AR(p), for the variable x_t is shown by

$$x_t = b_0 + b_1 x_{t-1} + b_2 x_{t-2} + \ldots + b_p x_{t-p} + \epsilon_t \tag{5}$$

In this equation, p past values of x_t are used to predict the current value of x_t. In the next section we discuss a key assumption of time-series models that include lagged values of the dependent variable as independent variables.

4.1 Covariance-Stationary Series

Note that the independent variable (x_{t-1}) in Equation 4 is a random variable. This fact may seem like a mathematical subtlety, but it is not. If we use ordinary least squares to estimate Equation 4 when we have a randomly distributed independent variable that is a lagged value of the dependent variable, our statistical inference may be invalid. To conduct valid statistical inference, we must make a key assumption in time-series analysis: We must assume that the time series we are modeling is **covariance stationary**.[10]

What does it mean for a time series to be covariance stationary? The basic idea is that a time series is covariance stationary if its properties, such as mean and variance, do not change over time. A covariance stationary series must satisfy three principal requirements.[11] First, the expected value of the time series must be constant and finite in all periods: $E(y_t) = \mu$ and $|\mu| < \infty$, $t = 1, 2, \ldots, T$. Second, the variance of the time series must be constant and finite in all periods. Third, the covariance of the time series with itself for a fixed number of periods in the past or future must be constant and finite in all periods. The second and third requirements can be summarized as follows:[12]

$$\text{Cov}(y_t, y_{t-s}) = \lambda, |\lambda| < \infty, t = 1, 2, \ldots, T; s = 0, \pm1, \pm2, \ldots, \pm T$$

---

[10] "Weakly stationary" is a synonym for covariance stationary. Note that the terms "stationary" or "stationarity" are often used to mean "covariance stationary" or "covariance stationarity," respectively. You may also encounter the more restrictive concept of "strictly" stationary, which has little practical application. For details, see Diebold (2004).

[11] In the first requirement, we will use the absolute value to rule out the case in which the mean is negative without limit (minus infinity).

[12] When s in this equation equals 0, then this equation imposes the condition that the variance of the time series is finite. This is so because the covariance of a random variable with itself is its variance: $\text{Cov}(y_t, y_t) = \text{Var}(y_t)$.

where λ signifies a constant. What happens if a time series is not covariance stationary but we model it using Equation 4? The estimation results will have no economic meaning. For a non-covariance-stationary time series, estimating the regression in Equation 4 will yield spurious results. In particular, the estimate of b_1 will be biased, and any hypothesis tests will be invalid.

How can we tell if a time series is covariance stationary? We can often answer this question by looking at a plot of the time series. If the plot shows roughly the same mean and variance through time without any significant seasonality, then we may want to assume that the time series is covariance stationary.

Some of the time series we looked at in Figures 1 to 4 appear to be covariance stationary. For example, the inflation data shown in Figure 3 appear to have roughly the same mean and variance over the sample period. Many of the time series one encounters in business and investments, however, are not covariance stationary. For example, many time series appear to grow (or decline) steadily through time and so have a mean that is nonconstant, which implies that they are nonstationary. As an example, the time series of Intel's quarterly sales in Figure 5 clearly shows the mean increasing as time passes. Thus Intel's quarterly sales are not covariance stationary.[13] Macroeconomic time series such as those relating to income and consumption are often strongly trending as well. A time series with seasonality (regular patterns of movement with the year) also has a nonconstant mean, as do other types of time series that we discuss later.[14]

Figure 2 showed that monthly retail sales (not seasonally adjusted) are also not covariance stationary. Sales in December are always much higher than sales in other months (these are the regular large peaks), and sales in January are always much lower (these are the regular large drops after the December peaks). On average, sales also increase over time, so the mean of sales is not constant.

Later in the reading, we will show that we can often transform a nonstationary time series into a stationary time series. But whether a stationary time series is original or transformed, a caution applies: Stationarity in the past does not guarantee stationary in the future. There is always the possibility that a well-specified model will fail when the state of the world changes and yields a different underlying model that generates the time series.

4.2 Detecting Serially Correlated Errors in an Autoregressive Model

We can estimate an autoregressive model using ordinary least squares if the time series is covariance stationary and the errors are uncorrelated. Unfortunately, our previous test for serial correlation, the Durbin–Watson statistic, is invalid when the independent variables include past values of the dependent variable. Therefore, for most time-series models, we cannot use the Durbin–Watson statistic. Fortunately, we can use other tests to determine whether the errors in a time-series model are serially correlated. One such test reveals whether the autocorrelations of the error term are significantly different from 0. This test is a *t*-test involving a residual autocorrelation and the standard error of the residual autocorrelation. As background for the test, we next discuss autocorrelation in general before moving to residual autocorrelation.

---

[13] In general, any time series accurately described with a linear or log-linear trend model is not covariance stationary, although a transformation of the original series might be covariance stationary.

[14] In particular, random walks are not covariance stationary.

The **autocorrelations** of a time series are the correlations of that series with its own past values. The order of the correlation is given by k where k represents the number of periods lagged. When $k = 1$, the autocorrelation shows the correlation of the variable in one period to its occurrence in the previous period. For example, the k**th order autocorrelation** (ρ_k) is

$$\rho_k = \frac{\text{Cov}(x_t, x_{t-k})}{\sigma_x^2} = \frac{E[(x_t - \mu)(x_{t-k} - \mu)]}{\sigma_x^2}$$

Note that we have the relationship $\text{Cov}(x_t, x_{t-k}) \leq \text{Var}(x_t)$ with equality holding when $k = 0$. This means that the absolute value of ρ_k is less than or equal to 1.

Of course, we can never directly observe the autocorrelations, ρ_k. Instead, we must estimate them. Thus we replace the expected value of x_t, μ, with its estimated value, $\bar{x}$, to compute the estimated autocorrelations. The kth order estimated autocorrelation of the time series x_t, which we denote $\hat{\rho}_k$, is

$$\hat{\rho}_k = \frac{\displaystyle\sum_{t=k+1}^{T} [(x_t - \bar{x})(x_{t-k} - \bar{x})]}{\displaystyle\sum_{t=1}^{T} (x_t - \bar{x})^2}$$

Analogous to the definition of autocorrelations for a time series, we can define the autocorrelations of the error term for a time-series model as[15]

$$\begin{aligned}
\rho_{\epsilon,k} &= \frac{\text{Cov}(\epsilon_t, \epsilon_{t-k})}{\sigma_\epsilon^2} \\
&= \frac{E[(\epsilon_t - 0)(\epsilon_{t-k} - 0)]}{\sigma_\epsilon^2} \\
&= \frac{E(\epsilon_t \epsilon_{t-k})}{\sigma_\epsilon^2}
\end{aligned}$$

where E stands for the expected value. We assume that the expected value of the error term in a time-series model is 0.[16]

We can determine whether we are using the correct time-series model by testing whether the autocorrelations of the error term (**error autocorrelations**) differ significantly from 0. If they do, the model is not specified correctly. We estimate the error autocorrelation using the sample autocorrelations of the residuals (**residual autocorrelations**) and their sample variance.

A test of the null hypothesis that an error autocorrelation at a specified lag equals 0 is based on the residual autocorrelation for that lag and the standard error of the residual correlation, which is equal to $1/\sqrt{T}$, where T is the number of observations in the time series.[17] Thus, if we have 100 observations in a time series, the standard error for each of the estimated autocorrelations is 0.1. We can compute the t-test of the null hypothesis that the error correlation at a particular lag equals 0, by dividing the residual autocorrelation at that lag by its standard error $(1/\sqrt{T})$.

How can we use information about the error autocorrelations to determine whether an autoregressive time-series model is correctly specified? We can use a

---

[15] Whenever we refer to autocorrelation without qualification, we mean autocorrelation of the time series itself rather than autocorrelation of the error term or residuals.

[16] This assumption is similar to the one made in the previous two readings about the expected value of the error term.

[17] This calculation is derived in Diebold (2004).

simple three-step method. First, estimate a particular autoregressive model, say an AR(1) model. Second, compute the autocorrelations of the residuals from the model.[18] Third, test to see whether the residual autocorrelations differ significantly from 0. If significance tests show that the residual autocorrelations differ significantly from 0, the model is not correctly specified; we may need to modify it in ways that we will discuss shortly.[19] We now present an example to demonstrate how this three-step method works.

EXAMPLE 4

Predicting Gross Margins for Intel Corporation

Having investigated the time-series modeling of Intel Corporation's sales, analyst Ray Benedict decides to use a time-series model to predict Intel's gross margin [(Sales − Cost of goods sold)/Sales]. His observations on the dependent variable are 2Q:1985 through 4Q:1999. He does not know the best model for gross margin but believes that the current-period value will be related to the previous-period value. He decides to start out with a first-order autoregressive model, AR(1): Gross margin$_t$ = $b_0 + b_1$(Gross margin$_{t-1}$) + ϵ_t. Table 4 shows the results of estimating this AR(1) model, along with the autocorrelations of the residuals from that model.

TABLE 4 Autoregression: AR(1) Model Gross Margin of Intel Quarterly Observations, April 1985–December 1999

Regression Statistics

R-squared	0.7784
Standard error	0.0402
Observations	59
Durbin–Watson	1.8446

	Coefficient	Standard Error	*t*-Statistic
Intercept	0.0834	0.0367	2.2705
Lag 1	0.8665	0.0612	14.1493

(Table continued on next page . . .)

---

[18] We can compute these residual autocorrelations easily with most statistical software packages. In Microsoft Excel, for example, to compute the first-order residual autocorrelation, we compute the correlation of the residuals from observations 1 through $T - 1$ with the residuals from observations 2 through T.

[19] Often, econometricians use additional tests for the significance of residual autocorrelations. For example, the Box–Pierce Q-statistic is frequently used to test the joint hypothesis that all autocorrelations of the residuals are equal to 0. For further discussion, see Diebold (2004).

TABLE 4   (continued)

Autocorrelations of the Residual

Lag	Autocorrelation	Standard Error	t-Statistic
1	0.0677	0.1302	0.5197
2	−0.1929	0.1302	−1.4814
3	0.0541	0.1302	0.4152
4	−0.1498	0.1302	−1.1507

Source: Compustat.

The first thing to note about Table 4 is that both the intercept ($\hat{b}_0 = 0.0834$) and the coefficient on the first lag ($\hat{b}_1 = 0.8665$) of the gross margin are highly significant in the regression equation.[20] The *t*-statistic for the intercept is about 2.3, whereas the *t*-statistic for the first lag of the gross margin is more than 14. With 59 observations and two parameters, this model has 57 degrees of freedom. At the 0.05 significance level, the critical value for a *t*-statistic is about 2.0. Therefore, Benedict must reject the null hypotheses that the intercept is equal to 0 ($b_0 = 0$) and the coefficient on the first lag is equal to 0 ($b_1 = 0$) in favor of the alternative hypothesis that the coefficients, individually, are not equal to 0. But are these statistics valid? We will know when we test whether the residuals from this model are serially correlated.

At the bottom of Table 4, the first four autocorrelations of the residual are displayed along with the standard error and the *t*-statistic for each of those autocorrelations.[21] The sample has 59 observations, so the standard error for each of the autocorrelations is $1/\sqrt{59} = 0.1302$. Table 4 shows that none of the first four autocorrelations has a *t*-statistic larger than 1.50 in absolute value. Therefore, Benedict can conclude that none of these autocorrelations differs significantly from 0. Consequently, he can assume that the residuals are not serially correlated and that the model is correctly specified, and he can validly use ordinary least squares to estimate the parameters and the parameters' standard errors in the autoregressive model.[22]

Now that Benedict has concluded that this model is correctly specified, how can he use it to predict Intel's gross margin in the next period? The estimated equation is Gross margin$_t$ = 0.0834 + 0.8665(Gross margin$_{t-1}$) + ϵ_t. The expected value of the error term is 0 in any period. Therefore, this model predicts that gross margin in period $t + 1$ will be

[20] The first lag of a time series is the value of the time series in the previous period.

[21] For seasonally unadjusted data, analysts often compute the same number of autocorrelations as there are observations in a year (for example, four for quarterly data). The number of autocorrelations computed also often depends on sample size, as discussed in Diebold (2004).

[22] Statisticians have many other tests for serial correlation of the residuals in a time-series model. For details, see Diebold (2004).

Gross margin$_{t+1}$ = 0.0834 + 0.8665(Gross margin$_t$). For example, if gross margin is 55 percent in this quarter (0.55), the model predicts that in the next quarter gross margin will increase to 0.0834 + 0.8665(0.55) = 0.5600 or 56.0 percent. On the other hand, if gross margin is currently 65 percent (0.65), the model predicts that in the next quarter, gross margin will fall to 0.0834 + 0.8665(0.65) = 0.6467 or 64.67 percent. As we show in the following section, the model predicts that gross margin will increase if it is below a certain level (62.50 percent) and decrease if it is above that level.

4.3 Mean Reversion

We say that a time series shows **mean reversion** if it tends to fall when its level is above its mean and rise when its level is below its mean. Much like the temperature in a room controlled by a thermostat, a mean-reverting time series tends to return to its long-term mean. How can we determine the value that the time series tends toward? If a time series is currently at its mean-reverting level, then the model predicts that the value of the time series will be the same in the next period. At its mean-reverting level, we have the relationship $x_{t+1} = x_t$. For an AR(1) model ($x_{t+1} = b_0 + b_1x_t$), the equality $x_{t+1} = x_t$ implies the level $x_t = b_0 + b_1x_t$, or that the mean-reverting level, x_t, is given by

$$x_t = \frac{b_0}{1 - b_1}$$

So the AR(1) model predicts that the time series will stay the same if its current value is $b_0/(1 - b_1)$, increase if its current value is below $b_0/(1 - b_1)$, and decrease if its current value is above $b_0/(1 - b_1)$.

In the case of gross margins for Intel, the mean-reverting level for the model shown in Table 4 is 0.0834/(1 − 0.8665) = 0.6250. If the current gross margin is above 0.6250, the model predicts that the gross margin will fall in the next period. If the current gross margin is below 0.6250, the model predicts that the gross margin will rise in the next period. As we will discuss later, all covariance-stationary time series have a finite mean-reverting level.

4.4 Multiperiod Forecasts and the Chain Rule of Forecasting

Often, financial analysts want to make forecasts for more than one period. For example, we might want to use a quarterly sales model to predict sales for a company for each of the next four quarters. To use a time-series model to make forecasts for more than one period, we must examine how to make multiperiod forecasts using an AR(1) model. The one-period-ahead forecast of x_t from an AR(1) model is as follows:

$$\hat{x}_{t+1} = \hat{b}_0 + \hat{b}_1x_t \qquad \textbf{(6)}$$

If we want to forecast x_{t+2} using an AR(1) model, our forecast will be based on

$$\hat{x}_{t+2} = \hat{b}_0 + \hat{b}_1x_{t+1} \qquad \textbf{(7)}$$

Unfortunately, we do not know x_{t+1} in period t, so we cannot use Equation 7 directly to make a two-period-ahead forecast. We can, however, use our forecast of x_{t+1} and the AR(1) model to make a prediction of x_{t+2}. The **chain rule of forecasting** is a process in which the next period's value, predicted by the forecasting equation, is substituted into the equation to give a predicted value two periods ahead. Using the chain rule of forecasting, we can substitute the predicted value of x_{t+1} into Equation 7 to get $\hat{x}_{t+2} = \hat{b}_0 + \hat{b}_1 \hat{x}_{t+1}$. We already know $\hat{x}_{t+1}$ from our one-period-ahead forecast in Equation 6. Now we have a simple way of predicting x_{t+2}.

Multiperiod forecasts are more uncertain than single-period forecasts because each forecast period has uncertainty. For example, in forecasting x_{t+2}, we first have the uncertainty associated with forecasting x_{t+1} using x_t, and then we have the uncertainty associated with forecasting x_{t+2} using the forecast of x_{t+1}. In general, the more periods a forecast has, the more uncertain it is.[23]

EXAMPLE 5

Multiperiod Prediction of Intel's Gross Margin

Suppose that at the beginning of 2000, we want to predict Intel's gross margin in two periods using the model shown in Table 4. Assume that Intel's gross margin in the current period is 65 percent. The one-period-ahead forecast of Intel's gross margin from this model is 0.6467 = 0.0834 + 0.8665(0.65). By substituting the one-period-ahead forecast, 0.6467, back into the regression equation, we can derive the following two-period-ahead forecast: 0.6438 = 0.0834 + 0.8665(0.6467). Therefore, if the current gross margin for Intel is 65 percent, the model predicts that Intel's gross margin in two quarters will be 64.38 percent.

EXAMPLE 6

Modeling U.S. CPI Inflation

Analyst Lisette Miller has been directed to build a time-series model for monthly U.S. inflation. Inflation and expectations about inflation, of course, have a significant effect on bond returns. Beginning with January 1971, she selects as data the annualized monthly percentage change in the CPI. Which model should Miller use?

The process of model selection parallels that of Example 4 relating to Intel's gross margins. The first model Miller estimates is an AR(1) model, using the previous month's inflation rate as the independent variable: $\text{Inflation}_t = b_0 + b_1 \text{Inflation}_{t-1} + \epsilon_t$, $t = 1, 2, \ldots, 359$. To estimate this model, she uses monthly CPI inflation data from January 1971 to December 2000 ($t = 1$ denotes February 1971). Table 5 shows the results of estimating this model.

---

[23] If a forecasting model is well specified, the prediction errors from the model will not be serially correlated. If the prediction errors for each period are not serially correlated, then the variance of a multiperiod forecast will be higher than the variance of a single-period forecast.

TABLE 5   Monthly CPI Inflation at an Annual Rate: AR(1) Model Monthly Observations, February 1971–December 2000

Regression Statistics

R-squared	0.3808
Standard error	3.4239
Observations	359
Durbin–Watson	2.3059

	Coefficient	Standard Error	t-Statistic
Intercept	1.9658	0.2803	7.0119
Lag 1	0.6175	0.0417	14.8185

Autocorrelations of the Residual

Lag	Autocorrelation	Standard Error	t-Statistic
1	−0.1538	0.0528	−2.9142
2	0.1097	0.0528	2.0782
3	0.0657	0.0528	1.2442
4	0.0920	0.0528	1.7434

Source: U.S. Bureau of Labor Statistics.

As Table 5 shows, both the intercept ($\hat{b}_0 = 1.9658$) and the coefficient on the first lagged value of inflation ($\hat{b}_1 = 0.6175$) are highly statistically significant, with large t-statistics. With 359 observations and two parameters, this model has 357 degrees of freedom. The critical value for a t-statistic at the 0.05 significance level is about 1.97. Therefore, Miller can reject the individual null hypotheses that the intercept is equal to 0 ($b_0 = 0$) and the coefficient on the first lag is equal to 0 ($b_1 = 0$) in favor of the alternative hypothesis that the coefficients, individually, are not equal to 0.

Are these statistics valid? Miller will know when she tests whether the residuals from this model are serially correlated. With 359 observations in this sample, the standard error for each of the estimated autocorrelations is $1/\sqrt{359} = 0.0528$. The critical value for the t-statistic is 1.97. Because both the first and the second estimated autocorrelation have t-statistics larger than 1.97 in absolute value, Miller concludes that the autocorrelations are significantly different from 0. This model is thus misspecified because the residuals are serially correlated.

If the residuals in an autoregressive model are serially correlated, Miller can eliminate the correlation by estimating an autoregressive model with more lags of the dependent variable as explanatory variables. Table 6 shows the result of estimating a second time-series model, an AR(2) model using the same data as in the analysis shown in Table 5.[24] With 358 observations and three parameters, this model has 355 degrees of freedom. Because the degrees of freedom are almost the same as those for the estimates shown in Table 5, the critical value of the t-statistic at the 0.05 significance level also is almost the same (1.97). If she estimates the equation with two lags, $\text{Inflation}_t = b_0 + b_1 \text{Inflation}_{t-1} + b_2 \text{Inflation}_{t-2} + \epsilon_t$, Miller finds that all three of the coefficients in the regression model (an intercept and the coefficients on two lags of the dependent variable) differ significantly from 0. The bottom portion of Table 6 shows that none of the first four autocorrelations of the residual has a t-statistic greater in absolute value than the critical value of 1.97. Therefore, Miller fails to reject the hypothesis that the individual autocorrelations of the residual equal 0. She concludes that this model is correctly specified because she finds no evidence of serial correlation in the residuals.

TABLE 6   Monthly CPI Inflation at an Annual Rate: AR(2) Model Monthly Observations, March 1971–December 2000

Regression Statistics

Multiple R	0.6479
R-squared	0.4197
Standard error	3.3228
Observations	358
Durbin–Watson	2.0582

	Coefficient	Standard Error	t-Statistic
Intercept	1.4609	0.2913	5.0147
Lag 1	0.4634	0.0514	9.0117
Lag 2	0.2515	0.0514	4.8924

Autocorrelations of the Residual

Lag	Autocorrelation	Standard Error	t-Statistic
1	−0.0320	0.0529	−0.6048
2	−0.0982	0.0529	−1.8574
3	−0.0114	0.0529	−0.2150
4	0.0320	0.0529	0.6053

Source: U.S. Bureau of Labor Statistics.

[24] Note that Table 6 shows only 358 observations in the regression because the extra lag of inflation requires the estimation sample to start one month later than the regression in Table 5. (With two lags, inflation for January and February 1971 must be known in order to estimate the equation starting in March 1971.)

In the previous example, the analyst selected an AR(2) model because the residuals from the AR(1) model were serially correlated. Suppose that in a given month, inflation had been 4 percent at an annual rate in the previous month and 3 percent in the month before that. The AR(1) model shown in Table 5 predicted that inflation in the next month would be $1.9658 + 0.6175(4) = 4.44$ percent approximately, whereas the AR(2) model shown in Table 6 predicts that inflation in the next month will be $1.4609 + 0.4634(4) + 0.2515(3) = 4.07$ percent approximately. If the analyst had used the incorrect AR(1) model, she would have predicted inflation to be 37 basis points higher (4.44 percent versus 4.07 percent) than using the AR(2) model. This incorrect forecast could have adversely affected the quality of her company's investment choices.

4.5 Comparing Forecast Model Performance

One way to compare the forecast performance of two models is to compare the variance of the forecast errors that the two models make. The model with the smaller forecast error variance will be the more accurate model, and it will also have the smaller standard error of the time-series regression. (This standard error usually is reported directly in the output for the time-series regression.)

In comparing forecast accuracy among models, we must distinguish between in-sample forecast errors and out-of-sample forecast errors. **In-sample forecast errors** are the residuals from a fitted time-series model. For example, when we estimated a linear trend with raw inflation data from January 1971 to December 2000, the in-sample forecast errors were the residuals from January 1971 to December 2000. If we use this model to predict inflation outside this period, the differences between actual and predicted inflation are **out-of-sample forecast errors**.

EXAMPLE 7

In-Sample Forecast Comparisons of U.S. CPI Inflation

In Example 6, the analyst compared an AR(1) forecasting model of monthly U.S. inflation with an AR(2) model of monthly U.S. inflation and decided that the AR(2) model was preferable. Table 5 showed that the standard error from the AR(1) model of inflation is 3.4239, and Table 6 showed that the standard error from the AR(2) model is 3.3228. Therefore, the AR(2) model had a lower in-sample forecast error variance than the AR(1) model, which is consistent with our belief that the AR(2) model was preferable. Its standard error is $3.3228/3.4239 = 97.05$ percent of the forecast error of the AR(1) model.

Often, we want to compare the forecasting accuracy of different models after the sample period for which they were estimated. We wish to compare the out-of-sample forecast accuracy of the models. Out-of-sample forecast accuracy is important because the future is always out of sample. Although professional forecasters distinguish between out-of-sample and in-sample forecasting performance, many articles that analysts read contain only in-sample forecast evaluations. Analysts should be aware that out-of-sample performance is critical for evaluating a forecasting model's real-world contribution.

Typically, we compare the out-of-sample forecasting performance of forecasting models by comparing their **root mean squared error (RMSE)**, which is the square root of the average squared error. The model with the smallest RMSE is judged most accurate. The following example illustrates the computation and use of RMSE in comparing forecasting models.

EXAMPLE 8

Out-of-Sample Forecast Comparisons of U.S. CPI Inflation

Suppose we want to compare the forecasting accuracy of the AR(1) and AR(2) models of U.S. inflation estimated over 1971 to 2000, using data on U.S. inflation from January 2001 to December 2002.

TABLE 7   Out-of-Sample Forecast Error Comparisons: January 2001–December 2002 U.S. CPI Inflation (Annualized)

Date	Infl(t)	Infl($t-1$)	Infl($t-2$)	AR(1) Error	Squared Error	AR(2) Error	Squared Error
2001							
January	7.8556	−0.6871	0.6918	6.3141	39.8681	6.5392	42.7611
February	4.9042	7.8556	−0.6871	−1.9122	3.6564	−0.0242	0.0006
March	2.7648	4.9042	7.8556	−2.2291	4.9689	−2.9440	8.6669
April	4.8729	2.7648	4.9042	1.1999	1.4399	0.8976	0.8058
May	5.5638	4.8729	2.7648	0.5892	0.3472	1.1497	1.3217
June	2.0448	5.5638	4.8729	−3.3564	11.2656	−3.2196	10.3660
July	−3.3192	2.0448	5.5638	−6.5475	42.8703	−7.1267	50.7892
August	0.0000	−3.3192	2.0448	0.0837	0.0070	−0.4369	0.1909
September	5.5446	0.0000	−3.3192	3.5788	12.8078	4.9183	24.1899
October	−3.9642	5.5446	0.0000	−9.3536	87.4891	−7.9944	63.9110
November	−2.0072	−3.9642	5.5446	−1.5252	2.3261	−3.0252	9.1519
December	−4.6336	−2.0072	−3.9642	−5.3600	28.7299	−4.1675	17.3685
2002							
January	2.7505	−4.6336	−2.0072	3.6459	13.2927	3.9416	15.5365
February	4.8476	2.7505	−4.6336	1.1834	1.4005	3.2772	10.7404
March	6.9619	4.8476	2.7505	2.0029	4.0118	2.5630	6.5692
April	6.9218	6.9619	4.8476	0.6573	0.4320	1.0158	1.0319
May	0.0000	6.9218	6.9619	−6.2397	38.9339	−6.4190	41.2034
June	0.6695	0.0000	6.9218	−1.2963	1.6804	−2.5319	6.4105
July	1.3423	0.6695	0.0000	−1.0369	1.0751	−0.4288	0.1839
August	4.0719	1.3423	0.6695	1.2773	1.6315	1.8207	3.3148
September	2.0105	4.0719	1.3423	−2.4694	6.0981	−1.6747	2.8047
October	2.0072	2.0105	4.0719	−1.2000	1.4400	−1.4092	1.9860
November	0.0000	2.0072	2.0105	−3.2051	10.2728	−2.8965	8.3900
December	−2.6157	0.0000	2.0072	−4.5814	20.9893	−4.5812	20.9876
				Average	14.0431	Average	14.5284
				RMSE	3.7474	RMSE	3.8116

Source: U.S. Bureau of Labor Statistics.

For each month from January 2001 to December 2002, the first column of numbers in Table 7 shows the actual annualized inflation rate during the month. The second and third columns show the rate of inflation in the previous two months. The fourth column shows the out-of-sample errors from the AR(1) model shown in Table 5. The fifth column shows the squared errors from the AR(1) model. The sixth column shows the out-of-sample errors from the AR(2) model shown in Table 6. The final column shows the squared errors from the AR(2) model. The bottom of the table displays the average squared error and the RMSE. According to these measures, the AR(1) model was slightly more accurate than the AR(2) model in its out-of-sample forecasts of inflation from January 2001 to December 2002. The RMSE from the AR(1) model was only $3.7474/3.8116 = 98.32$ percent as large as the RMSE from the AR(2) model. Therefore, even though the AR(2) model was more accurate in-sample, the AR(1) model was slightly more accurate out of sample. Of course, this was a small sample to use in evaluating out-of-sample forecasting performance. Although we seem to have conflicting information about whether to choose an AR(1) or an AR(2) model here, we must also consider regression coefficient stability. We will continue the comparison between these two models in the following section.

4.6 Instability of Regression Coefficients

One of the important issues an analyst faces in modeling a time series is the sample period to use. The estimates of regression coefficients of the time-series model can change substantially across different sample periods used for estimating the model. Often, the regression coefficient estimates of a time-series model estimated using an earlier sample period can be quite different from those of a model estimated using a later sample period. Similarly, the estimates can be different between models estimated using relatively shorter and longer sample periods. Further, the choice of model for a particular time series can also depend on the sample period. For example, an AR(1) model may be appropriate for the sales of a company in one particular sample period, but an AR(2) model may be necessary for an earlier or later sample period (or for a longer or shorter sample period). Thus the choice of a sample period is an important decision in modeling a financial time series.

Unfortunately, there is usually no clear-cut basis in economic or financial theory for determining whether to use data from a longer or shorter sample period to estimate a time-series model. We can get some guidance, however, if we remember that our models are valid only for covariance-stationary time series. For example, we should not combine data from a period when exchange rates were fixed with data from a period when exchange rates were floating. The exchange rates in these two periods would not likely have the same variance because exchange rates are usually much more volatile under a floating-rate regime than when rates are fixed. Similarly, many U.S. analysts consider it inappropriate to model U.S. inflation or interest-rate behavior since the 1960s as a part of one sample period, because the Federal Reserve had distinct policy regimes during this period. The best way to determine appropriate samples for time-series estimation is to look at graphs of the data to see if the time series looks stationary before estimation begins. If we know that a government policy changed on a specific date, we might also test whether the time-series relation was the same before and after that date.

In the following example, we illustrate how the choice of a longer versus a shorter period can affect the decision of whether to use, for example, a first- or second-order time-series model. We then show how the choice of the time-series model (and the associated regression coefficients) affects our forecast. Finally, we discuss which sample period, and accordingly which model and corresponding forecast, is appropriate for the time series analyzed in the example.

EXAMPLE 9

Instability in Time-Series Models of U.S. Inflation

In Example 6, analyst Lisette Miller concluded that U.S. CPI inflation should be modeled as an AR(2) time series. A colleague examined her results and questioned estimating one time-series model for inflation in the United States since 1971, given that Federal Reserve policy changed dramatically in the late 1970s and early 1980s. He argues that the inflation time series from 1971 to 2000 has two **regimes** or underlying models generating the time series: one running from 1971 through 1984, and another starting in 1985. Therefore, the colleague suggests that Miller estimate a new time-series model for U.S. inflation starting in 1985. Because of his suggestion, Miller first estimates an AR(1) model for inflation using data for a shorter sample period from 1985 to 2000. Table 8 shows her AR(1) estimates.

TABLE 8   Autoregression: AR(1) Model Monthly CPI Inflation at an Annual Rate, February 1985–December 2000

Regression Statistics

R-squared	0.1540
Standard error	2.4641
Observations	191
Durbin–Watson	1.9182

	Coefficient	Standard Error	t-Statistic
Intercept	2.1371	0.2859	7.4747
Lag 1	0.3359	0.0690	4.8716

(Table continued on next page . . .)

TABLE 8	(continued)		
Autocorrelations of the Residual			
Lag	**Autocorrelation**	**Standard Error**	**_t_-Statistic**
1	0.0284	0.0724	0.3922
2	−0.0900	0.0724	−1.2426
3	−0.0141	0.0724	−0.1955
4	−0.0297	0.0724	−0.4103

Source: U.S. Bureau of Labor Statistics.

The bottom part of Table 8 shows that the first four autocorrelations of the residuals from the AR(1) model are quite small. None of these autocorrelations has a *t*-statistic larger than 1.97, the critical value for significance. Consequently, Miller cannot reject the null hypothesis that the residuals are serially uncorrelated. The AR(1) model is correctly specified for the sample period from 1985 to 2000, so there is no need to estimate the AR(2) model. This conclusion is very different from that reached in Example 6 using data from 1971 to 2000. In that example, Miller initially rejected the AR(1) model because its residuals exhibited serial correlation. When she used a larger sample, an AR(2) model initially appeared to fit the data much better than did an AR(1) model.

How deeply does our choice of sample period affect our forecast of future inflation? Suppose that in a given month, inflation was 4 percent at an annual rate, and the month before that it was 3 percent. The AR(1) model shown in Table 8 predicts that inflation in the next month will be 2.1371 + 0.3359(4) = approximately 3.48 percent. Therefore, the forecast of the next month's inflation using the 1985 to 2000 sample is 3.48 percent. Remember from the analysis following Example 6 that the AR(2) model for the 1971 to 2000 sample predicts inflation of 4.07 percent in the next month. Thus, using the correctly specified model for the shorter sample produces an inflation forecast almost 0.6 percentage points below the forecast made from the correctly specified model for the longer sample period. Such a difference might substantially affect a particular investment decision.

Which model is correct? Figure 9 suggests an answer. Monthly U.S. inflation was, on average, so much higher and so much more volatile during the mid-1970s to early 1980s than it was after 1984 that inflation is probably not a covariance-stationary time series from 1971 to 2000. Therefore, we can reasonably believe that the data have more than one regime and Miller should estimate a separate model for inflation from 1985 to 2000, as shown above. As the example shows, judgment and experience (such as knowledge of government policy changes) play a vital role in determining how to model a time series. Simply relying on autocorrelations of the residuals from a time-series model cannot tell us the correct sample period for our analysis.

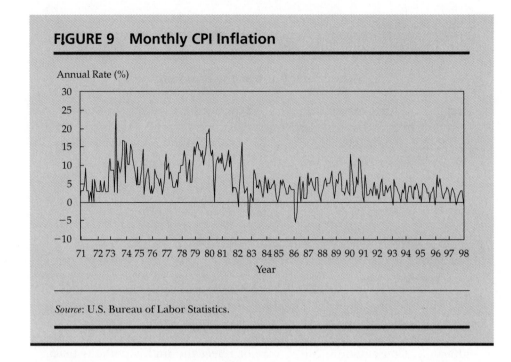

FIGURE 9   Monthly CPI Inflation

Source: U.S. Bureau of Labor Statistics.

5   RANDOM WALKS AND UNIT ROOTS

So far, we have examined those time series in which the time series has a tendency to revert to its mean level as the change in a variable from one period to the next follows a mean-reverting pattern. In contrast, there are many financial time series in which the changes follow a random pattern. We discuss these "random walks" in the following section.

5.1 Random Walks

A random walk is one of the most widely studied time-series models for financial data. A **random walk** is a time series in which the value of the series in one period is the value of the series in the previous period plus an unpredictable random error. A random walk can be described by the following equation:

$$x_t = x_{t-1} + \epsilon_t, \; E(\epsilon_t) = 0, \; E(\epsilon_t^2) = \sigma^2, \; E(\epsilon_t \epsilon_s) = 0 \text{ if } t \neq s \qquad (8)$$

Equation 8 means that the time series x_t is in every period equal to its value in the previous period plus an error term, ϵ_t, that has constant variance and is uncorrelated with the error term in previous periods. Note two important points. First, this equation is a special case of an AR(1) model with $b_0 = 0$ and $b_1 = 1$.[25] Second, the expected value of ϵ_t is zero. Therefore, the best forecast of x_t that can be made in period $t - 1$ is x_{t-1}. In fact, in this model, x_{t-1} is the best forecast of x in every period after $t - 1$.

Random walks are quite common in financial time series. For example, many studies have tested and found that currency exchange rates follow a ran-

---

[25] Equation 8 with a nonzero intercept added (as in Equation 9 given later) is sometimes referred to as a random walk with drift.

dom walk. Consistent with the second point made above, some studies have found that sophisticated exchange rate forecasting models cannot outperform forecasts made using the random walk model, and that the best forecast of the future exchange rate is the current exchange rate.

Unfortunately, we cannot use the regression methods we have discussed so far to estimate an AR(1) model on a time series that is actually a random walk. To see why this is so, we must determine why a random walk has no finite mean-reverting level or finite variance. Recall that if x_t is at its mean-reverting level, then $x_t = b_0 + b_1 x_t$, or $x_t = b_0/(1 - b_1)$. In a random walk, however, $b_0 = 0$ and $b_1 = 1$, so $b_0/(1 - b_1) = 0/0$. Therefore, a random walk has an undefined mean-reverting level.

What is the variance of a random walk? Suppose that in Period 1, the value of x_1 is 0. Then we know that $x_2 = 0 + \epsilon_2$. Therefore, the variance of $x_2 = \text{Var}(\epsilon_2) = \sigma^2$. Now $x_3 = x_2 + \epsilon_3 = \epsilon_2 + \epsilon_3$. Because the error term in each period is assumed to be uncorrelated with the error terms in all other periods, the variance of $x_3 = \text{Var}(\epsilon_2) + \text{Var}(\epsilon_3) = 2\sigma^2$. By a similar argument, we can show that for any period t, the variance of $x_t = (t - 1)\sigma^2$. But this means that as t grows large, the variance of x_t grows without an upper bound: It approaches infinity. This lack of upper bound, in turn, means that a random walk is not a covariance-stationary time series, because a covariance-stationary time series must have a finite variance.

What is the practical implication of these issues? *We cannot use standard regression analysis on a time series that is a random walk.* We can, however, attempt to convert the data to a covariance-stationary time series if we suspect that the time series is a random walk. In statistical terms, we can difference it.

We difference a time series by creating a new time series, say y_t, that in each period is equal to the difference between x_t and x_{t-1}. This transformation is called **first-differencing** because it subtracts the value of the time series in the first prior period from the current value of the time series. Sometimes the first difference of x_t is written as $\Delta x_t = x_t - x_{t-1}$. Note that the first difference of the random walk in Equation 8 yields

$$y_t = x_t - x_{t-1} = \epsilon_t, \; E(\epsilon_t) = 0, \; E(\epsilon_t^2) = \sigma^2, \; E(\epsilon_t \epsilon_s) = 0 \text{ for } t \neq s$$

The expected value of ϵ_t is 0. Therefore, the best forecast of y_t that can be made in period $t - 1$ is 0. This implies that the best forecast is that there will be no change in the value of the current time series, x_{t-1}.

The first-differenced variable, y_t, is covariance stationary. How is this so? First, note that this model ($y_t = \epsilon_t$) is an AR(1) model with $b_0 = 0$ and $b_1 = 0$. We can compute the mean-reverting level of the first-differenced model as $b_0/(1 - b_1) = 0/1 = 0$. Therefore, a first-differenced random walk has a mean-reverting level of 0. Note also that the variance of y_t in each period is $\text{Var}(\epsilon_t) = \sigma^2$. Because the variance and the mean of y_t are constant and finite in each period, y_t is a covariance-stationary time series and we can model it using linear regression.[26] Of course, modeling the first-differenced series with an AR(1) model does not help us predict the future, as $b_0 = 0$ and $b_1 = 0$. We simply conclude that the original time series is, in fact, a random walk.

Had we tried to estimate an AR(1) model for a time series that was a random walk, our statistical conclusions would have been incorrect because AR models cannot be used to estimate random walks or any time series that is not covariance stationary. The following example illustrates this issue with exchange rates.

---

[26] All the covariances are finite, for two reasons: The variance is finite, and the covariance of a time series with its own past value can be no greater than the variance of the series.

EXAMPLE 10

The Yen/U.S. Dollar Exchange Rate

Financial analysts often assume that exchange rates are random walks. Consider an AR(1) model for the Japanese yen/U.S. dollar exchange rate. Table 9 shows the results of estimating the model using month-end observations from January 1975 to December 2002.

TABLE 9   Yen/U.S. Dollar Exchange Rate: AR(1) Model Month-End Observations, January 1975–December 2002

Regression Statistics

R-squared	0.9914
Standard error	5.9006
Observations	336
Durbin–Watson	1.8492

	Coefficient	Standard Error	t-Statistic
Intercept	1.0223	0.9268	1.1092
Lag 1	0.9910	0.0050	196.4517

Autocorrelations of the Residual

Lag	Autocorrelation	Standard Error	t-Statistic
1	0.0706	0.0546	1.2930
2	0.0364	0.0546	0.6667
3	0.0864	0.0546	1.5824
4	0.0566	0.0546	1.0366

Source: U.S. Federal Reserve Board of Governors.

The results in Table 9 suggest that the yen/U.S. dollar exchange rate is a random walk because the estimated intercept does not appear to be significantly different from 0 and the estimated coefficient on the first lag of the exchange rate is very close to 1. Can we use the *t*-statistics in Table 9 to test whether the exchange rate is a random walk? Unfortunately, no, because the standard errors in an AR model are invalid if the model is estimated on a random walk (remember, a random walk is not covariance stationary). If the exchange rate is, in fact, a random walk, we might come to an incorrect conclusion based on faulty statistical tests and then invest incorrectly. We can use a test presented in the next section to test whether the time-series is a random walk.

Suppose the exchange rate is a random walk, as we now suspect. If so, the first-differenced series, $y_t = x_t - x_{t-1}$, will be covariance stationary. We present the results from estimating $y_t = b_0 + b_1 y_{t-1} + \epsilon_t$ in Table 10. If the exchange rate is a random walk, then $b_0 = 0$ and $b_1 = 0$ and the error term will not be serially correlated.

TABLE 10 First-Differenced Yen/U.S. Dollar Exchange Rate: AR(1) Model Month-End Observations, January 1975–December 2002

Regression Statistics

R-squared	0.0053
Standard error	5.9133
Observations	336
Durbin–Watson	1.9980

	Coefficient	Standard Error	*t*-Statistic
Intercept	−0.4963	0.3244	−1.5301
Lag 1	0.0726	0.0547	1.3282

Autocorrelations of the Residual

Lag	Autocorrelation	Standard Error	*t*-Statistic
1	−0.0045	0.0546	−0.0824
2	0.0259	0.0546	0.4744
3	0.0807	0.0546	1.4780
4	0.0488	0.0546	0.8938

Source: U.S. Federal Reserve Board of Governors.

In Table 10, neither the intercept nor the coefficient on the first lag of the first-differenced exchange rate differs significantly from 0, and no residual autocorrelations differ significantly from 0.[27] These findings are consistent with the yen/U.S. dollar exchange rate being a random walk. We have concluded that the differenced regression is the model to choose. Now we can see that we would have been seriously misled if we had based our model choice on an R^2 comparison. In Table 9, the R^2 is 0.9914, whereas in Table 10 the R^2 is 0.0053. How can this be, if we just concluded that the model in Table 10 is the one that we should use? In

---

[27] See Greene (2003) for a test of the joint hypothesis that both regression coefficients are equal to 0.

Table 9, the R^2 measures how well the exchange rate in one period predicts the exchange rate in the next period. If the exchange rate is a random walk, its current value will be an extremely good predictor of its value in the next period, and thus the R^2 will be extremely high. At the same time, if the exchange rate is a random walk, then changes in the exchange rate should be completely unpredictable. Table 10 estimates whether changes in the exchange rate from one month to the next can be predicted by changes in the exchange rate over the previous month. If they cannot be predicted, the R^2 in Table 10 should be very low. In fact, it is low (0.0053). This comparison provides a good example of the general rule that we cannot necessarily choose which model is correct solely by comparing the R^2 from the two models.

The exchange rate is a random walk, and changes in a random walk are by definition unpredictable. Therefore, we cannot profit from an investment strategy that predicts changes in the exchange rate.

To this point, we have discussed only simple random walks; that is, random walks without drift. In a random walk without drift, the best predictor of the time series in the next period is its current value. A random walk with drift, however, should increase or decrease by a constant amount in each period. The equation describing a random walk with drift is a special case of the AR(1) model:

$$x_t = b_0 + b_1 x_{t-1} + \epsilon_t$$
$$b_1 = 1, b_0 \neq 0, \text{ or}$$
$$x_t = b_0 + x_{t-1} + \epsilon_t, E(\epsilon_t) = 0 \tag{9}$$

A random walk with drift has $b_0 \neq 0$ compared to a simple random walk, which has $b_0 = 0$.

We have already seen that $b_1 = 1$ implies an undefined mean-reversion level and thus nonstationarity. Consequently, we cannot use an AR model to analyze a time series that is a random walk with drift until we transform the time series by taking first differences. If we first-difference Equation 9, the result is $y_t = x_t - x_{t-1}$, $y_t = b_0 + \epsilon_t$, $b_0 \neq 0$.

5.2 The Unit Root Test of Nonstationarity

In this section, we discuss how to use random walk concepts to determine whether a time series is covariance stationary. This approach focuses on the slope coefficient in the random-walk-with-drift case of an AR(1) model in contrast with the traditional autocorrelation approach which we discuss first.

The examination of the autocorrelations of a time series at various lags is a well-known prescription for inferring whether or not a time series is stationary. Typically, for a stationary time series, either autocorrelations at all lags are statistically indistinguishable from zero, or the autocorrelations drop off rapidly to zero as the number of lags becomes large. Conversely, the autocorrelations of a nonstationary time series do not exhibit those characteristics. However, this approach is less definite than a currently more popular test for nonstationarity known as the Dickey–Fuller test for a unit root.

We can explain what is known as the unit root problem in the context of an AR(1) model. If a time series comes from an AR(1) model, then to be covariance stationary the absolute value of the lag coefficient, b_1, must be less than 1.0. We could not rely on the statistical results of an AR(1) model if the absolute value of the lag coefficient were greater than or equal to 1.0 because the time series would not be covariance stationary. If the lag coefficient is equal to 1.0, the time series has a **unit root**: it is a random walk and is not covariance stationary.[28] By definition, all random walks, with or without a drift term, have unit roots.

How do we test for unit roots in a time series? If we believed that a time series, x_t, was a random walk with drift, it would be tempting to estimate the parameters of the AR(1) model $x_t = b_0 + b_1 x_{t-1} + \epsilon_t$ using linear regression and conduct a t-test of the hypothesis that $b_1 = 1$. Unfortunately, if $b_1 = 1$, then x_t is not covariance stationary and the t-value of the estimated coefficient, $\hat{b}_1$, does not actually follow the t-distribution; consequently, a t-test would be invalid.

Dickey and Fuller (1979) developed a regression-based unit root test based on a transformed version of the AR(1) model $x_t = b_0 + b_1 x_{t-1} + \epsilon_t$. Subtracting x_{t-1} from both sides of the AR(1) model produces

$$x_t - x_{t-1} = b_0 + (b_1 - 1)x_{t-1} + \epsilon_t$$

or

$$x_t - x_{t-1} = b_0 + g_1 x_{t-1} + \epsilon_t, \, E(\epsilon_t) = 0 \qquad \textbf{(10)}$$

where $g_1 = (b_1 - 1)$. If $b_1 = 1$, then $g_1 = 0$ and thus a test of $g_1 = 0$ is a test of $b_1 = 1$. If there is a unit root in the AR(1) model, then g_1 will be 0 in a regression where the dependent variable is the first difference of the time series and the independent variable is the first lag of the time series. The null hypothesis of the Dickey–Fuller test is H_0: $g_1 = 0$—that is, that the time series has a unit root and is nonstationary—and the alternative hypothesis is H_a: $g_1 < 0$, that the time series does not have a unit root and is stationary.

To conduct the test, one calculates a t-statistic in the conventional manner for $\hat{g}_1$ but instead of using conventional critical values for a t-test, one uses a revised set of values computed by Dickey and Fuller; the revised set of critical values are larger in absolute value than the conventional critical values. A number of software packages incorporate Dickey–Fuller tests.[29]

EXAMPLE 11

Intel's Quarterly Sales (1)

Earlier, we concluded that we could not model the log of Intel's quarterly sales using only a time-trend line (as shown in Example 3). Recall that the Durbin–Watson statistic from the log-linear regression caused us to reject the hypothesis that the errors in the regression were serially uncorrelated. Suppose, instead, that the analyst decides to model the

---

[28] When b_1 is greater than 1 in absolute value, we say that there is an explosive root. For details, see Diebold (2004).

[29] Dickey and Fuller developed three separate tests of the hypothesis that $g_1 = 0$ assuming the following models: random walk, random walk with drift, or random walk with drift and trend. The critical values for the Dickey–Fuller tests for the three models are different. For more on this topic, see Greene (2003) or Hamilton (1994).

log of Intel's quarterly sales using an AR(1) model. He uses ln Sales$_t$ = b_0 + b_1 ln Sales$_{t-1}$ + ϵ_t.

Before he estimates this regression, the analyst should use the Dickey–Fuller test to determine whether there is a unit root in the log of Intel's quarterly sales. If he uses the sample of quarterly data on Intel's sales from the first quarter of 1985 through the fourth quarter of 1999, takes the natural log of each observation, and computes the Dickey–Fuller t-test statistic, the value of that statistic might cause him to fail to reject the null hypothesis that there is a unit root in the log of Intel's quarterly sales.

If a time series appears to have a unit root, how should we model it? One method that is often successful is to first-difference the time series (as discussed previously) and try to model the first-differenced series as an autoregressive time series. The following example demonstrates this method.

EXAMPLE 12

Intel's Quarterly Sales (2)

Suppose you are convinced—from looking at the plot of the time series—that the log of Intel's quarterly sales is not covariance stationary (it has a unit root). So you create a new series, y_t, that is the first difference of the log of Intel's quarterly sales. Figure 10 shows that series.

If you compare Figure 10 to Figures 6 and 8, you will see that first-differencing the log of Intel's quarterly sales eliminates the strong upward trend that was present in both Intel's sales and the log of Intel's sales. Because the first-differenced series has no strong trend, you are

FIGURE 10   Log Difference, Intel Quarterly Sales

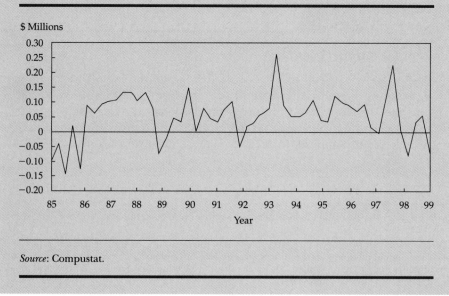

Source: Compustat.

better off assuming that the differenced series is covariance stationary rather than assuming that Intel's sales or the log of Intel's sales is a covariance-stationary time series.

Now suppose you decide to model the new series using an AR(1) model. You use $\ln(\text{Sales}_t) - \ln(\text{Sales}_{t-1}) = b_0 + b_1[\ln(\text{Sales}_{t-1}) - \ln(\text{Sales}_{t-2})] + \epsilon_t$. Table 11 shows the results of that regression.

TABLE 11   Log Differenced Sales: AR(1) Model Intel Corporation Quarterly Observations, January 1985–December 1999

Regression Statistics

R-squared	0.0946
Standard error	0.0758
Observations	60
Durbin–Watson	1.9709

	Coefficient	Standard Error	t-Statistic
Intercept	0.0352	0.0114	3.0875
Lag 1	0.3064	0.1244	2.4620

Autocorrelations of the Residual

Lag	Autocorrelation	Standard Error	t-Statistic
1	−0.0140	0.1291	−0.1088
2	−0.0855	0.1291	−0.6624
3	−0.0582	0.1291	−0.4506
4	0.2125	0.1291	1.6463

Source: Compustat.

The lower part of Table 11 shows that the first four autocorrelations of residuals in this model are quite small. With 60 observations and two parameters, this model has 58 degrees of freedom. The critical value for a t-statistic in this model is about 2.0 at the 0.05 significance level. None of the t-statistics for these autocorrelations has an absolute value larger than 2.0. Therefore, we fail to reject the null hypotheses that each of these autocorrelations is equal to 0 and conclude instead that no significant autocorrelation is present in the residuals.

This result suggests that the model is well specified and that we could use the estimates. Both the intercept ($\hat{b}_0 = 0.0352$) and the coefficient ($\hat{b}_1 = 0.3064$) on the first lag of the new first-differenced series are statistically significant. How can we interpret the estimated coefficients in the model? The value of the intercept (0.0352) implies that if sales have not changed in the current quarter ($y_t = \ln \text{Sales}_t - \ln \text{Sales}_{t-1} = 0$), sales will grow by 3.52 percent next quarter.[30] If sales have changed during this quarter, however, the model predicts that sales will grow by 3.52 percent plus 0.3064 times the sales growth in this quarter.

Suppose we wanted to use this model soon after the end of the fourth quarter of 1999 to predict Intel's sales for the first quarter of 2000. Let us say that t is the fourth quarter of 1999, so $t - 1$ is the third quarter of 1999 and $t + 1$ is the first quarter of 2000. Then we would have to compute $\hat{y}_{t+1} = 0.0352 + 0.3064\, y_t$. To compute $\hat{y}_{t+1}$, we need to know $y_t = \ln \text{Sales}_t - \ln \text{Sales}_{t-1}$. In the third quarter of 1999, Intel's sales were \$7,328 million, so $\ln (\text{Sales}_{t-1}) = \ln 7{,}328 = 8.8995$. In the fourth quarter of 1999, Intel's sales were \$8,212 million, so $\ln (\text{Sales}_t) = \ln 8{,}212 = 9.0134$. Thus $y_t = 9.0134 - 8.8995 = 0.1139$. Therefore, $\hat{y}_{t+1} = 0.0352 + 0.3064(0.1139) = 0.0701$. If $\hat{y}_{t+1} = 0.0701$, then $0.0701 = \ln (\text{Sales}_{t+1}) - \ln (\text{Sales}_t) = \ln (\text{Sales}_{t+1}/\text{Sales}_t)$. If we exponentiate both sides of this equation, the result is

$$
\begin{aligned}
e^{0.0701} &= (\text{Sales}_{t+1}/\text{Sales}_t) \\
\text{Sales}_{t+1} &= \text{Sales}_t\, e^{0.0701} \\
&= \$8{,}212 \text{ million} \times 1.0726 \\
&= \$8{,}808 \text{ million}
\end{aligned}
$$

Thus, based on fourth quarter sales for 1999, this model would have predicted that Intel's sales in the first quarter of 2000 would be \$8,808 million. This sales forecast might have affected our decision to buy Intel's stock at the time.

6   MOVING-AVERAGE TIME-SERIES MODELS

So far, many of the forecasting models we have used have been autoregressive models. Because most financial time series have the qualities of an autoregressive process, autoregressive time-series models are probably the most frequently used time-series models in financial forecasting. Some financial time series, however, seem to follow more closely another kind of time-series model called a moving-average model. For example, as we will see later, returns on the Standard & Poor's 500 Index can be better modeled as a moving-average process than as an autoregressive process.

In this section, we present the fundamentals of moving-average models so that you can ask the right questions when presented with them. We first discuss how to smooth past values with a moving average and then how to forecast a time series using a moving-average model. Even though both methods include the words "moving average" in the name, they are very different.

---

[30] Note that 3.52 percent is the exponential growth rate, not [(Current quarter sales/Previous quarter sales) − 1]. The difference between these two methods of computing growth is usually small.

6.1 Smoothing Past Values with an *n*-Period Moving Average

Suppose you are analyzing the long-term trend in the past sales of a company. In order to focus on the trend, you may find it useful to remove short-term fluctuations or noise by smoothing out the time series of sales. One technique to smooth out period-to-period fluctuations in the value of a time series is an ***n*-period moving average**. An *n*-period moving average of the current and past $n - 1$ values of a time series, x_t, is calculated as

$$\frac{x_t + x_{t-1} + \ldots + x_{t-(n-1)}}{n} \tag{11}$$

The following example demonstrates how to compute a moving average of Intel's quarterly sales.

EXAMPLE 13

Intel's Quarterly Sales (3)

Suppose we want to compute the four-quarter moving average of Intel's sales at the end of the fourth quarter of 1999. Intel's sales in the previous four quarters were 1Q:1999, $7,103 million; 2Q:1999, $6,746 million; 3Q:1999, $7,328 million; and 4Q:1999, $8,212 million. The four-quarter moving average of sales as of the first quarter of 2000 is thus (7,103 + 6,746 + 7,328 + 8,212)/4 = $7,347.25 million.

We often plot the moving average of a series with large fluctuations to help discern any patterns in the data. Figure 11 shows monthly real (inflation-adjusted) retail sales for the United States from January 1972 to December 2000, along with a 12-month moving average of the data.[31]

As Figure 11 shows, each year has a very strong peak in retail sales (December) followed by a sharp drop in sales (January). Because of the extreme seasonality in the data, a 12-month moving average can help us focus on the long-term movements in retail sales instead of seasonal fluctuations. Note that the moving average does not have the sharp seasonal fluctuations of the original retail sales data. Rather, the moving average of retail sales grows steadily, for example, from 1985 through 1990, then declines until 1993, and grows steadily thereafter. We can see that trend more easily by looking at a 12-month moving average than by looking at the time series itself.

Figure 12 shows monthly crude oil prices in the United States along with a 12-month moving average of oil prices. Although these data do not have the same sharp regular seasonality displayed in the retail sales data in Figure 11, the moving average smoothes out the monthly fluctuations in oil prices to show the longer-term movements.

---

[31] A 12-month moving average is the average value of a time series over each of the last 12 months. Although the sample period starts in 1972, data from 1971 are used to compute the 12-month moving average for the months of 1972.

FIGURE 11   Monthly U.S. Real Retail Sales and 12-Month Moving Average of Retail Sales

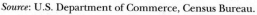

Source: U.S. Department of Commerce, Census Bureau.

Figure 12 also shows one weakness with a moving average: It always lags large movements in the actual data. For example, when oil prices fell sharply in late 1985 and remained relatively low, the moving average fell only gradually. When oil prices rose quickly in 1999, the moving average also lagged. Consequently, a simple moving average of the recent past, though often useful in smoothing out a time series, may not be the best predictor of the future. A main reason for this is that a simple moving average gives equal weight to all the periods in the moving average. In order to forecast the future values of a time series, it is often better to use a more sophisticated moving-average time-series model. We discuss such models below.

FIGURE 12   Monthly Oil Price and 12-Month Moving Average of Prices

Source: Dow Jones Energy Service.

6.2 Moving-Average Time-Series Models for Forecasting

Suppose that a time series, x_t, is consistent with the following model:

$$x_t = \epsilon_t + \theta\epsilon_{t-1}, E(\epsilon_t) = 0, E(\epsilon_t^2) = \sigma^2, E(\epsilon_t\epsilon_s) = 0 \text{ for } t \neq s \quad \boxed{(12)}$$

This equation is called a moving-average model of order 1, or simply an MA(1) model. Theta (θ) is the parameter of the MA(1) model.[32]

Equation 12 is a moving-average model because in each period, x_t is a moving average of ϵ_t and ϵ_{t-1}, two uncorrelated random variables that each have an expected value of zero. Unlike the simple moving-average model of Equation 11, this moving-average model places different weights on the two terms in the moving average (1 on ϵ_t, and θ on ϵ_{t-1}).

We can see if a time series fits an MA(1) model by looking at its autocorrelations to determine whether x_t is correlated only with its preceding and following values. First, we examine the variance of x_t in Equation 12 and its first two autocorrelations. Because the expected value of x_t is 0 in all periods and ϵ_t is uncorrelated with its own past values, the first autocorrelation is not equal to 0, but the second and higher autocorrelations are equal to 0. Further analysis shows that all autocorrelations except for the first will be equal to 0 in an MA(1) model. Thus for an MA(1) process, any value x_t is correlated with x_{t-1} and x_{t+1} but with no other time-series values; we could say that an MA(1) model has a memory of one period.

Of course, an MA(1) model is not the most complex moving-average model. A qth order moving-average model, denoted MA(q) and with varying weights on lagged terms, can be written as

$$x_t = \epsilon_t + \theta_1\epsilon_{t-1} + \ldots \theta_q\epsilon_{t-q}, E(\epsilon_t) = 0, E(\epsilon_t^2) = \sigma^2, \quad \boxed{(13)}$$
$$E(\epsilon_t\epsilon_s) = 0 \text{ for } t \neq s$$

How can we tell whether an MA(q) model fits a time series? We examine the autocorrelations. For an MA(q) model, the first q autocorrelations will be significantly different from 0, and all autocorrelations beyond that will be equal to 0; an MA(q) model has a memory of q periods. This result is critical for choosing the right value of q for an MA model. We discussed this result above for the specific case of $q = 1$ that all autocorrelations except for the first will be equal to 0 in an MA(1) model.

How can we distinguish an autoregressive time series from a moving-average time series? Once again, we do so by examining the autocorrelations of the time series itself. The autocorrelations of most autoregressive time series start large and decline gradually, whereas the autocorrelations of an MA(q) time series suddenly drop to 0 after the first q autocorrelations. We are unlikely to know in advance whether a time series is autoregressive or moving average. Therefore, the autocorrelations give us our best clue about how to model the time series. Most time series, however, are best modeled with an autoregressive model.

---

[32] Note that a moving-average time-series model is very different from a simple moving average, as discussed in Section 6.1. The simple moving average is based on observed values of a time series. In a moving-average time-series model, we never directly observe, ϵ_t or any other ϵ_{t-j}, but we can infer how a particular moving-average model will imply a particular pattern of serial correlation for a time series, as we discuss below.

EXAMPLE 14

A Time-Series Model for Monthly Returns on the S&P 500

Are monthly returns on the S&P autocorrelated? If so, we may be able to devise an investment strategy to exploit the autocorrelation. What is an appropriate time-series model for S&P 500 monthly returns?

Table 12 shows the first six autocorrelations of returns to the S&P 500 using monthly data from January 1991 to December 2002. Note that all of the autocorrelations are quite small. Do they reach significance? With 144 observations, the critical value for a t-statistic in this model is about 1.98 at the 0.05 significance level. None of the autocorrelations has a t-statistic larger in absolute value than the critical value of 1.98. Consequently, we fail to reject the null hypothesis that those autocorrelations, individually, do not differ significantly from 0.

TABLE 12   Annualized Monthly Returns to the S&P 500 January 1991–December 2002

Autocorrelations

Lag	Autocorrelation	Standard Error	t-Statistic
1	−0.0090	0.0833	−0.1083
2	−0.0207	0.0833	−0.2481
3	0.0020	0.0833	0.0240
4	−0.0730	0.0833	−0.8756
5	0.1143	0.0833	1.3717
6	−0.0007	0.0833	−0.0082
Observations	144		

Source: Ibbotson Associates.

If returns on the S&P 500 were an MA(q) time series, then the first q autocorrelations would differ significantly from 0. None of the autocorrelations is statistically significant, however, so returns to the S&P 500 appear to come from an MA(0) time series. An MA(0) time series in which we allow the mean to be nonzero takes the following form:[33]

$$x_t = \mu + \epsilon_t, E(\epsilon_t) = 0, E(\epsilon_t^2) = \sigma^2, E(\epsilon_t\epsilon_s) = 0 \text{ for } t \neq s \qquad \textbf{(14)}$$

---

[33] On the basis of investment theory and evidence, we expect that the mean monthly return on the S&P 500 is positive ($\mu > 0$). We can also generalize Equation 13 for an MA(q) time series by adding a constant term, μ. Including a constant term in a moving-average model does not change the expressions for the variance and autocovariances of the time series. A number of early studies of weak-form market efficiency used Equation 14 as the model for stock returns. See Garbade (1982).

which means that the time series is not predictable. This result should not be too surprising, as most research suggests that short-term returns to stock indexes are difficult to predict.

We can see from this example how examining the autocorrelations allowed us to choose between the AR and MA models. If returns to the S&P 500 had come from an AR(1) time series, the first autocorrelation would have differed significantly from 0 and the autocorrelations would have declined gradually. Not even the first autocorrelation is significantly different from 0, however. Therefore, we can be sure that returns to the S&P 500 do not come from an AR(1) model—or from any higher-order AR model, for that matter. This finding is consistent with our conclusion that the S&P 500 series is MA(0).

SEASONALITY IN TIME-SERIES MODELS   7

As we analyze the results of the time-series models in this reading, we encounter complications. One common complication is significant seasonality, a case in which the series shows regular patterns of movement within the year. At first glance, seasonality might appear to rule out using autoregressive time-series models. After all, autocorrelations will differ by season. This problem can often be solved, however, by using seasonal lags in an autoregressive model.

A seasonal lag is usually the value of the time series one year before the current period, included as an extra term in an autoregressive model. Suppose, for example, that we model a particular quarterly time series using an AR(1) model, $x_t = b_0 + b_1 x_{t-1} + \epsilon_t$. If the time series had significant seasonality, this model would not be correctly specified. The seasonality would be easy to detect because the seasonal autocorrelation (in the case of quarterly data, the fourth autocorrelation) of the error term would differ significantly from 0. Suppose this quarterly model has significant seasonality. In this case, we might include a seasonal lag in the autoregressive model and estimate

$$x_t = b_0 + b_1 x_{t-1} + b_2 x_{t-4} + \epsilon_t \qquad (15)$$

to test whether including the seasonal lag would eliminate statistically significant autocorrelation in the error term.

In Examples 15 and 16, we illustrate how to test and adjust for seasonality in a time-series model. We also illustrate how to compute a forecast using an autoregressive model with a seasonal lag.

EXAMPLE 15

Seasonality in Sales at Medtronic

We want to predict sales for Medtronic, Inc. Based on the previous results in this reading, we determine that the first difference of the log of sales is probably covariance stationary. Using quarterly data from the first quarter of 1985 to the last quarter of 2001, we estimate an AR(1) model using ordinary least squares on the first-differenced data. We estimate the following equation: $(\ln \text{Sales}_t - \ln \text{Sales}_{t-1}) = b_0 + b_1(\ln \text{Sales}_{t-1} - \ln \text{Sales}_{t-2}) + \epsilon_t$. Table 13 shows the results of the regression.

TABLE 13   Log Differenced Sales: AR(1) Model Medtronic, Inc., Quarterly Observations, January 1985–December 2001

Regression Statistics

R-squared	0.1619
Standard error	0.0693
Observations	68
Durbin–Watson	2.0588

	Coefficient	Standard Error	t-Statistic
Intercept	0.0597	0.0091	6.5411
Lag 1	−0.4026	0.1128	−3.5704

Autocorrelations of the Residual

Lag	Autocorrelation	Standard Error	t-Statistic
1	−0.0299	0.1213	−0.2463
2	−0.1950	0.1213	−1.6077
3	−0.1138	0.1213	−0.9381
4	0.4072	0.1213	3.3581

Source: Compustat.

The first thing to note in Table 13 is the strong seasonal autocorrelation of the residuals. The bottom portion of the table shows that the fourth autocorrelation has a value of 0.4072 and a t-statistic of 3.36. With 68 observations and two parameters, this model has 66 degrees of freedom.[34] The critical value for a t-statistic is about 2.0 at the 0.05 significance level. Given this value of the t-statistic, we must reject the null hypothesis that the fourth autocorrelation is equal to 0 because the t-statistic is larger than the critical value of 2.0.

In this model, the fourth autocorrelation is the seasonal autocorrelation because this AR(1) model is estimated with quarterly data. Table 13 shows the strong and statistically significant seasonal autocorrelation that

[34] Although the sample period begins in 1985, we use prior observations for the lags. Otherwise, the model would have fewer degrees of freedom because the sample size would be reduced with each increase in the number of lags.

occurs when a time series with strong seasonality is modeled without taking the seasonality into account. Therefore, the AR(1) model is misspecified, and we should not use it for forecasting.

Suppose we decide to use an autoregressive model with a seasonal lag because of the seasonal autocorrelation. We are modeling quarterly data, so we estimate Equation 15: $(\ln \text{Sales}_t - \ln \text{Sales}_{t-1}) = b_0 + b_1 (\ln \text{Sales}_{t-1} - \ln \text{Sales}_{t-2}) + b_2(\ln \text{Sales}_{t-4} - \ln \text{Sales}_{t-5}) + \epsilon_t$. The estimates of this equation appear in Table 14.

TABLE 14 Log Differenced Sales: AR(1) Model with Seasonal Lag Medtronic, Inc., Quarterly Observations, January 1985–December 2001

Regression Statistics

R-squared	0.3219
Standard error	0.0580
Observations	68
Durbin–Watson	2.0208

	Coefficient	Standard Error	t-Statistic
Intercept	0.0403	0.0096	4.1855
Lag 1	−0.2955	0.1058	−2.7927
Lag 4	0.3896	0.0995	3.9159

Autocorrelations of the Residual

Lag	Autocorrelation	Standard Error	t-Statistic
1	−0.0108	0.1213	−0.0889
2	−0.0957	0.1213	−0.7889
3	0.0075	0.1213	0.0621
4	−0.0340	0.1213	−0.2801

Source: Compustat.

Note the autocorrelations of the residual shown at the bottom of Table 14. When we include a seasonal lag in the regression, none of the t-statistics on the first four autocorrelations remains significant.

Now that we know that the residuals of this model do not have significant serial correlation, we can assume that the model is correctly specified. How can we interpret the coefficients in this model? To predict the current quarter's sales growth at Medtronic, we need to know two things: sales growth in the previous quarter and sales growth four quarters ago. If sales remained constant in each of those two quarters, the model in Table 14 predicts that sales will grow by 0.0403 (4.03 percent) in the current quarter. If sales grew by 1 percent last quarter and by 2 percent four quarters ago, then the model predicts that sales growth this quarter will be $0.0403 - 0.2955(0.01) + 0.3896(0.02) = 0.0451$ or 4.51 percent.[35] Notice also that the R^2 in the model with the seasonal lag (0.3219 in Table 14) was almost two times higher than the R^2 in the model without the seasonal lag (0.1619 in Table 13). Again, the seasonal lag model does a much better job of explaining the data.

EXAMPLE 16

Retail Sales Growth

We want to predict the growth in U.S. monthly retail sales so that we can decide whether to recommend discount store stocks. We decide to use non-seasonally adjusted data on retail sales, adjusted for inflation. To begin with, we estimate an AR(1) model with observations on the annualized monthly growth in real retail sales from February 1972 to December 2000. We estimate the following equation: Sales growth$_t = b_0 + b_1$ Sales growth$_{t-1} + \epsilon_t$. Table 15 shows the results from this model.

The autocorrelations of the residuals from this model, shown at the bottom of Table 15, indicate that seasonality is extremely significant in this model. With 347 observations and two parameters, this model has 345 degrees of freedom. At the 0.05 significance level, the critical value for a t-statistic is about 1.97. The 12th-lag autocorrelation (the seasonal autocorrelation, because we are using monthly data) has a value of 0.8739 and a t-statistic of 16.28. The t-statistic on this autocorrelation is larger than the critical value (1.97) implying that we can reject the null hypothesis that the 12th autocorrelation is 0. Note also that many of the other t-statistics for autocorrelations shown in the table differ significantly from 0. Consequently, the model shown in Table 15 is misspecified, so we cannot rely on it to forecast sales growth.

Suppose we add the seasonal lag of sales growth (the 12th lag) to the AR(1) model to estimate the equation Sales growth$_t = b_0 + b_1$(Sales growth$_{t-1}$) + b_2(Sales growth$_{t-12}$) + ϵ_t. Table 16 presents the results of estimating this equation. The estimated value of the seasonal autocorrelation (the 12th autocorrelation) has fallen to 0.0335. None of the first 12 autocorrelations has a t-statistic with an absolute value greater than the critical value of 1.97 at the 0.05 significance level. We can conclude that there is no significant serial correlation in the residuals from this model. Because we can reasonably believe that the model is correctly specified, we can use it to predict retail sales growth. Note that the R^2 in Table 16 is 0.8149, much larger than the R^2 in Table 15 (computed by the model without the seasonal lag).

---

[35] Note that all of these growth rates are exponential growth rates.

TABLE 15 Monthly Real Retail Sales Growth: AR(1) Model February 1972–December 2000

Regression Statistics

R-squared	0.0659
Standard error	2.3520
Observations	347
Durbin–Watson	2.1008

	Coefficient	Standard Error	*t*-Statistic
Intercept	1.2170	0.1357	8.9666
Lag 1	−0.2577	0.0522	−4.9349

Autocorrelations of the Residual

Lag	Autocorrelation	Standard Error	*t*-Statistic
1	−0.0552	0.0537	−1.0288
2	−0.1536	0.0537	−2.8619
3	0.1774	0.0537	3.3044
4	−0.1020	0.0537	−1.8996
5	−0.1320	0.0537	−2.4582
6	−0.2676	0.0537	−4.9841
7	−0.1366	0.0537	−2.5455
8	−0.0923	0.0537	−1.7186
9	0.1655	0.0537	3.0832
10	−0.1732	0.0537	−3.2273
11	−0.0623	0.0537	−1.1597
12	0.8739	0.0537	16.2793

Source: U.S. Department of Commerce.

How can we interpret the coefficients in the model? To predict growth in retail sales in this month, we need to know last month's retail sales growth and retail sales growth 12 months ago. If retail sales remained constant both last month and 12 months ago, the model in Table 16 predicts that retail sales will grow at an annual rate of approximately 15 percent this month. If retail sales grew at an annual rate of 5 percent last month and at an annual rate of 10 percent 12 months ago, the model in Table 16 predicts that retail sales will grow in the current month at an annual rate of $0.1516 - 0.0490(0.05) + 0.8857(0.10) = 0.2377$ or 23.8 percent.

**TABLE 16   Monthly Real Retail Sales Growth:
AR(1) Model with Seasonal Lag
February 1972–December 2000**

Regression Statistics

R-squared	0.8149
Standard error	1.0487
Observations	347
Durbin–Watson	2.4301

	Coefficient	Standard Error	*t*-Statistic
Intercept	0.1516	0.0669	2.2652
Lag 1	−0.0490	0.0239	−2.0484
Lag 12	0.8857	0.0237	37.3028

Autocorrelations of the Residual

Lag	Autocorrelation	Standard Error	*t*-Statistic
1	−0.0699	0.0537	−1.3019
2	−0.0107	0.0537	−0.1985
3	0.0946	0.0537	1.7630
4	−0.0556	0.0537	−1.0355
5	−0.0319	0.0537	−0.5936
6	0.0289	0.0537	0.5386
7	−0.0933	0.0537	−1.7382
8	0.0062	0.0537	0.1150
9	−0.0111	0.0537	−0.2059
10	−0.0523	0.0537	−0.9742
11	0.0377	0.0537	0.7026
12	0.0335	0.0537	0.6231

Source: U.S. Department of Commerce.

---

8   AUTOREGRESSIVE MOVING-AVERAGE MODELS

So far, we have presented autoregressive and moving-average models as alternatives for modeling a time series. The time series we have considered in examples have usually been explained quite well with a simple autoregressive model (with or without seasonal lags).[36] Some statisticians, however, have advocated using a more general model, the autoregressive moving-average (ARMA) model. The advocates of ARMA models argue that these models may fit the data better and provide better forecasts than do plain autoregressive (AR) models. However, as we discuss later in this section, there are severe limitations to estimating and using these models. Because you may encounter ARMA models, we provide a brief overview below.

An ARMA model combines both autoregressive lags of the dependent variable and moving-average errors. The equation for such a model with p autoregressive terms and q moving-average terms, denoted ARMA(p, q), is

$$x_t = b_0 + b_1 x_{t-1} + \ldots + b_p x_{t-p} + \epsilon_t + \theta_1 \epsilon_{t-1} + \ldots + \theta_q \epsilon_{t-q} \qquad \textbf{(16)}$$
$$E(\epsilon_t) = 0, \ E(\epsilon_t^2) = \sigma^2, \ E(\epsilon_t \epsilon_s) = 0 \text{ for } t \neq s$$

where b_1, b_2, . . ., b_p are the autoregressive parameters and θ_1, θ_2, . . ., θ_q are the moving-average parameters.

Estimating and using ARMA models has several limitations. First, the parameters in ARMA models can be very unstable. In particular, slight changes in the data sample or the initial guesses for the values of the ARMA parameters can result in very different final estimates of the ARMA parameters. Second, choosing the right ARMA model is more of an art than a science. The criteria for deciding on p and q for a particular time series are far from perfect. Moreover, even after a model is selected, that model may not forecast well.

To reiterate, ARMA models can be very unstable, depending on the data sample used and the particular ARMA model estimated. Therefore, you should be skeptical of claims that a particular ARMA model provides much better forecasts of a time series than any other ARMA model. In fact, in most cases, you can use an AR model to produce forecasts that are just as accurate as those from ARMA models without nearly as much complexity. Even some of the strongest advocates of ARMA models admit that these models should not be used with fewer than 80 observations, and they do not recommend using ARMA models for predicting quarterly sales or gross margins for a company using even 15 years of quarterly data.

AUTOREGRESSIVE CONDITIONAL HETEROSKEDASTICITY MODELS

9

Up to now, we have ignored any issues of heteroskedasticity in time-series models and have assumed homoskedasticity. **Heteroskedasticity** is the dependence of the error term variance on the independent variable; **homoskedasticity** is the independence of the error term variance from the independent variable. We have assumed that the error term's variance is constant and does not depend on the value of the time series itself or on the size of previous errors. At times, however, this assumption is violated and the variance of the error term is not constant. In such a situation, the standard errors of the regression coefficients in AR, MA, or ARMA models will be incorrect, and our hypothesis tests would be invalid. Consequently, we can make poor investment decisions based on those tests.

---

[36] For the returns on the S&P 500 (see Example 14), we chose a moving-average model over an autoregressive model.

For example, suppose you are building an autoregressive model of a company's sales. If heteroskedasticity is present, then the standard errors of the regression coefficients of your model are incorrect. It is likely that due to heteroskedasticity, one or more of the lagged sales terms may appear statistically significant when in fact they are not. Therefore, if you use this model for your decision making, you may make some suboptimal decisions.

In work responsible in part for his shared Nobel Prize in Economics for 2003, Robert F. Engle in 1982 first suggested a way of testing whether the variance of the error in a particular time-series model in one period depends on the variance of the error in previous periods. He called this type of heteroskedasticity autoregressive conditional heteroskedasticity (ARCH).

As an example, consider the ARCH(1) model

$$\epsilon_t \sim N(0, a_0 + a_1\epsilon_{t-1}^2) \qquad (17)$$

where the distribution of ϵ_t, conditional on its value in the previous period, ϵ_{t-1}, is normal with mean 0 and variance $a_0 + a_1\epsilon_{t-1}^2$. If $a_1 = 0$, the variance of the error in every period is just a_0. The variance is constant over time and does not depend on past errors. Now suppose that $a_1 > 0$. Then the variance of the error in one period depends on how large the squared error was in the previous period. If a large error occurs in one period, the variance of the error in the next period will be even larger.

Engle shows that we can test whether a time series is ARCH(1) by regressing the squared residuals from a previously estimated time-series model (AR, MA, or ARMA) on a constant and one lag of the squared residuals. We can estimate the linear regression equation

$$\hat{\epsilon}_t^2 = a_0 + a_1\hat{\epsilon}_{t-1}^2 + u_t \qquad (18)$$

where u_t is an error term. If the estimate of a_1 is statistically significantly different from zero, we conclude that the time series is ARCH(1). If a time-series model has ARCH(1) errors, then the variance of the errors in period $t + 1$ can be predicted in period t using the formula $\hat{\sigma}_{t+1}^2 = \hat{a}_0 + \hat{a}_1\hat{\epsilon}_t^2$.

EXAMPLE 17

Testing for ARCH(1) in Monthly Inflation

Analyst Lisette Miller wants to test whether monthly data on CPI inflation contain autoregressive conditional heteroskedasticity. She could estimate Equation 18 using the residuals from the time-series model. As discussed in Example 8, if she modeled monthly CPI inflation from 1971 to 2000, she would conclude that an AR(1) model was the best autoregressive model to use to forecast inflation out of sample. Table 17 shows the results of testing whether the errors in that model are ARCH(1).

Because the t-statistic for the coefficient on the previous period's squared residuals is greater than 7.5, Miller easily rejects the null hypothesis that the variance of the error does not depend on the variance of previous errors. Consequently, the test statistics she computed in

TABLE 17	Test for ARCH(1) in an AR(1) Model Residuals from Monthly CPI Inflation at an Annual Rate February 1971–December 2000

Regression Statistics

R-squared	0.1376
Standard error	26.3293
Observations	359
Durbin–Watson	1.9126

	Coefficient	Standard Error	t-Statistic
Intercept	7.2958	1.5050	4.8478
Lag 1	0.3687	0.0488	7.5483

Source: U.S. Bureau of Labor Statistics.

Table 5 are not valid, and she should not use them in deciding her investment strategy.

It is possible Miller's conclusion—that the AR(1) model for monthly inflation has ARCH in the errors—may have been due to the sample period employed (1971 to 2000). In Example 9, she used a shorter sample period of 1985 to 2000 and concluded that monthly CPI inflation follows an AR(1) process. (These results were shown in Table 8.) Table 17 shows that errors for a time-series model of inflation for the entire sample (1971 to 2000) have ARCH errors. Do the errors estimated with a shorter sample period (1985 to 2000) also display ARCH? For the shorter sample period, Miller estimated an AR(1) model using monthly inflation data.[37] Now she tests to see whether the errors display ARCH. Table 18 shows the results.

In this sample, the coefficient on the previous period's squared residual is quite small and has a t-statistic of only 1.4205. Consequently, Miller fails to reject the null hypothesis that the errors in this regression have no autoregressive conditional heteroskedasticity. This is additional evidence that the AR(1) model for 1985 to 2000 is a good fit. The error variance appears to be homoskedastic, and Miller can rely on the t-statistics. This result again confirms that a single AR process for the entire 1971–2000 period is misspecified (it does not describe the data well).

---

[37] The AR(1) results are reported in Example 9.

TABLE 18   Test for ARCH(1) in an AR(1) Model Monthly CPI Inflation at an Annual Rate February 1985–December 2000

Regression Statistics

R-squared	0.0106
Standard error	11.2593
Observations	191
Durbin–Watson	1.9969

	Coefficient	Standard Error	t-Statistic
Intercept	5.3939	0.9224	5.8479
Lag 1	0.1028	0.0724	1.4205

Source: U.S. Bureau of Labor Statistics.

Suppose a model contains ARCH(1) errors. What are the consequences of that fact? First, if ARCH exists, the standard errors for the regression parameters will not be correct. In case ARCH exists, we will need to use generalized least squares[38] or other methods that correct for heteroskedasticity to correctly estimate the standard error of the parameters in the time-series model. Second, if ARCH exists and we have it modeled, for example as ARCH(1), we can predict the variance of the errors. Suppose, for instance, that we want to predict the variance of the error in inflation using the estimated parameters from Table 17: $\hat{\sigma}_t^2 = 7.2958 + 0.3687\hat{\epsilon}_{t-1}^2$. If the error in one period were 0 percent, the predicted variance of the error in the next period would be $7.2958 + 0.3687(0) = 7.2958$. If the error in one period were 1 percent, the predicted variance of the error in the next period would be $7.2958 + 0.3687(1^2) = 7.6645$.

Engle and other researchers have suggested many generalizations of the ARCH(1) model, including ARCH(p) and generalized autoregressive conditional heteroskedasticity (GARCH) models. In an ARCH(p) model, the variance of the error term in the current period depends linearly on the squared errors from the previous p periods: $\sigma_t^2 = a_0 + a_1\epsilon_{t-1}^2 + \ldots + a_p\epsilon_{t-p}^2$. GARCH models are similar to ARMA models of the error variance in a time series. Just like ARMA models, GARCH models can be finicky and unstable: Their results can depend greatly on the sample period and the initial guesses of the parameters in the GARCH model. Financial analysts who use GARCH models should be well aware of how delicate these models can be, and they should examine whether GARCH estimates are robust to changes in the sample and the initial guesses about the parameters.[39]

---

[38] See Greene (2003).

[39] For more on ARCH, GARCH, and other models of time-series variance, see Hamilton (1994).

REGRESSIONS WITH MORE THAN ONE TIME SERIES

10

Up to now, we have discussed time-series models only for one time series. Although in the readings on correlation and regression and on multiple regression we used linear regression to analyze the relationship among different time series, in those readings we completely ignored unit roots. A time series that contains a unit root is not covariance stationary. If any time series in a linear regression contains a unit root, ordinary least squares estimates of regression test statistics may be invalid.

To determine whether we can use linear regression to model more than one time series, let us start with a single independent variable; that is, there are two time series, one corresponding to the dependent variable and one corresponding to the independent variable. We will then extend our discussion to multiple independent variables.

We first use a unit root test, such as the Dickey–Fuller test, for each of the two time series to determine whether either of them has a unit root.[40] There are several possible scenarios related to the outcome of these tests. One possible scenario is that we find that neither of the time series has a unit root. Then we can safely use linear regression to test the relations between the two time series. Otherwise, we may have to use additional tests, as we discuss later in this section.

EXAMPLE 18

Unit Roots and the Fisher Effect

In Example 8 in the reading on multiple regression, we examined the Fisher effect by estimating the regression relation between expected inflation and risk-free U.S. Treasury bill (T-bill) returns. We used a sample of 137 quarterly observations from the fourth quarter of 1968 until the fourth quarter of 2002 on the expected inflation and risk-free T-bill returns. We used linear regression to analyze the relationship between the two time series. The results of this regression would be valid if both the time series are covariance stationary; that is, neither of the two time series has a unit root. So, if we compute the Dickey–Fuller *t*-test statistic of the hypothesis of a unit root separately for each time series and find that we can reject the null hypothesis that the risk-free T-bill return series has a unit root and the null hypothesis that the expected inflation time series has a unit root, then we can use linear regression to analyze the relation between the two series. In that case, the results of our analysis of the Fisher effect would be valid.

A second possible scenario is that we reject the hypothesis of a unit root for the independent variable but fail to reject the hypothesis of a unit root for the dependent variable. In this case, the error term in the regression would not be covariance stationary. Therefore, one or more of the following linear regression

---

[40] For theoretical details of unit root tests, see Greene (2003) or Hamilton (1994). Unit root tests are available in some econometric software packages, such as EViews.

assumptions would be violated: 1) that the expected value of the error term is 0, 2) that the variance of the error term is constant for all observations, and 3) that the error term is uncorrelated across observations. Consequently, the estimated regression coefficients and standard errors would be inconsistent. The regression coefficients might appear significant, but those results would be spurious.[41] Thus we should not use linear regression to analyze the relation between the two time series in this scenario.

A third possible scenario is the reverse of the second scenario: We reject the hypothesis of a unit root for the dependent variable but fail to reject the hypothesis of a unit root for the independent variable. In this case also, like the second scenario, the error term in the regression would not be covariance stationary, and we cannot use linear regression to analyze the relation between the two time series.

EXAMPLE 19

Unit Roots and Predictability of Stock Market Returns by Price-to-Earnings Ratio

Johann de Vries is analyzing the performance of the South African stock market. He examines whether the percentage change in the Johannesburg Stock Exchange (JSE) All Share Index can be predicted by the price-to-earnings ratio (P/E) for the index. Using monthly data from January 1983 to December 2002, he runs a regression using $(P_t - P_{t-1})/P_{t-1}$ as the dependent variable and P_{t-1}/E_{t-2} as the independent variable, where P_t is the value of the JSE index at time t and E_t is the earnings on the index. De Vries finds that the regression coefficient is statistically significant and the value of the R-squared for the regression is quite high. What additional analysis should he perform before accepting the regression as valid?

De Vries needs to perform unit root tests for each of the two time series. If one of the two time series has a unit root, implying that it is not stationary, the results of the linear regression are not meaningful and cannot be used to conclude that stock market returns are predictable by P/E.[42]

The next possibility is that both time series have a unit root. In this case, we need to establish whether the two time series are **cointegrated** before we can rely on regression analysis.[43] Two time series are cointegrated if a long-term financial or economic relationship exists between them such that they do not diverge from each other without bound in the long run. For example, two time series are cointegrated if they share a common trend.

---

[41] The problem of spurious regression for nonstationary time series was first discussed by Granger and Newbold (1974).

[42] Barr and Kantor (1999) contains evidence that the P/E time series is nonstationary.

[43] Engle and Granger (1987) first discussed cointegration.

In the fourth scenario, both time series have a unit root but are not cointegrated. In this scenario, as in the second and third scenarios above, the error term in the linear regression will not be covariance stationary, some regression assumptions will be violated, the regression coefficients and standard errors will not be consistent, and we cannot use them for hypothesis tests. Consequently, linear regression of one variable on the other would be meaningless.

Finally, the fifth possible scenario is that both time series have a unit root, but they are cointegrated. In this case, the error term in the linear regression of one time series on the other will be covariance stationary. Accordingly, the regression coefficients and standard errors will be consistent, and we can use them for hypothesis tests. However, we should be very cautious in interpreting the results of a regression with cointegrated variables. The cointegrated regression estimates the long-term relation between the two series but may not be the best model of the short-term relation between the two series. Short-term models of cointegrated series (error correction models) are discussed in Engle and Granger (1987) and Hamilton (1994), but these are specialist topics.

Now let us look at how we can test for cointegration between two time series that each have a unit root as in the last two scenarios above.[44] Engle and Granger suggest this test: If y_t and x_t are both time series with a unit root, we should do the following:

1. Estimate the regression $y_t = b_0 + b_1 x_t + \epsilon_t$.

2. Test whether the error term from the regression in Step 1 has a unit root using a Dickey–Fuller test. Because the residuals are based on the estimated coefficients of the regression, we cannot use the standard critical values for the Dickey–Fuller test. Instead, we must use the critical values computed by Engle and Granger, which take into account the effect of uncertainty about the regression parameters on the distribution of the Dickey–Fuller test.

3. If the (Engle–Granger) Dickey–Fuller test fails to reject the null hypothesis that the error term has a unit root, then we conclude that the error term in the regression is not covariance stationary. Therefore, the two time series are not cointegrated. In this case any regression relation between the two series is spurious.

4. If the (Engle–Granger) Dickey–Fuller test rejects the null hypothesis that the error term has a unit root, then we conclude that the error term in the regression is covariance stationary. Therefore, the two time series are cointegrated. The parameters and standard errors from linear regression will be consistent and will let us test hypotheses about the long-term relation between the two series.

---

[44] Consider a time series, x_t, that has a unit root. For many such financial and economic time series, the first difference of the series, $x_t - x_{t-1}$, is stationary. We say that such a series, whose first difference is stationary, has a *single* unit root. However, for some time series, even the first difference may not be stationary and further differencing may be needed to achieve stationarity. Such a time series is said to have *multiple* unit roots. In this section, we consider only the case in which each nonstationary series has a single unit root (which is quite common).

EXAMPLE 20

Testing for Cointegration between Intel Sales and Nominal GDP

Suppose we want to test whether the natural log of Intel's sales and the natural log of GDP are cointegrated (that is, whether there is a long-term relation between GDP and Intel sales). We want to test this hypothesis using quarterly data from the first quarter of 1985 through the fourth quarter of 1999. Here are the steps:

1. Test whether the two series each have a unit root. If we cannot reject the null hypothesis of a unit root for both series, implying that both series are nonstationary, we must then test whether the two series are cointegrated.

2. Having established that each series has a unit root, we estimate the regression $\ln (\text{Intel Sales}_t) = b_0 + b_1 \ln \text{GDP}_t + \epsilon_t$, then conduct the (Engle–Granger) Dickey–Fuller test of the hypothesis that there is a unit root in the error term of this regression using the residuals from the estimated regression. If we reject the null hypothesis of a unit root in the error term of the regression, we reject the null hypothesis of no cointegration. That is, the two series would be cointegrated. If the two series are cointegrated, we can use linear regression to estimate the long-term relation between the natural log of Intel Sales and the natural log of GDP.

We have so far discussed models with a single independent variable. We now extend the discussion to a model with two or more independent variables, so that there are three or more time series. The simplest possibility is that none of the time series in the model has a unit root. Then, we can safely use multiple regression to test the relation among the time series.

EXAMPLE 21

Unit Roots and Returns to the Fidelity Select Technology Fund

In Example 3 in the reading on multiple regression, we used multiple linear regression to examine whether returns to either the S&P 500/BARRA Growth Index or the S&P 500/BARRA Value Index explain returns to the Fidelity Select Technology Fund using 60 monthly observations between January 1998 and December 2002. Of course, if any of the three time series has a unit root, then the results of our regression analysis may be invalid. Therefore, we could use a Dickey–Fuller test to determine whether any of these series has a unit root.

If we reject the hypothesis of unit roots for all three series, we can use linear regression to analyze the relation among the series. In that case the results of our analysis of the factors affecting returns to the Fidelity Select Technology Fund would be valid.

If at least one time series (the dependent variable or one of the independent variables) has a unit root while at least one time series (the dependent variable or one of the independent variables) does not, the error term in the regression cannot be covariance stationary. Consequently, we should not use multiple linear regression to analyze the relation among the time series in this scenario.

Another possibility is that each time series, including the dependent variable and each of the independent variables, has a unit root. If this is the case, we need to establish whether the time series are cointegrated. To test for cointegration, the procedure is similar to that for a model with a single independent variable. First, estimate the regression $y_t = b_0 + b_1 x_{1t} + b_2 x_{2t} + \ldots + b_k x_{kt} + \epsilon_t$. Then conduct the (Engle–Granger) Dickey–Fuller test of the hypothesis that there is a unit root in the errors of this regression using the residuals from the estimated regression.

If we cannot reject the null hypothesis of a unit root in the error term of the regression, we cannot reject the null hypothesis of no cointegration. In this scenario, the error term in the multiple regression will not be covariance stationary, so we cannot use multiple regression to analyze the relationship among the time series.

If we can reject the null hypothesis of a unit root in the error term of the regression, we can reject the null hypothesis of no cointegration. However, modeling three or more time series that are cointegrated may be difficult. For example, an analyst may want to predict a retirement services company's sales based on the country's GDP and the total population over age 65. Although the company's sales, GDP, and the population over 65 may each have a unit root and be cointegrated, modeling the cointegration of the three series may be difficult, and doing so is beyond the scope of this volume. Analysts who have not mastered all these complex issues should avoid forecasting models with multiple time series that have unit roots: The regression coefficients may be inconsistent and may produce incorrect forecasts.

OTHER ISSUES IN TIME SERIES   11

Time-series analysis is an extensive topic and includes many highly complex issues. Our objective in this reading has been to present those issues in time series that are the most important for financial analysts and can also be handled with relative ease. In this section, we briefly discuss some of the issues that we have not covered but could be useful for analysts.

In this reading, we have shown how to use time-series models to make forecasts. We have also introduced the RMSE as a criterion for comparing forecasting models. However, we have not discussed measuring the uncertainty associated with forecasts made using time-series models. The uncertainty of these forecasts can be very large, and should be taken into account when making investment decisions. Fortunately, the same techniques apply to evaluating the uncertainty of time-series forecasts as apply to evaluating the uncertainty about forecasts from linear regression models. To accurately evaluate forecast uncertainty, we need to consider both the uncertainty about the error term and the uncertainty about the estimated parameters in the time-series model. Evaluating this uncertainty is fairly complicated when using regressions with more than one independent variable.

In this reading, we used the U.S. CPI inflation series to illustrate some of the practical challenges analysts face in using time-series models. We used information on U.S. Federal Reserve policy to explore the consequences of splitting the inflation series in two. In financial time-series work, we may suspect that a time series has more than one regime but not have the information to attempt to sort the data into different regimes. If you face such a problem, you may want to investigate other methods, especially switching regression models, to identify multiple regimes using only the time series itself.

If you are interested in these and other advanced time-series topics, you can learn more in Diebold (2004) and Hamilton (1994).

12 SUGGESTED STEPS IN TIME-SERIES FORECASTING

The following is a step-by-step guide to building a model to predict a time series.

1. Understand the investment problem you have, and make an initial choice of model. One alternative is a regression model that predicts the future behavior of a variable based on hypothesized causal relationships with other variables. Another is a time-series model that attempts to predict the future behavior of a variable based on the past behavior of the same variable.

2. If you have decided to use a time-series model, compile the time series and plot it to see whether it looks covariance stationary. The plot might show important deviations from covariance stationarity, including the following:
   ▶ a linear trend;
   ▶ an exponential trend;
   ▶ seasonality; or
   ▶ a significant shift in the time series during the sample period (for example, a change in mean or variance).

3. If you find no significant seasonality or shift in the time series, then perhaps either a linear trend or an exponential trend will be sufficient to model the time series. In that case, take the following steps:
   ▶ Determine whether a linear or exponential trend seems most reasonable (usually by plotting the series).
   ▶ Estimate the trend.
   ▶ Compute the residuals.
   ▶ Use the Durbin–Watson statistic to determine whether the residuals have significant serial correlation. If you find no significant serial correlation in the residuals, then the trend model is sufficient to capture the dynamics of the time series and you can use that model for forecasting.

4. If you find significant serial correlation in the residuals from the trend model, use a more complex model, such as an autoregressive model. First, however, reexamine whether the time series is covariance stationary. Following is a list of violations of stationarity, along with potential methods to adjust the time series to make it covariance stationary:
   ▶ If the time series has a linear trend, first-difference the time series.
   ▶ If the time series has an exponential trend, take the natural log of the time series and then first-difference it.
   ▶ If the time series shifts significantly during the sample period, estimate different time-series models before and after the shift.
   ▶ If the time series has significant seasonality, include seasonal lags (discussed in Step 7).

5. After you have successfully transformed a raw time series into a covariance-stationary time series, you can usually model the transformed series with a short autoregression.[45] To decide which autoregressive model to use, take the following steps:

- ▶ Estimate an AR(1) model.

- ▶ Test to see whether the residuals from this model have significant serial correlation.

- ▶ If you find no significant serial correlation in the residuals, you can use the AR(1) model to forecast.

6. If you find significant serial correlation in the residuals, use an AR(2) model and test for significant serial correlation of the residuals of the AR(2) model.

- ▶ If you find no significant serial correlation, use the AR(2) model.

- ▶ If you find significant serial correlation of the residuals, keep increasing the order of the AR model until the residual serial correlation is no longer significant.

7. Your next move is to check for seasonality. You can use one of two approaches:

- ▶ Graph the data and check for regular seasonal patterns.

- ▶ Examine the data to see whether the seasonal autocorrelations of the residuals from an AR model are significant (for example, the fourth autocorrelation for quarterly data) and whether the autocorrelations before and after the seasonal autocorrelations are significant. To correct for seasonality, add seasonal lags to your AR model. For example, if you are using quarterly data, you might add the fourth lag of a time series as an additional variable in an AR(1) or an AR(2) model.

8. Next, test whether the residuals have autoregressive conditional heteroskedasticity. To test for ARCH(1), for example, do the following:

- ▶ Regress the squared residual from your time-series model on a lagged value of the squared residual.

- ▶ Test whether the coefficient on the squared lagged residual differs significantly from 0.

- ▶ If the coefficient on the squared lagged residual does not differ significantly from 0, the residuals do not display ARCH and you can rely on the standard errors from your time-series estimates.

- ▶ If the coefficient on the squared lagged residual does differ significantly from 0, use generalized least squares or other methods to correct for ARCH.

9. Finally, you may also want to perform tests of the model's out-of-sample forecasting performance to see how the model's out-of-sample performance compares to its in-sample performance.

Using these steps in sequence, you can be reasonably sure that your model is correctly specified.

---

[45] Most financial time series can be modeled using an autoregressive process. For a few time series, a moving-average model may fit better. To see if this is the case, examine the first five or six autocorrelations of the time series. If the autocorrelations suddenly drop to 0 after the first q autocorrelations, a moving-average model (of order q) is appropriate. If the autocorrelations start large and decline gradually, an autoregressive model is appropriate.

SUMMARY

▶ The predicted trend value of a time series in period t is $\hat{b}_0 + \hat{b}_1 t$ in a linear trend model; the predicted trend value of a time series in a log-linear trend model is $e^{\hat{b}_0 + \hat{b}_1 t}$.

▶ Time series that tend to grow by a constant amount from period to period should be modeled by linear trend models, whereas time series that tend to grow at a constant rate should be modeled by log-linear trend models.

▶ Trend models often do not completely capture the behavior of a time series, as indicated by serial correlation of the error term. If the Durbin–Watson statistic from a trend model differs significantly from 2, indicating serial correlation, we need to build a different kind of model.

▶ An autoregressive model of order p, denoted AR(p), uses p lags of a time series to predict its current value: $x_t = b_0 + b_1 x_{t-1} + b_2 x_{t-2} + \ldots + b_p x_{t-p} + \epsilon_t$.

▶ A time series is covariance stationary if the following three conditions are satisfied: First, the expected value of the time series must be constant and finite in all periods. Second, the variance of the time series must be constant and finite in all periods. Third, the covariance of the time series with itself for a fixed number of periods in the past or future must be constant and finite in all periods. Inspection of a nonstationary time-series plot may reveal an upward or downward trend (nonconstant mean) and/or nonconstant variance. The use of linear regression to estimate an autoregressive time-series model is not valid unless the time series is covariance stationary.

▶ For a specific autoregressive model to be a good fit to the data, the autocorrelations of the error term should be 0 at all lags.

▶ A time series is mean reverting if it tends to fall when its level is above its long-run mean and rise when its level is below its long-run mean. If a time series is covariance stationary, then it will be mean reverting.

▶ The one-period-ahead forecast of a variable x_t from an AR(1) model made in period t for period $t + 1$ is $\hat{x}_{t+1} = \hat{b}_0 + \hat{b}_1 x_t$. This forecast can be used to create the two-period ahead forecast from the model made in period t, $\hat{x}_{t+2} = \hat{b}_0 + \hat{b}_1 \hat{x}_{t+1}$. Similar results hold for AR(p) models.

▶ In-sample forecasts are the in-sample predicted values from the estimated time-series model. Out-of-sample forecasts are the forecasts made from the estimated time-series model for a time period different from the one for which the model was estimated. Out-of-sample forecasts are usually more valuable in evaluating the forecasting performance of a time-series model than are in-sample forecasts. The root mean squared error (RMSE), defined as the square root of the average squared forecast error, is a criterion for comparing the forecast accuracy of different time-series models; a smaller RMSE implies greater forecast accuracy.

▶ Just as in regression models, the coefficients in time-series models are often unstable across different sample periods. In selecting a sample period for estimating a time-series model, we should seek to assure ourselves that the time series was stationary in the sample period.

▶ A random walk is a time series in which the value of the series in one period is the value of the series in the previous period plus an unpredictable random error. If the time series is a random walk, it is not covariance stationary. A random walk with drift is a random walk with a nonzero intercept term. All random walks have unit roots. If a time series has a unit root, then it will not be covariance stationary.

▶ If a time series has a unit root, we can sometimes transform the time series into one that is covariance stationary by first-differencing the time series; we may then be able to estimate an autoregressive model for the first-differenced series.

▶ An n-period moving average of the current and past $(n - 1)$ values of a time series, x_t, is calculated as $[x_t + x_{t-1} + \ldots + x_{t-(n-1)}]/n$.

▶ A moving-average model of order q, denoted MA(q), uses q lags of a random error term to predict its current value.

▶ The order q of a moving average model can be determined using the fact that if a time series is a moving-average time series of order q, its first q autocorrelations are nonzero while autocorrelations beyond the first q are zero.

▶ The autocorrelations of most autoregressive time series start large and decline gradually, whereas the autocorrelations of an MA(q) time series suddenly drop to 0 after the first q autocorrelations. This helps in distinguishing between autoregressive and moving-average time series.

▶ If the error term of a time-series model shows significant serial correlation at seasonal lags, the time series has significant seasonality. This seasonality can often be modeled by including a seasonal lag in the model, such as adding a term lagged four quarters to an AR(1) model on quarterly observations.

▶ The forecast made in time t for time $t + 1$ using a quarterly AR(1) model with a seasonal lag would be $x_{t+1} = \hat{b}_0 + \hat{b}_1 x_t + \hat{b}_2 x_{t-3}$.

▶ ARMA models have several limitations: the parameters in ARMA models can be very unstable; determining the AR and MA order of the model can be difficult; and even with their additional complexity, ARMA models may not forecast well.

▶ The variance of the error in a time-series model sometimes depends on the variance of previous errors, representing autoregressive conditional heteroskedasticity (ARCH). Analysts can test for first-order ARCH in a time-series model by regressing the squared residual on the squared residual from the previous period. If the coefficient on the squared residual is statistically significant, the time-series model has ARCH(1) errors.

▶ If a time-series model has ARCH(1) errors, then the variance of the errors in period $t + 1$ can be predicted in period t using the formula $\hat{\sigma}_{t+1}^2 = \hat{a}_0 + \hat{a}_1 \hat{\epsilon}_t^2$.

▶ If linear regression is used to model the relationship between two time series, a test should be performed to determine whether either time series has a unit root:

   ▶ If neither of the time series has a unit root, then we can safely use linear regression.

   ▶ If one of the two time series has a unit root, then we should not use linear regression.

   ▶ If both time series have a unit root and the time series are cointegrated, we may safely use linear regression; however, if they are not cointegrated, we should not use linear regression. The (Engle–Granger) Dickey–Fuller test can be used to determine if time series are cointegrated.

PRACTICE PROBLEMS FOR READING 13

Note: In the Problems and Solutions for this reading, we use the hat (^) to indicate an estimate if we are trying to differentiate between an estimated and an actual value. However, we suppress the hat when we are clearly showing regression output.

1. The civilian unemployment rate (UER) is an important component of many economic models. Table 1 gives regression statistics from estimating a linear trend model of the unemployment rate: $UER_t = b_0 + b_1 t + \epsilon_t$.

TABLE 1   Estimating a Linear Trend in the Civilian Unemployment Rate Monthly Observations, January 1996–December 2000

Regression Statistics

R-squared	0.9314
Standard error	0.1405
Observations	60
Durbin–Watson	0.9099

	Coefficient	Standard Error	*t*-Statistic
Intercept	5.5098	0.0367	150.0363
Trend	−0.0294	0.0010	−28.0715

A. Using the regression output in the above table, what is the model's prediction of the unemployment rate for July 1996, midway through the first year of the sample period?

B. How should we interpret the Durbin–Watson (DW) statistic for this regression? What does the value of the DW statistic say about the validity of a *t*-test on the coefficient estimates?

2. Figure 1 compares the predicted civilian unemployment rate (PRED) with
the actual civilian unemployment rate (UER) from January 1996 to
December 2000. The predicted results come from estimating the linear
time trend model $UER_t = b_0 + b_1 t + \epsilon_t$.

What can we conclude about the appropriateness of this model?

FIGURE 1   Predicted and Actual Civilian Unemployment Rates

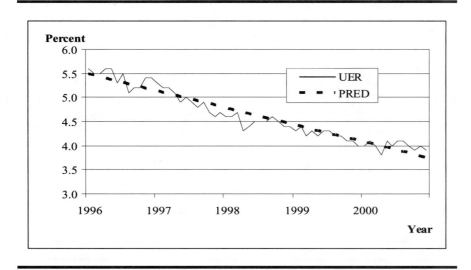

3. You have been assigned to analyze automobile manufacturers and as a first step
in your analysis, you decide to model monthly sales of lightweight vehicles to
determine sales growth in that part of the industry. Figure 2 gives lightweight
vehicle monthly sales (annualized) from January 1992 to December 2000.

FIGURE 2   Lightweight Vehicle Sales

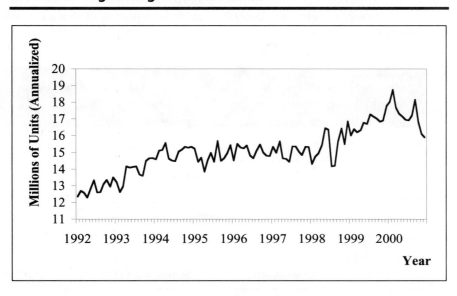

Monthly sales in the lightweight vehicle sector, $Sales_t$, have been
increasing over time, but you suspect that the growth rate of monthly sales
is relatively constant. Write the simplest time-series model for $Sales_t$ that is
consistent with your perception.

4. Figure 3 shows a plot of the first differences in the civilian unemployment rate (UER) between January 1996 and December 2000, $\Delta UER_t = UER_t - UER_{t-1}$.

FIGURE 3   Change in Civilian Unemployment Rate

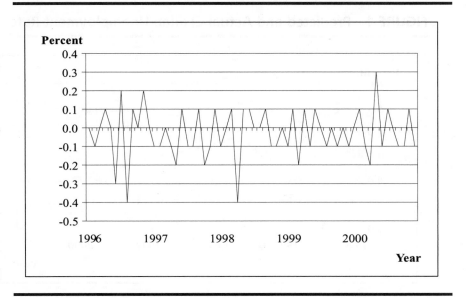

A. Has differencing the data made the new series, ΔUER_t, covariance stationary? Explain your answer.

B. Given the graph of the change in the unemployment rate shown in the figure, describe the steps we should take to determine the appropriate autoregressive time-series model specification for the series ΔUER_t.

5. Table 2 gives the regression output of an AR(1) model on first differences in the unemployment rate. Describe how to interpret the DW statistic for this regression.

TABLE 2   Estimating an AR(1) Model of Changes in the Civilian Unemployment Rate Monthly Observations, March 1996–December 2000

Regression Statistics

R-squared	0.2184
Standard error	0.1202
Observations	58
Durbin–Watson	2.1852

	Coefficient	Standard Error	t-Statistic
Intercept	−0.0405	0.0161	−2.5110
ΔUER_{t-1}	−0.4674	0.1181	−3.9562

6. Assume that changes in the civilian unemployment rate are covariance stationary and that an AR(1) model is a good description for the time series of changes in the unemployment rate. Specifically, we have $\Delta UER_t = -0.0405 - 0.4674\Delta UER_{t-1}$ (using the coefficient estimates given in the previous problem). Given this equation, what is the mean-reverting level to which changes in the unemployment rate converge?

7. Suppose the following model describes changes in the civilian unemployment rate: $\Delta UER_t = -0.0405 - 0.4674\Delta UER_{t-1}$. The current change (first difference) in the unemployment rate is 0.0300. Assume that the mean-reverting level for changes in the unemployment rate is -0.0276.

A. What is the best prediction of the next change?

B. What is the prediction of the change following the next change?

C. Explain your answer to Part B in terms of equilibrium.

8. Table 3 gives the actual sales, log of sales, and changes in the log of sales of Cisco Systems for the period 1Q:2001 to 4Q:2001.

TABLE 3			
Date **Quarter: Year**	**Actual Sales** **($ Millions)**	**Log of Sales**	**Changes in Log of Sales** $\Delta\ln(\text{Sales}_t)$
1Q:2001	6,519	8.7825	0.1308
2Q:2001	6,748	8.8170	0.0345
3Q:2001	4,728	8.4613	-0.3557
4Q:2001	4,298	8.3659	-0.0954
1Q:2002			
2Q:2002			

Forecast the first- and second-quarter sales of Cisco Systems for 2002 using the regression $\Delta\ln(\text{Sales}_t) = 0.0661 + 0.4698\Delta\ln(\text{Sales}_{t-1})$.

9. Table 4 gives the actual change in the log of sales of Cisco Systems from 1Q:2001 to 4Q:2001, along with the forecasts from the regression model $\Delta \ln (\text{Sales}_t) = 0.0661 + 0.4698 \Delta \ln (\text{Sales}_{t-1})$ estimated using data from 3Q:1991 to 4Q:2000. (Note that the observations after the fourth quarter of 2000 are out of sample.)

TABLE 4

Date	Actual Values of Changes in the Log of Sales $\Delta \ln (\text{Sales}_t)$	Forecast Values of Changes in the Log of Sales $\Delta \ln (\text{Sales}_t)$
1Q:2001	0.1308	0.1357
2Q:2001	0.0345	0.1299
3Q:2001	−0.3557	0.1271
4Q:2001	−0.0954	0.1259

   A. Calculate the RMSE for the out-of-sample forecast errors.

   B. Compare the forecasting performance of the model given with that of another model having an out-of-sample RMSE of 20 percent.

10. A. The AR(1) model for the civilian unemployment rate, $\Delta \text{UER}_t = -0.0405 - 0.4674 \Delta \text{UER}_{t-1}$, was developed with five years of data. What would be the drawback to using the AR(1) model to predict changes in the civilian unemployment rate 12 months or more ahead, as compared with one month ahead?

   B. For purposes of estimating a predictive equation, what would be the drawback to using 30 years of civilian unemployment data rather than only five years?

11. Figure 4 shows monthly observations on the natural log of lightweight vehicle sales, $\ln (\text{Sales}_t)$, for the period January 1992 to December 2000.

FIGURE 4   Lightweight Vehicle Sales

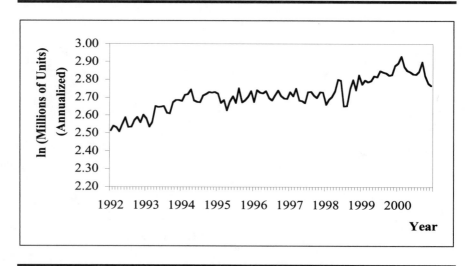

   A. Using the figure, comment on whether the specification $\ln (\text{Sales}_t) = b_0 + b_1 [\ln (\text{Sales}_{t-1})] + \epsilon_t$ is appropriate.

   B. State an appropriate transformation of the time series.

12. Figure 5 shows a plot of first differences in the log of monthly lightweight vehicle sales over the same period as in Problem 11. Has differencing the data made the resulting series, $\Delta \ln (\text{Sales}_t) = \ln (\text{Sales}_t) - \ln (\text{Sales}_{t-1})$, covariance stationary?

FIGURE 5 Change in Natural Log of Lightweight Vehicle Sales

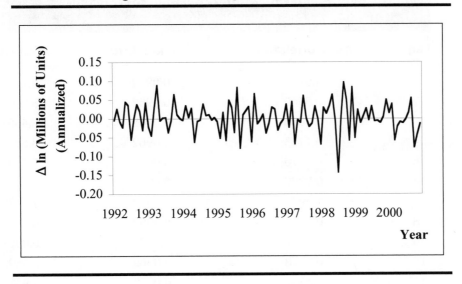

13. Using monthly data from January 1992 to December 2000, we estimate the following equation for lightweight vehicle sales: $\Delta \ln(\text{Sales}_t) = 2.7108 + 0.3987 \Delta \ln(\text{Sales}_{t-1}) + \epsilon_t$. Table 5 gives sample autocorrelations of the errors from this model.

TABLE 5   **Different Order Autocorrelations of Differences in the Logs of Vehicle Sales**

Lag	Autocorrelation	Standard Error	*t*-Statistic
1	0.9358	0.0962	9.7247
2	0.8565	0.0962	8.9005
3	0.8083	0.0962	8.4001
4	0.7723	0.0962	8.0257
5	0.7476	0.0962	7.7696
6	0.7326	0.0962	7.6137
7	0.6941	0.0962	7.2138
8	0.6353	0.0962	6.6025
9	0.5867	0.0962	6.0968
10	0.5378	0.0962	5.5892
11	0.4745	0.0962	4.9315
12	0.4217	0.0962	4.3827

A. Use the information in the table to assess the appropriateness of the specification given by the equation.

B. If the residuals from the AR(1) model above violate a regression assumption, how would you modify the AR(1) specification?

14. Figure 6 shows the quarterly sales of Cisco Systems from 1Q:1991 to 4Q:2000.

FIGURE 6   **Quarterly Sales at Cisco**

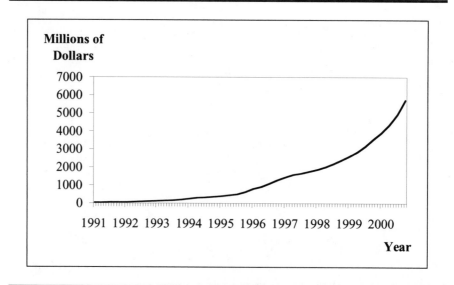

Table 6 gives the regression statistics from estimating the model $\Delta \ln (\text{Sales}_t) = b_0 + b_1 \Delta \ln (\text{Sales}_{t-1}) + \epsilon_t$.

TABLE 6   Change in the Natural Log of Sales for Cisco Systems Quarterly Observations, 3Q:1991–4Q:2000

Regression Statistics

R-squared	0.2899
Standard error	0.0408
Observations	38
Durbin–Watson	1.5707

	Coefficient	Standard Error	t-Statistic
Intercept	0.0661	0.0175	3.7840
$\Delta \ln (\text{Sales}_{t-1})$	0.4698	0.1225	3.8339

A. Describe the salient features of the quarterly sales series.

B. Describe the procedures we should use to determine whether the AR(1) specification is correct.

C. Assuming the model is correctly specified, what is the long-run change in the log of sales toward which the series will tend to converge?

15. Figure 7 shows the quarterly sales of Avon Products from 1Q:1992 to 2Q:2002. Describe the salient features of the data shown.

FIGURE 7   Quarterly Sales at Avon

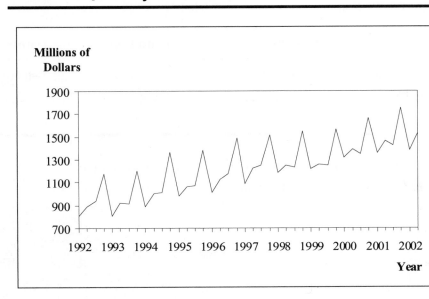

16. Table 7 below shows the autocorrelations of the residuals from an AR(1) model fit to the changes in the gross profit margin (GPM) of The Home Depot, Inc.

TABLE 7   Autocorrelations of the Residuals from Estimating the Regression $\Delta GPM_t = 0.0006 - 0.3330_1 \Delta GPM_{t-1} + \epsilon_t$ 1Q:1992–4Q:2001 (40 Observations)

Lag	Autocorrelation
1	−0.1106
2	−0.5981
3	−0.1525
4	0.8496
5	−0.1099

Table 8 shows the output from a regression on changes in the GPM for Home Depot, where we have changed the specification of the AR regression.

TABLE 8   Change in Gross Profit Margin for Home Depot 1Q:1992–4Q:2001

Regression Statistics

R-squared	0.9155
Standard error	0.0057
Observations	40
Durbin–Watson	2.6464

	Coefficient	Standard Error	t-Statistic
Intercept	−0.0001	0.0009	−0.0610
ΔGPM_{t-1}	−0.0608	0.0687	−0.8850
ΔGPM_{t-4}	0.8720	0.0678	12.8683

A. Identify the change that was made to the regression model.

B. Discuss the rationale for changing the regression specification.

17. Suppose we decide to use an autoregressive model with a seasonal lag because of the seasonal autocorrelation in the previous problem. We are modeling quarterly data, so we estimate Equation 15: $(\ln \text{Sales}_t - \ln \text{Sales}_{t-1}) = b_0 + b_1(\ln \text{Sales}_{t-1} - \ln \text{Sales}_{t-2}) + b_2(\ln \text{Sales}_{t-4} - \ln \text{Sales}_{t-5}) + \epsilon_t$. Table 9 shows the regression statistics from this equation.

TABLE 9   Log Differenced Sales: AR(1) Model with Seasonal Lag Johnson & Johnson Quarterly Observations, January 1985–December 2001

Regression Statistics

R-squared	0.4220
Standard error	0.0318
Observations	68
Durbin–Watson	1.8784

	Coefficient	Standard Error	t-Statistic
Intercept	0.0121	0.0053	2.3055
Lag 1	−0.0839	0.0958	−0.8757
Lag 4	0.6292	0.0958	6.5693

Autocorrelations of the Residual

Lag	Autocorrelation	Standard Error	t-Statistic
1	0.0572	0.1213	0.4720
2	−0.0700	0.1213	−0.5771
3	0.0065	0.1213	−0.0532
4	−0.0368	0.1213	−0.3033

A. Using the information in Table 9, determine if the model is correctly specified.

B. If sales grew by 1 percent last quarter and by 2 percent four quarters ago, use the model to predict the sales growth for this quarter.

18. Describe how to test for autoregressive conditional heteroskedasticity (ARCH) in the residuals from the AR(1) regression on first differences in the civilian unemployment rate, $\Delta \text{UER}_t = b_0 + b_1\Delta \text{UER}_{t-1} + \epsilon_t$.

19. Suppose we want to predict the annualized return of the five-year T-bill using the annualized return of the three-month T-bill with monthly observations from January 1993 to December 2002. Our analysis produces the data shown in Table 10.

TABLE 10	Regression with 3-Month T-Bill as the Independent Variable and 5-Year Treasury Bill as the Dependent Variable Monthly Observations, January 1993 to December 2002

Regression Statistics

R-squared	0.5829
Standard error	0.6598
Observations	120
Durbin–Watson	0.1130

	Coefficient	Standard Error	*t*-Statistic
Intercept	3.0530	0.2060	14.8181
Three-month	0.5722	0.0446	12.8408

Can we rely on the regression model in Table 10 to produce meaningful predictions? Specify what problem might be a concern with this regression.

SOLUTIONS FOR READING 13

1. A. The estimated forecasting equation is $UER_t = 5.5098 - 0.0294(t)$. The data begin in January 1996, and July 1996 is period 7. Thus the linear trend model predicts the unemployment rate to be $UER_7 = 5.5098 - 0.0294\,(7) = 5.3040$ or approximately 5.3 percent.

B. The DW statistic is designed to detect positive serial correlation of the errors of a regression equation. Under the null hypothesis of no positive serial correlation, the DW statistics is 2.0. Positive serial correlation will lead to a DW statistic that is less than 2.0. From the table in Problem 1, we see that the DW statistic is 0.9099. To see whether this result is significantly less than 2.0, refer to the Durbin–Watson table in Appendix E at the end of this volume, in the column marked $k = 1$ (one independent variable) and the row corresponding to 60 observations. We see that $d_l = 1.55$. Because our DW statistic is clearly less than d_l, we reject the null hypothesis of no serial correlation at the 0.05 significance level.

    The presence of serial correlation in the error term violates one of the regression assumptions. The standard errors of the estimated coefficients will be biased downward, so we cannot conduct hypothesis testing on the coefficients.

2. The difference between UER and its forecast value, PRED, is the forecast error. In an appropriately specified regression model, the forecast errors are randomly distributed around the regression line and have a constant variance. We can see that the errors from this model specification are persistent. The errors tend first to be above the regression line and then, starting in 1997, they tend to be below the regression line until 2000 when they again are persistently above the regression line. This persistence suggests that the errors are positively serially correlated. Therefore, we conclude that the model is not appropriate for making estimates.

3. A log-linear model captures growth at a constant rate. The log-linear model $\ln(Sales_t) = b_0 + b_1 t + \epsilon_t$ would be the simplest model consistent with a constant growth rate for monthly sales. Note that we would need to confirm that the regression assumptions are satisfied before accepting the model as valid.

4. A. The plot of the series ΔUER_t seems to fluctuate around a constant mean; its volatility appears to be constant throughout the period. Our initial judgment is that the differenced series is covariance stationary.

B. The change in the unemployment rate seems covariance stationary, so we should first estimate an AR(1) model and test to see whether the residuals from this model have significant serial correlation. If the residuals do not display significant serial correlation, we should use the AR(1) model. If the residuals do display significant serial correlation, we should try an AR(2) model and test for serial correlation of the residuals of the AR(2) model. We should continue this procedure until the errors from the final AR(p) model are serially uncorrelated.

5. The DW statistic cannot be appropriately used for a regression that has a lagged value of the dependent variable as one of the explanatory variables. To test for serial correlation, we need to examine the autocorrelations.

6. When a covariance-stationary series is at its mean-reverting level, the series will tend not to change until it receives a shock (ϵ_t). So, if the series ΔUER_t is at the mean-reverting level, $\Delta UER_t = \Delta UER_{t-1}$. This implies that $\Delta UER_t = -0.0405 - 0.4674\Delta UER_t$, so that $(1 + 0.4674)\Delta UER_t = -0.0405$ and $\Delta UER_t = -0.0405/(1 + 0.4674) = -0.0276$. The mean-reverting level is -0.0276. In an AR(1) model, the general expression for the mean-reverting level is $b_0/(1 - b_1)$.

7. A. The predicted change in the unemployment rate for next period is -5.45 percent, found by substituting 0.0300 into the forecasting model: $-0.0405 - 0.4674(0.03) = -0.0545$.

   B. If we substitute our one-period-ahead forecast of -0.0545 into the model (using the chain rule of forecasting), we get a two-period ahead forecast of -0.0150 or -1.5 percent.

   C. The answer to Part B is quite close to the mean-reverting level of -0.0276. A stationary time series may need many periods to return to its equilibrium, mean-reverting level.

8. The forecast of sales is \$4,391 million for the first quarter of 2002 and \$4,738 million for the second quarter of 2002, as the following table shows.

Date	Sales ($ Millions)	Log of Sales	Actual Values of Changes in the Log of Sales $\Delta\ln(\text{Sales}_t)$	Forecast Values of Changes in the Log of Sales $\Delta\ln(\text{Sales}_t)$
1Q:2001	6,519	8.7825	0.1308	
2Q:2001	6,748	8.8170	0.0345	
3Q:2001	4,728	8.4613	−0.3557	
4Q:2001	4,298	8.3659	−0.0954	
1Q:2002	4,391	8.3872		0.0213
2Q:2002	4,738	8.4633		0.0761

We find the forecasted change in the log of sales for the first quarter of 2002 by inputting the value for the change in the log of sales from the previous quarter into the equation $\Delta\ln(\text{Sales}_t) = 0.0661 + 0.4698\Delta\ln(\text{Sales}_{t-1})$. Specifically, $\Delta\ln(\text{Sales}_t) = 0.0661 + 0.4698(-0.0954) = 0.0213$, which means that we forecast the log of sales in the first quarter of 2002 to be $8.3659 + 0.0213 = 8.3872$.

Next, we forecast the change in the log of sales for the second quarter of 2002 as $\Delta\ln(\text{Sales}_t) = 0.0661 + 0.4698(0.0213) = 0.0761$. Note that we have to use our first-quarter 2002 estimated value of the change in the log of sales as our input for $\Delta\ln(\text{Sales}_{t-1})$ because we are forecasting past the period for which we have actual data.

With a forecasted change of 0.0761, we forecast the log of sales in the second quarter of 2002 to be $8.3872 + 0.0761 = 8.4633$.

We have forecasted the log of sales in the first and second quarters of 2002 to be 8.3872 and 8.4633, respectively. Finally, we take the antilog of our estimates of the log of sales in the first and second quarters of 2002 to get our estimates of the level of sales: $e^{8.3872} = 4,391$ and $e^{8.4633} = 4,738$, respectively, for sales of \$4,391 million and \$4,738 million.

9. A. The RMSE of the out-of-sample forecast errors is approximately 27 percent. Out-of-sample error refers to the difference between the realized value and the forecasted value of $\Delta\ln(\text{Sales}_t)$ for dates beyond the estimation period. In this case, the out-of-sample period is 1Q:2001 to 4Q:2001. These are the four quarters for which we have data that we did not use to obtain the estimated model $\Delta\ln(\text{Sales}_t) = 0.0661 + 0.4698\Delta\ln(\text{Sales}_{t-1})$.

The steps to calculate RMSE are as follows:

   i. Take the difference between the actual and the forecast value. This is the error.

   ii. Square the error.

   iii. Sum the squared errors.

   iv. Divide by the number of forecasts.

   v. Take the square root of the average.

We show the calculations for RMSE in the table below.

Actual Values of Changes in the Log of Sales $\Delta\ln(\text{Sales}_t)$	Forecast Values of Changes in the Log of Sales $\Delta\ln(\text{Sales}_t)$	Error (Column 1 − Column 2)		Squared Error (Column 3 Squared)
0.1308	0.1357	−0.0049		0.0000
0.0345	0.1299	−0.0954		0.0091
−0.3557	0.1271	−0.4828		0.2331
−0.0954	0.1259	−0.2213		0.0490
			Sum	0.2912
			Mean	0.0728
			RMSE	0.2698

B. The lower the RMSE, the more accurate the forecasts of a model in forecasting. Therefore, the model with the RMSE of 20 percent has greater accuracy in forecasting than the model in Part A, which has an RMSE of 27 percent.

10. A. Predictions too far ahead can be nonsensical. For example, the AR(1) model we have been examining, $\Delta\text{UER}_t = -0.0405 - 0.4674\Delta\text{UER}_{t-1}$, taken at face value, predicts declining civilian unemployment into the indefinite future. Because the civilian unemployment rate will probably not go below 3 percent frictional unemployment and cannot go below 0 percent unemployment, this model's long-range forecasts are implausible. The model is designed for short-term forecasting, as are many time-series models.

B. Using more years of data for estimation may lead to nonstationarity even in the series of first differences in the civilian unemployment rate. As we go further back in time, we increase the risk that the underlying civilian unemployment rate series has more than one regime (or true model). If the series has more than one regime, fitting one model to the entire period would not be correct. Note that when we have good reason to believe that a time series is stationary, a longer series of data is generally desirable.

11. A. The graph of ln (Sales$_t$) appears to trend upward over time. A series that trends upward or downward over time often has a unit root and is thus not covariance stationary. Therefore, using an AR(1) regression on the undifferenced series is probably not correct. In practice, we need to examine regression statistics to confirm visual impressions such as this.

   B. The most common way to transform a time series with a unit root into a covariance-stationary time series is to difference the data—that is, to create a new series Δln (Sales$_t$) = ln (Sales$_t$) − ln (Sales$_{t-1}$).

12. The plot of the series Δln (Sales$_t$) appears to fluctuate around a constant mean; its volatility seems constant throughout the period. Differencing the data appears to have made the time series covariance stationary.

13. A. In a correctly specified regression, the residuals must be serially uncorrelated. We have 108 observations, so the standard error of the autocorrelation is $1/\sqrt{T}$, or in this case $1/\sqrt{108} = 0.0962$. The t-statistic for each lag is significant at the 0.01 level. We would have to modify the model specification before continuing with the analysis.

   B. Because the residuals from the AR(1) specification display significant serial correlation, we should estimate an AR(2) model and test for serial correlation of the residuals of the AR(2) model. If the residuals from the AR(2) model are serially uncorrelated, we should then test for seasonality and ARCH behavior. If any serial correlation remains in the residuals, we should estimate an AR(3) process and test the residuals from that specification for serial correlation. We should continue this procedure until the errors from the final AR(p) model are serially uncorrelated. When serial correlation is eliminated, we should test for seasonality and ARCH behavior.

14. A. The series has a steady upward trend of growth, suggesting an exponential growth rate. This finding suggests transforming the series by taking the natural log and differencing the data.

   B. First, we should determine whether the residuals from the AR(1) specification are serially uncorrelated. If the residuals are serially correlated, then we should try an AR(2) specification and then test the residuals from the AR(2) model for serial correlation. We should continue in this fashion until the residuals are serially uncorrelated, then look for seasonality in the residuals. If seasonality is present, we should add a seasonal lag. If no seasonality is present, we should test for ARCH. If ARCH is not present, we can conclude that the model is correctly specified.

   C. If the model Δln (Sales$_t$) = b_0 + b_1[Δln (Sales$_{t-1}$)] + ϵ_t is correctly specified, then the series Δln (Sales$_t$) is covariance stationary. So, this series tends to its mean-reverting level, which is $b_0/(1 - b_1)$ or $0.0661/(1 - 0.4698) = 0.1247$.

15. The quarterly sales of Avon show an upward trend and a clear seasonal pattern, as indicated by the repeated regular cycle.

16. A. A second explanatory variable, the change in the gross profit margin lagged four quarters, ΔGPM$_{t-4}$, was added.

   B. The model was augmented to account for seasonality in the time series (with quarterly data, significant autocorrelation at the fourth lag indicates seasonality). The standard error of the autocorrelation coefficient equals 1 divided by the square root of the number of observations: $1/\sqrt{40}$ or 0.1581. The autocorrelation at the fourth lag

(0.8496) is significant: $t = 0.8496/0.1581 = 5.37$. This indicates seasonality, and accordingly we added ΔGPM_{t-4}. Note that in the augmented regression, the coefficient on ΔGPM_{t-4} is highly significant. (Although the autocorrelation at second lag is also significant, the fourth lag is more important because of the rationale of seasonality. Once the fourth lag is introduced as an independent variable, we might expect that the second lag in the residuals would not be significant.)

17. A. In order to determine whether this model is correctly specified, we need to test for serial correlation among the residuals. We want to test whether we can reject the null hypothesis that the value of each autocorrelation is 0 against the alternative hypothesis that each is not equal to 0. At the 0.05 significance level, with 68 observations and three parameters, this model has 65 degrees of freedom. The critical value of the t-statistic needed to reject the null hypothesis is thus about 2.0. The absolute value of the t-statistic for each autocorrelation is below 0.60 (less than 2.0), so we cannot reject the null hypothesis that each autocorrelation is not significantly different from 0. We have determined that the model is correctly specified.

B. If sales grew by 1 percent last quarter and by 2 percent four quarters ago, then the model predicts that sales growth this quarter will be $0.0121 - 0.0839(0.01) + 0.6292(0.02) = 0.0238$ or 2.38 percent.

18. We should estimate the regression $\Delta UER_t = b_0 + b_1 \Delta UER_{t-1} + \epsilon_t$ and save the residuals from the regression. Then we should create a new variable, $\hat{\epsilon}_t^2$, by squaring the residuals. Finally, we should estimate $\hat{\epsilon}_t^2 = a_0 + a_1 \hat{\epsilon}_{t-1}^2 + u_t$ and test to see whether a_1 is statistically different from 0.

19. To determine whether we can use linear regression to model more than one time series, we should first determine whether any of the time series has a unit root. If none of the time series has a unit root, then we can safely use linear regression to test the relations between the two time series. Note that if one of the two variables has a unit root, then our analysis would not provide valid results; if both of the variables have unit roots, then we would need to evaluate whether the variables are cointegrated.

ECONOMICS

STUDY SESSION

Study Session 4   Economics for Valuation

STUDY SESSION 4
ECONOMICS FOR VALUATION

This study session builds on the principles of economics from Level I and links them to the valuation process. The readings discuss how the economic environment affects a firm's performance. The first topic is alternative theories of economic growth, including capital investment, productivity, human capital, and technology. Governments can influence economic growth to an extent by applying different regulations, each of which has an associated cost for firms or consumers.

Most large firms do not exclusively trade within their own borders, but transact business with companies or individuals outside their own country. Foreign exchange fluctuations have an impact on the bottom line and hence on the valuation of a company. Buyers' decisions, however, are also based on parity relations; in other words, buyers will purchase goods and services where they can get the most for their money. Finally, the study session ends with a review of the measures of economic progress.

READING ASSIGNMENTS

Reading 14   Economic Growth
Economics, Eighth Edition, by Michael Parkin

Reading 15   Regulation and Antitrust Policy in a Globalized Economy
Economics Today, Fourteenth Edition, by Roger LeRoy Miller

Reading 16   Trading with the World
Economics, Eighth Edition, by Michael Parkin

Reading 17   The Exchange Rate and the Balance of Payments
Economics, Eighth Edition, by Michael Parkin

Reading 18   Currency Exchange Rates
Global Investments, Sixth Edition, by Bruno Solnik and Dennis McLeavey, CFA

Reading 19   Foreign Exchange Parity Relations
Global Investments, Sixth Edition, by Bruno Solnik and Dennis McLeavey, CFA

Reading 20   Measuring Economic Activity
Guide to Economic Indicators, Sixth Edition, by Richard Stutely

517

ECONOMIC GROWTH
by Michael Parkin

LEARNING OUTCOMES

The candidate should be able to:	Mastery
a. define the sources of economic growth, and discuss the preconditions for economic growth;	☐
b. discuss how the one-third rule can be used to explain the contributions of labor and technological change to growth in labor productivity;	☐
c. discuss how faster economic growth can be achieved by increasing the growth of physical capital, technological advances, and investment in human capital;	☐
d. compare and contrast classical growth theory, neoclassical growth theory, and new growth theory.	☐

TRANSFORMING PEOPLE'S LIVES 1

Real GDP *per person* in the United States almost tripled between 1960 and 2005. If you live in a dorm that was built during the 1960s, it is likely to have just two power sockets: one for a desk lamp and one for a bedside lamp. Today, with the help of a power bar (or two), your room bulges with a personal computer, television and DVD player, stereo system, microwave, refrigerator, coffeemaker, and toaster—and the list goes on. What has brought about this growth in production, incomes, and living standards?

We see even greater economic growth if we look at modern Asia. On the banks of the Li River in Southern China, Songman Yang breeds cormorants, amazing birds that he trains to fish and to deliver their catch to a basket on his simple bamboo raft. Songman's work, the capital equipment and technology he uses, and the income he earns are similar to those of his ancestors going back some 2,000 years. Yet all around Songman, in China's bustling cities, people are participating in an economic miracle. They are creating businesses, investing in new technologies, developing local and global markets, and transforming their lives. Why are incomes in China growing so rapidly?

In this reading, we study the forces that make real GDP grow, that make some countries grow faster than others, and that make our own growth rate sometimes slow down and sometimes speed up.

In *Reading Between the Lines* at the end of the reading, we return to the economic growth of China and see how it compares with that of the United States.

2   THE BASICS OF ECONOMIC GROWTH

Economic growth is a sustained expansion of production possibilities measured as the increase in real GDP over a given period. Rapid economic growth maintained over a number of years can transform a poor nation into a rich one. Such has been the stories of Hong Kong, South Korea, Taiwan, and some other Asian economies. Slow economic growth or the absence of growth can condemn a nation to devastating poverty. Such has been the fate of Sierra Leone, Somalia, Zambia, and much of the rest of Africa.

The goal of this reading is to help you to understand why some economies expand rapidly and others stagnate. We'll begin by learning how to calculate the economic growth rate and by discovering the magic of sustained growth.

Calculating Growth Rates

We express the **economic growth rate** as the annual percentage change of real GDP. To calculate this growth rate, we use the formula:

$$\text{Real GDP growth rate} = \frac{\text{Real GDP in current year} - \text{Real GDP in previous year}}{\text{Real GDP in previous year}} \times 100.$$

For example, if real GDP in the current year is $11 trillion and if real GDP in the previous year was $10 trillion, then the economic growth rate is 10 percent.

The growth rate of real GDP tells us how rapidly the *total* economy is expanding. This measure is useful for telling us about potential changes in the balance of economic power among nations. But it does not tell us about changes in the standard of living.

The standard of living depends on **real GDP per person** (also called *per capita* real GDP), which is real GDP divided by the population. So the contribution of real GDP growth to the change in the standard of living depends on the growth rate of real GDP per person. We use the above formula to calculate this growth rate, replacing real GDP with real GDP per person.

Suppose, for example, that in the current year, when real GDP is $11 trillion, the population is 202 million. Then real GDP per person is $11 trillion divided by 202 million, which equals $54,455. And suppose that in the previous year, when real GDP was $10 trillion, the population was 200 million. Then real GDP per person in that year was $10 trillion divided by 200 million, which equals $50,000.

Use these two real GDP per person values with the growth formula above to calculate the growth rate of real GDP per person. That is,

$$\begin{matrix} \text{Real GDP} \\ \text{per person} \\ \text{growth rate} \end{matrix} = \frac{\$54,455 - \$50,000}{\$50,000} \times 100 = 8.9 \text{ percent.}$$

The growth rate of real GDP per person can also be calculated (approximately) by subtracting the population growth rate from the real GDP growth rate. In the example you've just worked through, the growth rate of real GDP is 10 percent. The population changes from 200 million to 202 million, so the population growth rate is 1 percent. The growth rate of real GDP per person is approximately equal to 10 percent minus 1 percent, which equals 9 percent.

Real GDP per person grows only if real GDP grows faster than the population grows. If the growth rate of the population exceeds the growth of real GDP, real GDP per person falls.

The Magic of Sustained Growth

Sustained growth of real GDP per person can transform a poor society into a wealthy one. The reason is that economic growth is like compound interest.

Compound Interest

Suppose that you put $100 in the bank and earn 5 percent a year interest on it. After one year, you have $105. If you leave that $105 in the bank for another year, you earn 5 percent interest on the original $100 *and on the $5 interest that you earned last year.* You are now earning interest on interest! The next year, things get even better. Then you earn 5 percent on the original $100 and on the interest earned in the first year and the second year. You are even earning interest on the interest that you earned on the interest of the first year.

Your money in the bank is growing at a rate of 5 percent a year. Before too many years have passed, your initial deposit of $100 will have grown to $200. But after how many years?

The answer is provided by a formula called the **Rule of 70**, which states that the number of years it takes for the level of any variable to double is approximately 70 divided by the annual percentage growth rate of the variable. Using the Rule of 70, you can now calculate how many years it takes your $100 to become $200. It is 70 divided by 5, which is 14 years.

Applying the Rule of 70

The Rule of 70 applies to any variable, so it applies to real GDP per person. Figure 1 shows the doubling time for growth rates of 1 percent per year to 12 percent per year.

You can see that real GDP per person doubles in 70 years (70 divided by 1)—an average human life span—if the growth rate is 1 percent a year. It doubles in 35 years if the growth rate is 2 percent a year and in just 10 years if the growth rate is 7 percent a year.

FIGURE 1   The Rule of 70

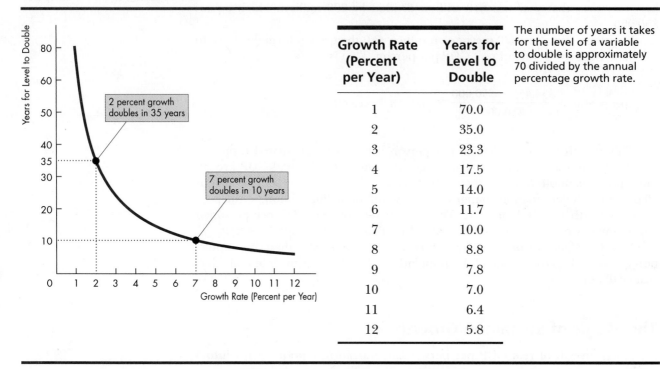

Growth Rate (Percent per Year)	Years for Level to Double
1	70.0
2	35.0
3	23.3
4	17.5
5	14.0
6	11.7
7	10.0
8	8.8
9	7.8
10	7.0
11	6.4
12	5.8

The number of years it takes for the level of a variable to double is approximately 70 divided by the annual percentage growth rate.

We can use the Rule of 70 to answer other questions about economic growth. For example, in 2000, U.S. real GDP per person was approximately 8 times that of China. China's recent growth rate of real GDP per person was 7 percent a year. If this growth rate were maintained, how long would it take China's real GDP per person to reach that of the United States in 2000? The answer, provided by the Rule of 70, is 30 years. China's real GDP per person doubles in 10 (70 divided by 7) years. It doubles again to 4 times its current level in another 10 years. And it doubles yet again to 8 times its current level in another 10 years. So after 30 years of growth at 7 percent a year, China's real GDP per person is 8 times its current level and equals that of the United States in 2000. Of course, after 30 years, U.S. real GDP per person would have increased, so China would still not have caught up to the United States.

3   ECONOMIC GROWTH TRENDS

You have just seen the power of economic growth to increase incomes. At a 1 percent growth rate, it takes a human life span to double the standard of living. But at a 7 percent growth rate, the standard of living doubles every decade. How fast is our economy growing? How fast are other economies growing? Are poor countries catching up to rich ones, or do the gaps between the rich and poor persist or even widen? Let's answer these questions.

Growth in the U.S. Economy

Figure 2 shows real GDP per person in the United States for the hundred years from 1905 to 2005. In the middle of the graph are two extraordinary events: the Great Depression of the 1930s and World War II of the 1940s. The fall in real GDP per person during the depression and the bulge during the war obscure any changes in the long-term growth trend that might have occurred within these years.

For the century as a whole, the average growth rate was 2 percent a year. But from 1905 to the onset of the Great Depression in 1929, the average growth rate was only 1.4 percent a year. Between 1930 and 1950, averaging out the depression and the war, the long-term growth rate was 2.2 percent a year. Then, after World War II, the average growth rate was 2 percent a year. Growth was especially rapid during the 1960s and late 1990s and slower during the period from 1973 to 1983.

Figure 2 shows the productivity growth slowdown of 1973–1983 in a longer perspective. It also shows that productivity growth slowdowns have occurred before. The early years of the 1900s and the mid-1950s had even slower growth than we had during the 1970s and 1980s. The rapid growth of the 1960s and 1990s is not unusual either. The 1920s were years of similarly rapid growth.

A major goal of this reading is to explain why our economy grows and why the long-term growth rate varies. Another goal is to explain variations in the economic growth rate across countries. Let's now look at growth rates in other countries.

FIGURE 2   A Hundred Years of Economic Growth in the United States

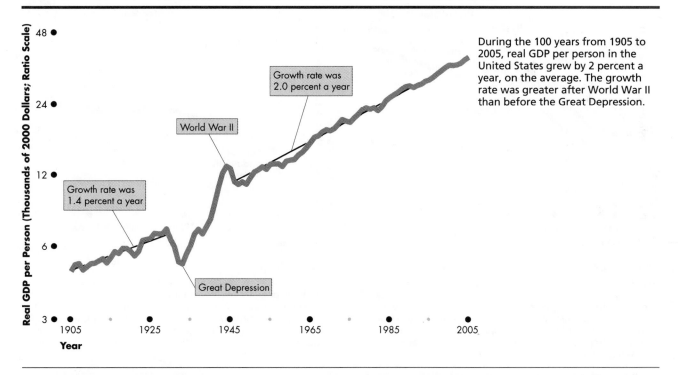

Sources: Christina D. Romer, "The Prewar Business Cycle Reconsidered: New Estimates of Gross National Product, 1869–1908," *Journal of Political Economy*, Vol. 97, 1989; Bureau of Economic Analysis; and author's calculations to link these two sources.

Real GDP Growth in the World Economy

Figure 3 shows real GDP per person in the United States and in other countries between 1960 and 2005. Part (a) looks at the seven richest countries—known as the G7 nations. Among these nations, the United States has the highest real GDP per person. In 2005, Canada had the second-highest real GDP per person, ahead of Japan and France, Germany, Italy, and the United Kingdom (collectively the Europe Big 4).

During the forty-five years shown here, the gaps between the United States, Canada, and the Europe Big 4 have been almost constant. But starting from a long way back, Japan grew fastest. It caught up to Europe in 1973 and to Canada in 1990. But during the 1990s, Japan's economy stagnated.

Many other countries are growing more slowly than, and falling farther behind, the United States. Figure 3(b) looks at some of these countries.

Real GDP per person in Central and South America was 28 percent of the U.S. level in 1960. It grew to 31 percent of the U.S. level by 1975 but then began to fall, and by 2005, real GDP per person in these countries had slipped to 22 percent of the U.S. level.

After a brief period of catch-up during the 1980s, the former Communist countries of Central Europe stagnated and fell increasingly behind the United States. More rapid growth resumed in these countries during the 1990s.

Real GDP per person in Africa, the world's poorest continent, slipped from 12 percent of the U.S. level in 1960 to 6 percent in 2005.

FIGURE 3   Economic Growth around the World: Catch-Up or Not?

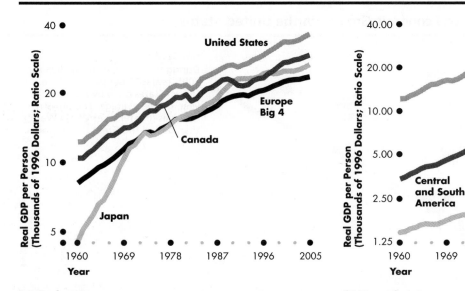

(a) Catch-up?

Real GDP per person has grown throughout the world economy. Among the rich industrial countries (part a), real GDP per person has grown slightly faster in the United States than in Canada and the four big countries of Europe (France, Germany, Italy, and the United Kingdom). Japan had the fastest growth rate before 1973 but then slowed and stagnated during the 1990s.

(b) No catch-up?

Among a wider range of countries shown in part (b), growth rates have been lower than that of the United States. The gaps between the real GDP per person in the United States and in these countries have widened. The gap between the real GDP per person in the United States and Africa has widened by a large amount.

Sources: (1960–2000) Alan Heston, Robert Summers, and Bettina Aten, Penn World Table Version 6.1, Center for International Comparisons at the University of Pennsylvania (CICUP), October 2002; and (2001–2005) International Monetary Fund, *World Economic Outlook*, April 2006.

A group of Asian economies provides a strong contrast to the persistent and growing gaps between the United States and other economies shown in Fig. 3(b). Hong Kong, Korea, Singapore, and Taiwan have experienced spectacular growth, which you can see in Fig. 4. During the 1960s, real GDP per person in these economies ranged from 13 to 30 percent of that in the United States. But by 2005, real GDP per person in Hong Kong and Singapore had reached 80 percent of that in the United States.

Figure 4 shows that China is catching up but from a long way behind. China's real GDP per person increased from 5 percent of the U.S. level in 1960 to 15 percent in 2005.

The Asian economies shown in Fig. 4 are like fast trains running on the same track at similar speeds and with a roughly constant gap between them. Hong Kong is the lead train and runs about 15 years in front of Korea and 40 years in front of the rest of China, which is the last train. Real GDP per person in Korea in 2005 was similar to that in Hong Kong in 1985, and real GDP in China in 2005 was similar to that of Hong Kong in 1965. Between 1965 and 2005, Hong Kong transformed itself from a poor developing economy into one of the richest economies in the world.

The rest of China is now doing what Hong Kong has done. If China continues its rapid growth, the world economy will change dramatically. China has a population 200 times that of Hong Kong and more than 4 times that of the United States.

FIGURE 4   Catch-Up in Asia

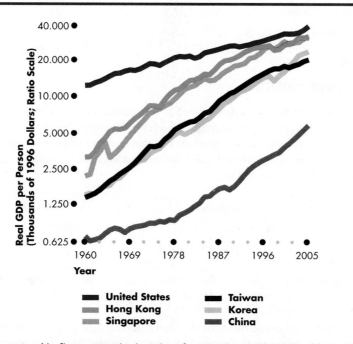

Catch-up has occurred in five economies in Asia. After starting out in 1960 with real GDP per person as low as 13 percent of that in the United States, Hong Kong, Korea, Singapore, and Taiwan have substantially narrowed the gap between them and the United States. And from being a very poor developing country in 1960, China now has a real GDP per person that equals that of Hong Kong in 1965. China is growing at a rate that is enabling it to continue to catch up with the United States.

Sources: See Fig. 3.

The facts about economic growth in the United States and around the world raise some big questions that we're now going to answer. We'll study the causes of economic growth in three stages. First, we'll look at the preconditions for growth and the activities that sustain it. Second, we'll learn how economists measure the relative contributions of the sources of growth—an activity called *growth accounting*. And third, we'll study three theories of economic growth that seek to explain how the influences on growth interact to determine the growth rate. Let's take our first look at the causes of economic growth.

4   THE SOURCES OF ECONOMIC GROWTH

For thousands of years, most human societies have lived like Li River fisherman Songman Yang, with no economic growth. Why?

Real GDP grows when the quantities of the factors of production grow or when persistent advances in technology make factors of production increasingly productive. So to understand what determines the growth rate of real GDP, we must understand what determines the growth rates of the factors of production and rate of increase in their productivity.

We are interested in real GDP growth because it contributes to improvements in our standard of living. But our standard of living improves only if we produce more goods and services per person. So our main concern is to understand the forces that make our labor more productive. We begin by dividing all the influences on real GDP growth into those that increase

▶ Aggregate hours
▶ Labor productivity

Aggregate Hours

Aggregate hours are the total number of hours worked by all the people employed during a year. We calculate aggregate hours as the number of people employed multiplied by average hours per worker. But the number of people employed equals the working-age population multiplied by the *employment-to-population ratio*. So aggregate hours change as a result of

1. Working-age population growth
2. Changes in the employment-to-population ratio
3. Changes in average hours per worker

Aggregate hours grow at the growth rate of the working-age population, adjusted for changes in the employment-to-population ratio and changes in average hours per worker.

With steady population growth, the working-age population grows at the same rate as the total population. But in the United States in recent years, the working-age population has grown faster than the total population because of the baby boom—the burst in the birth rate during the years that followed the end of World War II. Through the 1960s and early 1970s, an increasing number of "baby-boomers" entered the working-age group and the working-age population increased from 65 percent of the total population in 1960 to 77 percent in 2005.

The employment-to-population ratio has increased during the past few decades as the labor force participation rate has increased. But average hours per worker have decreased as the workweek has become shorter and more people have become part-time workers. The combined effects of a rising employment-to-population ratio and falling average hours per worker have kept the average hours per working-age person surprisingly constant at about 1,100 hours a year.

So the growth of aggregate hours comes from population growth rather than from changes in average hours per person.

Population growth increases aggregate hours and real GDP. But to increase real GDP per person, labor must become more productive.

Labor Productivity

Labor productivity is the quantity of real GDP produced by an hour of labor. It is calculated by dividing real GDP by aggregate labor hours. For example, if real GDP is $10,000 billion and aggregate hours are 200 billion, labor productivity is $50 per hour.

When labor productivity grows, real GDP per person grows and brings a rising standard of living.

The growth of labor productivity depends on three things:

▶ Physical capital growth

▶ Human capital growth

▶ Technological advances

These three sources of growth, which interact with each other, are the primary sources of the extraordinary growth in labor productivity during the past 200 years. Let's look at each in turn.

Physical Capital Growth

Physical capital growth results from saving and investment decisions. As the amount of capital per worker increases, labor productivity also increases. Labor productivity took the most dramatic upturn when the amount of capital per worker increased during the Industrial Revolution. Production processes that use hand tools can create beautiful objects, but production methods that use large amounts of capital per worker, such as auto plant assembly lines, are much more productive. The accumulation of capital on farms, in textile factories, in iron foundries and steel mills, in coal mines, on building sites, in chemical plants, in auto plants, in banks and insurance companies, and in shopping malls has added incredibly to the productivity of our economy. The next time you see a movie that is set in the Old West or colonial times, look carefully at the small amount of capital around. Try to imagine how productive you would be in such circumstances compared with your productivity today.

Human Capital Growth

Human capital—the accumulated skill and knowledge of human beings—is the most fundamental source of economic growth. It is a source of both increased labor productivity and technological advance.

The development of one of the most basic human skills—writing—was the source of some of the earliest major gains in productivity. The ability to keep written records made it possible to reap ever-larger gains from specialization and trade. Imagine how hard it would be to do any kind of business if all the accounts, invoices, and agreements existed only in people's memories.

Later, the development of mathematics laid the foundation for the eventual extension of knowledge about physical forces and chemical and biological processes. This base of scientific knowledge was the foundation for the technological advances of the Industrial Revolution 200 years ago and of today's information revolution.

But a lot of human capital that is extremely productive is much more humble. It takes the form of millions of individuals learning and repetitively doing simple production tasks and becoming remarkably more productive in those tasks.

One carefully studied example illustrates the importance of this kind of human capital. Between 1941 and 1944 (during World War II), U.S. shipyards produced some 2,500 units of a cargo ship, called the Liberty Ship, to a standardized design. In 1941, it took 1.2 million person-hours to build one ship. By 1942, it took 600,000 person-hours, and by 1943, it took only 500,000. Not much change occurred in the capital employed during these years. But an enormous amount of human capital was accumulated. Thousands of workers and managers learned from experience and accumulated human capital that more than doubled their productivity in two years.

Technological Advances

The accumulation of physical capital and human capital have made a large contribution to economic growth. But technological change—the discovery and the application of new technologies and new goods—has made an even greater contribution.

People are many times more productive today than they were a hundred years ago. We are not more productive because we have more steam engines and more horse-drawn carriages per person. Rather, it is because we have engines and transportation equipment that use technologies that were unknown a hundred years ago and that are more productive than the old technologies were. Technological change makes an enormous contribution to our increased productivity. Technological advance arises from formal research and development programs and from informal trial and error, and it involves discovering new ways of getting more out of our resources.

To reap the benefits of technological change, capital must increase. Some of the most powerful and far-reaching fundamental technologies are embodied in human capital—for example, language, writing, and mathematics. But most technologies are embodied in physical capital. For example, to reap the benefits of the internal combustion engine, millions of horse-drawn carriages and horses were replaced by automobiles; and to reap the benefits of digital music, millions of Walkmans were replaced by iPods.

Figure 5 summarizes the sources of economic growth that we've just described. It also emphasizes that for real GDP per person to grow, real GDP growth must exceed the population growth rate.

We began this account of the sources of economic growth by noting that for thousands of years, no growth occurred. You've seen that economic growth results from productivity growth. Why is productivity growth a relatively recent phenomenon?

FIGURE 5   The Sources of Economic Growth

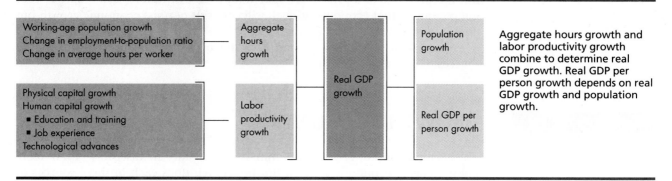

The reason is that early humans (like many people today) lacked the fundamental social institutions and arrangements that are essential preconditions for economic growth. Let's end our discussion of the sources of growth by examining its preconditions.

Preconditions for Economic Growth

The most basic precondition for economic growth is an appropriate *incentive* system. Three institutions are crucial to the creation of incentives:

1. Markets

2. Property rights

3. Monetary exchange

Markets enable buyers and sellers to get information and to do business with each other, and market prices send signals to buyers and sellers that create incentives to increase or decrease the quantities demanded and supplied. Markets enable people to specialize and trade and to save and invest. But markets need property rights and monetary exchange.

Property rights are the social arrangements that govern the ownership, use, and disposal of factors of production and goods and services. They include the rights to physical property (land, buildings, and capital equipment), to financial property (claims by one person against another), and to intellectual property (such as inventions). Clearly established and enforced property rights give people an assurance that a capricious government will not confiscate their income or savings.

Monetary exchange facilitates transactions of all kinds, including the orderly transfer of private property from one person to another. Property rights and monetary exchange create incentives for people to specialize and trade, to save and invest, and to discover new technologies.

No unique political system is necessary to deliver the preconditions for economic growth. Liberal democracy, founded on the fundamental principle of the rule of law, is the system that does the best job. It provides a solid base on which property rights can be established and enforced. But authoritarian political systems have sometimes provided an environment in which economic growth has occurred.

Early human societies, based on hunting and gathering, did not experience economic growth because they lacked these preconditions. Economic growth began when societies evolved the three key institutions that create incentives. But the presence of an incentive system and the institutions that create it does not guarantee that economic growth will occur. It permits economic growth but does not make that growth inevitable.

Next you'll learn how we measure the quantitative contributions of the sources of economic growth.

5   GROWTH ACCOUNTING

The accumulation of physical and human capital and the discovery of new technologies bring economic growth. But how much does each of these sources of growth contribute? The answer to this question is a crucial input in the design of policies to achieve faster growth. Edward F. Denison, an economist at the Brookings Institution, provided the answer by developing **growth accounting**, a tool that calculates the quantitative contribution to real GDP growth of each of its sources.

To identify the contributions of capital growth and separate it from the effect of technological change and human capital growth, we need to know how labor productivity changes when capital changes.

The *law of diminishing returns*, which states that as the quantity of one input increases with the quantities of all other inputs remaining the same, output increases but by ever smaller increments, applies to capital just as it applies to labor.

Applied to capital, the law of diminishing returns states that if a given number of hours of labor uses more capital (with the same technology), the *additional* output that results from the *additional* capital gets smaller as the amount of capital increases. One person working with two computers types fewer than twice as many pages a day as one person working with one computer. More generally, one hour of labor working with $40 of capital produces less than twice the output of one hour of labor working with $20 of capital. But how much less? The answer is given by the *one third rule*.

The One Third Rule

Using data on capital, labor hours, and real GDP in the U.S. economy, Robert Solow of MIT estimated the effect of capital on real GDP per hour of labor, or labor productivity. In doing so, he discovered the **one third rule**, that on the average, with no change in technology, a 1 percent increase in capital per hour of labor brings a *1/3 percent increase* in labor productivity. The one third rule is used to calculate the contributions of an increase in capital per hour of labor and technological change to the growth of labor productivity. Let's do such a calculation.

Suppose that capital per hour of labor grows by 3 percent a year and labor productivity grows by 2.5 percent a year. The one third rule tells us that capital growth contributed one third of 3 percent, which is 1 percent, to the growth of labor productivity. The rest of the 2.5 percent growth of labor productivity comes from technological change. That is, technological change contributed 1.5 percent, which is the 2.5 percent growth of labor productivity minus the estimated 1 percent contribution of capital growth.

Accounting for the Productivity Growth Slowdown and Speedup

We can use the one third rule to measure the contributions to U.S. productivity growth. Figure 6 shows the results for the years 1960 through 2005. Between 1960 and 1973, labor productivity grew by 3.7 percent a year and capital growth and technological change contributed equally to this growth.

Between 1973 and 1983, labor productivity growth slowed to 1.7 percent a year and a collapse of the contributions of human capital and technological change brought this slowdown. Technological change did not stop during the productivity growth slowdown. But its focus changed from increasing labor productivity to coping with energy price shocks and environmental protection.

FIGURE 6   Labor Productivity Growth

(a) Labor productivity growth

(b) The contributions to labor productivity growth

Labor productivity grew most quickly during the 1960s and most slowly between 1973 and 1983. Changes in the pace of technological change were the biggest source of fluctuations in labor productivity growth.

Sources: Bureau of Economic Analysis, Bureau of Labor Statistics, and author's calculations.

Between 1983 and 1993, labor productivity growth speeded to 2 percent a year, and between 1993 and 2005, it speeded to a bit more than 2.4 percent a year. Although growth in the "new economy" of the 1990s and 2000s was stronger than that of the 1970s, growth lagged a long way behind that of the booming sixties.

Achieving Faster Growth

Growth accounting tells us that to achieve faster economic growth, we must increase the growth rate of physical capital, the pace of technological advance, or the growth rate of human capital.

The main suggestions for achieving these objectives are

► Stimulate saving
► Stimulate research and development
► Target high-technology industries
► Encourage international trade
► Improve the quality of education

Stimulate Saving

Saving finances investment, which brings capital accumulation. So stimulating saving can increase economic growth. The East Asian economies have the highest growth rates and the highest saving rates. Some African economies have the lowest growth rates and the lowest saving rates.

Tax incentives can increase saving. Individual Retirement Accounts (IRAs) are a tax incentive to save. Economists claim that a tax on consumption rather than income provides the best saving incentive.

Stimulate Research and Development

Everyone can use the fruits of *basic* research and development efforts. For example, all biotechnology firms can use advances in gene-splicing technology. Because basic inventions can be copied, the inventor's profit is limited and the market allocates too few resources to this activity.

Governments can direct public funds toward financing basic research, but this solution is not foolproof. It requires a mechanism for allocating the public funds to their highest-valued use. The National Science Foundation is one possibly efficient channel for allocating public funds to universities to finance and stimulate basic research.

Target High-Technology Industries

Some people say that by providing public funds to high-technology firms and industries, a country can become the first to exploit a new technology and can earn above-average profits for a period while others are busy catching up. This strategy is risky and just as likely to use resources inefficiently as to speed growth.

Encourage International Trade

Free international trade stimulates growth by extracting all the available gains from specialization and trade. The fastest-growing nations today are those with the fastest-growing exports and imports.

Improve the Quality of Education

The free market produces too little education because it brings benefits beyond those valued by the people who receive the education. By funding basic education and by ensuring high standards in basic skills such as language, mathematics, and science, governments can contribute to a nation's growth potential. Education can also be stimulated and improved by using tax incentives to encourage improved private provision.

GROWTH THEORIES
6

You've seen that real GDP grows when the quantities of labor, physical capital, and human capital grow and when technology advances. Does this mean that the growth of labor and capital and technological advances *cause* economic growth? It might. But there are other possibilities. *Some* of these factors might be the causes of real GDP growth, and the others might be the *effect*. We must try to discover how the influences on economic growth interact with each other to make some economies grow quickly and others grow slowly. And we must probe the reasons why a country's long-term growth rate sometimes speeds up and sometimes slows down.

To explain economic growth, we need a theory of economic growth that explains the interactions among the several factors that contribute to it and disentangles cause and effect.

Economists seek a universal theory of economic growth. They want to understand the growth of poor countries and rich countries—why and how poor countries become rich and rich countries continue to get richer.

Economic growth occurs when real GDP increases. But a one-shot increase in real GDP in a recovery from recession isn't economic growth. Economic growth is a sustained, year-after-year increase in *potential GDP*.

We're going to begin our explanation of growth theory by studying the effects and interactions that occur when labor productivity increases.

Increase in Labor Productivity

How does an increase in labor productivity change real GDP? How does it change aggregate hours? And how does it influence the real wage rate—the income from labor?

We can answer these questions by using the classical model. This model of the full-employment economy is ideally suited to studying economic growth because sustained real GDP growth can occur only when potential GDP grows.

If labor productivity increases, production possibilities expand. The real GDP that any given quantity of labor can produce increases. The *marginal product of labor* also increases, which increases the demand for labor.

With an increase in the demand for labor and *no change in the supply of labor*, the real wage rate rises and the quantity of labor supplied increases. Employment (aggregate hours) increases.

Potential GDP increases for two reasons. First, because labor is more productive, a given amount of employment produces more real GDP. Second, equilibrium employment increases.

Illustrating the Effects of an Increase in Labor Productivity

Figure 7 illustrates the effects of an increase in labor productivity that results from an increase in physical capital or human capital or an advance in technology.

In part (a), the production function initially is PF_0. With 200 billion hours of labor employed, potential GDP is $12 trillion at point A.

In part (b), the demand for labor curve is LD_0 and the supply of labor curve is LS. The real wage rate is $35 an hour, and equilibrium employment is 200 billion hours a year.

Now an increase in capital or an advance in technology increases the labor productivity. In Fig. 7(a), the increase in labor productivity shifts the production function upward to PF_1. At each quantity of labor, more real GDP can be produced. For example, at 200 billion hours, the economy can now produce $17 trillion of real GDP at point B.

In Fig. 7(b), the demand for labor increases and the demand curve shifts rightward to LD_1. At the original real wage rate of $35 an hour, there is now a shortage of labor. So the real wage rate rises. In this example, the real wage rate keeps rising until it reaches $45 an hour. At $45 an hour, the quantity of labor demanded equals the quantity of labor supplied and aggregate hours at equilibrium employment increase to 225 billion a year.

Figure 7(a) shows the effects of the increase in labor productivity on potential GDP. There are two effects. At the initial quantity of labor, real GDP increases to point B on the new production function. But as aggregate hours increase from 200 billion to 225 billion, potential GDP increases further to $18 trillion at point C.

Potential GDP per hour of labor also increases. You can see this increase by dividing potential GDP by aggregate hours. Initially, with potential GDP at $12 trillion and aggregate hours at 200 billion, potential GDP per hour of labor was $60. With the increase in labor productivity, potential GDP is $18 trillion and aggregate hours are 225 billion, so potential GDP per hour of labor is $80.

You've now seen the effects of an increase in labor productivity. If labor productivity grows, potential GDP grows, the real wage rate rises, and aggregate hours increase.

There is a limit to the increase in aggregate hours and if the process of labor productivity growth continues with no change in the supply of labor, eventually, at some higher real wage rate, the labor supply curve becomes vertical. At this point, as labor productivity continues to grow, the real wage rate rises, potential GDP increases, but aggregate hours remain constant.

You've just seen that aggregate hours can increase as a consequence of an increase in labor productivity. This interaction of aggregate hours and labor productivity is an example of the interaction effects that economists seek to identify in their search for the ultimate causes of economic growth. In the case that we've just studied, aggregate hours increase but that increase is a consequence, not a cause, of real GDP growth. The source of the real GDP increase is an increase in capital or technological advances that increase labor productivity.

But aggregate hours can increase if the population increases. Let's now examine the effects of this source of an increase in aggregate hours.

FIGURE 7   The Effects of an Increase in Labor Productivity

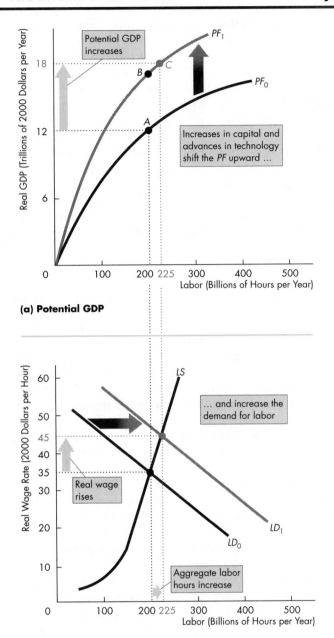

(a) Potential GDP

(b) The labor market

An increase in labor productivity shifts the production function upward from PF_0 to PF_1 in part (a) and shifts the demand for labor curve rightward from LD_0 to LD_1 in part (b). The real wage rate rises to $45 an hour, and aggregate hours increase from 200 billion to 225 billion. Potential GDP increases from $12 trillion to $18 trillion.

An Increase in Population

As the population increases and the additional people reach working age, the supply of labor increases. With more labor available, the economy's production possibilities expand. But does the expansion of production possibilities mean that potential GDP increases? And does it mean that potential GDP *per hour of labor* increases?

The answers to these questions have intrigued economists for many years. And they cause heated political debate today. In China, for example, families are under enormous pressure to limit the number of children they have. In other countries, such as France, the government encourages large families. In the United States and the United Kingdom, immigration and its effects on the population and the labor market are a big concern.

Again, we can analyze the effects of an increase in population by using the classical model of the full-employment economy.

If the population increases, the supply of labor increases. There is no change in the demand for labor and no change in the production function. The economy can produce more output by using more labor (a movement along the production function), but there is no change in the quantity of real GDP that a given quantity of labor can produce.

With an increase in the supply of labor and no change in the demand for labor, the real wage rate falls and equilibrium employment (aggregate hours) increases. The increased labor hours produce more output and potential GDP increases.

Illustrating the Effects of an Increase in Population

Figure 8 illustrates the effects of an increase in the population. In Fig. 8(a), the demand for labor curve is LD and initially the supply of labor curve is LS_0. The equilibrium real wage rate is $35 an hour and aggregate hours are 200 billion a year. In Fig. 8(b), the production function (PF) shows that with 200 billion hours of labor employed, potential GDP is $12 trillion at point A.

An increase in the population increases the number of people of working age, and the supply of labor increases. The supply of labor curve shifts rightward to LS_1. At a real wage rate of $35 an hour, there is now a surplus of labor. So the real wage rate falls. In this example, the real wage rate falls until it reaches $25 an hour. At $25 an hour, the quantity of labor demanded equals the quantity of labor supplied. Aggregate hours increase to 300 billion a year.

Figure 8(b) shows the effect of the increase in aggregate hours on real GDP. As aggregate hours increase from 200 billion to 300 billion, potential GDP increases from $12 trillion to $15 trillion at point B.

So an increase in the population increases aggregate hours, increases potential GDP, and lowers the real wage rate.

An increase in the population also decreases potential GDP per hour of labor. You can see this decrease by dividing potential GDP by aggregate hours. Initially, with potential GDP at $12 trillion and aggregate hours at 200 billion, potential GDP per hour of labor was $60. With the increase in the population, potential GDP is $15 trillion and aggregate hours are 300 billion. Potential GDP per hour of labor is $50. Diminishing returns are the source of the decrease in potential GDP per hour of labor.

Economic growth theory builds on the effects of labor productivity growth and population growth that you've just reviewed.

You're going to study three theories of economic growth, each of which gives some insights into the process of economic growth. But none provides a complete and definite answer to the basic questions: What causes economic growth and why do growth rates vary? Economics has some way to go before it

FIGURE 8   The Effects of an Increase in Population

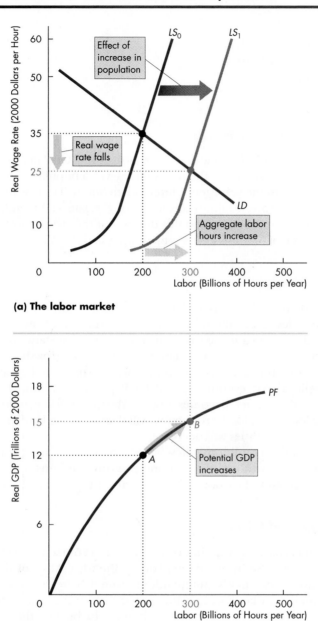

(a) The labor market

(b) Potential GDP

An increase in the population increases the supply of labor. In part (a), the real wage rate falls and employment (aggregate hours) increases. In part (b), the increase in aggregate hours increases potential GDP. Because the marginal product of labor diminishes, the increased population increases real GDP but real GDP per hour of labor decreases.

can provide a definite answer to these questions. The three growth theories we study are

▶ Classical growth theory
▶ Neoclassical growth theory
▶ New growth theory

Classical Growth Theory

Classical growth theory is the view that the growth of real GDP per person is temporary and that when it rises above the subsistence level, a population explosion eventually brings it back to the subsistence level. Adam Smith, Thomas Robert Malthus, and David Ricardo—the leading economists of the late eighteenth century and early nineteenth century—proposed this theory, but the view is most closely associated with the name of Malthus and is sometimes called the *Malthusian theory*.

Modern-Day Malthusians

Many people today are Malthusians! They say that if today's global population of 6.2 billion explodes to 11 billion by 2200, we will run out of resources, real GDP per person will decline, and we will return to a primitive standard of living. We must act, say the Malthusians, to contain the population growth.

Modern-day Malthusians also point to global warming and climate change as reasons to believe that eventually, real GDP per person will decrease. They believe that as the planet becomes hotter, the polar ice caps melt, and the oceans' water levels rise, food production will decrease, the land area will shrink, and production possibilities will decrease.

These doomsday conditions, they believe, arise as a direct consequence of today's economic growth and the vast and growing amounts of activity that are increasing the amount of carbon dioxide in the earth's atmosphere.

The Basic Classical Idea

To understand classical growth theory, let's transport ourselves back to the world of 1776, when Adam Smith is first explaining the idea. Most of the 2.5 million people who live in the newly independent United States of America work on farms or on their own land and perform their tasks using simple tools and animal power. They earn an average of 2 shillings (a bit less than 12 dollars in today's money) for working a 10-hour day.

Then advances in farming technology bring new types of plows and seeds that increase farm productivity. As farm productivity increases, farm production increases and some farm workers move from the land to the cities, where they get work producing and selling the expanding range of farm equipment. Incomes rise, and the people seem to be prospering. But will the prosperity last? Classical growth theory says it will not.

Advances in technology—in both agriculture and industry—lead to an investment in new capital, which makes labor more productive. More and more businesses start up and hire the now more productive labor. The greater demand for labor raises the real wage rate and increases employment.

At this stage, economic growth has occurred and everyone has benefited from it. Real GDP has increased, and the real wage rate has increased. But the classical economists believe that this new situation can't last because it will induce a population explosion.

Classical Theory of Population Growth

When the classical economists were developing their ideas about population growth, an unprecedented population explosion was under way. In Britain and other Western European countries, improvements in diet and hygiene had lowered the death rate while the birth rate remained high. For several decades, population growth was extremely rapid. For example, after being relatively stable for several centuries, the population of Britain increased by 40 percent between 1750 and 1800 and by a further 50 percent between 1800 and 1830. Meanwhile, an estimated 1 million people (about 20 percent of the 1750 population) left Britain for America and Australia before 1800, and outward migration continued on a similar scale through the nineteenth century. These facts are the empirical basis for the classical theory of population growth.

To explain the high rate of population growth, the classical economists used the idea of a **subsistence real wage rate**, which is the minimum real wage rate needed to maintain life. If the actual real wage rate is less than the subsistence real wage rate, some people cannot survive and the population decreases. In classical theory, when the real wage rate exceeds the subsistence real wage rate, the population grows. But an increasing population brings diminishing returns to labor. So labor productivity eventually decreases. This dismal implication led to economics being called the *dismal science.* The dismal implication is that no matter how much technological change occurs, real wage rates are always pushed back toward the subsistence level.

The dismal conclusion of classical growth theory is a direct consequence of the assumption that the population explodes if real GDP per hour of labor exceeds the subsistence level. To avoid this conclusion, we need a different view of population growth.

The neoclassical growth theory that we'll now study provides a different view.

Neoclassical Growth Theory

Neoclassical growth theory is the proposition that real GDP per person grows because technological change induces a level of saving and investment that makes capital per hour of labor grow. Growth ends only if technological change stops.

Robert Solow of MIT suggested the most popular version of neoclassical growth theory in the 1950s. But Frank Ramsey of Cambridge University in England first developed this theory in the 1920s.

Neoclassical growth theory's big break with its classical predecessor is its view about population growth. We'll begin our account of neoclassical theory by examining its views about population growth.

The Neoclassical Economics of Population Growth

The population explosion of eighteenth century Europe that created the classical theory of population eventually ended. The birth rate fell, and while the population continued to increase, its rate of increase became moderate. This slowdown in population growth seemed to make the classical theory less relevant. It also eventually led to the development of a modern economic theory of population growth.

The modern view is that although the population growth rate is influenced by economic factors, the influence is not a simple and mechanical one like that proposed by the classical economists. Key among the economic influences on population growth is the opportunity cost of a woman's time. As women's wage rates increase and their job opportunities expand, the opportunity cost of having children increases. Faced with a higher opportunity cost, families choose to have fewer children and the birth rate falls.

A second economic influence works on the death rate. The technological advance that brings increased productivity and increased incomes brings advances in health care that extends lives.

These two opposing economic forces influence the population growth rate. As incomes increase, both the birth rate and the death rate decrease. It turns out that these opposing forces almost offset each other, so the rate of population growth is independent of the economic growth rate.

This modern view of population growth and the historical trends that support it contradict the views of the classical economists. They also call into question the modern doomsday conclusion that the planet will one day be swamped with more people than it can support. Neoclassical growth theory adopts this modern view of population growth. Forces other than real GDP and its growth rate determine population growth.

Technological Change

In neoclassical growth theory, the rate of technological change influences the economic growth rate but economic growth does not influence the pace of technological change. It is assumed that technological change results from chance. When we're lucky, we have rapid technological change, and when bad luck strikes, the pace of technological advance slows.

Target Rate of Return and Saving

The key assumption in neoclassical growth theory concerns saving. Other things remaining the same, the higher the real interest rate, the greater is the amount that people save. But in the long run, saving is highly responsive to the real interest rate. To decide how much to save, people compare the real interest rate with a *target rate of return*. If the real interest rate exceeds the target rate of return, saving is sufficient to make capital per hour of labor grow. If the target rate of return exceeds the real interest rate, saving is not sufficient to maintain the current level of capital per hour of labor, so capital per hour of labor shrinks. And if the real interest rate equals a target rate of return, saving is just sufficient to maintain the quantity of capital per hour of labor at its current level.

The Basic Neoclassical Idea

To understand neoclassical growth theory, imagine the world of the mid-1950s, when Robert Solow is explaining his idea. Americans are enjoying post–World War II prosperity. Income per person is around $12,000 a year in today's money. The population is growing at about 1 percent a year. Saving and investment are about 18 percent of GDP, enough to keep the quantity of capital per hour of labor constant. Income per person is growing but not by much.

Then technology begins to advance at a more rapid pace across a range of activities. The transistor revolutionizes an emerging electronics industry. New plastics revolutionize the manufacture of household appliances. The interstate highway system revolutionizes road transportation. Jet airliners start to replace piston-engine airplanes and speed air transportation.

These technological advances bring new profit opportunities. Businesses expand, and new businesses are created to exploit the newly available profitable technologies. Investment and saving increase. The economy enjoys new levels of prosperity and growth. But will the prosperity last? And will the growth last? Neoclassical growth theory says that the *prosperity* will last but the *growth* will not last unless technology keeps advancing.

According to neoclassical growth theory, the prosperity will persist because there is no classical population growth to induce the wage rate to fall.

But growth will stop if technology stops advancing, for two related reasons. First, high profit rates that result from technological change bring increased saving and capital accumulation. But second, capital accumulation eventually results in diminishing returns that lower the real interest rate and that eventually decrease saving and slow the rate of capital accumulation.

A Problem with Neoclassical Growth Theory

All economies have access to the same technologies, and capital is free to roam the globe, seeking the highest available real interest rate. Given these facts, neoclassical growth theory implies that growth rates and income levels per person around the globe will converge. While there is some sign of convergence among the rich countries, as Fig. 3(a) shows, convergence is slow, and it does not appear to be imminent for all countries, as Fig. 3(b) shows.

New growth theory overcomes this shortcoming of neoclassical growth theory. It also explains what determines the rate of technological change.

New Growth Theory

New growth theory holds that real GDP per person grows because of the choices people make in the pursuit of profit and that growth can persist indefinitely. Paul Romer of Stanford University developed this theory during the 1980s, but the ideas go back to the work by Joseph Schumpeter during the 1930s and 1940s.

The theory begins with two facts about market economies:

▶ Discoveries result from choices.
▶ Discoveries bring profit, and competition destroys profit.

Discoveries and Choices

When people discover a new product or technique, they think of themselves as being lucky. They are right. But the pace at which new discoveries are made—and at which technology advances—is not determined by chance. It depends on how many people are looking for a new technology and how intensively they are looking.

Discoveries and Profits

Profit is the spur to technological change. The forces of competition squeeze profits, so to increase profit, people constantly seek either lower-cost methods of production or new and better products for which people are willing to pay a higher price. Inventors can maintain a profit for several years by taking out a patent or a copyright. But eventually, a new discovery is copied, and profits disappear.

Two further facts play a key role in the new growth theory:

▶ Discoveries are a public capital good.

▶ Knowledge is capital that is not subject to the law of diminishing returns.

Discoveries Are a Public Capital Good

Economists call a good a *public good* when no one can be excluded from using it and when one person's use does not prevent others from using it. National defense is one example of a public good. Knowledge is another.

When in 1992, Marc Andreesen and his friend Eric Bina developed a browser they called Mosaic, they laid the foundation for Netscape Navigator and Internet Explorer, two pieces of capital that have increased productivity unimaginably.

While patents and copyrights protect the inventors or creators of new products and production processes and enable them to reap the returns from their innovative ideas, once a new discovery has been made, everyone can benefit from its use. And one person's use of a new discovery does not prevent others from using it. Your use of a Web browser doesn't prevent someone else from using that same code simultaneously.

Because knowledge is a public good, as the benefits of a new discovery spread, free resources become available. These resources are free because nothing is given up when they are used. They have a zero opportunity cost. Knowledge is even more special because it is not subject to diminishing returns.

Knowledge Capital Is Not Subject to Diminishing Returns

Production is subject to diminishing returns when one resource is fixed and the quantity of another resource changes. Adding labor to a fixed amount of capital or adding capital to a fixed amount of labor both bring diminishing marginal product—diminishing returns.

But increasing the stock of knowledge makes labor and machines more productive. Knowledge capital does not bring diminishing returns.

The fact that knowledge capital does *not* experience diminishing returns is the central novel proposition of new growth theory. And the implication of this simple and appealing idea is astonishing. Unlike the other two theories, new growth theory has no growth-stopping mechanism. As physical capital accumulates, the return to capital—the real interest rate—falls. But the incentive to innovate and earn a higher profit becomes stronger. So innovation occurs, capital becomes more productive, the demand for capital increases, and the real interest rate rises again.

Labor productivity grows indefinitely as people discover new technologies that yield a higher real interest rate. This growth rate depends on people's ability to innovate.

Over the years, the ability to innovate has changed. The invention of language and writing (the two most basic human capital tools) and later the development of the scientific method and the establishment of universities and research institutions brought huge increases in the pace of innovation. Today, a deeper understanding of genes is bringing profit in a growing biotechnology industry. And advances in computer technology are creating an explosion of profit opportunities in a wide range of information-age industries.

A Perpetual Motion Economy

New growth theory sees the economy as a perpetual motion machine, which Fig. 9 illustrates.

No matter how rich we become, our wants will always exceed our ability to satisfy them. We will always want a higher standard of living.

In the pursuit of a higher standard of living, human societies have developed incentive systems—property rights and voluntary monetary exchange in markets—that enable people to profit from innovation.

Innovation leads to the development of new and better techniques of production and new and better products.

To take advantage of new techniques and to produce new products, new firms start up and old firms go out of business—firms are born and die.

As old firms die and new firms are born, some jobs are destroyed and others are created. The new jobs created are better than the old ones and they pay higher real wage rates. Also, with higher wage rates and more productive techniques, leisure increases.

New and better jobs and new and better products lead to more consumption goods and services and, combined with increased leisure, bring a higher standard of living.

But our insatiable wants are still there, so the process continues, going round and round a circle of wants, incentives, innovation, and new and better products, and a yet higher standard of living.

FIGURE 9   A Perpetual Motion Machine

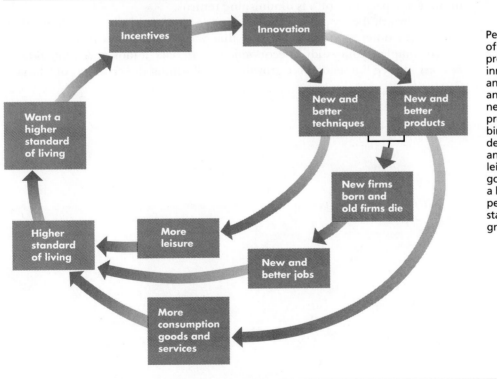

People want a higher standard of living and are spurred by profit incentives to make the innovations that lead to new and better techniques and new and better products. These new and better techniques and products, in turn, lead to the birth of new firms and the death of some old firms, new and better jobs, and more leisure and more consumption goods and services. The result is a higher standard of living. But people want a still higher standard of living, and the growth process continues.

Source: Based on a similar figure in *These Are the Good Old Days: A Report on U.S. Living Standards,* Federal Reserve Bank of Dallas 1993 Annual Report.

New Growth Theory versus Malthusian Theory

The contrast between the Malthusian theory and new growth theory couldn't be more sharp. Malthusians see the end of prosperity as we know it today and new growth theorists see unending plenty. The contrast becomes clearest by thinking about the differing views about population growth.

To a Malthusian, population growth is part of the problem. To a new growth theorist, population growth is part of the solution! People are the ultimate economic resource. A larger population brings forth more wants. But it also brings a greater amount of scientific discovery and technological advance. So rather than being the source of falling real GDP per person, population growth generates faster productivity growth and rising real GDP per person. Resources are limited, but the human imagination and ability to increase productivity are unlimited.

Sorting Out the Theories

Which theory is correct? Probably none tells us the whole story, but they all teach us something of value.

Classical growth theory reminds us that our physical resources are limited and that without advances in technology, we must eventually hit diminishing returns.

Neoclassical growth theory reaches the same conclusion but not because of a population explosion. Instead, it emphasizes diminishing returns to capital and reminds us that we cannot keep growth going just by accumulating physical capital. We must also advance technology and accumulate human capital. We must become more creative in our use of scarce resources.

New growth theory emphasizes the possible capacity of human resources to innovate at a pace that offsets diminishing returns.

New growth theory probably fits the facts of today's world more closely than either of the other two theories do. But that doesn't make it correct.

To complete your study of economic growth, take a look at *Reading Between the Lines* and see how economic growth is transforming the economy of China.

READING BETWEEN THE LINES

Economic Growth in Asia

THE NEW YORK TIMES, OCTOBER 21, 2005

China's Economy Surges 9.4% in 3rd Quarter

October 21, 2005

China's roaring economy grew 9.4 percent in the third quarter of this year, fueled by surging exports, strong investments in infrastructure and solid retail sales, according to government figures released Thursday.

The figures indicate that China's economy, the fastest-growing major economy in the world, shows no sign of moderating, despite repeated attempts by the government to ease growth as a way to head off inflation or overheating.

Economists and analysts who predicted late last year that China's growth would abate to about 8.5 percent in 2005 from about 9.5 percent in 2004 have repeatedly been forced to adjust their forecasts upward.

Thursday, more analysts raised their forecasts.

"This is much stronger growth than the market expected," said Hong Liang, an economist at Goldman Sachs, who expects the Chinese economy to grow 9.4 percent this year and 9 percent in 2006. . . .

Many experts say China seems to be locked into 9 percent economic growth—even after its economy has advanced at a faster pace over the last 20 years than any other major country in modern history, even outpacing the earlier decades long expansions of Japan and South Korea.

"It's not going to change," said Yiping Huang, an economist at Citigroup in Hong Kong. "At the moment, the government is trying to slow momentum a bit, but we're not seeing slowing." . . .

Essence of the Story

► Real GDP growth in China is running at more than 9 percent per year.

► China's economy is the fastest-growing major economy in the world.

► Economists who expected China's growth rate to slow have revised their forecasts upward.

► China is now expected to continue to achieve 9 percent economic growth.

► Government attempts to slow the growth rate are expected to have little effect.

Economic Analysis

► In 1949, when Mao Zedong established the People's Republic of China, incomes in China were among the lowest in the world.

► From 1949 until 1978, China operated a planned economy with little private enterprise. Economic growth was modest, and in some years, real GDP decreased.

► In 1978, under the leadership of Deng Xiaoping, China embarked on a program of economic reform.

► Gradually, state-owned monopolies were replaced by private competitive businesses, often financed with foreign capital and operated as joint ventures with foreign firms.

► By the early 1980s, China's real GDP was growing at one of the fastest rates in the world and the fastest ever known.

► In 2005, China's real GDP was more than $9 trillion (using U.S. dollars and PPP prices in 2000).

► U.S. real GDP in 2005 was almost $12 trillion (2000 dollars).

► Although China's real GDP was not far behind U.S. real GDP in 2005, China used much more labor than the United States used.

► Aggregate labor hours in the United States in 2005 were about 250 billion.

► We don't know what China's aggregate labor hours were. But employment was 790 million and with an average workweek of 40 hours (an assumption), aggregate hours would be around 1,650 billion—more than 6 times the U.S. hours.

► So real GDP per hour of labor in China in 2005 was around $5 compared to about $48 in the United States.

► But China's real GDP is growing at about 9 percent a year. In contrast, U.S. real GDP is growing at about 2.5 percent a year.

► If these growth rates persist, China's real GDP will surpass that of the United States within the next decade.

► But China's real GDP per hour of labor will continue to lag well behind that of the United States.

► The figure shows the situation in China and the United States in 2005.

► The U.S. production function is PF_{US05}, and China's production function is PF_{C05}.

► With employment of 250 billion hours, the United States produces $12 trillion of real GDP, and with employment of 1,650 billion hours, China produces $9 trillion of real GDP.

► That is, an hour of labor in the United States produces around 10 times as much as an hour of labor in China produces.

► The figure also shows the situation in the United States and China in 2015 if current growth rates persist.

► The U.S. production function will be PF_{US15}, and China's production function will be PF_{C15}.

► With population growth at about 1 percent a year in both countries, labor hours will increase and so will real GDP.

► In 2015, China will be producing a larger real GDP than the United States but real GDP per hour of labor in China will still lag that in the United States.

FIGURE 10   Growth in China and the United States

You're the Voter

► Do you think the United States can learn any lessons from China about how to make the U.S. economy grow faster?

► Can you think of any tax reforms that might increase the U.S. growth rate? Would you vote for these reforms? Why or why not?

SUMMARY

▶ Economic growth is the sustained expansion of production possibilities and is measured as the annual percentage rate of change of real GDP.

▶ Sustained growth transforms poor nations into rich ones.

▶ The Rule of 70 tells us the number of years in which real GDP doubles—70 divided by the annual percentage growth rate.

▶ Between 1905 and 2005, real GDP per person in the United States grew at an average rate of 2 percent a year. Growth was rapid during the 1960s and late 1990s.

▶ The gap in real GDP per person between the United States and Central and South America has persisted. The gaps between the United States and Hong Kong, Korea, Taiwan, and China have narrowed. The gaps between the United States and Africa and Central Europe have widened.

▶ The sources of economic growth are increases in aggregate hours and labor productivity. Labor productivity depends on physical capital and human capital growth and advances in technology.

▶ Economic growth requires an incentive system created by markets, property rights, and monetary exchange.

▶ Growth accounting measures the contributions of capital accumulation and technological change to the growth of labor productivity.

▶ Growth accounting uses the one third rule: A 1 percent increase in capital per hour of labor brings a 1/3 percent increase in labor productivity.

▶ During the productivity growth slowdown of the 1970s, technological change did not stop growing but its focus changed to coping with energy price shocks and environmental protection.

▶ Stimulating saving and research, targeting high-technology industries, encouraging international trade, and improving education might boost economic growth.

▶ An increase in labor productivity increases employment, the real wage rate, and potential GDP.

▶ An increase in the population increases employment and potential GDP, but the real wage rate and real GDP per hour of labor decrease.

▶ In classical theory, real GDP per person returns to the subsistence level.

▶ In neoclassical growth theory, without further technological change, diminishing returns to capital bring economic growth to a halt.

▶ In new growth theory, economic growth persists indefinitely at a rate determined by decisions that lead to innovation and technological change.

REGULATION AND ANTITRUST POLICY IN A GLOBALIZED ECONOMY

by Roger LeRoy Miller

LEARNING OUTCOMES

The candidate should be able to:	Mastery
a. explain the rationale for government regulation in the form of 1) economic regulation of natural monopolies and 2) social regulation of nonmonopolistic industries;	☐
b. discuss the potential benefits and possible negative side effects of social regulation;	☐
c. differentiate between the capture hypothesis and the share-the-gains, share-the-pains theory of regulator behavior.	☐

INTRODUCTION 1

In 1997, the U.S. government ruled out a proposed merger between the granddaddy of all telephone companies, American Telephone & Telegraph (AT&T), and Texas-based SBC, a regional phone-service provider. Such a combination, one government official stated, would cause an "unthinkable" reduction in the degree of competition in the telecommunications industry. Only eight years later, the government changed its tune and permitted AT&T and SBC to merge their operations. Why was this merger "unthinkable" in 1997 but entirely permissible in 2005? To understand this shift in the government's view of the social desirability of a telecommunications merger, you will have to learn more about *antitrust policy,* which is one of the key topics of this reading.

2   FORMS OF INDUSTRY REGULATION

The U.S. government began regulating social and economic activity early in the nation's history. The amount of government regulation began increasing in the twentieth century and has grown considerably since 1970. Figure 1 displays two common measures of regulation in the United States. Panel (a) shows regulatory spending by federal agencies (in 2005 dollars), which has generally trended upward since 1970. Panel (b) depicts the number of pages in the *Federal Register,* a government publication that lists all new regulatory rules. According to this measure, the scope of new federal regulations increased sharply during the 1970s, dropped off in the 1980s, and has generally increased since then.

There are two basic types of government regulation. One is *economic regulation* of natural monopolies and of specific nonmonopolistic industries. For instance, some state commissions regulate the prices and quality of services provided by electric power companies, which are considered natural monopolies that experience lower long-run average costs as their output increases. Financial services industries and interstate transportation industries are examples of nonmonopolistic industries that are subjected to considerable government regulation. The other form of government regulation is *social regulation,* which covers all industries. Examples include various occupational, health, and safety rules that federal and state governments impose on most businesses.

FIGURE 1   Regulation on the Rise

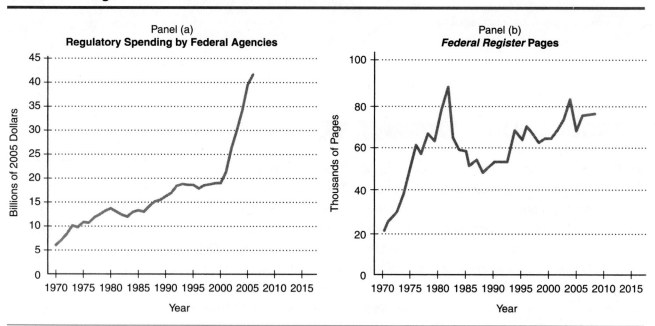

Panel (a) shows that federal government regulatory spending is now more than $40 billion per year. State and local spending is not shown. As panel (b) shows, the number of pages in the *Federal Register* per year rose from 1990 to 2000, dropped off somewhat, and then began to rise once more.

Sources: Institute for University Studies; *Federal Register*, various issues.

Economic Regulation

Initially, most economic regulation in the United States was aimed at controlling prices in industries considered to be natural monopolies. Over time, federal and state governments have also sought to influence the characteristics of products or processes of firms in a variety of industries without inherently monopolistic features.

Regulation of Natural Monopolies

The regulation of natural monopolies has tended to emphasize restrictions on product prices. Various public utility commissions throughout the United States regulate the rates (prices) of electrical utility companies and some telephone operating companies. This *rate regulation,* as it is usually called, has been aimed at preventing such industries from earning monopoly profits.

Regulation of Nonmonopolistic Industries

The prices charged by firms in many other industries that do not have steadily declining long-run average costs, such as financial services industries, have also been subjected to regulations. Every state in the United States, for instance, has a government agency devoted to regulating the prices that insurance companies charge.

More broadly, government regulations establish rules pertaining to production, product (or service) features, and entry and exit within a number of specific nonmonopolistic industries. The federal government is heavily involved, for instance, in regulating the securities, banking, transportation, and communications industries. The Securities and Exchange Commission regulates securities markets. The Federal Reserve, Office of the Comptroller of the Currency, and Federal Deposit Insurance Corporation regulate commercial banks. The Office of Thrift Supervision regulates savings banks, and the National Credit Union Administration supervises credit unions. The Federal Aviation Administration supervises the airline industry, and the Federal Motor Carrier Safety Administration regulates the trucking industry. The Federal Communications Commission has oversight powers relating to broadcasting and telephone and communications services.

Social Regulation

In contrast to economic regulation, which covers only particular industries, social regulation applies to all firms in the economy. In principle, the aim of social regulation is a better quality of life through improved products, a less polluted environment, and better working conditions. Since the 1970s, an increasing array of government resources has been directed toward regulating product safety, advertising, and environmental effects. Table 1 lists some major federal agencies involved in these broad regulatory activities.

The essential objectives of social regulation are to protect people from incompetent or unscrupulous producers. The *potential* benefits of more social regulations are many. For example, the water supply in some cities is known to be contaminated with cancer-causing chemicals, and air pollution contributes to many illnesses. Society would clearly benefit from cleaning up these pollutants. As we shall discuss, however, broad social regulations also entail costs that we all

TABLE 1 Federal Agencies Engaged in Social Regulation

Agency	Jurisdiction	Date Formed	Major Regulatory Functions
Federal Trade Commission (FTC)	Product markets	1914	Responsible for preventing businesses from engaging in misleading advertising, unfair trade practices, and monopolistic actions, as well as for protecting consumer rights.
Food and Drug Administration (FDA)	Food and pharmaceuticals	1938	Regulates the quality and safety of foods, health and medical products, pharmaceuticals, cosmetics, and animal feed.
Equal Employment Opportunity Commission (EEOC)	Labor markets	1964	Investigates complaints of discrimination based on race, religion, gender, or age in hiring, promotion, firing, wages, testing, and all other conditions of employment.
Environmental Protection Agency (EPA)	Environment	1970	Develops and enforces environmental standards for air, water, waste, and noise.
Occupational Safety and Health Administration (OSHA)	Health and safety	1970	Regulates workplace safety and health conditions.
Consumer Product Safety Commission (CPSC)	Consumer product safety	1972	Responsible for protecting consumers from products posing fire, electrical, chemical, or mechanical hazards or dangers to children.

pay, and not just as taxpayers who fund the regulatory activities of agencies such as those listed in Table 1.

3 REGULATING NATURAL MONOPOLIES

At one time, much government regulation of business aimed to solve the so-called monopoly problem. Of particular concern was implementing appropriate regulations for natural monopolies.

The Theory of Natural Monopoly Regulation

Recall that a natural monopoly arises whenever a single firm can produce all of an industry's output at a lower per-unit cost than other firms attempting to produce less than total industry output. In a natural monopoly, therefore, economies of large-scale production exist, leading to a single-firm industry.

The Unregulated Natural Monopoly

Like any other firm, an unregulated natural monopolist will produce to the point at which marginal revenue equals marginal cost. Panel (a) of Figure 2 depicts a situation in which a monopolist faces the market demand curve, D, and the marginal revenue curve, MR. The monopolist searches along the demand curve for the profit-maximizing price and quantity. The profit-maximizing quantity is at point A, at which the marginal revenue curve crosses the long-run marginal cost curve, LMC, and the unregulated monopolist maximizes profits by producing the quantity Q_m. Consumers are willing and able to pay the price P_m for this quantity at point F. This price is above marginal cost, so it leads to a socially inefficient allocation of resources by restricting production to a rate below that at which price equals marginal cost.

The Impracticality of Marginal Cost Pricing

What would happen if the government were to require the monopolist in Figure 2 to produce to the point at which price equals marginal cost, which is point B in panel (b)? Then it would produce a larger output rate, Q_1. Consumers, however, would pay only the price P_1 for this quantity, which would be less than the average cost of producing this output rate, AC_1. Consequently, requiring the monopolist to engage in marginal cost pricing would yield a loss for the firm equal to the shaded rectangular area in panel (b). The profit-maximizing monopolist would go out of business rather than face such regulation.

FIGURE 2 Profit Maximization and Regulation Through Marginal Cost Pricing

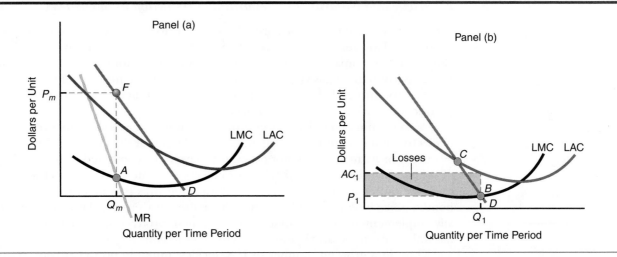

The profit-maximizing natural monopolist here would produce at the point in panel (a) where marginal costs equal marginal revenue—that is, at point A, which gives the quantity of production Q_m. The price charged would be P_m at point F, which is the price consumers would be willing to pay for the quantity produced. If a regulatory commission attempted to regulate natural monopolies so that price equaled long-run marginal cost, the commission would make the monopolist set production at the point where the marginal cost curve intersects the demand schedule. This is shown in panel (b). The quantity produced would be Q_1, and the price would be P_1. Average costs at Q_1 are equal to AC_1, however. Losses would ensue, equal to the shaded area. It would be self-defeating for a regulatory commission to force a natural monopolist to produce at an output rate at which MC = P without subsidizing some of its costs because losses would eventually drive the natural monopolist out of business.

Average Cost Pricing

Regulators cannot practically force a natural monopolist to engage in marginal cost pricing. Thus, regulation of natural monopolies has often taken the form of allowing the firm to set price at the point at which LAC intersects the demand curve. In panel (b) of Figure 2, this is point *C*. In this situation, the regulator forces the firm to engage in *average cost pricing*, with average cost including what the regulators deem a "fair" rate of return on investment. For instance, a regulator might impose **cost-of-service regulation**, which requires a natural monopoly to charge only prices that reflect the actual average cost of providing products to consumers. Alternatively, although in a similar vein, a regulator might use **rate-of-return regulation**, which allows firms to set prices that ensure a normal return on investment.

Natural Monopolies No More?

For years, the electricity, natural gas, and telecommunications industries have been subjected to regulations intended to induce firms in these industries to engage in average cost pricing. Traditionally, a feature common to all three industries has been that they utilize large networks of wires or pipelines to transmit their products to consumers. Federal, state, and local governments concluded that the average costs of providing electricity, natural gas, and telecommunications declined as the output rates of firms in these industries increased. Consequently, governments treated these industries as natural monopolies and established regulatory commissions to subject the industries to forms of cost-of-service and rate-of-return regulation.

Electricity and Natural Gas: Separating Production from Delivery

Today, 15 different companies provide electricity to homes, office buildings, and factories in Houston. Eight different firms compete to sell electricity in New York City, and six companies provide electricity in Philadelphia. Similarly, various producers of natural gas vie to market their product in a number of cities across the country. In nearly half of the U.S. states, there is active competition in the production of electricity and natural gas.

What circumstances led to this transformation? The answer is that regulators of electricity and natural gas companies figured out that the function of *producing* electricity or natural gas did not necessarily have to be combined with the *delivery* of the product. Until the mid-1980s, producers of natural gas and electricity had exclusive ownership of the pipeline and wire networks that provided energy for homes, office buildings, and factories. Since then, various regulators have gradually implemented policies that have separated production of electricity and natural gas from the distribution of these items to consumers.

Thus, in a growing number of U.S. locales, multiple producers now pay to use wire and pipeline networks to get their products to buyers. Economies of scale still exist in these distribution networks, and regulatory commissions impose cost-of-service or rate-of-return regulations on the network owners. Individual producers of electricity and natural gas openly compete, however, in the markets for the products that consumers actually utilize in their homes and businesses. The market clearing rates that consumers pay to consume electricity and natural gas reflect both the costs of producing these items and the transportation costs that producers pay to deliver them via regulated distribution networks.

Telecommunications Services Meet the Internet

As the production and sale of electricity and natural gas began to become more competitive undertakings, regulators started to apply the same principles to telecommunications services. In the 1980s, the Federal Communications Commission (FCC) required AT&T to open its existing phone networks to competing providers of long-distance phone services. Gradually, during the 1990s and early 2000s, federal, state, and local regulators applied the same principles to local telecommunications services. Today, many U.S. cities and towns are served by two or more competing producers of wired phone services.

At the same time, other forces reshaped the cost structure of the telecommunications industry. First, during the 1990s, significant technological advances drastically reduced the costs of providing wireless telecommunications. Most individuals and businesses regarded cellphone services as imperfect substitutes for wire-based telecommunications. Nevertheless, the growing use of cellphones slowed growth in the demand for services delivered over traditional wire networks.

Second, during the 2000s, internet phone service became more widely available. Most cable television companies that provide internet access now offer web-based telephone services as well. Many other companies also offer web phone services for purchase by anyone who already has access to the internet.

What lessons about cellular telecommunications have Irish regulators learned from the U.S. experience?

EXAMPLE 1

Time to Break Up the Irish Cellphone Duopoly?

Since the mid-1990s, two companies, Vodafone and mm02, have accounted for more than 95 percent of all sales of cellphone services in Ireland. Effectively, therefore, these two firms constitute a cellphone *duopoly*—the term economists use for a market with only two producers. The firms' ability to search for the profit-maximizing price enables them to receive 50 percent more revenues per customer than is received by firms in other nations with more competitive cellphone markets.

Ireland's telecommunications regulators recently decided to follow the U.S. example by proposing that Vodafone and mm02 open their exclusive cellular-service networks to competitors. Under the proposal, the Irish regulators would regulate the fees charged for use of these networks to ensure a "fair" rate of return to the owners of the two companies. Naturally, the two companies initially balked at giving up their duopoly arrangement. Nevertheless, it now appears likely that new entrants will eventually end the Irish cellphone duopoly.

For Critical Analysis

What key barrier to entry has enabled the Irish cellphone duopoly to survive for a decade?

Are Natural Monopolies Relics of the Past?

Clearly, the scope of the government's role as regulator of natural monopolies has decreased with the unraveling of conditions that previously created this market structure. In many U.S. electricity and natural gas markets, government agencies now apply traditional cost-of-service or rate-of-return regulations primarily to wire and pipeline owners. Otherwise, the government's main role in many regional markets is to serve as a "traffic cop," enforcing property rights and rules governing the regulated networks that serve competing electricity and natural gas producers.

In telecommunications, any natural monopoly rationale for a governmental regulator role is rapidly dissipating as more and more households and businesses substitute cellular and web-based phone services for wired phone services. Since 2000, consumers have stopped using 28 million land phone lines. At present, phone signals stop flowing on an additional 4 percent of existing lines each year. Telecommunications has become a technology-driven, competitive free-for-all. This industry is now far from a natural monopoly.

Just how much competition exists in the market for internet phone services?

EXAMPLE 2

Vying to Offer VOIP

The technical term for internet telephony is Voice Over Internet Protocol (VOIP), in which sounds are transformed into digital packets of information and transmitted across the internet much like e-mails. The digital information is then transformed back into sound when received by the recipient's web-connected phone service.

Initially, the main adopters of VOIP were businesses that chose to use it for internal phone communications while retaining traditional wired lines for external telecommunications services. Nevertheless, during the early 2000s, VOIP began to catch on for international calls, and today almost 25 percent of phone calls across national borders are completed using the internet. By the mid-2000s, technological improvements enabled cable and DSL providers of broadband internet service to roll out VOIP as an option for virtually all of their residential customers.

Today, all manner of companies have entered the market for VOIP services. Recently, America Online and eBay have joined the ranks of companies with names such as CallWave, Net2Phone, and VoiceGlo, which along with many other firms hope to profit from entering the VOIP market.

For Critical Analysis

Why is a single VOIP provider unlikely to emerge as a natural monopolist?

4   REGULATING NONMONOPOLISTIC INDUSTRIES

Traditionally, a fundamental purpose of governments has been to provide a coordinated system of safeguarding the interests of their citizens. Not surprisingly, protecting consumer interests is the main rationale offered for governmental regulatory functions.

Rationales for Consumer Protection in Nonmonopolistic Industries

The Latin phrase *caveat emptor,* or "let the buyer beware," was once the operative principle in most consumer dealings with businesses. The phrase embodies the idea that the buyer alone is ultimately responsible for assessing a producer and the quality of the items it sells before agreeing to purchase the firm's product. Today, various federal agencies require companies to meet specific minimal standards in their dealings with consumers. For instance, a few years ago, the U.S. Federal Trade Commission assessed monetary penalties on Toys "Я" Us and KB Toys because they failed to ship goods sold on their web sites in time for a pre-Christmas delivery. Such a government action would have been unheard of a few decades ago.

In some industries, federal agencies dictate the rules of the game for firms' interactions with consumers. The Federal Aviation Administration (FAA), for example, oversees virtually every aspect of the delivery of services by airline companies. The FAA regulates the process by which tickets for flights are sold and distributed, oversees all flight operations, and even establishes rules governing the procedures for returning luggage after flights are concluded.

Reasons for Government-Orchestrated Consumer Protection

Two rationales are commonly advanced for heavy government involvement in overseeing and supervising nonmonopolistic industries. One is the possibility of *market failures.* For example, the presence of negative externalities such as pollution may induce governments to regulate industries that create such externalities.

The second common rationale is *asymmetric information.* In the context of many producer-consumer interactions, this term refers to situations in which a producer has information about a product that the consumer lacks. For instance, administrators of your college or university may know that another school in your vicinity offers better-quality degree programs in certain fields. If so, it would not be in your college or university's interest to transmit this information to applicants who are interested in pursuing degrees in those fields.

For certain products, asymmetric information problems can pose special difficulties for consumers trying to assess product quality in advance of purchase. In unregulated financial markets, for example, individuals contemplating buying a company's stock, a municipality's bond, or a bank's certificate of deposit might struggle to assess the associated risks of financial loss. If the air transportation industry were unregulated, a person might have trouble determining if one airline's planes were considerably less safe than those of competing airlines. In an unregulated market for pharmaceuticals, parents might worry about whether one company's childhood-asthma medication could have more dangerous side effects than medications sold by other firms.

Asymmetric Information and Product Quality

In extreme cases, asymmetric information can create situations in which most of the available products are of low quality. A commonly cited example is the market for used automobiles. Current owners of cars that *appear* to be in good condition know the autos' service records. Some owners know that their cars have been well maintained and really do run great. Others, however, have not kept their autos in good repair and thus are aware that they will be susceptible to greater-than-normal mechanical or electrical problems.

Suppose that in your local used-car market, half of all used cars offered for sale are high-quality autos. The other half are low-quality cars, commonly called "lemons," that are likely to break down within a few months or perhaps even weeks. In addition, suppose that a consumer is willing to pay $20,000 for a particular car model if it is in excellent condition but is willing to pay only $10,000 if it is a lemon. Finally, suppose that people who own truly high-quality used cars are only willing to sell at a price of at least $20,000, but people who own lemons are willing to sell at any price at or above $10,000.

Because there is a 50–50 chance that a given car up for sale is of either quality, the average amount that a prospective buyer is willing to pay equals $(\frac{1}{2} \times \$20,000) + (\frac{1}{2} \times \$10,000) = \$15,000$. Owners of low-quality used cars are willing to sell them at this price, but owners of high-quality used cars are not. In this example, only lemons will be traded in the used-car market because most owners of cars in excellent condition will not sell their cars at a price that prospective buyers are willing to pay.

The Lemons Problem

Economists refer to the possibility that asymmetric information can lead to a general reduction in product quality in an industry as the **lemons problem**. This problem does not apply only to the used-car industry. In principle, any product with qualities that are difficult for consumers to fully assess is susceptible to the same problem. *Credence goods,* which are items such as pharmaceuticals, health care, and professional services, also may be particularly vulnerable to the lemons problem.

Market Solutions to the Lemons Problem

Firms offering truly high-quality products for sale can address the lemons problem in a variety of ways. They can offer product guarantees and warranties. In addition, to help consumers separate high-quality producers from incompetent or unscrupulous competitors, the high-quality producers may work together to establish industry standards.

In some cases, firms in an industry may even seek external product certification. They may, for example, solicit scientific reports supporting proposed industry standards and bearing witness that products of certain firms in the industry meet those standards. To legitimize a product-certification process, firms may hire outside companies or groups to issue such reports.

Implementing Consumer Protection Regulation

Governments offering asymmetric information and lemons problems as rationales for regulation presumably have concluded that private market solutions such as warranties, industry standards, and product certification are insufficient. To address asymmetric information problems, governments may offer legal remedies to consumers or enforce licensing requirements in an effort to provide minimum product standards. In some cases, governments go well beyond simple licensing requirements by establishing a regulatory apparatus for overseeing all aspects of an industry's operations.

Liability Laws and Government Licensing

Sometimes liability laws, which specify penalties for product failures, provide consumers with protections similar to guarantees and warranties. When the

Federal Trade Commission (FTC) charged Toys "Я" Us and KB Toys with failing to meet pre-Christmas delivery dates for internet toy orders, it operated under a mail-order statute Congress passed in the early 1970s. The mail-order law effectively made the toy companies' delivery guarantees legally enforceable. Although the FTC applied the law in this particular case, any consumer could have filed suit for damages under the terms of the statute.

Federal and state governments also get involved in consumer protection by issuing licenses granting only qualifying firms the legal right to produce and sell certain products. For instance, in an effort to ensure that bodies of deceased individuals are handled with care and dignity, governments of nearly half of the states give the right to sell caskets only to people who have a mortuary or funeral director's license.

Although government licensing may successfully limit the sale of low-quality goods, licensing requirements also often limit the number of providers. This can ease efforts by established firms to search for the profit-maximizing price, thereby enabling them to act as monopolists. In addition, if governments rely on the expertise of established firms for assistance in drafting licensing requirements, these firms may have strong incentives to recommend low standards for themselves but high standards for prospective entrants.

Direct Economic and Social Regulation

In some instances, governments determine that liability laws and licensing requirements are insufficient to protect the interests of consumers. A government may decide that lemons problems in banking are so severe that without an extensive banking regulatory apparatus, consumers will lose confidence in banks, and bank runs may ensue. It may rely on similar rationales to establish economic regulation of other financial services industries. Eventually, it may apply consumer protection rationales to justify the economic regulation of other industries such as trucking or air transportation.

The government may establish an oversight authority to make certain that consumers are protected from incompetent producers of foods and pharmaceuticals. Eventually, the government may determine that a host of other products should meet government consumer protection standards. It may also decide that the people who produce the products also require government agencies to ensure workplace safety. In this way, social regulation emerges, as it has in the United States and most other developed nations.

INCENTIVES AND COSTS OF REGULATION   5

Abiding by government regulations is a costly undertaking for firms. Consequently, businesses engage in a number of activities intended to avoid the true intent of regulations or to bring about changes in the regulations that government agencies establish.

Creative Response and Feedback Effects: Results of Regulation

Sometimes firms respond to a regulation in a way that conforms to the letter of the law but undermines its spirit. When they do so, they engage in **creative response** to regulations.

Consider state laws requiring male-female pay equity: The wages of women must be on a par with those paid to males who are performing the same tasks. Employers that pay the same wages to both males and females are clearly not in violation of the law. Yet wages are only one component of total employee compensation. Another component is fringe benefits, such as on-the-job training. Because on-the-job training is difficult to observe from outside the firm, employers could offer less on-the-job training to women and still not be in technical violation of pay-equity laws. This unobservable difference would mean that males were able to acquire skills that could raise their future income even though males and females were receiving the same current wages, in compliance with the law.

One type of creative response has been labeled a *feedback effect*. Individuals' behaviors may change after a regulation has been put into effect. If regulation requires fluoridated water, then parents know that their children's teeth have significant protection against tooth decay. Consequently, the feedback effect is that parents become less concerned about how many sweets their children eat.

How has a government regulation intended to reduce automobiles' contributions to urban air pollution generated a socially costly feedback effect?

EXAMPLE 3

How Dare You Get Ahead of Me in That HOV Lane!

To give people an incentive to carpool and thereby release less auto exhaust into the air, the federal government uses regulatory inducements and rules to encourage construction of high-occupancy-vehicle (HOV) lanes along highways in major cities. Typically, vehicles containing at least two or more passengers can use HOV lanes, and under normal conditions, they can travel faster than vehicles in non-HOV lanes. Since 1990, total stretches of HOV lanes nationwide have increased from about 600 miles to more than 2,500 miles.

There is growing evidence, however, that adding more HOV lanes to combat air pollution has had an unintended—and sometimes deadly—feedback effect. HOV lanes often run directly alongside other highway traffic so that drivers of vehicles in HOV lanes can merge into the regular highway to exit the highway. To merge safely from an HOV lane into a non-HOV lane, the driver of the merging vehicle often must slow down, while drivers of vehicles in the non-HOV lane yield to the merging vehicle. All too often, drivers of vehicles merging from an HOV lane drive faster than traffic conditions warrant. Furthermore, postaccident interviews indicate that drivers in non-HOV lanes often resent the fact that vehicles using HOV lanes can move at a faster pace. Acting on this resentment, they stubbornly refuse to yield to traffic merging from HOV lanes. The result is a regulatory feedback effect: higher accident rates along highways with HOV lanes. In many cities, accident rates along roadways with HOV lanes are more than two times higher than accident rates on comparable stretches without HOV lanes.

For Critical Analysis

Why do you suppose that the federal government is now contemplating new regulations requiring long stretches of concrete buffers to separate HOV lanes from regular highway traffic?

Explaining Regulators' Behavior

Those charged with enforcing government regulations operate outside the market, so their decisions are determined by nonmarket processes. A number of theories have emerged to describe the behavior of regulators. These theories explain how regulation can harm consumers by generating higher prices and fewer product choices while benefiting producers by reducing competitive forces and allowing higher profits. Two of the best-known theories of regulatory behavior are the *capture hypothesis* and the *share-the-gains, share-the-pains theory.*

The Capture Hypothesis

Regulators often end up becoming champions of the firms they are charged with regulating. According to the **capture hypothesis**, regardless of why a regulatory agency was originally established, eventually special interests of the industry it regulates will capture it. After all, the people who know the most about a regulated industry are the people already in the industry. Thus, people who have been in the industry and have allegiances and friendships with others in the industry will most likely be asked to regulate the industry.

According to the capture hypothesis, individual consumers of a regulated industry's products and individual taxpayers who finance a regulatory agency have interests too diverse to be greatly concerned with the industry's actions. In contrast, special interests of the industry are well organized and well defined. These interests also have more to offer political entrepreneurs within a regulatory agency, such as future employment with one of the regulated firms. Therefore, regulators have a strong incentive to support the position of a well-organized special-interest group within the regulated industry.

"Share the Gains, Share the Pains"

The **share-the-gains, share-the-pains theory** offers a somewhat different view of regulators' behavior. This theory focuses on the specific aims of regulators. It proposes that a regulator's main objective is simply to keep his or her job as a regulator. To do so, the regulator must obtain the approval of both the legislators who originally established and continue to oversee the regulatory agency and the regulated industry. The regulator must also take into account the views of the industry's customers.

In contrast to the capture hypothesis, which holds that regulators must take into account only industry special interests, the share-the-gains, share-the-pains theory contends that regulators must worry about legislators and consumers as well. After all, if industry customers who are hurt by improper regulation complain to legislators, the regulators might lose their jobs. Whereas the capture theory predicts that regulators will quickly allow electric utilities to raise their rates in the face of higher fuel costs, the share-the-gains, share-the-pains theory predicts a slower, more measured regulatory response. Ultimately, regulators will permit an increase in utility rates, but the allowed adjustment will not be as speedy or complete as predicted by the capture hypothesis. The regulatory agency is not completely captured by the industry; it also has to consider the views of consumers and legislators.

The Benefits and Costs of Regulation

As noted earlier, regulation offers many *potential* benefits. *Actual* benefits, however, are difficult to measure. Putting a dollar value on safer products, a cleaner environment, and better working conditions is a difficult proposition. Furthermore, the benefits of most regulations accrue to society over a long time.

The Direct Costs of Regulation to Taxpayers

Measuring the costs of regulation is also a challenging undertaking. After all, about 4,500 new federal regulations are issued each year. One cost, though, is certain: U.S. taxpayers pay more than $40 billion per year to staff regulatory agencies with more than 190,000 employees and to fund their various activities. Figure 3 displays the distribution of total federal government outlays for economic and social regulation of various areas of the economy.

The *total* cost of regulation is much higher than just the explicit government outlays to fund the administration of various regulations, however. After all, businesses must expend resources complying with regulations, developing creative responses to regulations, and funding special-interest lobbying efforts directed at legislators and regulatory officials. Sometimes companies find that it is impossible to comply with one regulation without violating another, and determining how to avoid the resulting legal entanglements can entail significant expenditures.

The Total Social Cost of Regulation

According to the Office of Management and Budget, annual expenditures that U.S. businesses must make solely to comply with regulations issued by various federal agencies amount to between $500 billion and $600 billion per year. Nevertheless, this estimate encompasses only explicit costs of satisfying regulatory demands placed on businesses. It ignores relevant opportunity costs. After all, owners, managers, and employees of companies could be doing other things with their time and resources than complying with regulations. Economists estimate that the opportunity costs of complying with federal regulations may be as high as $270 billion per year.

FIGURE 3   The Distribution of Federal Regulatory Spending

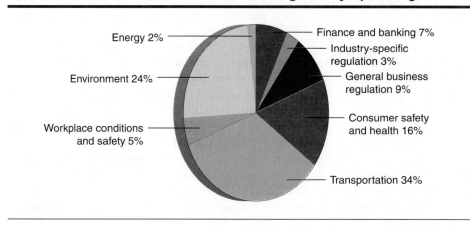

This figure shows the areas of the economy to which more than $40 billion of taxpayer-provided funds are distributed to finance economic and social regulation.

Source: Office of Management and Budget.

All told, therefore, the total social cost associated with satisfying federal regulations in the United States is probably between $800 billion and $900 billion per year. This figure, of course, applies only to federal regulations. It does not include the explicit and implicit opportunity costs associated with regulations issued by 50 different state governments and thousands of municipalities. Undoubtedly, the annual cost of regulation throughout the United States exceeds $1 trillion per year.

ANTITRUST POLICY   **6**

An expressed aim of the U.S. government is to foster competition. To this end, Congress has made numerous attempts to legislate against business practices it has perceived to be anticompetitive. This is the general idea behind antitrust legislation. If the courts can prevent collusion among sellers of a product, there will be no restriction of output, and monopoly prices will not result. Instead, the perfectly competitive solution to the price-quantity problem will emerge: The competitive output will prevail in each industry, producers will earn zero economic profits in the long run, and the price of each item will equal its marginal social opportunity cost.

Antitrust Policy in the United States

Congress has enacted four key antitrust laws, which Table 2 summarizes. The most important of these is the original U.S. antitrust law, called the Sherman Act.

The Sherman Antitrust Act of 1890

The Sherman Antitrust Act, which was passed in 1890, was the first attempt by the federal government to control the growth of monopoly in the United States. The most important provisions of that act are as follows:

> *Section 1:* Every contract, combination in the form of a trust or otherwise, or conspiracy, in restraint of trade or commerce among the several states, or with foreign nations, is hereby declared to be illegal.

> *Section 2:* Every person who shall monopolize, or attempt to monopolize, or combine or conspire with any other person or persons to monopolize any part of the trade or commerce . . . shall be guilty of a misdemeanor [now a felony].

Notice how vague this act really is. No definition is given for the terms *restraint of trade* or *monopolize*. Despite this vagueness, however, the act was used to prosecute the infamous Standard Oil Trust of New Jersey. This company was charged with and convicted of violations of Sections 1 and 2 of the Sherman Antitrust Act in 1906. At the time it controlled more than 80 percent of the nation's oil-refining capacity. In addressing the company's legal appeal, the U.S. Supreme Court ruled that Standard Oil's predominance in the oil market created "a *prima facie* presumption of intent and purpose to control and maintain dominancy . . . not as a result from normal methods of industrial development, but by means of combinations." Here the word *combination* meant entering into associations and preferential arrangements with the intent of restraining

TABLE 2 Key U.S. Antitrust Laws	
Sherman Antitrust Act of 1890	Forbids any contract, combination, or conspiracy to restrain trade or commerce within the United States or across U.S. borders. Holds any person who attempts to monopolize trade or commerce criminally liable.
Clayton Act of 1914	Prohibits specific business practices deemed to restrain trade or commerce. Bans discrimination in prices charged to various purchasers when price differences are not due to actual differences in selling or transportation costs. Also forbids a company from selling goods on the condition that the purchaser must deal exclusively with that company. In addition, prevents corporations from holding stock in other companies when this may lessen competition.
Federal Trade Commission Act of 1914 (and 1938 Amendment)	Outlaws business practices that reduce the extent of competition, such as alleged cutthroat pricing intended to drive rivals from the marketplace. Also established the Federal Trade Commission and empowered it to issue cease and desist orders in situations where it determines "unfair methods of competition in commerce" exist. The 1938 amendment added deceptive business practices to the list of illegal acts.
Robinson-Patman Act of 1936	Bans selected discriminatory price cuts by chain stores that allegedly drive smaller competitors from the marketplace. In addition, forbids price discrimination through special concessions in the form of price or quantity discounts, free advertising, or promotional allowances granted to one buyer but not to others, if these actions substantially reduce competition.

competition. The Supreme Court forced Standard Oil of New Jersey to break up into many smaller companies that would have no choice but to compete.

The Sherman Act applies today just as it did more than a century ago. In June 2001, the federal Court of Appeals for the District of Columbia determined that Microsoft Corporation had violated the Sherman Act. The court ruled that Microsoft had engaged in anticompetitive conduct in an effort to monopolize the market for operating systems for personal computers. Initially, the U.S. Justice Department proposed a Standard Oil–style remedy: splitting Microsoft into several companies. Ultimately, however, Microsoft reached a settlement that kept the company intact but required it to alter many of its business practices.

Other Important Antitrust Legislation

Table 2 lists three other important antitrust laws. In 1914, Congress passed the Clayton Act to clarify some of the vague provisions of the Sherman Act by identifying specific business practices that were to be legally prohibited.

Congress also passed the Federal Trade Commission Act in 1914. In addition to establishing the Federal Trade Commission to investigate unfair trade practices, this law enumerated certain business practices that, according to Congress, involved overly aggressive competition. A 1938 amendment to this law expressly prohibited "unfair or deceptive acts or practices in commerce" and empowered the FTC to regulate advertising and marketing practices by U.S. firms.

The Robinson-Patman Act of 1936 amended the Clayton Act by singling out specific business practices, such as selected price cuts, aimed at driving smaller competitors out of business. The act is often referred to as the "Chain Store Act" because it was intended to protect *independent* retailers and wholesalers from "unfair competition" by chain stores.

Exemptions from Antitrust Laws

Numerous laws exempt the following industries and business practices from antitrust legislation:

▶ Labor unions

▶ Public utilities—electric, gas, and telephone companies

▶ Professional baseball

▶ Cooperative activities among U.S. exporters

▶ Hospitals

▶ Public transit and water systems

▶ Suppliers of military equipment

▶ Joint publishing arrangements in a single city by two or more newspapers

Thus, not all U.S. businesses are subject to antitrust laws.

International Discord in Antitrust Policy

What, if anything, should U.S. antitrust authorities do if AT&T decides that it wishes to merge with British Telecommunications or if Germany's Deutsche Telecom wants to acquire Sprint Nextel? What, if anything, should they do if Time Warner, the largest U.S. entertainment company, attempts to merge with London-based EMI, one of the world's largest recorded-music companies? These are not just rhetorical questions, as U.S. and European antitrust authorities learned in the early 2000s when these issues actually surfaced. Growing international linkages among markets for many goods and services have increasingly made antitrust policy a global undertaking.

The international dimensions of antitrust pose a problem for U.S. antitrust authorities in the Department of Justice and the Federal Trade Commission. In the United States, the overriding goal of antitrust policies has traditionally been protecting the interests of consumers. This is also a formal objective of antitrust efforts of European Union (EU) antitrust authorities. In the EU, however, policymakers are also required to reject any business combination that "creates or strengthens a dominant position as a result of which effective competition would be significantly impeded."

This additional clause is creating tension between U.S. and EU policymaking. In the United States, increasing dominance of a market by a single firm arouses the concern of antitrust authorities. Nevertheless, U.S. authorities typically will remain passive if they determine that the larger market dominance arises from factors such as exceptional management and greater cost efficiencies that ultimately benefit consumers by reducing prices. In contrast, under EU rules antitrust authorities are obliged to block *any* business combination that increases the dominance of any producer. They must do so irrespective of what factors might have caused the business's preeminence in the marketplace.

7 | ANTITRUST ENFORCEMENT

How are antitrust laws enforced? In the United States, most enforcement continues to be based on the Sherman Act. The Supreme Court has defined the offense of **monopolization** as involving the following elements: "1) the possession of monopoly power in the relevant market and 2) the willful acquisition or maintenance of that power, as distinguished from growth or development as a consequence of a superior product, business acumen, or historical accident."

Monopoly Power and the Relevant Market

The Sherman Act does not define monopoly. Monopoly need not be a single entity. Also, monopoly is not a function of size alone. For example a "mom and pop" grocery store located in an isolated town can function as a monopolist.

It is difficult to define and measure market power precisely. As a workable proxy, courts often look to the firm's percentage share of the "relevant market." This is the so-called **market share test**. A firm is generally considered to have monopoly power if its share of the relevant market is 70 percent or more. This is only a rule of thumb, however, not an absolute dictum. In some cases, a smaller share may be held to constitute monopoly power.

What well-known U.S. firm captures more than 70 percent of total revenues in several different markets?

EXAMPLE 4

Microsoft's Market Shares

In the market for personal computer (PC) software, one company stands almost alone. Microsoft Corporation's market share in the market for operating software for PCs exceeds 95 percent. Microsoft's market share in the office-productivity software market stands at about 94 percent, and its market share in the web-browsing software market is just over 95 percent. In the market for operating software for computer servers, Microsoft faces increasingly tough competition from Linux. As a result, Microsoft's share of revenues in this market is "only" 85 percent. Thus, by the standard rule of thumb for gauging monopoly power, Microsoft possesses this power in four different software markets.

For Critical Analysis

Why might it be argued that Microsoft is not necessarily a computer software monopoly under the Sherman Act? (Hint: Recall the second of the two criteria that the U.S. Supreme Court has specified in defining the offense of monopolization.)

The relevant market consists of two elements: a relevant *product* market and a relevant *geographic* market. What should the relevant product market include? It must include all items produced by different firms that have identical attributes, such as sugar. Yet products that are not identical may sometimes be substituted for one another. Coffee may be substituted for tea, for example. In defining the relevant product market, the key issue is the degree to which products are interchangeable. If one product is sufficiently substitutable for another, then the two products are considered to be part of the same product market.

The second component of the relevant market is the geographic boundaries of the market. For items that are sold nationwide, the geographic boundaries of the market encompass the entire United States. If a producer and its competitors sell in only a limited area (one in which customers have no access to other sources of the product), the geographic market is limited to that area. A national firm may thus compete in several distinct areas and have monopoly power in one area but not in another.

Product Packaging and Antitrust Enforcement

A particular problem in U.S. antitrust enforcement is determining whether a firm has engaged in "willful acquisition or maintenance" of market power. Unfortunately, actions that appear to some observers to be good business look like antitrust violations to others. To illustrate why quandaries can arise in antitrust enforcement, let's consider two examples: *versioning* and *bundling*.

Product Versioning

A firm engages in product **versioning** when it sells an item in slightly altered forms to different groups of consumers. A typical method of versioning is to remove certain features from an item and offer what remains as a somewhat stripped-down version of the product at a different price.

Consider an office-productivity software program, such as Adobe Acrobat or Microsoft Word. Firms selling such programs typically offer both a "professional" version containing a full range of features and a "standard" version providing only basic functions. One perspective on this practice regards it as a form of price discrimination, or selling essentially the same product at different prices to different consumers. People who desire to use the full range of features in Adobe Acrobat or Microsoft Word are likely to be computing professionals. Compared to most other consumers, their demand for the full-featured version of an office-productivity software program is likely to be less elastic. In principle, therefore, Adobe and Microsoft can earn higher profits by offering "professional" versions at higher prices and selling a "standard" version at a lower price.

Price discrimination—charging varying prices to different consumers when the price differences are not a result of different production or transportation costs—is illegal under the Clayton Act of 1914. Are Adobe, Microsoft, and other companies engaging in illegal price discrimination? Another perspective on versioning indicates that they are not. According to this point of view, consumers regard "professional" and "standard" versions of software packages as imperfect substitutes. Consequently, each version is a distinctive product sold in a unique market. If so, versioning increases overall consumer satisfaction because consumers who are not computing professionals are able to utilize certain features of software products at a lower price. So far, antitrust authorities in the United States and elsewhere have been inclined toward this view of the economic effects of versioning, rather than perceiving it as a form of price discrimination.

Product Bundling

Antitrust authorities have been less tolerant of another form of product packaging, known as **bundling**, which involves the joint sale of two or more products as a set. Antitrust authorities usually are not concerned if a firm allows consumers to purchase the products either individually or as a set. They are more likely to investigate a firm's business practices, however, when it allows consumers to purchase one product only when it is bundled with another. Antitrust officials often view this form of bundling as a method of price discrimination known as **tie-in sales**, in which a firm requires consumers who wish to buy one of its products to purchase another item the firm sells as well.

To understand their reasoning, consider a situation in which one group of consumers is willing to pay $500 for a computer operating system but only $100 for an internet-browsing program. A second group of consumers is willing to pay only $250 for the same computer operating system but is willing to pay $350 for the same internet-browsing program. If the same company that sells both types of software offers the operating system at a price above $250, then only consumers in the first group will buy this software. Likewise, if it sells the internet-browsing program at a price above $100, then only the second group of consumers will purchase that program.

But if the firm sells both products as a bundled set, it can charge $600 and generate sales of both software products to both groups. One interpretation is that the first group pays $500 for the operating system, but for the second group, the operating system's price is $250. At the same time, the first group has paid $100 for the internet-browsing program, while the second group perceives the price of the program to be $350. Effectively, bundling enables the software company to engage in price discrimination by charging different prices to different groups.

Antitrust enforcers in the Justice Department applied this interpretation in their prosecution of Microsoft, which for years had bundled its internet-browsing program, Internet Explorer, together with its Windows operating system. Enforcement officials added another twist by contending that Microsoft also had monopoly power in the market for computer operating systems. By bundling the two products, they argued, Microsoft had sought both to price-discriminate and to extend its monopoly power to the market for internet-browsing software. The remedy that the courts imposed was for Microsoft to alter some of its business practices. As part of this legal remedy, Microsoft was required to unbundle its Windows and Internet Explorer products.

ISSUES AND APPLICATIONS

Identifying the Relevant Telecommunications Market

In 1997, two telecommunications companies, AT&T and SBC, the "Southwestern Bell" phone company that had separated from AT&T 13 years earlier, held preliminary talks about merging their companies again. The head of the Federal Communications Commission (FCC), the U.S. regulator charged with regulating U.S. telecommunications industries, quickly scotched the initiative. Before a Washington luncheon crowd of 100 people, including several representatives of the financial media, the FCC chief described the idea as "unthinkable." Such a merger, he suggested, would squelch the competition that breaking off SBC and other regional companies from AT&T had been intended to foster. Antitrust authorities at the U.S. Justice Department and the Federal Trade Commission also quietly raised concerns about the proposed combination.

Nevertheless, eight years later the two companies merged after all, and neither the FCC nor the U.S. antitrust authorities raised objections to the combination. Furthermore, the combined company, which kept the name AT&T, followed up by proposing a merger with BellSouth, another company that had separated from the old AT&T years before. What had happened? The answer is that the relevant market for SBC, AT&T, and other telecommunications companies had expanded considerably during those eight years.

Concepts Applied

▶ Antitrust Policy
▶ Relevant Market
▶ Market Share Test

Telephony, Television, Internet—All One Telecommunications Market?

A lot happened in the telecommunications industry between 1997 and 2005. Even as companies such as SBC and BellSouth began to branch out and compete with the initial providers of cellular phone services, they began to face competition in traditional phone services. Cable television companies, such as Comcast and Time Warner, discovered low-cost methods of providing regular phone services, which they could transmit through cables alongside television programming signals.

Furthermore, cable providers also began offering broadband internet access services. These cable services also competed directly with dial-up and digital-subscriber-line (DSL) services offered by telephone companies.

Hence, by the mid-2000s, AT&T, SBC, and BellSouth were not just competing with each other in the market for telephone services. They were also in direct competition with cable companies that provided these and other telecommunications services, including broadband internet access. Along all three dimensions—telephone services, television service, and internet access services—telephone and cable companies were trying to sell their products to the same sets of customers.

An Example: The Market for Broadband Access Services

To see how widened competition across telecommunications affected regulators' view of the relevant market for antitrust policy, let's focus exclusively on the broadband internet access services that telephone and cable companies provide. Take a look at Table 3. The left-hand column lists shares of total revenues from broadband access services provided via DSL by phone companies. The implied four-firm concentration ratio if these telephone companies were regarded as a single "DSL-access industry" would be 85.5 percent. The middle column lists market shares for cable companies that provide broadband internet access. If these companies were treated as a single "cable-access industry," the four-firm concentration ratio for this industry would be 76.2 percent.

Realistically, DSL and cable broadband internet access services are very close substitutes—so close that DSL and cable providers compete directly for the same customers. The right-hand column provides market shares if both types of providers are considered part of the same industry. The four-firm concentration ratio under this widened perspective of the relevant market for broadband internet access services drops to 61.9 percent.

TABLE 3 Shares of Industry Sales in Alternative Markets for Broadband Internet Access

This table provides the most recent market share figures available for DSL and cable providers of broadband internet access. These figures imply that if DSL access and cable access are viewed as different services, the four-firm concentration ratios for separate broadband DSL and broadband cable "industries" are 85.5 percent and 76.2 percent, respectively.

Broadband DSL	Market Share	Broadband Cable	Market Share	Total Broadband	Market Share
AT&T	37.2%	Comcast	34.6%	Comcast	21.5%
Verizon	26.3	Time Warner	19.3	AT&T	18.1
BellSouth	14.7	Cox	12.9	Time Warner	13.0
Qwest	7.3	Charter	9.4	Verizon	9.3
Sprint Nextel	3.6	Cablevision	6.9	Cox	8.1
Covad	3.6	Adelphia	6.4	Charter	6.6
Others	7.3	Others	10.5	Others	23.4
DSL Four-Firm Concentration Ratio	85.5%	Cable Four-Firm Concentration Ratio	76.2%	Combined Four-Firm Concentration Ratio	61.9%

Source: Federal Communications Commission.

In 1997, the FCC and antitrust regulators perceived that telephone companies and cable companies competed in separate markets. By 2005, these regulators recognized that the environment had changed. Telephone and cable companies all competed with one another in a variety of markets, including a single market for broadband internet access services. Consequently, in 2005 regulators raised no objections to a re-merger between SBC and AT&T.

OPTIONAL SEGMENT
ENDS

TRADING WITH THE WORLD
by Michael Parkin

LEARNING OUTCOMES

The candidate should be able to:	Mastery
a. explain comparative advantage and how countries can gain from international trade;	☐
b. compare and contrast tariffs, nontariff barriers, quotas, and voluntary export restraints;	☐
c. critique the arguments for trade restrictions.	☐

SILK ROUTES AND SUCKING SOUNDS

1

Since ancient times, people have expanded their trading as far as technology allowed. Marco Polo opened up the silk route between Europe and China in the thirteenth century. Today, container ships laden with cars and electronics and Boeing 747s stuffed with farm-fresh foods ply sea and air routes, carrying billions of dollars worth of goods. Why do people go to such great lengths to trade with those in other nations?

In 1994, the United States entered into a free trade agreement with Canada and Mexico—the North American Free Trade Agreement, or NAFTA. Some people predicted a "giant sucking sound" as jobs were transferred from high-wage Michigan to low-wage Mexico. Can we compete with a country that pays its workers a fraction of U.S. wages?

Workers in China earn even less than those in Mexico, and today, just about every manufactured object that we buy seems to be made in China. How can we compete with low-wage China and the other low-wage Asian nations? Are there any industries, besides perhaps making Hollywood movies and building large passenger jets, in which we have an advantage?

Would it be a good idea to limit imports from China and other countries by putting a tariff or a quota on those imports?

In this reading, we're going to learn about international trade and discover how all nations can gain from trading with other nations. You will discover that all nations can compete, no matter how high their wages. But you will also learn why, despite the fact that international trade brings benefits to all, governments restrict trade. In *Reading Between the Lines* at the end of the reading, we'll look at the growing trade with China and see why we all benefit from it.

2   PATTERNS AND TRENDS IN INTERNATIONAL TRADE

The goods and services that we buy from people in other countries are called **imports**. The goods and services that we sell to people in other countries are called **exports**. What are the most important things that we import and export? Most people would probably guess that a rich nation such as the United States imports raw materials and exports manufactured goods. Although that is one feature of U.S. international trade, it is not its most important feature. The bulk of our exports *and* imports is manufactured goods. We sell foreigners earth-moving equipment, airplanes, supercomputers, and scientific equipment, and we buy televisions, DVD players, blue jeans, and T-shirts from them. Also, we are a major exporter of agricultural products and raw materials. And we import and export a huge volume of services.

Trade in Goods

Manufactured goods account for 55 percent of our exports and 68 percent of our imports. Industrial materials (raw materials and semimanufactured items) account for 14 percent of our exports and 15 percent of our imports, and agricultural products account for only 8 percent of our exports and 4 percent of our imports. Our largest individual export and import items are capital goods and automobiles. But goods account for only 70 percent of our exports and 84 percent of our imports. The rest of our international trade is in services.

Trade in Services

You may be wondering how a country can "export" and "import" services. Here are some examples.

If you take a vacation in France and travel there on an Air France flight from New York, you import transportation services from France. The money you spend in France on hotel bills and restaurant meals is also classified as the import of services. Similarly, the money spent by a French student on vacation in the United States is a U.S. export of services to France.

When we import TV sets from South Korea, the owner of the ship that transports them might be Greek and the company that insures them might be British. The payments that we make for transportation and insurance are imports of services. Similarly, when an American shipping company transports California wine to Tokyo, the transportation cost is a U.S. export of a service to Japan. Our international trade in these types of services is large and growing.

Geographical Patterns of International Trade

The United States has trading links with every part of the world, but Canada is our biggest trading partner. In 2006, 20 percent of our exports went to Canada and 17 percent of our imports came from Canada. Japan is our second biggest trading partner, accounting for 8 percent of exports and 9 percent of imports in 2006. The regions in which our trade is largest are the European Union—with 24 percent of our exports and 23 percent of our imports in 2006—and Latin America—with 20 percent of our exports and 18 percent of our imports in 2006.

Trends in the Volume of Trade

In 1960, we exported 3.5 percent of total output and imported 4 percent of the goods and services that we bought. In 2006, we exported 10 percent of total output and imported 15 percent of the goods and services that we bought.

On the export side, capital goods, automobiles, food, and raw materials have remained large items and held a roughly constant share of total exports. But the composition of imports has changed. Food and raw material imports have fallen steadily. Imports of fuel increased dramatically during the 1970s but fell during the 1980s. Imports of machinery have grown and today approach 50 percent of total imports.

Net Exports and International Borrowing

The value of exports minus the value of imports is called **net exports**. In 2006, U.S. net exports were a negative $780 billion. Our imports were $780 billion more than our exports. When we import more than we export, as we did in 2006, we borrow from foreigners or sell some of our assets to them. When we export more than we import, we make loans to foreigners or buy some of their assets.

THE GAINS FROM INTERNATIONAL TRADE   3

The fundamental force that generates international trade is *comparative advantage*. And the basis of comparative advantage is divergent *opportunity costs*.

Most nations do not go to the extreme of specializing in a single good and importing everything else. But nations can increase the consumption of all goods if they redirect their scarce resources toward the production of those goods and services in which they have a comparative advantage.

To see how this outcome occurs, we'll begin by recalling how we can use the production possibilities frontier to measure opportunity cost. Then we'll see how divergent opportunity costs bring comparative advantage and gains from trade for countries as well as for individuals even though no country completely specializes in the production of just one good.

Opportunity Cost in Farmland

Farmland (a fictitious country) can produce grain and cars at any point inside or along its production possibilities frontier, *PPF*, shown in Fig. 1. (We're holding constant the output of all the other goods that Farmland produces.) The Farmers (the people of Farmland) are consuming all the grain and cars that they produce, and they are operating at point *A* in the figure. That is, Farmland is producing and consuming 15 billion bushels of grain and 8 million cars each year. What is the opportunity cost of a car in Farmland?

FIGURE 1   Opportunity Cost in Farmland

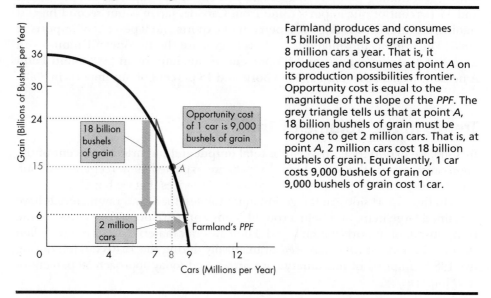

Farmland produces and consumes 15 billion bushels of grain and 8 million cars a year. That is, it produces and consumes at point *A* on its production possibilities frontier. Opportunity cost is equal to the magnitude of the slope of the *PPF*. The grey triangle tells us that at point *A*, 18 billion bushels of grain must be forgone to get 2 million cars. That is, at point *A*, 2 million cars cost 18 billion bushels of grain. Equivalently, 1 car costs 9,000 bushels of grain or 9,000 bushels of grain cost 1 car.

We can answer that question by calculating the slope of the production possibilities frontier at point *A*. The magnitude of the slope of the frontier measures the opportunity cost of one good in terms of the other. To measure the slope of the frontier at point *A*, place a straight line tangential to the frontier at point *A* and calculate the slope of that straight line. Recall that the formula for the slope of a line is the change in the value of the variable measured on the *y*-axis divided by the change in the value of the variable measured on the *x*-axis as we move along the line. Here, the variable measured on the *y*-axis is billions of bushels of grain, and the variable measured on the *x*-axis is millions of cars. So the slope is the change in the number of bushels of grain divided by the change in the number of cars.

As you can see from the grey triangle at point *A* in Fig. 1, if the number of cars produced increases by 2 million, grain production decreases by 18 billion bushels. Therefore the magnitude of the slope is 18 billion divided by 2 million, which equals 9,000. To get one more car, the people of Farmland must give up 9,000 bushels of grain. So the opportunity cost of 1 car is 9,000 bushels of grain. Equivalently, 9,000 bushels of grain cost 1 car. For the people of Farmland, these opportunity costs are the prices they face. The price of a car is 9,000 bushels of grain, and the price of 9,000 bushels of grain is 1 car.

Opportunity Cost in Mobilia

Figure 2 shows the production possibilities frontier of Mobilia (another fictitious country). Like the Farmers, the Mobilians consume all the grain and cars that they produce. Mobilia consumes 18 billion bushels of grain a year and 4 million cars, at point A'.

Let's calculate the opportunity costs in Mobilia. At point A', the opportunity cost of a car is equal to the magnitude of the slope of the grey line tangential to Mobilia's *PPF*. You can see from the grey triangle that the magnitude of the slope of Mobilia's *PPF* is 6 billion bushels of grain divided by 6 million cars, which equals 1,000 bushels of grain per car. To get one more car, the Mobilians must give up 1,000 bushels of grain. So the opportunity cost of 1 car is 1,000 bushels of grain, or equivalently, the opportunity cost of 1,000 bushels of grain is 1 car. These are the prices faced in Mobilia.

FIGURE 2   Opportunity Cost in Mobilia

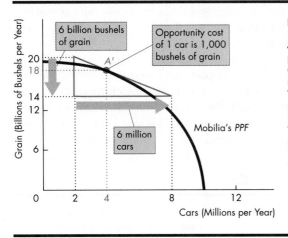

Mobilia produces and consumes 18 billion bushels of grain and 4 million cars a year at point A' on its production possibilities frontier. Opportunity cost is equal to the magnitude of the slope of the *PPF*. The grey triangle tells us that at point A', 6 billion bushels of grain must be forgone to get 6 million cars. That is, at point A', 6 million cars cost 6 billion bushels of grain. Equivalently, 1 car costs 1,000 bushels of grain or 1,000 bushels of grain cost 1 car.

Comparative Advantage

Cars are cheaper in Mobilia than in Farmland. One car costs 9,000 bushels of grain in Farmland but only 1,000 bushels of grain in Mobilia. But grain is cheaper in Farmland than in Mobilia—9,000 bushels of grain cost only 1 car in Farmland, while that same amount of grain costs 9 cars in Mobilia.

Mobilia has a comparative advantage in car production. Farmland has a comparative advantage in grain production. A country has a **comparative advantage** in producing a good if it can produce that good at a lower opportunity cost than any other country. Let's see how opportunity cost differences and comparative advantage generate gains from international trade.

The Gains from Trade: Cheaper to Buy than to Produce

If Mobilia bought grain for what it costs Farmland to produce it, then Mobilia could buy 9,000 bushels of grain for 1 car. That is much lower than the cost of growing grain in Mobilia, where it costs 9 cars to produce 9,000 bushels of grain. If the Mobilians can buy grain at the low Farmland price, they will reap some gains.

If the Farmers can buy cars for what it costs Mobilia to produce them, they will be able to obtain a car for 1,000 bushels of grain. Because it costs 9,000 bushels of grain to produce a car in Farmland, the Farmers would gain from such an opportunity.

In this situation, it makes sense for Mobilians to buy their grain from Farmers and for Farmers to buy their cars from Mobilians. But at what price will Farmland and Mobilia engage in mutually beneficial international trade?

The Terms of Trade

The quantity of grain that Farmland must pay Mobilia for a car is Farmland's **terms of trade** with Mobilia. Because the United States exports and imports many different goods and services, we measure the terms of trade in the real world as an index number that averages the terms of trade over all the items we trade.

The forces of international supply and demand determine the terms of trade. Figure 3 illustrates these forces in the Farmland–Mobilia international car market. The quantity of cars *traded internationally* is measured on the *x*-axis. On the *y*-axis, we measure the price of a car. This price is expressed as the *terms of trade*: bushels of grain per car. If no international trade takes place, the price of a car in Farmland is 9,000 bushels of grain, its opportunity cost, indicated by point *A*. The no-trade point *A* in Fig. 3 corresponds to point *A* in Fig. 1. The lower the price of a car in the international market (terms of trade), the greater is the quantity of cars that the Farmers are willing to import from the Mobilians. This fact is illustrated by the downward-sloping curve, which shows Farmland's import demand for cars.

FIGURE 3   International Trade in Cars

Farmland's import demand curve for cars is downward sloping, and Mobilia's export supply curve of cars is upward sloping. With no international trade, the price of a car is 9,000 bushels of grain in Farmland (point *A*) and 1,000 bushels of grain in Mobilia (point *A'*).

With free international trade, the price (terms of trade) is determined where the export supply curve intersects the import demand curve: 3,000 bushels of grain per car. At that price, 4 million cars a year are imported by Farmland and exported by Mobilia. The value of grain exported by Farmland and imported by Mobilia is 12 billion bushels a year, the quantity required to pay for the cars imported.

Again, if no trade takes place, the price of a car in Mobilia is 1,000 bushels of grain, its opportunity cost, indicated by point *A'*. The no-trade point *A'* in Fig. 3 corresponds to point *A'* in Fig. 2. The higher the price of a car in the international market, the greater is the quantity of cars that Mobilians are willing to export to Farmers. This fact is illustrated by Mobilia's export supply of cars—the upward-sloping line in Fig. 3.

The international market in cars determines the equilibrium terms of trade (price) and quantity traded. This equilibrium occurs where the import demand curve intersects the export supply curve. In this case, the equilibrium terms of trade are 3,000 bushels of grain per car. Mobilia exports and Farmland imports 4 million cars a year. Notice that the terms of trade are lower than the no-trade price in Farmland but higher than the no-trade price in Mobilia.

Balanced Trade

The number of cars exported by Mobilia—4 million a year—is exactly equal to the number of cars imported by Farmland. How does Farmland pay for the cars it imports? The answer is by exporting grain. How much grain does Farmland export? You can find the answer by noticing that for 1 car, Farmland must pay 3,000 bushels of grain. So for 4 million cars, Farmland pays 12 billion bushels of grain. Farmland's exports of grain are 12 billion bushels a year, and Mobilia imports this same quantity of grain.

Mobilia exchanges 4 million cars for 12 billion bushels of grain each year, and Farmland exchanges 12 billion bushels of grain for 4 million cars. Trade is balanced. For each country, the value received from exports equals the value paid out for imports.

Changes in Production and Consumption

We've seen that international trade makes it possible for Farmers to buy cars at a lower price than what it costs them to produce a car and to sell their grain for a higher price. International trade also enables Mobilians to sell their cars for a higher price and buy grain for a lower price than it costs them to produce grain. Both countries gain. How is it possible for *both* countries to gain? What are the changes in production and consumption that accompany these gains?

An economy that does not trade with other economies has identical production and consumption possibilities. Without trade, the economy can consume only what it produces. But with international trade, an economy can consume different quantities of goods from those that it produces. The production possibilities frontier describes the limits of what a country can produce, but it does not describe the limits to what it can consume. Figure 4 will help you to see the distinction between production possibilities and consumption possibilities when a country trades with other countries.

First, notice that Fig. 4 has two parts: part (a) for Farmland and part (b) for Mobilia. The production possibilities frontiers that you saw in Figs. 1 and 2 are reproduced here. The slopes of the two black lines represent the opportunity costs in the two countries when there is no international trade. Farmland produces and consumes at point *A*, and Mobilia produces and consumes at *A'*. The opportunity cost of a car is 9,000 bushels of grain in Farmland and 1,000 bushels of grain in Mobilia.

Consumption Possibilities

The grey line in each part of Fig. 4 shows the country's consumption possibilities with international trade. These two grey lines have the same slope, and the magnitude of that slope is the opportunity cost of a car in terms of grain on the world market: 3,000 bushels per car. The *slope* of the consumption possibilities line is common to both countries because its magnitude equals the *world* price. But the

FIGURE 4   Expanding Consumption Possibilities

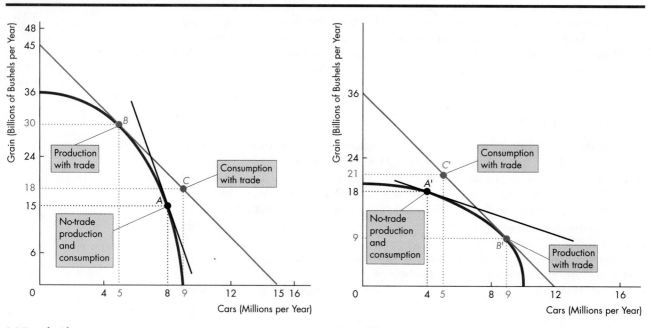

(a) Farmland   **(b) Mobilia**

With no international trade, the Farmers produce and consume at point *A* and the opportunity cost of a car is 9,000 bushels of grain (the slope of the black line in part a). Also, with no international trade, the Mobilians produce and consume at point *A'* and the opportunity cost of 1,000 bushels of grain is 1 car (the slope of the black line in part b).

   Goods can be exchanged internationally at a price of 3,000 bushels of grain for 1 car along the grey line in each part of the figure. In part (a), Farmland decreases its production of cars and increases its production of grain, moving from *A* to *B*. Farmland exports grain and imports cars, and it consumes at point *C*. The Farmers have more of both cars and grain than they would if they produced all their own consumption goods—at point *A*.

   In part (b), Mobilia increases car production and decreases grain production, moving from *A'* to *B'*. Mobilia exports cars and imports grain, and it consumes at point *C'*. The Mobilians have more of both cars and grain than they would if they produced all their own consumption goods—at point *A'*.

position of a country's consumption possibilities line depends on the country's production possibilities. A country cannot produce outside its production possibilities curve, so its consumption possibilities curve touches its production possibilities curve. So Farmland could choose to consume at point *B* with no international trade or, with international trade, at any point on its grey consumption possibilities line.

Free Trade Equilibrium

With international trade, the producers of cars in Mobilia can sell their cars for a higher price. As a result, they increase the quantity of cars they produce. At the same time, grain producers in Mobilia receive a lower price for their grain, and so they reduce the quantity of grain produced. Producers in Mobilia adjust their output by moving along their *PPF* until the opportunity cost in Mobilia equals the world price (the opportunity cost in the world market). This situation arises when Mobilia is producing at point *B'* in Fig. 4(b).

   But the Mobilians do not consume at point *B'*. That is, they do not increase their consumption of cars and decrease their consumption of grain. Instead, they sell some of the cars they produce to Farmland in exchange for some of Farmland's grain. They trade internationally. But to see how that works out, we first need to check in with Farmland to see what's happening there.

In Farmland, producers of cars now receive a lower price and producers of grain can sell their grain for a higher price. As a consequence, producers in Farmland decrease car production and increase grain production. They adjust their outputs by moving along the *PPF* until the opportunity cost of a car in terms of grain equals the world price (the opportunity cost on the world market). They move to point *B* in part (a). But the Farmers do not consume at point *B*. Instead, they trade some of their additional grain production for the now cheaper cars from Mobilia.

The figure shows us the quantities consumed in the two countries. We saw in Fig. 3 that Mobilia exports 4 million cars a year and Farmland imports those cars. We also saw that Farmland exports 12 billion bushels of grain a year and Mobilia imports that grain. So Farmland's consumption of grain is 12 billion bushels a year less than it produces, and its consumption of cars is 4 million a year more than it produces. Farmland consumes at point *C* in Fig. 4(a).

Similarly, we know that Mobilia consumes 12 billion bushels of grain more than it produces and 4 million cars fewer than it produces. Mobilia consumes at point *C'* in Fig. 4(b).

Calculating the Gains from Trade

You can now literally see the gains from trade in Fig. 4. Without trade, Farmers produce and consume at *A* (part a)—a point on Farmland's production possibilities frontier. With international trade, Farmers consume at point *C* in part (a)—a point *outside* the production possibilities frontier. At point *C*, Farmers are consuming 3 billion bushels of grain a year and 1 million cars a year more than before. These increases in consumption of both cars and grain, beyond the limits of the production possibilities frontier, are the Farmers' gains from international trade.

Mobilians also gain. Without trade, they consume at point *A'* in part (b)—a point on Mobilia's production possibilities frontier. With international trade, they consume at point *C'*—a point *outside* their production possibilities frontier. With international trade, Mobilia consumes 3 billion bushels of grain a year and 1 million cars a year more than they would without trade. These are the gains from international trade for Mobilia.

Gains for Both Countries

Trade between the Farmers and the Mobilians does not create winners and losers. Both countries are winners. Farmers selling grain and Mobilians selling cars face an increased demand for their products because the demand by foreigners is added to domestic demand. With an increase in demand, the price rises.

Farmers buying cars and Mobilians buying grain face an increased supply of these products because the foreign supply is added to domestic supply. With an increase in supply, the price falls.

Gains from Trade in Reality

The gains from trade between Farmland and Mobilia that we have just studied occur in a model economy—in a world economy that we have imagined. But these same phenomena occur every day in the real global economy.

Comparative Advantage in the Global Economy

We buy TVs and DVD players from Korea, machinery from Europe, and fashion goods from Hong Kong. In exchange, we sell machinery, grain and lumber, airplanes, computers, and financial services. All this international trade is generated by comparative advantage, just like the international trade between Farmland and Mobilia in our model economy. All international trade arises from comparative advantage, even when trade is in similar goods such as tools and machines. At first thought, it seems puzzling that countries exchange manufactured goods. Why doesn't each developed country produce all the manufactured goods its citizens want to buy?

Trade in Similar Goods

Why does the United States produce automobiles for export and at the same time import large quantities of automobiles from Canada, Japan, Korea, and Western Europe? Wouldn't it make more sense to produce all the cars that we buy here in the United States? After all, we have access to the best technology available for producing cars. Autoworkers in the United States are surely as productive as their fellow workers in Canada, Western Europe, and Asia. So why does the United States have a comparative advantage in some types of cars and Asia and Europe in others?

Diversity of Taste and Economies of Scale

The first part of the answer is that people have a tremendous diversity of taste. Let's stick with the example of cars. Some people prefer a sports car, some prefer a limousine, some prefer a regular, full-size car, some prefer a sport utility vehicle, and some prefer a minivan. In addition to size and type of car, there are many other dimensions in which cars vary. Some have low fuel consumption, some have high performance, some are spacious and comfortable, some have a large trunk, some have four-wheel drive, some have front-wheel drive, some have a radiator grill that looks like a Greek temple, others resemble a wedge. People's preferences across these many dimensions vary. The tremendous diversity in tastes for cars means that people value variety and are willing to pay for it in the marketplace.

The second part of the answer to the puzzle is *economies of scale*—the tendency for the average cost to be lower, the larger the scale of production. In such situations, larger and larger production runs lead to ever lower average costs. Production of many goods, including cars, involves economies of scale. For example, if a car producer makes only a few hundred (or perhaps a few thousand) cars of a particular type and design, the producer must use production techniques that are much more labor-intensive and much less automated than those employed to make hundreds of thousands of cars in a particular model. With short production runs and labor-intensive production techniques, costs are high. With very large production runs and automated assembly lines, production costs are much lower. But to obtain lower costs, the automated assembly lines have to produce a large number of cars.

It is the combination of diversity of taste and economies of scale that determines opportunity cost, produces comparative advantages, and generates such a large amount of international trade in similar commodities. With international trade, each car manufacturer has the whole world market to serve. Each producer can specialize in a limited range of products and then sell its output to the entire world market. This arrangement enables large production runs on the most popular cars and feasible production runs even on the most customized cars demanded by only a handful of people in each country.

The situation in the market for cars is also present in many other industries, especially those producing specialized equipment and parts. For example, the United States exports computer central processor chips but imports memory chips, exports mainframe computers but imports PCs, and exports specialized video equipment but imports DVD players. International trade in similar but slightly different manufactured products is profitable.

You've now seen how free international trade brings gains for all countries. But international trade is not free in our world. We'll now take a brief look at the history and the effects of international trade restrictions. We'll see that free trade brings the greatest possible benefits and that international trade restrictions are costly.

INTERNATIONAL TRADE RESTRICTIONS 　　4

Governments restrict international trade to protect domestic industries from foreign competition by using two main tools:

1. Tariffs
2. Nontariff barriers

A **tariff** is a tax that is imposed by the importing country when an imported good crosses its international boundary. A **nontariff barrier** is any action other than a tariff that restricts international trade. Examples of nontariff barriers are quantitative restrictions and licensing regulations limiting imports. First, let's look at tariffs.

The History of Tariffs

U.S. tariffs today are modest in comparison with their historical levels. Figure 5 shows the average tariff rate—total tariffs as a percentage of total imports. You can see in this figure that this average reached a peak of 20 percent in 1933. In that year, three years after the passage of the Smoot-Hawley Act, one third of our imports was subject to a tariff and on those imports the tariff rate was 60 percent. The average tariff in Fig. 5 for 1933 is 60 percent multiplied by 1/3, which equals 20 percent. Today, the average tariff rate is less than 2 percent.

In 1947, the United States and 22 other countries signed the **General Agreement on Tariffs and Trade** (GATT). From its formation, GATT organized a series of "rounds" of negotiations that resulted in a steady process of tariff reduction. The final round, the Uruguay Round, started in 1986 and completed in 1994, led to the creation of the **World Trade Organization** (WTO).

In 2001, the WTO embarked on an ambitious program known as the *Doha Development Agenda*, which seeks to create free world trade in all goods and services, including agriculture. The major challenge of this program is to open markets for developing countries in the developed world. Limited progress has been made in this program in conferences held in Cancún in 2003, Geneva in 2004, and Hong Kong in 2005, and this program is ongoing.

In addition to the agreements under the GATT and the WTO, the United States is a party to the **North American Free Trade Agreement** (NAFTA), which became effective on January 1, 1994, and under which barriers to international

FIGURE 5   U.S. Tariffs: 1930–2006

The Smoot-Hawley Act, which was passed in 1930, took U.S. tariffs to a peak average rate of 20 percent in 1933. (One third of imports was subject to a tariff rate of 60 percent.) Since the establishment of GATT in 1947, tariffs have steadily declined in a series of negotiating rounds, the most significant of which are identified in the figure. Tariffs are now as low as they have ever been.

Sources: U.S. Bureau of the Census, *Historical Statistics of the United States, Colonial Times to 1970*, Bicentennial Edition, Part 1 (Washington, D.C., 1975); Series U-212: updated from *Statistical Abstract of the United States*: various editions.

trade between the United States, Canada, and Mexico will be virtually eliminated after a 15-year phasing-in period.

In other parts of the world, trade barriers have virtually been eliminated among the member countries of the European Union, which has created the largest unified tariff-free market in the world. In 1994, discussions among the Asia-Pacific Economic Cooperation (APEC) led to an agreement in principle to work toward a free-trade area that embraces China, all the economies of East Asia and the South Pacific, Chile, Peru, Mexico, and the United States and Canada. These countries include the fastest-growing economies and hold the promise of heralding a global free-trade area.

The effort to achieve freer trade underlines the fact that trade in some goods is still subject to a high tariff. Textiles and footwear are among the goods that face the highest tariffs, and rates on these items average more than 10 percent. Some individual items face a tariff much higher than the average. For example, when you buy a pair of blue jeans for $30, you pay about $7 more than you would if there were no tariffs on textiles. Other goods that are protected by tariffs are agricultural products, energy and chemicals, minerals, and metals. The meat, cheese, and sugar that you consume cost significantly more because of protection than they would with free international trade.

The temptation for governments to impose tariffs is a strong one. First, tariffs provide revenue to the government. Second, they enable the government to satisfy special interest groups in import-competing industries. But, as we'll see, free international trade brings enormous benefits that are reduced when tariffs are imposed. Let's see how.

How Tariffs Work

To see how tariffs work, let's return to the example of trade between Farmland and Mobilia. Figure 6 shows the international market for cars in which these two countries are the only traders. The volume of trade and the price of a car are determined at the point of intersection of Mobilia's export supply curve of cars and Farmland's import demand curve for cars.

FIGURE 6   The Effects of a Tariff

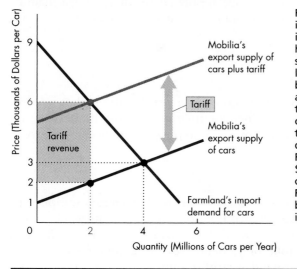

Farmland imposes a tariff on car imports from Mobilia. The tariff increases the price that Farmers have to pay for a car and shifts the supply curve of cars in Farmland leftward. The vertical distance between the original supply curve and the new one is the amount of the tariff, $4,000 per car. The price of a car in Farmland increases, and the quantity of cars imported decreases. The government of Farmland collects a tariff revenue of $4,000 per car—a total of $8 billion on the 2 million cars imported. Farmland's exports of grain decrease because Mobilia now has a lower income from its exports of cars.

In Fig. 6, these two countries trade cars and grain in exactly the same way that we saw in Fig. 3: Mobilia exports cars, and Farmland exports grain. The volume of car imports into Farmland is 4 million a year, and the world market price of a car is 3,000 bushels of grain. Figure 6 expresses prices in dollars rather than in units of grain and is based on a money price of grain of $1 a bushel. With grain costing $1 a bushel, the money price of a car is $3,000.

Now suppose that the government of Farmland, perhaps under pressure from car producers, decides to impose a tariff on imported cars. In particular, suppose that a tariff of $4,000 per car is imposed. (This is a huge tariff, but the car producers of Farmland are fed up with competition from Mobilia.) What happens?

► The supply of cars in Farmland decreases.

► The price of a car in Farmland rises.

► The quantity of cars imported by Farmland decreases.

► The government of Farmland collects the tariff revenue.

► Resource use is inefficient.

► The *value* of exports changes by the same amount as the *value* of imports, and trade remains balanced.

Change in the Supply of Cars

Farmland cannot import cars at Mobilia's export supply price. It must pay that price plus the $4,000 tariff. So the supply curve in Farmland shifts leftward. The new supply curve is labeled "Mobilia's export supply of cars plus tariff." The vertical distance between Mobilia's original export supply curve and the new supply curve is the tariff of $4,000 a car.

Rise in Price of a Car

A new equilibrium occurs where the new supply curve intersects Farmland's import demand curve for cars. That equilibrium is at a price of $6,000 a car, up from $3,000 with free trade.

Fall in Imports

Car imports fall from 4 million to 2 million cars a year. At the higher price of $6,000 a car, domestic car producers increase their production. Domestic grain production decreases as resources are moved into the expanding car industry.

Tariff Revenue

Total expenditure on imported cars by the Farmers is $6,000 a car multiplied by the 2 million cars imported ($12 billion). But not all of that money goes to the Mobilians. They receive $2,000 a car, or $4 billion for the 2 million cars. The difference—$4,000 a car, or a total of $8 billion for the 2 million cars—is collected by the government of Farmland as tariff revenue.

Inefficiency

The people of Farmland are willing to pay $6,000 for the marginal car imported. But the opportunity cost of that car is $2,000. So there is a gain from trading an extra car. In fact, there are gains—willingness to pay exceeds opportunity cost—all the way up to 4 million cars a year. Only when 4 million cars are being traded is the maximum price that a Farmer is willing to pay equal to the minimum price that is acceptable to a Mobilian. Restricting trade reduces the gains from trade.

Trade Remains Balanced

With free trade, Farmland was paying $3,000 a car and buying 4 million cars a year from Mobilia. Farmland was paying Mobilia $12 billion a year for imported cars. With a tariff of $4,000 a car, Farmland's imports have decreased to 2 million cars a year and the price paid to Mobilia has fallen to $2,000 a car. The total amount Farmland has paid to Mobilia for imports has fallen to $4 billion a year. Doesn't this fact mean that Farmland now has a balance of trade surplus? It does not.

The price of a car in Mobilia has fallen but the price of grain remains at $1 a bushel. So the relative price of a car has fallen, and the relative price of grain has increased. With free trade, the Mobilians could buy 3,000 bushels of grain for one car. Now they can buy only 2,000 bushels for a car.

With a higher relative price of grain, the quantity demanded by the Mobilians decreases and Mobilia imports less grain. But because Mobilia imports less grain, Farmland exports less grain. In fact, Farmland's grain industry suffers from two sources. First, there is a decrease in the quantity of grain sold to Mobilia. Second, there is increased competition for resources from the now-expanded car industry. The tariff leads to a contraction in the scale of the grain industry in Farmland.

It seems paradoxical at first that a country imposing a tariff on cars hurts its own export industry, lowering its exports of grain. It might help to think of it this way: Mobilians buy grain with the money they make from exporting cars to Farmland. If they export fewer cars, they cannot afford to buy as much grain. In fact, in the absence of any international borrowing and lending, Mobilia must cut its imports of grain by exactly the same amount as the loss in revenue from its export of cars. Grain imports into Mobilia are cut back to a value of $4 billion, the amount that can be paid for by the new lower revenue from Mobilia's car exports. Trade is still balanced. The tariff cuts the value of imports and exports by the same amount. The tariff has no effect on the *balance* of trade, but it reduces the *volume* of trade.

The result that we have just derived is perhaps one of the most misunderstood aspects of international economics. On countless occasions, politicians and others call for tariffs to remove a balance of trade deficit or argue that lowering tariffs would produce a balance of trade deficit. They reach this conclusion by failing to work out all the implications of a tariff.

Let's now look at nontariff barriers.

Nontariff Barriers

The two main forms of nontariff barriers are

1. Quotas

2. Voluntary export restraints

A **quota** is a quantitative restriction on the import of a particular good, which specifies the maximum amount of the good that may be imported in a given period of time. A **voluntary export restraint** (VER) is an agreement between two governments in which the government of the exporting country agrees to restrain the volume of its own exports.

Quotas are especially prominent in textiles and agriculture. VERs have been used in U.S. trade with Japan in a wide range of products, and more recently in textile trade with China (see *Reading Between the Lines* at the end of this reading).

How Quotas Work

Suppose that Farmland puts a quota on car imports of 2 million a year. Figure 7 shows the effects of this action. The quota is shown by the vertical grey line at 2 million cars a year. Farmland car importers buy that quantity from Mobilia and pay $2,000 a car. But because the quantity of cars imported is restricted to 2 million cars a year, people in Farmland are willing to pay $6,000 per car. This is the price of a car in Farmland.

The value of imports falls to $4 billion (the same as in the case of the tariff). With lower incomes from car exports and with a higher relative price of grain, Mobilians cut back on their imports of grain in exactly the same way that they did under a tariff.

The key difference between a quota and a tariff lies in who collects the gap between the exporter's supply price and the domestic price. In the case of a tariff,

FIGURE 7   The Effects of a Quota

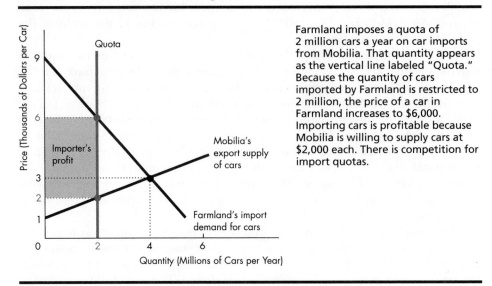

Farmland imposes a quota of 2 million cars a year on car imports from Mobilia. That quantity appears as the vertical line labeled "Quota." Because the quantity of cars imported by Farmland is restricted to 2 million, the price of a car in Farmland increases to $6,000. Importing cars is profitable because Mobilia is willing to supply cars at $2,000 each. There is competition for import quotas.

the government of the importing country receives the gap. In the case of a quota, it goes to the importer.

How VERs Work

A VER is like a quota allocated to each exporter. The effects of a VER are similar to those of a quota but differ from them in that the gap between the domestic price and the export price is captured not by domestic importers but by the foreign exporter. The government of the exporting country has to establish procedures for allocating the restricted volume of exports among its producers.

We're now going to look at some commonly heard arguments for restricting international trade and see why they are almost never correct.

5   THE CASE AGAINST PROTECTION

For as long as nations and international trade have existed, people have debated whether a country is better off with free international trade or with protection from foreign competition. The debate continues, but for most economists, a verdict has been delivered and is the one you have just seen. Free trade promotes prosperity for all countries; protection is inefficient. We've seen the most powerful case for free trade in the example of how Farmland and Mobilia both benefit from their comparative advantage. But there is a broader range of issues in the free trade versus protection debate. Let's review these issues.

Three arguments for restricting international trade are

► The national security argument
► The infant-industry argument
► The dumping argument

The National Security Argument

The national security argument for protection is that a country must protect the industries that produce defense equipment and armaments and those on which the defense industries rely for their raw materials and other intermediate inputs. This argument for protection does not withstand close scrutiny.

First, it is an argument for international isolation, for in a time of war, there is no industry that does not contribute to national defense.

Second, if the case is made for boosting the output of a strategic industry, it is more efficient to achieve this outcome with a subsidy to the firms in the industry, with the subsidy financed out of taxes. Such a subsidy would keep the industry operating at the scale judged appropriate, and free international trade would keep the prices faced by consumers at their world market levels.

The Infant-Industry Argument

The so-called **infant-industry argument** for protection is that it is necessary to protect a new industry to enable it to grow into a mature industry that can compete in world markets. The argument is based on the idea of *dynamic comparative advantage*, which can arise from *learning-by-doing*.

Learning-by-doing is a powerful engine of productivity growth, and comparative advantage does evolve and change because of on-the-job experience. But these facts do not justify protection.

First, the infant-industry argument is valid only if the benefits of learning-by-doing *not only* accrue to the owners and workers of the firms in the infant industry but also *spill over* to other industries and parts of the economy. For example, there are huge productivity gains from learning-by-doing in the manufacture of aircraft. But almost all of these gains benefit the stockholders and workers of Boeing and other aircraft producers. Because the people making the decisions, bearing the risk, and doing the work are the ones who benefit, they take the dynamic gains into account when they decide on the scale of their activities. In this case, almost no benefits spill over to other parts of the economy, so there is no need for government assistance to achieve an efficient outcome.

Second, even if the case is made for protecting an infant industry, it is more efficient to do so by a subsidy to the firms in the industry, with the subsidy financed out of taxes. Such a subsidy would encourage the industry to mature and to compete with efficient world producers and keep the prices faced by consumers at their world market levels.

The Dumping Argument

Dumping occurs when a foreign firm sells its exports at a lower price than its cost of production. Dumping might be used by a firm that wants to gain a global monopoly. In this case, the foreign firm sells its output at a price below its cost to drive domestic firms out of business. When the domestic firms have gone, the foreign firm takes advantage of its monopoly position and charges a higher price for its product. Dumping is usually regarded as a justification for temporary tariffs, which are called *countervailing duties*.

But there are powerful reasons to resist the dumping argument for protection. First, it is virtually impossible to detect dumping because it is hard to determine a firm's costs. As a result, the test for dumping is whether a firm's export price is below its domestic price. But this test is a weak one because it can be rational for a firm to charge a low price in markets in which the quantity demanded is highly sensitive to price and a higher price in a market in which demand is less price-sensitive.

Second, it is hard to think of a good that is produced by a natural *global* monopoly. So even if all the domestic firms in some industry were driven out of business, it would always be possible to find many alternative foreign sources of supply and to buy the good at prices determined in competitive markets.

Third, if a good or service were a truly global natural monopoly, the best way of dealing with it would be by regulation—just as in the case of domestic monopolies. Such regulation would require international cooperation.

The three arguments for protection that we've just examined have an element of credibility. The counterarguments are in general stronger, however, so these arguments do not make the case for protection. But they are not the only arguments that you might encounter. There are many other new arguments against globalization and for protection. The most common of them are that protection

▶ Saves jobs
▶ Allows us to compete with cheap foreign labor
▶ Brings diversity and stability
▶ Penalizes lax environmental standards
▶ Protects national culture
▶ Prevents rich countries from exploiting developing countries

Saves Jobs

The argument is that when we buy shoes from Brazil or shirts from Taiwan, U.S. workers in these industries lose their jobs. With no earnings and poor prospects, these workers become a drain on welfare and spend less, causing a ripple effect of further job losses. The proposed solution is to ban imports of cheap foreign goods and protect U.S. jobs. This argument does not withstand scrutiny for three reasons.

First, free trade does cost some jobs, but it also creates other jobs. It brings about a global rationalization of labor and allocates labor resources to their highest-valued activities. International trade in textiles has cost tens of thousands of jobs in the United States as textile mills and other factories closed. But tens of thousands of jobs have been created in other countries as textile mills opened. And tens of thousands of U.S. workers got better-paying jobs than textile workers because U.S. export industries expanded and created new jobs. More jobs were created than destroyed.

Second, imports create jobs. They create jobs for retailers that sell imported goods and firms that service those goods. They also create jobs by creating incomes in the rest of the world, some of which are spent on imports of U.S.-made goods and services.

Although protection does save particular jobs, it does so at a high cost. For example, until 2005, textile jobs in the United States were protected by an international agreement called the Multifiber Arrangement. The U.S. International Trade Commission (ITC) has estimated that because of quotas, 72,000 jobs existed in textiles that would otherwise have disappeared and that the annual clothing expenditure in the United States was $15.9 billion, or $160 per family, higher than it will be with free trade. Equivalently, the ITC estimated that each textile job saved cost $221,000 a year.

Allows Us to Compete with Cheap Foreign Labor

With the removal of tariffs in U.S. trade with Mexico, people said we would hear a "giant sucking sound" as jobs rushed to Mexico (shown in the cartoon). Let's see what's wrong with this view.

The labor cost of a unit of output equals the wage rate divided by labor productivity. For example, if a U.S. autoworker earns $30 an hour and produces 15 units of output an hour, the average labor cost of a unit of output is $2. If a Mexican auto assembly worker earns $3 an hour and produces 1 unit of output an hour, the average labor cost of a unit of output is $3. Other things remaining the same, the higher a worker's productivity, the higher is the worker's wage rate. High-wage workers have high productivity. Low-wage workers have low productivity.

Although high-wage U.S. workers are more productive, on the average, than low-wage Mexican workers, there are differences across industries. U.S. labor is relatively more productive in some activities than in others. For example, the productivity of U.S. workers in producing movies, financial services, and customized computer chips is relatively higher than their productivity in the production of metals and some standardized machine parts. The activities in which U.S. workers are relatively more productive than their Mexican counterparts are those in which the United States has a *comparative advantage*. By engaging in free trade, increasing our production and exports of the goods and services in which we have a comparative advantage and decreasing our production and increasing our imports of the goods and services in which our trading partners have a comparative advantage, we can make ourselves and the citizens of other countries better off.

Brings Diversity and Stability

A diversified investment portfolio is less risky than one that has all the eggs in one basket. The same is true for an economy's production. A diversified economy fluctuates less than does an economy that produces only one or two goods.

"I don't know what the hell happened—one minute I'm at work in Flint, Michigan, then there's a giant sucking sound and suddenly here I am in Mexico."

Source: © The New Yorker Collection 1993
Mick Stevens from Cartoonbank.com. All Rights Reserved.

But big, rich, diversified economies such as those of the United States, Japan, and Europe do not have this type of stability problem. Even a country such as Saudi Arabia that produces only one good (in this case, oil) can benefit from specializing in the activity at which it has a comparative advantage and then investing in a wide range of other countries to bring greater stability to its income and consumption.

Penalizes Lax Environmental Standards

Another argument for protection is that many poorer countries, such as Mexico, do not have the same environmental policies that we have and, because they are willing to pollute and we are not, we cannot compete with them without tariffs. So if they want free trade with the richer and "greener" countries, they must clean up their environments to our standards.

This argument for international trade restrictions is weak. First, not all poorer countries have significantly lower environmental standards than the United States has. Many poor countries and the former communist countries of Eastern Europe do have bad environmental records. But some countries enforce strict laws. Second, a poor country cannot afford to be as concerned about its environment as a rich country can. The best hope for a better environment in Mexico and in other developing countries is rapid income growth through free trade. As their incomes grow, developing countries will have the *means* to match their desires to improve their environment. Third, poor countries have a comparative advantage at doing "dirty" work, which helps rich countries to achieve higher environmental standards than they otherwise could.

Protects National Culture

The national culture argument for protection is not heard much in the United States, but it is a commonly heard argument in Canada and Europe.

The expressed fear is that free trade in books, magazines, movies, and television programs means U.S. domination and the end of local culture. So, the reasoning continues, it is necessary to protect domestic "culture" industries from free international trade to ensure the survival of a national cultural identity.

Protection of these industries is common and takes the form of nontariff barriers. For example, local content regulations on radio and television broadcasting and in magazines is often required.

The cultural identity argument for protection has no merit. Writers, publishers, and broadcasters want to limit foreign competition so that they can earn larger economic profits. There is no actual danger to national culture. In fact, many of the creators of so-called American cultural products are not Americans but the talented citizens of other countries, ensuring the survival of their national cultural identities in Hollywood! Also, if national culture is in danger, there is no surer way of helping it on its way out than by impoverishing the nation whose culture it is. And protection is an effective way of doing just that.

Prevents Rich Countries from Exploiting Developing Countries

Another argument for protection is that international trade must be restricted to prevent the people of the rich industrial world from exploiting the poorer people of the developing countries, forcing them to work for slave wages.

Child labor and near-slave labor is a serious problem that is rightly condemned. But by trading with poor countries, we increase the demand for the goods that these countries produce and, more significantly, we increase the demand for their labor. When the demand for labor in developing countries increases, the wage rate also increases. So, rather than exploiting people in developing countries, trade can improve their opportunities and increase their incomes.

We have reviewed the arguments that are commonly heard in favor of protection and the counterarguments against them. There is one counterargument to protection that is general and quite overwhelming. Protection invites retaliation and can trigger a trade war. The best example of a trade war occurred during the Great Depression of the 1930s when the Smoot-Hawley tariff was introduced in the United States. Country after country retaliated with its own tariff, and in a short period, world trade had almost disappeared. The costs to all countries were large and led to a renewed international resolve to avoid such self-defeating moves in the future. They also led to the creation of GATT and are the impetus behind NAFTA, APEC, and the European Union.

WHY IS INTERNATIONAL TRADE RESTRICTED?   6

Why, despite all the arguments against protection, is trade restricted? There are two key reasons:

▶ Tariff revenue
▶ Rent seeking

Tariff Revenue

Government revenue is costly to collect. In the developed countries such as the United States, a well-organized tax collection system is in place that can generate billions of dollars of income tax and sales tax revenues. This tax collection system is made possible by the fact that most economic transactions are done by firms that must keep properly audited financial records. Without such records, the revenue collection agencies (the Internal Revenue Service in the United States) would be severely hampered in the work. Even with audited financial accounts, some proportion of potential tax revenue is lost. Nonetheless, for the industrialized countries, the income tax and sales taxes are the major sources of revenue and the tariff plays a very small role.

But governments in developing countries have a difficult time collecting taxes from their citizens. Much economic activity takes place in an informal economy with few financial records, so only a small amount of revenue is collected from income taxes and sales taxes. The one area in which economic transactions are well recorded and audited is in international trade. So this activity is an attractive base for tax collection in these countries and is used much more extensively than it is in the developed countries.

Rent Seeking

Rent seeking is the major reason why international trade is restricted. **Rent seeking** is lobbying and other political activity that seek to capture the gains from trade. Free trade increases consumption possibilities *on the average*, but not everyone shares in the gain and some people even lose. Free trade brings benefits to some and imposes costs on others, with total benefits exceeding total costs. It is the uneven distribution of costs and benefits that is the principal source of impediment to achieving more liberal international trade.

Returning to our example of trade in cars and grain between Farmland and Mobilia, the benefits to Farmland from free trade accrue to all the producers of grain and to those producers of cars who do not bear the costs of adjusting to a smaller car industry. These costs are transition costs, not permanent costs. The costs of Farmland's move to free trade are borne by the car producers and their employees who have to become grain producers. In Mobilia, the benefits from free trade accrue to car producers and those grain producers who do not bear the transition costs to a small grain industry. The losers are the grain producers and their employees who have to produce cars.

The number of people who gain, in general, is large compared with the number who lose. So the gain per person is small but the loss per person to those who bear the loss is large. Because the loss that falls on those who bear it is large, it will pay those people to incur considerable expense to lobby against free trade. On the other hand, it will not pay those who gain to organize to achieve free trade. The gain from trade for any one person is too small for that person to spend much time or money on a political organization to achieve free trade. The loss from free trade will be seen as being so great by those bearing that loss that they *will* find it profitable to join a political organization to prevent free trade. Each group is optimizing—weighing benefits against costs and choosing the best action for themselves. The anti-free-trade group will, however, undertake a larger quantity of political lobbying than the pro-free-trade group.

Compensating Losers

If, in total, the gains from free international trade exceed the losses, why don't those who gain compensate those who lose so that everyone is in favor of free trade? To some degree, such compensation does take place. When Congress approved the NAFTA deal with Canada and Mexico, it set up a $56 million fund to support and retrain workers who lost their jobs as a result of the new trade agreement. During the first six months of the operation of NAFTA, only 5,000 workers applied for benefits under this scheme.

The losers from freer international trade are also compensated indirectly through the normal unemployment compensation arrangements. But only limited attempts are made to compensate those who lose. The main reason why full compensation is not attempted is that the costs of identifying all the losers and estimating the value of their losses would be enormous. Also, it would never be clear whether a person who has fallen on hard times is suffering because of free trade or for other reasons that might be largely under his or her control. Furthermore, some people who look like losers at one point in time might, in fact, end up gaining. The young autoworker who loses his job in Michigan and becomes a computer assembly worker in Minneapolis resents the loss of work and the need to move. But a year or two later, looking back on events, he counts himself fortunate. He has made a move that has increased his income and given him greater job security.

It is because we do not, in general, compensate the losers from free international trade that protectionism is such a popular and permanent feature of our national economic and political life.

You've seen why all nations gain from specialization and trade. By producing goods in which we have a comparative advantage and trading some of our production for that of others, we expand our consumption possibilities. Placing restriction on that trade reduces our gains from international trade. By opening our country up to free trade, the market for the things that we sell expands and their relative price rises. The market for the things that we buy also expands, and their relative price falls.

Reading Between the Lines looks at the globalization of production and the gains to Americans and Asians as production in China and trade between China and the United States expand.

7

READING BETWEEN THE LINES

The Gains from Globalization

THE NEW YORK TIMES, NOVEMBER 7, 2005

China and U.S. Expected to Reach Deal on Textiles

November 7, 2005

An agreement to limit for three years the surging growth of Chinese textile imports to the United States is expected to be completed as early as this week, Bush administration officials said yesterday.

. . . Worries that trade frictions could disrupt textile shipments from China have made some American retailers reluctant to place large orders. The deal is reportedly similar to an agreement reached last summer to limit Chinese clothing exports to the European Union, which followed disruption of supplies to retailers.

. . . China bought $278 million of American textile products in 2004, while selling 52 times that much, or $14.6 billion, to the United States, according to the United States trade representative's office. In 2002, the United States had 651,000 jobs in textile mills and apparel-making, less than half the number in 1990, data from the Census Bureau show.

. . . Overall Chinese textile exports to the United States surged 54 percent in the first eight months of this year, to $17.7 billion, the Chinese government reported last month. American officials put the figure at 46 percent.

. . . North Carolina had 350,000 textile jobs in 1972, but more than 90 percent of them will be gone by the end of this decade, Mark Vitner, a senior economist at Wachovia Bank in Charlotte, said yesterday. He said production had not declined as sharply because Chinese imports encouraged the state's companies to make investments in automated machinery, which cut payrolls.

China sold 700 million pairs of socks to the United States in the first eight months of this year, up from fewer than 12 million four years ago, and sales of jeans, underwear and other labor-intensive items are up as much as tenfold this year compared with 2004.

Essence of the Story

▶ China is expected to agree to limit textile exports to the United States.

▶ In 2004, for every $1 that China spent on U.S.-produced textiles, the United States spent $52 on textiles produced in China.

▶ Employment in textiles production in the United States has fallen, and it has done so especially strongly in North Carolina.

▶ Chinese textile exports to the United States grew by 54 percent in the first eight months of 2005.

▶ China sold 700 million pairs of socks to the United States in the first eight months of 2005, up from fewer than 12 million four years earlier.

▶ Sales of jeans and underwear were up tenfold in 2005 over 2004.

Economic Analysis

▶ With free trade, goods are produced where their opportunity cost of production is lowest.

▶ Clothing can be produced at a lower opportunity cost in China than in the United States.

▶ By specializing in items at which we have a comparative advantage and buying our clothes from China, we gain and China gains.

▶ We gain because our clothes cost less; China gains because it can sell clothing to us for a higher price than its cost of production.

▶ We also gain because we sell China items such as large passenger jets for more than our cost of production, and China gains because it can buy items like passenger jets for a lower price that its cost of producing them.

▶ Table 1 contains some illustrative numbers, and Fig. 8 shows these numbers graphically.

TABLE 1   Production Possibilities and Trading Possibilities for China and the United States

| | Other Goods and Services | | | |
| | Production Possibilities | | Trading Possibilities | |
Nike Outfits	United States	China	United States	China
0	100	20	100	30
20	80	10	85	15
40	60	0	70	0
100	0			

FIGURE 8   No Trade

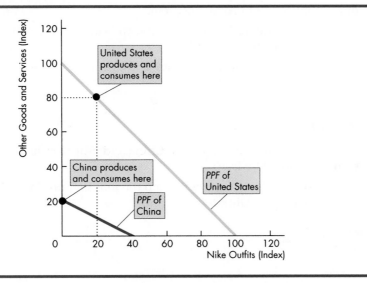

▶ The United States can produce Nike outfits or other goods and services. The opportunity cost in the United States of 1 unit of Nike outfits is 1 unit of other goods and services.

▶ China can also produce Nike outfits or other goods and services. The opportunity cost in China of 1 unit of Nike outfits is 0.5 unit of other goods and services.

▶ But if China produces Nike outfits and the United States produces other goods and services, the two countries can expand their consumption possibilities.

▶ In Fig. 9, China produces 40 units of Nike outfits and the United States produces 100 units of other goods and services.

FIGURE 9   Free Trade

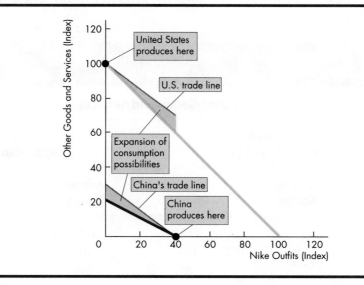

▶ If the two countries trade 1 unit of Nike outfits for 0.75 unit of other goods and services, the United States gets Nike outfits for less than its opportunity cost of producing them and China sells the outfits for more than its opportunity cost of producing them.

▶ Table 1 shows the trading possibilities, and each country can trade along its trade line in Fig. 9.

▶ The United States buys goods from China, but China also buys goods from the United States.

You're the Voter

▶ Do you think that U.S. trade with China and other low-income Asian countries should be free?

▶ Would you vote for measures to keep the jobs that produce clothing in the United States? Explain why or why not.

SUMMARY

► Large flows of trade take place between countries, most of which is in manufactured goods exchanged among rich industrialized countries.

► Since 1960, the U.S. international trade has almost tripled.

► Comparative advantage is the fundamental source of the gains from trade.

► Comparative advantage exists when opportunity costs between countries diverge.

► By increasing its production of goods and services in which it has a comparative advantage and then trading some of the increased output, a country can consume at points outside its production possibilities frontier.

► In the absence of international borrowing and lending, trade is balanced as prices adjust to reflect the international supply of and demand for goods and services.

► The world price balances the production and consumption plans of the trading parties. At the equilibrium price, trade is balanced.

► Comparative advantage explains the international trade that takes place in the world.

► But trade in similar goods arises from economies of scale in the face of diversified tastes.

► Countries restrict international trade by imposing tariffs, quotas, and voluntary export restraints.

► International trade restrictions raise the domestic price of imported goods, lower the volume of imports, and reduce the total value of imports.

► International trade restrictions also reduce the total value of exports by the same amount as the reduction in the value of imports.

► Arguments that protection is necessary for national security, to protect infant industries, and to prevent dumping are weak.

► Arguments that protection saves jobs, allows us to compete with cheap foreign labor, makes the economy diversified and stable, penalizes lax environmental standards, protects national culture, and prevents rich countries from exploiting developing countries are fatally flawed.

► Trade is restricted because tariffs raise government revenue and because protection brings a small loss to a large number of people and a large gain per person to a small number of people.

THE EXCHANGE RATE AND THE BALANCE OF PAYMENTS

by Michael Parkin

LEARNING OUTCOMES

The candidate should be able to:	Mastery
a. define an exchange rate, and differentiate between the nominal exchange rate and the real exchange rate;	☐
b. explain the factors that influence supply and demand in the foreign exchange market;	☐
c. discuss how the supply and demand for a currency changes the exchange rate;	☐
d. differentiate between interest rate parity and purchasing power parity;	☐
e. describe the balance of payments accounts;	☐
f. describe the following exchange rate policies: flexible exchange rates, fixed exchange rates, and crawling pegs.	☐

MANY MONIES! 1

The dollar ($), the yen (¥), and the euro (€) are three of the world's monies. But they are three among a world of more than 100 different monies. The dollar (the currency of the United States) and the yen (the currency of Japan) have been around for a long time. The euro (the currency of 12 members of the European Union) is new. It was created in the 1990s but didn't come into everyday use as notes and coins until January 1, 2002. Most of the world's international payments are made using these three currencies.

In August 2002, one U.S. dollar bought 1.02 euros. From 2002 through 2005, the dollar sank against the euro, and by August 2006, one U.S. dollar bought only 78 euro cents. But against the yen, the U.S. dollar held its value at about 117 yen per dollar.

Why did the dollar fall in value against the euro? Is there anything we can do or should do to stabilize the value of the dollar?

Before 1988, American ownership of foreign assets exceeded foreign ownership of U.S. assets. But in 1988, the value of foreign assets owned by Americans just equaled the value of the assets that foreigners owned in the United States. And every year since 1988, the balance has tipped increasingly the other way. Foreign entrepreneurs have roamed the United States with giant virtual shopping carts and loaded them up with Gerber, Firestone, Chrysler, Columbia Pictures, and Ben & Jerry's, all of which are now controlled by Japanese or European companies. Why have foreigners been buying U.S. businesses?

In this reading, you're going to discover why the U.S. economy has become attractive to foreign investors, what determines the amount of international borrowing and lending, and why the dollar fluctuates against other currencies. At the end of the reading, in *Reading Between the Lines*, we'll look at China's foreign exchange rate policy and see why many Americans are troubled by it.

2   CURRENCIES AND EXCHANGE RATES

When Wal-Mart imports DVD players from Japan, it pays for them using Japanese yen. And when Japan Airlines buys an airplane from Boeing, it pays using U.S. dollars. Whenever people buy things from another country, they use the currency of that country to make the transaction. It doesn't make any difference what the item is that is being traded internationally. It might be a DVD player, an airplane, insurance or banking services, real estate, the stocks and bonds of a government or corporation, or even an entire business.

Foreign money is just like U.S. money. It consists of notes and coins issued by a central bank and mint and deposits in banks and other depository institutions. When we describe U.S. money, we distinguish between currency (notes and coins) and deposits. But when we talk about foreign money, we refer to it as foreign currency. **Foreign currency** is the money of other countries regardless of whether that money is in the form of notes, coins, or bank deposits.

We get these foreign currencies and foreigners get U.S. dollars in the foreign exchange market.

The Foreign Exchange Market

The **foreign exchange market** is the market in which the currency of one country is exchanged for the currency of another. The foreign exchange market is not a place like a downtown flea market or a fruit and vegetable market. The foreign exchange market is made up of thousands of people—importers and exporters, banks, international travelers, and specialist traders called *foreign exchange brokers*.

The foreign exchange market opens on Monday morning in Sydney, Australia, and Hong Kong, which is still Sunday evening in New York. As the day advances, markets open in Singapore, Tokyo, Bahrain, Frankfurt, London, New York, Chicago, and San Francisco. As the West Coast markets close, Sydney is only an hour away from opening for the next day of business. The sun barely sets in the foreign exchange market. Dealers around the world are in continual contact by telephone and computer, and on a typical day in 2006, close to $2 trillion (of all currencies) were traded in the foreign exchange market—or more than $400 trillion in a year.

Exchange Rates

An **exchange rate** is the price at which one currency exchanges for another currency in the foreign exchange market. For example, on September 1, 2006, $1 would buy 117 Japanese yen or 78 euro cents. So the exchange rate was 117 yen per dollar or, equivalently, 78 euro cents per dollar.

The exchange rate fluctuates. Sometimes it rises and sometimes it falls. A rise in the exchange rate is called an *appreciation* of the dollar, and a fall in the exchange rate is called a *depreciation* of the dollar. For example, when the exchange rate rises from 117 yen to 130 yen per dollar, the dollar appreciates, and when the exchange rate falls from 117 yen to 100 yen per dollar, the dollar depreciates.

Figure 1 shows the U.S. dollar exchange rate against the five currencies that feature most prominently in U.S. imports—the Canadian dollar, the Chinese yuan, the European euro, the Mexican peso, and the Japanese yen—between 1995 and 2005.

FIGURE 1   The U.S. Dollar against Five Currencies

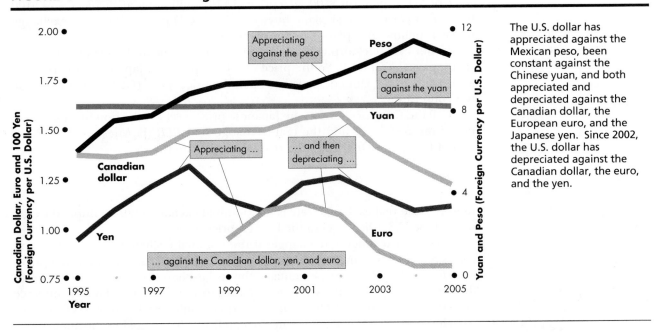

The U.S. dollar has appreciated against the Mexican peso, been constant against the Chinese yuan, and both appreciated and depreciated against the Canadian dollar, the European euro, and the Japanese yen. Since 2002, the U.S. dollar has depreciated against the Canadian dollar, the euro, and the yen.

Source: Federal Reserve Board.

The figure shows that the U.S. dollar has generally appreciated against the Mexican peso, been constant against the Chinese yuan, and fluctuated in both directions against the other three currencies. But since 2002, the dollar has depreciated against the currencies of Canada, Europe, and Japan.

The quantity of foreign money that we get for our dollar changes when the dollar appreciates or depreciates. But a change in the value of the dollar might not change what we *really* pay for our imports and earn from our exports. The reason is that prices might change to offset the change in the exchange rate and leave the terms on which we trade with other countries unchanged.

To determine whether a change in the exchange rate changes what we earn from exports and pay for imports, we need to distinguish between the *nominal* exchange rate and the *real* exchange rate.

Nominal and Real Exchange Rates

The **nominal exchange rate** is the value of the U.S. dollar expressed in units of foreign currency per U.S. dollar. It is a measure of how much of one money exchanges for a unit of another money.

The **real exchange rate** is the relative price of foreign-produced goods and services to U.S.-produced goods and services. It is a measure of the quantity of the real GDP of other countries that we get for a unit of U.S. real GDP.

The exchange rates that we've just discussed and that are graphed in Fig. 1 are *nominal* exchange rates. To understand the real exchange rate, suppose that Japan produces only DVD players and the United States produces only airplanes. The price of a DVD player is 10,000 yen, and the price of an airplane is $100 million. Also suppose that the exchange rate—the *nominal* exchange rate—is 100 yen per dollar. With this information, we can calculate the *real* exchange rate, which is the number DVD players that one airplane buys. Let's do this calculation.

At the price of 10,000 yen and an exchange rate of 100 yen per dollar, the price of a DVD player is $100. At a price of $100 million for an airplane and $100 for a DVD player, one airplane buys 1 million DVD players. The real exchange rate is 1 million DVD players per airplane.

In our example, airplanes represent U.S. real GDP, and DVD players represent Japanese real GDP. So the price of a DVD player in Japan and the price of an airplane in the United States represent the price levels (GDP deflators) in the two countries.

Call the U.S. price level P, the Japanese price level P^*, the nominal exchange rate E yen per dollar and the real exchange rate RER (Japanese real GDP per unit of U.S. real GDP). Then the real exchange rate is

$$RER = E \times (P/P^*).$$

In words, the real exchange rate is the nominal exchange rate multiplied by the ratio of the U.S. price level to the foreign price level.

The real exchange rate changes if the nominal exchange rate changes and prices remain constant. But if the dollar appreciates (E rises) and foreign prices rise (P^* rises) by the same percentage, the real exchange rate doesn't change. In the above example, if the exchange rate rises to 120 yen per dollar and the price of a DVD player rises to 12,000 yen, one airplane still buys 1 million DVD players.

How has the real exchange rate changed? Has it changed in the same way as the nominal exchange rate? We could answer these questions by calculating a real exchange rate in terms of each of the currencies in Fig. 1. But there is a more efficient way of measuring the real exchange rate. Instead of looking at the exchange rates between many different currencies, we can look at an average of the exchange rates against all the currencies in which the United States trades.

Trade-Weighted Index

The average exchange rate of the U.S. dollar against other currencies, with individual currencies weighted by their importance in U.S. international trade, is called the **trade-weighted index**. The trade-weighted index of major currencies is an index based on the currencies of Europe, Australia, Canada, Japan, Sweden, Switzerland, and the United Kingdom.

This index started in 1973, and it is defined to be 100 in that year. So the index tells us the value of the U.S. dollar against these currencies as a percentage of its 1973 value.

The blue line in Fig. 2 shows the nominal trade-weighted index since 1995. The index shows that the dollar appreciated from 1995 through 2000 and then started to depreciate in 2001. The grey line in Fig. 2 shows the real trade-weighted index. You can see that the nominal and real exchange rates moved in the same direction. But the nominal exchange rate appreciated less and depreciated more than the real exchange rate. The gap between the real exchange rate and the nominal exchange rate arises because the inflation rate in the rest of the world is below the U.S. inflation rate.

Questions about the Exchange Rate

The performance of the U.S. dollar in the foreign exchange market raises a number of questions that we address in the rest of this reading.

First, how are the nominal exchange rate and real exchange rate determined? Why did the dollar appreciate during the 1990s and depreciate during

FIGURE 2   The Trade-Weighted Index

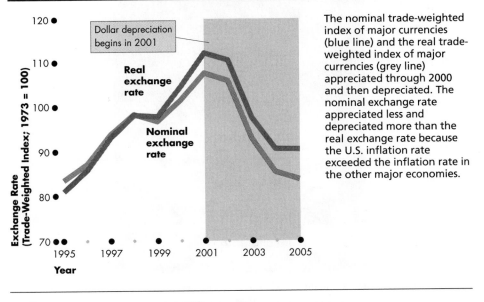

The nominal trade-weighted index of major currencies (blue line) and the real trade-weighted index of major currencies (grey line) appreciated through 2000 and then depreciated. The nominal exchange rate appreciated less and depreciated more than the real exchange rate because the U.S. inflation rate exceeded the inflation rate in the other major economies.

Source: Economic Report of the President, 2006.

the 2000s? And why did the dollar appreciate against the Mexican peso but depreciate against other currencies?

Second, how do exchange rate fluctuations influence our international trade and international payments? In particular, could we eliminate, or at least decrease, our international deficit by changing the exchange rate?

Third, how do the Fed and other central banks operate in the foreign exchange market? In particular, how was the exchange rate between the U.S. dollar and the Chinese yuan fixed and why did it remain constant for many years? Would an appreciation of the yuan change the balance of trade and payments between the United States and China?

We begin by learning how trading in the foreign exchange market determines the exchange rate.

THE FOREIGN EXCHANGE MARKET

An exchange rate is a price—the price of one currency in terms of another. And like all prices, an exchange rate is determined in a market—the foreign exchange market.

The U.S. dollar trades in the foreign exchange market and is supplied and demanded by tens of thousands of traders every hour of every business day. Because it has many traders and no restrictions on who may trade, the foreign exchange market is a *competitive market*.

In a competitive market, demand and supply determine the price. So to understand the forces that determine the exchange rate, we need to study the factors that influence demand and supply in the foreign exchange market. But there is a feature of the foreign exchange market that makes it special.

Dealers in the foreign exchange market.
Courtesy of AP Images/Katsumi Kasahara

The Demand for One Money Is the Supply of Another Money

When people who are holding the money of some other country want to exchange it for U.S. dollars, they demand U.S. dollars and supply that other country's money. And when people who are holding U.S. dollars want to exchange them for the money of some other country, they supply U.S. dollars and demand that other country's money.

So the factors that influence the demand for U.S. dollars also influence the supply of European Union euros, Canadian dollars, or Japanese yen. And the factors that influence the demand for that other country's money also influence the supply of U.S. dollars.

We'll first look at the influences on the demand for U.S. dollars in the foreign exchange market.

Demand in the Foreign Exchange Market

People buy U.S. dollars in the foreign exchange market so that they can buy U.S.-produced goods and services—U.S. exports. They also buy U.S. dollars so that they can buy U.S. assets such as bonds, stocks, businesses, and real estate or so that they can keep part of their money holding in a U.S. dollar bank account.

The quantity of U.S. dollars demanded in the foreign exchange market is the amount that traders plan to buy during a given time period at a given exchange rate. This quantity depends on many factors, but the main ones are

1. The exchange rate
2. World demand for U.S. exports
3. Interest rates in the United States and other countries
4. The expected future exchange rate

So that we can first isolate the exchange rate and see how it is determined, we'll look first at the relationship between the quantity of U.S. dollars demanded in the foreign exchange market and the exchange rate when the other three influences remain the same—the law of demand in the foreign exchange market. In the next section, we'll consider what happens when these other influences change.

The Law of Demand for Foreign Exchange

The law of demand applies to U.S. dollars just as it does to anything else that people value. Other things remaining the same, the higher the exchange rate, the smaller is the quantity of U.S. dollars demanded in the foreign exchange market. For example, if the price of the U.S. dollar rises from 100 yen to 120 yen but nothing else changes, the quantity of U.S. dollars that people plan to buy in the foreign exchange market decreases. The exchange rate influences the quantity of U.S. dollars demanded for two reasons:

► Exports effect
► Expected profit effect

Exports Effect

The larger the value of U.S. exports, the larger is the quantity of U.S. dollars demanded in the foreign exchange market. But the value of U.S. exports depends on the prices of U.S.-produced goods and services *expressed in the currency of the foreign buyer.* And these prices depend on the exchange rate. The lower the exchange rate, other things remaining the same, the lower are the prices of U.S.-produced goods and services to foreigners and the greater is the volume of U.S. exports. So if the exchange rate falls (and other influences remain the same), the quantity of U.S. dollars demanded in the foreign exchange market increases.

To see this effect at work, think about orders for Boeing's new 787 airplane. If the price of a 787 is $100 million and the exchange rate is 90 euro cents per U.S. dollar, the price of this airplane to KLM, a European airline, is €90,000,000. KLM decides that this price is too high, so it doesn't buy a new 787. If the exchange rate falls to 80 euro cents per U.S. dollar and other things remain the same, the price of a 787 now falls to €80,000,000. KLM now decides to buy a 787 and buys U.S. dollars in the foreign exchange market.

Expected Profit Effect

The larger the expected profit from holding U.S. dollars, the greater is the quantity of U.S. dollars demanded in the foreign exchange market. But expected profit depends on the exchange rate. For a given expected future exchange rate, the lower the exchange rate today, the larger is the expected profit from buying U.S. dollars today and holding them, so the greater is the quantity of U.S. dollars demanded in the foreign exchange market today.

To see this effect at work, suppose that Mizuho Bank, a Japanese bank, expects the exchange rate to be 120 yen per U.S. dollar at the end of the year. If today's exchange rate is also 120 yen per U.S. dollar, Mizuho Bank expects no profit from buying U.S. dollars and holding them until the end of the year. But if the exchange rate is 100 yen per U.S. dollar and Mizuho Bank buys U.S. dollars, it expects to sell those dollars at the end of the year for 120 yen per dollar and make a profit of 20 yen per U.S. dollar.

The lower the exchange rate today, other things remaining the same, the greater is the expected profit from holding U.S. dollars and the greater is the quantity of U.S. dollars demanded in the foreign exchange market today.

Demand Curve for U.S. Dollars

Figure 3 shows the demand curve for U.S. dollars in the foreign exchange market. A change in the exchange rate, other things remaining the same, brings a change in the quantity of U.S. dollars demanded and a movement along the demand curve as shown by the arrows.

We will look at the factors that change demand in the next section of this reading. But first, let's see what determines the supply of U.S. dollars.

Supply in the Foreign Exchange Market

People sell U.S. dollars and buy other currencies so that they can buy foreign-produced goods and services—U.S. imports. People also sell U.S. dollars and buy foreign currencies so that they can buy foreign assets such as bonds, stocks, businesses, and real estate or so that they can hold part of their money in bank deposits denominated in a foreign currency.

FIGURE 3 The Demand for U.S. Dollars

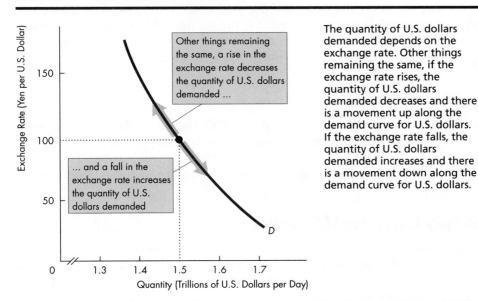

Other things remaining the same, a rise in the exchange rate decreases the quantity of U.S. dollars demanded ...

... and a fall in the exchange rate increases the quantity of U.S. dollars demanded

The quantity of U.S. dollars demanded depends on the exchange rate. Other things remaining the same, if the exchange rate rises, the quantity of U.S. dollars demanded decreases and there is a movement up along the demand curve for U.S. dollars. If the exchange rate falls, the quantity of U.S. dollars demanded increases and there is a movement down along the demand curve for U.S. dollars.

The quantity of U.S. dollars supplied in the foreign exchange market is the amount that traders plan to sell during a given time period at a given exchange rate. This quantity depends on many factors, but the main ones are

1. The exchange rate

2. U.S. demand for imports

3. Interest rates in the United States and other countries

4. The expected future exchange rate

Let's look at the relationship between the quantity of U.S. dollars supplied in the foreign exchange market and the exchange rate when the other three influences remain the same—the law of supply in the foreign exchange market.

The Law of Supply of Foreign Exchange

Other things remaining the same, the higher the exchange rate, the greater is the quantity of U.S. dollars supplied in the foreign exchange market. For example, if the exchange rate rises from 100 yen to 120 yen per U.S. dollar and other things remain the same, the quantity of U.S. dollars that people plan to sell in the foreign exchange market increases.

The exchange rate influences the quantity of dollars supplied for two reasons:

▶ Imports effect

▶ Expected profit effect

Imports Effect

The larger the value of U.S. imports, the larger is the quantity of U.S. dollars supplied in the foreign exchange market. But the value of U.S. imports depends on the prices of foreign-produced goods and services *expressed in U.S. dollars.* These prices depend on the exchange rate. The higher the exchange rate, other things remaining the same, the lower are the prices of foreign-produced goods and services to Americans and the greater is the volume of U.S. imports. So if the exchange rate rises (and other influences remain the same), the quantity of U.S. dollars supplied in the foreign exchange market increases.

Expected Profit Effect

This effect works just like that on the demand for the U.S. dollar but in the opposite direction. The higher the exchange rate today, other things remaining the same, the larger is the expected profit from selling U.S. dollars today and holding foreign currencies, so the greater is the quantity of U.S. dollars supplied.

Supply Curve for U.S. Dollars

Figure 4 shows the supply curve of U.S. dollars in the foreign exchange market. A change in the exchange rate, other things remaining the same, brings a change in the quantity of U.S. dollars supplied and a movement along the supply curve as shown by the arrows.

FIGURE 4   The Supply of U.S. Dollars

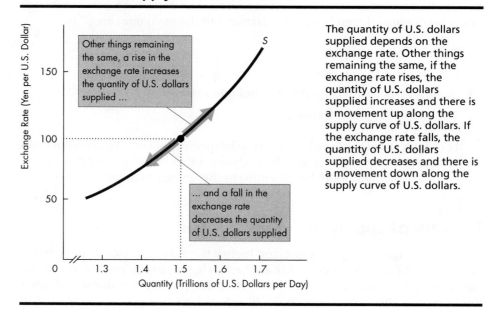

The quantity of U.S. dollars supplied depends on the exchange rate. Other things remaining the same, if the exchange rate rises, the quantity of U.S. dollars supplied increases and there is a movement up along the supply curve of U.S. dollars. If the exchange rate falls, the quantity of U.S. dollars supplied decreases and there is a movement down along the supply curve of U.S. dollars.

Market Equilibrium

Equilibrium in the foreign exchange market depends on how the Federal Reserve and other central banks operate. Here, we will study equilibrium when central banks keep out of this market. In a later section, we examine the effects of alternative actions that the Fed or another central bank might take in the foreign exchange market.

Figure 5 shows the demand curve for U.S. dollars, *D*, from Fig. 3 and the supply curve of U.S. dollars, *S*, from Fig. 4, and the equilibrium exchange rate.

FIGURE 5 Equilibrium Exchange Rate

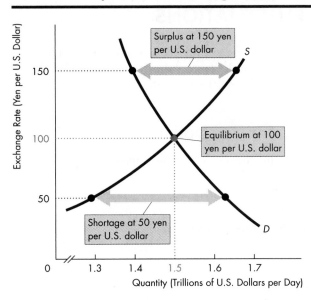

The demand curve for U.S. dollars is *D*, and the supply curve of U.S. dollars is *S*. If the exchange rate is 150 yen per U.S. dollar, there is a surplus of U.S. dollars and the exchange rate falls. If the exchange rate is 50 yen per U.S. dollar, there is a shortage of U.S. dollars and the exchange rate rises. If the exchange rate is 100 yen per dollar, there is neither a shortage nor a surplus of U.S. dollars and the exchange rate remains constant. The foreign exchange market is in equilibrium.

The exchange rate acts as a regulator of the quantities demanded and supplied. If the exchange rate is too high, there is a surplus—the quantity supplied exceeds the quantity demanded. For example, in Fig. 5, if the exchange rate is 150 yen per U.S. dollar, there is a surplus of U.S. dollars. If the exchange rate is too low, there is a shortage—the quantity supplied is less than the quantity demanded. For example, if the exchange rate is 50 yen per U.S. dollar, there is a shortage of U.S. dollars.

At the equilibrium exchange rate, there is neither a shortage nor a surplus. The quantity supplied equals the quantity demanded. In Fig. 5, the equilibrium exchange rate is 100 yen per U.S. dollar. At this exchange rate, the quantity demanded and the quantity supplied are each $1.5 trillion a day.

The foreign exchange market is constantly pulled to its equilibrium by the forces of supply and demand. Foreign exchange dealers are constantly looking for the best price they can get. If they are selling, they want the highest price available. If they are buying, they want the lowest price available. Information flows from dealer to dealer through the worldwide computer network, and the price adjusts minute by minute to keep buying plans and selling plans in balance. That is, the price adjusts minute by minute to keep the exchange rate at its equilibrium.

Figure 5 shows how the exchange rate between the U.S. dollar and the Japanese yen is determined. The exchange rates between the U.S. dollar and all other currencies are determined in a similar way. So are the exchange rates among the other currencies. But the exchange rates are tied together so that no profit can be made by buying one currency, selling it for a second one, and then buying back the first one. If such a profit were available, traders would spot it, demand and supply would change, and the exchange rates would snap into alignment.

4 ## CHANGES IN DEMAND AND SUPPLY: EXCHANGE RATE FLUCTUATIONS

When the demand for U.S. dollars or the supply of U.S. dollars changes, the exchange rate changes. We'll now look at the factors that make demand and supply change, starting with the demand side of the market.

Changes in the Demand for U.S. Dollars

The demand for U.S. dollars in the foreign exchange market changes when there is a change in

▶ World demand for U.S. exports
▶ U.S. interest rate relative to the foreign interest rate
▶ The expected future exchange rate

World Demand for U.S. Exports

An increase in world demand for U.S. exports increases the demand for U.S. dollars. To see this effect, think about Boeing's airplane sales. An increase in demand for air travel in Australia sends that country's airlines on a global shopping spree. They decide that the 787 is the ideal product, so they order 50 airplanes from Boeing. The demand for U.S. dollars now increases.

U.S. Interest Rate Relative to the Foreign Interest Rate

People and businesses buy financial assets to make a return. The higher the interest rate that people can make on U.S. assets compared with foreign assets, the more U.S. assets they buy.

What matters is not the *level* of the U.S. interest rate, but the U.S. interest rate minus the foreign interest rate—a gap that is called the **U.S. interest rate differential**. If the U.S. interest rate rises and the foreign interest rate remains constant, the U.S. interest rate differential increases. The larger the U.S. interest rate differential, the greater is the demand for U.S. assets and the greater is the demand for U.S. dollars in the foreign exchange market.

The Expected Future Exchange Rate

For a given current exchange rate, other things remaining the same, a rise in the expected future exchange rate increases the profit that people expect to earn by holding U.S. dollars and increases the demand for U.S. dollars today.

Figure 6 summarizes the influences on the demand for U.S. dollars. An increase in the demand for U.S. exports, a rise in the U.S. interest rate differential, or a rise in the expected future exchange rate increases the demand for U.S. dollars today and shifts the demand curve rightward from D_0 to D_1. A decrease in the demand for U.S. exports, a fall in the U.S. interest rate differential, or a fall in the expected future exchange rate decreases the demand for U.S. dollars today and shifts the demand curve leftward from D_0 to D_2.

FIGURE 6 Changes in the Demand for U.S. Dollars

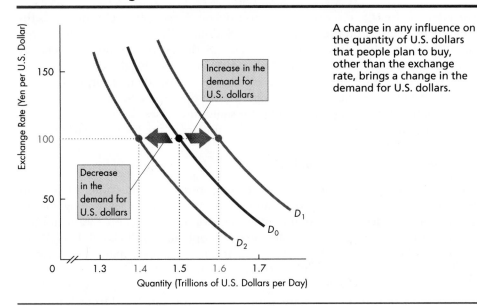

A change in any influence on the quantity of U.S. dollars that people plan to buy, other than the exchange rate, brings a change in the demand for U.S. dollars.

The Demand for U.S. Dollars

Increases if:	*Decreases if:*
► World demand for U.S. exports increases	► World demand for U.S. exports decreases
► The U.S. interest rate differential rises	► The U.S. interest rate differential falls
► The expected future exchange rate rises	► The expected future exchange rate falls

Changes in the Supply of U.S. Dollars

The supply of U.S. dollars in the foreign exchange market changes when there is a change in

► U.S. demand for imports
► U.S. interest rate relative to the foreign interest rate
► The expected future exchange rate

U.S. Demand for Imports

An increase in U.S. demand for imports increases the supply of U.S. dollars in the foreign exchange market. To see why, think about Wal-Mart's purchase of DVD players. An increase in the demand for DVD players sends Wal-Mart out on a global shopping spree. Wal-Mart decides that Panasonic DVD players produced in Japan are the best buy, so Wal-Mart increases its purchases of these players. The supply of U.S. dollars now increases as Wal-Mart goes to the foreign exchange market for Japanese yen to pay Panasonic.

U.S. Interest Rate Relative to the Foreign Interest Rate

The effect of the U.S. interest rate differential on the supply of U.S. dollars is the opposite of its effect on the demand for U.S. dollars. The larger the U.S. interest rate differential, the *smaller* is the supply of U.S. dollars in the foreign exchange market. The supply of U.S. dollars is smaller because the demand for *foreign* assets is smaller. If people spend less on foreign assets, the quantity of U.S. dollars they supply in the foreign exchange market decreases. So, a rise in the U.S. interest rate, other things remaining the same, increases the U.S. interest rate differential and decreases the supply of U.S. dollars in the foreign market.

The Expected Future Exchange Rate

For a given current exchange rate, other things remaining the same, a fall in the expected future exchange rate decreases the profit that can be earned by holding U.S. dollars and decreases the quantity of U.S. dollars that people want to hold. To lower their holdings of U.S. dollar assets, people must sell U.S. dollars. When they do so, the supply of U.S. dollars in the foreign exchange market increases.

Figure 7 summarizes the influences on the supply of U.S. dollars. If the supply of U.S. dollars decreases, the supply curve shifts leftward from S_0 to S_1. And if the supply of U.S. dollars increases, the supply curve shifts rightward from S_0 to S_2.

FIGURE 7   Changes in the Supply of U.S. Dollars

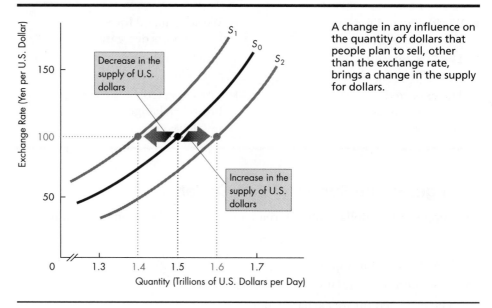

A change in any influence on the quantity of dollars that people plan to sell, other than the exchange rate, brings a change in the supply for dollars.

The Supply of U.S. Dollars

Increases if:	Decreases if:
▶ U.S. import demand increases	▶ U.S. import demand decreases
▶ The U.S. interest rate differential falls	▶ The U.S. interest rate differential rises
▶ The expected future exchange rate falls	▶ The expected future exchange rate rises

Changes in the Exchange Rate

If the demand for U.S. dollars increases and the supply does not change, the exchange rate rises. If the demand for U.S. dollars decreases and the supply does not change, the exchange rate falls. Similarly, if the supply of U.S. dollars decreases and the demand does not change, the exchange rate rises. If the supply of U.S. dollars increases and the demand does not change, the exchange rate falls.

These predictions are exactly the same as those for any other market. Let's now look at two episodes in the life of the U.S. dollar.

An Appreciating U.S. Dollar: 2000–2002

Between 2000 and 2002, the U.S. dollar appreciated against the yen. It rose from 108 yen to 127 yen per U.S. dollar. Figure 8(a) provides a possible explanation for this appreciation.

FIGURE 8   Exchange Rate Fluctuations

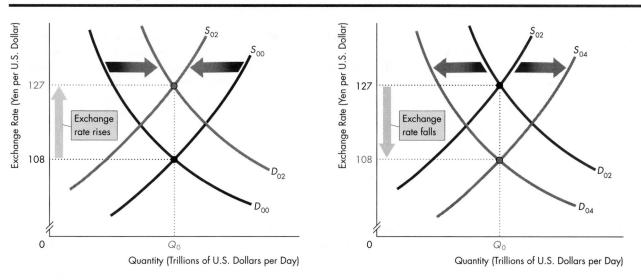

(a) 2000 to 2002   **(b) 2002 to 2004**

Between 2000 and 2002 (in part a), investors expected higher profits in the United States than in Japan and currency traders expected the U.S. dollar to appreciate. The demand for U.S. dollars increased, the supply of U.S. dollars decreased, and the U.S. dollar appreciated.

Between 2002 and 2004 (in part b), investors began to expect higher profits in Japan and currency traders expected the U.S. dollar to depreciate. The demand for U.S. dollars decreased, the supply of U.S. dollars increased, and the U.S. dollar depreciated.

In 2000, the demand and supply curves were those labeled D_{00} and S_{00}. The exchange rate was 108 yen per U.S. dollar.

During 2001, real GDP growth slowed in both the United States and Japan. But growth slowed by more in Japan. International investors believed that they would make a bigger profit from U.S. assets than from Japanese assets. So funds flowed into the United States. Also, currency traders, aware of these profit assessments, expected the dollar to appreciate against the yen. The demand for U.S. dollars increased, and the supply of U.S. dollars decreased.

In Fig. 8(a), the demand curve shifted rightward from D_{00} to D_{02} and the supply curve shifted leftward from S_{00} to S_{02}. The exchange rate rose to 127 yen per U.S. dollar. In the figure, the equilibrium quantity remained unchanged—an assumption.

A Depreciating U.S. Dollar: 2002–2004

Between 2002 and 2004, the U.S. dollar depreciated against the yen. It fell from 127 yen to 108 yen per U.S. dollar. Figure 8(b) provides a possible explanation for this depreciation.

In 2002, the demand and supply curves were those labeled D_{02} and S_{02}. The exchange rate was 127 yen per U.S. dollar.

During 2003, real GDP growth remained low in the United States but increased in Japan. Investors gradually changed their views about the profit they could earn from U.S. assets and Japanese assets and saw increasing profits in Japan. Also, the U.S. interest rate differential narrowed as the U.S. interest rate fell. Funds flowed into Japan. And assessing this situation, currency traders expected the U.S. dollar to depreciate against the yen. The demand for U.S. dollars decreased and the supply of U.S. dollars increased.

In Fig. 8(b), the demand curve shifted leftward from D_{02} to D_{04}, the supply curve shifted rightward from S_{02} to S_{04}, and the exchange rate fell to 108 yen per dollar.

Exchange Rate Expectations

The changes in the exchange rate that we've just examined occurred in part because the exchange rate was *expected to change*. This explanation sounds a bit like a self-fulfilling prophecy. So what makes expectations change? The answer is new information about the deeper forces that influence the value of one money relative to the value of another money. There are two such forces:

► Interest rate parity
► Purchasing power parity

Interest Rate Parity

One definition of what money is worth is what it can earn. Two kinds of money—U.S. dollars and Japanese yen, for example—might earn different amounts. For example, suppose a yen bank deposit in Tokyo earns 1 percent a year and a U.S. dollar bank deposit in New York earns 3 percent a year. In this situation, why does anyone deposit money in Tokyo? Why doesn't all the money flow to New York? The answer is because of exchange rate expectations. Suppose people expect the yen to appreciate by 2 percent a year. American investors expect that if they buy and hold yen for a year, they will earn 1 percent interest and 2 percent from the higher yen (lower dollar) to give a total return of 3 percent. So the interest rate in terms of U.S. dollars is the same in Tokyo and New York. This situation is one of **interest rate parity**, which means equal rates of return.

Adjusted for risk, interest rate parity always prevails. Funds move to get the highest return available. If for a few seconds a higher return is available in New York than in Tokyo, the demand for U.S. dollars increases and the exchange rate rises until expected rates of return are equal.

Purchasing Power Parity

Another definition of what money is worth is what it will buy. But two kinds of money—U.S. dollars and Japanese yen, for example—might buy different amounts of goods and services. Suppose a memory stick costs 5,000 yen in Tokyo and $50 in New York. If the exchange rate is 100 yen per dollar, the two monies have the same value. You can buy a memory stick in either Tokyo or New York for the same price. You can express that price as either 5,000 yen or $50, but the price is the same in the two currencies.

The situation we've just described is called **purchasing power parity**, which means *equal value of money*. If purchasing power parity does not prevail, some powerful forces go to work. To understand these forces, let's suppose that the price of a memory stick in New York rises to $60, but in Tokyo it remains at 5,000 yen. Further, suppose the exchange rate remains at 100 yen per dollar. In this case, a memory stick in Tokyo still costs 5,000 yen or $50. But in New York, it costs $60 or 6,000 yen. Money buys more in Japan than in the United States. Money is not of equal value in the two countries.

If all (or most) prices have increased in the United States and not increased in Japan, then people will generally expect that the value of the U.S. dollar in the foreign exchange market must fall. In this situation, the exchange rate is expected to fall. The demand for U.S. dollars decreases, and the supply of U.S. dollars increases. The exchange rate falls, as expected. If the exchange rate falls to 83.33 yen per dollar and there are no further price changes, purchasing power parity is restored. A memory stick that costs $60 in New York also costs the equivalent of $60 ($60 \times 83.33 = 5,000$) in Tokyo.

If prices increase in Japan and other countries but remain constant in the United States, then people will generally expect that the value of the U.S. dollar in the foreign exchange market is too low and that it is going to rise. In this situation, the exchange rate is expected to rise. The demand for U.S. dollars increases, and the supply of U.S. dollars decreases. The exchange rate rises, as expected.

Instant Exchange Rate Response

The exchange rate responds instantly to news about changes in the variables that influence demand and supply in the foreign exchange market. You can see why the response is immediate by thinking about the expected profit opportunities that such news creates.

Suppose that the Bank of Japan is reported to be considering raising the interest rate next week. If this move is regarded as likely, then traders expect the demand for yen to increase and the demand for dollars to decrease. They also expect the yen to appreciate and the dollar to depreciate.

But to benefit from a yen appreciation and to avoid the loss from a dollar depreciation, yen must be bought and dollars must be sold *before* the exchange rate changes. Each trader knows that all the other traders share the same information and have similar expectations. And each trader knows that when people begin to sell dollars and buy yen, the exchange rate will change. To transact before the exchange rate changes means transacting right away, as soon as the information that changes expectations is received.

The Nominal and Real Exchange Rates in the Short Run and in the Long Run

Earlier in this reading, we distinguished between the nominal exchange rate and the real exchange rate. So far we've explained only how the nominal exchange rate is determined. And we've focused on the day-to-day fluctuations in the nominal exchange rate. We're going to turn now to the real exchange rate and explain how it is determined. We're also going to distinguish between the short run and the long run.

Recall the equation that links the nominal and real exchange rates. That equation is

$$RER = E \times (P/P^*),$$

where *P* is the U.S. price level, *P** is the Japanese price level, *E* is the nominal exchange rate (yen per U.S. dollar), and *RER* is the real exchange rate (the quantity of Japanese real GDP per unit of U.S. real GDP).

In the short run, this equation determines the real exchange rate. The price levels in the United States and Japan don't change every time the nominal exchange rate changes. So a change in *E* brings an equivalent change in *RER*.

But in the long run, the situation is radically different. The classical dichotomy holds in the foreign exchange market just as it does in other markets. In the long run, the real exchange rate is determined by demand and supply in the markets for goods and services. If Japan and the United States produced identical goods (if GDP in both countries consisted only of memory sticks for example), purchasing power parity would make the real exchange rate equal 1. One Japanese memory stick would exchange for one U.S. memory stick. In reality, although there is overlap in what each country produces, U.S. real GDP is a different bundle of goods and services from Japanese real GDP. So the relative price of Japanese and U.S. real GDP—the real exchange rate—is not 1 and it fluctuates. But the forces of demand and supply in the markets for the millions of goods and services that make up real GDP determine these relative prices.

In the long run, with the real exchange rate determined by the real forces of demand and supply in markets for goods and services, the above equation must be turned around to determine the nominal exchange rate. That is, the nominal exchange rate is

$$E = RER \times (P^*/P).$$

This equation tells us that in the long run, the nominal exchange rate is determined by the equilibrium real exchange rate and the price levels in the two countries. A rise in the Japanese price level, *P**, brings dollar appreciation—a rise in *E*; and a rise in the U.S. price level, *P*, brings dollar depreciation—a fall in *E*.

In the long run, the quantity of money determines the price level. But the quantity theory of money applies to all countries. So the quantity of money in Japan determines the price level in Japan, and the quantity of money in the United States determines the price level in the United States.

A nominal exchange rate, then, in the long run, is a monetary phenomenon. It is determined by the quantities of money in two countries.

The long-run forces that we've just described explain the broad trends in exchange rates. For example, the U.S dollar has generally appreciated against the Mexican peso because Mexico has created money at a faster pace than has the United States and the price level in Mexico has risen more rapidly than the U.S. price level. The U.S. dollar has been depreciating since 2002 because U.S. prices have been rising faster, on the average, than European, Canadian, and Japanese prices.

5   FINANCING INTERNATIONAL TRADE

You have seen how the exchange rate is determined. But what is the effect of the exchange rate? How does currency depreciation or currency appreciation influence our international trade and payments? We're going to lay the foundation for addressing these questions by looking at the scale of international trading, borrowing, and lending and at the way in which we keep our records of international transactions. These records are called the balance of payments accounts.

Balance of Payments Accounts

A country's **balance of payments accounts** records its international trading, borrowing, and lending in three accounts:

1. Current account

2. Capital account

3. Official settlements account

The **current account** records receipts from exports of goods and services sold abroad, payments for imports of goods and services from abroad, net interest income paid abroad, and net transfers (such as foreign aid payments). The *current account balance* equals the sum of exports minus imports, net interest income, and net transfers.

The **capital account** records foreign investment in the United States minus U.S. investment abroad. (This account also has a statistical discrepancy that arises from errors and omissions in measuring capital transactions.)

The **official settlements account** records the change in **U.S. official reserves**, which are the government's holdings of foreign currency. If U.S. official reserves *increase*, the official settlements account balance is *negative*. The reason is that holding foreign money is like investing abroad. U.S. investment abroad is a minus item in the capital account and in the official settlements account.

The sum of the balances on the three accounts always equals zero. That is, to pay for our current account deficit, either we must borrow more from abroad than we lend abroad or our official reserves must decrease to cover the shortfall.

Table 1 shows the U.S. balance of payments accounts in 2005. Items in the current account and capital account that provide foreign currency to the United

TABLE 1   U.S. Balance of Payments Accounts in 2005

Current Account	Billions of Dollars
Exports of goods and services	+1,275
Imports of goods and services	−1,992
Net interest income	+11
Net transfers	−86
Current account balance	−792

Capital Account	
Foreign investment in the United States	+1,212
U.S. investment abroad	−444
Statistical discrepancy	10
Capital account balance	+778

Official Settlements Account	
Official settlements account balance	14

Source: Bureau of Economic Analysis.

States have a plus sign; items that cost the United States foreign currency have a minus sign. The table shows that in 2005, U.S. imports exceeded U.S. exports and the current account had a deficit of $792 billion. How do we pay for imports that exceed the value of our exports? That is, how do we pay for our current account deficit?

We pay by borrowing from the rest of the world. The capital account tells us by how much. We borrowed $1,212 billion (foreign investment in the United States) but made loans of $444 billion (U.S. investment abroad). Our *net* foreign borrowing was $1,212 billion minus $444 billion, which equals $768 billion. There is almost always a statistical discrepancy between our capital account and current account transactions, and in 2005, the discrepancy was $10 billion. Combining the discrepancy with the measured net foreign borrowing gives a capital account balance of $778 billion.

Our capital account balance plus our current account balance equals the change in U.S. official reserves. In 2005, our capital account balance of $778 billion plus our current balance of –$792 billion equaled –$14 billion. Our official reserves *decreased* in 2005 by $14 billion. This amount appears in Table 1 as +$14 billion. When our reserves *decrease*, we record this as a positive number in our international accounts because a decrease in our reserves is like borrowing from the rest of the world—the government decreases its deposits in foreign central banks.

The numbers in Table 1 give a snapshot of the balance of payments accounts in 2005. Figure 9 puts that snapshot into perspective by showing the balance of payments between 1980 and 2005. Because the economy grows and the price level rises, changes in the dollar value of the balance of payments do not convey much information. To remove the influences of growth and inflation, Fig. 9 shows the balance of payments as a percentage of nominal GDP.

FIGURE 9   The Balance of Payments: 1980–2005

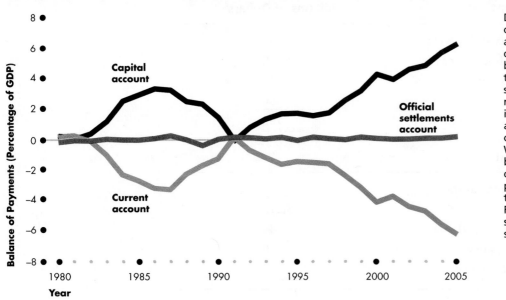

During the 1980s, a large current account deficit arose. That deficit decreased in the late 1980s but increased again through 2000, decreased slightly in the 2001 recession, and then increased again. The capital account balance mirrors the current account balance. When the current account balance is negative, the capital account balance is positive—we borrow from the rest of the world. Fluctuations in the official settlements balance are small.

Source: Bureau of Economic Analysis.

As you can see, the capital account balance is almost a mirror image of the current account balance. The official settlements balance is very small in comparison with the balances on these other two accounts. A large current account deficit (and capital account surplus) emerged during the 1980s but declined from 1987 to 1991. The current account deficit then increased every year through 2000, decreased slightly in 2001, and then increased again.

To see more clearly what the nation's balance of payments accounts mean, think about your own balance of payments accounts.

An Individual's Balance of Payments Accounts

An individual's current account records the income from supplying the services of factors of production and the expenditure on goods and services. Consider Jackie, for example. She worked in 2005 and earned an income of $25,000. Jackie has $10,000 worth of investments that earned her an interest income of $1,000. Jackie's current account shows an income of $26,000. Jackie spent $18,000 buying goods and services for consumption. She also bought a new house, which cost her $60,000. So Jackie's total expenditure was $78,000. Jackie's expenditure minus her income is $52,000 ($78,000 minus $26,000). This amount is Jackie's current account deficit.

To pay for expenditure of $52,000 in excess of her income, Jackie must either use the money that she has in the bank or take out a loan. Suppose that Jackie took out a loan of $50,000 to help buy her house and that this loan was the only borrowing that she did. Borrowing is an *inflow* in the capital account, so Jackie's capital account *surplus* was $50,000. With a current account deficit of $52,000 and a capital account surplus of $50,000, Jackie was still $2,000 short. She got that $2,000 from her own bank account. Her cash holdings decreased by $2,000.

Jackie's income from her work is like a country's income from its exports. Her income from her investments is like a country's interest income from foreigners. Her purchases of goods and services, including her purchase of a house, are like a country's imports. Jackie's loan—borrowing from someone else—is like a country's borrowing from the rest of the world. The change in Jackie's bank account is like the change in the country's official reserves.

Borrowers and Lenders

A country that is borrowing more from the rest of the world than it is lending to the rest of the world is called a **net borrower**. Similarly, a **net lender** is a country that is lending more to the rest of the world than it is borrowing from the rest of the world.

The United States is a net borrower, but it has not always been in this situation. Throughout the 1960s and most of the 1970s, the United States was a net lender to the rest of the world—the United States had a current account surplus and a capital account deficit. But from the early 1980s, with the exception of only a single year, 1991, the United States has been a net borrower from the rest of the world. And during the years since 1992, the scale of U.S. borrowing has mushroomed.

Most countries are net borrowers like the United States. But a few countries, including China, Japan, and oil-rich Saudi Arabia, are net lenders. In 2005, when the United States borrowed almost $800 billion from the rest of the world, these three countries lent $400 billion. China alone lent $160 billion.

Debtors and Creditors

A net borrower might be decreasing its net assets held in the rest of the world, or it might be going deeper into debt. A nation's total stock of foreign investment determines whether it is a debtor or creditor. A **debtor nation** is a country that during its entire history has borrowed more from the rest of the world than it has lent to it. It has a stock of outstanding debt to the rest of the world that exceeds the stock of its own claims on the rest of the world. A **creditor nation** is a country that during its entire history has invested more in the rest of the world than other countries have invested in it.

The United States was a debtor nation through the nineteenth century as we borrowed from Europe to finance our westward expansion, railroads, and industrialization. We paid off our debt and became a creditor nation for most of the twentieth century. But following a string of current account deficits, we became a debtor nation again in 1986.

Since 1986, the total stock of U.S. borrowing from the rest of the world has exceeded U.S. lending to the rest of the world. The largest debtor nations are the capital-hungry developing countries (such as the United States was during the nineteenth century). The international debt of these countries grew from less than a third to more than a half of their gross domestic product during the 1980s and created what was called the "Third World debt crisis."

Should we be concerned that the United States is a net borrower and a debtor? The answer to this question depends mainly on what the net borrower is doing with the borrowed money. If borrowing is financing investment that in turn is generating economic growth and higher income, borrowing is not a problem. It earns a return that more than pays the interest. But if borrowed money is used to finance consumption, to pay the interest and repay the loan, consumption will eventually have to be reduced. In this case, the more the borrowing and the longer it goes on, the greater is the reduction in consumption that will eventually be necessary.

Is U.S. Borrowing for Consumption?

In 2005, we borrowed almost $800 billion from abroad. In that year, private investment in buildings, plant, and equipment was $2,270 billion and government investment in defense equipment and social projects was $430 billion. All this investment added to the nation's capital, and much of it increased productivity. Government also spends on education and health care services, which increase *human capital*. Our international borrowing is financing private and public investment, not consumption.

Current Account Balance

What determines a country's current account balance and net foreign borrowing? You've seen that net exports (NX) is the main item in the current account. We can define the current account balance (CAB) as

$$CAB = NX + \text{Net interest income} + \text{Net transfers}.$$

We can study the current account balance by looking at what determines net exports because the other two items are small and do not fluctuate much.

Net Exports

Net exports are determined by the government budget and private saving and investment. To see how net exports are determined, we need to recall some of the things we know about the *National Income and Product Accounts*. Table 2 will refresh your memory and summarize some calculations.

TABLE 2 Net Exports, the Government Budget, Saving, and Investment

	Symbols and Equations	United States in 2006 (Billions of Dollars)
(a) Variables		
Exports*	X	1,395
Imports*	M	2,179
Government expenditures	G	2,474
Net taxes	T	2,161
Investment	I	2,270
Saving	S	1,799
(b) Balances		
Net exports	$X - M$	$1,395 - 2,179 = -784$
Government sector	$T - G$	$2,161 - 2,474 = -313$
Private sector	$S - I$	$1,799 - 2,270 = -471$
(c) Relationship among Balances		
National accounts	$Y = C + I + G + X - M$ $= C + S + T$	
Rearranging:	$X - M = S - I + T - G$	
Net exports equals:	$X - M$	-784
Government sector plus	$T - G$	-313
Private sector	$S - I$	-471

* The *National Income and Product Accounts* measures of exports and imports are slightly different from the balance of payments accounts measures in Table 1.

Source: Bureau of Economic Analysis. The data are for 2006, second quarter, seasonally adjusted at annual rate.

Part (a) lists the national income variables that are needed, with their symbols. Part (b) defines three balances. **Net exports** is exports of goods and services minus imports of goods and services.

The **government sector surplus or deficit** is equal to net taxes minus government expenditures on goods and services. If that number is positive, a government sector surplus is lent to other sectors; if that number is negative, a government deficit must be financed by borrowing from other sectors. The government sector deficit is the sum of the deficits of the federal, state, and local governments.

The **private sector surplus or deficit** is saving minus investment. If saving exceeds investment, a private sector surplus is lent to other sectors. If investment exceeds saving, a private sector deficit is financed by borrowing from other sectors.

Part (b) also shows the values of these balances for the United States in 2006. As you can see, net exports were –$784 billion, a deficit of $784 billion. The government sector's revenue from net taxes was $2,161 billion, and government expenditure was $2,474 billion. The government sector deficit was $313 billion. The private sector saved $1,799 billion and invested $2,270 billion, so it had a deficit of $471 billion.

Part (c) shows the relationship among the three balances. From the *National Income and Product Accounts*, we know that real GDP, Y, is the sum of consumption expenditure (C), investment, government expenditures, and net exports. It also equals the sum of consumption expenditure, saving, and net taxes. Rearranging these equations tells us that net exports is the sum of the government sector deficit and the private sector deficit. In the United States in 2006, the government sector deficit was $313 billion and the private sector deficit was $471 billion. The government sector deficit plus the private sector deficit equaled net exports of –$784 billion.

The Three Sector Balances

You've seen that net exports equal the sum of the government sector balance and the private sector balance. How do these three sector balances fluctuate over time? Figure 10 answers this question. It shows the government sector balance (the grey line), net exports (the blue line), and the private sector balance (the black line).

The private sector balance and the government sector balance move in opposite directions. When the government sector deficit increased during the late 1980s and early 1990s, the private sector surplus increased. And when the government sector deficit decreased and became a surplus during the 1990s and early 2000s, the private sector's surplus decreased and became a deficit.

Sometimes, when the government sector deficit increases, as it did during the first half of the 1980s, net exports become more negative. But after the early 1990s, net exports did not follow the government sector balance closely. Rather, net exports respond to the *sum* of the government sector and private sector balances. When both the private sector and the government sector have a deficit, net exports are negative and the combined private and government deficit is financed by borrowing from the rest of the world.

Where Is the Exchange Rate?

In explaining the current account balance, we have not mentioned the exchange rate. Doesn't the exchange rate play a role?

FIGURE 10   The Three Sector Balances

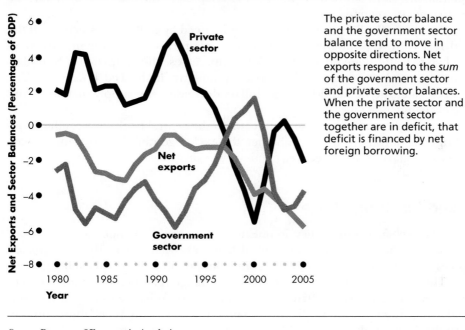

The private sector balance and the government sector balance tend to move in opposite directions. Net exports respond to the *sum* of the government sector and private sector balances. When the private sector and the government sector together are in deficit, that deficit is financed by net foreign borrowing.

Source: Bureau of Economic Analysis.

In the short run, a fall in the nominal exchange rate lowers the real exchange rate, which makes our imports more costly and our exports more competitive. A higher price of imported consumer goods might induce a decrease in consumption and an increase in saving. And a higher price of imported capital goods might induce a decrease in investment. Other things remaining the same, an increase in saving or a decrease in investment decreases the current account deficit.

But in the long run, a change in the nominal exchange rate leaves the real exchange rate and all other real variables unchanged. So in the long run, the nominal exchange rate plays no role in influencing the current account balance.

EXCHANGE RATE POLICY   6

Because the exchange rate is the price of a country's money in terms of another country's money, governments and central banks must have a policy toward the exchange rate. Three possible exchange rate policies are

► Flexible exchange rate

► Fixed exchange rate

► Crawling peg

Flexible Exchange Rate

A **flexible exchange rate** policy is one that permits the exchange rate to be determined by demand and supply with no direct intervention in the foreign exchange market by the central bank. Most countries—and the United States is among them—operate a flexible exchange rate, and the foreign exchange market that we have studied so far in this chapter is an example of a flexible exchange rate regime.

But even a flexible exchange rate is influenced by central bank actions. If the Fed raises the U.S. interest rate and other countries keep their interest rates unchanged, the demand for U.S. dollars increases, the supply of U.S. dollars decreases, and the exchange rate rises. (Similarly, if the Fed lowers the U.S. interest rate, the demand for U.S. dollars decreases, the supply increases, and the exchange rate falls.)

In a flexible exchange rate regime, when the central bank changes the interest rate, its purpose is not to influence the exchange rate. It is to achieve some other monetary policy objective.

Fixed Exchange Rate

A **fixed exchange rate** policy is one that pegs the exchange rate at a value decided by the government or central bank and that blocks the unregulated forces of demand and supply by direct intervention in the foreign exchange market. The world economy operated a fixed exchange rate regime from the end of World War II to the early 1970s. China had a fixed exchange rate until recently. And Hong Kong has had a fixed exchange rate for many years and continues with that policy today.

A fixed exchange rate requires active intervention in the foreign exchange market.

If the Fed wanted to fix the U.S. dollar exchange rate against the Japanese yen, the Fed would have to sell U.S. dollars to prevent the exchange rate from rising above the target value and buy U.S. dollars to prevent the exchange rate from falling below the target value.

There is no limit to the quantity of U.S. dollars that the Fed can *sell*. The Fed creates U.S. dollars and can create any quantity it chooses. But there is a limit to the quantity of U.S. dollars the Fed can *buy*. That limit is set by U.S. official holdings of foreign currency reserves. If reserves run dry, intervention to buy U.S. dollars would stop.

Let's look at the foreign exchange interventions that the Fed can make.

Suppose the Fed wants the exchange rate to be steady at 100 yen per U.S. dollar. If the exchange rate rises above 100 yen, the Fed sells dollars. If the exchange rate falls below 100 yen, the Fed buys dollars. By these actions, the Fed changes the supply of dollars and keeps the exchange rate close to its target rate of 100 yen per U.S dollar.

Figure 11 shows the Fed's intervention in the foreign exchange market. The supply of dollars is S and initially the demand for dollars is D_0. The equilibrium exchange rate is 100 yen per dollar. This exchange rate is also the Fed's target exchange rate, shown by the horizontal grey line.

When the demand for U.S. dollars increases and the demand curve shifts rightward to D_1, the Fed sells \$100 billion. This action increases the supply of U.S. dollars by \$100 billion and prevents the exchange rate from rising. When the demand for U.S. dollars decreases and the demand curve shifts leftward to D_2, the Fed buys \$100 billion. This action decreases the supply of U.S. dollars by \$100 billion and prevents the exchange rate from falling.

If the demand for U.S. dollars fluctuates between D_1 and D_2 and on the average is D_0, the Fed can repeatedly intervene in the way we've just seen. Sometimes the Fed buys and sometimes it sells but, on the average, it neither buys nor sells.

But suppose the demand for U.S. dollars *increases permanently* from D_0 to D_1. To maintain the exchange rate at 100 yen per U.S. dollar, the Fed must sell dol-

FIGURE 11   Foreign Exchange Market Intervention

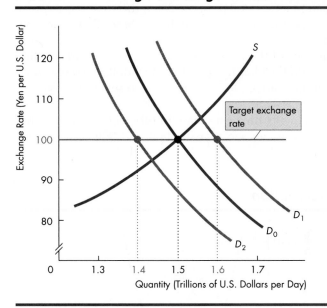

Initially, the demand for U.S. dollars is D_0, the supply of U.S. dollars is S, and the exchange rate is 100 yen per U.S. dollar. The Fed can intervene in the foreign exchange market to keep the exchange rate close to its target rate (100 yen in this example). If demand increases from D_0 to D_1, the Fed sells dollars to increase supply. If demand decreases from D_0 to D_2, the Fed buys dollars to decrease supply. Persistent intervention on one side of the market cannot be sustained.

lars and buy foreign currency, so U.S. official foreign currency reserves would be increasing. At some point, the Fed would abandon the exchange rate of 100 yen per U.S. dollar and stop piling up foreign currency reserves.

Now suppose the demand for U.S. dollars *decreases permanently* from D_0 to D_2. In this situation, the Fed cannot maintain the exchange rate at 100 yen per U.S. dollar indefinitely. To hold the exchange rate at 100 yen, the Fed must *buy* U.S. dollars. When the Fed buys U.S. dollars in the foreign exchange market, it uses U.S. official foreign currency reserves. So the Fed must decrease its foreign currency reserves. Eventually, the Fed would run out of foreign currency and would then have to abandon the 100 yen per U.S. dollar exchange rate.

Crawling Peg

A **crawling peg** exchange rate policy is one that selects a target path for the exchange rate with intervention in the foreign exchange market to achieve that path. The Fed has never operated a crawling peg. But some prominent countries do use this system. When China abandoned its fixed exchange rate, it replaced it with a crawling peg. Several other developing countries use a crawling peg.

A crawling peg works like a fixed exchange rate except that the target value changes. Sometimes the target changes once a month, and sometimes it changes every day.

The idea behind a crawling peg is to prevent fluctuating expectations from making the exchange rate fluctuate and to avoid the problems that can occur with a fixed exchange rate of running out of reserves or piling up reserves. (A crawling peg is also sometimes used to control inflation.)

The People's Bank of China in the Foreign Exchange Market

You saw in Fig. 1 that the exchange rate between the U.S. dollar and the Chinese yuan has been constant for several years. The reason for this near constant exchange rate is that China's central bank, the People's Bank of China, has intervened to operate a fixed exchange rate policy. From 1997 until 2005, the yuan was pegged at 8.28 yuan per U.S. dollar. Since 2005, the yuan has appreciated slightly but has not been permitted to fluctuate freely. Since 2005, the yuan has been on a crawling peg.

The immediate consequence of the fixed yuan exchange rate (and crawling exchange rate) is that since 2000, China has piled up U.S dollar reserves on a huge scale. By mid-2006, China's official foreign currency reserves approached $1 trillion!

Figure 12(a) shows the scale of China's increase in official foreign currency (mainly U.S. dollar) reserves. You can see that in 2004 and 2005, its reserves increased by $200 billion a year.

FIGURE 12   China's Foreign Exchange Market Intervention

(a) Increase in U.S. Dollar Reserves   **(b) Pegging the Yuan**

Part (a) shows the annual increase in China's reserves of U.S. dollars.

Part (b) shows the market for U.S. dollars in terms of the Chinese yuan. (Note that a higher exchange rate means a higher value of the U.S. dollar and a lower value of the yuan.) With demand curve *D* and supply curve *S*, the equilibrium exchange rate is below China's target exchange rate of 8.28 yuan per dollar. To keep the exchange rate pegged at its target level, the People's Bank of China must buy U.S. dollars and increase its foreign currency reserves.

Figure 12(b) illustrates what is happening in the market for U.S. dollars priced in terms of the yuan and explains why China's reserves have increased. The demand curve *D* and supply curve *S* intersect at 5 yuan per U.S. dollar. If the People's Bank of China takes no actions in the foreign exchange market, this exchange rate is the equilibrium rate. (This particular value is only an example. No one knows what the yuan–U.S. dollar exchange rate would be with no intervention.)

By intervening in the foreign exchange market and buying U.S. dollars, the People's Bank pegs the yuan at 8.28 yuan per U.S. dollar. But to do so, it must keep piling up U.S. dollars. In Fig. 12(b), the People's Bank buys $200 billion a year.

If the People's Bank stops buying U.S. dollars and piling up U.S. dollar reserves, the U.S. dollar will depreciate and the yuan will appreciate.

Why Does China Fix Its Exchange Rate?

The popular story is that China fixes its exchange rate to keep its export prices low and to make it easier to compete in world markets. You've seen that this story might have some truth in the short run. With prices in China and the rest of the world given, a low yuan–U.S. dollar exchange rate brings lower U.S. dollar prices for China's exports. But the yuan–U.S. dollar exchange rate has been fixed for almost 10 years. This long period of a fixed exchange rate has long-run, not short-run, effects. And in the long run, the exchange rate has no effect on competitiveness. The reason is that prices adjust to reflect the exchange rate and the real exchange rate is unaffected by the nominal exchange rate.

So why does China fix its exchange rate? The more convincing answer is that China sees a fixed exchange rate as a way of achieving a low inflation rate. By fixing the yuan against the U.S. dollar, China's inflation rate is anchored to the U.S. inflation rate and will not wander too far from that rate.

Similarly, countries that use a crawling peg keep their inflation rates close to that of the country against which they crawl. The bottom line is that exchange rate policy is monetary policy, not balance of payments policy. To change its balance of payments, a country must change its saving and investment.

Reading Between the Lines looks further at China's exchange rate policy.

7   READING BETWEEN THE LINES

The Sinking Dollar

THE NEW YORK TIMES, MAY 10, 2006

Bush Aides Struggling with Yuan

After nearly three years of pushing China to let its currency float more freely, with only modest results, the Bush administration still appears reluctant to accuse China of manipulating its exchange rate. . . .

American manufacturers and many members of Congress have complained for years that China has kept its currency, the yuan, at an artificially low exchange rate to the dollar as a way of selling its exports at cheap prices.

Treasury Secretary John W. Snow has resisted demands to threaten Beijing, arguing that Chinese leaders are making "progress" toward a more flexible exchange rate and a more open financial system.

This week, a Treasury official again emphasized China's steps toward openness.

"If you look at what China is doing in exercising their commitment on putting in place a foreign-exchange regime that has greater flexibility," Mr. Snow's principal spokesman, Tony Fratto, told reporters on Monday, "you see some evidence that they're doing that."

But changes in the yuan's value have been relatively minor. Chinese leaders let the yuan climb about 2 percent against the dollar last July, and another similarly small amount more recently.

When President Hu Jintao visited President Bush in Washington last month, top Chinese officials re-emphasized a need for "stability" and offered no hint of when they might let the yuan move more freely. . . .

The United States' trade deficit with China ballooned to $202 billion in 2005, an imbalance that might ordinarily have pushed up the value of the yuan in relation to the dollar. China has prevented the yuan from rising by buying hundreds of billions in dollar-denominated reserves. . . .

Essence of the Story

▶ U.S. producers and members of Congress complain that China has kept the yuan artificially low to sell exports at low prices.

▶ Treasury Secretary John W. Snow says that China is moving toward a more flexible exchange rate.

▶ Changes in the yuan–dollar exchange rate have been small.

▶ The yuan appreciated in July 2005 and by small amounts more recently.

▶ The U.S. trade deficit with China was $202 billion in 2005.

▶ This imbalance should have pushed up the value of the yuan, but China prevented that from happening and increased its U.S. dollar reserves.

Economic Analysis

▶ China's exchange rate was pegged at 8.28 yuan per U.S. dollar until July 2005.

▶ In July 2005, the yuan was appreciated (the dollar depreciated) by 2.1 percent.

▶ Since July 2005, the yuan has persistently but slowly risen against the dollar (the dollar has fallen against the yuan).

▶ Figure 13 shows the path of the falling dollar against the yuan.

FIGURE 13   The Yuan–U.S. Dollar Exchange Rate

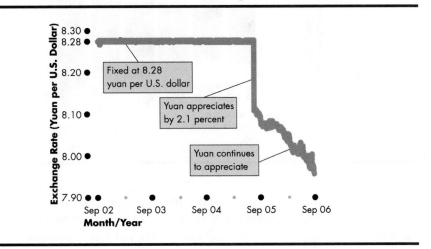

▶ To peg the yuan before July 2005 and to keep the exchange rate from rising more than it wants, the People's Bank of China buys U.S. dollars in the foreign exchange market.

▶ The result of these foreign exchange market transactions has been a strong growth in reserves.

▶ Figure 14 shows the buildup of China's reserves, which, by 2006, were almost $1 trillion.

FIGURE 14   China's Reserves Pile Up

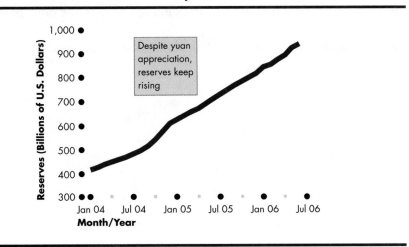

▶ Americans are concerned about the yuan because China has a large trade surplus with the United States.

▶ But China's overall current account surplus is not large and is a fraction of the large U.S. current account deficit.

▶ Figure 15 shows the U.S. current account deficit and China's current account surplus.

FIGURE 15   Current Account Balances

▶ The analysis in this reading explains that a current account deficit results from too little private and government saving relative to investment.

▶ China saves more than it invests, and the United States invests more than it saves.

▶ A change in the nominal exchange rate between the U.S. dollar and the Chinese yuan cannot make a large contribution to changing these imbalances.

▶ The main effect of the appreciation of the yuan will be to slow China's inflation rate relative to the U.S. inflation rate.

You're the Voter

▶ Do you think the United States should pressure China to raise the value of the yuan substantially?

▶ Do you think it would be in China's interest to raise the value of the yuan substantially?

▶ How would a substantially higher valued yuan affect world trade?

SUMMARY

► Foreign currency is obtained in exchange for domestic currency in the foreign exchange market.

► The nominal exchange rate is the value of one currency in terms of another currency.

► The real exchange rate is the price of one country's real GDP in terms of another country's real GDP.

► Demand and supply in the foreign exchange market determine the exchange rate.

► The higher the exchange rate, the smaller is the quantity of U.S. dollars demanded and the greater is the quantity of U.S. dollars supplied.

► The equilibrium exchange rate makes the quantity of U.S. dollars demanded equal the quantity of U.S. dollars supplied.

► Changes in the the world demand for U.S. exports, the U.S. interest rate differential, or the expected future exchange rate change the demand for U.S. dollars.

► Changes in U.S. demand for imports, the U.S. interest rate differential, or the expected future exchange rate change the supply of U.S. dollars.

► Exchange rate expectations are influenced by purchasing power parity and interest rate parity.

► In the long run, the nominal exchange rate is a monetary phenomenon and the real exchange rate is independent of the nominal exchange rate.

► International trade, borrowing, and lending are financed by using foreign currency.

► A country's international transactions are recorded in its current account, capital account, and official settlements account.

► The current account balance is similar to net exports and is determined by the government sector balance plus the private sector balance.

► An exchange rate can be flexible, fixed, or a crawling peg.

► To achieve a fixed or a crawling exchange rate, a central bank must intervene in the foreign exchange market and either buy or sell foreign currency.

CURRENCY EXCHANGE RATES

by Bruno Solnik and Dennis McLeavey, CFA

LEARNING OUTCOMES

The candidate should be able to:	Mastery
a. define direct and indirect methods of foreign exchange quotations, and convert direct (indirect) foreign exchange quotations into indirect (direct) foreign exchange quotations;	☐
b. calculate and interpret the spread on a foreign currency quotation, and explain how spreads on foreign currency quotations can differ as a result of market conditions, bank/dealer positions, and trading volume;	☐
c. calculate and interpret currency cross rates, given two spot exchange quotations involving three currencies;	☐
d. calculate the profit on a triangular arbitrage opportunity, given the bid–ask quotations for the currencies of three countries involved in the arbitrage;	☐
e. distinguish between the spot and forward markets for foreign exchange;	☐
f. calculate and interpret the spread on a forward foreign currency quotation, and explain how spreads on forward foreign currency quotations can differ as a result of market conditions, bank/dealer positions, trading volume, and maturity/length of contract;	☐
g. calculate and interpret a forward discount or premium and express it as an annualized rate;	☐
h. explain interest rate parity, and illustrate covered interest arbitrage;	☐
i. distinguish between spot and forward transactions, calculate the annualized forward premium/discount for a given currency, and infer whether the currency is "strong" or "weak."	☐

The international investor is faced with a complex task. The financial markets throughout the world are quite different from one another, and information on them is sometimes difficult to obtain. Trading in different time

Global Investments, Sixth Edition, by Bruno Solnik and Dennis McLeavey, CFA. Copyright © 2009 by Pearson Education. Reprinted with permission of Pearson Education, publishing as Prentice Hall.

633

zones and languages further complicates the task. But the most important aspect of international investment is the use of multiple currencies. An American investing in France must do so in euros; therefore, the performance (and risk) of the investment will depend in part on changes in the euro/U.S. dollar exchange rate. Because of the importance of exchange rates in international investment, this reading describes foreign exchange transactions.

This reading deals with foreign exchange quotes and the relationships between different types of quotes, as well as the nature of bid–ask spreads in the foreign exchange market. The exchange rate quotes for current and future delivery must be aligned with the risk-free interest rates in the two countries for which the quotes are given. This reading presents the basic facts of foreign exchange involving quotation interpretation and arbitrage.

1   CURRENCY EXCHANGE RATE QUOTATIONS

A currency exchange rate is the rate used to exchange two currencies. An exchange rate states the price of one currency in terms of units of another currency.

Before reviewing the international currency market, we will develop some basic notation. Over time, exchange rates change, so we will assume values for the current exchange rate, knowing that the actual values can be quite different by the time the reader views our printed page.

Suppose now that we are told that the current exchange rate between the dollar (\$) and the euro (€) is 0.8. That information is unhelpful because we have not been told whether this is a price quote for the dollar or for the euro.

By convention, we will present all quotes in this book as $a{:}b = S$ where

a is the quoted currency

b is the currency in which the price is expressed

S is the price of the quoted currency a in units of currency b

For example, \$:€ = 0.8 indicates that one dollar is priced at 0.8 euros. Sometimes newspapers will report this as 0.8 euros per dollar.

Conversely, we can also express the exchange rate between the dollar and the euro as €:\$ = 1.25, where the euro is the quoted currency in units of dollars. The euro is priced at 1.25 dollars. Hence, we have

€:\$ = 1.25 and

\$:€ = 0.80

Similarly, the dollar may be quoted as 120 Japanese yen (¥) per dollar, so that 100 yen are worth 0.8333 dollars. Quotations for the yen are usually indicated for 100 yen rather than for one yen because of the small value of the yen. Using the notation $a{:}b$, the quotations are

\$:¥ = 120 and

¥:\$ = 0.8333

Abbreviations are used to refer to the various currencies. These abbreviations could be commonly used symbols or "official" three-letter codes. Financial newspapers such as the *Financial Times* generally use symbols, while traders use three-letter codes. Symbols include $ (U.S. dollar), ¥ (Japanese yen), € (euro), £ (British pound), A$ (Australian dollar), and Sfr (Swiss franc). Three-letter codes for the same currencies are USD, JPY, EUR, GBP, AUD, and CHF. We will alternatively use in this reading the various currency abbreviations that are commonly encountered. For example, the Japanese yen can be referred to as ¥, JPY, or yen.

In our discussion so far, we have used the natural terminology *dollars per euro* when referring to €:$ = 1.25 because the quoted currency is the euro. However, newspaper and trader terminology varies, and it is useful to be aware of different exchange rate treatments. It must be stressed that different news and trading services use different notations to refer to the same exchange rate. Actually, the notation $/€ = 1.25, meaning 1.25 dollars per euro, is intuitive and we used this notation in previous editions, but we changed notation in the present edition to be consistent with what has become the most widely used convention. *Readers familiar with previous editions should be aware of the change in notation.* To repeat, we will use €:$ to mean the price of one euro in dollars (number of dollars per euro). With this notation, the *quoted currency* is the first one (here, €) and its price is measured in units of the second currency (here, $).

Direct and Indirect Quotations

As an exchange rate can be quoted with *a* as the domestic currency or with *a* as the foreign currency, it is useful to introduce the nationality of the investor.

If *a* in *a:b* is the foreign currency and *b* the domestic currency, then the quote is termed a *direct quote*—naturally enough, the price of the foreign currency in which we are interested. An American investor seeing a quote €:$ = 1.25 expects to pay $1.25 for one euro. He is viewing a direct quote, the price of the foreign currency. For the European investor, $:€ = 0.8 is the direct quote that the price of one dollar is 0.8 euros.

If *a* in *a:b* is the domestic currency and *b* the foreign currency, then the quote is termed an *indirect quote*, the amount of foreign currency that one unit of the domestic currency will purchase. To an American investor, $:€ = 0.8 indicates that one dollar (the domestic currency) will purchase 0.8 euros. To a European investor, €:$ = 1.25 indicates that one euro (the domestic currency) will buy $1.25.

A direct quote tells us how much it will cost to purchase amounts of foreign currency, and an indirect quote tells us how much foreign currency we can get for an amount of domestic currency. If a European must pay 100 dollars for an American product, he will use a direct quote $:€ = 0.8 to know that it will cost him 80 euros. If a European is making a donation to a U.S. charity and wants to donate 100 euros, he will use an indirect quote €:$ = 1.25 to know that he is contributing 125 dollars.

Direct quotes and indirect quotes are reciprocals of each other. The price per unit of the foreign currency is the reciprocal of the number of units of foreign currency received for a unit of the domestic currency. Just as €:$ = 1.25 tells an American investor that one euro costs 1.25 dollars, so the reciprocal 1/€:$ = 1/1.25 = $:€ = 0.8 tells her that one dollar will purchase 0.8 euros. Of course, the direct euro quote for an American is the indirect dollar quote for a European, and vice versa.

Direct quotes and indirect quotes have directional differences when it comes to price appreciation. Because the direct quote tells us the price of the foreign currency, an appreciation of the foreign currency causes an increase in the direct quote, but an appreciation of the foreign currency causes a decrease in the indirect quote. An appreciation of a currency is considered a strengthening and a depreciation of a currency is considered a weakening. The following table lays out these two alternatives for a foreign and domestic currency.

Domestic Currency	Foreign Currency	Direct Exchange Rate (Foreign Currency Quoted)	Indirect Exchange Rate (Domestic Currency Quoted)
Appreciates	Depreciates	Decreases	Increases
Depreciates	Appreciates	Increases	Decreases

Example 1 may help ensure familiarity with the terminology.

EXAMPLE 1

Direct and Indirect Exchange Rates

On April 1, the British pound is quoted as £:$ = 1.80. What are the direct and indirect quotes from the viewpoint of an American and a British investor? A month later, the exchange rate has moved to £:$ = 1.90. Which currencies appreciated or depreciated?

Solution: The pound is quoted in terms of dollars. This quote is a direct quote from the American viewpoint and an indirect quote from the British viewpoint. Conversely, $:£ = 0.55556 is an indirect quote from the American viewpoint and a direct quote from the British viewpoint.

In £:$, the pound is the quoted currency. Over a month, its price increased from $1.80 to $1.90, so the pound appreciated and the dollar depreciated.

Cross-Rate Calculations

A *cross rate* is the exchange rate between two currencies inferred from each country's exchange rate with a third currency, the reference currency. From the quotation of two currencies against a reference currency, we can derive a cross exchange rate. Of use for us in manipulating exchange rates will be the recognition that the : sign in a:b can be interpreted as a "divide" sign, and we interpret a:b as b/a.

Consider how two currencies, a and c, against a third, b, can give us a:c. In this form, a:b times b:c equals a:c. Of course, b:a times c:b then gives us c:a. Consider also how two currencies against a third a:b and a:c can give us c:b. In this form, a:b divided by a:c equals c:b. Our conclusion then is that

$$(a{:}b) \times (b{:}c) = a{:}c \text{ and}$$

$$(a{:}b) \div (a{:}c) = c{:}b$$

From the quotation of two currencies against the U.S. dollar, for example, we can derive the cross exchange rate between the two currencies: €:$ and $:¥ can give us €:¥. Assume that the euro is quoted as 1.25 dollars and the dollar is quoted as 120 Japanese yen (¥) per dollar. From these quotes, we can calculate the €:¥ rate.

€:$ = 1.25 and $:¥ = 120

implies that (€:$) × ($:¥) = €:¥, or

€:¥ = 1.25 × 120 = 150

In this example, one euro is worth 150 yen, or 100 yen are worth 0.6667 euros.

Now consider the a:b and a:c case in the following quotes for the Korean won and the Brazilian real against the dollar, with $:won = 1012.5 and $:R$ = 2.297. We calculate the won per real rate equal to the won per dollar rate (1012.50) divided by the real per dollar rate:

R$:won = ($:won) ÷ ($:R$) = 1012.5/2.297 = 440.79

Forex Market and Quotation Conventions

The international currency market can be seen as having two components:

► A worldwide *foreign exchange* (*Forex*) *market* where participants are major banks and specialized currency dealers (market makers). This is a "wholesale" interbank market for large transactions.

► A "retail" market where investors and corporations deal with local banks.

The Forex market is the driving force on the currency market. Banks quote foreign exchange rates to their clients based on the Forex quotations. The Forex market is a worldwide market in which dealers, mostly large commercial and investment banks, trade large orders (typically several million dollars). This is an *over-the-counter* (*OTC*) market in which trading is done by telephone and on electronic platforms. Trading takes place 24 hours a day, 5 days a week. A typical daily transaction volume is well above $1 trillion, making it the largest and most liquid market in the world.

In the Forex market, quotations are generally given with five significant digits and three-letter codes. For example, the USD:JPY quote could appear as 120.10 and the EUR:USD as 1.2515.[1]

The worldwide Forex market observes some specific trading conventions. *First,* there is no need to maintain a market in both euros against dollars and dollars against euros. For any pair of currencies, it is sufficient to trade in a single exchange rate. History mostly dictates the exchange rate direction that is selected. There is a decreasing order of seniority with the British pound as the senior currency. The Forex convention is to trade British pounds in units of other currencies, so the quote showing on Forex trading screens is the foreign exchange value of one GBP, that is, GBP:EUR, GBP:USD, or GBP:JPY. For exchange rates involving the British pound, the quoted currency is always the

---

[1] The most active currencies are sometimes quoted with six significant digits.

pound. For example, the exchange rate between the pound and the dollar is quoted as the dollar price of one pound. When the euro was introduced in 1999, it was given "seniority" just behind its British neighbor. Thus, the quote showing on Forex trading screens is the foreign exchange value of one euro, EUR:USD or EUR:JPY. For exchange rates involving the euro, the quoted currency is always the euro except for the exchange rate with the pound, where the quoted currency is the pound. Finally, the dollar is quoted in units of all other currencies, for example, USD:JPY.[2]

Second, not all exchange rates are traded. In a world with a large number of currencies, there are a very large number of cross exchange rates. For example, with 20 currencies, there are 380 bilateral exchange rates. The exchange rates between two minor currencies are not traded on the Forex market, so a Forex trader could not find on her trading screen the exchange rate between the South Korean won (won or KRW) and the Brazilian real (R$ or BRL). There would be too few transactions between the won and the real to maintain an active and liquid market. Actually, all currencies are simply traded against the U.S. dollar. To buy Korean won with Brazilian reals, an investor must do two Forex transactions: first buy dollars with reals, and then sell those dollars for won. To create liquidity on this interbank market, all transactions involving the Brazilian real are therefore conducted against the U.S. dollar. We can derive the cross rate won:R$ from the two exchange rates $:won and $:R$. Hence, all currencies are quoted against the U.S. dollar, which remains the dominant Forex currency of quotation, although there are such regional exceptions as the yen in Asia and the euro and pound in Europe.[3]

Third, Forex quotes always include a *bid price* and an *ask price* (or *offer* price), and there is no commission or fee added on a trade. The bid price is the price at which the foreign exchange dealer is willing to buy the quoted currency in exchange for the second currency. The ask price is the price at which the dealer is willing to sell the base currency in exchange for the second currency. The difference between the bid and the ask prices is referred to as the *spread*. As an example, assume that a dealer provides the following quote for the $:¥ (value of the dollar in yen):

$$\$:¥ = 120.17–120.19$$

The dealer is willing to buy dollars at a price of 120.17 yen per dollar (bid) and willing to sell dollars at a price of 120.19 yen per dollar (ask). We now provide more details on bid–ask quotes.

Bid–Ask (Offer) Quotes and Spreads

As mentioned above, the foreign exchange dealer quotes not one but two prices. The *bid* price is the exchange rate at which the dealer is willing to buy a currency; the *ask* (or *offer*) price is the exchange rate at which the dealer is willing to sell a currency. The *midpoint* price is the average of the bid and ask price: (*ask* + *bid*)/2. The *bid–ask spread* is the difference between the bid and ask prices. For example, a bank could quote the euro in dollars as

$$€:\$ = 1.2011–1.2014$$

---

[2] There is one exception, however. The Australian dollar (AUD) and New Zealand dollar (NZD) are traded in units of U.S. dollars (e.g., AUD:USD or NZD:USD). This is probably a remnant of the British Empire and there is pressure to change this convention for the AUD and NZD.

[3] For example, there are active markets between the euro and the Swiss franc and between the euro and the pound.

The dealer is willing to buy euros at a price of 1.2011 dollars per euro (bid) and willing to sell euros at a price of 1.2014 dollars per euro (ask). Forex traders would say that the spread is equal to 3 *pips*. A *pip*, which stands for *price interest point*, represents the smallest fluctuation in the price of a currency. Hence, a pip refers to one unit of the final digit of the quoted exchange rate. This is similar to the concept of "tick" for stocks. The spread is sometimes expressed as a percentage of the ask price (or midpoint price). In the example, the percentage spread is about 2.5 *basis points*:

$$\text{Percentage spread} = \frac{1.2014 - 1.2011}{1.2014} = 0.00025 = 0.025\% = 2.5 \text{ basis points}$$

Spreads differ as a result of market conditions and trading volume. The size of the bid–ask spread increases with exchange rate uncertainty (*volatility*) and lack of liquidity because of bank/dealer *risk aversion*. When a dealer posts a quote, she does not know whether the customer will buy or sell the quoted currency. Hence, the dealer could end up with an unexpected currency position, depending on the customer's decision. It could take some time for the dealer to offset that position with another customer or on the Forex market. When markets are volatile, there could be a large adverse price movement during that time period. Dealers increase their quoted spreads in volatile times. For thinly traded currencies, it will take longer to offset a currency position at reasonable prices. The length of that time period increases the risk of an adverse price movement. Dealers quote larger spreads for illiquid currencies relative to major currencies with active trading.

The bank/dealer position should not have a significant influence on the size of the bid–ask spread quoted by that dealer. Rather, the midpoint of the spread moves in response to dealer positions. For example, a dealer with excess supply of a specific foreign currency would move the midpoint of that quoted currency down rather than adjust the size of his spread. A dealer quoting a large spread relative to other dealers will basically not trade, so that would not help to reduce the position. Neither will the dealer want to quote a smaller spread because that would mean raising his bid price when he does not want to buy. Basically, the dealer will lower both his bid and ask prices in order to induce customers to buy this specific currency rather than sell it. For example, a dealer with excess euros will try to sell them and therefore lower his ask price of $1.2014 to, say, $1.2012 and will probably also lower his bid to avoid having to buy more euros, from $1.2011 to, say, $1.2009.

The Forex market quotes exchange rates only in one direction (e.g., €:$, not $:€). But it is easy to infer the bid–ask prices for the same pair of currencies quoted in the other direction. Two principles apply:

▶ The *$:€ ask* exchange rate is the reciprocal of the *€:$ bid* exchange rate.

▶ The *$:€ bid* exchange rate is the reciprocal of the *€:$ ask* exchange rate.

In the example above, the dealer is willing to buy euros for dollars at a bid price of 1.2011 dollars per euro. This would be equivalent of the dealer selling dollars for euros at a rate of $1/1.2011 = 0.83257$ euros per dollar. Hence, the €:$ quote of

€:$ = 1.2011–1.2014

is equivalent to a $:€ quote of

$:€ = 0.83236–0.83257

A customer wishing to convert $100,000 into euros could simply buy the euros from the dealer at the ask price of €:$ = 1.2014 and hence obtain 100,000/1.2014 = €83,236. This is identical to selling $100,000 at the bid $:€ = 0.83236.

A local bank will happily quote bid–ask exchange rates in any direction requested by a customer. Of course, spreads quoted to "retail" customers tend to be wider than those found on the "wholesale" Forex market.

Example 2 may help to show how a transaction is initiated.

EXAMPLE 2

Exchange Rate Quotes and French Bonds

A U.S. portfolio manager wants to buy $10 million worth of French bonds. The manager wants to know how many euros can be obtained to invest using the $10 million. The manager calls several banks to get their €/$ quotation, without indicating whether a sale or a purchase of euros is desired. Bank A gives the following quotation:

€:$ = 1.24969–1.25000

Bank A is willing to buy a euro for 1.24969 dollars or to sell a euro for 1.25000 dollars. These quotes are consistent with the following quotes for the $:€:

$:€ = 0.80000–0.80020

Note how the ask price for $:€ of 0.80020 is the reciprocal of the bid €:$, giving the ask price equal to 1/1.24969 = 0.80020.

To make the quote faster, only the last digits, called the *points*, are sometimes quoted. The preceding quote would often be given as follows:

$:€ = 0.80000–20

or even

$:€ = 000–020

Assume that the portfolio manager gets the following quotes from three different banks:

	Bank A	Bank B	Bank C
$:€ =	0.80000–20	0.79985–05	0.79995–15

Note that the ask for all three quotes adds 0.00020 to the bid. How many euros will the portfolio manager get to invest?

Solution: The manager will immediately choose Bank A and indicate that he will buy 8 million euros for $10 million. Both parties indicate where each sum should be transferred. The portfolio manager indicates that the euros should be transferred to an account with the Société Générale, the manager's business bank in Paris, whereas Bank A indicates that it will receive the dollars at its account with Citibank in New York. Electronic messages and faxes are exchanged to confirm the oral agreement. The settlement of the transaction takes place simultaneously in Paris and in New York two days later.

Cross-Rate Calculations with Bid–Ask Spreads

Recall that a cross rate is the exchange rate between two currencies inferred from each currency's exchange rate with a third currency, the reference currency.

Earlier we examined a case of $(a{:}b) \div (a{:}c) = c{:}b$, where we assumed that the exchange rate of the Brazilian real per dollar was \$:R\$ = 2.2970 and that the won per dollar rate was \$:won = 1012.50. We calculated the won per real cross rate by dividing the won per dollar rate (1012.50) by the real per dollar rate (2.2970):

$$R\${:}won = (\${:}won) \div (\${:}R\$) = 1012.50 / 2.2970 = 440.79$$

Let's now consider the case where currencies are quoted with a bid–ask spread, as follows:

$$\${:}R\$ = 2.2960\text{–}2.2980$$

$$\${:}won = 1012.0\text{–}1013.0$$

To compute bid–ask cross rates, we follow the same procedure but need to think of the direction of the money flow. For simplicity, assume that we are an investor interrogating a currency dealer. Hence, we take the view of a client, not of the dealer. First, think of the bid price as being the price when we (an investor) hold the quoted currency and want to sell it to the dealer, who is quoting us a price at which he is willing to purchase the quoted currency. Similarly, think of the ask price as the price when we want to buy the quoted currency from the dealer, who is quoting a price at which he will sell the quoted currency. In short, *bid* means we "have" the quoted currency (and wish to sell it) and *ask* means we "want" it as an investor.

For $(R\${:}won)_{bid}$ the dealer is willing to buy reals in exchange for won, and the investor desires to sell his reals to buy won. But, if we thought of the underlying two-step process, the investor would *use his reals to purchase dollars* (want dollars) at the $(\${:}R\$)_{ask}$ price and *use dollars* (have dollars) *to purchase won* at the $(\${:}won)_{bid}$ price. This means the investor faces the ask price for $(\${:}R\$)$ and the bid price for $(\${:}won)$.

$$(R\${:}won)_{bid} = (\${:}won)_{bid} \div (\${:}R\$)_{ask}$$

For $(R\${:}won)_{ask}$ the dealer is willing to sell reals in exchange for won, and the investor desires to buy reals using won. But in a two-step process, the investor would *use his won to purchase dollars* (want dollars) and then *use his dollars* (have dollars) *to purchase reals*. This means the investor faces the ask price for $(\${:}won)$ and the bid price for $(\${:}R\$)$.

$$(R\${:}won)_{ask} = (\${:}won)_{ask} \div (\${:}R\$)_{bid}$$

We first calculate the bid–ask cross rates when the Brazilian real is quoted in terms of won:

$$(R\$:won)_{bid} = (\$:won)_{bid} \div (\$:R\$)_{ask} = 1012.0/2.2980 = 440.38 \text{ won per real}$$

$$(R\$:won)_{ask} = (\$:won)_{ask} \div (\$:R\$)_{bid} = 1013.0/2.2960 = 441.20 \text{ won per real}$$

As an exercise, we now calculate the bid–ask cross rates when the won is quoted in terms of Brazilian reals:

$$(won:R\$)_{bid} = (\$:R\$)_{bid} \div (\$:won)_{ask} = 2.2960/1013.0 = 0.0022665 \text{ real per won}$$

$$(won:R\$)_{ask} = (\$:R\$)_{ask} \div (\$:won)_{bid} = 2.2980/1012.0 = 0.0022708 \text{ real per won}$$

Of course, it is much easier to calculate these second two quotes from the first two by using our relation that $(won:R\$)_{bid} = 1 \div (R\$:won)_{ask} = 1/441.20 = 0.0022677$ and $(won:R\$)_{ask} = 1 \div (R\$:won)_{bid} = 1 \div 440.38 = 0.002271$.

We have to be careful when different quotation conventions are used. For example, the euro is usually the quoted currency against the dollar in the Forex market. The equations given above should be adapted to reflect the quotation convention. Example 3 provides an illustration.

As mentioned above, it would be inefficient to maintain a market between two "minor" currencies (such as the won and the real). Because there would be too few direct transactions between them, the spread would need to be very large to induce a *market maker* to provide continuous quotes. Centralizing all transactions involving those two minor currencies against one single major currency (the dollar) is much more efficient from a cost viewpoint. However, there is a direct market between a few major currencies, meaning that the dollar is not necessarily used as the reference currency. For example, the spread quoted on a direct transaction from euros to Swiss francs could be less than the cross-rate spread.

EXAMPLE 3

Cross Rates with the Won, Euro, and Dollar

You wish to calculate the cross rate between the euro and the South Korean won (€:won). A major dealer on the Forex market provides the following quotes:

$$\$:won = 1012.0–1013.0$$

$$€:\$ = 1.24969–1.25000$$

Calculate the bid and ask cross exchange rate €:won.

Solution: Because the euro is quoted in terms of dollars, the won per euro exchange rate is given by

$$€:won = (€:\$) \times (\$:won)$$

Hence, the bid and ask cross rates are

$$(\text{€:won})_{\text{bid}} = (\text{€:\$})_{\text{bid}} \times (\text{\$:won})_{\text{bid}} = 1.24969 \times 1012.0$$

$$= 1264.69 \text{ won per euro}$$

$$(\text{€:won})_{\text{ask}} = (\text{€:\$})_{\text{ask}} \times (\text{\$:won})_{\text{ask}} = 1.25000 \times 1013.0$$

$$= 1266.25 \text{ won per euro}$$

To verify that the calculations have been made correctly, there are two checks.

The *first check* to make sure that you measure the cross rate in the right direction is to look at the symbols. Notice that the \$ symbol disappears in the equations above if you recall that $a{:}b$ times $b{:}c$ equals $a{:}c$.

A *second check* on the result is to make sure that you *maximize* the bid–ask spread. To get the bid cross rate, which is the smaller rate, you should use the combination of bid and ask exchange rates that yields the lowest cross rate.

No-Arbitrage Conditions with Exchange Rates

The foreign exchange market is highly liquid and efficient. If some riskless arbitrage became available, it would be quickly eliminated. Hence, quotes are immediately aligned. For example, several banks provide a market for the dollar in terms of euros, but it would be strange to see an *arbitrage* opportunity available between them. An arbitrage could be created if it were profitable to buy from one bank and sell to another. Such a profitable arbitrage would happen only if the ask price quoted by one bank were below the bid price quoted by another bank. If you saw the following quotes, what would look strangely attractive?

	Bank A	**Bank B**	**Bank C**
\$:€ =	0.80000–20	0.79985–95	0.79995–15

You could buy dollars from Bank B for 0.79995 euros per dollar and simultaneously sell them to bank A for 0.80000 euros per dollar. The gain per dollar is very small, but it is riskless and does not require any invested capital. Currency traders are careful that such arbitrage situations do not arise, and quotes are adjusted on a continuous basis. In highly volatile periods, the adjustment can take place every few seconds as the spread on exchange rates is very small compared to a typical exchange rate move.

Arbitrage aligns exchange rate quotes throughout the world. The quote for the €:\$ rate must be the same, at a given instant, in Frankfurt, London, Paris, and New York. If quotes were to deviate by more than the spread, a simple phone call would allow a trader to make enormous profits. There are enough professionals in the world watching continuous quote fluctuations to rule out such riskless profit opportunities.

Triangular arbitrage ensures consistency between exchange rates and cross rates, but spreads have to be taken into account, as suggested in Example 4.

EXAMPLE 4

Triangular Arbitrage on Cross Rates

On the Forex market, an American bank gives the following quotes:

$$€:\$ = 1.2000\text{--}1.2050$$

$$£:\$ = 1.7950\text{--}1.8000$$

A British bank gives the following quote:

$$£:€ = 1.5050\text{--}1.5070$$

Is there an arbitrage opportunity?

Solution: We can find the £:€ quotes implicit in the American bank's quotes:

$$(£:€)_{bid} = (£:\$)_{bid} \div (€:\$)_{ask} = 1.7950/1.2050 = 1.4896 \text{ euros per pound}$$

$$(£:€)_{ask} = (£:\$)_{ask} \div (€:\$)_{bid} = 1.8000/1.2000 = 1.5000 \text{ euros per pound}$$

The resulting cross-rate quote by the American bank is:

$$£:€ = 1.4896\text{--}1.5000$$

There is an arbitrage opportunity because the ask cross-rate of the American bank's quote is below the bid £:€ quoted by the British bank. An arbitrage sequence would be to

▶ Use 1.8 dollars to buy one pound from the American bank at $(£:\$)_{ask}$.

▶ Simultaneously sell the American bank 1.5 euros for dollars at $(€:\$)_{bid} = 1.2000$. This would yield 1.8 dollars. These first two transactions are equivalent to buying one pound with 1.5 euros at the American bank's cross rate of $(£:€)_{ask} = 1.5$ euros per pound.

▶ Sell one pound to the British bank at its $(£:€)_{bid}$ of 1.5050 euros per pound.

The net profit is 0.005 euro used in the arbitrage. This is a riskless profit that requires no initial investment. Such an arbitrage opportunity cannot remain on an efficient currency market.

2   FORWARD QUOTES

Spot exchange rates are quoted for immediate currency transactions, although in practice the settlement takes place 48 hours later. Spot transactions are used extensively to settle commercial purchases of goods as well as for investments.

Foreign exchange dealers also quote *forward exchange rates*. These are rates contracted today but with delivery and settlement in the future, usually 30 or 90 days hence. As with spot rates, forward rates are quoted by a bank with a bid and an ask price. For example, a bank may quote the one-month €:$ exchange rate as 1.24688–1.24719. This means that the bank is willing to commit itself today to buy euros for 1.24688 dollars or to sell them for 1.24719 dollars in one month. In a *forward contract* (or futures contract), a commitment is irrevocably made on the transaction date, but the exchange of currency takes place later on a date set in the contract. The origins of the forward currency market may be traced back to the Middle Ages, when merchants from all over Europe met at major trade fairs and made forward contracts for the next fair.

Forward exchange rates are commonly used by asset managers to manage their foreign currency positions. By investing in foreign assets, an investor takes a currency position that can suffer (or benefit) from exchange rate movements. For example, a German investor might wish to invest in attractive American stocks but fear a depreciation of the U.S. dollar. In order to hedge the dollar risk, the German investor will sell dollars forward against euros. It is important to get an understanding of the pricing of the forward exchange rate and its relation to the spot exchange rate.

Forward exchange rates are often quoted as a premium, or discount, to the spot exchange rate. With the convention of giving the value of the quoted currency (the first currency) in terms of units of the second currency, there is a premium on the quoted currency when the forward exchange rate is higher than the spot rate and a discount otherwise. Clearly, a negative premium is a discount. If the one-month forward exchange rate is €:$ = 1.24688 (1.24688 dollars per euro) and the spot rate is €:$ = 1.25000, the euro quotes with a discount of 0.00312 dollar per euro. In the language of currency traders, the euro is "weak" relative to the dollar, as its forward value is lower than its spot value. Conversely, the dollar is traded at a premium, as the forward value of one dollar ($:€ = 1/1.24688 = 0.80200) is higher than its spot value ($:€ = 0.80000).

Consequently, when a trader announces that a currency quotes at a premium, the premium should be added to the spot exchange rate to obtain the value of the forward exchange rate. If a currency quotes at a discount, the discount should be subtracted from the spot exchange rate to obtain the value of the forward rate.

The forward discount, or premium, is often calculated as an annualized percentage deviation from the spot rate. Given an exchange rate of *a:b*, the annualized forward premium (discount) on the quoted currency *a* is equal to

$$\left(\frac{\text{Forward rate} - \text{Spot rate}}{\text{Spot rate}}\right)\left(\frac{12}{\text{No. months forward}}\right)100\% \qquad \textbf{(1)}$$

If (Spot rate − Forward rate) replaces (Forward rate − Spot rate) in Formula 1, we have the forward discount (premium) on the measurement currency in which the price is expressed.

The percentage premium (discount) is annualized by multiplying by 12 and dividing by the length of the forward contract in months. For example, the annualized forward premium on the dollar as quoted above is

$$\left(\frac{0.802 - 0.800}{0.800}\right)\left(\frac{12}{1}\right)100\% = 3.0\%$$

Interbank quotations are often reported in the form of an annualized premium (discount) for reasons that will become obvious in the next section. However, forward rates quoted to customers are usually outright (e.g., €:$ = 1.24688−1.24719).

Spot and forward dollar exchange rates can be found in newspapers around the world, such as the London-based *Financial Times*. For example, the spot $:SFr exchange rate could be $:SFr = 1.2932−1.2939. The midpoint is equal to 1.2936.

At the same time, $:SFr for delivery three months later could be quoted at a midpoint of 1.2823. The dollar (the quoted currency) quotes at a discount and the Swiss franc at a premium. The annualized percentage premium of the Swiss franc would then be equal to 3.5 percent. Because the Swiss franc is the measurement currency in the quote, this premium is obtained by taking the difference between the spot and the forward rate and dividing it by the spot rate:

$$\text{Annualized three-month forward premium} = \left(\frac{0.0113}{1.2936}\right)\left(\frac{12}{3}\right)100\% = 3.5\%$$

CONCEPTS IN ACTION   STRONG CURRENCIES

The sign of the premium as reported in newspapers such as the *Financial Times* (FT) must be considered carefully. This is because the convention for quotation of the dollar exchange rate differs across currencies and because the layperson associates a premium with strength. For all currencies except the euro and British pound, the dollar is the quoted currency, and this leads the FT to reverse the formula and report a calculation based on *spot minus forward* so that a positive premium can indicate that the measurement currency on the line is "strong" relative to the dollar. For example, with $:Sfr, a dollar worth fewer future Swiss francs means a premium on the Sfr currency line. For the euro and the pound, the euro and the pound are the quoted currencies, so a euro worth fewer future dollars (a positive spot minus forward premium as reported) indicates that the currency on the line is "weak" relative to the dollar, while a discount (a negative premium) indicates that the currency is strong.

Foreign Exchange Quotations
Dollar Spot Forward Against the Dollar

Aug. 30		Closing Midpoint	Bid/Offer[1]	Three Months Rate	%PA[2]
Euro	(€)	0.9841	839–842	0.9802	1.6
UK	(£)	1.5492	490–494	1.541	2.1
Switzerland	(SFr)	1.4926	922–929	1.4887	1.1
Canada	(C$)	1.5612	610–614	1.566	−1.2
Japan	(¥)	118.185	160–210	117.655	1.8

[1]Bid/offer spreads show only the last three decimal places. UK £ and euro are quoted in U.S. currency.

[2]Means % per annum.

Source: Data from the *Financial Times* and WM/REUTERS.

Interest Rate Parity: The Forward Discount and the Interest Rate Differential

As mentioned earlier, arbitrage plays an important role in the worldwide currency market. Spot exchange rates, forward exchange rates, and interest rates are technically linked for all currencies that are part of the free international market.

Interest rate parity (*IRP*) is a relationship linking spot exchange rates, forward exchange rates, and interest rates. For two currencies, the IRP relationship is that the forward discount/premium equals the discounted interest rate differential between the two currencies. Stated more simply, the product of the forward rate multiplied by one plus the risk-free rate for the quoted currency equals the product of the spot exchange rate multiplied by one plus the risk-free rate for the measurement currency in which the price is expressed. The relation is driven by arbitrage as illustrated here. Assume that the following data exist for the dollar (quoted currency) and the euro:

Spot exchange rate	\$:€ = 0.8000
One-year forward exchange rate	\$:€ = 0.8080

One-year interest rates (purposely unrealistic at present to show numerical effects) are

$$r_€ = 14\% \text{ and } r_\$ = 10\%$$

To take advantage of the interest rate differential, a speculator could borrow dollars at 10 percent, convert them immediately into euros at the rate of 0.8 euros per dollar, and invest the euros at 14 percent. This action is summarized in Exhibit 1. The speculator makes a profit of 4 percent on the borrowing/lending position but runs the risk of a large depreciation of the euro.

In Exhibit 1, borrowing dollars means bringing money from the future to the present. Lending euros means the reverse. At the end of the period, at time 1, the speculator must convert euros into dollars at an unknown rate to honor the claim in dollars borrowed.

This position may be transformed into a covered (riskless) interest rate arbitrage by simultaneously buying a forward exchange rate contract to convert the euros into dollars in one year at a known forward exchange rate of \$:€ = 0.808. In the process shown in Exhibit 2, the investor still benefits on the interest rate differential (a gain of 4 percent) but loses on the conversion of euros to dollars. In one year, the rate of change in the exchange rate will be equal to

$$\frac{0.800 - 0.808}{0.800} = -0.01 \text{ for a loss of } 1\%$$

EXHIBIT 1	Currency Speculation

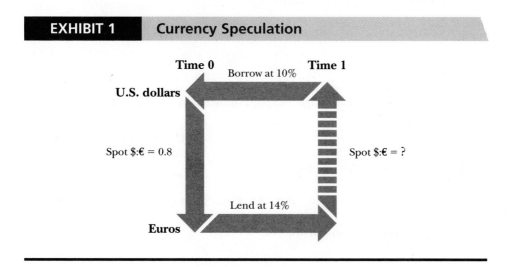

| EXHIBIT 2 | Covered Interest Rate Arbitrage |

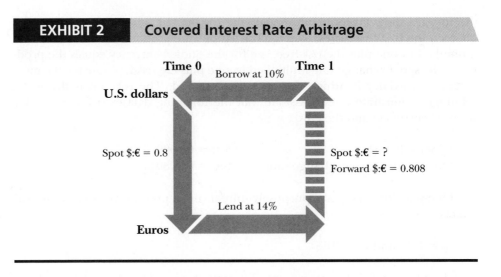

Per dollar borrowed, the net gain on the position is 3 percent. This gain is certain at time 0 because all interest rates and exchange rates are fixed at that time.

No capital is invested in the position, which is a pure *swap* with simultaneous borrowing and lending. If such rates were quoted in reality, banks would arbitrage to exploit this riskless profit opportunity. Enormous swaps could occur, because no capital needs to be invested. To prevent this obvious arbitrage (riskless profit), the forward discount (premium) must exactly equal the interest rate differential. The various rates must adjust so that interest rate parity holds. Note that if the forward discount (premium) were larger than the interest rate differential, the arbitrage would simply go the other way. Arbitrageurs would borrow euros and swap them for dollars.

The exact mathematical relationship is slightly more complicated, because one must buy a forward contract covering both the principal and the accrued interest in order to achieve a perfect arbitrage. In the previous example, for every dollar borrowed, the forward hedge should cover 0.8 euros plus the interest rate of 14 percent, that is, $0.80 (1.14) = 0.912$. The interest rate parity relationship is that the forward discount (premium) equals the discounted interest rate differential between two currencies:

$$(F - S)/S = (r_b - r_a)/(1 + r_a) \qquad \text{(2)}$$

where

r_a is the interest rate of the quoted currency

r_b is the interest rate of the measurement currency in which the price is expressed.

S and F are the spot and forward exchange rates; for example, $s = a{:}b$

Equivalently, we have the relation

$$F(1 + r_a) = S(1 + r_b) \quad \text{or} \quad F = S(1 + r_b)/(1 + r_a) \qquad \text{(3)}$$

Example 5 provides an illustration.

EXAMPLE 5

Interest Rate Parity

If the U.S. dollar is the quoted currency against the euro, arbitrage ensures that

$$F(1 + r_\$) = S(1 + r_€)$$

where S and F are the spot and forward exchange rates (euro price of one U.S. dollar) and $r_€$ and $r_\$$ are the interest rates in euros and U.S. dollars. This relation implies that the forward premium (discount) will be

$$\frac{F - S}{S} = \frac{r_€ - r_\$}{1 + r_\$}$$

If the spot exchange rate is \$:€ = 1.05 and the dollar and euro interest rates are 1.76 percent and 3.39 percent, what is the forward exchange rate, and what is the forward premium (discount)?

Solution: Using equation 3, we have

$$F = S(1 + r_€)/(1 + r_\$) = 1.05(1.0339/1.0176) = 1.0668,$$

or \$:€ = 1.0668

and

$$\frac{F - S}{S} = \frac{r_€ - r_\$}{1 + r_\$}$$

$$= \frac{0.0339 - 0.0176}{1.0176}$$

$$= 1.6\%$$

When the U.S. dollar trades with a forward premium relative to the euro—for example, as in the case above, in which the forward rate is €1.0668 and the spot rate is €1.0500—the dollar trades at a forward premium relative to the euro; conversely, the euro trades at a forward discount relative to the U.S. dollar. Notice that a forward premium is associated with a lower interest rate.

A similar arbitrage relation holds for maturities of less than a year, provided that the right interest rates are used. Whatever the maturity, the convention for interest rates and yields is to quote annualized rates. To perform the forward exchange rate calculations, annualized interest rates must first be converted into rates over the investment period. For a contract with n months' maturity, the quoted interest rate must be divided by 12 and multiplied by n. This is because short-term interest rates are quoted using a linear convention for annualization. Example 6 illustrates the calculations for maturities of less than one year.

EXAMPLE 6

Interest Rate Parity with Maturities of Less than One Year

Consider the following data:

Spot exchange rate $:€ = 1.058

Annual risk-free interest rates (three-month maturity)

3.39% for the euro

1.76% for the U.S. dollar

What is the three-month forward exchange rate $:€?

Solution: Three-month interest rates over the period are

$r_€$ 3.39%(3/12) = 0.8475%

$r_\$$ 1.76%(3/12) = 0.44%

The three-month forward exchange rate is equal to

$$\text{Forward exchange rate} = \text{Spot exchange rate} \times \frac{1 + r_€}{1 + r_\$}$$

$$= 1.058(1.008475/1.0044) = 1.0623$$

Thus, the three-month forward rate is €1.0623 per dollar, or $:€ = 1.0623.

One can also calculate forward exchange rates for maturities longer than a year, although that is more rarely done.[4] One should be aware that annual interest rates, or yields, for longer maturities are typically quoted using a compounding, or actuarial, convention, not a linear convention as for money rates.

Forward Exchange Rate Calculations with Bid–Ask Spreads

When an investor calls a bank to get a forward exchange rate quote, the bank will quote a bid and ask price. As with spot exchange rates, bid–ask spreads differ as a result of market conditions, bank/dealer positions, and trading volume. Unique to forward transactions is the feature that liquidity decreases with the increasing maturity of the forward contract. Consequently, bid–ask spreads increase with the increasing maturity of the contract.

Actually, a bank will usually construct a forward contract by doing the three transactions outlined above: a spot foreign exchange transaction, coupled with borrowing and lending in the two currencies. Hence, the spread

---

[4] As mentioned above, forward contracts are typically offered for maturities ranging from a day to three months, but it is easy to roll over 90-day contracts.

on a forward rate is derived from the spreads on the spot rate and on the two interest rates. As for exchange rates, banks quote interest rates with a bid–ask spread. The bid interest rate is the rate at which the bank is willing to borrow money from the client, and the ask interest rate is the rate at which the bank is willing to lend money to a client. Of course, the bid interest rate is lower than the ask interest rate. In what follows, we calculate the ask forward $:€ and then the bid forward $:€.

For example, a transaction in which an investor is buying forward dollars (having to pay the ask forward $:€) with euros is equivalent to $:€.

▶ Borrowing euros (and hence having to pay the ask interest rate, ask $r_€$)

▶ Using these euros to buy dollars spot (and hence having to pay the ask spot exchange rate, ask spot $:€)

▶ Lending those dollars (and hence receiving the bid interest rate, bid $r_$$)

To obtain the bid forward exchange rate, we perform the reverse calculations:

▶ Borrowing dollars (and hence having to pay the ask interest rate, ask $r_$$)

▶ Selling these dollars to buy euros spot (and hence receiving the bid spot exchange rate, bid spot $:€)

▶ Lending those euros (and hence receiving the bid interest rate, bid $r_€$)

The result will constitute the bid price of the forward exchange rate, bid forward $:€.

Example 7 illustrates the calculations.

EXAMPLE 7

Forward Quotations with Bid–Ask Spreads

Consider the following data:

Spot exchange rate $:Sfr = 1.2932–1.2939

Annual risk-free interest rates (one-year maturity) are

Swiss francs	1.42%–1.44%
U.S. dollar	4.50%–4.52%

What should be the bid–ask quote for the one-year forward exchange rate $:SFr?

Solution: Let's first make sure we calculate the forward rate in the proper direction. The one-year forward rate $:Sfr is given by Equation 3, where the dollar is the quoted currency measured in Swiss francs:

$$\text{Forward exchange rate} = \text{Spot exchange rate} \times \frac{1 + r_{\text{SFr}}}{1 + r_{\$}}$$

A bank will quote bid–ask forward rates, where the bid is lower than the ask. The ask forward rate (ask forward $:SFr) is the SFr price at which an investor can buy dollars forward, and the bid forward rate is the price that an investor can obtain for dollars. Buying dollars forward (paying the ask forward) is equivalent to

▶ Borrowing Swiss francs (and hence having to pay the ask interest rate, ask r_{SFr})
▶ Using these Swiss francs to buy dollars spot (and hence having to pay the ask exchange rate, ask spot $:SFr)
▶ Lending those dollars (and hence receiving the bid interest rate, bid $r_\$$)

The resulting ask forward exchange rate ($:SFr) is

$$\text{Ask forward}(\$:SFr) = 1.2939 \frac{1 + 1.44\%}{1 + 4.50\%} = 1.2560$$

The bid forward exchange rate ($:SFr) is

$$\text{Bid forward}(\$:SFr) = 1.2932 \frac{1 + 1.42\%}{1 + 4.52\%} = 1.2548$$

Thus, the one-year forward rate should be $:SFr = 1.2548–1.2560.

Finally, we note that interest rate parity is sometimes called *covered* interest rate parity (covered by a forward contract) to distinguish it from *uncovered interest rate parity*. *Uncovered interest rate parity* is based on economic theory rather than on arbitrage and involves expected exchange rates rather than forward rates. Uncovered interest rate parity is an economic theory that links interest rate differentials and the difference between the spot and expected exchange rate. We leave it and other parity theories for the reading on foreign exchange parity relations. On the other hand, interest rate parity, discussed in this reading, is a pure arbitrage condition imposed by efficient markets.

SUMMARY

- A direct exchange rate is the domestic price of foreign currency. An indirect exchange rate is the amount of foreign currency equivalent that one unit of the domestic currency purchases.

- The spread on a foreign currency transaction is the difference between the rate at which the bank is willing to commit itself today to buy (bid) foreign currency and to sell (ask). When given as a percentage, this spread is given as $100 \times (Ask - bid)/Ask$.

- Spreads differ as a result of market conditions and trading volume but not dealer positions. The size of the bid–ask spread increases with exchange rate uncertainty (volatility) because of bank/dealer risk aversion. Spreads are larger for currencies that have a low trading volume (thinly traded currencies).

- To work with currency cross rates and bid–ask spreads, we can use two principles: The ask exchange rate for the quoted currency is the reciprocal of the bid exchange rate for the measurement currency in which the price is expressed.

- To calculate the profit on a triangular arbitrage opportunity, the basic step is to determine whether the quoted cross rate is different from the implied cross rate.

- Spot exchange rates are quoted for immediate currency transactions, but forward change rates are rates contracted today for delivery and settlement in the future.

- As with spot rates, forward contract bid–ask spreads differ as a result of market conditions and trading volume but not bank/dealer positions. Bid–ask spreads increase with increasing maturity of the contract.

- The forward discount (negative) or premium (positive) is defined as the forward rate minus the spot rate expressed as a percentage of the spot rate.

- The forward discount or premium is often calculated as an annualized percentage deviation from the spot rate as given by the discount or premium multiplied by 12 over the number of months forward.

- The interest rate parity relationship is that the forward discount (premium) equals the interest rate differential between the two currencies: what is gained on the interest rate of a currency is lost on its discount.

- Covered interest arbitrage is the process of simultaneously borrowing the domestic currency, transferring it into foreign currency at the spot exchange rate, lending it, and buying a forward exchange rate contract to repatriate the foreign currency into domestic currency at a known forward exchange rate. The net result of such an arbitrage should be nil.

PRACTICE PROBLEMS FOR READING 18

1. If the exchange rate value of the British pound goes from U.S. $1.80 to U.S. $1.60, then:

   A. the pound has appreciated, and the British will find U.S. goods cheaper.

   B. the pound has appreciated, and the British will find U.S. goods more expensive.

   C. the pound has depreciated, and the British will find U.S. goods more expensive.

   D. the pound has depreciated, and the British will find U.S. goods cheaper.

2. If the exchange rate between the Australian dollar and the U.S. dollar, $:A$, changes from A$1.60 to A$1.50, then:

   A. the Australian dollar has appreciated, and the Australians will find U.S. goods cheaper.

   B. the Australian dollar has appreciated, and the Australians will find U.S. goods more expensive.

   C. the Australian dollar has depreciated, and the Australians will find U.S. goods more expensive.

   D. the Australian dollar has depreciated, and the Australians will find U.S. goods cheaper.

3. Over a period of time in the past, the exchange rate between the Swiss franc and the U.S. dollar, $:SFr, changed from about 1.20 to about 1.60. Would you agree that over this period, Swiss goods became cheaper for Americans?

4. Over a period of time in the past, you noticed that the exchange rate between the Thai baht and the dollar changed considerably. In particular, the $:baht exchange rate increased from 25 to 30.

   A. Did the Thai baht appreciate or depreciate with respect to the dollar? By what percentage?

   B. By what percentage did the value of the dollar change with respect to the Thai baht?

5. A foreign exchange trader with a U.S. bank took a short position of £5 million when the £:$ exchange rate was 1.45. Subsequently, the exchange rate changed to 1.51. Is this movement in the exchange rate good from the point of view of the position taken by the trader? By how much did the bank's liability change because of the change in exchange rate?

6. A financial newspaper provided the following midpoint spot exchange rates. Compute all the cross exchange rates based on these quotes.

   €:$ = 0.9119

   $:SFr = 1.5971

   $:¥ = 128.17

Practice Problems and Solutions: *Global Investments*, Sixth Edition, by Bruno Solnik and Dennis McLeavey, CFA, and *Solutions Manual* to accompany *Global Investments*, Sixth Edition, by Bruno Solnik and Dennis McLeavey, CFA. Copyright © 2009 by Pearson Education. Reprinted with permission of Pearson Education, publishing as Prentice Hall.

7. You visited the foreign exchange trading room of a major bank when a trader asked for quotes of the euro from various correspondents and heard the following:

Bank A   1.1210–15

Bank B   12–17

What do these quotes mean?

8. Do you think the dollar exchange rate of the British pound or the Polish zloty has a higher percentage bid–ask spread? Why?

9. Here are some historical quotes of the USD:JPY (yen per dollar) exchange rate given simultaneously on the phone by three banks:

Bank A   121.15–121.25

Bank B   121.30–121.35

Bank C   121.15–121.35

Are these quotes reasonable? Is there an arbitrage opportunity?

10. At a certain point in time, the euro is quoted as EUR:USD = 1.1610–1.1615, and the Swiss franc is quoted as USD:CHF = 1.4100–1.4120. What is the implicit EUR:CHF quotation?

11. At a certain point in time, a bank quoted the following exchange rates against the dollar for the Swiss franc and the Australian dollar.

$:SFr = 1.5960–70

$:A$ = 1.8225–35

Simultaneously, an Australian firm asked the bank for a A$:SFr quote. What cross rate would the bank have quoted?

12. At a certain point in time, a bank quoted the following exchange rates against the dollar for the Swiss franc and the Australian dollar.

$:SFr = 1.5960–70

$:A$ = 1.8225–35

Simultaneously, a Swiss firm asked the bank for an SFr:A$ quote. What cross rate would the bank have quoted?

13. Based on historical Japanese yen and Canadian dollar quotes by a bank, the implicit yen per Canadian dollar cross rate quotation was C$:¥ = 82.5150–82.5750. What would be the implicit Canadian dollar per yen cross rate quotation, ¥:C$?

14. Suppose that a quote for the dollar spot exchange rate of Danish kroner (symbol DKr or code DKK) is DKr8.25 per dollar, and a quote for the dollar spot exchange rate of Swiss Franc is SFr1.65 per dollar.

A. What should be the quote for the SFr:DKr cross rate so that there are no arbitrage opportunities (ignore transaction costs)?

B. Suppose a bank is offering a quote for the SFr:DKr cross rate as DKr5.20 per SFr. In this quote, which currency is overvalued with respect to the other?

15. Suppose that at a point in time, Barclays bank was quoting a dollars per pound exchange rate of £:$ = 1.4570. Industrial bank was quoting a Japanese yen per dollar exchange rate of $:¥ = 128.17, and Midland bank was quoting a Japanese yen per pound cross rate of £:¥ 183.

   A. Ignoring bid–ask spreads, was there an arbitrage opportunity here?

   B. If there was an arbitrage opportunity, what steps would you have taken to make an arbitrage profit, and how much would you have profited with $1 million available for this purpose?

16. Jim Waugh specializes in cross-rate arbitrage. At a point in time, he noticed the following quotes:

   U.S. dollar in Swiss francs = SFr1.5971 per $

   U.S. dollar in Australian dollars = A$1.8215 per $

   Swiss franc in Australian dollar = A$1.1450 per SFr

   Ignoring transaction costs, did Jim Waugh have an arbitrage opportunity based on these quotes? If there was an arbitrage opportunity, what steps would he have taken to make an arbitrage profit, and how much would he have profited with $1 million available for this purpose?

17. You notice the following hypothetical exchange rates in the newspaper.

   £:$ spot = 1.46

   £:$ three-month forward = 1.42

   $:SFr spot = 1.60

   $:SFr three-month forward = 1.65

   In the language of currency traders, would the £ be considered strong or weak relative to the dollar? What about the Swiss franc?

18. Suppose that the spot pound in dollars exchange rate is £:$ = 1.4570–1.4576 and the six-month forward pound exchange rate is $/£ = 1.4408–1.4434.

   A. Is the pound trading at a discount or at a premium relative to the dollar in the forward market?

   B. Compute the annualized forward discount or premium on the pound relative to the dollar.

19. Suppose that the spot Swiss francs per dollar exchange rate is $:SFr = 1.5960–70 and the three-month forward exchange rate is $:SFr = 1.5932–62.

   A. Is the Swiss franc trading at a discount or at a premium relative to the dollar in the forward market?

   B. Compute the annualized forward discount or premium on the Swiss franc relative to the dollar.

20. On the Forex market, you observe the following hypothetical quotes.

   Spot $:¥ = 110.00−110.10

   One-year interest rate $ = $4\%-4\frac{1}{4}\%$

   One-year interest rate ¥ = $1\%-1\frac{1}{4}\%$

   What should be the quote for the one-year forward exchange rate $:¥?

SOLUTIONS FOR READING 18

1. C is correct. Since the value of the British pound in U.S. dollars has gone down, it has depreciated with respect to the U.S. dollar. Therefore, the British will have to spend more British pounds to purchase U.S. goods.

2. A is correct. Since the number of Australian dollars needed to purchase one U.S. dollar has decreased from 1.60 to 1.50, the Australian dollar has appreciated with respect to the U.S. dollar. Therefore, the Australians will have to spend fewer Australian dollars to purchase U.S. goods.

3. The value of the dollar in Swiss francs has gone up from about 1.20 to about 1.60. Therefore, the dollar has appreciated relative to the Swiss franc, and the dollars needed by Americans to purchase Swiss goods have decreased. Thus, the statement is correct.

4. A. One baht was worth 1/25 or 0.04 dollars earlier. It is worth 1/30 or 0.0333 dollars now. Thus, the baht has depreciated with respect to the dollar. Percentage change in the dollar value of the baht = ((0.0333 − 0.04)/0.04)100% = −16.7%.

B. One dollar was worth 25 bahts earlier and is worth 30 bahts now. Percentage change in the value of the dollar = ((30 − 25)/25)100% = 20.0%.

5. The increase in £:$ exchange rate implies that the pound has appreciated with respect to the dollar. This is unfavorable to the trader since the trader has a short position in pounds.

Bank's liability in dollars initially was 5,000,0000 × 1.45 = $7,250,000
Bank's liability in dollars now is 5,000,0000 × 1.51 = $7,550,000

Thus, the bank's liability has increased by $300,000.

6. Three cross-exchange rates need to be computed: SFr/€, ¥/€, SFr/¥.

A. €:SFr = $:SFr × €:$ = SFr 1.5971 per $ × $ 0.9119 per € = 1.4564

B. €:¥ = $:¥ × €:$ = ¥ 128.17 per $ × $ 0.9119 per € = 116.88

C. ¥:SFr = $:SFr × ¥:$ = ($:SFr) ÷ ($:¥)
= (SFr 1.5971 per $)/(¥ 128.17 per $) = 0.0125

7. These quotations mean that Bank A is willing to buy one euro for 1.1210 dollars (bid rate) or to sell one for 1.1215 dollars (ask rate). Bank B's €:$ bid rate is 1.1212; its ask rate is 1.1217. That is, Bank B is willing to buy one euro for 1.1212 dollars or to sell one for 1.1217 dollars.

8. The percentage spread is considerably higher for the Polish zloty than for the British pound. The market for the Polish zloty is much less liquid than the market for the British pound. There is a lot more competition between market makers for the British pound than for the Polish zloty. Consequently, the percentage spread is considerably higher for the Polish zloty than for the British pound.

9. These quotes are unreasonable because they deviate from Bank A to Bank B by more than the spread; for example, Bank A's ask rate (121.25) is smaller than Bank B's bid rate (121.30). There is, therefore, an arbitrage opportunity. One can buy Bank A's dollars for 121.25 yen per dollar, sell these dollars to Bank B for 121.30 yen per dollar, and thereby make a profit of 0.05 yen per dollar traded. This is a riskless, instantaneous operation that requires no initial investment.

10. The €:SFr quotation is obtained as follows. In obtaining this quotation, we keep in mind that €:SFr = $:SFr × €:$, and that the price for each transaction (bid or ask) is the one that is more advantageous to the trader.

    The €:SFr bid price is the number of Swiss francs that a trader is willing to pay for one euro. This transaction (buy euro − sell Swiss francs) is equivalent to selling Swiss francs to buy dollars (at a bid rate of 1.4100), and then selling those dollars to buy euros (at a bid rate of 1.1610). Mathematically, the transaction is as follows:

$$(\text{Bid } \$:\text{SFr}) \times (\text{Bid } €:\$) = 1.4100 \times 1.1610 = 1.6370$$

The €:SFr ask price is the number of Swiss francs that a trader is asking for one euro. This transaction (sell euros − buy Swiss francs) is equivalent to buying Swiss francs with dollars (at an ask rate of 1.4120) and simultaneously purchasing these dollars against euros (at an ask rate of 1.1615). Mathematically, this can be expressed as follows:

$$(\text{Ask } \$:\text{SFr}) \times (\text{Ask } €:\$) = 1.4120 \times 1.1615 = 1.6400$$

So the resulting quotation by the trader is

$$€:\text{SFr} = 1.6370 - 1.6400$$

11. The A$:SFr quotation is obtained as follows. In obtaining this quotation, we keep in mind that A$:SFr = ($:SFr) ÷ ($:A$), and that the price (bid or ask) for each transaction is the one that is more advantageous to the bank.

    The A$:SFr bid price is the number of SFr the bank is willing to pay to buy one A$. This transaction (buy A$ − sell SFr) is equivalent to selling SFr to buy dollars (at a bid rate of 1.5960) and then selling those dollars to buy A$ (at an ask rate of 1.8235). Mathematically, the transaction is as follows:

$$\text{Bid A}\$:\text{SFr} = (\text{Bid } \$:\text{SFr}) \div (\text{Ask } \$:\text{A}\$) = 1.5960/1.8235 = 0.8752$$

The A$:SFr ask price is the number of SFr that the bank is asking for one A$. This transaction (sell A$ − buy SFr) is equivalent to buying SFr with dollars (at an ask rate of 1.5970) and simultaneously purchasing these dollars against A$ (at a bid rate of 1.8225). This may be expressed as follows:

$$\text{Ask A}\$:\text{SFr} = (\text{Ask } \$:\text{SFr}) \div (\text{Bid } \$:\text{A}\$) = 1.5970/1.8225 = 0.8763$$

The resulting quotation by the bank is

$$\text{A}\$:\text{SFr} = 0.8752 - 0.8763$$

12. The SFr:A$ quotation is obtained as follows. In obtaining this quotation, we keep in mind that SFr:A$ = ($:As) ÷ ($:SFr), and that the price (bid or ask) for each transaction is the one that is more advantageous to the bank.

The SFr:A\$ bid price is the number of A\$ the bank is willing to pay to buy one SFr. This transaction (buy SFr − sell A\$) is equivalent to selling A\$ to buy dollars (at a bid rate of 1.8225) and then selling those dollars to buy SFr (at an ask rate of 1.5970). Mathematically, the transaction is as follows:

Bid SFr:A\$ = (Bid \$:A\$)/(Ask \$:SFr) = 1.8225/1.5970 = 1.1412

The SFr:A\$ ask price is the number of A\$ that the bank is asking for one SFr. This transaction (sell SFr − buy A\$) is equivalent to buying A\$ with dollars (at an ask rate of 1.8235) and simultaneously purchasing these dollars against SFr (at a bid rate of 1.5960). This may be expressed as follows:

Ask SFr:A\$ = (Ask \$:A\$)/(Bid \$:SFr) = 1.8235/1.5960 = 1.1425

The resulting quotation by the bank is

SFr:A\$ = 1.1412 − 1.1425

13. The bid ¥:C\$ rate would be the inverse of the ask C\$:¥ rate, and the ask ¥:C\$ rate would be the inverse of the bid C\$:¥ rate. Therefore,

Bid ¥:C\$ = 1/Ask(C\$:¥) = 1/82.5750 = 0.01211
Ask ¥:C\$ = 1/Bid(C\$:¥) = 1/82.5150 = 0.01212

Thus, the quote is ¥:C\$ = 0.01211 − 0.01212.

14. **A.** There would be no arbitrage opportunities if cross rate SFr:DKr = \$:DKr × SFr:\$.

Because \$:SFr =1.65, SFr:\$ = 1/1.65 = 0.6061.

So, there would be no arbitrage opportunities if the cross rate SFr:DKr = 8.25 × 0.6061 = DKr 5 per SFr.

B. In the DKr 5.20 per SFr cross rate, one SFr is worth DKr 5.20. The implicit rate computed in Part A above indicates that one SFr should be worth DKr 5. Therefore, the SFr is overvalued with respect to the DKr at the exchange rate of DKr 5.20 per SFr.

15. The implicit cross rate between yen and pound is £:¥ = \$:¥ × £:\$ = 128.17 × 1.4570 = 186.74. However, Midland Bank is quoting a lower rate of ¥183 per £. So, triangular arbitrage is possible.

In the cross rate of ¥183 per £ quoted by Midland, one pound is worth 183 yen, whereas the cross rate based on the direct rates implies that one pound is worth 186.74 yen. Thus, pound is undervalued relative to the yen in the cross rate quoted by Midland, and your strategy for triangular arbitrage should be based on using yen to buy pounds from Midland. Accordingly, the steps you would take for an arbitrage profit are as follows:

A. Sell dollars to get yen: Sell \$1,000,000 to get \$1,000,000 × ¥128.17 per \$ = ¥128,170,000.

B. Use yen to buy pounds: Sell ¥128,170,000 to buy ¥128,170,000/(¥183 per £) = £700,382.51.

C. Sell pounds for dollars: Sell £700,382.51 for £700,382.51 × (\$1.4570 per £) = \$1,020,457.32.

Thus, your arbitrage profit is \$1,020,457.32 − \$1,000,000 = \$20,457.32.

16. A. The implicit cross rate between Australian dollars and Swiss francs is SFr:A\$ = \$:A\$ × SFr:\$ = (\$:A\$) ÷ (\$:SFr) = 1.8215/1.5971 = 1.1405. However, the quoted cross rate is higher at A\$1.1450 per SFr. So, triangular arbitrage is possible.

    B. In the quoted cross rate of A\$1.1450 per SFr, one Swiss franc is worth A\$1.1450, whereas the cross rate based on the direct rates implies that one Swiss franc is worth A\$1.1405. Thus, the Swiss franc is overvalued relative to the A\$ in the quoted cross rate, and Jim Waugh's strategy for triangular arbitrage should be based on selling Swiss francs to buy A\$ as per the quoted cross rate. Accordingly, the steps Jim Waugh would take for an arbitrage profit are as follows:

      i. Sell dollars to get Swiss francs: Sell \$1,000,000 to get \$1,000,000 × (SFr 1.5971 per \$) = SFr 1,597,100.

      ii. Sell Swiss francs to buy Australian dollars: Sell SFr 1,597,100 to buy SFr 1,597,100 × (A\$1.1450 per SFr) = A\$1,828,679.50.

      iii. Sell Australian dollars for dollars: Sell A\$1,828,679.50 for A\$1,828,679.50/ (A\$1.8215 per \$) = \$1,003,941.53.

    Thus, your arbitrage profit is \$1,003,941.53 − \$1,000,000 = \$3,941.53.

17. The value of the £ in \$ is worth less three months forward than it is now. Thus, the £ is trading at a forward discount relative to the \$. Therefore, the £ is "weak" relative to the \$. Because a \$ is worth SFr 1.60 now but worth SFr 1.65 three months forward, the \$ is "strong" relative to the SFr. That is, the SFr is "weak" relative to the \$.

18. The midpoint of the spot dollar to pound exchange rate is £:\$ = 1.4573. The midpoint of the six-month forward dollar to pound exchange rate is £:\$ = 1.4421.

    A. Based on the midpoints, the dollar value of a pound is 1.4573 now and only 1.4421 six months forward. Thus, the pound is worth less six months forward than now. That is, the pound is trading at a discount relative to the dollar in the forward market.

    B. Difference between midpoints of the forward and spot rates = 0.0152.

$$\text{Annualized discount} = \left(\frac{\text{Difference between forward and spot rates}}{\text{Spot rate}}\right)\left(\frac{12}{\text{No. months forward}}\right)100\%$$

$$= \left(\frac{0.0152}{1.4573}\right)\left(\frac{12}{6}\right)100\% = 2.09\%$$

19. The midpoint of the spot Swiss franc to dollar exchange rate is \$:SFr = 1.5965. The midpoint of the three-month forward Swiss franc to dollar exchange rate is \$:SFr = 1.5947.

    A. Based on the midpoints, a dollar is worth SFr 1.5965 now and only 1.5947 three months forward. So, the dollar is trading at a discount relative to the SFr in the forward market. That is, the SFr is trading at a premium relative to the dollar in the forward market.

B. Difference between midpoints of the forward and spot rates = 0.0018.

$$\text{Annualized premium} = \left(\frac{\text{Difference between forward and spot rates}}{\text{Spot rate}}\right)$$
$$\times \left(\frac{12}{\text{No. months forward}}\right) 100\%$$
$$= \left(\frac{0.0018}{1.5965}\right)\left(\frac{12}{3}\right) 100\% = 0.45\%$$

20. Let's first make sure we calculate the forward rate in the proper direction. The one-year forward rate $:¥ is given by Equation (3), where the dollar is the quoted currency (a) measured in yen (currency b):

$$\text{Forward exchange rate} = \text{Spot exchange rate} \times \frac{1 + r_¥}{1 + r_\$}$$

A bank will quote bid–ask forward rates, where the bid is lower than the ask. The ask forward rate (ask forward $:¥), is the ¥ price at which an investor can buy dollars forward and the bid forward rate is the ¥ price that an investor can obtain for dollars. Buying dollars forward (paying the ask forward) is equivalent to:

▶ Borrowing yen (and hence having to pay the ask interest rate: ask $r_¥$),
▶ Using these yen to buy dollars spot (and hence having to pay the ask exchange rate: ask spot $:¥),
▶ Lending those dollars (and hence receiving the bid interest rate: bid $r_\$$).

The resulting ask-forward exchange rate ($:¥) is

$$\text{Ask forward } (\$:¥) = 110.10 \frac{1 + 1.25\%}{1 + 4.00\%} = 107.19$$

The bid-forward exchange rate ($:¥) is

$$\text{Bid forward} (\$:¥) = 110 \frac{1 + 1.00\%}{1 + 4.25\%} = 106.57$$

Thus, the one-year forward rate should be: $:¥r = 106.57 − 107.19.

FOREIGN EXCHANGE PARITY RELATIONS

by Bruno Solnik and Dennis McLeavey, CFA

LEARNING OUTCOMES

The candidate should be able to:	Mastery
a. explain how exchange rates are determined in a flexible (or floating) exchange rate system;	☐
b. explain the role of each component of the balance of payments accounts;	☐
c. explain how current account deficits or surpluses and financial account deficits or surpluses affect an economy;	☐
d. describe the factors that cause a nation's currency to appreciate or depreciate;	☐
e. explain how monetary and fiscal policies affect the exchange rate and balance of payments components;	☐
f. describe a fixed exchange rate and a pegged exchange rate system;	☐
g. discuss absolute purchasing power parity and relative purchasing power parity;	☐
h. calculate the end-of-period exchange rate implied by purchasing power parity, given the beginning-of-period exchange rate and the inflation rates;	☐
i. discuss the international Fisher relation;	☐
j. calculate the real interest rate, given nominal interest rates and expected inflation rates, using the international Fisher relation and its linear approximation;	☐
k. discuss the theory of uncovered interest rate parity, and explain the theory's relation to other exchange rate parity theories;	☐
l. calculate the expected change in the exchange rate, given interest rates and the assumption that uncovered interest rate parity holds;	☐
m. discuss the foreign exchange expectation relation between the forward exchange rate and the expected exchange rate.	☐

663

Fluctuations in exchange rates are generated by a large variety of economic and political events. Exchange rate uncertainty adds an important dimension to the economics of capital markets. This reading starts with a review of foreign exchange fundamentals. In the flexible (or floating) exchange rate system of all major currencies, the foreign exchange rate is freely determined by supply and demand. Many international transactions affect foreign exchange demand and supply, and these are detailed in the country's balance of payments. After a brief review of the interaction between the two major components of the balance of payments (current account and financial account), we list the major factors that cause a currency to appreciate or depreciate.

Nevertheless, a detailed analysis of exchange rates and their importance in asset management requires a strong conceptual framework. Many domestic and foreign monetary variables interact with exchange rates. Before presenting the basic models of exchange rate determination, it is useful to recall well-known international parity conditions linking domestic and foreign monetary variables: inflation rates, interest rates, and foreign exchange rates. The relations among these are the basis for a simple model of the international monetary environment and are discussed in the second part of this reading. Given the complexity of a multicurrency environment, it is most useful to start by building a simplified model linking the various domestic and foreign monetary variables. The third part of this reading then discusses exchange rate determination theories and their practical implications.

1   FOREIGN EXCHANGE FUNDAMENTALS

Supply and Demand for Foreign Exchange

Just as the value of money is determined by supply and demand in the domestic economy, its value in relation to foreign currencies is also determined by supply and demand. Major currencies, such as the dollar, euro, yen, British pound, or Swiss franc, belong to a *flexible* or *floating* exchange rate system. These currencies are freely exchanged on the foreign exchange market, and their exchange rate depends on supply and demand.

Let's assume that the equilibrium exchange rate between the euro and the U.S. dollar is €:$ = 1.25. The $1.25 price of one euro results from the supply and demand for euros. American investors wishing to buy European goods or assets need to sell dollars to buy euros. Conversely, Europeans wishing to buy American goods or assets need to sell euros to buy dollars. If the exchange rate were artificially higher, say €:$ = 1.50, European goods would look more expensive to Americans. More dollars would be needed to spend the same amount of euros to buy European goods, and Americans would decrease their purchase of European goods and their quantity demanded of euros. American goods would look cheaper to Europeans, who would increase their purchase of American goods and the quantity of euros supplied.

In this two-country example, Exhibit 1 illustrates the demand and supply curves for euros. In the marketplace, the current exchange rate of $1.25 per euro is the

| EXHIBIT 1 | Foreign Exchange Market Equilibrium |

price that equilibrates demand and supply. If the exchange rate were set higher, say $1.50 per euro, there would be an excess supply of euros, a market disequilibrium.

The illustration presented in Exhibit 1 is simple, as we referred only to transactions motivated by trading demand between two countries. In general, there are many types of transactions that affect the demand and supply of one national currency. From an accounting viewpoint, each country keeps track of the payments on all international transactions in its balance of payments.

Balance of Payments

The *balance of payments* tracks all financial flows crossing a country's borders during a given period (a quarter or a year). It is an accounting of all cash flows between residents of a country (called the home country in the discussion that follows), and nonresidents. For example, an export creates a financial inflow for the home country, whereas an import creates an outflow (a negative inflow). A resident's purchase of a foreign security creates a negative financial inflow, whereas a loan made by a foreign bank to a resident bank creates a positive financial inflow. The convention is to treat all inflows (e.g., exports or sale of domestic assets) as a credit to the balance of payments.

For example, assume that a resident imports 100 currency units worth of goods from a foreign country and uses trade credit from the foreign exporter. There will be two accounting entries:

100 debit for the goods (imports)

100 credit for the loan obtained

International transactions such as these are further grouped into two main categories: the current account and the financial account.[1]

---

[1] We follow the 1993 International Monetary Fund (IMF) presentation and terminology, which is currently used by most countries. A revision in the IMF presentation is expected in 2008. A more detailed description of the balance of payments is given later in this reading.

Current Account

The *current account* covers all current transactions that take place in the normal business of residents of a country. It is dominated by the *trade balance*, the balance of all exports and imports. It also includes various other current transactions. To summarize, the current account is made up of

► Exports and imports (the trade balance)
► Services (such as services in transportation, communication, insurance, and finance)
► Income (interest, dividends, and a variety of investment income from cross-border investments)
► Current transfers (gifts and other flows without quid pro quo compensation)

The current account balance represents the net value of all these flows associated with current transactions, a country's resident's flows abroad and nonresidents' flows to the country.

Financial Account

The *financial account* covers a country's residents' investments abroad and nonresidents' investments in the country. It includes

► Direct investment made by companies
► Portfolio investments in equity, bonds, and other securities of any maturity
► Other investments and liabilities (such as deposits or borrowing with foreign banks and vice versa)

The financial account balance represents the net value of all these flows associated with investments and liabilities, a country's residents' flows abroad and nonresidents' flows to the country.

The sum of these two accounts, called the *overall balance*, should be zero.[2] If it is not zero, the monetary authority must use reserve assets to fill the gap. If the overall balance is negative, the central bank can use up part of its reserves to restore a zero balance. The *official reserves* account tracks all reserve transactions by the monetary authorities. By accounting definition, the sum of all the balance of payments accounts must be zero.

Current Account Deficits and Financial Account Surpluses

The trade balance, the primary component of the current account, receives major attention in the media of all countries. Monthly trade figures are widely discussed when they are released. The usual undertone is that a current account deficit is "bad." This simple value judgment is based on some economic arguments that are often incorrect. We now discuss the reasons that a current account deficit is not a bad thing in its own right.

---

[2] Two other small accounts also exist in the balance of payments terminology. They are the *capital account*, which tracks capital transfers (i.e., capital gifts to other countries, such as debt forgiveness), and *net errors and omissions* (to adjust for statistical discrepancies). These accounts are small in magnitude and are usually added to the financial account balance for analysis purposes. We follow this convention. A more detailed presentation of the balance of payments is proposed in the third part of this reading.

A Current Account Deficit Is Offset by a Financial Account Surplus

The current account is only one component of a country's balance of payments. A current account deficit should not be confused with an overall balance deficit. A current account deficit has to be offset by a financial account surplus. Of course, official reserves can be used to offset a current account deficit in a given quarter or year, but this can be only a temporary measure, as the country's reserves will quickly be depleted. To be sustained, a current account deficit must be financed by a financial account surplus. This has been the case for the United States since the mid-1990s. Exhibit 2 reports the 2004 balance of payments for the United States.

The large current account deficit of the United States is mostly caused by its trade deficit. But foreigners are large investors in the U.S. economy. They are attracted by a stable country with good investment opportunities and a major currency.

In Exhibit 2, we can see that domestic investments in the United States exceed domestic savings, and collaterally, imports exceed exports. The excess demand for investments is met by financial inflows from foreign countries. The exchange rate clears the market with respect to these other countries, for example China. China has a current account surplus (exports exceed imports) and is a net foreign investor (domestic savings exceed domestic investments).

EXHIBIT 2	**U.S. Balance of Payments for 2004**

Current Account (CA, in Billions of Dollars)			Capital Account (KA, in Billions of Dollars)		
Goods		−$665	Net capital transfers		−$2
Services	+$48		**Financial Account (FA)**		
Net income		+ $30	Net foreign direct investment	−$145	
Current transfers		−$81	Net portfolio investment		+$660
Total		−$668	Net banking and other flows	+ $67	
			Net statistical discrepancies	+ $85	
			Official Reserves		
			Net change in official reserve assets	+ $3	
			Total		+$668

U.S. Savings and Investment 2004 (in Billions of Dollars)

Gross domestic saving		+$1,572
Gross domestic investment	−$2,301	
Net other flows		+ $61
Total		−$668

Source: Modified from the *Economic Report of the President*, 2004.

Is a Current Account Deficit a Bad Economic Signal?

A country faces a trade deficit when its imports exceed its exports. As long as foreign investors are willing to finance this difference by net capital flows into the country, the situation poses no economic problem. The depreciation pressures from the current account deficit are balanced by the appreciation pressures from the financial account surplus.

A current account deficit is sometimes caused by economic growth. When a country grows faster than its trading partners, it tends to need more imports to sustain its output growth. Because other countries do not have the same growth rate, demand for exports does not grow as fast as that for imports. Higher economic growth also yields attractive returns on invested capital and attracts foreign investment. This capital inflow provides natural financing for the current account deficit.

Large current account imbalances can have social implications, however. Countries with trade deficits will face political pressures against free trade, and those with surpluses will be singled out as targets for tariffs.

Is a Large Current Account Deficit Sustainable?

First, we need to judge the size of a deficit relative to some benchmark. This deficit can be compared with total imports or *gross domestic product (GDP)*. Deficits ranging from 2 percent to 8 percent of GDP can be observed in different countries, but the sustainability question arises at the high end, particularly when foreign investment comes more from foreign government debt investments rather than from foreign private investors. Recall also that the income payments are part of the current account, so too large a foreign debt burden can exacerbate current account deficits. A large current account deficit can be sustained if nonresidents are willing to finance it continuously. As long as a country offers attractive investment opportunities and a stable "investment climate," it can keep attracting additional financial flows. The situation is no different for a corporation that relies on debt and equity financing to generate more activity. External financing is a normal recourse for a growing corporation. But as with corporations, external financing of a country also increases the risk of a crisis. As soon as foreign investors reduce their financial flows, or seek to repatriate their invested capital, the financing of the current account deficit will disappear and adjustments will need to take place, usually in the form of a depreciation of the currency to restore trade balances. We now detail factors that induce a financial account surplus.

Factors Affecting the Financial Account

Changes in Real Interest Rates

Financial flows are attracted by high expected return. For debt securities, investors search for high real interest rates. The *real interest rate* is the difference between the interest rate and expected inflation. If exchange rates do indeed adjust to inflation differentials, the country offering the highest real interest rate will provide the highest expected return after an exchange rate adjustment and will attract international loanable funds.

An increase in a country's real interest rate will lead to an appreciation of its currency, and a decrease in its real interest rate will lead to a depreciation of its currency. Of course, if the real interest rate movement is matched by a similar real interest rate movement in another country, the two currencies' exchange rates should stay unchanged. It is the relative movement in the real interest rate that is of importance for the exchange rate change. The influence of interest rates is detailed later in the reading.

Differences in Economic Performance

Financial flows are attracted by high expected return. For equity securities, investors search for high performance of individual firms and of the economy as a whole. So, good news on the prospect for growth of a nation should attract more international equity capital, and the nation's currency should appreciate.

Although growth should boost the financial account of a nation, there is also an opposite effect on the current account. As mentioned, a fast-growing economy has a fast-growing demand for imports. Demand for exports, however, does not grow at the same rate (because other countries are not growing as quickly). This situation will put a downward pressure on the current account, which could lead to a depreciation of the nation's currency.

The direction of the cumulative effect is unclear. In the early 1990s, Asian emerging countries grew at a very fast rate with stable currencies. Their imports grew rapidly to sustain the growth in production and to satisfy the consumption needs of their wealthier residents. But this deficit was offset by foreign financial flows, so the net result was a stable exchange rate.

It is important to stress that capital flows are motivated by *expected* returns. Thus, it is expected future long-run economic growth that affects investment flows. As indicated by its name, the *current* account reflects the influence of current economic growth on imports and exports. Current economic growth affects the current account; future economic growth affects the financial account (see Example 1).

EXAMPLE 1

Poor Relative Economic Performance and Depreciation

Suppose there are disappointing domestic economic data reports about a country that has a significant current account deficit and a relatively high level of foreign indebtedness. What are the likely effects on the domestic currency? To illustrate your answer, take the example of Thailand during the Asian crisis of 1997. In 1996, Thailand exhibited strong economic growth. Rapid growth created a large 1996 current account deficit equal to $15 billion, some 10 percent of its GDP. This was offset by large foreign capital inflows with a 1996 financial account surplus equal to $16 billion. The exchange rate was 25 Thai bahts per dollar. In 1997, some disappointing reports were published on the economic prospects in Thailand. What are the likely effects on the Thai baht?

Solution: The disappointing domestic economic data may lower expectations of future growth and hence put downward pressure on the financial account. At the same time, a significant current account deficit might not be reduced without some depreciation. The level of foreign indebtedness and the sensitivity of imports to economic conditions can reduce the sensitivity of the current account deficit to disappointing domestic economic data. The likely effects, then, are a depreciation of the domestic currency.

This deterioration of the economic prospects of Thailand in 1997 led to a rapid withdrawal of foreign capital and a negative financial flow balance. The overall balance became a huge deficit in 1997, as both the current account and financial account came in deficit. The baht was forced to be devalued to a level above 40 bahts per dollar. The financial crisis also affected the local real estate and stock markets, and a severe recession took place. Imports were cut back because of the economic recession and because of their increased price due to the baht depreciation. Exports increased as they became very competitive internationally with the large depreciation of the currency. By 1998, the current account had moved back to a $14 billion surplus, which helped absorb a continuing deficit in the financial account.

Changes in Investment Climate

Financial flows are attracted not only by high expected return but also by low risk. Investors favor countries with a good investment climate and dislike uncertainty. Among desired attributes are

▶ A stable political system

▶ A rigorous but fair legal system that protects the rights of all investors

▶ A tax system that is fair to foreign investors

▶ Free movements of capital

▶ Monetary authorities that favor price stability

An improvement in a country's investment climate will lead to increased financial inflows and a currency appreciation. Negative news will worsen investment risk perception and tend to lead to capital outflows and a depreciation of the currency.

Government Policies: Monetary and Fiscal

Many of the previously mentioned factors are affected by government policies, such as monetary and fiscal policies. In this section, we sketch the reaction of the exchange rate and components of the balance of payments to an unanticipated change in monetary or fiscal policy. This is a complex issue, and we have to assume that everything else remains the same, including policies of other governments.

Monetary Policy and the Foreign Exchange Rate

Suppose that a country decides to shift to a more expansionary monetary policy. This is a shift that was not anticipated. Most economists would agree that this monetary shock would have, at least, two effects on the domestic economy:

▶ The real interest rate will temporarily drop.

▶ There will be an upward pressure on the domestic price level, and inflation will accelerate.

As discussed, both factors would lead to a depreciation of the domestic currency relative to other currencies. Otherwise, both the current account (because of inflation) and the financial account (because of the low real interest rate) would be in deficit.

Whether an expansionary monetary policy creates economic growth in the short and long run is a matter of debate among economists. Many would argue that an unanticipated monetary expansion would induce a short-run boost in economic growth, but no long-run stimulation. Because this boost is not likely to be long-lived, it will hardly motivate additional foreign financial flows, but it will put additional pressures on the current account (imports will grow faster than exports).

For all these reasons, an expansionary monetary policy will lead to a depreciation of the home currency, while a restrictive monetary policy will lead to an appreciation of the home currency.[3]

Fiscal Policy and the Foreign Exchange Rate

Suppose that a country decides to use a mix of budget and fiscal policy to finance government expenditures. *Everything else equal,* a more restrictive fiscal policy means that a government increases the share of taxes and reduces the share of borrowing to finance government spending. A more expansionary fiscal policy means that a government reduces taxes while increasing the budget deficit.

A more restrictive fiscal policy implies less government borrowing, which should induce a reduction in the domestic real interest rate. In turn, this drop in the domestic real interest rate should lead to a depreciation of the home currency (investment outflows). However, a more restrictive fiscal policy should also slow down economic activity and inflation. These two factors should lead to an appreciation of the home currency (current account improvement).

These influences are conflicting, and it is hard to draw general conclusions on the link between fiscal policy and exchange rates. Many economists believe that the interest rate factor will dominate and that the net result of a more restrictive policy will be a depreciation of the home currency.

A more expansionary fiscal policy has the reverse effect. It will induce a higher domestic real interest rate, which should lead to an appreciation of the currency. However, this expansionary fiscal policy should also induce a rise in output and inflationary pressures, which tend to put depreciation pressure on the home currency. The net result is usually expected to be an appreciation of the home currency. The reaction will be somewhat stronger if the shift in fiscal policy is expected to be permanent rather than temporary.

Exchange Rate Regimes

The previous discussion was conducted assuming that exchange rates were flexible. Historically, exchange rates have operated under three different types of regimes:

► Flexible (or floating) exchange rates

► Fixed exchange rates

► Pegged exchange rates

---

[3] A detailed analysis of the dynamics of the exchange rate response to a monetary shock is given in the last part of this reading on the asset market approach.

Flexible (or Floating) Exchange Rates

A *flexible exchange rate regime* is one in which the exchange rate between two currencies fluctuates freely in the foreign exchange market. Today, all major currencies are freely traded, and their pairwise exchange rates fluctuate in the foreign exchange market in a flexible manner. A central bank can intervene on the foreign exchange market, but it is only one of the many players that contribute to total currency supply and demand, albeit an important one. A government can announce what it believes to be the "normal" exchange rate of its currency, and this announcement will be taken into account by the marketplace.[4] But governments have neither the power nor the will to set official exchange rates (usually called *parities*). In a "pure" floating exchange rate system, governments intervene in the foreign exchange market only to smooth temporary imbalances. If a government has some exchange rate target, it will try to achieve the target by adopting the proper macroeconomic policies.

The *advantage* of a flexible exchange rate system is that the exchange rate is a market-determined price that reflects economic fundamentals at each point in time. Governments do not intervene to defend some exchange rate level, so there is no incentive to speculate "against" them. Because exchange rates are flexible, governments are free to adopt independent domestic monetary and fiscal policies.

The *disadvantage* is that flexible exchange rates can be quite volatile. This volatility is unpleasant for agents engaged in trade and investment, but currency risk-hedging strategies are available.

Fixed Exchange Rates

A *fixed exchange rate regime* is one in which the exchange rate between two currencies remains fixed at a preset level, known as *official parity*. In a truly fixed system, the exchange rate is expected to remain at its fixed parity forever. It is not sufficient for a country to announce that it will keep a fixed exchange rate with other currencies. To be credible, it must put in place some disciplined system to maintain the official parity at all times.

Historically, the first international exchange rate regime was one of fixed exchange rates, in which all currencies had a value fixed in terms of gold content (*gold standard*). In such a gold standard, the domestic money supply is fully backed by an equivalent of gold reserves. This system worked well in the 1800s and up to the conclusion of World War I, but it progressively disappeared thereafter. Today, some countries still attempt to maintain a fixed exchange rate against the dollar or the euro. This is usually done by adopting a *currency board*. In a currency board, a country (say, Argentina) commits to keep a fixed exchange rate with a major currency (say, one peso per U.S. dollar), and the supply of home currency is fully backed by an equivalent amount of that major currency.

Suppose there is a deficit in the balance of payments of the home country. It must be financed out of reserves: The amount of dollars held as reserves will be reduced, and so will the domestic money supply (100 percent dollar backing). As the country's money supply is reduced, prices of goods must drop and interest rates must rise. In turn, these adjustments make domestic goods more competitive internationally, and the balance of payments equilibrium is restored.

---

[4] There is some similarity with a CEO announcing that a corporation's share price is undervalued. The company could decide to use cash reserves to buy back shares.

The *advantage* of a fixed exchange rate is that it eliminates exchange rate risk, at least in the short run. It also brings discipline to government policies; this is particularly useful for emerging countries, which are prone to running inflationary policies.

The *disadvantage* of a fixed exchange rate is that it deprives the country of any monetary independence: Its monetary policy is dictated by the "defense" of its parity. It also constrains the country's fiscal policy. A major problem with a fixed exchange rate is its long-term credibility. As soon as a country runs into economic problems, there will be strong speculatory and political pressures to remove the fixed rate system and a push toward a sizable devaluation, with major economic disruption (as happened in Argentina).

Pegged Exchange Rates

A *pegged exchange rate regime* is one characterized as a compromise between a flexible and a fixed exchange rate. A country decides to peg its currency to another major currency (the dollar or euro) or to a basket of currencies. A target exchange rate is set (the peg), but this is not a fixed exchange rate to be defended at all costs. First, the exchange rate is allowed to fluctuate within a (small) band around this target. Second, periodic changes in the target exchange rate can take place to reflect trends in economic fundamentals (mostly higher inflation in the home country).[5]

Smaller countries, especially emerging countries, frequently use a pegged exchange rate. To defend a target exchange rate against speculation pressures, a country can resort to a variety of measures. Central bank intervention, possibly coordinated with other countries, is one method. The demand and supply for its currency can also be constrained by imposing various restrictions on trade flows (tariffs and quotas) and on capital flows (capital and currency repatriation restrictions, taxes). In the end, aid from international agencies could be requested. But artificially defending a pegged exchange rate could be a costly process for a central bank if devaluation ultimately happened. Speculators would benefit, and this chain of events would also deter foreign investments in the future.

The *advantage* of a pegged exchange rate is that it reduces exchange rate volatility, at least in the short run. This is beneficial to international trade. Setting a fixed exchange rate target also encourages monetary discipline for the home country.

The *disadvantage* of a pegged exchange rate system is that it can induce destabilizing speculation. The more rigid the application of a pegged exchange rate system, the more likely it is that speculators will try to take advantage of the lack of adjustment in the exchange rate.

INTERNATIONAL PARITY RELATIONS

2

We now introduce a simple theoretical framework that is useful to understand the interplay between exchange rates, interest rates, and inflation rates. Traditionally, different nations use different currencies, allowing each nation some independence

---

[5] For example, Brazil had a "crawling peg" with the U.S. dollar for many years, whereby the target exchange rate (peg) was automatically adjusted for the inflation differential between Brazil and the United States.

in setting its national interest rate and monetary policy. Thus, inflation rates and interest rates can differ markedly among countries, implying that the currencies' exchange rates will not stay constant over time.

International parity relations detail how exchange rates, interest rates, and inflation rates would be linked in a simple and perfect world. The set of parity relations of international finance is as follows:

1. the *interest rate parity relation*, linking spot exchange rates, forward exchange rates, and interest rates

2. the *purchasing power parity relation*, linking spot exchange rates and inflation

3. the *international Fisher relation*, linking interest rates and expected inflation

4. the *uncovered interest rate parity relation*, linking spot exchange rates, expected exchange rates, and interest rates

5. the *foreign exchange expectation relation*, linking forward exchange rates and expected spot exchange rates

These theoretical relationships lead to predictions for exchange rate appreciation or depreciation in a simple world. This basic framework can then be enriched to accommodate more complex situations.

Some Definitions

First, we need to recall some notation introduced in the reading on currency exchange rates and introduce notation for the inflation rate.

► *The spot exchange rate S:* The rate of exchange of two currencies tells us the amount of one currency that one unit of another currency can buy. *Spot* means that we refer to the exchange rate for immediate delivery. For example, the €:$ spot exchange rate might be $S = \$1.25$, indicating that one euro is worth 1.25 dollars (one U.S. dollar is worth 0.8 euros).

► *The forward exchange rate F:* The rate of exchange of two currencies set on one date for delivery at a future specified date, the *forward* rate is quoted today for future delivery. For example, the €:$ forward exchange rate for delivery in one year might be $F = \$1.2061$, ($1.2061 per euro).

► *The interest rate r:* The rate of interest for a given time period is a function of the length of the time period and the denomination of the currency. Interest rates are usually quoted in the marketplace as an annualized rate. With the euro as the domestic currency and the U.S. dollar as the foreign currency, for example, the one-year rate in the domestic country (DC) might be $r_{DC} = 14\%$, and the one-year rate in the foreign country (FC) might be $r_{FC} = 10\%$. In this case, the *interest rate differential* is equal to -4 percent ($r_{FC} - r_{DC} = 10 - 14$).

► *The inflation rate I:* This is equal to the rate of consumer price increase over the period specified. The *inflation differential* is equal to the difference of inflation rates between two countries. For example, if the inflation in the FC is $I_{FC} = 8.91$ percent and the inflation in the DC is $I_{DC} = 12.87$ percent, the inflation differential over the period is approximately -4 percent ($I_{FC} - I_{DC} = 8.91 - 12.87 = -3.96\%$).

► *The forward discount or premium f:* This is equal to the forward minus spot rate as a percentage of the spot rate; $f = (F - S)/S = (1.20 - 1.25)/1.25 = -4\%$.

Interest Rate Parity

As discussed in the reading on currency exchange rates, spot exchange rates, forward exchange rates, and interest rates are linked by the interest rate parity relation

$$F/S = (1 + r_{FC})/(1 + r_{DC}) \text{ or } (F - S)/S = (r_{FC} - r_{DC})/(1 + r_{DC})$$

(1)

where S and F are quoted as DC:FC (the amount of foreign currency that one unit of domestic currency can buy) and r_{DC} and r_{FC} are the domestic and foreign risk-free interest rates, respectively.

Defining $f = (F - S)/S = (r_{FC} - r_{DC})/(1 + r_{DC})$, we have a linear approximation for interest rate parity:[6]

$$f \cong r_{FC} - r_{DC}$$

(1')

This relation states that the percentage difference between the forward and the spot exchange rates is equal to the interest rate differential. This parity relation results from riskless arbitrage and must be true at any point of time (within transaction cost band).

In practice, interest rate parity says that what we gain on the interest rate differential we lose on the discount in the forward contract. Calculations are illustrated in Example 2.

EXAMPLE 2

The Interest Rate Parity Relation

Suppose that the Eurozone is the domestic country and the United States is the foreign country. The spot exchange rate quote is $S = \$1.25$. Suppose further that the U.S. risk-free interest rate is 10 percent and the Eurozone risk-free interest rate is 14 percent. Calculate the forward rate and the forward discount.

Solution: With the domestic currency quoted (euro), we have $S = DC:FC = 1.25$.

Using Equation 1, we have $F/S = (1 + r_{FC})/(1 + r_{DC})$, and $F/1.25 = (1.10)/(1.14)$ gives $F = 1.2061$, \$1.2061 per euro. For a linear approximation with Equation 1', we have $f \cong r_{FC} - r_{DC} = 10\% - 14\% = -4\%$. The forward discount is -4%. Then we have the approximate forward rate given by $F = (1 + f) \times S = (1 - 0.04) \times 1.25 = 1.20$, \$1.20 per euro.

---

[6] All parity equations numbered with a prime are expressed in percentages rather than level. This presentation helps to gain an intuitive understanding of the various parity relations.

Purchasing Power Parity: The Exchange Rate and the Inflation Differential

Purchasing power parity (PPP) is a well-known relation in international finance.[7] It states that the spot exchange rate adjusts perfectly to inflation differentials between two countries. There are two versions of PPP: absolute PPP and relative PPP.

Absolute PPP

The version of PPP, inspired by a basic idea known as the law of one price, states that the real price of a good must be the same in all countries. If goods prices rise in one country relative to another, the country's exchange rate must depreciate to maintain a similar real price for the goods in the two countries. This argument is obvious for traded goods with no trade restrictions. Consider the following scenario: Suppose the price of wheat in the Eurozone is 2.68 euros per bushel, and the U.S. price is 2.55 dollars per bushel; the exchange rate is 1.05 euros per dollar. In the next year, suppose the euro price of wheat rises by 3.03 percent, whereas the U.S. dollar price of wheat rises by only 1.4 percent. If the euro depreciation does not offset this hypothetical 1.63 percent inflation differential, Eurozone wheat will be less competitive in the international market and trade flows from the United States to Europe will increase to take advantage of this price differential. If trade could take place instantaneously, at no cost and with no impediments, we would expect the law of one price to hold exactly for all traded goods.

If we take a weighted average of the prices of all goods in the economy, absolute PPP claims that the exchange rate should be equal to the ratio of the average price levels in the two economies. So absolute PPP is some "average" version of the law of one price. If the weights differ among countries, absolute PPP could be violated even if the law of one price held for each individual good. In practice, determining an average national price level is a daunting task that is never undertaken. Rather than calculating average price levels, expressed in euros in Europe and dollars in the United States, countries calculate movements in price indexes. A price index can be based on a representative sample of produced goods (GDP deflator) or a representative basket of consumed goods such as the *consumer price index (CPI)*. A price index is a pure number, without meaning in itself. Its purpose is to calculate price increases, or inflation rates, from one period to the next.

Relative PPP

Most economists are concerned with relative PPP when they talk about purchasing power parity. Because of domestic inflation, a currency loses some of its purchasing power. For example, a 6 percent annual inflation rate in a country implies that one unit of the country's currency loses 6 percent of its purchasing power over a year. Relative PPP focuses on the general, across-the-board inflation rates in two countries and claims that the exchange rate movements should exactly offset any inflation differential between the two countries.

---

[7] This theory was originally presented by Cassel (1916). A review of purchasing power parity may be found in Rogoff (1996).

The purchasing power parity relation might be written as

$$S_1/S_0 = (1 + I_{FC})/(1 + I_{DC}) \qquad \textbf{(2)}$$

where

S_0 is the spot exchange rate at the start of the period (the foreign price of one unit of the domestic currency)
S_1 is the spot exchange rate at the end of the period
I_{FC} is the inflation rate, over the period, in the foreign country
I_{DC} is the inflation rate, over the period, in the domestic country

Suppose the exchange rate is DC:FC = 2.235 and inflation rates are I_{FC} = 1.3 percent and I_{DC} = 2.1 percent. Then the end-of-period spot exchange rate "should" be equal to S_1, such that

$$S_1 = S_0(1 + I_{FC})/(1 + I_{DC})$$
$$S_1 = 2.235(1 + 0.013)/(1 + 0.021) = 2.2175$$

Thus, we have DC:FC = 2.2175. Here, the higher domestic country inflation rate means that the domestic currency depreciates as seen by a decline in the exchange rate from 2.235 to 2.2175.

The PPP relation is often presented as the linear approximation stating that the exchange rate variation is equal to the inflation rate differential. Let's define s to represent the exchange rate movement:

$$s = (S_1 - S_0)/S_0 = S_1/S_0 - 1$$
$$s = S_1/S_0 - 1 \cong I_{FC} - I_{DC} \qquad \textbf{(2')}$$

For the preceding example, we would have $I_{FC} - I_{DC}$ = 1.3 − 2.1 = −0.8, and we would expect the exchange rate to decline by 0.8 percent to give S_1 = (1 − 0.008) × 2.235 ≅ 2.2171, DC:FC = 2.2171 compared with 2.2175 from the exact formula. This is close to the exact figure, even though Equation 2′ gives us only a first-order approximation of the exact relation in Equation 1.

This PPP relation is of major importance in international portfolio management. If it holds, PPP implies that the real return on an asset is identical for investors from any country. For example, consider a foreign asset with an annual rate of return equal to 20 percent in a country with an inflation rate of 2.5 percent. If the domestic country has an inflation rate of 1.3 percent and PPP holds, the foreign currency should depreciate over the year by about 2.5 − 1.3 = 1.2 percent. With the linear approximation, the asset return for the domestic investor will be the foreign asset return (in foreign currency) minus the depreciation of the foreign currency relative to the domestic currency, or roughly 20 − 1.2 = 18.8 percent. PPP implies that the real return (or inflation-adjusted return) on the foreign asset is the same for investors in both countries. The real return on an asset is equal to the asset return minus the inflation rate of the investor. For the foreign investor the real return is 20 − 2.5 = 17.5 percent. For the domestic investor the real return is also 18.8 − 1.3 = 17.5 percent. Hence, the real return on a specific asset should be equal for investors from all countries. Of course, PPP is only an economic theory and the relation does not necessarily hold, especially in the short run.

In practice, purchasing power parity says that we should expect the foreign currency movement (appreciation or depreciation) to be equal to the inflation differential between the two countries. Calculations are illustrated in Example 3.

EXAMPLE 3

The Purchasing Power Parity Relation

Suppose that the Eurozone is the domestic country and the United States is the foreign country. The spot exchange rate quote is $S = $ €:$ = \$1.25$. Suppose further that the expected annual U.S. inflation rate is 8.91 percent and the expected Eurozone annual inflation rate is 12.87 percent. Calculate the expected spot rate and the approximate expected spot rate one year away.

Solution: Using Equation 2, we have $S_1/S_0 = (1 + I_{FC})/(1 + I_{DC})$, and $S_1/1.25 = (1.0891)/(1.1287)$ gives $S_1 = 1.2061$, or €:$ = 1.2061$. For a linear approximation with Equation 2′, we have $s \cong I_{FC} - I_{DC} = 8.91$ percent $- 12.87$ percent $= -3.96$ percent. This indicates that the exchange rate should decline by approximately 3.96 percent to $(1 - 0.0396) \times 1.25 = 1.20$, or €:$ = 1.20$.

International Fisher Relation: The Interest Rate and Expected Inflation Rate Differentials

Inspired by the *domestic* relation postulated by Irving Fisher (1930), the *international Fisher relation* states that the interest rate differential between two countries should be equal to the expected inflation rate differential over the term of the interest rate. In the domestic relation, the nominal interest rate r is the sum (or rather, the compounding) of the real interest rate ρ and expected inflation over the term of the interest rate $E(I)$:

$$(1 + r) = (1 + \rho)(1 + E(I)) \tag{3}$$

The nominal interest rate is observed in the marketplace and is usually referred to as *the interest rate*, while the real interest rate is calculated from the observed interest rate and the forecasted inflation. For example, consider a nominal interest rate of 10 percent and an expected inflation rate of 8.91 percent. The real interest rate is equal to 1 percent because

$$1 + 0.10 = (1 + 0.01)(1 + 0.0891)$$

This relation is often presented with the linear approximation stating that the interest rate is equal to a real interest rate *plus* expected inflation:

$$r \cong \rho + E(I) \tag{3'}$$

The economic theory proposed by Fisher is that real interest rates are stable over time. Hence, fluctuations in interest rates are caused by revisions in inflationary expectations, not by movements in real interest rates.[8] The *international*

---

[8] Many economists would disagree with this simple approach. They claim that real interest rates vary with liquidity conditions and with the business cycle. Real interest rates would be higher in periods of strong economic growth than in recession periods: High economic growth sustains high real interest rates. See Dornbusch, Fischer, and Startz (2001).

counterpart of this domestic relation is that the interest rate differential between two countries is linked to the difference in expected inflation:

$$(1 + r_{FC})/(1 + r_{DC}) = ((1 + \rho_{FC})/(1 + \rho_{DC}))$$
$$\times (1 + E(I_{FC}))/(1 + E(I_{DC}))$$

The international Fisher relation claims that real interest rates are equal across the world; hence, differences in nominal interest rates are caused only by differences in national inflationary expectations. The international Fisher relation can be written as

$$(1 + r_{FC})/(1 + r_{DC}) = (1 + E(I_{FC}))/(1 + E(I_{DC}))$$ **(4)**

or, with the linear approximation, as

$$r_{FC} - r_{DC} \cong E(I_{FC}) - E(I_{DC})$$ **(4')**

Suppose that the foreign country has a 4.74 percent interest rate and 2.3 percent expected inflation while the domestic country has 2.39 percent interest rate and zero expected inflation. The real interest rate will then be equal to 2.39 percent in both countries because

$$1 + \rho = (1 + r)/(1 + E(I)) = (1 + 0.0474)/(1 + 0.023)$$
$$= (1 + 0.0239)/(1 + 0) = 1 + 0.0239$$

With equal real rates, the ratio of the nominal rates equals the ratio of expected inflation rates:

$$(1 + r_{FC})/(1 + r_{DC}) = 1.0474/1.0239 = 1.023$$

and

$$(1 + E(I_{FC}))/(1 + E(I_{DC})) = 1.023/1 = 1.023$$

In practice, the international Fisher relation indicates that what we lose by having a higher domestic inflation rate, we can *expect* to gain on the nominal interest rate differential, leaving us with the same real rate of return regardless of whether we invest domestically or in the foreign country. Calculations of the real rate are illustrated in Example 4.

Again, many economists would not agree that real interest rates should be equalized worldwide, simply because national business cycles are not fully synchronized. Countries with different levels of economic growth could sustain different real interest rates.

EXAMPLE 4

The International Fisher Relation

Suppose that the Eurozone is the domestic country and the United States is the foreign country. The spot exchange rate quote is $S = $ €:\$ $= 1.25$. Suppose further that the expected annual U.S. inflation rate is 8.91 percent and the expected Eurozone annual inflation rate is 12.87 percent.

Interest rates are 10 percent in the U.S. and 14 percent in the Eurozone. Demonstrate how interest rates are related to expected inflation rates exactly and by approximation, and calculate the real interest rate for each country.

Solution: Using Equation 4, $(1 + r_{FC})/(1 + r_{DC}) = (1 + E(I_{FC}))/(1 + E(I_{DC}))$, we have

$$(1 + 0.10)/(1 + 0.14) = 0.96491 \text{ and } (1 + 0.0891)/(1 + 0.1287) = 0.96492$$

With Equation 4′, $r_{FC} - r_{DC} = E(I_{FC}) - E(I_{DC})$, we have

$$10 - 14 = -4\% \text{ and } 8.91 - 12.87 = -3.96\%$$

To calculate the real rate of interest, we use Equation 3 and solve for ρ: $(1 + r) = (1 + \rho)(1 + E(I))$. Arbitrarily using the Eurozone, we have $\rho = (1 + r)/(1 + E(I)) - 1 = 1$ percent. The real rates are the same in both countries by the international Fisher assumption.

Uncovered Interest Rate Parity

Purchasing power parity combined with the international Fisher relation implies that the expected currency depreciation should offset the interest differential between the two countries over the term of the interest rate. To see this, take the expected values of the future exchange rate and the inflation in the PPP equation (Equation 2). PPP applied to expected values implies

$$E(S_1)/S_0 = (1 + E(I_{FC}))/(1 + E(I_{DC}))$$

Combining with Equation 4, we get the theory of uncovered interest rate parity:

$$E(S_1)/S_0 = (1 + r_{FC})/(1 + r_{DC}) \tag{5}$$

or, with the linear approximation,

$$E(s) \cong r_{FC} - r_{DC} \tag{5'}$$

Example 5 demonstrates interest rate parity with Equations 5 and 5′. *Uncovered interest rate parity* refers to exchange rate exposure not covered by a forward contract. In practice, uncovered interest rate parity says that we expect the foreign currency movement (appreciation or depreciation) to be equal to the interest differential between the two countries. This parity relation is illustrated in Example 5. Although the relation looks similar to interest rate parity, the difference is dramatic. Interest rate parity must hold by arbitrage. Uncovered interest rate parity is an economic theory about expectations, and the theory's empirical validity can be tested.

From the linear approximation in Equation 5′, the expected movement in the exchange rate should offset the interest rate differential. The international Fisher relation assumes that differences in real interest rates among countries would moti-

EXAMPLE 5

The Uncovered Interest Rate Parity Relation

Suppose that the Eurozone is the domestic country and the United States is the foreign country. The spot exchange rate quote is $S = €:\$ = 1.25$, the one-year rate in the Eurozone $r_{DC} = 14$ percent, and the one-year rate in the United States is $r_{FC} = 10$ percent. Calculate the exact expected spot rate and the approximate expected spot rate one year forward.

Solution: $E(S_1) = 1.25 \times 1.1/1.14 = 1.2061$, using Equation 5. By linear approximation, $s = r_{FC} - r_{DC} = 10\% - 14\% = -4$ percent. This means that the spot rate is expected to decline by 4 percent to $(1 - 0.04) \times 1.25 = €:\$ = 1.20$.

vate capital flows between countries to take advantage of these real interest rate differentials. These capital flows would lead to an equalization of real interest rates across the world.

Consider for a moment a simple world in which goods and financial markets are perfect. Throughout the world, costless arbitrage can take place instantaneously for physical goods and financial assets. Further assume that all nationals consume the same goods and that there is *no uncertainty*. Hence, we know *exactly* what the inflation and the exchange rates will be in the future. In this simple world, arbitrage guarantees that the previous parity relations hold exactly. If the exchange rate does not adjust to the inflation differential as claimed by PPP, one would simply buy goods in the country with the lower real price and ship them for sale in the country with the higher real price to make a certain profit. In a perfect world with costless and instantaneous shipping, such attractive situations cannot exist for long; arbitrage will make the exchange rate movement adjust exactly to inflation in both countries. In the same spirit, if the interest rate differential does not reflect the anticipated and certain exchange rate movement exactly, an arbitrageur would simply borrow in one currency, transfer the amount to the other currency, and lend it at that currency interest rate. By doing so, the arbitrageur would make a certain profit with no capital investment. This riskless profit opportunity would attract huge arbitrage capital, and market rates would adjust to "prevent" such an arbitrage.

In reality, the future exchange rate is uncertain, and arbitrage in the goods market cannot be instantaneous and costless. So, the parity relations developed here are only *theories* claiming that real prices and interest rates should be equalized across the world.

Foreign Exchange Expectations: The Forward Premium (Discount) and the Expected Exchange Rate Movement

The *foreign exchange expectation* relation states that the forward exchange rate, quoted at time 0 for delivery at time 1, is equal to the expected value of the spot exchange rate at time 1. This can be written as

$$F = E(S_1) \tag{6}$$

This relation would certainly hold if the future values of exchange rates were known with certainty. If one were sure at time 0 that the exchange rate would be worth S_1 at time 1, the current forward rate for delivery at time 1 would have to be S_1; otherwise, a riskless arbitrage opportunity would exist.

Assume, for example, that we know for certain that the spot exchange rate will be €:$ = 1.2061 in a year but, surprisingly, the one-year forward rate is €:$ = 1.25. This arbitrage opportunity would be exploited (sell forward at €:$ = 1.25 and buy spot at the certain expiration rate of €:$ = 1.2061) until the forward exchange rate was established at €:$ = 1.2061.

Of course, this parity relation depends strongly on the certainty assumption. Some economists claim, however, that the forward exchange rate should be an unbiased predictor of the future spot exchange rate in the presence of uncertainty, thereby leading to Equation 6. Others claim the existence of a risk premium appended to this relation (see the reading on international asset pricing).

The foreign exchange expectation relation is often stated relative to the current spot exchange rate. If we subtract S_0 on both sides of Equation 6 (remember that the current spot exchange rate is known with certainty) and divide by S_0, we get

$$(F - S_0)/S_0 = E((S_1 - S_0)/S_0) = E(s) \qquad \textbf{(7)}$$

As mentioned in the reading on currency exchange rates, the left-hand side is usually referred to as the forward discount, or premium, and is denoted f. It is the percentage deviation of the forward rate from the current spot rate. This relation states that the forward discount (or premium) is equal to the expected exchange rate movement and can be written as

$$f = E(s) \qquad \textbf{(7')}$$

In practice, the foreign exchange expectation relation says that we expect the spot exchange rate to be equal to the current forward rate. This parity relation is illustrated in Example 6. If verified, it means that there is on average no reward for bearing foreign exchange uncertainty. If a risk premium were to be added to the relation, the symmetry of the exchange rate means the risk premium will be paid by some investors (e.g., those selling forward euros for dollars) and received by other investors (e.g., those buying forward euros for dollars). A zero-risk premium means that a forward hedge (the use of forward currency contracts to hedge the exchange risk of a portfolio of foreign assets) will be "costless" in terms of expected returns (except for commissions on the forward contracts).

EXAMPLE 6

The Foreign Exchange Expectation Relation

Suppose that the Eurozone is the domestic country and the United States is the foreign country. The spot exchange rate quote is $S = €:$ = 1.25. Suppose further that the U.S. risk-free interest rate is 10 percent and the Eurozone risk-free interest rate is 14 percent. Calculate the exact expected spot rate and the approximate expected spot rate one year away.

Solution: Using Equation 1, we have $F/S = (1 + r_{FC})/(1 + r_{DC})$, and $F/1.25 = (1.10)/(1.14)$ gives $F = 1.2061$. Using Equation 6, we have

$E(S_i) = F = 1.2061$, €:\$ = 1.2061, the expected spot rate. Using the linear approximation in Equation 1', $f \cong r_{FC} - r_{DC} = -4$ percent. Hence, using Equation 7', the exchange rate is expected to depreciate by 4 percent to $(1 - 0.4) \times 1.25 =$ €:\$ = 1.20.

Combining the Relations

The relations link the forward discount to the interest rate differential, the exchange rate movement to the inflation differential, the expected inflation differential to the interest rate differential, and the interest rate differential to the expected currency depreciation, and back to the forward discount.

▶ *Interest rate differential:* The forward discount (premium) equals the interest rate differential.

▶ *Interest rate differential:* The interest rate differential is expected to be offset by the currency depreciation.

▶ *Inflation differential:* The exchange rate movement should exactly offset any inflation differential.

▶ *Expected inflation rate differential:* The expected inflation rate differential should be matched by the interest rate differential, assuming (Fisher) real interest rates are equal.

▶ *Expected exchange rate movement:* The forward discount (or premium) is equal to the expected exchange rate movement.

These relations can also be organized in the following manner to show the linkages discussed.

Factor	Related to	By
Forward discount	Interest rates	Interest rate parity
Exchange rate movement	Inflation rates	Purchasing power parity
Interest rates	Expected inflation rates	Fisher relation
Expected exchange rate movement	Interest rates	Uncovered interest rate parity (PPP plus Fisher)
Forward discount	Expected exchange rate movement	Foreign exchange expectation

Recall that the *interest rate parity* relation states that the interest rate differential must equal the forward discount (or premium). This is a financial arbitrage condition that does not involve any economic theory. It must hold. Purchasing power parity also relies on some international arbitrage, but in the physical goods markets. Given the heterogeneity in goods and transaction costs, we cannot expect it to hold precisely. All other relations involve expectations on

EXHIBIT 3	International Parity Relations *Linear Approximation*

exchange rates and prices; they are based on simple economic theories about agent behavior. The various parity relations are illustrated in Exhibit 3 using the linear approximation.

International Parity Relations and Global Asset Management

The multicurrency dimension adds great complexity to global asset management. Interest rates differ among currencies. A foreign investment carries currency risk in addition to market risks. Because of exchange rate fluctuations, an investment could have a positive return when measured in one currency, but a negative one when measured in another currency. International parity relations provide the simplest framework to gain a better understanding of global investing in the presence of various exchange rates. From this basic framework, various complexities can be incorporated as done later.

International parity relations provide a useful base for the relationship among exchange rates, inflation, and interest rates. Using this simple framework as a starting point, an international investor can draw several practical implications:

► Interest rate differentials reflect expectations about currency movements. The expected return on default-free bills should be equal among countries whether measured in a common currency or in real terms.

► Investing in a country with a high interest rate is not necessarily an attractive option. The high interest rate is expected to be offset by currency depreciation. Nevertheless, the interest rate is a sure thing and the depreciation is only expected.

► Investors from different countries expect the same real return on a given asset, once currency is taken into account.

► Exchange risk reduces to inflation uncertainty if all these relationships hold perfectly, and, in this instance, an investor concerned with real returns would not be affected by exchange rate uncertainty.

► Currency hedging allows investors to eliminate currency risk without sacrificing expected return, because the forward exchange rate is equal to the expected spot exchange rate.

In this simplified world, currency risk is basically of little real importance; however, deviations from parity relations can introduce complexities. Of primary importance is the observation that currency fluctuations can have real effects if the exchange rate deviates from its PPP value, as illustrated in Example 7.

EXAMPLE 7

Are Foreign Risk-Free Investments Risk-Free to a Domestic Investor?

During June 2002, the U.S. dollar depreciated by 7 percent against the euro. One-month bills in euros and in dollars had the same interest rate of 3 percent (annualized), and annual inflation rates were about 2 percent in both regions. Would a European investor holding U.S. Treasury bills have the same return as U.S. investors?

Solution: A U.S. investor has a rate of return of 0.25 percent over the month (3%/12) and a real return of approximately 0.08 percent (1%/12). However, a European investor made a loss of 6.75 percent (7% currency loss minus 0.25% dollar interest rate) when measured in euro. The real return for European investors is −6.92 percent (−6.75% return in euro minus 0.17% monthly European inflation rate). The exchange rate movement has a dramatic real impact.

It could also be that real interest rates differ between two countries that are at different stages of the business cycle. Similarly, investors are not risk neutral and could append a risk premium to the foreign exchange expectations relation (see the reading on international asset pricing). We now go one step further and give a brief review of the simple economic models of the exchange rate that could induce deviations from the international parity relations.[9]

EXCHANGE RATE DETERMINATION   3

In this reading so far, the traditional view indicates that exchange rates should adjust the purchasing power of two currencies. After we discuss purchasing power parity in a long-term context, we will introduce other economic variables affecting the exchange rate.

---

[9] These models are detailed in standard international economics textbooks. See, for example, Dornbusch, Fischer, and Startz (2001).

Purchasing Power Parity Revisited

The short-run behavior of exchange rates does not conveniently conform to PPP. The empirical evidence demonstrates that yearly exchange rates can deviate significantly from the inflation differentials between countries. The *real exchange rate* is the observed exchange rate adjusted for inflation. Hence, movements in the real exchange rate are equal to movements in the exchange rate minus the actual inflation differential between the two countries. These movements in the real exchange rate are not explained by PPP. However, the theory, supported by extensive empirical evidence, claims that such real exchange rate movements (deviations from PPP) will be corrected in the long run. So, one approach to understanding the path of the exchange rate is to compute its long-run "fundamental" (or "equilibrium") value based on PPP, and to assume that any observed deviation of the current exchange rate from this fundamental value will be progressively corrected. To provide a forecast of the future short-run movement in exchange rates, we must first estimate the *fundamental PPP value* of a currency.

Fundamental Value Based on Absolute PPP

Ideally, we would like to compare directly the price of goods in two countries to see whether an exchange rate conforms to absolute PPP or whether it is overvalued or undervalued in real terms. This can only be done for some individual goods that are clearly comparable, and the estimation for different goods can lead to opposing conclusions.

For more than twenty years, *The Economist* has run a Big Mac Index, giving the price of the MacDonald's Big Mac hamburger in 120 countries. There is a wide dispersion in the dollar prices of the Big Mac throughout the world ranging from $1.45 in China to $5.20 in Switzerland. The article reprinted in the Concept in Action box, "Big Mac Index: Sizzling" shows the price of a Big Mac in local currency and in dollars. The implied PPP given in the third column is the exchange rate that makes the dollar price of a burger the same in each country. Let's take the example of China; the implied PPP exchange rate is simply the ratio of the Big Mac price in yuan divided by the Big Mac price in the United States, or $11/3.41 = 3.23$ yuan per dollar. The actual exchange rate in July 2007 is 7.60 yuan per dollar, which means that the yuan is undervalued by $(3.23 - 7.60)/7.60 = -58$ percent. Differences in taxes, rents, and labor costs partly contribute to these differences, but several studies have shown that Big Mac PPP is a useful predictor of future exchange rate movements because deviations tend to be corrected over the long run. This adjustment takes place either by a change in the exchange rate or by a change in the local-currency price of a Big Mac. For example, Cumby (1996) states that after correcting for currency-specific constants, "a 10 percent undervaluation according to the hamburger standard in one year is associated with a 3.5 percent appreciation over the following year" (p. 13).

In practice, no one would estimate the fundamental value of a currency by applying absolute PPP to a single good, especially a nontraded one, and the preceding discussion is only anecdotal. Some attempts have been made to compare the prices of baskets of goods, but goods consumed in different countries are seldom identical, so a direct comparison of their prices is not realistic. How, for example, can one directly compare the value of a nineteenth-century Parisian house and that of a suburban Dallas home?

CONCEPTS IN ACTION   BIG MAC INDEX: SIZZLING

American politicians bash China for its policy of keeping the yuan weak. France blames a strong euro for its sluggish economy. The Swiss are worried about a falling franc. New Zealanders fret that their currency has risen too far.

All these anxieties rest on a belief that exchange rates are out of whack. Is this justified? *The Economist's* "Big Mac Index," a light-hearted guide to how far currencies are from fair value, provides some answers. It is based on the theory of purchasing-power parity (PPP), which says that exchange rates should equalize the price of a basket of goods in any two countries. Our basket contains just a single representative purchase, but one that is available in 120 countries: a Big Mac hamburger. The implied PPP, our hamburger standard, is the exchange rate that makes the dollar price of a burger the same in each country.

Most currencies are trading a long way from that yardstick. China's currency is the cheapest. A Big Mac in China costs 11 yuan, equivalent to just $1.45 at today's exchange rate, which means China's currency is undervalued by 58%. But before China's critics start warming up for a fight, they should bear in mind that PPP points to where currencies ought to go in the long run. The price of a burger depends heavily on local inputs such as rent and wages, which are not easily arbitraged across borders and tend to be lower in poorer countries. For this reason PPP is a better guide to currency misalignments between countries at a similar stage of development.

The most overvalued currencies are found on the rich fringes of the European Union: in Iceland, Norway and Switzerland. Indeed, nearly all rich-world currencies are expensive compared with the dollar. The exception is the yen, undervalued by 33%. This anomaly seems to justify fears that speculative carry trades, where funds from low-interest countries such as Japan are used to buy high-yield currencies, have pushed the yen too low. But broader measures of PPP suggest the yen is close to fair value. A New Yorker visiting Tokyo would find that although Big Macs were cheap, other goods and services seemed pricey. A trip to Europe would certainly pinch the pocket of an American tourist: the euro is 22% above its fair value.

The Swiss franc, like the yen a source of low-yielding funds for foreign-exchange punters, is 53% overvalued. The franc's recent fall is a rare example of carry traders moving a currency towards its burger standard. That is because it is borrowed and sold to buy high-yielding investments in rich countries such as New Zealand and Britain, whose currencies look dear against their burger benchmarks. Brazil and Turkey, two emerging economies favoured by speculators, have also been pushed around. Burgernomics hints that their currencies are a little overcooked.

Cash and Carry: The Hamburger Standard

| | Big Mac Prices | | Implied PPP[†] of the | Actual Dollar Exchange Rate July 2nd | Under(−)/Over(+) Valuation against the Dollar, % |
	in Local Currency	in Dollars			
United States[‡]	$3.41	3.41			
Argentina	Peso 8.25	2.67	2.42	3.09	−22
Australia	A$3.45	2.95	1.01	1.17	−14
Brazil	Real 16.90	3.61	2.02	1.91	+6
Britain	£1.99	4.01	1.71[§]	2.01[§]	+18
Canada	C$3.88	3.68	1.14	1.05	+8
Chile	Peso 1,565	2.97	459	527	−13
China	Yuan 11.0	1.45	3.23	7.60	−58
Czech Republic	Koruna 52.9	2.51	15.5	21.1	−27
Denmark	Dkr 27.75	5.08	8.14	5.46	+49

(Continued on next page . . .)

CONCEPTS IN ACTION   (continued)

	Big Mac Prices		Implied PPP† of the	Actual Dollar Exchange Rate July 2nd	Under(−)/Over(+) Valuation against the Dollar, %
	in Local Currency	in Dollars			
Egypt	Pound 9.54	1.68	2.80	5.69	−51
Euro area**	€3.06	4.17	1.12††	1.36††	+22
Hong Kong	HK$12.0	1.54	3.52	7.82	−55
Hungary	Forint 600	3.33	176	180	−2
Indonesia	Rupiah 15,900	1.76	4,663	9,015	−48
Japan	¥280	2.29	82.1	122	−33
Malaysia	Ringgit 5.50	1.60	1.61	3.43	−53
Mexico	Peso 29.0	2.69	8.50	10.8	−21
New Zealand	NZ$4.60	3.59	1.35	1.28	+5
Peru	New Sol 9.50	3.00	2.79	3.17	−12
Phillippines	Peso 85.0	1.85	24.9	45.9	−46
Poland	Zloty 6.90	2.51	2.02	2.75	−26
Russia	Rouble 52.0	2.03	15.2	25.6	−41
Singapore	S$3.95	2.59	1.16	1.52	−24
South Africa	Rand 15.5	2.22	4.55	6.97	−35
South Korea	Won 2,900	3.14	850	923	−8
Sweden	SKr33.0	4.86	9.68	6.79	+42
Switzerland	SFr6.30	5.20	1.85	1.21	+53
Taiwan	NT$75.0	2.29	22.0	32.8	−33
Thailand	Baht 62.0	1.80	18.2	34.5	−47
Turkey	Lire 4.75	3.66	1.39	1.30	+7
Venezuela	Bolivar 7,400	3.45	2,170	2,147	+1

†Purchasing-power parity; local price divided by price in United States ‡Average of New York, Chicago, Atlanta and San Francisco §Dollars per pound **Weighted average of prices in euro area ††Dollars per euro

Source: From ECONOMIST. Copyright 2007 by Economist Newspaper Group. Reproduced with permission of Economist Newspaper Group.

Fundamental Value Based on Relative PPP

Instead, *relative PPP* is most commonly used to explain and forecast currency movements. Remember that relative PPP considers across-the-board movements in prices over time rather than absolute price levels. Several steps are required to implement this approach:

▶ Select an inflation index for each country.

▶ Select an historical period for which to compute long-run PPP.

▶ Determine the fundamental PPP value of the exchange rate and hence the current amount of over- or undervaluation of the currency.

The definition of a proper inflation index is open to question. The estimation of the inflation rate depends on the basket of goods chosen for the index. Different baskets of goods will exhibit different price increases as the relative prices of the goods change over time. An inflation rate measured from an index of consumed goods (CPI) will be different from an inflation rate measured from an index of produced goods (*wholesale price index* or *WPI*) because of differences in imported and exported goods.

Differences in price movements between tradable and nontradable goods can also make a difference as illustrated in the case of Japan. Japan has experienced remarkable growth in productivity in many manufacturing industries whose products trade internationally. However, productivity gains for nontradables, such as services and locally consumed agricultural products, have lagged considerably. Locally produced nontradables are a significant share of the Japanese consumption basket (CPI). Because of cultural and regulatory restrictions on imports of competing goods and services (including agricultural products), prices of Japanese nontradables can remain high in the long run. The relative price of nontradables versus tradables has also risen in other countries, but to a much smaller extent.

The historical period selected to compute the fundamental PPP exchange rate value is important. For example, assume that you are at the start of 2007 and you wish to determine the fundamental PPP value of the yen/dollar exchange rate. You can select December 31, 1972, as the base year. Then, the current fundamental PPP value will be equal to the December 1972 exchange rate, adjusted by the inflation differential over the period 1973–2006. As of the end of 2006, the fundamental PPP value would have been equal to the December 1972 spot exchange rate, $S_{1972} = ¥302$ per dollar, multiplied by the ratio of Japanese price indexes at the end of 2006 and at the end of 1972 ($CPI¥_{2006}/CPI¥_{1972}$), and divided by the ratio of U.S. price indexes at the end of 2006 and at the end of 1972 ($CPI\$_{2006}/CPI\$_{1972}$).

This yields a fundamental value of $\$:¥ = 130$ for year-end 2006, compared with an actual spot rate of ¥120 per dollar. This is shown in Exhibit 4, in which the solid line is the actual spot exchange rate at year-end, and the top dotted line is the PPP value using 1972 as base year. When the dotted line (PPP value) is above the solid line (actual value), the yen is overvalued (or the dollar is undervalued). Conversely, the yen is undervalued when the dotted line is below the solid line. The yen seemed slightly overvalued at the end of 2006. Based on PPP, you can only conclude that the yen should depreciate relative to the dollar.

If a different base year had been selected, however—for example, 1978—the conclusion would have been markedly different. The bottom dotted line in Exhibit 4 plots the PPP value using 1978 as base year: 1978 is a year in which the yen was strong relative to 1972. Hence, calculations using 1978 as a base year lead to a fundamental PPP value equal to only $\$:¥ = 69$ at the end of 2006, a value well below the actual spot rate of ¥120 per dollar at the end of 2006. The conclusion would have been that the yen was strongly undervalued in 2006. Clearly, the choice of base year can make a significant difference.

To summarize, estimating a currency's fundamental PPP value should help explain future short-term movements in the exchange rate. Such estimation is not an easy task, however, and exchange rates can become grossly misaligned and remain so for several years without a correction. This correction will take place, but it may take several years, and its timing is unclear. Additional models are needed to provide a better understanding of exchange rate movements.

EXHIBIT 4	Fundamental Value for Japanese Yen

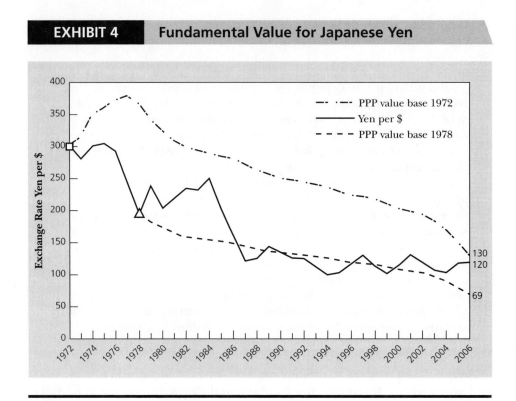

The Balance of Payments Approach

Historically, an analysis of the balance of payments provided the first approach to the economic modeling of the exchange rate. The balance of payments tracks all financial flows crossing a country's borders during a given period (a quarter or a year). For example, an export creates a positive financial inflow for the country, whereas an import creates a financial outflow (a negative financial inflow). A resident's purchase of a foreign security creates a negative financial inflow, whereas a loan made by a foreign bank to a resident bank creates a positive financial inflow. The balance of payments compiles all financial flows. The convention is to treat all financial inflows as a credit to the balance of payments and all financial outflows as debits.

A balance of payments is not an income statement or a balance sheet but a cash balance of the country relative to the rest of the world. The balance of all financial flows must be equilibrated because the foreign exchange market always clears. In other words, the final balance *must* be zero.

This concept can best be confirmed by a simple example. Consider a small country whose only international transactions consist of exports and imports of goods. Its central bank has a large reserve of foreign currencies accumulated over the years. Assume that in the year 2000, this country runs a trade deficit of $1 million (imports greater than exports). Then the central bank will need to use $1 million of reserves to offset this deficit. The net balance will then be zero. Of course, the importers could instead borrow $1 million abroad to finance the payment of the trade balance; this will create a financial inflow that will be recorded in the balance of payments as a positive inflow offsetting the trade deficit. Again, the balance of payments will be equilibrated.

A parallel can be drawn with an individual's cash balance. If expenses exceed receipts at the end of the month, an individual must use his reserves to cover the deficit, borrow money from the outside world, or sell some assets to the outside world. The net balance must be zero. Hence, what is interesting is to analyze and interpret the various components of the balance of payments because we know that the final balance must be zero.

The tradition is to separate the balance according to the type of transaction involved. There are many types of international transactions, including the following:

▶ International trade, leading to payment for goods imported and exported

▶ Payment for services such as tourism and consulting contracts

▶ Income received (and paid) on loans and existing investments

▶ Direct investments made by domestic corporations abroad and by foreign corporations at home

▶ Portfolio investments, such as purchase of foreign securities by domestic investors and purchase of domestic securities by foreign investors

▶ All types of short-term and long-term capital flows

▶ Sale of foreign currency reserves by the central bank

Several readings could be devoted to the accounting details of the balance of payments and to the controversy surrounding the various accounting conventions. The establishment of a balance of payments requires the collection of statistics from many sources, such as customs data, central bank statistics, and bank reports of transactions. Some countries, such as the United States, construct their balance of payments from a sampling of transactions. Most other countries attempt to trace every single international transaction. It is common to see the balance of payments figures revised periodically after a few months or years to reflect corrected data or changes in accounting conventions.

To simplify the presentation of a balance of payments, it is useful to consider four component groups of lines:

▶ Current account

▶ Capital account

▶ Financial account

▶ Official reserve account

The *current account* includes the balance of goods and services and income received or paid on existing investments. Exports, or income received from abroad, will appear as credits to the balance. It must be stressed that the current account does not include the amounts paid for investments abroad but only the income received on current holding of foreign assets, usually in the form of dividends or interest payments. Actual investments are reflected in the financial account section. The current account also includes current *transfers*, which are transactions without compensation, such as gifts to relatives living abroad, grants to foreign students, or government aid to developing countries.

An important component of the current account, often mentioned by the news media, is the *trade balance*, which is simply the balance of merchandise exports minus merchandise imports. Many economists believe that the merchandise trade balance is given too much importance and that services should be added to the trade balance. Altogether, the current account gives a more global view of all current (i.e., noninvestment) transactions. Introducing straightforward notation, the current account (*CA*) is the sum of the following:

Trade balance	*TB*
Balance of services	*BS*
Net income received	*NI*
Current transfers	*CT*
Current account	**CA**

The *capital account* (*KA*) section reflects unrequited (or unilateral) transfers corresponding to capital flows entailing no compensation (in the form of goods, services, or assets). These capital transfers are different from current transfers and cover, for example, investment capital given (without future repayment) in favor of poor countries, debt forgiveness, and expropriation losses. It is generally a very small account, whose title is a bit misleading.

The *financial account* (*FA*) includes all short-term and long-term capital transactions.[10] The definition in this textbook excludes transactions made by the central bank, which will be assigned to the official reserve account. The financial account includes direct investment, portfolio investment, other investment flows (especially short-term capital). Direct investment is the net amount of cross-border purchases of companies and real estate made by residents and foreigners. *Direct* means that the purchase did not go through the capital market and involves some form of control in the foreign company, as opposed to portfolio investment. The purchase (sale) of a foreign company by a resident is treated as a debit (credit) because it corresponds to a financial outflow (inflow). The purchase (sale) of a domestic company by a foreign resident is treated as a credit (debit) because it corresponds to a financial inflow (outflow). Portfolio investments correspond to the balance of investments made on financial markets by domestic and foreign investors.[11] The account called *other investment flows* captures many types of private and official capital flows, including short-term deposits made by foreigners at domestic banks and vice versa. Introducing straightforward notation, the financial account (*FA*) is the sum of these three items:

Direct investment	*DI*
Portfolio investment	*PI*
Other investment flows	*OI*
Financial account	**FA**

Net errors and omissions is very embarrassing for balance of payments accountants. At the end of the day, when all statistics are collected from many different sources, the balance of payments must balance, just as any cash balance. Net errors and omissions may include a few unaffected transactions but consists mostly of whatever is needed to equilibrate the final bal-

---

[10] Although the term *current account* is standard in the balance of payments literature, many terms have been used to refer to the sum of all capital flows, defined here as *financial account*. Hence, the reader should be careful in applying the concept of financial account to published balance of payments data. Here we use the IMF terminology adopted in 1993 and applied since 1995 by most countries (see IMF, 1995).

[11] The balance of payments tracks investment flows. It does not take into account changes in value of foreign investments or liabilities caused by changes in market prices of securities.

ance to zero. Apparently disliking this terminology, the United States in 1976 changed it to *statistical discrepancy*. This line is often assigned to the financial account because transactions in the current account are more reliably tracked than are capital transactions. Aggregating all these items in the *capital and financial account* (*KFA*), we get

Capital account	KA
Financial account	FA
Net errors and omissions	NE
Capital and Financial account	**KFA**

The sum of the current account, the capital account, and in IMF terminology the financial account is generally called the *overall balance* (*OB*):

$$OB = CA + KFA$$

The *official reserve account* reflects net changes in the government's international reserves.[12] These reserves can take the form of foreign currency holdings and loans to foreign governments. Conversely, liabilities that constitute foreign governments' reserves come in the deduction of the domestic reserves. When the U.S. Federal Reserve Bank sells foreign currencies to equilibrate a deficit in the current and financial accounts, it will receive dollars in exchange. This inflow of dollars is treated as a credit to the balance of payments. Thus, a *reduction* in the official reserves has a *positive* sign in the balance of payments accounting. This is often a source of confusion because most of us tend to regard a drop in reserves as "bad" or "negative." However, the convention is quite logical. If a country sells goods or services, it receives a financial inflow in exchange. If its government sells foreign currencies, the country also receives a financial inflow. Similarly, if a government is forced to borrow abroad to finance a deficit, the loan will induce a financial inflow and hence create a credit to the balance of payments. This credit is treated as an increase in official liabilities and therefore as a reduction in official reserves.

By definition of a balance of payments, the sum of the current account (*CA*), the capital and financial account (*KFA*), and the change in official reserves (*OR*) must be equal to zero:

$$CA + KFA + OR = 0$$

In other words, the change in official reserves simply mirrors the overall balance:

$$OR = -OB$$

The traditional approach to foreign exchange rate determination is to focus on the influence of balance of payments flows. Let's consider a country in which capital flows are restricted, as is often the case with developing nations. A trade deficit would lead to a reduction in the country's reserves and ultimately to a depreciation of the home currency. In turn, this depreciation would improve the terms of trade. National exports would become cheaper abroad and more competitive: Exports should increase. Imported goods would become more expensive: Imports should

---

[12] The official reserve account is sometimes included as a subcategory of the financial account.

drop. This should lead to an improvement in the trade balance, and the currency should stabilize.

For example, the drop in oil prices in 1985 and 1986 led to a Mexican trade balance deficit; the value of the oil that Mexico exported suddenly dropped, without a corresponding reduction in imports. This deficit forced the Mexican government to borrow abroad to offset the imbalance; it also led to a depreciation of the peso. This devaluation helped restore the terms of trade.

This analysis requires us to estimate the trade flow elasticities in response to a movement in the exchange rate: How will imports and exports react to an exchange rate adjustment? The answers have to be built on often complex models of the economy. For example, oil imports by an emerging country are necessary for the domestic production process, as well as other domestic needs. A devaluation of the home currency is unlikely to strongly affect the demand for oil. Conversely, the demand for some imported goods, such as liquor or luxury items, is going to decrease if such goods become more expensive in home-currency terms.

J-Curve Effect: Depreciation Means Trade Balance Gets Worse before It Gets Better

Furthermore, the model must be dynamic, because devaluation-triggered improvement in the trade balance will only be progressive. The immediate technical effect is not a quantity adjustment (more exports and less imports) but a price adjustment. Because imports are more expensive in terms of the home currency, as soon as the devaluation takes place, the trade deficit will immediately increase, given the new exchange rate. This is known as the *J-curve effect*: The trade balance will first deteriorate following devaluation before improving. Of course, this scenario is not always rosy: The rise in import prices can feed higher inflation at home, leading to further depreciation of the currency. The monetary authorities will have to adjust their monetary/fiscal policy to control this "imported" inflation.

The analysis becomes even more complex when we consider capital flows in a necessary look at the various components of the balance of payments. We must draw the line between flows that are autonomous—caused by current economic or political conditions—and those that are created to compensate for a potential imbalance.

The United States has run systematic, large trade deficits without a structural depreciation of its currency because of a financial account surplus. Foreign investors were happy to hold an increasing amount of dollar assets. The 1980s marked an important period for the United States as the dollar developed into the major international reserve currency: The U.S. dollar value swung widely, and the U.S. overall balance (*OB*) moved into a large deficit during the second half of the 1980s. Studying data from the late 1970s to the early 1990s leads to a better understanding of the current situation. The story is told in Exhibit 5, which gives the three major components of the U.S. balance of payments, as well as the real effective exchange rate index, as calculated by the IMF. The real effective exchange rate index is the weighted average of the currencies of selected U.S. trading partners, adjusted for relative inflation differentials. It is more representative of the value of the U.S. dollar than any single exchange rate. A real appreciation of the dollar would lead to an increase in the effective exchange rate index. To analyze Exhibit 5, remember that a positive official reserve account means a drop in reserves. In 1977 and 1978, the combined deficits of the current and capital accounts led to a drop in official reserves as well as a depreciation of the dollar. The improvement in the balance of payments (stable reserves, no trade deficit) from 1979 to 1982 led to an appreciation of the dollar. From 1983 to 1985, the

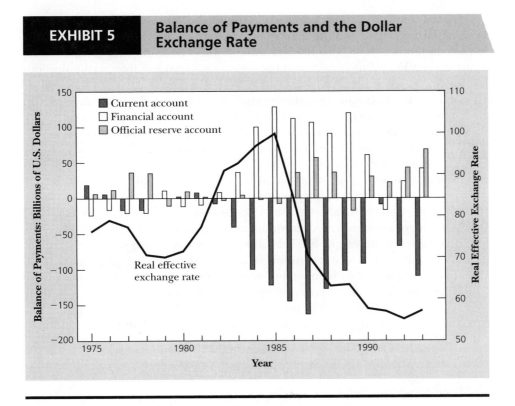

EXHIBIT 5 **Balance of Payments and the Dollar Exchange Rate**

United States started to run a huge trade and current account deficit. However, this current deficit was offset by fast-growing foreign investments, and the reserves did not deteriorate: The dollar kept rising. By 1986, the capital flows became insufficient to cover the current account deficit, the official reserve position deteriorated, and the dollar started to slide.[13] In 1990, the financial account began to deteriorate; it recovered in the mid-1990s. The big surge in capital investment in the 1980s came partly from Japanese investors who engaged in real estate and business acquisitions in the United States. The Japanese were running huge surpluses in their trade and current account balances, which allowed them to invest extensively in the United States and other countries (a Japanese deficit of the financial account). This situation of a huge U.S. trade deficit offset by foreign capital flows still prevails now.

The Asset Market Approach

The General Idea

Many economists reject the view that the short-term behavior of exchange rates is determined in flow markets. Exchange rates are financial prices traded in an efficient asset market. Indeed, an exchange rate is the relative price of two currencies and, therefore, is determined by the willingness to hold each currency. The exchange rate is determined by expectations about the future, not by current trade flows.

---

[13] Remember that the IMF changed its accounting convention for official reserves in 1997 and back-calculated all its balance of payments statistics. *Liabilities constituting foreign authorities reserves* were moved from official reserves to the financial flows account. This move has been questioned because its main implication is to drastically reduce the apparent overall balance deficit of the United States. Here, we use data under the old convention because it is better suited for our analysis.

A parallel with other asset prices may illustrate the approach. Consider the stock price of a winery traded on the Paris Bourse. A frost in late spring results in a poor harvest, in terms of both quantity and quality. After harvesting and a year of wine making, the wine is finally sold, and the income is much less than in the previous year. On the day of the final sale, there is no reason for the stock price to be influenced by this low cash flow. First, the unusually low level of income has already been discounted in the winery stock price since the previous spring. Second, the stock price is affected by future, in addition to current, prospects. The stock price is based on expectations of future earnings, and the major cause for a change in stock price is a revision of these expectations.

A similar reasoning applies to exchange rates: Contemporaneous international flows should have little effect on exchange rates to the extent that they are expected. Only news about future economic prospects will affect exchange rates. The mere announcement of some unexpected news is sufficient to trigger an immediate adjustment in market value, even if it will take several months or years to be fully reflected in economic data. Because economic expectations are potentially volatile and influenced by many variables, including those of a political nature, the short-run behavior of exchange rates is volatile.

Several types of news influence exchange rates, but many of them have to do with inflationary expectations and interest rates (see Example 8). The relationship between interest rates and exchange rates is often presented in a confusing fashion in the media. Hence, we will introduce some simple models to help explain this relationship. In particular, we need to distinguish between short-run and long-run effects.

EXAMPLE 8

Inflation-Pressure Ebb and Depreciation

Suppose a central bank chairman announces that inflation pressures have ebbed. Explain why such an announcement could lead to a depreciation of the domestic currency.

Solution: The return on investing in a currency is the sum of the (sure) interest rate plus the (uncertain) currency movement. So investors tend to be attracted to high interest rates (sure component of return), especially given the empirical evidence that subsequent depreciation is not necessarily associated with high interest rates. More importantly, inflation moves very slowly; on the other hand, central banks make serious adjustments to (real) interest rates to quell emerging inflation pressures. When a central bank raises short-term interest rates, it is not to adapt to current inflation (that would be a movement in nominal interest rate with no movement in real interest rate) but to slow down growth that could lead to an inflationary environment. Hence, most interest rate moves by a central bank are real, not nominal, moves in interest rates. A small increase in current inflation, then, could lead to a steep increase in the interest rate (mostly real). That would be attractive for domestic currency investments in real terms, at least in the short run. Conversely, the announcement that inflation pressures have eased means that the bank will not increase the real interest rate and might even lower it. The domestic currency investment becomes less attractive, hence the depreciation.

More on Interest Rates

As mentioned, the interest rate can be separated into an *expected inflation* component and a *real interest rate* component, as in Equation 3′:

$$r \cong \rho + E(I)$$

The relation introduced by Irving Fisher is a *long-run* equilibrium relation. It states that an increase in expected inflation causes a proportional increase in money rates. Over the long run, the real interest rate is assumed constant.

But monetary policy affects the real interest rate in the *short run*. To illustrate this point, it is useful to introduce a simple domestic monetary model. Equilibrium in the money market requires that money supply M^S equals money demand M^D. The money supply is provided by the central bank. Money demand by all agents can be written as the product of the price level P and real money demand. Real money demand M^D/P can be a function of many variables, but it is generally supposed to be an inverse function of the interest rate.[14] So we can write

$$M^D/P = L(r)$$

This inverse relation between money demand and interest rate is intuitive. Higher interest rates mean that it becomes more costly to hold money balances than to invest in interest-bearing assets. This opportunity cost reduces the demand for money. Equilibrium implies that money supply equals real money demand times the price level:[15]

$$M^S = P \times L(r) \tag{8}$$

The interest rate will adjust so that the quantity of money demanded by agents will equal the money supply. For example, assume that the central bank decides to provide more liquidity (unexpected increase in money supply). Agents will have additional cash balances to invest. The supply of loanable funds will increase and the interest rate will drop.

It must be stressed that the money equilibrium equation, Equation 8, is commonly used in two very different contexts:

▶ In the *long run*, monetarists use Equation 8 as an equilibrium relation between the money supply and the price level. Everything else equal, an increase in the money supply will cause a proportional increase in the price level. For example, if the money supply doubles, without any change in real output, the price level must also double. In the long run, goods prices adjust to a change in money supply, and real interest rates revert back to their normal equilibrium level.

▶ In the *short run*, goods prices are inelastic. They react only slowly to monetary shocks and changes in interest rates. An unexpected increase in money supply will not immediately translate into a proportional price increase for physical goods. Goods prices are generally slow to adjust ("sticky prices") and the price level will only increase progressively. This is

---

[14] Demand for real cash balances is also a function of economic activity. To simplify the analysis, we do not explicitly introduce the real sector here, but real output (real GDP) is implicit in L.

[15] M^S/P is called the real money supply.

quite different for financial prices, such as interest rates, which react immediately to new information that affect expectations. So, Equation 8 is used, assuming that the price level P remains unchanged in the short run. An increase in money supply translates immediately into a drop in the interest rate. This is a drop in the *real* interest rate because expected inflation has clearly not decreased (but rather increased).

This difference between short-run and long-run effects is equally important for the exchange rate.

Exchange Rate Dynamics: Asset Market Approach

The asset market approach is generally used to estimate the impact of some disturbance on the current value of a currency. Typically, a monetary shock (disturbance) such as a central bank intervention on the interest rate will take time to propagate through the economy, but its expected impact will be immediately reflected in current exchange rates. The asset market approach first determines the new equilibrium value of the exchange rate once the influence of the monetary shock has been fully reflected in the economy (long run). Then, knowing that this equilibrium exchange rate is expected to prevail in the long run, one can infer the current exchange rate using uncovered interest parity.

The typical asset market approach to the exchange rate assumes that the parity relations described previously will apply in the long run. The equilibrium value of the exchange rate is driven by PPP, but goods prices are sticky and PPP will not hold in the short run. Because exchange rates are financial prices, however, they will immediately reflect expected changes in this long-run equilibrium value. So, we must clearly differentiate between the long-run and short-run effects. Thus, the asset market approach studies the dynamics of the exchange rate and proceeds in two steps:

1. Determine the *long-run* expected value of the exchange rate, $E(S)$, based on PPP. This is its fundamental PPP value expected to prevail in the long run.

2. Infer the *short-run* value of the exchange rate S_0 assuming that the uncovered interest rate parity relation holds. Using Equation 5, we get Equation 9.

$$S_0 = E(S) \times (1 + r_{DC}) / (1 + r_{FC}) \qquad \textbf{(9)}$$

If the expected long-run exchange rate $E(S)$ were known with certainty, Equation 9 could be viewed as an arbitrage condition. S_0 would have to be equal to the expected exchange rate adjusted by the interest rate differential; otherwise, arbitrage would occur.[16]

Exchange Rate Dynamics: A Simple Model

A simple model reflects the economic reasoning behind the asset market approach. Assume that the foreign currency is the U.S. dollar and the domestic currency is the euro. $M_\$$ and $M_€$ are the money supplies, and $P_\$$ and $P_€$ are the

---

[16] Note that Equation 9 does not specify the time period necessary for the long-run adjustment. So, the interest rates r_{DC} and r_{FC} are compounded over the whole time period; they are not annualized. For example, assume that it takes two years for the exchange rate to reach its new fundamental value; then the interest rates should be equal to the annualized rates compounded over two years.

price levels in both countries. S is the €:$ spot exchange rate. For the sake of simplicity, assume that there is no inflation in either country and that the money supplies have been constant over time and are expected to remain so in the future. Further, assume that the yield curves are flat in both countries, with $r_\$ = r_€$.

An unexpected increase in money supply takes place in the United States, at time t_0, from $M_\$$ to $M_\$^*$. This is a one-time but permanent money expansion. In other words, the U.S. money supply is now expected to remain at $M_\$^*$ for the foreseeable future. Nothing has changed in Europe: the money supply, interest rate, and price level remain constant at $M_€$, $r_€$, and $P_€$. How should the exchange rate react to this money supply shock?

The time path of the various variables is described in Exhibit 6.

▶ The money supply jumps *permanently* from $M_\$$ to $M_\$^*$ at time t_0 (Exhibit 6a).

▶ The *long-run* equilibrium price level in the United States must increase proportionally to the increase in money supply. In the long run, it will reach a level $P_\$^* = P_\$ \times M_\$^*/M_\$$, as implied by Equation 8. Once the price level reaches $P_\$^*$, it will remain at that level because there is no expected monetary expansion beyond the one-time shock. The real money supply will get back to its equilibrium level: $M_\$^*/P_\$^* = M_\$/P_\$$. But goods prices are sticky in the short run, so it will take time for the price to reach the level $P_\$^*$. The increase in price level will be progressive (Exhibit 6b).

EXHIBIT 6 **Exchange Rate Dynamics**

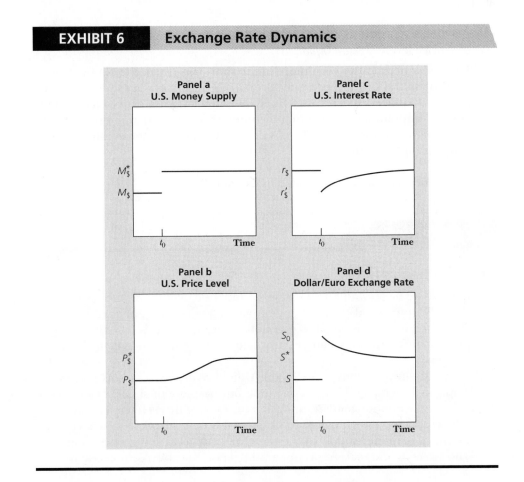

▶ Once the monetary shock is fully absorbed, the U.S. interest rate will revert, in the *long run*, to its normal level of $r_\$$. But in the *short run* the price level does not move, so the real money supply increases to $M_\$^*/P_\$$. This increase in money supply will lead to a drop in the U.S. interest rate (say, to a level $r_\$'$), which will progressively get back to its long-run equilibrium value in line with the increase in price level (Exhibit 6c).

▶ The exchange rate started at its PPP value of $S = P_\$/P_€$. In the long run it is expected to rise to its new equilibrium PPP value of $E(S) = S^* = P_\$^*/P_€$. The long-run exchange rate of the euro (number of dollars per euro) will appreciate in proportion to the increase in U.S. money supply, which is also the percentage increase in U.S. price level. Knowing what the exchange rate will be in the long run, we can infer its short-run value using uncovered interest parity. The short-run value (S_0) should be equal to the expected long-run value adjusted by the interest rate differential. Because the U.S. interest rate has dropped, the exchange rate will be higher than its new long-run expected value. The exchange rate will progressively move to its long-run PPP value (Exhibit 6d).

The immediate result of this U.S. monetary shock is a depreciation of the U.S. dollar (appreciation of the euro) beyond its new fundamental PPP value. This phenomenon, caused by the U.S. interest drop, is known as *overshooting*: The short-run reaction to a shock is larger than its long-run reaction. Here we see two phenomena at play:

▶ The dollar depreciates from S to S^* because of the long-run increase in the U.S. price level (*expected inflation*).

▶ The dollar depreciates even more in the short run (from S to S_0) because of the drop in the U.S. interest rate (drop in the *real interest rate*). As shown in Equation 9, the exchange rate S_0 is equal to the long-run expected exchange rate S^* compounded by the domestic interest rate (euro) and discounted at the foreign interest rate (dollar). A drop in the dollar interest rate implies that S_0 is higher than S^*.

A numerical illustration is provided in Example 9.

EXAMPLE 9

Exchange Rate Dynamics

The United States and Europe have no inflation, a constant money supply, and (annualized) interest rates equal to 3 percent for all maturities. The exchange rate is equal to one dollar per euro; this is its PPP value, and the price indexes can be assumed to be equal to one in both countries.

Suddenly and unexpectedly, the United States increases its money supply by 2 percent. This is a one-time but permanent shock. Immediately on the announcement, the U.S. interest rate drops from 3 percent to 2 percent for all maturities. It is expected that it will take two years for the shock in money supply to translate fully into a price increase. There is no effect on the real sector, nor any effect on Europe. Assume that the

Eurozone is the domestic country. What will be the exchange rate dynamics?

Solution: First, determine the long-run exchange rate. After two years, the U.S. price level will rise by 2 percent to 1.02. The exchange rate expected to prevail at that time, $E(S)$, is the new fundamental PPP value of the exchange rate:

$$S^* = 1 \times \frac{1.02}{1.000} = 1.02 \text{ dollars per euro}$$

After two years, the U.S. interest rate will be back to 3 percent. In the short run (immediately after the announcement), the exchange rate will move to

$$S_0 = E(S) \times (1 + r_{DC})/(1 + r_{FC}) = 1.02 \times \frac{(1 + 3\%)^2}{(1 + 2\%)^2}$$

$$= 1.04 \text{ dollars per euro}$$

Following the money supply shock, the short-run effect on the dollar is a depreciation of 4 percent. This is caused by two phenomena:

▶ The fundamental PPP value depreciates by 2 percent because of the 2 percent long-run increase in the U.S. price level.

▶ The drop in the U.S. interest rate leads to an additional 2 percent dollar depreciation (a total of 4 percent).

This second phenomenon is caused by the drop in U.S. interest rates. If the exchange rate S_0 had settled at its long-run value of $1.02 per €, an arbitrage could be constructed. Rather than investing dollars at a 2 percent interest rate, it is much more attractive to exchange dollars for euros spot at 1/1.02 euros, invest those euros at 3 percent, and repatriate the euros into dollars two years from now at the exchange rate of $S^* = \$1.02$ per €. This would enable a speculator to "pocket" the interest rate differential and put pressure on the spot exchange rate until it reaches $S_0 = \$1.04$ per €. Of course, such reasoning relies on the assumption that the future exchange rate S^* is known with certainty.

To summarize:

▶ An increase in expected inflation in the foreign country leads to a depreciation of the foreign currency.

▶ A drop in the real interest rate in the foreign country leads to a depreciation of the foreign currency.

This simple model illustrates how an exchange rate reacts immediately, and in a volatile fashion, to monetary news. More complex monetary expansion scenarios could be modeled. For example, we could consider an unexpected, but permanent, increase in the *rate of growth* in money supply rather than a quantity shock in its level. Then the long-run interest rate would rise because of the permanent increase in expected inflation, but there would also be short-run effects.

Difficulties

The challenge of the asset market approach is to specify the news that should affect the exchange rate and quantify its a priori influence in the short run and the long run. One of the important components of such an approach is modeling the behavior of monetary authorities, because investors will try to guess their reactions. Another important component is risk perception. Investors discount expected events, and a change in risk perception affects the pricing of the exchange rate, as in any forward-looking pricing model. The influence of uncertainty is particularly important for the currencies of weaker economies.

Central banks usually convey their attitude by interest rate announcements. We have to evaluate the content and credibility of interest rate announcements carefully. If the rise in interest rates simply reflects an increase in home inflation, not a rise in the real interest rate, it should not have a positive effect on the currency. Even worse, it could carry some negative information. For example, during currency crises, a rise in interest rates is often interpreted as evidence that the currency is under speculative attack, that the central bank has had serious problems defending the exchange rate, and that its foreign exchange reserves are being exhausted. This situation prompts other speculators to join the attack and basically sends a negative signal for the home currency.

SUMMARY

▶ In a flexible exchange rate regime, exchange rates are determined by supply and demand.

▶ In the balance of payments accounts, the current account includes the balance of goods and services, the income received or paid on existing investments, and current transfers. The financial account includes short-term and long-term capital transactions.

▶ Current account deficits can be balanced by financial account surpluses, and these deficits have a negative effect on the economy only if the country cannot attract financial inflows.

▶ Factors causing a country's currency to appreciate include lower inflation rates and higher real interest rates, but the effect of differences in economic performance is indeterminate.

▶ Expansionary monetary policy will generally lead to a depreciation of the home currency.

▶ Expansionary fiscal policy will generally lead to an appreciation of the home currency.

▶ A fixed exchange rate system is one in which the exchange rate between two currencies remains fixed at a preset level known as official parity.

▶ A pegged exchange rate system is one in which a target exchange rate (the peg) is set against a major currency, the exchange rate is allowed to fluctuate in a narrow band around the peg, and the peg is adjusted periodically to take account of economic fundamentals.

▶ Interest rate parity is the relation that the forward discount (premium) equals the interest rate differential between two currencies.

▶ Absolute purchasing power parity (PPP) claims that the exchange rate should be equal to the ratio of the average price levels in the two economies.

▶ Relative purchasing power parity claims that the percentage movement of the exchange rate should be equal to the inflation differential between the two economies.

▶ Purchasing power parity implies that the ratio of the end-of-period exchange rate to the beginning-of-period exchange rate (in indirect quotes) equals the ratio of one plus the foreign inflation rate to one plus the domestic inflation rate.

▶ The real interest rate can be approximated for all countries by subtracting the expected inflation rate from the nominal interest rate.

▶ The international Fisher relation claims that real interest rates are equal across the world, and hence differences in nominal interest rates are caused by differences in national inflationary expectations. Interest rate differences approximately equal expected inflation rate differences if the international Fisher relation holds.

▶ One plus the real interest rate for any country equals one plus the nominal rate divided by one plus the expected inflation rate for that country.

▶ Uncovered interest rate parity claims that the expected change in the exchange rate approximately equals the foreign minus the domestic interest rate.

▶ Uncovered interest rate parity is a theory combining purchasing power parity and the international Fisher relation.

► The forward exchange rate equals the expected exchange rate under the condition of no foreign currency risk premium.

► The forward exchange rate discount or premium equals the expected change in the exchange rate under the condition of no foreign currency risk premium.

► Combining all the parity relations indicates that the expected return on default-free bills should be the same in all countries, and exchange risk reduces to inflation uncertainty because there is no real foreign currency risk.

► Deviations from purchasing power parity should be corrected in the long run.

► The elements in the balance of payments are the current account, the capital account, the financial account, and the official reserves account; without central bank intervention, a current account deficit must be balanced by a financial account surplus. Exchange rate adjustments can be needed to restore balance of payments equilibrium.

► The asset market approach to pricing exchange rate expectations claims that the exchange rate is the relative price of two currencies, determined by investors' expectations about these currencies.

► The long-run exchange rate effect of a sudden and unexpected increase in the money supply is a depreciation of the currency so that purchasing power parity is maintained as the percentage increase in the price level matches the percentage increase in the money supply. Given sticky-goods prices, the short-run exchange rate effect is an immediate drop in the real interest rate and more depreciation of the currency than the depreciation implied by purchasing power parity.

PRACTICE PROBLEMS FOR READING 19

1. Consider two countries, A and B, whose currencies are α and β, respectively. The interest rate in A is greater than the interest rate in B. Which of the following is true according to the expected exchange rate movement relationship and interest rate parity, respectively?

   A. α is expected to appreciate relative to β, and α trades with a forward discount.

   B. α is expected to appreciate relative to β, and α trades with a forward premium.

   C. α is expected to depreciate relative to β, and α trades with a forward discount.

   D. α is expected to depreciate relative to β, and α trades with a forward premium.

2. Suppose that the spot €:$ is equal to 1.1795. The annual one-year interest rates on the Eurocurrency market are 4 percent in euros and 5 percent in U.S. dollars. The annualized one-month interest rates are 3 percent in euros and 4 percent in U.S. dollars.

   A. What is the one-year forward exchange rate?

   B. What is the one-month forward exchange rate?

3. You are given the following hypothetical quotes.

   Spot exchange rates:

   $$€:\$ = 1.1865-1.1870$$

   $$\$:¥ = 108.10-108.20$$

   Three-month interest rates (percent per year):

   in $ $5-5\frac{1}{4}$

   in € $3\frac{1}{4}-3\frac{1}{2}$

   in ¥ $1\frac{1}{4}-1\frac{1}{2}$

   What should the quotes be for the following?

   A. €:¥ spot exchange rate.

   B. €:$ *three-month forward ask exchange rate. Hint:* Buying euros forward is equivalent to borrowing dollars to buy euros spot and investing the euros.

   C. $:€ three-month forward bid exchange rate.

   D. $:¥ three-month forward bid and ask exchange rate.

4. Jason Smith is a foreign exchange trader. At a point in time, he noticed the following quotes.

Spot exchange rate	$:SFr = 1.6627
Six-month forward exchange rate	$:SFr = 1.6558
Six-month $ interest rate	3.5% per year
Six-month SFr interest rate	3.0% per year

   A. Ignoring transaction costs, was the interest rate parity holding?

   B. Was there an arbitrage possibility? If yes, what steps would have been needed to make an arbitrage profit? Assuming that Jason Smith was authorized to work with $1 million for this purpose, how much would the arbitrage profit have been in dollars?

5. At a point in time, foreign exchange arbitrageur noticed that the Japanese yen to U.S. dollar spot exchange rate was $:¥ = 108 and the three-month forward exchange rate was $:¥ = 107.30. The three-month $ interest rate was 5.20 percent per annum and the three-month ¥ interest rate was 1.20 percent per annum.

   A. Was interest rate parity holding?

   B. Was there an arbitrage possibility? If yes, what steps would have been needed to make an arbitrage profit? Assuming that the arbitrageur was authorized to work with $1 million for this purpose, how much would the arbitrage profit have been in dollars?

6. Suppose the following chart illustrates the domestic prices of three items in the United States and Mexico.

Items	United States (Dollars)	Mexico (Pesos)
Shoes	20	80
Watches	40	180
Electric motors	80	600

If one dollar exchanges for five Mexican pesos and transportation costs are zero, Mexico will import:

   A. shoes and watches, and the United States will import electric motors.

   B. shoes, and the United States will import watches and electric motors.

   C. all three goods from the United States.

   D. electric motors, and the United States will import shoes and watches.

7. A group of countries decides to introduce a common currency. What do you think would happen to the inflation rates of these countries after the introduction of the common currency?

8. Suppose that the current Swiss franc to U.S. dollar spot exchange rate is $:SFr = 1.60. The expected inflation over the coming year is 2 percent in Switzerland and 5 percent in the United States. According to purchasing power parity, what is the expected value of the Swiss franc to U.S. dollar spot exchange rate a year from now?

9. Let us consider a utopian world in which there are only three goods: sake, beer, and TV sets.

   ▶ Japanese consume only a locally produced food, called sake, and an industrially produced and traded good, called TV sets.

   ▶ Americans consume only a locally produced food, called beer, and an industrially produced and traded good, called TV sets.

   TV sets are produced in both countries and actively traded; their local prices follow the law of one price. Foods are produced only locally and are not traded. The consumption basket of a Japanese individual consists of two-thirds sake and one-third TV sets. The consumption basket of an American consists of one-half beer and one-half TV sets. Prices of beer and TV sets in the United States are constant over time in U.S. dollars. Japanese are very competitive and export a lot of TV sets. Japanese farmers want to share in the increased national wealth, and the price of sake is rising at a rate of 10 percent per year in yen. Assume that the yen/dollar exchange rate stays constant.

   A. What is the consumer price index inflation in Japan?

   B. Does relative PPP hold between Japan and the United States?

10. A. Explain the following three concepts of purchasing power parity:

   i. The law of one price.

   ii. Absolute PPP.

   iii. Relative PPP.

   B. Evaluate the usefulness of relative PPP in predicting movements in foreign exchange rates on a:

   i. short-term basis (e.g., three months).

   ii. long-term basis (e.g., six years).

11. A French company is importing some equipment from Switzerland and will need to pay 10 million Swiss francs three months from now. Suppose that the current spot exchange rate is €:SFr = 1.5543. The treasurer of the company expects the franc to appreciate in the next few weeks and is concerned about it. The three-month forward rate is €:SFr = 1.5320.

   A. Given the treasurer's expectation, what action can he take using the forward contract?

   B. Three months later, the spot exchange rate turns out to be €:SFr = 1.5101. Did the company benefit because of the treasurer's action?

12. Suppose the international parity conditions hold. Does that mean that the nominal interest rates would be equal among countries? Why or why not?

13. Suppose that you are given the following information about Australia, Switzerland, and the United States. The Australian dollar is expected to depreciate relative to the United States dollar. The nominal interest rate in the United States is greater than that in Switzerland. Can you say whether the Australian dollar is expected to depreciate or appreciate relative to the Swiss Franc?

14. Suppose that there were some statistics about the Swedish krona and the dollar:

	SKr	$
Inflation (annual rate)	6%	?%
One-year interest rate	8%	7%
Spot exchange rate ($:SKr)	?	
Expected exchange rate in one year ($:SKr)	6	
One-year forward exchange rate ($:SKr)	?	

Based on the linear approximations of the international parity conditions, replace the question marks with appropriate answers.

15. Suppose that the one-year interest rate is 12 percent in the United Kingdom. The expected annual rate of inflation for the coming year is 10 percent for the United Kingdom and 4 percent for Switzerland. The current spot exchange rate is £:SFr = 3. Using the precise form of the international parity relations, compute the one-year interest rate in Switzerland, the expected Swiss franc to pound exchange rate in one year, and the one-year forward exchange rate.

16. Following are some statistics for Malaysia, the Philippines, and the United States.

Inflation Rates: Annual Rates in Percent per Year

	1991	1992	1993	1994	1995	1996
Malaysia	4.40	4.69	3.57	3.71	5.28	3.56
Philippines	18.70	8.93	7.58	9.06	8.11	8.41
United States	4.23	3.03	3.00	2.61	2.81	2.34

Exchange Rate per U.S. Dollar: Annual Average

	1991	1992	1993	1994	1995	1996
Malaysia	2.75	2.55	2.57	2.62	2.50	2.52
Philippines	27.48	25.51	27.12	26.42	25.71	26.22

In 1997, Malaysia and the Philippines suffered a severe currency crisis. Use the numbers in the preceding tables to provide a partial explanation.

17. Paf is a small country whose currency is the pif. Twenty years ago, the exchange rate with the U.S. dollar was 2 pifs per dollar, and the inflation indexes were equal to 100 in both the United States and Paf. Now, the exchange rate is 0.9 pifs per dollar, and the inflation indexes are equal to 400 in the United States and 200 in Paf.

A. What should the current exchange rate be if PPP prevailed?

B. Is the pif over- or undervalued according to PPP?

18. Paf is a small country. Its currency is the pif, and the exchange rate with the United States dollar is 0.9 pifs per dollar. Following are some of the transactions affecting Paf's balance of payments during the quarter:

▶ Paf exports 10 million pifs of local products.

▶ Paf investors buy foreign companies for a total cost of $3 million.

▶ Paf investors receive $0.1 million of dividends on their foreign shares.

▶ Many tourists visit Paf and spend $0.5 million.

▶ Paf pays 1 million pifs as interest on Paf bonds currently held by foreigners.

▶ Paf imports $7 million of foreign goods.

▶ Paf receives $0.3 million as foreign aid.

Illustrate how the preceding transactions would affect Paf's balance of payments for the quarter, including the current account, the financial account, and the official reserves account.

19. The domestic economy seems to be overheating, with rapid economic growth and low unemployment. News has just been released that the monthly activity level is even higher than expected (as measured by new orders to factories and unemployment figures). This news leads to renewed fears of inflationary pressures and likely action by the monetary authorities to raise interest rates to slow the economy down.

A. Based on the traditional flow market approach, discuss whether this news is good or bad for the exchange rate.

B. Based on the asset market approach, discuss whether this news is good or bad for the exchange rate.

20. Even though the investment community generally believes that Country M's recent budget deficit reduction is "credible, sustainable, and large," analysts disagree about how it will affect Country M's foreign exchange rate. Juan DaSilva, CFA, states, "The reduced budget deficit will lower interest rates, which will immediately weaken Country M's foreign exchange rate."

A. Discuss the direct (short-term) effects of a reduction in Country M's budget deficit on:

   i. demand for loanable funds.

   ii. nominal interest rates.

   iii. exchange rates.

B. Helga Wu, CFA, states, "Country M's foreign exchange rate will strengthen over time as a result of changes in expectations in the private sector in country M." Support Wu's position that Country M's foreign exchange rate will strengthen because of the changes a budget deficit reduction will cause in:

   i. expected inflation rates.

   ii. expected rates of return on domestic securities.

SOLUTIONS FOR READING 19

1. **C is correct.** Because the interest rate in A is greater than the interest rate in B, α is expected to depreciate relative to β, and should trade with a forward discount.

2. Because the exchange rate is given in €:$ terms, the appropriate expression for the interest rate parity relation is

$$\frac{F}{S} = \frac{1 + r_\$}{1 + r_€}$$

($r_\$$ is a part of the numerator and $r_€$ is a part of the denominator).

A. The one-year €:$ forward rate is given by

$$€:\$ = 1.1795 \frac{1.05}{1.04} = 1.1908$$

B. The one-month €:$ forward rate is given by

$$€:\$ = 1.1795 \frac{1 + (0.04/12)}{1 + (0.03/12)} = 1.1805$$

Of course, these are central rates, and bid–ask rates could also be determined on the basis of bid–ask rates for the spot exchange and interest rates.

3. **A.** Bid €:¥ = (Bid $:¥) × (Bid €:$) = 108.10 × 1.1865 = 128.2607.
Ask €:¥ = (Ask $:¥) × (Ask €:$) = 108.20 × 1.1870 = 128.4334.

B. Because the exchange rate is in €:$ terms, the appropriate expression for the interest rate parity relation is $F/S = (1 + r_\$)/(1 + r_€)$.

$$€:\$ \text{ 3-month ask} = (\text{Spot ask } €:\$) \frac{1 + (\text{Ask } r_\$)}{1 + (\text{Bid } r_€)}$$

$$= 1.1870 \frac{1 + (0.0525/4)}{1 + (0.0325/4)} = 1.1929$$

Thus, the €:$3-month forward ask exchange rate is: 1.1929.

C. Bid $:€ = 1/Ask €:$ = 1/1.1929 = 0.8383.
Thus, the 3-month forward bid exchange rate is $:€ = 0.8383.

D. Because the exchange rate is in $:¥ terms, the appropriate expression for the interest rate parity relation is $F/S = (1 + r_¥)/1 + r_\$$.

$$\$:¥\text{3-month bid} = (\text{Spot bid } \$:¥) \frac{1 + (\text{bid } r_¥)}{1 + (\text{ask } r_\$)}$$

$$= 108.10 \frac{1 + (0.0125/4)}{1 + (0.0525/4)} = 107.03$$

$$\$:¥\text{3-month ask} = (\text{Spot ask } \$:¥) \frac{1 + (\text{ask } r_¥)}{1 + (\text{bid } r_\$)}$$

$$= 108.20 \frac{1 + (0.0150/4)}{1 + (0.0500/4)} = 107.26$$

Thus, the \$:¥ 3-month forward exchange rate is: 107.03 − 107.26. *Note*: The interest rates one uses in all such computations are those that result in a lower forward bid (so, bid interest rates in the numerator and ask rates in the denominator) and a higher forward ask (so, ask interest rates in the numerator and bid rates in the denominator).

4. A. For six months, $r_{SFr} = 1.50\%$ and $r_\$ = 1.75\%$. Because the exchange rate is in \$:SFr terms, the appropriate expression for the interest rate parity relation is

$$\frac{F}{S} = \frac{1 + r_{SFr}}{1 + r_\$}, \text{ or } \frac{F}{S}(1 + r_\$) = (1 + r_{SFr})$$

The left side of this expression is

$$\frac{F}{S}(1 + r_\$) = \frac{1.6558}{1.6627}(1 + 0.0175) = 1.0133$$

The right side of the expression is: $1 + r_{SFr} = 1.0150$. Because the left and right sides are not equal, IRP is not holding.

B. Because IRP is not holding, there is an arbitrage possibility: Because $1.0133 < 1.0150$, we can say that the SFr interest rate quote is more than what it should be as per the quotes for the other three variables. Equivalently, we can also say that the \$ interest rate quote is less than what it should be as per the quotes for the other three variables. Therefore, the arbitrage strategy should be based on borrowing in the \$ market and lending in the SFr market. The steps would be as follows:

▶ Borrow \$1,000,000 for six months at 3.5% per year. Need to pay back $\$1,000,000 \times (1 + 0.0175) = \$1,017,500$ six months later.

▶ Convert \$1,000,000 to SFr at the spot rate to get SFr 1,662,700.

▶ Lend SFr 1,662,700 for six months at 3% per year. Will get back $\text{SFr } 1,662,700 \times (1 + 0.0150) = \text{SFr } 1,687,641$ six months later.

▶ Sell SFr 1,687,641 six months forward. The transaction will be contracted as of the current date but delivery and settlement will only take place six months later. So, six months later, exchange SFr 1,687,641 for SFr 1,687,641/SFr 1.6558/\$ = \$1,019,230.

The arbitrage profit six months later is $1,019,230 − 1,017,500 = \$1,730$.

5. A. For three months, $r_\$ = 1.30\%$ and $r_¥ = 0.30\%$. Because the exchange rate is in \$:¥ terms, the appropriate expression for the interest rate parity relation is

$$\frac{F}{S} = \frac{1 + r_¥}{1 + r_\$}, \text{ or } \frac{F}{S}(1 + r_\$) = (1 + r_¥)$$

The left side of this expression is

$$\frac{F}{S}(1 + r_\$) = \frac{107.30}{108.00}(1 + 0.0130) = 1.0064$$

The right side of this expression is: $1 + r_¥ = 1.0030$. Because the left and right sides are not equal, IRP is not holding.

B. Because IRP is not holding, there is an arbitrage possibility. Because 1.0064 > 1.0030, we can say that the $ interest rate quote is more than what it should be as per the quotes for the other three variables. Equivalently, we can also say that the ¥ interest rate quote is less than what it should be as per the quotes for the other three variables. Therefore, the arbitrage strategy should be based on lending in the $ market and borrowing in the ¥ market. The steps would be as follows:

▶ Borrow the yen equivalent of $1,000,000. Because the spot rate is ¥108 per $, borrow $1,000,000 × ¥108/$ = ¥108,000,000. Need to pay back ¥108,000,000 × (1 + 0.0030) = ¥108,324,000 three months later.

▶ Exchange ¥108,000,000 for $1,000,000 at the spot exchange rate.

▶ Lend $1,000,000 for three months at 5.20% per year. Will get back $1,000,000 × (1 + 0.0130) = $1,013,000 three months later.

▶ Buy ¥108,324,000 three months forward. The transaction will be contracted as of the current date, but delivery and settlement will only take place three months later. So, three months later, get ¥108,324,000 for ¥108,324,000/(¥107.30 per $) = $1,009,543.

The arbitrage profit three months later is 1,013,000 − 1,009,543 = $3,457.

6. D is correct. At the given exchange rate of 5 pesos/$, the cost in Mexico in dollar terms is $16 for shoes, $36 for watches, and $120 for electric motors. Thus, compared with the United States, shoes and watches are cheaper in Mexico, and electric motors are more expensive in Mexico. Therefore, Mexico will import electric motors from the United States, and the United States will import shoes and watches from Mexico.

7. Consider two countries, A and B. Based on relative PPP,

$$\frac{S_1}{S_0} = \frac{1 + I_A}{1 + I_B}$$

where S_1 and S_0 are the expected and the current exchange rates between the currencies of A and B, and I_A and I_B are the inflation rates in A and B. If A and B belong to the group of countries that introduces the same currency, then one could think of both S_1 and S_0 being one. Then, I_A and I_B should both be equal for relative PPP to hold. Thus, introduction of a common currency by a group of countries would result in the convergence of the inflation rates among these countries. A similar argument could be applied to inflation among the various states of the United States.

8. Based on relative PPP,

$$\frac{S_1}{S_0} = \frac{1 + I_{\text{Switzerland}}}{1 + I_{\text{US}}}$$

where S_1 is the expected $:SFr exchange rate one year from now, S_0 is the current $:SFr exchange rate, and $I_{\text{Switzerland}}$ and I_{US} are the expected annual inflation rates in Switzerland and the United States, respectively. So,

$$\frac{S_1}{1.60} = \frac{1 + 0.02}{1 + 0.05} \quad \text{and} \quad S_1 = 1.60 \ (1.02/1.05) = \text{SFr}1.55/\$.$$

9. A. A Japanese consumption basket consists of two-thirds sake and one-third TV sets. The price of sake in yen is rising at a rate of 10% per year. The price of TV sets is constant. The Japanese consumer price index inflation is therefore equal to

$$\frac{2}{3}(10\%) + \frac{1}{3}(0\%) = 6.67\%$$

B. Relative PPP states that

$$\frac{S_1}{S_0} = \frac{1 + I_{FC}}{1 + I_{DC}}.$$

Because the exchange rate is given to be constant, we have $S_0 = S_1$, which implies $S_1/S_0 = 1$. As a result, in our example, PPP would hold if $1 + I_{FC} = 1 + I_{DC}$ (i.e., $I_{FC} = I_{DC}$). Because the Japanese inflation rate is 6.67% and the American inflation rate is 0%, we do not have $I_{FC} = I_{DC}$, and PPP does not hold.

10. A.   **i.** The law of one price is that, assuming competitive markets and no transportation costs or tariffs, the same goods should have the same real prices in all countries after converting prices to a common currency.

  ii. Absolute PPP, focusing on baskets of goods and services, states that the same basket of goods should have the same price in all countries after conversion to a common currency. Under absolute PPP, the equilibrium exchange rate between two currencies would be the rate that equalizes the prices of a basket of goods between the two countries. This rate would correspond to the ratio of average price levels in the countries. Absolute PPP assumes no impediments to trade and identical price indexes that do not create measurement problems.

  iii. Relative PPP holds that exchange rate movements reflect differences in price changes (inflation rates) between countries. A country with a relatively high inflation rate will experience a proportionate depreciation of its currency's value vis-à-vis that of a country with a lower rate of inflation. Movements in currencies provide a means for maintaining equivalent purchasing power levels among currencies in the presence of differing inflation rates.

      Relative PPP assumes that prices adjust quickly and price indexes properly measure inflation rates. Because relative PPP focuses on changes and not absolute levels, relative PPP is more likely to be satisfied than the law of one price or absolute PPP.

B.   **i.** Relative PPP is not consistently useful in the short run because of the following: 1) Relationships between month-to-month movements in market exchange rates and PPP are not consistently strong, according to empirical research. Deviations between the rates can persist for extended periods. 2) Exchange rates fluctuate minute by minute because they are set in the financial markets. Price levels, in contrast, are sticky and adjust slowly. 3) Many other factors can influence exchange rate movements rather than just inflation.

      ii. Research suggests that over the long term, a tendency exists for market and PPP rates to move together, with market rates eventually moving toward levels implied by PPP.

11. A. If the treasurer is worried that the franc might appreciate in the next three months, she could hedge her foreign exchange exposure by trading this risk against the premium included in the forward exchange rate. She could buy 10 million Swiss francs on the three-month forward market at the rate of SFr 1.5320 per €. The transaction will be contracted as of the current date, but delivery and settlement will only take place three months later.

    B. Three months later, the company received the 10 million Swiss francs at the forward rate of SFr 1.5320 per € agreed on earlier. Thus, the company needed (SFr 10,000,000)/(SFr 1.5320 per €), or €6,527,415. If the company had not entered into a forward contract, the company would have received the 10 million Swiss francs at the spot rate of SFr 1.5101 per €. Thus, the company would have needed (SFr 10,000,000) / (SFr 1.5101 per €), or €6,622,078. Therefore, the company benefited by the treasurer's action, because €6,622,078 − €6,527,415 = €94,663 were saved.

12. The nominal interest rate is approximately the sum of the real interest rate and the expected inflation rate over the term of the interest rate. Even if the international Fisher relation holds, and the real interest rates are equal among countries, the expected inflation can be very different from one country to another. Therefore, there is no reason why nominal interest rates should be equal among countries.

13. Because the Australian dollar is expected to depreciate relative to the dollar, we know from the combination of international Fisher relation and relative PPP that the nominal interest rate in Australia is greater than the nominal interest rate in the United States. Further, the nominal interest rate in the United States is greater than that in Switzerland. Thus, the nominal interest rate in Australia has to be greater than the nominal interest rate in Switzerland. Therefore, we can say from the combination of international Fisher relation and relative PPP that the Australian dollar is expected to depreciate relative to the Swiss franc.

14. According to the approximate version of the international Fisher relation, $r_{Sweden} - r_{US} = I_{Sweden} - I_{US}$. So, $8 - 7 = 6 - I_{US}$, which means that $I_{US} = 5\%$. According to the approximate version of relative PPP,

$$\frac{S_1 - S_0}{S_0} = I_{Sweden} - I_{US}$$

where, S_1 and S_0 are in \$:SKr terms. $I_{Sweden} - I_{US} = 6 - 5 = 1\%$, or 0.01. So, $(6 - S_0)/S_0 = 0.01$. Solving for S_0, we get $S_0 = $ SKr 5.94 per \$.

According to the approximate version of IRP,

$$\frac{F - S_0}{S_0} = r_{Sweden} - r_{US}$$

where, F and S_0 are in \$:SKr terms. $r_{Sweden} - r_{US} = 8 - 7 = 1\%$, or 0.01. So, $(F - 5.94)/5.94 = 0.01$. Solving for F, we get $F = $ SKr 6 per \$.

Because we are given the expected exchange rate, we could also have arrived at this answer by using the foreign exchange expectations relation.

15. According to the international Fisher relation,

$$\frac{1 + r_{\text{Switzerland}}}{1 + r_{\text{UK}}} = \frac{1 + I_{\text{Switzerland}}}{1 + I_{\text{UK}}}$$

So,

$$\frac{1 + r_{\text{Switzerland}}}{1 + 0.12} = \frac{1 + 0.04}{1 + 0.10}$$

therefore, $r_{\text{Switzerland}} = 0.0589$, or 5.89%.

According to relative PPP,

$$\frac{S_1}{S_0} = \frac{1 + I_{\text{Switzerland}}}{1 + I_{\text{UK}}}$$

where, S_1 and S_0 are in £:SFr terms.

So,

$$\frac{S_1}{3} = \frac{1 + 0.04}{1 + 0.10}$$

Solving for S_1 we get $S_1 = $ SFr 2.8364 per £.

According to IRP,

$$\frac{F}{S_0} = \frac{1 + r_{\text{Switzerland}}}{1 + r_{\text{UK}}}$$

where, F and S_0 are in £:SFr terms.

So,

$$\frac{F}{3} = \frac{1 + 0.0589}{1 + 0.12}.$$

Solving for F, we get $F = $ SFr 2.8363 per £. This is the same as the expected exchange rate in one year, with the slight difference due to rounding.

16. During the 1991–1996 period, the cumulative inflation rates were about 25 percent in Malaysia, 61 percent in the Philippines, and 18 percent in the United States. Over this period, based on relative PPP, one would have expected the Malaysian ringgit to depreciate by about 7 percent relative to the United States dollar (the inflation differential). In reality, the Malaysian ringgit *appreciated* by about 8 percent. Similarly, in view of the very high inflation differential between the Philippines and the United States, one would have expected the Philippine peso to depreciate considerably relative to the dollar. But it did not. Thus, according to PPP, both currencies had become strongly overvalued.

17. A. According to PPP, the current exchange rate should be

$$S_1 = S_0 \frac{PI_1^{\text{Pif}}/PI_0^{\text{Pif}}}{PI_1^{\$}/PI_0^{\$}}$$

where subscript 1 refers to the value now, subscript 0 refers to the value 20 years ago, PI refers to price index, and S is the \$:pif exchange rate. Thus, the current exchange rate based on PPP should be

$$S_1 = 2\left(\frac{200/100}{400/100}\right) = \text{pif } 1/\$.$$

B. As per PPP, the pif is overvalued at the prevailing exchange rate of pif 0.9 per \$.

18. Exports equal 10 million pifs and imports equal \$7 million (6.3 million pifs). Accordingly, the trade balance is $10 - 6.3 = 3.7$ million pifs.

▶ Balance of services includes the \$0.5 million spent by tourists (0.45 million pifs).

▶ Net income includes \$0.1 million or 0.09 million pifs received by Paf investors as dividends, minus 1 million pifs paid out by Paf as interest on Paf bonds (-0.91 million pifs).

▶ Unrequited transfers include \$0.3 million (0.27 million pifs) received by Paf as foreign aid.

▶ Portfolio investment includes the \$3 million or 2.7 million pifs spent by Paf investors to buy foreign firms. So, portfolio investment = -2.7 million pifs.

Based on the preceding,

▶ Current account = 3.24 (= 3.70 + 0.45 − 0.91)
▶ Capital account = 0.27
▶ Financial account = −2.7

The sum of current account, capital account, and financial account is 0.81. By definition of balance of payments, the sum of the current account, the capital account, the financial account, and the change in official reserves must be equal to zero. Therefore, official reserve account = −0.81.

The following summarizes the effect of the transactions on the balance of payments.

Current account		*3.24*
Trade balance	3.70	
Balance of services	0.45	
Net income	−0.91	
Capital account		*0.27*
Unrequited transfers	0.27	
Financial account		*−2.70*
Portfolio investment	−2.70	
Official reserve account		*−0.81*

19. **A.** A traditional flow market approach would suggest that the home currency should depreciate because of increased inflation. An increase in domestic consumption could also lead to increased imports and a deficit in the balance of trade. This deficit should lead to a weakening of the home currency in the short run.

B. The asset market approach claims that this scenario is good for the home currency. Foreign capital investment is attracted by the high returns caused by economic growth and high interest rates. This capital inflow leads to an appreciation of the home currency.

20. **A.** **i.** The immediate effect of reducing the budget deficit is to reduce the demand for loanable funds because the government needs to borrow less to bridge the gap between spending and taxes.

ii. The reduced public-sector demand for loanable funds has the direct effect of lowering nominal interest rates, because lower demand leads to lower cost of borrowing.

iii. The direct effect of the budget deficit reduction is a depreciation of the domestic currency and the exchange rate. As investors sell lower yielding Country M securities to buy the securities of other countries, Country M's currency will come under pressure and Country M's currency will depreciate.

B. **i.** In the case of a credible, sustainable, and large reduction in the budget deficit, reduced inflationary expectations are likely because the central bank is less likely to monetize the debt by increasing the money supply. Purchasing power parity and international Fisher relationships suggest that a currency should strengthen against other currencies when expected inflation declines.

ii. A reduction in government spending would tend to shift resources into private-sector investments, in which productivity is higher. The effect would be to increase the expected return on domestic securities.

MEASURING ECONOMIC ACTIVITY
by Richard Stutely

LEARNING OUTCOMES

The candidate should be able to:	Mastery
a. distinguish between the measures of economic activity (i.e., gross domestic product, gross national income, and net national income), including their components;	☐
b. differentiate between GDP at market prices and GDP at factor cost;	☐
c. differentiate between current and constant prices, and describe the GDP deflator.	☐

GDP should really stand for grossly deceptive product.

The Economist

INTRODUCTION ▬▬ 1

Total economic activity may be measured in three different but equivalent ways.

Perhaps the most obvious approach is to add up the value of all goods and services produced in a given period of time, such as one year. Money values may be imputed for services such as health care which do not change hands for cash. Since the output of one business (for example, steel) can be the input of another (for example, automobiles), double counting is avoided by combining only "value added," which for any one activity is the total value of production less the cost of inputs such as raw materials and components valued elsewhere.

A second approach is to add up the expenditure which takes place when the output is sold. Since all spending is received as incomes, a third option is to value producers' incomes.

Guide to Economic Indicators: Making Sense of Economics, Sixth Edition, by Richard Stutely, Copyright © 2007 by The Economist Newspaper Ltd. Reprinted with permission of Bloomberg, L.P.

Thus, Output = Expenditure = Incomes.

The precise definition of economic activity varies. The three main concepts are gross domestic product, gross national product, and net national product.

Gross domestic product. GDP is the total of all economic activity in one country, regardless of who owns the productive assets. For example, Britain's GDP includes the profits of a foreign firm located in Britain even if they are remitted to the firm's parent company in another country.

Gross national income or gross national product. GNI, a term which has replaced GNP in national accounts, is the total of incomes earned by residents of a country, regardless of where the assets are located. For example, Britain's GNI includes profits from British-owned businesses located in other countries.

Net national income. The "gross" in GDP and GNI indicates that there is no allowance for depreciation (capital consumption), the amount of capital resources used up in the production process due to wear and tear, accidental damage, obsolescence or retirement of capital assets. Net national income is GNI less depreciation.

The relationship between the three measures is straightforward:

GDP (gross domestic product)
+ Net property income from abroad (rent, interest, profits and dividends)
= GNI (gross national income)
− Capital consumption (depreciation)
= NNI (net national income)

Capital consumption. Capital consumption is not identifiable from a set of transactions; it can only be imputed by a system of conventions. For example, when investment spending of $1M on a new machine is included in GDP figures, national accounts statisticians pencil in depreciation of, say, $100,000 a year for each of the next ten years. This gives a stinted view of productive capacity. After five years the machine might still be producing at full capacity, but the national accounts would show it as capable of producing only half the volume that it could when new.

Choosing between GDP, GNI, and NNI

Net national income (NNI) is the most comprehensive measure of economic activity, but it is of little practical value due to the problems of accounting for depreciation. Gross concepts are more useful.

All the major industrial countries now use GDP as their main measure of national economic activity. America, Germany, and Japan, which had until the early 1990s focused on GNP, now use GDP. The difference between GDP and GNI or GNP is usually relatively small, perhaps 1% of GDP, but there are a few exceptions; for example, in 2001 Ireland's GDP was 19% bigger than its GNI, owing to the profits earned by foreign investors in the country. In the short term a large change in total net property income has only a minor effect on GDP. When reviewing longer-term trends, it is advisable to check net property income to see if it is making GNI grow faster than GDP.

Net Material Product

Some countries in the past, mainly centrally planned economies, used net material product (NMP) to measure overall economic activity. NMP was less comprehensive than GDP because it excluded "non-productive services," such as banking, government administration, health, and education, and was quoted net of capital consumption (depreciation). As a rule of thumb, NMP was roughly 80–90% of GDP.

Did the American economy start to recover in the second quarter of this year [1991], or was it stuck in recession? America's real gross national product (GNP), *the measure that is watched by the government and Wall Street and splashed across newspaper headlines, fell by 0.1% at an annual rate in the second quarter. However,* gross domestic product (GDP) *rose by 0.8% at an annual rate. By coincidence, the Department of Commerce has just decided that from November [1991], when the third-quarter figures will be released, it will concentrate more on GDP than on GNP.*

Cynics might claim that the switch to GDP is a bid to fiddle the figures. In fact it is America's first step to bring its national accounts into line with most of the rest of the world.

GNP is probably more useful in comparing the relative levels of income per head in different countries, but GDP provides a better guide to changes in domestic production—and hence is the better tool for steering economic policy. Because net income from abroad tends to be volatile, the two measures can often move in completely different directions from one quarter to another. Over longer periods, however, the two measures usually fall into step. Indeed, since the third quarter of last year [1990], America's GDP and GNP have both fallen by exactly the same amount. The government cannot boost its flagging growth rate simply by revising its figures; that requires a revision of its policies.

The Economist, September 21st 1991

OMISSIONS

Deliberate Omissions

There are many things which are not in GDP, including the following:

► **Transfer payments**. For example, social security and pensions.

► **Gifts**. For example, $10 from Aunt Agatha on your birthday.

► **Unpaid and domestic activities**. If you cut your grass or paint your house, the value of this productive activity is not recorded in GDP, but it is if you pay someone to do it for you.

► **Barter transactions**. For example, the exchange of a sack of wheat for a can of petrol.

► **Second-hand transactions**. For example, the sale of a used car (where the production was recorded in an earlier year).

► **Intermediate transactions**. For example, a lump of metal may be sold several times, perhaps as ore, pig iron, part of a component, and, finally, part of a washing machine (the metal is included in GDP once at the net total of the value added between the initial production of the ore and its final sale as a finished item).

► **Leisure**. An improved production process which creates the same output but gives more recreational time is recorded in the national accounts at exactly the same value as the old process.

► **Depletion of resources**. For example, oil production is recorded at sale price minus production costs and no allowance is made for the fact that an irreplaceable part of the nation's capital stock of resources has been consumed.

► **Environmental costs**. GDP figures do not distinguish between green and polluting industries.

► **Allowance for non-profit-making and inefficient activities**. The civil service and police force are valued according to expenditure on salaries, equipment, and so on (the appropriate price for these services might be judged to be very different if they were provided by private companies).

► **Allowance for changes in quality**. You can buy very different electronic goods for the same inflation-adjusted outlay than you could a few years ago, but GDP data do not take account of such technological improvements.

Some of the exclusions can be identified elsewhere. For example, environmental costs are seen in statistics on pollution and most countries report known oil or coal reserves (although these estimates may be over-optimistic or clouded by genuine ignorance about the size of underground reserves).

One other point to note is that the more advanced government statistical agencies include in GDP an allowance for the imputed rent paid by home owner-occupiers. This avoids an apparent change in national output because of any switch between owner-occupation and renting.

Surveys and Sampling

Many of the figures which go into GDP are collected by surveys. For example, governments ask selected manufacturing or retailing companies for details of their output or sales each month. This information is used to make inferences about all manufacturers or all retailers. Such estimates may not be correct, especially as the most dynamic parts of the economy are small firms constantly coming into and going out of existence, which may never be surveyed.

Sample evidence is supplemented by other information, including documentation required initially for bureaucratic purposes such as customs clearance or tax assessment. Such data take a long time to collect and analyse, which is why economic figures are frequently revised even when they are several years old.

Unrecorded Transactions

GDP may under-record economic activity, not least because of the difficulties of keeping track of new small businesses and because of tax avoidance or evasion.

Deliberately concealed transactions form the black, grey, hidden or shadow economy. This is largest at times when, and in countries where, taxes are high and bureaucracy is smothering. Estimates of the size of the shadow economy vary enormously. For example, differing studies put America's at 4–33%, Germany's at 3–28% and Britain's at 2–15%. What is agreed, though, is that among the industrial countries the shadow economy is largest in Greece, at perhaps 30% of GDP, followed by Italy, Portugal and Spain, while the smallest black economies are in Japan, Switzerland and America at around 10% of GDP.

The only industrial countries that adjust their GDP figures for the shadow economy are Italy and America, and they may well underestimate its size.

OUTPUT, EXPENDITURE, AND INCOME   3

Output

The output measure of GDP is obtained by combining value added (value of production less cost of inputs) by all businesses: agriculture, mining, manufacturing and services. Output data are usually presented in index form (that is, with a base year such as 2000 = 100).

Sectors In general countries have larger agricultural sectors in the early stages of economic development. The manufacturing sector's share of output increases as the economy develops and services take the largest share of output in mature economies.

Highly detailed data are often available. The production of tens or hundreds of goods and services industries may be recorded separately. For example, there will probably be an appropriate index in the GDP output breakdown to allow you to compare the performance of, say, a furniture manufacturing company with that of the industry as a whole. The industrialised countries generally publish more detailed (and more up-to-date) statistics than less developed countries.

Classifications Economic information has to be categorised, but the correct classification is not always self-evident. For example, should the production of man-made fibres from petroleum be recorded under textiles (as they generally used to be) or chemicals (as they are now)?

Standards have been introduced to deal with these problems and provide consistency. Industrial production, retail trade, imports and exports are classified according to standard themes. Many countries now follow the United Nations' international standard industrial classification (ISIC), while European countries tend to use the similar EU *Nomenclature générale des activités dans les Communautés Européennes* (NACE). These are fairly detailed and they need revision from time to time.

FIGURE 1   GDP per Sector (% of Total GDP, 2003)

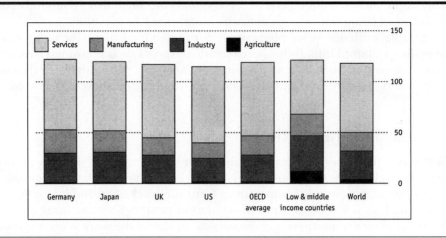

Source: World Bank.

For example, if the standard industrial classification (SIC), which was introduced in the U.K. in 1948, had not been revised several times, computer manufacturing would be classified under office equipment, which is part of non-electrical engineering.

When making sectoral comparisons between two or more countries, try to find out if the sectors are made up of the same industries, otherwise there may be inconsistencies in the comparison.

Expenditure

The expenditure measure of GDP is obtained by adding up all spending:

Consumption (spending on items such as food and clothing)
+ Investment (spending on houses, factories, and so on)
= Total domestic expenditure
+ Exports of goods and services (foreigners' spending)
= Total final expenditure
− Imports of goods and services (spending abroad)
= GDP

Government Consumption The level of government spending reflects the role of the state. Government consumption is generally 10–20% of GDP, although it is higher in countries such as Denmark and Sweden where the state provides many services. Changes in government spending tend to reflect political decisions rather than market forces.

Private Consumption This is also called personal consumption or consumer expenditure. It is generally the largest individual category of spending (but see exports, page 726). In the industrialized countries consumption is around 60% of GDP. The ratio is higher in poor countries which invest less and consume more.

FIGURE 2   Domestic Spending (% of GDP, 2003)

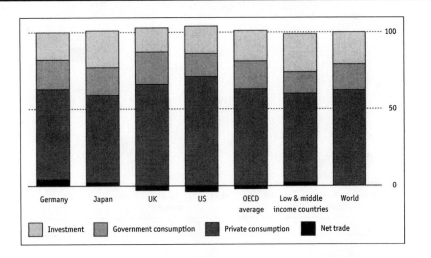

Note: Negative net trade as % of GDP indicates that the country is a net importer.
Source: World Bank.

Investment Investment is perhaps the key structural component of spending since it lays down the basis for future production. It covers spending on factories, machinery, equipment, dwellings and inventories of raw materials and other items. Investment averages about 20% of GDP in the industrialized countries (see Figure 2), but is over 30% of GDP in East Asian countries.

Consumption or Investment? There are some anomalies in the identification of consumption and investment. Government spending on roads, defence and education is generally scored as consumption rather than investment. Consumer spending on cars and other durable goods (items with a life of over one year) is considered to be consumption. Capital goods purchased by a financial institution and leased to an industrial company are also usually classified as consumption. Thus consumption tends to be overstated and investment under-recorded.

Total Domestic Expenditure (TDE) Consumption plus investment is known as total domestic expenditure. This is a useful concept because it measures domestic spending, some of which goes on imported goods and services. It under-records sales because it does not include those goods and services sold abroad (exports).

Total Final Expenditure/Output (TFE/TFO) Consumption and investment plus exports of goods and services is known as total final expenditure. This takes account of the fact that some consumer and investment goods and services are purchased by foreigners.

Another way of looking at this is as total final output: the value of home-produced and imported goods and services available for consumption, investment or export.

TFE and TFO are identical in coverage. The difference is in the terminology, which depends on whether the emphasis is on output or spending. Since some expenditure goes on goods and services originating overseas, TFE/TFO has to be reduced by the amount of imports of goods and services to give total output.

FIGURE 3   Trade in Goods and Services (% of GDP, 2003)

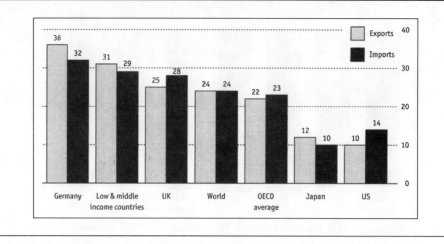

Source: OECD; World Bank.

Exports and Imports Exports generate foreign currency income, while imports are a leakage of domestic spending into another country's production. These external transactions can have an important effect on GDP.

Some countries have a low dependence on external trade. American imports are about 15% of GDP and exports over 10%. Other countries, especially those on the Pacific rim, are heavily dependent on external flows. Hong Kong and Singapore, both trading economies, have imports and exports each of which are 100–200% of GDP (many imports are reexported). These are open economies, while America and Japan are relatively closed (see Figure 3). Open economies have greater opportunity for export-led growth but are also more vulnerable to external shocks.

Income

The income measure of GDP is based on total incomes from production. It is essentially the total of:

► wages and salaries of employees;

► income from self-employment;

► trading profits of companies;

► trading surpluses of government corporations and enterprises; and

► income from rents.

These are known as factor incomes. GDP does not include transfer payments such as interest and dividends, pensions, or other social security benefits. The breakdown of incomes sheds additional light on economic behaviour because it is the counterpart to expenditure in what economists call the circular flow of money. It also provides a useful basis for forecasting inflation.

Accounting Conventions Incomes data are collected from figures which are based on common accounting conventions, rather than the principles of national accounting. One result is that reported company profits include any increase or decrease in the value of inventories. A value (as opposed to a volume) change does not represent any real economic activity, so this stock appreciation is deducted from total domestic income to arrive at GDP. Britain's Office for National Statistics now uses a definition of profits that excludes the change in the value of stocks, so no stock-appreciation adjustment is shown in national accounts.

Discrepancies

In a perfect world, the output, expenditure and income measures would be identical. In practice there are discrepancies owing to inevitable shortcomings in data collection, differences in the reported timing of transactions and the shadow economy. The discrepancy between any pair of measures is typically up to 1–2% of GDP. It can be much larger than this, as it was in many countries in the mid-1970s when data collection was complicated by sharp oil price increases and rapid inflation.

Since output, expenditure and income data are, by and large, collected independently, the safest approach is to take the average of the three as indicative of overall economic trends. Not many governments, however, publish such averages and it may not be practical to calculate them. Consequently it is usually necessary to focus on one.

The output measure is usually the most reliable indicator of short-term developments (that is, up to one year) as the survey data are fairly concrete. For longer periods the expenditure measure is probably better, mainly because the weights used to aggregate the output indicators are updated at infrequent intervals and they become out of date. The income measure is usually the last available and least reliable.

PRICES 4

Market Prices, Factor Cost, and Basic Prices

Many transactions are subject to taxes and subsidies. Sales tax or value-added tax (VAT) and subsidised housing are obvious examples. The expenditure measure of GDP records market prices, which includes these taxes and subsidies. The income and output measures are generally reported at factor cost (that is, they exclude taxes and subsidies). The relationship is simple:

> GDP at market prices
> − Indirect taxes ⎫
> + Subsidies ⎬ factor cost adjustment
> = GDP at factor cost ⎭

The Factor Cost Adjustment The factor cost adjustment (the net total of taxes and subsidies) enables the income, expenditure and output measures to be converted freely between factor cost and market prices. This allows consistent comparisons and highlights the effect of government intervention.

Basic Prices Britain's official statisticians now call the basic output measure of GDP "gross value added (GVA) at basic prices." This includes subsidies and excludes taxes (such as VAT) on products only. GVA or GDP at factor cost also excludes taxes on production, such as business property taxes. The statisticians consider GVA at basic prices to be a better measure of short-term movements in the economy than the old factor-cost measure.

National Conventions Americans tend to measure economic activity at market prices right through to the net national product stage. They then adjust for taxes and subsidies to reach national income at factor cost. Thus a reference to American GDP probably means GDP at market prices. In Britain, the "headline" measure of GDP is at market prices. However, GVA at basic prices is also reported. The only way to be sure is to check the basis of the figures in question.

Current and Constant Prices

GDP figures are reported in current and constant prices.

▶ Output data are generally collected in both current and constant prices. The constant price figures for each industry are obtained by valuing current output in the prices applicable in a given base year; say, 1990 or 2000.

▶ Expenditure data are mostly collected in current prices. They are converted into constant prices by the same adjustment process used with output data, or—slightly differently—by deflating each component by an estimated price indicator. Once the current and constant price versions of the expenditure measure are available, they are used to calculate an overall deflator (that is, the price index) which is used with the income measure.

▶ Income data are collected in current prices and converted into constant prices using deflators derived from the expenditure measure.

The Deflator The GDP deflator calculated from expenditure data at factor cost is also known as the implicit price deflator. This is a handy measure of economy-wide inflation trends, but it is affected by changes in the composition of GDP.

Adjusting for inflation is less reliable at times when prices are changing rapidly. Small errors in the measurements of current values and prices can combine to create large errors in the constant price series. Make it a rule to question the accuracy of price deflators. For example, 12% nominal GDP growth with inflation of 10% results in approximately 2% real growth in GDP. If inflation is actually slightly higher, at 11%, real GDP growth is halved to a mere 1%.

5   PUTTING IT IN CONTEXT

Population

The notes on omissions (Section 2) suggest that output figures are a dubious guide to the quality of life. Nevertheless, total output per head (that is, GDP divided by the size of the population) is used as a broad indicator of living standards. A rise in real GDP that is greater than any increase in population is taken to indicate an improvement in economic well-being. However, if, for example, real GDP increases by 3% while the population expands by 5%, the economy is "worse off" (that is, real GDP per head has declined).

Purchasing Power

Output per head in current prices is a useful guide to levels of economic activity when making snapshot comparisons between countries. Since it is necessary, however, to convert the figures into a common currency, the underlying message can be distorted by exchange-rate effects.

The best solution is to use output per head on a purchasing power parity (PPP) basis, which adjusts for national variations in the prices paid for goods and services. This is not easy to calculate accurately, but some intergovernmental agencies such as the World Bank and OECD produce estimates. Their figures show, for example, that although Britain's GDP per head is higher than that of Canada if converted into dollars at current exchange rates, after adjusting for variations in prices the spending power of the British is well below that of Canadians.

Employment

Another way of measuring relative activity is with output per person employed. This is an important measure of productivity.

RELIABILITY   6

Some problems of obtaining information by surveys and samples are outlined above. In addition, the rush to publish information often means that figures are revised several times as new information comes to hand, perhaps causing major changes in interpretation. For example, industrial production figures may be based initially on sales and output data and adjusted later to take account of changes in inventories not caught in the sales figures.

Statisticians go to great lengths to account for these and other problems. The techniques employed are reasonably reliable, at least in the more developed countries. It is important to remember, however, that published figures for GDP, average earnings, prices, and so on are only estimates.

Moreover, the basis on which some figures are calculated by less scrupulous governments does not stand up to close examination. Consumer-price indices are particularly vulnerable. They may include only selected subsidized goods and services and omit those which increase in price too rapidly.

The following information relates to Questions 1–6 and is based on "Economic Growth," "Regulation and Antitrust Policy in a Globalized Economy," "The Exchange Rate and the Balance of Payments," and this reading

Matthias Stefan is an investment analyst for Ng-Chang Capital Management. He is considering whether shares of Bricanian stocks should be included in his country allocation model portfolio. Stefan and a colleague, Aimee Liew, are discussing economic growth issues faced by Bricania, a developing country.

During their conversation, Liew makes the following statements:

Statement 1:   "With respect to productivity curves, a change in the capital stock leads to movements *along* the productivity curve. Changes in technology lead to *shifts* in the productivity curve."

Statement 2:   "In developed countries, growth accounting estimates indicate that capital growth explains the majority of productivity growth over time."

Later in their conversation, Liew and Stefan discuss the role of technology in fostering economic growth. Liew states:

Statement 3:   "Knowledge capital, unlike physical capital, does not experience diminishing returns because of the profit motive to advance technology."

Stefan comments, "Bricania's rate of technological change influences its rate of economic growth but Bricania's economic growth does not influence its pace of technological change."

After their conversation, Stefan reads a sell-side analyst's report on Bricania and the economic issues facing the country. The report notes that Bricania's capital per capita grew by 7.8 percent last year while real GDP per labor-hour grew at 6 percent. Stefan believes the one-third rule applies to Bricania and uses this information to calculate the contribution of technological change to the growth in real GDP per labor-hour.

Stefan notes the following excerpts from the report:

"Bricania has relatively large deposits of low-sulfur content coal. Low-sulfur coal is in demand as it generates less pollution than high-sulfur content coal. Electrical utilities in Bricania are the country's main purchasers of coal. Ten years ago, in the face of escalating energy demand and electricity prices, the Bricanian government instituted price controls on the electric utility industry by imposing rate-of-return regulation. Rates are set in a way so that fixed capital investors (mainly banks and some shareholders) can earn a fair return on their investment. But with a rising world price of low-sulfur coal, utility profits are being reduced as the Bricanian utilities are limited in the amount they can pay for coal. The price limits caused utilities' coal inventories to decline, leading to service restrictions including flow reduction ("brownouts") and interruptions ("blackouts"). Rather than pay the high world price for premium Bricanian low-sulphur coal, some utilities are finding it cost effective to import lower-cost high-sulfur coal from a neighboring country via train. Bricanian coal producers profit by shipping a similar quantity of their low-sulfur coal, via rail and sea, to other countries . . ."

"In our analysis we classify countries as 'developing' or 'developed' based on the proportion of agricultural output to overall GDP. Historically, developing countries have a higher proportion of agricultural output to GDP than do developed nations. Countries are classified as well by consumer spending; poorer countries have lower ratios of consumer spending to overall GDP. Note that the calculation of net national income is of little practical value because of problems with trying to account for depreciation. Measures of GDP include gains from domestically-owned business located outside the home country . . ."

"The recent bubble and subsequent sharp decline of price levels in the Bricanian residential real estate market harmed the wealth of many investors, leading to contraction of the important housing sector in Bricania's economy, and caused many to request that the government stabilize the market and economy. The foreign exchange value of Bricania's currency declined as well, as foreign investors withdrew from investments in domestic real estate-based debt securities. During the time when prices were rising, Bricania's central bank pursued a modestly restrictive monetary policy in an effort to avert speculative excess in real estate valuations. Bricania is now best served by shifting to a more expansionary monetary policy, even though such a shift might not be anticipated, because doing so would tend to increase the quantity of goods produced for export in the near-term and stabilize the exchange rate."

"Bricania has been a net borrower internationally in each of the past five years. Exhibit 1, below, gives data for the government budget, savings, and investment in 2008. Both government and private sector balances were negative. Government expenditures for defense equipment, public structures, education, and health care totaled 4.5 billion Bricanian pinnels (₽ 4,500 million) in 2008. The Official Settlements Account balance in 2008 was zero."

EXHIBIT 1	Net Exports, Government Budget, Savings, and Investment Bricanian Pinnels, in Millions	
Government Sector	Net tax receipts	₽ 12,387
	Expenditures	14,673
	Surplus (deficit)	(2,286)
Private Sector	Savings	₽ 11,398
	Investment	12,265
	Surplus (deficit)	(867)
Net Exports	Exports	₽ 6,203
	Imports	9,356
	Surplus (deficit)	(3,153)

Finally, Stefan consults Exhibit 2, which gives quotes for spot and one-month forward exchange rates for Bricanian pinnels per U.S. dollar.

EXHIBIT 2	Spot and One-Month Forward Exchange Rates Bricanian Pinnels per U.S. Dollar (₽/$)
Spot	1.6121–31
Forward	1.6087–97

1. Are Liew's first two statements correct?
   A. Yes.
   B. No, only Statement 1 is correct.
   C. No, only Statement 2 is correct.

2. Liew's Statement 3 is *most likely* based on which theory of economic growth?
   A. Classical.
   B. Neoclassical.
   C. New Growth theory.

3. Based on the data in the analyst's report and Stefan's belief regarding the one-third rule, the contribution of technological change was *closest* to:
   A. 2.6%.
   B. 3.4%.
   C. 4.0%.

4. The effects of the current electric utility regulation in Bricania *most likely* include:
   A. an improving trade balance.
   B. a lesser need for social regulation.
   C. decreased employment for transportation workers.

5. Are the sell-side analyst's statements concerning the use of agricultural output and consumer spending to classify countries *most likely* correct?
   A. Yes.
   B. Yes, for agricultural output only.
   C. Yes, for consumer spending only.

6. Based on the information provided by the sell-side analyst for Bricania's trade, private sector, and government expenditures, including Exhibit 1, which of the following statements is *most likely* correct?
   A. Bricania's international borrowing is financing private and public investment, not consumption.
   B. If Bricania continues to accumulate a deficit in its current account, consumption will eventually have to be reduced.
   C. Stefan must also obtain Bricania's Capital Account Balance for 2008 before evaluating its balance of payments.

SOLUTIONS FOR READING 20

1. B is correct. The first statement is a correct description of movements/shifts in the productivity curve but the second statement is incorrect as estimates are that most developed country productivity growth arises from technological change.

2. C is correct. Liew's statement is in agreement with new growth theory, which holds that growth can continue indefinitely because the profit motive leads to new discoveries.

3. B is correct. The contribution of capital growth to real GDP growth is $7.8\% \times 1/3 = 2.6\%$, meaning the contribution of technological change is $6\% - 2.6\% = 3.4\%$.

4. A is correct. High-priced coal is exported and low-priced coal is imported in approximately offsetting amounts; this will help to reduce a trade deficit (or increase a surplus).

5. B is correct. The reading states "in general countries have larger agricultural sectors in the early stages of economic development" and the ratio of private consumption to GDP is "much higher in poor countries that invest less and consume more." So the analyst's agricultural statement is correct and the analyst's second statement on consumer spending is incorrect.

6. A is correct. Government plus private investment (₱ 4,500 million and ₱ 12,265 million, respectively) total more than net international borrowing of ₱ 3,153 million. Net international borrowing is equal to the current account deficit (imports less exports) because the official settlements account balance is zero.

APPENDICES

www.cfainstitute.org/toolkit—Your online preparation resource

Appendix A — Cumulative Probabilities for a Standard Normal Distribution
$P(Z \leq x) = N(x)$ for $x \geq 0$ or $P(Z \leq z) = N(z)$ for $z \geq 0$

x or z	0	0.01	0.02	0.03	0.04	0.05	0.06	0.07	0.08	0.09
0.00	0.5000	0.5040	0.5080	0.5120	0.5160	0.5199	0.5239	0.5279	0.5319	0.5359
0.10	0.5398	0.5438	0.5478	0.5517	0.5557	0.5596	0.5636	0.5675	0.5714	0.5753
0.20	0.5793	0.5832	0.5871	0.5910	0.5948	0.5987	0.6026	0.6064	0.6103	0.6141
0.30	0.6179	0.6217	0.6255	0.6293	0.6331	0.6368	0.6406	0.6443	0.6480	0.6517
0.40	0.6554	0.6591	0.6628	0.6664	0.6700	0.6736	0.6772	0.6808	0.6844	0.6879
0.50	0.6915	0.6950	0.6985	0.7019	0.7054	0.7088	0.7123	0.7157	0.7190	0.7224
0.60	0.7257	0.7291	0.7324	0.7357	0.7389	0.7422	0.7454	0.7486	0.7517	0.7549
0.70	0.7580	0.7611	0.7642	0.7673	0.7704	0.7734	0.7764	0.7794	0.7823	0.7852
0.80	0.7881	0.7910	0.7939	0.7967	0.7995	0.8023	0.8051	0.8078	0.8106	0.8133
0.90	0.8159	0.8186	0.8212	0.8238	0.8264	0.8289	0.8315	0.8340	0.8365	0.8389
1.00	0.8413	0.8438	0.8461	0.8485	0.8508	0.8531	0.8554	0.8577	0.8599	0.8621
1.10	0.8643	0.8665	0.8686	0.8708	0.8729	0.8749	0.8770	0.8790	0.8810	0.8830
1.20	0.8849	0.8869	0.8888	0.8907	0.8925	0.8944	0.8962	0.8980	0.8997	0.9015
1.30	0.9032	0.9049	0.9066	0.9082	0.9099	0.9115	0.9131	0.9147	0.9162	0.9177
1.40	0.9192	0.9207	0.9222	0.9236	0.9251	0.9265	0.9279	0.9292	0.9306	0.9319
1.50	0.9332	0.9345	0.9357	0.9370	0.9382	0.9394	0.9406	0.9418	0.9429	0.9441
1.60	0.9452	0.9463	0.9474	0.9484	0.9495	0.9505	0.9515	0.9525	0.9535	0.9545
1.70	0.9554	0.9564	0.9573	0.9582	0.9591	0.9599	0.9608	0.9616	0.9625	0.9633
1.80	0.9641	0.9649	0.9656	0.9664	0.9671	0.9678	0.9686	0.9693	0.9699	0.9706
1.90	0.9713	0.9719	0.9726	0.9732	0.9738	0.9744	0.9750	0.9756	0.9761	0.9767
2.00	0.9772	0.9778	0.9783	0.9788	0.9793	0.9798	0.9803	0.9808	0.9812	0.9817
2.10	0.9821	0.9826	0.9830	0.9834	0.9838	0.9842	0.9846	0.9850	0.9854	0.9857
2.20	0.9861	0.9864	0.9868	0.9871	0.9875	0.9878	0.9881	0.9884	0.9887	0.9890
2.30	0.9893	0.9896	0.9898	0.9901	0.9904	0.9906	0.9909	0.9911	0.9913	0.9916
2.40	0.9918	0.9920	0.9922	0.9925	0.9927	0.9929	0.9931	0.9932	0.9934	0.9936
2.50	0.9938	0.9940	0.9941	0.9943	0.9945	0.9946	0.9948	0.9949	0.9951	0.9952
2.60	0.9953	0.9955	0.9956	0.9957	0.9959	0.9960	0.9961	0.9962	0.9963	0.9964
2.70	0.9965	0.9966	0.9967	0.9968	0.9969	0.9970	0.9971	0.9972	0.9973	0.9974
2.80	0.9974	0.9975	0.9976	0.9977	0.9977	0.9978	0.9979	0.9979	0.9980	0.9981
2.90	0.9981	0.9982	0.9982	0.9983	0.9984	0.9984	0.9985	0.9985	0.9986	0.9986
3.00	0.9987	0.9987	0.9987	0.9988	0.9988	0.9989	0.9989	0.9989	0.9990	0.9990
3.10	0.9990	0.9991	0.9991	0.9991	0.9992	0.9992	0.9992	0.9992	0.9993	0.9993
3.20	0.9993	0.9993	0.9994	0.9994	0.9994	0.9994	0.9994	0.9995	0.9995	0.9995
3.30	0.9995	0.9995	0.9995	0.9996	0.9996	0.9996	0.9996	0.9996	0.9996	0.9997
3.40	0.9997	0.9997	0.9997	0.9997	0.9997	0.9997	0.9997	0.9997	0.9997	0.9998
3.50	0.9998	0.9998	0.9998	0.9998	0.9998	0.9998	0.9998	0.9998	0.9998	0.9998
3.60	0.9998	0.9998	0.9999	0.9999	0.9999	0.9999	0.9999	0.9999	0.9999	0.9999
3.70	0.9999	0.9999	0.9999	0.9999	0.9999	0.9999	0.9999	0.9999	0.9999	0.9999
3.80	0.9999	0.9999	0.9999	0.9999	0.9999	0.9999	0.9999	0.9999	0.9999	0.9999
3.90	1.0000	1.0000	1.0000	1.0000	1.0000	1.0000	1.0000	1.0000	1.0000	1.0000
4.00	1.0000	1.0000	1.0000	1.0000	1.0000	1.0000	1.0000	1.0000	1.0000	1.0000

For example, to find the z-value leaving 2.5 percent of the area/probability in the upper tail, find the element 0.9750 in the body of the table. Read 1.90 at the left end of the element's row and 0.06 at the top of the element's column, to give 1.90 + 0.06 = 1.96. *Table generated with Excel.*

Quantitative Methods for Investment Analysis, Second Edition, by Richard A. DeFusco, CFA, Dennis W. McLeavey, CFA, Jerald E. Pinto, CFA, and David E. Runkle, CFA. Copyright © 2004 by CFA Institute. Reprinted with permission.

Appendix A (continued)	Cumulative Probabilities for a Standard Normal Distribution $P(Z \le x) = N(x)$ for $x \le 0$ or $P(Z \le z) = N(z)$ for $z \le 0$								
x or z	0	0.01	0.02	0.03	0.04	0.05	0.06	0.07	0.08	0.09
0.00	0.5000	0.4960	0.4920	0.4880	0.4840	0.4801	0.4761	0.4721	0.4681	0.4641
−0.10	0.4602	0.4562	0.4522	0.4483	0.4443	0.4404	0.4364	0.4325	0.4286	0.4247
−0.20	0.4207	0.4168	0.4129	0.4090	0.4052	0.4013	0.3974	0.3936	0.3897	0.3859
−0.30	0.3821	0.3783	0.3745	0.3707	0.3669	0.3632	0.3594	0.3557	0.3520	0.3483
−0.40	0.3446	0.3409	0.3372	0.3336	0.3300	0.3264	0.3228	0.3192	0.3156	0.3121
−0.50	0.3085	0.3050	0.3015	0.2981	0.2946	0.2912	0.2877	0.2843	0.2810	0.2776
−0.60	0.2743	0.2709	0.2676	0.2643	0.2611	0.2578	0.2546	0.2514	0.2483	0.2451
−0.70	0.2420	0.2389	0.2358	0.2327	0.2296	0.2266	0.2236	0.2206	0.2177	0.2148
−0.80	0.2119	0.2090	0.2061	0.2033	0.2005	0.1977	0.1949	0.1922	0.1894	0.1867
−0.90	0.1841	0.1814	0.1788	0.1762	0.1736	0.1711	0.1685	0.1660	0.1635	0.1611
−1.00	0.1587	0.1562	0.1539	0.1515	0.1492	0.1469	0.1446	0.1423	0.1401	0.1379
−1.10	0.1357	0.1335	0.1314	0.1292	0.1271	0.1251	0.1230	0.1210	0.1190	0.1170
−1.20	0.1151	0.1131	0.1112	0.1093	0.1075	0.1056	0.1038	0.1020	0.1003	0.0985
−1.30	0.0968	0.0951	0.0934	0.0918	0.0901	0.0885	0.0869	0.0853	0.0838	0.0823
−1.40	0.0808	0.0793	0.0778	0.0764	0.0749	0.0735	0.0721	0.0708	0.0694	0.0681
−1.50	0.0668	0.0655	0.0643	0.0630	0.0618	0.0606	0.0594	0.0582	0.0571	0.0559
−1.60	0.0548	0.0537	0.0526	0.0516	0.0505	0.0495	0.0485	0.0475	0.0465	0.0455
−1.70	0.0446	0.0436	0.0427	0.0418	0.0409	0.0401	0.0392	0.0384	0.0375	0.0367
−1.80	0.0359	0.0351	0.0344	0.0336	0.0329	0.0322	0.0314	0.0307	0.0301	0.0294
−1.90	0.0287	0.0281	0.0274	0.0268	0.0262	0.0256	0.0250	0.0244	0.0239	0.0233
−2.00	0.0228	0.0222	0.0217	0.0212	0.0207	0.0202	0.0197	0.0192	0.0188	0.0183
−2.10	0.0179	0.0174	0.0170	0.0166	0.0162	0.0158	0.0154	0.0150	0.0146	0.0143
−2.20	0.0139	0.0136	0.0132	0.0129	0.0125	0.0122	0.0119	0.0116	0.0113	0.0110
−2.30	0.0107	0.0104	0.0102	0.0099	0.0096	0.0094	0.0091	0.0089	0.0087	0.0084
−2.40	0.0082	0.0080	0.0078	0.0075	0.0073	0.0071	0.0069	0.0068	0.0066	0.0064
−2.50	0.0062	0.0060	0.0059	0.0057	0.0055	0.0054	0.0052	0.0051	0.0049	0.0048
−2.60	0.0047	0.0045	0.0044	0.0043	0.0041	0.0040	0.0039	0.0038	0.0037	0.0036
−2.70	0.0035	0.0034	0.0033	0.0032	0.0031	0.0030	0.0029	0.0028	0.0027	0.0026
−2.80	0.0026	0.0025	0.0024	0.0023	0.0023	0.0022	0.0021	0.0021	0.0020	0.0019
−2.90	0.0019	0.0018	0.0018	0.0017	0.0016	0.0016	0.0015	0.0015	0.0014	0.0014
−3.00	0.0013	0.0013	0.0013	0.0012	0.0012	0.0011	0.0011	0.0011	0.0010	0.0010
−3.10	0.0010	0.0009	0.0009	0.0009	0.0008	0.0008	0.0008	0.0008	0.0007	0.0007
−3.20	0.0007	0.0007	0.0006	0.0006	0.0006	0.0006	0.0006	0.0005	0.0005	0.0005
−3.30	0.0005	0.0005	0.0005	0.0004	0.0004	0.0004	0.0004	0.0004	0.0004	0.0003
−3.40	0.0003	0.0003	0.0003	0.0003	0.0003	0.0003	0.0003	0.0003	0.0003	0.0002
−3.50	0.0002	0.0002	0.0002	0.0002	0.0002	0.0002	0.0002	0.0002	0.0002	0.0002
−3.60	0.0002	0.0002	0.0001	0.0001	0.0001	0.0001	0.0001	0.0001	0.0001	0.0001
−3.70	0.0001	0.0001	0.0001	0.0001	0.0001	0.0001	0.0001	0.0001	0.0001	0.0001
−3.80	0.0001	0.0001	0.0001	0.0001	0.0001	0.0001	0.0001	0.0001	0.0001	0.0001
−3.90	0.0000	0.0000	0.0000	0.0000	0.0000	0.0000	0.0000	0.0000	0.0000	0.0000
−4.00	0.0000	0.0000	0.0000	0.0000	0.0000	0.0000	0.0000	0.0000	0.0000	0.0000

For example, to find the z-value leaving 2.5 percent of the area/probability in the lower tail, find the element 0.0250 in the body of the table. Read −1.90 at the left end of the element's row and 0.06 at the top of the element's column, to give −1.90 − 0.06 = −1.96. *Table generated with Excel.*

Appendix B　Table of the Student's t-Distribution (One-Tailed Probabilities)

df	p = 0.10	p = 0.05	p = 0.025	p = 0.01	p = 0.005
1	3.078	6.314	12.706	31.821	63.657
2	1.886	2.920	4.303	6.965	9.925
3	1.638	2.353	3.182	4.541	5.841
4	1.533	2.132	2.776	3.747	4.604
5	1.476	2.015	2.571	3.365	4.032
6	1.440	1.943	2.447	3.143	3.707
7	1.415	1.895	2.365	2.998	3.499
8	1.397	1.860	2.306	2.896	3.355
9	1.383	1.833	2.262	2.821	3.250
10	1.372	1.812	2.228	2.764	3.169
11	1.363	1.796	2.201	2.718	3.106
12	1.356	1.782	2.179	2.681	3.055
13	1.350	1.771	2.160	2.650	3.012
14	1.345	1.761	2.145	2.624	2.977
15	1.341	1.753	2.131	2.602	2.947
16	1.337	1.746	2.120	2.583	2.921
17	1.333	1.740	2.110	2.567	2.898
18	1.330	1.734	2.101	2.552	2.878
19	1.328	1.729	2.093	2.539	2.861
20	1.325	1.725	2.086	2.528	2.845
21	1.323	1.721	2.080	2.518	2.831
22	1.321	1.717	2.074	2.508	2.819
23	1.319	1.714	2.069	2.500	2.807
24	1.318	1.711	2.064	2.492	2.797
25	1.316	1.708	2.060	2.485	2.787
26	1.315	1.706	2.056	2.479	2.779
27	1.314	1.703	2.052	2.473	2.771
28	1.313	1.701	2.048	2.467	2.763
29	1.311	1.699	2.045	2.462	2.756
30	1.310	1.697	2.042	2.457	2.750

df	p = 0.10	p = 0.05	p = 0.025	p = 0.01	p = 0.005
31	1.309	1.696	2.040	2.453	2.744
32	1.309	1.694	2.037	2.449	2.738
33	1.308	1.692	2.035	2.445	2.733
34	1.307	1.691	2.032	2.441	2.728
35	1.306	1.690	2.030	2.438	2.724
36	1.306	1.688	2.028	2.434	2.719
37	1.305	1.687	2.026	2.431	2.715
38	1.304	1.686	2.024	2.429	2.712
39	1.304	1.685	2.023	2.426	2.708
40	1.303	1.684	2.021	2.423	2.704
41	1.303	1.683	2.020	2.421	2.701
42	1.302	1.682	2.018	2.418	2.698
43	1.302	1.681	2.017	2.416	2.695
44	1.301	1.680	2.015	2.414	2.692
45	1.301	1.679	2.014	2.412	2.690
46	1.300	1.679	2.013	2.410	2.687
47	1.300	1.678	2.012	2.408	2.685
48	1.299	1.677	2.011	2.407	2.682
49	1.299	1.677	2.010	2.405	2.680
50	1.299	1.676	2.009	2.403	2.678
60	1.296	1.671	2.000	2.390	2.660
70	1.294	1.667	1.994	2.381	2.648
80	1.292	1.664	1.990	2.374	2.639
90	1.291	1.662	1.987	2.368	2.632
100	1.290	1.660	1.984	2.364	2.626
110	1.289	1.659	1.982	2.361	2.621
120	1.289	1.658	1.980	2.358	2.617
200	1.286	1.653	1.972	2.345	2.601
∞	1.282	1.645	1.960	2.326	2.576

To find a critical t-value, enter the table with df and a specified value for α, the significance level. For example, with 5 df, $\alpha = 0.05$ and a one-tailed test, the desired probability in the tail would be $p = 0.05$ and the critical t-value would be $t(5, 0.05) = 2.015$. With $\alpha = 0.05$ and a two-tailed test, the desired probability in each tail would be $p = 0.025 = \alpha/2$, giving $t(0.025) = 2.571$. *Table generated using Excel.*

Quantitative Methods for Investment Analysis, Second Edition, by Richard A. DeFusco, CFA, Dennis W. McLeavey, CFA, Jerald E. Pinto, CFA, and David E. Runkle, CFA. Copyright © 2004 by CFA Institute. Reprinted with permission.

Appendix C   Values of χ^2 (Degrees of Freedom, Level of Significance)

Degrees of Freedom	Probability in Right Tail								
	0.99	0.975	0.95	0.9	0.1	0.05	0.025	0.01	0.005
1	0.000157	0.000982	0.003932	0.0158	2.706	3.841	5.024	6.635	7.879
2	0.020100	0.050636	0.102586	0.2107	4.605	5.991	7.378	9.210	10.597
3	0.1148	0.2158	0.3518	0.5844	6.251	7.815	9.348	11.345	12.838
4	0.297	0.484	0.711	1.064	7.779	9.488	11.143	13.277	14.860
5	0.554	0.831	1.145	1.610	9.236	11.070	12.832	15.086	16.750
6	0.872	1.237	1.635	2.204	10.645	12.592	14.449	16.812	18.548
7	1.239	1.690	2.167	2.833	12.017	14.067	16.013	18.475	20.278
8	1.647	2.180	2.733	3.490	13.362	15.507	17.535	20.090	21.955
9	2.088	2.700	3.325	4.168	14.684	16.919	19.023	21.666	23.589
10	2.558	3.247	3.940	4.865	15.987	18.307	20.483	23.209	25.188
11	3.053	3.816	4.575	5.578	17.275	19.675	21.920	24.725	26.757
12	3.571	4.404	5.226	6.304	18.549	21.026	23.337	26.217	28.300
13	4.107	5.009	5.892	7.041	19.812	22.362	24.736	27.688	29.819
14	4.660	5.629	6.571	7.790	21.064	23.685	26.119	29.141	31.319
15	5.229	6.262	7.261	8.547	22.307	24.996	27.488	30.578	32.801
16	5.812	6.908	7.962	9.312	23.542	26.296	28.845	32.000	34.267
17	6.408	7.564	8.672	10.085	24.769	27.587	30.191	33.409	35.718
18	7.015	8.231	9.390	10.865	25.989	28.869	31.526	34.805	37.156
19	7.633	8.907	10.117	11.651	27.204	30.144	32.852	36.191	38.582
20	8.260	9.591	10.851	12.443	28.412	31.410	34.170	37.566	39.997
21	8.897	10.283	11.591	13.240	29.615	32.671	35.479	38.932	41.401
22	9.542	10.982	12.338	14.041	30.813	33.924	36.781	40.289	42.796
23	10.196	11.689	13.091	14.848	32.007	35.172	38.076	41.638	44.181
24	10.856	12.401	13.848	15.659	33.196	36.415	39.364	42.980	45.558
25	11.524	13.120	14.611	16.473	34.382	37.652	40.646	44.314	46.928
26	12.198	13.844	15.379	17.292	35.563	38.885	41.923	45.642	48.290
27	12.878	14.573	16.151	18.114	36.741	40.113	43.195	46.963	49.645
28	13.565	15.308	16.928	18.939	37.916	41.337	44.461	48.278	50.994
29	14.256	16.047	17.708	19.768	39.087	42.557	45.722	49.588	52.335
30	14.953	16.791	18.493	20.599	40.256	43.773	46.979	50.892	53.672
50	29.707	32.357	34.764	37.689	63.167	67.505	71.420	76.154	79.490
60	37.485	40.482	43.188	46.459	74.397	79.082	83.298	88.379	91.952
80	53.540	57.153	60.391	64.278	96.578	101.879	106.629	112.329	116.321
100	70.065	74.222	77.929	82.358	118.498	124.342	129.561	135.807	140.170

To have a probability of 0.05 in the right tail when df = 5, the tabled value is $\chi^2(5, 0.05) = 11.070$.

Quantitative Methods for Investment Analysis, Second Edition, by Richard A. DeFusco, CFA, Dennis W. McLeavey, CFA, Jerald E. Pinto, CFA, and David E. Runkle, CFA. Copyright © 2004 by CFA Institute. Reprinted with permission.

Appendix D   Table of the F-Distribution

Panel A. Critical values for right-hand tail area equal to 0.05

Numerator: df_1 and Denominator: df_2

df2: \ df1:	1	2	3	4	5	6	7	8	9	10	11	12	15	20	21	22	23	24	25	30	40	60	120	∞
1	161	200	216	225	230	234	237	239	241	242	243	244	246	248	248	249	249	249	249	250	251	252	253	254
2	18.5	19.0	19.2	19.2	19.3	19.3	19.4	19.4	19.4	19.4	19.4	19.4	19.4	19.4	19.4	19.5	19.5	19.5	19.5	19.5	19.5	19.5	19.5	19.5
3	10.1	9.55	9.28	9.12	9.01	8.94	8.89	8.85	8.81	8.79	8.76	8.74	8.70	8.66	8.65	8.65	8.64	8.64	8.63	8.62	8.59	8.57	8.55	8.53
4	7.71	6.94	6.59	6.39	6.26	6.16	6.09	6.04	6.00	5.96	5.94	5.91	5.86	5.80	5.79	5.79	5.78	5.77	5.77	5.75	5.72	5.69	5.66	5.63
5	6.61	5.79	5.41	5.19	5.05	4.95	4.88	4.82	4.77	4.74	4.70	4.68	4.62	4.56	4.55	4.54	4.53	4.53	4.52	4.50	4.46	4.43	4.40	4.37
6	5.99	5.14	4.76	4.53	4.39	4.28	4.21	4.15	4.10	4.06	4.03	4.00	3.94	3.87	3.86	3.86	3.85	3.84	3.83	3.81	3.77	3.74	3.70	3.67
7	5.59	4.74	4.35	4.12	3.97	3.87	3.79	3.73	3.68	3.64	3.60	3.57	3.51	3.44	3.43	3.43	3.42	3.41	3.40	3.38	3.34	3.30	3.27	3.23
8	5.32	4.46	4.07	3.84	3.69	3.58	3.50	3.44	3.39	3.35	3.31	3.28	3.22	3.15	3.14	3.13	3.12	3.12	3.11	3.08	3.04	3.01	2.97	2.93
9	5.12	4.26	3.86	3.63	3.48	3.37	3.29	3.23	3.18	3.14	3.10	3.07	3.01	2.94	2.93	2.92	2.91	2.90	2.89	2.86	2.83	2.79	2.75	2.71
10	4.96	4.10	3.71	3.48	3.33	3.22	3.14	3.07	3.02	2.98	2.94	2.91	2.85	2.77	2.76	2.75	2.75	2.74	2.73	2.70	2.66	2.62	2.58	2.54
11	4.84	3.98	3.59	3.36	3.20	3.09	3.01	2.95	2.90	2.85	2.82	2.79	2.72	2.65	2.64	2.63	2.62	2.61	2.60	2.57	2.53	2.49	2.45	2.40
12	4.75	3.89	3.49	3.26	3.11	3.00	2.91	2.85	2.80	2.75	2.72	2.69	2.62	2.54	2.53	2.52	2.51	2.51	2.50	2.47	2.43	2.38	2.34	2.30
13	4.67	3.81	3.41	3.18	3.03	2.92	2.83	2.77	2.71	2.67	2.63	2.60	2.53	2.46	2.45	2.44	2.43	2.42	2.41	2.38	2.34	2.30	2.25	2.21
14	4.60	3.74	3.34	3.11	2.96	2.85	2.76	2.70	2.65	2.60	2.57	2.53	2.46	2.39	2.38	2.37	2.36	2.35	2.34	2.31	2.27	2.22	2.18	2.13
15	4.54	3.68	3.29	3.06	2.90	2.79	2.71	2.64	2.59	2.54	2.51	2.48	2.40	2.33	2.32	2.31	2.30	2.29	2.28	2.25	2.20	2.16	2.11	2.07
16	4.49	3.63	3.24	3.01	2.85	2.74	2.66	2.59	2.54	2.49	2.46	2.42	2.35	2.28	2.26	2.25	2.24	2.24	2.23	2.19	2.15	2.11	2.06	2.01
17	4.45	3.59	3.20	2.96	2.81	2.70	2.61	2.55	2.49	2.45	2.41	2.38	2.31	2.23	2.22	2.21	2.20	2.19	2.18	2.15	2.10	2.06	2.01	1.96
18	4.41	3.55	3.16	2.93	2.77	2.66	2.58	2.51	2.46	2.41	2.37	2.34	2.27	2.19	2.18	2.17	2.16	2.15	2.14	2.11	2.06	2.02	1.97	1.92
19	4.38	3.52	3.13	2.90	2.74	2.63	2.54	2.48	2.42	2.38	2.34	2.31	2.23	2.16	2.14	2.13	2.12	2.11	2.11	2.07	2.03	1.98	1.93	1.88
20	4.35	3.49	3.10	2.87	2.71	2.60	2.51	2.45	2.39	2.35	2.31	2.28	2.20	2.12	2.11	2.10	2.09	2.08	2.07	2.04	1.99	1.95	1.90	1.84
21	4.32	3.47	3.07	2.84	2.68	2.57	2.49	2.42	2.37	2.32	2.28	2.25	2.18	2.10	2.08	2.07	2.06	2.05	2.05	2.01	1.96	1.92	1.87	1.81
22	4.30	3.44	3.05	2.82	2.66	2.55	2.46	2.40	2.34	2.30	2.26	2.23	2.15	2.07	2.06	2.05	2.04	2.03	2.02	1.98	1.94	1.89	1.84	1.78
23	4.28	3.42	3.03	2.80	2.64	2.53	2.44	2.37	2.32	2.27	2.24	2.20	2.13	2.05	2.04	2.02	2.01	2.01	2.00	1.96	1.91	1.86	1.81	1.76
24	4.26	3.40	3.01	2.78	2.62	2.51	2.42	2.36	2.30	2.25	2.22	2.18	2.11	2.03	2.01	2.00	1.99	1.98	1.97	1.94	1.89	1.84	1.79	1.73
25	4.24	3.39	2.99	2.76	2.60	2.49	2.40	2.34	2.28	2.24	2.20	2.16	2.09	2.01	2.00	1.98	1.97	1.96	1.96	1.92	1.87	1.82	1.77	1.71
30	4.17	3.32	2.92	2.69	2.53	2.42	2.33	2.27	2.21	2.16	2.13	2.09	2.01	1.93	1.92	1.91	1.90	1.89	1.88	1.84	1.79	1.74	1.68	1.62
40	4.08	3.23	2.84	2.61	2.45	2.34	2.25	2.18	2.12	2.08	2.04	2.00	1.92	1.84	1.83	1.81	1.80	1.79	1.78	1.74	1.69	1.64	1.58	1.51
60	4.00	3.15	2.76	2.53	2.37	2.25	2.17	2.10	2.04	1.99	1.95	1.92	1.84	1.75	1.73	1.72	1.71	1.70	1.69	1.65	1.59	1.53	1.47	1.39
120	3.92	3.07	2.68	2.45	2.29	2.18	2.09	2.02	1.96	1.91	1.87	1.83	1.75	1.66	1.64	1.63	1.62	1.61	1.60	1.55	1.50	1.43	1.35	1.25
Infinity	3.84	3.00	2.60	2.37	2.21	2.10	2.01	1.94	1.88	1.83	1.79	1.75	1.67	1.57	1.56	1.54	1.53	1.52	1.51	1.46	1.39	1.32	1.22	1.00

With 1 degree of freedom (df) in the numerator and 3 df in the denominator, the critical F-value is 10.1 for a right-hand tail area equal to 0.05.

Quantitative Methods for Investment Analysis, Second Edition, by Richard A. DeFusco, CFA, Dennis W. McLeavey, CFA, Jerald E. Pinto, CFA, and David E. Runkle, CFA. Copyright © 2004 by CFA Institute. Reprinted with permission.

Appendix D Table of the F-Distribution

Panel B. Critical values for right-hand tail area equal to 0.025

Numerator: df_1 and Denominator: df_2

df2 \ df1	1	2	3	4	5	6	7	8	9	10	11	12	15	20	21	22	23	24	25	30	40	60	120	∞
1	648	799	864	900	922	937	948	957	963	969	973	977	985	993	994	995	996	997	998	1001	1006	1010	1014	1018
2	38.51	39.00	39.17	39.25	39.30	39.33	39.36	39.37	39.39	39.40	39.41	39.41	39.43	39.45	39.45	39.45	39.45	39.46	39.46	39.46	39.47	39.48	39.49	39.50
3	17.44	16.04	15.44	15.10	14.88	14.73	14.62	14.54	14.47	14.42	14.37	14.34	14.25	14.17	14.16	14.14	14.13	14.12	14.12	14.08	14.04	13.99	13.95	13.90
4	12.22	10.65	9.98	9.60	9.36	9.20	9.07	8.98	8.90	8.84	8.79	8.75	8.66	8.56	8.55	8.53	8.52	8.51	8.50	8.46	8.41	8.36	8.31	8.26
5	10.01	8.43	7.76	7.39	7.15	6.98	6.85	6.76	6.68	6.62	6.57	6.52	6.43	6.33	6.31	6.30	6.29	6.28	6.27	6.23	6.18	6.12	6.07	6.02
6	8.81	7.26	6.60	6.23	5.99	5.82	5.70	5.60	5.52	5.46	5.41	5.37	5.27	5.17	5.15	5.14	5.13	5.12	5.11	5.07	5.01	4.96	4.90	4.85
7	8.07	6.54	5.89	5.52	5.29	5.12	4.99	4.90	4.82	4.76	4.71	4.67	4.57	4.47	4.45	4.44	4.43	4.41	4.40	4.36	4.31	4.25	4.20	4.14
8	7.57	6.06	5.42	5.05	4.82	4.65	4.53	4.43	4.36	4.30	4.24	4.20	4.10	4.00	3.98	3.97	3.96	3.95	3.94	3.89	3.84	3.78	3.73	3.67
9	7.21	5.71	5.08	4.72	4.48	4.32	4.20	4.10	4.03	3.96	3.91	3.87	3.77	3.67	3.65	3.64	3.63	3.61	3.60	3.56	3.51	3.45	3.39	3.33
10	6.94	5.46	4.83	4.47	4.24	4.07	3.95	3.85	3.78	3.72	3.66	3.62	3.52	3.42	3.40	3.39	3.38	3.37	3.35	3.31	3.26	3.20	3.14	3.08
11	6.72	5.26	4.63	4.28	4.04	3.88	3.76	3.66	3.59	3.53	3.47	3.43	3.33	3.23	3.21	3.20	3.18	3.17	3.16	3.12	3.06	3.00	2.94	2.88
12	6.55	5.10	4.47	4.12	3.89	3.73	3.61	3.51	3.44	3.37	3.32	3.28	3.18	3.07	3.06	3.04	3.03	3.02	3.01	2.96	2.91	2.85	2.79	2.72
13	6.41	4.97	4.35	4.00	3.77	3.60	3.48	3.39	3.31	3.25	3.20	3.15	3.05	2.95	2.93	2.92	2.91	2.89	2.88	2.84	2.78	2.72	2.66	2.60
14	6.30	4.86	4.24	3.89	3.66	3.50	3.38	3.29	3.21	3.15	3.09	3.05	2.95	2.84	2.83	2.81	2.80	2.79	2.78	2.73	2.67	2.61	2.55	2.49
15	6.20	4.77	4.15	3.80	3.58	3.41	3.29	3.20	3.12	3.06	3.01	2.96	2.86	2.76	2.74	2.73	2.71	2.70	2.69	2.64	2.59	2.52	2.46	2.40
16	6.12	4.69	4.08	3.73	3.50	3.34	3.22	3.12	3.05	2.99	2.93	2.89	2.79	2.68	2.67	2.65	2.64	2.63	2.61	2.57	2.51	2.45	2.38	2.32
17	6.04	4.62	4.01	3.66	3.44	3.28	3.16	3.06	2.98	2.92	2.87	2.82	2.72	2.62	2.60	2.59	2.57	2.56	2.55	2.50	2.44	2.38	2.32	2.25
18	5.98	4.56	3.95	3.61	3.38	3.22	3.10	3.01	2.93	2.87	2.81	2.77	2.67	2.56	2.54	2.53	2.52	2.50	2.49	2.44	2.38	2.32	2.26	2.19
19	5.92	4.51	3.90	3.56	3.33	3.17	3.05	2.96	2.88	2.82	2.76	2.72	2.62	2.51	2.49	2.48	2.46	2.45	2.44	2.39	2.33	2.27	2.20	2.13
20	5.87	4.46	3.86	3.51	3.29	3.13	3.01	2.91	2.84	2.77	2.72	2.68	2.57	2.46	2.45	2.43	2.42	2.41	2.40	2.35	2.29	2.22	2.16	2.09
21	5.83	4.42	3.82	3.48	3.25	3.09	2.97	2.87	2.80	2.73	2.68	2.64	2.53	2.42	2.41	2.39	2.38	2.37	2.36	2.31	2.25	2.18	2.11	2.04
22	5.79	4.38	3.78	3.44	3.22	3.05	2.93	2.84	2.76	2.70	2.65	2.60	2.50	2.39	2.37	2.36	2.34	2.33	2.32	2.27	2.21	2.14	2.08	2.00
23	5.75	4.35	3.75	3.41	3.18	3.02	2.90	2.81	2.73	2.67	2.62	2.57	2.47	2.36	2.34	2.33	2.31	2.30	2.29	2.24	2.18	2.11	2.04	1.97
24	5.72	4.32	3.72	3.38	3.15	2.99	2.87	2.78	2.70	2.64	2.59	2.54	2.44	2.33	2.31	2.30	2.28	2.27	2.26	2.21	2.15	2.08	2.01	1.94
25	5.69	4.29	3.69	3.35	3.13	2.97	2.85	2.75	2.68	2.61	2.56	2.51	2.41	2.30	2.28	2.27	2.26	2.24	2.23	2.18	2.12	2.05	1.98	1.91
30	5.57	4.18	3.59	3.25	3.03	2.87	2.75	2.65	2.57	2.51	2.46	2.41	2.31	2.20	2.18	2.16	2.15	2.14	2.12	2.07	2.01	1.94	1.87	1.79
40	5.42	4.05	3.46	3.13	2.90	2.74	2.62	2.53	2.45	2.39	2.33	2.29	2.18	2.07	2.05	2.03	2.02	2.01	1.99	1.94	1.88	1.80	1.72	1.64
60	5.29	3.93	3.34	3.01	2.79	2.63	2.51	2.41	2.33	2.27	2.22	2.17	2.06	1.94	1.93	1.91	1.90	1.88	1.87	1.82	1.74	1.67	1.58	1.48
120	5.15	3.80	3.23	2.89	2.67	2.52	2.39	2.30	2.22	2.16	2.10	2.05	1.94	1.82	1.81	1.79	1.77	1.76	1.75	1.69	1.61	1.53	1.43	1.31
Infinity	5.02	3.69	3.12	2.79	2.57	2.41	2.29	2.19	2.11	2.05	1.99	1.94	1.83	1.71	1.69	1.67	1.66	1.64	1.63	1.57	1.48	1.39	1.27	1.00

Appendix D   Table of the *F*-Distribution

Panel C. Critical values for right-hand tail area equal to 0.01

Numerator: df$_1$ and Denominator: df$_2$

df1:\df2:	1	2	3	4	5	6	7	8	9	10	11	12	15	20	21	22	23	24	25	30	40	60	120	∞
1	4052	5000	5403	5625	5764	5859	5928	5982	6023	6056	6083	6106	6157	6209	6216	6223	6229	6235	6240	6261	6287	6313	6339	6366
2	98.5	99.0	99.2	99.2	99.3	99.3	99.4	99.4	99.4	99.4	99.4	99.4	99.4	99.4	99.5	99.5	99.5	99.5	99.5	99.5	99.5	99.5	99.5	99.5
3	34.1	30.8	29.5	28.7	28.2	27.9	27.7	27.5	27.3	27.2	27.1	27.1	26.9	26.7	26.7	26.6	26.6	26.6	26.6	26.5	26.4	26.3	26.2	26.1
4	21.2	18.0	16.7	16.0	15.5	15.2	15.0	14.8	14.7	14.5	14.5	14.4	14.2	14.0	14.0	14.0	13.9	13.9	13.9	13.8	13.7	13.7	13.6	13.5
5	16.3	13.3	12.1	11.4	11.0	10.7	10.5	10.3	10.2	10.1	10.0	9.89	9.72	9.55	9.53	9.51	9.49	9.47	9.45	9.38	9.29	9.20	9.11	9.02
6	13.7	10.9	9.78	9.15	8.75	8.47	8.26	8.10	7.98	7.87	7.79	7.72	7.56	7.40	7.37	7.35	7.33	7.31	7.30	7.23	7.14	7.06	6.97	6.88
7	12.2	9.55	8.45	7.85	7.46	7.19	6.99	6.84	6.72	6.62	6.54	6.47	6.31	6.16	6.13	6.11	6.09	6.07	6.06	5.99	5.91	5.82	5.74	5.65
8	11.3	8.65	7.59	7.01	6.63	6.37	6.18	6.03	5.91	5.81	5.73	5.67	5.52	5.36	5.34	5.32	5.30	5.28	5.26	5.20	5.12	5.03	4.95	4.86
9	10.6	8.02	6.99	6.42	6.06	5.80	5.61	5.47	5.35	5.26	5.18	5.11	4.96	4.81	4.79	4.77	4.75	4.73	4.71	4.65	4.57	4.48	4.40	4.31
10	10.0	7.56	6.55	5.99	5.64	5.39	5.20	5.06	4.94	4.85	4.77	4.71	4.56	4.41	4.38	4.36	4.34	4.33	4.31	4.25	4.17	4.08	4.00	3.91
11	9.65	7.21	6.22	5.67	5.32	5.07	4.89	4.74	4.63	4.54	4.46	4.40	4.25	4.10	4.08	4.06	4.04	4.02	4.01	3.94	3.86	3.78	3.69	3.60
12	9.33	6.93	5.95	5.41	5.06	4.82	4.64	4.50	4.39	4.30	4.22	4.16	4.01	3.86	3.84	3.82	3.80	3.78	3.76	3.70	3.62	3.54	3.45	3.36
13	9.07	6.70	5.74	5.21	4.86	4.62	4.44	4.30	4.19	4.10	4.02	3.96	3.82	3.66	3.64	3.62	3.60	3.59	3.57	3.51	3.43	3.34	3.25	3.17
14	8.86	6.51	5.56	5.04	4.70	4.46	4.28	4.14	4.03	3.94	3.86	3.80	3.66	3.51	3.48	3.46	3.44	3.43	3.41	3.35	3.27	3.18	3.09	3.00
15	8.68	6.36	5.42	4.89	4.56	4.32	4.14	4.00	3.89	3.80	3.73	3.67	3.52	3.37	3.35	3.33	3.31	3.29	3.28	3.21	3.13	3.05	2.96	2.87
16	8.53	6.23	5.29	4.77	4.44	4.20	4.03	3.89	3.78	3.69	3.62	3.55	3.41	3.26	3.24	3.22	3.20	3.18	3.16	3.10	3.02	2.93	2.84	2.75
17	8.40	6.11	5.19	4.67	4.34	4.10	3.93	3.79	3.68	3.59	3.52	3.46	3.31	3.16	3.14	3.12	3.10	3.08	3.07	3.00	2.92	2.83	2.75	2.65
18	8.29	6.01	5.09	4.58	4.25	4.01	3.84	3.71	3.60	3.51	3.43	3.37	3.23	3.08	3.05	3.03	3.02	3.00	2.98	2.92	2.84	2.75	2.66	2.57
19	8.19	5.93	5.01	4.50	4.17	3.94	3.77	3.63	3.52	3.43	3.36	3.30	3.15	3.00	2.98	2.96	2.94	2.92	2.91	2.84	2.76	2.67	2.58	2.49
20	8.10	5.85	4.94	4.43	4.10	3.87	3.70	3.56	3.46	3.37	3.29	3.23	3.09	2.94	2.92	2.90	2.88	2.86	2.84	2.78	2.69	2.61	2.52	2.42
21	8.02	5.78	4.87	4.37	4.04	3.81	3.64	3.51	3.40	3.31	3.24	3.17	3.03	2.88	2.86	2.84	2.82	2.80	2.79	2.72	2.64	2.55	2.46	2.36
22	7.95	5.72	4.82	4.31	3.99	3.76	3.59	3.45	3.35	3.26	3.18	3.12	2.98	2.83	2.81	2.78	2.77	2.75	2.73	2.67	2.58	2.50	2.40	2.31
23	7.88	5.66	4.76	4.26	3.94	3.71	3.54	3.41	3.30	3.21	3.14	3.07	2.93	2.78	2.76	2.74	2.72	2.70	2.69	2.62	2.54	2.45	2.35	2.26
24	7.82	5.61	4.72	4.22	3.90	3.67	3.50	3.36	3.26	3.17	3.09	3.03	2.89	2.74	2.72	2.70	2.68	2.66	2.64	2.58	2.49	2.40	2.31	2.21
25	7.77	5.57	4.68	4.18	3.86	3.63	3.46	3.32	3.22	3.13	3.06	2.99	2.85	2.70	2.68	2.66	2.64	2.62	2.60	2.53	2.45	2.36	2.27	2.17
30	7.56	5.39	4.51	4.02	3.70	3.47	3.30	3.17	3.07	2.98	2.91	2.84	2.70	2.55	2.53	2.51	2.49	2.47	2.45	2.39	2.30	2.21	2.11	2.01
40	7.31	5.18	4.31	3.83	3.51	3.29	3.12	2.99	2.89	2.80	2.73	2.66	2.52	2.37	2.35	2.33	2.31	2.29	2.27	2.20	2.11	2.02	1.92	1.80
60	7.08	4.98	4.13	3.65	3.34	3.12	2.95	2.82	2.72	2.63	2.56	2.50	2.35	2.20	2.17	2.15	2.13	2.12	2.10	2.03	1.94	1.84	1.73	1.60
120	6.85	4.79	3.95	3.48	3.17	2.96	2.79	2.66	2.56	2.47	2.40	2.34	2.19	2.03	2.01	1.99	1.97	1.95	1.93	1.86	1.76	1.66	1.53	1.38
Infinity	6.63	4.61	3.78	3.32	3.02	2.80	2.64	2.51	2.41	2.32	2.25	2.18	2.04	1.88	1.85	1.83	1.81	1.79	1.77	1.70	1.59	1.47	1.32	1.00

Appendix D Table of the F-Distribution

Panel D. Critical values for right-hand tail area equal to 0.005

Numerator: df_1 and Denominator: df_2

df2: \ df1:	1	2	3	4	5	6	7	8	9	10	11	12	15	20	21	22	23	24	25	30	40	60	120	∞
1	16211	20000	21615	22500	23056	23437	23715	23925	24091	24222	24334	24426	24630	24836	24863	24892	24915	24940	24959	25044	25146	25253	25359	25464
2	198.5	199.0	199.2	199.2	199.3	199.3	199.4	199.4	199.4	199.4	199.4	199.4	199.4	199.4	199.4	199.4	199.4	199.4	199.4	199.5	199.5	199.5	199.5	199.5
3	55.55	49.80	47.47	46.20	45.39	44.84	44.43	44.13	43.88	43.68	43.52	43.39	43.08	42.78	42.73	42.69	42.66	42.62	42.59	42.47	42.31	42.15	41.99	41.83
4	31.33	26.28	24.26	23.15	22.46	21.98	21.62	21.35	21.14	20.97	20.82	20.70	20.44	20.17	20.13	20.09	20.06	20.03	20.00	19.89	19.75	19.61	19.47	19.32
5	22.78	18.31	16.53	15.56	14.94	14.51	14.20	13.96	13.77	13.62	13.49	13.38	13.15	12.90	12.87	12.84	12.81	12.78	12.76	12.66	12.53	12.40	12.27	12.14
6	18.63	14.54	12.92	12.03	11.46	11.07	10.79	10.57	10.39	10.25	10.13	10.03	9.81	9.59	9.56	9.53	9.50	9.47	9.45	9.36	9.24	9.12	9.00	8.88
7	16.24	12.40	10.88	10.05	9.52	9.16	8.89	8.68	8.51	8.38	8.27	8.18	7.97	7.75	7.72	7.69	7.67	7.64	7.62	7.53	7.42	7.31	7.19	7.08
8	14.69	11.04	9.60	8.81	8.30	7.95	7.69	7.50	7.34	7.21	7.10	7.01	6.81	6.61	6.58	6.55	6.53	6.50	6.48	6.40	6.29	6.18	6.06	5.95
9	13.61	10.11	8.72	7.96	7.47	7.13	6.88	6.69	6.54	6.42	6.31	6.23	6.03	5.83	5.80	5.78	5.75	5.73	5.71	5.62	5.52	5.41	5.30	5.19
10	12.83	9.43	8.08	7.34	6.87	6.54	6.30	6.12	5.97	5.85	5.75	5.66	5.47	5.27	5.25	5.22	5.20	5.17	5.15	5.07	4.97	4.86	4.75	4.64
11	12.23	8.91	7.60	6.88	6.42	6.10	5.86	5.68	5.54	5.42	5.32	5.24	5.05	4.86	4.83	4.80	4.78	4.76	4.74	4.65	4.55	4.45	4.34	4.23
12	11.75	8.51	7.23	6.52	6.07	5.76	5.52	5.35	5.20	5.09	4.99	4.91	4.72	4.53	4.50	4.48	4.45	4.43	4.41	4.33	4.23	4.12	4.01	3.90
13	11.37	8.19	6.93	6.23	5.79	5.48	5.25	5.08	4.94	4.82	4.72	4.64	4.46	4.27	4.24	4.22	4.19	4.17	4.15	4.07	3.97	3.87	3.76	3.65
14	11.06	7.92	6.68	6.00	5.56	5.26	5.03	4.86	4.72	4.60	4.51	4.43	4.25	4.06	4.03	4.01	3.98	3.96	3.94	3.86	3.76	3.66	3.55	3.44
15	10.80	7.70	6.48	5.80	5.37	5.07	4.85	4.67	4.54	4.42	4.33	4.25	4.07	3.88	3.86	3.83	3.81	3.79	3.77	3.69	3.59	3.48	3.37	3.26
16	10.58	7.51	6.30	5.64	5.21	4.91	4.69	4.52	4.38	4.27	4.18	4.10	3.92	3.73	3.71	3.68	3.66	3.64	3.62	3.54	3.44	3.33	3.22	3.11
17	10.38	7.35	6.16	5.50	5.07	4.78	4.56	4.39	4.25	4.14	4.05	3.97	3.79	3.61	3.58	3.56	3.53	3.51	3.49	3.41	3.31	3.21	3.10	2.98
18	10.22	7.21	6.03	5.37	4.96	4.66	4.44	4.28	4.14	4.03	3.94	3.86	3.68	3.50	3.47	3.45	3.42	3.40	3.38	3.30	3.20	3.10	2.99	2.87
19	10.07	7.09	5.92	5.27	4.85	4.56	4.34	4.18	4.04	3.93	3.84	3.76	3.59	3.40	3.37	3.35	3.33	3.31	3.29	3.21	3.11	3.00	2.89	2.78
20	9.94	6.99	5.82	5.17	4.76	4.47	4.26	4.09	3.96	3.85	3.76	3.68	3.50	3.32	3.29	3.27	3.24	3.22	3.20	3.12	3.02	2.92	2.81	2.69
21	9.83	6.89	5.73	5.09	4.68	4.39	4.18	4.01	3.88	3.77	3.68	3.60	3.43	3.24	3.22	3.19	3.17	3.15	3.13	3.05	2.95	2.84	2.73	2.61
22	9.73	6.81	5.65	5.02	4.61	4.32	4.11	3.94	3.81	3.70	3.61	3.54	3.36	3.18	3.15	3.12	3.10	3.08	3.06	2.98	2.88	2.77	2.66	2.55
23	9.63	6.73	5.58	4.95	4.54	4.26	4.05	3.88	3.75	3.64	3.55	3.47	3.30	3.12	3.09	3.06	3.04	3.02	3.00	2.92	2.82	2.71	2.60	2.48
24	9.55	6.66	5.52	4.89	4.49	4.20	3.99	3.83	3.69	3.59	3.50	3.42	3.25	3.06	3.04	3.01	2.99	2.97	2.95	2.87	2.77	2.66	2.55	2.43
25	9.48	6.60	5.46	4.84	4.43	4.15	3.94	3.78	3.64	3.54	3.45	3.37	3.20	3.01	2.99	2.96	2.94	2.92	2.90	2.82	2.72	2.61	2.50	2.38
30	9.18	6.35	5.24	4.62	4.23	3.95	3.74	3.58	3.45	3.34	3.25	3.18	3.01	2.82	2.80	2.77	2.75	2.73	2.71	2.63	2.52	2.42	2.30	2.18
40	8.83	6.07	4.98	4.37	3.99	3.71	3.51	3.35	3.22	3.12	3.03	2.95	2.78	2.60	2.57	2.55	2.52	2.50	2.48	2.40	2.30	2.18	2.06	1.93
60	8.49	5.79	4.73	4.14	3.76	3.49	3.29	3.13	3.01	2.90	2.82	2.74	2.57	2.39	2.36	2.33	2.31	2.29	2.27	2.19	2.08	1.96	1.83	1.69
120	8.18	5.54	4.50	3.92	3.55	3.28	3.09	2.93	2.81	2.71	2.62	2.54	2.37	2.19	2.16	2.13	2.11	2.09	2.07	1.98	1.87	1.75	1.61	1.43
Infinity	7.88	5.30	4.28	3.72	3.35	3.09	2.90	2.74	2.62	2.52	2.43	2.36	2.19	2.00	1.97	1.95	1.92	1.90	1.88	1.79	1.67	1.53	1.36	1.00

Appendix E   Critical Values for the Durbin-Watson Statistic ($\alpha = .05$)

n	K = 1 d_l	K = 1 d_u	K = 2 d_l	K = 2 d_u	K = 3 d_l	K = 3 d_u	K = 4 d_l	K = 4 d_u	K = 5 d_l	K = 5 d_u
15	1.08	1.36	0.95	1.54	0.82	1.75	0.69	1.97	0.56	2.21
16	1.10	1.37	0.98	1.54	0.86	1.73	0.74	1.93	0.62	2.15
17	1.13	1.38	1.02	1.54	0.90	1.71	0.78	1.90	0.67	2.10
18	1.16	1.39	1.05	1.53	0.93	1.69	0.82	1.87	0.71	2.06
19	1.18	1.40	1.08	1.53	0.97	1.68	0.86	1.85	0.75	2.02
20	1.20	1.41	1.10	1.54	1.00	1.68	0.90	1.83	0.79	1.99
21	1.22	1.42	1.13	1.54	1.03	1.67	0.93	1.81	0.83	1.96
22	1.24	1.43	1.15	1.54	1.05	1.66	0.96	1.80	0.86	1.94
23	1.26	1.44	1.17	1.54	1.08	1.66	0.99	1.79	0.90	1.92
24	1.27	1.45	1.19	1.55	1.10	1.66	1.01	1.78	0.93	1.90
25	1.29	1.45	1.21	1.55	1.12	1.66	1.04	1.77	0.95	1.89
26	1.30	1.46	1.22	1.55	1.14	1.65	1.06	1.76	0.98	1.88
27	1.32	1.47	1.24	1.56	1.16	1.65	1.08	1.76	1.01	1.86
28	1.33	1.48	1.26	1.56	1.18	1.65	1.10	1.75	1.03	1.85
29	1.34	1.48	1.27	1.56	1.20	1.65	1.12	1.74	1.05	1.84
30	1.35	1.49	1.28	1.57	1.21	1.65	1.14	1.74	1.07	1.83
31	1.36	1.50	1.30	1.57	1.23	1.65	1.16	1.74	1.09	1.83
32	1.37	1.50	1.31	1.57	1.24	1.65	1.18	1.73	1.11	1.82
33	1.38	1.51	1.32	1.58	1.26	1.65	1.19	1.73	1.13	1.81
34	1.39	1.51	1.33	1.58	1.27	1.65	1.21	1.73	1.15	1.81
35	1.40	1.52	1.34	1.58	1.28	1.65	1.22	1.73	1.16	1.80
36	1.41	1.52	1.35	1.59	1.29	1.65	1.24	1.73	1.18	1.80
37	1.42	1.53	1.36	1.59	1.31	1.66	1.25	1.72	1.19	1.80
38	1.43	1.54	1.37	1.59	1.32	1.66	1.26	1.72	1.21	1.79
39	1.43	1.54	1.38	1.60	1.33	1.66	1.27	1.72	1.22	1.79
40	1.44	1.54	1.39	1.60	1.34	1.66	1.29	1.72	1.23	1.79
45	1.48	1.57	1.43	1.62	1.38	1.67	1.34	1.72	1.29	1.78
50	1.50	1.59	1.46	1.63	1.42	1.67	1.38	1.72	1.34	1.77
55	1.53	1.60	1.49	1.64	1.45	1.68	1.41	1.72	1.38	1.77
60	1.55	1.62	1.51	1.65	1.48	1.69	1.44	1.73	1.41	1.77
65	1.57	1.63	1.54	1.66	1.50	1.70	1.47	1.73	1.44	1.77
70	1.58	1.64	1.55	1.67	1.52	1.70	1.49	1.74	1.46	1.77
75	1.60	1.65	1.57	1.68	1.54	1.71	1.51	1.74	1.49	1.77
80	1.61	1.66	1.59	1.69	1.56	1.72	1.53	1.74	1.51	1.77
85	1.62	1.67	1.60	1.70	1.57	1.72	1.55	1.75	1.52	1.77
90	1.63	1.68	1.61	1.70	1.59	1.73	1.57	1.75	1.54	1.78
95	1.64	1.69	1.62	1.71	1.60	1.73	1.58	1.75	1.56	1.78
100	1.65	1.69	1.63	1.72	1.61	1.74	1.59	1.76	1.57	1.78

Note: K = the number of slope parameters in the model.

Source: From J. Durbin and G.S. Watson, "Testing for Serial Correlation in Least Squares Regression, II." *Biometrika* 38 (1951): 159-178. Reproduced by permission of Oxford University Press.

GLOSSARY

A priori probability A probability based on logical analysis rather than on observation or personal judgment.

Abandonment option The ability to terminate a project at some future time if the financial results are disappointing.

Abnormal earnings See *Residual income.*

Absolute dispersion The amount of variability present without comparison to any reference point or benchmark.

Absolute frequency The number of observations in a given interval (for grouped data).

Absolute valuation model A model that specifies an asset's intrinsic value.

Accelerated methods of depreciation Depreciation methods that allocate a relatively large proportion of the cost of an asset to the early years of the asset's useful life.

Account With the accounting systems, a formal record of increases and decreases in a specific asset, liability, component of owners' equity, revenue, or expense.

Account format A method of presentation of accounting transactions in which effects on assets appear at the left and effects on liabilities and equity appear at the right of a central dividing line; also known as T-account format.

Accounting estimates Estimates of items such as the useful lives of assets, warranty costs, and the amount of uncollectible receivables.

Accounting profit (income before taxes or pretax income) Income as reported on the income statement, in accordance with prevailing accounting standards, before the provisions for income tax expense.

Accounting risk The risk associated with accounting standards that vary from country to country or with any uncertainty about how certain transactions should be recorded.

Accounts payable Amounts that a business owes to its vendors for goods and services that were purchased from them but which have not yet been paid.

Accounts receivable turnover Ratio of sales on credit to the average balance in accounts receivable.

Accrual basis Method of accounting in which the effect of transactions on financial condition and income are recorded when they occur, not when they are settled in cash.

Accrued expenses (accrued liabilities) Liabilities related to expenses that have been incurred but not yet paid as of the end of an accounting period—an example of an accrued expense is rent that has been incurred but not yet paid, resulting in a liability "rent payable."

Accrued interest Interest earned but not yet paid.

Accumulated benefit obligation Under U.S. GAAP, a measure used in estimating a defined-benefit pension plan's liabilities, defined as "the actuarial present value of benefits (whether vested or non-vested) attributed by the pension benefit formula to employee service rendered before a specified date and based on employee service and compensation (if applicable) prior to that date."

Accumulated depreciation An offset to property, plant, and equipment (PPE) reflecting the amount of the cost of PPE that has been allocated to current and previous accounting periods.

Acquiring company, or acquirer The company in a merger or acquisition that is acquiring the target.

Acquisition The purchase of some portion of one company by another; the purchase may be for assets, a definable segment of another entity, or the purchase of an entire company.

Acquisition method A method of accounting for a business combination where the acquirer is required to measure each identifiable asset and liability at fair value. This method was the result of a joint project of the IASB and FASB aiming at convergence in standards for the accounting of business combinations.

Active factor risk The contribution to active risk squared resulting from the portfolio's different-than-benchmark exposures relative to factors specified in the risk model.

Active investment managers Managers who hold portfolios that differ from their benchmark portfolio in an attempt to produce positive risk-adjusted returns.

Active portfolio In the context of the Treynor-Black model, the portfolio formed by mixing analyzed stocks of perceived nonzero alpha values. This portfolio is ultimately mixed with the passive market index portfolio.

Active return The return on a portfolio minus the return on the portfolio's benchmark.

Active risk The standard deviation of active returns.

Active risk squared The variance of active returns; active risk raised to the second power.

Active specific risk or asset selection risk The contribution to active risk squared resulting from the portfolio's active weights on individual assets as those weights interact with assets' residual risk.

Active strategy In reference to short-term cash management, an investment strategy characterized by monitoring and attempting to capitalize on market conditions to optimize the risk and return relationship of short-term investments.

Activity ratios (asset utilization or operating efficiency ratios) Ratios that measure how efficiently a company performs day-to-day tasks, such as the collection of receivables and management of inventory.

Addition rule for probabilities A principle stating that the probability that A or B occurs (both occur) equals the probability that A occurs, plus the probability that B occurs, minus the probability that both A and B occur.

Add-on interest A procedure for determining the interest on a bond or loan in which the interest is added onto the face value of a contract.

Adjusted beta Historical beta adjusted to reflect the tendency of beta to be mean reverting.

Adjusted present value (APV) As an approach to valuing a company, the sum of the value of the company, assuming no use of debt, and the net present value of any effects of debt on company value.

Adjusted R^2 A measure of goodness-of-fit of a regression that is adjusted for degrees of freedom and hence does not automatically increase when another independent variable is added to a regression.

After-tax cash flow (ATCF) Net operating income less debt service and less taxes payable on income from operations.

After-tax equity reversion (ATER) Sales price less disposition costs, amortized mortgage loan balance, and capital gains taxes.

Agency costs Costs associated with the conflict of interest present when a company is managed by non-owners. Agency costs result from the inherent conflicts of interest between managers and equity owners.

Agency costs of equity The smaller the stake that managers have in the company, the less is their share in bearing the cost of excessive perquisite consumption or not giving their best efforts in running the company.

Agency problem, or **principal-agent problem** A conflict of interest that arises when the agent in an agency relationship has goals and incentives that differ from the principal to whom the agent owes a fiduciary duty.

Agency relationships An arrangement whereby someone, an agent, acts on behalf of another person, the principal.

Aging schedule A breakdown of accounts into categories of days outstanding.

Allowance for bad debts An offset to accounts receivable for the amount of accounts receivable that are estimated to be uncollectible.

Alpha (or **abnormal return**) The return on an asset in excess of the asset's required rate of return; the risk-adjusted return.

Alternative hypothesis The hypothesis accepted when the null hypothesis is rejected.

American Depositary Receipt A negotiable certificate issued by a depositary bank that represents ownership in a non-U.S. company's deposited equity (i.e., equity held in custody by the depositary bank in the company's home market).

American option An option contract that can be exercised at any time until its expiration date.

Amortization The process of allocating the cost of intangible long-term assets having a finite useful life to accounting periods; the allocation of the amount of a bond premium or discount to the periods remaining until bond maturity.

Amortizing and accreting swaps A swap in which the notional principal changes according to a formula related to changes in the underlying.

Analysis of variance (ANOVA) The analysis of the total variability of a dataset (such as observations on the dependent variable in a regression) into components representing different sources of variation; with reference to regression, ANOVA provides the inputs for an F-test of the significance of the regression as a whole.

Annual percentage rate The cost of borrowing expressed as a yearly rate.

Annuity A finite set of level sequential cash flows.

Annuity due An annuity having a first cash flow that is paid immediately.

Anticipation stock Excess inventory that is held in anticipation of increased demand, often because of seasonal patterns of demand.

Antidilutive With reference to a transaction or a security, one that would increase earnings per share (EPS) or result in EPS higher than the company's basic EPS—antidilutive securities are not included in the calculation of diluted EPS.

Arbitrage 1) The simultaneous purchase of an undervalued asset or portfolio and sale of an overvalued but equivalent asset or portfolio, in order to obtain a riskless profit on the price differential. Taking advantage of a market inefficiency in a risk-free manner. 2) A trading strategy designed to generate a guaranteed profit from a transaction that requires no capital commitment or risk bearing on the part of the trader. A simple example of an arbitrage trade would be the simultaneous purchase and sale of the same security in different markets at different prices. 3) The condition in a financial market in which equivalent assets or combinations of assets sell for two different prices, creating an opportunity to profit at no risk with no commitment of money. In a well-functioning financial market, few arbitrage opportunities are possible. 4) A risk-free operation that earns an expected positive net profit but requires no net investment of money.

Arbitrage opportunity An opportunity to conduct an arbitrage; an opportunity to earn an expected positive net profit without risk and with no net investment of money.

Arbitrage portfolio The portfolio that exploits an arbitrage opportunity.

Arithmetic mean The sum of the observations divided by the number of observations.

Arrears swap A type of interest rate swap in which the floating payment is set at the end of the period and the interest is paid at that same time.

Asian call option A European-style option with a value at maturity equal to the difference between the stock price at maturity and the average stock price during the life of the option, or $0, whichever is greater.

Asset beta The unlevered beta; reflects the business risk of the assets; the asset's systematic risk.

Asset purchase An acquisition in which the acquirer purchases the target company's assets and payment is made directly to the target company.

Asset retirement obligations (AROs) The fair value of the estimated costs to be incurred at the end of a tangible asset's service life. The fair value of the liability is determined on the basis of discounted cash flows.

Assets Resources controlled by an enterprise as a result of past events and from which future economic benefits to the enterprise are expected to flow.

Asset-based approach Approach that values a private company based on the values of the underlying assets of the entity less the value of any related liabilities.

Asset-based loan A loan that is secured with company assets.

Asset-based valuation An approach to valuing natural resource companies that estimates company value on the basis of the market value of the natural resources the company controls.

Assignment of accounts receivable The use of accounts receivable as collateral for a loan.

Asymmetric information The differential of information between corporate insiders and outsiders regarding the company's performance and prospects. Managers typically have more information about the company's performance and prospects than owners and creditors.

At the money An option in which the underlying value equals the exercise price.

Autocorrelation The correlation of a time series with its own past values.

Automated Clearing House An electronic payment network available to businesses, individuals, and financial institutions in the United States, U.S. Territories, and Canada.

Autoregressive (AR) model A time series regressed on its own past values, in which the independent variable is a lagged value of the dependent variable.

Available-for-sale investments Debt and equity securities not classified as either held-to-maturity or held-for-trading securities. The investor is willing to sell but not actively planning to sell. In general, available-for-sale securities are reported at fair value on the balance sheet.

Backtesting With reference to portfolio strategies, the application of a strategy's portfolio selection rules to historical data to assess what would have been the strategy's historical performance.

Backward integration A merger involving the purchase of a target ahead of the acquirer in the value or production chain; for example, to acquire a supplier.

Backwardation A condition in the futures markets in which the benefits of holding an asset exceed the costs, leaving the futures price less than the spot price.

Balance of payments accounts A country's record of international trading, borrowing, and lending.

Balance sheet (statement of financial position or statement of financial condition) The financial statement that presents an entity's current financial position by disclosing resources the entity controls (its assets) and the claims on those resources (its liabilities and equity claims), as of a particular point in time (the date of the balance sheet).

Balance sheet ratios Financial ratios involving balance sheet items only.

Balance-sheet-based accruals ratio The difference between net operating assets at the end and the beginning of the period compared to the average net operating assets over the period.

Balance-sheet-based aggregate accruals The difference between net operating assets at the end and the beginning of the period.

Band-of-investment method A widely used approach to estimate an overall capitalization rate. It is based on the premise that debt and equity financing is typically involved in a real estate transaction.

Bank discount basis A quoting convention that annualizes, on a 360-day year, the discount as a percentage of face value.

Bargain purchase When a company is acquired and the purchase price is less than the fair value of the net assets. The current treatment of the excess of fair value over the purchase price is different under IFRS and U.S. GAAP. The excess is never accounted for as negative goodwill.

Basic earnings per share (EPS) Net earnings available to common shareholders (i.e., net income minus preferred dividends) divided by the weighted average number of common shares outstanding during the period.

Basis point value (BPV) Also called *present value of a basis point* or *price value of a basis point* (PVBP), the change in the bond price for a 1 basis point change in yield.

Basis swap 1) An interest rate swap involving two floating rates. 2) A swap in which both parties pay a floating rate.

Bayes' formula A method for updating probabilities based on new information.

Bear hug A tactic used by acquirers to circumvent target management's objections to a proposed merger by submitting the proposal directly to the target company's board of directors.

Bear spread An option strategy that involves selling a put with a lower exercise price and buying a put with a higher exercise price. It can also be executed with calls.

Before-tax cash flow A measure of the expected annual cash flow from the operation of a real estate investment after all expenses but before taxes.

Benchmark A comparison portfolio; a point of reference or comparison.

Benchmark value of the multiple In using the method of comparables, the value of a price multiple for the comparison asset; when we have comparison assets (a group), the mean or median value of the multiple for the group of assets.

Bernoulli random variable A random variable having the outcomes 0 and 1.

Bernoulli trial An experiment that can produce one of two outcomes.

Beta A standardized measure of systematic risk based upon an asset's covariance with the market portfolio.

Bill-and-hold basis Sales on a bill-and-hold basis involve selling products but not delivering those products until a later date.

Binomial model A model for pricing options in which the underlying price can move to only one of two possible new prices.

Binomial random variable The number of successes in n Bernoulli trials for which the probability of success is constant for all trials and the trials are independent.

Binomial tree The graphical representation of a model of asset price dynamics in which, at each period, the asset moves up with probability p or down with probability $(1 - p)$.

Block Orders to buy or sell that are too large for the liquidity ordinarily available in dealer networks or stock exchanges.

Blockage factor An illiquidity discount that occurs when an investor sells a large amount of stock relative to its trading volume (assuming it is not large enough to constitute a controlling ownership).

Bond equivalent yield A calculation of yield that is annualized using the ratio of 365 to the number of days to maturity. Bond equivalent yield allows for the restatement and comparison of securities with different compounding periods.

Bond indenture A legal contract specifying the terms of a bond issue.

Bond option An option in which the underlying is a bond; primarily traded in over-the-counter markets.

Bond yield plus risk premium approach An estimate of the cost of common equity that is produced by summing the before-tax cost of debt and a risk premium that captures the additional yield on a company's stock relative to its bonds. The additional yield is often estimated using historical spreads between bond yields and stock yields.

Bond-equivalent basis A basis for stating an annual yield that annualizes a semiannual yield by doubling it.

Bond-equivalent yield The yield to maturity on a basis that ignores compounding.

Bonding costs Costs borne by management to assure owners that they are working in the owners' best interest (e.g., implicit cost of non-compete agreements).

Book value equity per share The amount of book value (also called carrying value) of common equity per share of common stock, calculated by dividing the book value of shareholders' equity by the number of shares of common stock outstanding.

Book value of equity (or book value) Shareholders' equity (total assets minus total liabilities) minus the value of preferred stock; common shareholders' equity.

Bootstrapping earnings An increase in a company's earnings that results as a consequence of the idiosyncrasies of a merger transaction itself rather than because of resulting economic benefits of the combination.

Bottom-up analysis With reference to investment selection processes, an approach that involves selection from all securities within a specified investment universe, i.e., without prior narrowing of the universe on the basis of macroeconomic or overall market considerations.

Bottom-up forecasting approach A forecasting approach that involves aggregating the individual company forecasts of analysts into industry forecasts, and finally into macroeconomic forecasts.

Bottom-up investing An approach to investing that focuses on the individual characteristics of securities rather than on macroeconomic or overall market forecasts.

Box spread An option strategy that combines a bull spread and a bear spread having two different exercise prices, which produces a risk-free payoff of the difference in the exercise prices.

Break point In the context of the weighted average cost of capital (WACC), a break point is the amount of capital at which the cost of one or more of the sources of capital changes, leading to a change in the WACC.

Breakeven point   The number of units produced and sold at which the company's net income is zero (revenues = total costs).

Breakup value or **private market value**   The value derived using a sum-of-the-parts valuation.

Breusch–Pagan test   A test for conditional heteroskedasticity in the error term of a regression.

Broker   1) An agent who executes orders to buy or sell securities on behalf of a client in exchange for a commission. 2) *See* Futures commission merchants.

Brokerage   The business of acting as agents for buyers or sellers, usually in return for commissions.

Build-up method   A method for determining the required rate of return on equity as the sum of risk premiums, in which one or more of the risk premiums is typically subjective rather than grounded in a formal equilibrium model.

Built-up method   A method of identifying the basic elements of the overall capitalization rate.

Bull spread   An option strategy that involves buying a call with a lower exercise price and selling a call with a higher exercise price. It can also be executed with puts.

Bundling   Offering two or more products for sale as a set.

Business risk   The risk associated with operating earnings. Operating earnings are uncertain because total revenues and many of the expenditures contributed to produce those revenues are uncertain.

Butterfly spread   An option strategy that combines two bull or bear spreads and has three exercise prices.

Buy-side analysts   Analysts who work for investment management firms, trusts, and bank trust departments, and similar institutions.

Call   An option that gives the holder the right to buy an underlying asset from another party at a fixed price over a specific period of time.

Cannibalization   Cannibalization occurs when an investment takes customers and sales away from another part of the company.

Cap   1) A contract on an interest rate, whereby at periodic payment dates, the writer of the cap pays the difference between the market interest rate and a specified cap rate if, and only if, this difference is positive. This is equivalent to a stream of call options on the interest rate. 2) A combination of interest rate call options designed to hedge a borrower against rate increases on a floating-rate loan.

Capital account   A record of foreign investment in a country minus its investment abroad.

Capital allocation line (CAL)   A graph line that describes the combinations of expected return and standard deviation of return available to an investor from combining the optimal portfolio of risky assets with the risk-free asset.

Capital asset pricing model (CAPM)   An equation describing the expected return on any asset (or portfolio) as a linear function of its beta relative to the market portfolio.

Capital budgeting   The allocation of funds to relatively long-range projects or investments.

Capital charge   The company's total cost of capital in money terms.

Capital market line (CML)   The line with an intercept point equal to the risk-free rate that is tangent to the efficient frontier of risky assets; represents the efficient frontier when a risk-free asset is available for investment.

Capital rationing   A capital rationing environment assumes that the company has a fixed amount of funds to invest.

Capital structure   The mix of debt and equity that a company uses to finance its business; a company's specific mixture of long-term financing.

Capitalization rate   The divisor in the expression for the value of a perpetuity.

Capitalized cash flow model (method)   In the context of private company valuation, valuation model based on an assumption of a constant growth rate of free cash flow to the firm or a constant growth rate of free cash flow to equity.

Capitalized inventory costs   Costs of inventories including costs of purchase, costs of conversion, other costs to bring the inventories to their present location and condition, and the allocated portion of fixed production overhead costs.

Caplet   Each component call option in a cap.

Capped swap   A swap in which the floating payments have an upper limit.

Captive finance subsidiary   A wholly-owned subsidiary of a company that is established to provide financing of the sales of the parent company.

Capture hypothesis   A theory of regulatory behavior that predicts that regulators will eventually be captured by special interests of the industry being regulated.

Carried interest   A share of any profits that is paid to the general partner (manager) of an investment partnership, such as a private equity or hedge fund, as a form of compensation designed to be an incentive to the manager to maximize performance of the investment fund.

Carrying amount (book value)   The amount at which an asset or liability is valued according to accounting principles.

Cash   In accounting contexts, cash on hand (e.g., petty cash and cash not yet deposited to the bank) and demand deposits held in banks and similar accounts that can be used in payment of obligations.

Cash basis   Accounting method in which the only relevant transactions for the financial statements are those that involve cash.

Cash conversion cycle (net operating cycle)   A financial metric that measures the length of time required for a company to convert cash invested in its operations to cash received as a result of its operations; equal to days of inventory on hand + days of sales outstanding − number of days of payables.

Cash equivalents   Very liquid short-term investments, usually maturing in 90 days or less.

Cash flow additivity principle   The principle that dollar amounts indexed at the same point in time are additive.

Cash flow at risk (CFAR)   A variation of VAR that reflects the risk of a company's cash flow instead of its market value.

Cash flow from operations (cash flow from operating activities or operating cash flow)   The net amount of cash provided from operating activities.

Cash flow statement (statement of cash flows)   A financial statement that reconciles beginning-of-period and end-of-period balance sheet values of cash; consists of three parts: cash flows from operating activities, cash flows from investing activities, and cash flows from financing activities.

Cash offering   A merger or acquisition that is to be paid for with cash; the cash for the merger might come from the acquiring company's existing assets or from a debt issue.

Cash price or **spot price**   The price for immediate purchase of the underlying asset.

Cash ratio   A liquidity ratio calculated as (cash + short-term marketable investments) divided by current liabilities; measures a company's ability to meet its current obligations with just the cash and cash equivalents on hand.

Cash settlement   A procedure used in certain derivative transactions that specifies that the long and short parties engage in the equivalent cash value of a delivery transaction.

Cash-flow-statement-based accruals ratio The difference between reported net income on an accrual basis and the cash flows from operating and investing activities compared to the average net operating assets over the period.

Cash-flow-statement-based aggregate accruals The difference between reported net income on an accrual basis and the cash flows from operating and investing activities.

Cash-generating unit The smallest identifiable group of assets that generates cash inflows that are largely independent of the cash inflows of other assets or groups of assets.

Catalyst An event or piece of information that causes the marketplace to re-evaluate the prospects of a company.

Central limit theorem A result in statistics that states that the sample mean computed from large samples of size n from a population with finite variance will follow an approximate normal distribution with a mean equal to the population mean and a variance equal to the population variance divided by n.

Centralized risk management or **companywide risk management** When a company has a single risk management group that monitors and controls all of the risk-taking activities of the organization. Centralization permits economies of scale and allows a company to use some of its risks to offset other risks. (See also *enterprise risk management*.)

Chain rule of forecasting A forecasting process in which the next period's value as predicted by the forecasting equation is substituted into the right-hand side of the equation to give a predicted value two periods ahead.

Chart of accounts A list of accounts used in an entity's accounting system.

Cheapest to deliver A bond in which the amount received for delivering the bond is largest compared with the amount paid in the market for the bond.

Cherry-picking When a bankrupt company is allowed to enforce contracts that are favorable to it while walking away from contracts that are unfavorable to it.

Classical growth theory A theory of economic growth based on the view that the growth of real GDP per person is temporary and that when it rises above subsistence level, a population explosion eventually brings it back to subsistence level.

Classified balance sheet A balance sheet organized so as to group together the various assets and liabilities into subcategories (e.g., current and noncurrent).

Clean surplus accounting Accounting that satisfies the condition that all changes in the book value of equity other than transactions with owners are reflected in income. The bottom-line income reflects all changes in shareholders' equity arising from other than owner transactions. In the absence of owner transactions, the change in shareholders' equity should equal net income. No adjustments such as translation adjustments bypass the income statement and go directly to shareholders equity.

Clean surplus relation The relationship between earnings, dividends, and book value in which ending book value is equal to the beginning book value plus earnings less dividends, apart from ownership transactions.

Clearinghouse An entity associated with a futures market that acts as middleman between the contracting parties and guarantees to each party the performance of the other.

Clientele effect The preference some investors have for shares that exhibit certain characteristics.

Closeout netting Netting the market values of *all* derivative contracts between two parties to determine one overall value owed by one party to another in the event of bankruptcy.

Coefficient of variation (CV) The ratio of a set of observations' standard deviation to the observations' mean value.

Cointegrated Describes two time series that have a long-term financial or economic relationship such that they do not diverge from each other without bound in the long run.

Collar An option strategy involving the purchase of a put and sale of a call in which the holder of an asset gains protection below a certain level, the exercise price of the put, and pays for it by giving up gains above a certain level, the exercise price of the call. Collars also can be used to provide protection against rising interest rates on a floating-rate loan by giving up gains from lower interest rates.

Combination A listing in which the order of the listed items does not matter.

Commercial paper Unsecured short-term corporate debt that is characterized by a single payment at maturity.

Committed lines of credit A bank commitment to extend credit up to a pre-specified amount; the commitment is considered a short-term liability and is usually in effect for 364 days (one day short of a full year).

Commodity forward A contract in which the underlying asset is oil, a precious metal, or some other commodity.

Commodity futures Futures contracts in which the underlying is a traditional agricultural, metal, or petroleum product.

Commodity option An option in which the asset underlying the futures is a commodity, such as oil, gold, wheat, or soybeans.

Commodity swap A swap in which the underlying is a commodity such as oil, gold, or an agricultural product.

Common size statements Financial statements in which all elements (accounts) are stated as a percentage of a key figure such as revenue for an income statement or total assets for a balance sheet.

Common-size analysis The restatement of financial statement items using a common denominator or reference item that allows one to identify trends and major differences; an example is an income statement in which all items are expressed as a percent of revenue.

Company fundamental factors Factors related to the company's internal performance, such as factors relating to earnings growth, earnings variability, earnings momentum, and financial leverage.

Company share-related factors Valuation measures and other factors related to share price or the trading characteristics of the shares, such as earnings yield, dividend yield, and book-to-market value.

Comparable company A company that has similar business risk; usually in the same industry and preferably with a single line of business.

Comparables (comps, guideline assets, guideline companies) Assets used as benchmarks when applying the method of comparables to value an asset.

Comparative advantage A person or country has a comparative advantage in an activity if that person or country can perform the activity at a lower opportunity cost than anyone else or any other country.

Compiled financial statements Financial statements that are not accompanied by an auditor's opinion letter.

Complement In probability, with reference to an event S, the event that S does not occur; in economics, a good that is used in conjunction with another good.

Completed contract A method of revenue recognition in which the company does not recognize any revenue until the contract is completed; used particularly in long-term construction contracts.

Component cost of capital The rate of return required by suppliers of capital for an individual source of a company's funding, such as debt or equity.

Compounding The process of accumulating interest on interest.

Comprehensive income All changes in equity other than contributions by, and distributions to, owners; income under clean surplus accounting; includes all changes in equity during a period except those resulting from investments by owners and distributions to owners; comprehensive income equals net income plus other comprehensive income.

Conditional expected value The expected value of a stated event given that another event has occurred.

Conditional heteroskedasticity Heteroskedasticity in the error variance that is correlated with the values of the independent variable(s) in the regression.

Conditional probability The probability of an event given (conditioned on) another event.

Conditional variances The variance of one variable, given the outcome of another.

Confidence interval A range that has a given probability that it will contain the population parameter it is intended to estimate.

Conglomerate discount The discount possibly applied by the market to the stock of a company operating in multiple, unrelated businesses.

Conglomerate merger A merger involving companies that are in unrelated businesses.

Consistent With reference to estimators, describes an estimator for which the probability of estimates close to the value of the population parameter increases as sample size increases.

Consolidation The combining of the results of operations of subsidiaries with the parent company to present financial statements as if they were a single economic unit. The assets, liabilities, revenues and expenses of the subsidiaries are combined with those of the parent company, eliminating intercompany transactions.

Constant dividend payout ratio policy A policy in which a constant percentage of net income is paid out in dividends.

Constant maturity swap or **CMT swap** A swap in which the floating rate is the rate on a security known as a constant maturity treasury or CMT security.

Constant maturity treasury or **CMT** A hypothetical U.S. Treasury note with a constant maturity. A CMT exists for various years in the range of 2 to 10.

Contango A situation in a futures market where the current futures price is greater than the current spot price for the underlying asset.

Contingent claims Derivatives in which the payoffs occur if a specific event occurs; generally referred to as options.

Contingent consideration Potential future payments to the seller that are contingent on the achievement of certain agreed on occurrences.

Continuing residual income Residual income after the forecast horizon.

Continuous random variable A random variable for which the range of possible outcomes is the real line (all real numbers between ($-\infty$ and $+\infty$) or some subset of the real line.

Continuous time Time thought of as advancing in extremely small increments.

Continuously compounded return The natural logarithm of 1 plus the holding period return, or equivalently, the natural logarithm of the ending price over the beginning price.

Contra account An account that offsets another account.

Contribution margin The amount available for fixed costs and profit after paying variable costs; revenue minus variable costs.

Control premium An increment or premium to value associated with a controlling ownership interest in a company.

Controlling interest An investment where the investor exerts control over the investee, typically by having a greater than 50 percent ownership in the investee.

Convenience yield The nonmonetary return offered by an asset when the asset is in short supply, often associated with assets with seasonal production processes.

Conventional cash flow A conventional cash flow pattern is one with an initial outflow followed by a series of inflows.

Conversion factor An adjustment used to facilitate delivery on bond futures contracts in which any of a number of bonds with different characteristics are eligible for delivery.

Convertible debt Debt with the added feature that the bondholder has the option to exchange the debt for equity at prespecified terms.

Corporate governance The system of principles, policies, procedures, and clearly defined responsibilities and accountabilities used by stakeholders to overcome the conflicts of interest inherent in the corporate form.

Corporate raider A person or organization seeking to profit by acquiring a company and reselling it, or seeking to profit from the takeover attempt itself (e.g., greenmail).

Corporation A legal entity with rights similar to those of a person. The chief officers, executives, or top managers act as agents for the firm and are legally entitled to authorize corporate activities and to enter into contracts on behalf of the business.

Correlation A number between -1 and $+1$ that measures the co-movement (linear association) between two random variables.

Correlation analysis The analysis of the strength of the linear relationship between two data series.

Cost approach to value A method of valuing property based on site value plus current construction costs less accrued depreciation.

Cost averaging The periodic investment of a fixed amount of money.

Cost leadership The competitive strategy of being the lowest cost producer while offering products comparable to those of other firms, so that products can be priced at or near the industry average.

Cost of capital The rate of return that suppliers of capital require as compensation for their contribution of capital.

Cost of carry The cost associated with holding some asset, including financing, storage, and insurance costs. Any yield received on the asset is treated as a negative carrying cost.

Cost of carry model A model for pricing futures contracts in which the futures price is determined by adding the cost of carry to the spot price.

Cost of debt The cost of debt financing to a company, such as when it issues a bond or takes out a bank loan.

Cost of equity The required rate of return on common stock.

Cost of goods sold For a given period, equal to beginning inventory minus ending inventory plus the cost of goods acquired or produced during the period.

Cost of preferred stock The cost to a company of issuing preferred stock; the dividend yield that a company must commit to pay preferred stockholders.

Cost recovery method A method of revenue recognition in which the seller does not report any profit until the cash amounts paid by the buyer—including principal and interest on any financing from the seller—are greater than all the seller's costs for the merchandise sold.

Cost structure The mix of a company's variable costs and fixed costs.

Cost-of-service regulation Regulation that allows prices to reflect only the actual average cost of production and no monopoly profits.

Covariance A measure of the co-movement (linear association) between two random variables.

Covariance matrix A matrix or square array whose entries are covariances; also known as a variance–covariance matrix.

Covariance stationary Describes a time series when its expected value and variance are constant and finite in all periods and when its covariance with itself for a fixed number of periods in the past or future is constant and finite in all periods.

Covered call An option strategy involving the holding of an asset and sale of a call on the asset.

Covered interest arbitrage A transaction executed in the foreign exchange market in which a currency is purchased (sold) and a forward contract is sold (purchased) to lock in the exchange rate for future delivery of the currency. This transaction should earn the risk-free rate of the investor's home country.

Crawling peg A policy regime is one that selects a target path for the exchange rate with intervention in the foreign exchange market to achieve that path.

Creative response Behavior on the part of a firm that allows it to comply with the letter of the law but violate the spirit, significantly lessening the law's effects.

Credit With respect to double-entry accounting, a credit records increases in liability, owners' equity, and revenue accounts or decreases in asset accounts; with respect to borrowing, the willingness and ability of the borrower to make promised payments on the borrowing.

Credit analysis The evaluation of credit risk; the evaluation of the creditworthiness of a borrower or counterparty.

Credit derivatives A contract in which one party has the right to claim a payment from another party in the event that a specific credit event occurs over the life of the contract.

Credit risk or **default risk** The risk of loss caused by a counterparty's or debtor's failure to make a promised payment.

Credit scoring model A statistical model used to classify borrowers according to creditworthiness.

Credit spread option An option on the yield spread on a bond.

Credit swap A type of swap transaction used as a credit derivative in which one party makes periodic payments to the other and receives the promise of a payoff if a third party defaults.

Credit VAR, **default VAR**, or **credit at risk** A variation of VAR that reflects credit risk.

Credit-linked notes Fixed-income securities in which the holder of the security has the right to withhold payment of the full amount due at maturity if a credit event occurs.

Creditor nation A country that during its entire history has invested more in the rest of the world than other countries have invested in it.

Creditworthiness The perceived ability of the borrower to pay what is owed on the borrowing in a timely manner; it represents the ability of a company to withstand adverse impacts on its cash flows.

Cross-product netting Netting the market values of all contracts, not just derivatives, between parties.

Cross-sectional analysis Analysis that involves comparisons across individuals in a group over a given time period or at a given point in time.

Cross-sectional data Observations over individual units at a point in time, as opposed to time-series data.

Cumulative distribution function A function giving the probability that a random variable is less than or equal to a specified value.

Cumulative relative frequency For data grouped into intervals, the fraction of total observations that are less than the value of the upper limit of a stated interval.

Currency forward A forward contract in which the underlying is a foreign currency.

Currency option An option that allows the holder to buy (if a call) or sell (if a put) an underlying currency at a fixed exercise rate, expressed as an exchange rate.

Currency swap A swap in which each party makes interest payments to the other in different currencies.

Current account A record of receipts from exports of goods and services, payments for imports of goods and services, net income and net transfers received from the rest of the world.

Current assets, or **liquid assets** Assets that are expected to be consumed or converted into cash in the near future, typically one year or less.

Current cost With reference to assets, the amount of cash or cash equivalents that would have to be paid to buy the same or an equivalent asset today; with reference to liabilities, the undiscounted amount of cash or cash equivalents that would be required to settle the obligation today.

Current credit risk The risk associated with the possibility that a payment currently due will not be made.

Current exchange rate For accounting purposes, the spot exchange rate on the balance sheet date.

Current liabilities Short-term obligations, such as accounts payable, wages payable, or accrued liabilities, that are expected to be settled in the near future, typically one year or less.

Current rate method Approach to translating foreign currency financial statements for consolidation in which all assets and liabilities are translated at the current exchange rate. The current rate method is the prevalent method of translation.

Current ratio A liquidity ratio calculated as current assets divided by current liabilities.

Current taxes payable Tax expenses that have been recognized and recorded on a company's income statement but which have not yet been paid.

Cyclical businesses Businesses with high sensitivity to business- or industry-cycle influences.

Daily settlement See *Marking to market*.

Data mining The practice of determining a model by extensive searching through a dataset for statistically significant patterns.

Day trader A trader holding a position open somewhat longer than a scalper but closing all positions at the end of the day.

Days of inventory on hand (DOH) An activity ratio equal to the number of days in the period divided by inventory turnover over the period.

Days of sales outstanding (DSO) An activity ratio equal to the number of days in period divided by receivables turnover.

Dead-hand provision A poison pill provision that allows for the redemption or cancellation of a poison pill provision only by a vote of continuing directors (generally directors who were on the target company's board prior to the takeover attempt).

Dealing securities Securities held by banks or other financial intermediaries for trading purposes.

Debit With respect to double-entry accounting, a debit records increases of asset and expense accounts or decreases in liability and owners' equity accounts.

Debt covenants Agreements between the company as borrower and its creditors.

Debt incurrence test A financial covenant made in conjunction with existing debt that restricts a company's ability to incur additional debt at the same seniority based on one or more financial tests or conditions.

Debt rating approach A method for estimating a company's before-tax cost of debt based upon the yield on comparably rated bonds for maturities that closely match that of the company's existing debt.

Debt ratings An objective measure of the quality and safety of a company's debt based upon an analysis of the company's ability to pay the promised cash flows, as well as an analysis of any indentures.

Debt with warrants Debt issued with warrants that give the bondholder the right to purchase equity at prespecified terms.

Debtor nation A country that during its entire history has borrowed more in the rest of the world than other countries have lent in it.

Debt-to-assets ratio A solvency ratio calculated as total debt divided by total assets.

Debt-to-capital ratio A solvency ratio calculated as total debt divided by total debt plus total shareholders' equity.

Debt-to-equity ratio A solvency ratio calculated as total debt divided by total shareholders' equity.

Decentralized risk management A system that allows individual units within an organization to manage risk. Decentralization results in duplication of effort but has the advantage of having people closer to the risk be more directly involved in its management.

Deciles Quantiles that divide a distribution into 10 equal parts.

Decision rule With respect to hypothesis testing, the rule according to which the null hypothesis will be rejected or not rejected; involves the comparison of the test statistic to rejection point(s).

Declaration date The day that the corporation issues a statement declaring a specific dividend.

Deductible temporary differences Temporary differences that result in a reduction of or deduction from taxable income in a future period when the balance sheet item is recovered or settled.

Deep in the money Options that are far in-the-money.

Deep out of the money Options that are far out-of-the-money.

Default risk premium An extra return that compensates investors for the possibility that the borrower will fail to make a promised payment at the contracted time and in the contracted amount.

Defensive interval ratio A liquidity ratio that estimates the number of days that an entity could meet cash needs from liquid assets; calculated as (cash + short-term marketable investments + receivables) divided by daily cash expenditures.

Deferred tax assets A balance sheet asset that arises when an excess amount is paid for income taxes relative to accounting profit. The taxable income is higher than accounting profit and income tax payable exceeds tax expense. The company expects to recover the difference during the course of future operations when tax expense exceeds income tax payable.

Deferred tax liabilities A balance sheet liability that arises when a deficit amount is paid for income taxes relative to accounting profit. The taxable income is less than the accounting profit and income tax payable is less than tax expense. The company expects to eliminate the liability over the course of future operations when income tax payable exceeds tax expense.

Defined benefit obligation Under IFRS, the liability of a defined benefit pension.

Defined-benefit pension plans Plan in which the company promises to pay a certain annual amount (defined benefit) to the employee after retirement. The company bears the investment risk of the plan assets.

Defined-contribution pension plans Individual accounts to which an employee and typically the employer makes contributions, generally on a tax-advantaged basis. The amounts of contributions are defined at the outset, but the future value of the benefit is unknown. The employee bears the investment risk of the plan assets.

Definition of value (or **standard of value**) A specification of how "value" is to be understood in the context of a specific valuation.

Definitive merger agreement A contract signed by both parties to a merger that clarifies the details of the transaction, including the terms, warranties, conditions, termination details, and the rights of all parties.

Degree of confidence The probability that a confidence interval includes the unknown population parameter.

Degree of financial leverage (DFL) The ratio of the percentage change in net income to the percentage change in operating income; the sensitivity of the cash flows available to owners when operating income changes.

Degree of operating leverage (DOL) The ratio of the percentage change in operating income to the percentage change in units sold; the sensitivity of operating income to changes in units sold.

Degree of total leverage The ratio of the percentage change in net income to the percentage change in units sold; the sensitivity of the cash flows to owners to changes in the number of units produced and sold.

Degrees of freedom (df) The number of independent observations used.

Delivery A process used in a deliverable forward contract in which the long pays the agreed-upon price to the short, which in turn delivers the underlying asset to the long.

Delivery option The feature of a futures contract giving the short the right to make decisions about what, when, and where to deliver.

Delta The relationship between the option price and the underlying price, which reflects the sensitivity of the price of the option to changes in the price of the underlying.

Delta hedge An option strategy in which a position in an asset is converted to a risk-free position with a position in a specific number of options. The number of options per unit of the underlying changes through time, and the position must be revised to maintain the hedge.

Delta-normal method A measure of VAR equivalent to the analytical method but that refers to the use of delta to estimate the option's price sensitivity.

Dependent With reference to events, the property that the probability of one event occurring depends on (is related to) the occurrence of another event.

Dependent variable The variable whose variation about its mean is to be explained by the regression; the left-hand-side variable in a regression equation.

Depreciation The process of systematically allocating the cost of long-lived (tangible) assets to the periods during which the assets are expected to provide economic benefits.

Deregulation The elimination or phasing out of regulations on economic activity.

Derivative A financial instrument whose value depends on the value of some underlying asset or factor (e.g., a stock price, an interest rate, or exchange rate).

Derivatives dealers   Commercial and investment banks that make markets in derivatives.

Descriptive statistics   The study of how data can be summarized effectively.

Designated fair value instruments   Financial instruments that an entity chooses to measure at fair value per IAS 39 or SFAS 159. Generally, the election to use the fair value option is irrevocable.

Diff swaps   A swap in which the payments are based on the difference between interest rates in two countries but payments are made in only a single currency.

Differential expectations   Expectations that differ from consensus expectations.

Differentiation   The competitive strategy of offering unique products or services along some dimensions that are widely valued by buyers so that the firm can command premium prices.

Diffuse prior   The assumption of equal prior probabilities.

Diluted earnings per share (diluted EPS)   Net income, minus preferred dividends, divided by the number of common shares outstanding considering all dilutive securities (e.g., convertible debt and options); the EPS that would result if all dilutive securities were converted into common shares.

Diluted shares   The number of shares that would be outstanding if all potentially dilutive claims on common shares (e.g., convertible debt, convertible preferred stock, and employee stock options) were exercised.

Dilution   A reduction in proportional ownership interest as a result of the issuance of new shares.

Diminishing balance method   An accelerated depreciation method, i.e., one that allocates a relatively large proportion of the cost of an asset to the early years of the asset's useful life.

Direct debit program   An arrangement whereby a customer authorizes a debit to a demand account; typically used by companies to collect routine payments for services.

Direct financing lease   A type of finance lease, from a lessor perspective, where the present value of the lease payments (lease receivable) equals the carrying value of the leased asset. The revenues earned by the lessor are financing in nature.

Direct format (direct method)   With reference to the cash flow statement, a format for the presentation of the statement in which cash flow from operating activities is shown as operating cash receipts less operating cash disbursements.

Direct income capitalization approach   Division of net operating income by an overall capitalization rate to arrive at market value.

Direct sales-comparison approach   Method of valuing property based on recent sales prices of similar properties.

Direct write-off method   An approach to recognizing credit losses on customer receivables in which the company waits until such time as a customer has defaulted and only then recognizes the loss.

Dirty surplus accounting   Accounting in which some income items are reported as part of stockholders' equity rather than as gains and losses on the income statement; certain items of comprehensive income bypass the income statement and appear as direct adjustments to shareholders' equity.

Dirty surplus items   Items that affect comprehensive income but which bypass the income statement.

Disbursement float   The amount of time between check issuance and a check's clearing back against the company's account.

Discount   To reduce the value of a future payment in allowance for how far away it is in time; to calculate the present value of some future amount. Also, the amount by which an instrument is priced below its face value.

Discount for lack of control   An amount or percentage deducted from the pro rata share of 100 percent of the value of an equity interest in a business to reflect the absence of some or all of the powers of control.

Discount for lack of marketability   An amount or percentage deducted from the value of an ownership interest to reflect the relative absence of marketability.

Discount interest   A procedure for determining the interest on a loan or bond in which the interest is deducted from the face value in advance.

Discount rate   Any rate used in finding the present value of a future cash flow.

Discounted cash flow analysis   In the context of merger analysis, it is an estimate of a target company's value found by discounting the company's expected future free cash flows to the present.

Discrete random variable   A random variable that can take on at most a countable number of possible values.

Discrete time   Time thought of as advancing in distinct finite increments.

Discriminant analysis   A multivariate classification technique used to discriminate between groups, such as companies that either will or will not become bankrupt during some time frame.

Dispersion   The variability around the central tendency.

Divestiture   The sale, liquidation, or spin-off of a division or subsidiary.

Dividend coverage ratio   The ratio of net income to dividends.

Dividend discount model (DDM)   A present value model of stock value that views the intrinsic value of a stock as present value of the stock's expected future dividends.

Dividend discount model based approach   An approach for estimating a country's equity risk premium. The market rate of return is estimated as the sum of the dividend yield and the growth rate in dividends for a market index. Subtracting the risk-free rate of return from the estimated market return produces an estimate for the equity risk premium.

Dividend displacement of earnings   The concept that dividends paid now displace earnings in all future periods.

Dividend imputation tax system   A taxation system which effectively assures that corporate profits distributed as dividends are taxed just once, at the shareholder's tax rate.

Dividend policy   The strategy a company follows with regard to the amount and timing of dividend payments.

Dividend payout ratio   The ratio of cash dividends paid to earnings for a period.

Dividend rate   The most recent quarterly dividend multiplied by four.

Dividends per share   The dollar amount of cash dividends paid during a period per share of common stock.

Double declining balance depreciation   An accelerated depreciation method that involves depreciating the asset at double the straight-line rate. This rate is multiplied by the book value of the asset at the beginning of the period (a declining balance) to calculate depreciation expense.

Double taxation system   Corporate earnings are taxed twice when paid out as dividends. First, corporate earnings are taxed regardless of whether they will be distributed as dividends or retained at the G-13 corporate level, and second, dividends are taxed again at the individual shareholder level.

Double-entry accounting   The accounting system of recording transactions in which every recorded transaction affects at least two accounts so as to keep the basic accounting equation (assets = liabilities + owners' equity) in balance.

Down transition probability The probability that an asset's value moves down in a model of asset price dynamics.

Downstream A transaction between two affiliates, an investor company and an associate company such that the investor company records a profit on its income statement. An example is a sale of inventory by the investor company to the associate.

Drag on liquidity When receipts lag, creating pressure from the decreased available funds.

Due diligence Investigation and analysis in support of a recommendation; the failure to exercise due diligence may sometimes result in liability according to various securities laws.

Dummy variable A type of qualitative variable that takes on a value of 1 if a particular condition is true and 0 if that condition is false.

Dumping The sale by a foreign firm of exports at a lower price than the cost of production.

DuPont analysis An approach to decomposing return on investment, e.g., return on equity, as the product of other financial ratios.

Duration A measure of an option-free bond's average maturity. Specifically, the weighted average maturity of all future cash flows paid by a security, in which the weights are the present value of these cash flows as a fraction of the bond's price. A measure of a bond's price sensitivity to interest rate movements.

Dutch Book theorem A result in probability theory stating that inconsistent probabilities create profit opportunities.

Dynamic hedging A strategy in which a position is hedged by making frequent adjustments to the quantity of the instrument used for hedging in relation to the instrument being hedged.

Earnings at risk (EAR) A variation of VAR that reflects the risk of a company's earnings instead of its market value.

Earnings expectation management Attempts by management to encourage analysts to forecast a slightly lower number for expected earnings than the analysts would otherwise forecast.

Earnings game Management's focus on reporting earnings that meet consensus estimates.

Earnings management activity Deliberate activity aimed at influencing reporting earnings numbers, often with the goal of placing management in a favorable light; the opportunistic use of accruals to manage earnings.

Earnings per share The amount of income earned during a period per share of common stock.

Earnings yield Earnings per share divided by price; the reciprocal of the P/E ratio.

Economic exposure The risk associated with changes in the relative attractiveness of products and services offered for sale, arising out of the competitive effects of changes in exchange rates.

Economic growth The expansion of production possibilities that results from capital accumulation and technological change.

Economic growth rate The annual percentage change in real GDP.

Economic order quantity–reorder point An approach to managing inventory based on expected demand and the predictability of demand; the ordering point for new inventory is determined based on the costs of ordering and carrying inventory, such that the total cost associated with inventory is minimized.

Economic profit See *Residual income.*

Economic sectors Large industry groupings.

Economic value added (EVA®) A commercial implementation of the residual income concept; the computation of EVA® is the net operating profit after taxes minus the cost of capital, where these inputs are adjusted for a number of items.

Economies of scale In reference to mergers, it is the savings achieved through the consolidation of operations and elimination of duplicate resources.

Effective annual rate The amount by which a unit of currency will grow in a year with interest on interest included.

Effective annual yield (EAY) An annualized return that accounts for the effect of interest on interest; EAY is computed by compounding 1 plus the holding period yield forward to one year, then subtracting 1.

Efficiency In statistics, a desirable property of estimators; an efficient estimator is the unbiased estimator with the smallest variance among unbiased estimators of the same parameter.

Efficient frontier The portion of the minimum-variance frontier beginning with the global minimum-variance portfolio and continuing above it; the graph of the set of portfolios offering the maximum expected return for their level of variance of return.

Efficient portfolio A portfolio offering the highest expected return for a given level of risk as measured by variance or standard deviation of return.

Elasticity A measure of sensitivity; the incremental change in one variable with respect to an incremental change in another variable.

Electronic funds transfer The use of computer networks to conduct financial transactions electronically.

Empirical probability The probability of an event estimated as a relative frequency of occurrence.

Enhanced derivatives products companies (EDPC) A type of subsidiary engaged in derivatives transactions that is separated from the parent company in order to have a higher credit rating than the parent company.

Enterprise risk management A form of *centralized risk management* that typically encompasses the management of a broad variety of risks, including insurance risk.

Enterprise value (EV) Total company value (the market value of debt, common equity, and preferred equity) minus the value of cash and investments.

Enterprise value multiple A valuation multiple that relates the total market value of all sources of a company's capital (net of cash) to a measure of fundamental value for the entire company (such as a pre-interest earnings measure).

Entry price The price paid to buy an asset.

Equilibrium The condition in which supply equals demand.

Equitizing cash A strategy used to replicate an index. It is also used to take a given amount of cash and turn it into an equity position while maintaining the liquidity provided by the cash.

Equity Assets less liabilities; the residual interest in the assets after subtracting the liabilities.

Equity carve-out A form of restructuring that involves the creation of a new legal entity and the sale of equity in it to outsiders.

Equity charge The estimated cost of equity capital in money terms.

Equity dividend rate Income rate that reflects the relationship between equity income and equity capital.

Equity forward A contract calling for the purchase of an individual stock, a stock portfolio, or a stock index at a later date at an agreed-upon price.

Equity method A basis for reporting investment income in which the investing entity recognizes a share of income as earned rather than as dividends when received. These transactions are typically reflected in Investments in Associates or Equity Method Investments.

Equity options Options on individual stocks; also known as stock options.

Equity risk premium   The expected return on equities minus the risk-free rate; the premium that investors demand for investing in equities.

Equity swap   A swap transaction in which at least one cash flow is tied to the return to an equity portfolio position, often an equity index.

Error autocorrelation   The autocorrelation of the error term.

Error term   The portion of the dependent variable that is not explained by the independent variable(s) in the regression.

Estimate   The particular value calculated from sample observations using an estimator.

Estimated (or **fitted**) **parameters**   With reference to regression analysis, the estimated values of the population intercept and population slope coefficient(s) in a regression.

Estimation   With reference to statistical inference, the subdivision dealing with estimating the value of a population parameter.

Estimator   An estimation formula; the formula used to compute the sample mean and other sample statistics are examples of estimators.

Eurodollar   A dollar deposited outside the United States.

European-style option or **European option**   An option contract that can only be exercised on its expiration date.

Event   Any outcome or specified set of outcomes of a random variable.

Excess kurtosis   Degree of peakedness (fatness of tails) in excess of the peakedness of the normal distribution.

Exchange for physicals (EFP)   A permissible delivery procedure used by futures market participants, in which the long and short arrange a delivery procedure other than the normal procedures stipulated by the futures exchange.

Exchange rate   The value of the U.S. dollar in terms of other currencies in the foreign exchange market.

Exchange ratio   The number of shares that target stockholders are to receive in exchange for each of their shares in the target company.

Ex-dividend   Trading ex-dividend refers to shares that no longer carry the right to the next dividend payment.

Ex-dividend date   The first date that a share trades without (i.e., "ex") the dividend.

Ex-dividend price   The price at which a share first trades without (i.e., "ex") the right to receive an upcoming dividend.

Exercise or **exercising the option**   The process of using an option to buy or sell the underlying.

Exercise date   The day that employees actually exercise the options and convert them to stock.

Exercise price (strike price, striking price, or **strike)**   The fixed price at which an option holder can buy or sell the underlying.

Exercise rate or **strike rate**   The fixed rate at which the holder of an interest rate option can buy or sell the underlying.

Exhaustive   Covering or containing all possible outcomes.

Exit price   The price received to sell an asset or transfer a liability.

Expanded CAPM   An adaptation of the CAPM that adds to the CAPM a premium for small size and company-specific risk.

Expectational arbitrage   Investing on the basis of differential expectations.

Expected holding-period return   The expected total return on an asset over a stated holding period; for stocks, the sum of the expected dividend yield and the expected price appreciation over the holding period.

Expected value   The probability-weighted average of the possible outcomes of a random variable.

Expensed   Taken as a deduction in arriving at net income.

Expenses   Outflows of economic resources or increases in liabilities that result in decreases in equity (other than decreases because of distributions to owners); reductions in net assets associated with the creation of revenues.

Expiration date   The date on which a derivative contract expires.

Exports   The goods and services that we sell to people in other countries.

Exposure to foreign exchange risk   The risk of a change in value of an asset or liability denominated in a foreign currency due to a change in exchange rates.

External growth   Company growth in output or sales that is achieved by buying the necessary resources externally (i.e., achieved through mergers and acquisitions).

Externality   The effect of an investment on other things besides the investment itself.

Face value (also **principal, par value, stated value,** or **maturity value**)   The amount of cash payable by a company to the bondholders when the bonds mature; the promised payment at maturity separate from any coupon payment.

Factor   A common or underlying element with which several variables are correlated.

Factor risk premium (or **factor price**)   The expected return in excess of the risk-free rate for a portfolio with a sensitivity of 1 to one factor and a sensitivity of 0 to all other factors.

Factor sensitivity (also **factor betas** or **factor loadings**)   An asset's sensitivity to a particular factor; a measure of the response of return to each unit of increase in a factor, holding all other factors constant.

Fair market value   The market price of an asset or liability that trades regularly.

Fair value   The amount at which an asset (or liability) could be bought (or incurred) or sold (or settled) in a current transaction between willing parties, that is, other than in a forced or liquidation sale; the price that would be received to sell an asset or paid to transfer a liability in an orderly transaction between market participants at the measurement date.

Fiduciary call   A combination of a European call and a risk-free bond that matures on the option expiration day and has a face value equal to the exercise price of the call.

Finance lease (capital lease)   Essentially, the purchase of some asset by the buyer (lessee) that is directly financed by the seller (lessor).

Financial analysis   The process of selecting, evaluating, and interpreting financial data in order to formulate an assessment of a company's present and future financial condition and performance.

Financial distress   Heightened uncertainty regarding a company's ability to meet its various obligations because of lower or negative earnings.

Financial flexibility   The ability to react and adapt to financial adversities and opportunities.

Financial futures   Futures contracts in which the underlying is a stock, bond, or currency.

Financial leverage   The extent to which a company can effect, through the use of debt, a proportional change in the return on common equity that is greater than a given proportional change in operating income; also, short for the financial leverage ratio.

Financial leverage ratio   A measure of financial leverage calculated as average total assets divided by average total equity.

Financial reporting quality   The accuracy with which a company's reported financials reflect its operating performance and their usefulness for forecasting future cash flows.

Financial risk   The risk that environmental, social, or governance risk factors will result in significant costs or other losses to a company and its shareholders; the risk arising from a company's obligation to meet required payments under its financing agreements.

Financial transaction   A purchase involving a buyer having essentially no material synergies with the target (e.g., the purchase of a private company by a company in an unrelated industry or by a private equity firm would typically be a financial transaction).

Financing activities   Activities related to obtaining or repaying capital to be used in the business (e.g., equity and long-term debt).

First-differencing   A transformation that subtracts the value of the time series in period $t - 1$ from its value in period t.

First-in, first-out (FIFO)   The first in, first out, method of accounting for inventory, which matches sales against the costs of items of inventory in the order in which they were placed in inventory.

First-order serial correlation   Correlation between adjacent observations in a time series.

Fixed asset turnover   An activity ratio calculated as total revenue divided by average net fixed assets.

Fixed charge coverage   A solvency ratio measuring the number of times interest and lease payments are covered by operating income, calculated as (EBIT + lease payments) divided by (interest payments + lease payments).

Fixed costs   Costs that remain at the same level regardless of a company's level of production and sales.

Fixed exchange rate   An exchange rate pegged at a value decided by the government or central bank and that blocks the unregulated forces of demand and supply by direct intervention in the foreign exchange market.

Fixed-income forward   A forward contract in which the underlying is a bond.

Fixed-rate perpetual preferred stock   Nonconvertible, noncallable preferred stock with a specified dividend rate that has a claim on earnings senior to the claim of common stock, and no maturity date.

Flexible exchange rate   An exchange rate is determined by demand and supply with no direct intervention in the foreign exchange market by the central bank.

Flip-in pill   A poison pill takeover defense that dilutes an acquirer's ownership in a target by giving other existing target company shareholders the right to buy additional target company shares at a discount.

Flip-over pill   A poison pill takeover defense that gives target company shareholders the right to purchase shares of the acquirer at a significant discount to the market price, which has the effect of causing dilution to all existing acquiring company shareholders.

Float   In the context of customer receipts, the amount of money that is in transit between payments made by customers and the funds that are usable by the company.

Float factor   An estimate of the average number of days it takes deposited checks to clear; average daily float divided by average daily deposit.

Floating-rate loan   A loan in which the interest rate is reset at least once after the starting date.

Floor   A combination of interest rate put options designed to hedge a lender against lower rates on a floating-rate loan.

Floor traders or **locals**   Market makers that buy and sell by quoting a bid and an ask price. They are the primary providers of liquidity to the market.

Floored swap   A swap in which the floating payments have a lower limit.

Floorlet   Each component put option in a floor.

Flotation cost   Fees charged to companies by investment bankers and other costs associated with raising new capital.

Focus   The competitive strategy of seeking a competitive advantage within a target segment or segments of the industry, either on the basis of cost leadership (**cost focus**) or differentiation (**differentiation focus**).

Foreign currency   The money of other countries regardless of whether that money is in the form of notes, coins, or bank deposits.

Foreign currency transactions   Transactions that are denominated in a currency other than a company's functional currency.

Foreign exchange market   The market in which the currency of one country is exchanged for the currency of another.

Forward contract   An agreement between two parties in which one party, the buyer, agrees to buy from the other party, the seller, an underlying asset at a later date for a price established at the start of the contract.

Forward dividend yield   A dividend yield based on the anticipated dividend during the next 12 months.

Forward integration   A merger involving the purchase of a target that is farther along the value or production chain; for example, to acquire a distributor.

Forward P/E (also **leading P/E** or **prospective P/E**)   A P/E calculated on the basis of a forecast of EPS; a stock's current price divided by next year's expected earnings.

Forward price or **forward rate**   The fixed price or rate at which the transaction scheduled to occur at the expiration of a forward contract will take place. This price is agreed on at the initiation date of the contract.

Forward rate agreement (FRA)   A forward contract calling for one party to make a fixed interest payment and the other to make an interest payment at a rate to be determined at the contract expiration.

Forward swap   A forward contract to enter into a swap.

Franking credit   A tax credit received by shareholders for the taxes that a corporation paid on its distributed earnings.

Free cash flow   The actual cash that would be available to the company's investors after making all investments necessary to maintain the company as an ongoing enterprise (also referred to as free cash flow to the firm); the internally generated funds that can be distributed to the company's investors (e.g., shareholders and bondholders) without impairing the value of the company.

Free cash flow hypothesis   The hypothesis that higher debt levels discipline managers by forcing them to make fixed debt service payments and by reducing the company's free cash flow.

Free cash flow method   Income approach that values an asset based on estimates of future cash flows discounted to present value by using a discount rate reflective of the risks associated with the cash flows.

Free cash flow to equity   The cash flow available to a company's common shareholders after all operating expenses, interest, and principal payments have been made, and necessary investments in working and fixed capital have been made.

Free cash flow to equity model   A model of stock valuation that views a stock's intrinsic value as the present value of expected future free cash flows to equity.

Free cash flow to the firm   The cash flow available to the company's suppliers of capital after all operating expenses (including taxes) have been paid and necessary investments in working and fixed capital have been made.

Free cash flow to the firm model   A model of stock valuation that views the value of a firm as the present value of expected future free cash flows to the firm.

Frequency distribution   A tabular display of data summarized into a relatively small number of intervals.

Frequency polygon A graph of a frequency distribution obtained by drawing straight lines joining successive points representing the class frequencies.

Friendly transaction A potential business combination that is endorsed by the managers of both companies.

Full price The price of a security with accrued interest.

Functional currency The currency of the primary economic environment in which an entity operates.

Fundamental beta A beta that is based at least in part on fundamental data for a company.

Fundamental factor models A multifactor model in which the factors are attributes of stocks or companies that are important in explaining cross-sectional differences in stock prices.

Fundamentals Economic characteristics of a business such as profitability, financial strength, and risk.

Future value (FV) The amount to which a payment or series of payments will grow by a stated future date.

Futures commission merchants (FCMs) Individuals or companies that execute futures transactions for other parties off the exchange.

Futures contract A variation of a forward contract that has essentially the same basic definition but with some additional features, such as a clearinghouse guarantee against credit losses, a daily settlement of gains and losses, and an organized electronic or floor trading facility.

Futures exchange A legal corporate entity whose shareholders are its members. The members of the exchange have the privilege of executing transactions directly on the exchange.

Gains Asset inflows not directly related to the ordinary activities of the business.

Gamma A numerical measure of how sensitive an option's delta is to a change in the underlying.

General Agreement on Tariffs and Trade An international agreement signed in 1947 to reduce tariffs on international trade.

Generalized least squares A regression estimation technique that addresses heteroskedasticity of the error term.

Geometric mean A measure of central tendency computed by taking the nth root of the product of n non-negative values.

Giro system An electronic payment system used widely in Europe and Japan.

Going-concern assumption The assumption that the business will maintain its business activities into the foreseeable future.

Going-concern value A business's value under a going-concern assumption.

Goodwill An intangible asset that represents the excess of the purchase price of an acquired company over the value of the net assets acquired.

Government sector surplus or **deficit** An amount equal to net taxes minus government expenditure on goods and services.

Grant date The day that options are granted to employees; usually the date that compensation expense is measured if both the number of shares and option price are known.

Greenmail The purchase of the accumulated shares of a hostile investor by a company that is targeted for takeover by that investor, usually at a substantial premium over market price.

Gross domestic product A money measure of the goods and services produced within a country's borders over a stated time period.

Gross income multiplier (GIM) A ratio derived from the market; sales price divided by annual gross income equals GIM.

Gross profit (gross margin) Sales minus the cost of sales (i.e., the cost of goods sold for a manufacturing company).

Gross profit margin The ratio of gross profit to revenues.

Grouping by function With reference to the presentation of expenses in an income statement, the grouping together of expenses serving the same function, e.g., all items that are costs of good sold.

Grouping by nature With reference to the presentation of expenses in an income statement, the grouping together of expenses by similar nature, e.g., all depreciation expenses.

Growth accounting A tool that calculates the contribution to real GDP growth of each of its sources.

Growth investors With reference to equity investors, investors who seek to invest in high-earnings-growth companies.

Growth option or **expansion option** The ability to make additional investments in a project at some future time if the financial results are strong.

Growth phase A stage of growth in which a company typically enjoys rapidly expanding markets, high profit margins, and an abnormally high growth rate in earnings per share.

Guideline public companies Public-company comparables for the company being valued.

Guideline public company method A variation of the market approach; establishes a value estimate based on the observed multiples from trading activity in the shares of public companies viewed as reasonably comparable to the subject private company.

Guideline transactions method A variation of the market approach; establishes a value estimate based on pricing multiples derived from the acquisition of control of entire public or private companies that were acquired.

Harmonic mean A type of weighted mean computed by averaging the reciprocals of the observations, then taking the reciprocal of that average.

Hedge ratio The relationship of the quantity of an asset being hedged to the quantity of the derivative used for hedging.

Hedging A general strategy usually thought of as reducing, if not eliminating, risk.

Held-for-trading securities (trading securities) Debt or equity financial assets bought with the intention to sell them in the near term, usually less than three months; securities that a company intends to trade.

Held-to-maturity investments Debt (fixed-income) securities that a company intends to hold to maturity; these are presented at their original cost, updated for any amortization of discounts or premiums.

Herfindahl–Hirschman Index A measure of market concentration that is calculated by summing the squared market shares for competing companies in an industry; high HHI readings or mergers that would result in large HHI increases are more likely to result in regulatory challenges.

Heteroskedastic With reference to the error term of a regression, having a variance that differs across observations.

Heteroskedasticity The property of having a nonconstant variance; refers to an error term with the property that its variance differs across observations.

Heteroskedasticity-consistent standard errors Standard errors of the estimated parameters of a regression that correct for the presence of heteroskedasticity in the regression's error term.

Histogram A bar chart of data that have been grouped into a frequency distribution.

Historical cost In reference to assets, the amount paid to purchase an asset, including any costs of acquisition and/or preparation; with reference to liabilities, the amount of proceeds received in exchange in issuing the liability.

Historical equity risk premium approach An estimate of a country's equity risk premium that is based upon the historical averages of the risk-free rate and the rate of return on the market portfolio.

Historical exchange rates For accounting purposes, the exchange rates that existed when the assets and liabilities were initially recorded.

Historical method A method of estimating VAR that uses data from the returns of the portfolio over a recent past period and compiles this data in the form of a histogram.

Historical simulation (or **back simulation**) Another term for the historical method of estimating VAR. This term is somewhat misleading in that the method involves not a *simulation* of the past but rather what *actually happened* in the past, sometimes adjusted to reflect the fact that a different portfolio may have existed in the past than is planned for the future.

Holder-of-record date The date that a shareholder listed on the corporation's books will be deemed to have ownership of the shares for purposes of receiving an upcoming dividend; two business days after the ex-dividend date.

Holding period return The return that an investor earns during a specified holding period; a synonym for total return.

Holding period yield (HPY) The return that an investor earns during a specified holding period; holding period return with reference to a fixed-income instrument.

Homogenization Creating a contract with standard and generally accepted terms, which makes it more acceptable to a broader group of participants.

Homoskedasticity The property of having a constant variance; refers to an error term that is constant across observations.

Horizontal analysis Common-size analysis that involves comparing a specific financial statement with that statement in prior or future time periods; also, cross-sectional analysis of one company with another.

Horizontal common-size analysis A form of common-size analysis in which the accounts in a given period are used as the benchmark or base period, and every account is restated in subsequent periods as a percentage of the base period's same account.

Horizontal merger A merger involving companies in the same line of business, usually as competitors.

Hostile transaction An attempt to acquire a company against the wishes of the target's managers.

Human capital The value of skills and knowledge possessed by the workforce.

Hurdle rate The rate of return that must be met for a project to be accepted.

Hypothesis With reference to statistical inference, a statement about one or more populations.

Hypothesis testing With reference to statistical inference, the subdivision dealing with the testing of hypotheses about one or more populations.

Identifiable intangible An intangible that can be acquired singly and is typically linked to specific rights or privileges having finite benefit periods (e.g., a patent or trademark).

If-converted method A method for accounting for the effect of convertible securities on earnings per share (EPS) that specifies what EPS would have been if the convertible securities had been converted at the beginning of the period, taking account of the effects of conversion on net income and the weighted average number of shares outstanding.

Illiquidity discount See *Liquidity discount.*

Impairment Diminishment in value as a result of carrying (book) value exceeding fair value and/or recoverable value.

Impairment of capital rule A legal restriction that dividends cannot exceed retained earnings.

Implied repo rate The rate of return from a cash-and-carry transaction implied by the futures price relative to the spot price.

Implied volatility The volatility that option traders use to price an option, implied by the price of the option and a particular option-pricing model.

Implied yield A measure of the yield on the underlying bond of a futures contract implied by pricing it as though the underlying will be delivered at the futures expiration.

Imports The goods and services that we buy from people in other countries.

Imputation In reference to corporate taxes, a system that imputes, or attributes, taxes at only one level of taxation. For countries using an imputation tax system, taxes on dividends are effectively levied only at the shareholder rate. Taxes are paid at the corporate level but they are *attributed* to the shareholder. Shareholders deduct from their tax bill their portion of taxes paid by the company.

Income Increases in economic benefits in the form of inflows or enhancements of assets, or decreases of liabilities that result in an increase in equity (other than increases resulting from contributions by owners).

Income approach Valuation approach that values an asset as the present discounted value of the income expected from it.

Income statement (statement of operations or **profit and loss statement)** A financial statement that provides information about a company's profitability over a stated period of time.

Income tax paid The actual amount paid for income taxes in the period; not a provision, but the actual cash outflow.

Income tax payable The income tax owed by the company on the basis of taxable income.

Income tax recoverable The income tax expected to be recovered, from the taxing authority, on the basis of taxable income. It is a recovery of previously remitted taxes or future taxes owed by the company.

Incremental cash flow The cash flow that is realized because of a decision; the changes or increments to cash flows resulting from a decision or action.

Indenture A written contract between a lender and borrower that specifies the terms of the loan, such as interest rate, interest payment schedule, maturity, etc.

Independent With reference to events, the property that the occurrence of one event does not affect the probability of another event occurring.

Independent and identically distributed (IID) With respect to random variables, the property of random variables that are independent of each other but follow the identical probability distribution.

Independent projects Independent projects are projects whose cash flows are independent of each other.

Independent variable A variable used to explain the dependent variable in a regression; a right-hand-side variable in a regression equation.

Index amortizing swap An interest rate swap in which the notional principal is indexed to the level of interest rates and declines with the level of interest rates according to a predefined schedule. This type of swap is frequently used to hedge securities that are prepaid as interest rates decline, such as mortgage-backed securities.

Index option An option in which the underlying is a stock index.

Indexing An investment strategy in which an investor constructs a portfolio to mirror the performance of a specified index.

Indirect format (indirect method) With reference to cash flow statements, a format for the presentation of the statement which, in the operating cash flow section, begins with net income then shows additions and subtractions to arrive at operating cash flow.

Industry structure An industry's underlying economic and technical characteristics.

Infant-industry argument The argument that it is necessary to protect a new industry to enable it to grow into a mature industry that can compete in world markets.

Inflation premium An extra return that compensates investors for expected inflation.

Information ratio (IR) Mean active return divided by active risk; or alpha divided by the standard deviation of diversifiable risk.

Initial margin requirement The margin requirement on the first day of a transaction as well as on any day in which additional margin funds must be deposited.

Initial public offering (IPO) The initial issuance of common stock registered for public trading by a formerly private corporation.

In-process research and development Research and development costs relating to projects that are not yet completed, such as have been incurred by a company that is being acquired.

In-sample forecast errors The residuals from a fitted time-series model within the sample period used to fit the model.

Instability in the minimum-variance frontier The characteristic of minimum-variance frontiers that they are sensitive to small changes in inputs.

Installment Said of a sale in which proceeds are to be paid in installments over an extended period of time.

Installment method (installment-sales method) With respect to revenue recognition, a method that specifies that the portion of the total profit of the sale that is recognized in each period is determined by the percentage of the total sales price for which the seller has received cash.

Intangible assets Assets lacking physical substance, such as patents and trademarks.

Interest coverage A solvency ratio calculated as EBIT divided by interest payments.

Interest rate A rate of return that reflects the relationship between differently dated cash flows; a discount rate.

Interest rate call An option in which the holder has the right to make a known interest payment and receive an unknown interest payment.

Interest rate cap or **cap** A series of call options on an interest rate, with each option expiring at the date on which the floating loan rate will be reset, and with each option having the same exercise rate. A cap in general can have an underlying other than an interest rate.

Interest rate collar A combination of a long cap and a short floor, or a short cap and a long floor. A collar in general can have an underlying other than an interest rate.

Interest rate floor or **floor** A series of put options on an interest rate, with each option expiring at the date on which the floating loan rate will be reset, and with each option having the same exercise rate. A floor in general can have an underlying other than the interest rate.

Interest rate forward See *Forward rate agreement.*

Interest rate option An option in which the underlying is an interest rate.

Interest rate parity A formula that expresses the equivalence or parity of spot and forward rates, after adjusting for differences in the interest rates.

Interest rate put An option in which the holder has the right to make an unknown interest payment and receive a known interest payment.

Interest rate swap A swap in which the underlying is an interest rate. Can be viewed as a currency swap in which both currencies are the same and can be created as a combination of currency swaps.

Intergenerational data mining A form of data mining that applies information developed by previous researchers using a dataset to guide current research using the same or a related dataset.

Internal rate of return (IRR) Rate of return that discounts future cash flows from an investment to the exact amount of the investment; the discount rate that makes the present value of an investment's costs (outflows) equal to the present value of the investment's benefits (inflows).

Interquartile range The difference between the third and first quartiles of a dataset.

Interval With reference to grouped data, a set of values within which an observation falls.

Interval scale A measurement scale that not only ranks data but also gives assurance that the differences between scale values are equal.

In-the-money Options that, if exercised, would result in the value received being worth more than the payment required to exercise.

Intrinsic value or **exercise value** The value of an asset given a hypothetically complete understanding of the asset's investment characteristics; the value obtained if an option is exercised based on current conditions.

Inventory The unsold units of product on hand.

Inventory blanket lien The use of inventory as collateral for a loan. Though the lender has claim to some or all of the company's inventory, the company may still sell or use the inventory in the ordinary course of business.

Inventory turnover An activity ratio calculated as cost of goods sold divided by average inventory.

Inverse floater A floating-rate note or bond in which the coupon is adjusted to move opposite to a benchmark interest rate.

Inverse price ratio The reciprocal of a price multiple, e.g., in the case of a P/E ratio, the "earnings yield" E/P (where P is share price and E is earnings per share).

Investing activities Activities which are associated with the acquisition and disposal of property, plant, and equipment; intangible assets; other long-term assets; and both long-term and short-term investments in the equity and debt (bonds and loans) issued by other companies.

Investment constraints Internal or external limitations on investments.

Investment objectives Desired investment outcomes; includes risk objectives and return objectives.

Investment opportunity schedule A graphical depiction of a company's investment opportunities ordered from highest to lowest expected return. A company's optimal capital budget is found where the investment opportunity schedule intersects with the company's marginal cost of capital.

Investment strategy An approach to investment analysis and security selection.

Investment value The value to a specific buyer, taking account of potential synergies based on the investor's requirements and expectations.

IRR rule An investment decision rule that accepts projects or investments for which the IRR is greater than the opportunity cost of capital.

Joint probability The probability of the joint occurrence of stated events.

Joint probability function A function giving the probability of joint occurrences of values of stated random variables.

Joint venture   An entity (partnership, corporation, or other legal form) where control is shared by two or more entities called venturers.

Justified (fundamental) P/E   The price-to-earnings ratio that is fair, warranted, or justified on the basis of forecasted fundamentals.

Justified price multiple (or warranted price multiple or intrinsic price multiple)   The estimated fair value of the price multiple, usually based on forecasted fundamentals or comparables.

Just-in-time method   Method of managing inventory that minimizes in-process inventory stocks.

kth order autocorrelation   The correlation between observations in a time series separated by k periods.

Kurtosis   The statistical measure that indicates the peakedness of a distribution.

Labor productivity   The quantity of real GDP produced by an hour of labor.

Lack of marketability discount   An extra return to investors to compensate for lack of a public market or lack of marketability.

Laddering strategy   A form of active strategy which entails scheduling maturities on a systematic basis within the investment portfolio such that investments are spread out equally over the term of the ladder.

Last-in, first-out (LIFO)   The last in, first out, method of accounting for inventory, which matches sales against the costs of items of inventory in the reverse order the items were placed in inventory (i.e., inventory produced or acquired last are assumed to be sold first).

Law of one price   The condition in a financial market in which two equivalent financial instruments or combinations of financial instruments can sell for only one price. Equivalent to the principle that no arbitrage opportunities are possible.

Leading dividend yield   Forecasted dividends per share over the next year divided by current stock price.

Leading P/E (or forward P/E or prospective P/E)   A stock's current price divided by the next year's expected earnings.

Legal risk   The risk that failures by company managers to effectively manage a company's environmental, social, and governance risk exposures will lead to lawsuits and other judicial remedies, resulting in potentially catastrophic losses for the company; the risk that the legal system will not enforce a contract in case of dispute or fraud.

Legislative and regulatory risk   The risk that governmental laws and regulations directly or indirectly affecting a company's operations will change with potentially severe adverse effects on the company's continued profitability and even its long-term sustainability.

Lemons problem   The potential for asymmetric information to bring about a general decline in product quality in an industry.

Leptokurtic   Describes a distribution that is more peaked than a normal distribution.

Lessee   The party obtaining the use of an asset through a lease.

Lessor   The owner of an asset that grants the right to use the asset to another party.

Level of significance   The probability of a Type I error in testing a hypothesis.

Leverage   In the context of corporate finance, leverage refers to the use of fixed costs within a company's cost structure. Fixed costs that are operating costs (such as depreciation or rent) create operating leverage. Fixed costs that are financial costs (such as interest expense) create financial leverage.

Leveraged buyout (LBO)   A transaction whereby the target company management team converts the target to a privately held company by using heavy borrowing to finance the purchase of the target company's outstanding shares.

Leveraged floating-rate note or leveraged floater   A floating-rate note or bond in which the coupon is adjusted at a multiple of a benchmark interest rate.

Leveraged recapitalization   A post-offer takeover defense mechanism that involves the assumption of a large amount of debt that is then used to finance share repurchases; the effect is to dramatically change the company's capital structure while attempting to deliver a value to target shareholders in excess of a hostile bid.

Liabilities   Present obligations of an enterprise arising from past events, the settlement of which is expected to result in an outflow of resources embodying economic benefits; creditors' claims on the resources of a company.

LIFO layer liquidation (LIFO liquidation)   With respect to the application of the LIFO inventory method, the liquidation of old, relatively low-priced inventory; happens when the volume of sales rises above the volume of recent purchases so that some sales are made from relatively old, low-priced inventory.

LIFO reserve   The difference between inventory reported as FIFO and inventory reported as LIFO (FIFO inventory value less LIFO inventory value).

Likelihood   The probability of an observation, given a particular set of conditions.

Limit down   A limit move in the futures market in which the price at which a transaction would be made is at or below the lower limit.

Limit move   A condition in the futures markets in which the price at which a transaction would be made is at or beyond the price limits.

Limit up   A limit move in the futures market in which the price at which a transaction would be made is at or above the upper limit.

Linear association   A straight-line relationship, as opposed to a relationship that cannot be graphed as a straight line.

Linear interpolation   The estimation of an unknown value on the basis of two known values that bracket it, using a straight line between the two known values.

Linear regression   Regression that models the straight-line relationship between the dependent and independent variable(s).

Linear trend   A trend in which the dependent variable changes at a constant rate with time.

Liquidation   To sell the assets of a company, division, or subsidiary piecemeal, typically because of bankruptcy; the form of bankruptcy that allows for the orderly satisfaction of creditors' claims after which the company ceases to exist.

Liquidation value   The value of a company if the company were dissolved and its assets sold individually.

Liquidity   A company's ability to satisfy its short-term obligations using assets that are most readily converted into cash; the ability to trade a futures contract, either selling a previously purchased contract or purchasing a previously sold contract.

Liquidity discount   A reduction or discount to value that reflects the lack of depth of trading or liquidity in that asset's market.

Liquidity premium   An extra return that compensates investors for the risk of loss relative to an investment's fair value if the investment needs to be converted to cash quickly.

Liquidity ratios   Financial ratios measuring the company's ability to meet its short-term obligations.

Liquidity risk   The risk that a financial instrument cannot be purchased or sold without a significant concession in price due to the size of the market.

Local currency   The currency of the country where a company is located.

Lockbox system A payment system in which customer payments are mailed to a post office box and the banking institution retrieves and deposits these payments several times a day, enabling the company to have use of the fund sooner than in a centralized system in which customer payments are sent to the company.

Locked limit A condition in the futures markets in which a transaction cannot take place because the price would be beyond the limits.

Logit model A qualitative-dependent-variable multiple regression model based on the logistic probability distribution.

Log-linear model With reference to time-series models, a model in which the growth rate of the time series as a function of time is constant.

Log-log regression model A regression that expresses the dependent and independent variables as natural logarithms.

London Interbank Offer Rate (LIBOR) The Eurodollar rate at which London banks lend dollars to other London banks; considered to be the best representative rate on a dollar borrowed by a private, high-quality borrower.

Long The buyer of a derivative contract. Also refers to the position of owning a derivative.

Longitudinal data Observations on characteristic(s) of the same observational unit through time.

Long-lived assets (or **long-term assets**) Assets that are expected to provide economic benefits over a future period of time, typically greater than one year.

Long-term contract A contract that spans a number of accounting periods.

Long-term debt-to-assets ratio The proportion of a company's assets that is financed with long-term debt.

Long-term equity anticipatory securities (LEAPS) Options originally created with expirations of several years.

Long-term liability An obligation that is expected to be settled, with the outflow of resources embodying economic benefits, over a future period generally greater than one year.

Look-ahead bias A bias caused by using information that was not available on the test date.

Losses Asset outflows not directly related to the ordinary activities of the business.

Lower bound The lowest possible value of an option.

Macaulay duration The duration without dividing by 1 plus the bond's yield to maturity. The term, named for one of the economists who first derived it, is used to distinguish the calculation from modified duration. (See also *modified duration*.)

Macroeconomic factor A factor related to the economy, such as the inflation rate, industrial production, or economic sector membership.

Macroeconomic factor model A multifactor model in which the factors are surprises in macroeconomic variables that significantly explain equity returns.

Maintenance margin requirement The margin requirement on any day other than the first day of a transaction.

Management buyout (MBO) A corporate transaction in which management repurchases all outstanding common stock, usually using the proceeds of debt issuance.

Managerialism theories Theories that posit that corporate executives are motivated to engage in mergers to maximize the size of their company rather than shareholder value.

Manufacturing resource planning (MRP) The incorporation of production planning into inventory management. A MRP analysis provides both a materials acquisition schedule and a production schedule.

Margin The amount of money that a trader deposits in a margin account. The term is derived from the stock market practice in which an investor borrows a portion of the money required to purchase a certain amount of stock. In futures markets, there is no borrowing so the margin is more of a down payment or performance bond.

Marginal investor An investor in a given share who is very likely to be part of the next trade in the share and who is therefore important in setting price.

Market approach Valuation approach that values an asset based on pricing multiples from sales of assets viewed as similar to the subject asset.

Market efficiency A finance perspective on capital markets that deals with the relationship of price to intrinsic value. The **traditional efficient markets formulation** asserts that an asset's price is the best available estimate of its intrinsic value. The **rational efficient markets formulation** asserts that investors should expect to be rewarded for the costs of information gathering and analysis by higher gross returns.

Market-extraction method Method used to estimate the overall capitalization rate by dividing the sale price of a comparable income property into the net operating income.

Market price of risk The slope of the capital market line, indicating the market risk premium for each unit of market risk.

Market rate The rate demanded by purchasers of bonds, given the risks associated with future cash payment obligations of the particular bond issue.

Market risk The risk associated with interest rates, exchange rates, and equity prices.

Market risk premium The expected excess return on the market over the risk-free rate.

Market share test The percentage of a market that a particular firm supplies; used as the primary measure of monopoly power.

Market timing Asset allocation in which the investment in the market is increased if one forecasts that the market will outperform T-bills.

Market value of invested capital The market value of debt and equity.

Marketability discount A reduction or discount to value for shares that are not publicly traded.

Market-oriented investors With reference to equity investors, investors whose investment disciplines cannot be clearly categorized as value or growth.

Marking to market A procedure used primarily in futures markets in which the parties to a contract settle the amount owed daily. Also known as the *daily settlement*.

Markowitz decision rule A decision rule for choosing between two investments based on their means and variances.

Mark-to-market The revaluation of a financial asset or liability to its current market value or fair value.

Matching principle The accounting principle that expenses should be recognized when the associated revenue is recognized.

Matching strategy An active investment strategy that includes intentional matching of the timing of cash outflows with investment maturities.

Materiality The condition of being of sufficient importance so that omission or misstatement of the item in a financial report could make a difference to users' decisions.

Matrix pricing In the fixed income markets, to price a security on the basis of valuation-relevant characteristics (e.g., debt-rating approach).

Mature growth rate The earnings growth rate in a company's mature phase; an earnings growth rate that can be sustained long term.

Mature phase   A stage of growth in which the company reaches an equilibrium in which investment opportunities on average just earn their opportunity cost of capital.

Maturity premium   An extra return that compensates investors for the increased sensitivity of the market value of debt to a change in market interest rates as maturity is extended.

Mean   The sum of all values in a distribution or dataset, divided by the number of values summed; a synonym of arithmetic mean.

Mean absolute deviation   With reference to a sample, the mean of the absolute values of deviations from the sample mean.

Mean excess return   The average rate of return in excess of the risk-free rate.

Mean reversion   The tendency of a time series to fall when its level is above its mean and rise when its level is below its mean; a mean-reverting time series tends to return to its long-term mean.

Mean–variance analysis   An approach to portfolio analysis using expected means, variances, and covariances of asset returns.

Measure of central tendency   A quantitative measure that specifies where data are centered.

Measure of location   A quantitative measure that describes the location or distribution of data; includes not only measures of central tendency but also other measures such as percentiles.

Measurement scales   A scheme of measuring differences. The four types of measurement scales are nominal, ordinal, interval, and ratio.

Median   The value of the middle item of a set of items that has been sorted into ascending or descending order; the 50th percentile.

Merger   The absorption of one company by another; two companies become one entity and one or both of the pre-merger companies ceases to exist as a separate entity.

Mesokurtic   Describes a distribution with kurtosis identical to that of the normal distribution.

Method based on forecasted fundamentals   An approach to using price multiples that relates a price multiple to forecasts of fundamentals through a discounted cash flow model.

Method of comparables   An approach to valuation that involves using a price multiple to evaluate whether an asset is relatively fairly valued, relatively undervalued, or relatively overvalued when compared to a benchmark value of the multiple.

Minimum-variance frontier   The graph of the set of portfolios that have minimum variance for their level of expected return.

Minimum-variance portfolio   The portfolio with the minimum variance for each given level of expected return.

Minority active investments   Investments in which investors exert significant influence, but not control, over the investee. Typically, the investor has 20 to 50% ownership in the investee.

Minority interest (noncontrolling interest)   The proportion of the ownership of a subsidiary not held by the parent (controlling) company.

Minority passive investments (passive investments)   Investments in which the investor has no significant influence or control over the operations of the investee.

Mismatching strategy   An active investment strategy whereby the timing of cash outflows is not matched with investment maturities.

Mispricing   Any departure of the market price of an asset from the asset's estimated intrinsic value.

Mixed factor models   Factor models that combine features of more than one type of factor model.

Mixed offering   A merger or acquisition that is to be paid for with cash, securities, or some combination of the two.

Modal interval   With reference to grouped data, the most frequently occurring interval.

Mode   The most frequently occurring value in a set of observations.

Model risk   The use of an inaccurate pricing model for a particular investment, or the improper use of the right model.

Model specification   With reference to regression, the set of variables included in the regression and the regression equation's functional form.

Modified duration   A measure of a bond's price sensitivity to interest rate movements. Equal to the Macaulay duration of a bond divided by one plus its yield to maturity.

Molodovsky effect   The observation that P/Es tend to be high on depressed EPS at the bottom of a business cycle, and tend to be low on unusually high EPS at the top of a business cycle.

Momentum indicators   Valuation indicators that relate either price or a fundamental (such as earnings) to the time series of their own past values (or in some cases to their expected value).

Monetary assets and liabilities   Assets and liabilities with value equal to the amount of currency contracted for, a fixed amount of currency. Examples are cash, accounts receivable, mortgages receivable, accounts payable, bonds payable, and mortgages payable. Inventory is not a monetary asset. Most liabilities are monetary.

Monetary/nonmonetary method   Approach to translating foreign currency financial statements for consolidation in which monetary assets and liabilities are translated at the current exchange rate. Nonmonetary assets and liabilities are translated at historical exchange rates (the exchange rates that existed when the assets and liabilities were acquired).

Money market   The market for short-term debt instruments (one-year maturity or less).

Money market yield (or CD equivalent yield)   A yield on a basis comparable to the quoted yield on an interest-bearing money market instrument that pays interest on a 360-day basis; the annualized holding period yield, assuming a 360-day year.

Moneyness   The relationship between the price of the underlying and an option's exercise price.

Money-weighted rate of return   The internal rate of return on a portfolio, taking account of all cash flows.

Monitoring costs   Costs borne by owners to monitor the management of the company (e.g., board of director expenses).

Monopolization   The possession of monopoly power in the relevant market and the willful acquisition or maintenance of that power, as distinguished from growth or development as a consequence of a superior product, business acumen, or historical accident.

Monte Carlo simulation method   An approach to estimating a probability distribution of outcomes to examine what might happen if particular risks are faced. This method is widely used in the sciences as well as in business to study a variety of problems.

Multicollinearity   A regression assumption violation that occurs when two or more independent variables (or combinations of independent variables) are highly but not perfectly correlated with each other.

Multiple linear regression   Linear regression involving two or more independent variables.

Multiple linear regression model   A linear regression model with two or more independent variables.

Multiple R   The correlation between the actual and forecasted values of the dependent variable in a regression.

Multiplication rule for probabilities   The rule that the joint probability of events A and B equals the probability of A given B times the probability of B.

Multi-step format   With respect to the format of the income statement, a format that presents a subtotal for gross profit (revenue minus cost of goods sold).

Multivariate distribution   A probability distribution that specifies the probabilities for a group of related random variables.

Multivariate normal distribution   A probability distribution for a group of random variables that is completely defined by the means and variances of the variables plus all the correlations between pairs of the variables.

Mutually exclusive events   Events such that only one can occur at a time.

Mutually exclusive projects   Mutually exclusive projects compete directly with each other. For example, if Projects A and B are mutually exclusive, you can choose A or B, but you cannot choose both.

n Factorial   For a positive integer n, the product of the first n positive integers; 0 factorial equals 1 by definition. n factorial is written as $n!$.

Negative serial correlation   Serial correlation in which a positive error for one observation increases the chance of a negative error for another observation, and vice versa.

Neoclassical growth theory   A theory of economic growth that proposes that real GDP per person grows because technological change induces a level of saving and investment that makes capital per hour of labor grow.

Net asset balance sheet exposure   When assets translated at the current exchange rate are greater in amount than liabilities translated at the current exchange rate. Assets exposed to translation gains or losses exceed the exposed liabilities.

Net book value   The remaining (undepreciated) balance of an asset's purchase cost. For liabilities, the face value of a bond minus any unamortized discount, or plus any unamortized premium.

Net borrower   A country that is borrowing more from the rest of the world than it is lending to it.

Net exports   The value of exports of goods and services minus the value of imports of goods and services.

Net income (loss)   The difference between revenue and expenses; what remains after subtracting all expenses (including depreciation, interest, and taxes) from revenue.

Net lender   A country that is lending more to the rest of the world than it is borrowing from it.

Net liability balance sheet exposure   When liabilities translated at the current exchange rate are greater than assets translated at the current exchange rate. Liabilities exposed to translation gains or losses exceed the exposed assets.

Net operating assets   The difference between operating assets (total assets less cash) and operating liabilities (total liabilities less total debt).

Net operating cycle   An estimate of the average time that elapses between paying suppliers for materials and collecting cash from the subsequent sale of goods produced.

Net operating profit less adjusted taxes, or **NOPLAT**   A company's operating profit with adjustments to normalize the effects of capital structure.

Net present value (NPV)   The present value of an investment's cash inflows (benefits) minus the present value of its cash outflows (costs).

Net profit margin (profit margin or **return on sales)**   An indicator of profitability, calculated as net income divided by revenue; indicates how much of each dollar of revenues is left after all costs and expenses.

Net realisable value   Estimated selling price in the ordinary course of business less the estimated costs necessary to make the sale.

Net revenue   Revenue after adjustments (e.g., for estimated returns or for amounts unlikely to be collected).

Netting   When parties agree to exchange only the net amount owed from one party to the other.

New growth theory   A theory of economic growth based on the idea that real GDP per person grows because of the choices that people make in the pursuit of profit and that growth can persist indefinitely.

Node   Each value on a binomial tree from which successive moves or outcomes branch.

No-growth company   A company without positive expected net present value projects.

No-growth value per share   The value per share of a no-growth company, equal to the expected level amount of earnings divided by the stock's required rate of return.

Nominal exchange rate   The value of the U.S. dollar expressed in units of foreign currency per U.S. dollar.

Nominal rate   A rate of interest based on the security's face value.

Nominal risk-free interest rate   The sum of the real risk-free interest rate and the inflation premium.

Nominal scale   A measurement scale that categorizes data but does not rank them.

Nonconventional cash flow   In a nonconventional cash flow pattern, the initial outflow is not followed by inflows only, but the cash flows can flip from positive (inflows) to negative (outflows) again (or even change signs several times).

Noncurrent   Not due to be consumed, converted into cash, or settled within one year after the balance sheet date.

Noncurrent assets   Assets that are expected to benefit the company over an extended period of time (usually more than one year).

Nondeliverable forwards (NDFs)   Cash-settled forward contracts, used predominately with respect to foreign exchange forwards.

Nonearning assets   Cash and investments (specifically cash, cash equivalents, and short-term investments).

Nonlinear relation   An association or relationship between variables that cannot be graphed as a straight line.

Nonmonetary assets and liabilities   Assets and liabilities that are not monetary assets and liabilities. Nonmonetary assets include inventory, fixed assets, and intangibles, and nonmonetary liabilities include deferred revenue.

Nonparametric test   A test that is not concerned with a parameter, or that makes minimal assumptions about the population from which a sample comes.

Nonstationarity   With reference to a random variable, the property of having characteristics such as mean and variance that are not constant through time.

Nontariff barrier   Any action other than a tariff that restricts international trade.

Normal backwardation   The condition in futures markets in which futures prices are lower than expected spot prices.

Normal contango   The condition in futures markets in which futures prices are higher than expected spot prices.

Normal distribution   A continuous, symmetric probability distribution that is completely described by its mean and its variance.

Normalized earnings   Earnings adjusted for nonrecurring, noneconomic, or other unusual items to eliminate anomalies and/or facilitate comparisons.

Normalized earnings per share (or normal earnings per share)   The earnings per share that a business could achieve currently under mid-cyclical conditions.

Normalized P/E   P/Es based on normalized EPS data.

North American Free Trade Agreement   An agreement, which became effective on January 1, 1994, to eliminate all barriers to international trade between the United States, Canada, and Mexico after a 15-year phasing-in period.

Notes payable Amounts owed by a business to creditors as a result of borrowings that are evidenced by (short-term) loan agreements.

***n*-Period moving average** The average of the current and immediately prior $n - 1$ values of a time series.

NPV rule An investment decision rule that states that an investment should be undertaken if its NPV is positive but not undertaken if its NPV is negative.

NTM P/E Next twelve months P/E: current market price divided by an estimated next twelve months EPS.

Null hypothesis The hypothesis to be tested.

Number of days of inventory An activity ratio equal to the number of days in a period divided by the inventory ratio for the period; an indication of the number of days a company ties up funds in inventory.

Number of days of payables An activity ratio equal to the number of days in a period divided by the payables turnover ratio for the period; an estimate of the average number of days it takes a company to pay its suppliers.

Number of days of receivables Estimate of the average number of days it takes to collect on credit accounts.

Objective probabilities Probabilities that generally do not vary from person to person; includes a priori and objective probabilities.

Off-balance sheet financing Arrangements that do not result in additional liabilities on the balance sheet but nonetheless create economic obligations.

Official settlements account A record of the change in official reserves, which are the government's holdings of foreign currency.

Off-market FRA A contract in which the initial value is intentionally set at a value other than zero and therefore requires a cash payment at the start from one party to the other.

Offsetting A transaction in exchange-listed derivative markets in which a party re-enters the market to close out a position.

One third rule The rule that, on the average, with no change in technology, a 1 percent increase in capital per hour of labor brings a 1/3 percent increase in labor productivity.

One-sided hypothesis test (or one-tailed hypothesis test) A test in which the null hypothesis is rejected only if the evidence indicates that the population parameter is greater than (smaller than) θ_0. The alternative hypothesis also has one side.

Operating activities Activities that are part of the day-to-day business functioning of an entity, such as selling inventory and providing services.

Operating breakeven The number of units produced and sold at which the company's operating profit is zero (revenues = operating costs).

Operating cycle A measure of the time needed to convert raw materials into cash from a sale; it consists of the number of days of inventory and the number of days of receivables.

Operating lease An agreement allowing the lessee to use some asset for a period of time; essentially a rental.

Operating leverage The use of fixed costs in operations.

Operating profit (operating income) A company's profits on its usual business activities before deducting taxes.

Operating profit margin (operating margin) A profitability ratio calculated as operating income (i.e., income before interest and taxes) divided by revenue.

Operating return on assets (operating ROA) A profitability ratio calculated as operating income divided by average total assets.

Operating risk The risk attributed to the operating cost structure, in particular the use of fixed costs in operations; the risk arising from the mix of fixed and variable costs; the risk that a company's operations may be severely affected by environmental, social, and governance risk factors.

Operations risk or **operational risk** The risk of loss from failures in a company's systems and procedures (for example, due to computer failures or human failures) or events completely outside of the control of organizations (which would include "acts of God" and terrorist actions).

Opportunity cost The value that investors forgo by choosing a particular course of action; the value of something in its best alternative use.

Opportunity set The set of assets available for investment.

Optimal capital structure The capital structure at which the value of the company is maximized.

Optimizer A specialized computer program or a spreadsheet that solves for the portfolio weights that will result in the lowest risk for a specified level of expected return.

Option A financial instrument that gives one party the right, but not the obligation, to buy or sell an underlying asset from or to another party at a fixed price over a specific period of time. Also referred to as contingent claims.

Option price, option premium, or **premium** The amount of money a buyer pays and seller receives to engage in an option transaction.

Orderly liquidation value The estimated gross amount of money that could be realized from the liquidation sale of an asset or assets, given a reasonable amount of time to find a purchaser or purchasers.

Ordinal scale A measurement scale that sorts data into categories that are ordered (ranked) with respect to some characteristic.

Ordinary annuity An annuity with a first cash flow that is paid one period from the present.

Ordinary least squares (OLS) An estimation method based on the criterion of minimizing the sum of the squared residuals of a regression.

Ordinary shares (common stock or **common shares)** Equity shares that are subordinate to all other types of equity (e.g., preferred equity).

Organic growth Company growth in output or sales that is achieved by making investments internally (i.e., excludes growth achieved through mergers and acquisitions).

Orthogonal Uncorrelated; at a right angle.

Other comprehensive income Changes to equity that bypass (are not reported in) the income statement; the difference between comprehensive income and net income.

Other post-employment benefits Promises by the company to pay benefits in the future, other than pension benefits, such as life insurance premiums and all or part of health care insurance for its retirees.

Other receivables Amounts owed to the company from parties other than customers.

Outcome A possible value of a random variable.

Outliers Small numbers of observations at either extreme (small or large) of a sample.

Out-of-sample forecast errors The differences between actual and predicted value of time series outside the sample period used to fit the model.

Out-of-sample test A test of a strategy or model using a sample outside the time period on which the strategy or model was developed.

Out-of-the-money Options that, if exercised, would require the payment of more money than the value received and therefore would not be currently exercised.

Overall capitalization rate A ratio in property valuation; net operating income divided by sale price. Also known as the going-in rate.

Overnight index swap (OIS)　A swap in which the floating rate is the cumulative value of a single unit of currency invested at an overnight rate during the settlement period.

Owners' equity　The excess of assets over liabilities; the residual interest of shareholders in the assets of an entity after deducting the entity's liabilities.

Paired comparisons test　A statistical test for differences based on paired observations drawn from samples that are dependent on each other.

Paired observations　Observations that are dependent on each other.

Pairs arbitrage　A trade in two closely related stocks that involves buying the relatively undervalued stock and selling short the relatively overvalued stock.

Pairs arbitrage trade　A trade in two closely related stocks involving the short sale of one and the purchase of the other.

Pairs trading　An approach to trading that uses pairs of closely related stocks, buying the relatively undervalued stock and selling short the relatively overvalued stock.

Panel data　Observations through time on a single characteristic of multiple observational units.

Parameter　A descriptive measure computed from or used to describe a population of data, conventionally represented by Greek letters.

Parameter instability　The problem or issue of population regression parameters that have changed over time.

Parametric test　Any test (or procedure) concerned with parameters or whose validity depends on assumptions concerning the population generating the sample.

Partial regression coefficients or **partial slope coefficients**　The slope coefficients in a multiple regression.

Partnership　A business owned and operated by more than one individual.

Passive portfolio　A market index portfolio.

Passive strategy　In reference to short-term cash management, it is an investment strategy characterized by simple decision rules for making daily investments.

Payables turnover　An activity ratio calculated as purchases divided by average trade payables.

Payer swaption　A swaption that allows the holder to enter into a swap as the fixed-rate payer and floating-rate receiver.

Payment date　The day that the company actually mails out (or electronically transfers) a dividend payment.

Payment netting　A means of settling payments in which the amount owed by the first party to the second is netted with the amount owed by the second party to the first; only the net difference is paid.

Payoff　The value of an option at expiration.

Payout policy　The principles by which a company distributes cash to common shareholders by means of cash dividends and/or share repurchases.

Payout ratio　The percentage of total earnings paid out in dividends in any given year (in per-share terms, DPS/EPS).

Pecking order theory　The theory that managers take into account how their actions might be interpreted by outsiders and thus order their preferences for various forms of corporate financing. Forms of financing that are least visible to outsiders (e.g., internally generated funds) are most preferable to managers and those that are most visible (e.g., equity) are least preferable.

PEG　The P/E-to-growth ratio, calculated as the stock's P/E divided by the expected earnings growth rate.

PEG ratio　The ratio of P/E-to-growth, calculated as the stock's P/E divided by the expected earnings growth rate in percent.

Per unit contribution margin　The amount that each unit sold contributes to covering fixed costs—that is, the difference between the price per unit and the variable cost per unit.

Percentage-of-completion　A method of revenue recognition in which, in each accounting period, the company estimates what percentage of the contract is complete and then reports that percentage of the total contract revenue in its income statement.

Percentiles　Quantiles that divide a distribution into 100 equal parts.

Perfect capital markets　Markets in which, by assumption, there are no taxes, transactions costs, or bankruptcy costs, and in which all investors have equal ("symmetric") information.

Perfect collinearity　The existence of an exact linear relation between two or more independent variables or combinations of independent variables.

Performance appraisal　The evaluation of risk-adjusted performance; the evaluation of investment skill.

Performance guarantee　A guarantee from the clearinghouse that if one party makes money on a transaction, the clearinghouse ensures it will be paid.

Performance measurement　The calculation of returns in a logical and consistent manner.

Period costs　Costs (e.g., executives' salaries) that cannot be directly matched with the timing of revenues and which are thus expensed immediately.

Periodic inventory system　An inventory accounting system in which inventory values and costs of sales are determined at the end of the accounting period.

Periodic rate　The quoted interest rate per period; the stated annual interest rate divided by the number of compounding periods per year.

Permanent differences　Differences between tax and financial reporting of revenue (expenses) that will not be reversed at some future date. These result in a difference between the company's effective tax rate and statutory tax rate and do not result in a deferred tax item.

Permutation　An ordered listing.

Perpetual inventory system　An inventory accounting system in which inventory values and costs of sales are continuously updated to reflect purchases and sales.

Perpetuity　A perpetual annuity, or a set of never-ending level sequential cash flows, with the first cash flow occurring one period from now.

Pet projects　Projects in which influential managers want the corporation to invest. Often, unfortunately, pet projects are selected without undergoing normal capital budgeting analysis.

Plain vanilla swap　An interest rate swap in which one party pays a fixed rate and the other pays a floating rate, with both sets of payments in the same currency.

Platykurtic　Describes a distribution that is less peaked than the normal distribution.

Point estimate　A single numerical estimate of an unknown quantity, such as a population parameter.

Point of sale　Systems that capture transaction data at the physical location in which the sale is made.

Poison pill　A pre-offer takeover defense mechanism that makes it prohibitively costly for an acquirer to take control of a target without the prior approval of the target's board of directors.

Poison puts　A pre-offer takeover defense mechanism that gives target company bondholders the right to sell their bonds back to the target at a pre-specified redemption price, typically at or above par value; this defense increases the need for cash and raises the cost of the acquisition.

Pooled estimate　An estimate of a parameter that involves combining (pooling) observations from two or more samples.

Pooling of interests accounting method   A method of accounting in which combined companies were portrayed as if they had always operated as a single economic entity. Called pooling of interests under U.S. GAAP and uniting of interests under IFRS. (No longer allowed under U.S. GAAP or IFRS.)

Population   All members of a specified group.

Population mean   The arithmetic mean value of a population; the arithmetic mean of all the observations or values in the population.

Population standard deviation   A measure of dispersion relating to a population in the same unit of measurement as the observations, calculated as the positive square root of the population variance.

Population variance   A measure of dispersion relating to a population, calculated as the mean of the squared deviations around the population mean.

Portfolio implementation problem   The part of the execution step of the portfolio management process that involves the implementation of portfolio decisions by trading desks.

Portfolio performance attribution   The analysis of portfolio performance in terms of the contributions from various sources of risk.

Portfolio possibilities curve   A graphical representation of the expected return and risk of all portfolios that can be formed using two assets.

Portfolio selection/composition problem   The part of the execution step of the portfolio management process in which investment strategies are integrated with expectations to select a portfolio of assets.

Position trader   A trader who typically holds positions open overnight.

Positive serial correlation   Serial correlation in which a positive error for one observation increases the chance of a positive error for another observation, and a negative error for one observation increases the chance of a negative error for another observation.

Posterior probability   An updated probability that reflects or comes after new information.

Potential credit risk   The risk associated with the possibility that a payment due at a later date will not be made.

Power of a test   The probability of correctly rejecting the null—that is, rejecting the null hypothesis when it is false.

Precautionary stocks   A level of inventory beyond anticipated needs that provides a cushion in the event that it takes longer to replenish inventory than expected or in the case of greater than expected demand.

Pre-investing   The strategy of using futures contracts to enter the market without an immediate outlay of cash.

Premise of value   The status of a company in the sense of whether it is assumed to be a going concern or not.

Prepaid expense   A normal operating expense that has been paid in advance of when it is due.

Present value (PV)   The present discounted value of future cash flows: For assets, the present discounted value of the future net cash inflows that the asset is expected to generate; for liabilities, the present discounted value of the future net cash outflows that are expected to be required to settle the liabilities.

Present (price) value of a basis point (PVBP)   The change in the bond price for a 1 basis point change in yield. Also called *basis point value* (BPV).

Present value of growth opportunities (or **value of growth**)   The difference between the actual value per share and the no-growth value per share.

Present value model or **discounted cash flow model**   A model of intrinsic value that views the value of an asset as the present value of the asset's expected future cash flows.

Presentation currency   The currency in which financial statement amounts are presented.

Pretax margin   A profitability ratio calculated as earnings before taxes divided by revenue.

Price discovery   A feature of futures markets in which futures prices provide valuable information about the price of the underlying asset.

Price limits   Limits imposed by a futures exchange on the price change that can occur from one day to the next.

Price momentum   A valuation indicator based on past price movement.

Price multiple   The ratio of a stock's market price to some measure of value per share.

Price relative   A ratio of an ending price over a beginning price; it is equal to 1 plus the holding period return on the asset.

Price to book value   A valuation ratio calculated as price per share divided by book value per share.

Price to cash flow   A valuation ratio calculated as price per share divided by cash flow per share.

Price to sales   A valuation ratio calculated as price per share divided by sales per share.

Priced risk   Risk for which investors demand compensation for bearing (e.g., equity risk, company-specific factors, macroeconomic factors).

Price-setting option   The operational flexibility to adjust prices when demand varies from forecast. For example, when demand exceeds capacity, the company could benefit from the excess demand by increasing prices.

Principal   The amount of funds originally invested in a project or instrument; the face value to be paid at maturity.

Prior probabilities   Probabilities reflecting beliefs prior to the arrival of new information.

Prior transaction method   A variation of the market approach; considers actual transactions in the stock of the subject private company.

Private sector surplus or **deficit**   An amount equal to saving minus investment.

Probability   A number between 0 and 1 describing the chance that a stated event will occur.

Probability density function   A function with non-negative values such that probability can be described by areas under the curve graphing the function.

Probability distribution   A distribution that specifies the probabilities of a random variable's possible outcomes.

Probability function   A function that specifies the probability that the random variable takes on a specific value.

Probit model   A qualitative-dependent-variable multiple regression model based on the normal distribution.

Production-flexibility   The operational flexibility to alter production when demand varies from forecast. For example, if demand is strong, a company may profit from employees working overtime or from adding additional shifts.

Profitability ratios   Ratios that measure a company's ability to generate profitable sales from its resources (assets).

Project sequencing   To defer the decision to invest in a future project until the outcome of some or all of a current project is known. Projects are sequenced through time, so that investing in a project creates the option to invest in future projects.

Projected benefit obligation   Under U.S. GAAP, a measure used in estimating a defined-benefit pension plan's liabilities, defined as "the actuarial present value as of a date of all benefits attributed by the pension benefit formula to employee service rendered prior to that date. The projected benefit obligation is measured using assumptions as to future compensation if the pension benefit formula is based on those future compensation levels."

Projected unit credit method Method used under IFRS to estimate the defined benefit obligation; for each period in which employees provide services, they earn a portion of the post-employment benefits that the company has promised to pay.

Proportionate consolidation A method of accounting for joint ventures where the venturer's share of the assets, liabilities, income and expenses of the joint venture are combined on a line-by-line basis with similar items on the venturer's financial statements.

Protective put An option strategy in which a long position in an asset is combined with a long position in a put.

Provision In accounting, a liability of uncertain timing or amount.

Proxy fight An attempt to take control of a company through a shareholder vote.

Proxy statement A public document that provides the material facts concerning matters on which shareholders will vote.

Pseudo-random numbers Numbers produced by random number generators.

Pull on liquidity When disbursements are paid too quickly or trade credit availability is limited, requiring companies to expend funds before they receive funds from sales that could cover the liability.

Purchase method A method of accounting for a business combination where the acquiring company allocates the purchase price to each asset acquired and liability assumed at fair value. If the purchase price exceeds the allocation, the excess is recorded as goodwill.

Purchased in-process research and development costs Costs of research and development in progress at an acquired company; often, part of the purchase price of an acquired company is allocated to such costs.

Purchasing power gain A gain in value caused by changes in price levels. Monetary liabilities experience purchasing power gains during periods of inflation.

Purchasing power loss A loss in value caused by changes in price levels. Monetary assets experience purchasing power losses during periods of inflation.

Purchasing power parity The equal value of different monies.

Pure discount instruments Instruments that pay interest as the difference between the amount borrowed and the amount paid back.

Pure factor portfolio A portfolio with sensitivity of 1 to the factor in question and a sensitivity of 0 to all other factors.

Pure-play method A method for estimating the beta for a company or project; it requires using a comparable company's beta and adjusting it for financial leverage differences.

Put An option that gives the holder the right to sell an underlying asset to another party at a fixed price over a specific period of time.

Put–call parity An equation expressing the equivalence (parity) of a portfolio of a call and a bond with a portfolio of a put and the underlying, which leads to the relationship between put and call prices.

Put–call–forward parity The relationship among puts, calls, and forward contracts.

p-Value The smallest level of significance at which the null hypothesis can be rejected; also called the marginal significance level.

Pyramiding Controlling additional property through reinvestment, refinancing, and exchanging.

Qualifying special purpose entities Under U.S. GAAP, a special purpose entity structured to avoid consolidation that must meet qualification criteria.

Qualitative dependent variables Dummy variables used as dependent variables rather than as independent variables.

Quality of earnings analysis The investigation of issues relating to the accuracy of reported accounting results as reflections of economic performance; quality of earnings analysis is broadly understood to include not only earnings management, but also balance sheet management.

Quantile (or **fractile**) A value at or below which a stated fraction of the data lies.

Quartiles Quantiles that divide a distribution into four equal parts.

Quick assets Assets that can be most readily converted to cash (e.g., cash, short-term marketable investments, receivables).

Quick ratio, or **acid test ratio** A stringent measure of liquidity that indicates a company's ability to satisfy current liabilities with its most liquid assets, calculated as (cash + short-term marketable investments + receivables) divided by current liabilities.

Quintiles Quantiles that divide a distribution into five equal parts.

Quota A quantitative restriction on the import of a particular good, which specifies the maximum amount that can be imported in a given time period.

Random number An observation drawn from a uniform distribution.

Random number generator An algorithm that produces uniformly distributed random numbers between 0 and 1.

Random variable A quantity whose future outcomes are uncertain.

Random walk A time series in which the value of the series in one period is the value of the series in the previous period plus an unpredictable random error.

Range The difference between the maximum and minimum values in a dataset.

Rate of return The proportional annual benefit that results from making an investment.

Rate-of-return regulation Regulation that seeks to keep the rate of return in the industry at a competitive level by not allowing excessive prices to be charged.

Ratio scales A measurement scale that has all the characteristics of interval measurement scales as well as a true zero point as the origin.

Ratio spread An option strategy in which a long position in a certain number of options is offset by a short position in a certain number of other options on the same underlying, resulting in a risk-free position.

Rational efficient markets formulation See *Market efficiency*.

Real exchange rate The relative price of foreign-made goods and services to U.S.-made goods and services.

Real GDP per person Real GDP divided by the population.

Real options Options that relate to investment decisions such as the option to time the start of a project, the option to adjust its scale, or the option to abandon a project that has begun.

Real risk-free interest rate The single-period interest rate for a completely risk-free security if no inflation were expected.

Realizable value (settlement value) With reference to assets, the amount of cash or cash equivalents that could currently be obtained by selling the asset in an orderly disposal; with reference to liabilities, the undiscounted amount of cash or cash equivalents expected to be paid to satisfy the liabilities in the normal course of business.

Recapture premium Provision for a return of investment, net of value appreciation.

Receivables turnover An activity ratio equal to revenue divided by average receivables.

Receiver swaption A swaption that allows the holder to enter into a swap as the fixed-rate receiver and floating-rate payer.

Reconciliation   Resolving differences in indications of value when estimating market value.

Regime   With reference to a time series, the underlying model generating the times series.

Regression coefficients   The intercept and slope coefficient(s) of a regression.

Regulatory risk   The risk associated with the uncertainty of how derivative transactions will be regulated or with changes in regulations.

Rejection point (or **critical value**)   A value against which a computed test statistic is compared to decide whether to reject or not reject the null hypothesis.

Relative dispersion   The amount of dispersion relative to a reference value or benchmark.

Relative frequency   With reference to an interval of grouped data, the number of observations in the interval divided by the total number of observations in the sample.

Relative strength (RSTR) indicators   Valuation indicators that compare a stock's performance during a period either to its own past performance or to the performance of some group of stocks.

Relative valuation models   A model that specifies an asset's value relative to the value of another asset.

Rent seeking   The pursuit of wealth by capturing economic rent—consumer surplus, producer surplus, or economic profit.

Reorganization   Agreements made by a company in bankruptcy under which a company's capital structure is altered and/or alternative arrangements are made for debt repayment; U.S. Chapter 11 bankruptcy. The company emerges from bankruptcy as a going concern.

Replacement value   The market value of a swap.

Report format   With respect to the format of a balance sheet, a format in which assets, liabilities, and equity are listed in a single column.

Reporting unit   An operating segment or one level below an operating segment (referred to as a component).

Reputational risk   The risk that a company will suffer an extended diminution in market value relative to other companies in the same industry due to a demonstrated lack of concern for environmental, social, and governance risk factors.

Required rate of return   The minimum rate of return required by an investor to invest in an asset, given the asset's riskiness.

Residual autocorrelations   The sample autocorrelations of the residuals.

Residual claim   The owners' remaining claim on the company's assets after the liabilities are deducted.

Residual dividend approach   A dividend payout policy under which earnings in excess of the funds necessary to finance the equity portion of company's capital budget are paid out in dividends.

Residual dividend policy   A policy in which dividends are paid from any internally generated funds remaining after such funds are used to finance positive NPV projects.

Residual income (or **economic profit** or **abnormal earnings**)   Earnings for a given time period, minus a deduction for common shareholders' opportunity cost in generating the earnings.

Residual income method (or **excess earnings method**)   Income approach that estimates the value of all intangible assets of the business by capitalizing future earnings in excess of the estimated return requirements associated with working capital and fixed assets.

Residual income model (RIM) (also **discounted abnormal earnings model** or **Edwards-Bell-Ohlson model**)   A model of stock valuation that views intrinsic value of stock as the sum of book value per share plus the present value of the stock's expected future residual income per share.

Residual loss   Agency costs that are incurred despite adequate monitoring and bonding of management.

Retail method   An inventory accounting method in which the sales value of an item is reduced by the gross margin to calculate the item's cost.

Return on assets (ROA)   A profitability ratio calculated as net income divided by average total assets; indicates a company's net profit generated per dollar invested in total assets.

Return on common equity (ROCE)   A profitability ratio calculated as (net income − preferred dividends) divided by average common equity; equal to the return on equity ratio when no preferred equity is outstanding.

Return on equity (ROE)   A profitability ratio calculated as net income divided by average shareholders' equity.

Return on invested capital (ROIC)   The after-tax net operating profits as a percent of total assets or capital.

Return on total capital   A profitability ratio calculated as EBIT divided by the sum of short- and long-term debt and equity.

Revaluation   The process of valuing long-lived assets at fair value, rather than at cost less accumulated depreciation. Any resulting profit or loss is either reported on the income statement and/or through equity under revaluation surplus.

Revenue   The amount charged for the delivery of goods or services in the ordinary activities of a business over a stated period; the inflows of economic resources to a company over a stated period.

Reverse stock split   A reduction in the number of shares outstanding with a corresponding increase in share price, but no change to the company's underlying fundamentals.

Reviewed financial statements   A type of non-audited financial statements; typically provide an opinion letter with representations and assurances by the reviewing accountant that are less than those in audited financial statements.

Revolving credit agreements   The strongest form of short-term bank borrowing facilities; they are in effect for multiple years (e.g., 3–5 years) and may have optional medium-term loan features.

Rho   The sensitivity of the option price to the risk-free rate.

Risk budgeting   The establishment of objectives for individuals, groups, or divisions of an organization that takes into account the allocation of an acceptable level of risk.

Risk governance   The setting of overall policies and standards in risk management.

Risk management   The process of identifying the level of risk an entity wants, measuring the level of risk the entity currently has, taking actions that bring the actual level of risk to the desired level of risk, and monitoring the new actual level of risk so that it continues to be aligned with the desired level of risk.

Risk premium   The expected return on an investment minus the risk-free rate.

Risk-neutral probabilities   Weights that are used to compute a binomial option price. They are the probabilities that would apply if a risk-neutral investor valued an option.

Risk-neutral valuation   The process by which options and other derivatives are priced by treating investors as though they were risk neutral.

Robust   The quality of being relatively unaffected by a violation of assumptions.

Robust standard errors   Standard errors of the estimated parameters of a regression that correct for the presence of heteroskedasticity in the regression's error term.

Root mean squared error (RMSE)   The square root of the average squared forecast error; used to compare the out-of-sample forecasting performance of forecasting models.

Roy's safety first criterion   A criterion asserting that the optimal portfolio is the one that minimizes the probability that portfolio return falls below a threshold level.

Rule of 70   A rule that states that the number of years it takes for the level of a variable to double is approximately 70 divided by the annual percentage growth rate of the variable.

Rule of 72   The principle that the approximate number of years necessary for an investment to double is 72 divided by the stated interest rate.

Safety stock   A level of inventory beyond anticipated needs that provides a cushion in the event that it takes longer to replenish inventory than expected or in the case of greater than expected demand.

Safety-first rules   Rules for portfolio selection that focus on the risk that portfolio value will fall below some minimum acceptable level over some time horizon.

Sales   Generally, a synonym for revenue; "sales" is generally understood to refer to the sale of goods, whereas "revenue" is understood to include the sale of goods or services.

Sales returns and allowances   An offset to revenue reflecting any cash refunds, credits on account, and discounts from sales prices given to customers who purchased defective or unsatisfactory items.

Sales risk   Uncertainty with respect to the quantity of goods and services that a company is able to sell and the price it is able to achieve; the risk related to the uncertainty of revenues.

Sales-type lease   A type of finance lease, from a lessor perspective, where the present value of the lease payments (lease receivable) exceeds the carrying value of the leased asset. The revenues earned by the lessor are operating (the profit on the sale) and financing (interest) in nature.

Salvage value   The amount the company estimates that it can sell the asset for at the end of its useful life.

Sample   A subset of a population.

Sample excess kurtosis   A sample measure of the degree of a distribution's peakedness in excess of the normal distribution's peakedness.

Sample kurtosis   A sample measure of the degree of a distribution's peakedness.

Sample mean   The sum of the sample observations, divided by the sample size.

Sample selection bias   Bias introduced by systematically excluding some members of the population according to a particular attribute—for example, the bias introduced when data availability leads to certain observations being excluded from the analysis.

Sample skewness   A sample measure of degree of asymmetry of a distribution.

Sample standard deviation   The positive square root of the sample variance.

Sample statistic or **statistic**   A quantity computed from or used to describe a sample.

Sample variance   A sample measure of the degree of dispersion of a distribution, calculated by dividing the sum of the squared deviations from the sample mean by the sample size minus 1.

Sampling   The process of obtaining a sample.

Sampling distribution   The distribution of all distinct possible values that a statistic can assume when computed from samples of the same size randomly drawn from the same population.

Sampling error   The difference between the observed value of a statistic and the quantity it is intended to estimate.

Sampling plan   The set of rules used to select a sample.

Sandwich spread   An option strategy that is equivalent to a short butterfly spread.

Sarbanes–Oxley Act   An act passed by the U.S. Congress in 2002 that created the Public Company Accounting Oversight Board (PCAOB) to oversee auditors.

Scaled earnings surprise   Unexpected earnings divided by the standard deviation of analysts' earnings forecasts.

Scalper   A trader who offers to buy or sell futures contracts, holding the position for only a brief period of time. Scalpers attempt to profit by buying at the bid price and selling at the higher ask price.

Scatter plot   A two-dimensional plot of pairs of observations on two data series.

Scenario analysis   Analysis that shows the changes in key financial quantities that result from given (economic) events, such as the loss of customers, the loss of a supply source, or a catastrophic event; a risk management technique involving examination of the performance of a portfolio under specified situations. Closely related to stress testing.

Screening   The application of a set of criteria to reduce a set of potential investments to a smaller set having certain desired characteristics.

Seats   Memberships in a derivatives exchange.

Sector neutral   Said of a portfolio for which economic sectors are represented in the same proportions as in the benchmark, using market-value weights.

Sector neutralizing   Measure of financial reporting quality by subtracting the mean or median ratio for a given sector group from a given company's ratio.

Sector rotation strategy   A type of top-down investing approach that involves emphasizing different economic sectors based on considerations such as macroeconomic forecasts.

Securities Act of 1933   An act passed by the U.S. Congress in 1933 that specifies the financial and other significant information that investors must receive when securities are sold, prohibits misrepresentations, and requires initial registration of all public issuances of securities.

Securities Exchange Act of 1934   An act passed by the U.S. Congress in 1934 that created the Securities and Exchange Commission (SEC), gave the SEC authority over all aspects of the securities industry, and empowered the SEC to require periodic reporting by companies with publicly traded securities.

Securities offering   A merger or acquisition in which target shareholders are to receive shares of the acquirer's common stock as compensation.

Security market line (SML)   The graph of the capital asset pricing model.

Segment debt ratio   Segment liabilities divided by segment assets.

Segment margin   Segment profit (loss) divided by segment revenue.

Segment ROA   Segment profit (loss) divided by segment assets.

Segment turnover   Segment revenue divided by segment assets.

Sell-side analysts   Analysts who work at brokerages.

Semideviation   The positive square root of semivariance (sometimes called semistandard deviation).

Semilogarithmic   Describes a scale constructed so that equal intervals on the vertical scale represent equal rates of change, and equal intervals on the horizontal scale represent equal amounts of change.

Semivariance   The average squared deviation below the mean.

Sensitivity analysis   Analysis that shows the range of possible outcomes as specific assumptions are changed.

Serially correlated   With reference to regression errors, errors that are correlated across observations.

Service period   The period benefited by the employee's service, usually the period between the grant date and the vesting date.

Settlement date or **payment date**   The date on which the parties to a swap make payments.

Settlement period   The time between settlement dates.

Settlement price   The official price, designated by the clearinghouse, from which daily gains and losses will be determined and marked to market.

Settlement risk   When settling a contract, the risk that one party could be in the process of paying the counterparty while the counterparty is declaring bankruptcy.

Share repurchase   A transaction in which a company buys back its own shares. Unlike stock dividends and stock splits, share repurchases use corporate cash.

Shareholders' equity   Total assets minus total liabilities.

Share-the-gains, share-the-pains theory   A theory of regulatory behavior that holds that regulators must take account of the demands of three groups: legislators, who established and oversee the regulatory agency; firms in the regulated industry; and consumers of the regulated industry's products.

Shark repellents   A pre-offer takeover defense mechanism involving the corporate charter (e.g., staggered boards of directors and supermajority provisions).

Sharpe ratio   The average return in excess of the risk-free rate divided by the standard deviation of return; a measure of the average excess return earned per unit of standard deviation of return.

Sharpe's measure   Reward-to-volatility ratio; ratio of portfolio excess return to standard deviation.

Short   The seller of a derivative contract. Also refers to the position of being short a derivative.

Shortfall risk   The risk that portfolio value will fall below some minimum acceptable level over some time horizon.

Simple interest   The interest earned each period on the original investment; interest calculated on the principal only.

Simple random sample   A subset of a larger population created in such a way that each element of the population has an equal probability of being selected to the subset.

Simple random sampling   The procedure of drawing a sample to satisfy the definition of a simple random sample.

Simulation   Computer-generated sensitivity or scenario analysis that is based on probability models for the factors that drive outcomes.

Simulation trial   A complete pass through the steps of a simulation.

Single-payment loan   A loan in which the borrower receives a sum of money at the start and pays back the entire amount with interest in a single payment at maturity.

Single-step format   With respect to the format of the income statement, a format that does not subtotal for gross profit (revenue minus cost of goods sold).

Sinking fund factor   Amount that must be set aside each period to have $1 at some future point in time.

Skewed   Not symmetrical.

Skewness   A quantitative measure of skew (lack of symmetry); a synonym of skew.

Sole proprietorship   A business owned and operated by a single person.

Solvency   With respect to financial statement analysis, the ability of a company to fulfill its long-term obligations.

Solvency ratios   Ratios that measure a company's ability to meet its long-term obligations.

Sovereign yield spread   An estimate of the country spread (country equity premium) for a developing nation that is based on a comparison of bonds yields in country being analyzed and a developed country. The sovereign yield spread is the difference between a government bond yield in the country being analyzed, denominated in the currency of the developed country, and the Treasury bond yield on a similar maturity bond in the developed country.

Spearman rank correlation coefficient   A measure of correlation applied to ranked data.

Special purpose entity (special purpose vehicle or **variable interest entity)**   A non-operating entity created to carry out a specified purpose, such as leasing assets or securitizing receivables; can be a corporation, partnership, trust, limited liability, or partnership formed to facilitate a specific type of business activity.

Specific identification method   An inventory accounting method that identifies which specific inventory items were sold and which remained in inventory to be carried over to later periods.

Spin-off   A form of restructuring in which shareholders of a parent company receive a proportional number of shares in a new, separate entity; shareholders end up owning stock in two different companies where there used to be one.

Split-off   A form of restructuring in which shareholders of the parent company are given shares in a newly created entity in exchange for their shares of the parent company.

Split-rate tax system   In reference to corporate taxes, a split-rate system taxes earnings to be distributed as dividends at a different rate than earnings to be retained. Corporate profits distributed as dividends are taxed at a lower rate than those retained in the business.

Spread   An option strategy involving the purchase of one option and sale of another option that is identical to the first in all respects except either exercise price or expiration.

Spreadsheet modeling   As used in this book, the use of a spreadsheet in executing a dividend discount model valuation, or other present value model valuation.

Spurious correlation   A correlation that misleadingly points towards associations between variables.

Stable dividend policy   A policy in which regular dividends are paid that reflect long-run expected earnings. In contrast to a constant dividend payout ratio policy, a stable dividend policy does not reflect short-term volatility in earnings.

Standard cost   With respect to inventory accounting, the planned or target unit cost of inventory items or services.

Standard deviation   The positive square root of the variance; a measure of dispersion in the same units as the original data.

Standard normal distribution (or **unit normal distribution)**   The normal density with mean equal to 0 and standard deviation (σ) equal to 1.

Standardized beta   With reference to fundamental factor models, the value of the attribute for an asset minus the average value of the attribute across all stocks, divided by the standard deviation of the attribute across all stocks.

Standardized unexpected earnings (SUE)   Unexpected earnings per share divided by the standard deviation of unexpected earnings per share over a specified prior time period.

Standardizing   A transformation that involves subtracting the mean and dividing the result by the standard deviation.

Stated annual interest rate or **quoted interest rate**   A quoted interest rate that does not account for compounding within the year.

Stated rate (nominal rate or **coupon rate)**   The rate at which periodic interest payments are calculated.

Statement of cash flows (cash flow statement)   A financial statement that reconciles beginning-of-period and end-of-period balance sheet values of cash; provides information about an entity's cash inflows and cash outflows as they pertain to operating, investing, and financing activities.

Statement of changes in shareholders' equity (statement of owners' equity)   A financial statement that reconciles the beginning-of-period and end-of-period balance sheet values of shareholders' equity; provides information about all factors affecting shareholders' equity.

Statement of retained earnings   A financial statement that reconciles beginning-of-period and end-of-period balance sheet values of retained income; shows the linkage between the balance sheet and income statement.

Static trade-off theory of capital structure   A theory pertaining to a company's optimal capital structure; the optimal level of debt is found at the point where additional debt would cause the costs of financial distress to increase by a greater amount than the benefit of the additional tax shield.

Statistic   A quantity computed from or used to describe a sample of data.

Statistical factor models   A multifactor model in which statistical methods are applied to a set of historical returns to determine portfolios that best explain either historical return covariances or variances.

Statistical inference   Making forecasts, estimates, or judgments about a larger group from a smaller group actually observed; using a sample statistic to infer the value of an unknown population parameter.

Statistically significant   A result indicating that the null hypothesis can be rejected; with reference to an estimated regression coefficient, frequently understood to mean a result indicating that the corresponding population regression coefficient is different from 0.

Statistics   The science of describing, analyzing, and drawing conclusions from data; also, a collection of numerical data.

Statutory merger   A merger in which one company ceases to exist as an identifiable entity and all its assets and liabilities become part of a purchasing company.

Stock grants   The granting of stock to employees as a form of compensation.

Stock options (stock option grants)   The granting of stock options to employees as a form of compensation.

Stock purchase   An acquisition in which the acquirer gives the target company's shareholders some combination of cash and securities in exchange for shares of the target company's stock.

Stock-out losses   Profits lost from not having sufficient inventory on hand to satisfy demand.

Storage costs or **carrying costs**   The costs of holding an asset, generally a function of the physical characteristics of the underlying asset.

Straddle   An option strategy involving the purchase of a put and a call with the same exercise price. A straddle is based on the expectation of high volatility of the underlying.

Straight-line method   A depreciation method that allocates evenly the cost of a long-lived asset less its estimated residual value over the estimated useful life of the asset.

Strangle   A variation of a straddle in which the put and call have different exercise prices.

Strap   An option strategy involving the purchase of two calls and one put.

Strategic transaction   A purchase involving a buyer that would benefit from certain synergies associated with owning the target firm.

Stratified random sampling   A procedure by which a population is divided into subpopulations (strata) based on one or more classification criteria. Simple random samples are then drawn from each stratum in sizes proportional to the relative size of each stratum in the population. These samples are then pooled.

Stress testing   A set of techniques for estimating losses in extremely unfavorable combinations of events or scenarios.

Strip   An option strategy involving the purchase of two puts and one call.

Structured note   A variation of a floating-rate note that has some type of unusual characteristic such as a leverage factor or in which the rate moves opposite to interest rates.

Subjective probability   A probability drawing on personal or subjective judgment.

Subsidiary merger   A merger in which the company being purchased becomes a subsidiary of the purchaser.

Subsistence real wage rate   The minimum real wage rate needed to maintain life.

Sum-of-the-parts valuation   A valuation that sums the estimated values of each of a company's businesses as if each business were an independent going concern.

Sunk cost   A cost that has already been incurred.

Supernormal growth   Above average or abnormally high growth rate in earnings per share.

Surprise   The actual value of a variable minus its predicted (or expected) value.

Survey approach   An estimate of the equity risk premium that is based upon estimates provided by a panel of finance experts.

Survivorship bias   Bias that may result when failed or defunct companies are excluded from membership in a group.

Sustainable growth rate   The rate of dividend (and earnings) growth that can be sustained over time for a given level of return on equity, keeping the capital structure constant and without issuing additional common stock.

Swap   An agreement between two parties to exchange a series of future cash flows.

Swap spread   The difference between the fixed rate on an interest rate swap and the rate on a Treasury note with equivalent maturity; it reflects the general level of credit risk in the market.

Swaption   An option to enter into a swap.

Synthetic call   The combination of puts, the underlying, and risk-free bonds that replicates a call option.

Synthetic forward contract   The combination of the underlying, puts, calls, and risk-free bonds that replicates a forward contract.

Synthetic index fund   An index fund position created by combining risk-free bonds and futures on the desired index.

Synthetic lease   A lease that is structured to provide a company with the tax benefits of ownership while not requiring the asset to be reflected on the company's financial statements.

Synthetic put   The combination of calls, the underlying, and risk-free bonds that replicates a put option.

Systematic factors   Factors that affect the average returns of a large number of different assets.

Systematic sampling   A procedure of selecting every kth member until reaching a sample of the desired size. The sample that results from this procedure should be approximately random.

Takeover   A merger; the term may be applied to any transaction, but is often used in reference to hostile transactions.

Takeover premium   The amount by which the takeover price for each share of stock must exceed the current stock price in order to entice shareholders to relinquish control of the company to an acquirer.

Tangible assets Long-term assets with physical substance that are used in company operations, such as land (property), plant, and equipment.

Tangible book value per share Common shareholders' equity minus intangible assets from the balance sheet, divided by the number of shares outstanding.

Target balance A minimum level of cash to be held available—estimated in advance and adjusted for known funds transfers, seasonality, or other factors.

Target capital structure A company's chosen proportions of debt and equity.

Target company, or target The company in a merger or acquisition that is being acquired.

Target payout ratio A strategic corporate goal representing the long-term proportion of earnings that the company intends to distribute to shareholders as dividends.

Target semideviation The positive square root of target semivariance.

Target semivariance The average squared deviation below a target value.

Tariff A tax that is imposed by the importing country when an imported good crosses its international boundary.

Tax base (tax basis) The amount at which an asset or liability is valued for tax purposes.

Tax expense An aggregate of an entity's income tax payable (or recoverable in the case of a tax benefit) and any changes in deferred tax assets and liabilities. It is essentially the income tax payable or recoverable if these had been determined based on accounting profit rather than taxable income.

Tax loss carry forward A taxable loss in the current period that may be used to reduce future taxable income.

Tax risk The uncertainty associated with tax laws.

Taxable income The portion of an entity's income that is subject to income taxes under the tax laws of its jurisdiction.

Taxable temporary differences Temporary differences that result in a taxable amount in a future period when determining the taxable profit as the balance sheet item is recovered or settled.

***t*-Distribution** A symmetrical distribution defined by a single parameter, degrees of freedom, that is largely used to make inferences concerning the mean of a normal distribution whose variance is unknown.

Technical indicators Momentum indicators based on price.

Temporal method A variation of the monetary/nonmonetary translation method that requires not only monetary assets and liabilities, but also nonmonetary assets and liabilities that are measured at their current value on the balance sheet date to be translated at the current exchange rate. Assets and liabilities are translated at rates consistent with the timing of their measurement value. This method is typically used when the functional currency is other than the local currency.

Tender offer A public offer whereby the acquirer invites target shareholders to submit ("tender") their shares in return for the proposed payment.

Tenor The original time to maturity on a swap.

Terminal price multiple The price multiple for a stock assumed to hold at a stated future time.

Terminal share price The share price at a particular point in the future.

Terminal value of the stock (or continuing value of the stock) The analyst's estimate of a stock's value at a particular point in the future.

Termination date The date of the final payment on a swap; also, the swap's expiration date.

Terms of trade The quantity of goods and services that a country exports to pay for its imports of goods and services.

Test statistic A quantity, calculated based on a sample, whose value is the basis for deciding whether or not to reject the null hypothesis.

Theory of contestable markets A hypothesis concerning pricing behavior that holds that even though there are only a few firms in an industry, they are forced to price their products more or less competitively because of the ease of entry by outsiders. The key aspect of a contestable market is relatively costless entry into and exit from the industry.

Theta The rate at which an option's time value decays.

Tie-in sales Purchases of one product that are permitted by the seller only if the consumer buys another good or service from the same firm.

Time series A set of observations on a variable's outcomes in different time periods.

Time to expiration The time remaining in the life of a derivative, typically expressed in years.

Time value decay The loss in the value of an option resulting from movement of the option price toward its payoff value as the expiration day approaches.

Time value of money The principles governing equivalence relationships between cash flows with different dates.

Time value or speculative value The difference between the market price of the option and its intrinsic value, determined by the uncertainty of the underlying over the remaining life of the option.

Time-period bias The possibility that when we use a time-series sample, our statistical conclusion may be sensitive to the starting and ending dates of the sample.

Time-series data Observations of a variable over time.

Time-weighted rate of return The compound rate of growth of one unit of currency invested in a portfolio during a stated measurement period; a measure of investment performance that is not sensitive to the timing and amount of withdrawals or additions to the portfolio.

Tobin's *q* The ratio of the market value of debt and equity to the replacement cost of total assets.

Top-down analysis With reference to investment selection processes, an approach that starts with macro selection (i.e., identifying attractive geographic segments and/or industry segments) and then addresses selection of the most attractive investments within those segments.

Top-down forecasting approach A forecasting approach that involves moving from international and national macroeconomic forecasts to industry forecasts and then to individual company and asset forecasts.

Top-down investing An approach to investing that typically begins with macroeconomic forecasts.

Total asset turnover An activity ratio calculated as revenue divided by average total assets.

Total invested capital The sum of market value of common equity, book value of preferred equity, and face value of debt.

Total probability rule A rule explaining the unconditional probability of an event in terms of probabilities of the event conditional on mutually exclusive and exhaustive scenarios.

Total probability rule for expected value A rule explaining the expected value of a random variable in terms of expected values of the random variable conditional on mutually exclusive and exhaustive scenarios.

Total return swap A swap in which one party agrees to pay the total return on a security. Often used as a credit derivative, in which the underlying is a bond.

Tracking error The standard deviation of the difference in returns between an active investment portfolio and its benchmark portfolio; also called tracking error volatility, tracking risk, and active risk.

Tracking portfolio A portfolio having factor sensitivities that are matched to those of a benchmark or other portfolio.

Tracking risk The standard deviation of the differences between a portfolio's returns and its benchmark's returns; a synonym of active risk.

Trade credit A spontaneous form of credit in which a purchaser of the goods or service is financing its purchase by delaying the date on which payment is made.

Trade receivables (commercial receivables or **accounts receivable)** Amounts customers owe the company for products that have been sold as well as amounts that may be due from suppliers (such as for returns of merchandise).

Trade-weighted index The average exchange rate, with individual currencies weighted by their importance in U.S. international trade.

Trading securities (held-for-trading securities) Securities held by a company with the intent to trade them.

Traditional efficient markets formulation See *Market efficiency*.

Trailing dividend yield Current market price divided by the most recent quarterly per-share dividend multiplied by four.

Trailing P/E (or current P/E) A stock's current market price divided by the most recent four quarters of earnings per share.

Transaction exposure The risk of a change in value between the transaction date and the settlement date of an asset or liability denominated in a foreign currency.

Transactions motive In the context of inventory management, the need for inventory as part of the routine production–sales cycle.

Transition phase The stage of growth between the growth phase and the mature phase of a company in which earnings growth typically slows.

Translation exposure The risk associated with the conversion of foreign financial statements into domestic currency.

Treasury shares Shares that were issued and subsequently repurchased by the company.

Treasury stock method A method for accounting for the effect of options (and warrants) on earnings per share (EPS) that specifies what EPS would have been if the options and warrants had been exercised and the company had used the proceeds to repurchase common stock.

Tree diagram A diagram with branches emanating from nodes representing either mutually exclusive chance events or mutually exclusive decisions.

Trend A long-term pattern of movement in a particular direction.

Trimmed mean A mean computed after excluding a stated small percentage of the lowest and highest observations.

Trust receipt arrangement The use of inventory as collateral for a loan. The inventory is segregated and held in trust, and the proceeds of any sale must be remitted to the lender immediately.

t-Test A hypothesis test using a statistic (t-statistic) that follows a t-distribution.

Two-sided hypothesis test (or two-tailed hypothesis test) A test in which the null hypothesis is rejected in favor of the alternative hypothesis if the evidence indicates that the population parameter is either smaller or larger than a hypothesized value.

Type I error The error of rejecting a true null hypothesis.

Type II error The error of not rejecting a false null hypothesis.

U.S. interest rate differential The U.S. interest rate minus the foreign interest rate.

U.S. official reserves The government's holding of foreign currency.

Unbiasedness Lack of bias. A desirable property of estimators, an unbiased estimator is one whose expected value (the mean of its sampling distribution) equals the parameter it is intended to estimate.

Unbilled revenue (accrued revenue) Revenue that has been earned but not yet billed to customers as of the end of an accounting period.

Unclassified balance sheet A balance sheet that does not show subtotals for current assets and current liabilities.

Unconditional heteroskedasticity Heteroskedasticity of the error term that is not correlated with the values of the independent variable(s) in the regression.

Unconditional probability (or marginal probability) The probability of an event *not* conditioned on another event.

Underlying An asset that trades in a market in which buyers and sellers meet, decide on a price, and the seller then delivers the asset to the buyer and receives payment. The underlying is the asset or other derivative on which a particular derivative is based. The market for the underlying is also referred to as the spot market.

Underlying earnings (or persistent earnings, continuing earnings, or **core earnings)** Earnings excluding nonrecurring components.

Unearned fees Unearned fees are recognized when a company receives cash payment for fees prior to earning them.

Unearned revenue (deferred revenue) A liability account for money that has been collected for goods or services that have not yet been delivered; payment received in advance of providing a good or service.

Unexpected earnings (also earnings surprise) The difference between reported earnings per share and expected earnings per share.

Unidentifiable intangible An intangible that cannot be acquired singly and that typically possesses an indefinite benefit period; an example is accounting goodwill.

Unit root A time series that is not covariance stationary is said to have a unit root.

Uniting of interests method A method of accounting in which combined companies were portrayed as if they had always operated as a single economic entity. Called pooling of interests under U.S. GAAP and uniting of interests under IFRS. (No longer allowed under U.S. GAAP or IFRS.)

Units-of-production method A depreciation method that allocates the cost of a long-lived asset based on actual usage during the period.

Univariate distribution A distribution that specifies the probabilities for a single random variable.

Unlimited funds An unlimited funds environment assumes that the company can raise the funds it wants for all profitable projects simply by paying the required rate of return.

Up transition probability The probability that an asset's value moves up.

Upstream A transaction between two affiliates, an investor company and an associate company such that the associate company records a profit on its income statement. An example is a sale of inventory by the associate to the investor company.

Valuation The process of determining the value of an asset or service on the basis of variables perceived to be related to future investment returns, or on the basis of comparisons with closely similar assets.

Valuation allowance A reserve created against deferred tax assets, based on the likelihood of realizing the deferred tax assets in future accounting periods.

Valuation ratios Ratios that measure the quantity of an asset or flow (e.g., earnings) in relation to the price associated with a specified claim (e.g., a share or ownership of the enterprise).

Value The amount for which one can sell something, or the amount one must pay to acquire something.

Value at risk (VAR) A money measure of the minimum value of losses expected during a specified time period at a given level of probability.

Value investors With reference to equity investors, investors who are focused on paying a relatively low share price in relation to earnings or assets per share.

Variable costs Costs that fluctuate with the level of production and sales.

Variance The expected value (the probability-weighted average) of squared deviations from a random variable's expected value.

Variation margin Additional margin that must be deposited in an amount sufficient to bring the balance up to the initial margin requirement.

Vega The relationship between option price and volatility.

Venture capital investors Private equity investors in development-stage companies.

Venturers The owners of a joint venture. Each is active in the management and shares control of the joint venture.

Vertical analysis Common-size analysis using only one reporting period or one base financial statement; for example, an income statement in which all items are stated as percentages of sales.

Vertical common-size analysis The most common type of common-size analysis, in which the accounts in a given period are compared to a benchmark item in that same year.

Vertical merger A merger involving companies at different positions of the same production chain; for example, a supplier or a distributor.

Versioning Selling a product in slightly altered forms to different groups of consumers.

Vested benefit obligation Under U.S. GAAP, a measure used in estimating a defined-benefit pension plan's liabilities, defined as the "actuarial present value of vested benefits."

Vested benefits Future benefits promised to the employee regardless of continuing service. Benefits typically vest after a specified period of service or a specified period of service combined with age.

Vesting date The date that employees can first exercise stock options; vesting can be immediate or over a future period.

Visibility The extent to which a company's operations are predictable with substantial confidence.

Volatility As used in option pricing, the standard deviation of the continuously compounded returns on the underlying asset.

Voluntary export restraint An agreement between two governments in which the government of the exporting country agrees to restrain the volume of its own exports.

Warehouse receipt arrangement The use of inventory as collateral for a loan; similar to a trust receipt arrangement except there is a third party (i.e., a warehouse company) that supervises the inventory.

Weighted average cost An inventory accounting method that averages the total cost of available inventory items over the total units available for sale.

Weighted harmonic mean See *Harmonic mean.*

Weighted mean An average in which each observation is weighted by an index of its relative importance.

Weighted-average cost of capital (WACC) A weighted average of the after-tax required rates of return on a company's common stock, preferred stock, and long-term debt, where the weights are the fraction of each source of financing in the company's target capital structure.

White knight A third party that is sought out by the target company's board to purchase the target in lieu of a hostile bidder.

White squire A third party that is sought out by the target company's board to purchase a substantial minority stake in the target—enough to block a hostile takeover without selling the entire company.

White-corrected standard errors A synonym for robust standard errors.

Winner's curse The tendency for the winner in certain competitive bidding situations to overpay, whether because of overestimation of intrinsic value, emotion, or information asymmetries.

Winsorized mean A mean computed after assigning a stated percent of the lowest values equal to one specified low value, and a stated percent of the highest values equal to one specified high value.

Working capital The difference between current assets and current liabilities.

Working capital management The management of a company's short-term assets (such as inventory) and short-term liabilities (such as money owed to suppliers).

Working capital turnover A comparison of revenues with working capital to produce a measure that shows how efficiently working capital is employed.

World Trade Organization An international organization that places greater obligations on its member countries to observe the GATT rules.

Write-down A reduction in the value of an asset as stated in the balance sheet.

Yield The actual return on a debt security if it is held to maturity.

Yield beta A measure of the sensitivity of a bond's yield to a general measure of bond yields in the market that is used to refine the hedge ratio.

Yield spread The difference between the yield on a bond and the yield on a default-free security, usually a government note, of the same maturity. The yield spread is primarily determined by the market's perception of the credit risk on the bond.

Yield to maturity The annual return that an investor earns on a bond if the investor purchases the bond today and holds it until maturity.

Zero-cost collar A transaction in which a position in the underlying is protected by buying a put and selling a call with the premium from the sale of the call offsetting the premium from the purchase of the put. It can also be used to protect a floating-rate borrower against interest rate increases with the premium on a long cap offsetting the premium on a short floor.